INNOVATION, ORGANIZATION AND ECONOMIC DYNAMICS

To G., who has changed my life

Innovation, Organization and Economic Dynamics

Selected Essays

Giovanni Dosi

Professor of Economics, St Anna School of Advanced Studies, Pisa, Italy

Edward Elgar

Cheltenham, UK • Northampton, MA, USA

Published by
Edward Elgar Publishing Limited
Glensanda House
Montpellier Parade
Cheltenham
Glos GL50 1UA
UK

Edward Elgar Publishing, Inc.
136 West Street
Suite 202
Northampton
Massachusetts 01060
USA

A catalogue record for this book
is available from the British Library

Library of Congress Cataloguing in Publication Data

Dosi, Giovanni, 1953–
    [Essays, Selections]
    Innovation, organization and economic dynamics : selected essays / Giovanni Dosi.
    Includes bibliographical references.
    1. Technological innovations—Economic aspects. 2. Economics. I. Title.
    HC79.T4 D67 2000
    338'.064—dc21   99–056230

ISBN 1 85898 591 9 (cased)

Printed in the United Kingdom at the University Press, Cambridge

Contents

Acknowledgements   ix

Innovation, Organization and Economic Dynamics: An Autobiographical
Introduction   1

PART I   OPPORTUNITIES OF INNOVATION, SEARCH PROCEDURES
          AND DIFFUSION

1   'Technological Paradigms and Technological Trajectories', *Research
     Policy*, **11**, 1982, 147–62   47
2   'Sources, Procedures, and Microeconomic Effects of Innovation',
     Journal of Economic Literature, **XXVI** (3), September 1988, 1120–71   63
3   'The Research on Innovation Diffusion: An Assessment' in *Diffusion of
     Technologies and Social Behavior*, Nebojša Nakićenović and Arnulf
     Grübler (eds), Springer-Verlag, 1991, 179–208   115
4   'Opportunities, Incentives and the Collective Patterns of Technological
     Change', *Economic Journal*, **107**, September 1997, 1530–47   145

PART II   ECONOMIC BEHAVIOURS, ORGANIZATIONS AND
          INNOVATION IN CHANGING ENVIRONMENTS

5   'Substantive and Procedural Uncertainty: An Exploration of Economic
     Behaviours in Changing Environments', with M. Egidi, *Journal of
     Evolutionary Economics*, **1** (2), 1991, 145–68   165
6   'Norms as Emergent Properties of Adaptive Learning: The Case of
     Economic Routines', with Luigi Marengo, Andrea Bassanini and Marco
     Valente, *Journal of Evolutionary Economics*, **9** (1), 1999, 5–26   189
7   'Some Elements of an Evolutionary Theory of Organizational
     Competences', with Luigi Marengo in *Evolutionary Concepts in
     Contemporary Economics*, Richard W. England (ed.), University of
     Michigan Press, 1994, 157–78, references   211
8   'Rational Entrepreneurs or Optimistic Martyrs? Some Considerations
     on Technological Regimes, Corporate Entries, and the Evolutionary
     Role of Decision Biases', with Dan Lovallo in *Technological
     Innovation: Oversights and Foresights*, Raghu Garud, Praveen Rattan
     Nayyar and Zur Baruch Shapira (eds), Cambridge University Press,
     1997, 41–68   236
9   'Understanding Corporate Coherence: Theory and Evidence', with
     David J. Teece, Richard Rumelt and Sidney Winter, *Journal of
     Economic Behavior and Organization*, **23**, 1994, 1–30   264

10   'Learning how to Govern and Learning how to Solve Problems: On the
Co-Evolution of Competences, Conflicts and Organizational Routines',
with Benjamin Coriat in *The Dynamic Firm: The Role of Technology,
Strategy, Organization, and Regions*, Alfred D. Chandler, Jr, Peter
Hagström and Örjan Sölvell (eds), Oxford University Press, 1998,
103–33   294

PART III   EVOLUTIONARY INTERPRETATIONS OF ECONOMIC
CHANGE

11   'An Introduction to Evolutionary Theories in Economics', with Richard
R. Nelson, *Journal of Evolutionary Economics*, **4**, 1994, 153–72   327
12   'The Institutional Embeddedness of Economic Change: An Appraisal of
the "Evolutionary" and "Regulationist" Research Programmes', with
Benjamin Coriat in *Institutions and Economic Change: New Perspectives
on Markets, Firms and Technology*, Klaus Nielsen and Björn Johnson
(eds), Edward Elgar Publishing, 1998, 3–32   347

PART IV   LEARNING AND MARKET SELECTION: EVOLUTIONARY
MODELS OF ECONOMIC CHANGE

13   'On "Badly Behaved" Dynamics: Some Applications of Generalized Urn
Schemes to Technological and Economic Change', with Y. Kaniovski,
Journal of Evolutionary Economics, **4** (2), 1994, 93–123   379
14   'Innovation, Diversity and Diffusion: A Self-Organisation Model', with
Gerald Silverberg and Luigi Orsenigo, *Economic Journal*, **98** (393),
December 1988, 1032–54   410
15   'Learning, Market Selection and the Evolution of Industrial Structures',
with Orietta Marsili, Luigi Orsenigo and Roberta Salvatore, *Small
Business Economics*, **7** (6), December 1995, 411–36   433
16   'Modeling Industrial Dynamics with Innovative Entrants', with
S.G. Winter and Y.M. Kaniovski, IIASA Report, May 1998   459
17   'Innovative Learning and Institutions in the Process of Development:
On the Microfoundation of Growth Regimes', with Francesca
Chiaromonte and Luigi Orsenigo in *Learning and Technological
Change*, Ross Thomson (ed.), Macmillan Press, 1993, 117–49   501
18   'The Dynamics of International Differentiation: A Multi-Country
Evolutionary Model', with Silvia Fabiani, Roberta Aversi and Mara
Meacci, *Industrial and Corporate Change*, **3** (1), 1994, 225–42   534
19   'Exploring the Unknown. On Entrepreneurship, Coordination and
Innovation Driven Growth', with Giorgio Fagiolo in *Advances in Self-
Organisation and Evolutionary Economics*, J. Lesourne and A. Orléan
(eds), Economica, 1998, reset   552

PART V   INSTITUTIONS AND ECONOMIC DYNAMICS

20   'Institutions and Markets in a Dynamic World', *The Manchester School*,
     LVI (2), June 1988, 119–46   593
21   'Finance, Innovation and Industrial Change', *Journal of Economic
     Behavior and Organization*, **13**, 1990, 299–319   621
22   'Corporate Organization, Finance and Innovation', with Masahiko Aoki
     in *Finance and the Enterprise*, Vera Zamagni (ed.), Academic Press,
     1992, 37–61, references   642
23   'Hierarchies, Markets and Power: Some Foundational Issues on the
     Nature of Contemporary Economic Organizations', *Industrial and
     Corporate Change*, **4** (1), 1995, 1–19   669

Works and publications of Giovanni Dosi   689
Name index   697

Acknowledgements

The publishers wish to thank the following who have kindly given permission for the use of copyright material.

Academic Press for: 'Corporate Organization, Finance and Innovation', with Masahiko Aoki in *Finance and the Enterprise*, Vera Zamagni (ed.), 1992, 37–61.

American Economic Association for: 'Sources, Procedures, and Microeconomic Effects of Innovation', *Journal of Economic Literature*, **XXVI** (3), September 1988, 1120–71.

Blackwell Publishers for: 'Opportunities, Incentives and the Collective Patterns of Technological Change', *Economic Journal*, **107**, September 1997, 1530–47; 'Innovation, Diversity and Diffusion: A Self-Organisation Model', with Gerald Silverberg and Luigi Orsenigo, *Economic Journal*, **98** (393), December 1988, 1032–54; 'Institutions and Markets in a Dynamic World', *The Manchester School*, **LVI** (2), June 1988, 119–46.

Cambridge University Press for: 'Rational Entrepreneurs or Optimistic Martyrs? Some Considerations on Technological Regimes, Corporate Entries, and the Evolutionary Role of Decision Biases', with Dan Lovallo in *Technological Innovation: Oversights and Foresights*, Raghu Garud, Praveen Rattan Nayyar and Zur Baruch Shapira (eds), 1997, 41–68.

Economica for: 'Exploring the Unknown. On Entrepreneurship, Coordination and Innovation Driven Growth', with Giorgio Fagiolo in *Advances in Self-Organisation and Evolutionary Economics*, J. Lesourne and A. Orléan (eds), 1998.

Elsevier Science b.v. for: 'Technological Paradigms and Technological Trajectories', *Research Policy*, **11**, 1982, 147–62; 'Understanding Corporate Coherence: Theory and Evidence', with David J. Teece, Richard Rumelt and Sidney Winter, *Journal of Economic Behavior and Organization*, **23**, 1994, 1–30; 'Finance, Innovation and Industrial Change', *Journal of Economic Behavior and Organization*, **13**, 1990, 299–319.

Kluwer Academic Publishers for: 'Learning, Market Selection and the Evolution of Industrial Structures', with Orietta Marsili, Luigi Orsenigo and Roberta Salvatore, *Small Business Economics*, **7** (6), December 1995, 411–36.

Macmillan Press Ltd for: 'Innovative Learning and Institutions in the Process of Development: On the Microfoundation of Growth Regimes', with Francesca Chiaromonte and Luigi Orsenigo in *Learning and Technological Change*, Ross Thomson (ed.), 1993.

Oxford University Press for: 'Learning how to Govern and Learning how to Solve Problems: On the Co-Evolution of Competences, Conflicts and Organizational Routines', with Benjamin Coriat in *The Dynamic Firm: The Role of Technology, Strategy, Organization, and Regions*, Alfred D. Chandler, Jr, Peter Hagström and Örjan Sölvell (eds), 1998, 103–33; 'The Dynamics of International Differentiation: A Multi-Country Evolutionary Model', with Silvia Fabiani, Roberta Aversi and Mara Meacci, *Industrial and Corporate Change*, 3 (1), 1994, 225–42; 'Hierarchies, Markets and Power: Some Foundational Issues on the Nature of Contemporary Economic Organizations', *Industrial and Corporate Change*, 4 (1), 1995, 1–19.

Springer Verlag for: 'The Research on Innovation Diffusion: An Assessment' in *Diffusion of Technologies and Social Behavior*, Nebojša Nakićenović and Arnulf Grübler (eds), 1991, 179–208; 'Substantive and Procedural Uncertainty: An Exploration of Economic Behaviours in Changing Environments', with M. Egidi, *Journal of Evolutionary Economics*, 1 (2), 1991, 145–68; 'Norms as Emergent Properties of Adaptive Learning: The Case of Economic Routines', with Luigi Marengo, Andrea Bassanini and Marco Valente, *Journal of Evolutionary Economics*, 9 (1), 1999, 5–26; 'An Introduction to Evolutionary Theories in Economics', with Richard R. Nelson, *Journal of Evolutionary Economics*, 4, 1994, 153–72; 'On "Badly Behaved" Dynamics: Some Applications of Generalized Urn Schemes to Technological and Economic Change', with Y. Kaniovski, *Journal of Evolutionary Economics*, 4 (2), 1994, 93–123.

The University of Michigan Press for: 'Some Elements of an Evolutionary Theory of Organizational Competences', with Luigi Marengo in *Evolutionary Concepts in Contemporary Economics*, Richard W. England (ed.), 1994, 157–78, references.

Every effort has been made to trace all the copyright holders but if any have been inadvertently overlooked the publishers will be pleased to make the necessary arrangements at the first opportunity.

Innovation, organization and economic dynamics: an autobiographical introduction[*]

An invitation to select and re-publish pieces of one's own work is at the same time flattering and challenging. The reasons to feel flattered are obvious; the challenge is that one is forced to put some distance between oneself and all of one's professional path so far, and to ponder achievements and failures as measured against both one's own research programme and the ever-changing 'state-of-the-art' of the discipline or disciplines to which one has been trying to contribute.

The exercise inevitably involves some indulgence as regards autobiography, interwoven with the intellectual history of the 'invisible college' wherein one perceives oneself to belong. This is also the way in which I shall begin the presentation of the essays which follow. These cover a span of around two decades, from 'Technological Paradigms and Technological Trajectories' (Chapter 1 of Part I), published in 1982 when I was still a PhD student at the University of Sussex, to articles published almost contemporaneously with this collection, in 1999.

In this introduction I shall discuss some of the main ideas which unify – at least in my mind – the contributions presented, notwithstanding their apparent variety of theme. In doing so, I shall try to outline also the underlying research programme (admittedly still largely unfulfilled but, in my view, still promising and well worth a fight). At the same time, I shall flag some items which I consider of high priority on the agenda, and some major policy implications.

The selection of work included in this collection has been primarily based on its congruence with four broad themes:

- Part I deals with the theory of and evidence on the processes of technological innovation and diffusion, their determinants, procedures and effects at the levels of individual firms and sectorial dynamics.
- The focus of Part II is much more explicitly on behaviours and organizational structures in complex and changing environments persistently characterized by the emergence of technological innovation, and more generally, of new ways of organizing economic activities.
- Part III presents a general appreciation of evolutionary theories in economics. In many respects, it concerns the statement of the 'grand' research programme – as a few colleagues and I see it.
- Part IV covers different attempts to model, on those grounds, economic dynamics, nested in the twin processes of learning and market selection and microfounded on persistently heterogeneous agents.

    Finally, Part V deals with various aspects of the institutional embeddedness of economic processes – including the relationships between financial structures, governance mechanism and industrial dynamics; more broadly, the institutional foundations of behaviours and economic organizations; and some policy implications.

Coherent presentation of these chosen themes has forced me (with significant reluctance!) to leave out a few other works, including those interpreting the evidence about trade and growth patterns (see for example Amendola, Dosi and Papagni (1993); Dosi and Kogut (1993) and Dosi, Freeman and Fabiani (1994)); on development (see Cimoli and Dosi (1995)); on the evidence and theory of consumption and demand dynamics (Aversi *et al.* (1999)) and, more broadly, on learning in evolutionary environments (Dosi, Marengo and Fagiolo (1996)). Possibly another, future, collection?

A few of the ideas explored in the following essays (and indeed some others) are already contained, at least in a preliminary form, in *Technical Change and Industrial Transformation* (Dosi (1984)) where they are also used to interpret the first three decades of life of the semiconductor industry, itself at the core of the so-called 'microelectronics revolution'. I have decided not to include here anything from the book: it is a self-contained work which one might want to read in its own right, and so is *The Economics of Technological Change and International Trade* (1990), written together with Keith Pavitt and Luc Soete, which attempts to provide a relatively comprehensive, alternative interpretation of trade patterns (with some implication for growth in open economies) grounded on technological and organizational asymmetries among firms and countries.

Finally, somewhat similar considerations apply to *Technical Change and Economic Theory* (1988) edited by Chris Freeman, Richard Nelson, Gerry Silverberg, Luc Soete and myself. It represents the outcome of an exciting collective endeavour and my contributions to it are best read in that context.

Some autobiographical notes: the formative years

Leaving aside 'prehistory' (High School in the little town of my birth, Fiorenzuola, Italy, halfway between Milan and Bologna, and, for one year, as an exchange student, in Buffalo, New York) let me start with the graduation years at the State University of Milan.

Undecided between physics and economics, I finally opted for philosophy. This was in the early 1970s with the big post-'68 wave still at full flood in Italy, with political fervour mixed with a rather naive but enthusiastic feeling of collective omnipotence. And for those of us who did not need some new church – whether provided by various breeds of Marxist-Leninist, Maoist or Trotskyist – it was also a time of intellectual subversion and discovery. For sure, the intellectual debate was to a good degree influenced by Marxism, and so was the teaching, but (re-reading my early essays) I realize with relief that, even then, I tended to give credit to Marx as a social analyst (which he certainly was, outstandingly) and as a political utopian, rather than as a founder of a faith or, worse still, as the hagiographic figure of Eastern European dictatorships.

In those years, the course of studies was very much *à la carte,* which allowed me to span German classical philosophy, epistemology, the classics of sociology and political science, and also a fair amount of political economy. (Incidentally, this same type of study has allowed a good share of a whole generation to graduate without any defined skills – but this is another issue!)

Not long after my graduation, I decided I wanted to become an economist, for various different reasons. At an intellectual level, at least as I rationalize it now, the drive was to explore, so to speak *sub specie scientiae*, a few of the enormous number of conjectures and 'visions of the world' stemming from classical philosophy and from the multiple founding traditions in the social sciences. These traditions addressed fundamental topics, ranging from cognition to the very roots of human identity, the relationship between agency and structures, the forces keeping the social fabric together and those instigating change – that is, basically, anything worth studying in the social domain, often wrapped up in appealing, but highly metaphorical, language. At another, more operational, level, I believed that understanding how contemporary economies worked was essential in order to contribute to social change. (The judgement on the naivety and/or hubris of this is left to the reader!)

Throughout the process (of course much less clearcut than in this *ex-post* reconstruction), Michele Salvati has been a precious and valued mentor (and with him, among my teachers, I would like to mention also Giorgio Lunghini, Salvatore Veca and the philosopher Enzo Paci, and, among my marginally older colleagues, Cristina Marcuzzo and Giorgio Pizzuto).

The graduation thesis, on Keynes' *General Theory* and the 'Keynesian syntheses' thereafter is extremely naive on the grounds of any current standard but underwrites in a nutshell some ideas which I still believe in, with my only regret that I have not had the time so far to explore them more thoroughly. (On macroeconomics, see also below.)

After graduation, I had to serve in the Italian Army. Next I attended the ISTAO Master programme in Ancona, founded and guided with an iron hand by Giorgio Fuà. There I was introduced to many previously ignored topics (ranging from industrial accounting to the basics of econometrics!) and I also had the opportunity to cooperate (and compete) with fellow students such as Aldo Rustichini, Franco Peracchi and a few others, probably less known in the international economic *milieu* but demonstrating no less an academic performance.

Fuà carried with him the experience and wisdom of that group of European economists, including Myrdal, Svenilsson, Kaldor and Tibor Barna (later my supervisor at the University of Sussex), partly grouped around the United Nations Economic Commission for Europe, heavily influenced also from across the Atlantic by Kuznets and collaborators (including notably Moe Abramovitz). Fuà believed in an extremely sound discipline to economic analysis, first and foremost characterized by the identification of major *stylized facts*, that is, robust statistical, cross-sectional and longitudinal, regularities, at different levels of aggregation, in economic structures and dynamics. (If anything, Fuà placed himself in extreme opposition to the current *ethos* in economics, with his heavy scepticism if not outright hostility to formal theory.)

In the late 1970s graduates who were beginning to go abroad to pursue a PhD tended to privilege Cambridge, England, as a location, and the theory of value (and related areas such as the critique of aggregate neoclassical theory of capital) as topics. Important as they are, at the time these topics were overloaded with enormous ideological connotations – as if they were the magic bullets capable of upsetting the whole economic theory, by exposing its 'apology of capitalism', and further burdened with some annoying nonsense (such as endless discussion on the difference between the 'transformation' and the *trans*-formation (!?) of values into prices in Marxian theory, or the statement that I heard more than once that 'linear algebra is leftwing and differential calculus is rightwing'!). Incidentally, I do think that attempting a partial disconnection between the theory of prices and income distribution, on the one hand, and the theory of technology and consumer preferences on the other (as for example Piero Sraffa intended to do) is indeed an important endeavour. And I also think that Cambridge, England (for example J. Robinson, Pasinetti, Garegnani, etc.) was dead right as opposed to Cambridge, Massachusetts (that is, P. Samuelson and colleagues) in stressing the logical contradictions involved in writing, within the aggregate production function, a variable (capital) supposed to contribute to the determination of relative prices and income distribution (via its absolute availability and its marginal productivity), when the magnitude of the variable itself depends upon income distribution (since in equilibrium it ought to depend on the capitalization of the generated stream of profits). In fact, it is somewhat sad as concerns our discipline to see that nowadays nobody cares, everyone innocently writes down aggregate production functions and the new generation have not even heard of the 'capital theory debate'.

Well, even at the time, I thought that there was much more to political economy than value theory, and, while trying to choose where to apply in the UK, I came across a paper prepared by Chris Freeman for the OECD on technology, structural change and employment. I thought that the area was much more interesting and I applied to the University of Sussex (possibly a personal example of path-dependency, with small stochastic events bearing long-term consequences?). The decision drew the scorn of some Italian colleagues who did not consider technical change a serious subject for research ('we thought you wanted to become an economist and not a mechanic', I was once told).

At the University of Sussex, Tibor Barna – normally feared as one of the most demanding of professors – offered his supervision, and represented thereafter a powerful, albeit sometimes invisible, intellectual challenge, mixing rigour and a healthy dose of scepticism toward theoretical results *per se*. As a (would-be) economist, I joined the Sussex European Research Center (SERC), headed by François Dûchene, where I found as senior colleagues Geoffrey Shepherd, Dan Jones and Jürgen Müller. The participation there in the project on 'Industrial adjustment in the European Community' forced me to learn quickly about industrial economics and policies. That project also taught me how crucial it is to link case studies, institutional details and theory: it is a lesson too often neglected simply in favour of the latter.

I joined the Science Policy Research Unit (SPRU) only around 1980, but from the very start Chris Freeman has been for me a fundamental 'intellectual father' who introduced me to the economics of innovation and has remained a major source of inspiration. And he has always been for me a contagious example of enthusiasm for research and of moral integrity (I hope he has been contagious enough!). Chris is mainly responsible also for my choice of semiconductors as the industrial case study of my PhD thesis. In that line of research, I was forced to measure the adequacy of, and possibly improve upon, the existing theories of technological change, industrial organization and international trade in the light of the evidence from an industry characterized by spectacular rates of technological change, rapid turnover of leading firms (at least in the first three decades of industry life), wide international technological gaps even among industrialized countries and diverse public policies.

As already mentioned, Dosi (1984) is the outcome of those years of work, presenting altogether a relatively unified theoretical contribution and its application to the analysis of the semiconductor industry. (Needless to say, the neat way one presents theory and evidence in a book is not the way the former actually emerges: all that, in reality, came out of many more 'inductive' and messy iterations between the two!)

In any case, the 1984 book is well down the line of the story of that period. When I arrived at Sussex, even though accepted to the doctoral programme – without any course requirement – I felt the need to follow a good deal of the Master programme in economics (in fact, quite mainstream, solid and thorough) and to that I added a significant investment of my own. Whether I invested enough into the understanding of the achievements and limitation of standard theory is a question that I leave to the reader: certainly, it is obvious that I did not end up converted to it!

At the Economics Department I tended to get involved in heated but engaging and fruitful controversies with teachers and young colleagues, while at SPRU the feeling was much more that of sharing an ambitious interdisciplinary enterprise centred upon the understanding of the multiple facets of the processes of generation and diffusion of innovation, their implications for firms, sectors and countries, and the role of institutions (see especially Part I and Part V in this volume).

For this endeavour, SPRU provided a unique environment: unable to list all the inspiring friends there, I want to mention (in addition to Chris Freeman) Keith Pavitt and William Walker, among the more senior ones, and Mick McLean (who soon deprived us of his sharp mathematical intuitions to go and manage the magazine *Electronic Times*), Luc Soete, Luigi Orsenigo – with whom I developed in almost symbiotic fashion most of the ideas thereafter – and a growing Italian colony of researchers, starting with Mario Cimoli, Fabio Arcangeli and Luigi Marengo.[1]

Outside the University of Sussex, I had the good fortune to be called to long-lasting collaboration with the Science, Technology and Industry Directorate of the OECD, working especially on innovation, trade and international investment: the interchanges there, especially with François Chesnais and Henry Ergas, and with the large international community which catalyzed around them, have been another essential part of my formative years. The OECD was also the vehicle whereby I began to work with the late Franco Momigliano, one of the founding fathers of industrial economics as a discipline in Italy, and one of my unforgotten mentors. The collaboration with Momigliano partly overlapped with my continuing association throughout the 1980s with the Istituto Ricerche Sociali (IRS), Milan, headed at the time by Pippo Ranci: it was within one of their projects – coordinated by Fabrizio Onida and sponsored by Umberto Colombo, chairman of the Energy Agency (ENEA) – that I was able to complete my share of the book on technical change and international trade (see Dosi, Pavitt and Soete (1990)).

During the fieldwork for my thesis, I met in France Jean-Louis Truel, a fellow PhD student, who introduced me to a largely neglected French 'institutionalist' approach to industrial economics, which – albeit in sometimes loose ways – has been trying to address important issues such as the dynamic role of both commodity- and knowledge-flows across clusters of inter-related sectors (that is, what the French call *filiéres* and what, in a similar perspective in Sweden, Eric Dahmen has named *development blocks*), and more generally, the importance of the institutional environment in the interpretation of the particular patterns of competition and industrial change.

That was also the beginning of my 'French connection'. Soon thereafter, the encounter with Robert Boyer, Pascal Petit and my future co-author Benjamin Coriat induced increasing interconnectedness between my research agenda and the so-called 'Regulation' approach (see also Chapters 10, 12 and 17).

During my PhD years, a decisive encounter was that with Dick Nelson, which came about through Franco Malerba, at the time one of his PhD students at Yale, who was also working on the semiconductor industry. Franco showed Dick some of my early drafts and Dick was kind enough to invite me to visit him. The influence of Nelson and of Sidney Winter (whom I first met a couple of years later) on my own intellectual trajectory should be obvious to all readers of the essays which follow. When I came into contact with their work I was immediately fascinated by the evolutionary theory which Nelson and Winter had been developing as a major step forward in the establishment of an alternative microfoundation of economic dynamics, which, as I was seeing it at the time, could be a crucial complement to the much more 'structuralist' (basically European) approaches I was familiar with. This is also one of the themes underlying the whole 1984 book (Dosi (1984)).

To illustrate the point concisely, consider for example the interpretation by Sylos Labini (1967) of industrial performances (in terms of, for example, prices and profit margins): this is mostly done on the grounds of the technological structure of the industry itself (for example, size-related asymmetries in productivity) plus a simple and (sometimes questionable) behavioural assumption – that is, limit pricing. I thought then, and I still think now, that starting from the technological and structural conditions of an industry is a sound point of departure which also sets the boundaries to the range of possible behaviours which firms can undertake. However, within these boundaries aggregate performances do also depend upon what firms actually do. And, further, one should ask how those observed technologies and structures came into existence and how they change over time.

Clearly, the first issue has to do with the behavioural microfoundations, while the second concerns the determinants of dynamics. One way to handle the former focuses almost entirely on the consistency conditions amongst sophisticated strategic behaviours: as known, this is the thrust of the currently almost entirely dominant 'New Industrial Organization' approach. Conversely, evolutionary theory – at least in the version that Nelson, Winter and I share – attempts to handle both issues (the behavioural microfoundations and the determinants of the dynamics in technologies and structures) on the grounds of (i) much simpler behavioural representations of what agents do – partly reducible to organizational routines (for example, Nelson and Winter (1982), Cohen *et al.* (1996) and Chapters 5, 6 and 7 in this volume); (ii) no commitment to any *ex ante* consistency of behaviours (that is, no postulation of market equilibrium) and (iii) heterogeneous processes of learning – including of course technological and organizational innovation/imitation. This basic evolutionary story is expanded upon in Chapters 11 and 12 while three models in this spirit are presented in Chapters 14, 15 and 16 (see also Dosi (1992b) and Dosi *et al.* (1997) for comparative discussions on the current state-of-the-art in industrial economics).

A broadly similar story can be told concerning aggregate economic growth. Take as the point of departure the (non-microfounded) aggregate models of growth developed in the Cambridge (England) tradition, such as those of Kaldor (1957), Kaldor and Mirrlees (1962) and the ambitious vision of Pasinetti (1981). At least this was *my* point of departure. The reference for Nelson and Winter was much more directly the Solow-type tradition (see Solow (1957) and (1970)) which, I must confess, I was finding rather unpalatable due to its heavy inbuilt commitments to purported but undemonstrated equilibrating mechanism in factor markets and input intensities (see also the above hints on the 'capital controversy').

However, two alternative ways forward happened to emerge. The dominant one turned out, again, to build a microfoundation of some sort upon an increasingly sophisticated, and utterly mythical, 'representative agent' (or variations thereupon, such as those with overlapping generations dynamics).

Alternative microfounding endeavours build on more or less explicit 'evolutionary' roots, with heterogeneous learning agents and growth fuelled by endogenously generated technological advances (see the Dosi-Orsenigo chapter in Dosi *et al.* (1988) and Chapters 11 and 12 – for general statements of the 'evolutionary' perspective – and Chapters 17 to 19 for some models of growth in that vein).

Some theoretical digressions
Since the foregoing points hint at some very general themes that also cut across most of the following chapters and throughout my whole work, let me briefly expand upon a few.

Microfoundations
One of these themes, as mentioned earlier, concerns indeed the microfoundations of propositions regarding economic aggregates, and relations amongst them. Here, in a very broad sense, by 'microfoundations', I mean the reconstruction of the dynamics of micro constituents of a system (be they molecules, animals of a specie, consumers, firms, cells, etc.) which yield the dynamics of some aggregate variables of the system under consideration (which could be temperatures, features of biological populations, GDPs, etc.). Incidentally, note also that the issue of 'microfoundations' is in principle separate from that of 'micro intentionality', although obviously in social sciences the relationship between the two is a tricky problem. However, contrary to the prevalent opinion amongst economists, I think it is healthy to keep the two matters separate. As no physicist in a right state of mind would claim that molecules tend in probability to some energy state because by doing so they 'maximize their utility', so some partial decoupling might help also investigators of socio-economic phenomena (see also Chapters 12 and 23).

With no doubt, I share the idea that the quest for such foundations ought to be a central and ubiquitous task of the economic discipline (and social sciences at large): more on this in Chapters 12 and 23. However, this applies with some important qualifications.

First, the establishment of *non*-microfounded aggregate properties is a fundamental activity in its own right. After all, the identification of a good deal of 'stylized facts' – concerning for example growth patterns (see the already mentioned work by Kuznets (1966) and Kaldor (1978), among others, and in my own work, Dosi, Freeman and

Fabiani (1994)), or industrial structures and dynamics (see the works surveyed in Chapter 15, below) belong to this genre and are an important part of what we know about the economic system. And so are a good deal of major conjectures and propositions on how the economic system works: from Adam Smith on, for example, the relationship between size of markets, division of labour and productivity growth, to Marx (right or wrong) on the secular tendency toward increasing 'organic composition of capital' and falling profit rates, to Keynes and the early Keynesians on the relations between investment, income and growth (that is, the 'multiplier' and the 'accelerator'). Note, in this respect, that the identification of *non*-microfounded regularities has been, and is, a respectable activity also throughout the natural sciences. The law of thermodynamics, or the properties of modern chemistry indeed came much earlier than their 'microfoundations' (with the later works of Boltzmann, Gibbs, Bose and Einstein, among others, in the former case, and, more generally, with quantum theory in the latter).

Second, one should prefer no microfoundation to a bad one. Indeed, I consider in general bad ones to be those which derive the aggregate properties directly from the behaviour of one single ('representative') agent. By doing this, one in fact assumes an unwarranted isomorphism between micro and aggregate dynamics (sometimes with a misplaced appeal to some law of large numbers). In fact, it has been shown conclusively at both theoretical and econometric levels (see Kirman (1989) and (1992) on the former and Forni and Lippi (1997) on the latter) that aggregation, except peculiar cases, does *not* preserve microdynamic properties. In a sense, it is a vindication of the old adage that 'the whole is different from the sum of its parts'. However, that pernicious 'microfounding' practice has become, if anything, a must in current theorizing.

I remember that, as a student, one of the sources of my unease with 'old' Keynesians was the imputation of the purported aggregate regularities to an implicit representative agent characterized by 'money illusions', 'liquidity traps' and the like. But, in this respect, the arrival of so-called 'new classical macroeconomics' (and similar tendencies in other fields, including industrial economics) only made things much worse. The 'representativeness' assumption is kept and strengthened. Simply, earlier, some behavioural features of such an agent were (questionable) generalizations from casual empiricism and common sense. The current representative agent has simply lost any common sense behavioural justification and performs unbelievable hyper-rational forward looking exercises, which even top level PhD students in economics find hard to solve!

Incidentally, note also that considering only *average* characteristics over population of agents might censor a crucial link between the description of the state of a system and its dynamics in so far as the latter are driven by 'deviants' traits (innovation being a case in point) which in certain circumstances become self-reinforcing. For a germane discussion of the importance of *symmetry breaking* in evolutionary phenomena, see Allen (1988). Among the works in this volume, Chapter 8 discusses the experimental evidence on entry games, arguing that 'irrational' non-average behaviours might have a crucial role as entrepreneurial drivers of change, and a similar theme is re-appraised more formally in Chapter 19.

As witnessed by most of the works included here, the notion of 'microfoundation' which I have been trying to explore has to bear the discipline of a painstaking investigation of *what agents actually do* (in multiple domains, concerning for example innovation, imitation, pricing, entry, etc.). It is an epistemological strategy which finds noble advocates in contemporary economics, starting with Herbert Simon and the 'Carnegie approach', and including Jim March, Richard Cyert, Dick Nelson and Sid Winter, among others, but it still represents a sort of deviant minority within economics *stricto sensu*.

Micro rationality and equilibrium as the end of (theoretical) history?

In a nutshell, the point, mostly contained already in Herbert Simon's argument (see for example Simon (1976)) is the following.[2] Suppose that:

(i)   The 'world' in which agents operate displays some sort of 'ontological transparency' (a curious assumption, indeed, shared only by economists and theologicians, suggesting that the basic working of any environment is 'naturally understood' in the same way by all actors).

(ii) Inter-agent differences in such understanding can only be imputed to imperfect/incomplete information (imperfect information is ultimately a sort of 'noise' on the signals stemming from the world, whose structure, to repeat, is perfectly understood and shared; 'incompleteness' is somewhat more difficult to summarize since it is often the garbage bag in which economists throw anything that is 'more than imperfect').

(iii) Given the available information, agents obviously (?) know what they want (that is, the function that they intend to maximize), and conditional on the available information, *possess the algorithm to achieve their objectives*.

Under these circumstances, of course there is no need to know how agents actually think and behave. It is enough to know what they want and the information available to them from the world, and we shall be able to predict their response without empirical observation of either behaviours or even more profoundly, of their individual and collective cognitive processes, mechanism of deliberation, preference formation, problem-solving, learning and so on.

Here is a basic methodological divide. Some (very many indeed!) believe that the foregoing assumptions hold. Others believe that they are often rather far-fetched and, correspondingly, demand to know how agents 'think, feel and behave' in order to interpret the dynamics of any one socio-economic environment. But this requirement, which would win the approval of most psychologists, sociologists, anthropologists, etc., (and be considered a scientific challenge in its own right) is not very trendy in current economics.

I have often wondered why this is so and I must confess to my continuing intellectual bewilderment and sociological uneasiness among my peers. In fact my current understanding (sincerely hoping to be proved wrong!) is that there are two basic tenets around which a good deal of current theoretic endeavours are organized, namely *micro-rationality* and *equilibrium* (with the partial caveat that one might give up, *temporarily*, the former – in its grand forward looking form – if it is restored as a property of equilibrium itself, such as in many 'evolutionary games').

Having heard the story so many times, I think one might identify some sort of pattern in the defence of these two 'core assumptions' (call them MR and E) which end up totally shielded from refutation, *even in principle*.

The pattern of such an archetypical discussion goes something like this:

Step 1   'Theoretical approximations are obviously approximations but MR and E are not too bad in highlighting the fundamental features of both *empirical* micro behaviours and collective outcomes'.

Answer   (Easy at least concerning MR): just check all micro evidence on *systematic* departures from MR, also in trivially simple environments (see the growing literature from experimental economics, even leaving aside the established contributions from other cognitive/psychological/social disciplines).

Step 2   'The assumptions might be empirically inadequate concerning MR but they are still powerful shorthand descriptions of equilibrium (microfounded) properties' – that is, some more sophisticated versions of Milton Friedman's 'as ... if' conjecture.

Answer   Show some powerful selection dynamics leading to the postulated equilibrium properties. But on that there are mostly negative results. (Note that multiple equilibria as such are sufficient to de-link equilibrium from unambiguous predictions on behaviours. More generally on the weaknesses of the 'as ... if' assumption, see Winter (1987) and (1988). See also Chapters 5, 6 and 23 below).

Step 3   'Consider the models based on MR plus E as theoretical *yardsticks*, notwithstanding the implausibility of the assumptions'.

Answer   I really do not know what a 'yardstick' is. I increasingly hear such a notion as the ultimate epistemology of the practice of most of our economist colleagues (and especially of young ones). Here it is difficult to find an answer to what I consider as an awkward rationalization of what the profession does, based on a somewhat perverse mixture between normative and descriptive approaches. Every time I hear the 'yardstick epistemology', I think of, for example, someone coming along in physics with the 'general theory of gravitation' suggesting that '... apples have a natural tendency to fly up in the air' (the yardstick?), while any observation of, for example, apples falling down is just evidence of 'imperfections' which we should normatively correct. I cannot imagine any falsification of such a proposition, even in principle.

A few, even among my students, suggest that this is indeed the 'winning format' – at least with regards to the presentation of academic outputs. I maintain on the contrary that this is too close to a pre-Galilean style of intellectual inquiry, even when successful in terms of collective recognition and publication in leading journals.

Be this as it may, without the possibility of exploring here at greater detail the epistemology of current dominant trends in economics, let me just add few brief remarks on the 'seeds' of the collective process which led us to where we are. Consider the case of General Equilibrium.

When confronting the 'founding fathers' of the theory – such as Kenneth Arrow whom I also came soon to appreciate as a (sometimes conflictual) intellectual reference, a highly respected friend and undoubtedly a great *maitre-à-penser* – one appreciates the enormous challenge of developing an extremely spare, elegant, institution-free representation of a fully interdependent economic system.

My impression is that the hope of the 'founding fathers' was to build incrementally upon such barebone construction and to relax the more demanding hypotheses – concerning for example the distribution of information – and achieve results on stability, dynamics and so on. It is fair to say that such a construction turned out to be too fragile and ill-suited for such an endeavour. And one of the reasons (although by no means the only one) is the inability of such a paradigm to account for a fundamental dynamic factor such as technical change.

As Joseph Stiglitz puts it:

> The standard Arrow–Debreu model (the competitive paradigm) not only does not include (endogenous) changes in technology but its framework is fundamentally inconsistent with incorporating technological change. What is more, it is not just that competition is imperfect – that firms are not price takers – but that the form and nature of competition – competition to develop new and different products – is simply not well captured by the standard Arrow–Debreu model (Stiglitz (1997), p.140).

What is also interesting is that the founding fathers themselves (such as Arrow and Frank Hahn) are well aware of the enormous gap between the basic model (a yardstick?) and most empirical phenomena, but much less so are many practitioners of the discipline, who even go so far as to empirically estimate 'computable general equilibria' (which, I must confess, sounds to me almost an oxymoron, and keeps reminding me of the title of a seminar I happened to see advertised around ten years ago at UC Berkeley called 'Applied Heidegger'!).

Approximately similar methodological considerations apply to game theory in refinements and empirical applications.

There is a more general point here: a number of economic models remain in the epistemological limbo of 'yardsticks' because they tend to lack robustness even to minor relaxations of their most demanding assumptions. One possible way to face the problem is of course to keep trying in the 'incrementalist' vein. (For a balanced argument supporting this view by a sophisticated scholar working close to the mainstream of the discipline but well aware of its limitations, see Kreps (1990)).

There is also another, more radical, alternative which suggests on the contrary that major impediments to the development of theories which would better account for both micro behaviours and aggregate regularities are precisely the two core assumptions of 'rationality' and equilibrium. Consequently, this alternative tries to develop an interpretation of economic phenomena grounded on a characterization of agents – individuals or organizations – much more directly 'inductive' – drawing also from cognitive sciences, organization theory, social psychology, etc. Moreover, in terms of system dynamics, it tries to explain the evidence as the outcome of far-from-equilibrium interactions amongst heterogeneous agents. It is this perspective that one has tried to explore, develop and put to use in many of the essays in this volume. (More in Chapters 11 and 12 and in Part IV.)

The evaluation of how successful such an approach has been and how promising it is for a future research agenda is of course left for the reader to judge. In any case, I want to emphasize two points.

First, I took particular care in showing, within both empirical and theoretical analyses, that the abandonment of the MR and E assumptions does not mean that 'anything goes'. On the contrary, it demands even more carefully disciplined observation (which, it is fair to say, is often lacking in apparently more elegant 'equilibrium' analyses). By the same token, one of the purposes of including in this selection a few modelling exercises is also to dispel the prejudice that one cannot do 'hard' (formal) analyses outside the equilibrium format. Indeed, many novel and interesting properties can be explored – sometimes through analytical methods, more often via computer simulations – in this alternative prospective.

Second, notwithstanding the thrust of the whole argument so far, I would not like the reader to end up with the impression that I suggest that all the results obtained under the MR & E tradition should be discarded. On the contrary, I believe that one should just assess their robustness in the light of two questions, namely (i) in the examined phenomenon, is there some evidence that the speed of adjustment of agents to given 'fundamentals' of the economy is fast enough as compared to the change of fundamentals themselves, such as to justify the appeal to an equilibrium analysis? and/or, (ii) does an investigation under the MR & E mode tell us something which can be 'carried over' to circumstances where such assumptions were abandoned? So, to illustrate, I have a great appreciation for the results obtained by Joe Stiglitz, Bruce Greenwald and colleagues on the economic consequences of different aspects of the distribution of information. They are generally obtained in an MR & E world, but most likely they would apply *even more so* were these assumptions abandoned (indeed, checking formally the validity of this proposition is an interesting research challenge ahead). This does not seem to apply, in my view, to many results obtained by game theory applied to IO, and even less so, to plenty of works whose results depend on a little footnote on page 2 claiming, say, that '... without loss of generality we assume a quadratic utility function ...', while in fact it is on that little detail that the result stands or falls (the point has been made already long ago by Herb Simon, but with little effect on the methodology of the profession).

Back to the intellectual biography: the SPRU years and after

Most of the foregoing digression concerned theory and the ways in which I began to elaborate on it in the early 1980s and thereafter. However, throughout the 1980s SPRU was probably the biggest centre in the world studying jointly the process of scientific discovery, technological change, innovation, diffusion, their institutional contexts and many other facets of knowledge accumulation in contemporary societies. As such, SPRU was also central to a large and growing 'invisible college' of scholars. Paraphrasing Dick Nelson, the common endeavour concerned a better understanding of the 'anatomy' of contemporary systems of innovation, ranging from the organizational architectures fostering and/or hindering it in individual corporations to institutions and science and technology policies. In fact, what we were trying to do was to identify the patterns of technological learning, and, even more ambitiously, trace their determinants and constraints within both the characteristics of *knowledge bases* themselves and the socio-economic organizations supporting their accumulation and exploitation.

It is a persistently fascinating, far from completed, exercise which only in the 1970s and 1980s saw the establishment of firmer methodologies of inquiry and relatively robust interpretative categories and 'appreciative theories' (that is, 'bottom-up', history-based, theorizing: see Nelson and Winter (1982) for a discussion of such a notion).

Keith Pavitt in the introduction to his selected essays (see Pavitt (1999)), broadly referring to the same collective research endeavour, mentions in particular as major sources of inspiration, amongst the classics, the analyses of technological change by Adam Smith, Karl Marx and Schumpeter, and, among contemporaries, Chris Freeman's pioneering 'innovation studies', Nathan Rosenberg's '... historical studies [which] began to unravel the importance of both the socio-economic and cognitive factors shaping the accumulation of knowledge' (see Pavitt (1999), p. 2), and, nearer the theoretical side, Richard Nelson and Sidney Winter. I entirely share this assessment, except that I would like to add Keith Pavitt himself as a major intellectual leader. And I would like to acknowledge also the important role of Paul David, whom I first met in person only in the mid-1980s, and who has been an endless mine of extremely bright ideas, intellectually provoking and challenging about almost anything concerning the links between the interpretation of any evidence, the role of history in it all and economic theory. (In fact, I often disagreed with him, but, in any case, an effective 'acid test' for a new idea is to check it against his witty criticisms!)

The intellectual atmosphere at SPRU even in the 1980s (and, as I understand it, more so in the 1990s) was profoundly 'empirical', deeply committed to the 'inductive' search for and interpretation of the evidence (which I find an extremely sound attitude, if it does not turn into any sort of collective *ethos* against theory – which might happen if the dialogue between the two styles of inquiry is not continuously encouraged). For the empirical part of my PhD dissertation I was studying, as mentioned earlier, the microelectronic industry, but I happened also to be involved in research projects concerning machine tools, process plants and chemicals. Among my friends and co-authors there, Luigi Orsenigo was studying bioengineering and pharmaceuticals, and Luc Soete was dealing with several data sources regarding, among other issues, the relationships between firm size and the propensity to innovate, between technology and trade, and between technology, employment and growth. Moreover, partly out of intellectual curiosity and even more because of binding financial constraints, I accepted the job of starting (with Keith Pavitt, later joined by Pari Patel) the effort of reclassifying US patent data – which ended up in the so-called OTAF-SPRU patent classes. I hated every moment of it, but I must admit I also learned a lot, being forced to elaborate in my mind all sorts of very rough 'knowledge metrics' across different technologies and industrial sectors.

In fact, within SPRU (although fortunately not within the broader 'invisible college'!) the emphasis on the theoretical implications of what we were doing was almost entirely confined to the 'Italian gang' (myself, Orsenigo and, later, Cimoli and Marengo), Luc Soete and, in a different role, Chris Freeman who was always able to extract the theoretical punchline out of both esoteric pieces of evidence and cryptic formal models, even when they were well beyond his technical skills (I hope I have learned something from him!). Econometrics was the almost exclusive domain of Luc Soete and to a lesser extent myself (!), before the arrival of Pari Patel, Nick von Tunzelman and Ian

Fagerberg (whose work at the time would be considered, by current standards, as very 'applied' and relatively simple econometrics).

It was in this climate that, relatively early on, I produced the paper that turned out to be quite influential, 'Technological Paradigm and Trajectories' (Chapter 1 in this volume).

One way of reading that paper – together with the later one, 'Sources, Procedures, and Microeconomic Effect of Innovation' (Chapter 2), and also the chapter on technical change in Dosi, Pavitt and Soete (1990) – is in terms of some broader underlying questions on the nature of technological knowledge and its accumulation. Let me mention some of them, with some concise hints at the types of answers (or, at least research agendas) that I (we) were pursuing (and we still try to explore).

The structure and dynamics of technological knowledge
An obvious issue in the first place is *whether there is any meaningful way of interpreting knowledge and its dynamics in their own right.*

Pathbreaking exercises by economic historians (see Rosenberg (1976) and (1984), the fascinating reconstructions of the technological drivers of modern industrial development in Landes (1969), and more recent works, among others, by Hughes (1982), Vincenti (1990), Mokyr (1990), Basalla (1988)) and preciously rare economists (see, notably, the contributions of Chris Freeman (1982)) suggested that this was indeed the case. And I agreed, possibly influenced by my inadequate indoctrination in standard economics, so that I never came near to the automatic belief that a convex production possibility set is everything one needs to know about production, by a lasting ('ideological'?) dislike of anything resembling standard production functions and by my training in philosophy (if one dares investigating the dynamics of knowledge regarding relatively abstract physical and mathematics objects, why shouldn't one do the same about *technological* knowledge?).

Indeed, as most readers probably know, a fair share of the *paradigm view* of the technological change freely borrows from, builds upon and modifies Thomas Kuhn's interpretation of the dynamics of knowledge in the scientific domain. Note that for the purposes of my (our) work it is not especially relevant to know to what extent Kuhn was right about science (some scholars suggest that indeed that prospective might end up to fit better technological, that is, 'applied', rather than 'pure' scientific knowledge).

The bottom line of my view in any case is that, *first*, there are powerful restrictions on the dynamics of technological knowledge stemming from the internal structure of each specific knowledge basis which yield some proximate cognitive coherence in what applied scientists, engineers and practitioners know about their *problem-solving tasks* and also in the ways they search for improvements.

Second, and relatedly, one might hope to identify sorts of archetypical structures (that is, 'technological paradigms'), differentiated according to: (a) the type of knowledge they rely upon; (b) the procedures through which such knowledge bases are learned and exploited; (c) possible invariances in the structures of the artefacts they generate; and, finally, (d) distinguishable patterns in search heuristics.

The examples that I briefly mention in Chapter 1 should be taken just as hints over a much richer empirical variety. In Chapter 2, I try to provide some generalizations on the grounds of a wider evidence. Still nowadays, more rigorous and comprehensive explorations of the structures of diverse knowledge bases and patterns of knowledge accumulation continue to be, in my view, an exciting research route.

Let me also add some further incidental remarks. 'Technological paradigms' are meant to be sorts of *theoretical* 'ideal types' of knowledge structures, sharing, more generally, the view (emphasized in the partly different field of organizations by Oliver Williamson and David Teece) that theoretical interpretations ought to be fruitfully pursued also by means of the identification of *discrete types of structural forms*. However, since I do not like them to remain solely 'theoretical yardsticks', I would like to see, together, the empirical exploration of their basic distinguishing features and their dynamics. That is, *cross-sectionally*, is discretization helpful in understanding the differences in production and innovation patterns between, say, textiles, aircrafts and pharmaceuticals? And, *longitudinally*, are there major discontinuities in any one knowledge base?

Concerning the latter, a long-lasting argument between Keith Pavitt and I is a good case in point (sometimes we over-emphasize it on purpose!) with Keith stressing 'incrementalism' and I pointing also at the existence of significant discontinuities. Everyone agrees that, for example, going from thermoionic valves to transistors represents a major discontinuity in the knowledge bases of producers of electrical/ electronic components. This is also what I studied at some detail for my PhD and represents a vivid illustration of a 'paradigm change'. But how frequent are such circumstances? And, even if they were, how relevant are they for the patterns of knowledge accumulation in related sectors (for example, computers, telecommuni- cations, industrial controls, etc. in the case of the 'semiconductor revolution')?

Obviously, in the real world there is no pure paradigm discontinuity and also no pure, linear, incrementalism in knowledge accumulation. But, still, what is the likely distribution of the historical evidence along this continuum? (Indeed an issue bearing major implications for both corporate management and public policies).

The (circumstantial) identification of 'technological paradigms', or whatever other name is chosen (often their meaning, as proposed here, significantly overlaps with notions like 'technological regimes', 'dominant designs' and others) is likely to entail interdisciplinary efforts involving engineers, applied scientists, students of organization and business history, and (why not?) ethnographers and industrial anthropologists tracing the evolution and establishment of specific 'technological cultures'.

In the last resort, however, some social scientists might well find an exciting task in the very discovery of the processes by which persistently dominant forms of knowledge exploration and/or exploitation – and related institutional set-ups – happen to emerge. Others, on the contrary, might deem it largely irrelevant for their own scientific purposes.

In particular most economists would wonder about the relevance of the investigation of the details of the processes of technological learning. Why should an economist care about the details of individual cognition, organizational coordination, corporate competences, patterns of collective learning and so on?

Trajectories in technological learning
The answer, rather explicit already in the 1982 article (Chapter 1), which I have tried

to articulate and operationalize since then, is that the regularities and discontinuities in the dynamics over a knowledge space intuitively defined over a large number of elementary knowledge dimensions and problem-solving procedures also yield powerful consequences when detected in the (much lower dimensional) spaces of economic outcomes – *in primis*, input coefficients and output ('hedonic') characteristics. Stating the same in its negative implications: the foregoing features of knowledge accumulation might be generally in conflict with either the assumption of well-behaved production sets over which producers may ('freely') pick according to relative prices, or with the (more implicit) assumption that consumers, heterogeneous in their tastes, are choosing amongst products without normally facing major (and somewhat abrupt) constraints over the fulfilment of the desired combinations in their hedonic preferences.

On the contrary, the 'paradigm view' finds no surprise in that (to illustrate by caricature) China under President Mao in the late 1950s miserably failed in its drive to develop labour-intensive 'farmer-friendly' steel-mills, or, more generally, that it is so hard to find 'appropriate technologies' (whatever that means) in developing countries notwithstanding huge relative price differentials.

The idea of technological trajectories, tries precisely to capture all the above phenomena. Specific, and path-dependently augmenting, knowledge bases (that is, 'paradigms') yield relatively coherent patterns of change in input coefficients and techno-economic characteristics of output, in ways that might be to different degrees independent from changes in relative prices and demand patterns. Hence, understanding the patterns of knowledge accumulation is essential also to the understanding of what shapes and constrains economic interactions (more on it in Chapter 4).

Even in the early 1980s there was puzzling evidence in this respect (from a few economists – like Devandra Sahal – and some students of technology), strengthened since then by some more rigorous longitudinal analyses – such as those by Paolo Saviotti. Again, further empirical evidence is still quite welcome.

Note also that if 'paradigms' (in the domain of knowledge and learning dynamics) and 'trajectories' (as the dynamic outcomes of the former concerning inputs productivities and relative intensities, and product performances) apply, then one might be forced to re-think also the theory of production to which economists normally subscribe.

Illustrations
- What is the 'production set', if any, available to any one firm, in the short term? (Indeed, it is probably the degenerate distribution comprising only the technique the firm is actually using.)
- And, over all firms, at any given time, and for given relative prices, what does the distribution of techniques look like?
  (The standard prediction economists should make is that the mass is around the 'profit maximizing' technique, possibly with some noise. Our view predicts, on the contrary, distributions spread over a large support – covering also unequivocally dominated, that is, less efficient, techniques – whose shapes depend upon the conditions of knowledge accumulation and their asymmetries across firms.)
- And, dynamically, how do techniques change?
  (The simplest conventional approximation – literally following textbook General

Equilibrium theory, Solow-type growth models, Real Business Cycle theories and so on – is that they are subject to exogenous shocks, without any remarkable characterization in patterns of change. On the contrary, the paradigm/trajectory view focuses on those very processes of change, trying to identify knowledge-related constraints to the search dynamics. And it also suggests the likely emergence of dynamic increasing returns in the search process itself. See Chapter 4 and Winter (1982).)

Since the early 1980s, a lot of work has promisingly gone into the operationalization of the foregoing knowledge-centred approach to the analysis of production and innovation.

First, one has attempted to identify characteristic variables of each knowledge-base (and learning dynamics) suitable in principle also of empirical measurement. So, notions like *technological opportunities, appropriability, cumulativeness*, degrees of knowledge *tacitness*, etc. (see Chapters 2 and 15) help in identifying taxonomies over paradigms and trajectories and in drawing predictions on their economic implications.

Second, a conjecture that we begin to explore in Chapter 15 is that such taxonomies of learning processes map also into diverse processes of industrial change and different industrial structures.

Third, the approach straightforwardly links with complementary analyses of the diverse institutions and organizational mechanisms governing the generation and diffusion of new knowledge, from public research laboratories to intra-organizational learning (see, among others, Freeman (1982), Nelson (1993), and (1996), Lundvall (1992), Pavitt (1999)).

These themes are repeatedly touched upon throughout the first section of the following essays, but, admittedly, a fully fledged theory of production in this perspective is still to come (for promising hints, see Winter (1982), Iwai (1984a, 1984b), Metcalfe (1998) and parts of Nelson and Winter (1982)).

A final incidental remark on 'paradigms' and related concepts. As it should be clear from the chapters that follow, I use such notions with a rather micro-technological meaning – the empirical reference being specific problem-solving activities and knowledge bases, such as, for example, synthetic chemistry, thermoionic valves, recombinant DNA bioengineering and semiconductor-based microelectronics. It happens that roughly in the same period, Chris Freeman and Carlota Perez proposed a notion of *techno-economic paradigms* which tries to capture broader, much more 'macro', regularities over technologies and over phases of economic development – for example, 'early mechanization', steam power and railways, electrical and heavy engineering, information and communication technologies, etc. (Freeman and Perez (1988)). It is impossible to discuss here the precise relationships between the two notions. This is just a *caveat*: let us keep them distinct since they entail different observational objects and levels of analysis.

Information, knowledge and incentives

A major theme cutting across several chapters below is whether 'knowledge' is equivalent to sheer information. As I shall argue in a short while, I believe that this is not generally the case. However, even neglecting for the time being the knowledge/information distinction, a fundamental aspect of the foregoing discussion on paradigms etc. (explored at length especially in the first two Parts of this book) is, to repeat, that the structure of knowledge and its dynamics ought to be an object of analysis in its own right, since it displays specific procedures and patterns which are not reducible just to 'responses' to whatever incentive structures.

In many respects the question overlaps with the issue of the extent to which one can understand how the economic system works solely on the grounds of the mechanism governing resource allocation, distribution, and accumulation. In fact, the issue entails a profound divide within economic theory which goes back all the way to the origin of the discipline.

Interestingly, among the classics one finds side by side the threads of the two stories, which in the current jargon could be taken to correspond roughly to (a) the theory of allocation, relative prices, etc., given the 'fundamentals' of the economy (endowments, preferences, technologies), versus (b) the theory of changes in the fundamentals themselves. So for example in Adam Smith and Karl Marx one has theories of value which pertain to the former and elements of theories of technological dynamics belonging to the latter. Concerning this latter domain, see, for example, in A. Smith, the famous pin factory parable or his quasi-sociological emphasis on the role of both learning-by-doing by 'practical men' and more theoretical advances by 'philosophers' (see also the re-appraisal by Pavitt (1998)). Or see in Marx the long and detailed analyses of the expropriation of knowledge from the workers and its incorporation into machinery as a major source of productivity growth and secular increase in the 'rates of exploitation'.

In a different vein, an analogous divide distinguishes Schumpeter's analysis of the innovation process (in fact, identified a bit too easily in his early works, with 'entrepreneurial creativity') as opposed to the purported powers of some Walrasian allocation process, given the new 'fundamentals'.

Amongst contemporary scholars, for an extreme illustration of the foregoing dichotomy, compare the contributions on growth theory by Luigi Pasinetti and those by Robert Solow and the ensuing tradition. Both focus upon the determinants of long-term growth patterns and both are in some sense equilibrium analysis (Solow's ones straightforwardly are such, but also Pasinetti mainly studies the conditions allowing some sort of 'super-golden-age' growth path: see also the review of Pasinetti (1981) in Harris (1988)). However, Pasinetti's perspective censors all the allocative and incentive-related aspects and entirely focuses upon highly stylized learning patterns, on the supply side, and 'anthropologically' shaped demand patterns. Conversely, the Solovian approach tries to squeeze everything one can (and more!) out of the optimal allocation process blackboxed in the aggregate production function, leaving technical progress to the famous 'residual'.

Indeed, a good deal of contemporary research concerning, loosely speaking, 'the sources of change' goes under the broad heading of the 'economics of information', whose seminal contributions feature, from diverse angles, the works of Arrow and Simon, include several works by Stiglitz and colleagues, and – in different perspectives – by Masahiko Aoki, George Akerlof, Leo Hurwicz, Roy Radner and many others. In short, the 'economics of information' impinges upon the drivers of dynamics in so far as it studies the role of specific institutional set-ups in the generation, distribution and economic exploitation of new 'information'.

In a narrow sense, also 'new-growth' theories take on board some, albeit very simple, properties of 'information' which distinguish them from 'normal' commodities: for example, information can be indefinitely re-used without depreciation, it can be utilized in non-rival ways by multiple agents and it is likely to be produced and augmented under conditions of increasing returns.

Indeed, I do believe that the whole domain of analysis of 'economics of information' has yielded some of the most important results in recent economic theorizing, especially when enriched by an explicit attention to the different institutional contexts in which information is generated and exploited. And it also has major overlaps with the perspective underlying the essays that follow (witness also Chapter 22, below, co-authored with Masa Aoki). Note also that many other economic implications of information-rich economies still wait to be theoretically analyzed.

As Arrow (1996) emphasized, 'it is surprising to find how poorly current theories apply to the situation of high fixed costs which arises when information acquisition becomes a major part of a firm's activity' (p. 646), with major unresolved consequences also for the theory of pricing and competition, when conducted under large fixed cost (p. 652), and for the analysis of information distribution and acquisition across multiple firms.

However, I also believe the study of the informational properties of specific institutional set-ups – important as they are – go only part of the way in building a bridge between the processes of allocation and the processes of learning.

There are two crucial issues here.

The first one addresses precisely the question posed at the beginning of this paragraph, namely, can one reduce knowledge to information? And, second, how responsive is knowledge accumulation to the incentive structure usually assumed to be associated with microeconomic decisions on resources allocation?

The distinction between knowledge and information is indeed one of the themes running through most chapters in Parts I and II and it is explored further in Dosi (1996) and Dosi, Marengo and Fagiolo (1996). As one argues at greater length in these works (upon which the following paragraph draws), information entails well-stated and codified propositions about (i) states-of-the-world (for example, 'it is raining'), (ii) properties of nature (for example, '... A causes B ...'); (iii) identities of the other agents ('I know Mr X and he is a crook ...') and (iv) explicit algorithms on how to do things. Conversely, *knowledge* includes (a) cognitive categories; (b) codes of interpretation of the information itself, (c) tacit skills, and (d) search and problem-solving heuristics irreducible to well-defined algorithms.

So for example, the few hundred pages of demonstration of the Fermat's last theorem would come under the heading of 'information'. Having said that, only some dozen mathematicians in the world will have adequate *knowledge* to understand and evaluate it.

Similarly a manual on 'how to produce microprocessors' is 'information', while knowledge concerns the pre-existing ability of the reader to understand and implement the instructions contained therein.

Moreover, in this definition, knowledge includes tacit and rather automatic skills like operating a particular machine or correctly driving a car to overtake another one (without stopping first in order to solve the appropriate system of differential equations!).

Finally, knowledge includes 'visions' and ill-defined rules of search, like those involved in most activities of scientific discovery, and in technological and organizational innovation (for example, proving a *new* theorem, designing a *new* kind of car, figuring out the behavioural patterns of a *new* kind of crook that appeared on the financial market).

In this definition, knowledge is to varying degrees tacit, at the very least in the sense that the agent itself, and even a very sophisticated observer, would find it very hard to state explicitly the sequence of procedures by which information is coded, behavioural patterns are formed, problems are solved and so on.

From this perspective, learning has three inter-related meanings.

First, rather obviously, it might involve, as in the conventional view, the acquisition of more information (conditional on the ability of correctly interpreting it).

Second, it entails various forms of augmentation of knowledge *stricto sensu* (which might well be independent from any arrival of new pieces of information).

Third, it might concern the articulation and codification of previously tacit knowledge (learning here involves, so to speak, 'knowing better what you know').

These features of knowledge, together with the specific characteristics of *technological* learning discussed earlier, imply also the *non-reducibility* of knowledge accumulation to a sheer matter of incentives and resource allocation. Rather, two themes lurking within several essays that follow – especially from Parts I, II and V – are those of (a) the *complementarity* between learning and accumulation of physical assets, and (b) the *co-evolution* between organizational and technological competences, on the one hand, and incentive structures, on the other.

Note that the former implies also the inseparability of the contributions to the growth among supposedly different 'factors'. The latter means also that allocative incentives are likely to be endogenous to the very process by which individuals, corporate organizations and other institutions augment and change their problem-solving competences. Unfortunately, yet again, all this appears to be at odds with the main thrust of a good deal of contemporary theory, eager to reduce learning issues to a matter of equilibrium resource allocation by extremely sophisticated, farsighted agents, in environments wherein learning opportunities are innocently supposed to be uniformly responsive to incentives to search. That is, putting it bluntly, not only 'money can buy everything', but also there is a basic equivalence among the notional 'supply functions' (?) of energy-saving cars, cures for AIDS, proofs of the Fermat's last theorem and so on.

This basic philosophy clearly applies to the case of those new growth theory models attempting to squeeze the Solovian 'residual' into a sort of 'meta-production function' incorporating knowledge as an intermediate (sometimes proprietary) input. And it obviously applies also to the case of many IO models dealing with technological change (for example, 'patent races' and R&D games). The essays in this volume attempt to explore a quite different route: at different levels of analysis – from the microeconomics of problem-solving knowledge and organizational competences (Parts I and II) all the way to the institutional embeddedness of economic behaviours (Part V)

– one fully acknowledges the irreducibility of the entire interpretation of economic dynamics solely to an incentives/allocation problem and correspondingly tries to give operational meaning to the notions of complementarity and co-evolution mentioned earlier. (This is also one of the distinguishing features of evolutionary accounts of aggregate growth as compared to New Growth Theories: more on that in Chapters 18 and 19; Dosi *et al.* (1994) and Nelson (1998).)

The route is still largely unexplored: in this respect, take the works that follow as a part of a painstaking beginning. Fundamental sources of inspiration include Herb Simon's path-breaking inquiries into the nature of problem-solving activities and, even earlier, von Hayek's fascinating conjectures on the distribution of knowledge in the economy, but a thorough understanding of how 'knowledge-intensive' economies work is far from achieved.

The (gradual) return to Italy and the 1990s

When in Brighton (UK), I always enjoyed a love-hate relationship with the place, but I guess I never meant seriously to pursue my professional future in England (in that, helped by the risk-aversion of the SPRU administration at the time). So, after the doctoral degree, I took up a post of 'ricercatore' in economics (more or less assistant professor, badly paid but tenured) at the Faculty of Architecture and Urban Planning in Venice, while keeping a part-time Fellowship at SPRU. However, in between (late-1983), I happily accepted an offer of a six-month's visiting professorship at the Federal University of Rio de Janeiro.

Rio (after five years in England!) was a badly needed culture shock, but has also been a precious intellectual and political experience which greatly sharpened my interests in many of the already mentioned issues such as the institutional embeddedness of economic process, and the coupled dynamics between knowledge accumulation, incentive structures and political institutions. Clearly, the South American record shows that something went wrong in that whole process, but the diagnosis is much harder.

The lenses through which many of my new colleagues were reading the situation at the time were heavily influenced by that variegated school of 'structuralist' political economists of development, including, among others, Gerchenkron, Prebish, Hirschman, Myrdal and Nurske. I felt then, and I feel now, a lot of sympathy for the basic ideas, notwithstanding some grand naivety on technological change and political processes and a disappointing lack of any theory of (yes!) microeconomic incentives. Some of the reflections on development presented in Cimoli and Dosi (1995) have been indeed influenced by that and subsequent visits to Brazil, Argentina, Mexico and Chile. (And in that connection I found a few long-lasting friends: among them, those who had the greatest influence on my thinking have probably been Fabio Erber – my first intellectual mentor in Brazil – Alejandra Herrera, Jorge Katz and Mario Possas.)

I just regret not having devoted far more time and effort to development topics. They are crucially important as such and for the related policy implications. And more so, given that for a couple of decades, I have had the continuing feeling of moral outrage *vis-à-vis* a conventional international wisdom that keeps obsessively repeating – no matter what the problem is – that the magic cure is '… more markets, more blood, more tears …'.

In 1987, I won a full professorship in Italy and, somewhat unexpectedly, I was called to a position in Rome. The Faculty of Statistics of the University 'La Sapienza', and the Department of Economic Sciences largely overlapping with it, were and are one of the best teaching and research institutions in Italy. In the domain of economics it lists scholars like Amendola, Lippi, Reichlin, Roncaglia, Spaventa and Sylos Labini (in strict alphabetical order!) – just mentioning those with whom I collaborated and/ or I fought the most – and a few others; and it provides a solid formal training for undergraduates (comparable with the best British and American universities). Teaching and undertaking research there for around a decade has been a consider-able challenge, with much of the impetus coming from my students who made me improve significantly upon a few formal skills necessary both to master the details of the state-of-the-art and explore some novel directions. Confining the list to those with whom I subsequently wrote scientific articles, let me mention Roberta Aversi, Andrea Bassanini, Francesca Chiaromonte, Silvia Fabiani, Giorgio Fagiolo, Orietta Marsili, Mara Meacci, Claudia Olivetti, Roberta Salvatore and Marco Valente – and many of them also appear as co-authors of the chapters that follow.

At the end of 1998, I left Rome to join the St Anna School of Advanced Studies in Pisa, largely lured by its Rector, Riccardo Varaldo, to construct an institutional environment able to form top level postgraduates and, together, support research with marginally less bureaucratic constraints than in the usual Italian university environment: so far with no regrets and a few dreams still to fulfil.

I shall return below to some other research themes cutting across my research work over the last fifteen years. First, let me just mention, however, some events starting with two that had, in my view, both major scientific and cultural significance, namely the Venice Conference on Innovation Diffusion and the book, *Technological Change and Economic Theory.*

The Venice Conference, put together in 1986 by Fabio Arcangeli, Paul David and myself, has proved, for many topics discussed in the essays below, a focal point of interaction among multiple research programmes, 'invisible colleges' and disciplines. A rather amazing four-day event brought together most scholars near the core of an emerging 'evolutionary' research programme – from Dick Nelson and Sid Winter to Chris Freeman, Stan Metcalfe, Gerry Silverberg, and Luc Soete, and many others; institutionalist economists from the French 'Regulation' approach – including Robert Boyer, Benjamin Coriat and Pascal Petit; but also outstanding economic theorists *tout-court* – first of all, Ken Arrow who contributed his insightful comments on innumerable subjects; regional economists and economic geographers; industrial economists and economic historians; business economists and political scientists. I dare say with some pride that the Venice Conference was a landmark event, firmly establishing the studies of innovation and diffusion on the map of multiple socio-economic disciplines.

The book on *Technological Change and Economic Theory*, edited by Chris Freeman, Dick Nelson, Gerry Silverberg, Luc Soete and myself, is much more integral to the development of a research programme organized around a few 'evolutionist' and 'institutional' ideas, but not less important.[3] Of course, not all pieces of the overall puzzle fit into the right place and many pieces are still missing. However, the book was meant as an ambitious attempt to move well beyond the boundaries of technical change and growth and to explore, in similar or at least mutually consistent perspectives, diverse areas such as the economics of organizations; the role of institutions in different 'phases' of economic development; the formal representation of boundedly rational behaviours; aggregation issues from 'micro' to 'macro'; the formal representation of innovation diffusion and evolutionary processes; and the economics of international trade and multinational investment.

Moreover, in 1990, at last, the book by Keith Pavitt, Luc Soete and myself on *The Economics of Technological Change and International Trade* was finally published. This tries to follow the whole thread of a story from the microeconomics of innovation to sector-specific and country-specific implications; to the determinants of absolute and comparative advantages in international trade; with some final suggestions on the consequences of all that for the stimuli and constraints to growth in interdependent economies characterized by persistent technological and institutional asymmetries.

Recent advances in 'evolutionary' theorizing

For a moment, I have been tempted to write that the 1980s were the decade of emergence of a fuzzy but ambitious 'evolutionary research programme', while the 1990s have seen the move towards its consolidation, refinement and expansion. However, the number and weight of the qualifications that such a statement would require are overwhelming.

First, there is not likely to be any exact sharing within the concerned community of what such a programme ought to be. And there are good reasons for this to be so: only *ex post* is one likely to reconstruct and, to some extent, rationalize what it is all about. A few close collaborators and I do have some ideas of what it is, presented in Chapters 11 and 12, but one should only expect a less than perfect sharing even by likeminded researchers. For the sake of illustration, this is likely to apply even to the invisible college which does put on an 'evolutionary' hat, from Geoff Hodgson to Gunnar Eliasson, from Horst Hanusch and colleagues to Ulrich Witt, from Dick Langlois to Jacques Lesourne, from Bart Verspagen to my close collaborators and friends Stan Metcalfe and Gerry Silverberg.

Second, and relatedly, the 'programme', at least as I see it – has been and is enormously enriched by contributors who would not particularly care to call themselves 'evolutionists' (from Paul David on the role of history in economic dynamics, to Michael Cohen and Massimo Egidi on problem solving heuristics and routines, to Buz Brock and Alan Kirman on the properties of decentralized markets, to Marco Lippi and colleagues on the econometrics of spatial and temporal aggregation. The list should be very long indeed.)

Needless to say, it is not the label that counts, but rather the fruitful convergence of a 'hundred blossoming flowers' – as the old Chinese saying goes.

The bottom line is that nobody knows *ex-ante* whether the ideas, conjectures or empirical generalizations presented in the following will end up as parts (amongst many more) of a relatively new theoretical construction, or, conversely, as one of the contributions that happened to stimulate more incremental progress within the incumbent one (or as wishful thinking colliding with the *status quo*?).

Come what may, it is also true that over the last two decades some notion of 'evolution' has begun to feature as a central concept in several current analytical perspectives. We examine some of them in Dosi and Winter (1998) (from which the coming paragraphs are partly drawn). In particular, there, we comparatively assess (a) *evolutionary theories of economic change* (ETEC), loosely in the genre pioneered by Nelson and Winter (1982), with some 'Schumpeterian' and 'Simonian' ascendencies; (b) *ecology of organizational populations* (EOP) approaches (see Chapter 12 for some basic references); (c) *evolutionary game theories* (EG);[4] (d) *artificial economies* models (AE);[5] and, (e) parts of that expanding literature on *adaptive learning* which is based on some evolutionary argument.

Notwithstanding the encouraging overlaps, emphasized also in Chapter 12, there are still quite a few difficult and controversial issues concerning the basic nature of evolutionary dynamics in the socio-economic domain. Partly repeating Dosi and Winter (1998), let me review some of them.

Small words versus open-ended dynamics

Evolutionary processes, in biology as well as in the social domain, clearly involve the emergence of novelty of various kinds along the evolutionary paths. Although novelties are constrained to some extent by past history, there is still ample room for unexpected emergent phenomena and surprises. But capturing this in models presents tricky modelling challenges.

Full-fledged evolutionary dynamics would most likely entail an endogenous explosion of the dimensionality of the state space explored by the system. As the complexity of functions and traits increases in biological evolution from unicellular entities to mammals, so it happens also in the socio-economic arena.

One possible modelling strategy for all this is to allow for a notionally infinite-dimensional space of search,[6] without being able to fully specify the 'laws of motion' over that space, except locally. But what might be the analytical objectives in studying such a system?

Clearly, there is by intended construction hardly any hope of finding some particular limit state where the system might end up – such a result would spell the failure of the attempt to capture the persistent emergence of novelty. Under such open-ended dynamics, one might aim at best to find some emergent regularities in the process itself, concerning, for example, the properties of emergent, metastable, structures; the temporal scaling of events – such as the 'punctuation' of (quasi) equilibria and major structural discontinuities;[7] and average dynamic properties such as rates of growth of some variables.[8] This is indeed the philosophy of a good deal of AEs, and is shared by a few ETEC models.[9]

However, EGs are in this respect located at the opposite extreme: they generally assume some closed and well-defined domain of exploration given from the start, allowing a rigorous characterization of the limit states of dynamics that primarily capture mechanisms of adaptation and selection over a *given* fitness landscape.

Ultimately, the appropriateness of the theoretical representation depends on the nature of the phenomena to be explained. The 'small world' is best suited to the interpretation of the properties of modelled environments where the rates of adjustment to given 'fundamentals', for example technologies and organizational forms (that is, to a given evolutionary landscape), is of orders of magnitude greater than the change in the fundamentals themselves (and thus in the selective environment).

Given the rate of technological and organizational innovation in modern economics, suitable targets would seem to be rare.

Limit versus 'transient' properties
Given whatever evolving system, what are the properties one primarily wishes to study? This issue overlaps with the previous point. Whenever one is pretty sure that adaptation is 'fast' compared to innovation, then one assumes that most empirical observations of the phenomenon at hand are close-to-equilibrium outcomes of the underlying adaptive dynamics: hence it should be *descriptively* fruitful to study the properties of the limit states of the dynamical systems that one models. Conversely, when the foregoing condition does not apply it might be of greater interest to study the *transient* ('disequilibrium') properties of the system, knowing that its fundamental parameters will be shocked well before it reaches anything approaching an equilibrium. This is indeed what most ETEC and AE modellers do.[10]

It seems to us (at the very least to Sid Winter and myself!) that the EG methodology too often subscribes cavalierly to the former assumption. And sometimes it does worse than that: it starts from some equilibrium notions which have 'nice' properties from the point of view of economic theory (for example because they correspond to micro-behaviours that can be supported by standard 'rationality' assumptions) and then searches for dynamical processes able to generate them. And, at bottom, it rests on unquestioning faith in the view that economic rationality is the only viable approach to understanding behaviour in the specific case – as distinguished from the less doctrinaire view that the rationality assumption is sometimes a fruitful approach.

More to the point, however, a general issue concerns what can we learn from the characterization of the asymptotic properties of the system about its finite-time behaviours. In some cases, empirically interesting propositions may be derived from the rates-of-convergence properties[11] since the latter allow to infer, loosely speaking, how 'similar' the finite time (disequilibrium) observation is going to look as compared to the limit prediction. However, even assuming a qualitatively correct dynamic model, empirically relevant conclusions on this point cannot be derived from purely analytical studies of convergence; the quantitative magnitudes always matter. It is also one of the points in favour of simulation modelling in that it offers the opportunity to explore the quantitative convergence behaviour of the model experimentally, drawing on rough evidence or intuitions concerning parameter magnitudes. (See also below.)

Interaction dynamics and selection
A minimal requirement, common to different genres of evolutionary approaches, and shared with a vast class of models of decentralized economies,[12] are microfoundations involving a large number of interacting agents. This requires the specification of (a) the *levels* at which interaction occurs (for example, does it concern product-market competition? Behavioural imitation? Mutual technological learning?); (b) the *mechanism of interaction* (who can do what to whom, when, and under what types of rules?); and, possibly, (c) some *topology* over which agents are distributed, which may shape also the actual interaction process (for example, by making interaction probabilities dependent upon some distance in an appropriately defined space).

As mentioned earlier, complete evolutionary models of economic change ought to account explicitly for the joint dynamics of learning and selection. Ideally, one should specify the 'physics' of interaction in both domains, together with the ways they are dynamically coupled. This is yet another item high on the research agenda, but actual practice typically remains well short of that ideal.

In many models, either learning or selection is bracketed, which as such is not necessarily a bad intellectual strategy since it allows exploration within some sort of 'reduced forms', the properties of single dynamic processes, holding the rest constant. So, for example, several models of stochastic, decentralized, adaptive economic agents – but without explicit market competition – offer very useful insights into the collective outcomes of mutual adjustments by boundedly rational agents. In a similar spirit, so do various models of innovation diffusion with heterogeneous agents increasing returns and/or network externalities, and sequential adoptions.[13] Within a distinctly different modelling style, also most AE models focus upon the collective properties of adaptive interactions (for example, in the simplest cases, some rudimentary forms of local learning). Nearer the ETEC philosophy, in Chapter 19 one studies the properties of a reduced form of evolutionary model wherein, absent any form of market competition, the whole dynamics are driven by decentralized activities of technological exploration, learning and imitation over a notionally unbounded opportunity space.

At the opposite extreme, quite a few models explore the properties of selection dynamics driven by competitive interactions in the absence of any explicit micro learning (see most EOP models). Within the ETEC perspective, among others, Metcalfe (1992), (1995) and (1998) refines the Fisher Law, originally developed with reference to populations in biology,[14] and insightfully applies it to industrial dynamics. See also Winter *et al.* (1997) and Chapter 16, which study some generic properties of market selection fed by the persistent arrival of technologically heterogeneous entrants, as compared to those more specific to particular learning dynamics by entrants themselves.

EGs, too, rely extensively upon selection dynamics of some sort. However many models in this perspective appear to fold together properties of population dynamics and properties involving, at least implicitly, some form of adaptive learning at the level of micro entities (see also below).

As Sid Winter and I see it, the basic shortcoming of most current modelling of interaction mechanisms does *not* concern the *ceteris paribus* assumptions typically made (to repeat, a possibly healthy style of preliminary exploration). Rather, our concerns primarily relate to the general lack of any disciplined mappings between theoretical constructs on interaction processes and empirical 'stylized facts' on those very processes.

Consider competitive selection dynamics. Most of us, practitioners in the economic discipline, have utilized on several occasions some blackboxed representation of an aggregate 'interaction law', be it, for example, an aggregate demand curve or a replicator dynamic of some sort. So, for example, in Nelson and Winter (1982) interactions in the product markets are compressed into an unmodelled market clearing process involving a standard demand curve. In turn, the outcome of that collective interaction feeds back upon the growth possibilities of each individual entity (and thus operates like a selection device) via the gross surplus each entity is able to invest, determined by the difference between the industry-wide price and firm-specific unit costs. Similarly, in other models, such as Chapter 14, selection is explicitly modelled via a replication dynamic, defining the 'law of change' in market shares as a function of the 'competitiveness' of each firm as compared to the industry average.

The point to be emphasized here is that it might be time to go beyond such 'black-box' assumptions on collective dynamics starting from an explicit account of the 'microphysics' of market interactions. This is indeed a challenge that has been powerfully brought to evolutionary modelling by the AE methodology, with its abhorrence for pre-defined 'laws of motion' and its emphasis on explicit rules for 'local' interactions among micro entities (see also Fagiolo (1998)).

I have already mentioned the connection between the AE modelling endeavours and some impressionistically defined 'Santa Fe philosophy'. As readers might guess, it refers to the Santa Fe Institute, New Mexico, founded by an extremely distinguished interdisciplinary group of scholars, from physics, biology, mathematics, economics and computer sciences, whose mission includes prominently the understanding of 'complex' phenomena in both natural and social domains, most often emerging from non-linear interactions among the constituent parts of the system under consideration.

Throughout the last ten years by lucky chance I repeatedly visited the institute and engaged in challenging, often cross-disciplinary, exchanges (at the very least, I would like to mention in this connection Ken Arrow, Brian Arthur, David Lane, Buz Brock, Steve Durlauf and John Geanakoplos as inspiring hosts in and around the economists' camp, and also Phil Anderson, Murray Gell-Mann, John Holland, Stue Kauffman, Jim Pelkey and especially Walter Fontana, from other disciplines).

One – out of quite a few – precious research paths that I came to appreciate has been the search for some relatively invariant 'orderly' features of complex dynamic processes typically crawling far from equilibrium (echoing in that similar suggestions by Ilya Prigogine and his numerous collaborators).

Another (somewhat more controversial) path has been the methodological urge to search for these invariances by means of the most 'reduced form' representation of the environment to be explained, stripped down as much as possible of its 'phenomenological' specificities. I do believe this is a challenge worth facing, which might well yield to the discovery of robust statistical and morphological invariances holding across diverse disciplines (Pareto/Zipf laws in the distributions of whatever entities one is measuring? Self-organized criticalities in the system dynamics? The obiquitous appearance of 'order on the edge of chaos'? Or, even more fascinating, emergence of 'higher level', self-sustained, structures out of 'lower-level' interactions?).

Granted all that (which is very much indeed, and still largely unexplored), I maintain that there continues to be a vast domain of phenomena which are context-specific, and, thus also require 'phenomenological' details to be properly understood. So, back to my earlier point, even if one were able to identify some generic properties of decentralized market interactions (already a daunting task!), one would still like to know how specific classes of interaction processes affect the detailed patterns of outcomes.

This in turn implies taking much more seriously the question of *how markets work*:[15] for example, what are the effects of the institutional architectures of particular markets upon the ensuing collective dynamics? How do they affect selection processes? In what circumstances, is something like a replicator dynamics a good approximation of collective selection patterns?[16]

A distinct, albeit overlapping, issue concerns the dimensions over which selection occurs. In the economic arena a fundamental dimension has obviously to do with output prices, but what about the non-price dimension of competition?[17] This is another domain where evolutionary modelling can be substantially enriched by empirical investigations into the actual determinants of competitiveness in different industries and under different institutional settings.

More generally, as argued in Chapter 11, and in Tordjman (1998), selection in the social arena – and its relationship with some notion of 'fitness' – must confront the question of the endogeneity of the selection criteria themselves.

Also in biological sciences what is selected (in favour or against) is likely to be determined in some complicated and non-linear way by the distributions of actual populations present at a point in time and by their history. However, one might still hold that the selection *criteria* (for example, the reproduction abilities or the food processing efficiencies) remain relatively invariant. On the contrary, this might not be so in many socio-economic circumstances: that is, not only is one likely to find 'dancing' fitness landscapes, but also the dimensions of the space over which such landscapes are defined are likely to change, too.[18]

What is conserved in the evolutionary process? And how?

A general feature of evolutionary interpretations of change (in biology but also in economics) is that selection ultimately operates upon a pool of 'fundamental traits' of some kind, also determining their probabilities of transmission over time. The common biological story is known: the 'fundamental units' of selection are the genes which shape the phenotypic characteristics of the individual entities upon which selection operates; inheritance is the mechanism of transmission; and selection by 'weeding out' over phenotypic distributions, affects over time the frequencies in the underlying genetic pool.

In fact the story is not so simple even in biology, and it is more complex still in the social domain. For example, one might lack a clear one-for-one mapping between the genes and their phenotypic manifestations affecting 'fitness' (for example, due to fitness-neutral genetic drifts). Or, one might often find forms of *epistatic correlation* (see Kauffman (1993)), so that different traits non-linearly combine in order to yield a particular environmental fitness.[19]

Further peculiarities are specific to the socio-economic domain (see Chapters 11 and 23, Winter (1987) and (1988)). First there is, and *rightly* so, much more ambiguity in the identification of what the 'fundamental units' are. Good candidates – depending on the problem at hand – are routines, technologies, organizational forms, behavioural patterns or even 'mental models'. Second, technologies, behavioural patterns and so on can be improved and modified over time in quite 'Lamarkian' fashions. Third, 'inheritance' takes diverse meanings. In some circumstances, the biological meta-phor on inter-generational transmission is not too much off the mark. In others, it should be mainly read as 'social imitation'. Yet, in others, there is no proper 'in-heritance' but rather the indefinite perpetuation (and possibly growth over time) of the 'phenotypic' expression of the underlying traits: this is the case of industrial evolution, where, at least in part, the frequency of particular technologies or organizational forms grow, shrink or die together with the organizational entities embodying them.

Finally note that, in biology – and even more in economics – the objects over which selection is exerted are not single elementary traits but structures of much higher dimensions in which they are nested. So, for example, markets choose relatively complex products or technological systems – not individual elements of technological knowledge. Therefore, even after assuming some underlying space of technological and organizational traits as the appropriate 'primitive' dimension of evolution, one still needs some interpretation of organizational development in order to relate 'evolution' and 'selection'. Putting it another way, one needs a much better grasp of the relationships between the 'genotypic' and 'phenotypic' level: this is so in biology and it is certainly a priority in economics. And this is also a major area of complementarity between evolutionary theories on the one hand, and business economics and experimental psychology, on the other.

Here let me just mention two points.

First, notions like those of 'organizational routines' and 'competencies' begin to forge that link, building on an ETEC perspective, and exploring for example the way organizational knowledge is stored and reproduced within organizations, the nature and origins of routines themselves, and so on.

Second, note also that the genotype/phenotype problem tends to be neglected within the EGs perspective – at least so far. In fact the biological interpretation of such a link is straightforwardly a genetic populations dynamic. Economic applications are much more ambiguous, but one may reasonably understand them as defining dynamics on some metaphorically equivalent space of strategies (the 'fundamental units of selection'). Here 'selection', which has (at least in principle) a clear meaning in biology as an environmental pressure toward/against the reproduction of particular traits, is taken to be equivalent to some payoff-driven pressure to adaptive learning by boundedly rational agents. As Larry Samuelson puts it

> I describe the forces guiding agents' strategy choice as 'selection' or 'learning'. I use these terms interchangeably, though the former has a more biological flavor, while the latter is commonly used in economic contexts; (L. Samuelson (1997), p. 22).

In a way this is like saying that there is a set of given strategies, and that agents 'climb' through them by means of some unspecified algorithm, which however, at least on the average of the population, yields results identical to genuine environmental selection operating upon different (pure strategy) types.[20] But ultimately this boils down to assumption that, one way or another, the 'selection landscape' in the black-boxed head of the agents is exactly isomorphic to 'true' selective ecology under which the whole population lives.

The distinction between selection and learning is, on the contrary, of paramount importance within the ETEC perspective, and certainly throughout the essays in this volume.

Selection, to repeat has to do with what actually happens to agents (that is at primarily *phenotypical* level) in terms of market share, profitability, survival probability and so on. Learning, loosely speaking, concerns what 'goes on in the mind'. However, once the idea that the latter is some mirror image of the former does not turn out to hold, even in very simple environments, then the obvious question is: what and how agents learn?

Learning in evolutionary environments
The issue is obviously too wide to be adequately handled in this introduction and even Chapters 5, 6 and 7 only begin to tackle it (see also Dosi *et al.* (1996) for a more extensive discussion).

Ultimately, the question concerns how agents (individuals and organizations) make sense of complex and changing environments and how they act in them. Different strands of 'evolutionary' thinking certainly have in common, as mentioned earlier, a hypothesis of some 'bounds' on agents' rationality. This should be taken just to mean that they are less omniscient than God (or than the local gods, the creators of the model at hand). However, there is not much agreement on where the 'bounds' are and what they imply.

Indeed, in Chapters 5, 6, 7 and 12 and Dosi *et al.* (1996), one argues *first*, that agents (including of course ourselves) are not only characterized by information-processing and memory limitations, but more fundamentally, by an intrinsic *competence-gap* concerning (a) the representation of the environment; (b) the problem-solving repertoire; (c) the detection of payoffs; and (d) the very nature of goals and preferences. Learning encompasses all four domains, and their co-evolution.

Second, as discussed in particular in Dosi *et al.* (1996), one is likely to obtain precious clues on such learning mechanisms by the observation of cognitive and behavioural patterns in circumstances which are not at all 'evolutionary' – the context is invariant and relatively simple, the payoffs are straightforward and the action menu is trivial – wherein, nevertheless, agents display systematic biases *vis-à-vis* the prescriptions of 'rational' decision making, as experiments have shown.

More generally, *third*, the evidence both on individual patterns of cognition/ behaviours and on regularities in organizational adjustments and learning should be considered as fundamental disciplining criteria for the micro foundations of evolutionary models.

At this level, the difference among alternative perspectives is indeed striking. At one extreme, ETEC models have attempted to represent agents reflecting some 'phenomenological' regularities, for example on pricing and R&D investment. At the other extreme, EGs – despite heroic simplifications in modelled environments – have almost entirely neglected an admittedly much more robust evidence from experimental economic and cognitive sciences. Indeed, Camerer's remarks that 'when game theory does aim to describe behaviour, it often proceeds with a disturbingly low ratio of careful observation to theorizing' (Camerer (1997), p. 167) apply equally to its EG version. As a case in point, compare Fudenberg and Levine (1998) and L. Samuelson (1997), on the one hand, with the experimental evidence discussed in Camerer (1995) and (1997), on the other. And even more striking, although more blurred, is the comparison between what modellers of Industrial Organization theorize (or prescribe?) and the evidence on corporate behaviours.[21]

As an illustration, consider the stimulating examples of interactions involving a strategic dimension, at least 'objectively' – irrespective of whether agents are aware of it and behave accordingly or not – presented in the path-breaking work of Schelling (1978). Certainly, the environments defining most of these games are *not* evolutionary in any specific sense: there is no dynamic in the 'fundamentals', there is a fixed menu of actions given from the start and fairly understandable to the agents; there is no replication dynamic of any sort. If there is a genuinely evolutionary part to them, it is in the way people come to understand such environments and develop their action repertoires – and Schelling offers precious insights and conjectures. Since Schelling's contribution, what have we learned in terms of *descriptive* theories? Certainly we have learned a lot about the structure, and implied incentives, of the interactions themselves by re-stating them in formal game-theoretic terms (but, in the view of Winter and I, at least, with rapidly decreasing returns from one refinement to the next of the equilibrium concepts). What else does one gain by postulating some variety of dynamics in the EG style? In fact, one suggests an implicit theory of adaptive learning. Whether it is sound theory or not depends, presumably, on the empirical check from the behavioural and cognitive disciplines. For example, do people actually learn via mechanisms that entail the self-seeking reinforcements postulated by most EGs? Roughly speaking, the experimental answer seems to be negative. Rather, as we argue at greater length in Dosi *et al.* (1996), a more promising avenue of research appears to be an explicit account of the nature and dynamics of *mental models* and *interpretative categories* through which agents make sense of the environment they are facing and adjust to it.[22] *A fortiori*, we suggest, this applies to fully evolutionary environments. But all that, in turn, demands *descriptive* theories of economic behaviours resting on empirically disciplined 'nanofoundations', taking on board the growing literature on the dynamics of cognition, 'reasoning', 'sentiments' and so on – at the individual level – and organizational behaviours at collective levels.

More than this, I strongly believe that one of the main research tasks ahead entails the development of microfoundations driven by the dialogue with experimental economics and cognitive sciences, on the one hand, and organizational sciences, on the other. Indeed, few of us have begun, at last, to move on the latter route (with an impressive lag *vis-à-vis* the early intuitions of Simon, Cyert, March), liberally drawing from the 'appreciative theorizing' of Nelson and Winter (1982) and trying to construct also some (admittedly still rudimentary) formalism for organizational 'knowledge' and learning (see among others, Marengo (1992) and, in this volume, Chapter 6). Conversely, the links between the overall perspective suggested here and experimental economics *plus* cognitive sciences appear *prima facie* enormously rich but remain a largely unexploited opportunity (with reference just to my own work, Chapter 8, Dosi *et al.* (1996) and Aversi *et al.* (1999) present rather timid inroads in this direction).

Increasing returns, path-dependency and evolution
The very nature of information, briefly discussed earlier, straightforwardly entails some form of increasing returns: the costs associated with its generation are basically upfront, sunk costs, while it can be generally reproduced and utilized at any scale with negligible marginal costs. This is so for, say, Pythagoras's theorem (whose 'production cost' was basically borne by Pythagoras himself) and it is also the case of engineering manuals, software programmes, etc. The distinction between sheer information and knowledge, introduced above, adds some qualification to these

general properties in that there might be significant costs associated with learning and decoding also notionally *available* information. (As in the foregoing examples, there is likely to be a cost in learning Pythagoras' theorem itself, in mastering a new software program, etc.). However, it remains true that knowledge is typically put to use under conditions of increasing returns, reinforced by the *cumulativeness* that learning typically entails (more in Chapters 1, 2 and 4). In turn, dynamic increasing returns tend to yield path-dependency (subject to the qualifications discussed in Bassanini and Dosi (1998a)): as generally in systems characterized by non-linearities and positive feedbacks, 'history matters' and the dynamics is likely to be affected by initial conditions and small stochastic events along the dynamic path (for a more thorough discussion, see also Bassanini and Dosi (1998b)).

This is a general property emphasized in the works of, among others, Brian Arthur (1994) and Paul David (see David (1975), (1985) and (1988), within a vast and imaginative production on related topics). Evolutionary environments too – at least the way I see them – tend to display path-dependent properties – associated, primarily but not exclusively, with knowledge accumulation, innovation and diffusion.

In the essays which follow, the path-dependency properties of evolutionary dynamics are addressed especially in Chapters 4 and 23; a general formalism – based on generalized Polya urns – is presented in Chapter 13; and path-dependency is also an outcome of other models of Part IV (see especially 14, 18 and 19).

Here let me add just a possibly redundant but important *caveat*. While non-linearities of various origins are likely to be a ubiquitous feature of evolutionary dynamics, the converse does not hold: the non-linearity of a system is not sufficient to qualify it as 'evolutionary'. To caricature the issue, spaghetti's cooking is a highly non-linear process, characterized by multiple phase transitions from cold to boiling water. However, one hardly says that one is 'evolving spaghetti' (!). In brief, in order to characterize a system as 'evolutionary', one ought to add also some forms of genuine novelty generation and collective adaptation.

Empirical investigations, 'stylized facts', formal theories: another methodological digression

In the foregoing paragraphs I have devoted a considerable attention to the formats, assumptions and formal methodologies of different, *lato sensu* 'evolutionary', theories because I do consider the formal exploration (that is, via analytical or simulation means) of basic theoretical propositions as a fundamental – albeit by no means exclusive – exercise.

This is witnessed also by the chapters in Part IV below.[23] As I see it, there are multiple reasons for that.

The first, most obvious (but, in my view, the least relevant) reason is a rhetorical one. Simply put, there happens to be a dominant language in the community whose neglect is likely to be paid in terms of peer recognition, visibility or even audibility to the others. As important as this social dynamic might currently be (which indeed it strikingly is!), I would not consider major methodological adjustments worth pursuing on the grounds of these considerations alone. Indeed, I have personally learned much more often from insightful case studies, 'appreciative' historical theories and humble statistical explorations than from sophisticated formal models. And I must also confess that, beyond certain reasonable pragmatic limits, I feel some sense of moral uneasiness watching plenty of (old and young) scholars adjusting for the above reason their style of inquiry and publication: To my taste, it is too close to the practices in the Soviet era when it was not uncommon even for mathematicians to start from the 'clever intuitions of Comrade Breznev'!

More to the point, second, I do believe that formalization is a powerful *disciplining device* which forces the analyst to extract some 'basic' elements from much more complex empirical objects and check for the coherence and robustness of the interpretation in the much simpler world of the constructed theory. This is not to suggest that all phenomena may or should be formally represented. On the contrary, in quite a few cases formal reduction might be either impossible or misleading. (For example I am not at all convinced that the imaginative efforts of an Italian colleague of mine to formalize Petrarch's poems in terms of frustrated oscillator dynamics add much to the understanding of the poems themselves! Similar considerations apply indeed to a fair share of models in economics). But the success in formalizing, in whatever way, an interpretative story might easily reveal the 'value added' of the theory itself.

Third, formalization – most often via means of computer simulations – might turn out to be particularly useful in the exploration of the properties of (loosely speaking, 'evolutionary') environments, typically characterized as discussed above, by positive feedbacks and non-linearities of different sorts. In these circumstances, the exclusive reliance on 'qualitative' intuitions by the analysts might turn out to be particularly poor, as most of us human beings are particularly bad in making 'thought experiments' over any multi-dimensional system especially when displaying some complex dynamics.

Finally, fourth, formalization is likely to be of crucial assistance in deriving empirically testable propositions, and, even better, propositions which might observationally discriminate across different theories.

Having said that, I also maintain that sound research can only be done through the painstaking dialogue between, so to speak, 'bottom up' generalizations – inductively building upon empirical phenomena – and 'top down' propositions – that is, more or less daring implications of inevitably 'abstract' theories. This is also the style of work that – admittedly with a lot of sweat, arm-twisting and efforts of translation across different methods of inquiry – Dick Nelson, Sid Winter and I tried to pursue with the project on 'Technological and Economic Dynamics' (TED) which I coordinated from 1993 to 1998 at the International Institute of Applied System Analysis (IIASA) (based in Laxenburg, near Vienna). In some ways it was a continuation of the 1988 collective book, but mainly focused on a few well-defined areas of research, namely:

(a) The formal representation of innovation diffusion processes with some forms of dynamic increasing returns (a field which had already seen some pathbreaking contributions by my deputy director and friend Yuri Kaniovski, developed together with Brian Arthur and Yuri Ermoliev: an overview, with some further results, is in Chapter 13);

(b) The nature and dynamics of organizational capabilities (see Dosi, Nelson and Winter (1999));

(c) The identification of the major 'stylized facts' (and their theoretical interpretation) concerning industrial structures and dynamics (see the special issue on these topics of *Industrial and Corporate Change*, 1997, and Chapters 15 and 16 in this volume);

(d) Some significant advancements in the understanding of the links between all the above, country-specific institutions and growth dynamics (and, on that, I must acknowledge the failure in producing so far any major research output: see also below);

(e) The development and computer implementation of a relatively user-friendly simulation environment, freely available on the Internet, able to lower significantly the 'access cost' to this form of evolutionary modelling for the community of interested researchers, and, at last, allowing easy replications of simulation experiments. In this huge enterprise, the main merits (and the possible blames too!) go to Marco Valente who built with very little resources and amazing enthusiasm what is now called the 'Laboratory for Simulation Development' (acronym – LSD!).[24]

(f) The incremental construction, in an LSD environment, of a family of 'artificial financial markets', characterized by different institutional architectures for trading processes and easily accommodating diverse microeconomic trading rules (Francesca Chiaromonte did most of this, with the precious collaboration of a younger Italian graduate, Mariele Bertè): now, we are finally beginning to put to use what we named the *Financial Toy-Room* (more details in Chiaromonte and Dosi (1998)).

The TED project (again) enthusiastically mobilized a large and diverse 'invisible college' well beyond the scope of IIASA financial support, but unfortunately, was forced to an end shortly after the departure of the former IIASA director, Peter de Janosi, whom we all remember with fond gratitude.

Opening-up the organizational blackbox

I have already discussed at length some aspects of those research endeavours which have been and are aimed at 'opening up the technological blackbox' (Rosenberg (1982)).

In the 1990s, a parallel effort has gone into opening up also the *'organizational blackbox'*, in ways consistent with what we were understanding about technological knowledge and learning. Of course, organization theory is much older than that and indeed the works of the genre presented in Part II below, and plenty of other works in germane perspectives, find their seminal sources – as already mentioned – in the preceding contributions by Cyert, March, Simon and also Edith Penrose (1959) and G.B. Richardson (1972).

However, it seems fair to say that only around the 1990s 'evolutionary theory met organization theory' (and business history). Certainly, many elements were already suggested in the analysis by Nelson and Winter (1982) of *firms as repositories of knowledge*, but that was only the beginning of a scientific enterprise attempting to understand more precisely what 'organizational knowledge' means and how it links with corporate structures and practices – including of course *organizational routines*.

It is a collective enterprise still in progress, to which Chapters 7, 9 and 10 try to contribute (see also Cohen *et al.* (1996) and Dosi, Nelson and Winter (1999)).

Part of that exercise involves the operationalization of notions such as *organizational capabilities* and the understanding of their generating processes.

My reflections on these subjects have been profoundly shaped throughout the last decade especially by the interchanges with my friends and co-authors Dick Rumelt, Sid Winter and David Teece. In particular, David offered me, twice, the opportunity to pay long visits to the Haas Business School, at UC Berkeley. It was during the first of such visits (overlapping with Sid Winter's one), in the late 1980s, that Chapter 9 took shape. With a lot of immodesty, let me claim that it is one of the first works to make the notion of organizational knowledge operational, to use it as a proximate predictor of the horizontal and vertical boundaries of firms, and to try to find a circumstantial corroboration in the data. Indeed, much more along these lines awaits to be done, both on the grounds of the micro statistical evidence that is currently becoming available, and through industry case studies.[25]

Likewise, one is only beginning to study the variegated evidence from business history from the point of view of the coupled dynamics between forms of organization of business enterprises and the patterns of knowledge accumulation that diverse organizational structures embodied/fostered/hindered (some insightful remarks in these directions are in Teece's review (Teece (1993)) of Chandler (1990) and in Alfred Chandler's assessment of the links between various strands of economic theorizing and his own research: see Chandler (1990) and also the discussion in Chandler *et al.* (1997).

Needless to say, all this bears major implications also in terms of comparative assessments of learning potentials across discretely different organizational arche-types that one tends to identify in the contemporary economic scene – for example, the 'Japanese firm', the 'lean-and-mean' (American?) model, the ('third-Italy'?) small 'district' enterprise, etc. The bottom line regards the ways in which the rates and directions of accumulation of problem-solving knowledge (including, of course, technological knowledge) are shaped by organizational structures: for example, relatively 'hierarchical' versus decentralized forms; 'functional' (U-form in Chandler's terminology) versus divisionalized ('M-form') structures; 'Japanese-type' versus 'American-type' organizations (see also Chapter 22). And, conversely, it regards the influence that specific invariances in the patterns of knowledge accumulation (roughly, 'paradigms' and 'trajectories' discussed earlier) exert on the development and revealed comparative success of particular organizational forms.

Let me open yet another parenthesis here.

First, note that this whole issue is historically and normatively relevant in so far as *both* organizational forms and learning patterns display enough inertia and path-dependency through time. Otherwise, one could easily adjust learning to any organizational form. Or conversely, easily re-shape organizations in the light of changing learning requirements. Either or both of these hypotheses are indeed held by many respectable contemporary perspectives. For example, it is straightforward that the spirit of Principal-Agent models suggests an overwhelming 'plasticity' of equilibrium (*read: observed*) organizational forms to the technological tasks at hand. And, at the opposite end of the ideological spectrum, this is also what analysts such as

Chack Sabel and Jonathan Zeitlin suggest, working at a controversial edge between business history, conterfactual thought experiments and political manifestos. Their claim is that both technologies and organizations tend to be highly malleable to individual and collective purposeful actions, without any powerful efficiency bound on the attainable combination between organizational forms and learning patterns (so that, admittedly in a caricature, an airplane can be designed and produced equally well within Boeing and Airbus complex organizations or in an Italian decentralized industrial district). The general hypothesis of relative inertia and path-dependent lock-ins is what, on the contrary, I suggest here (for further remarks, see Chapters 7, 10 and 23).

Second, note also that, for the reasons already mentioned above, by problem-solving knowledge I do not mean simply the information-processing features of an organization on the grounds of some – generally unspecified – processing algorithms. Rather, I mean primarily the evolving abilities of interpreting environmental signals, and, at least equally important, as Pavitt ((1999) p. 3), plainly puts it, 'knowing how to solve complex problems in designing, developing, testing and making artefacts that work, and that are useful ...'. Given all that, I am ready to risk accusations of 'technological determinism' (unjust ones: see Chapters 1, 2 and 3, and 23) by those who do not see technological learning as a distinct and patterned source of change; and also accusations of 'sociological determinism', by all those who deny that organizations *as such* are crucial determinants of their own future (as well as of microbehaviours) well beyond the microeconomic exchanges and contracts which they entail.

How does one formalize the emergence of particular problem-solving behaviours? Chapter 7 is an exploratory attempt to answer such a question, in the case of pricing behaviours, showing how adaptive learning processes in complex and changing environments might lead to the establishment of relatively invariant *routines*. The issue is much more general, though. In the last resort, the challenge still largely to be tackled is to show how mechanisms of *variation* (that is, *lato sensu*, 'mutation') and *recombination* over relatively elementary elements of knowledge yield coherent problem-solving procedures. Clearly, this is another area where economic analysis overlaps with cognitive and organizational disciplines and also with 'artificial sciences'.

Within organizations, the problem-solving dimension – as important as it is – is however coupled with particular incentive structures and mechanism of distribution of power and control.

The issue is introduced in Chapter 7, but, only in Chapter 10 do we begin to make operational the idea that an essential feature of organizations is their *double nature*, as both repositories of problem-solving knowledge and institutions governing potentially conflicting interests. The most recent elaborations of this view, as presented in this volume, owe a lot to several discussions with Ollie Williamson who (not surprisingly!) has been repeatedly urging the importance of potentially opportunistic exploitation of informational asymmetries within transactions and the role of organizations as devices to curb and govern 'self-interest with guile'. However, the primary influence has come from endless discussions with my friend Benjamin Coriat. With his long practice of analyses of industrial relations (influenced by both Marxism and industrial sociology) he was much keener in understanding the roots of conflicts even where it was much more natural for me to see, as a *first approximation*, primarily 'distributed knowledge' and organizational problem-solving procedures (and *vice versa* for Benjamin).

Chapter 10 is the outcome of these long exchanges, and, as I see it now, the beginning of an ambitious research task, trying to develop theories and empirical analyses of organizations grounded on the links (and, dynamically, the co-evolutionary processes) between knowledge/problem-solving dimensions and incentive/control dimensions (see also Chapter 22).

Some hints on a research agenda ahead, by way of a conclusion
In this long introductory essay I have already mentioned several topics of research readily following from the essays presented here, and, more generally, stemming from the underlying 'research programme'. They include the determinants, mechanism and effects of innovation and diffusion; the nature and dynamics of organizational structures; learning processes in evolutionary environments; the relationship between technological and organizational innovation; the behavioural microfoundations of economic processes, among others.

On the first item, I totally share Pavitt's indication that future directions of inquiry will have to prominently feature, first, further investigation on the *nature on technology*, and, second, progress in the *measurement of technological activities* (Pavitt (1999), p. 15). The other items could be summarized in the slogan 'evolutionary theory meets organization theory, experimental economics and cognitive sciences'.

Let me just suggest a few further priority areas, as I see them.

Growing attention has been recently paid to national and sectoral *systems of innovation* (and, to a lesser extent, of production). I do think that this is an area where a lot of work is still to be done, also on the grounds of the development of an improved theoretical framework. (Some sketchy remarks of mine are in Dosi (1992) and (1999), and Dosi and Kogut (1993); see also Chapter 10). In brief, the way I see it is that such 'systems' (at whatever level of observation, be they firms, sectors, regions or countries) involve complementarities (or 'mismatchings') among multiple institutional components, including the arrangements governing labour and financial markets, industrial relations, workforce training, non-profit research and so on. In a nutshell, it is some *combinatorics* between these elements which define discrete systems and shape their performances. It is a perspective which is currently pursued, in different vein, by David Soskice, Masa Aoki and is also germane to the spirit of the French Regulation School (see in particular the works by Michel Aglietta and Robert Boyer: Aglietta (1982) and Boyer (1988a, 1988b). Among the essays which follow, Chapters 21 and especially 22 are written in this spirit. (For an attempt to formalize the growth dynamics of different institutional regimes, see also Chapter 17). In fact, one ought to consider all that as a part of a broader endeavour which is encapsulated under the headings of *institutional embeddedness of economic processes* – paraphrasing the famous work of Marc Granovetter (1985) – and *comparative institutional analysis*. Some thoughts in this direction are presented in Chapters 10, 12, 20, 22 and 23, but it is fair to say that most of the work remains to be done for all of us who do not believe either that institutions are simply sorts of 'rules of the game' derivable for a (meta) game-theoretic exercise, or that their effects are simply reducible to the parametrization of otherwise standard economic processes. Around a century after the founding contributions to sociological thought (Durkheim, Weber, etc.), basic questions like 'What is precisely an institution?', 'Can one identify discrete types of them?', 'Are they suitable to some formal representation?' still remain largely unanswered. Relatedly, it is imperative for evolutionary theory to meet institutional theory, but major advances ought to be reached also on the side of the latter.

As already mentioned, I have devoted a whole section of this volume (Part IV) to various formal models addressing different phenomena such as innovation diffusion, industrial dynamics, macroeconomic growth and international trade. I wish they were considered, yet again, as parts of an ongoing enterprise through which the basic analytical apparatus described in Chapters 11 and 12 is put to use to interpret a growing set of 'stylized facts' at those different levels of observation. I see these developments as an important part of the research agenda, despite the fears by some friends that 'the effects of the largely empirically based research agenda (of innovation studies) on the developments in evolutionary theory have been diminishing over time, probably because practical problem-solving has been displaced by formal theory and model-building as the main drivers in its development. Hence the ever-present danger in the future of the co-existence of "numbers without theory" with "theory without numbers"' (Pavitt (1999) p. 16). I do not think that there are many reasons to hold this fear, although I do believe that one is only scratching the surface of the available evidence, especially with regard to industrial statistics, but also concerning growth patterns.

So, for example, what are the empirically testable predictions stemming from evolutionary models on industrial structures and firm growth? (Exploratory exercises in this spirit are in Chapter 15); What are the overlappings and the observational differences as compared to other interpretations such as John Sutton's 'bounds approach' (Sutton (1998))?; And, concerning aggregate dynamics, what are the implications of evolutionary theories in terms of the 'decomposition' of the time-series properties of entities such as GDP, productivity and employment? (For some hints, see Chapters 18 and 19.) All this is particularly urgent if one wants to dispel the scepticism of those practitioners who – even when relatively sympathetic – might be tempted to react as my friend Paul Geroski summarizes in his review of Metcalfe (1998): '*that is nice but so what?*'.

A major weakness of evolutionary theories so far is their almost complete neglect of *macroeconomic* issues. Possibly this is partly due to the implicit anti-Keynesian bias of the Schumpeterian heritage, and partly to the absence of explicit accounts of consumption and labour market dynamics (see, however, Aversi *et al.* (1999) on the former and Lesourne (1991) on the latter). Be that as it may, this is another, extremely ambitious but urgent, item on the research agenda.[26]

As I see it – in a telegraphic summary – a central task involves linking functional relations amongst aggregate variables with 'evolutionary' microfoundations of the sort discussed above and throughout the essays that follow.

In turn, this is likely to entail, *first*, a fresh and prejudice-free assessment of aggregate regularities themselves – e.g. old 'Keynesian' ones such as 'multipliers', 'accelerators', 'Phillips curves', 'Beveridge curves', aggregate consumption propensities', etc.; and, most likely, new ones still awaiting to be identified.

Second, given all that, a fascinating enterprise is going to be the analysis of the institutional and behavioural contexts under which particular macroeconomic propositions hold. Just an illustrative example: can one provide robust micro-foundations of IS/LM curves? And, if so, under what distributions of microbehaviours do they apply? How do they relate to the behavioural rules one is painstakingly trying to identify with reference to, e.g., pricing, investment, R&D, etc.?

Can one establish the occurrence of phase transitions, conditional on changes in the underlying institutional and technological regimes?

At the end of the road, it could well be that 'evolutionary theories meet (some version of) Keynesian macro theories'....

Last but not least, evolutionary approaches have tended to give more emphasis to the interpretative side of the theory at the expense of the normative one. Exploration is the beginning of implications for managerial strategies as well as for science, technology and competition policies (see among others, Teece (1998), Tidd *et al.* (1997), Pavitt (1999)). However, partly owing to its persistent macroeconomic weakness – mentioned above – there remains a big lag in tapping the rich policy consequences of the whole approach. So, just to give quick hints, while the conventional emphasis is on microeconomic incentives, evolutionary theorists – albeit not neglecting the latter – are keen to emphasize learning, competence accumulation and the effects of particular institutions on all that (for similar considerations, see Pavitt (1999)). Likewise, while standard views tend to look at the allocative efficiency of particular market forms, evolutionary approaches focus primarily on the selection role of competition and its dynamic outcomes. And, finally, while the prevalent inclination is to undertake policy analysis in terms of comparative statics (or, equivalently, comparative equilibrium dynamic paths), an evolutionary perspective will much more naturally bring into the picture the effects of particular policy measures upon learning and selection dynamics, and with that, also, take more seriously phenomena of path-dependency and increasing returns (preliminary conjectures on all that are in Chapter 20 and Dosi *et al.* (1990)).

Having said all that, I am fully aware that the essays which follow inevitably represent only a small fraction of what would be needed to accomplish the underlying research programme. I would consider it a major success if they could just provide some source of inspiration or simply issues for possibly tough, but civilized and empirically disciplined, controversies.

* I would like to thank my assistant, Elisa Zanobini, who painstakingly helped with the drafting of this work. Support by Dynacom Project (TSER Program, DG XII, European Union) is gratefully acknowledged.

Notes
1. Well beyond the disciplinary boundaries of economics, the University of Sussex in the late 1970s and early 1980s was also an exciting *locus* of dialogue with daring and somewhat unorthodox explorations in various other disciplines – including biology, chemistry, linguistics and cognitive psychology. It is impossible to acknowledge all my intellectual debts: let me just mention my friends Arthur Merin and Patrizia Tabossi, and the endless evenings of challenging discussions on cognition, rationality, sociology, philosophy....
2. For a more detailed discussion, see Dosi, Marengo and Fagiolo (1996).
3. It emerged under the sponsorship of the International Federation of Institutes for Advanced Studies – IFIAS, Sweden – which I want to take the chance here to thank.

4. For comprehensive presentation of the state-of-the-art at various dates, together with several original advancements, see Hofbauer and Sigmund (1988), D. Friedman (1991), Vega-Redondo (1996), Weibull (1995), L. Samuelson (1997), Young (1998).

5. An archetypical example is Epstein and Axtell (1996). See also a good deal of works in the 'Santa Fe' spirit and the insightful discussion in Lane (1993).

6. Or, talking of computer implementations, finite for obvious technical reasons, but with a dimensionality high enough to practically simulate the lack of dimensional boundaries.

7. For example, Eldredge and Gould (1972). See also Casti (1992) and the remarks in Lane (1993).

8. See for example, Winter *et al.* (1997) and Chapter 16 in this volume.

9. But also some 'reduced' forms models developed in the ETEC spirit: see Winter *et al.* (1997).

10. Without, however, any religious commitments to the methodology. So, for example, the ETEC perspectives fully draws from those works on innovation diffusion where suggestive empirical implications may be derived from the limit properties of dynamics *cum* heterogeneous agents and increasing returns, see, among others, David (1988), Arthur, Ermoliev and Kaniovski (1987), Bassanini and Dosi (1998a), and Chapters 13 and 19.

11. An example concerning the patterns of innovation diffusion is explored in Bassanini and Dosi (1998); convergence properties in stochastic EG are discussed in Vega-Redondo (1996).

12. See the critical surveys in Weisbuch *et al.* (1998) and Fagiolo (1998) and the references therein.

13. More on them in David (1992) and Bassanini and Dosi (1998a, 1998b), and in this volume, especially Chapters 3, 13 and 14.

14. In brief, Fisher Law establishes the *law of motion* of average 'fitness', and, thus, of the relative frequencies of the related traits, as a function of the higher moments of the distribution of the latter in the appropriate fitness space. Short of some (important) technical qualifications, one may interpret it as an approximate equivalent of the replicator dynamics often found in both theoretical biology and EGs in economics: relative frequencies change with monotonic dependence upon the relative 'fitness' of particular trait(s) as compared to the overall populations averages (for a germane critical discussion, see G. Silverberg (1988)).

15. One of the few notable works in this spirit is Kirman and Vignes (1991) on the Marseilles fish market, but – as fascinating as it is – it might not be a sufficient support for the entire economics discipline which keeps mentioning 'markets' as the general *deus-ex-machina*! A germane direction of analysis impinging both on the institutional architecture of markets and the patterns of competition/cooperation stemming from particular divisions of (cognitive and productive) labour draws from network analysis. (For some preliminary results in this vein, see Orsenigo *et al.* (1998) cf. also Marengo *et al.* (1999).)

16. On this and other issues – such as the nature and dynamics of financial markets – my debt to endless discussions with Helene Tordjman is enormous.

17. Here one is primarily talking about real markets (that is, markets for commodities and services). Financial markets are likely to embody quite different selection criteria, much more related to speculative phenomena: more on it in Marengo and Tordjman (1996).

18. Incidentally note that all this cast serious doubts on the monotonicity in the effects of selection forces which is generally assumed in EGs.

19. For a fruitful economic application to the theory of the firm, see Levinthal (1999).

20. 'The agents in biological applications of evolutionary game theory never choose strategic and never change their strategies. Instead, they are "hard-wired" to play a particular strategy, which they do until they die. Variations in the mix of strategies within a population are caused by differing rates of reproduction. In economic applications, we have a different process in mind. The players in the game are people, who choose and may change their strategies. An evolutionary approach in economics begins with a model of this strategy adjustment process' (L. Samuelson (1997), p. 18).

21. For some insightful remarks see the reviews by Loasby (1995) and Metcalfe (1995) of Milgrom and Roberts (1992).

22. I am glad to admit that, again, Helene Tordjman has been instrumental in introducing me to this domain of investigation. Since that initial curiosity in the early 1990s, my views on the subject have been significantly influenced by repeated interchanges with Dan Lovallo (see also Chapter 8), and, more recently, Massimo Warglien, Giovanna Devetag and Paolo Legrenzi (of course they do not bear any responsibility for my mistakes).

23. Incidentally note that given my intellectual pedigree, briefly sketched earlier, I freely admit that I am well short of resembling a professional mathematical economist: an indication is also the fact that most of my works in that vein have been undertaken with collaborators having a comparative advantage in the related skills.

24. This is accessible now from the Alborg University site (www.business.auc.dk/~mv/lsd1.1), Denmark, where Marco ended up to finish his PhD, under the protective wings of Esben Andersen.

25. I would like to mention David Teece also in connection with the establishment and management of

Industrial and Corporate Change, the journal published by OUP which we helped to establish and continue to run together with Glenn Carroll, Franco Malerba, Nate Rosenberg and Nick Von Tunzelmann and Josef Chytry (and relying on the precious secretarial skills of Adriana Mongelli). In its origins the journal was sponsored by the ASSI Foundation – an Italian group of economic historians eager to build a bridge with economics and management. Even if our relationship with them later went sour for reasons not worth explaining here, I would like to acknowledge their early help (and especially that of the general secretary at that time, Bruno Bezza), the subsequent support of LIUC, Castellanza, Italy, and the unchanging support from the Haas Business School, UC Berkeley and Oxford University Press which made possible such an ambitious interdisciplinary enterprise.

26.   In this connection, Dick Lipsey is one of the few noticeable exceptions who, coming from macroeconomics, has been recently trying, mostly alone, to build connection with an evolutionary microeconomics. The intuitive compatibility – as remarked also by Stiglitz (1997) – is certainly there but most of the work is still to be done.

Bibliography

Aghion, P. and P. Howitt (1998), *Endogenous Growth Theory*, Cambridge, MA: MIT Press.

Aglietta, M. (1982), *Regulation et Crise du Capitalisme*, (2nd edn), Paris: Calmann Levy.

Allen, P. (1988), 'Evolution, innovation and economics', in Dosi, G. *et al.* (1988), pp. 95–119.

Amendola, G., G. Dosi and B. Papagni (1993), 'The dynamics of international competitiveness', *Weltwirtschaftliches Archiv*, **129**(3), 451–71.

Arrow, K. (1962a), 'Economic welfare and the allocation of resources for invention', in Nelson, R.R. (ed.), *The Rate and Direction of Inventive Activity*, Princeton: Princeton University Press.

Arrow, K. (1962b), 'The economic implications of learning by doing', *Review of Economic Studies*, **29**(2), 155–73.

Arrow, K. (1996), 'Technical information and industrial structure', *Industrial and Corporate Change*, **5**(2), 645–52.

Arthur, B. (1994), *Increasing Returns and Path-Dependence in the Economy*, Ann Arbor: University of Michigan Press.

Arthur, B., Y. Ermoliev and Y. Kaniovski (1987), 'Path-dependent processes and the emergence of macrostructure', *European Journal of Operations Research*, **30**, 294–303.

Aversi, R., G. Dosi, G. Fagiolo, M. Meacci and C. Olivetti (1999), 'Demand dynamics with socially evolving preferences', *Industrial and Corporate Change*, **8**(2), 353–408.

Basalla, G. (1988), *The Evolution of Technology*, Cambridge: Cambridge University Press.

Bassanini, A. and G. Dosi (1998a), 'Competing technologies, international diffusion and the role of convergence to a stable market structure', IIASA, Laxemburg, Austria, IR-98-012, March.

Bassanini, A. and G. Dosi (1998b), 'When and how chance and human will can twist the arms of Clio', Pisa, Sant'Anna School of Advanced Studies, working paper, forthcoming in R. Garud *et al.* (eds), *Path Creation and Path Dependencies*, Mahwah, NJ: Lawrence Erlbaum Publishers.

Boyer, R. (1988a), 'Formalizing growth regime', in Dosi, G. *et al.* (eds) (1988), pp. 608–30.

Boyer, R. (1988b), 'Technical change and the theory of "Regulation"', in Dosi, G. *et al.* (eds) (1988), pp. 67–94.

Camerer, C. (1995), 'Individual decision making', in Kagel, J.H. and A.E. Roth (eds), *The Handbook of Experimental Economics*, Princeton, NJ: Princeton University Press, pp. 587–704.

Camerer, C. (1997), 'Progress in behavioural game theory', *Journal of Economic Perspectives*, **11**(4), 167–88.

Casti, J.L. (1992), *Reality Rules*, New York: Wiley.

Chandler, A. (1990), *Scale and Scope: The Dynamics of Industrial Capitalism*, Cambridge, MA/London: The Belknap Press of Harvard University Press.

Chandler, A. (1992), 'Organizational capabilities and the economic history of the industrial enterprise', *Journal of Economic Perspectives*, **6**(3), Summer, 79–100.

Chandler, A., F. Amatori and T. Hikino (eds) (1997), *Big Business and the Wealth of Nations*, Cambridge: Cambridge University Press.

Chiaromonte, F. and G. Dosi (1998), 'Modeling a decentralized asset market: an introduction to the financial "Toy-Room" ', Laxenburg, Austria, IIASA, Interim Report.

Cimoli, M. and G. Dosi (1995), 'Technological paradigms, patterns of learning and development: an introductory roadmap', *Journal of Evolutionary Economics*, **5**(3).

Cohen, M.D., K. Burkhart, G. Dosi, M. Egidi, L. Marengo, M. Warglien and S. Winter (1996), 'Routines and other recurring action patterns of organizations: contemporary research issues', *Industrial and Corporate Change*, **5**(3), 653–98.

David, P.A. (1975), *Technical Choice, Innovation and Economic Growth*, Cambridge: Cambridge University Press.

David, P.A. (1985), 'Clio and the economics of QWERTY', *American Economic Review, Papers and Proceedings*, **75**(2), 332–7.

David, P.A. (1988), 'Path-dependence: putting the past into the future of economics', Stanford, Institute for Mathematical Studies in Social Sciences, *Technical Report*, 533.

David, P.A. (1992), 'Heroes, herds and hysteresis in technological change: Thomas Edison and the battle of the systems', *Industrial Corporate and Change*, **1**(1), 129–80.

Dosi, G. (1984), *Technical Change and Industrial Transformation. The Theory and an Application to the Semiconductor Industry*, London: Macmillan and New York: St Martin Press.

Dosi, G. (1992a), 'Industrial organisation, competitiveness and growth', *Revue d'Economie Industrielle*, **59**(1), 27–45.

Dosi, G. (1992b), 'Performances, interactions and evolution in the theory of industrial organization', in A. Del Monte (ed.), *Recent Developmnents in Industrial Organization*, London: Macmillan.

Dosi, G. (1996), 'The contribution of economic theory to the understanding of a knowledge-based economy', in Foray and Lundvall (1996).

Dosi, G. (1999), 'Some notes on national systems of innovation and production, and their implications for economic analysis', in Archibugi, D., J. Howells and J. Michie (eds), *Innovation Policy in a Global Economy*, Cambridge: Cambridge University Press, pp. 35–48.

Dosi, G., C. Freeman, K. Nelson, G. Silverberg and L. Soete (eds) (1988), *Technical Change and Economic Theory*, London: Pinter and New York: Columbia University Press.

Dosi, G., K. Pavitt and L. Soete (1990), *The Economics of Technical Change and International Trade*, Brighton: Harvester Wheatsheaf and New York: New York University Press.

Dosi, G. and B. Kogut (1993), 'National specificities and the context of change: the co-evolution of organization and technology', in B. Kogut (ed.), *Country Competitiveness. Technology and Re-organization of Work*, Oxford/New York: Oxford University Press.

Dosi, G., C. Freeman and S. Fabiani (1994), 'The process of economic development. Introducing some stylized facts on technologies, firms and the institutions', *Industrial and Corporate Change*, **3**, pp. 1–45.

Dosi, G., L. Marengo and G. Fagiolo (1996), 'Learning in evolutionary environments', IIASA Working Paper, Laxemburg, Austria.

Dosi, G., F. Malerba, O. Marsili and L. Orsenigo (1997), 'Industrial structures and dynamics: evidence, interpretations and puzzles', *Industrial and Corporate Change*, **6**(1), 3–24.

Dosi, G. and S. Winter (1998), 'Interpreting economic change: evolution, structures and games', Pisa, St Anna School of Advanced Studies, Working Paper.

Dosi, G., R. Nelson and S. Winter (eds) (1999), *The Nature and Dynamics of Organizational Capabilities*, Oxford/New York: Oxford University Press (forthcoming).

Eldredge, N. and S. Gould (1972), 'Puntuacted equilibria: an alternative to phyletic gradualism', in T.J.M. Schopf (ed.), *Models in Paleobiology*, San Francisco: Freeman, Cooper and Co., pp. 82–115.

Epstein, J.M. and R. Axtell (1996), *Growing Artificial Societies: Social Science from Bottom-Up*, Washington DC: Brookings Institution and MIT Press.

Fagiolo, G. (1998), 'Spatial interaction in dynamics decentralized economics: a review' in P. Cohendet, P. Llerena, H. Stahn and G. Umbhauer (eds), *The Economics of Networks*, Berlin/New York: Springer Verlag, pp. 53–91.

Foray, D. and B.A. Lundvall (eds) (1996), *Knowledge, Employment and Economic Growth*, Paris: OECD.

Forni, M. and M. Lippi (1997), *Aggregation and the Microfoundations of Dynamic Macroeconomics*, Oxford: Clarendon Press.

Freeman, C. (1982), *The Economics of Industrial Innovation*, 2nd edn, London: Francis Pinter.

Freeman, C. (1994), 'The economics of technical change', *Cambridge Journal of Economics*, **18**, 463–514.

Freeman, C. (1995), 'The national systems of innovation in historical perspective', *Cambridge Journal of Economics*, **19**(1), 5–24.

Freeman, C. and C. Perez (1988), 'Structural crises of adjustment: business cycles and investment behaviour', in Dosi *et al.* (1988), pp. 38–66.

Friedman, D. (1991), 'Evolutionary games in economics', *Econometrica*, **59**(3), 637–66.

Fudenberg, D. and D.K. Levine (1998), *The Theory of Learning in Games*, Cambridge, MA: MIT Press.

Geroski, P.A. (1999), 'Review of J.S. Metcalfe, *Evolutionary Economics and Creative Destruction*', *Economic Journal*, **109**, 256–8.

Granovetter, M. (1985), 'Economic action and social structure: the problem of embeddedness', *American Journal of Sociology*, **91**(3), 481–510.

Harris, D.J. (1988), 'Structural change and economic growth: a review article', *Contributions to Political Economy*, **I**, 25–46.

Hofbauer, J. and K. Sigmund (1988), *The Theory of Evolution and Dynamical Systems*, Cambridge: Cambridge University Press.

Hughes, T.P. (1982), *Networks of Power: Electrification in Western Society, 1800–1930*, Baltimore, MD: Johns Hopkins University Press.

Iwai, K. (1984a), 'Shumpeterian dynamics:an evolutionary model of innovation and imitation', *Journal of Economic Behavior and Organization*, **5**(2), 159–90.

Iwai, K. (1984b), 'Shumpeterian dynamics Part II: technological progress, firm growth and economic selection', *Journal of Economic Behavior and Organization*, **5**(3–4), 379–92.

Kaldor, N. (1957), 'A model of economic growth', *Economic Journal*, **67**, 591–624.

Kaldor, N. (1978), *Further Essays in Applied Economics*, London: Duckworth.

Kaldor, N. and J.A. Mirrlees (1962), 'A new model of economic growth', *Review of Economic Studies*, **29**, 174–92.

Kauffman, S. (1993), *The Origins of Order*, New York: Oxford University Press.

Kirman, A. (1989), 'The intrinsic limits to modern economic theory: the emperor has no clothes', *Economic Journal*, **99**, 126–39.

Kirman, A. (1992), 'Whom or what does the representative agent represent?', *Journal of Economic Perspectives*, **6**, 126–39.

Kirman, A. and A. Vignes (1991), 'Price dispersion. theoretical considerations and empirical evidence from the Marseilles fish market', in K. Arrow (ed.), *Issues in Contemporary Economics*, London: Macmillan.

Kirman, A.P. and G. Weisbuch (1998), 'Market organization', in Lesourne and Orléan (1998).

Kreps, D. (1990), *A Course in Microeconomic Theory*, Princeton: Princeton University Press.

Kuznets, S. (1966), *Modern Economic Growth: Rate, Structure and Spread*, New Haven, CT: Yale University Press.

Landes, D. (1969), *The Unbound Prometheus*, Cambridge: Cambridge University Press.

Lane, D. (1993), 'Artificial worlds and economics', Parts I and II, *Journal of Evolutionary Economics*, **3**, 89–107 and 177–97.

Lesourne, J. (1991), *L'Economie de l'Ordre et du Désordre*, Paris: Economica.

Lesourne, J. and A. Orlean (eds) (1998), *Advances on Self-Organization and Evolutionary Economics*, Paris: Economica.

Levinthal, D. (1999), 'Organizational capabilities in complex worlds', in Dosi, Nelson and Winter (1999).

Loasby, B.J. (1995), 'Running a business: an appraisal of *Economics, Organization and Management* by Paul Milgrom and John Roberts', *Industrial and Corporate Change*, **4**(2), 471–90.

Lundvall, B.-Å. (ed.) (1992), *National Systems of Innovation*, London: Francis Pinter.

March, J. and H.E. Simon (1993), *Organizations*, 2nd edn, Oxford: Basil Blackwell.

Marengo, L. (1992), 'Coordination and organizational learning in the firm', *Journal of Evolutionary Economics*, **2**, 313–26.

Marengo, L. and Tordjman (1996), 'Speculation, heterogeneity and learning: a model of exchange rate dynamics', *Kyklos*, **49**(3), 407–38.

Marengo, L., G. Dosi, P. Legrenzi and C. Pasquali (1999), 'The structure of problem-solving knowledge and the structure of organizations', Sant'Anna School of Advanced Studies, Pisa, working paper.

Metcalfe, J.S. (1992), 'Variety, structure and change: an evolutionary perspective on the competitive process', *Revue d'Economie Industrielle*, **59**(1), 46–61.

Metcalfe, J.S. (1995), 'Economies, organizations and management: a review of Milgrom and Roberts', *Industrial and Corporate Change*, **4**(2), 491–7.

Metcalfe, J.S. (1998), *Evolutionary Economics and Creative Construction*, London and New York: Routledge.

Milgrom, P. and J. Roberts (1992), *Economics, Organization and Management*, Englewood Cliffs: Prentice-Hall.

Mokyr, J. (1990), *The Level of Riches*, Oxford: Oxford University Press.

Nelson, R.R. (ed.) (1993), *National Innovation Systems: A Comparative Study*, Oxford/New York: Oxford University Press.

Nelson, R.R. (1996), *The Sources of Economic Growth*, Cambridge, MA: Harvard University Press.

Nelson, R. (1998), 'The agenda for growth theory: a different point of view', *Cambridge Journal of Economics*, **22**(3), 497–520.

Nelson, R.R. and S. Winter (1982), *An Evolutionary Theory of Economic Change*, Cambridge, MA: The Belknap Press and Harvard University Press.

Orsenigo, L., F. Pammolli, M. Riccaboni and A. Bonaccorsi (1998), 'The dynamics of knowledge and the evolution of an industry network', *Journal of Management and Governance*, **2**(1), 144–75.

Pasinetti, L.L. (1981), *Structural Change and Economic Growth: A Theoretical Essay on the Dynamics of the Wealth of Nations*, Cambridge: Cambridge University Press.

Pasinetti, L.L. (1993), *Structural Economic Dynamics: A Theory of the Economic Consequences of Human Learning*, Cambridge: Cambridge University Press.

Pavitt, K. (1998), 'Technologies, products and organization in the innovating firm: what Adam Smith tells us and Joseph Schumpeter doesn't', *Industrial and Corporate Change*, **7**(3).

Pavitt, K. (1999), *Technology, Management and Systems of Innovation*, Cheltenham: Edward Elgar (forthcoming).

Penrose, E. (1959), *The Theory of the Growth of the Firm*, Oxford: Oxford University Press, 3rd edn.

Radner, R. (1992), 'Hierarchy: the economics of managing', *Journal of Economic Literature*, **30**(4), 1382–415.

Richardson, G.B. (1972), 'The organization of industry', *Economic Journal*, **82**, 883–96.

Romer, P.M. (1990), 'Endogenous technological change', *Journal of Political Economy*, **98**(5), 71–102.

Rosenberg, N. (1976), *Perspectives on Technology*, Cambridge: Cambridge University Press.

Rosenberg, N. (1984), *Inside the Blackbox: Technology and Economics*, Cambridge: Cambridge University Press.

Samuelson, L. (1997), *Evolutionary Games and Equilibrium Selection*, Cambridge, MA: MIT Press.

Schelling, T.C. (1978), *Micro Motives and Macro Behaviors*, New York: Norton.

Silverberg, G. (1988), 'Modelling economic dynamics and technical change', in Dosi *et al.* (1988), pp. 531–59.

Simon, H.A. (1957), *Models of Man*, New York, Wiley.

Simon, H.A. (1965), *Administrative Behavior: A Study of Decision-making Processes in Administrative Organization*, 2nd edn, New York: The Free Press.

Simon, H.A. (1976), 'From substantive to procedural rationality', in Latsis, S.J. (ed.), *Method and Appraisal in Economics*, Cambridge: Cambridge University Press.

Simon, H.A. (1981), *The Sciences of the Artificial*, 2nd edn, Cambridge, MA: MIT Press.

Simon, H.A. (1983), *Reason in Human Affairs*, Stanford: Stanford University Press.

Solow, R.M. (1957), 'Technical change and the aggregate production function', *Review of Economics and Statistics*, **39**(4), August, 312–20.

Solow, R.M. (1970), *Growth Theory: An Exposition*, Oxford: Oxford University Press.

Stiglitz, J.E. (1997), *Whither Socialism?*, Cambridge, MA, MIT Press.

Sutton, J. (1998), *Technology and Market Structure*, Cambridge, MA: MIT Press.

Sylos Labini, P. (1967), *Oligopoly and Technical Progress*, Cambridge, MA: Harvard University Press, 2nd edn.

Teece, D.J. (1993), 'The dynamics of industrial capitalism: perspectives on Alfred Chandler's scale and scope', *Journal of Economic Literature*, **31**(1), March, 199–225.

Teece, D.J. (1998), *Strategy, Technology and Public Policy*, Cheltenham: Edward Elgar.

Tidd, J., J. Bessant and K. Pavitt (1997), *Managing Innovation: Integrating Technological, Organizational and Market Change*, Chichester/New York: Wiley.

Tordjman, H. (1998), 'Evolution: history, change and progress', in Lesourne and Orléan (1998).

Vega-Redondo, F. (1996), *Evolution, Games and Economic Behaviours*, Oxford/New York: Oxford University Press.

Vincenti, W. (1990), *What Do Engineers Do and How Do They Know It?*, Baltimore: Johns Hopkins University Press.

Weibull, J.W. (1995), *Evolutionary Game Theory*, Cambridge, MA: MIT Press.

Weisbuch, G., A. Kirman and D. Herreiner (1998), 'Market organization', in Lesourne and Orlean (1998), pp. 160–82.

Williamson, D.E. (1985), *The Economic Institutions of Capitalism*, New York: Free Press.

Winter, S.G. (1982), 'An essay in the theory of production', in S.H. Hymans (ed.), *Economics and the World Around It*, Ann Arbor: University of Michigan Press.

Winter, S.G. (1984), 'Schumpeterian competition under alternative technological regimes', *Journal of Economic Behaviour and Organisation*, (5), 287–320.

Winter, S.G. (1987), 'Competition and natural selection', in J. Eatwell *et al.* (eds), *The New Palgrave: a Dictionary of Economics*, New York: Stockton Press and London: Macmillan, pp. 614–17.

Winter, S.G. (1988), 'Economic natural selection and the theory of the firm', in P.E. Earl (ed.), *Behavioural Economics*, Aldershot: Edward Elgar.

Winter, S.G., Y. Kaniovski and G. Dosi (1997), *A Baseline Model of Industrial Evolution*, IIASA, Laxenburg, Austria, Working Paper.

Young, P. (1998), *Individual Strategy and Social Structure*, Princeton: Princeton University Press.

PART I

OPPORTUNITIES OF INNOVATION, SEARCH PROCEDURES AND DIFFUSION

[1]

Technological paradigms and technological trajectories

A suggested interpretation of the determinants and directions of technical change

GIOVANNI DOSI *

Science Policy Research Unit, University of Sussex, Brighton U.K.

The procedures and the nature of "technologies" are suggested to be broadly similar to those which characterize "science". In particular, there appear to be "technological paradigms" (or research programmes) performing a similar role to "scientific paradigms" (or research programmes). The model tries to account for both continuous changes and discontinuities in technological innovation. Continuous changes are often related to progress along a technological trajectory defined by a technological paradigm, while discontinuities are associated with the emergence of a new paradigm. One-directional explanations of the innovative process, and in particular those assuming "the market" as the prime mover, are inadequate to explain the emergence of new technological paradigms. The origin of the latter stems from the interplay between scientific advances, economic factors, institutional variables, and unsolved difficulties on established technological paths. The model tries to establish a sufficiently general framework which accounts for all these factors and to define the process of selection of new technological paradigms among a greater set of notionally possible ones.

The history of a technology is contextual to the history of the industrial structures associated with that technology. The emergence of a new paradigm is often related to new "schumpeterian" companies, while its establishment often shows also a process of oligopolistic stabilization.

* Previously at the Sussex European Research Centre. I am grateful to R. Nelson, W. Walker, D. Jones, M. Salvati, A. Merin, L. Bucciarelli and two anonymous referees for their comments and criticisms on previous drafts. The responsibility for this draft is obviously mine. A version of this research, more focussed on the effects of technical change upon long-run patterns of growth, is appearing in C. Freeman (ed.), *Technical Innovation and Long Waves in World Economic Development*, IPC Press, Guildford, 1982 (forthcoming).

Research Policy 11 (1982) 147–162
North-Holland Publishing Company

0048-7333/82/0000–0000/$02.75 © 1982 North-Holland

1. Introduction

The strict relationship between economic growth and change, on the one hand, and technical progress on the other is a rather evident and well recognized "fact" in economic thought. The nature of the relationship between the two, however, has been a much more controversial issue of economic theory. The theoretical problem concerns the direction of causal relationship, the degree of independence of technical change vis-a-vis endogenous market mechanisms – both in the short and long run, – the role played by institutional factors, the determinants of the "rate and direction" of innovative activity. Theories of technical change have generally been classified into two broad categories, namely "demand-pull" and "technology-push" theories. The distinction is self-explanatory and relates to the degree of autonomy of the innovative activity from short-run changes in the economic environment. Section 2 of this paper will attempt a brief critical review of the main difficulties of both approaches and in particular of demand-pull theories. We will try to show that these latter interpretations present a rather crude conception of technical change, as an essentially reactive mechanism, based on a "black box" of readily available technological possibilities. Moreover this conception contradicts substantial pieces of empirical evidence. On the other hand, extreme forms of technology-push approaches, allowing for a one-way causal determination (from science to technology to the economy) fail to take into account the intuitive importance of economic factors in shaping the direction of technical change.

Section 3 will attempt an interpretation of the process of innovative activity, suggesting that there are strong similarities between the nature and the procedures of "science" – as defined by modern epistemology – and those of "technology". The parallel is still rather impressionistic, but leads to the definition of technological paradigms (or technological research programmes) with many features in common with scientific paradigms (or scientific reseach programmes).

We shall define a "technological paradigm" broadly in accordance with the epistemological definition as an "outlook", a set of procedures, a definition of the "relevant" problems and of the specific knowledge related to their solution. We shall argue also that each "technological paradigm" defines its own concept of "progress" based on its specific technological and economic trade-offs. Then, we will call a "technological trajectory" the direction of advance witin a technological paradigm.

Moreover, we shall analyze the role played by economic and institutional factors in the selection and establishment of those technological paradigms and the interplay between endogenous economic mechanisms and technological innovations, once a "technological paradigm" has been established.

Section 4 will consider some implications of the model with respect to industrial structures. In particular, we shall try to translate the logical distinction between the process of search for new technological patterns and their establishment into an historical distinction, along the development of an industry, between a "schumpeterian" phase of emergence of that industry and its "maturity". We do not provide in this work any empirical backing (or very little). An application of the model to the semiconductor industry can be found in another work by the author [7]. Even that cannot be considered an adequate test of its interpretative capability which should be tried upon different technologies and longer time spans. The conclusions in section 5 suggest some of the possible directions of inquiry, together with some implications in terms of economic theory and of public policies.

This paper does not aspire to provide a "general theory" of technical change. It simply attempts to focus on questions like "why did certain technological developments emerge instead of others?" "Are there regularities in the process of generation of new technologies and in technical progress thereafter?" "Is there any regularity in the func-

tional relationship between the vast number of economic, social, institutional, scientific factors which are likely to influence the innovative process?" Our answers to these questions are necessarily tentative. In some ways our model could be considered in itself as an "outlook", an interpretative grid, focussing on questions often neglected by orthodox economic theory which is mainly concerned with questions of instantaneous adjustments instead of problems of long-run transformation of the economic and institutional environment.

2. A critical review of the theories of technical change

Although everyone recognises, that there can be – and generally are – different and contextual origins of inventive activity, in the economic literature there has been a substantial effort to define the common elements among a wide range of inventions and/or innovations, [1] together with the search for some kind of "prime mover" of inventive activity. In the literature on the subject, one used to define two different basic approaches, the first pointing to market forces as the main determinants of technical change ("demand-pull" theories) and the second defining technology as an autonomous or quasi-autonomous factor, at least in the short run ("technology-push" theories). Such a clear-cut distinction is of course hard to make in practise but remains useful for the sake of exposition: there is indeed a fundamental distinction between the two approaches and that is the role attributed to market signals in directing innovative activity and technical changes. It seems to us that this distinction (the role attributed to market signals), although overlapping a great deal with the distinction "demand-pull" versus "technology-push" theories, is indeed the main core of the discussion.

---

[1] "In this schumpeterian distinction an "*invention*" is an idea, a sketch or a model for a new or improved device, product, process of system. Such inventions ... do not necessarily lead to technical *innovations* ... . An innovation in the economic sense is accomplished only with the first *commercial* transaction involving the new product, process ... ", Freeman [12], p. 22. Accepting this distinction, the borderline is in that the new device or process is not only potentially *marketable* but actually *marketed*. I will recall the distinction when discussing the role of the market.

Let us consider first a "pure" demand-pull theory. As discussed exhaustively in a comprehensive critical paper by Rosenberg and Mowery [31], the causal prime mover in those theories is some supposed "recognition of needs" by the productive units in the market, to which follows their attempts to fulfill those needs through their technological efforts. This "pure" market-pull theory would run more or less as follows (both causally and chronologically). (1) There exists a set of consumption and intermediate goods, at a given time, on the market, satisfying different "needs" by the purchasers. In passing, one must notice – as we shall recall below – that the same definition of "needs" is quite ambiguous: at the one extreme one may define them in very general "anthropological" terms (the needs to eat, have shelter, communicate, etc.) but then they express a total indifference to the way they are satisfied and do not have any economic relevance; or, at the other extreme, "needs" are expressed in relation to the specific means of their satisfaction, but then each "need" cannot emerge before the basic invention to which it is related.[2] (2) Consumers (or users) express their preferences about the features of the goods they desire (i.e. the features that fulfill their *needs* the most) through their patterns of demand. This is another way of saying that demand functions are determined by the existence and the forms of utility functions. We may assume now that pattern of demand change (i.e. that the demand function shifts upward or downward) or just that – which is basically the same – in a growing economy, given the relative prices of the considered commodities, the income elasticities of demand of the latter are different. (3) The theory would argue that, with a growing income relaxing the budget constraint of the consumers/users, the latter demand proportionally more of the goods which embodied some relatively preferred characteristics (i.e. those which more adequately satisfy their needs). (4) At this point the producers enter into the picture, realising – through the movements in demand and prices – the revealed needs of the consumers/users: some "utility dimensions" have a higher weight (there is more *need* for them).

(5) Here the proper innovative process begins, and the successful firms will at the end bring to the market their new/improved goods, letting again the "market" (as above defined) monitor their increased capability to fulfill consumers' needs.

Of course not even the most extremist "demand-pull" theorist would support entirely this crude view.[3] The basic argument however maintains that there *generally exist* a *possibility* of *knowing a priori* (before the invention process takes place) the *direction* in which the market is "pulling" the inventive activity of producers and furthermore that an important part of the "signalling process" operates through movements in relative prices and quantities. Thus, in this perspective, the innovative process can be placed – although with consistent difficulties – inside the neo-classical framework.[4] With respect to producers, this viewpoint implies that the "choice sets are given and the outcomes of any choice known".[5] The assumption of "known outcomes" could perhaps be relaxed to introduce risk and stochastic variables, but the first assumption has to be maintained (given and finite sets of choices).

The viewpoints outlines above might be criticised on different levels, namely: (1) the general theory of prices as determined by supply and demand functions; (2) the difficulties of defining demand functions as determined by utility functions and the same feasibility of a "utility" concept; and (3) the logical and practical difficulties in interpreting the innovative process through this approach.

The first question is undoubtedly the biggest one because it could undermine the entire theory

---

[2] In other words, in the first definition, the "need" to move around can be satisfied either through a horse or a space-shuttle. In the second definition, obviously the "need" for a space-shuttle cannot emerge before the space-shuttle itself is conceived.

[3] But this "one-directional" determination of the innovative activity from consumers/users to producers' innovative output appears clearly in studies like that of Myers and Marquis [21].

[4] In a "weaker sense", it is apparent that within this approach the innovative mechanism operates in the same way as the usual mechanism of determination of prices and quantities in a general equilibrium analysis. In a "stronger sense", it does not appear impossible – given restrictive assumptions – to construct a neoclassical general equilibrium analysis which takes account of this kind of innovative activity. For the difficulties of this approach, see below.

[5] Nelson and Winter [24] in Belassa and Nelson [4]. This work, to which I will refer again later, is, as far as I know, one of the first attempts to formalise a non-neoclassical model of technical progress, embodying rather complex assumptions about firms' attitudes toward, and responses to the innovative activity.

on which this approach is based upon. This is not the place though to deal with that issue [6] and the discussion will be restricted to the third point.

With respect to this more circumscribed question, some significant problems throw doubts on the entire adequacy of demand-based theories of innovations. (1) A theory of innovation is supposed to explain not only (and not even primarily) "incremental" technical progress on the existing products/processes, but first of all it is meant to interpret major and minor technological breakthroughs. As far as the latter are concerned the range of "potential needs" is nearly infinite and it is difficult to argue that these would-be demands can explain why, in a definite point in time, an invention/innovation occurs (see Rosenberg [30] and Rosenberg and Mowery [31]).

(2) Even after allowing *a priori* recognition of a "need", it is difficult to explain with this approach what happens between that recognition by producers and the final outcome of a new product. Either we have to assume a set of technological possibilities already in existence (but then we must wonder why those possibilities have not been exploited before [7]) or we must assume a limited time lag between research and the outcomes of that research. The concept of technology (and, at least indirectly, of science) underlying this appraoch is of a very versatile and "responsive" mechanism which can be directed with limited effort and cost in one direction or another. To avoid a crude conception of technology as a "freely available blackbox", there have been some efforts in the theory to consider information as an expensive commodity. [8] Those attempts, while representing a big advance in that they account for the microeconomic aspects of technological efforts (which have a cost and an expected return for each single firm)

and also in that they somehow account for the interrelation science-technology-production, do not seem to be able to consider the entire complexity of scientific and technological procedures. [9]

To summarize, there appear to be three basic weaknesses in "strong" versions of demand-pull approaches: first, a concept of passive and mechanical "reactiveness" of technological changes vis-a-vis market conditions; second, the incapability of defining the *why* and *when* of certain technological developments instead of others and of a certain timing instead of others; third, the neglect of changes over time in the inventive capability which do not bear any *direct* relationship with changing market conditions.

The theoretical ambiguities of demand-pull theories seem inevitably reflected in the empirical studies on the determinants of innovation (critically reviewed in Rosenberg and Mowery [31]). Not surprisingly, most of the studies find that "market is important in determining successful innovations". I find myself in agreement with Rosenberg and Mowery though, in that most of the studies with a demand-pull approach fail to produce sufficient evidence that "needs expressed through market signalling" are the prime movers of innovative activity (see [31]). And this is precisely the question at stake. Other important empirical works on the contrary point to multi-variables explanations of innovative activity [10] and

---

[6] For our purposes it is enough to mention that if we assume, at any point in time, fixed coefficient of production and constant return to scale, variations in the quantities do not affect relative prices. Therefore we are bound to loose an important part of the "signalling" mechanism. On the other hand a demand/supply theory of prices might be abandoned for the unavoidable difficulties of its theory of factor prices and distribution.

[7] Except in the cases in which an already existing *invention* can become a marketable *innovation*, at a certain point in time, due to changes in income distribution, or in relative prices.

[8] Generally with particular features such as limited appropriability, indivisibility, etc. See Arrow [2 and 3].

[9] The effort of "endogenising" the production of knowledge, equated to the production of a commodity, accounts for the evident trend, at least in this century, toward a greater contribution to the innovative activity by institutional centres directly related to production of scientific and technological advances (and first of all by R&D facilities of big corporations). This schumpeterian view (Schumpeter [39]) is challenged by some scholars, for example Jewkes et al. [16] who maintain that a great percentage of innovation is still attributable to private inventors. For an exhaustive discussion of this issue, see Freeman [12]. The problem crucial to our discussion, however, still remains: how do technological efforts operate? Can the direction of technological advances be pushed almost frictionless in any direction? Can the lags between an assumed "market demand" and the technological response be considered fairly limited in time? etc. For a critical discussion of the "black-box approach" to technology, see again Rosenberg [30 and 31].

[10] See project SAPPHO [36] Teubal, Arnon, Trachtenberg [44] and Teubal [45]. Those studies, and especially the first are primarily concerned with determinants of success and failures in industrial innovations and not so much with the determinants of the direction of the innovative activity as such.

to the role of science and technology in fostering innovation along a path leading from initial scientific advances to the final innovative product/process. [11]

On a more general level, an analysis of the technology and generally "supply-side" factors of innovative process can be found in Freeman [12], Pavitt and Wald [28] and Pavitt and Soete [29]. [12] Some aspects of the innovative process can, in our view, be considered rather established. Among them:

(1) The increasing role (at least in this century) of scientific inputs in the innovative process.

(2) The increased complexity of R & D activities which makes the innovative process a matter of long-run planning for the firms (and not only for them) and witnesses against an hypothesis of prompt innovative answer by producers vis-a-vis changes in market conditions.

(3) A significant correlation between R & D efforts (as proxy of the inputs in the innovative process) and innovative output (as measured by patent activity) in several industrial sectors [13] and the absence, in *cross-country* comparisons, of evident correlations between market and demand patterns on the one hand, and innovative output, on the other.

(4) The intrinsically *uncertain* nature of the inventive activity which plays against an hypothesis of limited and known sets of choices and outcomes.

The difficulties incurred by strong versions of "technology-push" theories are in some respects opposite to those discussed above: there, it was the difficulty to take into account the complexity, the relative autonomy and the uncertainty associated with technological change and innovation. Here, the problem arises in relation to the obvious fact that "economic factors are important indeed" in shaping the direction of the innovative process. The process of growth and economic change, variations in distributive shares and in relative prices are all affecting the direction of the innovative activity and one feels quite uneasy in accepting a view of technical progress – paraphrasing Joan Robinson – as "given by God, scientists and engineers". The main theoretical task with respect to supply-side approaches is the avoidance of a one-directional conception "science – technology – production" in which the first would represent a sort of exogenous and neutral *deus-ex-machina*. One realises that, in actual fact, there is a complex structure of feed-backs between the economic environment and the directions of technological changes. A tentative theory of technical change should define – in a form as general as possible – the nature of these inter-active mechanisms. In different ways demand-pull and technology-push theories appear to fail to do so. In the former, technical change and innovation are a basically *reactive* mechanism which certainly shows some consistency with the traditional assumptions of neo-classical economics (consumer sovereignty, optimising behaviours, general equilibrium, etc.) but presents also unavoidable logical and empirical difficulties. On the other hand, if supply-side factors manifest some independence – at least in the short-run – from market changes, it must be possible to show how they are affected in the long run by the economic transformation.

---

[11] See the TRACES Project [15].

[12] In the first study, an analytical examination of various innovations in the fields of process plant, synthetic materials and electronics considers the role of scientific and organised technological efforts in determining innovation, while the second, in a cross-country analysis, compares demand and market-related factors with technological organisational and supply-related factors. Finally, the third relates indicators of economic performance to indicators of technical efforts and innovativeness (in a causal relationship which goes from the latter to the former).

[13] See also the important findings by Pavitt and Soete [29] and Soete [42]. Moreover, if we measure innovative output in terms on increase in productivity (as a proxy of technical progress) the impact of research efforts is significant (see for example Mansfield [19] and Terleckyi [43]).

3. A proposed interpretation: Technological paradigms and technological trajectories

Economic theory usually represents *technology* as a given set of factors' combination, defined (qualitatively and quantitatively) in relation to certain outputs. Technical progress is generally defined in terms of a moving production possibilities curve, and/or in terms of the increasing number of producable goods. The definition we suggest here is, on the contrary, much broader. Let us define technology as a set of pieces of knowledge, both directly "practical" (related to concrete problems and devices) and "theoretical" (but practically applicable although not necessarily already applied), know-how, methods, procedures, experience of successes and failures and also, of course, physical devices and equipment. Existing physical devices embody – so to speak – the achievements in the development of a technology in a defined problem-solving activity. At the same time, a "disembodied" part of the technology consists of particular expertise, experience of past attempts and past technological solutions, together with the knowledge and the achievements of the "state of the art". Technology, in this view, includes the "perception" of a limited set of possible technological alternatives and of notional future developments. This definition of technology is very impressionistic, but it seems useful to explore the patterns of technical change. One can see that the conceptual distance between this definition and the attributes of "science" – as suggested by modern epistemology – is not so great.

We shall push the parallel further and suggest that, in analogy with scientific paradigms (or scientific research programmes), there are "technological paradigms" (or technological research programmes). [14]

A "scientific paradigm" could be approximately defined as an "outlook" which defines the relevant problems, a "model" and a "pattern" of inquiry.

"The success of a paradigm ... is at the start largely a promise of success discoverable in selected and still incomplete examples. Normal science consists in the actualization of that promise, an actualization achieved by extending the knowledge of those facts that the paradigm displays as particularly revealing, by increasing the extent of match between those facts and the paradigm's predictions, and by further articulation of the paradigm itself" (Kuhn [14], pp. 23–41).

In broad analogy with the Kuhnian definition of a "scientific paradigm", we shall define a "technological paradigm" as "model" and a "pattern" of solution of *selected* technological problems, based on *selected* principles derived from natural sciences and on *selected* material technologies.

First of all, the similarities relate to the mechanism and procedures of "science", on the one hand, and those of technology, on the other. [15] As a scientific paradigm determines the field of enquiry, the problems, the procedures and the tasks (the "puzzles", in Kuhn's words), so does "technology" in the sense defined above (it would perhaps be better to talk of "cluster of technologies", e.g. nuclear technologies, semiconductor technologies, organic chemistry technologies, etc.).

As "normal science" is the "actualization of a promise" contained in a scientific paradigm, so is "technical progress" defined by a certain "technological paradigm". We will define a *technological trajectory* as the pattern of "normal" problem solving activity (i.e. of "progress") on the ground of a technological paradigm.

More precisely, if the hypothesis of technological paradigm is to be of some use, one must be able to assess also in the field of technology the existence of something similar to a "positive heuristic" and a "negative heuristic". [16] In other words a technological paradigm (or research programme)[17] embodies strong prescriptions on the *directions* of technical change to pursue and those to neglect. Given some generic technological tasks (one could call them generic "needs") such as, for example, those of transporting commodities and passengers, producing chemical compounds with certain properties or switching and amplifying electrical signals, certain specific technologies emerged, with their own "solutions" to those problems and the exclusion of other notionally possible ones: in our three examples, historically these

---

[14] On scientific paradigms, see Kuhn [14] and on scientific research programmes, Lakatos [17]; for a thorough discussion Musgrave and Lakatos [22]. One does not have any ambition here to argue "what science is" or tackle the epistemological disputes on the differences between the Kuhnian approach and Lakatos' one. For our purposes the degreee of overlap between the two approaches is great enough to borrow from them a few basic definitions of science which they have in common.

[15] A very stimulating paper by Bonfiglioli [5] defines "science" as a "particular technology". Although the aims of that paper are different from ours here, there is in common the strict similarity and overlapping between "science" and "technology" and the role of institutional factors in determining the direction of both (see below).

[16] "... The continuity evolves from a genuine research programme adumbrated at start. The programme consists of methodological rules: some tell us what paths of research to avoid (*negative heuristic*) and others what paths to pursue (*positive heuristic*)". Lakatos [17], p. 47.

[17] Note that here one is impressionistically using the two concepts as equivalent.

technologies were the internal combustion engine, petrochemical processes and semiconductors, respectively. Technological paradigms have a powerful *exclusion effect*: the efforts and the technological imagination of engineers and of the organizations they are in are focussed in rather precise directions while they are, so to speak, "blind" with respect to other technological possibilities. At the same time, technological paradigms define also some idea of "progress". Again in analogy with science, this can hardly be an absolute measure but has some precise meaning within a certain technology. The identification of a technological paradigm relates to generic tasks to which it is applied (e.g. amplifying and switching electrical signals), to the material technology it selects (e.g. semiconductors and more specifically silicon), to the physical/chemical properties it exploits (e.g. the "transistor effect" and "field effect" of semiconductor materials), to the technological and economic dimensions and trade-offs it focusses upon (e.g. density of the circuits, speed, noise-immunity, dispersion, frequency range, unit costs, etc.). Once given these technological and economic dimensions, it is also possible to obtain, broadly speaking, an idea of "progress" as the improvement of the trade-offs related to those dimensions.

The broad analogy between "science" and "technology" we have been drawing should clearly not be taken as an identity. In addition to the obvious difference related to the different nature of the "problem solving" activity, technological "knowledge" is much less well articulated than is scientific knowledge; much of it is not written down and is implicit in "experience", skills, etc. This implies also that the definition of a "technological paradigm" is bound to be much looser while the distinction between "normal activity" and "problem-shifts" is likely to be hard to make in practice. The same idea of a "technological paradigm" should be taken as an approximation, adequate in some cases but less so in others. In our view, however, the analogy keeps its validity in that both ("scientific" and "technological") activities represent strongly selective *gestalten* embodying powerful heuristics.

A crucial question relates to how an established technological paradigm emerged in the first place and how it was "preferred" to other possible ones. Let us consider "downward" the sequence science –technology–production, remembering that it is meant to be just a *logical* simplification which neglects the crucial long-run influence of the economic and technological environments upon science itself.

Even within "science", the problems and the "puzzles" *actually* tackled (and those solved) are of course much more limited in number than the total number of problems and puzzles that the scientific theories potentially allow, and even more so the pieces of theory, puzzles, possibilities of development, "passed-on" from scientific theory to "applied science" and to technology (the last two, at least, being significantly overlapping). Leaving aside temporarily the problems of feedbacks, the hypothesis is that along the stream science–technology– production, the "economic forces" (that I will define below) together with institutional and social factors, operate as a *selective device* (the "focussing device" of Rosenberg [30]). Within a large set of *possibilities* of directions of development, notionally allowed by "science", a first level of selection (at least in the overwhelming majority of research activity in the enterprise sector) operates on the basis of rather general questions like: "Is any practical application conceivable?"; "Is there some possibility of the hypothesised application being marketable?", etc. Along the down-stream from "Big Science" to production (on a path which is much easier to conceive as a continuum instead of a strictly defined discrete set of steps), the *determinateness* of the selection increases: at one end we have the "puzzle-solving activity" (Kuhn [14]) defined by scientific paradigms *stricto sensu*; at the other end we have a technology totally embodied in devices and equipment. In between, in a field that we must already call technology because it is specifically ("economically") finalised, the activities aimed at "technical progress" have still many procedures and features similar to "science", namely the problem solving activity along lines defined by the nature of the paradigm. The economic criteria acting as selectors define more and more precisely the *actual* paths followed inside a much bigger set of possible ones.

On the other hand, once a path has been selected and established, it shows a momentum of its own (Nelson and Winter [24], Rosenberg [30]), which contributes to define the directions toward which the "problem solving activity" moves: those are what Nelson and Winter [25] define as *natural trajectories* of technical progress [18]. A technological trajectory, i.e. to repeat, the "normal" problem solving activity determined by a paradigm, can be represented by the movement of multi-dimensional trade-offs among the technological variables which the paradigm defines as relevant. Progress can be defined as the improvement of these trade-offs. [19] One could thus imagine the trajectory as a "cylinder" in the multidimensional space defined by these technological and economic variables. (Thus, a technological trajectory is a cluster of possible technological directions whose outer boundaries are defined by the nature of the paradigm itself). Some features of these technological trajectories, defined on the basis of technological paradigms are worth considering:

1. There might be more general or more circumscribed as well as more powerful or less powerful [20] "trajectories".

2. There generally are *complementarities* among trajectories (i.e., out of the metaphor, there are strong complementarities between different forms of knowledge, experience, skills, etc.) (see Rosenberg [30 and 48]). Furthermore developments or lack of development in one technology might foster or prevent developments in other technologies.

3. In terms of our model one can define as the "technological frontier" the highest level reached upon a technological path with respect to the relevant technological and economic dimensions. [21]

4. "Progress" upon a technological trajectory is likely to retain some cumulative features: the probability of future advances is in this case related also to the position that one (a firm or a country) already occupies vis-a-vis the existing technological frontier. This is strictly consistent with Nelson and Winter's representation of technical progress at firm and industry levels, with Markovian chains. (Nelson and Winter [24]).

5. Especially when a trajectory is very "powerful", it might be difficult to switch from one trajectory to an alternative one. Moreover, when some comparability is possible between the two (i.e. when they have some "dimensions" in common), the frontier on the alternative ("new") trajectory might be far behind that on the old one with respect to some or all the common dimensions. In other words, whenever the technological paradigm changes, one has got to start (almost) from the beginning in the problem-solving activity.

6. It is doubtful whether it is possible *a priori* to compare and assess the superiority of one technological path over another. There might indeed be some objective criteria, once chosen some indicators, but only *ex post*. [22] This is one of the reasons behind the intimate uncertain nature of

---

[18] They suggest two general dimensions of these "natural trajectories", toward progressive exploitation of latent economies of scale and toward increasing mechanisation of operations, quoting as supporting evidence – among others – the studies by Hughes on electric power equipment, Levin on various petrochemical processes and Rosenberg [30].

[19] To take obvious examples, the trade-offs between energy consumption and horsepower in internal combustion engines or that between speed and density of the circuits in semiconductors (this refers to the comparison between bipolar and MOS technologies). A definition of technical progress in terms of multi-dimentional trade-offs is sometimes used in technological forecasting models. For a short overview, see Martino [20]. Sahal [33 and 34] utilize a similar definition of technology and technical progress, applied to individual industries and products.

After the first draft of this paper was completed, an important article by Sahal [47] was published. He suggests a "system approach" to technology and technical change, seeing it as an evolutionary and continuum process. Moreover he suggests the existence of "technological guide-posts". One can easily see the consistence of his thesis with what is argued here. We hope, in this paper, to throw some light also on the definition, emergence and selection of his "technological guide-posts" and on the implications in terms of evolution of industrial structures.

[20] Again one uses the term in analogy with epistemology: in our case a trajectory is more powerful the bigger the set of technologies which it excludes. For instance it seems that the technological paths defined by nuclear or oil power-generation equipment is very powerful, meaning that many other sources of energy (many other technologies) are excluded.

[21] One may figure that "frontier" as a set of points in a multidimensional space.

[22] For some examples on semiconductors, Dosi [7]. An important attempt to define some precise criteria of "progress" is in Sahal [34]. As should be clear from the discussion above, an unequivocal criterion can be easily identified only *within* a technological paradigm (i.e. *along* a technological trajectory). Comparisons (even *ex post*) between different trajectories might yield sometimes, although not always, to ambiguous results. In other words, it might occur that the "new" technology is "better" than the "old" one in several chosen dimensions, but it might still be "worse" in some others. One can see here a loose analogy with the epistemological discussion (whereby an "extreme" Kuhnian approach claims strict incomparability and a Popper-like approach suggests some progressive continuity).

research activity (even leaving aside the market evaluations of the results, but just considering purely technological indicators).

The role of economic, institutional and social factors must be considered in greater detail. A first crucial role – as already mentioned – is the *selection* operated at each level, from research to production-related technological efforts, among the possible "paths", on the ground of some rather obvious and broad criteria such as feasibility, marketability and profitability.

On these very general grounds, there might still be many possible technological paradigms that could be chosen. Given the intrinsic uncertainty associated with their outcomes, in terms of both technological and economic success, it is hardly possible to compare and rank them *ex ante*. [23] Other more specific variables are likely to come into play such as (1) the economic interests of the organizations involved in R & D in these new technological areas, (2) their technological history, the fields of their expertise, etc; (3) institutional variables *stricto sensu* such as public agencies, the military, etc. All these factors are likely to operate as focussing forces upon defined directions of technological development. In particular one must stress the role often played in the establishment of a particular technological trajectory by public ("political") forces. An obvious example is electronics, especially in the fields of semiconductors and computers during the first two decades of the post-war period. Military and space programmes operated then as a powerful focussing mechanism toward defined technological targets, while at the same time providing financial support to R & D and guaranteeing public procurement. [24] Other similar cases can be found throughout the modern history of technology: for example, the emergence of synthetic chemistry in Germany bears a close relationship with the "political" drive of that country towards self-sufficiency in the post-Bismarck period (see Freeman [12] and Walsh et al. [46]).

These kinds of institutional effects upon the emergence of new technologies are not a general rule: the point we want to stress, however, is the general weakness of market mechanisms in the *ex*

ante selection of technological directions especially at the initial stage of the history of an industry. This is, incidentally, one of the reasons that militates for the existence of "bridging institutions" between "pure" science and applied R & D. [25]. Even when a significant "institutional focussing" occurs, there are likely to be different technological possibilities, an uncertain process of search, with different organizations, firms and individuals "betting" on different technological solutions. Proceeding in our parallel with epistemology, this resembles a world *à la* Feyerabend [11] with different competing technological paradigms: competition does not only occur between the "new" technology and the "old" one which it tends to substitute but also among alternative "new" technological approaches.

We did not say very much about *positive ex ante* criteria of selection among potential technological paradigms apart from rather general ones such as marketability or potential profitability. Another powerful selecting criterion in capitalist economies is likely to be the cost saving capability of the new technology and in particular its labour saving potential: this is obviously consistent with Nelson and Winter's suggestion of "natural trajectories" toward mechanisation and exploitation of economies of scale. Certainly in societies where industrial conflict and conflict over income distribution are structural features, substitution of machines for labour must be a powerful determinant in the search process for new technologies. [26]

More generally, the patterns of industrial and social conflict are likely to operate, within the process of selection of new technological paradigms, both as negative criteria (which possible developments to exclude) and as positive criteria (which technologies to select). In this respect, one might be able to define some long-run relationship between patterns of social development and actually chosen technological paradigms (one quite clear example could be the relationship between industrial relations at the turn of the last century and the selection and development of "tayloristic"

---

[23] For a discussion of uncertainty in R&D projects' evaluation, see Freeman [12].

[24] A more detailed discussion is in [7].

[25] A convincing and thorough discussion is in Freeman [12].

[26] The discussion of possible biases in cost-saving technical change, long-run cycles, etc. is clearly beyond the scope of this work. Our hypotheses on the procedures of technical change and innovation might, however, provide a possible framework for the analysis of these questions.

patterns of technical change in mechanical engineering).

Let us consider the final stage of this logical sequence from science to production, when – in cases of product innovations – a commodity is produced and sold: at this final stage markets operate again as the selective environment.[27] It must be noted that this "final selection" has a different nature from the previous stages. In the choices of the technological paths some kinds of economic indicators were operating as *a priori* directing devices among a big number of possible and wide technological choices. Here the market operates *ex post* as a selecting device, generally among a range of products already determined by the broad technology patterns chosen *on the supply side*. To further clarify the distinction, R. Nelson suggested in his comments on a previous draft of this paper, a biological analogy. The final market selection may be equated to the environmental selection on mutations (Nelson and Winter models describe mainly this "evolutionary" mechanism within the economic environment). The discussion above relates, on the contrary, to the selection of the "mutation generating" mechanisms. Thus economic and social environment affects technological development in two ways, first selecting the "direction of mutation" (i.e. selecting the technological paradigm) and then selecting among mutations, in a more darwinian manner (i.e. the *ex post* selection among "schumpeterian" trials and errors). At times when new technologies are emerging, one can often observe new ("schumpeterian") companies trying to exploit different technological innovations. Markets perform as a system of rewards and penalizations, thus checking and selecting amongst different alternatives. In this respect, the existence of a multiplicity of risk-taking actors, in non-planned economies, is crucial to the trial-and-error procedures associated with the search for new technological paths. These "actors" take risks, of course, because there are markets which allow high rewards (i.e. profits) in case of commercial success.

Incidentally, one should note that if our interpretation of the process of technical change is correct, the emergence of new technological paradigms is *contextual* to the explicit emergence of economically defined "needs". In other words, the supply-side determines, so to speak, the "universe"

of possible modalities through which generic "needs" or productive requirements (which as such do not have any direct economic significance) are satisfied. (In this, one can see the element of truth contained in those sociologically-based theories suggesting needs "induced" by corporate strategies).

Changing economic conditions clearly interact with the process of selection of new technologies, with their development and finally with their obsolescence and substitution. One has therefore to analyze the feed-back mechanisms, "upward", from the economic environment to the technology (one should also consider the long-run influence of economic and technological factors upon scientific change: this is however well beyond the scope of this article). Changing relative prices and distributive share are bound to affect demand for the various commodities and the relative profitabilities in manufacturing them. Producers certainly react to these signals from the economic environment, trying to respond through technical advances. However, this often occurs within the boundaries of a given technological trajectory, which might either be conducive or place increasing constraints to any development consistent with the "signals" the economic environment is delivering.[28] Difficulties and unsolved technological puzzles and problems, to use again the Kuhnian language, operate upward as focussing devices, sometimes put pressure on other technological fields to go further in their problem solving, and finally facilitate or hinder the switch to other technological trajectories. It must be stressed, however, that unsolved technological difficulties do not automatically imply a change to another "path".[29] Of course, changes in market conditions and opportunities (among which changes in demand patterns, in relative distributive shares, in costs of production, etc. are very important) continuously bring pressures "upward", at various levels, upon technological trajectories, and upon the same selection criteria on the basis of which those trajectories are chosen. But this fact does not imply by

[27] See Nelson and Winter [24].

---

[28] Take the example of the oil-powered internal combustion engine. Changing oil prices put an increasing pressure on oil substitution and energy saving. The scope for substitution however is limited by the technology which itself defines the range of possible technological advances.

[29] Precisely as unsolved puzzles or ("falsifications") in a scientific paradigm do not imply an alternative paradigm.

any means an assumption of malleable "ready-to-use" alternative technological paths, or, even more so, instantaneous technological responses to changes in market conditions. Furthermore an implicit consequence of what was just said is that the "upward" impact of changing economic conditions on technological research patterns seems directly proportional to the *technological determinateness* of the economic stimuli themselves.[30] So one would generally expect this determinateness to increase as one moves from consumers' goods to investment goods and to other kinds of non-properly-market goods (such as military equipment).

Note that changes in the economic environment are a permanent feature of the system: those changes often simply stimulate technical progress (as defined above) *along* one technological trajectory. Again in parallel with epistemology we can call it the "normal" technological activity. "Extraordinary" technological attempts (related to the search for new technological directions) emerge either in relation to new opportunities opened-up by scientific developments or to the increasing difficulty in going forward on a given technological direction (for technological or economic reasons or both).[31]

4. Technical change and industrial structures: From a schumpeterian phase to industrial maturity

We tried above to make a logical distinction between the process of search and selection on new technological paradigms and technical progress along a defined path. New technologies are selected through a complex interaction between some fundamental economic factors (search for new profit opportunities and for new markets, tendency toward cost saving and automation, etc.), together with powerful institutional factors (the interests and the structure of the existing firms, the

effects of government agencies, etc.). Technical change along established technological paths, on the contrary, becomes more endogenous to the "normal" economic mechanism. This distinction between two technological phases is likely to correspond historically to two different sets of features of an industry, related to its emergence and its maturity. In the phase of economic *trial and error*, primary importance must be attributed to (1) the *institutions* which produce and direct the accumulation of knowledge, experience, etc., and (2) the existence of a multiplicity of risk-taking actors, ready to try different technical and commercial solutions. The "schumpeterian" features properly refer to this second aspect.[32] Note that breakthroughs and innovations, in this phase, need not be developed by those schumpeterian companies themselves. There is evidence, on the contrary, that often in this century the production of major technological advances has been the result of organized R&D efforts as opposed to the "inventiveness" of individuals.[33] What matters are the attempts (either by new companies or old ones), in the first phase, to implement and commercially exploit "extraordinary technology", driven by the search for new profit and market opportunities. Often this period of emergence of new technologies is actually characterized by newly emerging firms, even in cases when the major technological advances were originally produced in established firms and institutions (semiconductors for example).[34]

In the second phase, which may often correspond to an *oligopolistic maturity*, the production, exploitation and commercial diffusion of innovations are much less divorced and technical change often becomes itself part of the pattern of "oligopolistic competition". The more a fundamental technological pattern becomes established, the more the mechanism of generation of innovations

---

[30] This broadly corresponds to Teubal's concept of *market determinateness* [45].

[31] It can be (and has been) reasonably argued that scientific developments themselves are fostered in the long-run by technological and economic "foci" of attention and that they are somewhat directed by the *weltanschauungen* that economic systems provide. This very wide issue concerns fields like epistemology, sociology of knowledge, etc., and it is not possible to discuss it here.

[32] Here one refers to the "first" Schumpeter of the *Theory of Economic Development* [38].

[33] A review of the discussion on the subject is in Freeman [12]. Some, however, still hold the opposite view (Jewkes et al. [16]). The history of chemical innovations is analyzed by Walsh et al. [46]. On the role of established firms in semiconductors, see [7].

[34] We try to analyze the factors which allow it, related to different attitudes toward risk, constraints facing a quick diffusion of innovations by existing firms, taxation regimes, in [9].

and of technological advances appears to become endogenous to the "normal" economic mechanism. In this respect, the possibility of enjoying temporary monopolistic (and long-run oligopolistic) positions on new products and processes appears to act as a powerful incentive to the innovative activity, improvement of existing products, etc. The perspective differential advantages accruing to successful technological and market leaders, in my view, are likely to influence and stimulate the process of innovation much more than the *ex ante* market structure as such.[35] The process of innovation itself is, of course, bound to affect the industrial structure and shape its transformation.

The establishment of a defined technological paradigm is likely to be parallelled by a process of "internalization" within companies of the so-called "externalities" related to the innovative activity, capitalizing on the previous experience of attempts, successes and failures, etc.: within an established technological paradigm the fluid market structure characterized by the "heroic entrepreneurship" often described in the literature on new industries is likely to disappear.

Both phases are likely to show some "oligopolistic power",[36] although the sources of it differ

significantly: whereas in the first one, oligopolistic positions mainly relate to *dynamic* economies ("learning curve", etc.) and temporary asymmetries in relation to the capability of successfully innovating, in the second stage the origins of oligopolistic structures would relate not only to the technological progressiveness of firms but also to some *static* entry barriers (economies of scale, etc.).

5. Conclusions: Some theoretical and policy implications

We should stress, first of all, the limitations of the suggested model: the analogy between science and technology is, in some respects, "impressionistic" and the parallel should not be pushed too far without reaching decreasing returns. This notwithstanding, the model might prove useful in interpreting some important questions related to the process of technical change. First, it can explain – in rather general terms – the role of *continuity* versus *discontinuity* in technical change. "Incremental" innovation versus "radical" innovations can be reinterpreted in terms of "normal" technical progress as opposed to new emerging technological paradigms. The distinction might still be in practice difficult to draw, but nonetheless can account for the conditions which allow either "normal" progress or "extraordinary" innovative effort to take place. Second, it can throw some light on the *procedures* through which technical change occurs. The search for new products or processes is never a random process on the entire set of notional technological opportunities. Paradigms are also an "outlook" which focusses the eye and the efforts of technologists and engineers in defined directions. (This, incidentally, might have interesting implications in terms of the sociology of the firms and it would be worth studying the origins and the backgrounds of "revolutionary" engineers as compared with "normal" ones).

[35] The relationship between market structure and incentives to innovate has produced significant discussion in the literature. See among other, Arrow [2], Needham [49], Shrieves [40], Scherer [50] and Salvati [35]. Salvati shows, under rather general assumptions that the incentive to *introduce innovations* is not generally lower under oligopolistic conditions than in competitive ones. Arrow, in his seminal article, states the opposite view (at least as far as process innovations are concerned), with respect to the incentive to *produce* innovations. Two implicit and rather questionable assumptions are, however, crucial to his argument. First, one must assume that there are no economies of scale and no minimum threshold in R&D activities, no cumulativeness of technical progress, or, alternatively, that market mechanisms induce an allocation of innovative activities amongst competitive actors, *as if* they were a simple monopolist. Second, one must assume that the "degree of private appropriability" of the innovations is the same under competitive and oligopolistic conditions. Needham offers a thorough and rigorous treatment of R&D and innovation decisions under neo-classical behavioural assumptions on firms' conduct. He shows that, depending on elasticities and expected rivals' reactions, more or less everything may be expected to happen (i.e. that structural variables like concentration, demand elasticities, etc. may have effects of opposite signs upon firms' propensity to innovate).

One can find in Soete [41] a critical analysis of the available evidence on the subject and a strong support for a

"Schumpeterian view". Nelson and Winter [24] interpret, in a genuinely dynamic framework, the process of innovation under oligopolistic conditions and market structure itself, in their models, as an endogenous variable.

[36] I try to assess the existence of the determinants of oligopolistic margins in the semiconductor industry in [9].

Third, the idea of paradigms and trajectories can account for the often observable phenomenon of *cumulativeness* of technical advances (within an established trajectory). At the same time the intrinsic *uncertainty* associated with technological shifts can be clearly appreciated. The same idea of "technical progress' might be rigorously defined within one technological path (as the improvements of the trade-offs between the technological and economic dimensions it embodies) but it might prove impossible to compare *ex ante* two different technological paradigms and even *ex post* there might be overwhelming difficulties in doing it on solely technological grounds.[37]

We tried to suggest some interacting mechanisms between technological factors and economic factors, the latter performing as selective criteria, as final ("market") checking and as a continuous form of incentives, constraints and "feed-back" stimuli. The evidence on market-induced innovative activity (see Schmookler [37]) which survives a closer scrutiny of its empirical foundations[38] may indeed be consistent with our model: economic growth and transformation of the economy involves a permanent re-allocation of resources as well as of research efforts among different sectors, and it is plausible to assume that a greater effort will be put into those areas which offer relatively higher growth and profit opportunities (although the two might not necessarily coincide). This process, however, relates much more to *normal* technology than to discontinuous technological advances. In other words: suppose there are two sectors, both defined by rather stable technological trajectories, which allow broadly similar possibili-

ties of technological advance,[39] but one experiences higher rates of growth of demand than the other. It is plausible that a firm will put greater research efforts into the first rather than the second sector. Moreover, if there is some relationship between research input and innovative output, one may find a higher number of technical innovations (as measured, say, by patents) in the former sector. This induced effect, however, does *not* explain the emergence of significantly radical innovations, which is precisely what one tried to do above. This is not to say that the emergence of new technological paradigms is independent of the evolution and the changes in the social system (of which the economic structure is a crucial component). A reconstruction of the history of technology and history of science would almost certainly show the long-run influences of the evolution of the social and economic structure upon the emergence of new scientific and technological opportunities. Simply, what we want to stress is their relative autonomy vis-a-vis short-run adjustment and inducement mechanisms of the economic system (changes in prices, quantities, profitabilities, etc.).

Various hypotheses on the determinants and directions of technical changes have been proposed, during the past two decades, in a revived attention to the schumpeterian problematique of the long-run relationship between technical change and economic growth (one should actually refer also to Marx as the other classical economist who focussed on the issue). It is worth mentioning these models and hypotheses, not only to acknowledge our theoretical debts, but also to discuss briefly the reciprocal consistency. We refer in particular to Freeman [18], Nelson and Winter [24–26], Rosenberg [30], Abernathy and Utterback [1], Sahal [34 and 7]. In different ways, and with different analytical aims, one may consider these contributions as part of a painstaking attempt to construct a non-neoclassical theory of technical change capable of giving a satisfactory account of (1) the relationship between economic forces and the relatively autonomous momentum that techni-

---

[37] Another example from the semiconductor industry: how could it have been possible to compare in the 1950s the thermionic valve technology and the emerging semiconductor technology? Even *ex post* (i.e. now) when most of the common dimensions (e.g. size and density, speed, costs, energy consumption, etc.) show the striking superiority of semiconductor technology, valves still maintain in some narrow technological dimensions their advantage. Note that we took here one of the most extreme examples of a new clear-cut "superior" technology: in many other cases even an *ex post* comparison between the different technologies may prove rather difficult.

[38] Walsh et al. [46] examine Schmookler's hypothesis of a dependence of innovative activity upon market growth and in the case of chemical innovations find abundant falsifying evidence.

[39] Note that within stable technologies the possibilities of advances (so to speak, the potential rate of technical progress compatible with that technology) might radically differ. A low possibility of further advances and unsolved (or "badly" solved) technical problems might indeed be a stimulus for the search for a new technological paradigm.

cal progress appears to maintain, (2) the role of supply-side factors, (3) the role and effects of technical change in oligopolistic environments, (4) its relationship with company behaviour and organizational structures, (5) the relevance of non-market organizations and first of all of public institutions in shaping the patterns of technical change.

Broadly speaking, the interpretation of the procedures, progresses and shifts in the innovative process proposed here are, in my view, consistent with the approach of the above cited works, for what they have in common. Few features need mention. In particular, the continuity (and partial overlapping) between our hypothesis and Nelson and Winter's models should be clear enough. The existence of technological paradigms, with the attributes one tried to describe, support the existence of "natural trajectories" of technical change suggested by Nelson and Winter. Their models focus primarily on the *endogenous dynamics* of technical progress in oligopolistic environments (and differential innovative success is, in their simulations of the model, one of the main driving forces toward oligopolistic structures). Translated in the definitions used above, their model [24] gives us a fascinating (and rich in terms of firms' behavioural variables) account of the transition to oligopolistic maturity and of the technology-based oligopolistic competition thereafter, upon a given technological path. On the other hand, the weakness of simple market mechanisms (together with the likely inadequacies of institutional intervention) in the innovative process are discussed by Nelson in [27].

Two incidental remarks related to economic theory: first, if technological paradigms and technological trajectories prove to be a general case in the modern history of technology, then it becomes more plausible to assume – in terms of "aggregate" technical progress in the economy as defined by input coefficients of production – one discrete (and limited) set of input combinations. Technical change should then be strictly associated with their movement "outward" (using the traditional representation of production functions) along something like a cone, rather than the movement along and of, a smooth curve. Second, this idea of technological paradigms and trajectories bear some relevance within the revived discussion concerning the existence and the determinants of Kondratief's

long-waves (see Clark, Freeman and Soete [6]). One of the variables affecting long-run cycles of capitalist development may be the *establishment* of broad new technological trajectories, which could explain the "clustering" of groups of innovations and, even more important, the "clustering" in time of their economic impact.

The innovative process – both in its "normal" procedures and in its "extraordinary" breakthroughs – is shaped by the interplay of economic and institutional factors. One can distinguish, however, the role of public policies related to the search for new technological paths, from that aimed at technological advances along a broadly defined technology. In the former case policies concern what one may call "the burden of the first comer". Throughout the process of selection and emergence of new technologies, three crucial institutional factors appear to be crucial: (1) the accumulation of knowledge in both "scientific" and "applied" forms (in this respect the existence of "bridging institutions" between proper "science" and technology is of the utmost importance (see Freeman [12]).; (2) forms of institutional intervention which allow "a hundred flowers to blossom and a hundred schools to compete" – both in terms of technological explorations and manufacturing attempts; (3) the selective and focussing effect induced by various forms of *stricto sensu* non-economic interests (such as, for example, military technological requirements and procurement, specific energy saving programmes, the national drive toward self-sufficiency in a particular sector, etc.). One must notice that even when technological paths are well established, the above-mentioned variables may contribute to shape and determine the rate at which technical advances occur. Moreover, even at this stage when technical advances are in many ways endogenous to the economic dynamics, both the uncertainty related to the R&D process and the existence of untraded aspects of technical change do not disappear. Under these circumstances even traditional economics suggest normatively some form of public intervention to correct what it calls "market failures" related to differences between social and private rates of return and between social and private discounts of risks, and to "externalities".

A particularly interesting case refers to countries lagging behind vis-a-vis the technological frontier on a certain technology. If technical advances maintain their cumulative (although stochastic) nature, and if oligopolistic structures tend to appropriate those technological leads, the process of technical change as such is not likely to yield to convergence between countries starting from different technological levels.[40] Imitative technological policies in this case might not be sufficient and public intervention aimed at catching-up might have to affect trade flows, foreign investment, and the structure of the domestic industry (I discuss at some length those policies in Europe and Japan for electronics in [8]).

I wish to make our final comment on the heuristic capability of this interpretation of the process of technical change and innovation. For our suggestion to prove useful, one should be able to (1) identify with sufficient precision the "dimensions" which characterize each broad technological paradigm and differentiate it from others, (2) separate the periods of "normal" technology from extraordinary search, (3) define the "difficult puzzles" and unsolved difficulties of a technology which are often a necessary (although not sufficient) condition for the search for other ones; (4) describe the transition from one technological path to another and assess the factors which allow the emergence of a "winning" technology. Probably this exercise will be possible in some instances and not in others.

Technological paradigms and trajectories, are in some respects metaphors of the interplay between continuity and ruptures in the process of incorporation of knowledge and technology into industrial growth: the metaphor, however, should help to illuminate its various aspects and actors and to suggest a multi-variables approach to the theory of innovation and technical change.

References

[1] W.J. Abernathy and J.M. Utterback, *Innovation and the Evolution of the Firm*, Harvard University, mimeo, 1976.
[2] K. Arrow, Economic Welfare and the Allocation of Resources for Invention, in NBER [23].

---

[40] Of course there are other factors which induce technological diffusion and convergence. A discussion of variables such as differential labour costs, international investments, market "imperfections" which allow countries to develop domestic manufacturing, etc. can be found in [10].

[3] K. Arrow, The Economic Implications of Learning by Doing, *Review of Economic Studies*, 1962.
[4] B. Belassa and R. Nelson (eds.), *Economic Progress, Private Values and Public Policies: Essays in honour of William Fellner* (North-Holland, Amsterdam, 1977).
[5] A. Bonfiglioli, *Universal Science, Appropriate Technology and Underdevelopment: A Reprise of the Latin-American Case*, SPRU, University of Sussex, mimeo, 1979.
[6] J. Clark, C. Freeman and L. Soete, *Long Waves and Technological Developments in the 20th Century*, paper prepared for the Bochum Conference on *Wirtschafliche Wechsellagen und Sozialer Wandel*, SPRU, University of Sussex, mimeo, 1980.
[7] G. Dosi, *Institutional Factors and Market Mechanisms in the Innovative Process*, SERC, University of Sussex, mimeo, 1979.
[8] G. Dosi, *Technical Change and Survival: Europe's Semiconductor Industry*, Sussex European Papers, University of Sussex, 1981.
[9] G. Dosi, *Structure of the Industry and Pricing Policies – Some Theoretical Hypotheses and the Evidence from Semiconductor Industry*, SERC, University of Sussex, mimeo, 1980.
[10] G. Dosi, *Transmission Mechanisms of Technical Change, Adjustment Problems and Their International Implications*, SERC, University of Sussex, mimeo, 1981.
[11] P.K. Feyerabend, *Against Method* (New Left Books, London, 1975).
[12] C. Freeman, *The Economics of Industrial Innovation* (Penguin, Harmondsworth, 1974).
[13] R. Gilpin, *Technology, Economic Growth and International Competitiveness* (U.S. Government Printing Office, Washington, 1975).
[14] T. Kuhn, *The Structure of Scientific Revolutions* (Chicago University Press, Chicago, 1962).
[15] Illinois Institute of Technology, *Report on Project TRACES* (National Science Foundation, Washington, 1969).
[16] J. Jewkes, D. Sawers and R. Stillerman, *The Sources of Invention* (Macmillan, London, 1958).
[17] I. Lakatos, *The Methodology of Scientific Research Programmes* (Cambridge University Press, Cambridge, 1978).
[18] R. Levin, *Toward an Empirical Model of Schumpeterian Competition*, Yale University, mimeo, 1980.
[19] E. Mansfield, *Industrial Research and Technological Innovation* (Norton, New York, 1968).
[20] J.P. Martino, Technological Forecasting – An Overview, *Management Science*, January, 1980.
[21] S. Meyers and D.G. Marquis, *Successful Industrial Innovation*, (National Science Foundation, Washington, 1969).
[22] R.A. Musgrave and I. Lakatos (eds.) *Criticism and Growth of Knowledge* (Cambridge University Press, Cambridge, 1973).
[23] National Bureau and Economic Research, *The Rate and Direction of Inventive Activity* (Princeton University Press, Princeton, NJ, 1962).
[24] R. Nelson and S. Winter, Dynamic Competition and Technical Progress, in [4].
[25] R. Nelson and S. Winter, In Search of a Useful Theory of Innovation, *Research Policy*, 6 (1977).
[26] R. Nelson and S. Winter, *The Schumpeterian Trade-offs Revisited*, Yale University, mimeo, 1980.

[27] R. Nelson, *Balancing Market Failure and Government In-adequacy: The Case of Policy Toward Industrial R&D*, Working Paper no. 840, Yale University, 1980.

[28] K. Pavitt and S. Wald, *The Conditions for Success in Technological Innovation*, (OECD, Paris, 1971).

[29] K. Pavitt and L. Soete, Innovative Activities and Export Shares: Some Comparisons between Industries and Countries, in K. Pavitt (ed.) *Technical Innovation and British Economic Performance* (Macmillan, London, 1980).

[30] N. Rosenberg, *Perspectives on Technology* (Cambridge University Press, Cambridge, 1976).

[31] N. Rosenberg and D. Mowery, The Influence of Market Demand upon Innovation: A Critical Review of some Recent Empirical Studies, *Research Policy*, 8 (1978).

[32] D. Sahal, *Recent Advances in a Theory of Technological Change* (International Institute of Management, Berlin, 1979).

[33] D. Sahal, On the Conception and Measurement of Trade-offs in Engineering Systems, *Technological Forecasting and Social Change* (1974).

[34] D. Sahal, *Law-like Aspects of Technological Development* (International Institute of Management, Berlin, 1978).

[35] M. Salvati, *Monopolio Sviluppo e Distribuzione* (Edizioni dell'Ateneo, Rome, 1971).

[36] Science Policy Research Unit (SPRU), *Report on Project SAPPHO* (SPRU, University of Sussex, 1971).

[37] J. Schmookler, *Invention and Economic Growth* (Harvard University Press, Cambridge, MA 1966).

[38] J. Schumpeter, *The Theory of Economic Development* (OUP, New York, 1961)(first ed. 1919).

[39] J. Schumpeter, *Capitalism, Socialism and Democracy* (Harpers, New York, 1947).

[40] R. Shrieves, Market Structure and Innovation: A New Perspective, *Journal of Industrial Economics*, June (1978).

[41] L. Soete, Firm Size and Inventive Activity: The Evidence Reconsidered, *European Economic Review*, 12 (1979).

[42] L. Soete, A General Test of Technology Gap Theory, *Weltwirtschaftliches Archiv* (1981).

[43] N. Terleckyj, *The Effects of R&D on Productivity Growth in Industry* (National Planning Association, Washington, 1974).

[44] M. Teubal, N. Arnon and M. Trachtenberg, The Performance in the Israeli Electronics Industry: A Case Study of Biomedical Instrumentation, *Research Policy* (1976).

[45] M. Teubal, *On Users Needs and Need Determination: Aspects of the Theory of Technological Innovation*, Maurice Falk Institute for Economic Research in Israel, Discussion Paper No. 774, 1977.

[46] V.M. Walsh, J.F. Townsend, B.G. Achilladelis and C. Freeman, *Trends in Invention and Innovation in the Chemical Industry*, Report to SSRC, SPRU, University of Sussex, mimeo, 1979.

[47] D. Sahal, Alternative Conceptions of Technology, *Research Policy* (1981).

[48] N. Rosenberg, Technological Interdependence in the American Economy, *Technology and Culture* (1978).

[49] D. Needham, Market Structure and Firms; R&D Behaviour, *Journal of Industrial Economics* (1975).

[50] R. Scherer, Firm Size, Market Structure, Opportunity and the Output of Patented Inventions, *American Economic Review* (1965).

[2]

Journal of Economic Literature
Vol. XXVI (September 1988), pp. 1120–1171

Sources, Procedures, and Microeconomic Effects of Innovation

By Giovanni Dosi

University of Sussex and University of Rome

Fabio Arcangeli, Paul David, Frank Engelman, Christopher Freeman, Massimo Moggi, Richard Nelson, Luigi Orsenigo, Nathan Rosenberg, Michele Salvati, G. N. von Tunzelman, two anonymous referees, and the participants at the meeting of the Committee on Distribution, Growth, and Technical Progress of the Italian National Research Council (CNR), Rome, November 16, 1985, have helped with various redraftings. A particularly grateful acknowledgment is for the insightful and patient help of Moses Abramovitz.

This work has been undertaken at the Science Policy Research Unit (SPRU), University of Sussex, as part of the research program of the Designated Research Centre, sponsored by the Economic and Social Research Council (ESRC). Earlier support to the research that led to this paper by the Italian National Research Council (CNR) is also gratefully acknowledged. The statistical research has been undertaken with the assistance of Stephano Brioschi, Ilaria Fornari, and Giovannu Prennushi.

I. Introduction

THIS ESSAY concerns the determinants and effects of innovative activities in contemporary market economies. In the most general terms, private profit-seeking agents will plausibly allocate resources to the exploration and development of new products and new techniques of production if they know, or believe in, the existence of some sort of yet unexploited scientific and technical opportunities; if they expect that there will be a market for their new products and processes; and, finally, if they expect some economic benefit, net of the incurred costs, deriving from the innovations. In turn, the success of some agents in introducing or imitating new products and production processes changes their production costs, their market competitiveness and, ultimately, is part of the evolution of the industries affected by the innovations.

It is the purpose of this essay to analyze the processes leading from notional technological opportunities to actual innovative efforts and, finally, to changes in the structures and performance of industries.

Thus, I shall discuss the sources of innovation opportunities, the role of markets in allocating resources to the exploration of these opportunities and in determining the rates and directions of technological advances, the characteristics of the processes of innovative search, and the nature of the incentives driving private agents to commit themselves to innovation.

It is not my purpose to review the whole body of innovation-related literature.[1] Rather I limit my discussion to a selected group of (mostly empirical) contributions and focus on the microeconomic nature of innovative activities and the effects of innovation upon techniques of production, product characteristics, and patterns of change of industrial structures. The discussion will aim to identify (a) the main characteristics of the innovative process, (b) the factors that are conducive to or hinder the development of new processes of production and new products, and (c) the processes that determine the selection of particular innovations and their effects on industrial structures.

There are two major sets of issues here: first, the characterization, *in general,* of the innovative process, and, second, the interpretation of the factors that account for observed differences in the modes of innovative search and in the rates of innovation between different sectors and firms and over time.

Typically, the search, development, and adoption of new processes and products in noncentrally planned economies are the outcome of the interaction between (a) capabilities and stimuli generated within each firm and within industries and (b) broader causes external to the individual industries, such as the state of science in different branches; the facilities for the communication of knowledge; the supply of technical capabilities, skills, engineers, and so on; the conditions controlling occupational and geographical mobility and/or consumer promptness/resistance to change; market conditions, particularly in their bearing on interfirm competition and on demand growth; financial facilities and patterns and criteria of allocation of funds to the industrial firms; macroeconomic trends, especially in their effects on changes in relative prices of inputs and outputs; public policies (e.g., tax codes, patent laws, industrial policies, public procurement). It is impossible to consider here each of these factors in detail and the survey will focus upon the procedures, determinants, and effects of the innovative efforts of business firms; however, at each step of the analysis, I will try to show how those broader factors affect the opportunities, incentives, and capabilities of innovating in different firms and industries.

The empirical evidence rests on studies of several industries and technologies; however, particular attention is devoted to the characteristics and effects of microelectronics-based innovations. The obvious reason is the pervasiveness of these technologies and the scope of the transformations that-they are inducing in the contemporary economic system.

Various forms of innovations affect all sectors of economic activity. The present discussion, however, concentrates on the production of goods (in primis, manufacturing) and it emphasizes the efforts concerned with the improvements of the techniques of production and the search for new products.

---

[1] An extensive survey of the literature on innovation and technical change can be found in Freeman (1982). See also National Science Foundation (1983). A more specific survey on technical change and productivity growth is in Nelson (1981a). Other surveys of the economics of technological change, oriented more to the theoretical literature, include Charles Kennedy and Anthony Thirlwall (1981), and Paul Stoneman (1983).

TABLE 1
R & D EXPENDITURE BY COUNTRY AND BY SOURCE OF FINANCE, R & D REAL GROWTH AND R & D EMPLOYMENT

Country:	USA	Japan	West Germany	United Kingdom	France	Italy
Yearly Percentage Growth of Total National (R & D) Expenditures (at Constant Prices)						
1969–75	−0.6	8.3	6.2	1.3	2.3	4.9
1975–81	4.2	7.9	4.7	3.1	4.2	4.6
1981–83	3.8	8.2	1.9	−0.7	4.7	4.9
Total R & D as Percentage of GDP:						
1983	2.7	2.8	2.8	2.8	2.5	1.6
Total R & D Employment per Thousand of Total Labor Force:						
1983	6.6	5.8	4.7[a]	3.6[a]	3.9	2.3
Business-financed R & D as a Percentage of Total R & D: 1983	49.0	65.3	58.1	42.1	42.0	45.5
Business-performed R & D as a Percentage of Total R &D: 1983	71.1	63.5	69.8	61.0	56.8	57.0
Military R & D as Percentage of Total R &D: 1983[b]	27.8	0.6		13.5[c]		

Sources: National Science Foundation (1986), OECD (1986), Peri Patel and Keith Pavitt (1986) and elaborations by the author (in terms of ratios to GDP and total labor force).
Note: i) Unless otherwise specified, the data of rows 4 to 8 refer to 1983; ii) despite normalization efforts, stimulated in particular by the OECD, some discrepancies are still likely to appear among the various countries in coverage and definitions; iii) some caution should be used in comparing rows 4 and 5: the differences are the likely result of both statistical discrepancies and different relative wages of research workers to average workers in each country.
[a] 1981 (Source for R & D employment: National Science Foundation).
[b] Calculated by Patel and Pavitt (1986).
[c] All Western Europe.

In Part II I recall some stylized evidence on the allocation of resources to research and on the patterns of innovation across countries and sectors. The interpretation of these observed patterns will begin in Part III with an analysis of the characteristics of the search process aimed at the discovery and development of innovations. Part IV discusses the nature of the opportunities and knowledge on which innovations draw and the incentives leading profit-motivated actors to innovate and/or imitate other people's innovations. I argue that the suggested interpretation of the innovation process helps to explain why sectors differ in their modes and rates of innovation. Moreover, firms within each industry differ,

too, in their propensity to innovate. Part V discusses this phenomenon. Finally, Part VI considers the relationship between innovative activities and the dynamics of industrial structures and performances.

II. *Searching for Innovations—The General Patterns*

Modern industrial countries devote a significant share of their income and labor force to formalized activities of pure and applied research and technological development, within both nonprofit institutions (universities, government laboratories, etc.) and business enterprises. Table 1 provides an overview of employ-

TABLE 2

United States R & D Expenditures by Type and by Sources of Finance, Various Years (Percentages)

	1960	1970	1980	1983
Total R & D	100	100	100	100
Basic research financed by	8.9 (100)	13.6 (100)	12.9 (100)	12.6 (100)
Federal government	5.3 (59.7)	9.5 (70.1)	8.9 (68.8)	8.4 (66.4)
Industry	2.5 (28.6)	2.0 (14.9)	2.0 (15.7)	2.3 (18.4)
University and colleges[b]	0.5 (6.0)	1.3 (10.0)	1.3 (10.0)	1.3 (10.0)
Other nonprofit institutions	0.5 (5.7)	0.7 (5.1)	0.7 (5.6)	0.7 (5.3)
Applied research financed by	22.3 (100)	21.9 (100)	22.4 (100)	23.4 (100)
Federal government	12.5 (55.9)	11.8 (53.8)	10.5 (47.0)	10.6 (45.4)
Industry	9.1 (40.6)	9.3 (42.4)	10.7 (47.7)	11.6 (49.6)
University and colleges[b]	0.5 (2.1)	0.4 (1.7)	0.7 (3.0)	0.7 (2.0)
Other nonprofit institutions	0.3 (1.3)	0.3 (2.0)	0.5 (2.3)	0.5 (2.0)
Development financed by	68.9 (100)	64.5 (100)	64.6 (100)	64.0 (100)
Federal government	46.8 (68.1)	35.7 (55.3)	27.6 (42.7)	27.6 (43.1)
Industry	21.8 (31.7)	28.6 (44.4)	36.7 (56.7)	36.0 (56.3)
University and colleges[b]	0.01 (0.1)	0.0 (0.1)	0.1 (0.2)	0.02 (0.2)
Other nonprofit institutions	0.01 (0.1)	0.2 (0.2)	0.2 (0.3)	0.02 (0.3)

Source: National Science Foundation (1986).

Note: i) Data in parentheses are percentages of each research category subtotal; ii) Subdivisions between "pure" research, "applied" research, and "development," are taken from NSF classifications.

[a] Based on preliminary estimates.

[b] Federally funded university-based research is included in the "federal government" source.

ment and expenditures on R & D by country, shares of business-performed research, and sources of finance.[2]

As regards the composition of R & D

[2] In an effort to standardize definitions and data collection on research expenditures, the Organization of Economic Cooperation and Development (OECD) has proposed, in the so-called "Frascati Manual," that "Research and Experimental Development comprise creative work undertaken on a systematic basis in order to increase the stock of knowledge . . . and the use of this stock of knowledge to devise new applications" (OECD 1981, p. 25). Within that general definition, "pure" research broadly corresponds to activities aimed at knowledge growth, "applied" research involves the search for "applications," and "development" concerns the activities of design, implementation, and prototype manufacturing of the "new applications" themselves. Still the details of the activities actually surveyed in different countries—in terms of both expenditures and employment—are often not strictly homogeneous and some caution should be used in comparing the investment figures on R & D among different countries. For an in-depth discussion of R & D measurement problems, see Freeman (1982).

expenditures (see Table 2 for evidence on the USA), about one-tenth is devoted to pure research, more than one-fourth to applied research, and the rest to development. Not surprisingly, pure research, with its character of relative publicness, is financed mainly by the federal government, universities, and other nonprofit institutions, while industry meets about one-half the cost of applied research and development; however, private industry also devotes roughly 20 percent of its total R & D expenditures to pure research.

Moreover, within the broad picture of national R & D investments, one observes marked intersectoral differences in the allocation of resources to research (see Table 3). As regards the sources of these investments and their institutional location, in contemporary market economies roughly half of the total investment in R & D is, as said, financed by business

TABLE 3

EXPENDITURES ON RESEARCH AND DEVELOPMENT AS A PERCENTAGE OF VALUE ADDED BY SECTOR AND BY COUNTRY
AND SECTORAL RATIOS OF R & D USE TO EXPENDITURE

Sector	USA	Japan	West Germany	France	United Kingdom	Italy	Estimated USA Ratio of Use to Generation of R & D[a]
Electric and electronics industries	12.7	8.5	8.8	13.7	16.2	5.7	0.34
Chemicals	6.5	7.7	5.8	7.0	6.8	5.5	
Organic and inorganic chemicals	4.3	8.0	} 8.4	} 7.6	5.3	} 6.0	0.50
Drugs	12.1	10.0			17.8		0.17
Petroleum refineries	6.4	3.0	0.6	3.4	2.0	4.6	1.31
Instruments	20.5	(8.6)[b]	8.3	(5.4)[b]	8.5	(1.2)[b]	0.14
Office machinery and computers	21.7	7.5	} 4.2	} 2.4	19.8	} 2.7	0.11
Industrial nonelectrical machinery	2.5	2.9			2.5		0.17
Aerospace	32.6	} 7.2	30.8	} 10.0	30.9	} 6.6	0.37
Transport equipment	10.0		5.5		3.1		
Motor vehicles	12.6	6.5	5.9	n.a.	4.2	n.a.	0.20
Ships	n.a.	7.8	1.2	n.a.	0.8	n.a.	} 0.32
Other transport equipment	n.a.	n.a.	1.6	n.a.	0.0	n.a.	
Food, drink, and tobacco	0.7	1.3	0.5	0.3	0.8	2.4	1.18
Textile and clothing	2.7	1.3	0.5	0.5	0.3	0.3	1.31
Rubber and plastic products	2.5	2.8	1.9	4.4	1.1	1.8	1.12
Ferrous metals	1.6	2.9	1.6	1.1	1.1	0.5	1.63
Nonferrous metals	2.4	4.3	1.8	2.4	2.1	3.2	1.06
Fabricated metal products	1.1	1.2	1.4	1.0	0.8	0.0	0.49
Lumber, wood products, and furniture	.7	—[c]	—[c]	—[c]	—[c]	—[c]	1.33
Paper and printing	.7	—[c]	—[c]	—[c]	—[c]	—[c]	1.31
Stone, clay, and glass	1.9	—[c]	—[c]	—[c]	—[c]	—[c]	0.86
Total manufacturing	8.1	4.9	5.4	(4.6)[d]	6.6	(2.9)[d] (1.7)[e]	0.42

Sources: OECD (1986), National Science Foundation (1986), OECD, *Industrial Structures Statistics*, various years, and Scherer (1982); data of R & D expenditures and value added have been aggregated, whenever necessary, by the author for comparability purposes.

Notes: The sectoral R & D intensities are calculated as the ratio of business-performed R & D to sectoral value added.

Special caution must be taken in comparing the data along any one row: The coverage of value-added data differ among countries (e.g., for Italy, it includes only firms with more than 20 employees).

[a] Ratio of the total R & D used to the R & D performed by the sector as estimated by Frederick M. Scherer (1982).

[b] Professional instruments include photographic equipment.

[c] No comparable data available.

[d] Estimates based on the subset of manufacturing for which sectoral data are available.

[e] Based on aggregate OECD data on the Italian economy.

and roughly between half and two-thirds of R & D is carried out by business firms (cf. Table 1).

Of course, Tables 1 through 3 show only the commitment of resources to innovation that fund formalized research activities, typically in R & D laboratories; however, in addition to formalized R & D, and in many ways complementary to it, a significant amount of innovation and improvements is originated through design improvements, "learning by doing," and "learning by using" (see, for example, Kenneth Arrow 1962a; Rosenberg 1982; David 1975; Samuel Hollander 1965; Louis Yelle 1979). Such informal effort is generally embodied in people and organizations (primarily firms) (David Teece 1977, 1986; Keith Pavitt 1986a), and its cost is hard to trace. Again, sectors differ in the relative importance of the four basic modes of technological advance, namely (*a*) economically expensive and formalized processes of search whose costs are measured in the tables; (*b*) informal processes of diffusion of information and of technological capabilities (e.g., via publications, technical associations, watch-and-learn processes, personnel transfers); (*c*) those particular forms of "externalities," internalized within each firm, associated with learning by doing and learning by using; and (*d*) the adoption of innovation developed by other industries and embodied in capital equipment and intermediate inputs (cf. Pavitt 1984).

In the interpretation of the evidence on innovative activities in contemporary economies, one faces, first, the question of the nature of the process leading from a perception of an economically exploitable opportunity to its actual development: That is, what do people actually do? How do they search? Why do sectors differ in their search procedures?

Second, one should account for the observed directions of technological change: To what extent do such observed patterns represent reactions to market signals? Are there other factors that influence the patterns of technological change?

Third, one should explain why sectors differ in their commitment of resources to search activities and in the rates at which they generate new products and processes of production. In short, I call "propensity to innovate" the empirical outcome of both sets of phenomena

and try to disentangle its determinants.

In the following, I deal, in turn, with these questions.

III. *Innovation: The Characteristics of the Search Process*

Over the past 20 years, various analyses have been made of the process of innovation, concerned with both the relationship between inputs and outputs of innovative activities (that is, the relationship between the resources devoted to innovative search and rates of generation of innovations, however measured) and the nature of the innovation process itself. In this section I focus first on the second issue.

These analyses, which can be classified under the broad heading of "innovation studies" (Zvi Griliches 1984b), include those of William Abernathy and James Utterback (1975, 1978), E. W. Constant (1980), David (1975), Freeman (1982), Burton Klein (1977), Nelson and Sidney Winter (1977, and 1982), Rosenberg (1976, 1982), Devandra Sahal (1979, 1981, 1985), Pavitt (1979, 1984), Eric von Hippel (1979, and 1982), and Dosi (1982, 1984). The analytical aims of these studies are different and their contributions quite heterogeneous. Nonetheless, most of them point toward some common characteristics of innovation which, in my view, are of crucial importance in the economics of technological change.

A. *Innovation as Problem-solving: Technological Paradigms*

In very general terms, technological innovation involves *the solution of problems*—for example, on transformation of heat into movement, shaping materials in certain ways, producing compounds with certain properties—meeting at the same time some cost and marketability requirements. Typically, the problems are "ill structured," in that the available information (e.g., on the limits in the cutting speed of a certain machine, the physical reasons it breaks at higher speed) does not provide by itself a solution to the problem (relevant discussions of this class of problems are in Herbert Simon 1973, 1979; and Nelson and Winter 1982; see also Massimo Egidi 1986 and Dosi and Egidi 1987). In other words, an "innovative solution" to a certain problem involves "discovery" and "creation," since no general algorithm can be derived from the information about the problem that generates its solution "automatically" (more on this in Dosi and Egidi 1987). Certainly, the "solution" of technological problems involves the use of information drawn from previous experience and formal knowledge (e.g., from the natural sciences); however, it also involves specific and *uncodified* capabilities on the part of the inventors. Following Nelson and Winter (1982) and Winter (1984), I use the term *knowledge base* for the set of information inputs, knowledge, and capabilities that inventors draw on when looking for innovative solutions. A first characterization that can be made of different technologies is in terms of the degrees of "publicness" and universality versus tacitness and specificity of their knowledge bases (Winter 1984). Following Michael Polanyi (1967), *tacitness* refers to those elements of knowledge, insight, and so on that individuals have which are ill defined, uncodified, unpublished, which they themselves cannot fully express and which differ from person to person, but which may to some significant degree be shared by collaborators and colleagues who have a common experience. Conversely, scientific inputs are typically universal and public. Nelson (1986) cites the results of the Yale questionnaire, showing that in 30 sectors out of 130, university research—especially in chemistry, materials science, computer science, and

metallurgy—is considered to be very important for sectoral innovativeness; in the cases of biotechnologies François Chesnais (1986) analyzes a complex thread of joint ventures between university and industry. Also the knowledge base in several chemical sectors is directly linked to scientific knowledge on chemical/physical properties of complex organic molecules.

However, even in these rather science-based activities and, more so, in other technologies, public knowledge is complementary to more specific and tacit forms of knowledge generated within the innovating units (for evidence, see Freeman 1982; SPRU 1972; J. Langrish 1972; Michael Gibbons and Ron Johnston 1974; and Pavitt 1984). For example, in mechanical engineering (e.g., machine tools) an important part of the knowledge base consists of tacit knowledge about the performance of previous generations of machines, their typical conditions of use, the productive requirements of the users, and so on. In the case of microelectronics, one finds three major and complementary forms of knowledge, namely (a) advances in solid-state physics (e.g., electrical properties of semiconductors at the micron/submicron level) (b) knowledge related to the construction of semiconductor manufacturing and testing equipment, and (c) programming logics. As regards the applications of microelectronics, embodied in components and equipment, the fundamental forms of knowledge consist of (a) systems architectures and systems engineering; (b) programming logics (ranging from the logics embodied in the "firmware" of computers, to the proper applicative software), (c) the interfaces between information processing and the mechanical or chemical processes to which it is applied (e.g., the interfaces between an electronic control and the mechanical movements of a machine tool or the flows in a chemical plant), and (*d*) the interacting devices (e.g., sensors).

The crucial point is that this (technology-specific and sector-specific) variety in the knowledge base of innovative search implies also different degrees of *tacitness* of the knowledge underlying innovative success and, as will be discussed below, also helps explain the differences across sectors in the typical organization of research activities. Whatever the knowledge base on which innovation draws, each problem-solving activity implies the development and refinement of "models" and specific procedures.

Elsewhere (Dosi 1982, 1984), I suggest a broad similarity, in terms of definition and procedures, between *science* and *technology*. More precisely, as modern philosophy of science suggests the existence of scientific paradigms (or scientific research programs), so there are *technological paradigms*. Both scientific and technological paradigms embody an *outlook*, a definition of the relevant problems, a pattern of enquiry. A "technological paradigm" defines contextually the needs that are meant to be fulfilled, the scientific principles utilized for the task, the material technology to be used. In other words, a technological paradigm can be defined as a "pattern" of solution of selected technoeconomic problems based on highly selected principles derived from the natural sciences, jointly with specific rules aimed to acquire new knowledge and safeguard it, whenever possible, against rapid diffusion to the competitors. Examples of such technological paradigms include the internal combustion engine, oil-based synthetic chemistry, and semiconductors. A closer look at the patterns of technical change, however, suggests the existence of "paradigms" with different levels of generality, in several industrial sectors.

A technological paradigm is both an *exemplar*—an artifact that is to be developed and improved (such as a car, an integrated circuit, a lathe, each with its particular technoeconomic characteristics)—and a *set of heuristics* (e.g., Where do we go from here? Where should we search? What sort of knowledge should we draw on?).

These aspects of technological change which relate to the improvement of some typical performance attributes of exemplars (e.g., four-wheeled internal-combustion cars, jet aircraft) underlie Sahal's idea of "technological guide posts" (Sahal 1981, 1985), a guidepost being the basic artifact whose technoeconomic characteristics are progressively improved. Basic artifacts (such as car) are also functionally specified (e.g., a car's locomotive attributes) in relation to some use in the socioeconomic system (a car is used jointly with human time for household mobility and also in market production activities). (For an attempt to map characteristics of technological paradigms and socioeconomic uses or "needs," see Paolo Saviotti and J. Stanley Metcalfe 1984.) In this respect, technological paradigms define "bundles" of characteristics of the various commodities. If, following Kevin Lancaster (1971), the latter are defined in terms of combination of hedonic attributes, technological paradigms restrict the actual combinations in a notional characteristics space to a certain number of prototypical bundles.

On the other hand, the development and improvement of these basic "exemplars" involve the development of specific competences and "rules." Rosenberg (1976) highlights the importance of "focusing devices," that is, typical problems, opportunities, and targets that tend to focus the search process in particular directions.

Of course, the procedures, competences, and heuristics involved in the search process are, to varying degrees, specific to each technology. In other words, each technological paradigm involves a specific "technology of technical change."[3] For example, in some sectors (such as organic chemicals), these procedures relate to the ability of coupling basic scientific knowledge with the development of new molecules that present the required characteristics. Thus, one often searches around the existing compounds, helped by the scientific knowledge of the relationship between chemical structures and physical properties, by previous experience, and by chance. In other sectors (such as microelectronics devices) the methods of innovative search involve scientific advances on submicron electrical flows in semiconductors, the development of more sophisticated hardware capable of "writing" the chips at the desired level of miniaturization, and advances in the programming logic to be built into the chips. In mechanical engineering, the search process is generally "focused" by trade-offs involved in the use of machines (e.g., between speed, flexibility to different uses, and cutting precision). The skills required by this search process typically involve also unwritten and relatively tacit experience in design and use of mechanical equipment, and more recently, in the interface between electronic controls and mechanical movements. Yet in other sectors (e.g., the top end of textile, clothing, leather, and shoemaking) fundamental "search skills" are the capabilities of understanding/anticipating/influencing the trends in tastes and fashion.

It quite often happens that prototypical problem-solving models, rules on how to search and on what targets to focus, and beliefs as to "what the market wants" become the shared view of the engineering community. A paradigm is economically

exploited and reproduced over time also through the development of institutions that train the would-be practitioners in methods for the improvement of basic exemplars, and peers' judgments are also based on the success achieved in the refinement and use of these methods (in this respect, Noble's history of the development of American engineering schools and their relationship with industry and Hughes' history of electrification are vivid illustrations of the institutional process that goes together with the establishment of "technological paradigms;" see David Noble 1987, and Thomas Hughes 1982).

B. *Technological Paradigms and Patterns of Innovation: Technological Trajectories*

A crucial implication of the general paradigmatic form of technological knowledge is that innovative activities are strongly *selective, finalized* in quite precise directions, *cumulative* in the acquisition of problem-solving capabilities. This accounts also for the relatively ordered patterns of innovation that one tends to observe at the level of single technologies, as shown by several studies of "technological forecasting" (for a comprehensive review and discussion, see Joseph Martino 1976). Let us define as a *technological trajectory* (Nelson and Winter 1977; Sahal 1981, Dosi 1982, Theodore Gordon and Thomas Munson 1981; Saviotti and Metcalfe 1984) the activity of technological process along the economic and technological trade-offs defined by a paradigm.

Thus, for example, technological progress in aircraft technology has followed two quite precise trajectories (one civilian and one military) characterized by log-linear improvements in the trade-offs between horsepower, gross takeoff weight, cruise speed, wing loading, and cruise range (Sahal 1985 and an oral com-

---

[3] This was also the title of an important conference, coordinated by R. Nelson at the Royal College of Arts, London, July 1985. See also Nelson (1981b).

munication of P. Saviotti on ongoing research at Manchester University). In microelectronics, technical change is accurately represented by an exponential trajectory of improvement in the relationship between density of the electronic chips, speed of computation, and cost per bit of information (Dosi 1984). More generally, there is growing evidence that specific "innovation avenues" are a widespread feature of the observed patterns of technical change (Sahal 1985). Of course, there is no a priori economic reason why one should observe limited clusters of technological characteristics at any one time and ordered trajectories over time. Indeed, given consumers with different preferences and equipment users with different technical requirements, if technology had the malleable attributes of information and if the innovative search were a purely random process, one would tend to observe sorts of "technological indifference curves" at any one time, and, over time, random search all over the n-dimension characteristics space. Of course, "how different" are consumers and users of goods, pieces of equipment, intermediate components, is, in principle, an empirical question. However, relatively wide differences (given the high dimensionality of the space of characteristics/technical requirements demanded by consumers/users of commodities) cannot be ruled out by either casual empiricism or general theoretical arguments. Moreover, for whatever distribution of characteristics at any arbitrary time t, one should expect that income growth and division of labor among different productive activities would increase such diversity of micro demands. Were technologies simply pieces of information (or "recipes") that could be added, convexly combined, etc., one would also tend to observe an increasingly dispersed variety of technical and performance combinations in ac-

tual products and production inputs. Over time, this would lead toward the exploration of the entire characteristics space of final products, machine tools, components, etc. Indeed, the evidence surveyed suggests that one still observes "explorations" limited to some, much smaller, subsets of the notional characteristics space. It is precisely the paradigmatic cumulative nature of technological knowledge that accounts for the relatively ordered nature of the observed patterns of technological change.

Engineers typically try to improve the desirable characteristics that are specific to a certain product, tool, or device, keeping in mind the trade-offs among them. Relatedly, historical evidence strongly suggests that a major impulse to innovation has derived from *imbalances* between the technical dimensions that characterize a "trajectory" (or "avenue") e.g., between cutting speed and tool resistance in machine tools or shuttle speed in eighteenth century looms and spinning speed in spindles. For a discussion of several examples of this process of solution of technical imbalances, which Hughes (1987) calls "adverse salients" and "critical problems," see Rosenberg (1976, especially chapter 6). Arguments broadening the scope of "imbalances" to the relationships between technical change and social roles and behaviors of different groups of workers are in William Lazonick (1979, 1987), and von Tunzelmann (1982). Other examples can be drawn from David Landes (1969).

Conversely, a change in the paradigm generally implies a change in the trajectories: Together with different knowledge bases and different prototypes of artifacts, the technoeconomic dimensions of innovation also vary. Some characteristics may become easier to achieve, new desirable characteristics may emerge, some others may lose importance. Relatedly, the engineers' vision of future technological advances changes, together with a changing emphasis on the various trade-offs that characterize the new artifacts. Thus, for example, the technological trajectory in active electrical components based on thermionic valves had, as fundamental dimensions, heat-loss parameters, miniaturization, and reliability over time. With the appearance of solid-state components, heat loss became much less relevant, while miniaturization increased enormously in importance and also the rates at which progress could be achieved shot up. More generally, it has also been suggested that major clusters of prevailing technological paradigms (e.g., those related to oil-based synthetic chemistry, or, to electromechanical production, or, more recently, to microelectronics) involve the intensive utilization of some crucial input abundantly available at low cost (e.g., energy in the former two examples, and information-processing in the latter; Carlota Perez 1987).

C. *Technology: Freely Available Information or Specific Knowledge?*[4]

The view of technology just presented is very different from the concept of technology as information that is generally applicable, and easy to reproduce and reuse (Arrow 1962b), one where firms can produce and use innovations by dipping freely into a general "stock" or "pool" of technological knowledge. It implies that firms produce things in ways that are differentiated technically from the products and methods of other firms and that they make innovations largely on the basis of in-house technology, but with some contributions from other firms, and from public knowledge. In such circumstances, the search process of industrial firms to improve their tech-

nology is *not* likely to be one where they survey the whole stock of notional technological knowledge before making their technical choices (see Nelson and Winter 1982). Given its highly differentiated nature, firms will instead seek to improve and to diversify their technology by searching in zones that enable them to use and to build on their existing technological base and also on their existing markets, distribution arrangements, and so on (Teece 1982, 1986). In other words, technological search processes in each firm are cumulative processes too. What the firm can hope to do technologically in the future is narrowly constrained by what it has been capable of doing in the past.

The distinction between *technology* and *information*—with the latter being only a subset of the former—entails important analytical consequences for the theory of production. To illustrate that distinction let us take a scientific analogy (note also that *science* is somewhat closer to *information* in that the ethos of the scientific community is to disclose results, while in privately generated technology it is to withhold and appropriate them, see Partha Dasgupta and David 1985). Certainly, a good part of "science" can be embodied in "information." There are freely available journals, textbooks, and university lectures that disseminate this information. Moreover, there are market conditions of access to it; for example, there is a market for textbooks and economic conditions of access to higher education (e.g., the level of registration fees, the availability or scarcity of grants for students unable to support themselves); however, in any proper sense of the word, getting a PhD is not simply acquiring information, and it is even less true to say that there is a market for PhDs. In this analogy, "information" stands vis-à-vis innovative technological capabilities as a subscription to the *American Economic Review* stands vis-à-vis

---

[4] This paragraph is partly based on Dosi, Pavitt, and Soete (1988), which in turn draws from Pavitt (1984d).

winning the Nobel Prize in economics: In both cases there is an irreducible element that is not information and cannot be bought and sold, but rather depends on cumulatively augmented abilities and skills. In each technology there are elements of *tacit and specific* knowledge that are not and *cannot* be written down in a "blueprint" form, and cannot, therefore, be entirely diffused either in the form of public or proprietary information (see Polanyi 1967 and the discussion of this same issue in Nelson and Winter 1982).[5] Of course, this does not imply that such skills and forms of tacit knowledge are entirely immobile: People can be hired away from one firm to another or can start their own firms (and sometimes supply goods and knowledge to competitors of their own original firm), learning procedures of one firm may be imitated by other firms, and so on. It still holds, however, that the innovative activities present—to different degrees—firm-specific, local, and cumulative features. This is borne out by empirical studies.

It has been found that *information* about what other firms are doing spreads quite quickly (Edwin Mansfield 1985); however, the ability to produce or replicate innovative results is much more sticky. Successful innovations are more closely related to firms' existing ranges of technological and marketing skills than unsuccessful ones (Robert Cooper 1983; Modesto Maidique 1983); they tend to occur in product fields proximate to firms' current fields; the activities that firms undertake entail initial learning costs that are recovered later as a consequence of cumulative improvements in product performance and in wider market applications (John Enos 1962; David 1975; Rosenberg 1976, 1982; Sahal 1981; Morris Teubal 1982; Paul Gardiner 1984; Roy Rothwell and Gardiner 1984).

Once the cumulative and firm-specific nature of technology is recognized, its development over time ceases to be random, but is constrained to zones closely related technologically and economically (e.g., related markets and distribution networks) to existing activities. If those zones can be identified, measured, and explained, it also is possible to predict likely future patterns of innovative activities in firms, industries, and countries (see David 1975; Sahal 1981, 1985; Pavitt 1984; Dosi, Pavitt, and Luc Soete 1988).

Each technological paradigm, I suggest, entails a specific balance between exogenous determinants of innovation (e.g., university-based advances in pure science) and determinants that are endogenous to the process of competition and technological accumulation of particular firms and industries. Moreover, each paradigm involves specific *search modes, knowledge bases, and combinations between proprietary and public forms of technological knowledge.*

Given these features of technology and technological innovation, how are search processes organized? Who are the actors that undertake them? How do they relate to the rest of the economic system?

D. *How Organizations Build Knowledge Bases*

The increasing complexity of technologies and research activities in this cen-

---

[5] Egidi (1986) develops an analogy between "technology" and linguistic structures: As the semantics and syntax of natural languages shapes what is said and how it is said, so technology involves coherent chains of routines (". . . first take a piece of iron and the hammer, then do so and so, then place it under the lathe, . . ." etc.). In turn, these routines involve abilities that cannot be deduced either from the nature of the inputs (the piece of iron, the hammer, the lathe, etc.) nor by the sequence of operations. This is obviously the case also of linguistic production: the knowledge of the Oxford Dictionary (the semantics) and of English grammar (the syntax) constrains and shapes what can be said but is by no means sufficient to generate the ability to write *Hamlet*. In a different perspective, changes in technologies as a creative process of generation of new skills are discussed in Mario Amendola (1983) and Amendola and Jean-Luc Gaffard (1986).

tury militates in favor of formal organizations (R & D laboratories of big firms, government and university labs, etc.) as opposed to individual innovators, as the most conducive environments to the production of innovations. This is also shown by the secular growth in the share of corporate as opposed to individual patents registered in the USA as well as other western economies.

David Mowery (1980, 1983) has reconstructed the growth of research and development activities in American industry from the beginning of this century. Notably, he finds that industry-performed R & D—which grows at a much higher rate than industrial output or employment—also tends to be internalized within manufacturing companies. In other words, contrary to Stigler's hypothesis (George Stigler 1956), R & D growth has not led to a comparable process of market-based division of labor and the emergence of specialized "innovation suppliers." Inhouse R & D is the dominant form of organization for corporate technological search (on this point, see also Leonard Reich 1985; Rosenberg 1985; and Nelson 1986). As Richard Nelson puts it, "the modern industrial R & D laboratory, linked within the firm with production and often marketing, had a number of advantages over reliance on outside research and development laboratories, particularly when aspects of the relevant technologies were somewhat idiosyncratic and tacit, and R & D needed to be tailored to those idiosyncracies and to particular firm strategies. In addition to the general advantage of integration in such circumstances stressed by Oliver Williamson (1985), here, as Mowery has stressed, integration had the additional advantages of facilitating better information flow from the R & D laboratory to those who would have to implement the new technology, and from the latter to the former. It also served to limit cross-organization information leaks" (Nelson 1986, p. 10). Of course, one often observes also market transfers of innovations and technical competences—such as licensing and consultancy deals; however, "the predominant mode of industrial research in the private sector, at least in the United States, is the integrated research organization, part of a business enterprise which engages in at least one other activity vertically related to research and development such as manufacturing, marketing, distribution, sales and service" (Teece 1986, p. 1). Moreover, even when licensing and other forms of interfirm transfer of technology occur, they do not stand as an all-or-nothing substitute for in-house search: One needs to have substantial in-house capacity in order to recognize, evaluate, negotiate, and finally adapt the technology potentially available from others.

Williamson's analysis (1975, 1985) of the costs of transactions involving informational asymmetries, monitoring problems, and possibilities of opportunistic behavior is clearly part of the interpretation of this phenomenon: Market transactions involving research activities generally imply (a) incomplete specifications of contracts, given the uncertainty about the research outcomes; (b) lack of adequate protection of proprietary information; (c) possibilities of "lock-in" phenomena with research suppliers, who can subsequently earn rents from that asymmetric advantage; (d) weak incentives to least cost performance; (e) monitoring costs (on all these points, see Teece 1988).

In addition (and complementary) to these transaction-related factors, however, the foregoing discussion of the nature of technology and innovative search suggests another set of factors related to the characteristics of knowledge and problem solving. Indeed, the heuristics on "how to do things" and "how to improve them" are often embodied in *organizational routines,* which, through practice, repetition, and more or less incremental improvements make certain firms "good" at exploring certain technical opportunities and translating them into specific marketable products. In such matters, there is a significant amount of organizational indivisibility, because organizational learning may well not be additive in the learning of individuals or groups who compose the organization: indeed, it was Adam Smith who first emphasized the possible dichotomy between "system learning" (e.g., the beneficial effects on economic efficiency of the division of labor), on the one hand, and the degrading brutality which repetitive and mindless tasks could imply for some groups of workers, on the other. Intrafirm processes of specialization and division of labor are good examples of this possibility. Individuals and groups may well decrease the scope of knowledge and competences that they are required to put into production or innovative search (in a sense, they may be required to "forget"), while at the same time these same individuals and groups become linked through routines that increase organizational efficiency (on whatever criterion the latter is evaluated). For example, the emergence of the modern factory has also implied "deskilling" of particular categories of craftsmen; the abilities of several groups of artisan-like workers became redundant, the skills of *making* particular machines became increasingly separated from the skills involved in *using* them; the introduction of electromechanical techniques of automated mass production in big plants has further reduced the knowledge required of significant portions of the work force. These same processes, however, have been associated with major increases in the abilities of (more and more complex) business organizations to learn, that is to "store" and develop internally, procedures for a growing production efficiency.

The exploration of the characteristics of the organizational competences with specific reference to research an innovation is still at an early stage (see Pavitt 1986a; Teece 1986, 1988; Winter 1987a, 1987b Neil Kay 1979, 1982); however, in my view, they are a fundamental ingredient (together with transaction costs and monitoring factors emphasized by Williamson 1985) of the explanation of both the integration of research within production/marketing units and, more generally, of the *boundaries of the firms* in contemporary market economies. More precisely, Teece (1986) and Pavitt, Mike Robson and Joe Townsend (1987) have independently put forward the conjecture that these boundaries are defined by the scope of their "core competences," that is, loosely speaking, by the scope of what "they are good at" and the relevance of this specific knowledge to the activities of innovation, production, and marketing of a certain commodity. This—it is suggested—affects also the scope of efficient vertical integration and diversification of any one firm (more on this in Dosi, Teece, and Winter 1987).

Organizational routines and higher-level procedures to alter them in response to environmental changes and/or to failures in performance embody a continuous tension between efforts to improve the capabilities of doing *existing* things, monitor *existing* contracts, allocate *given* resources, on the one hand, and the development of capabilities for doing new things or old things in new ways. This tension is complicated by the intrinsically uncertain nature of innovative activities, notwithstanding their increasing institutionalization within business firms. The technical (and, even more so, the commercial) outcome of research activities can hardly be known ex ante (for empirical evidence on individual research projects, see Mansfield 1968 and Mansfield et al. 1977). In general, the uncertainty associated with innovative activities is much stronger than that with which familiar economic model deals. It involves not only lack of knowledge of the precise cost and outcomes of different alternatives, but often also lack of knowledge of what the alternatives are (see Freeman 1982; Nelson 1981a; Nelson and Winter 1982). In fact, let us distinguish between (*a*) the notion of uncertainty familiar to economic analysis defined in terms of imperfect information about the occurrence of a *known list of events* and (*b*) what we could call *strong uncertainty* whereby the list of possible events is unknown and one does not know either the consequences of particular actions for any given event (more on this in Dosi and Egidi 1987). I suggest that, in general, innovative search is characterized by strong uncertainty. This applies, in primis to those phases of technical change that could be called *pre-paradigmatic:* During these highly exploratory periods one faces a double uncertainty regarding both the practical outcomes of the innovative search and also the scientific and technological principles and the problem-solving procedures on which technological advances could be based. When a technological paradigm is established, it brings with it a reduction of uncertainty, in the sense that it focuses the directions of search and forms the grounds for formating technological and market expectations more surely. (In this respect, technological trajectories are not only the ex post description of the patterns of technical change, but also, as mentioned, the basis of heuristics asking "where do we go from here?") However, even in the case of "normal" technical search (as opposed to the "extraordinary" exploration associated with the quest for new paradigms)

strong uncertainty is present. Even when the fundamental knowledge base and the expected directions of advance are fairly well known, it is still often the case that one must first engage in exploratory research, development, and design before knowing what the outcome will be (what the properties of a new chemical compound will be, what an effective design will look like, etc.) and what some manageable results will cost, or, indeed, whether very useful results will emerge (Mansfield et al. 1977).

As a result, firms tend to work with relatively general and event-independent routines (with rules of the kind ". . . spend x% of sales on R & D," ". . . distribute your research activity between basic research, risky projects, incremental innovations according to some routine shares . . ." and sometimes metarules of the kind "with high interest rates or low profits cut basic research," etc.). This finding is corroborated by ample managerial evidence and also by recent more rigorous econometric tests; see Griliches and Ariel Pakes (1986) who find that "the pattern of R & D investment within a firm is essentially a random walk with a relatively low error variance" (pp. 10–11). In this sense, Schumpeter's hypothesis about the routinization of innovation (Joseph Schumpeter 1942) and the persistence of innovation-related uncertainty must not be in conflict but may well complement each other. As suggested by the "late" Schumpeter, one may conjecture that large-scale corporate research has become the prevailing form of organization of innovation because it is most effective in exploiting and internalizing the tacit and cumulative features of technological knowledge (Mowery 1980; Pavitt 1986). Moreover, companies tend to adopt steady policies (rules), because they face complex and unpredictable environments where they cannot forecast future states of the world, or even "map" notional events into actions, and outcomes (Dosi and Orsenigo 1986; Heiner 1983, 1988). Internalized corporate search exploits the cumulativeness and complexity of technological knowledge. Together with steady rules, firms try to reduce the uncertainty of innovative search, without, however, eliminating it.

Internalization and routinization in the face of the uncertainty and complexity of the innovative process also point to the importance of particular organizational arrangements for the success or failure of individual innovative attempts. This is what was found by the SAPPHO Project (cf. Science Policy Research Unit 1972 and Rothwell et al. 1974), possibly the most extensive investigation of the sources of *commercial* success or failure of innovations: Institutional traits, both internal to the firm—such as the nature of the organizational arrangements between technical and commercial people, or the hierarchical authority within the innovating firm—and between a firm and its external environment—such as good communication channels with users, universities, and so on—turn out to be very important. Moreover, it has been argued (Pavitt 1986; Robert Wilson, Peter Ashton, and P. Thomas Egan 1984) that, for given incentives and innovative opportunities, the various forms of internal corporate organization (U form versus M form, centralized versus decentralized, etc.) affect innovation and commercial success positively or negatively, according to the particular nature of each technological paradigm and its stage of development.

In general, each organizational arrangement of a firm embodies procedures for resource allocation to particular activities (in our case, innovative activities), and for the efficient use of these resources in the search for new products, new processes, and procedures for improvements in existing routines; however, the specific nature of these procedures differs across firms and sectors. For example, the typical degrees of commitment of resources vary by industry and so do the rates at which learning occurs. I now turn to the interpretation of these phenomena.

IV. *Opportunities, Incentives, and the Intersectoral Patterns of Innovation*

Clearly, the commitment of resources by profit-motivated agents must involve both the perception of some sort of opportunity and an effective set of incentives. Are the observed intersectoral differences in innovative investment the outcome of different incentive structures, different opportunities, or both? Jacob Schmookler, in his classic work, argued that the serendipity and universality of modern science provide a wide and *intersectorally indifferent* pool of opportunities that are exploited to different degrees in each economic activity according to differential economic incentives, and, in particular, to different patterns of demand growth (Schmookler 1966). (In fact, he was not so much concerned with innovative investments as with innovative outputs, which he measured by patents. However, the same argument applies: For identical opportunities, the elasticity of innovative outputs to R & D inputs should be the same.) Schmookler's thesis has been criticized on both theoretical and empirical grounds (see Rosenberg 1976, chapter 15, and Freeman 1982). The foregoing analysis of the innovation process supports these criticisms and helps to clarify the merits and limitations of Schmookler's hypothesis.

A. *Technological Opportunities: Exogenous Science and Specific Learning*

I first discuss the role of science-related opportunities for innovation and, then, the importance of other sources of opportunities.

Scientific knowledge plays a crucial role in opening up new possibilities of major technological advances. In this century, the emergence of major new technological paradigms has frequently been directly dependent and *directly linked* with major scientific breakthroughs; see, for example, the origin of synthetic chemistry (John Beer 1959; Freeman 1982), the transistor (Nelson 1962; H. S. Kleiman 1977; Dosi 1984), and bioengineering (Orsenigo 1988). Certainly, in western civilization there is a long history of linkages between science and technology, hinting at rather close feedbacks, at least since Leonardo da Vinci and Galileo. What is new and increasingly important in this century is that the generation and utilization of part of the scientific knowledge is internal to, and often a necessary condition of, the development of new technological paradigms. Until the end of the nineteenth century, technological innovations were typically introduced by imaginative craftsmen; for example, engines were developed by practical-minded inventors well before the works of Carnot on thermodynamics. In this century, as far as major innovations are concerned, one moves somewhat closer to the "transistor archetype," whereby the discovery of certain quantum mechanics properties of semiconductors, yielding a Nobel Prize for physics, and the technological development of the first microelectronics device have been one and the same thing (Nelson 1962; Ernest Braun and Stuart MacDonald 1978; Dosi 1984).

Prima facie, the increasing role of scientific inputs in the innovative process can be taken as evidence of the importance of factors exogenous to competitive processes among private economically motivated actors. This is true, subject, however, to two qualifications.

First, the link between science and technology runs also from the latter to the former. It has been noted, for example, that the development of scientific instruments has exerted a major impact on subsequent scientific progress. In general, however, the scope, timing, and channels of influence of technological advances on science have a different nature from the more direct influence of scientific discoveries on technological opportunities. A detailed discussion is beyond the limits of this survey. (On these topics, see John Bernal 1939; Rosenberg 1982; and Derek de Solla Price 1984.) Second, scientific advances play a major *direct* role, especially at an early phase of development of new technological paradigms. It is often the case that the establishment of a major new paradigm involves also the solution of problems of a theoretical nature and/or the development of devices, compounds, molecules, and so on which are themselves challenging tests for the scientists (the transistor, polypropylene, and genetic engineering are obvious examples).

In a sense, progress in general scientific knowledge yields a widening pool of *potential* technological paradigms. In another work (Dosi 1984), I analyze the specific mechanisms through which a few of these potential paradigms are actually developed, economically applied, and often become dominant. Here, suffice it to say that this process of selection depends, in general, on (*a*) the nature and the interests of the "bridging institutions" (Freeman 1982) between pure research and economic applications (these institutions, which can be private establishments, such as Bell Labs, or public organizations, are instrumental in applying theoretical advances to the development of practical devices even under remote or nonexistent direct economic incentives); (*b*) quite often, especially in this century, strictly institutional factors, such as public agencies (e.g., the military); (c) the trial-and-error mechanisms of exploration of the new technologies, often associated with "Schumpeterian" enterpreneurship; (d) the selection criteria of markets and/or the technoeconomic requirements of early users (e.g., the technical specification of NASA and the Pentagon in the early days of integrated circuits, FDA requirements in the case of bioengineering, and the technical needs of the American navy in the case of nuclear reactors).

Once a technological paradigm becomes established, the objectives and heuristics of technological search often tend to diverge from those of scientific inquiry. This is partly due to the different ethos of the technological and scientific communities. (For example, the development of a first transistor had a deep scientific interest; a "better" transistor might have had a great interest for the engineer, but very little for the scientist); however, particular scientific activities (especially of an applied nature) often become part of the technological search along the "trajectories" defined by a particular paradigm. In other words, part of the scientific activity becomes "endogenized" within the activities of technological accumulation and search of profit-motivated firms (consider, for example, the applied scientific research of drug and chemical companies; for an analysis of the relationship between "endogenous" and "exogenous" research with regard to this case, see Chesnais 1986 and Orsenigo 1988).

All this has to do with the science-related opportunities of innovative activity; however, it has already been mentioned that, even in technologies that draw more directly on scientific advances, the knowledge base underlying innovative search also includes more specific forms of technical knowledge. A fortiori, this applies to technologies less directly dependent on science. These considerations have important implications for technological opportunities.

First, the specificity, cumulativeness, and tacitness of part of the technological knowledge imply that both the realized opportunities of innovation and the capabilities for pursuing them are to a good extent *local* and firm-specific. Second, the opportunity for technological advances in any one economic activity (and, thus, also the "innovative productivity" —were we able to measure it—of a dollar investment in R & D) can also be expected to be specific to and constrained by the characteristics of each technological paradigm and its degree of maturity. Moreover, the innovative opportunities in each economic sector will be influenced by the degree to which it can draw from the knowledge base and the technological advances of its suppliers and customers. The sectoral specificity of technological opportunities is also consistent with Scherer's findings that in econometric cross-firm, cross-industry estimates of rates of innovation—approximated by patenting—42.5 percent of the total variance must be attributed to the interindustry component: Frederick Scherer suggests that a good part of such variance is likely to relate to interindustry differences in opportunity (admittedly, despite the lack of any quantitative measure of it; Scherer 1986, ch. 9) other analyses confirm such sectoral specificities (e.g., Pakes and Mark Schankerman 1984).

In many respects, the idea that technological opportunities are *paradigm-bound* is also consistent with the historical evidence and interpretive conjectures put forward earlier by Simon Kuznets (1930) and Arthur Burns (1934) about a "secular retardation" in the growth of output and productivity, by commodity and industry, stemming—in the terminology suggested here—from the gradual exhaustion of technological opportunities along particular trajectories.

New paradigms reshape the patterns of opportunities of technical progress in terms of both the *scope* of potential innovations and the *ease* with which they are achieved. Moreover, they generally spread their effect well beyond their sector of origin and provide new sources of opportunity, via input-output flows and technological complementaries, to otherwise stagnant activities. The emergence of new paradigms and the diffusion of their effects throughout the economy are possibly the main reasons why in modern economies we have not seen an approach to a "stationary state." More precisely, one tends to observe two broad phenomena which reinforce each other. First, new technological paradigms have continuously brought forward new opportunities for product developments and productivity increases. Second, a rather uniform characteristic of the observed technological trajectories is their wide scope for mechanization, specialization, and division of labor within and among plants and industries (Nelson and Winter 1977). Contrary to the pessimistic expectations of classical economists and contrary also to many prevailing contemporary formalizations of problems of allocation of resources in decentralized markets, decreasing returns historically did not emerge even in those activities involving a given and "natural" factor such as agriculture or mining: Mechanization, chemical fertilizers and pesticides, new breeds of plants and animals and improved techniques of mineral extraction and purification prevented "scarcity" from becoming the dominant functional feature of these activities. A fortiori, this applies to manufacturing. Similarly, new technological paradigms, directly and indirectly—via their effects on "old" ones—generally prevent the establishment of decreasing returns in the

search process for innovations. Think of the effects of biotechnology on the search efficiency for new drugs or the effects of electronics controls and computers on the innovative opportunities in machine building.

Contemporary studies of technological effort and progress, indeed support the conjecture that (*a*) at any point in time, technological opportunities vary according to the sectors and the degrees of development of the various paradigms under which they work, and (*b*) this is an important part of the explanation of why the commitment to innovative investment varies across sectors. (These hypotheses are supported on both empirical and theoretical grounds by Michael Gort and Richard Wall 1986.) Another—complementary—reason for interindustry differences in R & D investment relates to the different *modes of innovative search* that each paradigm entails. For example, in some technologies (e.g., electronics, organic chemicals, drugs, aerospace) innovation involves laboratory research and/or complex development and testing of prototypes. In other technologies (e.g., several kinds of nonelectrical machinery) innovation is much more "informal," often embodied in incremental improvement in design, and as such neither recorded nor, often, perceived as the result of an "investment" in R & D.

As argued by Rosenberg (1976, pp. 277–79), differentiated scientific and technological opportunities determine different cost structures of technological advance (for example, the cost of a *x* percent improvement in the trade-offs implied by a particular technological trajectory). The cross-sectoral distribution of technological opportunities is far from homogeneous (Scherer 1982, republished in 1986; Pavitt 1984; Louise Dulude 1983). The appearance of new paradigms is unevenly distributed across sectors and so are (a) the degrees of technical difficulties in advancing production efficiency and product performance, and (b) the technological competence to innovate, embodied in people and firms. These distributions of opportunities and competence, in turn are not random, but depend on (a) the nature of the sectoral production activities, (b) their technological distance from the "revolutionary core" where new paradigms are originated, and (c) the knowledge base that underpins innovation in any one sector. As regards the effects of demand levels and changes upon sectoral rates of innovation (Schmookler's "demand pull" hypothesis, whose discussion introduced this section), all the foregoing considerations need not conflict with the hypothesis that, *other things being equal,* market size and market growth may exert a positive influence on the propensity to innovate. However, the ceteris paribus clause is indeed a crucial one, since—it has been argued in this section—technological opportunities may vary widely across sectors and also over the history of individual technologies.

Given any one level of notional opportunities for innovation, the incentive to commit resources to their discovery and development will depend, of course, on the incentives that interest-motivated agents perceive in terms of expected economic returns. Let us consider the nature of these incentives.

B. *Appropriability of Technological Innovations*

As suggested by the classical and—even more so—Schumpeterian traditions, varying degrees of private appropriation of the benefits of innovation are both the incentive to and the outcome of the innovative process. To put it another way, each technology embodies a specific balance between public-good aspects and private (i.e., economically appropriable) features (see Arrow 1962b; Nelson 1984; and for an empirical analysis, Richard Levin et al. 1984 and Chesnais 1986). Call *appropriability* those properties of technological knowledge and technical artifacts, of markets, and of the legal environment that permit innovations and protect them, to varying degrees, as rent-yielding assets against competitors' imitation.

Appropriability conditions differ among industries and among technologies: Levin et al. (1984) study the varying empirical significance as appropriability devices of (a) patents, (b) secrecy, (c) lead times, (d) costs and time required for duplication, (e) learning-curve effects, (f) superior sales and service efforts. To these one should add more obvious forms of appropriation of differential technical efficiency related to scale economies. In an extreme synthesis, Levin et al. (1984) find that for most industries, "lead times and learning curve advantages, combined with complementary marketing efforts, appear to be the principle mechanisms of appropriating returns for product innovations" (p. 33). Learning curves, secrecy and lead times are also the major appropriation mechanisms for process innovations. Patenting often appears to be a *complementary* mechanism which, however, does not seem to be the central one, with some exceptions (e.g., chemicals and pharmaceutical products). Moreover, by comparing the protection of processes and products, one tends to observe that lead times and learning curves are relatively more effective ways of protecting process innovations, while patents are a relatively better protection for product innovations. Finally, there appears to be quite significant interindustrial variance in the importance of the various ways of protecting innovations and in the overall degrees of appropriability: Some three-quarters of the industries surveyed by the study reported the existence of at least one effective means of protecting process innovation, and more than 90 percent of the industries reported the same regarding product innovations (Levin et al. 1984, p. 20).[6]

Take, as an example, the case of microelectronics. Here one should distinguish between patterns of appropriability in the "core" technologies (semiconductors, computers, telecommunications, industrial controls) and in the technologies where it is applied (e.g., machine tools, consumer durables, cars). In the former, appropriability is a function of cumulative R & D (Franco Momigliano 1985); lead times; quite often, economies of scale in production (e.g., semiconductors and computers) and in R & D (minimum thresholds are sometimes very high, as in telecommunications); marketing and servicing networks (as in mainframe computers). Conversely, in the sectors where microelectronics is introduced as part of processes and products, the patterns of appropriability continue to correspond broadly to the "traditional" sector-specific features (see below for a more detailed taxonomy). An additional source of appropriability, however, relates to the capability of internalizing and/or efficiently exploiting the interfaces and synergies between microelectronics and applicative processes, for example, the capability of mastering both innovation in electronic equipment and the design of mechanical machinery. In fact, the latter is an example of a more general phenomenon, discussed by Teece (1986), whereby the control of complementary

technologies becomes a rent-earning firm-specific asset.

In general, it must be noticed that the partly tacit nature of innovative knowledge and its characteristics of partial private appropriability makes imitation, as well as innovation, a creative process, which involves search, which is not wholly distinct from the search for "new" development, and which is economically expensive—sometimes even more expensive than the original innovation (for evidence on the cost of imitation relative to innovation, see Mansfield, Mark Schwartz, and Samuel Wagner 1981; Mansfield 1984; and Levin et al. 1984). This applies to both patented and non-patented innovations.

C. *The Driving Forces of Technical Change*

I have argued that opportunities—stemming partly from "exogenous" scientific advances and partly from the knowledge endogenously accumulated by the firms—and appropriability conditions account for the varying degrees of commitment of business enterprises to innovation. It is important to remark that what has just been said does *not* imply that market-determined inducement mechanisms are irrelevant to the propensity to search for new products and new techniques. The levels and changes in demand (market size and growth, income elasticities of the various products), and the levels and changes in relative prices, in particular the price of labor to the price of machines[7] and also to the price of energy are influential factors. Indeed, they are likely to be fundamental ones, influencing (*a*) the rate and also the direction of technical progress, particularly within the boundaries defined by the nature of each technological paradigm, and (*b*) the selection of potential paradigms

[6] For detailed discussions of appropriability mechanisms, see also Christopher Taylor and Aubrey Silberston (1973), von Hippel (1978, 1980, 1982) and Terje Christian Buer (1982). The relative costs of innovation versus imitation—which is clearly a good proxy for appropriability—are studied by Levin et al. (1984) and Edwin Mansfield (1984). A detailed company-level study of patenting strategies is presented in Sally Wyatt and Gille Bertin (1985).

[7] On this point compare Paolo Sylos Labini (1984).

for exploration and thus for eventual appearance and dominance. My general point, however, is that the observed sectoral patterns of technical change are the result of the interplay between various sorts of market-inducements, on the one hand, and opportunity and appropriability combinations, on the other.

As an illustration of these points take, first, the case of automobiles. Throughout the seventies there was a clear inducement to produce energy-saving cars. Moreover, the more general demand conditions appear to be supportive (a very large market, although not growing very fast in advanced countries). Finally the appropriability conditions seemed favorable (relatively few producers with extensive distribution networks, marketing a complex product that is not so easy to copy). However, despite these favoring conditions, and leaving aside a significant change in the composition of output and demand (from big to smaller cars) progress in energy saving was rather modest: The technical opportunities on the internal combustion engine trajectory were certainly the major limiting factor. (Energy saving in U.S.-manufactured cars was, indeed, quite substantial, but this was due to the fact that American products were behind the "best-practice frontier" already reached by European and Japanese producers.)

Conversely, one can cite examples of a relatively low commitment to research and innovation, despite significant scientific and technological opportunities, due to the lack of satisfactory appropriability conditions. A case in point is part of agricultural research (until the advent of bioengineering) (Nelson 1986). There, the atomistic structure of production did not provide any incentive to research on seed variety, and so on, for individual farmers and lack of sufficient appropriability hindered industry-based research. Thus, most of the research in these fields

has been publicly sponsored (e.g., in the USA, by the Department of Agriculture): the exceptions are hybrid sterile varieties, in addition, of course, to most industrial inputs to agriculture—pesticides, fertilizers, machinery—whose appropriability conditions have been broadly similar to the rest of manufacturing industry.

Finally, one can find examples of industries where both opportunities and notionally adequate appropriability conditions are there, but the firms generally lack the appropriate skills and technical competence to undertake research and innovation (to my knowledge, this is, for example, the case of Italian ceramic producers with respect to advanced ceramic materials or, more generally, of most firms in developing countries).

The conceptualization of technology and technical change based on "paradigms," "guideposts" or whatever name is chosen, also helps in resolving the long debate in the innovation literature about the relative importance of "market pull" (cf., again, Schmookler 1966) versus "technology push" (for critical review, see Mowery and Rosenberg 1979). As known, in the former approach innovation is represented as a choice/allocation process on some sort of metaproduction function (the innovation possibility frontier) driven by market signals. In the latter, innovation drops from an exogenous domain (typically, it is a freely available by-product of scientific advances) and thus can be treated parametrically; however, the evidence from diverse technologies, such as aircraft (Constant 1980; Sahal 1981), agricultural technology and farm equipment (David 1975; Sahal 1981), synthetic chemicals (Freeman 1982), and semiconductors (Dosi 1984) is at odds with both accounts.

It is often the case that environment-related factors (such as demand and relative prices) are instrumental in shaping (a) the selection criteria among new potential technological paradigms; (*b*) the rates of technical progress; (*c*) the precise trajectory of advance, within the set allowed by any given paradigm. However, it is useful to distinguish between what I call "normal" technical progress (i.e., those processes of innovation within the bounds of a *given* technological paradigm) and "extraordinary" technical progress (associated with the development of new paradigms). As regards the former, I suggest, unlike market-pull accounts, the set of possible trajectories is quite limited, bounded by the rules, technical imperatives, and specific scope of advance of each technology (Mowery and Rosenberg 1979)—which in the short term are to a good extent invariant to market conditions.

On a generally broader time horizon, market conditions exert a powerful influence on the conduct of technological search, but they do so primarily by stimulating, hindering, and focusing the search for new technological paradigms. When established, however, each paradigm—even when at the origin of its selection there were direct market stimuli—remains quite "sticky" in its basic technical imperatives, rules of search, and input combinations. For example, the number of ways of making polymers from fossil fuels is far from unlimited and so are the input intensities, irrespective of input prices. Even the substitution among different fuels (e.g., oil versus coal) often present major technical problems. Certainly, market changes may stimulate the search for new products and new "ways of doing things." I suggest, however, that environmental factors are going to succeed in radically changing the directions and procedures of technical progress only *if* and *when* they are able to foster the emergence of new paradigms (for example, in the earlier example, new materials that substitute for plastics, bioengineering pro-

cesses to produce inputs that are alternative to fossil hydrocarbons).

Moreover, unlike both market-pull and "exogenous" accounts of technical progress, it appears misleading to consider innovation simply as a *reactive* process (to relative prices and demand, in one case, to new exogenous opportunities, in the other). On the contrary, technical progress is largely endogenously driven by a competitive process whereby firms continously try to improve on their basic technologies and artifacts. Whether market signals change or not, firms try to perfect their products and processes, by trial-and-error mechanisms of search and imitations of the results already achieved by other firms, motivated by the competitive edge that innovations are expected to offer. Thus, according to this interpretation, each body of knowledge, expertise, selected physical and chemical principles, and so on (that is, each paradigm) constrains both the opportunities of technical progress and the boundaries within which "inducement effects" can be exerted by the market, while appropriability conditions motivate the economic agents to explore these technological opportunities as a rent-yielding competitive device. Finally, the evolution of the economic environment, in the longer term, is instrumental in the selection of new technological paradigms, and, thus, in the long-term selection of the fundamental directions and procedures of innovative search.

D. *Inducement Factors, Patterns of Technical Change, and Irreversibility*

Whatever the nature of the stimuli to change products and production processes exerted by an economic environment on microeconomic agents, ". . . they are naturally led to search the technological horizon . . . within the framework of [their] current activities and to attack the most restrictive constraint . . ." (Rosenberg 1976, p. 11). "Most mechanical productive processes throw off signals of a sort which are both compelling and fairly obvious; indeed, these processes when sufficiently complex and interdependent, involve an almost compulsive formulation of problems" (Rosenberg 1976, p. 11). The foregoing discussion on the general "paradigm-bound" nature of technical change allows the extension of Rosenberg's thesis to most contemporary innovative processes and also reconciles it with those historical interpretations of different national/sectoral patterns of innovation that trace a cause of different rates of technical progress down to different environmental inducements, especially relative prices, availability or scarcity of natural resources (a *locus classicus* is the debate on the relative degrees of mechanization in the United States and England in the nineteenth century; see Erwin Rothbarth 1946; Hrothgar Habakkuk 1962; Peter Temin 1966; David 1975; Rosenberg 1976, especially chapters 3, 4, and 6).

As known, if one sticks to a general equilibrium framework and a representation of technology based on well-behaved production functions or convex production possibility sets, it is very difficult and often logically incoherent to attribute any observed bias in the rates and direction of technical change to particular biases in relative input prices (see David 1975 for a critical overview of a long debate). In the last instance, "economic incentives to reduce costs always exist in business operations, and precisely because such incentives are so diffuse and general, they do not explain very much in terms of the *particular sequence and timing of innovative activity*" (Rosenberg 1976, p. 110); however, specific incentives, *coupled with the paradigm-bound, cumulative, and local nature of technological learning can* explain particular

rates and directions of technological advance (David 1975, 1986a and 1986b; Nelson and Winter 1982; Anthony Atkinson and Joseph Stiglitz 1969; W. Brian Arthur 1983, 1988).

To illustrate this point, consider the following story. Suppose that, once upon a time, when an imaginary technological history began, there were production possibility sets with all the right properties of continuity, convexity, and so on. Then, people started learning in a particular direction (to make it easy, suppose that this particular direction was triggered by an exogenous relative-price shock). With the help of some cumulativeness in technological knowledge and in search skills, *local* technological capabilities (that is, capabilities associated with the neighborhood of particular input combinations and output characteristics) developed more than proportionally to the "general" growth of knowledge on other notional portions of the production possibility set. Thus, other things being equal, technological progress became easier in this direction than in others. Then, with or without further shocks, people proceeded in this direction of search, which, in turn, further increased specific knowledge and skills. It is easy to see the moral of the story: One ends up with dynamic increasing returns along specific trajectories that channel also the response to particular environmental incentives to innovate. (A formal equivalent of this story is told in Arthur 1983, 1988).

A fundamental implication of this view is that, even when technical change is "triggered," say, by relative price changes, the new techniques developed as a result are likely to be or become superior to the old ones irrespective of relative prices—immediately, as in the case of several microelectronics-based innovations (Soete and Dosi 1983), or after some learning time as in agricultural machinery (David 1975). In other words, if they had existed before, they would also have often been adopted at the "old" relative prices. That is to say, technical progress generally exhibits strong *irreversibility features*.[8]

Let us consider in greater detail the example of microelectronics. As discussed at greater length in Freeman and Soete (1985), Momigliano (1985), Soete and Dosi (1983), and Benjamin Coriat (1983, 1984), electronics-based production technologies are (*a*) labor-saving; (*b*) fixed-capital saving (i.e., they often induce a fall in the capital/output ratio; for sectoral evidence in the U.K., see Soete and Dosi 1983); (*c*) circulating-capital saving (i.e., the optimization of production flows allows a fall in the stocks of intermediate inputs per unit of output); (*d*) quality improving (i.e., they increase the accuracy of production processes, allow quality testing, etc.); (*e*) energy saving (in so far as the energy use generally is also a function of mechanical movements of the various machineries, the substitution of information-processing equipment for electromechanical parts reduces the use of energy). Taking all these characteristics together, it is clear that electronics-based production techniques are generally unequivocally superior to electromechanical ones irrespective of relative prices. That is, the new wage/profit frontiers associated with the new techniques do not generally intersect the "old" ones for any positive value (see Dosi, Pavitt, and Soete 1988). Remarkably, this example illustrates also the complex intersectoral linkages in the innovative process and their bearing on the "exogeneity versus endogeneity" issue in technical change. In the example of electronics technologies, unequivocally "superior" techniques and pieces of equipment appear, for several users' sectors, as "dropping from an exogenous domain" (see Section IV C concerning "technology-push" accounts of technical change). In actual fact, they are generated through processes of exploration of technological opportunities *endogenous to some other industrial sectors* (in the example here, semiconductors, computers, industrial controls, etc.). Moreover, even in these cases, the full and efficient utilization of these potentially superior technologies (e.g., electronics-based automation as compared to electromechanical automation) relies on a painstaking process of learning on the side of the users, which is favored/hindered by the technological capabilities of the users themselves and the market conditions in which they operate. (It is an issue that relates also to the economics of innovation diffusion and that is impossible to discuss length in this work: For more historical evidence see Rosenberg 1975, 1982; a highly stylized attempt to model these learning processes is in Dosi, Orsenigo and Gerald Silverberg 1986.)

In other cases, the irreversibility properties of innovation emerge more slowly. At the start, the process of development/diffusion of new technologies may indeed involve choice-of-technique issues (see David 1975 on agricultural machinery). In the long term, the outcome of the rivalry between old and new technologies clearly depends also on the "latent opportunities" in the background, implicit in the two alternative paradigms; however, the degrees to which these opportunities are perceived, exploited, and expanded is likely to show path-dependent, cumulative, and irreversible features (for discussions and examples, see again David 1975, 1986b; Arthur 1983). Learning-by-

[8] For microeconomic accounts of the local and irreversible features of technological learning, see David (1975, 1986b). On more general grounds, the study by Anne Carter (1970) on the technological coefficients of the American economy shows (a) the unequivocal superiority of the 1958 coefficients with respect to 1947 coefficients and (b) the dominance of a labor-saving trend on other variations of input coefficients. My informed guess is that this continues to remain true today.

doing and by-using, incremental improvements on the new technologies, and economies of scale in their production tend to improve their performance and lower their cost. Moreover, if adopted, a new product or process then attracts R & D efforts to itself, which, in turn, tend to improve costs and performance further. As a result, whenever the new technological trajectory is established, it is likely *to dominate* the old one (in the sense that, to repeat, it is economically superior, irrespective of relative prices).

Whatever the case, it is important to distinguish between the factors that *induce, stimulate, or constrain* technical change from the *outcomes* of the changes themselves. As analyzed in Dosi, Pavitt, and Soete (1988), drawing upon Rosenberg (1976), inducement mechanisms relate to a broad set of factors, including (a) technological bottlenecks in interrelated activities; (b) scarcities of critical inputs; or, conversely, (c) abundance of particular inputs (e.g., energy, raw materials); (d) major shocks in prices/supplies; (e) composition, changes, and rate of growth of demands; (f) levels and changes in relative prices (first of all, as mentioned, the relative price of machines to labor); (g) patterns of industrial conflict. Where the critical stimuli come from depends on the nature of the technologies and on the economic and institutional context of each country: One can find plenty of evidence on the role of each of these factors (for evidence and references on different technologies and countries, see Rosenberg 1976, 1982; Dosi, Pavitt, and Soete 1988; Ergas 1984). However, irrespective of the immediate triggering factor, I suggest that the patterns of innovation tend to follow rather irreversible "trajectories" defined by specific sets of knowledge and expertise. Moreover, irreversibility in the technological advances also means that, using neoclassical language, the changes

of the production possibility sets are likely to *dominate* changes *within* any given set. More precisely, at any given time, instead of a well-behaved set we are likely to observe only one (or very few) points corresponding to the best-practice techniques, while, over time, the dominant process of change will imply improvements in these (very few) best-practice techniques, rather than processes of "static" interfactoral substitution. Admittedly, this interpretative conjecture is going to require more evidence and tests (which will not be easy) in order to corroborate its levels of empirical generality. (And there are also more subtle but normatively crucial issues: For example, in the historical evidence, how irreversible and local are learning processes? How powerful are "dynamic increasing return" phenomena? How can we measure, for normative purposes, the likely emergence of nonconvexities, despite the obvious impossibility of making counterfactual historical experiments?) In any case, my assessment of the state of the art in innovation studies suggests, at the very least, that significant path dependencies, nonlinearities, and processes of specific, cumulative learning should be taken very seriously also at the level of the general, theoretical representations.

Finally, the irreversibility features of technical progress tend to be reinforced by the likely emergence of various sorts of externalities and specific infrastructures and institutions associated with the generation and/or exploitation of specific skills. I will now consider these latter aspects of innovation.

E. *The Externalities of the Innovation Process*

It has already been mentioned above that technology typically involves "public" aspects and "private" ones. The appropriability of the economic returns from innovation clearly relates to the latter. Conversely, the "public" aspects essentially take two forms.

First, there are certainly "free-good" elements, in technological progress, essentially stemming from the free flow of information, readily available publications, and so on. As mentioned earlier, economic theory tends to assume this to be the dominant feature of technology (save for institutionally granted rights to appropriation, such as patent rights). Of course, I do not suggest that models such as Arrow's (Arrow 1962a) hinted at such a narrow equivalence of technology and information; however, it is fair to say that it provided some legitimacy for several contemporary formulations that have assumed it as least as a "workable hypothesis". The foregoing survey of the characteristics of technology and technical progress implies a rejection of such a view as, at best, incomplete.

Moreover, the "public" characteristics of technology relates to the information flows and the *untraded interdependencies* among sectors, technologies, and firms and takes the form of technological complementarities, "synergies," flows of stimuli, and constraints that do not entirely correspond to commodity flows. For example, knowledge and expertise about continuous chemical processing may allow technological innovations in food processing even when the latter do not involve any chemical inputs; "arms-length" relationships between producers and users of industrial equipment (such as informal exchanges of information, exchanges of technical specifications, and manpower mobility) are often a fundamental element in the innovation process even if sometimes no economic transaction is involved; at its origins the production of bicycles drew technological knowledge from the production of shotguns, even if obviously neither product is an output or an input in the other activity. All these phenomena represent a

structured set of technological externalities that can sometimes be a *collective asset* of groups of firms/industries within countries or regions (see Bengt-Ake Lundvall 1984 and 1988) or else, tend to be internalized within individual companies (e.g., Teece 1982 and Pavitt 1986a). By a "structured set" of externalities, I mean some sort of consistent, and sometimes hierarchical, pattern linking different industries and technologies (such as different kinds of machinery production and users and producers of particular types of equipment). In other words, technological bottlenecks and opportunities (Rosenberg 1976) and experiences and skills embodied in people and organizations, capabilities, and "memories" overflowing from one economic activity to another tend to organize *context conditions* that (*a*) are country-specific, region-specific, or even company-specific and (*b*) as such, determine different incentives/stimuli/constraints to innovation, for any given set of strictly economic signals.

Relatedly, technological progress along any one trajectory is linked with (*a*) the development of *specific infrastructures;* (*b*) *system scale economies;* (*c*) *complementary technologies;* and (*d*) *particular technical standards* that positively feed upon specific patterns of innovation David (1986) and Hughes (1982), for example, discuss the interrelation between the development of the electricity-grid infrastructure and what, in the terminology suggested here, are electricity-based technological trajectories. Other obvious examples of "infrastructure technologies" that perform as an externality to a wide range of innovative activities are transport systems and telecommunications. Arthur (1983) and David (1985) illustrate the latter two points in the case of the development of the QWERTY keyboard in typewriters (QWERTY refers to the first top letters in the standard American keyboard). Although it was designed to meet problems which subsequent developments have overcome, and though it is no longer the optimal keyboard, the QWERTY standard has remained dominant as a result of cumulative development on an early lead: The specific skill of typists in QWERTY fostered QWERTY standards on the manufacturing side, which in turn increased the incentive to acquire QWERTY typing skills. Moreover, the interrelatedness between different technologies that compose a technological system or a complex product helps us understand why companies and countries may be "locked" into technologies—see the classic work by incumbent Marvin Frankel (1956) linking this point to development topics. Finally, Teece (1982, 1986) discusses a somewhat similar issue from the point of view of firms' structures and strategic management, identifying the crucial role of internalized complementary technologies in firms' competitive performances.

Untraded interdependences and context conditions are, to different degrees, the *unintentional* outcome of decentralized, but irreversible, processes of environmental organization (one obvious example is Silicon Valley) and/or the result of explicit strategies of public and private institutions.

The evolution over time and the spatial differences in these untraded interdependences also represent an important link between innovation studies and the regional economics of technical change (see Edward Malecki 1983 and Morgan Thomas 1985). Whenever these technological externalities—in the form of specific infrastructures, skill availability, competences embodied in local firms, easier information about new production inputs—reproduce through time as a sort of dynamic increasing returns (Arthur 1986), they also help explain the differentiation in the technological capabilities,

rates of innovation, and rates of diffusion among regions and countries (see Alfred Thwaites and Ray Oakey 1985). In this field, an original tradition of studies has developed particularly in France: the analysis of "filieres" (literally "webs"), linking groups of industries and technologies via input-output flows and technological complementarities, is a promising way of relating the microeconomic process of innovation with the evolution of the wider economic environments (on "filieres," see Joel Toledano 1978; Alexis Jacquemin and Michael Rainelli 1984; Richard Arena, Michael Rainelli, and Andre Torre 1984; Ehud Zuscovitch 1984; Patrick Cohendet, Regis Larue de Tournemine, and Zuscovitch 1982; Jean-Louis Truel 1980).[9]

F. *Determinants and Patterns of Investment in Innovation: Toward a Sectoral Taxonomy*

Let me summarize the discussion of the foregoing five subsections. As analyzed in detail by Nelson (1986, 1988), the process of innovation in Western economies embodies complex and varying balances between public and proprietary forms of knowledge, and different combinations between notional opportunities of innovation, firm-based capabilities to reap these opportunities, and economic incentives to do so (related to appropriability mechanisms, market conditions, relative prices, broader socioeconomic conditions such as industrial relations). Moreover, the specific opportunities that are seized, the appropriability mechanisms that are developed, and the actual capabilities that are used tend to grow with each other. Phenomena of hysteresis are likely to emerge:

[9] The concept of "filieres" partly overlaps with Hirschman's insights on "backward" and "forward" linkages (Albert Hirschman 1958).

The exploration of particular technologies and the development of particular problem-solving methods increase the capabilities of firms and industries in these specific directions and thus increase the incentive to do so also in the future. These technology-specific forms of dynamic increasing returns tend' to "lock in" the processes of technical change into particular trajectories, entailing a mutual reinforcement (a positive feedback) between a certain pattern of learning and a pattern of allocation of resources into innovative activities where learning has already occurred in the past (for general discussions of these path-dependent processes, see David 1975, 1986a; and Arthur 1983, 1988).

In line with Nelson (1986), I suggest that the different combinations among these factors explain the "rich and variegated institutional structures supporting technical advance that have grown up in capitalist countries" (p. 1). They also constitute the rather complicated constellation of factors by which a significant group of contemporary economists seek to explain the pace and characteristics of technological progress, and its international, interindustry, and intertemporal changes. Certainly, while this outlook appears to be the most promising approach we have, and while it appears to be consistent with some blocks of experience, far more empirical and historical work will be needed to establish its validity and the manner in which the different elements of the new outlook operate. A first step is to generalize on some common empirical characteristics of technologies and sectors (which I do below) and, then, try tentatively to "map" these characteristics into the features of technologies and innovative processes discussed so far (see Section VI).

Scherer, as mentioned, has recently developed an intersectoral matrix of the origin and use of R & D in the U.S. economy, based on the intersectoral generation and use of a large sample of patents (Scherer 1982). The sectoral ratios of (direct plus indirect) use of R & D to performed R & D are shown in the last column of Table 3. On the grounds of a data base on innovations in the U.K. from 1945 to 1979 collected at the Science Policy Research Unit of the University of Sussex, Pavitt (1984) has developed a sectoral taxonomy of sectors of production/use of innovation. The two data sets appear to be in many ways complementary and provide interesting insights into the "anatomy" of contemporary economic systems and their major inner *loci* of innovation generation (the Yale questionnaire—partly discussed in Levin et al. (1984) and summarized in Nelson (1986)—adds further, and broadly consistent, evidence). Pavitt (1984) identified four major groups of manufacturing industries, namely:

1. *"Supplier-dominated" Sectors.* Innovations are mainly process innovations, embodied in capital equipment and intermediate inputs and originated by firms whose principal activity is outside these sectors proper. Supplier-dominated industries include agriculture, textiles, clothing, leather, printing and publishing, wood products, and the simplest metal products. In these sectors the process of innovation is primarily a process of diffusion of best-practice capital goods and of innovative intermediate inputs (such as synthetic fibers) while endogenously generated opportunities are rather limited and so are R & D expenditures. The knowledge base of these technologies tends to relate to incremental improvements in the equipment produced elsewhere and/or to its efficient use, and to organizational innovations. Cumulativeness and appropriability of technological capabilities are relatively restricted and firms are typically not very big (with some exceptions in those activi-

ties characterized by some significant economies of scale in production, such as part of textiles, or in marketing and distribution networks, such as in clothing).

2. *"Specialized Suppliers."* Innovative activities relate primarily to product innovations that enter most other sectors as capital inputs. Firms tend to be relatively small, operate in close contact with their users and embody a specialized and partly tacit knowledge in design and equipment building. Typically, this group includes mechanical and instruments engineering. Opportunities for innovation are generally abundant, but are often exploited through "informal" activities of design improvement (thus, formal R & D is often rather low). Idiosyncratic and cumulative skills make for a relatively high appropriability of innovation (think of the secular advantage of German machine-tool makers).

3. *"Scale-intensive"* Sectors. Innovation relates to both processes and products, and production activities generally involve mastering complex systems (and, often, manufacturing complex products); economies of scale of various sorts (in production and/or design, R & D, distribution networks) are significant; firms tend to be big, produce a relatively high proportion of their own process technologies, often devote a relatively high proportion of resources to innovation, and tend to integrate vertically into manufacturing their own equipment. This group includes transport equipment, several electric consumer durables, metal manufacturing, food products, glass, and cement.

4. *"Science-based"* Sectors. Innovation is directly linked to new technological paradigms made possible by scientific advances; technological opportunity is very high; innovative activities are formalized in R & D laboratories; investments in innovative search are quite high; a high proportion of their product innovation enters a wide number of sectors as capital or intermediate inputs; firms tend to be big (with the exception of new "Schumpetarian" ventures and highly specialized producers). This group includes the electronics industries, most of the organic chemical industries, drugs, and bioengineering. (Aerospace and some military-related activities share with science-based sectors the importance of inputs from scientific advances and of formalized research, while sharing with the production-intensive sectors the importance of economies of scale and of an efficient organization of complex production systems.)

Taxonomic exercises on the intersectoral differences in the sources, procedures, and intensity of innovative search are rather new and a lot of comparative work is still to be done; however, let me briefly mention the importance of these analyses on both positive and normative grounds. As regards the former, the fact that innovations are located at different places within the "capitalist engine" (Nelson 1986, p. 20) demands a better understanding of the factors that tend to concentrate innovative opportunities and investments in some activities more than in others. Taxonomic efforts help in this understanding and also in answering puzzling comparative questions such as, How did Germany and Sweden become so good in mechanical engineering? How does this relate to their productive structure and international competitiveness? Why is the United States relatively strong in science-based industries? (some tentative answers to these comparative questions are attempted in Pavitt 1988; Pavitt, Dosi, and Soete 1988; Ergas 1984). On normative grounds, a more detailed understanding of the intersectoral patterns of innovation directs attention to questions of importance for industrial and development policies. Given the objective of an acceleration of the rate of technical progress, would R & D incentives be well suited for science-based industries but not for "supplier-dominated" industries? Would the development of a large internal market be important for scale-intensive industries but not so much for "specialized suppliers"?

G. *Some Conclusions*

In this section, I have focused on the broad differences in opportunities, incentives, R & D investments, and innovative procedures among industries. The thrust of the argument has been that these differences exist, are important, and help explain the internal structure of the complex engine which in modern noncentrally planned economies continuously generates new products and production processes. Moreover, intertechnological differences in opportunity, appropriability conditions, knowledge bases, and search procedures help explain what Nelson (1986) calls the "problem of institutional assignment," that is, the location within the socioeconomic system of specific search and development activities to particular actors, for example, why certain activities are undertaken by nonprofit institutions and others by business firms, why some sectors produce their own process innovations and others buy them from the market (more on the latter in Williamson 1985; Buer 1982), and why some economic activities contribute a disproportionate share of innovations while others are mainly recipients. Relatedly, the input-output structure of the economy, together with information flows and intersectoral flows of knowledge embodied in people and organizations, diffuses through the system the economic effects of particular innovations, thus amplifying the opportunities for productivity growth and new product development.

There is a yet finer level of analysis, however. After all, industry-specific characteristics are averages of cross-firm distributions. The fact that these averages show recognizable patterns that are relatively stable over time and across countries entails the relative stability of the industry-specific and technology-specific factors analyzed above. Still, one must explain also the intra-industry variance in innovative investments and degrees of innovative success. Moreover, innovation and imitation continuously modify the relative performance and competitiveness of firms and thus affect also the dynamics of industrial structures. Parts V and VI will discuss these topics.

V. *Intrasectoral Differences in Innovativeness and Economic Performance*

One of the most common features of industrial case studies is the description of significant differences among firms not only in terms of size, but also in terms of technological capabilities, product-market strategies, degrees of innovativeness and competitive success, costs of productions, and profitability. Putting it another way, nothing similar to the "representative firm" stylized by economic theory seems to emerge from the empirical accounts (to see this, consult a random sample of articles in, say, the *Harvard Business Review* and the *California Management Review*, or, for more detail of industrial histories, Alan Altshuler et al. 1984 on automobiles, Dosi 1984 and Franco Malerba 1985 on semiconductors, and Enos 1962 on petroleum refining). With reference to the foregoing discussion, one is led to ask what are the relationships between the characteristics of innovation analyzed earlier, on the one hand, and the intrasectoral differences in firm structures (e.g., in size) and performance (e.g., rates of innovation and production costs), on the other. In this section I focus mainly on the general features of *interfirm, intrasectoral* differences in innovativeness, and, more generally, economic performance, leaving to Section VI a more detailed account of the *processes* that generate them. The empirical reference upon which this section is based is rather commonsensical, for example, the fact that firms can be generally found to be widely different, in terms of various performance indicators and also of behaviors, structures, and strategies. However, these simple ideas might be usefully conceptualized in the sense that meaningful classifications might help, first, in providing empirically sound hypotheses for theoretical modeling and, second, in moderating the innocent acceptance—widespread in the economic literature—of "representative firms," "equilibrium conditions of production," "technological identity of producers," and so on. Thus, in the following, I attempt a classification of the factors that account for *intrasectoral* differences in both structures (e.g., size) and performances (e.g., degrees of innovativeness).

I start from the intrasectoral, interfirm differences in innovative investment as shown by their R & D expenditures.

A. *Interfirm Differences in R & D*

A long debate has taken place in industrial economics on the relationship between size of firm and innovation (both R & D investments and innovative output, typically patents). I shall not enter the details of the discussion that concern both the meaning of particular measures (it has been argued that patenting underestimates the innovation output of big firms—which appear to show a lower propensity to patent; the R & D expenditures are likely to underestimate innovative contributions of small firms—which

sometimes innovate on an "informal" basis, etc.) and the degrees of empirical corroboration of the improperly termed *Schumpeterian hypothesis* (i.e., that bigness is relatively more conducive to innovation, that concentration and market power affect the propensity to innovate). For reviews and (partly conflicting) findings, see Scherer (1988), Soete (1979), Griliches (1984a), Griliches and Pakes (1986), Morton Kamien and Nancy Schwartz (1982), Wesley Cohen and Levin (1988), and Pavitt, Robson, and Townsend (1987). For the purposes of the present work, it is enough to mention three major regularities that come out of empirical studies.

First, there appears to be a *roughly* log-linear relation within industries between firm size and R & D expenditures (or patenting). This is, however, a rather crude approximation. On closer inspection, subject to industry differences and different measures of innovativeness, one finds better fits of quadratic and cubic relationships between size (i.e., sales or employment) and innovativeness (R & D expenditure, R & D employment, number of patents, or number of innovations); however, irrespective of the form of the econometric model, the estimates show *roughly* nondecreasing returns of innovative proxies to firm size (Scherer 1986 argues in favor of a lower degree of innovativeness for the greatest size classes; Soete 1979, using partly different data, shows the opposite for about a third of his industry sample).

Second, the size distribution of innovating firms *within sectors* depends on the technological characteristics of the sectors themselves. Pavitt, Robson, and Townsend (1987), using the SPRU sample of innovation mentioned earlier, conclude that in sectors with high technological opportunities (chemicals, electrical/electronics) the innovating firms "can be found heavily represented among those that are very large and those that are small" (p. 16). Conversely, in machinery and mechanical engineering (approximately those "specialized suppliers" with the characteristics identified earlier) a relatively greater proportion of innovation is undertaken by small firms (which, however, are "small" in comparison with the size of distribution of the manufacturing firms' universe, but not necessarily in relation to the specific national or world market in which they operate).

Third, irrespective of the statistical proxy for innovativeness (and in particular, irrespective of the choice between an investment measure or an output measure), after allowing for the effect of firm size, one still generally observes a substantial unexplained interfirm, intrasectoral variance, in terms of both R & D investments and, even more so, innovative output. (Moreover, note that a significant proportion of firms in each industry do *not* patent and do *not* produce significant innovations; for evidence, see John Bound et al. 1984.)

There are three obvious caveats for the interpretation of these results. The first relates to the fact that the statistical proxies for innovativeness cannot capture those aspects of technical change, discussed above, based on "informal" learning (thus, independent of measured R & D investments) and/or yielding incremental innovations (hence, unrecorded in patents or discrete innovation counts). The second is that some (generally undetermined) part of the *intra*sectoral variance in innovative performance must be attributed to differences in the actual lines of business (and, thus, in opportunity, appropriability) which are, nevertheless, statistically classified within the "same" industry. Third, some firms may not patent or innovate but still engage in substantial R & D which is simply devoted to keeping up and adapting to what other competitors are doing.

Despite such limitations, however, these empirical regularities tell a story that, in my view, is consistent with the characteristics of the innovative process discussed earlier. More precisely, the intra- and intersectoral differences in the size distribution of firms in general and in particular of innovating firms are linked with the characteristics of different technological paradigms and the ways innovative capabilities develop and can be competitively exploited by individual firms. After all, any particular distribution of firms' characteristics (e.g., size, R & D propensities, unit costs) at any one time is itself the result of processes of corporate learning and market competition whereby certain corporate features turned out to yield a competitive advantage. The general interpretations suggested here are that (*a*) the sectoral distributions of characteristics such as firms' sizes are affected by the specific characteristics of the technological paradigms on which the production of that sector is based, in terms of appropriability, technological opportunities, scope for automation, and economies of scale; however, (*b*) any observed bias in the size distribution of firms in a particular sector is not sufficient evidence to make inferences on the "true" effect of size upon innovativeness. For example, an industry may show a relative bias toward "bigness" even if the latter does not confer particular innovative advantages (or disadvantages); it may be due simply to technical requirements on the production side (such as economies of scale in production and marketing). Alternatively, size may actually be conducive to innovation (because of indivisibilities of R & D projects, high R & D minimum thresholds) or detrimental to it (e.g., if it induces organizational inflexibilities). Finally, there may be cases in which the correlation between size and innovativeness reflects a causal process in the reverse direction: Big firms happened to grow big because they innovated successfully in the past and continue to do so in the present without, however, finding a differential advantage in "bigness" as such. In general, the relationship between industrial structures and degrees of innovativeness runs both ways and the understanding of particular intrasectoral distributions of firms' structural and performance characteristics implies the understanding of the (technology-specific) effects of innovation on firms' economic performance and competitiveness. Some of these effects obviously relate to the scope for economies of scale that each technological paradigm entails. Others relate to the impact that the differential innovative capabilities of certain firms exert on their ability to acquire a lead in efficiency and/or product quality vis-à-vis other firms. Let me start with the former.

B. *Flexibility and Economies of Scale*

Most technological trajectories since the Industrial Revolution involved increasing mechanization of production and increasing exploitation of economies of scale (see Nelson and Winter 1977 and the works cited therein); however, each technological paradigm is characterized by different trade-offs between flexibility (with respect to production runs and variety of outputs, for a given equipment) and economies of scale. Thus, a first determinant of any observed sectoral distribution of firms (and/or plants), by size, relates to the degrees to which individual firms have explored and possibly improved along a particular technological trajectory. Take the contemporary example of the transition from electromechanical patterns of automation to electronics-based ones. As compared to "classical" (electromechanical) automation of mass production, numerically controlled machine tools, flexible manufacturing systems, and robots allow a much greater

flexibility of production in terms of (*a*) acceptable variance of throughputs (defined in terms of number of cost-effectively produced homogeneous items per unit of time), (*b*) acceptable variances in output varieties, and (*c*) minimum scale of production (see Coriat 1983, 1984; Michael Piore and Charles Sabel 1984).

This has two consequences. First, it increases the efficiency of small-scale productions. Second, it is likely to decrease the importance of plant-related economies of scale that were one of the main sources of both productivity growth and production rigidity in "classical" Fordist automation.

Within the electromechanical paradigm, higher efficiency of production (stemming from standardization, economies of scale, etc.), generally associated with "Taylorist" and "Fordist" principles of organization and production, is also correlated with very high degrees of inflexibility—in terms of acceptable variance in production runs and mixes. Figure 1 illustrates such a case. Suppose that, in the "old" technology, the line *AA* represents the technical relationship between "normal" average total unit costs (*c*) and rates of throughput (*q*), while the line *FF* represents the corresponding relationship between unit costs and degrees of flexibility (*F*), say, approximated by the standard deviation in the rate and mixes of throughput that does not significantly increase "normal" unit costs. Fundamental dimensions of technical progress along the old technological trajectory are the increasing exploitation of economies of scale and economies of standardization. Thus, any increase of the flexibility requirements (due, for example, to increasing uncertainty about the levels and composition of demand) indirectly represents a retardation factor of technological innovation/diffusion within the electromechanical paradigm, insofar as technical advances are also

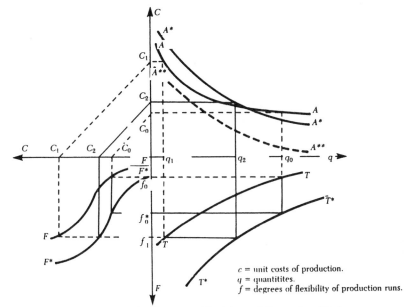

Figure 1. The Trade-off Between Flexibility and Economies of Scale

scale biased; however, different technological paradigms embody different trade-offs between flexibility and scale. Suppose for example that, in Figure 1, the line $A*A*$ represents the relationship costs/quantities for a new electronics-based paradigm, while the line $F*F*$ is the corresponding relationship flexibility costs. Thus, the trade-off quantity/flexibility is TT for the old technology and $T*T*$ for the new one.[10] Now, consider again an increase in the desired flexibility. Remarkably, this is likely to have two effects: First, it is likely to hinder "normal" technical progress/diffusion along the "old" technological trajectory while, second, fostering innovation/diffusion in the new technological paradigm. Suppose we start from production runs equal to q_0, normal total costs at c_0 and a degree

of flexibility f_0. Now, say, an increasing instability of economic growth, an increasing uncertainty about consumers' demand and rivals' strategies increases the required flexibility of production from f_0 to f_1. On the grounds of the "old" technological paradigm, this would mean very short production runs (q_1) and very high costs (c_1). The new paradigm (e.g., electronics-based automation) changes the nature of the trade-offs, allowing, for example, the required flexibility to be achieved at throughput q_2 and unit costs c_2. Moreover, I suggest, the higher technological opportunities of the new paradigm (with its scope for learning, decreasing costs of capital equipment, etc.) in the long term will shift the technoeconomic relation between costs and quantities, say, down to $A**A**$.

In contemporary economies one often observes a fall in plant sizes (see, for example, Fabrizio Barca 1984 on Italy),

[10] This example owes a lot to the discussions with B. Coriat on automation in general and, in particular, on the car industry.

somewhat analogous to the change in the scale of production from q_0 to q_2 in Figure 1; however, this empirical observation per se does not allow any conclusion on either the "optimal" or "equilibrium" relationship between characteristics of the technology and size, or on the long-term trends in technical opportunities for economies of scale. As illustrated above, the actual change in production scale is the joint outcome of (a) differences in the scope for economies of scale of the two technological paradigms, (b) (sector-specific) differences in the trade-offs between flexibility and scale economies that they imply, and (c) different degrees of technical progress along the two trajectories defined by the two paradigms.

One can see here a first link going *from* the characteristics of each technology *to* industrial structure (and its changes): The observed intra-industry distributions of firms by size are obviously affected by the sector-specific opportunities for various kinds of economies of scale and the trade-offs between the latter and production flexibility. If different firms position themselves differently on the notional trade-offs between flexibility and scale economies and/or explore and exploit the opportunities of automation at different paces, one should observe a distribution of varying plant sizes and firm sizes even when the propensity to innovate is neutral with respect to size. As an historical example, I suggest we are currently observing, at least in the industrialized countries, a process of change in the size distribution of plants and firms that is significantly influenced by (a) the new flexibility-scale trade-offs associated with electronic production technologies, and (b) the painstaking attempts to learn how to use them efficiently and slowly explore the (still largely unknown) potential for economies of scale that they entail (for some highly preliminary and impressionistic evidence, see Mehmet Gonenc 1984; Fabio Arcangeli, Dosi and Moggi

1986 and Giancarlo Cainarca, Massimo Colombo, and Sergio Mariotti 1987); and, possibly (c) an increasing variety of demanded characteristics of products, greater refinement and tolerance for (or desire for) novelty, associated with market segmentation and higher consumers' income. As general outcome of all these factors, in line with Pavitt (1986b), I conjecture that changes in the size distribution (by plant and especially by firm) in the "specialized supplier" industries—machine making, etc.—will tend to be biased toward the bigger size classes, because of R & D indivisibilities, economies of scope based on electronics flexible manufacturing systems, and so on. Conversely, in mass-production industries the higher flexibility of the new forms of automation is likely to allow the efficient survival also of relatively smaller firms (as compared to the past).

More generally, on the grounds of sectoral, and still scattered, evidence, it is plausible to conjecture that, at any one time, there may be a certain number of (technology-specific) size distributions (by plant and by firm), that represent, so to speak, notional "evolutionary equilibria," in the sense that a variety of firms and plants coexist at roughly similar levels of economic performance, by exploiting more economies of scale with less flexibility, more economies of scope and lesser economies of scale, and so on.

This is not the only source of difference among firms. Other differentiating mechanisms relate even more directly to innovation and innovative strategies.

C.   *Innovation, Variety, and Asymmetries Among Firms*

A major implication of the characteristics of cumulativeness, tacitness, and partial appropriability of innovation is the permanent existence of *asymmetries* among firms, in terms of their process technologies and quality of output. That is, firms can be ranked as "better" or "worse" according to their distance from the technological frontier. As discussed in another work (Dosi, Pavitt, and Soete 1988), one can see here an interesting convergence between the findings from international trade analyses suggesting widespread technology gaps between countries (see Freeman 1963; Freeman, C. J. Harlow, and J. K. Fuller 1965; Gary C. Hufbauer 1966; Dosi and Soete 1983; OECD 1968; Soete 1981; and Mario Cimoli 1988) and the evidence from industrial economics within each country on similarly wide gaps in technology among firms as measured by their costs of production (see, for example, Tsung-Yuen Shen 1968; Nelson 1968, 1981a; Bela Gold 1969; and Dosi 1984. This confirms earlier findings by the U.S. Bureau of Labor Statistics, cited in Nelson 1981a). Moreover, some recent studies in industrial economics have begun to explore the existence and intertemporal persistence of above- or below-average profitabilities of individual firms (see Paul Geroski and Alexis Jacquemin 1986; Bruno Contini 1986; Dennis Mueller 1977; and Yiroyoki Odogiri and Hideki Yamawaki 1986); incidentally, note that interfirm profitability differences are likely to underestimate the differences in production efficiency and product technology insofar as their "quasi-rents" are distributed as differential wages and salaries.

Call *degrees of asymmetry* of an industry its dispersions of (a) input efficiencies for a given (homogeneous) output and (b) price-weighted performance characteristics of firms' (differentiated) outputs—were we able to measure them with precision. Certainly, part of these interfirm asymmetries in production efficiency are due to (a) economies of scale in production (see Cliff Pratten 1971; Aubrey Silberston 1972; and Donald Hay and Derek Morris 1979), and (b) different vintage distributions of the equipment of each firm (Wilfred Salter 1969); how-

ever—perhaps more important—these asymmetries are also the effect of different innovative capabilities, that is, different degrees of technological accumulation and different efficiencies in the innovative search processes. Other things being equal, one would expect that the higher the potential that a technological paradigm entails for creating asymmetries in product quality and production efficiency (that is, the higher are, *jointly*, technological opportunities *and* appropriability of innovative advantages), the higher the scope for the "best" firms to enjoy a competitive advantage and grow bigger, irrespective of any possible bias in the "returns" of innovativeness to size (I come back to this issue in Section VI). Of course, any observed pattern of asymmetry among firms depends also on many other features of the markets in which firms operate. For example, varying degrees of demand elasticity affect the degrees of protection that any firm enjoys against the greater efficiency of rivals, or conversely, the ease with which technological leaders can grow at the expense of less efficient rivals. In fact, there is here an obvious complementarity between the findings and conceptualizations emerging from innovation studies, on the one hand, and the analyses of entry and mobility barriers in industrial economics, on the other (see, for example, Richard Caves and Michael Porter 1977 and 1978; Scherer 1980; Sylos Labini 1967).

If such asymmetries are a factor of diversity among firms that correspond, in a loose biological analogy, to different degrees of "fitness," there is yet another source of diversity which, in the same analogy, corresponds to roughly equal fitness and "polymorphism." Take, for example, two firms that show identical unit costs and produce the same good. Thus, they do not show any asymmetry, in the sense defined above; however, they might still show differences in their input combinations, which are the particular result of firm-specific histories of technological accumulation (Nelson and Winter 1982; Nelson 1985; Metcalfe 1985; Gibbons and Metcalfe 1986; Dosi, Orsenigo, and Silverberg 1986). Similarly, firms might well search for their product innovations in different product spaces, embodying different characteristics and aimed at different corners of the markets. Call this second set of sources of diversity *technological variety,* to mean all those technological differences that do not correspond to unequivocal hierarchies (i.e., "better" and "worse" technologies and products).

Finally, empirical studies often show the coexistence, within the same industry and for identical environmental incentives, of widely different strategies related to innovation, pricing, R & D, investment and so on. Specifically with regard to innovation one notices a range of strategies concerning whether or not to undertake R & D; being an inventor or an early imitator, or "wait and see"; the amount of investment in R & D; the choice between "incremental" and risky projects, and so on (see Charles Carter and Bruce Williams 1957; Freeman 1982 and the bibliography cited therein). Call these differences *behavioral diversity.*

I suggest that technological asymmetries, varieties, and behavioral diversities manifest themselves also in the "unexplained" variances in R & D, patenting, and a number of discrete innovations cited earlier (Section V A).

To summarize: Each production activity is characterized by a particular distribution of firms according to their R & D investments, innovative output, size, degrees of asymmetries in product quality, and production efficiency. However, the picture of an industry that emerges at any time is itself the result of a competitive process which selected survivors within the technological variety and behavioral diversity of firms, put a premium or a penalty on early innovators and allowed varying degrees of technological imitation and diffusion. Thus, a satisfactory understanding of the relationship between innovation and distribution of firms' structural and performance characteristics also implies an analysis of the learning and competitive process through which an industry changes. I turn now to these topics.

VI. Innovation and Industrial Change: Learning and Selection

A. The Innovative Process and Industrial Structures

Over time, as innovation proceeds, new products are introduced and later imitated by other firms, better methods of production are developed or adopted in the form of new types of capital equipment, and, relatedly, some firms are able to obtain below-average costs of production and/or a monopolistic/oligopolistic position, in the manufacturing of some new products. In turn, they can exploit these differential advantages by increasing their rates of profit, their market shares, or, of course, a combination of the two. Conversely, some firms find themselves with above-average costs and/or lower-quality products and, through various strategies of imitation, search, and attempts to "leapfrog," must try to catch up in order to improve their profitabilities and market competitiveness. One version or another of this basic process is what determines the sectoral "snapshots" discussed in the previous section and is revealed, over time, also by the changes in the averages and distributions of firms' inputs, productivity, unit costs, product performances, profit rates, and sizes. Putting it another way, industrial performance and industrial structures are *endogenous* to the process of innovation, imitation, and competition.

Nelson and Winter (1982), Winter (1971), Katsushito Iwai (1981), Gunnar Eliasson (1986a), Gerald Silverberg (1987), Dosi, Orsenigo, and Silverberg (1986), Gibbons and Metcalfe (1986) and Öve Granstrand (1986) have tried to formalize this process in an evolutionary perspective: "Market structure and technological performance are endogenously generated by three underlying sets of determinants: the structure of demand, the nature and strength of opportunities for technological advance and the ability of firms to appropriate the returns from private investment in research and development" (Levin et al. 1984, p. 1). (Treatments of the endogeneity of market structures have been recently developed also within an "equilibrium" framework; see Dasgupta and Stiglitz 1980a, 1980b.) Case studies of individual industries confirm both the endogenous nature of market structures and the causal link going *from* technological success *to* changes in firm size and degree of industrial concentration; in addition to Gort and Steven Klepper (1982) and Gort and Akira Konakayama (1982) who provide comparative intertechnological evidence, see for example, some cross-sectoral evidence in Levin, Cohen and Mowery (1985); and the more qualitative sectoral evidence in Almarin Phillips (1971) on aircraft; Barbara G. Katz and Phillips (1982) on data processing; Wilson, Ashton, and Egan (1980), Dosi (1984), John Tilton (1971), Ed Sciberras (1977), and Malerba (1985) on semiconductors; Altschuler et al. (1984) on automobiles; Chesnais (1986) on drugs and bioengineering; and Momigliano (1983) for a cross-company international econometric analysis of the relationship between levels and changes in various indicators of innovativeness and changes in performance of computer firms.

Broadly speaking, the growing (but still largely inadequate) evidence on the dynamics of industries and technologies highlights complex and varied learning processes whereby firms explore specific domains of perceived technological opportunity, improve their search procedures, and refine their skills in developing and manufacturing new products, drawing partly on their internal accumulated knowledge, partly on artifacts and knowledge developed elsewhere, and partly by copying their competitors. In turn, market interactions select, to different degrees, particular directions of technological development, allowing some firms to grow bigger and penalize others. Note also that in this dynamics, technological asymmetries and technological and behavioral variety *are both the outcome and a driving force* of technological and organizational change. That they are the *outcome* of innovation is straightforward from the earlier discussion: Firms generally learn at different rates, and with modes and behavioral rules specific to their history, internal organization, and institutional context. These interfirm differences are also a major driving force of the process of change in that they underlie the competitive incentive (for the "winners") and the competitive threat (for the "losers") to innovate/imitate products, processes, and organizational arrangements.

Each observed industrial history is, in an essential sense, the outcome of a particular form of this general process; however, in order to account for the specific differences in the patterns shown by individual industries, one should move one step further and, so to speak, "map" the varied characteristics of innovation, as discussed in Sections II to IV, into empirically recognizable classes of evolutionary processes. So, for example, one should be able to link the characteristics of opportunity, appropriability, and so on, of each technological paradigm and the patterns of change in, for example, firms' sizes, market concentration, and degrees of asymmetries. Here the evidence is still highly unsatisfactory and some conjectures can be related only to single case studies and to the plausibility of simulation results; however, the issue is worth pursuing for its analytical (and also normative) relevance.

B. *Characteristics of Innovation and Patterns of Industrial Change*

In general, the observed changes in industrial structures and the observed dynamics of industrial performance (e.g., rates of introduction of new products and rates of change in sectoral productivities) are the outcome of (a) *innovative learning* by single firms (together with that contributed by universities, government agencies, and so on); (b) *diffusion* of innovative knowledge and innovative products and processes, and (c) *selection* among firms. Relatedly, my general interpretative conjectures are the following. First, the empirical variety in the patterns of industrial change is explained by different combinations of selection, learning, and diffusion and different learning mechanisms (e.g., "informal" learning by doing, learning through formalized R & D, and experience in marketing). Second, the nature of each technological paradigm, with its innovative opportunities, appropriability conditions, and so on (jointly with other economic and institutional factors) helps explain the observed intersectoral differences in the relative importance of the three processes. (Some further discussion of these conjectures can be found in Dosi, Orsenigo, and Silverberg 1986 and Dosi, Winter, and Teece 1987.) I will proceed by making some broad remarks on the nature of the three processes and then highlight the ways in which they are affected by the characteristics of innovation, by means of some "ideal examples," simulation results, and case studies.

To begin, note that each successful innovation—whether related to process technology, products, or organizational arrangements—entails ceteris paribus, an *asymmetry-creating* effect, which allows one or some firm(s) to enjoy some improvement in its competitive position (e.g., lower prices or better products). Of course, changes in the asymmetries among individual firms do not necessarily correspond to changes in the overall degrees of asymmetry in any one industry. For example, a firm that was previously inefficient, or relatively unsuccessful because its product line was unattractive, now succeeds in devising better processes of products. Other things being equal, this might well reduce the dispersion in the general distribution of the industry; however, it still generates an asymmetry between the considered firm and its laggard competitors. Certainly, the possibility of imitation holds out a greater potential for gain (in productivity, etc.) to firms that are relatively laggard than to firms that are relatively advanced. Ceteris paribus, therefore, there is reason to think that the process of imitation and diffusion makes for *convergence*. But asymmetries in the capabilities of firms impose limits on this tendency and its strength remains to be determined. (I am obviously unable to deal here with the vast literature on diffusion which would require a work of its own and I will mention only a few results relevant to the present discussion.) In turn, the higher the asymmetries among firms, the higher also is the possibility for the technological leaders (or, in any case, the most efficient producers) to modify the industrial structure in their favor, and also improve aggregate industrial performance, by eliminating the laggard producers. Vice versa, the lower the degrees of interfirm asymmetries, the more the improvements of whatever indicator of industrial performance have to rely on widespread learning and diffusion processes.

Moreover, note that the concepts of appropriability, cumulativeness, and tacitness of technological capabilities—introduced earlier—bear a direct link with those concepts developed in industrial economics such as entry and mobility barriers in that the former entails forms of competitive differentiation both between incumbents and potential entrants and among incumbents. In this respect, the "degree of asymmetry" of an industry is a synthetic representation of both sets of phenomena.

With these remarks in mind, let me consider in more detail the relationship between features of the innovative process and patterns of industrial dynamics.

Consider, first, differences in technological *opportunity*, holding other characteristics of innovation (such as appropriability) constant. It is straightforward that, ceteris paribus, one would expect the rates of performance improvement over time (e.g., productivity growth) to be positively correlated with the levels of technological opportunities; however, what can one say about the characteristics of the underlying evolutionary process driven by high technological opportunities? Of course, one would expect that, the higher the opportunities are, the higher also will be the innovative learning by some producers and the selective pressures against laggard firms. That is, the higher the opportunities are, the higher also is the probability that some firms will "learn a lot," a lot more than other competitors, and that—on the grounds of their vastly superior performance—they will, so to speak, drive forward the industry by eliminating backward producers. The simulation exercises in Nelson and Winter (1982) broadly

corroborate these conjectures about the relationship between degrees of technological opportunities, possibilities of differential innovative learning, and selection, leading, ceteris paribus, to rather concentrated industrial structures. One must stress, recalling the discussion in Section IV, that "opportunity" is only a necessary but not sufficient condition for its actual exploitation, while the speed of sectoral performance improvements (in productivity and product characteristics) depend on the latter. Given any notional technological opportunity, its effective exploitation by business firms will depend, as mentioned, on factors such as appropriability conditions, and, also on market variables such as the size of the market, the elasticity of demand to price and quality changes, and the degrees of industrial concentration. The rates at which opportunities are actually exploited (in terms of new/better products and more efficient processes of production) by, at least, some firms, and the rates at which these new products and processes diffuse to other firms obviously affect also the rates of change of industrial performance over time—e.g., the rates of productivity growth or the changes in output prices. In this respect, the case studies cited in paragraph V A also present some evidence on the impressive record of productivity growth and real price fall in sectors characterized by promising new paradigms and high technological opportunities, e.g., computers and semiconductors. Moreover, as regards cross-industry analyses, the evidence that one often finds on the statistical link between sectoral R & D intensity and sectoral innovative performance (e.g., sectoral productivity growth) should, in the light of this discussion, be considered as evidence that relatively high technological opportunities tend to be associated with a formalized, R & D–based mode of technological learning (Nelson 1981a).

Second, consider the impact of *cumulativeness* of innovative capabilities. Here, the implications are straightforward. The more technical progress is cumulative at a firm level, the more success breeds success. Firm-level cumulativeness of technological capabilities entails a nonrandom distribution of probabilities of innovative advance and path dependence: Firms that achieve higher levels of innovativeness (competitiveness) increase also their probability of maintaining or increasing their levels of competitiveness (innovativeness). Technological variety and diffusion are then likely to play only minor roles in industrial dynamics, while the rates of innovative learning of the technological leader(s) directly determine rates of change in the aggregate performance of (often highly concentrated) industries. The converse is the case where cumulativeness is relatively low, as has often been true in "supplier-dominated" sectors. Innovations are mainly embodied in equipment and components bought from other sectors, and while technological opportunities might be significant, they are mainly generated *exogenously* to these industrial activities. In fact, they are the result of opportunities of developing, for example, new seeds, fungicides, pesticides, tractors, and textile machinery that can be efficiently adopted in agriculture, textile, clothing, and so on. Under these circumstances, one would expect diffusion of new vintages of equipment to be the main source of industrial dynamics, while selection processes leading to market concentration are likely to be relatively weak. The evidence on the structure of these sectors (for a discussion, see for example Pavitt 1984) is in line with this hypothesis. Suppliers of new types of machinery, components, seeds, and so on have an interest in the most rapid possible diffusion of their outputs, and thus the rates of change in average performance (productivity, etc.) in the user sectors depends jointly on (*a*) the pace of innovation in the supplier sectors and (*b*) the variant conditions governing adoption. The former, clearly, puts the upper ceiling to such rates of performance improvement. The latter are especially important in explaining the average gaps between faster- and slower-moving countries (again, for an historical illustration of American versus English agriculture in the nineteenth century, see David 1975).

Third, consider the role of appropriability conditions. Of course, the "ease" of imitation of a certain innovation (and, thus, of its diffusion into the output or the production process of other firms) or the ease with which rival firms may succeed in introducing a competitive product stands, ceteris paribus, in an inverse relationship with its appropriability.

In general, the overall degrees of appropriability, the relative effectiveness of the various sources of appropriability (e.g., patenting, innovative leads, and firm-specific learning by doing), the technological opportunities and their sources (e.g., internally generated by incumbents versus external to the industry and "public"), the size and rates of growth of the market all change significantly over the trajectory of development of a technology (its "life cycle"). These factors, jointly with the conditions governing market competition (e.g., various other sorts of entry barriers, necessary minimum scale, difficulties of breaking into or enlarging markets—both domestic and foreign, price and quality elasticity of demand) govern the evolution of both industrial performances and structures.

Certainly, from an empirical standpoint, the concepts emphasized in this work (such as opportunity and appropriability) do not have obvious and objective counterparts, because they are not directly measurable and empirical studies

Number of
Producers

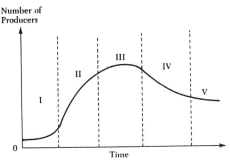

Figure 2. New Products and Number
of Producers

Source: Gort and Klepper (1982), based on a sample of
46 product innovations.

are still difficult and uncertain; however, in my view, statistical difficulties do not detract from their crucial interpretative importance. And, despite all practical drawbacks, it seems to me that the empirical studies now available are quite consistent with this framework of analysis. For example, it has been shown that, along what has been defined here as paradigm-specific "technological trajectories," the net rate of entry of new firms changes. Gort and Klepper (1982) find rather robust cross-innovations evidence (based on 46 innovations) of a five-stage cycle as depicted in Figure 2. It might be worth summarizing their major conclusions: ". . . there is no equilibrium number of firms in an industry"; ". . . [the] ultimate number of producers . . . and the number at each preceding point in time depends upon the sequence of events to that point"; ". . . technical change (innovations) plays a critical role in determining both entry rates and the eventual number of firms in the market"; ". . . the number of firms in product markets technologically adjacent to those of a new product—that is, the number of potential entrants—influence the entry rates"; ". . . the onset of Stage III [flattening net entry rates] and the ensu-

ing net exit in Stage IV is not associated with the maturity of the market as measured by market size or the growth rate in demand"; "rather it corresponds to a decrease in the rate of innovations external to the industry, a compression of profit rates, and the accumulation of valuable experience by incumbent producers" (p. 634). Of course, there is no general necessity for an innovation to pass through all five stages. Whenever radically new (and competing) innovations emerge, one may observe "truncated cycles" (on semiconductors, see Dosi 1984). Still, the major conclusion holds: The net rate of entry and, more generally, the structure of production of any one innovation (the number and size of firms, degrees of industrial concentration, entry barriers, etc.) are endogenous to the technological dynamics, and depend also on rates and modes of innovative learning and on the extent to which this learning is appropriated and internalized within firms as a rent-earning asset.

Empirical and theoretical research on the properties of different modes of industrial evolution is still at a rather early stage; however, the foregoing conjectures and findings highlight the very promising link between the studies of the microeconomic features of the processes through which people and firms search for new products and processes—the domains of the "economics of innovation"— on the one hand, and the analyses of the competitive process, and of the structures, performance, and change of industries—a typical domain of industrial economics—on the other. Innovative learning, of course, is an important competitive weapon. Moreover, the ways economic actors learn also influence the degrees to which they can exploit such a weapon competitively and ultimately change the environment in which they operate. Such a process is inherently "evolutionary," at least in the sense that various economic actors are forced to search for technological changes whose success will only be determined ex post by market selection. Thus, there is inevitably a distribution of "mutations" of which at least some are destined to be "mistakes." In that model, markets select both among firms and among specific technological advances (more on this in Gibbons and Metcalfe 1986); however, such an evolutionary process, unlike a strict biological analogy, is not driven by any purely random change-generating mechanism. Agents learn—from the environment, from their rivals, from their own successes and mistakes—in ways that are specific to the body of knowledge that characterizes each technology, that is, each "technological paradigm." As a consequence, the features of the evolution of each industry are, so to speak, "ordered" by the patterns of learning, and by the ways the latter influence the competitive process; The understanding of the variety of observable industrial structures, performances, and their changes implies, I suggest, a sort of "microfoundation" in the underlying modes by which economic agents accumulate knowledge and competencies on how to solve technological and organizational problems. This, possibly, remains as one of the major fields of analysis of the variegated structures and dynamics by which noncentrally planned economies search for, generate, and select technological innovations. Still, I believe, a fundamental ingredient of the explanation of such variegated industrial structures (and of why in some sectors innovating firms are small and in others large, why some innovating firms diversify beyond the boundaries of their original activities and others do not, why some firms continue to innovate and others slow down, etc.) derives from the equally variegated nature of the evolutionary processes that generated them. Finally, in this perspective, one might

also try to explain (*a*) the levels and changes of economic performance of different countries as the joint outcome of movements of the "technological frontiers" (that is, unequivocal improvements in best-practice production techniques and production inputs), (*b*) processes of learning/diffusion to more "backward"/imitative firms (and countries), and (*c*) processes of selection associated with higher competitiveness or higher international market shares of the most successful innovators (or imitators). Clearly, in considering international differences, factors that go beyond those that differentiate firms within a common national environment need to be considered (e.g., education, financial facilities, legal institutions, cultural traits, forms of social organization). However, it will be interesting to see, first, how far the factors that emerge from the present survey can take us, and, second, how such factors interact with those broader national characteristics which I have just mentioned.

VII. *Some Conclusions*

The number, variety, and scope of the studies that have been reviewed (albeit a subset of the recent literature on technological change) reveal the progress that has been made over the last 20 years in the conceptualization and, to some extent, in the empirical analysis of the process of generation of innovations and their effects. Some of the themes can be considered as developments on insights and hypotheses already present in the writings of classical economists, and, after them, Schumpeter. Other elements of analysis add novel understanding of the characteristics of technical progress. Certainly, the empirical analysis of the innovative process within and across industries and countries has made a promising beginning and is pursued with vigor. Progress in this area is often constrained by scarcity of the relevant data, but possibly also by the "vision" and approach to empirical analysis of economists who are generally trained to consider technology among the preanalytical data of their models.

In the new view, appropriability; partial tacitness; specificity; uncertainty; variety of knowledge bases, search procedures, and opportunities; cumulativeness; and irreversibility (all concepts defined in Sections II and III) have been recognized as *general features* of technological progress. Relatedly, the endogenous nature of market structures associated with the dynamics of innovation, the asymmetries among firms in technological capabilities, various phenomena of nonconvexity, history dependence, dynamic increasing returns, and the evolutionary nature of innovation/diffusion processes are some of the main elements of the process of technological change.

My impression is that there is a significant gap between the wealth of findings by economic historians, students of technology, applied industrial economists, on the one hand, and the (more limited) conceptualization of these findings in economic theory, on the other. Clearly, there will always be a difference between the "empirical stories" and the "analytical stories" of the theoreticians. The former tend inevitably to focus on the uniqueness of the details while the latter are bound to involve varying degrees of simplification and abstraction.[11] However, the core hypotheses made by the theory should not openly conflict with empirical phenomena that show enough persistence over time and/or across eco-

nomic environments. If one believes this, then some questions immediately come to mind: For example, how does one translate the features of the innovative process, outlined above, into theory-level propositions on microeconomic behaviors, production theory, adjustment processes, and so on? Are these propositions consistent with the corresponding assumptions that one generally makes in economic analysis? Or, putting it another way, can we build incrementally upon standard assumptions in order to account for the foregoing properties of the innovative process? Whatever one's answer to these questions, the field of innovation is, in my view, particularly fascinating and challenging. Innovation and technical change have been a privileged focus of attention also for those who have been trying to model economic dynamics in unorthodox fashion, based on "evolutionary" assumptions, a much looser concept of "equilibria," a characterization of behaviors that leave great room for institutional traits and a big emphasis on competition as a selective mechanism (notably, Nelson and Winter 1982; see also Dosi et al. 1988). However, the challenge that innovative processes pose to this approach is equally formidable. It must show that assumptions which, with little doubt, are empirically more plausible, can also generate models with levels of generality somewhat comparable with those based on a more conventional approach; explore the robustness of results that so far have been obtained mainly through simulations; achieve, despite an admittedly higher complexity, that threshold of elegance that makes models appealing to the professional community.

Almost certainly, competing theories in social sciences are somewhat like competing phenotypes in complex evolutionary environments: There is no way of telling ex ante which one will be "fitter."

---

[11] This is not the place to engage in a discussion of economic methodology. A rich exchange of views on "theory versus history" which directly touches on many issues involving technical change is in William Parker (1986). A pertinent methodological argument, which, again, is impossible to tackle here, despite several suggestive points and disagreements, is in John Elster (1983).

It is hard to doubt, however, that the domain of innovation, with the characteristics discussed in this review, are a major—and still largely unexplored—frontier of economic analysis.

REFERENCES

ABERNATHY, WILLIAM J. AND UTTERBACK, JAMES M. "A Dynamic Model of Product and Process Innovation," *Omega*, 1975, 3(6), pp. 639–56.
_____. "Patterns of Industrial Innovation," *Tech. Rev.*, June–July 1978, 7, pp. 2–9.
ALTSHULER, ALAN ET AL. *The future of the automobile.* Cambridge: MIT Press, 1984.
AMENDOLA, MARIO. "A Change of Perspective in the Analysis of the Process of Innovation," *Metroecon.*, Oct. 1983, 35(3), pp. 261–74.
AMENDOLA, MARIO AND GAFFARD, JEAN-LUC. "Innovation as Creation of Technology: A Sequential Model"; see Venice 1986.
ANTONELLI, CRISTIANO. "The International Diffusion of New Information Technologies," *Res. Policy*, 1986a, 15, pp. 139–47.
ARCANGELI, FABIO. "Innovation Diffusion: A Cross-Tradition State of the Art." SPRU, U. of Sussex, Brighton, 1958.
ARCANGELI, FABIO; DOSI, GIOVANNI AND MOGGI, MASSIMO. "The Patterns of Diffusion of Microelectronic Technologies." DRC Discussion Paper, SPRU, U. of Sussex, Brighton; presented at the Conference on Programmable Automation, Paris, Apr. 1987.
ARENA, RICHARD; RAINELLI, MICHEL AND TORRE, ANDRE. "Du Concept à l'Analyse de Filière: Une Tentative d'Eclaircissment Theorique." Discussion Paper, LATAPSES, Nice, 1984.
ARROW, KENNETH. "The Economic Implications of Learning by Doing," *Rev. Econ. Stud.*, June 1962a, 29, pp. 155–73.
_____. "Economic Welfare and the Allocation of Resources for Invention," see NBER 1962, pp. 609–25.
ARTHUR, W. BRIAN. "Competing Techniques and Lock-in by Historical Events. The Dynamics of Allocation Under Increasing Returns." IIASA, Laxemburg, 1983; rev. ed. CEPR, Stanford U., 1985.
_____. "Industry Location and the Importance of History." CEPR paper no. 43, Stanford U., 1986.
_____. "Competing Technologies: An Overview," in DOSI ET AL. 1988.
ATKINSON, ANTHONY B. AND STIGLITZ, JOSEPH E. "A New View of Technological Change," *Econ. J.*, Sept. 1969, 79(315), pp. 573–78.
BAILY, MARTIN W. AND CHAKRABARTI, A. K. "Innovation and Productivity in U.S. Industry," *Brookings Pap. Econ. Act.*, Dec. 1985, 2, pp. 609–32.
BAKER, MICHAEL J., ed. *Industrial innovation.* London: Macmillan, 1979.
BARCA, FABRIZIO. "Modello della specializzazione flessibile. Fondamenti teorici ed evidenza empirica," in *Contributi alla ricerca economica.* Rome: Banca d'Italia, 1984.

LE BAS, CHRISTIAN. *Economie des innovations techniques.* Paris: Economica, 1981.
BEER, JOHN J. *The emergence of the German dye-industry.* Champaign-Urbana: U. of Ill. Press, 1959.
BERNAL, JOHN D. *The social function of science.* London: Routledge and Kegan Paul, 1939.
BOUND, JOHN ET AL. "Who Does R&D and Who Patents?" in GRILICHES 1984, pp. 21–45.
BRAUN, ERNEST AND MACDONALD, STUART. *Revolution in miniature: The history and impact of semiconductor electronics.* Cambridge: Cambridge U. Press, 1978.
BURNS, ARTHUR F. *Production trends in the United States since 1870.* NY: NBER, 1934.
BRESNAHAN, TIMOTHY AND DAVID, PAUL A. "The Diffusion of Automatic Teller Machines Across US Banks." CEPR, Stanford U.; see Venice 1986.
BUER, TERJE CHRISTIAN. "Investigation of Consistent Make or Buy Patterns of Selected Process Machinery in Selected US Manufacturing Industry." Sloan School of Management, MIT, PhD diss., 1982.
CAINARCA, GIANCARLO; COLOMBO, MASSIMO AND MARIOTTI, SERGIO. "An Evolutionary Pattern of Innovation Diffusion: The Case of Flexible Automation." Dept. of Electronics Discussion paper; Milan Politecnico; presented at the 14th EARIE Conference, Madrid, Sept. 1987.
CARTER, ANNE. *Structural change in the American economy.* Cambridge: Harvard U. Press, 1970.
CARTER, CHARLES AND WILLIAMS, BRUCE. *Industry and technical progress.* Oxford: Oxford U. Press, 1957.
_____. *Investment in innovation.* Oxford: Oxford U. Press, 1958.
CAVES, RICHARD E. AND PORTER, MICHAEL E. "From Entry Barriers to Mobility Barriers: Conjectural Decisions and Contrived Deterrence to New Competition," *Quart. J. Econ.*, May 1977, 91(2), pp. 241–61.
_____. "Market Structure, Oligopoly, and Stability of Market Shares," *J. Ind. Econ.*, June 1978, 26(4), pp. 289–313.
CHESNAIS, FRANÇOIS. "Some Notes on Technological Cumulativeness, the Appropriation of Technology and Technological Progressiveness in Concentrated Market Structures." OECD, Paris; see Venice 1986.
CIMOLI, MARIO. "Technological Gaps and Institutional Asymmetries in a North-South Model with a Continuum of Goods," *Metroecon.*, June 1988.
CLARK, KIM B. AND GRILICHES, ZVI. "Productivity Growth and R & D at the Business Level: Results from the PIMS Data Base," in GRILICHES 1984, pp. 393–416.
COHEN, STEPHEN ET AL. "Competitiveness." BRIE Working Paper, U. of California, Berkeley, 1984.
COHEN, WESLEY N. AND LEVIN, RICHARD C. "Empirical Studies of Innovation and Market Structure," in *Handbook of industrial organization.* Eds: RICHARD SCHMALENSEE AND ROBERT WILLIG. Amsterdam: North-Holland, 1988.
COHENDET, PATRICK; TOURNEMINE, REGIS LARUE DE AND ZUSCOVITCH, EHUD. "Progrès Technique et

Perculation." BETA, U. Louis Pasteur, Strasbourg, 1982.

CONSTANT, EDWARD W. *The origins of the turbojet revolution.* Johns Hopkins U. Press, 1980.

CONTINI, BRUNO. "Organizational Change and Performance in the Italian Industry." Discussion paper, U. of Turin; see Venice 1986.

COOPER, ROBERT. "A Process Model for New Industrial Product Development," *IEE Transaction on Engineering Management*, 1983, 30(1), pp. 2–11.

CORIAT, BENJAMIN. *La robotique.* Paris: La Decouverte/Maspero, 1983.

_____. "Crise et Electronisation de la Production: Robitisation d'Atelier et Modele Fordien d'Accumulation du Capital," *Critiques de l'economie politique*, 1984.

CUNEO, PHILLIPPE AND MAIRESSE, JACQUES. "Productivity and R & D at the Firm Level in French Manufacturing Industry," in GRILICHES 1984, pp. 375–92.

CYERT, RICHARD M. AND MARCH, JAMES G. *A behavioral theory of the firm.* Englewood Cliffs, NJ: Prentice-Hall, 1963.

DASGUPTA, PARTHA D. AND DAVID, PAUL A. "Information Disclosure and the Economics of Science and Technology." CEPR Pub. No. 48, Stanford U., 1985.

DASGUPTA, PARTHA D. AND STIGLITZ, JOSEPH E. "Industrial Structure and the Nature of Innovative Activity," *Econ. J.*, June 1980a, 90(358), pp. 266–93.

_____. "Uncertainty, Industrial Structure and the Speed of R & D," *Bell J. Econ.*, Spring 1980b, 11(1), pp. 1–28.

DAVID, PAUL A. "A Contribution to the Theory of Diffusion." Center for Research in Economic Growth, Memo No. 71, Stanford U., 1969.

_____. *Technical choice, innovation and economic growth.* Cambridge: Cambridge U. Press, 1975.

_____. "Clio and the Economics of QWERTY," *Amer. Econ. Rev.*, May 1985, 75(2), pp. 332–37. (An extended version is published in Parker 1986.)

_____. "Narrow Windows, Blind Giants and Angry Orphans: The Dynamics of Systems Rivalries and Dilemmas of Technology Policy." CEPR Working Paper No. 10, Stanford U.; see Venice 1986a.

_____. "Some New Standards for the Economics of Standardization in the Information Age." CEPR Working Paper No. 11, Stanford U., 1986b.

DAVID, PAUL A. AND OLSEN, TROND E. "Anticipated Automation: A Rational Expectation Model of Technological Diffusion." CEPR Pub. No. 24, Stanford U., 1984.

_____. "Equilibrium Dynamics When Incremental Technological Innovations Are Foreseen." CEPR, Stanford U.; see Venice 1986.

DAY, RICHARD AND ELIASSON, GUNNAR, eds. *The dynamics of market economies.* Amsterdam: North-Holland, 1986.

DAVIES, STEPHEN. *The diffusion of process innovations.* Cambridge: Cambridge U. Press, 1979.

DOSI, GIOVANNI. "Technological Paradigms and Technological Trajectories: A Suggested Interpretation of the Determinants and Directions of Technical Change," *Res. Policy*, June 1982, 11(3), pp. 147–62.

_____. *Technical change and industrial transformation.* London: Macmillan, 1984.

_____. "Institutions and Markets in a Dynamic World," *The Manchester School*, May 1988.

DOSI, GIOVANNI AND EGIDI, MASSIMO. "Substantive and Procedural Uncertainty. An Exploration of Economic Behaviours in Complex and Changing Environments." DRC Discussion paper, SPRU, U. of Sussex, Brighton; presented at the Conference on Programmable Automation, Paris, Apr. 1987

DOSI, GIOVANNI AND ORSENGIO, LUIGI. "Coordination and Transformation: An Overview of Structure, Performance and Change in Evolutionary Environments," in DOSI ET AL. 1988.

DOSI, GIOVANNI; ORSENIGO, LUIGI AND SILVERBERG, GERALD. "Innovation, Diversity and Diffusion: A Self-Organisation Model." DRC Discussion Paper, SPRU, U. of Sussex, Brighton; see Venice 1986.

DOSI, GIOVANNI; PAVITT, KEITH AND SOETE, LUC. *The economics of technical change and international trade.* Brighton: Wheatsheaf, forthcoming.

DOSI, GIOVANNI AND SOETE, LUC. "Technology Gaps and Cost-based Adjustment: Some Explorations on the Determinants of International Competitiveness," *Metroecon.*, Sept. 1983, 12(3), pp. 357–82.

DOSI, GIOVANNI; TEECE, DAVID AND WINTER, SIDNEY. "Toward a Theory of Corporate Coherence." Presented at the Conference on Technology and the Enterprise in an Historical Perspective, Terni, Italy, Oct. 1987.

DOSI, GIOVANNI; FREEMAN, CHRISTOPHER; NELSON, RICHARD; SILVERBERG, GERALD AND SOETE, LUC, eds. *Technical change and economic theory.* London: Francis Pinter; NY: Columbia U. Press, 1988.

DULUDE, LOUISE S. "Les Flux Technologiques Interindustriels: Une Analyse Exploratoire du Potential Canadien," *L'Actualite Economique*, Sept. 1983, 3, pp. 259–81.

EGIDI, MASSIMO. "The Generation and Diffusion of New Market Routines." Torino, Laboratorio di Economia Politica; paper; see Venice 1986.

ELIASSON, GUNNAR. "Innovative Change Dynamic Market Allocation and Long Term Stability of Economic Growth." Industrial Institute for Economics and Social Research, Stockholm; paper; see Venice 1986.

_____. "Micro Heterogeneity of Firms and Stability of Industrial Growth," in DAY AND ELIASSON 1986a.

ELSTER, JOHN. *Explaining technical change: A case study in the philosophy of science.* Cambridge: Cambridge U. Press, 1983.

ENOS, JOHN L. *Petroleum progress and profits: A history of process innovation.* Cambridge: MIT Press, 1962.

ERBER, FABIO. "Microelectronica: Reforma ou Revolucao?" Instituto de Economia Industrial, UFRJ, Rio de Janeiro, 1983.

ERGAS, HENRY. "Why do Some Countries Innovate More Than Others?" Center for European Policy Studies paper no. 5, Bruxelles, 1984.

ERNST, DIETER. *The global race in microelectronics.* Frankfurt and NY: Campus Verlag, 1983.

FARRELL, JOSEPH AND SALONER, GARTH. "Standardization, Compatibility, and Innovation," *Rand J. Econ.*, Spring 1985, *16*(1), pp. 70–83.

FRANKEL, MARVIN. "Obsolescence and Technological Change in a Maturing Economy," *Amer. Econ. Rev.*, May 1956, *45*(3), pp. 94–112.

FREEMAN, CHRISTOPHER. "The Plastics Industry, a Comparative Study on Research and Innovation," *Nat. Inst. Econ. Rev.*, 1963.

————. *The economics of industrial innovation.* 2nd ed. London: Francis Pinter, 1982. (1st ed., Penguin, 1974)

————, ed. *Design, innovation, and long cycles in economic development.* London: Royal College of Arts, 1984. (2nd ed., London: Francis Pinter, 1986).

FREEMAN, CHRISTOPHER; CLARK, JOHN AND SOETE, LUC. *Unemployment and technical innovation.* London: Francis Pinter, 1982.

FREEMAN, CHRISTOPHER; HARLOW, C. J. AND FULLER, J. K. "Research and Development in Electronics Capital Goods," *Nat. Inst. Econ. Rev.*, Nov. 1965, *34*, pp. 40–91.

GARDINER, PAUL. "Design Trajectories for Airplanes and Automobiles During the Past Fifty Years," and "Robust and Lean Designs," in FREEMAN 1984, pp. 121–68.

GEROSKI, PAUL A. AND JACQUEMIN, ALEXIS. "The Persistence of Profits: A European Comparison." Dept. of Economics discussion paper, U. of Southampton, 1986.

GIBBONS, MICHAEL AND JOHNSTON, RON. "The Role of Science in Technological Innovation," *Res. Policy*, 1974, *3*, pp. 220–42.

GIBBONS, MICHAEL AND METCALFE, J. STANLEY. "Technological Variety and the Process of Competition." U. of Manchester paper; see Venice 1986.

GIERSCH, HERBERT, ed. *Emerging technologies.* Tübingen: Mohr, 1982.

GOLD, BELA. *Productivity, technology, and capital.* Lexington, MA: Heath, 1979.

————. "Technological Diffusion in Industry: Research Needs and Shortcomings," *J. Ind. Econ.*, Mar. 1981, *29*(3) pp. 247–69.

GONENC, MEHMET R. "Electronisation et Reorganisation Verticale dans l'Industrie." Thèse de Troisieme Cycle, U. of Paris X, Nanterre, 1984.

GORDON, THEODORE J. AND MUNSON, THOMAS R. "Research into Technology Output Measures." The Future Group, Glanstonbury, CT, 1981.

GORT, MICHAEL AND KLEPPER, STEVEN. "Time Paths in the Diffusion Product Innovations," *Econ. J.*, Sept. 1982, *92*(367), pp. 630–53.

GORT, MICHAEL AND KONAKAYAMA, AKIRA. "A Model of Diffusion in the Production of an Innovation," *Amer. Econ. Rev.*, Dec. 1982, *72*(5), pp. 1111–20.

GORT, MICHAEL AND WALL, RICHARD A. "The Evolution of Technologies and Investment in Innovation," *Econ. J.*, Sept. 1986, *96*(393), pp. 741–57.

GRANSTRAND, OVE. "The Modelling of Buyer/Seller Diffusion Processes. A Novel Approach to Modelling Diffusion and Simple Evolution of Market Structure." Göteborg, Chalmers U. of Technology; see Venice 1986.

GRILICHES, ZVI. "Hybrid Corn: An Exploration in the Economics of Technological Change," *Econometrica*, Oct. 1957, *25*(4), pp. 501–22.

————. "Issues in Assessing the Contribution of Research and Development to Productivity Growth," *Bell J. Econ.*, Spring 1979, *10*(1), pp. 92–116.

————, ed. *R & D, patents, and productivity.* Chicago: Chicago U. Press for NBER, 1984.

————. "R & D, Patents, and Productivity, Introduction," in *R & D, patents and productivity.* Chicago: Chicago U. Press, 1984, pp. 1–19.

GRILICHES, ZVI AND LICHTENBERG, F. "R & D and Productivity Growth at the Industry Level: Is There Still a Relationship?" in GRILICHES 1984, pp. 465–96.

GRILICHES, ZVI AND MAIRESSE, JACQUES. "Productivity and R & D at the Firm Level," in GRILICHES 1984, p. 339–74.

GRILICHES, ZVI AND PAKES, ARIEL. "The Value of Patents as Indicators of Inventive Activity." Presented at the Conference on the Economic Theory of Technology Policy, London, Centre for Economic Policy Research, Sept. 1986.

HABAKKUK, HROTHGAR J. *American and British technology in the nineteenth century.* Cambridge: Cambridge U. Press, 1962.

HAY, DONALD A. AND MORRIS, DEREK, J. *Industrial economics: Theory and evidence.* Oxford: Oxford U. Press, 1979.

HEINER, RONALD. "The Origin of Predictable Behavior," *Amer. Econ. Rev.*, Sept. 1983, *73*(4), pp. 560–95.

————. "Imperfect Decisions, Routinized Behaviour and Inertial Technical Change." Provo, Brigham Young U.; in DOSI, ET AL. 1988.

VON HIPPEL, ERIC. "A Customer Active Paradigm for Industrial Product Idea Generation," *Res. Policy*, 1978, *7*, pp. 240–66.

————. "A Customer Active Paradigm for Industrial Product Idea generation," in BAKER 1979.

————. "The User's Role in Industrial Innovation," in *Management of research and innovation.* Eds.: BURTON DEAN AND JOEL GOLDHAR. Amsterdam: North-Holland, 1980.

————. "Appropriability of Innovation Benefit as a Predictor of the Source of Innovation," *Res. Policy*, 1982, *11*(2), pp. 95–115.

HIRSCHMAN, ALBERT O. *The strategy of economic development.* New Haven, CT: Yale U. Press, 1958.

HOLLANDER, SAMUEL. *The source of increased efficiency: A study of Du Pont rayon plants.* Cambridge: MIT Press, 1965.

HUFBAUER, G. C. *Synthetic materials and the theory of international trade.* London: Duckworth, 1966.

HUGHES, THOMAS P. *Networks of power: Electrification in Western society, 1880–1930.* Baltimore, MD: Johns Hopkins U. Press, 1982.

————. "Reverse Salients and Critical Problems: The Dynamics of Technological Change." U. of Pennsylvania paper; presented at the Conference on Technology and the Enterprise in an Historical Perspective, Terni, Italy, Oct. 1987.

IRELAND, N. J. AND STONEMAN, PAUL. "Technological Diffusion, Expectations and Welfare," *Oxford Econ. Pap.*, July 1986, *38*(2), pp. 283–304.

IWAI, KATSUSIIITO. "Schumpeterian Dynamics, Part I: An Evolutionary Mode of Innovation and Imitation and Part II: Technological Progress, Firm Growth and 'Economic Selection.'" Cowles Discussion Papers, Yale U., New Haven, CT, 1981. (rev. ed., *J. Econ. Behav. Organ.*, June 1984, *5*(2), pp. 159–90; Sept.-Dec. 1984, *5*(3–4), pp. 321–51.)

JACQUEMIN, ALEXIS AND RAINELLI, MICHEL. "Filières de la Nation et Filières de l'Entreprise," *Revue Econ.*, Mar. 1984, *35*(2), pp. 379–92.

JENSEN, RICHARD A. "Adoption and Diffusion of an Innovation of Uncertain Profitability," *J. Econ. Theory*, June 1982, *27*(1), pp. 182–99.

KAMIEN, MORTON AND SCHWARTZ, NANCY. *Market structure and innovation.* Cambridge: Cambridge U. Press, 1982.

KATZ, BARBARA G. AND PHILLIPS, ALMARIN. "Government, Technological Opportunities and the Emergence of the Computer Industry," in GIERSCH 1982, pp. 419–66.

KATZ, MICHAEL L. AND SHAPIRO, CARL. "Network Externalities, Competition and Compatibility," *Amer. Econ. Rev.*, June 1985, *75*(3), pp. 424–40.

KAY, NEIL. *The innovating firm.* London: Macmillan, 1979.

_____. *The evolving firm.* London: Macmillan, 1982.

KENNEDY, CHARLES AND THIRLWALL, ANTHONY P. "Surveys in Applied Economics: Technical Progress," *Econ. J.*, Mar. 1981, *82*(1), pp. 11–63.

KLEIMAN, H. S. *The U.S. government role in the integrated circuit innovation.* Paris: OECD, 1977.

KLEIN, BURTON. *Dynamic economics.* Cambridge, MA: Harvard U. Press, 1977.

KUZNETS, SIMON. *Secular movements in production and prices.* Boston: Houghton Mifflin, 1930.

LANCASTER, KEVIN J. *Consumer demand: A new approach.* NY: Columbia U. Press, 1971.

LANDAU, RALPH AND ROSENBERG, NATHAN, eds. *The positive sum society: Harnessing technology for economic growth.* Washington, DC: National Academy Press, 1986.

LANDES, DAVID. *The unbound Prometheus.* Cambridge: Cambridge U. Press, 1969.

LANGRISH, J. *Wealth from knowledge.* London: Macmillan, 1972.

LAZONICK, WILLIAM. "Industrial Relations and Technical Change: The Case of the Self-Acting Mule," *Cambridge J. Econ.*, Sept. 1979, *3*(3), pp. 231–62.

_____. "The Social Determinants of Technological Innovation." Presented at the Conference on Technology and the Enterprise in an Historical Perspective, Terni, Italy, Oct. 1987.

LEVIN, RICHARD; COHEN, WESLEY M. AND MOWERY, DAVID C. "R & D Appropriability, Opportunity, and Market Structure: New Evidence on some Schumpeterian Hypotheses," *Amer. Econ., Rev.*, May 1985, *75*(2), pp. 20–24.

LEVIN, RICHARD ET AL. *Survey research on R & D appropriability and technological opportunity.*

Part 1: Appropriability. New Haven, CT: Yale U. Press, 1984.

LUNDVALL, BENGT-AKE. "User/Producer Interaction and Innovation." TIP Workshop Paper, Stanford U., 1984. (Rev. ed Denmark: Aalborg U. Press, 1985)

_____. "Innovation as an Interactive Process: User-Producer Relations," in DOSI ET AL. 1988.

MAIDIQUE, MODESTO A. "The Stanford Innovation Project," in *Strategic management of technology innovation.* Eds.: ROBERT A. BURGELMAN AND MODESTO A. MAIDIQUE. Worchester Polytechnic Institute, 1983.

MALECKI, EDWARD J. "Technology and Regional Development: A Survey," *Int. Reg. Sci. Rev.*, Oct. 1983, *8*(2), pp. 89–125.

MALERBA, FRANCO. *The semiconductor business: The economics of rapid growth and decline.* Madison: U. of Wis. Press, 1985.

MANSFIELD, EDWIN. "Technical Change and the Rate of Imitation," *Econometrica*, Oct. 1961, *29*(2), pp. 741–66.

_____. *Industrial research and technological innovation.* NY: Norton, 1968, pp. 127–48.

_____. "R & D and Innovation: Some Empirical Findings," in GRILICHES 1984, pp. 127–48.

_____. "How Rapidly Does New Industrial Technology Leak Out?" *J. Ind. Econ.*, Dec. 1985, *34*(2), pp. 217–23.

MANSFIELD, EDWIN ET AL. *Research and innovation in the modern corporation.* NY: Norton, 1971.

_____. *The production and application of new industrial technology.* NY: Norton, 1977.

MANSFIELD, EDWIN; SCHWARTZ, MARK AND WAGNER, SAMUEL. "Imitation Costs and Patents: An Empirical Study," *Econ. J.*, Dec. 1981, *91*(364), pp. 907–18.

MARRIS, ROBIN M. AND MUELLER, DENNIS C. "Corporation, Competition and the Invisible Hand," *J. Econ. Lit.*, Mar. 1980, *18*, pp. 32–63.

MARTINO, JOSEPH. *Technological forecasting for decision making.* NY: American Elsevier, 1976.

MENSCH, GERHARD. *Das technologische Patt.* [Stalemate in Technology] Frankfurt: Umschau, 1975.

METCALFE, J. STANLEY. "Diffusion of Innovation in the Lancashire Textile Industry," *Manchester Sch. Econ. Soc. Stud.*, June 1970, *38*(2) pp. 145–62.

_____. "On Technological Competition," Mimeo. Dept. of Economics, U. of Manchester, 1985.

METCALFE, J. STANLEY AND GIBBONS, MICHAEL. "On the Economics of Structural Change and the Evolution of Technology." Manchester U. Paper presented at the 7th World Congress of the International Economics Assoc., Madrid, Sept. 1983.

MOMIGLIANO, FRANCO. "Determinanti ed Effetti della Ricerca e Sviluppo in una Industria ad Alta Opportunità Tecnologica: una Indagine Econometrica," *L'Industria*, 1983, *4*(1), pp. 61–109.

_____. "Le Tecnologie dell'informazione: Effetti Economici e Politiche Pubbliche," in *Tecnologia Domani.* Ed.: A. RUBERTI. Bari: Laterza-Sat, 1985.

MOMIGLIANO, FRANCO AND DOSI, GIOVANNI. *Tecnologia e organizzaione industriale internazionale.* Bologna: Il Mulino, 1983.

MOWERY, DAVID C. "The Emergence and Growth of Industrial Research in American Manufacturing—1899–1946." PhD diss., Stanford U., 1980.

_____. "The Relationship Between Intrafirm and Contractual Forms of Industrial Research in American Manufacturing, 1900–1940," *Exploration Econ. Hist.*, Oct. 1983, 20(4), pp. 351–74.

MOWERY, DAVID C. AND ROSENBERG, NATHAN. "The Influence of Market Demand upon Innovation: A Critical Review of Some Recent Empirical Studies," *Res. Policy*, 1979, 8, pp. 102–53.

MUELLER, DENNIS. "The Persistence of Profits above the Norm," *Economica*, Nov. 1977, 44(176), pp. 369–80.

NABSETH, L. AND RAY, G. F. *The diffusion of new industrial processes.* Cambridge: Cambridge: U. Press, 1974.

NATIONAL BUREAU OF ECONOMIC RESEARCH. *The rate and direction of inventive activity.* Princeton: Princeton U. Press, 1962.

NATIONAL SCIENCE FOUNDATION. *The process of technological innovation: Reviewing the literature.* Washington, DC: NSF, 1983.

NATIONAL SCIENCE FOUNDATION. *Science indicators.* Washington, DC: U.S. GPO, 1986.

NELSON, RICHARD R. "The Link Between Science and Invention: The Case of the Transistor," in NBER 1962, pp. 549–83.

_____. "A 'Diffusion' Model of International Productivity Differences in Manufacturing Industry," *Amer. Econ. Rev.*, Dec. 1968, 58(5), pp. 1219–48.

_____. "Production Sets, Technological Knowledge and R&D: Fragile and Overworked Constructs for Analysis of Productivity Growth?" *Amer. Econ. Rev.*, May 1980, 70(2), pp. 62–67.

_____. "Research on Productivity Growth and Productivity Difference: Dead Ends and New Departures," *J. Econ. Lit.*, Sept. 1981a, 19(3), pp. 1029–64.

_____. "Assessing Private Enterprise," *Bell J. Econ.*, Spring 1981b, 12(1) pp. 93–111.

_____ "The Role of Knowledge in R & D Efficiency," *Quart. J. Econ.*, Aug. 1982, 97(3), pp. 453–70.

_____. "Policies in Support of High Technology Industries." Working Paper No. 1011, Institution for Social and Policy Studies, Yale U., 1984.

_____. *Industry growth accounts and cost functions when techniques are proprietary.* New Haven: Yale U. Press, 1985.

_____. "Institutions Generating and Diffusing New Technology." see Venice 1986.

_____. "Capitalism as an Engine of Growth," in DOSI ET AL. 1988.

NELSON, RICHARD R. AND WINTER, SIDNEY G. "In Search of a Useful Theory of Innovations," *Res. Policy*, Jan. 1977, 6(1), p. 36.

_____. *An evolutionary theory of economic change.* Cambridge, MA: Belknap Press of Harvard U. Press, 1982.

NOBLE, DAVID. *America by design.* NY: Knopf, 1977.

NORTHCOTT, JIM; KUETSCH, WERNER AND DE LESTAPIS, BERENGERE. "Microelectronics Industry: An International Comparison." Policy Study Institute, London, 1985.

NORTHCOTT, JIM AND ROGERS, PETRA. "Microelectronics in British Industry: Patterns of Change." Policy Study Institute, London, 1984.

ODAGIRI, HIROYUKI AND YAMAWAKI, HIDEKI. "A Study of Company Profit-Rate Time Series: Japan and the United States," *Int. J. Ind. Organ.*, Mar. 1986, 4(1), pp. 1–23.

OECD. *Gaps in technology.* Paris: OECD, 1968.

OECD. *The measurement of scientific and technical activities: Proposed standard practice for surveys of research and experimental developments.* Paris: OECD, 1981.

_____. "Committee for Scientific and Technological Policy, Science, Technology and Competitiveness: Analytical Report of the ad hoc Group." Paris: OECD/STP (84) 26, 1984.

_____. *Science and technology indicators.* Paris: OECD, 1986.

ORSENIGO, LUIGI. "Institutions and Markets in the Dynamics of Industrial Innovation. The Theory and the Case of Biotechnology." D Phil thesis; SPRU, U. of Sussex, Brighton, 1988.

PAKES, ARIEL AND SCHANKERMAN, MARK. "An Exploration into the Determinants of Research Intensity," in GRILICHES 1984, pp. 209–32.

PARKER, WILLIAM N., ed. *Economic history and the modern economist.* Oxford: Blackwell, 1986.

PATEL, PARI AND PAVITT, KEITH. "Is Western Europe Losing the Technological Race?" *Res. Policy*, 1987, 16(2), pp. 59–85.

PAVITT, KEITH. "Technical Innovation and Industrial Development: The New Causality," *Futures*, Dec. 1979, 11(6), pp. 458–70.

_____. "Patterns of Technical Change: Towards a Taxonomy and a Theory," *Res. Policy*, 1984, 13(6), pp. 343–73.

_____. "Technology, Innovation and Strategic Management," in *Strategic managment research: A European perspective.* Eds.: J. McGEE AND H. THOMAS. NY: Wiley, 1986a.

_____. "Chips and 'Trajectories': How Will the Semiconductor Influence the Sources and Directions of Technical Change?" in *Technology and the human prospect.* Ed.: R. MACLEOD. London: Francis Pinter, 1986.

_____. "Technological Accumulation, Diversification and Organization in UK companies, 1945–83." DRC Discussion Paper, SPRU, U. of Sussex, Brighton, 1988.

PAVITT, KEITH; ROBSON, MICHAEL AND TOWNSEND, JOE. "The Size Distribution of Innovative Firms in the UK: 1945–1983," *J. Ind. Econ.*, Mar. 1987, 35(3), pp. 297–319.

PEREZ, CARLOTA. "Microelectronics, Long Waves and the World Structural Change. New Perspectives for Developing Countries," *World Devel.*, Mar. 13, 1985, 13(3), pp. 441–63.

_____. "The New Technologies: An Integrated View." SPRU, U. of Sussex, Brighton English Trans.; originally in *La tercera revolucion industrial.* Ed.: C. OMINAMI. Buenos Aires, Argentina: 1987.

PHILLIPS, ALMARIN. *Technology and market structure.* Lexington, MA: Heath, 1971.

PIORE, MICHAEL AND SABEL, CHARLES F. *The second industrial divide.* NY: Basic Books, 1984.

POLANYI, MICHAEL. *The tacit dimension.* Garden City, NY: Doubleday Anchor, 1967.

PRATTEN, CLIFFORD F. *Economies of scale in manufacturing industry.* Cambridge: Cambridge U. Press, 1971.

PRICE, DEREK DE SOLLA. "The Science/Technology Relationship, the Craft of Experimental Science and Policy for the Improvement of High Technology Innovation," *Res. Policy,* Feb. 1984, *13*(1), pp. 3–20.

RAY, GEORGE. *The diffusion of mature technologies.* Cambridge: Cambridge U. Press, 1984.

REICH, LEONARD. *The making of American industrial research: Science and business at G.E. and Bell, 1876–1926.* NY: Cambridge U. Press, 1985.

REINGANUM, JENNIFER F. "On the Diffusion of New Technology: A Game Theoretic Approach," *Rev. Econ. Stud.,* July 1981a, *48,* pp. 395–405.

_____. "Market Structure and the Diffusion of New Technology," *Bell J. Econ.,* Autumn 1981b, *12*(2), pp. 618–24.

ROMEO, ANTHONY A. "Interindustry and Interfirm Differences in the Rate of Diffusion of an Innovation," *Rev. Econ. Statist.,* Aug. 1975, *57*(3) pp. 311–19.

RONEN, JOSHUA. "Some Insights into the Entrepreneurial Process," in *Entrepreneurship.* Ed.: JOSHUA RONEN. Lexington, MA: Heath, 1983, pp. 137–73.

ROSENBERG, NATHAN. *Perspectives on technology.* Cambridge: Cambridge U. Press, 1976.

_____. *Inside the black box.* Cambridge: Cambridge U. Press, 1982.

_____. "The Commercial Exploitation of Science by American Industry," in *The uneasy alliance: Managing the productivity-technology dilemma.* Ed.: KIM B. CLARK, ROBERT H. HAYES AND CHRISTOPHER LORENZ. Cambridge, MA: Harvard Business School Press, 1985.

ROTHBARTH, ERWIN. "Causes of the Superior Efficiency of USA Industry as Compared with British Industry," *Econ. J.,* Sept. 1946, *56,* pp. 383–90.

ROTHWELL, ROY ET AL. "SAPPHO Updated. Project SAPPHO, Phase 2," *Res. Policy,* Nov. 1946, *3*(5), pp. 258–91.

ROTHWELL, ROY AND GARDINER, PAUL. "The Role of Design in Product and Process Change," *Design Studies,* July 1984, *4*(3), pp. 161–70.

SAHAL, DEVENDRA. *Recent advances in the theory of technological change.* Berlin: International Institute of Management, 1979.

_____. *Patterns of technological innovation.* NY: Addison-Wesley, 1981.

_____. *The transfer and utilization of technical knowledge,* Lexington, MA: Heath, 1982.

_____. "Technology Guide-Posts and Innovation Avenues," *Res. Policy,* 1985, *14*(2), pp. 61–82.

SALTER, WILFRED E. G. *Productivity and technical change.* 2nd ed. Cambridge: Cambridge U. Press, 1969.

SAVIOTTI, PAOLO P. AND METCALFE, J. STANLEY. "A Theoretical Approach to the Construction of Technological Output Indicators," *Res. Policy,* June 1984, *13*(3) pp. 141–51.

SHEN, TSUNG-YUEN. "Competition, Technology and Market Shares," *Rev. Econ. Statist.,* Feb. 1968, *50*(1), pp. 96–102.

SCHERER, FREDERICK M. *Industrial market structure and economic performance.* 2nd ed. Chicago: Rand McNally, 1980.

_____. "Inter-Industry Technology Flows in the US," *Res. Policy,* 1982, *11*(4), pp. 227–45.

_____. *Innovation and growth. Schumpeterian perspectives.* Cambridge: MIT Press, 1986.

_____. "Inter-industry Technology Flows in the US," *Res. Policy.* 1982,

SCHMOOKLER, JACOB. *Invention and economic growth.* Cambridge: Harvard U. Press, 1966.

SCHUMPETER, JOSEPH A. *The theory of economic development.* Cambridge: Harvard U. Press, 1934 (English translation from 1919 German ed.).

_____. *Capitalism, socialism and democracy.* NY: McGraw-Hill, 1942.

SCIBERRAS, ED. *Multinational electronic companies and national economic policies.* Greenwich, CT: JAI Press, 1977.

(SPRU) SCIENCE POLICY RESEARCH UNIT. *Success and failure in industrial innovation.* London: Centre for the Study of Industrial Innovation, 1972.

SIMON, HERBERT. "The Structure of Ill-Structured Problems," *Artificial Intelligence,* 1973, *4*(3), pp. 181–201.

_____. "Rational Decision Making in Business Organizations," *Amer. Econ. Rev.,* Sept. 1979, *69*(4), pp. 493–513.

SILBERSTON, AUBREY. "Economies of Scale in Theory and Practice," *Econ. J.,* Mar. 1972, *86,* pp. 369–91.

SILVERBERG, GERALD. "Technical Progress, Capital Accumulation and Effective Demand: A Self-Organisation Model," in *Economic evolution and structural change.* Ed.: D. BATTEN. Berlin, Heidelberg, New York: Springer, 1987.

SOETE, LUC. "Firm Size and Innovative Activity: The Evidence Reconsidered," *European Econ. Rev.,* 1979, *12*(4), pp. 319–40.

_____. "A General Test of Technological Gap Trade Theory," *Weltwirtsch. Arch.,* 1981, *117*(4) pp. 638–60.

_____. "Firm Size and Innovative Activity: The Evidence Reconsidered," *Europ. Econ. Rev.,* 1982.

SOETE, LUC AND DOSI, GIOVANNI. *Technology and employment in the electronics industry.* London: Francis Pinter, 1983.

SOETE, LUC AND TURNER, ROY. "Technology Diffusion and the Rate of Technical Change," *Econ. J.,* Sept. 1984, *94*(375) pp. 612–23.

STIGLER, GEORGE J. "Industrial Organisation and Economic Progress," in *The state of social sciences.* Ed.: LEONARD D. WHITE. Chicago: Chicago U. Press, 1956.

STIGLITZ, JOSEPH E. "Information and Economic Analysis: A Perspective," *Econ. J.* Conference Papers, 1984, *95,* pp. 21–41.

STONEMAN, PAUL. *Technological diffusion and the*

computer revolution. Oxford: Clarendon Press, 1976.

_____. *The economic analysis of technological change.* Oxford: Oxford U. Press, 1983.

_____. "Technological Diffusion: The Viewpoint of Economic Theory." see Venice, Mar. 1986.

SYLOS LABINI, PAOLO. *Oligopoly and technical progress.* 2nd ed. Cambridge: Harvard U. Press, 1967.

_____. *Le forze dello sviluppo e del declino.* Bari: Laterza (*The forces of development and decline.* Cambridge: Cambridge U. Press, 1984).

TAYLOR, CHRISTOPHER AND SILBERSTON, AUBREY. *The economic impact of the patent system.* Cambridge: Cambridge U. Press, 1973.

TEECE, DAVID J. "Technology Transfer by Multinational Firms: The Resource Cost of Transferring Technological Know-how," *Econ. J.,* June 1977, 87(346), pp. 242–61.

_____. "Toward an Economic Theory of the Multiproduct Firms," *J. Econ. Behaviour Organ.* 1982a, 3(1), pp. 39–63.

_____. "Profiting from Technological Innovation," *Res. Policy.* 1986, 15(6), pp. 285–306.

TEECE, DAVID J. "The Nature and the Structure of Firms," in DOSI ET AL. 1988.

TEMIN, PETER. "Labor Scarcity and the Problem of American Industrial Efficiency in the 1850's," *J. Econ. Hist.,* Sept. 1966, 26, pp. 277–98.

TERLECKYJ, NESTER E. "R & D and the US Industrial Productivity," in SAHAL 1982.

TEUBAL, MORRIS. "The R & D Performance Through Time of High Technology Firms," *Res. Policy,* 1982.

THOMAS, MORGAN D. "Regional Economic Development and the Role of Innovation and Technological Change," in THWAITES AND OAKEY 1985, pp. 13–35.

THWAITES, ALFRED T. AND OAKEY. RAY P., eds. *The regional economic impact of technological change.* London: Francis Pinter, 1985.

TILTON, JOHN. *International diffusion of technology: The case of semiconductors.* Washington, DC: Brookings Inst., 1971.

TOLEDANO, JOEL. "A Propos des Filières Industrielles," *Revue d'Economie Industrielle,* 1978.

TRUEL, JEAN-LOUIS. "L'Industrie Mondiale de Semi-

Conducteurs." PhD thesis. U. of Paris-Dauphine, 1980.

VON TUNZELMANN, G. N. *Steam power and British industrialisation to 1860.* Oxford: Clarendon Press, 1978.

_____. "Britain 1900–1945: A Survey," in *Economic history of Britain since 1870.* Vol. II. Eds.: RODERICK FLOUD AND DONALD MCCLOSKEY. Cambridge: Cambridge U. Press, 1982.

VENICE, Conference on Innovation Diffusion, 17–21 Mar., 1986. in *Frontiers in innovation diffusion.* Eds.: FABIO ARCANGELI, PAUL DAVID AND GIOVANNI DOSI. Oxford: Oxford U. Press, forthcoming.

WILLIAMSON, OLIVER. *Markets and hierarchies.* NY: Free Press, 1975.

_____. *The economic institutions of capitalism.* NY: Free Press, 1985.

WILSON, ROBERT W.; ASHTON, PETER K. AND EGAN, P. THOMAS *Innovation, competition, and government policy in the semiconductor industry.* Lexington, MA: Heath, 1980.

WINTER, SIDNEY G. "Satisficing, Selection and the Innovating Remnant," *Quart. J. Econ.,* May 1971, 85(2), pp. 237–61.

_____. "An Essay on the Theory of Production," in *Economics and the world around it.* Ed.: S. H. HYMANS. Ann Arbor: U. of Mich. Press, 1982.

_____. "Schumpeterian Competition in Alternative Technological Regimes," *J. Econ. Behav. Organ.,* Sept./Dec. 1984, 5(3–4), pp. 287–320.

_____. "Competition and Selection" in *The New Palgrave: A dictionary of economics.* London: Macmillan, 1987a.

_____. "Natural Selection and Evolution," in *The New Palgrave: A dictionary of economics.* London: Macmillan, 1987b.

WYATT, SALLY AND BERTIN, GILLE. *The role of patents in multinational corporations strategies for growth.* Paris: AREPIT, 1985.

YELLE, LOUIS E. "The Learning Curve: Historical Review and Comprehensive Survey," *Decision Science,* 1979.

ZUSCOVITCH, EHUD. *Une approche meso-economique du progress technique: Diffusion de l'innovation et apprentissage industriel.* Doctoral thesis, Strasbourg, U. Louis Pasteur, 1984.

[3]

The Research on Innovation Diffusion: An Assessment

Giovanni Dosi

7.1 The Role of Innovation Diffusion in Economic and Social Change

In recent years, innovation diffusion has attracted increasing attention within the economic discipline as well as from other social sciences, such as sociology, organization theory, economic geography, and political science.

Some of the reasons for the growing attention are likely to be found within the internal patterns of enquiry of the various disciplines themselves. Others are more obviously related to a general awareness of the importance of innovations and innovation diffusion – in products, processes of production, and forms of economic organization – for economic growth and, more generally, social change.

Certainly, the so-called *microelectronics revolution* has provided a powerful focus on the widespread economic and social consequences of major technological innovations. In this respect, fundamental, and still largely unanswered, questions concern, for example, its impact on employment and growth, the consequences for business organization, the induced changes in the patterns of consumption, the implications for educational requirements, the possible demand for new public policies, and many others. Moreover, in addition to microelectronics, other new technologies, such as bioengineering and new materials raise somewhat different but equally broad interpretative and normative issues.

The importance of changing patterns of innovation and diffusion has also emerged as a controversial issue in the interpretation of the trends in productivity growth within several OECD countries. Can the observed statistical slowdown be attributed to a parallel slowdown in the rates of innovation? Or, rather, to a slowdown in the rates of innovation *diffusion* and, thus, to an increasing gap between average and best-practice techniques? How can all this be reconciled with the intuitive evidence on the far-reaching productivity improvements which apparently the *microelectronics revolution* produces?

There is also an international aspect of innovation and diffusion. The most striking phenomenon has probably been the impressive Japanese capability of quickly adopting, improving, and – more recently – introducing new technologies. These capabilities, together with somewhat different organizational arrangements, have also meant a rapid growth of Japanese international competitiveness. More generally, many analysts suggest that the changing competitive strengths of the USA, the EEC countries, Japan and the newly industrializing countries, must also be attributed to a differential promptness of these countries in introducing and/or adopting technological and organizational innovations.

Another major issue, somewhat related to the previous one, concerns the relationship between innovativeness and the capability of appropriating economic benefits from the innovations themselves. This is the subject of great debat in the USA. To what extent is it necessary to be an innovator in order to enjoy relatively high per capita incomes? Under what circumstances is the innovator able to enjoy a quasi-rent on its technological achievements?

From a longer historical perspective, a view with respectable consensus holds that all the processes of economic growth and social change – at least since the English Industrial Revolution – cannot be explained without reference to the introduction and diffusion of major technological innovations – from the steam engine to electricity, the internal combustion engine, railroads, fertilizers, plastics, jet engines, and uncountable minor innovations.

Finally, very broad interpretative questions which are well beyond the domain of the economic discipline concern, for example, the relationship between new technologies and labor processes; the cultural and social structures which favor or hinder the introduction and diffusion of new technologies; the scientific and educational context within which innovation and innovation diffusion take place.

The list of questions could be much longer. Indeed, all the foregoing issues highlight the crucial importance of the phenomena of innovation and innovation diffusion in the interpretation of how economic and social structures keep together and change, sometimes in a rather orderly manner, and at other times with more abrupt discontinuities.

In a fundamental sense, the empirical evidence on the permanent process of technological and organizational change in contemporary societies confronts most social sciences such as, for example, economics, sociology, political science, and psychology, and demands theoretical explanations of its causes, patterns, and consequences.

The aim of this chapter is simply to sketch an overview of the state of the art, primarily in *the economics of innovation diffusion* highlighting some common themes and (often controversial) issues which underlie most other chapters of this book (see also, Arcangeli *et al.*, 1990, on whose introduction this chapter partly draws).

7.2   Invention, Innovation, and Diffusion

One of the contributions of J. Schumpeter's work that is often cited with reference to technological change concerns his distinction between invention, innovation, and diffusion. According to his definition, invention concerns the first development of a new artifact or process. Innovation entails its economic application. Diffusion describes its introduction by buyers or competitors. It is a rough and "heroic" conceptual distinction, which can hardly be found in practice, since the empirical processes are usually never quite like this. The *invention* is often introduced from the start as an *innovation* by economically-minded research establishments. *Diffusion* entails further innovation on the part of both developers and users. All three activities are often associated with changes in the characteristics of, and incentives for, potential innovators/adopters. However, Schumpeter's distinction between invention, innovation, and diffusion is still a useful theoretical point of departure. For example, *invention* is suggestive of some sort of exploited *potential* for technological progress, while *innovation* and *diffusion* hint at the economic, social and organizational incentives and impediments to the incorporation of technological advances into economic products and processes.

What progress has recently been made in the conceptualization of such phenomena? It is tempting to compare the contributions that follow with those presented almost thirty years ago at the Conferences of the National Bureau on Economic Research on *The Rate and Directions of Inventive Activities* (NBER, 1962). Significant elements of continuity as well as further developments appear.

7.2.1   Inventive opportunities

What is an *inventive opportunity*? Do all "new opportunities" emerge from apparently exogenous scientific progress? What shapes the dynamics of their actual exploitation? The analysis of *technology* as a quite specific sort of *information* characterized by indivisibilities and, at least some, *public-good* features in the sense of being able to be potentially transmitted and reused repeatedly without loss, certainly drew also from the seminal contributions of Arrow (*cf.*, for example, Arrow, 1962a and 1962b) and a few of the roots of such an approach are already witnessed by the cited NBER reading. That approach easily fostered widening streams of later analyses on "the economics of R&D" as a subset of the economics of imperfect and asymmetric information (for reviews of recent developments, see Stiglitz, 1985; Stoneman, 1990; Tirole, 1988). In an extreme synthesis, all the variegated contributions that can be joined under the "imperfect information" perspective have explored the properties of innovative worlds whereby *notional opportunities* are either given or are subject to the exogenous dynamics of scientific discoveries, but their *actual* exploitation depends on the particular incentive structures (related, e.g., to the forms of market competition, etc.) and possibly also on the *past* available information on which the agents can draw (*cf.* David, 1975; Atkinson and Stiglitz, 1969; Stiglitz, 1987).

Conversely, a somewhat different approach has drawn a sharper distinction between information and prior knowledge, the latter being the rather elusive set of cognitive structures, search rules, "tacit" capabilities guiding inventive activities (*cf.* Nelson and Winter, 1982; Pavitt, 1988; Dosi, 1988), all implicitly or explicitly linking with Simon's views on behaviors and decisions (see, e.g., Simon, 1965 and 1979). From such a perspective, *information* is still imperfect – indeed, *largely* imperfect – but, in addition, the rates and directions of inventive activities are shaped and constrained also by specific skills and heuristics of the searching agents, the activities in which "they are good", their past experiences, etc. The recent attempts to conceptualize the procedures and directions of innovative activities in terms of *technological paradigms* and *trajectories* clearly fits within this perspective (Dosi, 1988).

Relatedly, significant progress has been made in the empirical understanding of the varying balances between *private* and *public* aspects of technological knowledge, between new opportunities that are generated in non-profit institutions (such as universities, public research establishments, etc.) and those which are created within the business sector (in private R&D laboratories, but also through the more informal activities such as experimentation and learning) (on all this, see Nelson, 1988 and 1990).

7.2.2   Invention and innovation incentives

Irrespectively of the specific theoretical representations of inventive opportunities and their exploitation, the economic discipline has increasingly attempted to understand and conceptualize the effects of different economic incentives upon the actual rates of invention and innovation. Plainly, the issue goes back to the highly plausible fact that economically-motivated agents will undertake the costs and risks of innovating only in so far as there is, or they believe in, some differential economic returns from innovation. In other words, for whatever notional opportunities, the actual rates of innovation are going to be affected by the *appropriability conditions*. In fact, the recent economic literature has increasingly tried to explore the nature and effects of varying appropriability conditions (see Levin *et al.*, 1985 and 1987); a mainly empirical survey is in Dosi (1988); the review in Kamien and Schwartz (1982) concerns the relationship between market structures and incentives to innovate discussed within a relatively orthodox perspective; a discussion of some of the current theoretical literature is in Dasgupta (1988).

7.2.3   History and path-dependency

Both the theoretical and empirical literature reflect the growing recognition that *history counts*: past technological achievements influence future achievements via the specificity of knowledge that they entail, the development of specific infrastructures, the emergence of various sorts of increasing returns and non-convexities in the notional set of technological options. On theoretical grounds, this has led to the development of *path-dependent* models (*cf.* Arthur, 1988; David, 1985 and 1990); for some discussion of the general importance of this class of models for economic theory see Dosi and Orsenigo, 1988).

Certainly, over the last three decades, empirical analyses and theoretical modeling has made significant advances in the unfolding of the *black box* by which the economic discipline had traditionally represented technology and technological change (Rosenberg, 1982), by unfolding the determinants and nature of invention and innovation, and the driving forces, patterns and consequences of innovation diffusion (reviews and some evidence can be found in Dosi, 1988; Arcangeli *et al.*, 1990).

Below, I shall first sketch some empirical *stylized facts* and, second, try to present an overview of the diverse streams of analysis, organized around their methodological analogies, their basic assumptions on the diffusion process, and the characteristics of the adopters.

7.3   Some "Stylized Facts" on Innovation Diffusion

Even after a new product or production process or form of organization is developed, its economic and/or social significance is still going to depend on its acceptance amongst potential customers and the degrees to which it is imitated by competitors. The study of innovation diffusion concerns these phenomena. Not surprisingly these phenomena have been of interest to several social disciplines. For example, rural sociology has studied the circumstances which affect the pace of adoption of agricultural innovations. Other areas of sociology have investigated the diffusion of social innovations, such as particular forms of health care, pension funds, etc., and the social characteristics that influence the acceptance of new products. The latter have obviously also been the concern of marketing studies. Economic geography has studied innovation diffusion in its spatial dimension (somewhat overlapping with regional economics). A thorough review of these areas of research is in Rogers (1983). Innovation diffusion studies also have a relatively long tradition in economics, pioneered by the investigation on the diffusion of hybrid corn by Griliches (1957) and of a few industrial processes by Mansfield (1961). (For surveys, see Stoneman, 1983 and 1990; Metcalfe, 1988).

One can find in the literature different definitions of diffusion. However, whatever the definition, one of the basic *stylized facts* of the diffusion process is that it is never instantaneous. Innovation diffusion always takes time and occurs at rates that plausibly depend on the features of those technologies which are to be adopted; possibly on the features of those technologies which are to be substituted; on the incentives that the economic environment provides for adoption; on the characteristics of the would-be adopters; on the information available to them; on their technological competence; possibly, on their size. For example, the evidence from Mansfield (1968), Romeo (1975), Nasbeth and Ray (1974), von Tunzlemann (1978), and Ray (1984) show indeed quite a high inter-firm, inter-industry and inter-technology variance in the speed of diffusion (irrespective of the measures chosen).

7.3.1 Diffusion patterns

In general, as Rosenberg puts it,

> in the history of diffusion of many innovations, one cannot help being struck by two characteristics of the diffusion process: its apparent overall slowness on the one hand, and the wide variations in the rates of acceptance of different inventions, on the other [Rosenberg, 1976, p. 191].

Typically, one observes roughly S-shaped diffusion curves, whose precise form varies considerably across innovations (*cf.* Davies, 1979; and several contributions to this book). That the empirical curves are S-shaped should not be surprising: many time-dependent processes with some kind of asymptotic value present such a form. However, an important interpretative question concerns the determinants of particular diffusion patterns.

In one way or another diffusion analyses attempt to explain such empirical variety in the observed rates and patterns of adoption of new products, processes, and forms of organization:

- Why is adoption not instantaneous? Why is adoption distributed over time?
- What keeps the sequence of adoptions going forward through time, rather than stopping after the first or n-th firm or household has adopted?

At a more detailed level of empirical investigation, several studies, as mentioned, highlight the differences in the patterns of innovation diffusion and, also, in the origins of innovations themselves. For example, some innovations are embodied in specific artifacts produced somewhere else in the economic system (for example by machine or intermediate component manufacturers). Other innovations take the form of disembodied knowledge which diffuses via people's mobility and/or via competitive R&D.

In general, the *speed of diffusion* is inherently hard to judge because there is no precise way to define the ultimate scope of application or use of a new method of production or a new method of production or a new product (Rosenberg, 1976; Gold, 1981). In fact, whatever empirical definition of *potential adopters* one takes, their number tends to increase over a certain time after the introduction of the original innovation. At an early stage, new methods of production and new pieces of equipment "are of necessity, badly adapted to many of the ultimate uses to which they will eventually be put" (Rosenberg, 1976, p. 195). Diffusion is generally interlinked with more or less incremental improvements of the innovation itself which (a) enhance the technical/economic superiority of the new product or process *vis-à-vis* older ones, and (b) enlarge its scope of application (a detailed illustration of these processes for agricultural machinery is in David, 1975).

7.3.2 Potential adopters

The universe of potential adopters cannot be realistically assumed to be composed of identical units. One of the clearest cases is that discussed in David (1975) where the set of potential adopters of agricultural equipment were farms of different sizes and different configurations of the land. In turn, this affected the scope and the profitability of the mechanization of agricultural production. So, for example, the larger and on average flatter and regularly shaped American farms help to explain a faster rate of diffusion of agricultural mechanization in the USA as compared to, for example, the UK (of course in these international comparisons, differences in wage rates also determine differential incentives to the diffusion of mechanized equipment).

Another straightforward case is whenever the incentive of adopting an innovation is somewhat *scale-based*, or at least there is a minimum scale at which adoption is profitable (this general conjecture is argued in Sylos-Labini, 1967). Hence, the differences in size of potential adopters affect the incentive to adopt. A wealth of empirical evidence suggests, in fact, that the size of the firm is positively correlated to the speed of adoption (Mansfield, 1968; Metcalfe, 1970; Davies, 1979; see also Chapter 14 by Kelley and Brooks). This is not necessarily the case in inter-industrial, cross-innovation comparisons: that is, *ceteris paribus*, an innovation does not diffuse quicker simply because it is introduced into an industry where the average size of the firm is larger (Romeo, 1975; Davies, 1979). That the scale of firms matters, is also shown by the finding that the absolute cost of innovation affects, *ceteris paribus*, its rate of diffusion (Mansfield, 1968; Davies, 1979). Of course, from a theoretical point of view, one may attribute the phenomenon to various sorts of *imperfections* on the financial markets, etc. However, the expense of introducing and using an innovation does not include only the price tag on the new equipment, but also the costs of reorganization needed to take advantage of the new equipment or method. In turn, there is a fixed element in these costs, which can be spread, according to the size of the firm, over different volumes of production. More generally, a whole approach to innovation and diffusion studies would argue that it is often the case that the adopting firms differ in their technological capabilities, and that some of the potential adopters may not adopt because they do not have the technological and organizational capabilities to do so. To put it simply, they do not adopt since they lack the appropriate skills, internal knowledge, or managerial capabilities. Diffusion processes generally involve learning, modifications in the existing organization of production, and, sometimes, even modifications in the products, i.e., essentially, diffusion involves innovation for the user (Freeman, 1982; Rosenberg, 1976 and 1982; Gold, 1981; Lundvall, 1988). In brief, this second set of factors, which influence the patterns of diffusion, relates to the nature and distribution of *technological asymmetries* between firms. Conversely, each process of diffusion is matched by the development of skills among users, the solution of specific technical bottlenecks which hinder adoption, and the development of complementarities with other ancillary technologies (for detailed illustrations of these points, see Rosenberg, 1976, Chapter 11).

Over time, post-innovation changes in the price of the innovative goods (e.g., new machines) affect the incentive to adopt them, in general, and differentially for different sets of users (see again, Rosenberg, 1976; David, 1975).

7.3.3   Profitability and expectations

It is not surprising that there is robust evidence indicating that the rates of diffusion of innovation are influenced by the differential profitability of the new process of equipment as compared to the existing one (Mansfield, 1968; Mansfield *et al.*, 1977; Davies, 1979). It can plausibly be argued that this is indirect evidence of the *disequilibrium nature* (or at least a high degree of uncertainty) of many diffusion processes, since one would expect that according to most definitions of equilibrium, any firm for which the innovation is profitable – no matter *to what extent* profitable – would adopt it.

Certainly, part of the explanation of a discrete time lag in the diffusion of, e.g., a superior (i.e., unequivocally more profitable) machine is a "vintage effect" (Salter, 1969): given the general irreversibility of investment decisions, adoption decisions are to some extent scrapping decisions, which in turn depend on the "technological vintage" of the equipment currently in use.

Moreover, *technological expectations* matter, in the sense that the expected stream of future revenues from, e.g., a new type of machine of today's type, depends also on the expectations about the technical characteristics, productivity, and costs of future machines. In a way, the rate of adoption of innovation is implicitly influenced by expectations about future technological developments and also about the second order (how will that rate of change vary in the future). On empirical grounds, the evidence suggests very complex and often hardly formalizable processes of formation of these expectations: the decision rules of adoption may be highly *imperfect* in a neoclassical sense – heavily based on firm-specific and sector-specific institutional traits and *animal spirits* (for evidence, see Carter and Williams, 1957; Stoneman, 1976; Kleine, 1983).

7.3.4   Appropriability

The typical process of diffusion discussed so far, fits particularly well the description of the factors which drive or hinder the purchase and use of, say, a new type of machinery by a (changing) population of potential adopters. That is, it concerns primarily the introduction of a *process innovation* which is often a *product innovation* manufactured somewhere else in the economic system: for example, it can be the decision of a textile firm whether to introduce an automatic loom which in turn is a new product of a machine-building firm. However, the symmetric complement to this process is the diffusion of product innovations amongst potential suppliers (e.g., machine tool builders, etc.). After all, *product*-related R&D is estimated to account for 75 to 90% of total R&D expenditures in manufacturing (see Le Bas, 1981, for a discussion of the various sources of evidence). What affects the patterns of diffusion in supply (e.g., the number of machine tool builders which produce numerically controlled machines of a certain type or the number of drug firms which manufacture a new antibiotic)? Empirical research in this field is relatively young. However, some important findings emerge from the works of Gort and Klepper (1982) and Gort and Konakayama (1982) as well as from industrial case studies.

First, diffusion in supply – which implies more or less creative imitation of the original innovative product by other producers – relates directly to the *appropriability conditions* of innovations. Of course, a notional innovation with total appropriability would never be imitated by any other producers. Conversely, very low degrees of appropriability would allow, other things being equal, easy imitation and a quick diffusion in supply.

Second, note the double role that appropriability plays in diffusion in production. On the one hand, it acts as an incentive to imitation and entry since it is, *ceteris paribus*, correlated with a differential profitability in the production of the innovation good. On the other hand, it performs as an *entry barrier*, since appropriability is almost by definition based on some kind of appropriable asset, cumulated experience, differential technological capabilities or legal devices such as patents (see on these issues, Chesnais, 1990; Teece, 1986; Levin *et al.*, 1987; Philips, 1971; Gort and Klepper, 1982; Dosi, 1984). The net effect upon the rates of diffusion in production (that is, the rates of entry) are likely to depend on (a) the perceived opportunities of technical progress (a high opportunity with high appropriability conditions is likely to be a powerful incentive to enter and make a *better* product and/or innovate further along the same technological trajectory); (b) the nature of the knowledge-base on which a particular technology draws and, relatedly, the degree of specificity to the incumbent producers of their innovative capability (see Gort and Klepper, 1982, for empirical evidence).

7.4 Innovation Diffusion: Drawing Together Diverse Streams of Analysis

Let us first introduce a classification of diffusion models by means of some underlying dichotomies in the analytical hypotheses and *stylized facts* which they assume.

(1) *Heterogeneity versus uniformity of potential adopters of innovations*. Are all agents the same? Do they have similar *incentives* to innovation adoption? Or, conversely, do they differ in some structural characteristics, or in their *capabilities* of efficiently acquiring new products and processes of production, or in their technological *expectations*?

(2) *Perfect versus imperfect information*. Can the adopting agents be assumed to have adequate information – at least for interpretative purposes – about the nature and future developments of any one technology? Or,

rather, should we suppose that an essential determinant of innovation diffusion concerns information diffusion about the existence and attribute of particular innovations?

(3) *Non-increasing versus increasing returns in new technological developments.* Under what circumstances can we expect the *use* and/or the *production* of innovations to exhibit constant or decreasing returns? Conversely, are there factors which may yield size-related economies of scale, various sorts of learning processes and, generally, dynamic increasing returns?

(4) *The importance of history for the patterns of diffusion.* Clearly, the issue relates also to points (2) and (3). The higher the uncertainty about the technical and economic characteristics of innovation, the higher the importance of the *learning history* of individual agents is likely to be with respect to their adoption decisions. But does this also affect the general patterns of diffusion, or can one assume that the final "attractor" or stationary state of a diffusion process will still be independent of individual vicissitudes? Most is going to depend on the existence of dynamic increasing returns [point (3)] and on the feedback processes between the number of adopters of the technology, on the one hand, and the changing incentives to further adopt it, on the other. Whenever these circumstances occur we are clearly in the domain of path-dependent, non-ergodic processes, briefly recalled in Section 7.2 of this work. In all these cases, history counts, not only for individual patterns of behavior, but also in terms of the general long-term dynamics of the system.

(5) *The interaction between supply and demand of innovation.* When can one reasonably assume that the innovation to be adopted is supplied once-and-for-all, and conversely, when is it correct to assume a continuous process of improvement in its technical characteristics – which also make adoption easier and enlarges the set of potential users? How important are changes in supply conditions, *in primis* prices, for the changing pace of innovation diffusion?

(6) *Diffusion in demand versus diffusion in supply.* The way diffusion processes are often represented typically concerns a new good (say, a new type of production machinery) whose manufacturer is keen on selling to as many customers as possible. However, another side of the diffusion process concerns, as mentioned, the diffusion of the manufacturing capacity of this new good amongst the producers themselves. The theoretical representation of this kind of *diffusion in production* clearly relates to the *conditions of imitation* of an innovation and thus with the

theoretical analysis of technological appropriability, possibly entry- and mobility-barriers, "tacitness" versus "universality" of technical knowledge. Ultimately, it is an area where diffusion analysis joins with the economics of innovation and the economics of industrial dynamics.

(7) *The forces driving diffusion.* Are these forces mainly *exogenous* to the context in which the diffusion of a particular innovation takes place, such as general changes in relative prices and macro demand growth? Or rather do they mainly relate to factors that are *endogenous* to the supplying and adopting industries, such as for example, learning in the manufacturing of the innovation, learning by using, network externalities?

In addition to these basic dichotomies on the "stylized facts" that the analyses assume, some other fundamental alternatives concern directly the analytical methodology, and in particular:

(8) *Behaviors and choice processes of individuals or individual organizations.* At one extreme, one may represent decision processes about adoption/non-adoption of new technologies as a standard optimization exercise, whereby the agents explicitly form expectations about the returns on the new technologies, confronts the entire payoff matrix reachable through their actions, and choose by maximizing some objective function. Following an economist's convention, call this "rational" or "optimizing" behavior. At the other extreme, a few authors attribute much less "rationality" to individual choice processes, according to a methodological option grounded in the empirical observation and in some theoretical reasons for the impossibility of literally maximizing behaviors in environments that are sufficiently complex and nonstationary. Thus, in this other approach, behaviors are likely to be rather "routinized", influenced by specific "visions" and norms. Call this "institutionalized behavior".

(9) *Equilibrium versus disequilibrium dynamics of diffusion.* In the following, I shall use the convention that diffusion dynamics is an "equilibrium one" whenever micro decisions are postulated to be *reciprocally consistent* and "rational" microbehaviors all turn out to be fulfilled in their objectives. Conversely, I shall call "disequilibrium" diffusion processes all those dynamics wherein (a) the "attractors" of the process change themselves as a result of the very actions of the agents – such as when there are system-level increasing returns to technology adoption and/or (b) the diffusion process is explicitly represented in terms of the trial-

and-error efforts of the agents, which exhibit "disequilibrium behaviors" and deliver "disequilibrium signals" to other agents. (I refer here to equilibrium and disequilibrium diffusion dynamics as "macro level" analysis even when it refers to "macro behaviors" of single industries or groups of forms. The proper meaning of "macroeconomics" will be restated in the final section.)

As can be easily seen, the foregoing dichotomies in assumptions, in the postulated *stylized facts*, and in the theoretical methodologies have a crucial importance well beyond the area of innovation diffusion. Indeed, issues like the diversity amongst agents, the access to information that the latter have, the consequences of increasing returns and non-convexities, the status of maximization and equilibrium assumptions, and the postulated processes which bring consistency among a multiplicity of agents, all raise challenging questions which are at the core of economic analysis in general. In fact, this is probably one of the reasons for the general importance of innovation diffusion: it does, after all, concern the processes by which the economy generates and accommodates "the new", and thus directly touches all those questions on coordination and change that have puzzled economists since the beginning of economics as a discipline.

7.5 Diffusion as Information Spread and Adaptation

Before adding some comments of my own, let me suggest a taxonomical guide through the state of the art in the field by mapping the various approaches found in the literature according to some of the earlier dichotomies. In *Table 7.1* diffusion analyses are grouped according to their methodological differences [points (8) and (9), above]. Four broad groups are given based on a two-dimensional classification based on whether the equilibrium or disequilibrium approach is used and on whether the particular model deals with optimizing or institutionalized behavior.

7.5.1 Equilibrium approaches

"Institutionalized" Behavior

The top-right corner of *Table 7.1* includes all equilibrium models with institutionalized behavior, developed with a strong *descriptive* emphasis, that

Table 7.1.   Methodological classification of diffusion models.

Macro level	Micro behaviors	
	Optimizing behaviors	Institutionalized behaviors
Equilibrium		
Steady-states	Neoclassical models, e.g., David (1969); Stoneman (1983); Reinganum (1981)	*Traditional* models with adjustment lags, e.g., Griliches (1957); Mansfield (1968)
	Davies (1979)[a]	
	Marshallian models in Metcalfe (1988)[a]	
Disequilibrium		
Traverses or *self-organization* processes	*Increasing returns* models of diffusion, cum. innovation, e.g., David and Olsen (1984, 1986); David (1985, 1986); Farrell-Saloner (1985)	Evolutionary models, e.g., Nelson and Winter (1982); self-organizational models, e.g., Silverberg, Dosi, and Orsenigo (1988)
	Arthur (1983, 1988)[a]	

[a]These models do not make explicit assumptions on microbehaviors and are, in principle, consistent with either hypothesis.

investigate the empirical relevance of various economic and social variables as favorable or retarding factors in the adoption of innovation. The starting point is generally the *empirical regularity*, mentioned earlier, on diffusion patterns often presenting an S-shaped profile. Indeed, it is generally found that time-patterns fit rather well rate equations of the generic form

$$\frac{dx_t}{dt} = f(N, x_t) \tag{7.1}$$

where x_t stands for the number of adopters at time t and N is the total number of potential adopters. Hence the analysis primarily concerns the factors determining the rates of change in adoption and the primary focus is about how people and organizations become exposed to novelty and react by rejecting or embracing change. The analysis of the diffusion of new technologies, in this approach, could in a way be considered as part of the study of more general behavioral patterns of humans and organizations.

Both in the economic and sociological literatures, primary attention is given to the propagation of information about novelties, which may come as *stimuli, surprises* or *threats* to individuals and corporations. The stimuli elicit responses, which come with varying lags, depending upon socio-psychological attributes of individuals, their position in the social system, or, somewhat analogously, on corporate cultures and organizational structures.

I classified this approach under "equilibrium" because it still generally treats diffusion as a process of convergence to some long-term, steady-state (say $X^* = N$ in equation 7.1) with non-instantaneous adoption primarily accounted by frictions, lack of information, response lags, and "out-of-equilibrium" behaviors of micro agents. The various studies that come under this heading are thoroughly reviewed in Rogers (1983). They have certainly provided rich insights into the empirical variety of socioeconomic determinants of diffusion patterns. However, if one looks for a *deeper explanation*, then it does not exist. In particular, economists often consider such a *deeper level* to rest in the *microfoundations* of any one aggregate process and most often are only satisfied when, in turn, micro behaviors can be grounded deductively into some "rational" choice procedure. This kind of theoretical diffidence toward simply descriptive models is probably also one of the explanations for the appeal of the class of models that we are going to consider next, those at the top-left of *Table 7.1*.

"Optimizing" Behavior

The top-left corner of *Table 7.1* includes "optimizing" equilibrium models. In many respects equilibrium diffusion models *cum* micro optimization represent the extension of neoclassical economic theory to diffusion phenomena. In this class of models diffusion is seen as the outcome of rational goal-directed choices, made by more or less fully informed firms and consumers, among the set of available technologies – particularly the choice between new technologies and those previously available. Here the focus is upon modeling the choice-process, and assimilating innovation-adoption into the larger corpus of (decision-theoretic or game-theoretic) microeconomic theory. This theory, when it is employed as a *positive* model (and not simply as a normative exercise) asserts a correspondence between the central (average) tendencies in individual behaviors and the (theoretically-derived) equilibrium.

Given the above, why, then do not all the agents adopt at the same time? One of the simplest answers is that the agents are "rational", but less-than-perfectly informed: there are objective costs in information acquisition, adjustment costs, etc. In a way this is the most straightforward "rationalization" (in terms of "rational agent" micro theory) of the evidence put forward by the studies reviewed in the previous section.

Another route is to assume that agents are "rational" *and different* in some structural characteristics. P.A. David long ago started exploring this route whereby thresholds to efficient innovation adoption are determined by the scale of output of adopters, and consequently, the benefits of adoption for each agent do not reach a maximum at the same time (David, 1969).

Consider the basic model:

- The users of the innovation belong to a competitive industry.
- They are heterogeneous with respect to output scale.
- There is perfect information about the characteristics and economic benefits of the innovation.
- The innovation is embodied in some fixed, lumpy piece of equipment (e.g., continuous rolling, annealing machines, tractors, etc.).
- Adopters are "myopic" in that they ignore the future acquisition costs of the technology.
- The scale of the firms is fixed and does not adjust in response to the innovations.

This *scale-constrained* world (as from David, 1969) is depicted in *Figure 7.1*, where $g(z)$ is the frequency distribution of some agents' characteristics (z, in our case, size). If we specify a time-path of the threshold level of the characteristics index $z^*(t)$ above which adoption becomes profitable, we re-map the characteristics distribution into the time domain. We can derive a so-called "Probit model" of diffusion.

Consider for example lognormal size distributions (as in David, 1969 and Davies, 1979) and some alternative time patterns of the threshold (for example, exponential relative decline in fixed-factor/variable factor price ratio, as in David, 1969, or linear time-paths with retardation in the decline of the threshold, as in Davies, 1969). Distributions of heterogeneous agents with a moving threshold for efficient adoption can generate a sigmoid diffusion curve. The time-profile of the threshold can obviously be given exogenously, but can also be derived from the diffusion-dynamics itself: for example, Stoneman and Ireland (1983) and David and Olsen (1984) derive it explicitly by specifying *learning effects* in the supply of the new technology.

Of course, size is by no means the only source of differentiation amongst adopters and equilibrium – "rational" models can accommodate other forms of heterogeneity, such as, for example, location and transport costs, regional wage levels, information costs, etc. For example, David and Olsen (1984)

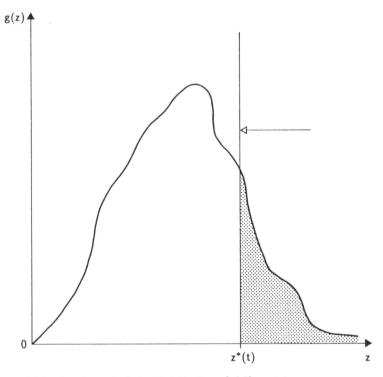

Objective characteristics distributions [g(z)] models:

- Vintage-distribution of fixed capital (Salter).
- Size-distribution of firms (output) (David, Davies).
- "Priors" on benefits (uncertain) (Stoneman, Jensen, Reinganum).
- Risk-aversion distribution.

Figure 7.1. "Equilibrium diffusion" with heterogeneous agents.

move beyond probit-type (or "threshold") models – in which the scale of output is not influenced by the new technology and the firm size distribution remains invariant with respect to the diffusion process – and allow for a competitive firm's choice of output jointly with its technology adoption decision. Hence, the heterogeneity which determines the time-distribution of adoptions must come from factors other than output size.

Equilibrium models with heterogeneous firms have typically assumed a competitive industry (with competitive or monopolistic suppliers of the innovation). Conversely, another stream of equilibrium analysis has explored diffusion in the context of *strategic oligopolistic* interactions *cum homogeneous agents* (e.g., Reinganum, 1981; Fudenberg and Tirole, 1985).

A closely related approach describes equilibrium diffusion with homogeneous, perfectly forward-looking agents *cum* non-appropriable learning (Jovanovic and Lach, 1989).

A taxonomy of equilibrium – "rational" models, categorized according to the heterogeneity versus homogeneity of the agents and endogeneity versus exogeneity of the *driving forces* of diffusion is presented in *Table 7.2*.

Table 7.2. A taxonomy of equilibrium models of technology diffusion.

Nature of dynamic driving process	Objective characteristics of potential adopters	
	Heterogeneous	Homonogeneous
Exogeneous	Competitive industry adoption, driven by: • market demand growth • output distribution changes • input price trends	Interdependent adopters with: pre-commitment (Reinganum, 1981) or strategic interaction (Fudenberg and Tirole, 1985) • exogeneous drivers
Endogeneous	Competitive industry adoption, driven by: • learning in innovation supply • learning in use • network externalities which are unbounded or bounded	Oligopolistic or duopolistic rivalry with *learning* or *system-scale* effects

One of the general questions addressed by equilibrium models with interdependent adopters is: can one conceive a *consistent* pattern of adoption whereby identical agents adopt at different times? Technically, an answer to such a question generally corresponds to the exploration of the existence of Nash equilibria in the domain of adoption decisions, thus extending the application of a methodology increasingly used by mainstream industrial economics with respect to, e.g., price and quantity variables in oligopolistic settings.

Certainly, these various versions of equilibrium-rational analyses have generated an increasing number of contributions, highlighting the implication for the diffusion process of different subsidiary assumptions (e.g., "myopic" versus "rational" expectations, strategic interactions with or without pre-committed choices, competitive versus monopolistic supply of the innovations, etc.). (A review of these developments is in Stoneman, 1990.) It is much harder to assess the heuristic value of this class of models for the *positive* interpretation of empirical phenomena of innovation diffusion. Any evaluation also involves a general judgement on the tool-box of the economic discipline as a whole, the status, and interpretative power of methodological assumptions such as equilibrium, rationality, etc. It is a judgement which certainly divides the economic discipline. However, irrespective of disciplinary preferences and the particular beliefs on "how much of the real world equilibrium-rational models can illuminate", there are phenomena which they can hardly handle, ultimately related to diffusion processes involving various forms of increasing returns, *circular feedbacks* between innovation and diffusion and environments where "rational behavior" is not only empirically unlikely but theoretically impossible to define. The models classified in the bottom half of *Table 7.1* try precisely to deal with some or all of these phenomena. I shall now turn to them.

7.5.2   Disequilibrium approaches

Increasing Returns, Path-dependency, and Evolutionary Processes in Innovation Diffusion

Many students of technology diffusion processes have arrived at the view, argued, for example, by Rosenberg (1972); Freeman (1982); Sahal (1981); Freeman and Perez (1988), that innovation and diffusion are continuously interlinked. Over time, technology adoption, and the creation of new technologies are mutually dependent. Moreover, the innovation-diffusion process must be seen as "macro-disequilibrium dynamics" (in the meaning of *macro* defined earlier), characterized by the exploration of various sorts of increasing returns along particular "trajectories" of technical progress (Nelson and Winter, 1977; Dosi, 1982), and the evolution of various institutions within the economy (including firms) along with the exploitation of the new technologies.

Of course, if *positive feedbacks* between adoption of innovations, their further improvements, and the cost of acquiring them are important enough, this implies, in technical terms, a source of non-convexity in the technological opportunities at the level of the firm, the industry or the whole economy. We leave the world of *convergence* to macro-level *solutions* and of equilibrium paths which can be defined independently of the *actual* technological and economic history of particular clusters of innovations. On the contrary, we are in the path-dependent world of Arthur (1983 and 1988) and David (1985), wherein the long-term positions of the system may well depend on even minor initial *fluctuations*, individual choices, institutions, and policy measures. (On these issues, *cf.*, in particular, the chapters by David; Amendola and Gaffard; Dosi *et al.* in Arcangeli *et al.*, 1990.)

In a different vein, all the models classified in the bottom half of *Figure 7.1* deal with diffusion processes that are implicitly or explicitly *historical* with multiple notional end-state and endogenously-generated opportunities (dynamic increasing returns). However, they differ in their approach to micromodeling.

Those on the bottom-left (e.g., David, 1985 and 1990; David and Olsen, 1990; Farell and Saloner, 1985) maintain a micro "rationality" assumption: agents still make their optimizing choices which collectively yield some sort of externality that in turn affects future returns and future options.

Conversely, the "evolutionary" and "self-organization" models on the bottom-right of *Figure 7.1* depart also from the standard micro-rationality and explicitly represent diffusion as the outcome of diverse behaviors of agents exhibiting "institutionalized" (so-called "bounded rationality") behaviors. Indeed, the supporters of this analytical approach do claim that the difference between "evolutionary" and "equilibrium" approaches to innovation diffusion is much deeper than the difference between the explicit (but somewhat unelegant) representation of a process and the description of the final state to which *that same process* is converging. Rather, evolutionary theory claims that (a) only under particular circumstances can "rational equilibria" be postulated to be the "attractor" or end-states of empirically more plausible "disequilibrium" trial-and-error processes, and relatedly, (b) actual end-states may well depend on non-average behaviors, so that an explicit account of the distributions of specific choice rules and of the specific mechanisms of competitive selection are theoretically required (these issues are discussed, in this perspective, in Nelson and Winter, 1982, and Dosi *et al.*, 1988, in particular the chapters therein by Silverberg, Allen, Dosi, and Orsenigo.

Broadly speaking, many "rational" and evolutionary/self-organization models of innovation diffusion overlap in the endeavor to *explain* theoretically *open-ended* (history-bound) processes. They do also sometimes overlap in the questions that they ask. For example: are there micro strategies that are stable in an evolutionary sense? How does dynamic mutual consistency come about? However, they depart in the relative faith that they place on the rational power of microagents as an "ordering factor". In a way, all micro-rational models look for order by investigating the conditions of existence of consistent rational strategies (whether pure or mixed strategies, in game-theoretic settings) that could support a diffusion process. Conversely, evolutionary/self-organization models rest their emphasis on diversity, learning and environmental selection as the main ordering factors, which *ex post, but not necessarily ex-ante* produce recognizable regularities in the diffusion process.

7.5.3   Optimizing equilibrium compared to institutionalized behaviors and disequilibrium

The reader may find a vivid illustration of the analogies and differences between the basic equilibrium and disequilibrium approaches by comparing Jovanovic and Lach (1989) and Silverberg *et al.* (1988). Loosely speaking, they could be considered as somewhat extreme archetypes of the two categories of models. In fact, they both start with quite similar technological assumptions: adoption of a capital-embodied innovation drives fixed and variable costs down and, therefore, the efficiency gains are a sort of collective result of adoption decisions. However, the analogies stop here. Jovanovic and Lach assume perfect micro technological forecasting and an *ex-ante* "equilibrium ordering" of entry decisions which, I must confess, I keep finding rather obscure in its microeconomic plausibility. (What is the mechanism generating the proper "queue"? How does one learn that he got an epsilon-wrong in this queue? What are the collective results of several epsilon mistakes?) Conversely, Silverberg *et al.* (1988) assume that people get it systematically wrong. This is not because they are "more stupid" than the Jovanovic-Lach (1989) agents. In principle, they form their expectations the best way they can. However, the end-results are truly collective phenomena, emerging from complex nonlinear interactions amongst all of them. What difference do the alternative analytical approaches make? In my view, one of the basic differences is that the "rational-equilibrium" approach loses interpretative significance the more the diffusion process is influenced by particular distributions of the expectational and technological characteristics of individual agents. In this sense, "equilibrium approaches" show the same limitations, and more so, than so-called rational expectation models in macroeconomics: "equilibrium paths" – whenever they exist – are not independent of the distribution of beliefs, technological capabilities, and learning processes of individual agents. In fact, one may simply check the robustness of the properties of a unique equilibrium diffusion path – from Jovanovic-Lach – allowing for different stochastic disturbances on, e.g., expectations: in general, one cannot presume the equilibrium path to be even *locally* stable; hence also the conclusions based on the properties of "perfect" equilibrium diffusion processes cannot be presumed to hold. In particular, it seems to me, equilibrium-"rational" analyses of diffusion must rule out *ex hypothesi* the possibility of (imperfect) out-of-equilibrium adjustment and learning from mistakes, which, I would argue, are an essential part of diffusion processes and affect also the specific path that is empirically observed.

It is indeed a major methodological difference which cuts across most fields of economic analysis: it is particularly evident with respect to innovation diffusion probably because, as mentioned, it is a crucial domain where novelties emerge in the economic system with an intrinsic tension between economic coordination and change. The supporters of methodological rationality believe that the calculating and planning powers of the agents can be stretched to also embrace highly complex, uncertain and non-stationary environments. Others suggest that for interpretative purposes this is a research program that despite unreasonable demands on individual calculating powers is bound to end up in rather indeterminate conclusions, and that institutions, together with more "impersonal" selection mechanisms can be part of a more promising microfoundation.

Moreover, innovation diffusion obviously bears major implications also in terms of macroeconomic growth of income, productivity, and employment (meaning here the proper "macro" level of the whole economy); industrial structures and organizational forms (including size, degrees of integration of business firms, etc.), and, finally, public policies. Let me now also briefly introduce also these broader issues.

7.6   Innovation Diffusion, Economic Dynamics, and Public Policies

Most diffusion models focus upon the determinants of innovation diffusion. However, a somewhat symmetric question concerns the *effects* of innovation diffusion upon changes in industrial structures and, more generally, on economic development.

In a genuinely dynamic framework, different capabilities, degrees of success or simply luck in innovation adoption by the various firms, affect firms' competitiveness, continuously generate *asymmetries* among them, and ultimately modify industrial structure (relative firm size, degrees of industrial concentration, etc.). It is probably a rather uncontroversial claim of "Schumpeterian"/"evolutionary" economics to have initiated this kind of investigation, albeit now paralleled by other approaches that rely more on optimizing microfoundations and equilibrium dynamics (see, for example, Dasgupta and Stiglitz, 1980a and 1980b).

Yet, irrespective of the specific analytical assumptions, any world where structural conditions and innovation diffusion are *dynamically-coupled*, that is wherein structural conditions influence innovation adoption and innovation adoption changes industrial structures, is going to exhibit nonlinear dynamics and path-dependency (hence, also multiplicity of dynamic paths and irreversibilities).

A crucial corollary of all this is that *institutions and policies matter in shaping economic dynamics*. Some of the contributions in Arcangeli *et al.* (1990) (especially Volume III) go further and conjecture some general "mappings" between (a) characteristics of diffusing technologies (or clusters of them), (b) institutions also shaping their adoption (and economic coordination, in general), and (c) patterns of economic growth. For example, Freeman and Perez (1988) argue that it is the "matching" or "mismatching" between broad "techno-economic paradigms" (such as electromechanic automation, microelectronics, etc.) and forms of socioeconomic organization which accounts for long-term historical regularities in economic growth intertwined by significant periods of instabilities and crises. On a somewhat similar level of analysis, contributions like Boyer (1988a and 1988b), Boyer and Coriat (1990), Coricelli *et al.* (1989), attempt some sort of explanation of the changing macrocoefficients (e.g., in the rates of change of income, employment, labor productivity, etc.) also in terms of plausible changes in the underlying trends in innovation and diffusion.

It is a formidable task, still at a very early stage of development, but it hints at the possibility of "microfounding" macrodynamics *cum non-stationarity* (at the very least in the available technologies, and most likely also in institutions and "preferences"). Some are keener on searching for these microfoundations through multiple equilibrium-rational dynamics. Others prefer to explore evolutionary/self-organization processes. Still, there seems a common quest for a micro-macro link that withholds (indeed, endogenously generates) non-stationarity in the so-called "fundamentals" and accommodates micro-diversity.

Another major consequence of differentiated patterns of innovation and diffusion concerns its regional and international dimensions. If regions and countries innovate and adopt at different rates, *first*, that very phenomenon must be explained, which in principle is a task of some sort of diffusion model *cum heterogeneous adopters*. *Second*, its implications for regional growth, international trade, and development must be explored. Several works have started to address these issues (see again, Volume III of Arcangeli *et al.*, 1990). Some increase the understanding of the "microcircularities" between technological advantages, patterns of international location, and international trade (such as the chapter by Cantwell and Dunning in Arcangeli *et al.*, 1990). Others (e.g., Cimoli *et al.*, 1990; Dosi *et al.*, 1990) link international diffusion with international institutional differences and "technology-gap" trade theories. Still a few others develop the tradition of regional economic studies in a fruitful parallelism between those models where *time* is the dimension of diffusion (such as, typically, in industrial economics), and those where it is *space*. Finally, all these complex and intertwined features of innovation diffusion have equally crucial normative (policy) dimensions.

Path-dependency and irreversibilities of diffusion patterns also imply the fundamental role of (plausibly less-than-perfectly informed) policies in the choice of major technological *trajectories*. But one side of the dilemma is that with *local* increasing returns, markets could most likely be more "myopic" and dynamically inefficient than approximate policy measures. However, somewhat symmetrically, it is hard to define the circumstances under which public policies can *plan* with more foresight toward notionally *superior* technologies. *Prima facie*, all this is a powerful argument for technological *pluralism* or at least for economic set-ups which allow for a sufficient diversity at the beginning of any new *technological paradigm* (Dosi, 1982 and 1988; David, 1990; Nelson, 1988). It remains also a major area of historical and theoretical exploration.

Micro-macro links add further complexity to the normative puzzles. If there are "multiple possible macro worlds" and institutions count in the determination of the one which finally emerges, then also very subtle questions come out concerning how individual agents, social groups, and public policies can influence such outcomes. Putting it another way, no matter whether one represents the world as multiple equilibrium dynamics *cum* non-convexities or as multiple *open-ended* evolutionary processes, one is still left with the questions on how and in which direction should the *initial conditions* be influenced – in one case – or how and in which form should micro diversities, selection processes, and economic institutions be shaped – in the other case.

All this, in our view, is another major frontier of research, which brings history, social disciplines, and policy analysis somewhat nearer to each other. Needless to say, it is an enormous task, but I believe, worth the endeavor.

References

Arcangeli, F., David, P.A., and Dosi, G., eds., 1990, *Frontiers on Innovation Diffusion*, Oxford University Press, Oxford, UK (forthcoming).

Arrow, K., 1962a, The economic implications of learning by doing, *Review of Economic Studies* 29:155–173.

Arrow, K., 1962b, Economic welfare and the allocation of resources for invention, in NBER, *The Rate and Direction of Inventive Activity*, Princeton University Press, Princeton, NJ, USA.

Arthur, B., 1983, *Competing technologies and lock-in by historical events: the dynamic of allocation under increasing returns*, WP-83-90, International Institute for Applied Systems Analysis, Laxenburg, Austria.

Arthur, B., 1988, Competing technologies, in G. Dosi *et al.*, eds., *Technical Change and Economic Theory*, Pinter Publishers, London and New York.

Atkinson, A. and Stiglitz, J., 1969, A new view of technological change, *Economic Journal* 79(315):573–578.

Boyer, R., 1988a, Technical change and the theory of regulation, in G. Dosi *et al.*, eds., *Technical Change and Economic Theory*, Pinter Publishers, London and New York.

Boyer, R., 1988b, Formalizing growth regimes, in Dosi *et al.* (*ibid*).

Boyer, R. and Coriat, B., 1990, Technical flexibility and macro stabilization: some preliminary steps, in F. Arcangeli *et al.*, eds., *Frontiers on Innovation Diffusion*, Oxford University Press, Oxford, UK (forthcoming).

Carter, C. and Williams, B., 1957, *Industry and Technical Progress*, Oxford University Press, Oxford, UK.

Cimoli, M., Dosi, G., and Soete, L., 1990, Technological gaps, institutional differences and patterns of trade: a North-South model, in F. Arcangeli *et al.*, eds., *Frontiers on Innovation Diffusion*, Oxford University Press, Oxford, UK (forthcoming).

Coricelli, F., Dosi, G., and Orsenigo, L., 1989, *Microeconomic dynamics and macro regularities: an "evolutionary" approach to technological and institutional change*, OECD-DSTI-SPR-89.7, Paris, France.

Chesnais, F., 1990, Some notes on technological cumulativeness, appropriation of technology and technological progressiveness in concentrated market structures, in F. Arcangeli *et al.*, eds., *Frontiers on Innovation Diffusion*, Oxford University Press, Oxford, UK (forthcoming).

Dasgupta, P., 1988, Patents, priority and imitation or, the economics of races and waiting games, *Economic Journal* **98**(389):66–80.

Dasgupta, P. and Stiglitz, J., 1980a, Industrial structure and the nature of innovative activity, *Economic Journal* **90**(358):266–293.

Dasgupta, P. and Stiglitz, J., 1980b, Uncertainty, industrial structure and the speed of R&D, *Bell Journal of Economics* **11**(1):1–28.

Dasgupta, P. and Stoneman, P., eds., 1987, *The Economic Theory of Technology Policy*, Cambridge University Press, Cambridge, UK.

David, P., 1969, *A Contribution to the Theory of Diffusion*, Memorandum No. 71, Stanford Center for Research in Economic Growth, Stanford University, Stanford, CA, USA.

David, P., 1975, *Technical Choice, Innovation and Economic Growth*, Cambridge University Press, Cambridge, UK.

David, P., 1985, Clio and the economics of QWERTY, *American Economic Review* **75**(2):332–337.

David, P., 1990, Narrow windows, blind giants and angry orphans: The dynamics of systems rivalries and dilemmas of technology policy, in F. Arcangeli *et al.*, eds., *Frontiers on Innovation Diffusion*, Oxford University Press, Oxford, UK (forthcoming).

David, P. and Olsen, T.A., 1984, *Anticipated Automation: A Rational Expectation Model of Technological Diffusion*, CEPR Working Paper No. 11, Stanford University, Stanford, CA, USA.

David, P. and Olsen, T.A., 1990, Equilibrium dynamics when incremental technological innovations are foreseen, in F. Arcangeli *et al.*, eds., *Frontiers on Innovation Diffusion*, Oxford University Press, Oxford, UK (forthcoming).

Davies, S., 1979, *The Diffusion of Process Innovations*, Cambridge University Press, Cambridge, UK.

Dosi, G., 1982, Technological paradigms and technological trajectories: a suggested interpretation of the determinants and directions of technical change, *Research Policy* **11**,(3):147–162.

Dosi, G., 1984, *Technical Change and Industrial Transformation*, Macmillan, London, UK and St. Martin's Press, New York, NY, USA.

Dosi, G., 1988, Sources, procedures and microeconomic effects of innovation, *Journal of Economic Literature* **26**(3):1120–1171.

Dosi, G. and Orsenigo, L., 1988, Coordination and transformation: An overview of structures, performance and change in evolutionary environments, in G. Dosi *et al.*, eds., *Technical Change and Economic Theory*, Pinter Publishers, London and New York.

Dosi, G., Orsenigo, L., and Silverberg, G., 1990, Innovation diffusion: A self-organization approach, in F. Arcangeli *et al.*, eds., *Frontiers on Innovation Diffusion*, Oxford University Press, Oxford, UK (forthcoming).

Dosi, G., Freeman, C., Nelson, R., Silverberg, G., and Soete, L., eds., 1988, *Technical Change and Economic Theory*, Pinter Publishers, London and New York.

Dosi, G., Pavitt, K., and Soete, L., 1990, *The Economics of Technological Change and International Trade*, Wheatsheaf, Brighton, UK.

Farrell, J. and Saloner, G., 1985, Standardization, compatibility and innovation, *Rand Journal of Economics* 16(1):70–83, Spring.

Freeman, C., 1982, *The Economics of Industrial Innovation*, 2nd edition, Frances Pinter, London, UK.

Freeman, C. and Perez, C., 1988, Structural crisis of adjustment: business cycles and investment behavior, in G. Dosi *et al.*, eds., *Technical Change and Economic Theory*, Pinter Publishers, London and New York.

Fudenberg, D. and Tirole, J., 1985, Pre-emption and rent equalization in the adoption of new technology, *Review of Economic Studies* 52(3):383–401.

Gort, M. and Klepper, S., 1982, Time paths in the diffusion of product innovations, *Economic Journal* 92(367):630–653.

Gort, M. and Konakayama, A., 1982, A model of diffusion in the production of an innovation, *American Economic Review* 72(5):1111–1120.

Gold, B., 1981, Technological diffusion in industry: Research needs and shortcomings, *Journal of Industrial Economics* 29(3):247–269.

Griliches, Z., 1957, Hybrid corn: An exploration in the economics of technological change, *Econometrica* 25:501–522.

Jensen, R.A., 1982, Adoption and diffusion of an innovation of uncertain profitability, *Journal of Economic Theory* 27(1):182–193.

Jovanovic, B. and Lach, S., 1989, Entry, exit and diffusion with learning by doing, *American Economic Review* 79:690–699.

Kamien, M. and Schwartz, N., 1982, *Market Structure and Innovation*, Cambridge University Press, Cambridge, UK.

Kleine, P., 1983, *Investitionsverhalten bei Prozeßinnovationen*, Campus Verlag, Frankfurt and New York.

Le Bas, C., 1981, *Economie des Innovations Techniques*, Economica, Paris, France.

Levin, R., Cohen, W.M., and Mowery, D.C., 1985, R&D appropriability, opportunity and market structure: New evidence on some Schumpeterian hypotheses, *American Economic Review* 75(2):20–24.

Levin, R., Klevorick, A., Nelson, R., and Winter, S., 1987, Appropriating the returns from industrial research and development, *Brookings Papers on Economic Activity* (3):783–831.

Lundvall, B.A., 1988, Innovation as an interactive process: From user-producer interaction to the national system of innovation, in G. Dosi *et al.*, eds., *Technical Change and Economic Theory*, Pinter Publishers, London and New York.

Mansfield, E., 1961, Technical change and the rate of imitation, *Econometrica* 29:741–766.

Mansfield, E., 1968, *Industrial Research and Technological Innovation: An Econometric Analysis*, Norton & Co., New York, NY, USA.

Mansfield, E., Rapoport, J., Romeo, A., Villani, E., Wagner, S., and Husic, F., 1977, *The Production and Application of New Industrial Technology*, Norton & Co., New York, NY, USA.

Metcalfe, S., 1970, Diffusion of innovation in the Lancashire textile industry, *The Manchester School of Economic and Social Studies* **38**(2):145–162.

Metcalfe, S., 1988, The diffusion of innovations: An interpretative survey, in G. Dosi *et al.*, eds., *Technical Change and Economic Theory*, Pinter Publishers, London and New York.

Nasbeth, L. and Ray, G.F., 1974, *The Diffusion of New Industrial Processes*, Cambridge University Press, Cambridge, UK.

NBER (National Bureau of Economic Research), 1962, *The Rate and Direction of Inventive Activity*, Princeton University Press, Princeton, NJ, USA.

Nelson, R., 1981, Research on productivity growth and productivity difference: dead ends and new departures, *Journal of Economic Literature* **19**(3):1029–1064.

Nelson, R., 1988, Institutions supporting technical change in the United States, in G. Dosi *et al.*, eds., *Technical Change and Economic Theory*, Pinter Publishers, London and New York.

Nelson, R., 1990, Institutions generating and diffusing new technology, in F. Arcangeli *et al.*, eds., *Frontiers on Innovation Diffusion*, Oxford University Press, Oxford, UK (forthcoming).

Nelson, R. and Winter, S., 1977, In search of a useful theory of innovation, *Research Policy* **6**(1):36–76.

Nelson, R. and Winter, S., 1982, *An Evolutionary Theory of Economic Change*, The Belknap Press of Harvard University Press, Cambridge, MA, USA.

Pavitt, K., 1988, International patterns of technological accumulation, in N. Hood and J.E. Vahlne, eds., *Strategies in Global Competition*, Croom Helm, London, UK.

Phillips, A., 1971, *Technology and Market Structure*, D.C. Heath, Lexington, MA, USA.

Ray, G., 1984, *The Diffusion of Mature Technologies*, Cambridge University Press, Cambridge, UK.

Reinganum, J.F., 1981, On the diffusion of new technology: A game theoretic approach, *Review of Economic Studies* **48**(3):395–405.

Rogers, E.M., 1983, *Diffusion of Innovations*, 3rd edition, The Free Press, New York, NY, USA.

Romeo, A.A., 1975, Interindustry and interfirm differences in the rate of diffusion of an innovation, *Review of Economics and Statistics* **57**(3):311–319.

Rosenberg, N., 1972, Factors affecting the diffusion of technology, *Explorations in Economic History* **10**:3–33, Fall.

Rosenberg, N., 1976, *Perspectives on Technology*, Cambridge University Press, Cambridge, UK.

Rosenberg, N., 1982, *Inside the Black Box*, Cambridge University Press, Cambridge, UK.

Sahal, D., 1981, *Patterns of Technological Innovation*, Addison-Wesley, Reading, MA, USA.

Salter, W.A.G., 1969, *Productivity and Technical Change*, 2nd edition, Cambridge University Press, Cambridge, UK.

Silverberg, G., Dosi, G., and Orsenigo, L., 1988, Innovation, diversity and diffusion: A self-organization model, *Economic Journal* 98(393):1032–1054.

Simon, H., 1965, *Administrative Behavior*, 2nd edition, The Free Press, New York, NY, USA.

Simon, H., 1967, *Models of Man*, John Wiley & Sons Inc., New York, NY, USA.

Simon, H., 1979, Rational decision making in business organizations, *American Economic Review* 69(4):493–513.

Stiglitz, J., 1985, Information and economic analysis: A perspective, *Economic Journal* 95(5):21–41.

Stiglitz, J., 1987, Learning to learn, in P. Dasgupta and P. Stoneman, eds., *The Economic Theory of Technology Policy*, Cambridge University Press, Cambridge, UK.

Stoneman, P., 1976, *Technological Diffusion and the Computer Revolution*, Clarendon Press, Oxford, UK.

Stoneman, P., 1983, *The Economic Analysis of Technological Change*, Oxford University Press, Oxford, UK.

Stoneman, P., 1990, Technological diffusion: The viewpoint of economic theory, in F. Arcangeli *et al.*, eds., *Frontiers on Innovation Diffusion*, Oxford University Press, Oxford, UK (forthcoming).

Stoneman, P. and Ireland, N., 1983, The role of supply factors in the diffusion of new process technology, *Economic Journal Conference Papers* 93:66–78.

Sylos-Labini, P., 1967, *Oligopoly and Technical Progress*, 2nd edition, Harvard University Press, Cambridge, MA, USA.

Teece, D., 1986, Profiting from technological innovation: implications for integration, collaboration, licensing and public policy, *Research Policy* 15(6):285–305.

Tirole, J., 1988, *The Theory of Industrial Organization*, MIT Press, Cambridge, MA, USA.

Trachtenberg, M., 1987, *The Welfare Analysis of Product Innovations with an Application to CT Scanners*, Department of Economics, Tel-Aviv University, Tel-Aviv, Israel.

von Tunzlemann, N., 1978, *Steam Power and British Industrialization to 1860*, Clarendon Press, Oxford, UK.

[4]

The Economic Journal, 107 (*September*), 1530–1547. © Royal Economic Society 1997. Published by Blackwell
Publishers, 108 Cowley Road, Oxford OX4 1JF, UK and 350 Main Street, Malden, MA 02148, USA.

OPPORTUNITIES, INCENTIVES AND THE COLLECTIVE PATTERNS OF TECHNOLOGICAL CHANGE*

Giovanni Dosi

In a few pages, in the introductory article for this debate, Vernon Ruttan succeeds in the unlikely task of flagging many issues at the core of the economic interpretation of technological change (and by doing so he implicitly addresses also a few sensitive spots for the economic discipline at large). Here I will not attempt to provide any thorough view of what I consider the achievements and limitations of the current state-of-the-art (see, however, Freeman (1994) for a critical survey which I largely share). Rather, I shall put forward a series of remarks which, hopefully, could be seen as part of a much wider, and still largely unexplored, research programme.

As a premise, just note that some form of attention to technology-related phenomena has spread over the last 20–30 years from small enclaves of heterodox economists and economic historians to become an important concern even for quite mainstream theories of e.g. the firm, industrial organisation, macroeconomics, trade, growth, etc. From 'patent races' all the way to 'New Trade' and 'New Growth' theories and even Real Business Cycle macro models, technical change has drawn a consideration which is less by default than it was, say, in Robert Solow's original growth models or Joe Bain's barriers-to-entry views on industrial structures. And, in parallel, empirical studies – at the levels of specific technologies, firms, sectors and countries – have boomed (for overviews cf. Dosi (1988), Nelson (1993), Freeman (1982, 1994), Cohen (1995) and Granstrand (1994), among others). So, at least in this sense, those 'decreasing returns' to the economics of technical change suggested by Ruttan do not seem to have set in. However, Ruttan's paper raises also substantive questions about the relative success of three interpretative perspectives – which he calls 'induced', 'evolutionary' and 'path-dependent'. In the following I shall argue that an evolutionary perspective, broadly defined, can easily accommodate both inducement effects and path-dependent patterns of technical change.

Let me start from what I consider the major building blocks of an

* Support to the research by the International Institute of Applied Systems Analysis (IIASA), Laxenburg, Austria and the Italian National Research Council (CNR) is gratefully acknowledged.

Comments by Vernon Ruttan and Huw Dixon (Editor) and discussions with Andrea Bassanini, Valerie Revest, and Marco Valente have contributed to mould the paper to the present shape. The usual caveats apply.

evolutionary theory (admittedly in its maximal form: most models and empirical analysis cited below share only a subset of these features).[1]

I. EVOLUTIONARY THEORIES OF ECONOMIC CHANGE

1. As Sidney Winter used to summarise it, the methodological imperative of evolutionary theories is *dynamics first*! That is, the explanation to why something exists intimately rests on how it became what it is. Or putting it in terms of negative prescriptions: never take as a good 'explanation' either an existence theorem or a purely functionalist claim (entity x exists because it performs function y...).

2. *Theories are explicitly microfounded*, in the sense that they must involve or at least be consistent with a story of what agents do and why they do it.[2]

3. Agents have at best an *imperfect understanding* of the environment they live in, and, even more so, of what the future will deliver. Hence, 'bounded rationality' in a very broad sense is generally assumed.

4. Imperfect understanding and imperfect, path-dependent, learning entails persistent *heterogeneity* among agents, even when facing identical information and identical notional opportunities.

5. Agents are always capable of discovering new technologies, new behavioural patterns, new organisational set-ups. Hence, also the *continuous appearance of various forms of novelty* in the system.

6. Relatedly, while (imperfect) adaptation and discovery generate variety (possibly in seemingly random fashions), collective interactions within and outside markets, perform as *selection mechanisms*, yielding also differential growth (and possibly also disappearance) of different entities which are so to speak 'carriers' of diverse technologies, routines, strategies, etc.

7. As a result of all this, aggregate phenomena (e.g. regularities in the growth process or in industrial structures, etc.) are 'explained' as *emergent properties*. They are the collective outcome of *far-from-equilibrium interactions* and heterogeneous learning. Finally, they often have a *metastable nature*, in the sense that while persistent on a time-scale longer than the processes generating them, tend to disappear with probability one as time goes to infinity.[3]

This is not the place to review the growing number of contributions which share some or all of these seven broad methodological building blocks.[4] For the purposes of these comments it will suffice to mention the flourishing number of formal models and historical interpretations of economic growth as an evolutionary process propelled by technical change which have followed the

---

[1] More detailed discussions of evolutionary theories, following the seminal work of Nelson and Winter (1982), are in e.g. Coriat and Dosi (1995), Hodgson (1993), Dosi and Nelson (1994), Nelson (1995), Silverberg and Verspagen (1995).

[2] Note, however, that there are a few 'aggregate' (i.e. non-microfounded) models which are nonetheless 'evolutionary' in spirit (for a survey, Silverberg and Verspagen (1995)).

[3] On the notions of 'emergence' and 'metastability' cf. the discussion in Lane (1993). (The most noticeable exception to 'metastable' properties are irreversible lock-in phenomena, taken literally, so that collective regularities are limit properties of adaptation/learning process: see also below.)

[4] Note that, given the above quite broad definition of the 'evolutionary research programme', it may well cover also the contributions of authors who would not call themselves 'evolutionist' in any strict sense.

work of Nelson and Winter (1982). (See among others Dosi *et al.* (1988), Day and Eliasson (1986), Silverberg and Verspagen (1994), Conlisk (1989), Chiaromonte and Dosi (1993), Silverberg and Soete (1993) and the discussion in Nelson (1995) Coriat and Dosi (1995) and Silverberg and Verspagen (1995).)

Formal models have gone together with a rapidly growing number of empirical studies – inspired to different degree by evolutionary ideas – aimed at the understanding of the processes by which knowledge is produced, diffused and economically exploited. Since the characteristics of these processes bear major consequences also in terms of possible 'inducement' mechanisms and path-dependency, let me consider them at some length.

II. SOURCES AND DRIVERS OF TECHNICAL CHANGE: WHAT HAVE WE OBSERVED INSIDE THE 'BLACK BOX'?

In order to assess better what one has found so far 'inside the blackbox' of technological change,[5] it is useful to distinguish between four (albeit interrelated) objects of analysis, namely, first, (the changes in) innovative *opportunities* (strictly speaking, the 'sources' of technical change pertain to this domain); secondly, the *incentives* to exploit those opportunities themselves; thirdly, the *capabilities* of the agents to achieve whatever they try to do, conditional on their perceptions of both opportunities and incentives, and, fourthly, the *organisational arrangements* and *mechanisms* through which technological advances are searched for and implemented.

Telegraphically,

'the picture which emerges from numerous studies of innovation in firms is one of continuous interactive learning. Firms learn both from their own experience of design, development, production and marketing... *and* from a wide variety of external sources at home and abroad – their customers, their supplies, their contractors..., and from many other organisations – universities, governments laboratories and agencies, consultants, licensors, licencees and others' (Freeman (1994), p. 470).

Complementarity between sources internal and external to the firm is the general property (cf. for example Cohen and Levinthal (1989), Malerba (1992) and the overview in Freeman (1994)). And in fact a good deal of empirical work has gone into the understanding of the inter-sectoral and inter-technological differences in the relative importance of these various forms of opportunities – including, of course, those provided by scientific advances (cf. Klevorick *et al.* (1993), Rosenberg (1982), Freeman (1982)). I shall turn below to modeling-related issues. However, note already that the evidence here is quite far from any view of exogenous shift in the opportunity set. (In fact, it is sometimes the case that even scientific advances are triggered by firm-sponsored technological developments and not the other way round, cf. Rosenberg (1994) and Freeman (1982).)

---

[5] *Inside the Blackbox* is the title of an influential book by Nathan Rosenberg (1982).

Relatedly, one observes a variety of learning processes, ranging from institutionalised search processes formally placed in R & D labs all the way to much more informal procedures of 'learning-by-interacting' with customers and suppliers (Lundvall, 1992; Freeman, 1994): again one is beginning to draw up sectoral maps of the typical learning patterns, conditional on their knowledge bases.

Another robust 'stylised fact' emerging from studies on innovation and diffusion is the persistent heterogeneity in the knowledge and problem-solving capabilities that firms embody, their relative stickiness over time, together with wide asymmetries in performances, highlighted also by the persistence of 'inferior' techniques and product characteristics – given the prevailing relative prices and demand patterns – and of significant profitability differentials. (More on these points in Dosi (1988) and Dosi *et al.* (1995), Nelson (1981), Winter (1987), Malerba and Orsenigo (1996).)[6]

Regarding incentives to innovate, a lot (in my view possibly even too much!) attention has been given to the conditions of appropriability of the rent streams coming from successful innovations. (An extensive intersectoral analysis of the various appropriation mechanism in the US industry from patents to secrecy, etc. – is in Levin *et al.* (1987).) While it is straightforward that some expected differential profitability is a necessary condition for private actors to undertake expensive and uncertain search efforts, to my knowledge, one lacks any convincing evidence that the intensity of search grows monotonically with the expected value of the rent streams: on the contrary, it seems, inter-sectoral and inter-temporal differences in the propensity of innovating are better accounted for, in a first approximation, by differences in opportunities and firm-specific capabilities rather than fine variations in profitability incentives (above a minimum threshold).

Finally, one often observes relatively ordered patterns of technical change in both spaces of input coefficients and product characteristics (i.e. what I have called elsewhere technological trajectories) grounded in rather invariant, incrementally augmenting, knowledge bases (i.e. technological paradigms), every now and then intertwined by major discontinuities in both the sources of knowledge and the directions of change (Dosi, 1982, 1988).

How can these findings, together with the evolutionary perspective sketched above, help in explaining also possible inducement mechanisms on the rates and directions of technological change?

III. INDUCEMENTS, SEARCH AND EVOLUTION

The classic inducement story, recalled in Ruttan's article, had the pioneering merit of trying to provide some analytical link between today's prevailing economic conditions (be they relative prices or demand patterns), allocative

---

[6] Incidentally note also that technology-focused studies have recently found fruitful interchanges with firm-focused ones highlighting organisation-specific problem-solving capabilities as part of the answer to the questions of (i) why firms exist, (ii) why do they have the boundaries which one observes, and (iii) why are they different in behaviours and performances. See, among others, the special issue of *Industrial and Corporate Change*, no. 1, 1994, on 'Dynamic Capabilities' edited by David Teece and Gary Pisano; Teece *et al.* (1994); Montgomery (1995).

decisions by the economic agents and tomorrow's technological possibilities.[7] However, it does so with pitfalls already mentioned by Ruttan and others. It blackboxes notional opportunities of innovation into the rather farfetched notion of an Innovation Possibility Frontier (IPF). It is rather cavalier on the ways relative prices (or demand patterns) affect incentives to search in particular factor-saving directions (unless one introduces quite *ad hoc* hypotheses on the shape of the IPF, on elasticities of substitutions, etc.). It is rather shaky in its microfoundations. And, finally, by folding together sources and incentives to innovate, it implicitly assumes a smooth response of knowledge-creation to market-signals.[8]

Conversely, there is an evolutionary story of 'inducement' which, in my view, sounds much more convincing. It runs more or less as follows.

Abandon the idea that there is any well defined IPF anywhere. Rather, each body of knowledge specific of particular technologies (each 'paradigm') determines the notional opportunities of future technical advance and also the boundaries of the set of input coefficients which are feasible on the grounds of that knowledge base. So, for example, the semiconductor-based paradigm in microelectronics or the oil-based paradigm in organic chemicals broadly determine the scope and directions of technical progress – i.e. the 'trajectories' in both product and process technologies (for example, miniaturisation and increasing chip density in semiconductors; polymerisation techniques in organic chemicals, etc.). Together, technological paradigms bind the scope for dynamic interfactoral substitution (so that, for example, irrespectively of the relative price of energy, it is difficult to imagine, given our current knowledge base, a technology for the production of hyperpure silicon which would not be very energy-intensive...).

It follows also from the foregoing remarks that the ways opportunities are tapped and the degrees of success in doing so depend to a good extent upon the capabilities and past achievements of economic agents. So, more technically, think of 'opportunities' as some measure on the set of input coefficients which are reachable at time t, with positive probability, conditional on the vector $\mathbf{x}_j(t)$ of coefficients that agent j ($j = 1, ..., n$) masters at t. And, straightforwardly, capabilities can be seen as the transition probabilities, specific to each j for any given search effort.[9] 'Inducement', *lato sensu*, can work in four ways.[10]

First, changes in relative prices and demand or supply conditions may well affect search heuristics. This is what Rosenberg (1976) has called *focusing devices*, and historically documented in a few cases of supply shocks and technological bottlenecks, from the continental blockade during Napoleonic

---

[7] In a different fashion, the endogenisation of technical advances resulting from explicit investment in knowledge-augmentation is of course also a central theme of New Growth theories, but its simpler (one-dimensional) account of technical progress cannot address the question of the directions of change.

[8] For a thorough critique of that particular version of inducement theories which treat innovation as 'demand-pulled', cf. Mowery and Rosenberg (1979). See also below.

[9] This to make things simple: in a more complicated but realistic account, allowing for imitation, transition probabilities of each j should depend also on the states achieved but all other agents and some metrics on their distances (cf. Nelson and Winter (1982) and Chiaromonte and Dosi (1993)).

[10] Most elements of this basic story can be found in Nelson and Winter (1982), Chapter 7.

wars to late nineteenth century history of mechanical technologies... (Bounded rationality and lack of 'rational' technological expectations stand behind the relevance of these behaviourally-mediated inducements effects. But, of course, evolutionary theories – quite in tune with empirical evidence – are at ease with these assumptions, see also below.)

In this case, 'inducement' stands for the influences that the perception of environmental conditions exert upon the problem-solving activities which agents decide to undertake.

Formally, it is like saying that market shocks induce different partitions of the notional search space attainable at t, and focus search in those regions where one is more likely to find, say, savings on the inputs which are perceived as scarce and more expensive. Note that, for example, part of the (highly convincing) interpretation of inducements to mechanisation in the American nineteenth century economy suggested by Paul David (1975) can be rephrased in this way without any analytical loss, except the dubious commitments to rational choice with reference to a mysterious IPF.

The earlier caveat that knowledge bases constrain the directions of search is crucial as well, and this applies to both single technologies and broad technological systems (or 'techno-economic paradigms' in the sense of Freeman and Perez (1988)) which dominate in the economy over particular phases of development (e.g. steam power, electricity and electromechanical technologies, microelectronics and information technologies, etc.). Consider for example, Moses Abramovitz's proposition that 'in the nineteenth century, technological progress was heavily biased in a physical capital-using direction [and] it could be incorporated into production only by agency of a large expansion in physical capital per worker... [while]... in the twentieth century... the bias weakened [and] may have disappeared all together' (Abramovitz, 1993, p. 224). As I read it, it is a proposition on the nature of the knowledge available at a certain time in the society and the ways it constrains its economic exploitation, irrespectively of relative prices. That is, the proposition concerns the boundaries of the opportunity set attainable on the grounds of the available paradigms[11] and the limits to possible 'inducement effects'.

Second, inducement may take the form of an influence of market conditions upon the relative allocation of search efforts to different technologies or products. Note that while the former inducement process concerned the directions of search (e.g. in the input space), this second form regards the intensity of search and, other things being equal, the rates of advance. In the literature, it has come to be known as 'Schmookler's hypothesis' (Schmookler, 1966), suggesting that cross-product differences in the rates of innovation (as measured by patenting) could be explained by differences in the relative rates of growth of demand. While it is no *a priori* reason why the perception of demand opportunities should not influence the allocation of technological efforts, the general idea of 'demand-led' innovation has been criticised at its

---

[11] A pale image of all that appear even after blackboxing the whole process into aggregate production functions, via different elasticities of substitution and factor saving biases. A pertinent discussion is the cited work by Abramovitz (1993). Relatedly see also Nelson (1981).

foundations for its theoretical ambiguities (does one talk about observed demand? expected demand? and how are these expectations formed?) (Mowery and Rosenberg, 1989). The empirical evidence is mixed. The review in Freeman (1994) concludes that 'the majority of innovation characterized as "demand led"... were actually relatively minor innovations along established trajectories", while as shown by Walsh (1984) and Fleck (1988), "counter-Schmookler"-type patterns was [the] characteristic of the early stage of innovation in synthetic material, drugs, dyestuff...', and robotics (Freeman, 1984, p. 480).

As emphasised by Freeman himself and by Kline and Rosenberg (1986), the major step forward here is the abandonment of any 'linear' model of innovation (no matter whether driven by demand or technological shocks) and the acknowledgement of a co-evolutionary view embodying persistent feedback loops between innovation, diffusion and endogenous generation of further opportunities of advancement (see the empirical remarks above).

Both mechanisms of 'inducement' discussed so far ultimately rest on the ways changing market conditions influence incentives, and in turn, the way the latter affect behavioural patterns – either in terms of search heuristics or allocation rules. However, changing relative prices can easily 'induce' changes in the directions of technical change, even holding search behaviour constant, via the selection of the (stochastic) outcomes of search itself. This is the *third* inducement process that I shall consider. Let me illustrate it by recalling the very basics of the Markov model of factor substitution from Nelson and Winter (1982, pp. 175–92).

It has been mentioned earlier that 'innovative opportunities', when talking about process innovations, can be seen as the (bounded) set of states in the space of inputs (per unit of output) attainable starting from an arbitrary technique in use at time t. Suppose that search is a random process invariant in t (this implies that one excludes both decreasing returns to innovative efforts and those inducement effects upon search rules, discussed earlier). When a new technique is drawn, it is compared with the one currently in use, given the prevailing input prices, and the minimum cost one is obviously chosen. The sequence of factor ratios displayed by a firm can be described by a Markov process characterised by the transition probability matrix $\mathbf{F} = [f_{ik}]$, where f_{ik} is the probability that state i follows state k.[12] Note that the transition matrix is time invariant but transition probabilities depend on relative input prices. This is because of the 'comparison check': holding constant the initial technique and the one drawn, whether the latter will be adopted or not might depend on relative prices,[13] and that choice will set different initial conditions for the next draw, etc. The intuition on dynamic-choice-of-technique inducement suggests that if the relative price of some input increases, the

[12] Nelson and Winter, quite in tune with the general idea that there are 'paradigm-based' constraints to the scope of factor substitution, assume that factor ratios can assume only N possible values; thus $i, k = 1, \ldots, N$.

[13] It obviously does not whenever the newly discovered technique is more efficient in terms of every input – a case which evolutionary theories easily allow.

transition probabilities, loosely speaking, of 'getting away' from the techniques which intensively use that input will also increase. And in fact, Nelson and Winter (1982, pp. 180–92) establish the result, in a two-input case, that, with the appropriate ordering in terms of relative input intensities, the transition matrix $\hat{F}$ (based on the new relative prices) stochastically dominates the 'old' one, F. It is an appealing result, resting so far on many formal qualifications, but certainly worth further exploration.[14] The bottom line is the following. Even if opportunities do not change and agents do not perceive variations in relative prices as incentives to change their search rules, it is enough that relative prices enter into the criteria of choice between what has been found by search and what is already in use, in order to determine – in probability – 'induced' changes in the patterns of factor use, at the level of individual firms and whole industries.[15]

Fourth, and complementarily, assume that agents are totally inertial in their production routines (i.e. in fact there is no innovative search): even in this extreme case, market selection will increase the frequency in supply – i.e. the market shares of agents who happen to embody the 'better' techniques, conditional on prevailing prices – via their differential ability to invest in production capacity.

It is revealing to compare the foregoing interpretation of 'inducement' with the more conventional ones, reviewed in Ruttan's article (in this issue of this JOURNAL). In the evolutionary view, to summarise, one tries to disentangle three sources of 'inducement' related to (a) changes in microeconomic rules of search, affecting the direction of exploration in the notional opportunity space; (b) changes in the allocation of resources to search efforts (irrespectively of its 'directions'); and (c) market-induced changes in the selection criteria by which some techniques or products are compared with alternative varieties. And, (d) it does that in ways that easily allow for endogenous interactions (i.e. 'co-evolution') between the incentive structure (stemming from relative prices and demand patterns), on the one hand, and learning capabilities, on the other. In this respect, the article by Gavin Wright, in this issue of this JOURNAL is an excellent illustration of the point. Even in the case of mineral resources – i.e. the nearest one can get to a 'naturally' determined opportunity set – Wright shows opportunities themselves have been the outcome of both public and private search efforts (see also David and Wright (1997)). Conversely, more conventional views of inducement, by making stronger commitments to both optimising rationality and equilibrium, obscure – in my opinion – the distinctions between behavioural effects and system level ('selection') effects, and, together, render very difficult any account of the sector-specific and

[14] Among other points, the clarity of representation in terms of a time-invariant finite-state Markov process has its inevitable downside in that, – taking seriously the question of 'what happens as time goes to infinity?' – all persistent states return infinitely often in the limit (see also below on path-dependency). However, it should not be formally impossible to make transition probabilities phase-space dependent, thus giving also more persistence to the weight of past 'inducements'.

[15] I do not dare extend this conjecture to whole economies, since no evolutionary model has so far adventured seriously into the exploration of multi-sectoral systems, linked by input–output relations, checking also the empirical plausibility of phenomena like reswitching of techniques, etc. – which appeared prominently in the theoretical debates in the 1970s and disappeared by magic later on.

period specific patterns of knowledge accumulation. The blackboxing under unobservable constructs like IPF's, 'elasticities of substitution', etc. just helps to rationalise the dynamic outcome while obscuring the processes driving it.

IV. PATH-DEPENDENCIES

In the broadest sense, one should expect path-dependency whenever in presence of nonlinearities and increasing returns of some kind. And, indeed, an evolutionary world characterising the endogenous generation of innovative opportunities is inevitably rich in positive feedbacks.[16]

The very possibility that agents can access new information and knowledge[17] through their own actions already entails the possibility of some form of increasing returns. It is a point repeatedly emphasised by Kenneth Arrow (1962, 1974, 1987) and it has become one of the starting point of New Growth Theories (cf. Romer (1986, 1990, 1994); Grossman and Helpman (1991)). Briefly, this is because the main cost of acquisition of information is upfront, but thereafter information can be utilised at any scale of output, it is not used up through production itself (but if anything increased through phenomena like learning-by-doing) and it has non-rival use (if I use it, this does not prevent you from using it too...).

Other (related) sources of increasing returns have been recognised since the origin of the economic discipline, like the famous proposition by Adam Smith, revisited by A. Young and neglected for another fifty years, on the positive feedback between size of the market, division of labour and specialisation-driven increases in productivity.[18] Moreover, classic contributors to growth and development theories, including Gerschenkron, Hirschman, Kaldor, and Myrdal when suggesting processes of 'cumulative causation' and 'virtuous' or 'vicious cycles', clearly had self-reinforcing dynamics in mind.

Contemporary analyses of the patterns of technological change add other potential sources of increasing returns, associated, for example, with what have been called the 'cumulativeness' of technological advances (i.e. the probability of future discovery being positively influenced by past realisations), network externalities, learning-by-using, etc.

In brief, one is at last acknowledging a wide set of positive feedbacks (and, thus, nonlinearities, and, thus, path-dependencies) in economics in general, and in particular in the domain of technical change.[19] How important they are and what form they take is primarily an empirical question (and the answer is likely to be conditional on particular sectors, technologies, etc.). However, one

---

[16] Note that evolutionary worlds (in the earlier definition) are almost by necessity nonlinear, but the converse does not hold (for example putting spaghetti to boil involves highly nonlinear dynamics, path-dependencies in the ways bubbles form in the water, phase-transitions, etc., but one would hardly call it an evolutionary process!).

[17] I discuss the difference between the two in Dosi (1995).

[18] It should be clear that increasing-returns phenomena may well be (and often are) quite distinct from sheer economies of scale. The example of division of labour is a good case to the point.

[19] As known, non-linear dynamics (with the related dependence on initial conditions) have been found to be a frequent occurrence also in otherwise highly orthodox models in macroeconomics, international trade, etc., but in these short notes it is impossible to discuss in general how far one can stretch standard neoclassical models in order to account for history.

would like to have some 'theoretical tales' – as George Akerlof would put it – providing some guidance on the nature of the processes involved, and also helping in answering questions like: how important path-dependency itself is? Does it involve phenomena of irreversible lock-in? What are the consequences in terms of efficiency? And, moreover, can one reconcile path-dependency/ positive feedbacks with individual forward-looking rationality?

At a first glance, the ways evolutionary models *à la* Nelson–Winter treat increasing returns to knowledge appear to be quite different from the story on path-dependency that emerges, say, from Arthur *et al.* (1987), Arthur (1989) or David (1985). The interpretation that I want to suggest here, however, is that the two basic stories are to a good extent complementary, and that the remaining differences highlight major theoretical issues worth further exploration.

In the barebone Nelson–Winter (NW) story (and in many others, cited above), heterogenous agents are so to speak 'carriers' of different behavioural and technological traits and interact in some collective environment, typically a market which rewards or penalises them on the grounds of some revealed performance, ultimately related to their profitabilities. In turn, the latter influence the ability of each agent to grow and its survival probabilities. In the discrete time formulation, next 'period', each agent may well search again for new technologies and new behavioural rules, undertakes production, and, again, faces its competitors in the market. And so on.[20] In the last resort, dynamics rests on some learning processes (search, innovation, imitation by individual agents), on the one hand, and some selection mechanism on the other. Within the philosophy of the story (although not always in models that have been already implemented), path-dependency can arise at least at three levels. First, it may regard the patterns of technological learning of individual agents. Secondly, it may concern their behavioural' rules.[21] Thirdly, path-dependency may be a collective property of the time profile of aggregate rates of growth of output, average productivities, factor intensities, product characteristics, etc.

Conversely, take what I shall call in a shorthand the Arthur–David (AD) story.[22] It is essentially a story of diffusion (although in the background there are implicitly incremental innovation of the products or technologies candidates to be adopted). In its simplest version, multiple producers offer two or n alternative technologies and the adoption choices feedback upon the incentive of the next adopter via (a) sheer imitation effects and endogenous preferences; (b) network externalities; or (c) learning 'induced' upon the producers of the chosen technology which then improve their quality and/or price.

Said like that, one can see a nice complementarity between behaviourally

---

[20] The story can in principle be extended by allowing, for example, for multiple selection environments, e.g. both product – and financial markets; enlarging the dimensionality of the selection space, e.g. by introducing diverse output characteristics; testing for different interaction mechanisms....

[21] Organisational adaptation, inertia and lock-in is a theme widely discussed in organisational disciplines: for a suggestive discussion of the evolutionary roots of these phenomena cf. Levinthal (1992).

[22] That story also has many ancestors, in economic history and even in formal economic theory (cf. Atkinson and Stiglitz, 1969).

richer evolutionary models (the former) and sort of reduced-form ones (the latter), which, however, vividly highlight dynamic-increasing-return inter-actions between demand and supply of alternative technologies. And, with that, also (a) how 'history matters' (small initial fluctuations bear long-term macro effects); and (b) the possibility of lock-in into notionally inferior technologies. More subtle issues, however, differentiate the two stories, and disentangling them is the challenge that the evolutionary research programme ought to face urgently. Let me end by outlining some of them.

V. MICROFOUNDATIONS AND PATH-DEPENDENCY

It happens that evolutionary models in the NW model spell out a set of control variables which agents are in principle asked to master, together with some empirically-derived hypotheses on how they do it. The general acknow-ledgement of bounded rationality and heterogeneity comes as a natural corollary of the fact that even the sophisticated theorist would have overwhelming difficulties in finding out the appropriate intertemporal optimisation schedules, given the complexity of the problem. But, of course, the inevitable consequence is that the dynamics are not only path-dependent – in the sense of initial conditions and early stochastic fluctuations – but also behaviour-dependent – in the sense that the nature and distributions of agents' behaviour affects long-term outcomes, for identical initial conditions, oppor-tunities and incentives. Here come also the full challenge for evolutionary models to map classes of behaviours robustly into classes of collective long-term outcomes. (And this is also where an evolutionary perspective links with studies of organisational behaviour, on the one side, and analyses of economic institutions, on the other.) Works developed in the 'AD mode',[23] on the contrary, are most agnostic on the behavioural foundations – a task made easier by the fact that generally the decision setting is simple enough as to make redundant any theoretical commitment on the degrees of 'rationality' of the agents... (would you choose A or B, given that the majority of your sample has chosen A and it is convenient for you to choose with a majority/minority rule?...). So given the simplicity of the decision problem, decision rules can either be interpreted as based on some (stochastically perturbed) routine or alternatively as the outcome of (myopic) optimisation. But, beyond those simple set-ups, the type of chosen microfoundation matter, and, of course, the inclination of evolutionary theorists is that of setting them 'phenomenologi-cally' by abstracting some invariances from what agents actually do in circumstances similar to those purported by the model.[24]

In this respect, note that the evolutionary story – based on heterogeneity of

[23] The fact that these are modelling styles and not deeper methodological commitments is shown, at least in the case of the author of these notes, by the fact that, according to the different objects of analysis, one has chosen either set of instruments: compare for example Chiaromonte and Dosi (1993), Silverberg *et al.* (1988), Dosi, Fabiani *et al.* (1994) with Dosi, Ermoliev and Kaniovski (1994), and Dosi and Kaniovski (1994).

[24] More detailed discussion of decision and learning in evolutionary environments are in Nelson and Winter (1982), Winter (1975), Dosi, Marengo and Fagiolo (1996).

expectations, competences and behaviours – and the alternative maximising agent/equilibrium story may often be rendered observationally equivalent at aggregate level by inventing the appropriate restrictions on opportunity sets, elasticities, risk-aversions, intertemporal preferences, etc. However, such observational equivalence breaks down at more micro-levels of analysis.

To begin with, the 'stylised' facts, briefly mentioned above concerning persistent performances asymmetries across firms are, in my view, a robust circumstantial evidence against 'rational'/equilibrium microfoundations of technological search.[25]

More direct computations of any assumption that agents involved in technological innovation/imitation are in some sense 'rational', and in particular hold 'rational technological expectations' are widespread in the applied literature, although not likely to convince the religious believers in 'rationality' – whatever that means in this context.[26] For example, Rosenberg (1996) – cited also in the companion article by Wright – highlights systematic mistakes of most major innovators in forecasting the economic impact of what they are doing. And, this is fully supported by many longitudinal case studies. For example, from what I have learned from the history of the semiconductor industry (Dosi (1984); see also Malerba (1985)), search efforts – in terms of both size of investments and direction of investigation – have been a far cry from what a rational (or, often even modestly reasonable) agent should have expected about outcomes. More generally, Freeman (1982) presents over-whelming evidence that grossly 'boundedly rational' criteria for evolution of R & D projects are often involving systematic underestimation of costs, cognitive path-dependencies, irresponsiveness to environmental feedbacks, etc.[27]

Even more broadly, most of applied business economics insists that the very notion of 'strategy' is at best an ensemble of fuzzy and often contradictory heuristics (within an enormous literature, see for example, Starbuck (1989)).

Having said that, this should not be taken at all as a support for the idea that 'outside full rationality anything goes...'. On the contrary, two complementary tasks are high on the evolutionary research agenda, namely first, a more precise identification of the empirical regularities regarding business behaviour in general and in particular with regard to innovative search; and, secondly, the

---

[25] Certainly, all this makes any 'representative agent' reduction of the underlying search dynamics utterly implausible. However, these are imaginative attempts to account together for heterogeneity in capabilities, individual forward-looking rationality and equilibrium. See, for example, Joranovic and MacDonald (1994).

[26] Notice incidentally that this is not meant as an outright objection to the usefulness in some circumstances, of sort of thought experiments grounded on fully 'rational' agents. For example, the way I understand the spirit of Paul Romer's exercises on endogenous growth is to show, among other things, that even if one had forward-looking representative agents, still one would get systematic divergences between endogenously generated and socially optional ratios of growth. And, *a fortiori* this applies when the underlying 'rationality' requirement is absent. All this, however, is quite different from taking seriously such microfoundations as descriptively pertinent.

[27] In the same spirit, in Dosi and Lovallo (1995), we argue that a good deal of evidence on corporate entry can be explained in terms of decision biases such as 'overconfidence' and 'illusion of control'.

analysis of the statistical conditions under which a heterogenous and messy microeconomics yields nonetheless relatively stable aggregate properties.[28]

VI. SELECTION DYNAMICS AND THE NOTION OF 'FITNESS'

I have already mentioned that an evolutionary interpretation of technical change (and more generally economic dynamics) has one of its building blocks in some selection process – whether it is done by markets or by other institutional arrangements (e.g. hospital authorities in the case of medical technologies, of defence ministries for military equipment...). Selection is important, of course, because agents are assumed to carry with them different technical and economic solutions to similar problems. Some of them turn out to 'get it right' and others to 'get it wrong'.

But what does 'wrong' or 'right' mean? The question bears, more technically, on the dimensions of the selection landscape and its functional form. Take the simplest case (which is not very far from the first generation of models in the NW mode) where technological search is about producing a homogeneous output as cheaply as one can, given input prices. Therefore, costs (or better the difference between industry-level output prices and firm-specific costs) define the selection landscape, which determines also the 'fitness' (and relatedly the potential to grow, shrink or die) of individual entities, and of the techniques that they embody. Assuming that innovative opportunities are notionally unlimited, and with some further restriction on the shape of the demand curve, it is easy to construct a landscape which has no fitness maximum (with costs that go to zero as time goes to infinity).

Note two things. First, at each arbitrary time the 'fitness' of individual entities or techniques is a contingent notion, because it depends on the distribution of all entities and techniques at that time, which in turn is the outcome of all the stochastic history of arrivals, plus selection, up to that time. Secondly, the implied idea of path-dependency is only a weak one, since one knows where the process will converge to in the limit, irrespectively of initial conditions. Moreover, given relative prices, one is able to say what is 'better' and what is 'worse' in a history-independent fashion (because that depends unequivocally on lower or higher costs of production).

This basic story, however, can be refined and easily take on board more path-dependent phenomena. For example, on the grounds of the same basic process, the interaction between search patterns and relative prices can produce long-term path-dependencies, e.g. whenever some initial input prices 'focus' search in a particular region of the technology space, which in turn affects search competences and probabilities of discovery the next round, etc.[29] In this example, and in many possible variations on the same theme, what can

---

[28] This links with the attempts of doing the same thing on the demand side: see the inspiring work by Hildebrand (1994).

[29] One cannot discuss here the formal issues involved in the different representations and their analytical tractability (for example the fact that the simpler dynamics described above can be sketched as a time-invariant Markov process, while time-invariancy is likely to be lost when accounting for many forms of path-dependent learning).

generate path-dependent trajectories of innovation is the local and cumulative nature of learning, involving dynamic increasing returns to particular bodies of knowledge. Still, one can have path-dependency on the learning side together with path-independent attributes of the various technologies over which selection operate.

The AD modelling style pushes path-dependency even further and implicitly suggests that both selection criteria and 'fitness landscapes' ought to be considered entirely endogenous: whether the technological winner turned out to be the internal combustion engine or the steam engine or the electrical car – so the story goes – depended primarily on a series of small events early on in the diffusion history, which got amplified by dynamic increasing returns. In these circumstances, of course, there is no way to define what is 'good' or 'bad', either for producers or adopters, without knowing the whole history of the process up to the time when the question is asked (and, even less so, ahead in time).

VII. DETECTING PATH-DEPENDENCE

How strong path-dependency is, to repeat, seems to me to be mainly an empirical question, and a major one for both economic historians and students of technology. There is, however, the tricky methodological issue of 'how do you recognise path-dependency when you see it?'. After all, we just observe *one* sample path, since we can only see the one history that actually occurred. And, of course, in order to know whether the occurrence of what you see now is path-dependent or not one ought to be able to 're-run history' repeatedly – which is very rarely the case in human affairs.[30]

An extreme perspective on this issue is what I shall provocatively call Mr Pangloss' view. Its main claim is the analytical irrelevance of the nature of the process leading to the observed state $s(t)$ of the system at t, in all circumstances when (a) that state is not remediable (in the sense that, at t, there is no state $s'(t)$ which is preferable and can be achieved with a net welfare gain), and (b) agents made the best use of their information along the whole path leading to $s(t)$. (A thorough presentation of the view is in Liebowitz and Margolis (1995), but of course the basics are already in Voltaire's *Candide*.) In this perspective the two main tasks of theorists and historians are, first, the rationalisation of whatever one observes as an equilibrium, and secondly, the attribution of rational purposefulness to all actions which led to the present state.[31]

The evolutionary view in most respects is the opposite one: it tries to understand the processes which have led to whatever observed phenomenon

---

[30] Dosi and Metcalfe (1991) discusses these issues at greater length.

[31] Note that even if one granted all that, path-dependency in the sense used in these notes cannot be ruled out at all: under conditions of network externalities, dynamic increasing returns, etc., individually purposeful decisions may collectively lead to both satisfactory outcomes or irremediable disasters.

And, more generally, what does it mean to be individually 'rational' in a path-dependent world (except for omniscient beings who know with infinite precision initials conditions and the full sequence of choices that all other agents will make)?

Note also that path-dependent worlds are likely to violate a notion much weaker than full forward-looking rationality, namely *no-regret* criteria: if I could go back (and, even more so, if we could collectively go back in time) would we have done something different? And the answer is possibly positive.

(with much lower commitments to rationality of the actors involved along the path), and, also with the help of formal tales, attempt counterfactual experiments ('what would have happened if...'). In doing that it also tries to establish, from a normative point of view, the leverages and 'windows of opportunities' – as Paul David puts it – for individual and collective actors to influence the selection of future paths.

VIII. SOME ISSUES AHEAD

Contrary to the rather pessimistic tone of Ruttan's essay, my assessment of the current state-of-the-art is the beginning of a very promising interaction between empirical analyses, 'appreciative theories' and formal modelling which is possibly going to bear fruits well outside the domain of technological change.

More than twenty years ago, when Chris Freeman was writing the first edition of his classic *Economics of Industrial Innovation*, he was correctly lamenting the poverty of empirical studies in the field. Now the situation is very different and, if anything, the bottlenecks are on the ability of the theory to digest observations and 'stylised facts'.

An illustrative example is growth theory. Despite the nearly universal recognition that 'knowledge is important', the ways knowledge-generation is generally accounted for is strikingly at odds with the evidence I tried to summarise earlier. New Growth models attack the issue more directly, and current evolutionary models, in my biased view, go even further (at the expense of elegance and analytical tractability). But still there is a long way to go in order to incorporate path-dependent learning, micro-heterogeneity, out-of-equilibrium interactions, etc. into a robust aggregate story of trade, growth, international convergence, divergence, forging ahead and falling behind (more on this in Dosi, Freeman and Fabiani (1994)).

Even more striking is macroeconomics (that area arbitrarily carved out of growth theory with the justification, in good Keynesian times, that it handled the 'short-term', and, nowadays, on the basic assumption that the future all the way to infinity is correctly understood by our representative agent). In this area, despite the general perceptions that technology (together with institutions) have a lot to do with the nature of macro adjustments – and *vice versa*, that macro variables influence the rates and directions of knowledge accumulation –, very little has been done so far to explore the implications of all that.

Similar considerations apply to the theory of industrial organisation: one is often struck by conflict between the acknowledgement of the empirical evidence and the baroque attempts to force it within an equilibrium/forward-looking strategic-rationality framework.

The list of examples is much longer. One of the points that I have tried to argue is that an interpretation of technological dynamics which significantly relaxes the commitments to equilibrium, rationality and inter-agent homogeneity is straightforwardly born by the current evidence, and is also beginning to generate formalised theoretical tales – with implications well beyond technical change itself, addressing basic issues like how the future is linked to the past, how individual (possibly mistaken-ridden) decisions aggregate into collective outcomes, and how problem-solving knowledge is accumulated in a society. I am not sure that nowadays younger generations of scientists have the 'Kuhnian' spirit of paradigm-subversion, the courage and the integrity to take up the challenge. But certainly there are enough empirical evidence and theoretical tools to begin with.

University of Rome 'La Sapienza' and University of Sussex

REFERENCES

Abramovitz, M. (1993). 'The search for the sources of growth: areas of ignorance, old and new.' *Journal of Economic History*, vol. 53, pp. 217–43.
Arrow, K. J. (1962). 'Economic welfare and the allocation of resources for invention.' In Nelson *et al.* (1962).
Arrow, K. J. (1974). *The Limits of Organisation*. New York: Norton.
Arrow, K. J. (1987). *Technical Information, Returns to Scale, and the Existence of Competitive Equilibrium*, Stanford, Stanford Institute for Mathematical Studies in the Social Sciences. Reprint Series, no. 385.
Arthur, B. W. (1989). 'Increasing returns and lock-in by historical events.' ECONOMIC JOURNAL, vol. 99, pp. 116–31.
Arthur, B., Ermoliev, Y. and Kaniovski, Y. (1987). 'Path-dependent processes and the emergence of macrostructures.' *European Journal of Operation Research*, vol. 30, pp. 294–303.
Atkinson, A. and Stiglitz, J. (1969). 'A new view of technological change.' ECONOMIC JOURNAL, vol. 79, pp. 573–578.
Chiaromonte, F. and Dosi, F. (1993). 'Heterogeneity, competition and macroeconomic dynamics.' *Structural Change and Economic Dynamics*, vol. 4, pp. 39–6.
Cohen, W. and Levinthal, D. (1989). 'Learning and innovation: the two faces of R & D.' ECONOMIC JOURNAL, vol. 99, p. 569
Cohen, W. (1995). 'Empirical studies of innovative activities.' In *Handbook of the Economics of Innovation and Technological Change* (ed. P. Stoneman). Oxford: Basil Blackwell.
Conlisk, J. (1989). 'An aggregate model of technical change.' *Quarterly Journal of Economics*, vol. 104, pp. 787–821.
Coriat, B. and Dosi, G. (1995). 'The institutional embeddedness of economic change. An appraisal of the 'evolutionary' and 'regulationist' research programmes.' IIASA Working Paper, WP-95-117, IIASA, Laxenburg, Austria.
David, P. (1975). *Technical Choice, Innovation and Economic Growth*. Cambridge: Cambridge University Press.
David, P. (1985). 'Clio and the economics of QWERTY.' *American Economic Review*, vol. 75, pp. 332–7.
David, P. (1988). 'Path-dependence: putting the past into the future of economics.' Stanford, Institute for Mathematical Studies in the Social Sciences, Technical Report 533.
David, Paul A. and Wright, Gavin (1997). 'Increasing returns and the genesis of American resource abundance.' *Industrial and Corporate Change* (forthcoming).
Day, R. and Eliasson, G. (1986). (eds.), *The Dynamics of Market Economies*. Amsterdam: North-Holland.
Dosi, G. (1982). 'Technical paradigms and technical trajectories, the determinants and directions of technical change and the transformation of the economy.' *Research Policy*. vol. 11, pp. 147–162.
Dosi, G. (1984). *Technical Change and Industrial Transformation*. London: Macmillan and New York: St. Martin's Press.
Dosi, G. (1995). 'The contribution of economic theory to the understanding of a knowledge-based economy.' IIASA, WP-56-95, Laxenburg, Austria; forthcoming. In *Knowledge, Employment and Growth* (ed. D. Foray and B. A. Lundvall). Paris: OECD, 1996.
Dosi, G. (1988). 'Sources, procedures and microeconomic effects of innovation.' *Journal of Economic Literature*, vol. 26, pp. 1120–71.
Dosi, G., Ermoliev, Y. and Kaniovski, Y. (1994). 'Generalized urn schemes and technological dynamics.' *Journal of Mathematical Economics*, vol. 23, pp. 1–19.
Dosi, G., Fabiani, S., Aversi, R. and Meacci, M. (1994). 'The dynamics of international differentiation. A multi-country evolutionary model.' *Industrial and Corporate Change*, vol. 3, pp. 225–42.
Dosi, G., Freeman, C. and Fabiani, S. (1994). 'The process of economic development. Introducing some stylized facts and theories on technologies, firms and institutions.' *Industrial and Corporate Change*, vol. 3, pp. 1–28.

Dosi, G., Freeman, C., Nelson, R. R., Silverberg, G. and Soete, L. (eds.) (1988). *Technical Change and Economic Theory.* London: Francis Pinter; New York: Columbia University Press.

Dosi, G. and Kaniovski, Y. (1994). 'On "badly-behaved" dynamics. Some applications of generalized urn schemes to technological and economic change.' *Journal of Evolutionary Economics*, vol. 4, pp. 93–123.

Dosi, G. and Lovallo, D. (1995). 'Rational entrepreneurs or optimistic martyrs? Some considerations on technological regimes, corporate entries and the evolutionary role of decision biases', Working Paper, IIASA, Laxenburg, Austria; forthcoming. In *Foresight and Oversight in Technological Change* (ed. R. Garud, R. Nayyar and Z. Shapiro). New York/Cambridge: Cambridge University Press, 1997.

Dosi, G., Marengo, L. and Fagiolo, G. (1996). 'Learning in evolutionary environments.' IIASA, WP-96-124, Laxenburg, Austria; forthcoming. In *Principles of Evolutionary Economics* (ed. K. Dopfer). Cambridge: Cambridge University Press.

Dosi, G., Marsili, O., Orsenigo, L. and Salvatore, R. (1995). 'Learning, market selection and the evolution of industrial structures.' *Small Business Economics*, vol. 7, pp. 411–36.

Dosi, G. and Metcalfe, S. (1991). 'On some notions of irreversibility in economics.' In Saviotti and Metcalfe (1991).

Dosi, G. and Nelson, R. R. (1994). 'An introduction to evolutionary theories in economics.' *Journal of Evolutionary Economics*, vol. 4, pp. 153–72.

Dosi, G., Pavitt, K. and Soete, L. (1990). *The Economics of Technological Change and International Trade.* Brighton: Wheatsheaf and New York: New York University Press.

Fleck, J. (1988). 'Innofusion or diffusation? The nature of technological development in robotics.' GSRC Programme on Information and Communication Technologies, University of Edinburgh, Working Paper.

Freeman, C. (1982). *The Economics of Industrial Innovation.* London: Francis Pinter, 2nd ed.

Freeman, C. (1994). 'The economics of technical change.' *Cambridge Journal of Economics*, vol. 18, pp. 463–514.

Freeman, C. and Perez, C. (1988). 'Structural crises of adjustment.' In Dosi *et al.* (1988).

Granstrand, O. (ed.) (1993). *The Economics of Technology.* Amsterdam/New York: North-Holland.

Grossman, G. N. and Helpman, E. (1991). *Innovation and Growth in the Global Economy.* Cambridge, MA: MIT Press.

Hildebrand, W. (1994). *Market Demand.* Princeton: Princeton University Press.

Hodgson, A. (1993). *Economics and Evolution.* Cambridge: Polity Press and Ann Arbor: University of Michigan Press.

Jovanovic, B. and MacDonald, G. M. (1994). 'The life cycle of a competitive industry.' *Journal of Political Economy*, vol. 102, pp. 322–47.

Klevorick, A. K., Levin, R. C., Nelson, S. and Winter, S. (1993). 'On the sources and significance of interindustry differences in technological opportunities.' New Haven: Yale University, Working Paper.

Kline, S. J. and Rosenberg, N. (1986). 'An overview of innovation.' In *The Positive Sum Strategy* (eds. R. Landau and N. Rosenberg). Washington, DC: National Academy Press.

Lane, D. (1993). 'Artificial worlds and economics.' Parts I and II. *Journal of Evolutionary Economics*, vol. 3, pp. 89–107 and 177–97.

Levin, R., Klevorick, A. K., Nelson, R. and Winter, S. (1987). 'Appropriating the returns from industrial research and development.' *Brookings Papers on Economic Activity*, pp. 783–820.

Levinthal, D. (1992). 'Surviving in Schumpeterian environments.' *Industrial and Corporate Change*, vol. 1, pp. 427–43.

Liebowitz, S. J. and Margolis, S. E. (1995). 'Path-dependence, lock-in and history.' *Journal of Law, Economics and Organization*, vol. 11, pp. 205–26.

Lundvall, B. A. (ed.) (1992). *National Systems of Innovation.* London: Francis Pinter.

Malerba, F. (1985). *The Semiconductor Business. The Economics of Rapid Growth and Decline.* Madison: University of Wisconsin Press.

Malerba, F. (1992). 'Learning by firm and incremental technical change.' ECONOMIC JOURNAL, vol. 102, pp. 845–59.

Malerba, F. and Orsenigo, L. (1996). 'The dynamics and evolution of industries.' *Industrial and Corporate Change*, vol. 5, pp. 51–87.

Metcalfe, S. (1995). 'The economic foundations of technology policy: equilibrium and evolutionary perspectives.' In *Handbook of the Economics of Innovation and Technological Change* (ed. P. Stoneman). Oxford: Basil Blackwell.

Montgomery, C. (ed.) (1995). *Resource-Based and Evolutionary Theories of the Firm.* Boston; Dordrecht; London: Kluwer.

Mowery, D. C. and Rosenberg, N. (1989). 'The influence of market demand upon innovation: a critical review of some recent empirical studies.' *Research Policy*, vol. 8, pp. 102–53.

Nelson, R. R. (ed.) (1962). *The Rate and Direction of Inventive Activity.* Princeton: NBER, Princeton University Press.

Nelson, R. R. (1981). 'Research on productivity, growth and productivity differences: dead ends and new departures.' *Journal of Economic Literature*, vol. 19, pp. 1029–64.

Nelson, R. R. and Winter, S. (1982). *An Evolutionary Theory of Economic Change.* Cambridge, MA: Bellkap Press of Harvard University Press.

Nelson, R. R. (ed.) (1993). *National Innovation Systems. A Comparative Study.* Oxford/New York: Oxford University Press.

Nelson, R. R. (1995). 'Recent evolutionary theorizing about economic change.' *Journal of Economic Literature*, vol. 33, pp. 48–90.

Romer, P. M. (1986). 'Increasing returns and long-run growth.' *Journal of Political Economy*, vol. 94, pp. 71–102.

Romer, P. M. (1990). 'Endogenous technical change.' *Journal of Political Economy*, vol. 98, pp. 71–102.

Romer, P. M. (1994). 'The origins of endogenous growth.' *Journal of Economic Perspectives*, vol. 8, pp. 3–22.

Rosenberg, N. (1976). *Perspectives on Technology.* Cambridge/New York: Cambridge University Press.

Rosenberg, N. (1982). *Inside the Black Box.* Cambridge/New York: Cambridge University Press.

Rosenberg, N. (1993). *Exploring the Black Box.* Cambridge/New York: Cambridge University Press.

Rosenberg, N. (1994). 'Science-technology-economy interactions.' In Granstrand (ed.) (1994).

Rosenberg, N. (1996). 'Uncertainty and technological change.' In *The Mosaic of Economic Growth* (ed. Ralph Landau, Timothy Taylor and Gavin Wright). Stanford: Stanford University Press.

Saviotti, P. and Metcalfe, S. (eds.) (1991). *Evolutionary Economics.* London/Chur: Harwood Academic Press.

Schmookler, T. (1966). *Invention and Economic Growth.* Cambridge, MA: Harvard University Press.

Silverberg, G., Dosi, G. and Orsenigo, L. (1988). 'Innovation, diversity and diffusion. a self-organisation model.' ECONOMIC JOURNAL, vol. 98, pp. 1032–54.

Silverberg, G. and Soete, L. (eds.) (1993). *The Economics of Growth and Technical Change: Technologies, Nations, Agents.* Aldershot: Edward Elgar.

Silverberg, G. and Verspagen, B. (1994). 'Learning, innovation and economic growth. A long-run model of industrial dynamics.' *Industrial and Corporate Change*, vol. 3, pp. 199–223.

Silverberg, G. and Verspagen, B. (1995). 'Evolutionary theorizing on economic growth', IIASA Working Paper, WP-95-78; forthcoming in (Dopfer, K., ed.), *The Evolutionary Principles of Economics.* Norwell, MA: Kluwer Academic Publishers.

Starbuck, W. H. (1993). 'Strategizing in the real world.' *International Journal of Technology Management*, vol. 8, pp. 77–85.

Teece, D., Rumelt, R., Dosi, G. and Winter, S. (1994). *Journal of Economic Behaviour and Organisation*, vol. 23, pp. 1–30.

Walsh, V. (1984). 'Invention and innovation in the chemical industry: demand pull or discovery push.' *Research Policy*, vol. 13, pp. 211–34.

Winter, S. G. (1975). 'Optimization and evolution in the theory of the firm.' In *Adaptive Economic Models* (ed. R. Day and Groves). New York: Academic Press.

Winter, S. G. (1986). 'The research program of the behavioural theory of the firm: orthodox critiques and evolutionary perspectives.' In *Handbook of Behavioural Economics* (ed. B. Gilad and S. Kaish). Greenwich, CT: JAI Press.

Winter, S. (1987). 'Knowledge and competences as strategic assets.' In *The Competitive Challenge. Strategies for Industrial Innovation and Renewal* (ed. D. J. Teece). Cambridge, MA: Ballinger.

PART II

ECONOMIC BEHAVIOURS, ORGANIZATIONS AND INNOVATION IN CHANGING ENVIRONMENTS

[5]

J Evol Econ (1991) 1:145–168

——Journal of——
Evolutionary
Economics
© Springer-Verlag 1991

Substantive and procedural uncertainty

An exploration of economic behaviours in changing environments

G. Dosi[1] and M. Egidi[2]

[1] University of Rome "La Sapienza", Rome, Italy and Visiting Fellow, SPRU, University of Sussex, Brighton, UK
[2] University of Trento, Italy

Abstract. Different sources of uncertainty are analysed and a representation of decision-making in principle consistent with behavioural evidence is proposed. The endogenous emergence of "innovations", in the forms of unexpected events and novel behaviours is also examined.

Key words: Innovation – Uncertainty – Problem-solving – Rationality

1. Introduction

In a very general sense, uncertainty in human behaviours stems from incompleteness of the knowledge necessary to forecast future events, undertake any one course of action and control its results. In order to analyse how economic agents behave under uncertainty, one obviously needs to understand how they can reduce their lack of knowledge. In turn, a central aspect of decision making under uncertainty concerns learning processes, involving also the ability of the economic agents of reducing their uncertainty by framing their choices.

Uncertainty may have two origins, i.e. 1) the lack of all the information which would be necessary to make decisions with certain outcomes, and 2) limitations on the computational and cognitive capabilities of the agents to pursue unambiguously their objectives, given the available information.

The former source of uncertainty comes from the *incompleteness of the information set*, and the latter from the inability of the agents to recognise and interpret the relevant information, even when available. In other words, from their *knowledge incompleteness* rather than information incompleteness.

Notably the traditional axiomatic approach to choice under uncertainty implicitly ignores the second of uncertainty: on the contrary, in this work we focus on this aspect of decision.

Of course, different environments and different decision problems entail also different forms of uncertainty of the two types. As a consequence, according to the circumstances, the agents may be expected to show different kinds of behaviours and different decisional procedures leading to these behaviours.

The traditional point of departure of the axiomatic theory of choice under uncertainty assumes that agents can exhaustively represent all possible events. As known, the theory defines the choice problem in terms of (1) a set of states of the world (or events), (2) actions, and (3) consequences of actions (conditional on the occurrence of each event). The decision problem is then formulated as the choice of the course of action which maximises some sort of goal (or utility) of the decision-maker given his beliefs on the probability distributions of the events [1].

Of course, the beliefs may not be correct and the model – in the case of repeated choices – involves the updating of the subjective probabilities, generally through Bayesian learning.

With respect to such as axiomatic decision theory, there are two sides to the work that follows, a critical one and a propositive one.

On the critical side, we shall argue that in the usual treatment of decision under uncertainty as a straightforward maximisation problem, seemingly innocent assumptions, such as the stationarity of the "world" and the competence of the agents to process the information that the world delivers, constrain its interpretative power to particular classes of decision problems.

On the propositive side, we shall suggest an interpretation of decision processes which holds also (indeed, especially) when environmental conditions or limitations on the "rational" capabilities of the agents (which we shall define) make the usual decision-theoretic models an inadequate representation of economic behaviours under uncertainty.

In Section 2 we shall analyse different sources of uncertainty which affect decisions and behaviours. Some of them can be treated within a maximising decision-theoretic framework, but some cannot. In particular, those cases which cannot be treated relate to environmental complexity or non-stationarity, on the one hand, and to the nature of the problem-solving which particular classes of decisions require, on the other.

In analogy with H. Simon's distinction between "substantive" and "procedural" rationality we shall introduce the notions of *substantive and procedural uncertainty*. The former is related to some lack of information about environmental events, while the latter concerns the competence gap in problem-solving. We shall argue that most cases of decisions involving procedural uncertainty cannot be dealt with on the grounds of the traditional decision theory. These cases include, we shall see, most things that have to do *lato sensu* with "innovation".

As a further point, we must acknowledge that theories of "rational" behaviour in economics are sometimes given a different epistemological status, namely as part of a positive theory of economic environments, used in order to define the equilibrium conditions of some variable (prices, quantitites, etc.), without, however, any assumption on the actual behaviour of individual agents. Thus, we must also discuss under what circumstances, "as ... if" assumptions on microeconomic behaviours are legitimate devices to analyse the state or dynamics of the economic system.

---

[1] The classical references are Arrow (1951, 1951 a, 1970, 1971), von Neumann and Morgenstern (1953), Savage (1954); for an overview of subsequent developments, Diamond and Rothschild (1978).

To what extent and under which circumstances can the market surrogate the (uncertainty-bound) fallibility of individual agents? We shall address this question in Section 3, concluding that the most circumstances actual (possibly, non-optimizing) behaviours do matter in terms of aggregate performance of the system.

Then, what do people actually do? How do they make their decisions, and which decisions do they make? In Section 4, we shall suggest a theoretical interpretation of behaviours in these circumstances. In particular, we shall analyse the relationship between decisions and problem-solving in environmental conditions where "uncertainty" stems indeed from the limitations intrinsic to the computational and recursive features of a "rational" decision process. We shall develop upon the notion of procedural rationality and make use of results of computation theory – especially those derived since the '30s by Turing, Markov and Godel in relation to the problem of formalisation of natural reasoning.

Our argument applies, first of all, to decisions and behaviours in environments where procedural and substantive uncertainty jointly appear.

In the framework that we propose, decisions are represented as specific problem-solving procedures in formal languages, which (1) are developed on the grounds of competences that logically pre-exist the acquisition of information from the environment; (2) involve particular rules for the search and selection of information; and, (3) can evolve, generating new languages and new behaviours.

Our interpretation seems quite consistent with the evidence on judgement and behaviour under risk and uncertainty from experimental psychology. Certainly, some of our predictions overlap with (and are distinguishable from) those of the "rational" decision-theoretic models. The simpler the environment or the decision problem, the more redundant our interpretation is (and the more parsimonious is the "rational choice" model). Conversely, the more complex the environment or the decision problem, the less adequate is the "rational" approach: with sufficient problem-solving complexity, the latter does not apply, either because it would be self-contradictory or because it would run against a finite computational limit of empirical agents.

In Section 5 we shall suggest some examples of empirical phenomena and theoretical fields to which our interpretation can be fruitfully applied. The theory of production, the theory of the firm and innovation belong to this category.

2. Nature of the uncertainty, information and choice procedures: substantive and procedural uncertainty

A very common metaphor of uncertainty, at least since the time of Bernoulli, is expressed in terms of flipping a coin, throwing dice, etc. The general applicability of the metaphor to other uncertain situations has been questioned, among others, by Knight, Keynes and Schackle. However, in somewhat more refined formulations, it underpins the general axiomatic model of choice under uncertainty. Flipping coins, gambling, weather forecasts or – in the economic domain – things like life insurance, etc. have some characteristics in common.

First, "events" are states of nature which can hardly be affected by the decision-maker (or, for that matter, other decision-makers). Second, the list of events is known (and preferably finite). Third, the process of attribution of consequences to actions and events is procedurally trivial (... if tomorrow it will rain my harvest will get wet ...; ... if I gamble on the red, and black comes out, I lose ...). Thus,

preferences, states of nature, actions, consequences are easily separable and procedurally can be easily mapped into each other. Uncertainty simply comes from
lack of information about the occurrence of future events. Using Heiner's terminology we have here an information gap, but no competence gap of the agents
(Heiner 1983, 1987). Call this case, *substantive uncertainty and procedural certainty*. An axiomatic theory of choice easily applies.

Consider now the case of a strategic interaction, say an n-person game. Suppose also that we (as analysts of that environment) know that all the usual
assumptions "objectively" hold: the rules of the game are given, there is a pay-off
matrix which depends on the states of nature and on the actions of the other
players. Theoretically, the uncertainty facing each agent strongly resembles that
of the former case, and in fact there is a strong theoretical resemblance between
the ways one generally treats "games against nature" and "strategic games".

Let us define *weak substantive uncertainty* (analogous to "risk") as all those
circumstances where uncertainty simply derives from lack of information about
the occurrence of a particular event within a known list of events, in principle
representable as a random drawing by "nature", with a certain known (or at least
knowable) probability distribution.

Consider next the case whereby the "events" are not in any proper sense
"states of nature" but are partly endogenous to the decision process of the agents,
so that events are not independent from actions. Here the metaphor of uncertainty in terms of random natural variables (the weather, etc.) is inappropriate
even as a theoretical approximation. We believe this to be a quite general case in
economic affairs: externalities, increasing returns, most forms of technical
change, path-dependent processes imply, to different degrees, endogeneity of
events and *bi-directional interactions between actions, events and outcomes*[2].

In particular consider the case of non-stationary environments, meaning environments that change, either endogenously or through exogenous shocks, their
structural characteristics (technology, tastes, commodities, etc.). Innovation is
obviously a phenomenon which implies non-stationarity. In turn, non-stationarity implies that each agent may expect an unknown number of unknown events
to occur in the future. Whether the agents interact in strategic fashion or perfect
competition prevails, endogeneity of events and non-stationarity introduce a
strategic dimension of a higher order in the decision process[3].

We define *strong substantive uncertainty* as all those cases involving unknown
events or the impossibility, even in principle, of defining the probability distributions of the events themselves.

Clearly, this latter notion of uncertainty closely resembles the earlier suggestions of Keynes, Knight and Schackle, and from a standard informational point,
involves near ignorance.

Note also that the boundaries between "weak" and "strong" uncertainty are
not so clear-cut. Einhorn and Hogarth fruitfully define a domain of ambiguity
defined as "... an intermediate state between ignorance (no distributions of ex-

---

[2] An appealing discussion of some cases is in Shelling (1978). Arthur (1985) and Silverberg,
Dosi, and Orsenigo (1988) formalise cases of environmental dynamics where this occurs; Silverberg (1988) discusses the general subject.
[3] Note, incidentally, that even under these conditions, experimental evidence shows significant
departures from "rationality": cf. Tversky and Kahnemann (1974, 1988), Hogarth and Reder
(1988); on some results of experimental economics interpretable – in our view – in this perspective, see Plott (1982), V. Smith (1982), Hey (1982).

pected probabilities of events are ruled out) and risk (all distributions but one are ruled out). Thus, ambiguity results from the uncertainty associated with specifying which of a set of distributions is appropriate in a given situation" (Einhorn and Hogarth 1988, p. 45).

So far, we have discussed different categories of uncertainty from a purely informational point of view, which we have called *substantive* forms of uncertainty. Indeed, this has also been the perspective in which its economic analysis has been mostly undertaken, generally limited to "weak" uncertainty, or risk.

Relatedly, a quite diffused theoretical presumption in the economic analysis of information is that agents make the best possible use of the available information, which is generally taken to mean both that they utilize maximisation procedures and that these procedures are somewhat "naturally" associated with their normal cognitive competences. That is, there is no competence gap in their *information processing*. We shall call all the conditions in which this applies as *procedural certainty*.

Of course, one can easily identify a lot of empirical circumstances characterized by weak substantive uncertainty *cum* procedural certainty. From gambling to deciding whether to subscribe an insurance, one can list several choices under uncertainty, whose procedures are nonetheless relatively trivial and can be theoretically assumed to be generally known[4].

However, even weak substantive uncertainty may well involve competence gaps, notwithstanding the availability of information which would theoretically allow a "rational" solution[5].

Experimental psychology has provided robust evidence on such departures from "rational" choice procedures essentially related to (1) the ways the problem is posed (whether it is "transparent" or "opaque"); (2) outcomes that are delayed and not easily attributable to particular actions; (3) variability in the environment which degrades the reliability of feedbacks, especially when outcomes of low probability are involved; (4) lack of information about the outcomes of other possible actions (Tversky and Kahnemann 1988, pp. 90–91).

Similar properties of choice under uncertainty can be analysed at a theoretical level. Consider, for example, the case of a strategic interaction whereby we (the analysts) can represent the decision problem within the axiomatic theory of choice. Suppose also that we know that some Nash-equilibria exist (because we have proved some theorem on their existence). Can we expect that, in general, the agents will actually behave according to the choice-theoretic model? A "rational" agent who knows the rules of the game and the list of state of nature would, of course, exhaustively explore all the decision tree, form his beliefs on the probability distributions of the states of nature and choose the strategy accordingly (the

---

[4] Note also that this case of procedural certainty is the only one where the analyst can, so to speak, interpret behaviours "working backward" (Arrow 1983, especially p. 23) from revealed actions to the agents beliefs and priors (on probability distributions, degrees of risk-aversion, etc.) and postulate a (conscious or "automatic") maximising choice, given the information structure and some generic goal (e.g. "make as much money as possible"). Finally, note that only with procedural certainty, maximisation and "revealed" consistency of plans may be considered to be equivalent.

[5] As an illustration, let us just recall the dramatic increase in computational complexity required to re-establish coherent plans after the re-opening of a spot market in an Arrow-Debreu-Hahn economy in inter-temporal equilibrium (Radner 1968). A fortiori the argument applies to our case.

von Neumann algorithm for a two-person game is the procedural representation of this process). However, the "rational" procedure may quickly run against the computational constraints of empirical agents.

Interestingly, computability may not only be a problem for empirical agents, but also for the theoretician: for example, Nash-equilibria may exist but may not be recursively realisable[6].

However, the complexity of the decision task (for example, many-person games, non-linearities in the relationships between events, actions and consequences, etc.) may easily determine a competence gap, in addition to the information gap associated with substantive uncertainty, and in addition to computational limitations. Heiner (1988) defines such a competence gap in terms of the difficulties of the agents to map information into the "true" events (that is, as a positive probability of "wrongly" interpreting an environmental message).

More generally, we propose that in most decision problems, "choice" is nothing but the terminal act of a problem-solving activity, preceded by the formulation of the problem itself, the identification of the relevant information, the application of pre-existing competences or the development of new ones to the problem solution and, finally, the identification of alternative courses of action.

In the analysis of this process, we suggest, the focus of the decision task is not on choice as such, but, rather, on problem-solving procedures. Building on Tversky and Kahnemann (1984) and (1988), we call "problem framing" all those activities leading from the identification of the problem to the selection of possible actions. Relatedly, we call cognitive competences the abilities of the agents to "frame" a decision problem and derive a course of action.

With the exception of the simplest decision tasks, nothing allows us to assume that the agents are naturally endowed with cognitive competences sufficient to the identification of solutions of a particular problem, let alone the "optimal" ones. Neither, can one assume that such competences are uniformly distributed amongst the different agents.

We shall define all those circumstances whereby the solution of choice problems is constrained by the computational and cognitive capabilites of the agents as characterized by *procedural uncertainty*.

With both substantive and procedural uncertainty, the agents will certainly try to find "rational" procedures, in the sense of Simon (1957) and (1959), but "rational" may not mean more than robust and computationally efficient. Typically, one is likely to find relatively stable "rules", and, indeed, Heiner has shown that whenever any competence gap exists, routinized behaviours are more efficient than optimizing procedures (Heiner 1983, 1988).

Are these "rules", whatever they are, approximations to an optimising behaviour? *Prima facie* the answer is that this will depend on the nature of the environment and the decision problem. Winter (1988) quotes Schumpeter arguing that this is likely to occur only when "things have had time to hammer logic into men". Certainly, necessary conditions are environmental stationarity, persistence of near-equilibrium conditions and existence of a computable optimal procedure. In turn, these conditions are a sub-set of those which arise under weak substantive uncertainty (risk).

---

[6] For a thorough formal analysis of the choice functions which are effectively computable from a theoretical point of view, see A. Lewis (1985, 1986).

More so, strong substantive uncertainty will always be associated with procedural uncertainty. In non-stationary environments, agents are always bound to try to understand – via procedures that almost by definition cannot be derived from the information delivered by the markets – future behaviours of other agents or future events that had never occurred in the past [7]. Those same capabilities which allow some agents to generate unforeseeable changes (e.g., developing a new product, opening a new market, etc.) are endogenous sources of uncertainty for the other agents.

Note that non-stationary environments may not be generally expected to satisfy the completeness-of-events description, and moreover can give rise to *computational failures* of the agents.

Under these circumstances, we suggest, the usual axiomatic theory of choice is neither an approximation to empirical behaviours nor a legitimate theoretical "stylisation". Not only will agents not behave as literal maximisers, but it will be impossible to construct a theoretical model based on maximising agents, since the theory should construct a model where events are conditional on unknown (unpredictable) behaviours, and, of course, behaviours are also conditional on expectations on events. An infinite regress. Indeed, the very notion of "optimality" becomes an ambiguous theoretical notion.

In these cases, substantive and procedural sources of uncertainty are obviously related. Very little of the "mechanical" nature of the decision process is left.

A typical maximisation problem under uncertainty in standard decision theory is a well structured problem with a well defined solution and a known algorithm leading to it. On the contrary, in the situations we are considering here, one often finds ill-structured problems, which – irrespective of the actual information available and the actual computational complexity – continuously require also the generation of "representations" (models) of the world and models for the analysis and solutions of problems. Expanding upon Simon (1957), we suggest that this is the general case underlying choice/action in most empirical economic environments. Strong procedural uncertainty implies that the main activities involved in the process leading to action are neither choice (in the sense of some kind of comparison among well-defined alternatives) nor updating of probability distributions of know random variables (via some sort of Bayesian procedure), but model-building and problem-solving.

Under these circumstances, a positive theory of decision and behaviour entails the analysis of problem-solving procedures and of the forms of knowledge underlying it. Before turning to these issues, however, let us consider to what extent, in such decision processes, markets can surrogate the agent fallibility.

3. Rational choice as an analytical device, or, can the market surrogate individual fallibility under uncertainty?

The empirical evidence on economic behaviours, it is often conceded, is messy and subject to various sorts of disturbances. Especially under uncertainty, people may

---

[7] Possibly the extreme attempt of applying a "rational" choice theoretic model, while recognising the requirement of some sort of "special skills" in information processing and decision-making, is Stiglitz (1986), where maximising agents "learn to learn". However, the "orthodox agent" faces the same problems of procedural uncertainty discussed here also at the second order information-processing, and so on: an infinite regress is unavoidable.

well make mistakes on their expected probability distributions and in their actions; indeed, they may not literally maximise (in the sense that they do not consciously go through the decision procedures outlined, say, in Arrow (1951 a)) but follow different kinds of – more or less automatic – "rules". However, it is sometimes argued, the standard representation of agents as literal maximisers (and, perhaps, learners in the sense of Bayes' theorem) still retains a useful theoretical content since it underpins the analysis of the equilibrium states which characterise the system (the obvious implication being that these states are attained irrespectively of the procedures through which empirical agents make their decisions). In the economic literature, one finds three major arguments in favour of this "as ... if" assumption, namely:

1. Behaviours may neither come close to literal maximisation in terms of decision procedures, nor even in terms of choices and actions that are undertaken, but markets perform as selection environments so that in the asymptotic state of the system only "maximisers" survive, whether they know to be maximisers or not (see in particular Alchian 1950 and Friedman 1953). This is clearly the strongest version of the "as ... if" hypothesis.
2. The actual attempts of empirical agents to make the best use of the available information are such that the maximising choice-theoretic models can be considered as approximations to empirical behaviours. However, with uncertainty, information is imperfect and possibly asymmetric, agents hold different beliefs and "priors", and their knowledge of the future is limited. They can interpret correctly the signals that they receive (and try to do so), but they do not receive all the signals necessary to make those optimal choices that would have been taken under perfect information. The markets surrogate – to greater or lesser extents – the fallibility of individuals in so far as they allow the exchange of commodities (and claims on them) contingent on particular events. This is of course the theoretical approach of contemporary General Equilibrium Analysis (as in Arrow and Hahn 1971).
3. Empirical behaviours may well show "rules" with varying degrees of automaticity: thus, the actors may not be procedurally maximisers. However, their behaviour may still be fruitfully represented in the standard choice-theoretic way, in so far as the observed "rules" are those which actually lead to optimal actions (see Machlup 1946 and Friedman 1953) (Of course, point (3) may well overlap with point (2), and also coincide with point (1), whenever the world is in that particular "selection equilibrium").

The "as ... if" assumptions have been critically discussed, in a perspective which we broadly share, in Nelson and Winter (1982) and Winter (1986 and 1988). Here, we shall simply recall some theoretical properties and results which will be useful for our subsequent argument. Of course, the strongest version of the "as ... if" argument is sub (1). In order to substantiate that claim one would ideally need a proof of global stability of the equilibrium model that one is talking about. Lacking that (as one does), one would need at least proofs of local stability of a sufficiently small number of equilibria under rather general conditions and some rather robust ideas on the nature of the adjustment process leading there. In general, none of these has been provided, neither with respect to the level of analysis which is proper to this conjecture, i.e., General Equilibrium, nor even in selection environments where agents do behave rationally and strategically (for a discussion, see Silverberg 1988). At the very least, one should show that the end point(s) of an unspecified market process (the "as ... if" equilibria) are recursively realisable, which, note, is a much less demanding proof than global stability. Loosely speaking, it simply requires the existence of a finite logical process leading from individual preferences, etc. to the aggregate outcomes: however, exactly the opposite has been proved (Lewis 1986).

Take this argument the other way round: since the strongest version of the "as ... if" hypothesis does not hold, some characterisation of actual behaviours is required, because particular types of microeconomic decision processes and actions do affect the states which the system attains: in fact, a widening theoretical literature shows that equilibria are often path-dependent, behaviour-dependent and institution-dependent.

Consider now the heuristic status and the theoretical domain of applicability of the "weaker" "as ... if" assumption, sub point (2) and, to some extent, (3), above. That approach entails "uncertainty", meaning the lack of part of the relevant information about the occurrence of future events; complete procedural rationality (the agents solve without particular difficulties the computational problems involved in the relevant choice/action task) and, finally, markets which surrogate fallibility by trading "conditional commodities". Of course, the obvious boundary on its positive applicability is the existence of the complete set of future markets, which we all know are in fact very rare. However, this is not our point. Consider, indeed, the case when all future markets exist, contingent on the complete set of known events (which are random variables) and known commodities. Even in this case, the "surrogation" of individual fallibility via the market holds under the strict condition that no unpredictable change is allowed to occur in the future, and this must be also believed by the agents. (In this respect change may be a new commodity, a new technology, etc.) To illustrate it, suppose that, on the contrary, new commodities (or technologies) may appear. Then, we have two possibilities.

First, one may add from the start to the commodity space and the event space the "unknown" dimensions corresponding to the exogenous future "shocks". In other words, it must be possible to (and indeed the agents must – consciously or "automatically") represent a terminal economy, T, whose commodity space N' strictly includes the initial space N, containing n'-n "present" commodities (here, meaning, simply, commodities that exist also at the present). However, this implies a "complete future" which exhausts all humanly conceivable possibilities. In turn, this takes away a lot of the "exogeneity" and randomness of future changes. In a sense, as Winter (1988) puts it quoting the Ecclesiastes, one must assume (both the theoretician and the agent) that "there is no new thing under the sun".

Second, and alternatively, one may postulate that the economy is sequential, so that, in each period, new events, new technologies, new commodities are generated, through, say, a random draw from a quite wide and largely unknown set. Thus, starting from the initial economy, one would generate sequences of economies characterised by an increasing number of "dimensions" (in the commodity-space, the event-space, etc.), without a unique terminal economy. Thus, one would have to represent the future (the "terminal economy") in a space with infinite dimensions[8]. Though this might not be a problem from a mathematical

---

[8] A "sequential" approach to economic analysis has recently produced interesting insights into economic dynamics characterised by unpredictable technological change (see Amendola and Gaffard 1988).

point of view, it is certainly one from the point of view of the "rationality" of individual agents, since at each step of an infinite sequence they must be able to recognise correctly "the new": for example, they must be able to recognise a "new event", even if, of course, they could still be "uncertain" on its probability distribution.

Under both these theoretical alternatives, uncertainty about the possibility of something new (new commodities, technologies, etc.) seems hardly reconcilable with the "maximising rationality plus market surrogation" hypothesis. In the former case, one must drastically reduce the domain of "newness" to an identifiable set of possible events. Whether they are finite or not, the set must be complete and "realisable". In the latter case, the constraint is on the computational and interpretative capabilities of the agents: a sequential economy, which the agents know it is sequential, impose on each "rational" agent an increasing (quickly, an infinite) computational burden and/or require some "hidden" or "creative" capability of recognising "newness", which certainly the decision-theoretical model does not specify.

This is the fundamental point. Irrespective of whether or not contingency markets empirically exist, the domain of theoretical applicability of an axiomatic theory of "rational choice" is that whereby uncertainty regards incomplete information about the occurrence of a *known list* of events [9].

In other words, axiomatic representations of microeconomic behaviours under uncertainty as straightforward "rational choice" problems are theoretically legitimate (irrespectively of the existence of the relevant contingency markets), only under suitable (and quite strong) restrictions on the nature of uncertainty itself and on the nature of the choice-problem. Thus, one should, first, assess the sources and nature of uncertainty in different choice settings. Second, "[a]n analysis of behaviour under uncertainty must answer [the following] questions": (i) how are uncertain prospects formulated by the unit of decision? (ii) How does the actual occurrence of contemplated events affect the estimation of prospects? ... (iii) How is the choice between uncertain prospects arrived at?" (Hahn 1985, p. 211). We add, (iv) how does the possibility of uncontemplated events affect behaviours? Putting it another way, "How is knowledge acquired? ... How is knowledge acted upon?" [Ibid.]. These are precisely the issues we shall discuss in the following.

4. Procedural uncertainty: representation, interpretation, rules and problem-solving

In order to highlight the fundamental problem-solving nature of the decision process with procedural uncertainty, let us consider first those simplest cases where uncertainty emerges only as a result of the complexity of the decision task, despite substantive certainty (that is, despite complete information on "events").

---

[9] Another way of interpreting the foregoing argument is with reference to Shackle's view of uncertainty (Shackle 1969) in terms of ignorance about "residual" events and (related) "surprise". Katzner (1986) shows that a behavioural theory of "surprise" (with unknown events) cannot be reduced (i.e., is not formally equivalent to) an axiomatic theory of choice with subjective probabilities about a known list of events. As one shall see, that interpretation of behaviours under uncertainty is easily consistent with our argument and, indeed, possibly also a fruitful conjecture on the empirical regularities in signal-detection and response under several uncertainty conditions.

Take strategic games with complete and perfect information (chess, nim, etc.) and also "puzzles" (e.g., Rubik cube).

In these strategic games and puzzles the procedure of search for a strategy (a winning one in the former case, an efficient one in the latter) may be represented by formal rules. We have "states" or "configurations" (the position of the various pieces on the chess-board, the position of the different colours on each side of the Rubik cube, etc.) and we have "rules" – perfectly known to the players – for the transformation of one state into another one. Each player must solve the problem of choosing a strategy made of a sequence of transformations leading from the initial state to the desired one (Nillson 1980). Reaching a (the) winning configuration is generally a complex procedure, given the high number of combinatorial possibilities ("states") that may be generated and must be examined (this applies to both strategic games and puzzles like the Rubik cube).

In two-persons games a winning strategy for either player exists, and, as already mentioned earlier, may be expressed through the well-known von Neumann algorithm. However, such an algorithm requires the generation of all the game-tree and creates problems of computational complexity. The same holds for puzzles, like the Rubik cube. An algorithm for the generation of all final states starting from any initial (scrambled) one exists. In fact, as we shall see later, there are more than one.

Suppose however that an agent faces a *new* problem: say, he is given for the first time a Rubik cube, taught the rules and told the solution concept.

He can follow three procedures, namely:

1. Explore extensively the game-tree according to a general search algorithm (Nillson 1971) (assuming that this does not exceed his computational capabilities). Remarkably, this is the procedure which in general would correspond to that implied by standard maximising choice-theoretic models. Call this as the *orthodox player*. As well known, an agent behaving accordingly with the procedure may easily fail to reach the task, because of the high computational effort and memory storage generally required.
2. Use locally the algorithm orienting the search through *ad hoc* criteria. He will examine sub-trees and attribute empirical static evaluators to the intermediate positions (states) that are reached. This is the way many people seem to play, for example, chess. It is also the way "artificial players" do it (i.e., chess-playing computer programmes). Finally, it is the way that, in the economic literature, the "bounded rationality" of empirical agents is often interpreted, as an approximation – imperfect for quantitative limitations on computational capabilities – to the complete rationality of the choice-theoretic model (see, for example, Baumol and Quandt 1964). Call this the *satisficing player*.
3. Try to find a new problem-specific algorithm. He will temporarily give up the solution of the problem and try to solve sub-problems, moving in the sub-problem space, i.e., attempt to create new representations of the problem (Newell & Simon 1972). The problem is posed in a very incomplete way (a rather limited number of positions is explored), and the actual sequence of configurations may be redundant (an analyst with the unlimited computational capability apt to pursue procedure (1) could find a shorter sequence), but the level of abstraction is higher than that of both the orthodox and the satisficing players: the problems that he tries to solve do not hold only for a specific state but for an entire class which share the same property. Call this the *innovative player*.

As we will see in the following, neither of the three procedures can be considered "the best", independently from the nature and conditions of the game (e.g., the complexity of the game-tree, its rules, the number of times that the game is played, etc.). Moreover, it is in principle impossible to establish *ex-ante* (even for an external analyst, more so for the players) whether a procedural choice is better than another one, e.g., in terms of time and costs of search. The knowledge of the set of events which must be generated or explored is necessarily incomplete and so also is the knowledge of the elements which will lead to the solution (types of mental operations, transformation sequences, time, etc.).

Formally, procedures (1) and (2) do not present particular problems of interpretation. However, procedure (3) does involve somewhat subtle issues related to knowledge and capabilities that the agent must pre-possess and that cannot be derived from what he was told on the rules of the game, the solution concepts, etc. In order to analyse them, it might be worthwhile to describe briefly how the "solution of problems" can represented in formal terms.

Let us assume that the problems are representable in an appropriate formal language. First, each subject (agent) will pre-possess a set of elementary symbols, such as the words in language through which the problem can be described. In the case of the Rubik cube, the elementary symbols may represent the little coloured squares of which the cube is made. A sequence of these symbols, a string, will represent a configuration (a state) of the cube. Second, there are transformation rules, through which each phrase of the language, each string, can be modified to generate other strings. In our example, the rules specify how to rotate the mobile parts of the cube. Solving the problem (reaching the solution) means finding a sequence of transformations which get to a final given state. Thus the agents must have the capability of exploring the tree generated from the initial configuration by applying the transformation rules. The initial string may be formally called an "axiom", in the sense of Computation Theory, since it is the only initial "postulation" from which the strings (theorems) that belong to the system are generated (see for example Cutland 1980).

Let us summarise the main characteristics of the problem-solving framework that we have defined for strategic games and puzzles. We may establish: (1) an alphabet $S = (A, B, C, D \ldots)$ whose strings depict states or configurations of the problem (states of the game); (2) some rules of transformation which act upon the strings of alphabet S, each of which is symbolised by a latter of a second alphabet $P(= a, b, c, d \ldots)$.

One usually indicates with S^* the set of all the strings of finite length that can be constructed with letters of alphabet S, and with P^* the set of all the strings of finite length that can be constructed with letters of alphabet P.

Note also that to pass from a position $s_1 \in S^*$ of the problem to another state $s_2 \in S^*$ it is necessary to write a sequence of P symbols, which constitutes a *procedure* describing the solution of the game (we will term such procedures as *routines* of *programmes*).

It is easy to recognise that in general not all the sequences of P^* constitute a programme, because there will be sequences which one cannot apply to certain configurations of the problem. The set of admissible sequences or programmes, i.e. those sequences that can be applied to a state of the game to produce a new position, constitute a *formal language*.

Any strategic situation which can be described in the normal terminology of games theory can be translated into the terms of a formal language. Such a language which characterises it is defined by the set of all the programmes which can be put into practise in the context of the given strategic situation.

In fact, what we have described is a special case of a *Post axiomatic system*. All puzzles (like the Rubik cube) can be represented as Post systems, i.e., can be interpreted in a problem-solving specific framework [10]. Moreover, we can represent the problem of finding a strategy in a game (with two or more players) by means of a Post System.

Having posed a problem, if a solution exists, will there be a programme (procedure) that represents that solution? How can one reach such a procedure?

Recall the Rubik cube. The initial position is given by chance and the transformation rules are elementary rotations around the vertical and horizontal axes. The solution is a sequence apt to reach a final configuration. Consider the solution procedures of the "orthodox", "satisficing" and "innovative" players. The "orthodox" one will orderly examine all the possible sequences, i.e., will write all the possible procedures which can be generated from the initial position. Obviously, he needs sufficient memory in order to compare the new sequences with the previous ones and avoid the generation of an infinite tree. The "satisficer" will basically follow the same procedure but explore only a limited number of branches of the tree and perhaps "stop" and "go back" according to ad hoc evaluators. The "innovative" player will try to reach a more synthetic representation of the problem and a more powerful language (which implies more general transformation rules). When the search is successful, this reduces the procedural uncertainty by reducing the computational complexity of the problem.

Let us analyze how this task can be performed, by way of an illustration. Consider an hyper-simplified Rubik cube made of two juxtaposed squares (back and front). Each square is composed of four elements (four little squares) of four different colours. Denote the colours as A, B, C, D. Each element has the same colour in the front and in the back. Adopt the convention of calling the position of an element, clockwise from the top-left element as 1, 2, 3, 4. So, for example, the string ABCD represents a configuration where colour A is in position 1, B in position 2, etc. The rules of transformation are rules of 180 degrees rotation around the two axes with four possibilities, "up" (u) (rotation of the top half of the square around the vertical axis); "down" (d) (rotation of the bottom half around the vertical axis); "left" (l) (rotation of the left half of the square around

---

[10] Let $\Sigma = \{a_1, a_2, \ldots a_n\}$ be a finite set of symbols, called an *alphabet*. A *string* from Σ is, as we previously stated, any sequence $a_{i1}, a_{i2}, \ldots a_{in}$ of symbols from Σ. For any alphabet Σ we denote as Σ^* the set of all the strings from Σ. Let $S, S_1, \ldots S_n$ be strings from Σ^*. Post called *Production* a general rule of transformation between strings, which takes the form

(a) $g_1 S_1, g_2 S_2, \ldots g_{m-1} S_{m-1}, g_m S_m \rightarrow h_1 S_{i1}, h_2 S_{i2}, \ldots h_n S_{in}$

where

(i) $g_1, g_2, \ldots g_m, h_1, h_2 \ldots h_n$ are given (fixed) strings
(ii) the subscript $i_1, i_2, \ldots$ in stand for strings all derived from 1, 2, ... m and which need not to be distinct.

A Post (canonical) system consists of

(1) a finite alphabet Σ
(2) a finite subset of Σ^*, (the subset A of the *axioms*)
(3) a finite set of *Productions* of the form (a) above, whose fixed strings are in Σ^*. It can be shown that a system of Post is equivalent to a Turing machine (Cutland 1980, 3rd chapter; M. Minsky 1967).

Rules of transformation

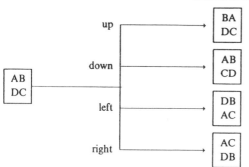

Fig. 1

the horizontal axis); "right" (r) (rotation of the right half of the square around the horizontal axis). Of course, with each rotation, half of the back face comes to the front, and vice versa. The game is easily represented in a system of Post. Each string with the four letters (symbols) A, B, C, D is a configuration of the game. For example, reading clockwise, the string ABCD is depicted in Fig. 1.

One can easily see that each transformation exchanging adjacent letters is admissible (e.g., ABCD into DCBA). One can also consider as adjacent the first and the last letter of each string, by representing each string on a ring divided in four sections. Thus we have:

(1) an axiom, say, an initial position ABCD
(2) the rules of transformation. The are
   a) exchanges between adjacent letters:

      ABCD → BACD (by applying the up rule)
      ABCD → ACBD (left)
      ABCD → ABDC (down)

   b) exchanges between the leftmost and the rightmost letter

      ABCD → DBCA (right)

(3) An objective: a certain arbitrary final configuration.

A procedure (a programme) establishes a sequence of transformations (for example **rrlul**). Each procedure can be obtained by combining the four elementary procedures, **u, d, l, r**.

Consider in detail the strategy of the "innovative player". Suppose he faces with the following:

Problem 0: ⟨reach the configuration ABCD starting from any one scrambled configuration⟩

This problem can be immediately divided into the following sub-problems:

(1) move A from the initial position in the string to position 1 (top left)
(2) examine the element in position 3 (bottom right). If it is not C, then move C (which can only be in positions 2 or 4) to position 3
(3) if B and D are not in the required places 2 and 4, exchange them.

In order to solve the sub-problems 1 he must solve the following:

(a) Move a colour from any one position to any other position. This involves in turn sub-problems, i.e., (a1) move a colour to an adjacent position, and (a2) move a colour to the diagonal opposite position on the square.

Programmes with length one (**u, d, l, r**) solve the first sub-problem. Obviously, one solves the second by applying the first transformation twice (hence, procedures of length two, e.g. **ud, ul, …**). Note that repetitive procedures (**uu, dd, …**) do not yield any configuration change and the procedures **ud, lr, rl, du** invert the square to its symmetric opposite. Call all the procedures which solve problem (a) *adjacent change routines*.

The problem (a) is now reduced to elementary sub-problems which can be solved with *adjacent change routines*. Problem (2) is trivially solved by an adjacent change routine.

Sub-problem (3) can be solved if the player is able to:

(b) Exchange two colours along a diagonal *leaving the rest unchanged*. In turn this involves two sub-problems, i.e., first, (b1) exchange along the north-west/south-east diagonal, and (b2) exchange along the north-east/south-west diagonal.

One can easily see that the procedures **uru** and **dld** solve the first sub-problem and the procedures **ulu** and **drd** solve the second one. Call all the procedures which solve problem (b), *diagonal routines*.

Finally, the player has reduced the original problem to a set of sub-problems which can easily be solved by means of simple routines. It is easy to recognize that any problem like Problem 0 can be solved by a combination of the routines (procedures) which solve problems (a) and (b).

Let us verify this "theorem", supposing for simplicity that we want to transform any initial scrambled configuration into the final configuration ABCD.

Starting from the scrambled configuration, move A into position 1 (top left). In order to do so, use the adjacent change routines. Then examine the element in position 3 (bottom right). If it is not C, then move C (which can only be in positions 2 or 4) to position 3 using an adjacent routine (**d** or **r**). Finally, if B and D are not at the desired place, use the diagonal routines **ulu** or **drd**. Thus, by simply using the two ("adjacent" and "diagonal") routines, it is possible to obtain the solution, ABCD, or whatever other desired final configuration.

The entire class of problems of reaching a final configuration starting from a scrambled one is then solved by *recursive decomposition* of the original problem in sub-problems.

However, one must notice that this is not the only way to solve them. We leave to the reader the demonstration that the same result (e.g., configuration ABCD) can be obtained by decomposing the original problem into the following sub-problems:

(1) Move A to position 1 with adjacent routines;
(2) Move B to position 2 with adjacent routines, leaving A in position 1.
(3) If C and D are not in the required place, exchange them using the adjacent routine d.

Note that in this case the routines are not the same as the previous "theorem": no use is made of "diagonal routines" but only a sequence of "adjacent routines".

It is important to notice that the analysis of the problem has led to a new, more synthetic, representation of the same problem. The *solution of the sub-problems led in fact to the construction of routines, that are the building-blocks of a new, more abstract, language.* In addition to the elementary routines **u, d, l, r** – defined earlier – we can define:

q (= **ulu** = **drd** = **rur** = **ldl**)
(exchange of colours on the right diagonal)

w (= **uru** = **dld** = ...)
(exchange of colours on the left diagonal)

v (= **uu** = **dd** = ...)
(null operation)

s (= **ud** = **lr** = ...)
(specular inversion of the entire square)

The new routines define new "elementary transformations" whose combinations easily allow *any* problem of the class of the previous Problem 0 to be solved and also the general Problem 00: ⟨transform any initial scrambled configuration into any final configuration⟩.

Note that starting from the original system which operated on strings like ABCD, etc., we have defined a new set of transformation rules by means of an "intelligent", *inductive* procedure based on problem decomposition. This new language is able to represent the original problem in a more tractable fashion, from the point of view of its complexity.

As we have seen, there are at least two different ways to decompose the original problem, and consequently players can generate at least two different languages. How can a player find a "good" decomposition? Is there a general algorithm which allows us to decompose a problem? Are there many different algorithms for the decomposition such that we can choose the best one?

To answer these questions, let us recall that what we have described is a special example of a Post axiomatic system, i.e., a system which generates "theorems" (new strings of characters) from "axioms" by the application of "transformation rules". Post used it to describe the working of a *formal logical system*. Puzzles are special examples of Post systems: then, the properties of Post systems can be applied to them and generally to any formalized problem-solving framework.

In general, one can formalize the notion of *problem solving* by means of Post system: solving a problem is simply to reach a final configuration starting from a given one. If it is possible to transform the latter into the former by means of repeated applications of the transformation rules – as in the Rubik simplified puzzle – then one obtains the solution of the problem: one is able to write a "programme".

However, a fundamental implication of the equivalence between a Post system and a Turing machine (see for example (Cutland 1980; Traktenbrot 1963) is that to both applies the so-called *unsolvibility* of *the word problem*, i.e.: Given two strings from the same alphabet, and a finite set of transformation rules, there is *no* general algorithm that can say if the two strings *are* derivable one from the other or not.

Here a "general algorithm" means an algorithm valid for any possible Post system. As in the previous example, it is possible to solve the *word problem* for a specific Post system, or a set of them; but not for the entire class of Post systems.

It follows that it is impossible to generate a programme which solves a given formalized problem by using a general problem-solver algorithm. In other words, the players who look for efficient algorithms for the solution of specific games *cannot draw on general rules for construction of algorithms, because they do not and cannot exist.*

This is the intrinsic element of procedural uncertainty. In a general problem-solving framework one does not know and cannot know *ex-ante* which or how many algorithms can be generated, or if they can be generated at all. Relatedly, this search for new algorithms involves "true" uncertainty and cannot be simply interpreted as "risk" with a cost and a probability of success.

As a consequence of all this, the main characteristics of the problem solving search, when successful, are the following:

(1) It produces routines which apply to entire classes of problems (they are higher-level rules of transformation).
(2) There may be more than one routine (more than one sequence of elementary operations) which solve the problem. Generally, it is impossible to establish which one is "better" independently from the initial configuration of the problem.
(3) Even if the routines are "derived" from the original system, there is no general algorithm of derivation. That is, the procedure of derivation cannot be automatised.

Let us discuss some consequences of these results in terms of "rational" decision making. We have argued earlier that the theoretical boundary of applicability of a rational choice-theoretical model as a positive theory of behaviour is set by the recursive computability of choice functions. It has been shown (Lewis 1985, 1986) that this condition may not be expected to hold in general also in stationary environments (General Equilibrium models, certain Nash-type models of strategic interaction).

Further restrictions emerge if we formalise the decision problem in a general problem-solving framework: since the problem of generating a solution for *any* class of problems is unsolvable one must also rule out the possibility of automatically deriving uniform decision rules from a general principle of "rationality". Many classes of problems are of course solvable, but any new class (not included in a previously solved one) requires a solution which can be found only by means of an *inductive search process.*

What do people generally do, then? They use routines which imply "higher level" representations of the problem, de-composition into familiar sub-problems, powerful "rules of transformation" that lead from the information about "the problem" to its "solution" (i.e., to the decision) and that do not only apply to single problems but to entire classes of them.

As we saw, in a general problem-solving framework even when "routines" are "derived" from the original information about the problem, they entail more "information" than that contained in its original formulation. Their "derivation" involves some inductive ability – which the agent must possess – of generating new knowledge which is not contained in the original information.

In line with the description of discovery as a result of a search in the problem-space (Simon 1981), we suggest that this behaviour, based on higher-level representation of problems and routines, can be generally attributed also to the problem-solving/decision activity of economic agents.

Of course, the agents most often use these routines automatically. Indeed, their efficiency and their robustness stems partly from the very fact that they can be used automatically. However, repetition automates an original "creative" act. If we are allowed a metaphor, "mechanical stupidity" hints at an original product of intelligence[11]. "Routinised" decision processes – in the sense discussed here – reduce procedural uncertainty. Further, the more general the routines are, the more capable they are to deal with variations in the nature of the problem to be solved (i.e., the class of problems that they can efficiently tacke is wide). With sufficient "generality" or "abstraction" they can tackle ill-structured problems which typically arise with strong substantive uncertainty (defined earlier). Conversely, the search for new routines is, as argued, characterised by an intrinsic procedural uncertainty.

Whether the choice/behaviour which one can expect on the grounds of our interpretation correspond to that which could be predicted on the grounds of the "rational" choice theoretic-model (within the limits of its applicability) depends on the nature of the decision-problem. Of course, the nearer one gets to substantive certainty, computational simplicity and tautology, the more likely it is that the two coincide. In the other cases, there is no a priori reason to expect that they generally will. The foregoing interpretation of the relationship between various forms of uncertainty and decision-making, we believe, has important implications in terms of economic analysis. We shall briefly consider some examples in the following section.

5. Routines, production and innovation

One of the direct applications of this analysis of behaviours under substantive and procedural uncertainty is to the theory of production[12]. If one recognises the essential problem-solving nature of production activities (certainly infinitely more complex than a Rubik cube, even leaving aside substantive uncertainty), one can easily represent them in the formal language suggested earlier – strings, rules of transformation, etc. The production routines (the technology) codify the procedure and the knowledge involved in the solution of particular classes of production problems. These routines are – to different degrees – specific to these classes and to the people and the organisations (typically, firms) who have developed them. Of course, the transferability of these routines from one organisation to another has to do also with their degrees of tacitness, the nature of the knowledge that their original generation and their implementation involve, etc. The tree of the possible techniques which can nationally be generated on the grounds of a certain set of initial information, skills, chemical/physical principles is plausibly infinite. So, our earlier considerations on the impossiblity of automatic derivation of the actual routines strictly applies. Some routines are "stored" in individual

---

[11] Vercelli (1986) quotes Husserl, saying that "... tradition is forgetting the origins...".
[12] More on this point in Egidi (1986). This analysis is broadly complementary to that of Winter (1982) and Nelson and Winter (1982). What follows is also strictly consistent with the analysis of technology in terms of "technological paradigms" of Dosi (1982 and 1984).

people, many others in organizations, which often reproduce and improve them through their use (Nelson and Winter 1982).

In the framework proposed here, the representation of technical change is straightforward: it is the generation of new routines. These new routines may relate to a new production process – different, hopefully more efficient, rules of transformation of certain inputs and information into a given output – or to the conception of a new product, or a new organizational set-up. Again, the automatic underivability of new routines highlights the meaning of technological uncertainty. There is not, and there cannot be, a general rule which leads innovative search. Indeed, there can only be specific search heuristics, strongly characterised by procedural uncertainty.

The model allows also a theoretically easy distinction between what one of us calls "normal" technical change (i.e., technical change along a certain "technological trajectory") as distinguished from "extra-ordinary" (paradigm-) changes (Dosi 1982).

In the language introduced earlier, "normal" innovations are generated, although not automatically, by "derivation", analogy, refinement from a basic set of "axioms" and transformation rules and an underlying specific knowledge, i.e., a given paradigm. A paradigm change occurs when it involves also a change of "axioms" and transformation rules. (Alexander the Great's solution to the problem of the Gordian Knot is one of the simplest examples of a radically new system of Post leading to a new routine that in turn solves a problem for which no efficient routine could be derived on the grounds of another set of axioms and transformation rules.)

The development, improvement and modification over time of specific routines on the grounds of a certain body of knowledge accounts also for the cumulative and local nature of technical change. That is, one empirically finds that firms and industries do not explore the entire "production possibility set", whatever that means, but typically improve and develop upon the areas of their existing competence, yielding to quite defined "trajectories" of technical progress[13].

Both "radical" and "normal" innovations yield routines – of varying degrees of generality – which reduce the procedural uncertainty of the innovators themselves, but, other things being equal, increase the substantive uncertainty of the other agents, in that they continuously introduce novelty ("new events") in the environment.

In this interpretation, the flexibility of a particular technology (a particular body of knowledge) means, at one level, the opportunity that it offers of generating a wide set of efficient routines (of course, this, strictly speaking, can be assessed only ex post). At another level, the flexibility of a particular routine relates to its generality and robustness (i.e., its "abstraction"), and, thus, the width of the set of problems to which it can be successfully applied (this obviously includes the set of products that can be made and the different environmental conditions that it can meet)[14]. That is, the flexibility of a technological routine relates to its robustness in dealing with the substantive uncertainty stemming

---

[13] For a survey of the evidence, Dosi (1988). On cumulative and local technical progress see also Atkinson and Stiglitz (1969) and David (1975). On the related nature of search processes, Nelson (1981).
[14] An analysis of the relationship between production routines, flexibility and economies of scope is in Colombo and Mariotti (1986).

from the high dimensionality of the event-space, and the incompleteness of the ex-ante knowledge that agents have of them.

One can establish a natural link between the characterisation of production activities in terms of specific knowledge and routines, on the one hand, and the nature of business firms, on the other. Certainly, an important part of the explanation of the existence and forms of internal organisation of modern corporations resides in the problems of performance control and transaction costs (Williamson 1975, 1985). However, equally important, firms – or whatever other form of productive organisation – must exist in so far as the complexity of routines (and related specific knowledge) required by a particular problem-solving activity is beyond the capabilities of an individual agent (for more on the relationship between knowledge specificities and the boundaries of firms see Dosi, Teece and Winter 1991).

Note also the dual characteristics of problem-solving. On the one hand, it implies identification of sub-problems, their codification and, as a consequence, specialisation and division of labour. On the other hand, it involves strict coordination among the different tasks. Those reasons which account for the impossibility of automatic derivability of the routines make also very problematic and inefficient the complete separation of the various pieces of knowledge leading to the solution of a particular task (it would be as if, in the example of the Rubik cube discussed earlier, one would study the movements of colour A, another those of colour B and then trade the results). Indeed, organizations embody, to varying degrees, both specialisation and coordination within company-specific competences.

In our interpretation, it generally happens that, for sufficiently complex problem-solving tasks, in non-stationary environments, the specific knowledge which is required cannot be defined independently from the organisation in which it is developed and applied. Obviously, there are pieces of people-embodied knowledge which are clearly identifiable and traded on the markets for labour or for *specific services*. If a firm needs to solve a problem of basic semiconductor properties of a certain material, of course, it is more likely to hire a physicist than a carpenter. However, several problem-solving routines are embodied in the way the organisation works rather than in precisely identifiable competences of individual people, even if clearly it makes use of these competences. The indeterminacy of labour contracts (on what is actually "delivered") has partly to do with this phenomenon. So has the interpretation of "de-skilling" which has often been observed in the history of labour-processes: what were previously specific people-embodied competences – and thus traded as such, on the labour market – become attributes of organisational routines, well beyond the knowledge-inputs of the individual performers of certain tasks.

Hence, as argued at greater length in Dosi, Teece and Winter (1991), the general conjecture is that the scope of the firm is defined by the domain of applicability of its specific knowledge and problem-solving routines[15]. Innovation, of course, changes (1) the routines, (2) the forms of specific knowledge required for their development and/or implementation and (3) the degree to which a certain problem-solving task can be subdivided into relatively autonomous and general "sub-problems". Therefore, it changes also the scope of the firm. Seeing it from the mirror opposite angle, it changes the scope for "Smithian" intra- and inter-firm division of labour.

---

[15] Teece's analysis of the co-specialised assets which underpin a firm's competitiveness is clearly consistent with this interpretation (see Teece, 1982 and 1986).

6. Conclusions

Possibly one of the most heard common sense arguments in favour of a "rational" choice-theoretic model of behaviour is that it is simply the theoretical representation of the attempt of empirical agents to make the best use of information that they can, and that, conversely, a routine representation would imply some sort of "mechanicity" or "stupidity" on the part of the agents. We showed that under most circumstances involving various sorts of substantive and procedural uncertainty, precisely the opposite holds true. With sufficiently complex problem-solving tasks as, we argued, most human activities within and without the economic sphere are, "intelligent" actors will look for problem-solving routines which are "abstract" and robust, in the sense that they will not only apply to single problems but classes of them. In fact, the development of these routines involves forms of specific, inductive and synthetic knowledge which is not implied in the "information" about the problem itself. In the most general sense, innovation is the process of discovery of new routines. The nature and, indeed, the *necessity* of such routines can be founded in a quite general theory of problem solving, as pioneered by Simon and, earlier, by the theories of computation and formalization of natural languages. Indeed, such results are highly complementary to the findings on the evolutionary emergence of norms in complex biological and social environments (cfr. Holland 1975; Holland et al. 1987).

In this interpretation, *innovation is an endogenous mechanism of generation of uncertainty in the environment,* since each innovation is in act the appearance of a new, unexpected event. At the same time it is a *procedure through which the innovator,* when successful, solves more efficiently, with greater generality, a particular set of problems, and, hence, *through the resulting routines, reduces complexity and procedural uncertainty. Given strong uncertainty,* defined earlier, the main activity of each agent will not reasonably be a Bayesian updating of probability distributions upon a set of events that he considers as entirely "external" and natural. On the contrary, he will try to find, in ways which are agent-specific, new and, so to speak, "deterministic" procedures of control upon, and generation of, new events. The entire process inevitably produces endogenous non-stationarity of the environments. More general routines are developed and, to different degrees, diffused and imitated by other agents and firms. In turn, the general opportunity of development of new routines yields environmental complexity and strong substantive uncertainty[16]. The permanent gap between the notionally efficiency of the currently existing routines and those which could be developed on the grounds of all the existing information and knowledge defines the (uncertain) domain of "Schumpeterian" innovative behaviours.

Putting it another way, there are possibly in economics two extreme mirror opposite views. The first is that, the R. Lucas' words, "there are no $ 100 bills on the sidewalk", or a bit more extremely, as a member of a committee encharged to decide whether to invite a Rational Expectation economist as a professor, once

---

[16] If we are correct in this representation of innovation and, more generally, non-stationarity, one might wonder what is the interpretative status of a growing stream of literature which represents the innovative process (e.g., R & D investments and innovative outputs) in terms of the usual maximisation procedure under uncertainty. As argued in Dosi and Orsenigo (1988), they often yield important "negative" or "a fortiori" results (..."even if the agents could be literal maximisers, the equilibria would be multiple, would not generally be Pareto-optima...", etc.). However, we believe they offer only limited insights in the processes leading to innovation.

ironically said, "if it were a good idea he would already be here". The world always runs on the edge of its possibilities and everything worth happening has already happened. At the other extreme, there is the view that "intelligent" processes of discovery, and the intimately associated processes of routinisation and automatic application of routines, always create notional unexploited opportunities.

We stand by this latter view: Yes, there always are $ 100 bills on the sidewalk, even if it is impossible to axiomatise the process leading to their discovery. The changing focus that we have proposed here from a purely informational notion of uncertainty to another – procedural – one, associated with the problem-solving competences of the agents, allows precisely the analysis of economic behaviours that often appear "patterned" and routinized, but also present recognisable changes and discoveries.

Acknowledgements. Comments on an earlier draft by the participants at the International Workshop on "Programmable Automation and New Work Modes", Paris, 2–4 April 1987 and at the International Political Science Workshop, Dubrovnick, October 1988 are gratefully acknowledged. Support to one of the authors (G.D.) by the Designated Research Centre of the ESRC at the Science Policy Research Unit (SPRU), University of Sussex, and to both by the Italian Ministery of Education (Progetti M.P.I. 40%), is gratefully acknowledged.

References

Akerlof G (1970) The market for lemons: qualitative uncertainty and the market mechanism. Quarterly Journal of Economics 84:488–500

Alchian AA (1951) Uncertainty, evolution and economic theory. Journal of Political Economy 57:211–221

Amendola M, Gaffard JL (1988) The innovative choice, Oxford, Basil Blackwell

Arbib MA (1969) Theories of abstract automata, Englewood-Cliffs, NJ, Prentice-Hall

Arrow KJ (1951) Alternative approaches to the theory of choice in risk-taking situations. Econometrica 19:404–437

Arrow KJ (1951a) Social choice and individual values. New York, Wiley

Arrow KJ (1970) Essays in the theory of risk-bearing. Amsterdam, North-Holland

Arrow KJ (1971) Exposition of the theory of choice under uncertainty. In: McGuire and Radner

Arrow KJ (1982) Risk perception in psychology and economics. Economic Inquiry 20:1–9

Arrow KJ (1983) Innovation in large and small firms. In: Ronen

Arrow KJ, Hahn F (1971) General competitive analysis. San Francisco, Holden-Day

Arthur WB (1985) Competing technologies and lock-in by historical events. The dynamics of allocation under increasing returns. Stanford, Stanford University, CEPR Discussion Paper

Arthur WB (1988) Competing technologies. In: Dosi, Freeman, Nelson, Silverberg, Soete

Atkinson AB, Stiglitz JE (1969) A new view of technological change. Economic Journal: Sept. 1979:573–578

Baumol WJ, Quandt RE (1964) Rules of thumb and optimally imperfect decisions. American Economic Review

Cass D, Shell K (1983) Do sunspots matter? Journal of Political Economy 91:193–227

Colombo MG, Mariotti S (1986) Flexible automation, idle times and economies of scope. Milan, Politecnico, Department of Electronics, Rapporto Interno no 86-009

Coricelli F, Dosi G (1988) Coordination and order in economic change and the interpretative power of economic theory. In: Dosi, Freeman, Nelson, Soete, Silverberg

Cutland NJ (1980) Computability. An introduction to recursive function theory. Cambridge, MA, Cambridge University Press

David PA (1975) Technical choice, innovation and economic growth. Cambridge, MA, Cambridge University Press

Davies M (1958) Computability and unsolvability. New York, McGraw-Hill

Debreu G (1959) Theory of value. New York, Wiley

Diamond P, Rothschild M (eds) (1978) Uncertainty in economics. Orlando, FL, Academic Press

Dosi G (1982) Technological paradigms and technological trajectories. A suggested interpretation of the determinants and directions of technical change. Research Policy 11: 147–162

Dosi G (1984) Technical change and industrial transformation. London, Macmillan

Dosi G (1988) Sources, procedures and microeconomic effects of innovation. Journal of Economic Literature

Dosi G, Orsenigo L (1988) Structures, performance and change in evolutionary environments. In: Dosi, Freeman, Nelson, Soete, Silverberg

Dosi G, Freeman C, Nelson R, Soete L, Silverberg G (eds) (1988), Technical change and economic theory, London, Francis Pinter

Dosi G, Teece D, Winter S (1991) Toward a theory of corporate conference. In: Dosi G, Giannetti R and Toninelli PA (eds), Technology and the enterprise in a historical perspective. Oxford, Oxford University Press (Forthcoming)

Egidi M (1986) The generation and diffusion of new market routines. Presented at the International Conference on Innovation Diffusion, Venice, 17–21 March

Friedman M (1953) Essays in positive economics. Chicago, University of Chicago Press

Gaffard JL (1986) Mutations technologiques et choix strategiques des entreprises. Nice, University of Nice, LATAPSES, mimeo

Hahn F (1984) Equilibrium and macroeconomics. Oxford, Basil Blackwell

Hahn F (1985) Money, growth and stability. Oxford, Basil Blackwell

Heiner RA (1983) The origin of predictable behaviours. American Economic Review

Heiner RA (1988) Imperfect decisions, routinized behaviour and intertial technical change. In: Dosi, Freeman, Nelson, Soete, Silverberg

Hey JD (1982) Search for rules for search. Journal of Economic Behaviour and Organisation 3: 65–81

Hirshleifer J, Riley J (1979) The analytics of uncertainty and information: A survey. Journal of Economic Literature 17: 1375–1421

Hogart RM, Reder MW (eds) (1987) Rational choice. Chicago, The University of Chicago Press

Holland JH (1975) Adaptation in a natural and artificial systems. Ann Arbor, MI, Univ. Michigan Press

Holland JH, Holyoak KJ, Nisbett RE, Thaeard PR (1986) Induction: Processis of inference learning and discovering, Cambridge, MA, MIT Press

Hopcroft J, Ullman JD (1969) Formal language in their relation to automata. New York, Addison-Wesley

Hopcroft J, Ullman JD (1979) Introduction to automata theory, languages, and computation. New York, Addison-Wesley

Kahneman D, Tversky A (1979) Prospect theory: an analysis of decision under risk. Econometrica 47: 263–291

Kahneman D, Tversky A (1986) Rational choice and the framing of decisions. In: Hogard and Reder (1987)

Katzner DW (1986) Potential surprise, potential confirmation, and probability. Journal of Post-Keynesian Economics 9: 58–78

Lewis AA (1985) On Effectively computable realisations of choice functions. Mathematical Social Science 10

Lewis AA (1986) Structure and complexity. The use of recursion theory in the foundations of neo-classical mathematical economics and the theory of games. Ithaca, Cornell University, Dept. of Mathematics

Machlup F (1946) Marginal analysis and empirical research. American Economic Review 36: 519–554

Marschak J (1950) Rational behaviour, uncertain prospects and measurable utility. Econometrica 43: 111–141

McGuire CB, Radner R (eds) (1971) Decision and organisation. Amsterdam, North-Holland

Merin A (1985) Elementary social relations, duality principles and model paradigmata. Sociomorphic structures of english grammar. Brighton, University of Sussex, Dept of Linguistics, DPhil Thesis

Minsky M (1967) Computation. Finite and infinite machines. Englewood Cliffs, NJ, Prentice-Hall

Nelson RR (1981) The role of knowledge in R&D efficiency. Quarterly Journal of Economics

Nelson RR, Winter SG (1982) An evolutionary theory of economic change. Cambridge (MA), The Belknap Press of Harvard University Press

von Neumann J, Morgenstern O (1953) Theory of games and economic behaviour. Princeton, Princeton University Press, 3rd ed

Newell A, Simon HA (1972) Human problem solving. Englewood Cliffs, NJ, Prentice-Hall

Nillson NJ (1971) Problem solving methods in artificial intelligence. New York, McGraw Hill

Nillson NJ (1980) Principles of artificial intelligence. Palo Alto, Tioga Publishing Company

Radner R (1968) Competitive equilibrium under uncertainty. Econometrica 36:31–58

Ronen J (ed) (1983) Entrepreneurship. Lexington (MA), DC Heath

Savage LJ (1954) The foundations of statistics. New York, Wiley

Shackle GLS (1969) Decision, order and time in human affairs. Cambridge, Cambridge University Press

Sharples M et al. (1989) Computers and thought. Cambridge (MA), MIT Press

Shelling TC (1978) Micromotives and macrobehaviours. New York, Norton

Silverberg G (1987) Technical progress, capital accumulation and effective demand: A self-organisation model. In: Batten D, Casti J (ed) Economic evolution and structural change. Berlin/New York, Springer-Verlag

Silverberg G (1988) Modelling economic dynamics and technical change: mathematical approaches to self-organisation and evolution. In: Dosi, Freeman, Nelson, Soete and Silverberg (1988)

Simon HA (1957) Models of man. New York, Wiley

Simon HA (1959) Theories of decision making in economics. American Economic Review 49:253–383

Simon HA (1973) The structure of ill-structured problems. Artificial Intelligence 4

Simon HA (1979) Rational decision making in business organisations. American Economic Review 69:493–513

Simon HA (1981) The science of artificial. Cambridge (MA), MIT Press, 2nd ed

Sternberg RJ (ed) (1984) Mechanisms of cognitive development. New York, Freeman and Co

Stiglitz J (1984) Information and economic analysis: A perspective. Economic Journal, Conference Papers

Stiglitz J (1986) Lerning to learn. Presented at the Conference on the Economic Theory of Technology Policy, CEPR, London, September 1986

Taylor M, Tayler P (1986) The surprise game: An exploration of constrained relativism. Coventry, Warwick University, Institute for Management, Aston-Warwick Scale Papers n 4

Teece D (1982) Toward an economic theory of multi-product firms. Journal of Economic Behaviour and Organisation

Teece D (1986) Profiting from innovation. Research Policy

Trakhtenbrot BA (1963) Algorithms and automatic computing machines. Boston, DC Heath (English trans. from Russian original)

Turing AM (1936) On computable numbers, with an application to the Entscheidungsproblem. Proceedings of the London Mathematical Society 42:230–265

Tversky A, Kahneman D (1974) Judgement under uncertainty: heuristics and biases. Science 185:1124–1131

Tversky A, Kahneman D (1981) The framing of decisions and the psychology of choce, Science 221:453–458

Vercelli A (1986) Technological flexibility, financial fragility and the recent revival of Schumpeterian enterpreneurship. Siena, University of Siena. Presented at the International Conference on Technological and Social Factors in Long Term Fluctuations, December 1986

Williams EF, Findlay MC (1986) Risk and the role of failed expectations in an uncertain world. Journal of Post-Keynesian Economics 9:32–47

Williamson O (1975) Markets and hierarchies. New York, Free Press

Williamson O (1985) The economic institutions of capitalism. New York, Free Press

Winter SG (1982) An essay on the theory of production. In: Hymans SH (ed) Economics and the world around it. Ann Arbor, Michigan University Press

Winter SG (1986) Adaptive behaviour and economic rationality. Comments on Arrow and Lucas. In Hogart and Reder

Winter SG (1988) Competition and selection. The New Palgrave

J Evol Econ (1999) 9: 5–26

—Journal of—
**Evolutionary
Economics**
© Springer-Verlag 1999

Norms as emergent properties of adaptive learning: The case of economic routines*

Giovanni Dosi[1,2], Luigi Marengo[3], Andrea Bassanini[4], Marco Valente[5]

[1] Scvola Superiore S. Anna, Pisa, Italy
[2] IIASA, Laxenburg, Austria
[3] Department of Economics, University of Trento, Via Inama 1, I-38100 Trento, Italy
(e-mail: lmarengo@gelso.unitn.it)
[4] Faculty of Statistics, University "La Sapienza", Rome, Italy, and OECD, Paris, France
[5] Aalborg University, Aalborg, Denmark

Abstract. Interaction among autonomous decision-makers is usually modelled in economics in game-theoretic terms or within the framework of General Equilibrium. Game-theoretic and General Equilibrium models deal almost exclusively with the existence of equilibria and do not analyse the processes which might lead to them. Even when existence proofs can be given, two questions are still open. The first concerns the possibility of multiple equilibria, which game theory has shown to be the case even in very simple models and which makes the outcome of interaction unpredictable. The second relates to the computability and complexity of the decision procedures which agents should adopt and questions the possibility of reaching an equilibrium by means of an algorithmically implementable strategy. Some theorems have recently proved that in many economically relevant problems equilibria are not computable. A different approach to the problem of strategic interaction is a "constructivist" one. Such a perspective, instead of being based upon an axiomatic view of human behaviour grounded on the principle of optimisation, focuses on algorithmically implementable "satisfycing" decision procedures. Once the axiomatic approach has been abandoned, decision procedures cannot be deduced

* Support to the research at different stages has been provided by the International Institute of Applied Systems Analysis (IIASA), Laxenburg, Austria, the Italian Ministry of University and Research (Murst 40%), the Italian Research Council (CNR, Progetto Strategico "Cambiamento Tecnologico e Sviluppo Economico") and the Center for Research in Management, University of California, Berkeley. Comments by an anonymous referee and by the participants at seminars at the Cerisy Association (Cerisy, France), the Santa Fe Institute (Santa Fe, New Mexico), and in particular Kenneth Arrow, are gratefully acknowledged. This work was awarded the "International A. Kapp Prize" for 1994 by the European Association of Political and Evolutionary Economics.
Correspondence to: L. Marengo

6   G. Dosi et al.

from rationality assumptions, but must be the evolving outcome of a process of learning and adaptation to the particular environment in which the decision must be made. This paper considers one of the most recently proposed adaptive learning models: Genetic Programming and applies it to one the mostly studied and still controversial economic interaction environment, that of oligopolistic markets. Genetic Programming evolves decision procedures, represented by elements in the space of functions, balancing the exploitation of knowledge previously obtained with the search of more productive procedures. The results obtained are consistent with the evidence from the observation of the behaviour of real economic agents.

Key words: Computability – Genetic Programming – Oligopoly

JEL-classification: C63; D43; D83

1 Introduction

As Kenneth Arrow – himself one of the major contributors to rational decision theory – puts it, a system of literally maximizing norm-free agents "... would be the end of organized society as we know it" (Arrow, 1987, p. 233). And indeed one only rarely observes behaviours and decision processes which closely resemble the canonical view from decision theory as formalized by von Neumann, Morgenstern, Savage and Arrow.

What are then the characteristics of norm-guided behaviours? And where do norms come from? Can they be assumed to derive from some higher-level rational choice? Or can one show different kinds of processes accounting for their emergence?

In this work we shall discuss these issues and present an evolutionary view of the emergence of norm-guided behaviours (i.e. routines[1]) in economics.

We shall call *rules* all the procedures linking actions and some representation of the environment. In turn, representations are likely to involve relations between environmental states and variables and require the fulfilment of certain conditions (IF-THEN rules). It is a familiar definition in Artificial Intelligence and cognitive psychology (see Newell and Simon, 1972; Holland et al., 1986). Of course representations may encompass both environmental states and internal states of the actor; and the action part may equally be a behaviour in the environment or an internal state, such as a cognitive act.[2]

Further, we shall call *norms* that subset of rules which pertain to socially interactive behaviours and, in addition, have the following characteristics:

1) they are context-dependent (in ways that we shall specify below), and

2) given the context, they are, to varying degrees, event independent, in the sense that, within the boundaries of a recognised context, they yield

---

[1] For a general discussion on organizational routines and their role in economics see Nelson and Winter (1982) and Cohen et al. (1995).

[2] Clearly, this very general definition of rules includes as particular cases also the procedures for decision and action postulated by "rational" theories.

patterns of behaviour whose selection is not itself contingent on particular states of the world.[3]

This definition of norms is extremely broad in scope and encompasses also behavioural routines, social conventions and morally constrained behaviours.[4] Thus our definition includes the norm of not robbing banks, but excludes robbing or not robbing banks according to such criteria as expected utility maximization; it includes the "rules of the games" in game theoretical set-ups, but excludes the highly contingent strategies which rational players are supposed by that theory to engage in thereafter.

Our argument is divided into two parts. First, we ask what is the link between norms, so defined, and the "rational" decision model familiar in the economic literature. In particular we shall address the question whether, whenever one observes those types of norm-guided behaviours, they can be referred back to some kind of higher-level rational act of choice among alternative patterns of action. We shall claim that this is not generally the case. The empirical evidence, even in simple contexts, of systematic departures of judgements and actions from the predictions of the rationality model is now overwhelming.[5] Here however we are not going to discuss such evidence, rather we shall pursue a complementary line of enquiry and show that, with respect to an extremely broad set of problems, a 'rational' choice procedure cannot even be theoretically - constructed, let alone adopted by empirical agents. Drawing from computation theory, it can be shown that many choice set-ups involve algorithmically insoluble problems: in other words, there is not and there cannot be a universal rational procedure of choice. An optimization procedure cannot be devised even in principle: this is the negative part of the argument.

But what do people do, then? We shall suggest precisely that agents employ problem-solving rules and interactive norms, which: 1) cannot be derived from any general optimization criterion and, 2) are "robust", in the sense that they apply to entire classes of events and problems (Dosi and Egidi, 1991).

The second part of this work considers the origin and nature of these rules. The cases we shall consider regard the emergence of corporate routines applied to the most familiar control variables in economics, i.e. prices and quantities. However, there appear to be no a priori reason to restrict the applicability of the argument to economic behaviours. In fact, a similar

---

[3] Note that this definition as such does not imply any restriction on the use of information by the norms themselves. Some might be extremely simple and parsimonious in their handling of information (like those we shall show emerging in the exercises below). Others might imply sophisticated information-processing (such as, e.g. accounting routines in a firm). Both types, however, share the property that the *behavioural patterns*, although not necessarily the single actions, once established, are rather invariant throughout the whole set of contingencies that might occur in that context.

[4] These finer categorization are quite familiar in political sciences: see for example the discussion in Koford and Miller (1991). On the contrary, the broader notion of norms adopted here includes both moral constraints and positive behavioural prescriptions (i.e. both "morality" and "ethics" in the sense of Hegel).

[5] Cf., for instance, Kahneman, Slovic and Tversky (1982), Kahneman and Tversky (1979), Herrnstein and Prelec (1991).

8

analytical approach could be applied to several other forms of patterned behaviour in social interactions.

Concerning the origin of behavioural norms, we develop a model broadly in the perspective outlined by Holland (1975) and Holland et al. (1986): various forms of inductive procedures generate, via adaptive learning and discovery, representations or "mental models" and, together, patterns of behaviour: "the study of induction, then, is the study of how knowledge is modified through its use" (Holland et al., 1986, p. 5). In our model, artificial computer-simulated agents progressively develop behavioural rules by building cognitive structures and patterns of action, on the grounds of initially randomly generated and progressively improved symbolic building blocks and no knowledge of the environment in which they are going to operate. The implementation technique is a modified version of Genetic Programming (c.f. Koza, 1992, 1993), in which agents (firms) are modelled by sets of symbolically represented decision procedures which undergo structural modifications in order to improve adaptation to the environment. Learning takes place in an evolutionary fashion, and is driven by a selection dynamics whereby markets reward or penalise agents according to their revealed performances.[6]

A major point in the analysis which follows is that representations of the world in which agents operate and behavioural patterns co-evolve through the interaction with the environment and the inductive exploratory efforts of agents to make sense of it.[7] Indeed, we show that, despite the complexity of the search space (technically, the space of λ-functions), relatively coherent behavioural procedures emerge. Of course, none of us would claim that empirical agents do learn and adapt in a way which is anything like Genetic Programming, or, for that matter, any other artificially implementable formalism (but, similarly, we trust that no supporter of more rationalist views of behaviour would claim that human beings choose their course of action by using fixed-point theorems, Bellman equations, etc.). We do however conjecture that there might be a sort of "weak isomorphism" between artificial procedures of induction and the ways actual agents adapt to their environment.

The final question that we address concerns the nature of the behavioural patterns that emerge through our process of learning and market selection. In particular, in the economic settings that we consider, are these patterns algorithmic approximation to the purported rational behaviours which the theory simply assumes? Or, do they have the features of relatively

---

[6] A similar exercise has been recently proposed by Curzon-Price (1997). Like us he considers firms which adaptively learn their price and/or quantity fixation strategies in monopolistic and oligopolistic industries. But this paper employs standard Genetic Algorithms: as Curzon-Price himself argues in his conclusions, Genetic Programming is a richer modelling tool, which offers a much more appealing analogue to decision-making routines implemented by real firms.

[7] On the evolution of representations, see also Margolis (1987). In economics, such a co-evolutionary perspective is held by a growing minority of practitioners. More on it can be found in Nelson and Winter (1982), Dosi et al. (1988), March (1988), Marengo (1996), Dosi and Marengo (1994), Arthur (1992).

invariant and context-specific norms (or routines) as defined earlier? It turns out that, in general, the latter appears to be the case: surviving agents display routines, like mark-up pricing or simple imitative behaviour (of the type "follow-the-leader") in all environments that we experimented, except the simplest and most stationary ones. Only in the latter do we see the emergence of behaviours not far from what supposedly rational agents would do (and, even then, cooperative behaviours are more likely to come out than what simple Nash equilibria would predict[8]). The context dependence of emerging routines can be given a rather rigorous meaning: the degrees of complexity of the environment and of the problem-solving tasks can be mapped into the characteristics of the emerging routines. Interestingly enough, it appears that the higher the complexity, the simpler behavioural norms tend to be and the more potentially relevant information tends to be neglected. In that sense, social norms seem to be the typical and most robust form of evolutionary adaptation to uncertainty and change.

In Section 2 we shall show that, in general, it is theoretically impossible to assume that the rationality of behaviours could be founded in some kind of general algorithmic ability of the agents to get the right representation of the environment and choose the right course of action. Section 3 presents a model of inductive learning where representations and actions co-evolve. Finally, in Section 4 we present some results showing the evolutionary emergence of behavioural routines, such as mark-up pricing.

2 Rational vs. norm-guided behaviour

Let us start from the familiar view of rational behaviour grounded on some sort of linear sequence leading from 1) representations to 2) judgement, 3) choice and, finally, 4) action. Clearly, that ideal sequence can apply to pure problem-solving (for example proving a theorem, discovering a new chemical compound with certain characteristics, etc.), as well as to interactive situations (how to deal with competitors, what to do if someone tries to mug you, etc.).

At least two assumptions are crucial to this 'rationalist' view, namely, first, that the linearity of the sequence strictly holds (for example one must rule out circumstances in which people act and then adapt their preferences and representations to what they have already done) and, second, that at each step of the process agents are able to build the appropriate algorithm in order to tackle the task at hand. Regarding the first issue, the literature in sociology and social psychology is rich of empirical counterexamples and alternative theories.[9] Indeed, in the next section of this work, we shall present a model whereby representations and actions co-evolve.

---

[8] This is of course in line with the findings of Axelrod (1984) and Miller(1988).

[9] In addition to the references from footnote 4, see for discussions, among the others, Sen (1977), Simon (1986), Hodgson (1988), Elster (1986), Luhmann (1979), and, closer to the spirit of this paper, Nelson and Winter (1982), March (1994) and Dosi and Metcalfe (1991). For a more general discussion of these issues, cf. Dosi, Marengo and Fagiolo (1996).

The second issue is even more at the heart of the 'constructivist' idea of rationality so widespread in economics, claiming that agents are at the very least procedurally rational.[10] In turn this implies that they could algorithmically solve every problem they had to face, if they were provided with the necessary information about the environment and the degrees of rationality of their possible opponents or partners. Conversely, the very notion of rational behaviour would turn out to be rather ambiguous if one could show that, *even in principle*, the appropriate algorithms cannot be constructed.

It happens in fact that computability theory provides quite a few impossibility theorems, i.e. theorems showing examples of algorithmically insoluble problems. Many of them bear direct implications also for the micro assumptions of economic theory and, particularly, for the possibility of 'naturally' assuming the algorithmic solvability of social and strategic interaction problems.[11] We can distinguish between two kinds of impossibility results. First, it is possible to show the existence of classes of problems which are not solvable by means of a general recursive procedure (c.f. Lewis, 1985a,b). This implies that economic agents who look for efficient procedures for the solution of specific problems cannot draw on general rules for the construction of algorithms, because such general rules do not and cannot exist (c.f., also, Dosi and Egidi, 1991). Broadly speaking, we can say that nobody may be assumed to be endowed with the meta-algorithm for the generation of every necessary algorithm.

Second, it is possible to prove the existence of single problems whose optimal solution cannot be implemented by means of *specific* algorithms. Hence one faces truly algorithmically insoluble problems: economic agents cannot have readily available algorithms designing optimal strategies to tackle such problems. Therefore, unless they have been told what the optimal solutions are by an omniscient entity, they have actually to find other criteria and procedures to solve them in a 'satisfactory' way. In fact, they need novel criteria to define what a satisfactory solution is and inductively discover new procedures to accomplish their tasks (see again Dosi and Egidi, 1991).

Let us briefly examine these two kinds of impossibility results.

Lewis (1985a, b) proves a general result about the uncomputability of rational choice functions. Let $P(X)$ be the set of all subsets of a space of alternatives X where an asymmetric and transitive preference relation has been identified, we can roughly define a rational choice function as a set function

$C:P(X) \rightarrow P(X)$ such that, for every $A \in P(X)$, $C(A)$ is the set of acceptable alternatives.[12]

---

[10] The central reference on the distinction between 'substantive' and 'procedural' rationality is of course Herbert Simon: see especially Simon (1976, 1981, 1986).

[11] See Lewis (1985a), Casti (1992) and Rustem and Velupillai (1990). Note that, loosely speaking, algorithmic solvability means that one is able to define a recursive procedure that will get you, say, to a Nash equilibrium. This turns out to be a question quite independent from proving a theorem which shows the existence of such an equilibrium.

[12] Given a preference relation $>$ on a set of objects X and a non-empty set A belonging to X, the set of acceptable alternatives is defined as: $c(A, >) = \{x \in A:$ there is no $y \in A$ such that $y > x\}$.

Lewis considers some compact, convex subset of $R^n\backslash\{0\}$ as the space X of alternatives. Among these alternatives he takes into account only the set of recursive real numbers in the sense of Kleene and Post, i.e. the set of real numbers which can be codified as natural numbers by means of a particular Gödel numbering (for more details see Lewis, 1985a). Moreover, one operates directly on the codified values (which are called R-indices). Given a preference relation defined only on the space of R-indices and numerically representable by a computable function and given some non-triviality conditions, Lewis does not only show that the related rational choice function is uncomputable but also that so is its restriction over the sole decidable subsets.[13] Even more important than the proposition on undecidable sets (since in this case it may seem that the uncomputability of the function necessarily derives from the undecidability of the subsets), the result concerning only its restriction to the decidable subsets of R^n is quite powerful. It means in fact that the functions are uncomputable even if their domains are computable.

Obviously this result does not imply that the optimal solution cannot be algorithmically determined for every $A \in P(X)$. Lewis' theorems actually prove only that no automatic procedure can generate uniformly optimal solutions over the whole family of optimization problems identified by the set of all recursive subsets of R-indices of elements of X. This would be true even if there existed some specific solution algorithm for every single problem of this family (see Lewis, 1985a, p. 67). This result shows actually that there exist small enough classes (i.e. not so broad to be meaningless from a decision-theoretic point of view) of well-structured choice problems whose solution cannot be obtained by means of a general recursive procedure.

In economic theory, environmental or social interactions are usually represented by using subsets of R^n as spaces of alternative strategies. Thus, Lewis' results can be naturally extended to prove the generic uncomputability of the class of General Economic Equilibria and, relatedly, of the class of Nash equilibria for games (see Lewis, 1987).

Concerning the second type of uncomputability results, examples can be found in game theory: Rabin (1957) and Lewis (1985a) show that there is at least one two-person, zero-sum game with perfect information whose optimal strategies are uncomputable.[14] On the same token, similar uncomputability results concerning Post systems (Post, 1943; Thrakhtenbrot, 1963) directly bear upon production theory as they show that there is no guarantee that optimal productive processes can be algorithmically identified (even, as economists would say, under exogenous technical progress). Therefore it is impossible to assume that economic agents make always use of optimal processes without giving a context-specific proof.

---

[13] Broadly speaking, we call a set decidable if there exist an algorithm which is always able to completely identify its elements, i.e. if the membership function which characterises the set is computable.

[14] This result has been proven for a particular class of Gale-Stewart games: such games have infinite Nash equilibria with at least one sub-game perfect among them, nevertheless they admit no computable winning strategy.

It is worth emphasising that these impossibility results entail quite disruptive implications not only for the 'constructivist' concept of rationality, but also for the so-called *as-if* hypothesis (see Friedman, 1953; discussion in Winter, 1986). In order to assume that agents behave as if they were rational maximizers, one needs to represent a thoroughly autonomous selection process which converges to an optimal strategy equilibrium, i.e. one must be able to formalise something like an automatic procedure which ends up with the elimination of every non-optimizing agent (or behaviour).

However, the first group of results mentioned above, implies that, for some classes of problems, we are not allowed to assume the existence of a general and algorithmically implementable selection mechanism leading in finite time to the exclusive survival of optimal behaviours. In addition, the second group of results provides examples where one can definitely rule out the existence of every such a selection mechanism.

Moreover, the minimal prerequisite one needs for a selection-based *as-if* hypothesis on behavioural rationality is the existence of some agents whose behaviour is consistent with optimization in the first place (cf. Winter, 1971). But, if the set of optimal strategies is undecidable, how can we be sure of having endowed some agent with one optimal strategy? An approximate easy answer could be that if we consider a sufficiently large population of differentiated agents, we can safely suppose that some of them play optimal strategies and will be eventually selected. But how big should our population be, given that we cannot have any idea about the size of the set of possible strategies?

Finally there is also a problem of complexity which arises in connection with rational behaviour (both under a "constructivist" view and under the *as-if* hypothesis). Broadly speaking, we can roughly define the complexity of a problem as the speed of the best computation processes we could theoretically use to solve it (c.f., e.g., Cutland, 1980). But then the speed of environmental change becomes a crucial issue: as Winter (1986) and Arthur (1992) pointed out, the *as-if* view is primarily connected with a situation without change. In fact, even when the only kind of change we allow is an exogenous one, a necessary, albeit by no means sufficient condition for the hypothesis to hold is that the speed of convergence be higher than the pace of change. However, it is easy to find many examples of games whose optimal strategies, while existing and being computable, require too much time to be effectively pursued even by a modern computer.[15]

Moreover, if the environment is not stationary, it is unlikely that behaviour consistent with optimization in one environmental state will be so also in another one, unless we assume that the agent is actually using the optimizing algorithm (but this amounts to denying the "as-if" thesis one wants to prove).

We do not want to make too much out of these impossibility results: one of the reasons is that generic uncomputability might tell us little on the

---

[15] Think for instance to the game of Chess or to the Rubik cube.

average complexity of any one particular problem.[16] However, in our view, they do establish a sort of upper bound to the algorithmic rationality with which we may innocently endow the empirical agents whose behaviour we want to describe. These impossibility proofs, together with more familiar results on the indeterminacy of learning processes even under quite restrictive cognitive assumptions (such as "rational expectation" and Bayesian learning) add to the importance of an explicit analysis of the *processes of formation of representations and behavioural rules*. This is what we shall do in the next section, by considering the emergence of rules of cognition/action in some familiar economic examples of decision and interaction.

3 Genetic programming as a model of procedural learning

With a lag of at least two decades after Herbert Simon's repeated invitations to tackle "bounded rationality", a few recent models have finally begun also in economics to represent agents who adaptively improve their representations of the environment in which they operate and their repertoire of actions.

Some of the most promising modelling techniques are based on John Holland's Genetic Algorithms (Holland, 1975) and Classifiers Systems (Holland et al., 1986). Despite their variety, what this class of "adaptive learning" models has in common is the assumption that agents, at least at the start, are characterized by some sort of competence gap, as Ronald Heiner has put it (cf. Heiner, 1983, 1988). That is, beyond imperfect information and uncertainty about the states of the world, they are less than perfectly able to interpret whatever information they have and to establish the appropriate courses of action conditional on that information.[17] Having said that, the different adaptive learning models which have been produced so far differ quite a lot in the nature of the "competence gap" that they allow, in the environments that they depict, and in the spirit of the whole exercise. At one extreme, models such as Arifovic (1994) attempt to show how adaptive learning based on Genetic Algorithms in quite simple environmental set-ups yield convergence to the "optimal" behaviour generally assumed by economic theory. Conversely, Lindgren (1991), Miller (1988) and Marengo (1996), among others, study the properties of emergent behaviours in more complex interactive environments (prisoner's dilemma and intra-firms coordination problems, respectively).

In any case, irrespectively of the modelling philosophy, all these adaptive learning models allow for some mechanism of search and recombina-

---

[16] We owe this observation to Kenneth Arrow, who pointed to us the example of linear programming and the difference between "normal" and maximum computational complexity of simplex methods as compared to other ones.

[17] This is what in Dosi and Egidi (1991) we have called *procedural uncertainty*. As illustrations, think of the exercises of proving a theorem or solving a Rubik cube. There is no "substantive uncertainty" (i.e. no unknown move of nature) and the information might well be perfect. Still, "procedural uncertainty" remains, regarding what to do with the information and how to achieve the desired result.

tion of the initial knowledge apt to reduce the competence gap of the agents and improve their performances in the decision tasks at hand. However, quite a few problems of cognition, within and outside the economic arena, regard the discovery of the purported structure of the environment, i.e. the functional relations among environmental variables (being them e.g. the possible correlation between stochastic trend in some fundamental variable; the effect of investment on income growth, etc.). And also many procedural problems of decision/action involve the discovery of specific functions (whether it is the identification of a function to maximize, its first order condition, or also stationary rules such as "invest a given percentage of sales in R&D"). But, then, can one model artificial agents which explore and learn in some *space of functions*? This is precisely what we shall do next, applying a modified version of Genetic Programming (cf. Koza, 1992, 1993). Genetic Programming – GP henceforth – is a computational model which simulates learning and adaptation through a search in the space of representations/procedures. Similarly to John Holland's Genetic Algorithms, Genetic Programming pursues learning and adaptation by processing in an evolutionary fashion a population of structures which are represented by fixed length binary strings in the case of Genetic Algorithms and by symbolic functions in the case of GP.

In GP, the learning system (an artificial learning agent) is endowed with a set of basic "primitive" operations (such as the four arithmetic operations, Boolean operators, if-then operators) and combine them in order to build complex procedures (functions) which map environmental variables into actions. Each artificial agent is represented by a set of such procedures and learns to adapt to the environment through an evolutionary process which involves both fitness-driven selection among existing procedures and generation of new ones through mutation and genetic recombination (crossover) of the old ones.

General features of this model are the following:

1. *Representations and rule behaviour*: A common feature to many computational models of learning, including the one presented here, is that of modeling the learning process not just as acquisition of information and probability updating, but as modification of representations and models of the world. But contrary to other similar models (such as genetic algorithms and classifiers systems), genetic programming models learning and adaptation as an explicit search in the space of procedures, i.e. functions in their symbolic representation, which define functional relations among environmental and decision variables.[18]

2. *Adaptive selection*: Each artificial agent stores in its memory a set of alternative procedures of representation/action and selects at each moment of time a preferred one according to its fitness, i.e. the payoff cumulated by each procedure in the past.

---

[18] A more general formal tool in the same spirit and which we intend to apply in the near future is presented in Fontana (1992) and Fontana and Buss (1994), applied in the domain of biology to self-reproducing systems.

3. Generation of new rules: Learning does not involve only adaptive selection of the most effective decision rules among the existing ones, but also generation of new ones. Learning and adaptation require a calibration of the complicated trade-off between exploitation and refinement of the available knowledge and exploration of new possibilities. GP uses genetic recombination to create new sequences of functions: sub-procedures of the existing most successful ones are re-combined with the cross-over operator in order to generate new and possibly more effective combinations.

In GP symbolic functions are represented by trees, whose nodes contain either operators or variables. Operators have connections (as many as the number of operands they need) to other operators and/or variables, if they are variables they do not have, of course, any further connection and constitute therefore the leaves of the tree.

Thus, every node can be chosen in a set of basic function (e.g. the arithmetic, Boolean, relation, if-then operators) plus some variables and constants:

BF =

$$\{+, -, *, /, \ldots\ldots, OR, AND, NOT, >, <, =, \ldots v_1, v_2, v_3, \ldots c_1, c_2, c_3, \ldots\ldots\}$$

But basic functions can be freely defined depending on the kind of problem which is being faced (see Koza, 1993, for a wide range of examples of applications in different problem domains).

The execution cycle of a GP system proceeds along the following steps:

0) An initial set of function/trees is randomly generated. Each tree is created by randomly selecting a basic function; if the latter needs parameters, other basic functions are randomly selected for each connection. The operation continues until variables (which can be considered as zero-parameter functions) close every branch of the tree.

1) Once a population of trees is so created, the relative strength of each function is determined by calculating its own fitness in the given environment.

2) A new generation of functions/trees is generated. Two mechanisms serve this purpose: selection and genetic operators. Selection consists in preserving the fittest rules and discarding the less fit ones. Genetic operators instead generate new rules by modifying and recombining the fittest among the existing ones. The generation of new (possibly better) functions/trees in GP is similar to the genetic operators proposed by Holland for the Genetic Algorithms and is mainly based on the cross-over operators.[19] Cross-over operates by selecting randomly two nodes in the parents' trees and swapping the sub-trees which have such nodes as roots.

Consider for example the two parents functions:

$$P_1 := X + (Y*Z) - Z \quad \text{and} \quad P_2 := Z/(Y*X) - A$$

---

[19] For a discussion of the power of cross-over as a device for boosting adaptation, see Holland (1975) and Goldberg (1989).

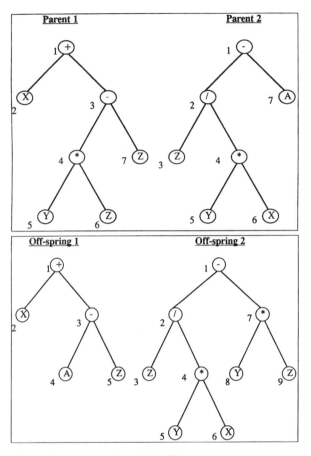

Fig. 1. Tree representation of the GP

which are depicted in Fig. 1 in their tree representation. Suppose that node 4 in the first function and node 7 in the second one are randomly selected: cross-over will generate two new 'off-spring' trees which correspond to the functions:

$$OS_1 := X + (A - Z) \quad \text{and} \quad OS_2 := Z/(Y*X) - (Y*Z)$$

Such off-spring substitute the weakest existing rules, so that the number of rules which are stored at every moment in time is kept constant.
      3) Go back to 1).

4 Learning pricing procedures in oligopolistic markets

Here we shall consider one of the most typical problems of economic interaction, namely, an oligopolistic market.

Think of a small group of firms who sell their product (a homogeneous one, for simplicity) in a decentralized market where customers are imperfectly informed about the prices of other suppliers, there are search costs and/or customers exhibit some inertia (or "loyalty") in their purchasing behaviours.

In a full-fledged representation of such type of market interactions – indeed quite common in contemporary industrial economics – one would of course try to model "artificial markets" entailing the dynamics of search and purchases by multiple customers. However, here we want to focus primarily on the evolution of pricing rules by suppliers. Therefore, for the sake of simplicity, we accept the usual economists' convention of "black-boxing" the collective behaviour of customers into a downward-sloped industry demand curve, unknown to all suppliers, who have to set simultaneously their prices at discrete time intervals. To do so they can observe both the past values taken by the relevant market variables (quantity and prices) and the current value of such firm-specific variables as costs. However, they do not know either the parameters of the demand function or the prices competitors are about to set. Once all prices have been simultaneously set, the corresponding aggregate demand can be determined and individual market shares are updated according to relative prices.

This interactive set-up and the substantive uncertainty about both the exogenous environment (i.e. the demand function) and the competitors' behaviour require agents to perform a joint search in the space of representations and in the space of decision functions.

Let us examine more precisely the structure of the market we analyse in our simulations. There exist an exogenous linear demand function:

$$p = a - bq \qquad a, b > 0 \tag{1}$$

and n firms which compete in this market by choosing a price p_i. Firms are supposed to start up all with the same market share s_i:

$$s_i(0) = 1/n \qquad i = 1, ..., n$$

Price decisions are taken independently (no communication is possible between firms) and simultaneously at regular time intervals (t = 1,2,........). Each firms is supposed to incur into a constant unitary cost c_i for each unit of production. Once all decisions have been taken, the aggregate market price can be computed as the average of individual prices:

$$p(t) = \Sigma_i s_i(t) p_i(t) \tag{2}$$

and the corresponding demanded quantity is thus determined. Such a quantity is divided up into individual shares which evolve according to a sort of replicator dynamics equation in discrete time:

$$s_i(t) = \eta [p(t)/p_i(t) - 1] s_i(t - 1) \tag{3}$$

if $s_i(t) \geq 0.01$, otherwise the firm is declared "dead" and a new one enters with a 0.01 market share.

The parameter η is the reciprocal of the degree of inertia of the market.

Such a replicator-type dynamics of shares has to be taken as the simplest approximation to an imperfect adjustment of consumer behaviour to price differentials, in which customers stick to their previous suppliers or move to cheaper ones as a function of price differentials.[20]

Finally, individual profits are given by:

$$\Pi_i(t) = [p_i(t) - c_i(t)] \, s_i(t)q(t) - F_i \tag{4}$$

where F_i are fixed costs, independent of the scale of production, but small enough to allow the firms to break-even for an excess of prices over variable costs, were they to pursue Bertrand-type competition.

We model these firms as artificial agents, each represented by an autonomous GP system, which, at each time step t, must select one pricing rule among those which it currently stores. Each artificial agent can observe at each moment of time t the following past (i.e. the values taken at time t−1) variables:

– average industry price $p(t-1)$,
– aggregate demanded quantity $q(t-1)$,
– individual prices of each agent $p_i(t-1)$, for $i = 1,2,...n$
– own unitary cost $c_i(t-1)$
– own market share $s_i(t-1)$

moreover it can observe its current unitary cost $c_i(t)$.

Each agent is then endowed with a few basic "elementary" operations, i.e. the four arithmetic operations, if-then operators, Boolean operators and equality/inequality operators, in addition a few integers are given as constant to each GP system.

Each agent's decision rules are randomly generated at the outset, and a preferred one is chosen for action in a random way, with probabilities proportional the payoffs cumulated by each rule in the previous iterations. Periodically, new rules are generated through cross-over and replace the weaker ones.

In order to test the learning capabilities of an economic artificial agent represented by a GP, we started with a very simple model of a single agent in a monopolistic market. In such an environment, there is one and only one optimal behaviour for the agent, that is to set its price to the value which maximises its profit. As shown in Fig. 2, in this case with constant costs and stable demand curve, price rapidly converges to the optimal one. The optimal value can be computed from the available parameters of the

---

[20] Clearly, the stochastic version of eq. (3) form would be more adequate to describe the mechanism, but, for our purposes, the main property that we want to capture – namely, inertial adjustment of the market to price differential – is retained also by the simpler deterministic dynamics. Were agents to behave as in conventional Bertrand models, eq. (3) would still converge, in the limit, to canonical Bertrand equilibria. It must be also pointed out that our model is not concerned with the population dynamics of the industry but primarily with the evolution of pricing rules. Therefore we artificially set a minimum market share (1%) under which firms cannot shrink. According to the past performance record, firms may die, in which case they are replaced by a new agent which stochastically recombines some of the behavioural rules of the incumbents.

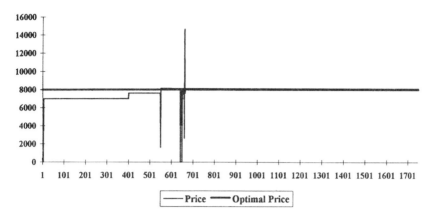

Fig. 2. Monopoly in a stationary environment

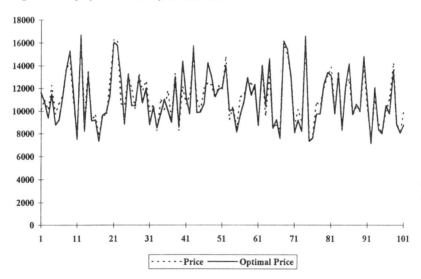

Fig. 3. Monopoly: random costs and demand

environment (demand curve) as the result of a maximisation process. But, this same result can be obtained by a wide variety of different functions. In Fig. 3 [21] the same monopolistic agent faces a more complex environment: both the parameters of the demand function and cost vary. Again, the selected procedures can be completely different from the "theoretical" optimal one in their functional forms but, their outcomes are hardly

---

[21] Since the pay-off of each function depends on random factors, we tested each function over 100 trials and the pay-off is the average of the values obtained. To show the level of performance, in the figure we plot only 100 iterations of the best emerging rule.

20   G. Dosi et al.

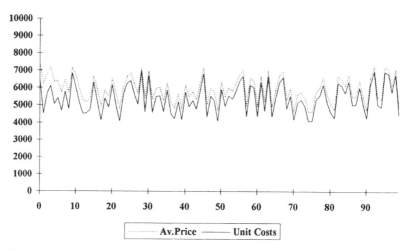

Fig. 4. Oligopoly: inertial learning case av. price and average unit costs

distinguishable. To conclude, these preliminary tests show that GP is able to reproduce an optimising behaviour in simple "non-strategic" situations.

Let us now consider an oligopolistic market. We explore two different environmental and learning scenarios. In the first one we suppose that the demand function is fixed and equal to:

$$p = 10\,000 - 10q$$

Moreover, unitary costs, identical for every agent, are a random variable uniformly distributed on a finite support. Finally, on the representation/action side, our artificial agents are allowed to experiment each set of rules for 100 iterations.

We will present the result of a typical run of the simulation. Since we do not have the possibility either to compare the results to theoretical predictions in this context (because none exist) or to explore formally the functions produced, because of their complexity, we did not carry over a formal statistical analysis about the robustness of our result. We systematically observed in different runs of the models that agents basically used behavioural rules which can be referred to two types.

In Fig. 4 we report the average price plotted against costs for an oligopolistic market with 9 firms. In Fig. 5a,b we report the price series for two typical firms: in Fig. 5a we observe a pricing strategy which strictly follows cost variations.

Although emerging rules are usually quite complex,[22] they behave "as if" they were simple mark-up rules. Another typical behaviour that we

---

[22] The complexity of the rules is at least partly due to the fact that our agents have to produce constants (such as mark-up coefficients) that they do not possess in their set of primitives and have therefore to be obtained by means of operations on variables (e.g. $(X + X)/X = 2$).

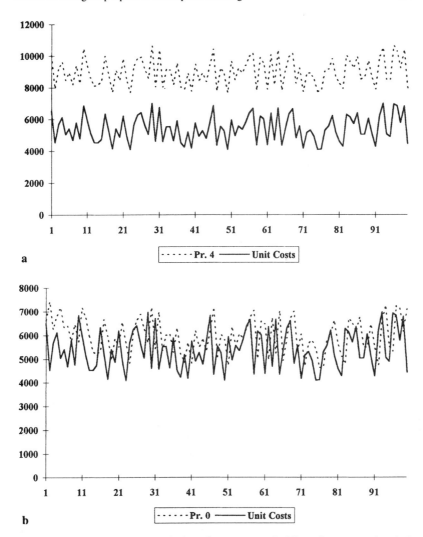

Fig. 5. a Oligopoly: costs and typical mark-up strategy. **b** Oligopoly: costs and typical follower strategy

observe is a follower type of pricing rule: in Fig. 5b, we present the plot of the pricing decisions of an agent using a typical follower strategy. Given the basic functions available to the agents, the follower strategy involves setting the price equal to the value of a past variable. The tree representing the function is a single node containing the name of the variable to follow. This strategy can produce low profits, but it is extremely persistent, since the cross-over cannot break such degenerate tree. Moreover, with a higher number of firms, the complexity of the coordination task increases and this, in turn, favours the emergence of simple imitative behaviour.[23]

Under a second scenario, the intercept of the demand function randomly fluctuates, drawing from a uniform distribution on the support [8000–12 000]. In addition, the individual unitary costs are given by the ratio between two variables: a component which is common to the entire industry and is represented by a random variable uniformly distributed over the interval [0;8000] and an individual productivity component, different for each firm, which is a random walk with a drift. Moreover, we allow agents to change stochastically their sequences of rule at each period, i.e. to switch among the procedures of representation/action which they store. In this way, one forces behavioural variability (and, of course, this decreases predictability of each and every competitor). This extreme learning set-up prevents any rule from settling down and from proving its value in the long term, while facing rather stable behaviours of the competitors. Despite all this, the main conclusions reached under the former scenario hold: mark-up type policies still turn out to be the most frequent and most efficient response to environmental uncertainty.[24] Figures 6 and 7 illustrate costs and price dynamics for the industry

In other exercises, not shown here, we consider similar artificial agents whose control variables are quantities rather than prices. Again, as in the example presented above, a monopolist facing a stationary environment does discover the optimal quantity rule. However, under strategic interactions the agents do not appear to converge to the underlying Cournot-Nash equilibrium, but, rather, cooperative behaviours emerge. In particular, in the duopoly case, the decision rule has "Tit-for-tat" features (cf. Axelrod, 1984) and displays a pattern of the type "do at time t what your opponent did at time t−1".

It has been already mentioned that a straightforward "semantic" interpretation of the procedures which emerge is often impossible. However, their inspection – in the simplest cases – together with the examination of

---

[23] Econometric estimates of the form:

$$\ln p_t = \alpha + \beta \ln p_{t-1} + \cdots + \gamma_0 \ln c_t + \gamma_1 \ln c_{t-1} + \cdots$$

for the industry as a whole, always yield R^2 above 0.90 with significant coefficients for current costs and the first lag on prices only, and always insignificant lagged costs. Conversely, for the majority of the firms, no lagged variable significantly adds to the explanation: firms appear to follow a stationary rule of the simplest mark-up type, $p_i^t = m_i(c^t)$. However, for some firms (the "imitators") current prices seem to be set as a log-linear combination between costs and lagged average prices of the industry, or the lagged price of one of the competitors (as in the example presented in Fig. 5b).

[24] As may be expected, estimates of the form presented in footnote 23 yield somewhat lower R^2 as compared to the previous case – both for the industry aggregate and for the individual firms –, but still most often in the range between 0.6 and 0.8.

Also the other properties of individual pricing procedures stand, and in particular simple stationary rules characterize the most successful players, as assessed in terms of cumulated profits or average market shares. Finally, in analogy to the previous learning scenario, the adjustment dynamics in aggregate prices – where the first lag on prices themselves turns out to be significant – appear to be due primarily to an aggregation effect over most often stationary rules (for a general theoretical point on this issue, cf. Lippi, 1988).

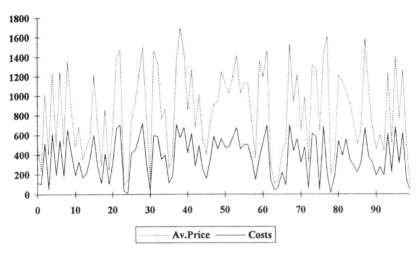

Fig. 6. Oligopoly: continuous adjustment case average costs and prices

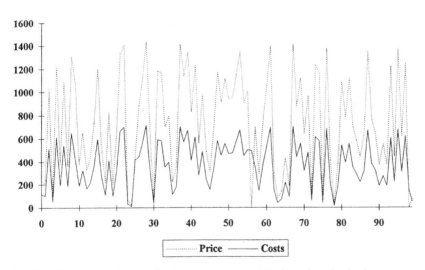

Fig. 7. Oligopoly: continuous adjustment case costs and prices of market leader

the behavioural patterns that they entail, allows an assessment of their nature. Some remarkable patterns appear. First, procedures which "look like" optimization rules emerge only in rather simple and stationary environments. Second, as the complexity of the representation/decision problem increases, rules evolve toward simpler ones, involving the neglect of notionally useful information and very little contingent behaviour. More precisely, the procedure which the evolutionary dynamics appear to select either neglect the strategic nature of the interactive set-up – thus transforming the decision problem into a game "against nature" – or develop very simple imitative behaviours. In all these circumstances the resulting collective outcomes of the interaction significantly depart from the equilibria prescribed by a theory of behaviour grounded on standard rationality assumptions (this applies both to the Cournot-Nash and to the Bertrand set-ups, corresponding to quantity-based and price-based decision rules).

5 Conclusions

In this work we have begun to explore the properties of the procedures of representation/decision which emerge in an evolutionary fashion via adaptive learning and stochastic exploration in a space of elementary functions. Following a negative argument on the general impossibility of endowing agents with some generic and natural optimization algorithms, we presented some preliminary exercises on the co-evolution of cognition and action rules. The results highlight the evolutionary robustness of procedures which – except for the simplest environments – have the characteristics of norms or routines, as defined earlier. Of course one can easily object that real agents indeed base their understanding of the world on a pre-existing cognitive structure much more sophisticated than the elementary functions we have assumed here, and that therefore our result might not bear any implication for the understanding of the actual evolution of norms. On the other hand, the problem solving tasks that empirical agents (and, even more so, real organizations) face are several orders of magnitude more complex than those depicted in this work. Indeed, we would like to consider the exercise presented in this work as a beginning of an answer to the challenge most often confronting the non-believers in (unbounded) rationality assumptions, namely, what do you substitute the latter with? How do you avoid *ad-hocery* and casual empiricism? There is indeed no claim of realism in the model we have presented: however, we suggest that some basic features of the evolution of the rules for cognition and action presented here might well hold in all those circumstances where a "representation gap" exists between the ability that agents pre-possess in interpreting their environment and the "true" structure of the latter. This is obviously a field of analysis where stylized modelling exercises on evolutionary learning can only complement more inductive inquiries from e.g. social psychology and organizational sciences.

References

Arifovic J (1994) Genetic algorithm learning and the cobweb model. Journal of Economic Dynamics and Control 18: 3–25
Arrow K (1987) Oral history: an interview. In: Feiwel GR (ed) Arrow and the ascent of modern economic theory. MacMillan, London
Arthur WB (1992) On learning and adaptation in the economy. Santa Fe NM, Santa Fe Institute, working paper 92-07-038
Axelrod R (1984) The evolution of cooperation. Basic Books, New York
Casti JL (1992) Reality rules. Wiley, New York
Cohen D (1987) Computability and logic. Ellis Horwood, Chichester

Cohen M, Burkhart R, Dosi G, Egidi M, Marengo L, Warglien M, Winter S, Coriat B (1995) Routines and other recurring action patterns of organizations: Contemporary Research Issues. Santa Fe, Santa Fe Institute, WP 95-11-101, Industrial and Corporate Change (forthcoming)

Cutland NJ (1980) Computability: an introduction to recursive function theory. Cambridge University Press, Cambridge

Curzon-Price T (1997) Using co-evolutionary programming to simulate strategic behaviour in markets. Journal of Evolutionary Economics 7: 219–254

Dosi G, Egidi M (1991) Substantive and procedural uncertainty. An exploration of economic behaviours in complex and changing environments. Journal of Evolutionary Economics 1: 145–168

Dosi G, Freeman C, Nelson R, Silverberg G, Soete L (eds) (1988) Technical change and economic theory. Pinter, London

Dosi G, Marengo L (1994) Some elements of an evolutionary theory of organizational competences. In England RW (ed) Evolutionary concepts in contemporary economics, pp 157–78. University of Michigan Press, Ann Arbor

Dosi G, Marengo L, Fagiolo G (1996) Learning in evolutionary environments. Laxenburg, Austria, International Institute for Applied Systems Analysis, Working Paper

Dosi G, Metcalfe JS (1991) On some notions of Irreversibility in Economics. In Saviotti PP, Metcalfe JS (eds) Evolutionary theories of economic and technological change. Harwood Academic Press, Chur

Elster J (1986) The multiple self. Cambridge University Press, Cambridge

Fontana W (1992) Algorithmic chemistry. In: Langton C, Farmer JD, Rasmussen S (eds) Artificial life. Addison Wesley, Redwood City, CA

Fontana W, Buss LW (1994) What would be conserved if "the tape were played twice"? Proceedings of the National Academy of Sciences USA, vol 91, pp 757–761

Friedman M (1953) Essays in positive economics. University of Chicago Press, Chicago

Goldberg DE (1989) Genetic algorithms in search. Optimization and learning. Addison Wesley, Reading, MA

Heiner RA (1983) The origin of predictable behavior. American Economic Review 73: 560–595

Heiner RA (1988) Imperfect decisions in organizations: toward a theory of internal structure. Journal of Economic Behavior and Organization 9: 25–44

Herrnstein RJ, Prelec D (1991) Melioration: a theory of distributed choice. Journal of Economic Perspectives 5: 137–156

Hodgson G (1988) Economics and institutions. Polity Press, London

Hogart RM, Reder MW (eds) (1986) Rational choice. Chicago University Press, Chicago

Holland JH (1975) Adaptation in natural and artificial systems. University of Michigan Press, Ann Arbor

Holland JH, Holyoak KJ, Nisbett RE, Thagard PR (1986) Induction: processes of inference, learning and discovery. MIT Press, Cambridge, MA

Kahneman D, Slovic P, Tversky A (eds) (1982) Judgment under uncertainty: heuristics and biases. Cambridge University Press, Cambridge, MA

Kahneman D, Tversky A (1979) Prospect theory: an analysis of decision under risk. Econometrica 47: 263–291

Koford KJ, Miller JB (eds) (1991) Social norms and economic institutions. University of Michigan Press, Ann Arbor

Koza JR (1992) The genetic programming paradigm: genetically breeding populations of computer programs to solve problems. In: Soucek B (ed) Dynamic, genetic and chaotic programming. Wiley, New York

Koza JR (1993) Genetic programming. MIT Press, Cambridge, MA

Lewis A (1985a) On effectively computable realization of choice functions. Mathematical Social Sciences 10: 43–80

Lewis A (1985b) The minimum degree of recursively representable choice functions. Mathematical Social Sciences 10: 179–188

Lewis A (1986) Structure and complexity. The use of recursion theory in the foundations of neoclassical mathematical economics and the theory of games. Cornell University, Department of Mathematics, Ithaca, mimeo

Lewis A (1987) On turing degrees of walrasian models and a general impossibility result in the theory of decision-making. Technical report n. 512, Institute for Mathematical Studies in the Social Sciences, Stanford University

Lindgren K (1991) Evolutionary phenomena in simple dynamics. In: Langton CG et al. (eds) Artificial life II. Addison Wesley, Redwood City, CA

Lippi M (1988) On the dynamics of aggregate macro equations: from simple micro behaviours to complex macro relationships. In: Dosi G et al. (eds) Technical change and economic theory, pp 170–196. Pinter, New York

Luhmann N (1979) Trust and power. Wiley, Chichester

March JG (1988) Decisions and organizations. Blackwell, Oxford

March JG (1994) A primer on decision making. Free Press, New York

Marengo L (1996) Structure, competences and learning in an adaptive model of the firm. In: Dosi G, Malerba F (eds) Organization and strategy in the evolution of the enterprise. MacMillan, London

Margolis H (1987) Patterns, thinking and cognition: A theory of judgement. Chicago University Press, Chicago

Miller JH (1988) The evolution of automata in the repeated prisoner's dilemma. Santa Fe Institute, working paper

Nelson RR, Winter SG (1982) An evolutionary theory of economic change. Harvard University Press, Cambridge MA

Newell A, Simon H (1972) Human problem solving. Prentice-Hall, Englewood Cliffs, NJ

Post E (1943) Formal reductions of the general combinatorial decision problem. American Journal of Mathematics 65: 197–215

Rabin MO (1957) Effective computability of winning strategies: contributions to the theory of games III. Annals of Mathematics Studies 39: 147–157

Rustem B, Velupillai K (1990) Rationality, computability and complexity. Journal of Economics Dynamics and Control 14: 419–432

Sen A (1977) Rational fools: a critique of the behavioral foundations of economic theory. Philosophy and Public Affairs 6: 317–344

Simon HA (1976) From substantive to procedural rationality. In: Latsis SJ (ed) Method and appraisal in economics, pp 129–148. Cambridge University Press, Cambridge

Simon HA (1981) The sciences of the artificial. MIT Press, Cambridge MA

Simon HA (1986) Rationality in psychology and economics. Journal of Business 59: supplement

Thrakhtenbrot DA (1963) Algorithms and automatic computing machines. Heath, Boston, MA

Winter SG (1971) Satisficing, selection and innovating remnant. Quarterly Journal of Economics 85: 237–261

Winter SG (1986) Adaptive behaviour and economic rationality: comments on Arrow and Lucas. Journal of Business 59: supplement

[7]

Some Elements of an Evolutionary Theory of Organizational Competences

Giovanni Dosi and Luigi Marengo

Only recently has the economic theory of the firm begun to address the issue of the role of different organizational structures. Traditionally, the neoclassical theory explained all economic phenomena in terms of individual agents (households or firms) and markets, which through the price mechanism convey all the information necessary to individual decision making and therefore coordinate all interactions among individuals.

The basic tenets of neoclassical theory are summarized with remarkable clarity by Arrow (1974a, 1–3):

> The neoclassical model is founded on two concepts, which are considerably different in nature. One is the notion of the individual economic agent, whose behavior is governed by a criterion of optimization under constraints which are partly peculiar to the agent, such as production functions, and partly terms of trade with the economic system as a whole. The other is the market; here the aggregate of individual decisions is acknowledged, and the terms of trade adjusted until the decisions of the individuals are mutually consistent in the aggregate, i.e., supply equals demand.

Indeed, the reduction of rationality to maximization makes it possible for the neoclassical economist to ignore the psychological and cognitive aspects of decision making (Simon 1976): the rationality of a decision resides solely in the optimality of the decision itself, regardless of the procedure that led to it. Symmetrically, the reduction of all coordination modes to the market— exemplified by the general equilibrium theory but also, in strategic contexts, by most game-theoretical models—brings the issue of organization outside the domain of economic theory: organizations such as firms might indeed exist, but their internal structure is immaterial for the allocation of resources at the level of the entire economic system.

Recent streams of research, e.g., Williamson (1975, 1985), Sah and Stiglitz (1986), Crémer (1980), and Aoki (1986, 1988), have progressively challenged the latter assumption and analyzed coordination modes different from that of the market. Aoki, in particular, has extensively studied the potential for learning within and resource generation of different organizational setups. However, the primary emphasis of most of these studies is upon learning in activities involving information processing, which can be fundamentally reduced to Bayesian estimation of random variables with stationary means and finite variance. Certainly, along these lines of research, major progress has been made in highlighting the different efficiency properties of alternative combinations of market mechanisms and hierarchies in the organization of economic activities.

In essence, whenever one abandons the most restrictive assumptions on information perfectness and symmetry among agents, organizational forms do matter because incentives, information flows, and behaviors differ according to the particular "institutional architecture" of each system. In particular, if each system's performance rests on specific learning dynamics by individuals or groups of them (such as "firms"), the institutional architecture affects the scope and rate at which such learning can occur. Even more so, all of this applies whenever one considers environments characterized by permanent opportunities for technological and organizational innovation.

As argued elsewhere, for example, Dosi (1988) and Dosi and Egidi (1991), innovative activities involve also a kind of learning quite different from Bayesian probability updating and regression estimation: it requires agents to build new representations of the environment they operate in (and that remains largely unknown) and develop new skills enabling them both to explore and to exploit this world of ever-expanding opportunities (Nelson and Winter 1982).

The Notion of Competence

To introduce the notion of competence, one may begin with the puzzle posed by the quite robust piece of empirical evidence that suggests that firms do *persistently* differ in their characteristics, behaviors, and performances. It is a piece of evidence that has been intuitively obvious for a long time to managers, business analysts, and consultants alike. However, these phenomena are also increasingly "tested" according to criteria that satisfy the requirements of the economic profession, and efforts are being made to explain them with a variety of theoretical tools.

Mentions of the evidence here need only be very telegraphic. For example, firms—*even within the same industry*—differ in terms of their propensities to commit resources to innovation and imitation. They differ in their revealed successes in developing and adopting new products, new production processes, and new organizational setups (Freeman 1982; Dosi 1988). They also differ—*also within the same line of business*—in terms of unit costs of production and their profitabilities (Rumelt 1988 and, for a somewhat different interpretation, Schmalensee 1985). Moreover, among firms (often operating in different lines of business) profit differentials are quite persistent over time (Geroski and Jacquemin 1984; Mueller 1986). Finally, differences in innovativeness and production efficiency, although not necessarily in profitability, are even more pronounced and persistent in international comparisons (Patel and Pavitt 1988).

What has economic theory to say about these observations? As is well known, many theoretical accounts with some bearing on this evidence have been proposed over the last decade or so. In a rather sketchy way, we could group them into two different streams. A first class of theoretical interpretations suggests that either asymmetries among firms are wrongly inferred from the data or that they are indeed epiphenomena. For example, interfirm differences in innovation and timing of adoption are explained primarily as the outcome of *equilibrium* strategic interactions. If this were the case, one could account for residual diversity as temporary disequilibrium phenomena. However, persistence of technological or economic asymmetries is strikingly at odds with this kind of interpretation. A second stream of analysis, often in combination with the former, acknowledges various forms of interfirm diversity and explains them in terms of: (1) different utility functions—mainly intertemporal preferences and risk-aversions; (2) different endowments in some production and innovating skills; and (3) asymmetric information.

Let us focus primarily on points (2) and (3) of the latter interpretation. Suppose that the comparison between the performance of two firms (or groups of them) shows a systematic difference. For example, one of them could show systematically higher rates of innovation. But this would not be sufficient to suggest an asymmetry between the two: the other firm could follow an equilibrium strategy of imitation, given some appropriate difference between average costs of innovation and imitation. However, the first one could also be systematically more profitable, while the second subsisted permanently on the verge of bankruptcy. What do we make of all that? Most likely there is an underlying asymmetry between them. Ruling out differences in utility functions and expectations—easy to claim but also ad hoc unobservable—most economists would base their explanation on differences in endowments and/or asymmetric information.

The main points of the "endowments" explanation could be summarized as follows. Individuals and organizations are highly bounded in their performances by their inner features (something analogous to their "genes") but they do not exhibit, ex ante, what they are. The actual process of interaction among agents is in fact a sort of tournament that allows the "inherently best" to emerge as winners (Jovanovic 1982; Lucas 1978). Alternatively, the "asymmetric information" explanation would roughly claim that individuals and organizations, though having virtually similar performance potentials, happen to face asymmetric access to information and therefore reveal, ex post, systematically different performances.

We do not intend to deny the importance of asymmetries in endowments and in access to information. However, we believe that a large class of features exists that characterizes and distinguishes firms that cannot be reduced to either category. Indeed, we propose that competences cannot be reduced to either endowments or information partitions, but represent the *problem-solving features of particular sets of organizational interactions, norms, and*—to some extent—*explicit strategies*. Competences present a significant degree of inertia and firm-specificity. Thus, as a first approximation, they could be considered as firm-specific assets but unlike "endowments" are subject to learning and change through their very application to actual problem solving. Similarly, they share with information partitions the fact that being more competent also implies, loosely speaking, a greater control upon the environment wherein the firm operates. However, competences do not necessarily increase as information becomes more perfect. There are fundamental elements of learning and innovation that concern much more the *representation* of the environment in which individuals and organizations operate and *problem solving* rather than simple information gathering and processing.

Let us illustrate these points by means of a metaphor. What does being a good soccer player mean? Certainly there is a strong "endowment" component. However, the number of those who succeed is most likely much lower than the set of those endowed with an adequate potential. Ultimately, success depends on training, the sequence of teams the individual has played for, his or her coaches, and, last but not least, on chance. In this example one can easily identify some basic features: (1) the existence of some learning process, (2) a puzzling difficulty in stating the exact procedures of this learning, and (3) different performance outcomes that can hardly be attributed to ex-ante recognizable differences in the features of the agents or differences in the environmental stimuli to which they have been exposed.

Competence and Decision Making

In order to clarify what a "competence" is, it might be useful to start from a relatively standard decision-theoretic representation of an agent or a firm. The existing theory of decision making, on which most of the economic theories of the firm are based, characterizes each decision maker by his or her own information partition, which constitutes the decision maker's information processing capabilities. In other words, this information partition embodies the agent's knowledge about the environment in which he or she is operating, his or her "model of the world." Such an information partition is the frame through which the agent can classify the information received from the environment and compute the probabilities according to which conceivable events are expected to take place. Bayes's rule is the rational way of coherently incorporating new information within such a frame, and maximization of expected utility is the rational criterion for taking a decision that is coherent with the probability distribution.

Two key, but often implicit, hypotheses are made about this information partition. First, it is assumed, by definition, to be a partition, which involves postulating consistency and even isomorphism between the real world and the agent's model of it. Agents may differ only because they have "finer" or "coarser" partitions, meaning that they can be more or less precise in responding to events. However, mistakes, surprises, and inconsistencies are all ruled out. Second, the partition is assumed as given, and the study of the decision process is limited to the study of the rules that optimize the use of information within such a frame. It can be contended instead that a crucial part of the decision process is the construction, evaluation, and modification of the frame of reference itself. This very process can be defined as *learning*. Bayesian learning is instead the use of new information in order to update the present probability distribution, within a given and constant frame of reference.[1]

As far as decision making is concerned, this perspective clearly implies a shift of attention away from the objective validity of the rules that determine the optimum use of information and the optimum action toward the *procedures* used by the agents to improve their understanding of reality (Simon 1976). Moreover, whereas with information partitions, more information always means better decisions (or at least not worse ones), without partitions, more information can also lead to worse decisions (Geanakoplos 1990).

This applies to individuals and, a fortiori, to organizations such as firms. Basically, the firm is seen in most of present-day economic theory as an information-processing unit, although the presence of a multiplicity of agents with information asymmetries raises complex questions about the design of coordination and incentive schemes that can efficiently allocate information

---

1. Bayesian decision making reduces all uncertainty to mere risk. It cannot account therefore for another fundamental source of uncertainty: ignorance. On one side there is the uncertainty deriving from the intrinsic randomness of the phenomena the decision maker faces: this kind of uncertainty cannot be entirely eliminated by the decision maker and is adequately handled within the framework of probability theory. But, on the other hand, there exists also the uncertainty that derives from the agent's ignorance of the characteristics of the world he or she is facing. This kind of uncertainty instead can be reduced by the agent through the improvement of his or her own state of knowledge, that is, by what we properly call "learning" in this work.

among them. Thus, differences in efficiency among firms are reduced to differences in their "endowments," i.e., in the information partitions of their members and in the ability of their executives to efficiently allocate information by designing and running appropriate coordination and incentive schemes.

Our perspective characterizes instead firms mainly as *learning organizations*, where the set of "opportunities" open to the organization is not assumed as being known to the decision makers and, therefore, where the members' and the organization's information-processing capabilities and the very decision rules cannot be postulated but are generated and coevolve in a process of learning and adaptation. In other words, organizational knowledge is neither presupposed nor derived from the available information but rather emerges as a property of the learning system and is shaped by the interaction among the various learning processes that constitute the organization.

This interpretation implies a radical shift in the object of analysis. Rather than analyzing the signals that the environment delivers to the unit of decision, it focuses on the inner features of the response mechanisms of the unit itself. It is a perspective that clearly goes back to Simon, Cyert, March, Nelson, and Winter—i.e., to what is often referred to as "bounded rationality" and the "behavioral theory of the firm." As these and other authors have repeatedly emphasized, the very definition of what information is relevant (before its collection, classification, and interpretation) might turn out to be highly problematic and "framed." Individuals and organizations most likely have only a modest control over the world and there may often be an essential ambiguity in the relationship between events, actions, and outcomes (March 1988a). Given all this, it is hard to postulate some invariant optimizing algorithm and to define it.

However, even when the existence of such an optimizing algorithm can be established, its derivation from the available (even perfect) information might still prove problematic. In Dosi and Egidi (1991) the solution of a Rubik cube is considered as a simple and archetypical example. Given the initial configuration, the solution concept and the admissible rules ("information" in the sense of the foregoing decision-theoretic setup) are perfect: there is no environmental uncertainty and indeed there notionally exists a function that maps information into actions that maximize utility (say, by minimizing the number of moves leading to the solution). However, *finding* that optimal procedure or, for that matter, any procedure is precisely the crucial task.

The following should be noted: (1) This is a pure problem-solving task quite independent of any further interaction with the external environment. (2) Despite the known existence of an algorithm, it is no trivial task and in fact many people do give up. (3) It can be shown that human subjects develop *higher-level rules* in order to solve it—rules that are underivable from the original information about the problem itself, that apply to a whole set of initial configurations (i.e., they are *robust* to changes in the initial information), and that can be automatized as *routines*. We believe that this is a highly simplified metaphor of individual problem solving and, even more so, of firms as problem solvers.

"Competences" here are viewed as the properties of the solution procedures. Each set of rules or algorithm may well be different, with different revealed efficiencies, without, however, the possibility of defining ex ante the optimal one and without even the possibility of determining *in general* whether any such algorithm exists before having found it. Both, in fact, are well-known results of computation theory on problem solving. In the foregoing representation of the decision problem, the partition on the set of states of the world and the solution concept are formally equivalent to finite strings of information.

Finding maps from states of the world into action means finding a Turing machine that rewrites the information string into the solution string with a finite set of transformations (Dosi and Egidi 1991). A powerful impossibility theorem from computation theory states that there is no general algorithm that can always decide whether two strings are derivable one from another after a finite sequence of admissible transformations. In other words, there cannot be any general problem-solving algorithm (Cutland 1980). Or, putting it in yet another way, information about states of the world, solution concepts, and admitted rules—no matter how "perfect"—are by themselves insufficient to automatically derive *in general terms* any solution algorithm and hence, a fortiori, the optimal one. In order to do so, one requires also some form of preexisting *knowledge* and some imperfectly definable procedures, which are usually the product of inferential induction, analogy, and problem framing but also of socially constructed norms and bodies of knowledge.

What do we make of all this from the point of view of positive theories of behavior and decision making of individuals and organizations? One epistemology consists in postulating that individuals and organizations do prepossess all the knowledge appropriate to most relevant economic decisions and also that they have already worked out the problem-solving algorithm. Hence, no issue of "competence" arises. The heavy assumption here is that proving an existence theorem requires some innate cognitive and computational endowment of the agents to work out the appropriate algorithm in order to get to the place where the theorem states it is optimal for the agents to be, given the available information.[2]

A second possible approach is to explicitly acknowledge "bounded rationality": memory and the other computational resources are finite, and recur-

---

2. Incidentally, an increasing stream of theoretical results shows that many familiar equilibrium concepts are recursively noncomputable (Lewis 1985, 1986).

sive computability represents the "upper bound" to the perfection of the decision procedures that agents are allowed to possess. Indeed, suggestive results have been recently achieved on the grounds of this methodology, especially in game theory. For example, by assuming that agents are bound to choose sets of algorithmic rules in their interactions,[3] it can be shown that the set of possible equilibria significantly changes as compared to unrestricted rationality setups (e.g., Rubinstein 1986; Abreu and Rubinstein 1988).

This notwithstanding, a lingering issue concerns the procedure by which agents "choose" their appropriate algorithm (i.e., their automaton). In a sense, the question of whether or not agents possess the "competence" appropriate to the solution of the problem they face is only pushed to some meta-level. By assuming that agents possess different and well-constructed (albeit computationally finite) procedures and can choose among them, one attributes to them all the appropriate "competence" to work them out and select them. From a computational point of view, this implies that agents are assumed to possess some unspecified "correct" heuristics of choice among different automata. In turn, this implies—at the very least—a very strong interpretation of Simonian "procedural rationality." Comparisons among alternative algorithms plausibly ought to imply that "problem solving is viewed as *nearly decomposable*, meaning that for the most part each subgoal can be solved without knowledge of the other subgoals of the system" (Forrest 1990, 7).

We want to argue here for a third perspective implying an even more radical departure from the standard representation of rationality. It develops recent modeling on "emergent computation" (Holland et al. 1986; Forrest 1990) and in its spirit directly connects with the analyses of corporate decisions and behaviors by March, Nelson and Winter, and many organizational theorists.

To put it briefly, suppose that—no matter how perfect information is—agents do not prepossess the appropriate "problem solver." Suppose also that the space of "opportunities" is incompletely known by the agents and is possibly modified by their own actions. Finally, suppose that agents start from very simple and rudimentary rules, by themselves inadequate to the solution tasks. Our conjecture is that the problem-solving procedures are emergent properties of interactions, involving also mutation and recombination of these distributed basic rudimentary rules, often drawing on related but hardly codifiable knowledge, experience, and interpretation frames.

The crucial point of this perspective is that learning involves adaptation and discovery of problem-solving procedures that cannot be automatically derived either from the information about the states of the world or from the

---

3. This assumption is usually formalized by such finite automata as "Moore machines."

solution concept. The empirical counterpart of these problem-solving procedures comprises organizational tasks ranging from how to design a product
and manufacture it efficiently to how to penetrate new markets—that is, most
of the activities of business firms. A few important implications follow from
this view of the firm.

First, the difference between the *process* and the *content* of learning is a
blurred one, a point repeatedly emphasized by Nelson and Winter (1982) and
also in Dosi, Teece, and Winter (1991) and Pavitt (1990a). What a firm
"knows" is mainly stored in its behavioral rules and is reproduced, augmented, changed via the actual implementation of such problem-solving
routines.

Second, "competences" summarize the effectiveness of firm-specific
problem-solving procedures. The "dynamic competences" discussed by Teece
et al. (1990) concern higher-level procedures, namely those related to the
search for *new problems* and *new problem-solving procedures* (after all, this is
an essential part of technological and organizational innovation). Hence,
loosely speaking, competences relate to both "being good at doing certain
things" and "being good at learning certain things."

Third, this focus on firms as problem solvers may be taken as somewhat
complementary to the view of Williamson (1990) that firms are economizers
on the costs of transactions. The fundamental divide is between a representation of firms primarily in terms of strategizing versus a representation in terms
of learning and economizing. The first view in its essence proposes that firms,
by assumption, have got their problem-solving procedures and their hierarchical structure right and, therefore, that their primary activity involves playing
complicated and devious games with each other. On the contrary, we would
argue the latter view to the extreme and claim that most of firms' activities
concern *games against nature*, in which strategic interactions induce only
relatively minor fluctuations.[4]

The strategic view concentrates on equilibrium interactions among firms,

---

4. Similar remarks were made by Sidney Winter during the conference on "Fundamental
Issues in Strategy: A Research Agenda for the 1990's," Napa Valley, California, 1990. To
illustrate, in the latter perspective a car manufacturer tries primarily to develop a new type of car
with a quality as high as possible and costs as low as possible: the primary activities involve
understanding changing consumers' preferences, developing new electronic gadgets, building
and learning how to use new machinery, organizing production, etc. Looking at competitors is
important mainly to learn from their own problem-solving procedures, but in a first approximation everyone is playing games against nature wherein subtle strategizing has only second-order
effects. Conversely, the "strategizing view" would suggest that every competitor notionally
knows how to make a new car or a new microprocessor equally well (or at least knows equally
well how to draw from a stochastic process such as the "patent race"). Differences are mainly the
outcome of complicated strategizing (e.g., preemptive investment) or chance.

on the assumption that each of them is *internally* optimally adjusted, while in the learning perspective the primary explanation of what firms do relates to what goes on *within* them.

Some of these analytically conflicting views could be settled, in principle, on empirical grounds: e.g., what is the variance of interfirm, intraindustry performance that is left unexplained after allowing for the effect of different governance structures? How far can one go in explaining different competences by assimilating them to identifiable assets, however defined? But, of course, even if one subscribes, in a first approximation, to a "learning" or "dynamic competence" view of the firm, a more satisfactory picture would be a model that embodies other corporate functions that have traditionally been the major focus of other theories.

The model of the firm described here suggests that it is a *behavioral entity* (Kreps 1990a) embodying highly *idiosyncratic, specific, and inertial compromises* between different functions, namely: (1) resource allocation; (2) information processing; (3) incentives to individual performance; (4) control and power exercise; and (5) learning.

Remarkably, most breeds of economic theory focus primarily upon one single function, often trying to explain it on the grounds of the usual maximization cum equilibrium assumptions. The perspective proposed here, on the contrary, embodies fundamental trade-offs between the functions mentioned above (e.g., Aoki and Dosi 1991). To illustrate them in a somewhat caricatural way, think of the possible trade-offs between performance control and learning. While the former is likely to imply rigid task specification, the latter generally involves a lot of experimentation, trial and error, and "deviant" behavior.

Competence, Learning, and Organization

We would like to suggest that the notion of competence does not involve only problem-solving skills, concerning the relationship between the firm and the outside environment, but also skills and rules governing internal relationships. The two are strictly interconnected: the rates and direction of learning are shaped by the internal norms of behavior of individual organizations.

Holland et al. (1986) examine the key characteristics of a learning process. As already pointed out, learning takes place in the space of *representations* and cannot be reduced to mere information gathering. In a complex and ever-changing world, agents must define sets of states that they consider as equivalent for the purpose of action. In other words, they have to build representations of the world in order to discover regularities that can be exploited by their actions. These representations have a pragmatic nature and are contingent upon the particular purpose the routine is serving. Second, learning is essentially driven by the search for a better performance. The learning agent must therefore use some system of *performance assessment*. Finally, if rules of behavior have to be selected, added, modified, and deleted, there must exist a procedure for the *evaluation of the usefulness* of the rules. This problem might not have a clear solution when the performance of the system may be assessed only as a result of a long and complex sequence of interdependent rules (such as in the game of chess).

These questions arise in every learning system, individual or organizational. But when learning takes place within a multiagent setting, it requires the coordination of the learning processes of many individuals. This poses some additional questions about representations, performance assessment, and rule evaluation within an organizational context.

Members of an organization will in general have different representations of the environment they are facing. This multiplicity of representations requires the implementation of some mechanisms whose task is to reconcile actual or potential conflicts.

Mechanisms of this kind can be considered from at least two perspectives. The first is a "cognitive" one. From this perspective, conflict resolution requires the definition of a common knowledge basis, a "shared representation" of some parts of the environment that takes the form of a collection of organizational facts, codes, and languages whose meaning is clear to all members of the organization and that enables communication and coordination among them. As with individual representations, organizational common knowledge and languages will also be contingent upon the particular purposes they serve.

The second perspective is a "political" one and encompasses all the procedures that define and govern hierarchical relations inside the organization.[5] It is important to stress that the cognitive and the political aspects of coordination mechanisms are strictly interconnected and cannot be distinguished: the relations that shape the organizational knowledge basis are the same as those that define the hierarchical structure of the organization.

If the multiplicity of representations, on the one hand, raises the problem of coordination in organizational learning, it might also be a source of learning if the resulting variety of organizational knowledge can be exploited. In general there will be a trade-off between the two aspects of multiplicity: on the one side, coordination benefits from a large and consistent "shared representation"; on the other side, commonality of knowledge reduces the scope for learning from diversity.

In addition to a multiplicity of representations, collective decision mak-

---

5. This perspective lies behind the conception of organizational routines as a "truce" among conflicting intraorganizational interests (Nelson and Winter 1982, 107–12).

ing is usually characterized by a multiplicity of systems of preferences. Members of an organization have different goals, which must be harmonized in some way.

It is worth mentioning that assuming multiplicity of representations complicates even more the problem of the multiplicity of preferences. Not only do preferences among states vary across members, but the same state might be differently perceived by different members, making performance assessment highly complicated. Cohen (1987) provides an example: the present state of the firm may be perceived by a functional unit as "we are in our third successive quarter of increasing market share" and by another as "we are in our third successive quarter of decreasing return on capital." Even if the two functional units shared the same system of preferences, their assessments of the present performance of the firm would turn out to be divergent.

Similar problems arise when one tries to evaluate the contribution of single decisions to a complex and interconnected set of actions leading to a certain organizational outcome. Divergent representations and divergent systems of preferences make this evaluation even more complex than in the case of individual decision makers, where already no unique solution seems possible.

As Cohen (1984) pointed out, looking at the incentive problem from a static optimizing or a learning point of view may lead to very different conclusions. From the former perspective, diversity of representations and goals leads to inefficiency and suboptimality ("loss of control"), whereas from the latter perspective diversity of representations and preferences enhances organizational adaptability and learning. All in all, there is no reason why, in general, efficient design of hierarchical structures for allocation and control should coincide with effective design for learning.

Organizations achieve coordination through the definition of a common set of rules, codes, and languages that are well understood and shared by all the members of the organization involved in a given interaction. Such a set is termed by Crémer (1990, 54) "corporate culture" and defined as "the stock of knowledge which is common to a substantial portion of the employees of the firm, but not to the general population from which they are drawn." Organizations are social institutions that shape, preserve, and modify this common knowledge basis.

Let us consider an organizational decision problem where the outcome for the organization depends on the actions of several agents in a nonadditive way. The information-processing capabilities of the members of the organization do not necessarily represent a partition of the set of states of the world but are, more generally, a subset of the power set of the states of the world.[6] A

---

6. Recent critiques of and extensions to the theory of probability, such as fuzzy probabilities and the theory of evidence (e.g., Dubois and Prade 1987), which provide a formal

fortiori, the information-processing capabilities of different members of the organization generally will neither coincide nor be compatible (meaning that given two information partitions, either they are equal or one can be obtained from the other by simply refining or coarsening some information cells).

If agents shared the same model of the world or knew each other's model, the only obstacle to effective coordination would derive from some form of lack, bias, or strategic use of information. In a world instead where decision makers do not entirely share a given model and do not know a priori each other's models, a common knowledge basis must be developed that enables agents to communicate effectively and eventually achieve coordination. If, for instance, one part of the organization communicates to another that, to the best of its knowledge, the present state of the world is X and such communication is truthful (and known as such to the other), the meaning of such a piece of information can still be misunderstood because the receiver has a different information-processing capability than the sender.[7] For example, the proposition "the state of the world is X" can have for the receiver a different meaning (when the considered subset of the states of the world's power set is not the same for the two agents) or even no meaning at all (when X does not exist in the receiver's information-processing capabilities).

As far as organizational decision making is concerned, the problem is therefore first of all to build a common knowledge basis, a common language that enables communication and coordination. At the same time members of the organization, who are involved in learning, do modify their own knowledge basis. Individual knowledge and organizational knowledge *coevolve* through a process of *mutual adaptation*.

In game theory, common knowledge expresses the concept that a group of people know some facts, each of them knows that the others know, each of them knows that the others know that they know, and so on ad infinitum. It is well known that such a chain of conditions leads either to an infinite regress or to a logical contradiction (Gilboa 1988) and that therefore this kind of common knowledge can ultimately only be postulated and not deduced from the agents' information-processing capabilities.

These considerations cast strong doubts on the validity of the neoclassical reduction of the firm to an optimum bundle of contracts that can be entirely deduced from the members' rational interaction. The firm appears on the contrary as a social institution, formed indeed by individuals, but not entirely "transparent" to their rational introspection. People do coordinate their actions and base such coordination on a common knowledge basis that allows them to form correct expectations about each other's behavior and to

---

framework for the treatment of subjective uncertain knowledge, are based on this very representation of the subjective state of knowledge.

7. Similar concepts are expressed in Arrow's (1974b) discussion of the issue of "coding."

"close" the chain of speculations on each other's actions that would be unsolvable on the grounds of mere rationality. Such a common knowledge basis is formed by and *evolves* through the interaction of individual knowledge bases but cannot be reduced entirely to them. It takes the form of social institutions, such as conventions, rules, languages, culture, etc., which embed, preserve, and modify the amount of social knowledge that makes coordination possible.

Marengo (1992) has developed a simulation model of organizational decision making and learning in which the members of the organization do not possess any prior knowledge of the environment they are facing, let alone a given common partition of the states of the world. At every moment in time, each member's state of knowledge is represented by a subset of the power set of states of the world. This very state of knowledge is modified through a process of learning and adaptation, which is driven exclusively by the search for a higher organizational payoff, according to a methodology derived from the classifier systems (Holland 1986; Holland et al. 1986).

Suppose that the members of the organization observe independently the state of the world and do not communicate among themselves. Simulations show that coordination cannot emerge, even in the simplest case where the state of the world is held constant throughout the entire simulation. Such a negative result is obvious when we consider that agents cannot, in these conditions, make any connection between states of the world, action, and payoff, since the latter depends on the other agents' actions as well.

But consider now another agent, whose task is to observe and forecast the state of the world and send a unique message to the other agents, who will now receive only this message and will not directly observe the state of the world. Let us again suppose that this higher-level agent (let us call it "management"[8]) is, like the other ones, completely ignorant at the outset and refines its knowledge according exclusively to the organizational payoff.

Simulations show that in this case coordination can indeed emerge. It may appear as surprising that such a different behavior can emerge since in both cases the members of the organization still observe a unique external message and do not communicate with each other. (Actually in both cases they are not even aware of each other's existence.) The difference is that now the message that is received is not fixed but adapts to the receivers' capabilities of interpreting and using the message itself. In other words, the system builds an internal *language*, a *common knowledge* basis that adapts to and coevolves with the information-processing capabilities of both the management and the other decision units.

A few observations are due on the nature of this language. First, the language has a pragmatic nature. It is developed to help solve a particular

---

8. It could be called, more generally, "institution."

problem and to serve a particular state of cognitive capabilities of both the broadcaster and the receiver. Therefore, the language cannot be directly transferred to another problem or another organization. Second, the very semantic content of the language and the level of understanding of reality that the common knowledge basis embeds are themselves strictly adapted to the problem that is being faced and to the characteristics of the agent's cognitive capabilities. For example, if the state of the world remains constant and the agents are not pursuing a refinement of their information-processing capabilities, they develop a "minimal" language—a single message for all the possible situations—that embeds no understanding at all of the environment but is perfectly apt to promote coordination in the case.

Marengo (1992) considers the role of the structure of the organization in shaping and modifying such an organizational knowledge basis. Organizational structures are characterized by their degrees of centralization/ decentralization in the formation and use of knowledge. Suppose again that the organization must adapt its decisions to an environment whose characteristics are not known a priori and that the organizational outcome depends on the actions of all the members in some nonadditive way. At the same time, suppose also that comprehensive detailed planning is not feasible, so that the members of the organization always have some degree of discretion in their decisions.

One way of achieving coordination is by centralizing the formation of an organizational model of the world coadapted with the members' capabilities to interpret it. On the other hand, the formation of such a model can be entirely decentralized, by allowing all the members to observe independently the environment and exchange messages in order to negotiate a common interpretation. Between these two cases—complete centralization and complete decentralization—there exists a range of intermediate ones. For instance, it is possible to centralize the formation of the model of the world but allow subordinate units to communicate and coordinate actions via horizontal communication. Or it is possible both to allow subordinate units to form their own autonomous model of the world and to have at the same time a competing centralized model that preserves the coherence of the organization.

Simulations allow us to test the learning performance of these different organizational structures in different environmental conditions, characterized by varying degrees of being stationary and regular. If the state of the world remains stationary, "simpler" structures such as the completely centralized and the completely decentralized ones are faster in achieving coordination, while changing environmental conditions and the need for reorganizing routines that have already been accumulated through past experience favor structures where forms of centralization and decentralization coexist.

In particular, when environmental changes follow some regular and detectable pattern, the discovery and exploitation of such regularities seem to require organizational structures that allow subordinate units to form autonomous models of the world but make them coherent through a centrally defined organizational model. In fact, to exploit a regularly changing environment, a large amount of knowledge about the environment is required: the organizational knowledge basis must distinguish between the states of the world and connect them diachronically. By partly decentralizing the acquisition of knowledge about the environment, it is possible to achieve higher levels of sophistication in the organizational model of the world, provided the coordination mechanisms—which are centralized—are powerful enough to enable the organization to solve conflicts of representations.

On the other hand, this very decentralization of the acquisition of knowledge can be a source of loss when it is more profitable for the organization to cling to a robust, stable set of routines. Therefore, when environmental changes are unpredictable but within predictable limits, decentralization of the accumulation of knowledge can only disrupt organizational coherence around a robust set of routines. This situation requires strong coordination in order to make the entire organization implement coherently such a set of robust routines and favors structures that centralize the accumulation of knowledge and emphasize horizontal coordination around a unique central body of knowledge.

Ultimately there appears to be a tension between the necessity of "keeping together" the organization and allowing diversity of experimentation. This topic will be further examined in the next section.

Exploitation vs. Exploration in Organizational Learning

We have already hinted at the fact that one of the crucial problems in organizational learning is the trade-off between exploitation of the available knowledge and exploration of new possibilities. Exploitation of the available knowledge involves refinement of the available technology, learning by doing, improvement of the division of labor, and all the activities oriented toward the search for higher efficiency. Exploration involves innovation, search for novelty, risk-taking, and all the activities oriented toward the discovery of new opportunities.

Successful organizations must combine exploitation and exploration, since both of them are vital. As March (1990, 1) puts it: "[Organizations] that engage in exploration to the exclusion of exploitation are likely to find that they suffer the costs of experimentation without gaining many of its benefits. They exhibit too many undeveloped new ideas and too little distinctive competence. Conversely, . . . [organizations] that engage in exploitation to the exclusion of exploration are likely to find themselves trapped in suboptimal stable equilibria."

Exploration and exploitation activities compete for scarce resources, and only in a few circumstances is it possible to discern clearly which organizational functions are oriented toward the exploitation of existing knowledge and which are instead oriented toward the generation of new competences. The problem has been tackled by statistical decision theory by means of such models as the "two-armed bandit" problem. Suppose we have a slot machine with two arms, A and B, and suppose that we know that one of the two arms—but we do not know which one—gives a higher average reward. The player therefore faces the problem of collecting information in order to infer which arm is associated with the higher payoff. Two possible sources of loss can merge: on the one hand the collection of information involves the allocation of some trials to the inferior arm, and on the other hand, there is always the risk of choosing as the most profitable arm the one that is actually inferior. If the decision maker tries to reduce the first source of loss by decreasing the number of experiments and clinging to the best observed arm, he will inevitably increase the chances of selecting the inferior arm. Vice versa, the chances of selecting the inferior arm can be reduced only by collecting more information about both arms and thus increasing the loss that derives from the trials allocated to the inferior arm.

Statistical decision theory has approached this trade-off by dichotomizing exploration and exploitation: the agent first performs a series of trials whose purpose is to collect information and then sticks irreversibly to the arm that appears to be the best one according to collected information. There exist several problems with this decision-theoretic approach. First of all, it assumes that the decision maker knows the alternatives among which the choice has to be made. In most real-life situations the problem of exploration is not just one of computing the statistics that characterize the distribution of some variables known as relevant, but rather one of discovery and definition of the alternatives themselves. Furthermore, the probability distributions may themselves depend on the actions of the decision makers: positive feedbacks, network externalities, and learning by doing make the profitability of the various alternatives depend on the decision maker's and other agents' actions. Finally, in most economic decisions there exist strong irreversibilities: the resources committed to an alternative cannot be cheaply redeployed.

All these complications make the maximization approach inadequate to give an account of most actual economic decisions. Another approach is instead based on bounded rationality and explains the balance between exploitation and exploration by referring to targets and aspiration levels. This approach is at the heart of the evolutionary theory of the firm presented in

Nelson and Winter (1982): firms stick to the present routine whenever the economic result remains above a certain target level. Only when the payoff falls below the target do firms engage in exploration for better alternatives. Targets and aspiration levels may in turn be subject to adaptation and change according to experience and imitation of other agents (March 1988a).

Actually, the separation between routine and search behavior can be somewhat misleading, especially when we consider organizational learning. Ultimately, the problem of the balance between exploitation and exploration becomes one of balance between the process of *selection* and the process of *mutation* in an evolutionary system. Within organizations, these two processes normally coexist and interact at different levels: one of the strengths of organizations is their capability of flexibly combining procedures for selection and procedures for innovation. Fast-learning and slow-learning individuals and departments can coexist. Innovation itself can become a largely routinized process, though uncertain in its outcome. Learning by doing can add exploratory value to normally exploitive activities.

March (1990, 7–8) stresses the importance of the social context in which organizational learning takes place. A "distinctive feature of the social context . . . is the mutual learning of an organization and the individuals in it. Organizations store knowledge in their procedures, norms, rules, and forms. They accumulate such knowledge over time, learning from their members. At the same time, individuals in an organization are socialized to organizational beliefs."

Such mutual learning is fundamental for the trade-off between exploration and exploitation in organizations. A high degree of differentiation of knowledge among the members of an organization increases the total amount of knowledge possessed by the organization. But differentiation makes coordination more difficult and ultimately can inhibit the social exploitation of this knowledge basis. On the contrary, a widely held body of organizational knowledge facilitates coordination and specialization but reduces the scope for decentralized experimentation, which could prove a vital source of organizational learning.

The framework outlined so far can help cast some light on the relevance of this trade-off. Consider an organizational structure where subordinate units receive and interpret two kinds of messages: one from the environment, which allows them to build their own independent knowledge about the world in which the firm operates, and one from the management, which instead defines the organizational state on which they should coordinate their actions. The weights with which these two types of messages enter the shops' decision processes define the organizational balance between differentiation and commonality of knowledge. Simulations show (Marengo 1992) that flexible adaptation to a slowly and regularly changing environment requires local experimentation and differentiation of learning processes, provided that a minimum coordination is guaranteed by a simple set of commonly known rules. On the contrary, when environments are unpredictably changing within predictable limits, organizational performance increases with the increase of the degree of attention to the managerial messages, while it decreases with the degree of decentralized experimentation.

Hence, there exists a tension between centralization and decentralization in the organizational learning process. Firms require both centralization and decentralization to operate successfully in changing environments. Decentralization in the acquisition of knowledge is a source of variety and experimentation and, ultimately, a fundamental source of learning. But, eventually, knowledge has to be made available for exploitation to the entire organization. When agents differ with regard to their representations of the environment and their cognitive capabilities, there must exist an organizational body of knowledge that guarantees the coherence of the various learning processes. In order to cope with changing environments, the process of generation and modification of such a body of knowledge, although fed by the decentralized learning processes, has to undergo some form of centralization. Thus, a tension inevitably arises between the forces that keep the coherence of the organization and the forces that promote decentralized learning.

Some examples may help illustrate this point. Consider the development of the M-form corporate organization, especially in Anglo-Saxon countries, analyzed by Chandler (1962). Clearly, the "divisionalization" of activities grouped according to product/market characteristics implies decentralization of decision making and learning. However, note also that one requires a parallel centralization of strategic activities—and of the related learning process—in order to reproduce the long-term coherence of the firm and its ability to discover and exploit new opportunities for innovation and growth. In turn, as argued at greater length in Aoki and Dosi (1991), this involves a fundamental informational and competence dilemma. The ability to develop innovation with some bearing on the general organization and strategies of the firm differs from and indeed is likely to be separated from the ability to conduct "business as usual."

Thus, in the Anglo-Saxon M-form organization, with its high degrees of functional hierarchy and specialization, decisions concerning the direction of innovation search must be placed quite high in the ranks of strategic management. But, if this is so, where should one place, for example, R&D activities, given the relative *nonspecificity* that some innovative knowledge implies? Should one set them within divisions, making them more responsive to product/market learning, but possibly missing broader innovative opportunities? Or should one centralize them in corporate laboratories, which depend directly on strategic management? And in turn, how do strategic managers learn the required "special skills" of detecting and selecting technological and organizational innovations? In this respect, Pavitt (1990b) has argued that the very rigidity of Anglo-Saxon divisionalized profit centers and the lack of technical competence of most strategic managers in the Anglo-Saxon countries help to explain the weak performance of British and U.S. industries. However, even if this is the case, no easy alternative prescription can be suggested without having a more general model that connects changes in organization, innovative competences, and corporate performance.

Ideally, one would like to see this dynamics of competences and organizational forms explicitly embedded in an evolutionary model wherein firms both interact with each other and change their internal structures and behaviors. Admittedly, no one has fully done it yet. We can, however, put forward some conjectures and preliminary results.

Conclusions: Patterns of Learning and Selection

Let us recall three major "stylized facts." First, in cross-national comparisons, one observes significant differences in the typical patterns of corporate organization with respect to information flows, the structure of the incentives to the members of the organization, and, ultimately, the rates and directions of learning.

However, and second, individual sectors of economic activities seem to display rather typical forms of organization of production and learning, which appear to be rather invariant across countries.[9] So, for example, the organization of innovation and production in, say, machine tools is different from that in textiles and seems to proceed along patterns that seem to hold in Europe as well as in Japan and the United States. Third, firms show persistent differences in their internal organization and competences even within the same countries and the same production activities.

We suggest that the above analysis of the nature of competences and their relationships with organizational forms helps us to interpret all three sets of phenomena. Firms are behavioral entities whose competences, decision rules, and internal governance structures coevolve with the environment in which they are embedded. Nonetheless, organizational change, as well as technological learning, is highly path-dependent. The strength of norms, routines, and "corporate cultures" resides precisely in their persistence and reproduction over time. As sociologists and organizational theorists tell us, this inertia provides some degree of consistency among individual behaviors and motivation to action even if incentive compatibilities are much weaker than those prescribed by economic theory, and even if information partitions border

---

9. For evidence and taxonomical exercises, see Pavitt (1984) and Patel and Pavitt (1991).

complete ignorance. But precisely that same inertia makes organizational arrangements quite differentiated and often highly suboptimal in their ability to seize technological and market opportunities.

Environmental selection, in the form of differential economic performances, together with technological and organizational imitation, tend to reduce the variety of both technological and organizational innovations that emerge. However, the locality of learning, the "opaqueness" of the environment, and the positive feedbacks linking particular directions of technological learning with particular organizational setups all imply the persistence of different forms of corporate and industrial organization, even when, ex post, they yield different competitive performances. In a jargon more familiar to economists: as one can easily generate multiple equilibria stemming from nonconvexities and increasing returns in the space of technologies, so one can also easily conjecture multiple "organizational trajectories" stemming from organizational learning about norms, competences, and corporate structures.

These properties, of course, are consistent with the earlier observation on persistent diversity among firms. However, the observed variations in organizational and behavioral traits are not unbounded: the institutional and market environment in which each firm operates is likely to set some viability constraint on such a variety. In this respect, for instance, Aoki's interpretation of the differences between the "American" and the "Japanese" firm is nested in the conditions under which the incentive structure and information flows occurring within the firm appropriately match the incentives and information flows stemming from the relations between the firm and the markets for labor, products, and finance. In turn, the properties of the latter depend on their institutional design. Hence, as Aoki (1988) shows, the viability of each organizational form is determined by the incentive compatibility of the various notional combinations between internal governance structures and industry-finance links, mechanisms of labor mobility, and user-producer links. So, for example, decentralized learning within the firm in order to be incentive-compatible, as in the Japanese archetype, has to be matched by rank hierarchies in internal labor mobility and a relatively lower reliance on labor market mobility as compared to firms that rely on more centralized forms of information processing and decision making, as in the American archetype.

Our analysis of competence building and innovative exploration—as distinguished from sheer information processing—adds a new dimension to these viability requirements. In fact, in an innovative world, evolutionary viability[10] ought to imply also some incentives either within the firm or, more generally, in the economic system to "break the rules" and explore new

---

10. A somewhat similar notion of "viability" is used in a sequential neo-Austrian model by Amendola and Gaffard (1988).

technologies and forms of organization. In fact, in contemporary Western economies this is done by various combinations between specific provisions for innovative efforts within incumbent firms and via the birth of new firms (Aoki and Dosi 1991; Dosi 1990).

Note that the foregoing analysis of competence-building implies at a normative level a strong argument in favor of pluralism and variety of organizations. Since there is not and *there cannot be* a simple invariant "one best way of doing things," only institutional setups of production and innovation allowing for diverse organizational and technological trajectories are likely to allow any one system to navigate that permanent tension between exploitation and exploration.

Moreover, at both descriptive and normative levels, our competence-based description of firms allows us in principle to analyze the limits of the set of "possible worlds," that is, of organizational structures and market dynamics that are evolutionary viable. Dosi, Teece, and Winter (1991) attempt to map the fundamental characteristics of possible *learning regimes* and possible *selection regimes* into particular modes of corporate organizations and strategies. It is argued that the mechanisms and speed by which product markets select among different products and different firms, coupled with the characteristics of the learning regimes (such as levels of technological opportunities, emulativeness, nature and applicability of knowledge bases, etc.), combine to determine the organizational features (e.g., specialization, horizontal diversification, etc.) that can be effectively selected.

Still a lot of work has to be done in this direction, but it seems a promising avenue to link a competence-based theory of the firm with a positive theory accounting for: (1) why firms differ; (2) why, despite these differences, they tend to show some organizational regularities, conditional on their principal activities and knowledge base; and (3) why sectors differ in their typical modes of corporate organization.

From a normative point of view, this may be a sound basis from which to derive prescriptions on R&D organization, intersectoral diversification, organizational change, and vertical integration/disintegration. It may be also a good starting point for sectoral industrial policies and, more generally, for the sort of "institutional engineering" that former centrally planned economies are undertaking in order to build viable market mechanisms.

References

Abreu, D., and A. Rubinstein. 1988. "The Structure of Nash Equilibrium in Repeated Games with Finite Automata." *Econometrica* 56 (November): 1259–81.

Amendola, M., and J. Gaffard. 1988. *The Innovative Choice*. Oxford: Basil Blackwell.

Aoki, M. 1986. "Horizontal vs. Vertical Information Structure of the Firm." *American Economic Review* 76 (December): 971–83.

Aoki, M. 1988. *Information, Incentives and Bargaining in the Japanese Economy*. Cambridge: Cambridge University Press.

Aoki, M., and G. Dosi. 1991. "Corporate Organization, Finance and Innovation." In V. Zamagni, ed., *Finance and the Enterprise*. New York: Academic Press.

Arrow, K. 1974a. *The Limits of Organization*. New York: W.W. Norton.

Arrow, K. 1974b. "On the Agenda of Organizations." In R. Marris, ed., *The Corporate Society*. London: Macmillan.

Chandler, A., Jr. 1962. *Strategy and Structure: Chapters in the History of Industrial Enterprise*. Cambridge: MIT Press.

Cohen, M. 1984. "Conflict and Complexity: Goal Diversity and Organizational Search Effectiveness." *American Political Science Review* 78 (June): 435–54.

Crémer, J. 1980. "A Partial Theory of Optimal Organization of a Bureaucracy." *Bell Journal of Economics* 11 (Autumn): 683–93.

Crémer, J. 1990. "Common Knowledge and the Co-Ordination of Economic Activities." In M. Aoki, B. Gustafsson and O. E. Williamson, eds., *The Firm as a Nexus of Treaties*. London: Sage.

Cutland, N. 1980. *Computability: An Introduction to Recursive Function Theory*. Cambridge: Cambridge University Press.

Dosi, G. 1988. "Sources, Procedures and Microeconomic Effects of Innovation." *Journal of Economic Literature* 26 (September): 1120–71.

Dosi, G. 1990. "Finance, Innovation and Industrial Change." *Journal of Economic Behavior and Organization* 13 (June): 299–319.

Dosi, G. and M. Egidi. 1991. "Substantive and Procedural Uncertainty. An Exploration of Economic Behaviours in Complex and Changing Environments." *Journal of Evolutionary Economics* 1 (April): 145–68.

Dosi, G., D. Teece, and S. Winter. 1991. "Toward a Theory of Corporate Coherence." In G. Dosi, R. Giannetti, and P. A. Toninelli, eds., *Technology and the Enterprise in a Historical Perspective*. Oxford: Oxford University Press.

Dubois, D., and H. Prade. 1987. *Defense et illustration des approaches non-probabilistes de l'imprecis et de l'incertain*. Université Paul Sabatier, Toulouse. Rapport L.S.I. No. 269.

Forrest, S. 1990. "Emergent Computation: Self-Organizing Collective and Cooperative Phenomena in Natural and Artificial Computing Networks." *Physica* D 42 (June): 1–11.

Freeman, C. 1982. *The Economics of Industrial Innovation*. 2nd ed. London: Pinter.

Geanakoplos, J. 1990. *Game Theory without Partitions, and Applications to Speculation and Consensus*. Santa Fe Institute, Working paper no. 90-018.

Geroski, P., and A. Jacquemin. 1984. "Dominant Firms and Their Alleged Decline." *International Journal of Industrial Organization* 2 (March): 1–27.

Gilboa, I. 1988. "Information and Meta Information." In M. Vardi, ed., *Theoretical Aspects of Reasoning about Knowledge*, 227–43. Los Altos, Calif.: Morgan Kaufmann.

Holland, J. 1986. "Escaping Brittleness: The Possibilities of General Purpose Learning Algorithms Applied to Parallel Rule-Based Systems." In R. Michalski, J. Carbonell, and T. Mitchell, eds., *Machine Learning II*, 593–623. Los Altos, Calif.: Morgan Kaufmann.

Holland, J., K. Holyoak, R. Nisbett, and P. Thagard. 1986. *Induction: Processes of Inference, Learning and Discovery*. Cambridge: MIT Press.

Jovanovic, B. 1982. "Selection and Evolution of Industry." *Econometrica* 50: 649–70.

Kreps, D. 1990a. *A Course in Microeconomic Theory*. New York: Harvester Wheatsheaf.

Lewis, A. 1985. "On Effectively Computable Realization of Choice Functions." *Mathematical Social Sciences* 10.

Lewis, A. 1986. *Structure and Complexity. The Use of Recursive Theory in the Foundations of Neoclassical Mathematical Economics and the Theory of Games*. Ithaca: Cornell University Department of Mathematics. Mimeo.

Lucas, R. 1978. "On the Size Distribution of Business Firms." *Bell Journal of Economics* 9 (Autumn): 508–23.

March, J. 1988a. *Decisions and Organizations*. Oxford: Basil Blackwell.

March, J. 1990. *Exploration and Exploitation in Organizational Learning*. Stanford, Calif.: Stanford University. Mimeo.

Marengo, L. 1992. *Structure, Competence and Learning in an Adaptive Model of the Firm*. Papers on Economics and Evolution, edited by the European Study Group for Evolutionary Economics. Freiburg.

Mueller, D. 1986. *Profits in the Long Run*. Cambridge: Cambridge University Press.

Nelson, R. R., and S. Winter. 1982. *An Evolutionary Theory of Economic Change*. Cambridge: Harvard University Press.

Patel, P., and K. Pavitt. 1988. "The International Distribution and Determinants of Technological Activities." *Oxford Review of Economic Policy* 4.

Patel, P., and K. Pavitt. 1991. "Large Firms in Western Europe's Technological Competitiveness." In L. G. Mattson and B. Stymme, eds., *Corporate and Industry Strategies for Europe*. Amsterdam: Elsevier.

Pavitt, K. 1984. "Sectoral Patterns of Technical Change: Towards a Taxonomy and a Theory." *Research Policy* 13: 343–74.

Pavitt, K. 1990a. "What We Know about the Strategic Management of Technology." *California Management Review* 32 (Spring): 17–26.

Pavitt, K. 1990b. *Some Foundations for a Theory of the Large Innovating Firm*. Sussex, England: Science Policy Research Unit, University of Sussex. Mimeo.

Rubinstein, A. 1986. "Finite Automata Play the Repeated Prisoner's Dilemma." *Journal of Economic Theory* 36 (June): 83–96.

Rumelt, R. 1988. *How Much Does Industry Matter?* UCLA Anderson School of Management. Mimeo.

Sah, R., and J. Stiglitz. 1986. "The Architecture of Economic Systems: Hierarchies and Polyarchies." *American Economic Review* 76 (September): 716–27.

Schmalensee, R. 1985. "Do Markets Differ Much?" *American Economic Review* 75 (March): 341–51.

Simon, H. 1976. "From Substantive to Procedural Rationality." In S. J. Latsis, ed., *Method and Appraisal in Economics*, 129–48. Cambridge: Cambridge University Press.

Teece, D., et al. 1990. *Firms' Capabilities, Resources and the Concept of Strategy.* University of California at Berkeley, Centre for Research in Management. Working paper no. 90-8.

Williamson, O. 1975. *Markets and Hierarchies*. New York: Free Press.

Williamson, O. 1985. *The Economic Institutions of Capitalism*. New York: Free Press.

4 Rational entrepreneurs or optimistic martyrs? Some considerations on technological regimes, corporate entries, and the evolutionary role of decision biases

Giovanni Dosi and Dan Lovallo

I. Introduction

This is a rather conjectural report on the evolutionary role of decision bias-es—at both the level of individuals and of organizations—and, in particular, on their importance to the processes of corporate entry and the evolution of industrial structures. A growing and quite robust body of evidence high-lights the pervasiveness of various types of biases in individual decision making, which accounts for systematic departures from predictions of the canonical model of rational choice (see, for example, Kahneman & Tversky, 1973, 1986, Shafir & Tversky, 1992). For our purposes, we will mainly con-cern ourselves with *overconfidence* or optimism, which frequently leads to bold forecasts of the consequences of one's own actions. Also, by way of ex-ample, we will examine risk seeking in the domain of losses, which often yields escalating commitments in the face of failures. Interestingly, these bi-ases appear to carry over from the level of individuals to that of groups and organizations and, indeed, might even be amplified in the latter circum-stances (see, for example, Kahneman & Lovallo, 1993, Lovallo, 1996a, and the literature discussed there). In this respect, a challenging domain of in-vestigation – with vast ramifications into the analyses of the nature of entre-preneurship, technological change, and industrial dynamics – is that of cor-porate entry into an industry.

Numerous studies have shown that the vast majority of entrants fail (see, for example, Dunne, Roberts, & Samuelson, 1988). Furthermore, there are significant interindustry differences in failure rates. Evidence of high-level firm failure rates appears to be consistent with experimental data showing that, typically, people are unrealistically optimistic, exhibit illusions of con-trol in even modestly complex environments, and systematically neglect the statistics of previously observed performances.

In this study, we report some preliminary results and conjectures from an ongoing investigation of corporate entry, postentry performances, and the collective outcome of innovative successes and failures. First, we propose that persistent *intra*industry differences in firm performances are the joint outcome of a) heterogeneous patterns of organizational learning and b) cognitive mechanisms such as unrealistic optimism and "competitive blind spots" – areas where agents insufficiently consider the contingent decisions of their opponents.

Second, we suggest some hypotheses on *inter*industry differences in relative entry rates and postentry performances using a taxonomy of technological and market regimes. The basic idea is that knowledge and learning – concerning new products, new techniques, and new markets – are specific to distinct production activities. In turn, "technological paradigms" map expectations and corporate behaviors into diverse patterns of entry behaviors that are at least partly independent of the standard measures of profitability and risk. Of course, were we to find robust corroboration of this conjecture, it would be witness against any naive "rational-expectation" hypothesis on entrepreneurial behavior.

Our third conjecture takes this argument a step further. We propose that *micro "irrationalities"* – in terms of unrealistic optimism, etc – *are likely to be a fundamental ingredient in the collective development of new knowledge bases and new industries*. The development of new technological paradigms and the related emergence of new industries and new "technological communities" might be intimately associated with seemingly wasteful mistakes, rough search heuristics, and even "irrational" hubris, rather than sober forecasts.

Our empirical evidence is diverse. We will draw both on a few experimental studies, on the growing evidence on the economics of innovation, and on what we know from some statistical surveys and longitudinal samples of firms in manufacturing industries in various countries. (Research aimed at testing the foregoing conjectures, in collaboration with John Balwin, Statistics Canada, is currently underway).

In sections II to IV we briefly review the relevant evidence from behavioral decision research, identify analogous biases in organizational decision patterns, and present some experimental evidence on entry decisions. Section V discusses the evidence on corporate entry, postentry performances, exit, and the puzzles that all this entails. In section VI we outline some elements of an evolutionary interpretation and suggest some promising links with complementary exercises in evolutionary modeling as well as some possible further developments.

II. From individual biases to organizational errors

In economics, the use of psychological assumptions other than rationality to make predictions about organizational behavior is relatively rare, although the company is quite good – including John Maynard Keynes, Herbert Simon, Richard Nelson, Oliver Williamson, and Sidney Winter, among others. Certainly, from an empirical point of view, there is massive evidence that individuals do deviate from the behavioral patterns prescribed by rational models. Furthermore, these deviations are systematic – the errors tend to be in the same direction – which implies that nonrational behavior is often not random but predictable.

However, one of the major hurdles to incorporating alternative psychological assumptions into economic models is a healthy skepticism about how individual decision biases are likely to "scale up" to organizational outcomes. While it is beyond the scope of this work to examine the vast literature on individual and organizational decision making, there are good reasons to believe that organizations, in many instances, reinforce rather than mitigate individual decision biases (see, for example, March & Shapira, 1987, Kahneman & Lovallo, 1993, and Lovallo, 1996a). "Escalation" situations are a very good example of the consistency of psychological phenomena in various contexts and at widely different units of analysis (ranging from individual choices under experimental conditions all the way to enormous collective tragedies such as the Vietnam War). Two basic psychological principles lay at the foundation of "escalation phenomena," at the level of *both* individuals and organizations, namely: (i) people respond to changes rather than absolute levels, and, (ii) they exhibit diminishing sensitivity to quantities of various items, including money.

As is known, drawing on these two principles, Kahneman and Tversky (1979) constructed *prospect theory*, a descriptive theory of risk taking, in which individuals, due to diminishing sensitivity for absolute quantities, are both risk averse for gains and risk seeking in the domain of losses. Risk-seeking preferences for losses imply that when people have not made peace with their losses they are likely to place lower than expected value bets in order to break even. On average, these bets will fail and lead to even greater losses. Fox and Staw (1979) show that considering an important aspect of social context – the need for accountability – enhances individual willingness to "throw good money after bad." Using managers as subjects, Bateman and Zeithami (1989) also observe escalation behavior. Finally, Bazerman et al (1984) find that groups escalate less frequently but more dramatically than individuals. At each point along the path from individual-choice behavior to individual choice embedded in a social context to group decision making, there is reason to suspect that economic organizations will also escalate commitments to *losing courses of action*. The consistency of the findings mentioned above and others (for example, the cases that Janis, 1982 and Ross and Staw, 1986) recount of the Vietnam War and the Vancouver World Fair) indicate that these suspicions are valid.

Quite similar considerations apply to the widespread phenomena of overconfidence and "framing effects" in the interpretation of the available information. For example, March and Shapira (1987) suggest that managers tend to interpret uncertainty simply in terms of "challenges" to their abilities and commitments to the pursuit of their goals. "Groupthink" has been identified as a cause of organizational optimism (Janis, 1982). Moreover, groups are prone to use "representative heuristics" – the tendency to formulate probabilities on uncertain events based on the similarity of the event itself with some salient property of its parent population (Kahneman & Tversky, 1973, Argote, Seabright & Dyer, 1986).

There is extensive literature on overoptimism in project evaluation (for example, Merrow et al., 1981) and with regard to R&D (see discussion in Freeman, 1982). Grossly optimistic errors are especially likely if the project involves new technology or otherwise places the firm in an unfamiliar territory. In an interesting discussion of the cause of failure in capital investment projects, Arnold (1986) finds:

> Most companies support large capital expenditure programs with a worst case analysis that examines the projects' loss potential. But the worst case forecast is almost always too optimistic. . . . When managers look at the downside they generally describe a mildly pessimistic future rather than the worst possible future.

Standard operating procedures and decision methods, ranging from discounted cash flows and net present value methods in investment evaluation to cost accounting, often involve framing effects, overconfidence, preference for confirming evidence (for a discussion, especially with regard to technological innovation, see Schoemaker and Marais, 1995).

More generally, the acknowledgment of the specificities of technological and organizational competences embodied in each firm (Teece et al., 1994, Dosi & Marengo (1993) also entails the recognition of specific heuristics, problem-framing, and, ultimately, of diverse collective structures of cognition defining what the organization can do, how it does it, and where and how it can search for novel technologies and products. Clearly, competence specificity, other things being equal, will tend to strengthen an *inside view* in forecasts and decisions. That view – as detailed in Kahneman and Tversky (1979) and Kahneman and Lovallo (1993) – draws on knowledge of the case at hand and constructs an ideal history of the future conditional on the sequences of actions by the decision makers. (In contrast, an "outside view" is statistical and comparative, drawing from past experiences of analogous cases.)

In brief, organizational decision making in general, and, a fortiori, relatively unique "strategic" activities concerning innovation, diversification, and entry – grounded in firm-specific knowledge – is often likely to involve biased assessments of one's own technological and competitive abilities (stemming from overconfidence, the "inside view," and illusion of control), and inertial and escalating commitments (with neglect of potentially relevant information and "sunk-cost fallacies"). We suggest that entrepreneurial decisions of entry are no exception. In particular, it is worth reporting some experiments by one of us (Lovallo) indicating how "inside-view" thinking is likely to lead to excess entry. We refer to the prediction that there will be excess entry as the *optimism hypothesis*. The experiments reported below serve three purposes. First, one would like to test whether the relative optimism that we see in noncompetitive environments survives in the face of competitive interaction. Second, the controlled environment allows us to unpack the effects that various types of inside-view thinking have on entry. Third, these experiments may provide clearer insights into the psychology of competition, which would lead to more informative field surveys of entrants.

III. Experimental design

The isomorphism between the experiment and the industrial activity that we model is illustrated in Figure 4.1. It is reasonable to assume that one of the first steps towards entry is for a firm to undertake some kind of market assessment in order to determine if there is sufficient opportunity in terms of probability and the size of a market to warrant entry. In the experiments, subjects are provided with information about the market capacity – the number of entrants that can earn positive amounts of money in any given period. The next step in the entry process is competitor analysis. In an industrial setting, this procedure involves multiple dimensions including estimating the likely number and quality of potential entrants. In these experiments we explicitly ask subjects to estimate the number of entrants they expect to enter in each period. Implicitly, they make their entry decision, which is the next step in the process. Finally, in both environments there is competition and diverse performances that result in differential payoffs based on relative skills.

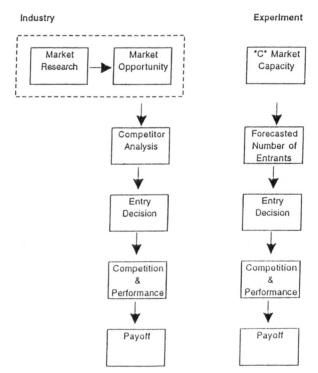

Figure 4.1. Experimental model.

Given this broad overview of the experimental model, let us be more specific about particular experiments where we manipulate several factors in the competitive environment. One of the most important manipulations is whether subjects self-selected themselves into a particular experiment or not. In some experiments, subjects are recruited to participate in entry games and no particular information is given about the dimension on which the subjects will compete. In other experiments, we explicitly ask for subjects who consider themselves to be above the median in terms of their knowledge of sports or current events. The subjects share common knowledge about the method in which they were recruited. In addition to the self-selection manipulation, the entry games occur in three different competitive environments: simultaneous entry without feedback, simultaneous entry with feedback, and sequential entry. In the simultaneous-entry condition, all of the subjects make their entry decisions at the same time. The feedback that the subjects receive is about the number of entrants that entered in the previous period. In the sequential-entry condition, each subject is given an entry order number that remains constant throughout the experiment. For example, the subject with entry order number one makes his entry decision first, subject two goes second, etc. All of the entry decisions are public knowledge.

In all of the experiments, we use an identical payoff table (Table 4.1). The amounts listed are the payoffs for the successful entrants for each market capacity. Unsuccessful entrants always lose $10. Consider the following example. If market capacity is two, then the highest-ranked entrant receives $33, the second-highest-ranked entrant receives $17, and anyone else that enters the market loses $10. In any case, the maximum total possible profit in the market is $50. This means that if five more entrants in excess of market capacity enter, the total profit in the market will be $0. For example, if there are seven entrants when the market capacity is two, the total profit for the entrants as a group will be $0, since the two top-ranked entrants will split $50 according to the payoff table and the third-through-seventh-

Table 4.1. *Payoff for sucessful entrants as a function of* C *(market capacity)*

| | | C | | |
Rank	2	4	6	8
1	33	20	14	11
2	17	15	12	10
3		10	10	8
4		5	7	7
5			5	6
6			2	4
7				3
				2

ranked entrants will each lose $10. If there were eight entrants when the market capacity was two total profits would be –$10.

In each experiment there, are two different ranking procedures: random rank and skill-based rank. In the random-rank procedure, subjects' ranks are predetermined by a random-number generator. Subjects do not know their ranks prior to making their entry decisions. After all the entry decisions have been made, a tournament starts, to be played for real money. It is only at that point subjects learn of their randomly assigned ranks. In the skill-based rank condition, subjects are shown examples of the types of questions on which their ranks will be based. However, they do not answer the questions until all of the entry decisions have been made. Then, subjects are given a quiz and their ranks are based on the number of questions they answer correctly. The purpose of the random-ranked condition is to control for risk preferences. In games with asymmetric payoff functions, such as the one described here, there is no way ex-ante to determine the equilibrium number of entrants without knowing subjects' risk preferences. Since the subjects not change across the different versions of the experiment, if we assume that their risk preferences do not change from one condition to the next, the only reason for greater entry in the skill-ranked condition is that subjects have more sanguine views of their probability of success than in the random-ranked condition. It is the difference in the number of entrants in the two conditions that will be the primary measure of interest throughout the experiments. Table 4.2 contains an example of the actual form subjects use to record their responses.

If, for example, there are 12 periods in each condition, balls numbered 1–24 will be placed in a bingo cage at the end of the experiment; the period corresponding to the chosen ball will be played for real money. The experimental procedure is summarized below.

1. Read instructions aloud
2. Comprehension test on the payoff
3. Explanation of the two types of ranking
4. Subjects are shown examples of the skill question
5. Subjects are informed that one period will be played for real money
6. Subjects make their forecasts and entry decisions in the random-rank condition
7. Subjects make their forecasts and entry decisions in the skill-rank condition
8. After all of the entry decisions are made, subjects take the quiz
9. A randomly drawn period is chosen to be played
10. Subjects' earnings are computed and immediately paid

IV. Summary of the results

Without going into too much detail, which can be found in Lovallo (1996b), this section summarizes the results from the experiments. There are four findings that are of interest. First, it is clear that there is excess entry in the

Table 4.2. *Market experiment A—random rank*

NAME _____   DATE _____

Payoff for Successful Entrants as a function of C

Rank	C			
	2	4	6	8
1	33	20	14	11
2	17	15	12	10
3		10	10	8
4		5	7	7
5			5	6
6			2	4
7				3
8				2

How much would you earn if C = 6, you entered, and your rank was 5 among the entrants? _____

How much would you earn if C = 2, you entered, and your rank was 4 among the entrants? _____

Round	C	Expected number of entrants	Enter	Not enter	Number of entrants
1					
2					
3					
4					
5					
6					
7					
8					
9					
10					
11					
12					

skill condition as compared to the risk-controlling, random-rank condition. This was true in each and every experiment. Furthermore, the expected value of entering in the random-rank condition was significantly positive in all of the experiments, while it was significantly negative in all of the skill-ranked conditions. Second, the excess entry that we observe in these experiments is not caused by "blind spots" – on average, subjects' forecasts of the number of entrants are accurate. This means that subjects in the skill condition are saying, "I realize that on average people are going to lose money in this market, but I'm not. I'm in!"

The next finding is the most surprising. In experiments without self-selection, we find a significant divergence between the number of entrants in the skill-versus random-rank conditions. However, this divergence is dwarfed by the magnitude of the divergence in markets with self-selection. This suggests that a large amount of excess entry is caused by reference-group neglect (Lovallo 1996a), rather than some variant of optimism. Reference-group neglect refers to the tendency of people to underappreciate the group with which they are competing. It is a competitive manifestation of inside-view thinking. For example, suppose that you are a phenomenally good cook and you are thinking of opening a restaurant. If you are asked to evaluate yourself as a cook in comparison to the general population, you might say that you are in the top 5%, and you might be right. However, a more pertinent question is how good of a cook are you in comparison to others in the restaurant business, almost all of whom consider themselves to be, and probably are, in the top of 5% of cooks. Reference group neglect implies that you will insufficiently regress your prediction of your relative ability in this more competitive group.

Finally, it is useful to point out that the effect that we are discussing is robust across many different types of competitive environments. The effect is significant with feedback and without self-selection and is even more robust without feedback and with self-selection. Furthermore, the effect works in both simultaneous- and sequential-entry games. Indeed, there is no significant difference between the effect in these two environments, which is rather astonishing. This means that in a sequential-entry environment, people are making a decision to enter knowing with probability one that the value of the game to the player as a group is already negative!

Our general conjecture is that this experimental evidence on cognitive and decision-biased entry also bears important implications for the understanding of *actual* entry processes of new firms in industry. In order to argue the point, let us begin by considering some available evidence on corporate entry and entrants' performances.

V. Patterns of entry, post-entry performance, and exit in manufacturing

Geroski (1991) identifies four major "stylized facts" on the entry process. First, "many firms attempt to enter each year, but [. . .] few survive for more than a year or two. The average entrant is, it seems, basically a tourist and not an immigrant, enjoying a life that is often nasty, brutish, and, above all, short" (p. 283). Second, "different measures of entry (net and gross entry measures, entry based on sales or on number of firms) are not very highly related to each other" (p. 287). Third, "there are a range of different types of entrants, and some are more successful at penetrating markets or surviving than others" (p. 290). Fourth, "the effects of entry [on market performance] – like the lives of most entrants – are fairly modest" (p. 293).

Dunne et al. (1988) examine the patterns of firm entry, growth, and exit of different types of firms over the period 1963–1982, using plant-level data from the U.S. Census of Manufacturers. For the 1967 entrant cohort, 63.8% of all new-firm, new-plant entrants exited within 5 years, while 49.6% of all diversifying-firm, new-plant entrants exited. The difference in failure rates is similar to the cohort's age. Within 15 years, 87.9% of the new-firm, new-plant entrants exited, whereas 74.6% of the diversifying-firm, new-plant entrants exited. The differences between de novo and diversifier exit rates are substantial for all the cohorts in the sample at any of the time periods measured.

The high mortality of entrants is corroborated by longitudinal studies on industrial life cycles (see Hannan and Freeman, 1989, Carroll and Swaminathan, 1992, Klepper, 1992), and so are the differences in post-entry performances according to different types of entrants and the timing of entry.

Consider, for example, Lane's investigation of ATM manufacturers (Lane, 1989). The ATM market began shortly before 1969. The first firm to enter the market was Money Machine Inc. in 1967. An interesting pattern of entry develops over the life cycle of this industry. The earliest entrants into the industry were almost all de novo entrants; the next group of entrants were the diversifying firms; the final wave of entry came from foreign firms. The average entry date for the three groups of firms were 1970, 1975, and 1979, respectively. The reasonably distinct partition between the entry dates for the three entrant types suggests that there is a systematic difference between the firm types that drive entry behavior. De novo firms, obviously, are start-up firms without any prior production experience. All of the diversifying firms that entered this industry had prior production experience in a related domestic industry. Specifically, diversifying firms had production experience in either cash-handling products, security products (safes and vaults), or computers. The foreign firms all had prior experience producing ATMs abroad prior to entering the U.S. market, although the degree to which they were selling other products in the U.S. market varied. (The question of whether prior U.S. market experience is a significant contributor to success is an interesting one that is not addressed in the Lane study.)

Docutel, a de novo entrant, was the dominant firm in the early years of the industry. However, as time went on, the de novo entrants lost market share to the diversifying entrants. In the middle to late 1970s, Diebold, an early diversifier became the dominant firm and held that position until the end of the sample period, 1986. The rise of Diebold coincided with the period when the overall size of the ATM market grew most rapidly. Eventually, in October

1986 when Docutel exited, all of the de novo entrants were a memory. Furthermore, the average life span for all of the de novo and diversifying firms that entered after the median entry date for their respective groups, except for the lone surviving firm (Concord), was less than 2.5 years. Whether these firms made or lost money cannot be determined from the available data. However, given that sunk costs play a significant role in this industry, it does not seem likely that such a brief visit would be profitable.

The big winners in this market in terms of market share were Diebold, NCR, and IBM – all early diversifying entrants. The experience that these firms had in safes and computers appeared to provide production advantages that increased market share and the likelihood of survival. Firm-wide production experience unrelated to the ATM industry did not confer an advantage either in terms of market share or survival. Furthermore, previous safe and computer experience with banks has greater advantages for survival and market share than nonbank-related safe and computer experience.

A somewhat similar story emerges from Mitchell's account of the medical diagnostic imaging industry (Mitchell 1989, 1991, 1993): one observes waves of new entrants (both de novo and diversifying entrants) linked with the introduction of new major technologies (nuclear imaging scanners, ultrasound equipment, etc.), mortality rates especially high among new comers, and incumbents regaining relatively quickly their dominant market shares. In fact, newcomer market share fell to 10% or less by 1988 in all of the subfields except for ultrasound. Even in ultrasound, where newcomers are a majority, their market share was less than 50% in 1988. In the subfields there have been waves of fluctuations in newcomer market share associated with newcomer product innovations. However, in all but the most recent upsurge of newcomer share in the ultrasound segment, incumbents recovered their market position.

Incumbents were also much more likely to survive (84%) in comparison to diversifying (44%) and de novo firms (29%) as of 1988. The method of exit also differs systematically between the firm types. 70% of the de novo firms that exit do so by closing down, whereas 70% of the diversifying or incumbent firms sell their business when they exit. Even the early newcomers to industries, one of the first three newcomers in each subfield, performed relatively poorly. Only two of 15 early newcomers still existed in 1990 and neither of these firms was in the top three in market share. This performance stands in sharp contrast to the early incumbent entrants – ten of 15 survived until 1990 and five of the 10 survivors were market-share leaders in 1988. In the medical diagnosis imaging industry it seems that de novo and diversifying firms' innovations contribute more to the evolution of the industry than to these firms' own success.

Other industries, however, suggest quite different patterns. In semiconductors (Dosi, 1984, and Malerba, 1985), some de novo entrants have indeed become the industry leaders while most diversifiers from seemingly related industries have failed. Likewise, in the computer-communication industry, the main actors have been new firms (Pelkey, 1993). Somewhat similarly, in photolithographic alignment equipment, incumbents have fared rather poorly, and each reconfiguration of product technologies has been associated with the emergence of new industry leaders (Henderson, 1988, 1993, Henderson & Clark, 1990).

At broader levels of description – often 2- to 4-digit industries – some intersectoral regularities in the process of entry, growth, and mortality appear to emerge. So, for example, entry, while being a very pervasive phenomenon, appears to be positively correlated with the number of incumbents and the growth of shipments in the industry and its variability, whereas there seems to be little correlation with industry profitability. Entry in concentrated industries seems to be lower in terms of number of firms but entrants tend to be bigger and have a higher life expectancy. The probability of survival of new small firms appear to be lower in capital-intensive and innovation-intensive industries. Hazard rates do not appear to be affected by scale economies in low-tech industries but they are in high-tech ones. The instantaneous effect of entry on output in terms of shares is generally low, but the medium-term one (of those surviving) is quite significant.[1] Moreover, hazard rates and post-entry performances seem to be significantly influenced by the nature of the entrant (whether de novo start-up or diversifying from other sectors). Finally, other more detailed traits of the entrants (such as educational attributes of the founders and the organizational strategies) seem to influence survival probabilities (Brüderl, Preisendorfer, & Ziegler, 1992).

What do we make of all this evidence on entry, performance, and mortality? How do we relate it to the cognitive and decision biases discussed in the previous section? And what is the importance of these biases for technical change and industrial dynamics?

VI. An evolutionary view of knowledge and biases in economic change

There are three major building blocks in our argument. First, cognitive biases are widespread attributes of adaptation and discovery in complex and evolving environments. Second, the nature of such biases – or, more generally of decision rules – can be inferred to a large extent from the characteristics of the knowledge upon which agents draw. This applies also to entry decisions. Third, at least with regard to entry, biases might often have a positive collective effect, in that they might be necessary to trigger exploratory behaviors, contribute to the development of commonly shared "technological paradigms," and ultimately foster the establishment and diffusion of new knowledge and new organizational forms.

Learning, competence traps, and biases

One of the remarkable features of most of the evidence discussed in sections II to IV is that biases are also prone to emerge in circumstances where the decision problem is sufficiently transparent to allow the unequivocal identification of "rational" decision procedures. A fortiori, one can expect them to emerge in more opaque and changing environments. Of course, an interpretation of such phenomena could be simply in terms of human fallibility, due, for example, to some underlying computational limitation, attention economizing, and inertial reinforcement of past behavioral responses. Far from denying that all these factors are at work, the line of inquiry that we want to pursue here is that, more fundamentally, these biases might be an unavoidable corollary of the ways agents form their interpretative models of the world and their behavioral routines in evolutionary environments.

It seems to us that a growing number of contributions from different camps – evolutionary economics, organization theory, cognitive psychology, and artificial intelligence sciences – are starting to converge in their analyses of learning processes in all circumstances when the environment continuously changes or in any case is sufficiently complex to entail some *competence gap* between the skills notionally required for decision and those "naturally" available to the agents (Heiner, 1983, 1988). It is clearly a perspective that goes back to the research program of Simon, Cyert, March, Nelson, and Winter on the nature and implications of "bounded rationality" and has been recently enriched by experimental evidence and computer-simulated models. To make a long story very short, this perspective implies a radical shift in the object of analysis: rather than focusing on the signals that the environment delivers to the unit of decision, it emphasizes the inner features of the response mechanism of the unit itself and the ways internal representations of the world are constructed.[2]

There are some quite general implications that come out of this perspective. First, facing an essential ambiguity in the relationships between events actions and outcomes,[3] agents are bound to search for appropriate categories that frame cognition and actions. Second, action rules often take the form of relatively event-invariant routines, which are nonetheless "robust," in the sense that they apply to entire classes of seemingly analogous problems. Third, adaptive learning, involving interrelated units of knowledge (that is, some sort of cognitive system), tend to lead to lock-in phenomena. For example, Dosi and Egidi (1991) discuss these learning dynamics in the simple case of the Rubik cube, and Dosi et al. (1994) show, in a simulated model of adaptive learning, the emergence of economic rules such as mark-up prices. Levinthal (1993) studies organizational adaptation on a "rugged landscape" (a selection environment characterized by interdependent and nonlinear contributions of various organizational attributes to the "fitness" of the organization). He shows the adaptive emergence of a few archetypes of organizations and behavioral patterns which, depending on the interdependence among traits, tend to lock organizational evolution even when the external environment changes in ways that are unfavorable to the existing setups. Marengo (1992) presents a model of co-evolution between organizational representations of the environment and its behavioral responses in a changing environment.

For our purposes here, what is important to notice is that by switching the analytical emphasis from agents as "information processors" to agents as "imperfect explorers" and "problem-solvers," it is easy to appreciate the widespread emergence of cognitive frames and decision routines. They are, in a sense, the inevitable outcome of imperfect adaptation to ever-changing and potentially surprising environments, even if they appear as "biases" whenever the environment is simple enough as to notionally allow more refined and orthodox rational decision procedures. All this applies, we suggest, to individuals and even more so, to organizations. But seeing organizations as problem solvers naturally leads to acknowledgement of the role of their internal knowledge, competences and "visions" as prime determinants of their behaviors. As Levinthal puts it

The ability of firms to evaluate and utilize outside knowledge is a function of their level of prior related knowledge. [The latter] confers an ability to recognize the value of new information, assimilate it, and apply it to commercial ends which . . . collectively constitute a firm's "absorptive capacity." (Levinthal, chapter 10, this volume)

Moreover, as emphasized in Cohen and Levinthal (1989, 1990), such absorptive capacity is path-dependent, given its cumulative nature and its coevolution with expectation formation (see also Dosi, 1988a). From an evolutionary point of view, the development of specific problem-solving competence is a necessary condition for survival, but such competences are inevitably "local," reinforced by past history but not necessarily relevant today.[4] Indeed, our general conjecture is that it is precisely these features of knowledge that tend to produce many of the biases discussed above. For example, cumulative and idiosyncratic knowledge may easily imply an "inside view" of future outcomes. Previously successful problem-solving routines can be expected to lead to overconfidence on their future applicability. And the Schumpeterian perception of the permanent existence of unexploited opportunities of innovation are likely to result in "destrategizing" of behaviors – actions whose outcomes also depend on interacting firms are seen on the contrary, as part of a "game against nature" (Dosi & Marengo, 1993). Putting it more vividly, as a senior officer of Intel told one of us when asked about their strategies, ". . . strategies might be a concern for our competitors; we are just better than the others and our, only goal is to remain that way. . . ."

In summary, we suggest that decision biases are to a large extent the downside of competence building, Schumpeterian processes of discovery, and the implementation of cognitive frames and routines, which are used to make sense of and control imperfectly understood environments.

Knowledge bases, entry and post-entry performances

A "knowledge-centered" view of organizational behaviors also makes a nice contrast to "information-centered" or "incentive-centered" ones with respect to entry decisions. Drastically simplifying, an "incentive story" on the entry process would start with the identification of proxies for expected profitabilities, then make some assumptions based on the information to which would-be entrants have access (rational expectation being the most extreme one), and then make predictions on entry dynamics microfounded on rational and unbiased decision processes.[5] A similar modeling strategy can obviously be applied to, for example, the propensity to innovate of incumbents versus entrants (cf. Arrow; 1962, Reinganum, 1983, and the critical discussion in Henderson, 1993). The major point, in any case, is that some hypothesis of an unbiased rationality and a fine perception of the "objective" incentive structure allows the theorist to work, so to speak, "backward" from future outcomes to past entry decisions. Conversely, the "knowledge-centered" (or "evolutionary") story only needs to assume, on the incentive side, what elsewhere we have called *weak incentive compatibility* (Dosi & Marengo, 1993), that is, put very roughly, the perception (no matter how biased, self-condescending, etc.) that ". . . there are some unexploited opportunities out there and if I'm good I can derive some economic benefit from them. . . ."[6] Rather, the core of the story relates expected behaviors to some specific characteristics of the knowledge bases on which agents are likely to draw and to some internal characteristics of the agents themselves, including, of course, their problem-solving competences. In this perspective, the predictions of the theory rest on exercises of "mapping" between a) modal learning processes approximately shared by the entire relevant population of agents or some subsets of them; b) the institutional arrangements under which agents interact; and, c) their revealed performances.

A good deal of work has already been done along these lines, at both empirical and theoretical levels. In terms of empirical investigation, and related "appreciative theorizing," as Nelson and Winter would call it, one finds, for example, Pavitt's taxonomy of the sectoral patterns of generation and use of innovation (Pavitt, 1984). The basic exercise there is to identify the fundamental sources and procedures of innovative activities specific to each sector. For example does innovative knowledge draw heavily on scientific advances? Or is it much more informal and, for example, rely on tacit design skills? Is innovation mainly related to the introduction of new products or to the adoption and efficient use of inputs produced by someone else? etc. Next, it derives propositions on the characteristics of the innovating firms (whether they will be typically big or small; single-product firms or diversified ones; etc.).[7] Another exercise in a similar spirit is that by Dosi, Teece, and Winter (1992) and Teece et al. (1994) who derive predictions on the boundaries of the firm – conditional on their principal activities – from the nature of the competences which their principal activities imply.

From a dynamic point of view, several studies have analyzed the typical patterns of evolution of industries following the emergence and establishment of a "technological paradigm" (for example, Dosi, 1984) or "dominant designs" (for example, Utterback & Suarez, 1993), often identifying some invariant features along a "technological life cycle" (Gort & Klepper, 1982, Klepper, 1992). Moreover, continuities or breaks in the process of knowledge accumulation – yielding "competence-enhancing" or "competence-destroying" technical progress – have been found to be robust predictors of the relative performance of incumbents versus new entrants (Henderson & Clark, 1990, Henderson, 1993).

At the level of more formal theory, diverse *regimes of learning and market selection* – have been used to explain different patterns of evolution of industrial structures, including changes in industrial concentration, size distributions, turbulence in market shares, growth and death probabilities conditional on size and age (Winter, 1984, Dosi & Salvatore, 1992, Dosi et al. 1994). Basically, the exercise involves some stylized representation of the learning regime (formally captured by a particular stochastic process driving the access to new firm-specific technologies), the analysis of the collective outcomes of competitive interactions, and their comparison under different regimes.[8]

Our general conjecture – which unfortunately we are still unable to substantiate in this preliminary report – is that the characteristics of learning regimes are also major predictors of (i) the rates of entry into an industry, (ii) the relative frequencies of different types of entrants (new started versus diversifiers), and (iii) post-entry performances.

Among the discriminating features of each regime the evolutionary literature has identified 1) the richness of innovative opportunities, 2) the degrees of codifiability of knowledge (versus its "tacitness"), 3) its serendipity versus specificity to a particular activity; 4) the levels of "cumulativeness" of technological and organizational learning. We predict these factors to be discriminating also in terms of patterns of entry and performances. So, for example, one may derive propositions like the following. a) Other things being equal, the higher the perceived technological opportunities, the higher will be entry rates, irrespective of post-entry performances. b) Knowledge serendipity positively affects entry rates but not necessarily survival probabilities. c) The rates of failures of de novo entrants are a positive function of the cumulativeness of technological learning. (And indeed, there is a much longer list of empirically testable propositions that can be derived with respect to corporate entry and mortality from evolutionary theories of learning and market selection.)

The way these theories link up with the evidence discussed earlier on decision biases is that they fully acknowledge them and in a sense try to predict their importance and impact on the grounds of some generalizations regarding the patterns of knowledge accumulation, the sources of competitive advantage, and the modes of market interaction. So, for example, evolutionary ("knowledge-centered") theories of industrial dynamics are perfectly at ease with the finding that entrants – and, most likely, also incumbents – tend to take an "inside view" in their strategic choices; having recognized it, they will try to predict under what circumstances the outcomes will turn out to be, with a reasonable probability, brave self-fulfilling prophecies, or, conversely, miserable delusions. Not only that, decisions that turn out to be biased from the point of view of individual forecasting rationality might have, collectively, a positive evolutionary value.

Heroes and martyrs in the dynamics of collective exploration

Entry dynamics are most often analyzed in terms of their effects on competition (which are generally rather modest), the waste of resources associated with the frequent failures (which appear to be significant), or long-term impact of successful entrants on industrial efficiency (again, quite important). On the first two points, cf. Geroski (1991) and on the latter, Baldwin (1994).

Here, however, we want to look at entry from a complementary point of view, namely the collective effect of *both successes and failures* upon industrial learning. A suggestive way to put the question is, following March (1991), in terms of the fundamental dichotomy in evolutionary environments between "exploitation" and "exploration." Briefly, "exploitation" concerns adaptation to a given environment and efficiency (improvements made in reaction to a given set of perceived opportunities). Conversely, "exploration" implies the discovery of novelties; for example, in the domains of products, processes, or organizational forms.[9] It is straightforward that in a "knowledge-centered," evolutionary view such a dichotomy might easily emerge. First, the knowledge bases required for "exploitation" might be quite different from those most conducive to "exploration." Second, we have mentioned earlier that learning generally entails path-dependency and locks in phenomena into particular regions of a high-dimensional, and quite ill-defined, search space. For both reasons, the search for novelty – and in particular, those forms of novelty that are not contemplated by the competences embodied into incumbent organizations – requires "deviant" behaviors often associated with new start-ups.[10] As argued at greater length in Dosi (1990), the distribution of mutations might be heavily biased in favor of mistakes; hence, search efforts are likely to turn out to be, on average, disappointing economic failures for the individual actors who undertake them. Nonetheless, collectively, they might be a crucial ingredient of change. In this sense, *the biases* reviewed in sections II to IV – especially overconfidence, inside view thinking, and illusions of control – *are essential to sustain exploration, even when the latter is not individually rewarding.*[11]

There is another, related, way in which individual mistakes are an essential part of collective learning. This occurs whenever "mistakes" also contribute to increased collective knowledge. In that case they represent a sort of externality for the whole system.

These propositions are finding increasing corroboration in the evolutionary literature in the domains of both natural and social systems. The general requirement of variety generation is, indeed, a quite established proposition (in economics, see Metcalfe, 1991 and Saviotti, 1992).[12] And it is also well established that, apart from the most restrictive cases, it is hard to identify – for the theorist and a fortiori for the empirical agents – any equilibrium distribution of "exploratory" versus "exploitative" behaviors. More technically, only under highly demanding assumptions on the nature of the environment, it is theoretically fruitful to interpret such dynamics in terms of (mixed) evolutionary stable strategies (ESS). This is so for different reasons. First, innovation, almost by definition, involves uniqueness and surprise. As a consequence, it is misleading to assume that the strategic pattern learned in the past will necessarily be the optimal one for the future. Second, successful exploration inevitably adds to the menu of available strategies and thus deforms the shape of the "fitness landscape" in ways that may well be unpredictable to individual agents.[13]

An illustration of the collective role of "Schumpeterian sacrificial lambs" is presented in Silverberg, Dosi, and Orsenigo (1988). There, the diffusion of a new technology under the assumption that learning-by-using is partly appropriated by individual adopters and partly leaks out as an externality was studied. Under some parametrizations of the learning process, they showed that unequivocally superior innovations might diffuse *only* if there were overoptimistic entrepreneurs who pay the price of the initial exploration: their failure opens the way to the takeoff of the industry. Somewhat similarly, one of the properties of the model in Chiaromonte and Dosi (1992) is that a necessary condition for sustained aggregate growth is some degree of diversity of macroeconomic behaviors (related to, for example, the propensity to innovate and imitate).

This theoretical argument easily relates also with the empirical evidence on the multiple contributions of a growing number of actors (quite a few firms, but also public agencies, universities, etc.) to the rise of new technologies and new industries. At one level, the process can be described in some technology space in terms of emergence and establishment of "technological paradigms," "dominant designs," etc. However, at a more behavioral level, the dynamics are driven by a network of diverse agents who, via trial and error, increasingly develop a commonly shared knowledge base, recognizable modes of interactions, collective institutions, etc.[14] The construction of a socially distributed knowledge base inevitably rests also upon a multitude of failed entrepreneurial efforts, in addition to a few impressive jackpots hit by the most ingenious or the luckiest.[15] In spite of that, we suggest that the stubborn pursuits of unlikely courses of search, together with the other biases, might well be a wasteful, imperfect, but crucial ingredient.

VII. Some conclusions

We have emphasized from the start the preliminary nature of this work. Still, if our interpretation is correct, it promises to provide closer and more coherent links among four domains of empirical investigation that so far have proceeded along quite separate paths, namely:

1. the nature of cognitive and decision biases of individuals and organizations;

2. the regularities and patterns in the processes of innovation and diffusion (associated with the emergence of "technological paradigms" and "dominant technological trajectories");
3. the (related) social dynamics underlying the development of technological systems by communities of firms, technical societies, universities, etc.;
4. the patterns of corporate entry, exit, and industrial dynamics.[16]

In a nutshell, our argument is that various forms of cognitive and decision biases are likely to be *intrinsic ingredients* of technological development and corporate strategies, including those concerning start-ups of new firms and diversification.[17]

This view easily links up with several other contributions to this volume. For example, it is certainly consistent with Langlois' "cognitive" analysis of corporate competences and behaviors (chapter 5). Indeed, the "inside view" – with associated biases of "illusion of control," etc., discussed above – might be considered as essential corollary of cumulative and local learning, as analyzed by Levinthal (chapter 10). And it is also consistent with the *systematic* errors of oversight of potentially rich opportunities, stubborn pursuit of past commitments, or, conversely, overconfidence in novelty and change considered in chapter 3 by Garud, Nayyar and Shapira. Having recognized this sort of inevitability of errors – grounded in the very nature of individual and collective learning, and in the decision procedures of single humans and aggregates of them – there is little scope, in our view, to develop any sort of positive (or normative) theory able to accurately predict (or correct) these biases. However, we have suggested – largely in the form of a research agenda – that it might be possible to undertake taxonomic exercises mapping particular types of behavior into particular characteristics of the knowledge bases upon which agents draw. We have outlined an example, linked to research in progress, and concerning entry decisions. Of course, the first task is to show that entry patterns – as observed both cross-sectionally and longitudinally – are systematically affected by persistent decision biases. Second, we conjecture that the biases themselves (and, relatedly, post-entry performances) can be partly understood on the grounds of the *learning regimes* characteristic of specific industries and of their degrees of development (for example, whether a dominant technological paradigm has emerged or not). In a somewhat similar spirit, Bercovitz, Figuercido, and Teece, (chapter 13, this volume) attempt to map corporate strategies onto characteristics of the decision problems facing the firms and the competences that they embody.

In any case, are decision biases necessarily "bad"? At first glance, an affirmative answer is based on the intuition that biases tend to degrade the future performances of the decision-maker, compared – as economists would easily do – with an agent endowed with "rational expectations" and unbiased decision algorithms. However, in the final part of this work we have argued that what might hold for the individual agent (or organization) might not hold for the whole population of them, even for each of them over longer time spans.

In the evolutionary interpretation we proposed, mistakes – *and biases that make these mistakes more frequent* – are likely to be a necessary ingredient of the exploration of technological and organizational novelties. Paraphrasing David (1992), collective change might generally require heroes, herds and a lot of failures. And hence, biases and mistakes might be considered as a sort of powerful externality through which society learns. We want to emphasize that there is no teleological connotation in that statement (biases exist because they are collectively useful). Rather, this is primarily a conjecture on the collective dynamics of a particular form of social organization – call it "capitalism" – which, for reasons well beyond the scope of investigation of this paper, have been able to steadily generate these forms of "animal spirits." Indeed it might even be that, in one form or another,., the strongest individual biases survive both heightened incentives and organizational processes across different cultures because they might have to do with some basic features of human cognition. This is clearly the view of the evolutionary biologist Lionel Tiger, who discusses the evolutionaly useful role optimism likely played in our ancestors' ability to proceed with the hunt and find new territory in spite of numerous dangers. He argues that

Thinking rosy futures is as biological as sexual fantasy. Optimistically calculating the odds is as basic a human action as seeking food when hungry or craving fresh air in dump. Making deals with uncertainty marks us as plainly as bipedalism. This has very practical outcomes. It is relatively easy to cater to and exploit this "psychological sweet tooth." I believe that optimism, not religion, is the opiate of the people. Religion is only one expression of the optimistic impulse. As well, exploitation based on optimism occurs in a wealth of places, not only religious ones; it occurs as much in betting shops as cathedrals and stock exchanges as confessionals." (Tiger, 1979, p. 35)

However, irrespective of whether one entirely subscribes to this general anthropological view, and sticking nearer home, major implications follow from the foregoing argument, in terms of both theory and normative prescriptions.

To end provocatively on the latter: are we sure that we want to teach any sort of "rational" decision making in business schools? How can one avoid the risk that less-biased assessment of any one decision environment yields more conservatism and slower collective change? Should one not emphasize the heuristics of knowledge accumulation capable of increasing the probability that biased gambles turn out to be self-fulfilling prophecies, rather than improving the "quality" of decisions as such?

Acknowledgments

Support to this research, at different stages, by the Center for Research in Management, U.C. Berkeley; the Italian National Research Council (CNR); the Italian Ministry of Universities and Research ("MURST 40%"), International Institute of Applied System Analysis (IIASA), Laxenburg, Austria;

and the Huntsman and Jones Centers at the Wharton School, University of Pennsylvania is gratefully acknowledged. This version benefited from the comments of the participants and organizers of the conference on "Technological Oversights and Foresights," L. N. Stern School of Business, New York University, March 1994, in particular,·Raghn Garud, Praaven Nayyar, Zur Shapira, and Jim Utterback. This work is partly based on ongoing research with John Baldwin, Analytical Studies, Statistics Canada.

Notes

1   On all these properties, see Dunne, Roberts, and Samuelson (1988), Baldwin and Gorecki (1990, 1991), Cable and Schwalbach (1991), Bianco and Sestito (1992), Aldrich and Auster (1986), Acs and Audretsch (1990, 1991), Phillips and Kirchoff (1989), Audretsch and Mahmood (1991), Mahmood (1992), Geroski and Schwalbach (1991), Baldwin (1994), Baldwin and Rafiquzzaman (1994).

2   Holland (1975), Holland et al. (1986), Dosi and Egidi (1991), Schrader, Riggs, and Smith (1993), March (1988), Dosi and Marengo (1993), Marengo (1992), Levinthal (1994), among others.

3   On the notion of ambiguity as distinct from uncertainty, see Einhorn and Hogarth (1985), March (1988), Marengo (1992), Schrader, Riggs and Smith (1993).

4   On the notion of organizational competence and its characteristics, see Dosi, Teece, and Winter (1992), Teece et al. (1994), Dosi and Marengo (1993), Teece, Pisano, and Schuen (1992).

5   More sophisticated variants of this same story would also allow for incomplete information on one's own ability relative to the other competititors, as in Jovanovic (1982).

6   Of course there are cases in which not even such weak incentive requirements are fulfilled. Think, for example, of many features of the past Soviet innovation system, or think of circumstances with zero appropriability of innovation, such as long-time, seed-related agricultural innovations. (See Dosi (1988a) for more on appropriability issues.

7   For further evidence on this point, see Malerba and Orsenigo (1995a,b,c).

8   A discussion of diverse corporate behaviors under different technological regimes in evolutionary models of industrial change is in Malerba and Orsenigo (1995b,c).

9   The trade-offs and dichotomies between "exploration" and "exploitation" also carry over to a more aggregate level, in terms of average or modal behaviors of the population of firms embedded in particular national institutions, collective competencies, perceived opportunities, and constraints. For discussions at this broader level of notions like "dynamic" or "Schumpeterian" efficiency as opposed to "static" or "allocative" efficiency, cf. Klein (1977) and Dosi (1988b).

10 It is a matter of debate to what degrees incumbents are able to internalize search for radical novelties and endogenize, in a biological metaphor, the generation of "mutations." It has been suggested, for example, that the institutional organization of markets influences such an ability. In particular, it is claimed that "market-based" financial systems, such as those of most Anglo-Saxon countries, induce strong pressures towards short-termism and "exploitation," thus relying much more on new firms for exploratory activities. Conversely, "bank-based"

systems – such as Japan or Germany – might confer on incumbents much greater room for time-consuming and uncertain attempts to search for new trajectories of learning. For discussions, cf. Zysman (1994), Dosi (1990), Aoki and Dosi (1991).

11   Note that this argument is quite distinct from the hypothesis that "explorers" are rational and risk-loving. Our point is that, irrespective of whether they are risk-lovers, they certainly have also to be biased in their decision making in order to do what they do. Or, putting it in another way, given their risk preference, if they were endowed with "rational expectations" about the future, they would do otherwise.

12   See also Allen (1988) and Allen and McGlade (1988) for a suggestive model of the dynamics of fishery driven by the interaction between "Cartesian" fishermen ("exploiters") and "stochasts" ("explorers").

13   Interrelatedness of the contribution to "fitness" by different traits, coevolutionary effects and nonlinearities are clearly sufficient to induce unpredictability. (See Levinthal (1993, 1994) and Dosi and Metcalfe (1991).

14   For analyses from different angles see Rip (1992), Rip, Misa, and Schot (1994), Metcalfe and Boden (1991), Garud and Rappa (1994), Garud and Van De Ven (1989), Callon (1993), Nelson (1994), Appod, Harrison, and Kelley (1993), Miller and Blais (1992). In general, the view presented here is highly complementary with the idea of coevolution between cognitive traits, artifacts, and routines outlined in Garud and Rappa (1994) and Garud and Ahlstrom (1995).

15   This statement is in principle consistent with formal investigation of "distributed learning models" (cf., for example, Huberman and Hogg, 1988, Huberman and Glance, 1992) as well as with the experimental evidence on cooperative learning in new problem-solving activities (some suggestive results are in Egidi, 1993).

16   The diversity between these fields and their relatively low degrees of communication with each other also motivates the choice of providing a rather extensive bibliography at the end of this chapter, which might help the reader in unfamiliar territories.

17   Throughout the text, as a first approximation, we took a rather naive and anthropomorphic view of "organizational decisions" (and related biases). In fact, our approach does not have any difficulty in accommodating a more complex view whereby organizational behavior is also the outcome of processes of political negotiation within the organization itself, grounded in the specific pieces of knowledge embodied in various "experts" (e.g. the "engineer," the marketing person, etc.) (see Lane et al., 1995). Also "experts," our argument would go, are likely to display the biases discussed above. In fact, insofar as these experts share the knowledge of broader communities (software specialists, copyright lawyers, chemical engineers, etc.) they might partly curb the "inside view" associated with each individual firm, but at the expense of bringing in the "inside view" dominant in the expert community to which they belong.

References and bibliography

Acs, Z. J. and Audretsch, D. B. (1990). *Innovation and the Small Firm*. Cambridge, MA: MIT Press.

Acs, Z. J. and Audretsch, D. B. (1991). New-firm startups, technology and macroeconomic fluctuations. Discussion Paper, FS IV 91–17, Wissenschaftszentrum, Berlin.

Aldrich, H. and Auster, E. (1986). Even giants started as dwarves. *Research in Organizational Behaviour*, 8.

Aldrich, H. and Fiol, C. M. (1992). Fools rush in? The institutional context of industrial creation. Working paper.

Allen, P. M. (1988). Evolution, innovation and economics. In Dosi et al. (eds.), *Technical Change and Economic Theory*. London: Pinter, and New York: Columbia University Press.

Allen, P. M. (1991). Modeling evolution and creativity in complex systems. *World Futures*, 34, 105–123.

Allen, P. M. and McGlade, J. M. (1988). Dynamics of discovery and exploitation: The case of the Scotian Shelf groundfish fisheries. *Canadian Journal of Fishery and Aquatic Sciences*.

Aoki, M. and Dosi, G. (1991). Corporate organization, finance and innovation. In V. Zamagni (ed.), *Finance and the Entreprise*. San Diego: Academic Press.

Appod, S. J., Harrison, B. and Kelley, M. R. (1993). Spacially distributed and proximate inter-organizational networks, agglomeration and technological performance in U.S. manufacturing. Paper delivered to the annual meeting of the Association of American Geographers, Atlanta, April.

Argote, L., Seabright, M. A. and Dyer, L. (1986) Individual versus group: Use of base-rate and individuating information. *Organizational Behavior and Individual Decision Processes*, 38, 65–75.

Arnold, J. III, (1986). Assessing capital risk: You can't be too conservative. *Harvard Business Review*, 113–121.

Arrow, K. J. (1962). Economic welfare and the allocation of resources for inventions. In R. Nelson (ed.), *The Rate and Direction of Inventive Activity: Economic and Social Factors*. Princeton, NJ: Princeton University Press.

Audretsch, D. B. and Mahmood, T. (1991). The rate of hazard confronting new firms and plants in U.S. manufacturing. Discussion Paper, FS IV 91–7, Wissenschaftszentrum, Berlin.

Baldwin, J. R. (1994). *The Dynamic of Industrial Competition, A North American Perspective*. New York: Cambridge University Press.

Baldwin, J. R. and Goreki, P. K. (1990). *Structural Change and the Adjustment Process*. A study prepared for Statistics Canada and the Economic Council of Canada, 1990.

Baldwin, J. R. and Goreki, P. K. (1991). Firms entry and exit in the Canadian Manufacturing Sector. *Canadian Journal of Economics*, 24, 300–323.

Baldwin, J. R. and Rafiquzzaman, M. (1994). Selection versus learning as determinants of post-entry performance. Ottawa: Statistics Canada, Working Paper.

Bateman, T. and Zietham, C. (1989). The psychological context of strategic decisions: A test of relevance to practitioners. *Strategic Management Journal*, 10, 587–92.

Bazerman, M. H., Giuliano, T. and Appleman, A. (1984). Escalation in individual and goup decision making. *Organizational Behavior and Human Decision Processes*, 33, 141–152.

Bianco, M. and Sestito, P. (1992). Entry, growth and market structure. A preliminary analysis of the Italian case. Presented at the International Conference on "Birth and Start-up of Small Firms," Milano.

64   DOSI AND LOVALLO

Brüderl, J., Preisendorfer, P. and Ziegler, R. (1992). Survival changes of newly founded business organizations. *American Sociological Review*, 57, 227–242.

Cable, J. and Schwalbach, J. (1991). International comparison of entry and exit. In P.
Geroski and J. Schwalbach (eds.), *Entry and Market Contestability: An International Comparison*. Basil Oxford: Blackwell, pp. 257–281.

Callon, M. (1993). Variety and irreversibility in network of technique conception and
adoption. In D. Foray and C. Freeman (eds.), *Technology and the Wealth of Nations*. London: Pinter.

Carroll, G. R. and Swaminathan, A. (1992). The organizational ecology of strategic groups in the american brewing industry from 1975 to 1990. *ICC*, 1,
65–97.

Chiaromonte, F. and Dosi, G. (1992). The microfoundations of competitiveness and
their macroeconomic implications. In D. Foray and C. Freeman (eds.), *Technology and the Wealth of Nations*, London: Pinter.

Cohen, W. and Levinthal, D. (1989). Innovation and learning: The two faces of R&D.
Economic Journal, 99, 657–674.

Cohen, W. and Levinthal, D. (1990). Absorptive capacity: A new perspective on
learning and innovation. *Administrative Science Quarterly*, 35, 128–152.

David, P. (1992). Heroes, herds and hysteresis in technological history. Thomas Edison and the battle of the systems reconsidered. *Industrial and Corporate Change*,
I.

Dosi, G., (1984). *Technical Change and Industrial Transformation, The Theory and an Application to the Semiconductor Industry*. London: Macmillan.

Dosi, G., (1988a). Sources, procedures and microeconomic effect of innovation. *Journal of Economic Literature*, 26, 1120–1171.

Dosi, G., (1988b). Institutions and markets in a dynamic world. *The Manchester
School*.

Dosi, G., (1990). Finance, innovation and industrial change. *Journal of Economic Behavior and Organization*.

Dosi, G. and Egidi, M. (1991). Substantive and procedural uncertainty. An exploration of economic behaviors in complex and changing environment. *Journal of
Evolutionary Economics*, 1, pp. 145–168.

Dosi, G., Freeman, C., Nelson, R., Silverberg, G., Soete, L. (eds.) (1988). *Technical
Change and Economic Theory*, London: Pinter, and New York, Columbia University Press.

Dosi, G. and Malerba, F. (eds.) (1995). *Organization and Strategy in the Evolution of the
Entreprise*. London: Macmillan.

Dosi, G. and Marengo, L. (1993). Some elements of an evolutionary theory of organizational competences. In W. England (ed.), *Evolutionary Concepts in Contemporary Economics*. Ann Arbor: University Michigan Press.

Dosi, G., Marengo, L., Bassanini, A., and Valente, M. (1994). *Norms as Emergent Properties of Adaptive Learning The Case of Economic Routines*. Laxemburg, Austria:
IIASA. Working Paper.

Dosi, G., Marsili, O., Orsenigo, L. and Salvatore, R. (1995). Learning, Market Selection and the Evolution of Industrial Structures. *Small Business Economics*, 7,
1–26.

Dosi, G. and S. Metcalfe (1991). On some notions of irreversibility in economics. In P.
P. Saviotti and S. Metcalfe (eds.), *Evolutionary Economics*. London: Harwood
Academic Press.

Rational entrepreneurs or optimistic martyrs?   65

Dosi, G. and Salvatore, R. (1992). The structure of industrial production and the boundaries between organization and markets. In A. Scott and M. Stolper (eds.), *Pathways to Regional Development*. Boulder, CO: Westview Press.

Dosi, G., Teece, D. J. and Winter, S. (1992). Towards a theory of corporate coherence: Preliminary remarks. In G. Dosi, R. Giannetti, and P. A. Toninelli (eds.), *Technology and Enterprises in a Historical Perspective*. New York: Oxford University Press.

Dunne, T., Roberts, M. J. and Samuelson, L. (1988). Patterns of firm entry and exit in U.S. manufacturing Industries. *Rand Journal of Economics*, 19, 495–515.

Egidi, M. (1993). Routines, hierarchies of problems, procedural behaviours: Some evidence from experiments. Laxemburg, Austria, IIASA, Working Paper.

Einhorn, H. J. and Hogarth, R. M. (1985). Ambiguity and Uncertainty in Probabilistic Inference. *Psychological Review*, 86, 433–461.

Foray, D. and Freeman, C. (eds.). (1993). *Technology and the Wealth of Nations*. London: Pinter.

Fox, F. V. and Staw, B. (1979). The trapped administrator: Effects of job insecurity and policy resistance upon commitment to a course of action. *Administrative Science Quarterly*, 40.

Freeman, C. (1982). *The Economics of Industrial Innovation*. London: Pinter,.

Garud, R. and Ahlstrom, D. (1995). Technology assessment: A socio-cognitive perspective. New York: New York University, L. N. Stern School of Business, Working Paper.

Garud, R. and Nayyar, P. R. (1994). Transformative capacity: Continual structuring by intertemporal technology transfer. *Strategic Management Journal*, 15, 365–385.

Garud, R. and Rappa, M. (1994). A socio-cognitive model of technology evolution: The case of cochlear implants. *Organization Science*, 5, 344–362.

Garud, R. and Van de Ven, A. H. (1989). Development of the cochlear implant program at 3M Corporation. *Strategic Management Research* Center, University of Minnesota, Minneapolis.

Garud, R. and Van de Ven, A. H. (1992). An empirical evaluation of the internal corporate venturing process. *Stategic Management Journal*, 13, 93–109.

Geroski P., (1991). Innovation and the Sectoral Sources of UK Productivity Growth. *Economic Journal*, 101, 1438–1451.

Geroski, P. and Schwalbach, J. (eds.). (1991). *Entry and Market Contestability: An International Comparison*. Oxford: Basil Blackwell.

Gort, M. and Klepper, S. (1982). Time paths in the diffusion of product innovation. *The Economic Journal*.

Hannan, M. T. and Carroll, G. R. (1991). *Dynamics of Organizational Populations: Density, Competition and Legitimation*. New York: Oxford University Press.

Hannan, M. T. and Freeman, J. (1989). *Organizational Ecology*. Cambridge, MA: Harvard University Press.

Heiner, R. (1983). On the origin of predictable behavior. *American Economic Review*.

Heiner, R. (1988). "Imperfect decisions, routinized behavior and inertial change. In Dosi et al. (1988).

Henderson, R. M. (1988). The failure of established firms in the face of technical change: A study of photolothographic alignment equipment. Dept. of Business Economics, Harvard University, Cambridge, MA.

Henderson, R. M. (1993). Underinvestment and incompetence as responses to radical innovation: Evidence from the photolithographics alignment equipment industry. *Rand Journal of Economics*, 24, 2.

Henderson, R. M. and Clarck, K. B. (1990). Architectural innovation: The reconfiguration of existing product technologies and the failure of established firms. *Administrative Science Quarterly*, 35, 9–30.

Holland, (1975). *Adaptation in Natural and Artificial Systems*. Ann Arbor: University of Michigan Press.

Holland, K. Holyook, R. Nesbatt and Thagard, P. (1986). *Induction: Processes of Inference, Learning and Discovery*. Cambridge, MA: MIT Press.

Huberman, B. A. and Glance, N. S. (1992). Diversity and collective action. Palo Alto: Xerox Palo Alto Research Center, Working Paper.

Huberman, B. A. and Hogg, T. (1988). The behavior of computational ecologies. Palo Alto: Xerox Palo Alto Research Center, Working Paper.

Janis, I. L., (1982). *Groupthink*. 2nd Edition. Boston: Houghton Mifflin.

Jovanovic, B. (1982). Selection and evolution of industry. *Econometrica*, 50, 649–670.

Kahneman, D. and Lovallo, D. (1993). Timid choice and bold forecast: A cognitive perspective on risk taking. *Management Science*, 39, 1.

Kahneman, D. and Tversky, A. (1973). On the psychology of prediction. *Psychological Review*, 80, 237–251.

Kahneman, D. and Tversky, A. (1979). Intuitive prediction: Biases and corrective procedures. *TIMS Studies in Management Sciences*, 12, 313–327.

Kahneman, D. and Tversky, A. (1986). Rational choice and the framing of decisions. *Journal of Business*, 59, S251–S278.

Klein, B. (1977). *Dynamic Competition*. Cambridge, MA: Harvard University Press.

Klepper, S. (1992). Entry, exit and innovation over the product life cycle: The dynamics of first mover advantages, declining product innovation and market failure. Paper presented at the International J. A. Schumpeter Society, Kyoto, August.

Klepper, S. and Miller, J. H. (1994). Entry, exit and shakeouts in the United States in new manufactured products. Carnegie-Mellon University, Working Paper.

Lane, S. J. (1989). *Entry and Industry Evolution in the ATM Manufacturers Market*. Stanford University, UMI.

Lane, D., Malerba, F. and Maxwell, R. (1995). Choice and action. *Journal of Evolutionary Economics*. forthcoming.

Levinthal, D. (1992). Surviving Schumpeterian environments: An evolutionary perspective. *Industrial and Corporate Change*, 1, 427–443.

Levinthal, D. A. (1993). Learning and Schumpeterian Dynamics. Philadelphia: The Warton School, Working Paper.

Levinthal, D.A. and March, J. G. (1994). The myopia of learning. *Strategic Management Journal*.

Lovallo, D. (1996a). From Individual Biases to Organizational Errors. In G. Dosi and F. Malerba (eds.), *Organization and Strategy in the Evolution of the Enterprise*. London: Macmillan.

Lovallo, D. (1996b). *Entry Decision: A Psychological Perspective*. Unpublished doctoral dissertation, University of California at Berkeley.

Mahmood, T. (1992). Does the hazard rate of new plants vary between low and high-tech industries? *Small Business Economics*, 4, 201–209.

Malerba, F. (1985). *The Semiconductor Business*. London: Pinter .

Malerba, F. and Orsenigo, L. (1993). Technological regimes and firm behaviour. *Industrial and Corporate Change*, 2(1), 74–89.

Malerba, F. and Orsenigo, L. (1995a). On new innovators and ex-innovators. Laxemburg, Austria, IIASA, working paper.

Malerba, F. and Orsenigo, L. (1995b). Schumpeterian patterns of innovation. *Cambridge Journal of Economics*.

Malerba, F. and Orsenigo, L. (1995c). Schumpeterian patterns of innovation are technology-specific. *Research Policy*.

March, J. (1988). *Decision and Organizations*. Oxford: Blackwell.

March, J. (1991). Exploration and exploitation in organizational learning. *Organization Science*, 2, 71–87.

March, J. and Olsen, J. P. (1976). Organizational learning and the ambiguity of the past. In J. G. March and J. P. Olsen (eds.), *Ambiguity and Choice in Organizations*. Bergen: Universitetsforlaget.

March, J. and Shapira, Z. (1987). Managerial perspectives on risk and risk taking. *Management Science*, 33, 1404–1418.

Marengo, L. (1992). Structure, competence and learning in an adaptive model of the firm. *Papers on Economic and Evolution*, edited by the European Study Group for Evolutionary Economics, Freiburg, no. 9203.

Merrow, E. et al. (1981). *Understanding Cost Growth and Performance Shortfalls in Pioneer Plants*. Santa Barbara, CA: Rand Corporation.

Metcalfe, S. (1991). *Variety, structure and change: An economic perspective on the competitive process*. Manchester: University of Manchester, Discussion Paper.

Metcalfe, S. and Bodem, M. (1991). Innovation strategy and the epistemic connection: An essay on the growth of technological knowledge. *Journal of Scientific & Industrial Research*, 50, 707–717.

Miller, R. and Blais, R. A. (1992). Configuration of innovation: Predictable and maverick modes. *Technology Analysis & Strategic Management*, 4, 4, 363–386.

Mitchell, W. (1989). Whether and when? Probably and timing of incumbents entry into emerging industrial subfields. *Administrative Science Quarterly*, 34, 208–230.

Mitchell, W. (1991). Dual clocks: Entry order influences on incumbent and newcomer market share and survival when socialized assets retain their value. *Strategic Management Journal*, 12, 85–100.

Mitchell, W. (1993). Invasion of the subfield snatchers: Newcomer and incumbent entry and success in new technical subfields of the medical diagnostic imaging equipment industry. Working Paper: University of Michigan.

Nelson, R. R. (1994). The co-evolution of technology, industrial structure and supporting institutions. *Industrial and Corporate Change*, 3, 1.

Nelson, R. R. and Winter, S. G. (1982). *An Evolutionary Theory of Economic Change*, Cambridge MA: The Belknap Press of Harvard University Press.

Pavitt, K. (1984). Sectoral patterns of innovation: Towards a taxonomy and a theory. *Research Policy*, 13, 343–373.

Pelkey, J. (1993). *Economic Growth and Technological Innovation: The Computer Communications Market Structure 1968–1988*. Santa Fe: SFI.

Philips, B. D. and Kirchoff, B. A. (1989). Formation, growth and survival: Small firm dynamic in the U.S. economy. *Small Business Economics*, 1, 65–74.

Reid, G. C. (1991). Staying in business. *International Journal of Industrial Organization*, 9.

Reinganum, J. F. (1983). Uncertain innovation and the persistence of monopoly. *AER*, 73, 741–748.

Reinganum, J. F. (1984). Uncertain innovation and the persistence of monopoly: re-play. *AER*, 74, 243–245.

Rip, A., (1992). *Cognitive Approaches to Technology Policy*. University of Twente, The Netherlands.

Rip, A., Misa, T. and Schot, J. (1994). *Managing Technology in Society. New Forms for the Control of Technology*. University of Twente, The Netherlands.

Ross, J. and Staw, B. (1986). EXPO 86: An escalation prototype. *Administrative Science Quarterly*, 31 p. 274—297.

Saviotti, P. P. (1992). Variety, economic and technological development. Presented at the 1992 Conference of the International Schumpeter Society.

Saviotti, P. P. and Metcalfe, S. (eds.). (1991). *Evolutionary Economics*. London: Harwood Academic Press.

Schoemaker, P. J. H. and Marais, M. L. (1995). Technological innovation and firm inertia. In G. Dosi and F. Malerba (eds.), *Organization and Strategy in the Evolution of the Enterprise*. London: Macmillan.

Schrader, S., Riggs, W. and Smith, R. P. (1993). Choice over uncertainty and ambiguity in technical problem solving. *Journal of Engineering and Technology Management*, 10, 73–99.

Shafir, E. and Tversky, A. (1992). Thinking through uncertainty: Non-consequential reasoning and choice. *Cognitive Psychology*, 24, 449–474.

Silvelberg, G., Dosi, G., and Orsenigo, L. (1988). Innovation, diversity and diffusion. A self-organization model. *The Economic Journal*, 98, 1032–1054.

Simon, H. A. (1982). *Models of Bounded Rationality*, vols. 1 and 2. Cambridge, MA: MIT Press.

Sterman, J. D. (1989). Modeling managerial behavior: Misperceptions of feedback in a dynamic decision making experiment. *Management Science*, 35, 321–338.

Teece, D. J., Pisano, G. and Schuen, A. (1992). Dynamic capabilities and strategic management. Center for Research in Management, University of California at Berkeley, CCC Working Paper.

Teece, D. J., Rumelt, R., Dosi, G., and Winter, S. (1994). Understanding corporate coherence: Theory and evidence. *Journal of Economic Behavior and Organization*.

Thaler, R. H. (1992). *The Winner's Curse: Paradoxes and Anomalies of Economic Life*. New York: The Free Press.

Tiger, L. (1979). *Optimism: The Biology of Hope*. New York: Simon and Schuster.

Utterback, J. M. (1994). *Mastering the Dynamics of Innovation*. Cambridge, MA: Harvard Business School Press.

Utterbark, J. and Suarez, F. (1993). Innovation, competition and market structure. *Research Policy*.

Winter, S. G. (1984). Schumpeterian competition in alternative technological regimes. *Journal of Economic Behavior and Organization*, 5, 287–320.

Zysman, J. (1994). How institutions create historically rooted trakectories of growth. *Industrial and Corporate Change*, 3, 1.

[9]

Journal of Economic Behavior and Organization 23 (1994) 1-30. North-Holland

Understanding corporate coherence
Theory and evidence*

David J. Teece

University of California, Berkeley, CA, USA

Richard Rumelt

University of California, Los Angeles, CA, USA

Giovanni Dosi

University of Rome, Rome, Italy

Sidney Winter

General Accounting Office, Washington, DC, USA

Received July 1990, final version received October 1992

Multiproduct firms are perceived to be coherent in their scope, yet there is no strong theoretical foundations to explain coherence in modern industrial organization theory. This paper shows that as U.S. manufacturing firms grow more diverse, they maintain a constant level of coherence between neighboring activities. This finding runs counter to the idea that firms with many activities are generally more 'incoherent'. A framework is then presented which appeals to the nature of enterprise learning, path dependencies, and the nature of the selection environment to explain the ubiquity of coherent diversifiers.

Correspondence to: Professor David J. Teece, Center for Research in Management, University of California, 554 Barrows Hall, Berkeley, CA 94720, USA.

*The views developed here were first presented by David J. Teece and Giovanni Dosi at Terni, Italy, October 1987. We are most grateful for an expansive and helpful anonymous review provided by *JEBO*. We are also grateful for comments by Connie Helfat of the Wharton School. Earlier versions of the paper containing some of our initial thinking appeared in: Les Frontièrs des Enterprises: Vers une Théorie de la Cohérence de la Grande Enterprise, Revue d'Economie Industrielle 51, 1ᵉʳ trimestre 1990, 128–254; and Dosi, Teece and Winter, Toward a theory of corporate coherence: Preliminary remarks, in: Dosi, Giannetti and Toninelli, eds., Technology and enterprise in a historical perspective (Clarendon Press of Oxford University Press, Oxford, 1992).

1. Introduction

There are three relatively unexplored characteristics of the boundaries of the modern corporation that deserve an explanation: (i) their multiproduct scope, (ii) the non-random (coherent) distribution of product portfolios inside firms, and (iii) the relative stability in the composition of firms' product portfolio over the long run.[1] In short, it appears that there is some coherence in the ways firms diversify, and this coherence is relatively stable over time. Thus Shell Oil Company has been in the oil business – exploration, production, refining, and marketing of crude oil and petroleum products – for almost a century. It has diversified into petrochemicals and little else. IBM has been in information technologies for almost half a century; Intel is focussed in semiconductors; ICI and DuPont are primarily in chemicals; and Boeing is in aerospace. Put differently, it is intriguing, from a theoretical perspective if not from a practical one, that Boeing does not make buses, DuPont does not make airplanes, ICI does not own supermarkets, IBM does not make cars, and Shell Oil does not make jewelry.

The standard neoclassical theory of industrial organization [e.g., Tirole (1988)] is almost completely silent with respect to the matter of corporate coherence, despite its obvious salience in industrial organization. In this paper we attempt to measure the coherence of business firms, and then outline a theory of corporate coherence. In order to do so, we pay explicit attention to enterprise learning and the development of competences, but also to complementary assets, technological opportunities and the strength of competition in product and capital markets. These concepts are alien to much of the received industrial organization literature, but we suggest that they have utility in unlocking a significant conundrum in modern industrial organization theory.

2. The concept of coherence

Firms are coherent to the extent that their constituent businesses are related to one another. In the language of economics, businesses are related if there are economies to their joint operation and/or ownership. In this paper we focus not on why firms diversify,[2] but on why they diversify coherently.[3] Setting aside for the moment the conglomerate form of business

---

[1] Pavitt, Robson and Townsend (1989, table 5, p. 91) show that the sectoral priorities of U.K. firms have been relatively stable over a 40-year period. Chandler's (1990) appendices suggest the same is true for U.S. and German firms.

[2] Teece (1980, 1982) has articulated a plausible theory of the multiproduct firm based on transaction costs, excess resources, and scope economies. But in these earlier papers he is not concerned explicitly with the coherence issue.

[3] In this paper we are not explicitly interested in vertical integration questions, which have been handled elsewhere, most notable in Williamson (1985).

organization, what is remarkable about firms, as we will show, is the relative 'coherence' in their business activities.[4] Admittedly, the boundaries of the firms are sometimes quite fuzzy, with interfirm agreements, joint ventures, and consortia rendering precise delineations of a firms' activities imprecise.

Few if any business firms are literally single product. In many cases, however, diversification is a straightforward consequence of micro-level diversity in the demands of the buyer population, such as that which exists for different ice cream flavors, shoe sizes, pizza toppings, and airline destinations. Much of this diversity is so readily accommodated on the production side that we find it useful to view such firms as being single product. It is the more variegated product diversity that we wish to explain, such as when a manufacturer of microprocessors also makes memory devices.

A salient attribute of diversification is that, as we shall show, firms over time add activities that relate to some aspect of existing activities. They build laterally on what they have got. New product lines bear certain technological and market similarities with the old. Thus the sequence is generally for firms to begin as single product and subsequently become multiproduct, rather than the other way around; and new product lines very often, though certainly not always, utilize capabilities common with existing product lines. Indeed, many prescriptions with respect to diversification strategies are characterized by their emphasis on the desirability for firms to 'stick to their knitting',[5] though such prescriptions rarely specify what the knitting is to which firms should stick.

Corporate diversification is also a phenomenon that can expand and contract. Firms not only add businesses, they also commonly divest. In the United States, the 1980s witnessed firms actively engaged in divestitures, including ITT, Allegis, and RJR Nabisco. Indeed, there often appears to be a degree of circularity to the fashion in which new businesses are added and subsequently divested. This is particularly so when corporations diversify through acquisition.[6] On the other hand, corporations often display remarkable similarities with respect to their diversification strategies. Almost everywhere the auto companies have diversified into a wide range of vehicles, e.g., Mercedes, Fiat, GM, and Renault all make cars, trucks, buses, and tanks. And, with few exceptions, aerospace companies have remained relati-

---

[4]We recognize that in the popular press the scope of diversification is frequently remarked upon; but unless one has a preconceived view of what the corporation ought to look like, one should find coherence equally remarkable. Certainly in the standard textbook on microeconomic analysis of firms there is usually nothing to explain why firms are diversified, let alone the nature of their diversification.

[5]See Peters and Waterman (1982).

[6]Thus the conglomerate ITT was put together by Harold Geneen, only to be dismantled by his successors. Similarly, Richard Ferris put together the Allegis Group, starting with United Airlines, only to have it undone months later by his successors.

vely focussed. The challenge is to develop a theory to explain not only coherence, but also similarities and differences in the nature of coherence across firms and industries.

In this regard, it is useful to differentiate between coherence at the business level and coherence at the corporate level. There is obviously much greater coherence and stability at the former level. Since its formation in 1918, Hertz has had at least five different corporate parents, yet its car rental business has been basically impervious to the identity of its 'parents'. In this paper we are interested in both business unit coherence and corporate coherence. The latter will necessarily take us into a consideration of various corporate forms, including the conglomerate.

Coherence, we should point out, is different from 'specialization'. Specialization refers to the performance of particular tasks in a particular setting. This is the manner in which Adam Smith implicitly defined the concept, and it is the way we will use it. Thus in the famous pin making example, Smith referred to specialization in terms of particular tasks, like grinding the point. Thus a firm may exhibit coherence though it may not necessarily be specialized. Specialization is a special case of coherence when the coherence is confined to a single product line. We are, accordingly, defining coherence in a multi-product sense.

A firm exhibits coherence when its lines of business are related, in the sense that there are certain technological and market characteristics common to each. A firm's coherence increases as the number of common technological and market characteristics found in each product line increases. Coherence is thus a measure of relatedness. A corporation fails to exhibit coherence when common characteristics are allocated randomly across a firm's lines of business.

3. Measuring the coherence of business firms

3.1. Prior literature

A great deal of work has been carried out on the measurement of corporate diversification,[7] but much less has been directed at the measurement of inter-business relatedness. One approach, developed by Caves (1981), is to use the hierarchy implicit in the SIC system, so that businesses in different 4-digit industries but the same 3-digit industry are 1 'unit' apart, whereas businesses whose closest connection is their 2-digit industry memberships are 2 'units' apart, and so forth. Lemelin (1982) measured inter-industry related-

---

[7]Gort (1962) used specialization measures, Rumelt (1972) combined specialization with adjudged relatedness, Berry (1971) developed the Herfindahl measure, which Palepu (1975) identifies as entropy.

ness as the correlation coefficient across input structures taken from the input-output table. Klavans' (1989) index of technology relatedness is also based on input patterns, but he uses the amount of overlap in occupational categories as an index. A fairly noisy measure of relatedness has been developed by Gollop and Monahan (1989): they compute the dissimilarity between the patterns of input shares, using nine classes of input (i.e., production wages, fuel, purchased services, etc.). Working with Census of Manufacturers data, Gollop and Monahan argue that because the data are 'filtered through the SIC system, the underlying notion of product dissimilarity must have a supply-side orientation ... differences in distribution systems and/or marketing patterns are ignored. It follows that the formulation of product heterogeneity must be based wholly on technical considerations' (1989:4).

One of the contributions of the present study is to develop an index using SIC data that goes beyond input considerations and overturns Gollop and Monahan's dictum. This is accomplished by moving away from associating the properties of SIC industries, and instead looking directly at the frequencies with which they are combined in firms.

3.2. A survivor measure of relatedness

The *survivor principle* is that economic competition will lead the disappearance of relatively inefficient organizational forms. Stigler (1968) argued in favor of using this principle to measure economies of scale (or estimate optimum firm size), noting that 'not only is the survivor technique more direct and simpler than the alternative techniques for the determination of the optimum size of the firm, it is also more authoritative' (1968:74). To apply the spirit of this principle to the study of relatedness, we assume that *activities which are more related will be more frequently combined within the same corporation.* Thus, if corporations which engage in activity *A* almost always also engage in activity *B*, we would conclude that these activities are highly related. Conversely, activities that are rarely or never combined are unrelated.

To be explicit, let the universe being studied consist of K corporations each active in *two or more of* I industries. Because undiversified companies shed no direct light on the relatedness of industries, they are omitted from consideration. To describe this data let $C_{ik} = 1$ if corporation k is active in industry i, and 0 otherwise. We call the operations of a corporation in an industry an activity. Thus, both corporations and industries are comprised of activities. The number of activities in corporation k is $m_k = \sum_i C_{ik}$ and the number of diversified activities in industry i is $n_i = \sum_k C_{ik}$.

Now consider the number J_{ij} of corporations which are active in both industry i and industry j, where

$$J_{ij} = \sum_k C_{ik} C_{jk}. \tag{1}$$

This count of joint occurrences of industries i and j can be used to construct a measure of relatedness. One initially appealing choice is $P(j/i)/J_{ij}/n_i$, the conditional probability that a corporation is active in industry j given that it is active in industry i. Unfortunately, $P(j/i) = P(i/j)$ because (in general) $n_i = n_j$.

The approach taken here is to compare the observed value of J_{ij} to the value that would be expected under the hypothesis that diversification is *random*. The intuition is straightforward: J_{ij} increases with the relatedness of i and j, but it also can be expected to increase with n_i and with n_j. Thus, if n_i and n_j are large, one would expect to see fair number of corporations active in both industries even if there was little relatedness between them. Conversely, if n_i or n_j is small, one would not expect to see very many linkages even if there were substantial synergy. Hence, the information in J_{ij} about relatedness can be extracted by comparing it to the number of linkages that would be observed for a given n_i, n_j and K were there no relatedness, i.e., if industries were randomly assigned to companies.

To operationalize the random hypothesis, assume that n_i and n_j are fixed. A sample (without replacement) of size n_i is drawn from the population of K corporations and those chosen are assigned activities in industry i. A second independent sample (without replacement) of size n_j is then drawn from the population of K corporations. Those chosen are assigned activities in industry j. Given this scheme, the number x_{ij} of corporations active in both industry i and j is a hypergeometric random variable (population K, special members n_i, and sample size n_j). That is,

$$\Pr[X_{ij} = x] = f_{hg}(x, N, n_i, n_j) = \frac{\binom{n_i}{x}\binom{K - n_i}{n_j - x}}{\binom{K}{n_i}}. \tag{2}$$

The mean and variance of X_{ij} are

$$\mu_{ij} = E(X_{ij}) = \frac{n_i n_j}{K}, \tag{3}$$

$$\sigma_{ij}^2 = \mu_{ij}\left(1 - \frac{n_i}{K}\right)\left(\frac{K}{K-1}\right). \tag{4}$$

If the actual number J_{ij} of linkages observed between industry i and industry *j* greatly exceeds the expected number, μ_{ij}, the two industries are highly 'related'. Accordingly, the measure of relatedness is taken to be

$$t_{ij} = \frac{J_{ij} - \mu_{ij}}{\sigma_{ij}}. \tag{5}$$

In analogy to a *t*-statistic, i_{ij} measures the degree to which the observed linkage between the two industries exceeds that which would be expected were the assignments of industries to companies simply random.

3.3. The data

The data used in this study were obtained from the 1987 Trinet Large Establishment tape. On this tape Trinet attempts to provide information on every establishment in the United States with over 20 employees. Each of the approximately one-half million records on the tape describes an establishment: its name, address, telephone number, employee count, its primary four-digit SIC (1987 standard), estimated value of shipments, and corporate parent, if any. After aggregating a parent's establishments in the same industry, deleting administrative units, deleting government and non-profit 'industries', and deleting corporations that were not diversified, 18,620 companies remained. These diversified firms were active in 958 different 4-digit SIC industries, with a total of 66,688 activities represented.

Of the 448,403 possible linkages between pairs of industries, 128,338 were observed. A t_{ij} measure of relatedness was calculated for each such pair. It ranged from -4.02 to 111.3. The average relatedness was 4.33 and the standard deviation was 5.41.

The highest observed relatedness was between SIC 5181 and SIC 5182; between beer & ale wholesalers and wine & spirits wholesalers. In this case, there were 307 SIC 5181 activities and 316 SIC 5182 activities in multi-activity firms; 255 of these appearances were joint. Some other examples of high relatedness illustrate how the measure overcomes the vagaries of the SIC system:

1. The 9 cane sugar refining (SIC 2061) activities and 7 beet sugar refining (SIC 2062) activities appeared jointly 7 times, inducing a relatedness of 85.9.
2. The 33 ordnance & accessories (SIC 3489) activities and the 16 military tanks (SIC 3795) activities appeared jointly 10 times, inducing a relatedness of 59.3.
3. The 81 fabric gloves manufacturing (SIC 2381) activities and the 13 leather glove manufacturing activities (SIC 3151) appeared jointly 6 times, inducing a relatedness of 50.7.
4. The 81 natural gas liquids (SIC 1321) activities and the 117 petroleum

refining (SIC 2911) activities appeared jointly 39 times, inducing a relatedness of 54.2.

3.4. Measures of the coherence of firms

A diversified (multi-activity) corporation consists of m activities.[8] Activity i has e_i employees and relatedness[9] τ_{ij} with activity j. The weighted-average relatedness WAR_i of activity i to all other activities within the firm is defined as

$$WAR_i = \frac{\sum_{j \neq i} \tau_{ij} e_j}{\sum_{j \neq i} e_j}. \tag{6}$$

This measure indicates the degree to which activity i is related to all of the other activities of the firm, where relatedness is weighted by employee count. Another interpretation is that WAR_i is as the expected relatedness between activity i and the activity housing an employee randomly selected from elsewhere in the firm.

The second measure of intra-firm relatedness captures the strength of association between activity i and its closest neighbors. In a corporation with m activities there are $m(m-1)/2$ different pairs of relatedness measures among activities. However, only $m-1$ links among activities need be drawn to create a connected graph that includes them all. The graph with $m-1$ links such that the sum of the relatedness measures on each link is largest is called the *maximum spanning tree*. Such a tree is defined by $\lambda_{ij} = 1$ if a link between activity i and activity j is part of the tree, and 0 otherwise. Given the maximum spanning tree of a company's activities, the weighted average relatedness of neighbors to activity i is defined by

$$WARN_i = \frac{\sum_{j \neq i} \tau_{ij} e_j \lambda_{ij}}{\sum_{j \neq i} e_j \lambda_{ij}}. \tag{7}$$

3.5. Findings

These measures were computed for each of the 41,857 activities in a Trinet multi-activity manufacturing company.[10] Table 1 shows average values of WAR_i and $WARN_i$, as well as standard deviations, for various values of m.

[8]The kth corporation has m_k activities; the subscript is suppressed here to focus on the relationships among activities within a single firm.

[9]Note that $\tau_{ij} = t_{q(i)q(j)}$, where the corporation's ith activity is in industry $q(i)$.

[10]Characterizing companies by the 2-digit SIC receiving the most employment, manufacturing companies have 2-digit SIC codes in the range 20–39.

Table 1

Relatedness of activities, establishments with over 20 employees.

Number of activities (m). 1987	Obs.	Coherence measures			
		$WARN_i$		WAR_i	
		Avg.	Std. Dev.	Avg.	Std. Dev.
2	13,944	19.8	17.6	19.8	17.6
3	4,434	21.5	17.6	18.1	15.4
4	2,748	24.7	18.8	19.0	15.5
5	2,010	24.1	17.5	17.1	13.5
6	1,386	23.4	16.7	15.5	12.2
7	1,183	24.7	16.4	15.5	11.4
8	1,016	23.6	15.4	14.6	10.9
9	801	23.5	15.5	13.4	10.2
10	760	23.4	14.6	13.0	8.9
11	594	24.0	15.3	12.8	9.3
12	588	23.6	15.2	11.7	8.0
13	455	24.9	16.2	11.3	8.5
14	616	23.7	13.5	12.0	8.4
15	345	23.9	15.2	12.1	8.7
16	448	22.2	13.3	10.5	8.1
17	306	20.6	11.0	10.0	6.4
18	378	23.4	13.5	11.3	8.1
19	342	25.8	13.5	11.7	7.6
20–29	2,975	25.0	13.9	10.2	7.0
30–39	2,032	24.0	12.8	9.0	5.6
40–49	1,598	25.4	13.3	8.5	5.4
50–59	921	28.3	13.8	8.9	5.4
60–69	773	28.2	14.7	9.1	5.7
≥ 70	1,204	26.8	14.2	6.8	3.8

As expected, the value of WAR_i falls with m: the regression[11] of m on WAR_i yields $R^2 = 0.0118$ and a slope coefficient of 0.091.

These results suggest that as U.S. manufacturing firms grow more diverse, they maintain a constant level of (local) coherence between neighboring activities. This finding runs counter to the idea firms with many activities are necessarily unrelated or incoherent. Taking the dyadic firm (a firm active in only two activities) as the standard, the 6,972 dyadic manufacturing firms have an average inter-activity relatedness of 19.8 (table 1). In firms with 3 activities, the average relatedness among neighbors increases slightly to 21.5. 10 activities increases average relatedness among neighbors to 23.4 and with 70 or more activities it increases to 27.5

These data reveal an industrial fine structure that does not vary a great deal (on average) with the diversity of the corporation. A useful analogy would be to a residential neighborhood, where $WARN_i$ measures the inverse of the average distance from a house to its neighbors and WAR_i measures

[11]All regression results reported are significant at the 0.0001 level. The high level of significance reflects the impact of 41,857 observations rather than large effects.

the inverse of the average distance from a house to all other houses in the area. As the area covered is increased, the distance to nearest neighbors does not change, but the average distance to all other homes does rise. In the industrial landscape, one sees that in a more diverse firm, just as in a larger neighborhood, the average distance to other activities increases, but the average distance to neighbors does not.

Our findings suggest that if firms grow more diverse, they add activities that relate to some portion of existing activities. Furthermore, the data suggest that the strength of relatedness between new and old business does not change much as firms grow more diverse. Coherence is indeed a salient characteristic of the American business enterprise. However, there is variability in the data, and much of the rest of this paper will attempt to build a theory to explain differing levels of coherence across firms by appealing to aspects of a firm's learning, history, and selection environment.

4. Elements of a theory of corporate coherence

4.1. The limitations of existing theories of the firm

Neoclassical theories of industrial organization, including the so-called new industrial organization [e.g., Tirole (1988)], have little to say about coherence and do not readily explain the findings identified in section 3. They neither explain coherence nor its absence. While there is some development of market power and economies of scope explanations for diversification, these theories are without strong organizational implications. Thus one can 'explain' diversification through notions of 'full line forcing' or 'economies of scope', but such theories rarely explain why a set of contractual relationships among specialist firms could not accomplish the same objectives. For instance, consider economies of scope. If the production of x_1 and x_2 involves scope economies, then $c(x_1, x_2) < c_1(x_1, 0) + c_2(0, x_2)$. However, in standard treatments the organizational dimensions of the joint cost function $c(x_1, x_2)$ are never explained. The amalgamation implied by the cost function could be accomplished by a variety of organizational mechanisms, including contracts [Teece (1980, 1982)]. A theory of multiproduct organization cannot be built on the concept of economies of scope. Nor can a theory of corporate coherence.

Other approaches are almost equally as barren. For instance, ecological theories of economic organization provide little mileage, though they may provide a starting point. Ecological approaches are sometimes quite explicit about the limited ability of firms to diversify. Thus, Freeman and Boeker (1984) remark, '[I]ndividual firms are not often entirely free to generate unique strategies. There is a strategic choice involved when one decides to open one kind of business or another. This choice is more or less fixed at firm founding and is constrained by an environment which permits less than free will in strategic choice. A bank selling hamburgers at some of its teller windows would be viewed by all as inconsistent' (p. 71). Likewise, transaction cost economics does not provide much of a foundation for a theory of diversification. Rather, it is from the organizational economics[12] perspective that we draw our theory of corporate coherence. Fig. 1 maps various theories of the firm and identifies the intellectual thrusts associated with different approaches.

We advance the fundamental proposition that the boundaries of the corporation can be understood in terms of learning, path dependencies, technological opportunities, the selection environment, and the firm's position in complementary assets. (Figs. 2a and 2b indicate the degree of coherence we expect to see in different business environments with different technological trajectories). To come to grips with coherence issues, we find it necessary to put to the side theories of the firm which consider it as a nexus of contracts involving labor, management, and suppliers; we also find theories which model the firm as a production function quite unhelpful. The former characterization puts zero weight on the organizational and administrative capabilities of firms; the latter assumes the existence of organizational and administrative capabilities which in our view need to be explained. This is because while the production function purports to be a technological relationship between inputs and outputs, unless the production relationship so described is contained wholly within a machine, issues of organizational and individual skills will necessarily be involved. Each of the key elements of a theory of corporate coherence will now be explained.

4.2. Enterprise learning[13]

A fundamental characteristic of economic activity is that it provides the opportunity for learning. Learning is a process involving repetition and experimentation which enables tasks to be performed better and quicker, and new production opportunities to be identified. As Simon (1991) notes, 'All learning takes place inside individual human heads; an organization learns in only two ways: (a) by the learning of its members, or (b) by ingesting new members who have knowledge the organization didn't previously have. But what is stored in any one head in an organization may not be unrelated to what is stored in other heads; and the relation between those two (and other) stores may have a great 'bearing on how the organization operates' (p. 125). Enterprise learning has several key characteristics.

First, it is generally cumulative. What is learned in one period builds upon

---

[12]See Barney and Ouchi (1986), chapter 1.

[13]A useful compendium of the literature on organizational learning is the special issue of *Organizational Sciences*, 2:1 (1991).

School	Representative Authors	Intellectual Thrust	Coherence Addressed
Neoclassical Economics	Fama (1980); Fama & Jensen (1983)	Principal agent/contract nexus	No
	Grossman & Hart (1982)	Residual claimant	No
	Milgrom & Roberts (1987)	Influence costs	No
	Baumol, Panzar & Willig (1982)	Subadditive cost function	No
	Alchian & Demsetz (1972)	Information, monitoring	No
Ecological Theory	Hannan & Freeman (1977)	Environmental selection	No
Evolutionary Theory	Nelson & Winter (1982)	Routines/selection	No
Transaction Cost Economics	Coase (1937)	Transaction and communcation cost	No
	Williamson (1975, 1985)	Asset specificity, incentive limits	No
Organizational Economics	Chandler (1977, 1990)	Historical process & path dependencies	Yes
	Teece (1980, 1982, 1986)	Technology transfer costs, learning, specific assets, technological opportunities, appropriability	Yes

Fig. 1. Authors and theories of the firm.

		Tight Selection	
		Slow Learning/ Restricted Opportunities	Rapid Learning/ Rich Opportunities
Evolutionary Path**	Wide	Coherent Diversifiers (low growth)	Coherent Diversifiers* (high growth)
	Narrow	Single Product and Vertical Integration (low growth)	Single Product (high growth)
	Converging	Lateral and Vertical Network Firms (low growth)	Lateral and Vertical Network Firms (high growth)

*   Coherent diversifiers might be thought of as laterally integrated firms.
** Note: Evolutionary paths are considered to be shaped by a multitude of factors discussed in section IV.B, including the firm's core competences, its complementary assets, and the technological opportunities lying ahead. Because learning is seen as local, all paths are seen at a point in time as being narrow; over time, firms may be able to diversify quite broadly, all the while preserving the local coherence identified in III.E.

Fig. 2a. Corporate coherence matrix (tight selection environment).

		Weak Selection	
		Slow Learning/ Restricted Opportunities	Rapid Learning/ Rich Opportunities
Evolutionary Path	Wide	Conglomerate (low growth)	Hollow Corporation (high growth)
	Narrow	Conglomerate (low growth)	Hollow Corporations (high growth)
	Converging	Conglomerate (low growth)	Hollow Corporations (high growth)

The organizational forms depicted here can co-exist with the more robust forms in Figure 2a because the selection environment is assumed to be weak.

Fig. 2b. Corporate coherence matrix (weak selection environment) (additive with fig. 2a*).

what was learned in an earlier period. Individual and group knowledge gained through learning must, however, be constantly used in order to be preserved. There may be switching costs associated with moving among tasks due to the set-up time associated with moving to a new task and 'forgetting' which occurs before returning to the old.

Business learning involves organizational rather than individual skills.[14] While individual skills are of relevance, their value depends upon their employment in particular organizational settings. Learning processes are intrinsically social and collective phenomena. Learning occurs not only through the imitation and emulation of individuals as with teacher-student or master-apprentice, but also because of joint contributions to the understanding of complex problems. Learning requires common codes of communication and coordinated search procedures.

The knowledge generated by such activity may be thought of as residing in organizational 'routines' [Nelson and Winter (1982)] and standard operating procedures. These are patterns of interactions which represent successful solutions to particular problems and which are resident in group behavior, though certain subroutines may be resident in individual behavior. Because of the complexity of such behavior, knowledge embedded in routines cannot be fully captured in codified form. That is, it has a tacit dimension that often cannot be readily articulated. Hence, it is the routines themselves, and the ability of management to call upon the organization to perform them, that represents an enterprise's essential capability.

Routines can be of several kinds. *Static routines* embody the capacity to replicate certain previously performed tasks. Needless to say, such routines are never entirely static, because with repetition routines can be constantly improved. The presence of standard learning curve economies often indicate the operation of static routines. *Dynamic routines* are directed at learning, and new product-process development. Thus R & D activity proceeds through the employment of routines to ascertain where to probe, how to probe, and how much to probe.

Because routines involve a strong tacit dimension, they may not be easy to imitate. To the extent that this is so, routines contribute to a firm's distinctive competences and capabilities. Such capabilities, by virtue of their evolution in particular environment and organizational contexts, are likely to differentiate firms from each other and provide the basis for differential performance vis-a-vis competitors.

As discussed below, the rate and direction of enterprise learning is partly a function of the technological opportunities which are available to a firm. These may be rich because of recent breakthroughs in basic science. Upstream innovation by supplier firms might also enrich the environment for firms downstream, and vice versa, as is true in the personal computer industry. Here innovation in microprocessors and in memory devices con-

---

[14]Simon (1991) also notes that 'human learning in the context of an organization is very much influenced by the organization, has consequences for the organization, and produces phenomena at the organizational level that go beyond anything we would simply infer by observing learning processes in isolated individuals' (p. 126).

stantly expands the price performance of products which embody them. Enterprise learning may have a strong 'public' element – as is the case when independent suppliers are responsible for innovation – thereby supplementing proprietary learning. When learning has a strong proprietary element, individual firms can significantly pull away from the public knowledge base in terms of their own capabilities.

Needless to say, learning is rarely entirely exogenous. While the external opportunity set may be driven primarily by public investments in basic science, individual firms can themselves push their own and the industries' opportunity through investment in early stage (basic and applied) research. Furthermore, firms in the same industry may have rather different rates of learning because of differences in the human skill base as well as differences in managerial and organizational systems.

A property of organizational learning is that it enables the enterprise as a whole to surmount the bounded rationality of particular individuals. This does not come automatically. Enterprises need to set up mechanisms for the timely capture of performance feedback so that success and failures become identified and provide the foundation of learning experiences. Furthermore, a corporate culture which identifies, supports, and rewards learning is almost a prerequisite for rapid learning to occur.

4.3. Path dependencies

Local Learning and the Textbook Paradigm. The local nature of enterprise learning significantly restricts what firms can do. Their future activities are highly dependent on what they have done in the past. Yet in economics textbooks firms have an infinite range of technologies from which they can choose, and markets they can occupy. Changes in product or factor prices will be responded to instantaneously, with technologies moving in and out according to value maximization criterion. Only in the short run are irreversibilities recognized. Fixed costs – such as equipment and overhead – cause firms to price below fully amortized costs but never constrain future investment choices. 'Bygones are bygones' in this conceptualization, and firms are able to strike out in directions which market signals suggest are attractive, no matter how distant those directions from a firm's current line of business.

Oliver Williamson (1975, 1985) has done much to enrich the standard treatment by introducing transaction-specific assets. Such assets have idiosyncratic uses and cannot be redeployed without substantial loss of value. Williamson demonstrates how the need for such assets generates particular requirements with respect to an industry's governance apparatus. Generally vertical integration or some other form of organizational safeguard is necessary to facilitate such investments and accomplish efficient supply. He is interested in how specific assets impact organizational design; his framework does not directly address how the presence of specific assets molds the market options open to the firm.

The notion of path dependencies goes even further than notions of irreversibilities employed in transaction cost economics. It recognizes that 'history matters'. Thus a firm's previous investments and its repertoire of routines (its 'history') constrains its future behavior. This follows because learning tends to be local. That is, opportunities for successful new developments will be 'close in' to previous activities and will thus be transaction and product specific [Teece (1988)]. This is because learning is a process of trial, feedback, and evaluation. If too many parameters are changed simultaneously, the ability of firms to conduct meaningful natural quasi experiments is attenuated. If many aspects of a firm's learning environment change simultaneously, the ability to ascertain cause-effect relationships is confounded because cognitive structures will not be formed and rates of learning diminish as a result.

Two key aspects of the learning environment for new product development are the technologies being employed, and the market into which the new product is to be launched. If firms attempt to enter new markets with new technologies, failure is likely to be the norm because the effort is likely to be outside the firm's learning range. Fig. 3 attempts to characterize this diagrammatically. This possibly explains why firms which are defense contractors have problems competing in civilian markets even if they are technologically sophisticated. Northrup provides a good example. Either technological or market distance can keep a firm penned up.

Moreover, a firm stationary for some period in the rapid learning range will of course be able to subsequently migrate (incrementally) to products and activities at greater technological and market distance. Where it can go will, however, be a function of where it has been. This is contrary to conventional economics treatments. In textbook treatments one is in theory able to forecast accurately the activity of the firm as a smoothly shifting solution to the analytical equations governing prices and factor costs. History, in the conventional treatments, is not particularly important; the firm is not constrained by where it has been [David (1988)].

What is true at the operational level is also true at the strategic level. The cognitive limits of managers and the costliness of information systems restrict the range of businesses and products that most managers can understand.[15] The limited capability of information systems to render useful information and the limited ability of managers to understand multiple competitive

---

[15]This phenomena perhaps forms the foundation of Quinn's (1980) focus on 'logical incrementalism' in which executives bring about step-by-step movements towards ends which initially are broadly conceived, but which are then constantly refined and reshaped as new information appears.

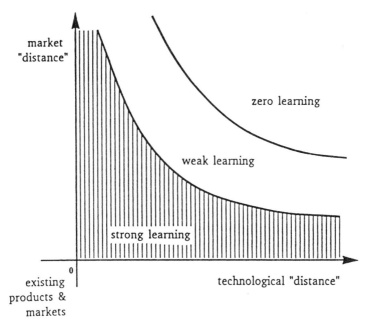

Fig. 3. Firms' (one period) learning domain.

environments appears to be a binding constraint, particularly in dynamically competitive markets. This is not only because the dynamics of technological change and market evolution are always complex, but also because the dynamics are likely to vary markedly across industries and product lines and because long lags may be necessary to capture the performance feedback necessary for learning.

The Concept of Competence.   A firm's competence [Teece (1988)] is a set of differentiated technological skills, complementary assets, and organizational routines and capacities that provide the basis for a firm's competitive capacities in one or more businesses. 'These people are good at X' summarizes external perceptions as to the nature of these competences. In essence, competence is a measure of a firm's ability to both solve technical and organizational problems. It isn't product specific. The presence of such competences open possibilities for multiproduct activity.[16]

A core competence will typically have both an organizational/economic

[16]Whether a firm has a sufficient foundation for efficient multiproduct activity will depend on the ease with which the competence in question can in fact be transferred across product lines [Teece (1980)], the complementary assets the firm possesses, and the opportunity cost of the activity. The latter will depend in part on the technological and market opportunities lying ahead in the firm's traditional lines of business.

and a technical dimension. Unfortunately, economic analysis typically separates the two. Thus Frank Knight (1921) insisted that economic problems be split from technical ones, with only the former being the proper domain for economic analysis. The profession appears to have agreed. However, since the two are initially interwoven in practice, splitting the two will stunt if not cripple efforts to theorize meaningfully about the firm and economic organization more generally.[17]

Organizational/economic competence involves: (1) allocative competence – deciding what to produce and how to price it; (2) transactional competence – deciding whether to make or buy, and whether to do so alone or in partnership; and (3) administrative competence – how to design organizational structures and policies to enable efficient performance. Technical competence, on the other hand, includes the ability to develop and design new products and processes, and to operate facilities effectively. It also involves the ability to learn. Typically, such competences have an important tacit dimension, making replication by others difficult but not impossible. Indeed, when a core competence exists, its replication proceeds either through deliberate efforts directed at internal expansion or through the exit of key individuals who collectively take certain competences with them, and then raise capital to buy the necessary complementary assets.

In our view, the competitive strength of a particular corporation is a function of its underlying technical and organizational competences.[18] The existence of organizational competences explains why plant and equipment produces more when owned by one company rather than another. The value of Tobin's Q – the difference between the market value of a firm's securities and the replacement cost of its assets – may reflect the presence of either technical or organizational competences. Technical competences may be more product specific than organizational ones.

Great companies like Hewlett Packard, DuPont, Exxon and Toyota consist of clusters of such technical-organizational competences. Successful companies must possess both organizational and technological competences.

---

[17]Economic theory almost always assumed economic competence. It is embedded in the implicit (and sometimes explicit) assumption that economic agents are generally omniscient, or at least hyper-rational. To admit that organizational/economic competence may be scarce undermines a very large body of neoclassical economic theory. For an excellent discussion of this and economic competence more generally, see Pelikan (1988). Pelikan's treatment has helped shape our views on economic competence.

[18]Numerous recent studies compare the operating performance across companies with respect to quality, speed, capital utilization and other measures of efficiency. Examples include Garvin's (1988) study of room air conditioners that showed dramatic differences among firms in defect rates. Such differences appear to be the result of different systems and procedures. Clark and Fujimoto (1991) in studying the auto industry found high variation in the efficiency of product development process and the quality of the resulting product. Jakumar (1988) showed significant differences in performance between flexible manufacturing systems (FMS) in Japanese and American firms.

As described below, hollow corporations lack technical competences; business is performed through contractual agreements struck with others. When the contracts terminate, the firm's ability to deliver value evaporates. We define a hollow corporation as a business entity that does not have any core technical competences and uses contractual mechanisms to link particular market requirements with productive capacities. Thus a hollow corporation may manage a nexus of contracts for design, manufacture, distribution, and service. Such enterprises often turn out to have weak survival properties because the basis of their initial advantage is easy-to-imitate organizational competences.

Likewise, a conglomerate is a portfolio of autonomous business units held together in a holding company. It is a 'mutual fund' of businesses without organizational competences at the corporate (holding company) level.[19] As discussed later, we do not believe that organizations such as these have survival properties unless they are somehow shielded from product and capital market competition. They are likely to survive longer than hollow corporations, not because they are more efficient, but because they are likely to be able to utilize cash flows generated by other divisions; hollow corporations more quickly become unglued if a subunit fails to perform.

Complementary Assets. The existence of complementary assets [Teece (1986)] helps contour evolutionary paths, and evolutionary paths help determine the composition of a firm's portfolio of complementary assets. Prior commercialization activities require and enable firms to build complementary assets. Such assets, built to support firm's prior activities, may have other uses as well. Rarely are such assets completely specialized to a particular product. Examples include distribution systems, manufacturing plant and equipment, and complementary technologies. Complementary assets typically lie downstream from product-process development in the value-added chain.

New products and processes can either enhance or destroy the value of complementary assets [Tushman and Anderson (1986)]. Thus the development of computers enhanced the value of IBM's direct sales force developed for other office products, while disc brakes destroyed the value of the auto industries' investment in drum brake facilities.

The presence of complementary assets, particularly those that can be enhanced by innovation, helps steer the evolution of new technologies [Teece (1986), Mitchell (1989)]. The reason why Singer Sewing machine got into the furniture business was in large measure due to the fact that it had designed and manufactured sewing machine cabinets to help facilitate the sale of sewing machines. Thus, a particular firm's path dependencies are not just

[19]By definition, a conglomerate has a limited headquarters function and so cannot have significant organizational competence at the corporate level.

technological determined. Paths are identified by technological paradigms and trajectories [Dosi (1982)] and constrained further by the complementary assets the firm has already built or can readily acquire.

In the world of neoclassical microeconomic theory, sunk costs, whether core or complementary, often do not matter. We suggest that in reality they do because they suggest a strategy for rapidly improving earnings – namely to increase the utilization rate. This steers firms with excess capacity in their complementary assets toward searching for value-creating opportunities to take up the slack [Teece (1980, 1982)]. Put differently, the existence of slack is likely to trigger search processes directed at raising the utilization rates of existing assets, simply because the cognitive path associated with doing this is likely to be clearer than other alternatives.

Technological Opportunities.   The concept of path dependencies can be given forward meaning through the consideration of an industry's technological opportunities. It is well recognized that how far and how fast a particular area of industrial activity can proceed is in part due to the technological opportunities that lie before it. Such opportunities are usually a lagged function of foment and diversity in basic science, and the rapidity with which new scientific breakthroughs are being made. They may also lie with customer-user inventiveness.

However, technological opportunities may not be completely exogenous to industry, not only because some firms have the capacity to engage in or at least support basic research, but also because technological opportunities are often fed by innovative activity itself. Moreover, the identification of such opportunities is affected by the organizational structures that link the institutions engaging in basic research (primarily the university) to the business enterprise. Hence, the existence of technological opportunities is a necessary but not a sufficient condition for innovation.

More important for our purposes is the rate and direction in which relevant scientific frontiers are being rolled back. Firms engaging in R & D may find the path dead ahead closed off, though breakthroughs in related areas may be sufficiently close to be attractive. Likewise, if the path dead ahead is extremely attractive, there may be no incentive for firms to shift the allocation of resources away from traditional pursuits. The depth and width of technological opportunities in the neighborhood of a firm's prior research activities thus are likely to impact a firm's options with respect to both the amount and level of R & D activity that it can justify.

Convergence of Paths.   Technological paths are shaped not only by a firm's history, but also by changes in the public knowledge base. These changes, often driven by developments in basic science, may be such that the technological foundations of businesses shift dramatically. This may cause the technological knowledge base of industries to converge or diverge. Thus digital electronics is presently causing a convergence in the public knowledge base supporting computer and telecommunications firms. This has implications for corporate coherence because products which may be aimed at rather different customer groups might suddenly develop common technological and production roots.

4.4. Selection

Selection is the process by which inefficient firms or businesses get weeded out. At the firm level, selection is accomplished primarily through market processes involving entry and exit; growth and decline provide a second mechanism. Neither mechanism works instantaneously so that firms with different capabilities may exist side-by-side attempting to serve the same customer needs. Indeed, bankruptcy laws in certain countries may slow selection processes.[20] However, 'market rationality' eventually prevails, and less competent firms can be expected to decline and exit.[21]

Thus the survivability of business activity depends on the selection environment and, in particular, the level of competition (both product market and capital market), public policy, and the frequency of technological discontinuities. In weak selection environments, firms and business units are buffered from market rationality. Less efficient firms may be able to survive and possibly even prosper for quite some time. The selection environment for a particular business may be stronger or weaker than that for the corporation as a whole, depending on how corporate management treats internal divisions and products that are not performing up to par.

The availability of free cash flows is perhaps the key regulator of selection inside the firm. If a firm or a business is generating sufficient cash flow to sustain itself and take care of reinvestment needs and opportunities, it will typically be able to survive. If it does not, then it will need additional debt or equity financing. To obtain funding of either kind exposes the firm to capital market discipline that might not otherwise intervene. Hence, initial capitalization, the 'inherited' capital structure of the firm, and subsequent financial restructuring are likely to affect the strength of selection processes with respect to particular business units. We predict the boundaries of the corporation are likely to be drawn 'close in' to core competencies the tighter the selection environment.

5. Propositions from the theory

The above framework has powerful implications for business strategy. It

[20]In the early 1990s in the United States, both TWA and Continental Airlines operated for long periods with the protection of Chapter 11 of the Bankruptcy Code. This protection enabled the companies to continue operations despite the fact that they were not able to cover their full costs of operation.

[21]There are often exceptions, depending on the selection environment itself.

suggests that the circumstances under which various organizational forms (implying certain strategic choices) will be viable. It implies that firms can be thought of as integrated clusters of core competences and supporting complementary assets and that the degree of coherence one would expect to observe among the parts at a particular point in time depends on the relationship between learning, path dependencies, opportunities, inherited complementary assets, and selection. We advance the following hypotheses:

Hypothesis one: specialist firms

With rapid learning, rich technological opportunities, and tight path dependencies, one will observe 'single' product (specialist) firms growing rapidly. Compaq Computer, Sun Microsystems, Intel, and possibly Boeing and Airbus are good examples. Specialist firms are likely to be young because the probability that technological opportunities in a given area remain rich is likely to decline over time, in part because of new entry.

Hypothesis two: vertically integrated firms

With slow learning but high path dependencies and specialized assets, one can expect specialist firms with some degree of lateral integration and significant vertical integration emerging over time[22] [e.g. Exxon, Shell, DuPont]. Older firms are likely to be more vertically integrated than young firms because start-ups are less common in industries where learning is slow.[23]

Hypothesis three: coherent diversifiers

With rapid learning, broad path dependencies due to the presence of generic technologies, and tight selection, one can expect to see coherent diversifiers like IBM, BMW, Hewlett Packard, W.R. Gore, and Raychem. Since older firms are likely to have experienced many recessions and periods of retrenchment, they are likely to be coherent diversifiers. Indeed, our findings reported in section 3 suggest this is so. Firms do indeed diversify over time but the modal form across the economy displays diversity but local coherence.

---

[22]Note that vertical integration in this framework stems mainly from a growth/'diversification' motive.

[23]If a firm is innovating in a regime of weak appropriability, it may find it essential to develop certain complementary assets (vertically integrate) into manufacturing and distribution. This is because with easy imitation of technological competences, marketplace success will swing on the relative positioning of innovator and imitators in the relevant complementary assets and technologies [Teece (1986)]. Thus the best defence of a new product is often a new manufacturing process. The former may be exposed to imitation; the latter may not.

Hypothesis four: conglomerates

With low path dependencies, slow learning, and weak selection, we predict the emergence of conglomerates or other highly diversified companies displaying few intracorporate transactions. As selection tightens, such as during recessions, we expect that the most egregious examples of this form will get weeded out. Conglomerates are thus a transitional form.

Hypothesis five: network firms

With rapid learning, colliding technological trajectories and tight selection, one can expect to see incumbent firms becoming enveloped in a dense skein of inter-corporate relationships involving partial equity holdings and joint ventures.[24] Such firms might be called 'network' firms. For example, because of the convergence of telecommunications and computers, AT & T is becoming embedded in a thicket of inter-corporate relationship. So are biotechnology firms like Genentech and Chiron because the biotechnology research paradigm yields products and processes competitive with pharmaceuticals and chemicals, to name just two examples [Pisano, Shan and Teece (1988), Orsenigo (1989)]. If learning were slower, then there is a good possibility that firms could diversify internally without the assistance of interfirm agreements. Unlike conglomerates, network firms are likely to exhibit survival properties so long as particular technologies continue to collide.

Hypothesis six: hollow corporations

With converging path dependencies, opportunities may arise for entrepreneurs to use contractual mechanisms to quickly assemble diverse capabilities directed at the development and commercialization of a particular product. We refer to such entities as hollow corporations. Unless capabilities develop to undergird these structures, and unless distinctive organizational routines emerge to 'glue' such organizations together, such organizations will not survive, except where the selection environment is weak. If they do survive, it is likely because they are constantly configuring and reconfiguring their alliances.[25]

These hypotheses are summarized in figs. 2a and 2b which are an obvious

---

[24]As compared to hollow corporations, network firms are assumed to have a core competence.

[25]Miles and Snow (1986) describe what they call 'dynamic networks' and suggest they are a new organizational form created in the 1980s. We concur; but except in limited circumstances such as the fashion industry doubt they are viable.

simplification of the theory we have tried to outline. Note that we have suggested that coherence is a function of several classes of variables: (a) enterprise learning (which we posit is necessarily local in scope); (b) path dependencies, which we see being shaped both by where the firm is currently situated (its existing competences and supporting complementary assets) and the technological opportunities which lie ahead or to one side or the other; and (c) the selection environment, which is a rough measure of the external and internal competition facing the various products the firm produces. We have collapsed these classes of variables in order to represent the predictions of the theory in a fashion which is easy to follow. Note that fig. 2b (weak selection environment) incorporates the organizational forms of fig. 2a – because organizational forms that can exist with tight selection can surely exist with weak selection. Hence, fig. 2b contains only the additional, and in our view ultimately nonsustainable, organizational forms – the conglomerate and the hollow corporation. The conglomerate is not associated with environments in which there is rapid learning and innovation because hierarchical structures are incompatible with quick (decentralized) decision making and high power incentives. Clearly, we are assuming weak competition and not its complete absence, because with the complete absence of competition any organizational form would be possible.

6. Remarks on organizational mutations

The conglomerate is not viewed especially favorably in our framework. There remains a class of highly diversified conglomerate firms that warrant further comment. The histories of such firms are invariably marked by a long sequence of mergers. Since, however, similar histories exist for many firms that are not highly diversified, growth by merger is not by itself an anomalous fact. The anomaly is the extreme degree of the diversification itself, as illustrated by firms like Tenneco, ITT and LTV. Such examples certainly appear to challenge an evolutionary interpretation of large firms as being, typically, the results of a historical process that involved the success, replication, modification and extension of the competence embedded in some set of routines.

Two responses to this challenge may be offered. The first is to raise the question of the (theoretically relevant) boundaries of the firm. Vesting the ownership of a diverse range of businesses in a common corporate parent may have few effects of real significance as regards the evolution of productive competence. The individual businesses, or sub-units within them, may be the packages of competence that matter.

The history of the Hertz Corporation provides some suggestive evidence in this regard. Hertz has had quite a number of different owners in its approximately 70 year history. Within recent years it was bought by United

Airlines (later renamed Allegis Corporation) from RCA, then was sold to Park Ridge Corporation, an entity formed by Hertz management and the Ford Motor Company to effect a leveraged buyout of Hertz.[26] Yet during this period Hertz operated under its various corporate owners in much the same fashion that it did when it was a freestanding company (1954–1967).

Under RCA, for example, Hertz paid out 50 percent of net income to RCA as dividends and kept the remainder for reinvestment. RCA's management and board were periodically apprised of Hertz's activities and plans. RCA was concerned with personnel policy issues at Hertz and, in particular, wanted Hertz to fill high-level managerial and staff positions with people from its own divisions. Matters of direct relevance to the car rental business remained Hertz's province throughout. RCA bought Hertz when conglomerate diversification was in favor, and sold it in a retreat to the 'core business' when such diversification fell out of favor. If one asks where the competence in the car rental business resided and what shaped its evolution, the answers seem clear: the competence resided in Hertz. Rivals, other environmental factors, and Hertz's own innovative efforts shaped the evolution of that competence much more strongly than Hertz's corporate parents did.

One major school of thought on the conglomerate corporation holds that its primary economic function is to serve as a 'miniature capital market' [Williamson (1975, 1985)], reallocating funds from lines of activity that generate high current cash flow to those whose future prospects and current investment needs outstrip currently available resources. Under this interpretation, relations between corporate headquarters and the individual business units within the conglomerate structure largely involve financial flows and financial monitoring. To the extent that the ownership relation facilitates monitoring and appraisal of future prospects relative to what is possible for the external capital market, the conglomerate form may have a secure niche in the long-term institutional ecology of capitalism.[27]

This appraisal is not obviously in conflict with the view that it is individual business units that are the important repositories of technical-productive competence, as illustrated by the example of Hertz. No judgment is implied as to the quality of the financial management of conglomerates in any absolute sense; there is only a claim that they may be sufficiently effective relative to the available institutional alternatives to account for their existence. Although the selection process would function differently than if there were no conglomerates, no judgment is implied as to how much

---

[26]An interesting contrast in the durability of transacting patterns is provided by the case of O.J. Simpson who has been doing Hertz commercials for over a decade.

[27]In periods when tax preferences for capital gains or other institutional factors impede the functioning of the external capital markets, conglomerates may be expected to play a larger role than at times when such biases are absent.

different it would be. On this view, the clearest implication of conglomerates for evolutionary analysis is that they impede investor research: instead of individual financial statements for each of a number of independent businesses, we encounter a single set of financial statements for the conglomerate. This certainly tends to hamper efforts to assess the performance of the individual businesses.

The alternative response to the analytical challenge represented by large conglomerates involves a more negative appraisal of the conglomerate form and its future prospects. Biologists have employed the term 'hopeful monsters' to refer to new types arising as a result of a fundamental 'systematic mutation', among which a few occasionally have characteristics that are compatible with survival and result in the founding of a new species. Nothing in the laws of biological evolution precludes the appearance of such types; on the other hand, one does not expect to see the fossil record strewn with examples because natural selection promptly eliminates all but a tiny fraction of them. On the average, there is not much hope per monster. The same may be true of large conglomerate corporations.

Techniques of financial control and monitoring are, on this view, good enough to lend a temporary surface plausibility to the conglomerate form but not good enough to assure its long-term viability in competition with more specialized organizations. In contrast to its biological analogues, the typical conglomerate monster does not expire soon after its creation. Its odd morphology is nonfatal precisely because it is so remote from being an integrated whole; it involves the binding together of entities that are viable, or approximately so, on their own. Furthermore, the power of corporate headquarters in the financial realm carries with it a significant amount of discretion regarding the reporting of results (not to speak of the discretion to make headquarters, at least, look prosperous). A long-term unfavorable trend in performance may be disguised for an extended period. The fundamental question is whether headquarters is paying its way, and the suggestion here is that it is not.[28]

To sort out the evidence regarding the performance of the conglomerate form, and the broader issues regarding diversification generally, is a larger undertaking than can be attempted here.[29] The 'hopeful monsters' interpretation is most congenial to evolutionary economic theory. A demonstration

---

[28]In the terms used in Williamson's (1985, pp. 286–290) discussion of conglomerates, the suggestion here is that the extension of M-form managerial techniques to the control of higher diverse activities may typically be unsuccessful – though an occasional monster may do well, at least for a while.

[29]Evidence available as of the mid-1980s in the United States suggests that conglomerates are divesting significant assets. The average number of business centered in conglomerates was declining, while business relatedness in the conglomerate was increasing [Williams, Paez and Sanders (1986)].

of its validity would, on the one hand, tend to support our view of the firm as a package of technical and organizational competences. When the contents of the package lack an organizational competence, the twine of financial control will rarely suffice to bind together a successful enterprise.

We likewise view the hollow corporation as an organizational mutation. If a firm is in fact merely a nexus of contracts, there is little opportunity for the various pieces to engage in mutual learning. This is because the contracting units are likely to have multiple contractual partners, further complicating transaction specific learning. A good example of a hollow corporation was Worlds of Wonder, an electronic toy company founded in Hayward, California in 1984. The company employed a strategy of contracting for almost everything – manufacturing, new product development, distribution, and marketing. The company grew to over $100 million in sales in record time, and then disappeared. There were a variety of reasons for the company's failure, not least of which was its absence of follow-along products. But the company's extreme dependency on contracts helps explain both its rapid growth and its rapid demise. It may have briefly possessed organizational competence, but it had no technical-productive competence of its own, and the former was not enough to sustain it in the business in which it ever so briefly competed.

7. Conclusion

We have shown that as firms grow more diverse, overall coherence does not change much in the United States. However, there are large differences among firms with respect to the degree of their coherence. We hypothesize that some of these differences can be explained as a complex interaction between three classes of factors: (1) enterprise learning, which we suggest is a 'local' phenomena; (2) evolutionary paths, which we see being shaped both by where firms have been (in terms of their scope of their past activities), where they are now (their current competences and complementary assets), and the opportunities which lie ahead; and (3) the strength of competition and the mechanism firms have to shield themselves from it, whether in the product market or the capital market. We have shown how these factors can be expected to mold the scope of a firm's activities. Given tight selection environments, we conclude that coherent diversifiers, who expand by adding related activities, are likely to be the most common corporate mode. Indeed, we find for the U.S. economy as a whole that diversification is of this kind.

We suggest that we have provided a framework to explain central tendencies in the growth of the business enterprise. We have assembled what we believe are provocative hypotheses, as well as some suggestive evidence. Our hope is that others will be both intrigued and challenged by our findings and our theorizing, and that as a consequence we will soon have a deeper understanding of one of the great theoretical conundrums in industrial organization – the coherence of the multiproduct business firm.

References

Alchian, A. and H. Demsetz, 1972, Production, information costs, and economic organization, American Economic Review 62, Dec., 777–795.

Baney, J. and W. Ouchi, 1986, Organizational economics (Jossey-Bass, San Francisco, CA).

Baumol, W.J., J. Panzer and R. Willig, 1982, Contestable markets (Harcourt Brace Jovanovich, New York).

Berry, C.H., 1971, Corporate growth and diversification, Bell Journal of Economics 14, 371–383.

Caves, R.E., 1981, Diversification and seller concentration: Evidence from changes, Review of Economics and Statistics 63, 289–293.

Chandler, A.D. Jr., 1977, The visible hand: The managerial revolution in American business (Harvard University Press, Cambridge, MA).

Chandler, A.D. Jr., 1990, Scale and scope: The dynamics of industrial capitalism (Harvard University Press, Cambridge, MA).

Clark, K.B. and T. Fujimoto, 1991, Product development and performance: Strategy, management and organization in the world auto industry (Harvard Business School Press, Boston, MA).

Coase, R.H., 1952, The nature of the firm, Economics N.S. 4 (1937) 386–405. Reprinted in: G.J. Stigler and K.E. Boulding, eds., Readings in price theory (Richard D. Irwin, Homewood, IL).

David, P., 1988, Path dependence: Putting the past into the future of economics, I.M.S.S.S. technical report no. 533 (Stanford University) Nov.

Dosi, G., 1982, Technological paradigms and technological trajectories, Research Policy.

Fama, E.F., 1980, Agency problems and the theory of the firm, Journal of Political Economy 88, April, 288–307.

Freeman, J. and W. Boeker, 1984, The ecological analysis of strategy, in: G. Carroll and D. Vogel, eds., Strategy and organization (Pitman, Boston, MA).

Garvin, D.A., 1988, Managing quality (Harvard Business School Press, Boston, MA).

Gollop, F.M. and J.L. Monahan, 1989, From homogeneity to heterogeneity: An index of diversification, Technical paper no. 60 (U.S. Department of Commerce, Bureau of the Census).

Hannan, M.T. and J. Freeman, 1977, The population ecology of organizations, American Journal of Sociology 82, Mar., 929–964.

Jakumar, R., 1989, Japanese flexible manufacturing systems, Japan and the World Economy, 113–143.

Klavans, R., 1989, Business relatedness and business performance, FTC Line of Business Program Research Paper no. 83.

Knight, F., 1921, Risk, uncertainty, and profit (Houghton-Mifflin, Boston, MA).

Lemelin, A., 1982, Relatedness in the patterns of interindustry diversification, Review of Economics and Statistics 64, 646–657.

Miles, R.E. and C.C. Snow, 1986, Organizations: New concepts for new forms, California Management Review 38, 62–73.

Milgram, P. and J. Roberts, 1987, Bargaining and influence costs and the organization of economic activity, Working paper no. 8731 (Department of Economics, Stanford University) Feb.

Mitchell, W., 1989, Whether and when? Probability and timing of incumbents' entry into emerging industrial subfields, Administrative Science Quarterly 34, 208–230.

Montgomery, C.A. and B. Wernerfelt, 1988, Diversification, Ricardian rents, and Tobin's q, Rand Journal of Economics 19, 623–632.

Nelson, R.R. and S.G. Winter, 1982, An evolutionary theory of economic change (Harvard University Press, Cambridge, MA).

Orsenigo, L., 1989, The emergence of biotechnology (Pinter, London).

Palepu, K., 1985, Diversification strategy, profit performance, and the entropy measure, Strategic Management Journal 6, 239–255.

Pavitt, K., M. Robson and J. Townsend, 1989, Technological accumulation, diversification and organization of U.K. companies, 1945–1983, Management Science 35, no. 1, Jan.

Pelikan, P., 1988, Can the innovation system of capitalism be outperformed, in: G. Dosi, C. Freeman, R. Nelson, G. Silverberg and L. Soete, eds., Technical change and economic theory (Ballinger, Cambridge, MA).

Peters, T.J. and R.H. Waterman, 1982, In search of excellence (Harper and Row, New York).

Pisano, G., W. Shan and D. Teece, 1988, Joint ventures and collaboration in the biotechnology industry, in: D. Mowery, ed., International collaborative ventures in U.S. manufacturing (Ballinger, Cambridge, MA) 183–222.

Quinn, J.B., 1980, Strategies for change: Logical incrementalism (Irwin, Homewood, IL).

Rumelt, R.P., 1972, Strategy, structure and economic performance (Harvard University Press, Cambridge, MA).

Stigler, G.J., 1968, The organization of industry (Irwin, Homewood, IL).

Teece, D.J., 1980, Economics of scope and the scope of an enterprise, Journal of Economic Behavior and Organization 1, 223–247.

Teece, D.J., 1982, Towards an economic theory of the multiproduct firm, Journal of Economic Behavior and Organization 3, 39–63.

Teece, D.J., 1986, Profiting from technological innovation, Research Policy 15, 286–305. Republished in Ricerche Economiche 4, Oct./Dec., 1986, 607–643, and as Innovazione technologica e successo imprenditoriale, L'Industria 7, no. 4, Oct./Dec., 1986, 605–643. Abstracted in The Journal of Product Innovation Management 5, no. 1, Mar. 1988.

Teece, D.J., 1988, Technological change and the nature of the firm, in: G. Dosi et al., eds., Technical Change and Economic Theory.

Tirole, J., 1989, The theory of industrial organization (MIT Press, Cambridge, MA).

Tushman, M. and P. Anderson, 1986, Technological discontinuities and organizational environments, Administrative Science Quarterly 31, 439–465.

Williams, J., B. Paez and L. Sanders, 1987, Conglomerates revisited, Working paper no. 64-85-86 (Graduate School of Industrial Administration, Carnegie-Mellon University) Nov.

Williamson, O.E., 1975, Markets and hierarchies (Free Press, New York).

Williamson, O.E., 1985, The economic institutions of capitalism (Free Press, New York).

Winter, S.E., 1988, On Coase, competence, and the corporation, Journal of Law Economics and Organization 4, no. 1, Spring.

[10]

Learning how to Govern and Learning how to Solve Problems: On the Co-Evolution of Competences, Conflicts and Organizational Routines*

BENJAMIN CORIAT AND GIOVANNI DOSI

1. INTRODUCTION

This work is meant as an exploration of the origins and roles of different organizational routines which sustain diverse corporate structures and reproduce over time different "strategies" and performances.

There is indeed quite robust evidence that firms—despite obvious regularities—persistently differ in their characteristics, behaviors and revealed performances. For example, they clearly differ in their sizes, their forms of internal organization, their degrees of vertical integration and intersectoral diversification, etc. But they also differ in their revealed performances—in terms, for example, of innovative success, speed of adoption of new technologies, inputs productivities and profitabilities. Relatedly, a major puzzle concerns the reasons of persistence of these asymmetries. Why apparently "superior" organizational forms diffuse very slowly, if at all, within industries and, even more so, across national borders?

A good part of the answer, in our view, certainly rests upon the specificities of organizational competences. In fact, the first building block in our argument, directly developing on evolutionary theories, is that firms are crucial (although not exclusive) repositories of knowledge, to a large extent embodied in their operational routines, and modified through time by their "higher level" rules of behavior and strategies (such as their "metarules" for innovative search, diversification, etc.). In this view, competences are the collective property of the routines of an organization, and—due to their partial tacitness—are often hard to transfer or copy.

* We gratefully acknowledge support of this research by the French Ministry for Foreign Affairs, the Italian Ministry of University and Research, the Italian National Research Council (CNR, Progetto Strategico) and the International Institute of Applied System Analysis (IIASA, Laxenburg, Austria). The draft has benefited from conversations with Sidney Winter, and from the comments of several participants at the Prince Bertil Symposium (Stockholm, June 1994) and in particular of Nathan Rosenberg.

Competence specificity leads straightforwardly to an easy possibility of "lock-in" and thus also to persistent diversity at firm-level and, moreover, to specificities at the level of "national trajectories."[1]

In this work we shall focus primarily on the non-random distribution of competences across countries (and, relatedly, on the differences in the national patterns of organizational evolution).

In order to interpret these international (or, also, interregional) differences, one must account, first for the properties of the networks in which firms are embedded: these linkages with other firms—within and outside their primary sectors of activity—and with other organizations (such as public agencies) shape and constrain the opportunities facing each firm to improve its problem-solving capabilities. Second, "national systems" of production and innovation entail also a broader notion of embeddedness of microeconomic behaviors into a set of social relationships, rules and institutional constraints (Granovetter 1985). In turn, these embeddedness properties contribute to determine the evolution of organizational structures and, together, competences and strategies.

There are, however, two complementary aspects of this embeddedness argument (as well as to the earlier "lock-in" one). These two aspects also correspond to two perspectives on the nature and function of business firms themselves.

The first one—which has been highly emphasized in the evolutionary literature—concerns the *coordination* and *problem-solving* nature of organizational routines. Hence, their specificities are shown to be related to the "cognitive" features of the operational or search tasks at hand.

Indeed, one of the authors in earlier works has claimed that, in a first approximation, one could start with the assumption that a "weak incentive compatibility" among individual agents could be taken for granted, and directly analyze the collective problem-solving features of particular ensembles of routines composing the repertoire of each organization (Dosi and Marengo 1994).[2] It is proving to be a fruitful investigative strategy. However, it neglects the second major role of organization and organizational routines, namely their being a *locus of conflict, governance, and a way of codifying microeconomic incentives and constraints*—as often emphasized by the other author (Coriat 1979 and 1990).

In this work we begin an exploration of this double—"cognitive" and "governance"—role of organizational routines.

Just to mention a few archetypal examples, the "Chandlerian" (primarily American) modern large corporation embodies the development of novel competences of managerial problem solving, as recently Teece (1993) and Chandler (1992) himself have convincingly argued. At the same time, however, that organizational form embodies equally specific forms of internal governance of conflicts and incentives, which, in a shorthand, can be identified with "Taylorism" and "Fordism."

Conversely, in an archetypal "Japanese" corporation (Aoki 1988 and 1990; Coriat 1991*b*), the patterns of competence accumulation are nested in quite different forms of governance and conflict management. Many other historical examples could be cited, from Germany to Italy to Britain.

Of course, governance mechanisms are today a quite familiar domain of economic analysis, but, most often, elegant equilibrium rationalizations have assumed away the crucial problem-solving tasks associated with the development of routinized, inertial and conflictual behaviors. Here, we take a rather different route, and move some steps toward an appreciation of the co-evolution of (highly imperfect) *mechanisms of governance*, on the one hand, and *"what a firm is able to do and to discover,"* on the other.

In this preliminary work, we aim to identify the properties, in both the "cognitive" and "governance" domains, of some distinctive set of routines—or *protocols*—of different organizational forms, and suggest a coevolutionary story regarding their origins.

The embeddedness argument clearly comes out enhanced. Particular patterns of conflict, "truces" and mechanisms of incentive governance present an intrinsic collective nature, grounded in the institutions of each country. Together with the cumulative nature of learning processes, they contribute to explain the persistence of national specificities in organizational setups and corporate routines.

2. SOME BACKGROUND FINDINGS AND HYPOTHESES ON LEARNING, CORPORATE ORGANIZATIONS AND GROWTH

Let us start by placing the discussion that follows concerning the relationships between processes of learning and mechanisms of organizational governance in the perspective of a broader set of questions and findings regarding the linkages between technological change, specificities in the institutional organization of economic activities and growth.

A useful point of departure are a few findings that evolutionary-inclined practitioners in economics, but also many economists of other intellectual origins, economic historians and organizational theorists would consider robust stylized facts (although of course this is a theory-ridden and by no means uncontroversial evaluation).

For our purposes, the preliminaries of our argument are: (a) even within commonly shared organizational patterns, the persistent heterogeneity across firms—and, even more so, across countries—in their abilities to develop, imitate, adopt technological innovations; (b) roughly similar persistent differences across countries in their input productivities and incomes; (c) the long-term correlation between the two sets of phenomena (which, indeed, a few economists would theoretically interpret in causal manners, in terms of co-evolutionary processes).

Many more details on the evidence and the causality linkages have been discussed elsewhere (cf. Dosi, Pavitt and Soete 1990). For example, there is an emerging evolutionary view on the microeconomics of technological innovation, grounded in the specificities of the learning processes which characterize particular classes of problem-solving activities. In turn, this view naturally leads to predictions of intersectoral heterogeneity in innovative patterns, asymmetries in innovative performance across firms, possible path-dependency and "lock-ins."[3]

At a more aggregate level, a few scholars have attempted to show— both at theoretical and empirical levels—that growth can be viewed as a process fueled by heterogeneous efforts of innovation checked by some market selection.[4] One is also able to show that these same processes in multieconomy settings may yield convergence but also (and more often) divergence, forging ahead and falling behind in relative per capita income.[5] Complementary empirical findings highlight the crucial importance of technological change as apparent determinant of trade patterns and growth.[6]

As annoying as it might be for economists of other entrenched beliefs, here we shall take these phenomena for granted while investigating their microeconomic foundations and some implications for "national trajectories" and possible lock-in phenomena.

Indeed, a few implications are prima facie observationally indistinguishable from those derived from other modeling assumptions. For example, "new growth" and "evolutionary" theories at least in a first approximation overlap in their prediction of, first, innovation-driven self-sustained growth, and, second, long-term differentiation in growth patterns across countries.[7] Most likely, one encounters here a generic property of learning: technological learning, no matter how roughly represented, tends to imply the possibility of international differentiation, even when embedded into equilibrium dynamics and scarcity constraints on underlying endowments (e.g. in the labor force, skills, capital, etc.). It is, indeed, an important theoretical result, already implicit in the pioneering work of Arrow (1974) on the peculiar nature of "information"—even when neglecting those differences between "information" and agent-specific "knowledge" emphasized by evolutionary theorists (Pavitt 1984; Winter 1981 and 1987; Dosi and Egidi 1991).

As argued at greater length elsewhere,[8] a distinctive feature of evolutionary models is the attempt to represent the possible emergence of relatively ordered and differentiated economic systems as self-organizing processes floating in a world where "endowments" and "available technological blueprints" are seldom functionally binding constraints. Rather, technological learning within a notionally unlimited space of opportunities, at the levels of both individual firms and whole industries and countries, determines economic performances. "Endowments" are seldom binding because one can continuously improve their quality and efficiency, while one can hardly separate the contribution of individual factors to growth, because of a rich structure of positive feedbacks. In this respect the evidence on the microeconomics of innovation (cf. Dosi 1988), shows a highly variegated pattern of search and development of new products and production processes, which nonetheless manifest a general inseparability between what firms do to allocate their resources to production and the processes through which they learn how to do better what they already do, or how to do new things.

First, learning is to a good extent a sort of joint production with manufacturing activities themselves. Obviously, this includes phenomena of learning by doing, but it is also likely that search activities, such as R&D, will occur within firms and industries in fields related to what they are currently good at doing. Second, part of the technological knowledge is often tacit, specific to particular problem-solving activities, somewhat idiosyncratic, embodied in people and organizations, cumulative in its developments. Third, there are sorts of general knowledge inputs (often related to "dominant" and pervasive technologies, such as mechanical engineering, electricity and more recently microelectronics) which enter most manufacturing activities, irrespectively of one country's specializations, so that the rates at which these general competences grow influence the overall efficiency of each country.

As a consequence, current allocative processes influence future opportunities of learning in ways that, to a good extent, are not and *cannot* be signaled and traded through the market.

The coupled dynamics between learning and resource allocations may entail "virtuous circles" of sustained learning and efficient allocation of resources, or conversely, in "vicious circles," whereby, irrespective of the efficiency by which available resources are used, the system generates relatively low rates of innovation and, thus, also relatively low rates of increase in input efficiencies. This conjecture, already expressed in a quite confused fashion by some Continental European writers on trade of the nineteenth century (e.g. Ferrier, List, etc.), is quite akin to the Kaldor–Myrdal idea of "circular causation." A contemporary, more rigorous formalization is in terms of path-dependent processes wherein "localized" learning and dynamic increasing returns amplify microfluctuations and may "lock" the system-dynamics into trajectories that may well be "inferior" from a normative point of view, but still be stable over time (cf. Arthur 1988; Arthur, Ermoliev and Kaniovski 1987; David 1975 and 1985). One can also see intuitively how international trade may reinforce polarization among countries and lock-in into particular patterns of growth: competition on the world market and specialization influence the rates and direction of innovative learning by firms and countries, which in turn affect international competitiveness and specialization.

Both the evolutionary story and the "equilibrium story" on endogenous technical change, trade and growth, it has already been mentioned, easily generate international differentiation in income levels and rates of growth. In addition, in our view, the former is capable of generating a richer variety of dynamic patterns (albeit trading it off against lower formal elegance), and also mapping them into the underlying characteristics of technological learning (e.g. its features of cumulativeness, partial tacitness, appropriability, etc.). However, this is not the issue we want to discuss here. Rather, let us consider the nature and importance of alternative micro-economic assumptions.

As is obvious, in the standard aggregate-production-function story on growth, organizational specificities of firms and countries are entirely absent. The most natural way of interpreting its microfoundations is in terms of an underlying General Equilibrium. In several of the "new trade" and "new growth" models there is indeed an explicit microfoundation, based on imperfectly competitive equilibria. However, precisely because of the equilibrium assumption, it is hard to account for any influence of particular forms of corporate and industrial organization upon competitiveness and growth. Putting it another way, one senses a striking conflict between any equilibrium account of trade and growth and, say, Porter's analysis of the specific organizational and technological features underlying, for example, the Italian competitiveness in ceramic tiles or the British failures in mechanical engineering (cf. Porter 1990), or, even more so, the stories that business economists usually tell about painstakingly discovered "superior" competitive strategies.

Empirically, corporate organizations embody specific innovative search heuristics, modes of internal management, production rules, strategies for dealing with suppliers and customers (e.g. vertical integration, arm's-length relationships, collaborative agreements, reliance on the markets, etc.), patterns of labor-relations, strategies toward multinational investment, etc., but do these differences affect *aggregate* competitiveness and growth?

One hypothesis could be, of course, that the microeconomic links between organizational forms and competitiveness identified by business economists are local disequilibrium phenomena which cancel out in the aggregate.

An alternative hypothesis to the same effect is to assume that, in general, organizational specificities are only epiphenomena without any long-lasting consequences on performance.[9]

Conversely, we build here on the ideas that specific problem-solving competences deeply affect the ability of both individual firms and whole countries to generate and adopt new technologies and that these competences are not orthogonal to the forms of corporate organization. Indeed, an emerging view on firm-specific "dynamic capabilities" supports this view (cf. Teece *et al.* 1992 and 1994), naturally overlapping with a much longer tradition of business studies pointing at the two-way causality between corporate strategies and structures, and their effects on performances. A *locus classicus* here is Chandler's interpretation of the emergence of the modern multidivisional corporation in the United States and the specificities of its development in other countries (Chandler 1962, 1990 and 1992). And, as forcefully emphasized by Teece 1993, a major distinguishing feature of the Chandlerian corporation rested in its ability to accumulate specific managerial competences in the domains of innovative search, production coordination and marketing.

At a microeconomic level, all this implies also that given any set of technological competences and techniques of production which a firm can master, particular organizational structures and strategies affect both the actual efficiency that a firm displays and the rates and direction of accumulation of innovative knowledge (and, relatedly, the patterns of competitiveness over time).

A growing empirical evidence corroborates this view. For example, Patel and Pavitt (1994) find that "a firm's existing product mix and associated competences strongly constrain the directions in which it seeks to exploit technological opportunities and acquire competences"; and that "... the firm's home country will influence its rate of technological accumulation" (p. 20). (See also Cantwell 1989; Nelson 1994; Porter 1990.)

At an aggregate level, the argument implies that the international distribution of organizational structures and strategies is not random but reflects some country-specific characteristics which display persistence over time. In open economies, this means also that, given the patterns of technological and cost-related advantages/disadvantages of any one country, the degree to which these advantages are exploited in terms of international competitiveness[10] depends also on the organization forms and strategies of the domestic firms. Size, degrees of diversification and vertical integration, propensity to invest abroad, etc. are obviously indicators, but at least equally important are the attitudes toward growth, profitability, market shares, uncertainty, innovation, the nature of internal hierarchies, the relationship between industry and finance, the ways conflict is managed, etc.

Finally, this implies that country-specific organizational characteristics may reproduce over time despite the selective pressures of international competition.

The general interpretative perspective, as discussed in Dosi (1992), might be summarized in four general propositions:

Proposition 1

In contemporary economies, *a good deal of knowledge about technology and exchange governance is embodied in organizations (primarily business firms), which reproduce and augment it via institutionalized procedures and "routines"* that are only limitedly subject to strategic decision at each point in time.

Another way of saying the same is that a lot of what is commonly considered as part of the "control variables" of corporate decision-makers is in fact part of the "state variables" of individual business units—possibly modifiable only in the long term (more on this in Winter 1987).

Proposition 2

Since the prevalent forms of market interaction are generally quite different from pure competition, agents plausibly engage in strategic behaviors. However, *the environments are complex and non-stationary, so that the high-dimensionality of the state—and control—spaces renders strategic behavior quite "opaque."* The mapping between information, actions and outcomes is, at best, imprecise—often undertaken on the grounds of roughly calibrated heuristics and sheer untested beliefs. Hence, *behavioral discretionality is very high.* In general, neither "backward inductive" rationality nor environmental selective pressures and adaptive learning are able to render behaviors uniform. Putting it another way, neither learning nor selection are likely to induce anything resembling symmetric Nash equilibria, or, for that matter, equilibrium behavior of any sort.

Proposition 3

Technological and organizational learning within each firm is to a good extent local and path-dependent. Agents learn, building upon previous knowledge and are often also "blind" vis-à-vis other learning trajectories. They are rather good at solving particular classes of problems but not others, irrespectively of the economic incentives that an ideal external analyst would be able to identify.[11]

The model of the firm telegraphically hinted here suggests that a firm is a behavioral entity (we borrow the definition from Kreps 1990) embodying highly idiosyncratic, specific and inertial compromises between different functions, namely: (i) resource allocation; (ii) information processing; (iii) incentives to individual performance; (iv) control and power exercise; (v) learning. Remarkably, most breeds of economic theories focus primarily upon one single function, often trying to "explain" it on the grounds of the usual maximization cum equilibrium assumptions (for an impressionistic map, see Table 6.1). In the picture of the firm proposed here on the contrary, we broaden the analysis of its evolutionary features accounting also for fundamental tradeoffs between the functions mentioned above.

To illustrate them in a somewhat caricatural way, think of the possible tradeoffs between performance control and learning. While the former is

TABLE 6.1. Representations of the firm in economic theories

Functions	Theories	
Allocations of resources.	Marshallian firms.	
Information processing. Incentives to individual performance	Team theories, principal/agent, cooperative games, transaction costs.	French theories of "Regulation" and "Conventions"
Control and power exercise.	"Radical" (Anglosaxon) theories.	
Learning and problem solving.	Evolutionary theories.	

likely to imply rigid task specifications, the latter generally involves a lot of experimentation, trial-and-error, "deviant" behaviors. (More on this below.) In fact, it is easy to imagine a lot of different organizational arrangements on an ideal continuum between the Prussian army and a university department full of crazy scientists. Indeed, some of these functional tradeoffs are discussed at length in, for example, the microanalytic part of Nelson and Winter (1982), or, from a diverse angle, in the works of Simon, Cyert and March. Moreover, the organizational and management literature is rich with taxonomies describing the specificities of the sociological and "cultural" architecture of firms and the way they affect internal relations, behaviors toward the external environment and performances.

One of the points of this paper is precisely to expand on the notion of "competence" and suggest that it also involves specific patterns of governance of the functions hinted earlier. That is, competences do not only involve problem-solving skills concerning the relationship between the firm and the outside environment, but also skills and rules governing internal relationships. The two are not disjoint: the rates and direction of learning are shaped by the internal structure and the internal norms of behaviour of individual organizations. In this respect Aoki's suggestive comparison between two "ideal types"—the "Japanese firm" and the "American firm"— is a good case in point: different internal governance structures affect learning and performance, even in the presence of identical economic opportunities (Aoki 1988).

More generally, this leads us to our last proposition.

Proposition 4

Firms are behavioural entities embodying specific and relatively inertial competences, decision rules and internal governance structures *which, in the longer term, co-evolve with the environment in which they are embedded.*

The strength of norms, routines, "corporate cultures" resides precisely in their persistence and reproduction over time. As sociologists and organizational theorists tell us, such an inertiality provides some degree of consistency among individual behaviors and motivations to action even if incentive compatibilities are much weaker than those prescribed by economic theory, and even if information about a changing and complex world borders pure ignorance. But precisely that same inertiality makes organizational arrangements quite differentiated, and, often highly suboptimal in their ability to seize technological and market opportunities. (A more detailed discussion is in Dosi and Marengo 1994.)

All four propositions, taken together, imply that, certainly, learning and environmental selection tend to reduce the variety of both technological and organizational innovations that continuously emerge. However, the "locality" of learning, the "opaqueness" of the environment and the positive feedbacks linking particular directions of technological learning with particular organizational setups all imply persistence of different forms of corporate and industrial organization, even when *ex post* they yield different competitive performances. In a jargon nearer to economists: as one can easily generate multiple equilibria stemming from non-convexities and increasing returns in the technology space, so one can easily conjecture multiple "organizational trajectories" stemming, in a loose analogy, from organizational learning about norms, competences, corporate structures.

Moreover, if these propositions are correct, one can identify a possible bridge between (evolutionary) modeling of growth and the rich and variegated account of the patterns of industrialization and growth provided by historians and industrial sociologists alike. Just to give some hints. Ronald Dore's fascinating anatomy of the Japanese industrial system (Dore 1973), Albert Hirschman's analyses of the emergence and role of markets (Hirschman 1977 and 1982), Lazonick's account of the relationship between industrial relations and patterns of industrial development (Lazonick 1993), all appear indeed compatible in principle with an evolutionary "explanation" of growth embedded in the dynamics of changing behavioral entities (firms, but also other social actors, for example banks, workers, public agencies, etc.) and in a technological dynamics with path-dependent learning and widespread increasing returns.[12]

In this respect, we share Zysman's view that collective social entities—such as nations—grounded in specific institutions and commonly shared norms of behavior, shape the patterns of opportunities and constraints facing micro agents and, as a consequence, also the aggregate paths of economic change (Zysman 1994).

However, while a lot of promising investigations have focused on technologies and firms as units of analysis, much less attention has been devoted so far in this perspective to the detailed anatomy of corporate organizations, the ways this links up with economy-wide institutions, and, ultimately their effect on economic performances.

3. COMPETENCES AND FORMS OF ORGANIZATIONAL GOVERNANCE: A PRELIMINARY LOOK INTO THE ORGANIZATIONAL BLACKBOX

As already mentioned, evolutionary economists and business analysts alike most often share the inclination to look at the repertoire of behavioral norms and practices—or routines—within each organization in order to identify "what a firm is good at," how it differs from other firms and also its proximate domains of future change.

Indeed, there are good reasons for the widespread presence of routinized behaviors which we do not need to repeat here:[13] suffice to say that they appear to be robust forms of adaptive learning in complex and changing environments.[14] Moreover, as Nelson and Winter (1982) thoroughly argue, the ensemble of organizational routines, to a large extent, stores and reproduces the problem-solving knowledge of the organization itself. Together with the hypothesis on the widespread emergence of routinized behaviors, a common feature of most evolutionary analyses is the emphasis on their problem-solving properties. This is indeed a major distinguishing building-block of this perspective—and of the earlier pioneering contributions of Herbert Simon—as compared to more orthodox interpretations of organizational arrangements, primarily focused upon the relationships between distribution of information, incentives and resulting equilibrium outcomes. Putting it in a somewhat extremist way, "evolutionists" tend to assume that some, rather rough, incentive compatibility is sufficient to motivate individual efforts and then get down to the analysis of how the set of particular individual actions painstakingly combine in order to solve some equally specific problems, say, building cars and, moreover, doing it at competitive costs, search for better varieties of them, etc. Conversely, e.g. a "principal/ agent" theorist would more easily assume that everyone is naturally able to build the "optimal" car—whatever that means—conditional on the available information, and then point at the details of sophisticated self-seeking interactions which could be undertaken by the members of the organization on the grounds of asymmetric access to information. Elsewhere (Dosi and Marengo 1994), one argues at greater length that the former approach is indeed a much more promising first approximation to organizational behaviors.

Relatedly, a growing effort has gone also into formal representations of processes of search, recombination, reinforcement of sequences of elementary operations yielding particular problem-solving procedures. (See Marengo 1992.) However, routines emerge and are implemented in organizations composed of a plurality of individuals who might have diverging interests. Certainly, a "firm can be understood in terms of hierarchy of practiced organizational routines, which define lower order organizational skills and how these skills are coordinated, and higher-order decision procedures for choosing what is to be done at lower level" (Nelson 1994: 234–5). This hierarchy, however, also entails a mechanism of exercise of authority and governance of the admissible behaviors by which individual members can pursue their interests. This is indeed acknowledged by Nelson and Winter (1982) who suggest that routines can be seen also as "truces" amongst potentially conflicting interests, but this complementary nature of routines has been so far relatively neglected in that literature which explicitly builds upon evolutionary ideas.[15] The double nature of routines as problem-solving skills and as mechanisms of governance appears with particular clarity when analyzing the emergence and establishment of new principles of management and work practices.

Here, we shall consider two archetypal examples, namely "Taylorism" and "Fordism" on the one hand and "Ohnism" and "Toyotism," on the other.

4. TAYLORISM, "SCIENTIFIC MANAGEMENT" AND ROUTINES

Much has been written about Taylor's "Scientific Management" principles based on the systematic subdivision of organizational tasks and grounded in so-called "Time and Motion Studies" (Taylor 1911/1967 and 1971): however, except for the work of a few historians, largely unknown to economists, the implications of that approach to management has been largely underestimated in organization theory, let alone economics.

That underestimation appears also in the pioneering work of March and Simon (1958). While they acknowledge Taylor's as one of the classic contributions to organizational theory (and practice)[16] they primarily emphasize, ". . . the use of men as adjuncts of machines in the performance of routine productive tasks . . . ," aimed to ". . . the goal (of using) the rather inefficient human organism in the productive process in the best way possible" (March and Simon 1993).[17] On the contrary, we shall argue that, first, Taylor had the pioneering understanding that questions of organization of production are essentially questions of know-how and competence; and second, that the distribution of knowledge is intimately connected with the distribution of power. Third, the establishment of Tayloristic practices is a paradigmatic example of coevolution between forms of incentive governance, routines, competences, under circumstances of acute interest conflict.

In all this, it is certainly true that one of Taylor's major contributions to management practices have been Time and Motion Studies (TMS), but the latter have been the precondition of an epochal wave of codification of previously tacit knowledge of working operatives in a set of elementary procedures and acts. In turn, such a codification was a prerequisite for a changing control upon such knowledge itself, previously embodied in its "aggregate" form into the specific experience of skilled workers, whose abilities to bargain on the condition of its use had been a major obstacle to productivity growth in the nineteenth century.

Some historical examples and some references to Taylor's own analysis might help in illustrating these points.

At the beginning of the twentieth century a prevalent form of production organization was still the system of "inside contractors/helpers."[18] Under that practice, the owner of a firm would entrust production to a set of skilled workers, operating on its premises, who acted as "inside contractors", hiring in turn their own "helpers." The contractors directly supervised and rewarded the helpers, either with a fixed salary or in proportion to their own gains.

Under the system, the possibility of control of the owner upon the contractors was quite limited: only the latter knew the methods of production, and times and rates of remuneration had to be painstakingly negotiated. Hiring directly the skilled workers as waged employees did not improve very much the outcome, since worker-specific, and tacit, knowledge allowed workers to master the pace of work. "Soldiering" (nowadays one would say "shirking") was a normal pattern of behavior:

Underworking, that is deliberately working slowly so as to avoid doing a full day's work, "soldiering" as it is called in this country, "hanging it out" as it is called in England, "ca'canny" as it is called in Scotland is almost universal in industrial establishments and prevails to a large extent in the building trades; and ... this constitutes the greatest evil by which the working people of both England and America are now affected. (Taylor 1911/1967: 13–14)

And moreover,

So universal is soldiering ... that hardly a competent workman can be found in a large establishment, whether he works by the day or on piecework, contract work, or under any of the ordinary system, who does not devote a considerable part of his time to studying just how slow he can work and still convince his employer that he is going at a good pace. (ibid. 20)

Taylor's description of the phenomenon in terms of "initiative and incentives" is surprisingly near the current parlance of principal/agent theorists, although he does not at all share with the latter the faith in the existence of some incentive-compatible equilibrium contract, irrespectively of the chosen reward system. The diagnosis is that

... as the cause for soldiering—the relations which exist between employers and employees under almost all systems of management which are in common use—it is impossible to make clear to one not familiar with this problem why it is the ignorance of employers as to the proper time in which work of various kind should be done—makes it the interest of the workman to "soldier." (ibid. 18)

In turn, this ignorance concerns the tacit knowledge associated with each trade.[19]

Incidentally note that—unlike most current representations of incentive-compatibility issues—one finds here an explicit emphasis on problem-solving knowledge as distinguished from sheer information,[20] and also an implicit assumption that particular social groups (e.g. skilled workers), independently of the fine tuning of incentive mechanisms, share particular forms of collective behaviors (in this case, rendering de facto collusion easier).

Rather than attempting to adjust the incentive structure, the general Tayloristic programme involves a major redefinition of the nature of productive knowledge and a novel distribution of it within the organization. Time and Motion Studies aim precisely at the control of the knowledge of working operatives themselves, yielding the development of detailed operational protocols, that were to become the elementary production routines of modern corporations.

This transformation required also a major organizational transformation, namely the establishment of a specific corporate function, the Department of Planning—as repository of the general "production intelligence" of the factory. The Department analyzes the elementary tasks, allocates them to the individual workers and establishes the coordinating procedures. A major transfer of knowledge occurs, from individual workers to the management; a good deal of tacit knowledge is decomposed, codified and made easily transmissible via operational protocols.

The end result has been that the tasks of the Tayloristic organization, "first are repetitive; second, these tasks do not require complex problem-solving activity by the workers who handle them . . ." (March and Simon 1993: 32). But this is so precisely because the overall problem-solving and coordinating activity had been taken in charge by a specific managerial institution, the Department of Planning. Indeed, the story of "Scientific Management"—and, at its core, TMS procedures—is precisely the story of the transformation of individual skills into organizational competences codified into hierarchies of routines.

This transformation, we suggest, had the same importance for the emergence of the modern (archetypal "American") corporation as the Chandlerian emergence of the managerial divisionalized organization. In fact, the two can be seen, to a large extent, as different levels of descriptions of the same major organizational innovation. The "Tayloristic revolution" describes at the level of production routines a process which co-evolves with the reshaping of the organizational structure of the firm, entrusting the general knowledge on coordination and strategies upon professional managers—as described by Chandler.[21]

Later on, we shall also argue that the rates and modes of international adaptation of such "American" (Chandlerian and Tayloristic) corporations have deeply affected for a long period the growth patterns of each country.

First, however, let us focus on the nature of the emerging Tayloristic routines and their birthmarks stemming from the conflict that they triggered.

At a social level, the introduction of Scientific Management has been accompanied by the *open-shop campaign*, in the effort by the managers to hire non-unionized workers. Here is another element of the co-evolutionary dynamics between transformation of the knowledge bases and transformation of the collective institutions—*in primis*, the labor market—in which firms are embedded. The organizational transfer of tasks from skilled workers to "specialized" ones has been painfully accompanied by the formation of new rules of hiring, firing and labor mobility which sustained the implementation of the new working procedures inside the organizations.

Not surprisingly, the process was ridden with conflict. The case of the Watertown Arsenal (documented by Aitken 1985) is only one of the many examples of the resistance of the labor movement to the diffusion of Scientific Management.[22]

Tayloristic routines as they finally emerged fully displayed their double nature as sets of problem-solving protocols and as devices of social control. TMS methods defined a new "economy of time" together with a new "economy of control." This implied also a new production paradigm whose implicit but fundamental assumption was that the productivity of any industrial unit is a positive direct function of the productivity of the individual worker considered at his work station; and "productivity" itself is measured by the number of elementary units of work performed by the individual worker during a given unit of time (e.g. the hour or the working-day). This production paradigm performed also for a long time as a "focusing device"—in Nathan Rosenberg's terminology—shaping the direction of routine improvement and competence accumulation.

As argued at greater length elsewhere (Coriat 1979/1994, 1992, 1993*a*), this led to a very specific trajectory of production learning, whereby an increasing fragmentation of tasks proved to be conducive to efficient manufacturing of high volume, standardized, low-cost products but is likely to be less suitable for differentiated high-quality products.

It is important to notice that this particular paradigm of organization of collective competence and of social control embodies also a specific mechanism of incentive governance. The approach Taylor suggested was twofold: on the one hand, he designed a new pay system (the so-called "differential piece-rate system"); on the other hand, incentives had to be matched by direct visual control upon work practices by foremen.

Patterns of problem solving and patterns of governance and control turned out to be intimately linked within a structure of organizational routines which constrained also the patterns of learning (the "trajectory" of technological and organizational change).

In order to highlight the specificities of these routines and their internal consistency requirements between problem solving and governance, let us compare "Taylorism" with another organizational archetype, namely "Ohnism" and "Toyotism"—as the new Japanese production practices are often called.

5. "OHNISM" AND JAPANESE PRODUCTION ROUTINES

As it is handy to identify an archetype of labour management practices with Taylor's original vision and normative programme—notwithstanding the obvious nuances in the fulfillment of such a model—so it is easy to point at T. Ohno for the general statement of an alternative set of "Japanese" production practices (cf. Ohno 1988).

The two major specificities of "Ohnism" might be identified with (a) "Just-in-time" organization of production flows, and (b) production routines based on the principle of "auto-activation" (for more on this see Coriat 1991a). Briefly, just-in-time coordination methods consist of just producing what can actually be sold, catering for orders insofar as they appear, rather than producing and stocking on the grounds of expectations of future sales.[23] "Auto-activation" or "autonomation" (*jidoka*) is a complementary organizing criterion for production tasks based on the idea that each worker has the time needed to complete his assignments and pass on a flawless product to his partner at the next stage of production. Moreover, "autonomation" entails the possibility—and, indeed the duty—to apply "local intelligence," identify anomalies, and, in case, stop the entire production flow. In turn, "autonomation" implies (i) a multiplicity of skills of each worker; (ii) some discretionality and autonomy in decision making; and (iii) patterns of coordination between production tasks smoothly flowing in temporal sequences from inputs to outputs.[24]

A casual observer, and especially an economist, might consider all this as belonging to the domain of diverse and ephemeral managerial practices. On the contrary, one of us has argued elsewhere (Coriat 1991a) that these two basic principles of production entail organizational forms significantly different from the "Tayloristic" (or "American") archetype sketched above, and with that, also different patterns of organization of knowledge.

The "seeding" of the evolutionary process which yielded these organizational outcomes, can be identified—as in the earlier Tayloristic example—into complementary problem-solving and incentive-compatibility dilemmas, most likely embedded in broader, more inertial institutions and cultures. Japan, in its industrializing and reconstruction efforts, especially after World War II, was forced to find ways of achieving productivity gains other than classic "Fordist" methods based on the exploitation of economies of scale. To a good extent, it shared also the requirement, felt earlier so acutely by the Tayloristic philosophy, to place operatives' knowledge under management control (a lag most likely due also to the previous authoritarian regime which tended to surrogate for incentive incompatibility with loyalty and force). In any case, the crux of the matter was, as in other modernizing countries, to reshape the distribution of knowledge away from variegated groups of highly skilled workers. And on the conflict-of-interest side, social polarization, in the decade following World War II, was certainly at a rather critical level. The course that labor relations and working organization actually took—by no means the only notional one[25]— was a specific and original way of work rationalization which did not stop at the Tayloristic breakdown of complex workers skills, but recomposed the tasks for multifunctional workers, with flexible working standards.[26] A major consequence of this organizational innovation was that it implied a production engineering approach (concerning design and layout of production lines, programming principles, etc.) radically different from that which has prevailed in America amid the numerous Ford-inspired recommendations.[27]

For our purposes, we want to emphasize that the combination of "just-in-time" with "auto-activation" has given rise to a novel series of routines, both at the level of intra- and inter-organization practices.

A first crucial difference from the "American" theory and practice can be sketched as follows. Whereas the Tayloristic approach has been aimed to separate the functions of production, maintenance, quality control, planning, etc. and to fragment the tasks required by each function, the Japanese way on the contrary has been to create work stations where the different tasks are to different degrees reaggregated.[28] Thus, one can observe that the fundamental significance of the Japanese approach consists of a reconstitution at shop-floor level of something like a general and reaggregated function of manufacturing, the main characteristic of which is that it puts together again tasks which Taylor's approach recommended be carefully and systematically kept apart.[29] On this basis, one observes the introduction of specific protocols entailing permanent manipulation of *kanban* and used either to command or to deliver "just-in-time" the internal flows of semifinished products.

One can wonder how it is possible to reaggregate general functions in manufacturing without losing control of productivity, i.e. can the Taylorian legacy be so deeply abandoned?

The answer to this question (crucial for the understanding of the "control" dimension of the Japanese routines) is twofold.

First, TMS is not abandoned at all. As has been pointed out by a very attentive and pertinent commentator, TMS has been "regained" (see Adler

1993), i.e. the idea of fragmenting tasks is maintained but, the jobs are now broken down into basic "transferable work components." Such a component is defined as: "the smallest practical combination of acts that can be transferred from one worker to another." Thus flexible work standards and reaggregation of elementary tasks are made compatible with the objective of maintaining workers' knowledge and work standards under control.[30] Second, the Japanese methods embed specific practices of controlling workers' tasks and activities, one of the most important being what is termed "management by eyes," elaborated and designed by T. Ohno himself. This principle is indeed very simple and consists in organizing the workshops, and the work on the lines, in such a way that everything can be very easily (physically) visible. For example, any worker has the right (and in fact more than the right, the duty) to stop the line any time he thinks it necessary to guarantee the quality of his performance; at the same time, each stop is signaled by a red light appearing on an electronic panel hanging above the line (It is the so-called "andon" system).

More generally, Ohno explains the principle of "managing by eyes" as follows:

In order to allow "autoactivation" to detect anomalies, one needs that anything "abnormal" appears immediately to the naked eye. The principle ought to apply to quality (every faulted product should immediately surface) as well as to quantity (progress of work vis-à-vis previous plans should be effortlessly measured at the very work place). This should not only apply to the machines but also to the methods of production, the circulation of kanbans, the levels of stocks, etc. (Ohno 1988)

Note again the learning side of this set of routines—as well as those associated with "just-in-time": far from being simple devices to minimize faulty pieces of output or inventories, they fulfill primarily the task of immediately highlighting the presence of a problem and allowing or forcing operatives to handle it.

6. MICROROUTINES, INCENTIVES AND INSTITUTIONAL EMBEDDEDNESS

More generally, a crucial implication of each distinct pattern of organization of production is that it involves a specific set of problem-solving routines *and equally specific, and broadly consistent, forms of incentive governance and control*. In a telegraphic summary, Taylorism introduces also a new reward mechanism based on a piece-wage system, made of a fixed part—corresponding to a minimum number of pieces per day, and a variable part—triggered by above minimum output and pushing upward the whole per-piece wage rates (also, on the part below, the minimum threshold).[31]

"Fordism" further modifies the reward mechanism, introducing the famous "five-dollar day" wage (well above the current wage at the time), but,
together, eliminates workers' discretionality in the choice of working pace
by incorporating it into the predetermined speed of conveyors along the
assembly line. Finally, it introduces systematic screening and testing of
workers themselves, in terms of their social attitudes, their loyalty and
obedience. This task is delegated to a special institution: the so-called
"Sociological Department."[32]
Conversely, "Ohnism" implies a complex reward structure involving (a)
a base salary; b) individual bonuses; and c) collective performance bonuses.
As M. Aoki has forcefully shown on several occasions, the two stylized
and archetypal organizational forms, called the "American" and the
"Japanese" enterprises, differing in the internal architecture with respect to
both information-processing and incentive-governance, are likely to yield
also systematically different performances.[33] Our argument indeed strengthens the point. The set of "Japanese" (or "Ohnist") production routines
does not only embody different channels of information processing but also
distributes knowledge within the organization in ways remarkably different
from the "Tayloristic"/"Chandlerian" enterprise. And at the same time,
on the governance side, individual incentives to efficiently perform and
learn are sustained by company-specific rank—hierarchies, delinked from
functional assignments (Aoki 1990).
The collective "embeddedness" dimension is equally important. We
mentioned earlier that the establishment of "Tayloristic" organizational
routines coevolved with the development of what one could shorthandedly
call the "American labor market." Symmetrically, radically different institutional norms (such as life-time employment, etc.) became established
with respect to large Japanese corporations. Yet at another level, different
corporate strategies (with respect to investment growth, diversification,
R&D, etc.) appear to taxonomically match specific institutional relationships between financial and industrial actors.[34]
At a much finer level of detail, these modal patterns of relationship
between diverse economic agents, again, are entangled into identifiable sets
of behavioral routines. For example in Coriat (1994), one tries to identify
typical protocols of interfirm transactions, conditional on the internal
modes of governance and problem solving.
A revealing illustration is the relationship between "core" companies and
their suppliers. Under the Japanese system of organizational routines,
Asanuma (1987 and 1989) sharply illustrates the protocols for information-
flows, competition/cooperation—"relational rent-sharing" as Aoki (1988)
would phrase it. Among this specific set of routines, those concerning
quality selection are clearly of crucial importance. Producing almost without inventories (of either inputs or outputs) implies that product quality of
the semi-finished products either ordered or received by core companies

must be very high. As a consequence, the process of selection of subcontractors implies very detailed protocols (in the case of the French auto industry they are discussed in Coriat 1994).[35]

Similar exercises could fruitfully be done (and, indeed, ought to be done) with respect to other types of interactive procedures (e.g. with respect to the labor market, financial investors, etc.) Just to mention an example, it seems to us that Lorenz' argument on the importance of trust (or rather the lack of it) in British production practices belongs precisely to this domain of analysis: the "truces" that emerged codified in particular sets of routines tended to foster conservatism, and hinder the diffusion of technological and organizational innovation (Lorenz 1994). In any case, for the little we know about the behaviors of enterprises with respect to their external environment, the evidence seems to corroborate our conjectures (i) that somewhat typical and rather inertial behavioral patterns tend to emerge, (ii) that these patterns can be roughly mapped into distinctive internal hierarchies of routines within the organization; (iii) that broader collective institutions— e.g. on the labor or financial markets—constrain and shape the sustainable routines; and (iv) that also in the relationships amongst legally independent actors, interactive routines enfold problem-solving complementarities and asymmetric mechanisms of control.[36]

"Taylorism," the Chandlerian M-form organization, "Fordism" or for that matter, "Ohnism" and "Toyotism" represent major organizational innovations, with—in principle—a universal character. And, indeed, at least the former three spread internationally, well beyond the countries where they were originally introduced, spurring deep modifications in industrial structures and shaping long-term productivity growth (on "Taylorism" and the M-form, see Kogut 1992, and Chandler 1990). It is possibly too early to evaluate the international diffusion of Japanese practices, but rich case-study evidence already suggests their widespread impact.

However, the rates and patterns of diffusion of all these major organizational paradigms have been shaped by the institutional context of each country, which implied also some inevitable "hybridization." This, in some cases, also yielded major modifications further down the road. In this respect, Japanese practices may indeed be considered as a profound organizational innovation originally grounded in the local adaptation of Taylorism and Fordism, which eventually led to a distinct archetype of organizational routines for problem solving and governance of industrial relations.

One can see here a good example of the notions of embeddedness, (limited) lock-in, and potential invadability. Embeddedness implies that earlier patterns of industrial organization, labour practices, etc. carry their influence over the ways new forms are introduced: it applies to the original adaptations of Taylorism and Fordism to Japan or Sweden, as well as to that of the M-form corporation in e.g. the UK, Germany or Japan. Lock-in entails the prediction of progressive dominance of some specific patterns of governance and problem solving and their rather inertial reproduction over time. However, each "national system" remains potentially "invadable"— to use the jargon of current evolutionary games: it might be unable to generate internally radically new organizational experiments, but is not immune to the progressive adoption of organizational innovations developed elsewhere.

7. FROM CORPORATE ROUTINES TO PATTERNS OF DEVELOPMENT: PRELIMINARY CONCLUSIONS AND MANY RESEARCH ITEMS ON LEARNING, INCENTIVES AND PATTERNS OF CHANGE

We began this work by presenting what we consider to be a few "stylized facts" on the relationship between technical change and growth, together with some microeconomic evidence on innovative activities. In turn, many of these "facts" entail challenging puzzles for the theory. Old ones like "why levels and growth rates of income differ" demand—it is increasingly acknowledged—the dissection of the black box of technological change, as Nathan Rosenberg urged us quite a while ago. Investigations in this perspective have recently increased momentum and, in our view, are significantly adding novel insights into the processes by which knowledge is augmented, to a good extent also as a result of exploratory endeavors of profit-motivated agents, together with those of other institutions. While one progresses in opening up the "technological black box," however, there is yet another black box—the organizational one—whose anatomy is plausibly quite important also for every macro economist who does not consider the specificities of corporate organizations simply as veils covering deeper and invariant economic mechanisms.

The proposition that organizational structures matter in terms of performances, in fact, can be quite easily supported even in term of otherwise quite orthodox theories, whenever one abandons the most restrictive assumptions on perfect information, complete markets, etc. (see, within an enormous literature, Aoki 1990; Sah and Stiglitz 1985; Radner 1992). Even more so, if one accounts for the endemic occurrence of transaction costs as Oliver Williamson (1985*a,b*) emphasizes.

Of course, the learning dimension that evolutionary and organizational economists add to the picture further reinforces the point. The path-dependent, often organization-embodied, nature of knowledge makes corporate structures the prime carriers of diverse problem-solving skills, to a good extent stored and reproduced via organizational routines.

However, routines do not only represent problem-solving procedures but are at the same time control and governance devices. In this work we have analyzed precisely this double nature of theirs. Moreover, we have argued, specific sets of routines often bear the mark of the conflicts which accompanied their emergence and establishment.

The two archetypal sets of routines which we have outlined in this work namely "Tayloristic" and "Ohnistic" (loosely speaking, "Japanese") production methods vividly illustrate these points. More precisely, we have tried to show that the explanation of particular sets of routines can be traced back to the coevolution between corporate patterns of knowledge distribution and mechanisms of coordination and governance.

All this, most likely, reinforces phenomena of path-dependence and international differentiation, generally sustained by mutually shared conventions, norms and implicit or legally enforced institutions.

There are several rather general implications of the perspective outlined in this work, which can only be sketched out in this paper.

As we have emphasized above, the multiple facets of organizational arrangements and the forms of their institutional embeddedness are, in our view, an integral part of the explanation of the diversity of development patterns that one observes: in fact, we suggest they are among the core elements of those diverse "social capabilities" identified by Abramovitz (1989) as "deeper causes" of contemporary growth.

Other, more theoretical implications, have only been briefly limited. For example, the foregoing interpretation of the nature of organizational routines encompasses the tasks of incentive governance analyzed by, for example, principal agent models. But it radically departs from the latter in that it considers "what the agents believe to be their interests," the ways they pursue them and the knowledge that they possess to be the evolutionary outcome of search, conflict and mutual adjustment sanctioned thereafter by rather inertial rules and organizational structures. Corollaries of this view are also the predictions that (a) might be generally misleading and reduce whatever pattern of intra- or interorganizational relations to a set of "contracts" (whether optimal or not); b) given the organizational routines, individual performances are likely to be rather insensitive to any fine tuning of incentives; and c) path-dependency phenomena will tend frequently to carry over the reproduction of particular organizational arrangements well beyond the time of their possible usefulness.

Other implications—nearer the concerns of the economics of innovation—regard the effect of established sets of routines upon the "trajectories" of technical progress (and here is also where the economics of innovation can meet analyses from other disciplinary camps which have emphasized the aspects of "social construction" of technical change).

Indeed, we see ahead a promising research agenda.

NOTES

1. Cf. Coriat (1994*b*), Lazonick (1990; 1993), Zysman (1994).
2. This assumption is in the same spirit as Nelson and Winter (1992).
3. Within a rapidly growing literature, see Freeman (1982); Nelson and Winter (1982); Pavitt (1984); Rosenberg (1985); Dosi (1988); Dosi *et al.* (1988); David (1985); Arthur (1988); Saviotti and Metcalfe (1992).
4. See the pioneering work of Nelson and Winter (1982), and, among others, Silverberg *et al.* (1988); Eliasson (1986); Chiaromonte, Dosi and Orsenigo (1993); Silverberg and Verspagen (1994).
5. Dosi *et al.* (1994*a*).
6. Cf. Dosi, Pavitt and Soete (1990), Fagerberg (1987; 1988), Soete and Verspagen (1993), and the broad discussion in Abramovitz (1989).
7. Cf. Romer (1986, 1990*a,b*); Helpman and Krugman (1989); Grossman and Helpman (1991); Aghion and Howitt (1992).
8. Dosi and Orsenigo (1988); Dosi (1992).
9. Indeed, the irrelevance of organizational forms can be argued from quite different theoretical points of view. Take, for example, an extreme version of a transaction-cost model of corporate organization. The model would suggest that observed institutional setups (e.g. within and between firms) are the organizational response to a requirement of efficient governance of exchanges. Hence, any observed international difference in the typical modes of organizing transactions would be primarily attributed to lags and leads in diffusion of more efficient forms of organization (if transaction costs do not dramatically differ across countries, which is likely to apply to developed economies, although it might not to comparisons among countries at different stages of development). In the long term, an extreme version of a transaction-cost theory of organization would suggest that one should observe *convergence in institutional setups*, driven by the differential efficiency of various organizational modes.

    At the symmetric opposite, consider an extreme version of the Marglin–Piore–Sabel interpretation of industrial organization (more faithful and sophisticated arguments along these lines are in Marglin (1974), Piore and Sabel (1984); needless to say, we are purposefully overemphasizing in order to clarify the point). Here, in a first approximation, the cross-sectional and intertemporal differences in the modes of organization of firms and industries would be simply responses to power criteria, and reproduce with the inertia that institutions generally entail. The set of *equally efficient* organizational regimes, this interpretation would suggest, is wide, and the observed variety results from a selection within such a set, driven primarily by considerations of social control and income distribution. Hence, again, national specificities in corporate and industrial organization would not be among the fundamental variables explaining "why levels and growth rates of income differ across countries."
10. On this notion of "competitiveness" cf. Dosi, Pavitt and Soete (1990).
11. Promising explorations of the idea are in Levinthal (1992), and Levinthal and March (1994). See also Dosi and Lovallo (1994).

12. And, at a more aggregate level of description, this interpretation is highly complementary with a "Regulationist" view—in the French institutionalist sense of the patterns of "socio-economic tuning" characterizing particular countries and phases of development (Boyer 1988*a,b*; Boyer and Coriat 1986).

13. Cf. Nelson and Winter (1982); March (1994); Dosi and Egidi (1991); Dosi and Marengo (1994); Dosi *et al.* (1994); Cohen (1987).

14. Like Nelson and Winter (1982), Dosi *et al.* (1994) and Teece *et al.* (1994), we include under the broad heading of "routines" relatively invariant norms of behavior which are context-dependent and approximately event-independent (in the sense that they are rather insensitive to the information on changes in the states of the world, given a particular context). Moreover, routines might be straightforwardly stationary rules (such as ". . . close the door of the factory every day at 7 p.m. . . .") or higher-level "dynamic rules" (such as ". . . search for new techniques in such and such directions . . ."; ". . . when something goes wrong do *x* and send a message to *y* . . .", etc.).

15. Important exceptions are Postrel and Rumelt (1992) and Kogut (1992).

16. The other being that by Guklick and Urwick, concerned with "the grand organizational problems of departmental division of work and coordination."

17. Hence they characterize the approach as "physiological organization theory," because it encompasses primarily physiological variables (p. 32) and add "Traditional Time and Motion Study Methods have avoided problem-solving tasks, and thus have not dealt with the aspects of human behaviour that will concern us throughout most of this volume" (p. 33).

18. Cf. Montgomery (1979); Hounshell (1984); S. Meyer, III (1982).

19. "The managers recognize frankly the fact that the 500 to 1,000 workmen included in the twenty or thirty trades who are under them, possess this mass of traditional knowledge, a large part of which is not in the possession of the management." "This mass of rules of thumb or traditional knowledge may be said to be the principle asset or possession of every tradesman" (ibid. 32).

20. That distinction is of course a major building block of the analyses of production and innovation of Nelson and Winter (1982); Winter (1981); Dosi (1988) and Pavitt (1984).

21. On the importance of routines and competences underlying the Chandlerian corporation, see Chandler himself (1992) and Teece (1993).

22. Taylor himself had also to justify his practices before a Special Committee of the House of Representatives, cf. Taylor (1971).

23. The so-called *Kanban* approach, originally named after a procedure of dropping paper orders of components "upstream" of the production chain, has been a well-known implementation.

24. Note that this does not apply to "Taylorist"/"Fordist" patterns of organization of production whereby each elementary "shop" (e.g. "the drilling shop," "the boring shop," etc.) produces for a buffer stock of intermediate goods.

25. To make a more general theoretical point: as with path-dependent models with multiple attainable limit states, conditional on the initial setups, we are far from claiming that the Japanese initial conditions telegraphically sketched here "determined" in any strong sense the observed outcome. Rather we just suggest that they contributed to select the feasible evolutionary path, together with

broader social circumstances, analyzed from different perspectives by Aoki (1988); Dore (1973); Gerlach (1993); among others.

26. Cf. Monden (1983). The linearization of the production processes hinted above is associated with these more flexible production standards and also permits switching from some predetermined production time to a "shared" time: cf. Monden (1983) and Coriat (1991).

27. Broadening the field of observation from the shop-floor level to the enterprise as a whole, the same principle of relative despecialization can be observed, particularly with the establishment of horizontal lines of communications between marketing, R&D and manufacturing. These flexible interdepartmental communications make it possible to get closer to the market as regards quality trends and at the same time to reduce lead times (cf. Clark and Fujimoto 1989, for example).

28. In more detail, this process of despecialization and reaggregation of tasks affects four domains. The first of these reaggregations concerns the reassociation of tasks within direct manufacturing itself: "versatility" and multispecialization are the norm and stand in opposition to the principles of compartmentalization and repetitivity featured by American Tayloristic patterns. The second consists of the reacquisition by direct operatives of the tasks of diagnostics, repair and light maintenance; self-management and self-inspection make sense and prove effective only if the front-line operatives are also in charge of the routine maintenance of the plant and machinery. The third is the reintroduction of quality control at the work stations. Here again, the be-all and end-all of the principle of self-management and self-inspection is to tackle product quality at the work stations themselves. Lastly, there is also a reaggregation of programming and manufacturing tasks, which constitutes the necessary condition of the *Kanban* method (Coriat 1991*a*, 1992).

29. In its spirit and in its practical details, the method appears as the implementation of principles of despecialization, not only in terms of the employee's work, but in a more global perspective as a despecialization of the "general work of the enterprise," reaggregating on the shop floor the tasks (production, programming or quality control, etc.) systematically kept apart by Taylorism.

30. For a number of very convincing illustrations of this kind of practices in Japanese transplants in the USA see Parker and Slaughter (1988).

31. So for example, suppose that the minimum output is 200 pieces per day corresponding to wages of $2 (i.e. 1 cent per piece): output up to 10% higher would entail, says, a 10% upward adjustment of the whole wage; a 20% higher output a wage 40% higher, etc. Incidentally, note that the principle appears in violation of "marginal productivity" criteria but seems more akin to a modified version of an "efficiency wage" principle.

32. The "Sociological Department" goes as far as checking on the workers' families, their social habits, etc. On the story of the Five-Dollar Day, and the role attributed to the "sociological department," see S. Meyer, III (1992).

33. Aoki (1988; 1990).

34. For example, "market-based" and "bank-based" forms of finance of investment and interfirm selection: cf. Zysman (1994), Aoki (1988), Dosi (1990). A tentative combinatorial exercise among the viable forms of governance among

internal routines, labor-market interactions, modes of finance and innovative strategies is presented in Aoki and Dosi (1992).

35. Briefly, they typically show a five-stage procedure of selection and relationship construction, going from the "assessment of quality aptitude"; to tentative efforts of knowledge transfer to the contractors; evaluation of the preliminary outcomes; acceptance into the core company "product quality assurance circle"; and, finally, permanent "real time" assessment of deliveries.

36. For example, with respect to this latter point, in Coriat (1994) we argue that networking routines, while being certainly a mechanism of collective learning, generally imply also persistent asymmetries and interfirm hierarchies. The embeddedness argument is formulated, in quite general terms in Granovetter (1985), and more specifically with regards to corporate strategies of production and innovation, in Lazonick (1990 and 1993), Soskice (1993) and Zysman (1994). See also Boyer (1988*a*) and Dosi, Pavitt and Soete (1990).

REFERENCES

Abramovitz, M. (1989), *Thinking About Growth* (Cambridge: Cambridge University Press).

Adler, P. (1993), "Time-and-Motion Study Regained," *Harvard Business Review*, Jan.–Feb., no. 93101.

Aghion, P. and Howitt, P. (1992), "A Model of Growth Through Creative Destinction," in Foray and Freeman (eds.), *Technology and the Wealth of Nations*.

Aitken, H. G. J. (1985), *Scientific Management in Action: Taylorism at Watertown Arsenal, 1908–1915* (Princeton: Princeton University Press).

Aoki, M. (1988), *Information, Incentives, and Bargaining Structure in the Japanese Economy* (Cambridge: Cambridge University Press).

——(1990), "Towards an Economic Theory of the Japanese Firm," *Journal of Economic Literature*, 26/1.

—— and Dosi, G. (1992), "Corporate Organization, Finance and Innovation," in V. Zamagni (ed.), *Finance and the Enterprise* (New York: Academic Press).

Arrow, K. (1974), *The Limits of Organizations* (New York: Norton).

Arthur, B. (1988), "Competing Technologies," in Dosi *et al.* (eds.), *Technical Change and Economic Theory*.

——Ermoliev, Y. and Kaniovski, Y. (1987), "Path-dependent Processes and the Emergence of Macro Structures," *European Journal of Operational Research*, 30/3 (June), 294–303.

Asanuma, B. (1987), "Transactional Structure of Parts Supply in the Japanese Automobile and Electric Machinery Industries: A Comparative Analysis," Working Paper, Kyoto University.

——(1989), "Manufacturer-Supplier Relationships in Japan and the Concept of Relation Specific Skill," *Journal of the Japanese and International Economies*, 3/1: 1–30.

Berggren, C. (1988), "The Swedish Experience with 'New Work Concepts' in Assembly Operations," in B. Dunkbaar, U. Jurgens and T. Munch, *Die Zukunft der Arbeit in der Automobilindustrie* (Berlin: Ed. Sigma).

Boyer, R. (1988a), "Technical Change and the Theory of Regulation," in Dosi *et al.* (eds.), *Technical Change and Economic Theory*.

——(1988b), "Formalizing Growth Regimes," in Dosi *et al.*, *Technical Change*.

——(1989), "New Directions in Management Practices and Work Trajectories," paper presented for the OECD Conference on "Technical Change as a Social Progress," Helsinki, 11–13. Dec.

—— and Coriat, B. (1986), "Technical Flexibility and Macro Stabilisation," *Ricerche Economiche*, 40/4 (Oct.–Dec.), 771–835.

Cantwell, J. (1989), *Technological Change and Multinational Corporations* (Oxford Blackwell).

Chandler, A. D. (1962), *Strategy and Structure* (Cambridge, Mass.: MIT Press).

——(1990), *Scale and Scope* (Cambridge, Mass.: The Belknap Press of Harvard University Press).

——(1992), "Organizational Capabilities and the Economic History of the Industrial Enterprise," *Journal of Economic Perspectives*, 6: 79–100.

Chiaromonte, F., Dosi, G. and Orsenigo, L. (1993), "Innovative Learning and Institutions in the Process of Development: On the Microfoundations of Growth Regimes," in Thomson (ed.), *Learning and Technological Change*.

Clark, K. B. and Fujimoto, T. (1989), "Product Development and Competitiveness," paper presented to the International Seminar on Science, Technology and Growth, OECD, Paris, April.

Cohen, M. (1987), "Adaptation and Organizational Routines," Working Paper, Ann Arbor, Michigan Institute of Public Policy Studies.

Cole, R. E (1989), *Strategies for Learning* (Berkeley: University of California Press).

Coriat, B. (1979), *L'Atelier et le Chronomètre: Essai sur le Taylorisme, le Fordisme et la Production de Masse*, 1st edn. (Paris: Christian Bourgois), paperback edn. 1994 (Paris: Collection Bourgois/Choix).

——(1990), *L'Atelier et le Robot: Essai sur le Fordisme et la Production de Masse à l'Age de l'Electronique*, 1st edn. (Paris: Christian Bourgois) paperback edn. 1994 (Paris: Collection Bourgois/Choix).

——(1991a), *Penser à l'Envers, Travail et Organisation dans l'Entreprise Japonaise* (Paris: Édition C. Bourgois).

——(1991b), "Technical Flexibility and Mass Production: Flexible Specialization and Dynamic Flexibility," in G. Benko and M. Dunford (eds.), *Industrial Change and Regional Development* (London: Belhaven Press).

——(1992), "The Revitalization of Mass Production in the Computer Age," in M. Torper and J. Scott (eds.), *Pathways to Industrialization in Regional Development* (London: Routledge).

——(1993a), "Incentives, Bargaining and Trust: Alternatives Scenarii for the Future of Work," Communication to the Conference on "Maastricht Revisited" (MERIT: Limburg University).

——(1993b), "Globalisation, Variety and Networks: The metamorphosis of the Fordist Firms," paper presented at the Conference "Hierarchies, Markets, Power in the Economy: Theories and Lessons from History," Fifth International Week on the History of the Enterprise, Castellanza, 15–17 Dec.

Coriat, B. (1994), "Taylor, Ford et Ohno: Nouveaux développements dans l'analyse du Ohnisme," *Japon in Extenso Revue.* 31 (Mar.–Apr.), 7–23.

Cremer, J. (1993), "Corporate Culture and Shared Knowledge," *Industrial and Corporate Change,* 2/3: 351–86.

David, P. A. (1975), *Technical Choice, Innovation and Economic Growth* (Cambridge: Cambridge University Press).

——(1985), "Clio and the Economics of QWERTY," *American Economic Review, Papers and Proceedings,* 75/2 (May), 332–7.

Dertouzos, M. L., Lester, R. K. and Solow, R. M. (1989), *Made in America* (Cambridge, Mass.: MIT Press).

Dore, R. (1973), *British Factory, Japanese Factory* (London: Allen & Unwin).

Dosi, G. (1988), "Sources, Procedures and Microeconomic Effects of Innovation," *Journal of Economic Literature,* 26/3 (Sept.), 1120–71.

——(1992), "Industrial Organization, Competitiveness and Growth," *Revue d'Economie Industrielle,* 59 (Jan.–Mar.), 27–45.

——and Egidi, M. (1991), "Substantive and Procedural Uncertainty," *Journal of Evolutionary Economics* 1/1: 145–68.

——and Lovallo, D. (1994), "Rational Entrepreneurs of Optimistic Martyrs? Some Considerations on Technological Regimes, Corporate Entries and the Evolutionary Role of Decision Biases," paper presented at the Conference on Technological Foresights and Oversights, Stern Business School, New York University, Mar. 1994.

——and Marengo, L. (1994), "Some Elements of an Evolutionary Theory of Corporate Competences," in R. W. England (ed.), *Evolutionary Concepts in Contemporary Economics* (Ann Arbor: University of Michigan Press).

——and Orsenigo, L. (1988), "Coordination and Transformation: An Overview of Structures, Behaviours and Change in Evolutionary Environments," in Dosi *et al* (eds.), *Technical Change and Economic Theory.*

——Freeman, C. and Fabiani, S. (1994), "The Process of Economic Development: Introducing Some Stylized Facts and Theories on Technologies, Firms and Institutions," *Industrial and Corporate Change,* 3/1: 1–46.

——Pavitt, K. and Soete, L. (1990), *The Economies of Technological Change and International Trade* (Brighton: Wheatsheaf/Harvester, and New York: New York University Press).

——Fabiani, S., Aversi, R. and Meacci, M. (1994), "The Dynamics of International Differentiation: A Multi-Country Evolutionary Model," *Industrial and Corporate Change,* 3/1: 225–42.

——Marengo, L., Bassanini, A. and Valente, M. (1994), "Norms as Emergent Properties of Adaptive Learning: The Case of Economic Routines," CCC Working Paper, Center for Research in Management, Graduate Business School, U. C. Berkeley.

——Marsili, O., Orsenigo, L. and Salvatore, R. (1993), "Learning, Market Selection and the Evolution of Industrial Structures," CCC Working Paper, CRM, Grodmate Business School, U. C. Berkeley, 93–3.

——Freeman, C., Nelson, R., Silverberg, G. and Soete, L. (1988), (eds.), *Technical Change and Economic Theory* (London: Pinter, and New York: Columbia University Press).

Eliasson, G. (1986), "Microheterogeneity of Firms and the Stability of Industrial

Growth," in R. Day and G. Eliasson (eds.), *The Dynamics of Market Economies* (Amsterdam and Oxford: North Holland with the Industrial Institute for Economic and Social Research, Stockholm; distributed in USA and Canada by Elsevier Science, New York), 79–104.

Fagerberg, I. (1987), "A Technology Gap Approach to Why Growth Rates Differ," *Research Policy*, 16/2–4 (Ang.), 87–99.

——(1988), "Why Growth Rates Differ," in Dosi *et al.* (eds.), *Technical Change and Economic Theory*.

Foray, D. and Freeman, C. (1992), (eds.), *Technology and the Wealth of Nations* (London: Pinter).

Freeman, C. (1982), *The Economics of Industrial Innovation*, 2nd edn. (London: Pinter).

Gerlach (1993), *Alliance Capitalism* (Berkeley: California University Press).

Granovetter, M. (1995), "Economic Action and Social Structure: A Theory of embeddedness," *American Journal of Sociology*, 19: 481–510.

Grossman, G. M. and Helpman, E. (1991), *Innovation and Growth* (Cambridge, Mass.: MIT Press).

Helpman, E. and Krugman, P. (1989), *Trade Policy and Market Structure* (Cambridge, Mass.: MIT Press).

Hirschman, A. (1977), *The Passion and the Interest* (Princeton, Princeton University Press).

——(1982), "Rival Interpretations of Market Societies: Civilizing, Destructive or Feeble?" *Journal of Economic Literature*, 20/4 (Dec.), 1463–84.

Hounshell, D. A. (1984), *The Development of Manufacturing Technology in the United States* (Baltimore: The Johns Hopkins University Press).

Kogut, B. (1992), "National Organizing Principles of Work and the Erstwhile Dominance of the American Multinational Corporation," *Industrial and Corporate Change*, 1: 285–317.

——(1993) (ed.), *Country Competitiveness* (Oxford: Oxford University Press).

Koike, K. (1988), *Understanding Industrial Relations in Modern Japan* (London: Macmillan).

Kreps, David (1990), *A Course in Microeconomic Theory* (Princeton: Princeton University Press).

Lazonick, W. (1990), *Competitive Advantage on the Shopfloor* (Cambridge, Mass.: Harvard University Press).

——(1993), "Industry Clusters in Global Webs: Organizational Capabilities in the American Economy", *Industrial and Corporate Change*, 2: 1–24.

Levinthal, D. A. (1992), "Surviving Schumpeterian Environments: An Evolutionary Perspective," *Industrial and Corporate Change*, 1: 427–43.

——and March, J. G. (1994), "The Myopia of Learning," *Strategic Management Journal* (forthcoming).

Lorenz, E. (1994), "Organizational Inertia and Competitive Decline: The British Cotton, Shipbuilding and Car Industries, 1945–1975," *Industrial and Corporate Change*, 3/2: 379–404.

March, J. G. (1994), *A Primer on Decision-Making* (New York: Free Press) (forthcoming).

——and Simon, H. (1958), *Organization* (New York: John Wiley).

————(1993), *Organization*, 2nd edn. (Oxford: Blackwell).

Marengo, L. (1992), "Coordination and Organizational Learning in the Firm," *Journal of Evolutionary Economics*, 2/4 (Dec.), 313–26.

Marglin, S. (1974), "What do Bosses Do? The Origins and Functions of Hierarchies in Capitalist Production," *Review of Radical Political Economy*, 6/2 (Summer), 60–112.

Meyer, S., III (1992), *The Five-Dollar Day* (Princeton: Princeton University Press).

Monden, Y. (1983), "Toyota Production System," (Atlanta: Institute of Industrial Engineers,).

Montgomery, D. (1979), *Worker's Control in America* (London: Cambridge University Press).

Nelson, R. (1993), *National Innovation Systems* (Oxford: Oxford University Press).

——(1994), "The Role of Firm Differences in an Evolutionary Theory of Technical Advance," in L. Magnusson (ed.), *Evolutionary and Neo-Schumpeterian Approaches to Economics* (Boston: Kluwer).

——and Winter, S. (1982), *An Evolutionary Theory of Economic Change* (Cambridge, Mass.: The Belknap Press of Harvard University Press).

Nomura, M. (1993), "Farewell to Toyotism," Working Paper no. 17, Cahiers du GERPISA, Paris.

Ohno, T. (1988), *L'Esprit Toyota* (Paris: Ed Masson).

——and Mito (1993), *Présent et avenir du Toyotisme* (Paris: Ed Masson).

Parker, M. and Slaughter, J. (1988), *Choosing Sides: Union and the Team Concept, A Labor Note-Book* (South End Press).

Patel, P. and Pavitt, K. (1994), "Technological Competences in the World's Largest Firms: Characteristics, Constraints and Scope for Managerial Choice," Working Paper, SPRU, University of Sussex.

Pavitt, K. (1984), "Sectoral Patterns of Innovation: Toward a Taxonomy and a Theory," *Research Policy*, 13/6: 343–73.

Piore, M. and Sabel, C. (1984), *The Second Industrial Divide* (New York: Basic Books).

Porter, M. E. (1990), *The Competitive Advantage of Nations* (London: Macmillan).

Postrel, S. and Rumelt, R. P. (1992), "Incentives, Routines and Self-Command," *Industrial and Corporate Change*, 1: 397–425.

Radner, R. (1992), "Hierarchy: The Economics of Managing," *Journal of Economic Literature*, 30: 1382–415.

Romer, P. (1986), "Increasing Returns and Long-Run Growth," *Journal of Political Economy*, 91: 1001–37.

——(1990*a*), "Are Non-Convexities Important for Understanding Growth?" *American Economic Review*, 80: 97–103.

——(1990*b*), "Endogenous Technological Change," *Journal of Political Economy*, 98: 71–102.

Rosenberg, N. (1985), *Inside the Blackbox* (Cambridge: Cambridge University Press).

Sah, R. K. and Stiglitz, J. (1985), "Human Fallibility and Economic Organization," *American Economic Review, Papers and Proceedings*.

Sandberg, Ä. *et al.* (1993), *Technical Change and Co-Determination in Sweden* (Philadelphia: Temple University Press).

Saviotti, P. and Metcalfe, S. (1992), (eds.), *Evolutionary Theories of Economic and Technological Change* (Reading: Harwood Publishers).

Silverberg, G. and Verspagen, B. (1994), "Learning, Innovation and Economic Growth: A Long-run Model of Industrial Dynamics," *Industrial and Corporate Change*, 3/1: 199–224.

——Dosi, G. and Orsenigo, L. (1988), "Innovation, Diversity and Diffusion: A Self-Organization Model," *Economic Journal*, 98/393 (Dec.), 1032–54.

Soete, L. and Verspagen, B. (1993), *Technology and Growth: The Complex Dynamics of Catching Up, Falling Behind and Taking Over*, (MERIT: University of Limburg).

Soskice, D. (1993), "Innovation Strategies of Companies: A Comparative Institutional Explanation of Cross Country Differences," Berlin, WZB, mimeo.

Taddei, D. and Coriat, B. (1993). "Made in France: L'Industrie française dans la compétition mondiale," éd. du Livre de Poche (Paris: Hachette).

Taylor, F. W. (1911), *The Principles of Scientific Management*, Norton Library, (New York: Harper and Row), Ist edn. 1911, paperback edn. 1967.

——(1971), "Testimony Before the Special Comittee, House of Representatives," in F. W. Taylor, *Scientific Management* (New York: Greenwood).

Teece, D. (1993), "The Dynamics of Industrial Capitalism: Perspectives on Alfred Chandler's *Scale and Scope*," *Journal of Economic Literature*, 31: 199–225.

——Pisano, G. and Shunen, A. (1992), "Dynamic Capabilities and Strategies Management," CCC Working Paper, CRM, Graduate Business School, U.C., Berkeley, Calif.

——Rumelt, R., Dosi, G. and Winter, S. (1994), "Understanding Corporate Coherence: Theory and Evidence," *Journal of Economic Behavior and Organization*, 23/1 (Jan.), 1–30.

Thomson, R. (1992), (ed.), *Learning and Technological Change* (London: Macmillan).

Williamson, O. (1985a), *Markets and Hierarchies* (New York: Free Press).

——(1985b), *The Economic Institutions of Capitalism* (New York: Free Press).

Winter, S. (1981), "An Essay on the Theory of Production," in S. Hymans (ed.), *The Economy and the World Around it* (Ann Arbor: University of Michigan Press).

——(1987), "Knowledge and Competences as Strategic Assets," In D. Teece (ed.), *The Competitive Challenge* (Cambridge, Mass.: Ballinger).

Womack, J., Jones, D. and Roos, D. (1991), *The Machine that Changed the World* (Cambridge, Mass.: MIT Press).

Zysman, J. (1994), "How Institutions Create Historically Rooted Trajectories of Growth," *Industrial and Corporate Change*, 3/1: 243–83.

PART III

EVOLUTIONARY INTERPRETATIONS OF ECONOMIC CHANGE

[11]

J Evol Econ (1994) 4:153-172

——Journal of——
Evolutionary
Economics
© Springer-Verlag 1994

An introduction to evolutionary theories in economics*

Giovanni Dosi[1] and Richard R. Nelson[2]

[1] Department of Economics, University of Rome "La Sapienza" and Visiting Scholar, Center for Research in Management, University of California, Berkeley, California, USA
[2] Columbia University and NBER, Stanford, California, USA

Abstract. This paper presents the basic ideas and methodologies of a set of contemporary contributions which are grouped under the general heading of "evolutionary economics". Some achievements – especially with regard to the analysis of technological change and economic dynamics – are illustrated, some unresolved issues are discussed and a few promising topics of research are flagged.

Key words: Evolutionary economics – Technological change – Economic change

JEL-classification: O0-O3-B4

1. Introduction

There are signs that evolutionary analysis and models may be making a comeback in economics. Just over the last decade, the book by Nelson and Winter (1982) has been followed by several other works also exploring evolutionary theory in economics (among others, Dosi et al. (1988), Saviotti and Metcalfe (1991), Anderson, Arrow and Pines (1989), Day and Eliasson (1986), Winter (1984) and (1987), Witt (1992), DeBresson (1988), Langlois and Everett (1992), Metcalfe (1992), Stiglitz (1992). This new *Journal of Evolutionary Economics* has been founded and several other new ones have advertised their interest in evolutionary analyses. In fact, evolutionary arguments are not at all new in economics. They go back at least to Malthus[1] and Marx and appear also among economists who have otherwise

---

* This article draws on a chapter prepared for the book Market and Organization: The Competitive Firm and its Environment, edited within an EEC/Tempus Programme by LATAPSES, Nice, France, and Iside, Rome.
[1] For a recent reappraisal of Malthus as an "evolutionary economist", cf. von Tunzelmann (1991).
Correspondence to: G. Dosi, Università degli Studi di Roma, Dipartimento di Science Economiche, Via Nomentana 41, I-00161 Roma, Italy

contributed to equilibrium theories: for example one often cites Alfred Marshall on "the Mecca of economics [lying] in economic biology rather than economic mechanics" (Marshall 1948, p. xiv); and also the "as... if" argument by Milton Friedman (1953) can be considered the most rudimentary use of an evolutionary point of view in order to justify the assumptions of equilibrium and rationality. In addition, of course scholars like Veblen, von Hayek and, even more so, Schumpeter, have anticipated many of the ideas that contemporary evolutionary economists are struggling with.[2]

However, the wave of current evolutionary theorizing is probably fostered by several convergent factors. There is certainly a growing recognition of the difficulties that equilibrium theories which presume perfectly rational agents face in interpreting wide arrays of economic phenomena – ranging from the generation of technological change all the way to the diversity of long-term patterns of growth. But, of course, we know from the history of science that anomalies and falsifications alone are not sufficient to spur alternative theories. In addition, a rich empirical literature, concerning the nature of the processes of innovation and the institutions supporting them, to a good extent inspired by evolutionary ideas, has shown that an evolutionary theoretical perspective can provide useful heuristics for applied research. Not only that: the empirical work has suggested fruitful inductive generalizations and taxonomies from which evolutionary theories can draw behavioral assumptions and "stylized facts."[3] Finally, the development of quite general formal machineries able to account for the properties of dynamical systems displaying various forms of non-linearities increasingly allows rigorous analytical treatments of evolutionary processes.[4] This, together with the possibility of computer implementations of formal *gedankenexperiment* concerning diverse "artificial economies" (Lane 1993a, b), holds the promise of establishing also formally sound bases for evolutionary analyses of economic change.

2. Evolutionary theory: principle characteristics and applications to the social domain

In order to present an evolutionary view of economics, it is obvious that we have to explain what an evolutionary theory is and work out general concepts and variables. For the purpose of this special issue let us first mention that we use the term "evolutionary" to define a class of theories, or models, or arguments, that have the following characteristics.[5] First, their purpose is to explain the movement of something over time, or to explain why that something is what it is at a moment in time in terms of how it got there; that is, the analysis is expressly dynamic. Second, the explanation involves both random elements which generate or renew some variation in the variables in question, and mechanisms that systematically winnow on extant variation. Evolutionary models in the social domain involve some

---

[2] For discussions of the role of evolutionary ideas in the history of economic thought, see Hodgson (1993) and Clark and Juma (1988).
[3] On the economics of innovation, cf. Freeman (1982) and Dosi (1988).
[4] More detailed surveys and discussions of economic applications are in Silverberg (1988) and Dosi and Kaniovski (1994). For a general appraisal, Nicolis and Prigogine (1989), and for economic applications, Rosser (1991).
[5] For a thorough discussion of this point we refer to Nelson and Winter (1982) and Dosi et al. (1988).

processes of imperfect (mistake-ridden) *learning and discovery*, on the one hand, and some *selection mechanism*, on the other. With respect to the latter an evolutionary theory includes a specification of the determinants of some equivalent of a notion of fitness – implying the identification of a unit of selection and certain mechanisms through which selection operates. Moreover, in analogy with evolutionary biology[6] one is able to identify four more concrete principal building blocks of an evolutionary theory: (i) a fundamental unit of selection (the genes); (ii) a mechanism linking the genotypic level with the entities (the phenotypes) which actually undergo environmental selection; (iii) some processes of interaction, yielding the selection dynamics; and, finally, (iv) some mechanisms generating variations in the population of genotypes and, through that, among phenotypes.

It is quite straightforward that one cannot construct a satisfactory theory of economic evolution simply by way of analogy with the biological model. Still, a reference to these four major building blocks of the biological model might help in illustrating the specificities of evolution in the social domain.

2.1 Units of selection

First, consider the nature of the fundamental unit of selection. In a very intuitive fashion, one may spot quite a few potential candidates to be loose equivalents of the genes in biological theory. For example, technologies, policies, behavioral patterns, cultural traits are obviously influential in determining what the agents embodying them – either individuals or organizations – do. (The "agents" here should impressionistically map into the phenotypic level). And technologies, cultural traits, etc. are also something that can be modified, and improved, from generation to generation, and which has its own rules of transmission. In fact, several scholars have proposed arguments of an evolutionary type in the domains of culture, law, institutional history, science and, of course, economics (for a critical appraisal, see Nelson 1993). We do not have any problem with the attribution of the role of "fundamental unit" to different entities according to the objects under consideration. For example, when one talks about the "ecology of the mind" one refers to the changes of some underlying cognitive structures occurring along the history of interactions with other human beings and the environment of artifacts. Here the "primitives" which the evolutionary process is supposed to structure, modify and select are not genes but plausibly mental categories, representations, rules. In domains nearer to our concerns here, evolutionary processes have often been represented as dynamics in some technology-space and, less often, a space of behaviors or organizational forms (we shall come back to some examples later on). But in all these instances of applications of an evolutionary perspective to social change, a crucial issue – in our view, not yet sufficiently explored – concerns the relationship between the level of the "primitives" (so to speak, the genotypic level) and the behaviors of the units which embody them and upon which selection is supposed to operate. The example of "technological evolution," which we shall consider at some detail, is a good illustration of this point.

It does not always happen that one can say that the economy or the society directly "select" among competing technologies (hence also the models based on this premise should be considered as a first approximation to more complex

---

[6] Note, here and throughout, that, while using sometimes biological analogies for illustrative convenience, we are not at all claiming any precise isomorphism between biological and economic theories of evolution.

dynamics). Sometimes, societies do directly select on technologies: for example, in many medical technologies it occurs through professional judgments based on the peer review system; somewhat similarly, procurement agencies in military technologies perform as direct selectors among alternative technological systems. However, quite often alternative technologies are incorporated within organizations, typically firms – whose relative competitiveness (i.e., "fitness") is mediated through their behavioral patterns – e.g., their decision rules concerning investment, R&D, pricing, scrapping, diversification, etc.[7] Moreover, one typically observes a multiplicity of selection environments affecting the probability of growth and survival of each organization – first, of all, the product-markets and the market for finance. Indeed, it happens in biology and even more so in social dynamics that the objects of selection are not single elementary traits but structures of much higher dimensions in which they are nested. So, for example, markets choose relatively complex products or technological systems, and not individual elements of technological knowledge; and penalize or reward whole organizations and not specific behaviors. Therefore, assuming some underlying space of technology and organizational traits as the appropriate "primitive" dimensions of evolution, one still needs some theory of organizational development in order to relate "evolution" and "selection." This is also a major area of complementarity between evolutionary theories and business economics. Notions like those of "organizational routines" and "competencies" begin to forge that link, but, certainly, an item high on the research agenda is the emergence and evolution of routines themselves.[8]

2.2 Mechanisms and criteria of selection

Another obvious building block of evolutionary theories concerns the mechanisms and criteria of selection. It has already been mentioned that "fitness" is likely to be judged on different and possibly conflicting criteria. For example, firms might be rationed to different degrees on the financial markets according to their cash-flow, or their accounting profits, or the expectations that investors hold about future profits; and in the product markets, the opportunities of growth and survival may be determined on the grounds of the relative quality of their products, their prices, after-sale servicing, delivery delays, marketing networks, etc.[9] This multidimensionality of selection criteria clearly demands that evolutionary models of e.g., technological or economic change specify the interactive mechanisms through which selection occurs.

Selection in the social arena and its relationship with some notion of "fitness" immediately confronts the question of the endogeneity of the selection criteria themselves. It has been mentioned earlier that also in natural sciences it is the general case that what is selected – in favor or against – might be determined in

[7] Evolutionary models such as Nelson and Winter (1982), Silverberg et al. (1988), Chiaromonte and Dosi (1991), Metcalfe (1992), all illustrate this complementarity of technological and behavioral features in determining competitiveness, and also, admittedly, the rudimentary nature of some behavioral assumptions.

[8] Some preliminary ideas and models are in Marengo (1992), Dosi and Marengo (1993), Dosi et al. (1993a).

[9] Admittedly, most evolutionary models developed so far in economics are based on relatively simple selection criteria, e.g., profits (Nelson and Winter 1982) or prices and delivery details (Silverberg, Dosi and Orsenigo 1988). However, they should be understood as first approximations to more complex selection dynamics.

some complicated and nonlinear ways by the distribution of actual populations present at a point in time and by their history. However, one might still hold that the selection criteria – that is, the variables ultimately affecting probabilities of survival – remain relatively invariant: for example, the rates of reproduction, or the efficiency in accessing food. On the contrary, this might not be so in many economic and social circumstances.

2.3 Adaptation and variation

The last fundamental building block of evolutionary theories concerns the processes by which agents adapt, learn and at the same time novelties are always produced in the system. We shall argue that, at this level, a natural ingredient is a representation of decisions and actions – of individuals and organizations – which departs in most respects from "rational" neoclassical models. Our basic hypothesis is that agents follow various forms of *rule-guided* behaviors which are *context-specific* and, to some extent, *event-independent* (in the sense that actions might be invariant to fine changes in the information regarding the environment). On the other hand, agents are always capable of experimenting and discovering new rules and, thus, they continue to introduce behavioral novelties into the system. (More in Nelson and Winter 1982, Dosi and Egidi 1991, March and Simon 1993). In order to illustrate these points, it is useful to compare evolutionary and neoclassical behavioral assumptions.

The central presumption in neoclassical theory is that the observed configuration of economic variables can be explained as the result of rational actors – individuals, households, firms, other formal organizations – having made choices that maximize their utility, given the constraints they face, and that they have made no systematic mistakes about that. The question of how these optimal decisions came to be is not a basic part of the theory. Sometimes the theory is rationalized in terms of the actors actually having correctly thought through the decision context. Sometimes the rationalization is that the optimal response has been learned or has evolved rather than having been in some sense precalculated, but in any case can be understood "as if" the actor had actually calculated.

Uncertainty and unfortunate results (from the point of view of the actor) that come about because of bad luck of the draw can be admitted under this theory, under either interpretation. The theory also can handle actor errors that occur because the actor has only limited information about certain key parameters which determine the outcomes of making various decisions, and in effect bets wrong regarding these parameters. However, systematic mistakes associated with ignorance, or wrong headed understanding, of the basic features of the situation are not admitted. The theory "works" by presuming the actors have a basically correct understanding of their actual choices and their consequences, as the theorist models that choice context. It is not a theory that tries to get "inside the actor's head," as does, for example, psychiatric theory. Put another way, the rationality assumed by the theory is objective not subjective.

An associated notion is that of equilibrium. In most economic analyses there are a number of actors. Each is assumed to optimize, and the optimization decisions are presumed to be consistent with each other, in that each actor's action is optimizing in the sense above, given the other actor's optimizing actions.

This basic mode of explaining behavior, including the making of predictions about how various possible developments might change behavior, has been employed regarding a vast range of human and organizational action, from analyses of the effects of the oil price shocks of the 1970s, to analyses of the effects of the presence of the death penalty upon crime.

There are several different (but not inconsistent) kinds of reasons why evolutionary theorists have backed away from rational choice theory, and adopted a quite different alternative. First, it can be argued that while rational choice theory provides useful insights into certain kinds of situations and phenomena, it sheds only limited light on others. An important motivation for evolutionary theorizing about, for example, technological advance is that most authors in this field believe that the canons of rational choice theory provide only limited guidance for study of that subject. Second, in many cases models possess multiple equilibria. In each, one can specify the optimizing choice, but behavior and achievement differ greatly across the possible equilibria. A key question then is why the particular equilibrium turned out to be the operative one, and one way of trying to answer this question is to appeal to evolutionary arguments. Third, in any case rational choice theory provides an explanation for behavior that takes the actor's objectives and constraints as given. One can argue that an explanation that considers how social values and institutions have evolved and affect the choices presently available to actors may provide a deeper and more illuminating understanding of behavior than a rational choice explanation alone, even if the latter can explain at one level.

Let us first consider the issue of the limits of the plausible domain of rational choice theory. It is important to recognize, precisely because it is usually repressed, that most economists understand very well how dubious, in any complex context, is the rationale for rational choice theory that presumes the "actors have correctly thought it all through." Beneath the surface faith that actions "optimize" is an understanding that actors are only "boundedly rational," to use Herbert Simon's term (1986). The other rationalization – that the actors have somehow eliminated behavior that was not up to standard – is the argument most economists really believe. (For a good discussion of this point see Winter 1986).

But when put this way, rational choice theory would seem applicable to contexts to which the actors can be presumed familiar, and evolutionary theoretic arguments can be understood as an attempt to deal with situations where this presumption does not seem applicable. In particular, evolutionary theory can be argued to be needed for analyses of behavior in contexts that involve significant elements of novelty, so that it cannot be presumed that good responses already have been learned, but rather that they are still to be learned.

More generally, evolutionary theory can be viewed as a theory about how society, or the economy, learn: in very special cases learning leads to the convergence to some repertoires of "optimal behaviors"; normally it entails more or less temporary, and highly suboptimal, adaptation to what are perceived to be the prevailing environmental constraints and opportunities, and also a lot of systematic errors, trials, and discoveries.

This line of argument would appear to preserve for neoclassical theory the analysis of decision making in situations that are relatively stable and actions repetitive. However, if one bases rational choice theory on accumulated learning, there are apparent limitations to the explanatory power of the theory even in these cases. In particular, learning processes may be very path dependent. Where they end up may depend to a considerable degree on how they got there. While in the steady state actual behavior may be locally optimal, there might be other behavior patterns that would be locally optimal too, some of these in fact much better from the actor's point of view than the actual behavior. Thus a "rational choice" explanation is, at best, incomplete, because it does not explain how the particular local context which frames choices came to be the point of rest. As we shall see, this point of view is a major motivation for evolutionary modeling of "path dependent" dynamic processes.

What about the argument that competition will force firms either to learn the best way of doing things or go out of business? Cannot one argue that, if competitive forces are very strong, firms that are not as efficient as the best firms may be forced out of business? Perhaps one can. But note that the standard here is defined by the most efficient existing firms, not the efficiency that is theoretically possible. And that benchmark level of efficiency may be determined by the actual learning processes that are operative and how far they have proceeded. Thus analyses that do not deal explicitly with learning paths may provide, at best, a quite limited analysis of prevailing equilibrium.

In addition, in many industries there are strong reasons to doubt that selection pressures are strong enough to drive out all firms that are not as efficient as the leader. Empirical studies show that the distribution of firms in an industry at any time often contains very considerable diversity of productivity and profitability.

Further, many of the actors in the economy are not firms. There are universities, legal systems, labor institutions, etc. And these generally are not subject to sharp selection pressures, at least not of a "market" variety.

From a similar but slightly different angle, the neoclassical way of explaining behavior and action can be faulted not so much for exaggerating the power of human and organizational intelligence – as argued above most economists believe the theoretical case for "rational choice" is experiential learning not calculating capabilities – but not for recognizing the extent to which learned behaviors are guided and constrained by socially held and enforced values, norms, beliefs, customs, and generally accepted practices. This argument joins with the one above in proposing that to understand behavior one must come to grips with the forces that have molded it, and in rejecting that such analysis can be short cut by a simple argument that, however learning happened, the ultimate result can be predicted and explained as optimizing behavior.

Conversely, evolutionary theories in economics comfortably match those analyses from social psychology, sociology, organization theory, suggesting the general occurrence of various rule-guided behaviors, often taking the form of relatively invariant *routines* (Nelson and Winter 1982), whose origin is shaped by the learning history of the agents, their pre-existing knowledge and, most likely, also their value systems and their prejudices.[10] Precisely because there is nothing which guarantees, in general, the optimality of these routines, notional opportunities for the discovery of "better" ones are always present. Hence, also the permanent scope for search and novelty (i.e., in the biological analogy, "mutations"). Putting it another way, the behavioral foundations of evolutionary theories rest on learning processes involving *imperfect adaption and mistake-ridden discoveries*. This applies equally to the domains of technologies, behaviors and organizational setups.

With these considerations in mind on the basic "building blocks" of evolutionary theories, let us turn to some applications to technological and economic dynamics.

---

[10] On these points, see also Winter (1986) and (1987), Dosi and Egidi (1991), Dosi and Marengo (1993).

3. Technological and economic change: some examples of evolutionary dynamics

3.1 Technical and organizational change

A number of analysts have proposed that technology evolve. The analyses of Freeman (1982), Rosenberg (1976, 1982), Basalla (1988), Mokyr (1990), Nelson and Winter (1977), Dosi (1982, 1984) and Vincenti (1990) are strikingly similar in many respects. (A survey is in Dosi 1988). As an illustration let us consider the discussion of Vincenti.

In Vincenti's theory, the community of technologists at any time faces a number of problems, challenges, and opportunities. He draws most of his examples from aircraft technology. Thus, in the late 1920s and early 1930s, aircraft designers knew well that the standard pattern of hooking wheels to fuselage or wings could be improved upon, given the higher speeds planes were now capable of, with the new body and wing designs and more powerful engines that had come into existence. They were aware of several different possibilities for incorporating wheels into a more streamlined design. Vincenti argues that trials of these different alternatives were somewhat blind. It turned out that having the wheel be retractable solved the problem better than did the other alternatives explored at that time. Thus, search and learning lead to what *ex-post* may be considered as differential "fitness". The latter here is defined in terms of solving particular technological problems better.

But, identification of this criterion also pushes the analytical problem back a stage. What determines whether one solution is better than another? At times, Vincenti writes as if the criterion were innate in the technological problem, or determined by consensus of a technological community who are cooperatively involved in advancing the art.

However, Vincenti also recognizes, explicitly, that the aircraft designers are largely employed in a number of competing aircraft companies, where profitability may be affected by the relative quality and cost of the aircraft designs they are employing, comparing with those employed by their competitors. But then what is better or worse in a problem solution is determined at least partially by the "market," the properties of an aircraft customers are willing to pay for, the costs associated with different designs solutions, the strategies of the suppliers, the changes in the requirements of the buyers, etc.[11]

As already mentioned in the previous section, the link between evolution in the space of technological characteristics and market dynamics rests to a great extent on the organizational and behavioral traits of firms, which in much of evolutionary literature is approximated with *routines*. More specifically, Nelson and Winter (1982) distinguish between three different kinds of routines.

First, there are those that might be called "standard operating procedures," those that determine and define how and how much a firm produces under various circumstances, given its capital stock and other constraints on its actions that are fixed in the short run. Second, there are routines that determine the investment behavior of the firm, and more generally the behaviors which affect its growth or decline (measured in terms of its capital stock) as a function of its profits, and perhaps other variables. Third, the deliberative processes of the firm, those that

---

[11] This co-evolutionary argument regarding technologies and organizations is prominently illustrated in the work by Alfred Chandler (1962, 1990). A reappraisal of Chandler's contribution in the light of contemporary theories of the firm' is in Teece (1993).

involve searching for better ways of doing things, also are viewed as guided by routines.

The concept of a technological paradigm (Dosi 1982, 1988; Nelson and Winter 1977, 1982) attempts to capture both the nature of the technological knowledge upon which innovative activities draw and the organizational procedures for the search and exploitation of the innovations. First, it refers to the set of understandings about particular technologies that are shared by firms and engineering communities about its present and innate limitations. Second, and relatedly, it embodies the prevailing views and heuristics on "how to make things better." And, third, it is often associated with shared ideas of "artifacts" which are there to be improved in their performances and made cheaper in their production.

We have used the term *technological trajectory* to refer to the path of improvement taken by that technology, given technologists' perceptions of opportunities, and the market and other evaluation mechanisms that determined what kinds of improvements would be profitable. (Sahal 1981 employs analogous concepts.) Note also that the fundamental dimensions of the trajectory in the appropriate technology space are analogous to the "fitness criteria" discussed earlier. By the *technological regime* we mean the complex of firms, professional disciplines and societies, university training and research programs, and legal and regulatory structures that support and constrain development within a regime and along particular trajectories.

3.2 Evolutionary models of growth fuelled by technical advance

Let us now consider a set of models of economic growth in which technical advance is the driving force, and within which technologies and industrial structures co-evolve. The outcomes of this processes are aggregate phenomena such as the growth of labor productivity and per capita incomes, relatively regular patterns of innovation diffusion, persistent fluctuations in the rates of income growth, a secular increase in capital intensities, and other "stylized facts" which traditionally pertain to the economics of growth and development (no single evolutionary model is able alone to account for all these regularities at the same time, but the degree of consistency between the different models focussing on subsets of them is quite remarkable).

Virtually all serious scholars of technical advance have stressed the uncertainty, the differences of opinion among experts, the surprises that mark the process. Mechanical analogies involving moving competitive equilibria in which the actors always behave "as if" the scene were familiar to them seem quite inappropriate. Most scholars agree that the process must be understood as an evolutionary one, in the sense sketched earlier.

The problem addressed by the authors considered in this section has been to devise a theory of growth capable of explaining the observed macroeconomic patterns, but on the basis of an evolutionary theory of technical change rather than one that presumes continuing neoclassical equilibrium.

It would seem inevitable that, in any such theory, firms would be key actors, both in the making of the investments needed to develop new technologies and bring them into practice, and in the use of technologies to produce goods and services. Indeed it is not hard to tell a quite compelling story about economic growth based on firms who compete with each other largely through the technologies they introduce and employ. Joseph Schumpeter laid out that analysis over fifty years ago, and modern analyses largely build upon his conjectures.

Let us concentrate on the first formalized evolutionary model of growth, microfounded into an explicit process of search and competition among heterogeneous actors (Nelson and Winter 1974 and the developments in 1982).

The central actors in this model are business firms. Firms are, from one point of view, the entities that are more or less "fit," in this case more or less profitable. But, from another point of view, firms can be regarded as merely the carriers of "technologies," in the form of particular practices or capabilities that determine "what they do" and "how productively" in particular circumstances. While in principle, within the model, search behaviors could be focussed on any one of the firms' prevailing routines described earlier, – its technologies, or other standard operating procedures, its investment rules, or even its prevailing search procedures – in practice, in all of the Nelson–Winter models, search is assumed to uncover new production techniques or to improve prevailing ones. It is therefore convenient to call such search R&D. Other authors of similar models have invoked the term "learning" to describe analogous improvement processes.

Firms search processes both provide the source of differential fitness – firms whose R&D turn up more profitable processes of production or products will grow relative to their competitors – and also tend to bind them together as a community. In the models in question a firm's R&D partly is focussed on innovating, coming up with something better than what its competitors are doing. But its R&D activities also attend to what its competitors are doing, and profitable innovations are, with a lag, imitated by other firms in the industry.

The firm, or rather the collection of firms in the industry, perhaps involving new firms coming into the industry and old ones exiting, is viewed as operating within an exogenously determined environment. The profitability of any firm is determined by what it is doing, and what its competitors do. Generally the environment can be interpreted as a "market," or set of markets.

The logic of the model defines a dynamic stochastic system. It can be modeled as a complex Markov process. A standard iteration can be described as follows. At the existing moment of time all firms can be characterized by their capital stocks and prevailing routines. Decision rules keyed to market conditions look to those conditions' "last period." Inputs employed and outputs produced by all firms then are determined. The market then determines prices. Given the technology and other routines used by each firm, each firm's profitability then is determined, and the investment rule then determines how much each firm expands or contracts. Search routines focus on one or another aspect of the firm's behavior and capabilities, and (stochastically) come up with proposed modifications which may or may not be adopted. The system is now ready for the next period's iteration.

The model described above can be evaluated on a number of different counts. One is whether the view of behavior it contains, in abstract form, is appealing given the context it purports to analyse. The individuals and organizations in the model act, as humans do in the models of most other social disciplines except economics, on the basis of habits or customs or beliefs; in the Nelson–Winter model all these define routines. There certainly is no presumption, as there is in neoclassical theory, that what they do is "optimal" in any way, save that metaphorically the actors do the best they know how to do. Some scholars, while recognizing a need to pull away from neoclassical canons, might argue that the model sees humans and human organizations as far less "rational" than they are. Indeed, it is quite possible to build more foresight into the actors of an evolutionary theory (see also below). Of course, if one wants a model in which it is presumed that the actors fully understand the context, one might as well use a rational choice model. But then the formidable challenge facing the "rational" models, let alone a supposedly "rational" actors is what it means to "fully understand" the context, whenever the latter depends in some complex, nonlinear ways on the distribution of microdecisions, and on chance, and is always full of surprises.

The model can be judged by the appeal of the theory of technical progress built into it. The view is certainly "evolutionary," and in that regard squares well with the accounts given by scholars of technical advance like Vincenti. However, it contains two "economist" kinds of presumptions. One is that profitability determines the "fitness" of a technology. The other is the central role played by "firms". In any case, the central purpose of this type of models is to explain economic growth at a macroeconomic level. Thus, a fundamental question about them is this: Can they generate, hence in a sense explain, e.g., the rising output per worker, growing capital intensity, rising real wages, and a relatively constant rate of return on capital, that have been the standard pattern in advanced industrial nations? The answer is that they can, and in ways that make analytic sense.

Within Nelson–Winter models a successful technological innovation generates profits for the firm making it, and leads to capital formation and growth of the firm. Firm growth generally is sufficient to outweigh any decline in employment per unit of output associated with productivity growth, and hence results in an increase in the demand for labor, which pulls up the real wage rate. This latter consequence means that capital using but labor saving innovations now become more profitable, and when by chance they appear as a result of a "search," they will be adopted, thus pulling up the level of capital intensity in the economy. At the same time that labor productivity, real wages, and capital intensity are rising, the same mechanisms hold down the rate of return on capital. If the profit rate rises, say because of the creation of especially productive new technology, the high profits will induce an investment boom, which will pull up wages, and drive capital returns back down.

At the same time that the model generates "macro" time series that resemble the actual data, beneath the aggregate at any time there is considerable variation among firms in the technologies they are using, their productivity, and their profitability. Within this simple model (which represses differences in other aspects of firm capabilities and behavior), the technologies employed by firms uniquely determine their relative performance. And within this model more productive and profitable techniques tend to replace less productive ones, through two mechanisms. Firms using more profitable technologies grow. And more profitable technologies tend to be imitated and adopted by firms who had been using less profitable ones.

Soete and Turner (1984), Metcalfe (1988, 1992), Silverberg (1987) and Metcalfe and Gibbons (1989) have developed sophisticated variants on this theme. These authors repress the stochastic element in the introduction of new technologies that was prominent in the model described above and, in effect, work with a given set of technologies. However, within these models each of the individual technologies may be improving over time, possibly at different rates. At the same time, firms are tending to allocate their investment portfolios more heavily towards the more profitable technologies than towards the less. As a result, productivity in the industry as a whole, and measured aggregated "technical advance," is the consequence of two different kinds of forces. One is the improvement of the individual technologies. The other is the expansion of use of the more productive technologies relative to the less productive ones.

Both groups of authors point out that the latter phenomenon is likely to be a more potent source of productivity growth when there is large variation in the productivity across technologies in wide use, than when the best technology already dominates in use. Thus the aggregate growth performance of the economy is strongly related to the prevailing sources of variation across technologies and their levels of diffusion, beneath the aggregate.

The model of Silverberg et al. (1988) develops the basic notions of evolutionary theory in another direction. In that model there are only two technologies. One is potentially better than the other, but that potential will not be achieved unless effort is put into improving current practice. Rather than incorporating a separate "search" activity, in Silverberg et al. a firm improves its prevailing procedures (technologies) through learning associated with operation. What a firm learns is reflected in its increased productivity in using that technology, but some of the learning "leaks out" and enables others using that technology to improve their productivity for free, as it were.

In contrast with Nelson–Winter models where firms do not "look forward" to anticipate future developments, in the model considered here firms, or at least some of them, recognize that the technology that initially is behind in productivity is potentially the better technology, and also that they can gain advantage over their competitors if they invest in using and learning with it. Also in contrast with Nelson–Winter models, a firm may employ some of both technologies, and hence may use some of its profits from using the prevailing best technology to invest in experience with presently inferior technology that is potentially the best. If no firms does this, then of course the potential of the potentially better technology never will be realized.

An early "innovator" may come out a winner, if it learns rapidly, and little of its learning "spills out," or its competitors are sluggish in getting into the new technology themselves. On the other hand, it may come out a loser, if its learning is slow and hence the cost of operating the new technology remains high, or most of its learning "spills out" and its competitors adopt it in a timely manner, taking advantage for free of the spillover.[12]

3.3 Evolution of industries

A joint account of the analyses focussed on the evolution of technology and those focussed on the history of business organizations also appear to suggest that some "typical" evolutionary patterns often appear at industry level (this does not rule out significant exceptions, and one still does not know enough on when and why other dynamics emerge).[13]

The basic model of the evolution of firms and industrial structures (what is sometimes called the "industry life cycle") goes this way. In the early stages of an industry – say automobiles – firms tend to be small, and entry relatively easy, reflecting the diversity of technologies being employed, and their rapid change. However, as a "dominant design" (or a technological "paradigm") emerges, barriers to entry begin to rise as an established scale and capital needed for competitive

---

[12] Another difference between Nelson–Winter and Silverberg–Dosi–Orsenigo models is that in the latter who "wins" and who "loses" is determined by a selection process captured by a replicator-type dynamics where market shares change according to the relative values of a vector of characteristics, synthetically called "competitiveness."

[13] Contributions from the field of "organizational ecology" also tackle similar life-cycle phenomena, albeit from a different angle; see Hannan and Freeman (1989) and Hannan and Carroll (1991).

production grows. Also, with the basic technological knowledge, learning becomes cumulative, and incumbent firms are advantaged relative to potential entrants for that reason as well. After a shakeout, industry structure settles down to a collection of established largish firms.

Part of this analysis stems from the work by Abernathy and Utterback (1975), done nearly two decades ago, who argued that with basic product configuration stabilized, R & D tends to shift towards improving production processes. When the market is divided up among a large variety of variants, and new products are appearing all the time, product specific process R & D is not particularly profitable. But with the emergence of a dominant design, the profits from developing better ways of producing it can be considerable.

Opportunities for operating on a large scale raise the profitability of exploiting latent economies of scale. Generally, large scale production is capital intensive, and thus capital intensity rises for this reason, as well as because with the stabilization of product design it is profitable to try to devise ways to mechanize production. Since highly mechanized production is profitable only at large scale of output, growth of mechanization and larger scale production go together for this reason as well.

Abernathy and Utterback argue that these dynamics cause major changes in the organization of firms and of the industry after a dominant design is established, and as the technology matures. Mueller and Tilton (1969) made the same argument about the evolution of industry structure some years before Abernathy and Utterback, based on a somewhat less detailed theory of the evolution of technology. Over the last decade articles by Gort and Klepper (1982), Klepper and Grady (1990), Utterback and Suarez (1992), and a recent analytic survey piece by Klepper (1992), have greatly enriched the analysis. However, it still remains to be seen how general are these "life cycles" patterns of industrial evolution. There are two major unsettled issues here, both linked with the characteristics of the learning processes underlying the "competitive advantages" (or disadvantages) of firms.

A first issue concerns the influence that particular "paradigms" and "regimes," as defined earlier, exert on industrial dynamics. The findings in Pavitt (1984) on the size and principal activities of innovating firms, suggest that significant groups of industrial sectors might not conform to the "life cycle" description, due for example to the specificity and tacitness of the knowledge that individual firms embody and to the absence of strong tendencies toward economies of scale (these groups include, for different reasons, machine-tools, scientific instruments, textile and several others). The potential variety in the evolutionary patterns of industries, interpretable on the grounds of different learning and selection regimes is also corroborated by the simulation exercises in Winter (1984) and Dosi et al. (1993). A second major issue concerns the degrees of disruption induced upon industrial structures by discontinuities in the knowledge base and in the "established ways of doing things" (i.e., discontinuities in the technological trajectories of that industry).

While much of the literature on technology and product cycles stops the narrative after a dominant design has emerged and industry structure stabilizes, there is a number of recent theoretical and empirical studies that ask the question, "What happens to a settled industry structure when a new technology comes along that has the promise of being significantly superior to the old?". Thus transistors and later integrated circuit technology ultimately came to replace vacuum tubes and wired-together circuits. At the present time, biotechnology promises a radically new way to create and produce a wide variety of pharmaceuticals, and industrial and agricultural chemicals. The term "competence destroying technical advance" has been coined by Tushman and Anderson (1986) to characterize such new technologies when the skills needed to deal with them are different than the skills and experience that were relevant to the old technologies they threaten to replace.

A considerable body of empirical work now has grown up which persuasively documents that certain new technologies were competence destroying in the above sense. (See, e.g., Tushman and Anderson 1986, and Henderson and Clark 1990). In such instances, the old established firms have had great difficulty in acquiring the new competencies they needed in order to survive in the new regime. New companies built around the new needed competencies tend to come in and grab a significant share of the new market, or firms who have established the needed competencies in other lines of business where they had been appropriate now shift over to the new area to employ their skills there. The extent to which technological discontinuities are associated with *organizational* discontinuities is yet another topic of research in common between evolutionary analyses of industrial change and business economics.

3.4 Chance and structures: path-dependencies and dynamic increasing returns

The discussion above leads naturally to another cluster of analytic and empirical issues coming up in evolutionary theorizing about long run economic change – path dependency, dynamic increasing returns, and their interaction. Path dependencies are built into all of the models considered above, and dynamic increasing returns into some.

Thus, in all of the models, the particular entities that survive in the long run are influenced by events, to a considerable extent random, that happen early in a model's run. To the extent that firms specialize in particular kinds of technology, what technologies survive is influenced similarly by early random events. In some of the models, "dynamic increasing returns" makes path dependency particularly strong. Thus, in Silverberg et al. (1988), the more a firm uses a technology the better it gets at that technology. More, some of the learning "spills over" to benefit other firms using that particular technology. Thus, the more a technology is used, the better it becomes vis-à-vis its competitors.

But while path dependencies and dynamic increasing returns are built into most of the models we already have considered, this was not the center of attention of the authors. Over the past few years, however, a considerable literature in evolutionary economics has grown, focussed on these topics. The works of Arthur (1988, 1989), Arthur et al. (1987) and David (1985, 1992) are particularly interesting, and probably the best known and noted. The simplest versions of these path-dependent models follow a somewhat different analytical strategy from those discussed in the previous section.[14]

There, firms were considered explicitly. They were the "carriers" of technology, and the technology they used affected their "fitness." In the models considered in this section, firms tend to be repressed, and "technologies" per se are the units of analysis. In the former set of models the behavioral description tends to be quite articulated (obviously involving also a few "inductive" generalizations on behavioral

---

[14] Here we refer mainly to differences in the modelling philosophy rather than in the formal instruments utilized – e.g., generalized Polya urns vs. ordinary differential equations, etc.: a discussion of the more technical aspects of different formal machineries is in Silverberg (1988), Rosser (1991) and Dosi and Kaniovski (1994).

rules). The latter set, on the contrary, tends to focus on some general system properties while being rather agnostic on behavioral assumptions (see Foray's chapter in Foray and Freeman 1992). The simplest version of the latter model basically works through the assumption that each time one technology is used, or bought (and others not), the probability that it will be used or bought next time increases (and the other probabilities decrease). Under conditions of unbounded increasing returns it can be shown that one of the technologies ultimately drives out all its competitors with probability one. But the winning technology is (a) ex ante unpredictable, and (b) might not be the "potential best" of those that competed.

Before discussing the various mechanisms that are argued to lie behind dynamic increasing returns, let us highlight why these analytic arguments are not simply interesting, but provocative. Let us consider the relationship between evolutionary success, intrinsic "fitness," and chance (i.e., unpredictable historical events) in the development and diffusion of innovations.

Students of technical advance long have noted that, in the early stages of a technology's history, there usually are a number of competing variants. Thus in the early history of automobiles, some models were powered by gasoline-fuelled internal combustion engines, some by steam engines, some by batteries. As we know, gradually gasoline-fuelled engines came to dominate and the other two possibilities were abandoned. The standard explanation for this, and it is a quite plausible one, is that gasoline engines were the superior mode, at that time, and with experience that was found out. The Silverberg–Dosi–Orsenigo model contains a variant of this mechanism. In their analysis a potentially superior new alternative requires some development – learning – before its latent superiority becomes manifest. It can take time before that development occurs and, with bad luck, it even is possible that it never occurs. However, one could argue, on the grounds of that model, that given sufficient heterogeneity among adopters (and thus also in expectations, initial skills, etc.) the potentially better technology is likely to win out, albeit at the cost of many "microeconomic tragedies" (unfulfilled expectations, mistakes that nonetheless produce system-level externalities, death of firms etc.).

In the Arthur and David models, one can see a different explanation for why the internal combustion engine won out. It need not have been innately superior. All that would have been required was that, because of a run of luck, it became heavily used or bought, and this started a rolling snowball mechanism.

What might be behind an increasing returns rolling snowball? Arthur, David, and other authors suggest several different possibilities.

One of them is that the competing technologies involved are what Nelson and Winter (1982), Dosi (1988) and others have called cumulative technologies. In a cumulative technology, today's technical advances build from and improve upon the technology that was available at the start of the period, and tomorrow's in turn builds on today's. The cumulative effect is like the technology specific learning in the Silverberg et al. model.

Thus, let us return to the history of automobile engine technology. According to the cumulative technology theory, in the early history of automobiles, gasoline engines, steam engines, and electrical engines, all were plausible alternative technologies for powering cars, and it was not clear which of these means would turn out to be superior. Reflecting this uncertainty, different inventors tended to make different bets, some working on internal combustion engines, others on steam engines, still others on electric power. Assume, however, that simply as a matter of chance, a large share of these efforts just happened to focus on one of the variants – the internal combustion engine – and, as a result, over this period there was much more overall improvement in the design of internal combustion engines than in the design of the two alternative power sources. Or, alternatively, assume that while the distribution of inventive efforts were relatively even across the three options, simply as a matter of chance significantly greater advances were made on internal combustion engines than on the other ones.

But then, at the end of the first period, if there were a rough tie before, gasoline powered engines now are better than steam or electric engines. Cars embodying internal combustion engines will sell better. More inventors thinking about where to allocate their efforts now will be deterred from allocating their attention to steam or electric engines because large advances in these need to be achieved before they would become competitive even with existing internal combustion engines. Thus, there are strong incentives for the allocation of inventive efforts to be shifted toward the variant of the technology that has been advancing most rapidly. The process is cumulative. The consequences of increased investment in advancing internal combustion engines, and diminished investment in advancing the other two power forms, are likely to be that the former pulls even further ahead. Relatively shortly, a clear dominant technology has emerged. And all the efforts to advance technology further in this broad area come to be concentrated on improving that particular "paradigm".

There are two other dynamic increasing returns stories that have been put forth. One stresses network externalities or other advantages to consumers or users if what different individuals buy are similar, or compatible, which lends advantage to a variant that just happened to attract a number of customers early. The other stresses systems aspects where a particular product has a specialized complementary product or service, whose development lends that variant special advantages. Telephone and computer networks, in which each user is strongly interested in having other users have compatible products, are commonly employed examples of the first case. Video cassette recorders which run cassettes that need to be specially tailored to their particular design, or computers that require compatible programs, are often used examples of the second. Paul David's story (1985) of the reasons why the seemingly inefficient "QWERTY" typewriter keyboard arrangement has persisted so long as a standard involves both its familiarity to experienced typists and the existence of typewriter training programs that teach QWERTY.

As in the QWERTY story, the factors leading to increasing returns often are intertwined, and also linked with the processes involved in the development of cumulative technologies. Thus, to return to our automobile example, people who learned to drive in their parents' or friends' car powered by an internal combustion engine naturally were attracted to gas powered cars when they themselves came to purchase one, since they knew how they worked. At the same time the ascendancy of automobiles powered by gas burning internal combustion engines made it profitable for petroleum companies to locate gasoline stations at convenient places along highways. It also made it profitable for them to search for more sources of petroleum, and to develop technologies that reduced gasoline production costs. In turn, this increased the attractiveness of gasoline powered cars to car drivers and buyers.

Note that, for those who consider gas engine automobiles, large petroleum companies, and the dependence of a large share of the nation's transportation on petroleum, a complex that spells trouble, the story spun out above indicates that "it did not have to be this way." If the toss of the die early in the history of automobiles had come out another way, we might today have had steam or electric cars. A similar argument recently has been made about the victory of A.C. over D.C. as the "system" for carrying electricity. The story also invites consideration of possibly biased professional judgments and social or political factors as major elements in the shaping of long run economic trends. After all, in these stories all it takes may be just a little push.

On the other hand, other analysts may see the above account as overblown. Steam and battery powered car engines had major limitations then and still do now; gasoline clearly was better. A.C. had major advantages over D.C., and still does. According to this point of view, dynamic increasing returns is an important phenomenon, but it is unlikely that it has greatly influenced which technology won out, in most important cases.

Indeed, the relative importance of unique historical circumstances in determining long-term evolution is likely to remain a lively topic of empirical research and argument over the coming years. This is by no means restricted to technological change. It applies as well to fields like the development of particular institutions, the growth of industries or the dynamics of financial markets.[15]

4. Conclusions

In this paper we have attempted to present some major distinguishing features of evolutionary models in general, and, with more detail, in economics. The examples of applications that we presented are only a small subset of the potential research agenda that one is only beginning to explore both via computer-implemented simulation models and via "reduced form" models that have become increasingly amenable to analytical treatments due to the advance in non-linear dynamics and system theory. And, of course, complementary to the theoretical endeavors there is a rich empirical agenda concerning the identification of the regularities in economic structures and in the process of change which are the natural objects of evolutionary explanations. Particularly promising areas of application of evolutionary models include the nature of learning process; the mechanisms of adaptation, discovery and selection underlying economic growth; the theory of the firm and the dynamics of industrial organization.

Acknowledgments. Support to one of the authors (G.D.) by the Italian National Research Council (CNR) and to both by the International Institute of Applied System Analysis (IIASA, Laxenburg, Austria) is greatfully acknowledged.

References

Abernathy W, Utterback J (1975) A Dynamic Model of Process and Product Innovation. Omega, pp 639–656

Anderson P, Arrow K, Pines D (1989) The Economy as an Evolving Complex System. Addison-Wesley, Redwood City, Calif

---

[15] In these other domains see for example Kuran (1991), Kirman (1991), Dosi and Kaniovski (1994).

Arthur B, Ermoliev Y, Kaniovski Y (1987) Path Dependent Processes and the Emergence of Macrostructure. Eur J Operational Res 30: 294–303

Arthur B (1988) Competing Technologies: An Overview. In: Dosi G, Freeman C, Nelson R, Silverberg G, Soete L (eds) Technical Change and Economic Theory. Frances Pinter, London

Arthur B (1989) Competing Technologies, Increasing Returns, and Lock-In by Historical Events. Econ J 99: 116

Basalla G (1988) The Evolution of Technology. Cambridge University Press, Cambridge, Mass

Chandler A (1962) Strategy and Structure: Chapters in the History of American Industrial Enterprise. Harvard University Press, Cambridge, Mass

Chandler A (1990) Scale and Scope: The Dynamics of Industrial Capitalism. Harvard University Press, Cambridge, Mass

Chiaromonte F, Dosi G (1991) The Microfoundations of Competitiveness and Their Macroeconomic Implications. In: Foray D, Freeman C (eds) (1992). Technology and the Wealth of Nations. Frances Pinter, London

Clark N, Juma C (1988) Evolutionary Theories in Economic Thought. In: Dosi G et al (eds) Technical Change and Economic Theory. Frances Pinter, London

David P (1985) Clio and the Economics of QWERTY. Am Econ Rev Papers Proc 75: 332–337

David P (1992) Heroes, Herds and Hysterisis in Technological Theory: Thomas Edison and the Battle of the Systems' Reconsidered. Industrial Corporate Change 1: 129–180

Day R, Eliasson G (eds) (1986) The Dynamics of Market Economics. North-Holland, Amsterdam

DeBresson C (1988) The Evolutionary Paradigm and the Economics of Technological Change. J Econ Issues: 751–761

Dosi G (1982) Technological Paradigms and Technological Trajectories: A Suggested Interpretation of the Determinants and Directions of Technical Change. Res Policy 11: 147–162

Dosi G (1984) Technical Change and Industrial Transformation. The Theory and an Application to the Semiconductor Industry. MacMillan, London

Dosi G (1988) Sources, Procedures, and Microeconomic Effects of Innovation. J Econ Lit 26: 126–171

Dosi G, Egidi M (1991) Substantive and Procedural Uncertainty: An Exploration of Economic Behaviours in Changing Environments. J Evol Econ 1: 145–168

Dosi G, Kaniovski Y (1994) On "badly" behaved dynamics. Some applications of generalized urn schemes to technological economic change. J Evol Econ 4: 93–123

Dosi G, Marengo L (1993) Toward an Evolutionary Theory of Organizational Competencies. In: England R W (ed) Evolutionary Concepts in Contemporary Economics, University of Michigan Press, Ann Arbor, Mich

Dosi G, Marsili O, Orsenigo L, Salvatore R (1993) Learning, Market Selection and the Evolution of Industrial Structures. Berkeley, Center for Research in Management, CCC Working Paper

Dosi G, Marengo L, Bassanini A, Valente M (1993a) The Evolutionary Emergence of Norms. Rome, Department of Economics, Berkeley, CA. Center for Research in Management, mimeo

Dosi G, Freeman C, Nelson R, Silverberg G, Soete L (1988) Technical Change and Economic Theory. Frances Pinter, London

Foray D, Freeman C (eds) (1992) Technology and the Wealth of Nations. Frances Pinter, London

Freeman C (1982) The Economics of Industrial Innovation 2nd edn. Frances Pinter, London

Friedman M (1953) Essays in Positive Economics. University of Chicago Press, Chicago

Gort M, Klepper S (1982) Time Paths in the Diffusion of Product Innovations. Econ J 92: 630–653

Hannan MT, Carroll GR (1991) The Dynamics of Organizational Populations. Oxford University Press, Oxford

Hannan M, Freeman J (1989) Organizational Ecology. Harvard University Press, Cambridge, Mass

Henderson R, Clark K (1990) Architectural Innovation: The Reconfiguration of Existing Product Technologies and the Failure of Established Firms, Admin Sc Q, pp 9–30

Hodgson G (1993) Economics and Evolution: Bringing Life Back Into Economics. Basil Blackwell, Oxford

Kirman A (1991) Epidemics of Opinion and Speculative Bubbles in Financial Markets. In: Taylor M (ed), Money and Financial Markets. Macmillan, London

Klepper S, Grady E (1990) The Evolution of New Industries and the Determinants of Market Structure. Rand Journal of Economics 21: 27–44

Kuran T (1991) Cognitive Limitations and Preference Evolution. J Inst Theor Econ 143: 241–273

Lane D (1993a) Artificial Worlds and Economics. Part I. J Evol Econ 3: 89–107

Lane D (1993b) Artificial Worlds and Economics, Part II. J Evol Econ 3: 177–197

Langlois R, Everett M (1992) What is Evolutionary Economics. Storrs, University of Connecticut, unpublished paper

March J, Simon H (1993) Organizations, 2nd edn. Basil Blackwell, Oxford

Marengo L (1992) Coordination and Organizational Learning in the Firm, J Evol Econ 2: 313–326

Marshall A (1948) Principles of Economics, 5th edn. Macmillan, London

Metcalfe S (1988) The Diffusion of Innovations: An Interpretative Survey. In: Dosi G et al (eds) Technical Advance and Economic Theory. Frances Pinter, London

Metcalfe S (1992) Variety, Structure and Change: An Evolutionary Perspective on the Competitive Process. Revue d'Economie Industrielle 65: 46–61

Metcalfe S, Gibbons M (1989) Technology, Variety, and Organization. Research on Technological Innovations – Management and Policy, Vol 4. JAI Press, pp 153–193

Mokyr J (1990) The Lever of Riches. Oxford University Press, Oxford

Mueller D, Tilton J (1969) Research and Development as Barriers to Entry. Can J Econ 2: 570–579

Nelson R (1982) The Role of Knowledge in R & D Efficiency, Q J Econ 97: 453–470

Nelson R (1993) Evolutionary Theorizing about Economic Change. NBER, Columbia University, New York, working paper

Nelson R, Winter S (1982) An Evolutionary Theory of Economic Change, Belknap Press, Cambridge

Nelson R, Winter S (1974) Neoclassical Versus Evolutionary Theories of Economic Growth: Critique and Perspective. Econ J, pp 886–905

Nelson R, Winter S (1977) In Search of Useful Theory of Innovation. Res Policy 7: 36–76

Nelson R, Winter S (1977) An Evolutionary Theory of Economic Change. Harvard University Press, Cambridge, Mass

Nicolis G, Prigogine I (1989) Exploring Complexity: An Introduction. Freeman, New York

Pavitt K (1984) Sectoral Patterns of Innovation: Toward a Taxonomy and a Theory. Res Policy 13: 343–375

Rosenberg N (1976) Perspectives on Technology. Cambridge University Press, Cambridge

Rosenberg N (1982) Inside the Black Box: Technology and Economics. Cambridge University Press, Cambridge

Rosser Jr JB (1991) From Catastrophe to Chaos: A General Theory of Economic Discontinuities. Kluwer, Boston Dordrecht

Sahal D (1981) Patterns of Technological Innovation. Addison-Wesley, Reading

Saviotti P, Metcalfe JS (eds) (1991) Evolutionary Theories of Economic and Technological Change. Harwood Academic Publishers, Reading

Silverberg G (1987) Technical Progress, Capital Accumulation and Effective Demand: A Self-Organization Model. In: Batten D, Casti J, Johansson B (eds) Economics Evolution and Structural Adjustment. Springer, Berlin Heidelberg New York

Silverberg G (1988) Modelling Economic Dynamics and Technical Change: Mathematical Approaches to Self-Organizaion and Evolution. In: Dosi G et al (1988) Technical Change and Economic Theory. Frances Pinter, London

Silverberg G, Dosi G, Orsenigo L (1988) Innovation, Diversity, and Diffusion: A Self Organizing Model. Econ J 98: 1032-1054

Simon H (1986) On the Behavioural and Rational Foundations of Economic Dynamics. In: Day R, Eliasson G (eds) The Dynamics of Market Economics. North-Holland, Amsterdam

Soete L, Turner R (1984) Technological Diffusion and the Rate of Technical Change, Econ J 94: 612–623

Stiglitz J (1992) Notes on Evolutionary Economics: Imperfect Capital Markets Organizational Design and Long Run Efficiency. Mimeo, Dept. of Economics, Stanford, Calif

Teece DJ (1993) Perspectives on Alfred Chandler's Scale and Scope. J Econ Lit 31: 199–225

Tunzelmann N von (l991) Malthus as an Evolutionary Economist. J Evol Econ 1: 273–291

Tushman M, Anderson D (1986) Technological Discontinuities and Organizational Environments. Admin Sc Q, pp 439–465

Utterback J, Suarez F (1992) Innovation, Competition, and Market Structure. Research Policy 21: 1–21

Vincenti W (1990) What Do Engineers Know and How Do They Know It? Johns Hopkins Press, Baltimore
Winter S (1984) Schumpeterian Competition under Alternative Technological Regimes. J Econ Behavior Organization 5: 287–320
Winter S (1986) The Research Program of the Behavioral Theory of the Firm: Orthodox Critiques and Evolutionary Perspectives. In: Gilad B, Kaish S (eds) Handbook of Behavioral Economics, vol A. JAI Press, Greenwich, Conn
Winter S (1987) Natural Selection and Evolution, The New Palgrave. Macmillan, London
Witt U (1992) Evolutionary Economics. Edward Elgar, London

[12]

1. The institutional embeddedness of economic change: an appraisal of the 'evolutionary' and 'regulationist' research programmes

Benjamin Coriat and Giovanni Dosi

1. INTRODUCTION

There are at least two complementary ways to present the ideas which follow. One is with reference to some 'grand' questions that have faced social sciences since their inceptions, namely, how do institutions shape the behaviour of individual agents, within and outside the economic arena? And what are institutions in the first place? How do they come about and how do they change? What are the relationships between 'agency' and structure? And also, nearer economic concerns, what is the role of institutions in economic coordination and change?

Another, more modest, way of tackling some of these grand issues is to see how this is done in practice by different research programmes which nonetheless share a common preoccupation with understanding economic change as a historical, institutionally embedded process.

This is what we shall attempt to do in this work, by discussing the links, overlapps, tensions and possible interbreedings between an emerging evolutionary theory of economic dynamics and various strands of institutionalist theories, with particular attention to the regulation approach.

Some definitions of what we mean by those terms and of where we put the boundaries of different theories are in order. We shall introduce these, in a rather telegraphic fashion, in Sections 2–4. In Section 5 we sketch, as an illustration, interpretations of the growth process in general, and, in particular, the case – very familiar to institutionalist macroeconomists – of the so-called 'Fordist' phase of development experienced by Western countries after World War II, and we assess the different 'styles' of explanation of evolutionary and regulation theories, respectively. In turn, these differences in 'style' partly hide different levels of observation – hence, probably, entailing fruitful complementarities – and partly also reveal genuine differences in the choice of explanatory variables and causal relationships. We shall discuss some of these issues with respect to the nature of institutions and behavioural microfoundations in Section 6. Finally, in Section 7 we propose a sort of taxonomy of potentially complementary levels of descriptions and analytical methodologies and, together, we suggest some items that in our view are high on both evolutionist and institutionalist research agendas.

2.   EVOLUTIONARY THEORIES: SOME DEFINITIONS

For the purposes of this work we will restrict our discussion to evolutionary theories of *economic* change. In brief, a sort of 'archetypical' evolutionary model possesses, in our view, the following characteristics (much more detailed discussions of the state-of-the-art are in Hodgson (1993), Dosi and Nelson (1994), Nelson (1995), and Silverberg and Verspagen (1995a))

1.   As Sidney Winter used to summarize it, the methodological imperative is dynamics first! That is, the explanation of why something exists rests intimately on how it became what it is. Or putting it in terms of negative prescriptions: never take as a good 'explanation' either an existence theorem or a purely functionalist claim (entity x exists because it performs function y . . .).
2.   Theories are explicitly microfounded, in the sense that they must involve or at least be consistent with a story of what agents do and why they do it.[1]
3.   Agents have at best an imperfect understanding of the environment they live in, and, even more so, of what the future will deliver. Hence, 'bounded rationality' in a very broad sense is generally assumed.
4.   Imperfect understanding and imperfect, path-dependent learning entails persistent heterogeneity among agents, even when facing identical information and identical notional opportunities.
5.   Agents are always capable of discovering new technologies, new behavioural patterns, and new organizational set-ups. Hence, also, the continuous appearance of various forms of novelty in the system.
6.   Related to the last point, while (imperfect) adaptation and discovery generate variety (possibly in seemingly random fashion), collective interactions within and outside markets perform as selection mechanisms, yielding also differential growth (and possibly also disappearance) of different entities which are, so to speak, 'carriers' of diverse technologies, routines, strategies, etc.
7.   As a result of all this, aggregate phenomena (e.g. regularities in the growth process or in industrial structures, etc.) are 'explained' as emergent properties. They are the collective outcome of far-from-equilibrium

interactions and heterogeneous learning. Finally, they often have a metastable nature, in the sense that while persistent on a time-scale longer than the processes generating them, tend to disappear with probability one.[2]

This is not the place to review the growing number of contributions which share some or all of these seven broad methodological building blocks[3].

Suffice it to mention, first, the flourishing number of formal models and historical interpretations of economic growth as an evolutionary process propelled by technical change which have followed the seminal work of Nelson and Winter (1982): see among others Dosi *et al.* (1988), Day and Eliasson (1986), Silverberg and Verspagen (1994), Conlisk (1989), Chiaromonte and Dosi (1993), Silverberg and Soete (1993) and the discussion in Nelson (1995) and Silverberg and Verspagen (1995a).

Second, the diffusion of innovations has been fruitfully analysed, from different angles, as an evolutionary path-dependent process (cf. among others David (1985 and 1992), Silverberg *et al.* (1988), Arthur *et al.* (1987), Nakicenovic and Grübler (1992), and Metcalfe (1992)).

Third, the very development of an evolutionary perspective has been deeply intertwined with the historical analysis of the processes by which technical change is generated, ranging from the microeconomic level all the way to 'national systems of innovation' (within an enormous literature, see Freeman (1982), David (1975), Rosenberg (1976 and 1982), Basalla (1988), Mokyr (1990), Granstrand (1994), Vincenti (1990), Nelson (1992), and the reviews in Dosi (1988) and Freeman (1994)).

Fourth, a growing number of industrial case studies and models of industrial change fits quite well the evolutionary conjectures outlined above (again, just as examples, see Pavitt (1984), Utterback and Suarez (1992), Klepper (1993), Malerba and Orsenigo (1994), Winter (1984), and Dosi *et al.* (1995)).

Fifth, one is starting to explore learning itself as an evolutionary process at the levels of both individuals and organizations (limiting ourselves to economic applications, see Marengo (1992), Marengo and Tordjman (1996), Lindgren (1992), Dosi *et al.* (1995b), Levinthal (1990), Warglien (1995), and Palmer *et al.* (1994)). This links also with a wide tradition of studies in the fields of organizational economics which is impossible to review here (but see the remarks in Winter 1986 and 1995).

Finally, there is a good overlap between the evolutionary perspective as we have defined it and various types of 'self-organization' models (see Lesourne (1991)), and also with the expanding field of evolutionary games (see for example Young (1993), Kandori *et al.* (1993), and Kaniovski and Young (1994)). Short of any detailed discussion of analogies and differences (which will be briefly mentioned below), let us just mention that certainly they have in common the emphasis on dynamics (point 1 above) and bounded rationality assumptions (point 3), but much less so the role of novelty (point 5) and the focus on non-equilibrium, finite time, properties (point 7)·[4]

So, yes: indeed, we do have a rich and growing body of economic literature which at last tackles change and evolution, whereby increasing returns are the norm rather than the exception (and, with that, also the possibility of 'lock-ins'), history counts, and agents are presumed to be less than perfectly rational and knowledgeable. But where do institutions fit in this picture?

Let us now turn to this issue.

3.   INSTITUTIONS AND EVOLUTION

Again, for the sake of clarity, starting with some definitions helps.

Here we use the term 'institution' with a broad meaning to include

(a) formal organizations (ranging from firms to technical societies, trade unions, universities, all the way to state agencies);
(b) patterns of behaviours that are collectively shared (from routines to social conventions to ethical codes);
(c) negative norms and constraints (from moral prescriptions to formal laws).

Distinctions between the three subcategories will be made in the following when necessary.

The proposition that in a sense 'institutions count' in shaping economic coordination and change is certainly shared by all breeds of 'evolutionists' mentioned earlier with various strands of 'neo-institutionalists' (see for example Williamson (1985 and 1995), and North (1990 and 1991)), and also, of course, with 'old' institutionalism (drawing back to Veblen, Commons, and so on). But, clearly, the tricky issue is *in which sense* they count.

Simplifying to the extreme, two archetypical, opposing views can be found in all this literature. At one end of the spectrum, the role of institutions can be seen as that of (i) parameterizing the environmental state variables (say the comparative costs of markets, hybrids and hierarchies in Williamson or, nearer to evolutionary concerns, technological opportunities and appropriability conditions); and (ii) constraining the menus of actions available to the agents (which in some game-theoretic versions reduces to 'the rules of the game'). Conversely, at the opposite end, let us put under the heading of embeddedness view all those theories which claim, in different fashions, that institutions not only 'parameterize' and 'constrain', but, given any one environment, also shape the 'visions of the world', the interaction networks, the behavioural patterns, and, ultimately, the very identity of the agents. (In the contemporary literature, under this heading come, for example, Granovetter (1985), and also

March and Olsen (1989) and DiMaggio and Powell (1991), just to name a few, and has a close relative in 'cultural theory': cf. Schwartz and Thompson (1990) and Grendstad and Jelle (1995)). Note that where a theory is placed along this spectrum has significant implications in terms of the predictions that it makes with respect to the collective outcomes of interactions and to the directions of change. On the grounds of the former view, the knowledge (by the analyst) of the (institutionally shaped) system parameters is sufficient to determine the collective outcomes (precisely, under 'perfect' rationality with the caveat of multiple equilibria; and approximately, under 'bounded' rationality). Conversely, the embeddedness view implies that in order to understand 'what happens' and the directions of change over time much richer institutional details are needed. (First of all, one is likely to require to know much more about the multiple institutions of which the agents are part, and also much more of their histories.)

As discussed at greater length in Dosi (1995), three other dichotomies are relevant here. The first concerns the origin of the institutions. Briefly put, are institutions themselves a *primitive* of the theory or is *self-seeking rationality* the primitive and institutions are a derived concept? Under the latter view, whatever institution one observes, one has to justify it, asking the question how self-seeking agents have come to build it (with an answer that could be either via forward-looking rationality or myopic adaptation). Conversely, under the former view, the existence of an institution is 'explained' relying much more heavily on the institutions that preceded it and the mechanisms which led to the transition. One is also entitled to ask why people embedded in certain institutions behave the way they do (that is, how institutions shape their specific 'rationality' and equally specific perceptions of their interests).

The second dichotomy regards the degrees of intentionality of institutional constructions, that is, whether they are purposefully built according to some sort of collective *constitutional* activity or, conversely, are mainly the outcome of an unintentional *self-organization* process.

The third dichotomy concerns the efficiency properties (and the equilibrium nature) of institutions themselves. Do they exist *because* they 'perform a function' and, thus, are the equilibrium outcome of some process that selected in favour of that function? Or conversely, paraphrasing Paul David (1994), are they mainly 'carriers of history', in the sense that they tend to path-dependently reproduce themselves well beyond the time of their usefulness (if they ever had one)?

The four dichotomies together define the distance between any one institutionalist view and the standard 'neoclassical' paradigm (institution-free, with perfectly rational agents, well formed and invariant preferences, etc.). As shown in Table 1.1, one may identify different *gradations* of institutionalism, ranging from *weak* forms retaining a lot of the canonic microfoundations to *strong*

8   *Prospects for evolutionary and institutional theory*

forms wherein institutions have much more life of their own and also much more influence on what microentities think and do.

Table 1.1   Weak and strong varieties of institutionalism

	'Weak' Institutionalism	'Strong' Institutionalism
(1) Role of institutions	Parameterize system variables; contain menu of strategies	Also 'embed' cognitive and behavioural patterns; shape identities of actors
(2) 'Primitives' of the theory	(Perfectly or boundedly) rational self-seeking agents; institutions as derived entities	Institutions as 'primitives'; forms of 'rationality' and perceptions of self-interest as derived entities
(3) Mechanisms of institution-formulation	Mainly intentional, 'constitutional', processes	Mainly unintentional self-organization processes
(4) Efficiency properties	Institutions perform useful coordinating and governance functions; may be considered equilibria in some selection space	Institutions as 'carriers of history'; reproduce path-dependently, often irrespectively of this functional efficiency

How does the evolutionary research programme (as we have defined it) relate to the various strands of institutionalism, if it does at all? It is our view that the links are indeed profound (the famous plea for an evolutionary approach to economic analysis by one of the founding figures of institutionalism, T. Veblen (1898), is a historical symbol of this intuitive relationship). However, it seems to us also true that the linkages so far still are to a large extent implicit.

Certainly there are a lot of institutional assumptions in evolutionary reasoning. So, for example, it is quite natural to assume that the particular behavioural rules, interaction mechanisms and learning patterns that one finds in evolutionary models are embedded into particular institutions. In fact, markets themselves are viewed as specific, history-contingent, institutions.

Moreover, it is plain that *routines* – which play a prominent role in evolutionary theorizing of economic behaviours – are shaped by the history of the organizations in which they have developed and also by a broader institutional history. (For example, one is quite at ease with the idea that the routines and strategies of a firm from Victorian Manchester are likely to be quite different from those of American multidivisional corporations analysed by Alfred Chandler; that differences in the institutional contexts contribute to explaining the behavioural differences between contemporary Japanese, American, and European firms, etc.).

Finally, a lot of effort has gone into the understanding of the specificities of the institutions supporting technological change (see, for example, Nelson (1993), Lundvall (1992) and the chapters by Nelson and Freeman in Dosi *et al.* (1988)).

However, it is fair to say that the institutional embeddedness of technological opportunities, routines, forms of market interactions and selection mechanisms, etc., while abundantly acknowledged, has received little attention on its own (with the exception of those institutions more directly linked with innovative activities and notwithstanding the suggestions in Lundvall (1992) aiming to provide a broader institutional meaning for the notion of 'national systems of innovation'). So, for example, one is still lacking any systematic mapping between classes of institutional arrangements of the economy and classes of interaction mechanisms/adjustment rules that one finds in evolutionary theories. As a consequence, one is equally still unable to map institutional arrangements into particular dynamic properties of aggregate variables such as income and productivity growth, employment, etc. (See, however, Chiaromonte *et al.* (1992) for an initial, still quite preliminary attempt.) Conversely, these types of mapping are precisely the *starting point* of 'strong' institutionalist approaches as defined above. As a term of comparison, let us consider in particular the 'regulation' school.

4.   AN INSTITUTIONALIST VIEW OF THE ECONOMIC SYSTEM: THE 'REGULATION' APPROACH

For those who are not familiar with this tradition of studies, which originally developed in France (see Aglietta (1982), Boyer and Mistral (1978), Boyer (1987, 1988a, 1988b and 1990), Coriat (1991), Jessop (1990), and Boyer and Saillard (1995)). First note that by 'regulation', in French, one does not mean the legal regulatory apparatus as understood by the same term in English. Rather, its meaning is nearer the notion from system theory of different parts or processes that under certain conditions reciprocally adjust yielding some orderly dynamics. Hence *regulation* stands for the relatively coherent socio-economic tuning of any one economic system, and different *regimes of regulation* capture the specificities in the 'mechanisms and principles of adjustment associated with

10   *Prospects for evolutionary and institutional theory*

a configuration of wage relations, competition, State interventions and hierarchisation of the international economy' (Boyer 1987, p. 127).

In this perspective, and unlike evolutionary models, the description of the system is immediately institutional and taxonomic, attempting to identify some sort of archetypical structural forms which distinguish alternative socio-economic regimes.[5]

For our purposes here, let us define different regimes of accumulation in terms of the institutional arrangements concerning six domains, namely:

1. *The wage-labour nexus.* Under this heading come the nature of the social division of labour; the type of employment and the mechanism of governance of industrial conflict; the existence and nature of union representation; the systems of wage formation; and so on.
2. The forms of *competition* in the product markets (whether nearly-competitive or oligopolist: the related mechanism of price formation; and so on).
3. The institutions governing *financial markets* and monetary management (including the relationships between banks and industry, the role of stock exchanges in industrial financing, the mechanisms of liquidity creation in the system, etc.).
4. The norms of *consumption* (that is, the composition and changes in the baskets of consumption and their differences across social groups).
5. The forms of *state intervention* in the economy (for example, monetary and fiscal policies; 'state as arbiter' versus state as an active player with respect to social conflict, income distribution, welfare and so on).
6. The organization of the *international system* of exchanges (for example, the rules of international trade; the presence/absence of a single hegemonic power; the patterns of specialization; and so on).

The identification of discrete regimes implies, then, a sort of combinatorial exercise among these six domains; the historically informed identification of dominant ones in particular periods; the assessment of the conditions of their viability and eventual crises; the specific realizations of a dominant regime in different countries. So a lot of work has been done in order to identify the nature of the 'classical' (or 'competitive') regime which ran through most of the nineteenth century, as opposed to a 'Fordist' (or 'monopolistic') regime coming to maturity in the developed West after World War II (cf. Aglietta (1982), Boyer and Mistral (1978) and the works reviewed in Boyer and Saillard (1995)). The focus of the analysis is to a great extent the *long term*, influenced by Marxism and the French historical tradition of the *Annales*, and the emphasis is macroinstitutional: it is centred, for example, on the institutions governing 'social compromises' among major social groups (Delorme and André (1983),

Coriat (1982 and 1990)), educational institutions (Caroli (1995)), financial institutions, and so on.

One could say that the regulation approach is an ambitious attempt – paraphrasing John Hicks – to develop a 'theory of contemporary history'. It has proved indeed to be a very rich source of heuristics and categories for historical analyses and comparative studies (a thorough survey of the state of the art is in Boyer and Saillard (1995)). But there are also a few exercises of formalization of types of reduced forms of the theory whereby the (institutionally-shaped) regularities in the above six domains are summarized by some functional relations linking aggregate variables (for example, wages with prices, productivity and employment; productivity growth with the growth of output, investments and R&D; output growth with investment and exports: see in particular Boyer (1988b) and the contributions by Billandot, Juillard and Amable in Boyer and Saillard (1995)). The models have a strong Keynesian/Kaldorian ascendency, but certainly expand upon the ancestors, and, more important, attempt to capture the differences across regimes in terms of different parametrizations and functional specifications of those aggregate relationships (for example, do wages depend mainly on unemployment, as in the 'competitive' regime, or are they basically linked to consumer prices and productivity, as in the 'Fordist' regime? Does some sort of 'Verdoorn–Kaldor law' apply to productivity growth? How sensitive are investments to profits as opposed to 'accelerator' effects? and so on). In these reduced forms, the stability of 'regimes' is investigated in terms of the existence of stable steady states engendered by particular ranges of parameters. Moreover, by specifying dynamic couplings across these same aggregate variables one is able to identify quite rich long-term patterns including bifurcations (Lordon (1993)) and phase transitions.

At this point, readers not too familiar with both the evolutionary and the regulation approaches might reasonably wonder what they have in common. *Prima facie,* they do indeed share some methodological commitment to the understanding of dynamic patterns which do not simply involve 'more of the same'. They both also depart from the canonic view of the economy as a 'naturally' self-regulating system. Moreover, their microfoundations (explicit in most 'evolutionary' contributions, implicit in most of the 'regulationist' ones) imply much less than perfect rationality and foresight. And, finally they share a deep commitment to the idea that 'institutions matter'. But what else beyond that? Are they talking about the same objects of analysis? And, when they do, how do their interpretations overlap or diverge? In order to clarify these issues for the discussion, let us briefly check the two perspectives against an object of inquiry that both have abundantly addressed, namely growth, and in particular the observed patterns during the period after World War II.

5.   SOME DIFFERENT THEORETICAL STORIES ON GROWTH, IN GENERAL, AND THE POST-WAR PERIOD, IN PARTICULAR

It is revealing to compare the bare bones of the interpretative stories that 'evolutionists' and 'regulationists' would be inclined to put forward about the basics of the growth process, were they forced to summarize them in a few sentences.

Most likely, the story provided within an evolutionary perspective would start with a multitude of firms searching for more efficient techniques of production and better-performing products, and competing in the markets for products and finance. Differential success in search, together with different behavioural rules and strategies (concerning, for example, pricing, investment, and so on) would then determine their differential revealed performances (in terms, for example, of their profitability, market shares, or survival probabilities) and hence their ability to grow in the next 'period'. Aggregate growth, in this view, is essentially driven by technological advances. Similarly, the eye of the analyst is naturally led to look for the origins, nature and accessability of technological opportunities; the ease with which firms can imitate each other (that is, appropriability conditions); the ways firms are able to store and augment their knowledge (that is, the relationships between organizational routines and competences); and finally the mechanisms and speed of market selection.

As already emphasized, such an evolutionary story is comfortable with complementary institutional factors. Most straightforwardly, for example, it is consistent with (and indeed demands) an institutionally grounded explanation of the mechanisms of generation of 'opportunities' to be tapped by private agents; of the legal framework contributing to shape appropriability conditions; of the origins of particular sets of corporate routines; of the nature of market interactions; of the ways wages react to the changes in the demand for labour induced by technical change and growth; and so on.

However, compare this story with the much more directly institution-based story within a regulation perspective. In the latter, plausibly, the starting point would be an analysis of the factors which render a particular regime of accumulation viable (note incidentally that while it was possible to tell a caricature of an evolutionary story of capitalist growth in general, here one needs history-contingent specifications from the start). One part of the story would concern the institutions governing wage formation, the labour process and income distribution – determining labour productivity and the surplus available for investment. Another part of the story would focus on the mechanisms of generation of aggregate demand (including the ways income distribution and social institutions affect the composition and dynamics of consumption baskets).

Yes another part would address the ways the state intervenes into the economy (is it a 'Keynesian'/welfare state or is it a laisser-faire one?, and so on) Moreover, one would look at the ways products and financial markets are organized. In a nutshell, the answer to the question of 'what drives growth' is found in the consistency conditions among those major pieces of institutional organization of the socio-economic fabric. Hence, consistent matching fosters sustained growth, while mismatching engenders instability, crises and macroeconomic depression.

Having focused, *in primis,* on the institutional features of the system, the approach in manners somewhat symmetrically opposite to the 'evolutionary' interpretation is complementary to detailed specifications of the patterns of technological change. For example, it is easily acknowledged that technological innovation is a major determinant of the division of labour and work organization; of the importance of economics of scale (and thus of the aggregate relationships between productivity growth and income growth); of demand patterns; of international competitiveness; and so on. However, it is fair to say that what appears as the major driver of growth in the evolutionary account, here (in the regulation approach) tends to feature more in the background among the necessary or constraining conditions for growth, while the opposite applies to the thread of country-specific and period-specific institutions.

A similar difference (which might be just a matter of emphasis or might be much more; see below) emerges when handling the interpretation of specific historical circumstances. Compare, as an illustration, Nelson and Wright (1992) and Aglietta (1982) on American performance in this century (notwithstanding the only partial overlap between the two, with the former focused on technological performance and the latter, more broadly, on growth patterns). In brief, the Nelson–Wright story reconstructs the origins of American leadership after World War II, tracing it back to

> two conceptually distinct components. There was, first of all, the longstanding strength in mass production industries that grew out of unique conditions of resource abundance and large market size. There was, second, a lead in 'high technology' industries that was new and stemmed from investment in higher education and in research and development, far surpassing the levels of other countries at the time. (Nelson and Wright, 1992, p. 1960)

The erosion of that leadership is then analysed in terms of the factors which allowed a more or less complete technological catching-up by other OECD countries over the last four decades (subject to the qualifications put forward by Patel and Pavitt (1994) on the long-term specificities in the patterns of technological accumulation by individual countries).

Nelson and Wright do not explicitly talk about the impact of technology on growth, but a strong evolutionary conjecture is that innovation and imitation have a major importance in explaining both trade patterns and growth patterns (for some empirical tests see Dosi *et al.* (1990), Verspagen (1993), Amendola *et al.* (1993), and Fagerberg (1994)). Conversely, the Aglietta story, directly concerning American (and international) *growth* patterns, is an archetypical application of the regulation framework sketched above. The conditions for a sustained regime of growth are identified into the 'virtuous' complementarity (i) mechanization/automation/standardization of production (entailing also ample opportunities for the exploitation of economics of scale); (ii) the development of 'Fordist' patterns of management of industrial relations; (iii) mechanisms of governance of the labour market on the grounds of implicit or explicit conventions indexing wages on productivity and consumer prices (with the effect, among others, of smoothing business cycles and sustaining effective demand); (iv) symmetrically, relatively stable forms of oligopolistic organization of product markets (which, combined with the wage dynamics described above, sustained rather stable patterns of income distribution and easy 'accelerator-driven' investment planning); (v) the diffusion in consumption of mass-produced durables; (vi) 'welfare' and 'Keynesian' fiscal policies; (vii) the development of an international monetary regime conducive to international exchanges (the Bretton Woods set-up) under the hegemony of one economic and technological leader (the USA).

Correspondingly, the end of the 'Golden Age' following World War II is seen as the outcome of 'mismatched dynamics', for institutional and technological reasons, at all the foregoing seven levels: the exhaustion of the potential for economies of scale; inflationary pressures amplified by wage formation mechanism; the entry of new competitors destabilizing cosy oligopolistic arrangements; increasing social conflict favoured by near-full-employment conditions; the collapse of the Bretton Woods regime; and so on.

Are these two basic stories essentially two complementary ways of looking at a broadly similar object? But in this case where does the complementarity precisely rest? Or do they entail competing explanations of the same phenomena? As we shall see, it is our conjecture that there is a bit of both – and sorting out what is what would be already a significant step ahead.

6. DIFFERENT LEVELS OF ANALYSIS OR COMPETING INTERPRETATIONS?

Certainly, part of the difference in the 'building blocks' of the basic stories outlined above relates to different levels of observation and different primary phenomena to be explained (and this, of course, militates for a would-be complementarity). In many respects, a much greater parsimoniousness on institutional assumptions that one finds in evolutionary models is due to the higher level of 'historical abstraction' in which they are set. Metaphorically speaking, this is the level at which one investigates the properties of an (imperfect) Invisible (or oligopolistically visible) Hand operating in presence of the Unbound Prometheus – as David Landes puts it – of technological change. In other words, evolutionary models – at least the first generation of them – start by addressing, in a first approximation, some stylized properties of capitalist dynamics in general, such as the possibility of self-sustained growth driven by the mistake-ridden search by self-seeking agents. Relatedly, the primary objects of interpretation are broad statistical regularities (or 'stylized facts') at aggregate level, such as exponential growth, the rough constancy of distributive shares, the secular increase in capital/labour ratios, the degrees of persistency in macro fluctuations and more generally the spectral density of time series; the broad patterns of divergence/convergence of per capita income in the world economy; etc. (see Nelson and Winter (1982), Dosi *et al.* (1994a), Silverberg and Verspagen (1994) and the (far too modest!) overview in Silverberg and Verspagen (1995a)). Similarly, at 'meso' level – that is, that of single industries – evolutionary models have proved to be quite capable of interpreting statistical phenomena such as skewed distributions of firms by size, 'life cycle' patterns of evolution, inter-sectoral differences in industrial structures grounded in different 'technological regimes', and so on (cf. Dosi *et al.* (1995)).

With respect to this level of observation, in many ways, the degree of abstraction of regulation theories *is* much lower and the interpretative ambition is higher, in the sense that the aim goes well beyond the account of broad statistical invariances but points at the understanding of discrete forms of development and the transitions across them. Similarly, the degree of institutional specification is bound to be much higher and, as it happens, the 'microfoundations' much more implicit (when they are there at all).

So we have here a potentially fruitful complementarity concerning two different levels of description (see also below). As we see it, the aggregate functional and institutional regularities which are the starting point of most regulation models[6] could possibly be shown to be emergent properties of underlying, explicitly microfounded, evolutionary models, appropriately enriched in their institutional specifications.

Take for example the Verdoorn–Kaldor functional form relating productivity growth and income growth which is postulated in regulation models. Evolutionary models are in principle suited to establishing the microeconomic conditions under which it emerges in the aggregate as a stable relation: for example what are the micro-learning processes that sustain it? What happens to its form and parametrizations if one varies the underlying mechanisms of search and sources of technological opportunities? Under what circumstances can one identify phenomena of 'symmetry breaking' engendered by microfluctuations and yielding the transition to different structural forms?

Similarly, with respect to wage formation mechanisms, the 'structural forms' in the regulation account tend to postulate aggregate invariances, say in the elasticities of wages to unemployment, prices and productivity. Conversely, evolution-inspired models of the labour market and labour processes (still to be built!) might well account for the conditions of their emergence, stability and crises. And the same could be said for most other primary building blocks of regulation models.

Of course we do not want to push the 'emergence philosophy' too far. It would be naive to think that straightforward links between levels of description can be made without resorting to a lot of further 'phenomenological', history-based, specifications. Jokingly, we illustrate all this with the parallel of the cow. If anyone is asked to describe what a cow is, it would be silly to start from a quantum mechanics account of the atoms composing it, and then move on to the levels of atoms, molecules, cells ... all the way to the morphological description of the cow. However the example is handy because it illustrates, first, the consistency in principle between the different levels of description; second, the fact that a good deal of higher-level properties (for example, concerning cells' self-maintenance) can be understood as emerging properties from lower-level dynamics; and, third, that without a lot of additional 'phenomenological' information, generic emergent properties are not enough to determine why that animal is a cow and not an elephant or a bird.

Admittedly, in economics we are very far from such a consistency across levels of descriptions (and certainly the compression to one single ahistorical level that the neoclassical tradition has taught us did not help). However, we want to suggest that a theory-informed dialogue between bottom-up (microfounded, and so on) evolutionary approaches and more top-down (aggregate, albeit institutionally richer) regulation ones is likely to be a formidable but analytically promising challenge.[7] Not only would it help to rigorously define the bridges between micro behaviours and entities at different levels of aggregation, but it would also highlight potential conflicts of interpretation which are currently often confused by level-of-description issues. Having said that, a few unresolved questions and areas of possible conflict come to mind.

The Descriptive Counterparts of Socio-Economic Regimes

We have already mentioned earlier that, in a sense, the regulation approach sets itself the ambitious task of dissecting the anatomy of discrete regimes of growth. But then, it seems to us, a unavoidable task is the empirical *and statistical* identification of these regimes. Some work has been done in this direction, concerning especially long-term wage dynamics, but also labour productivity and demand formation (for surveys, see Chapter 10 by C. Leroy, Chapter 22 by M. Juillard and Chapter 23 by B. Amable in Boyer and Saillard

(1995), and also Boyer (1988b)). However, a lot remains to be done – difficult as it is. For example, if phases of development and crises are traced back to the properties of underlying regimes, how are they revealed by the dynamics of statistical aggregates? And which ones? And at which level of aggregation? (for example, are GDP series too noisy and unprecise so that one should look at sectoral data?) Or is one forced to the conclusion that current econometric methods are ill-suited to detect changes which appear very important when inspecting qualitatively 'how the economy works', but are blurred by statistical noise in the reported series?

An answer to these questions will help a lot in pinning down the common objects of interpretation (and also in revealing the comparative merits of an institutionalist approach to macroeconomics as compared to more traditional ones). Moreover, a crucial part of the regulationist exercise involves the mapping of socio-economic regimes into dynamic properties of the system. But then a lot more work is required to find statistical proxies for those regimes themselves (this mirrors the effort that scholars in the evolutionary tradition have started putting into the statistical identification of 'technological regimes'; cf. Malerba and Orsenigo (1994)).

The Institutional Specifications of the Evolutionary Model

In a sort of complementary way, in order to start talking about (roughly) the same things, it is urgent that a new generation of evolutionary models begins experimenting systematically with variations in the institutional contexts in which evolutionary processes are embedded. One can think of different ways of doing it (corresponding also to different degrees of difficulty). First, holding constant the system parameters concerning, for example, notional technological opportunities, one may ask what happens to aggregate dynamics if one changes behavioural routines (an early example is in Chiaromonte *et al.* (1992)), and the constraints on those routines themselves (well expanding upon the exercise of Nelson and Winter (1982) regarding different financial constraints on borrowed funds). Second, even holding routines constant, one should experiment with different interaction environments (for example, centralized versus pairwise forms of interaction; price-based competition versus selection based on multidimensional product attributes; bank-based versus market-based access to finance; and so on). In fact a major claim of both evolutionary and regulation theories is that markets are themselves institutional constructions whose organizational details deeply affect collective outcomes. However one knows very little of how markets actually work[8] and even less does one have taxonomies of sort of 'archetypes' of markets which can thereafter be stylized and formally explored. Third, one might allow for routines themselves to be learnt in different institutional environments.[9] That would imply, in turn, the identification of distinct learning procedures in different environments. Fourth (and harder), it might be time to explore in an evolutionary perspective other domains of economic activity (for example, the labour market, financial markets, the endogenous dynamics of consumer preferences, and so on).

Some Possible Misunderstandings: Microfoundations, Representative Agents and Methodological Individualism

In the argument so far, an implicit assumption has been that the degrees of 'bottom-up-ness' or 'top-down-ness' (including the presence and details of interactions among lower-level entities with emergence of higher-level properties) is essentially conditional on the levels and modes of description themselves.

So, for example, we do not have any problem in acknowledging the descriptive power of the now-discredited Keynesian 'income multipliers', as a concise way of accounting – under historical conditions to be specified – for a specific relationship between modal behaviours of 'firms' and 'consumers'. In turn, such an aggregate description implies, of course, that functional roles in society count. (Here there should be little disagreement between the evolutionary and regulation approaches). The underlying idea is that an economic agent, Mr Jones – even when he is at the same time a worker at factory X, a shareholder of company Y which owns that factory, and a consumer of the products of that factory and of many other ones will behave according to modal patterns deriving from an institution-shaped logic of appropriateness, as James March puts it (how should Jones, as a consumer or as a worker, behave?). Most likely what Mr Jones does as a worker ought to be interpreted on the grounds of the collective history of many Mr Joneses, their experiences at the workplace, their successes and failures in industrial bargaining, etc. Analogously, the same should apply to his behaviour as a consumer or a shareholder. The basic point here is that a reduction of Mr Jones' behaviour to a coherent exercise of utility-maximization in a largely institution-free environment misses the point and is interpretatively misleading or, at best, void of any descriptive content. Mr Jones might, for example, feel safe to buy shares of very conservative companies in order to ensure a rosy retirement age, fight in the meantime at the workplace against the very practices that these same companies try to implement, and buy Japanese products even when that endangers the wealth possibly stemming from the companies whose shares he bought.

Having said that, however, it seems to us that the hypothesis of institutional embeddedness of social behaviours – largely shared by the evolutionary and regulationist approaches – cannot be pushed to the dangerous borders of some renewed functionalism. There is some echo of all that when one finds a too cavalier use of sorts of 'functional representative agents' in regulationist interpretations ('the behaviour of the Fordist firm', 'the unionized worker', and so on). If anything, those stylized behavioural archetypes ought to be considered as rough first approximations, demanding further investigations into their microfoundations and the conditions of their sustainability over time. For example, under what context conditions will the behaviours of many Mr Joneses (or, for that matter, of many firms 'Jones Inc.') remain relatively invariant over time? What are the conditions on interactions and statistical aggregation which sustain relatively invariant mean behaviours? And, conversely, under what circumstances do non-average behaviours induce symmetry-breaking and, possibly, phase transitions? (Note that this last issue is particularly relevant when accounting for the dynamics across different regimes). Certainly, we share Boyer and Saillard's general conjecture that

> a mode of *regulation* elicits a set of procedures and individual and collective behaviours which ought at the same time to reproduce [particular] social relations . . . and sustain the prevailing regime of accumulation. Moreover, a mode of regulation must assure the compatibility among a collection of decentralized decisions, without necessarily requiring the acknowledgment by the agents of the principles which govern the dynamics of the system as a whole. (Boyer and Saillard (1995), p. 64, our translation)

Work to support this claim (at both levels of empirical investigations and formal modelling) is urgently needed, and in our view is also another area of fruitful complementarity between 'evolutionists' and 'regulationists'.

In this respect, a possible misunderstanding has to be dispelled. The requirement of microfoundations of aggregate statements (that is, foundations in what a multitude of agents actually do and, possibly, think), which we have emphasized throughout this work, must not at all be considered equivalent to any advocacy for foundations into any 'methodological individualism'. The latter, in its canonic form, requires, first, that any collective state of the system ought to be explained on the grounds of what people contributing with their actions to determine that state think and do; and, second, that these micro 'thoughts', strategies and actions are the primitives of the theory. Our claim is much weaker. We share, in principle, the first requirement,[10] but we strongly deny the second. So for example, we are perfectly happy with 'microfoundations' which are themselves macrofounded, that is, where what 'people think and do' is *deeply but imperfectly* shaped by the organization and states of the system itself.

As an illustration consider the following toy model. Take a competitive world (as similar as possible to a Temporary General Equilibrium, of pure exchange – in order to make things simple). Suppose the state of the system, $s(0)$ at time $t(0)$ is defined by a price vector $p(0)$ and allocations $\omega_i(0)$ to each agent $i, (\omega_i \varepsilon \Omega(0))$. As usual, given prices and allocations, preference relations will determine the demand functions. If we specify a mechanism of exchange (which indeed the theory seldom does) this yields well-defined transition laws to the price sequence p(1), p(2) . . . and $\Omega(1)$, $\Omega(2)$ . . . (the subsequent allocations). This is obviously a microfounded story. However, add to the story that the *preference relations themselves* depend, imperfectly, on the lagged p( ) and $\Omega( )$, for example, because of phenomena of reduction of cognitive dissonance ('. . . don't desire what you were not able to get . . . '), social imitation, learning-how-to-like-what-you-have, and so on. In this case, we still have a microfounded story, but of course (a) individual preferences stop being a 'primitive' of the explanation, and (b) we have here a sort of 'macrofoundation of the micro', in the sense that what micro entities do is to a good extent determined by the collective history of the system itself.[11] This metaphor, we suggest, is of wide applicability, well-beyond the foregoing caricatural example.

A Crossroad for Dialogue (or Conflict): The Nature of Economic Routines

We have mentioned earlier that both evolutionary and regulation approaches share the idea that a good deal of individual and collective behaviours are 'boundedly rational', context-dependent and relatively inertial over time, shaped as they are by equally inertial institutions in which they are embedded. In a word, both approaches share the view that a good deal of the reproduction of the socio-economic fabric rests on the development and implementation of organizational routines. However, as we discuss at much greater length in Coriat and Dosi (1995), most organizational routines entail a double nature: on the one hand, they store and reproduce problem-solving competences, while, at the same time, they are also mechanisms of governance of potentially conflictual relations.

As it happens, the evolutionary approach has focused almost exclusively on the 'cognitive' aspects of routines (and by doing that has begun to open interesting avenues of dialogue with disciplines like cognitive psychology and artificial intelligence), but it has largely neglected the dimensions of power and control intertwined into the routines themselves.[12]

Almost the opposite applies to the regulation approach, which has tended to emphasize the requirements of social coherence implied by routines, but has not paid much attention to their knowledge content.

All this might be all right again as a first approximation but it is clearly unsatisfactory as an end result in either approach. Pushing it to the extreme, in the former perspective, an answer to the question of 'how Renault (or GM or United Biscuits ...) behaves' is inclined to account for operating procedures, mechanisms of knowledge accumulation, learning strategies, and so on leaving in the background phenomena like the conflict between different social groups, the links that particular organizational rules bear with income distribution and the exercise of power (well beyond their knowledge content), and so on. Conversely, the regulationist answer, by putting most of the emphasis on the latter phenomena, tends to convey the idea that governance is the paramount role of routines, quite irrespectively of the fact that Renault or GM have to know how to produce cars and United Biscuits cakes, and they have got to do it well, and better over time. The risks of one-sided accounts are particularly great when accounting for the *origins* of routines themselves, with an evolutionary inclination to trace them back to cognitive dynamics only, and the regulationists feeling a bit too comfortable with a reduction of the problem to a selection dynamics among well-specified menus of actions/strategies/conventions.[13]

We argue in Coriat and Dosi (1995) that the double nature of routines, and related to this the double marks on their origins, are challenging points of encounter between the evolutionist and institutionalist research programmes. Or, conversely, it could be the crossroad where the former take some sort of 'hypercognitive' route, whereby microeconomics and cognitive psychology tend to simply merge, and regulationists could well discover that 'methodological individualism' and weaker forms of 'neo-institutionalism' (cf. Table 1.1) are not so bad after all.

7. SOME CONCLUSIONS: TOWARDS A DEMANDING AND EXCITING INTERBREEDING?

Notwithstanding a series of important analytical issues – which might indeed be a source of serious interpretative conflict, and of which we have provided some illustrations – we do see an ideal sequence of modes of interpretation and levels of description in which both the evolutionist and regulationist programmes could ambitiously fit. As sketched in Table 1.2, they run from a sort of 'nano-economics', wherein the abandonment of any magic of a perfect and invariant rationality forces a dialogue with cognitive and social psychology, organization theory, and sociology, all the way to grand historical conjectures on the long-term destinies of contemporary forms of socio-economic organization. Even a quick look at the table highlights the enormous gaps between what we know and what such an ideal evolutionary-institutionalist research programme would demand. These gaps are high at all levels but in our view four issues are particularly urgent on the agenda.

A first one concerns co-evolutionary processes. The essence of the co-evolutionary point is that what happens in each partly autonomous domain of the system (for example, technology or institutional structures) shapes and constrains what is going to happen in the other ones. Hence, the overall dynamics is determined by the ways each domain evolves but also by the ways the various domains are coupled with each other.[14] We have listed 'co-evolution' under a separate level or description in order to demarcate that broad area

Table 1.2 Levels of analysis

	Objects of analysis (some still to be explored)	Examples of 'analytical styles'
Level 0 – From nanoeconomics to micro-economics	(i) Nature and origins of routines and, generally, behavioural norms (ii) Learning processes (iii) Mechanisms of expectation formation (iv) Nature and evolution of microorganiza-tions (e.g. business firms) (v) Embedding mechanisms of individual behaviours into the institutional context (vi) The evolution of criteria of actions and 'visions of the world'	From H. Simon to Holland *et al.* (1986); microanalytic part of Nelson and Winter (1982); Cohen and Bacdayan (1994); Egidi (1994); organizational economic 'compe-tences', and so on; Coriat (1994b); Dosi *et al.* (1994b); Marengo (1992); Warglien (1995); Marengo and Tordjman (1996); Possible economic applications of Fontana and Buss (1994a and b); and a lot to be done
Level 1 – From microeconomics to aggregate properties	(i) Generic properties of growth fuelled by technical changes (ii) Industrial evolution (iii) Self-organizing properties of labour markets (iv) The dynamics of consumption patterns	Explicit microfounded models with aggregate emergent statistical properties, for example, Nelson and Winter (1982); Silverberg and Verspagen (1994); Lesourne (1991); Dosi *et al.* (1995)
Level 2 – Aggregate dynamics	(i) Functional relations among aggregate variables (ii) Socio-economic regimes: consistency conditions among processes of economic adjustment and institutions	More 'stylized' but (hopefully) institutionally richer macro models (necessarily micro-founded): from Keynesian/Kaldorian models to Boyer (1988a/b) and Silverberg (1987)
Level 3 – 'Co-evolution'	(i) Co-evolutionary patterns between tech-nologies, corporate organizations and broader institutions (ii) Coupled institutional dynamics (iii) 'Political discretionality' and institutional inertias	A lot of appreciative theorizing from historians but relatively little modelling (but see the suggestion in Nelson (1994) on industrial dynamics); a vast regulation-inspired empirical literature (cf. Boyer and Saillard (1995))
Level 4 – 'Grand history'	General interpretative conjectures on long-term historical patterns	From Karl Marx to ... Schumpeter ... to Freeman and Perez (1988) ... to Aglietta (1982) and Boyer and Mistral (1978) (just to name the perspectives discussed in the work)

covering, for example, the interactions between the forms of economic organization, social and political institutions and technical change. However, co-evolutionary issues appear at all levels of description. For example, the emergence and development of each industry ought to be seen as a co-evolutionary process between technologies, corporate organizations and supporting institutions (Nelson (1994)). Analogously, the origins of organizational routines (cf. above) is intimately a co-evolutionary process, shaped by diverse and probably conflicting selection criteria (that is, problem-solving versus governance requirements).

A second (and related) item which is high on the research agenda considers the transition across different socio-economic regimes of growth: for example, at which level can such transitions be detected? (This will probably be conditional on the type of transition one is talking about.) What are the effects of 'higher-level' changes (for example, in the institutional set-ups or in the policy environment) upon microeconomic behaviour? And, conversely, under what circumstances do non-average microbehaviours become 'autocatalytic' and eventually induce higher-level phase transitions? What kind of co-evolutionary processes do particular classes of transitions entail?

A third priority item, in our view, concerns what could be called, in shorthand, the relationships between emergence and embeddedness, or, putting it another way, the role of 'bottom-up' processes shaping/generating higher-level entities (or at least aggregate statistical patterns) versus 'top-down' processes by which higher-level entities (for example, institutions, established mechanisms of interaction, etc.) shape/generate 'lower level' behaviours. One of the claims underlying this whole chapter is that the links work both ways and that one ought to account for 'macrofoundation of the micro' as well as 'microfoundations of the macro'. But how does one get beyond suggestive metaphors and elaborate more rigorous, albeit highly simplified, models which nonetheless capture the intuition? (Note that what we mean is something more than a feedback between a system-level state variable (say, a price or a market share) and the argument of an individual decision algorithm (say, pricing or investment rules): somewhat deeper, we think it is not beyond reach to develop models whereby micro decision algorithms themselves are shaped by macro states and, conversely, possibly non-linear interactions among the former change collective interaction rules/constraints/perceived payoffs/perceived opportunities.) But in turn, all this involves difficult issues concerning, again, coordination; relative time-scales of change; relative invariances of 'structures' and conditions of their stability.

Fourth, we suggest that the nature of learning processes, too, ought to deserve priority attention. As Lundvall (in this volume) emphasizes the *objects of learning* ('know what', 'know why', 'know how', 'know who' . . .) are likely to discriminate among classes of learning processes. And, certainly, the competence gap between the intrinsic complexity of any one cognition/decision problem at hand and the pre-existing abilities of (individual or collective) agents fundamentally shapes learning processes (for a discussion, cf. Dosi and Egidi (1991)). But, in turn, it is only a weird twist of contemporary economic thought that gives credibility to the idea that incrementalist procedures, either based on sophisticated hypothesis testing (such as in Bayesian models) or stimulus–response reinforcements, are the general paradigm of learning (note that this applies to 'evolutionary games', but also to most evolutionary models in general) that one has developed so far.[15]

As a way forward, we suggest, possibly building upon preliminary (and still very rudimentary) attempts by, among others, Marengo (1992), Egidi (1994), Cohen and Bacdayan (1994), Marengo and Tordjman (1996) and also Dosi *et al.* (1994c), a priority task is to account for the formation and collective establishment of cognitive categories, problem-solving procedures (routines?) and expectations about the identities and behaviours of other social actors.[16]

Yes, all this is an enormous task. Very fascinating and extremely difficult. The way we see it pursued, it involves tight and troublesome interchanges between empirical investigations, 'appreciative theorizing' and formal modelling efforts. It is likely also to involve major adjustments in the building blocks of institutionalist/evolutionary theories themselves.

We are probably now witnessing a rare window of opportunity for fulfilling the promise of making economics an 'evolutionary/institutionalist discipline'. The blame for failing to do so will fall mainly on ourselves, rather than the sectarian attitudes of chair committees or international journal editors.

NOTES

Support for this research from the Italian Ministry of Universities and Research (MURST, 'Progetti 40%') and from the International Institute for Applied Systems Analysis (IIASA), Laxenburg, Austria, is gratefully acknowledged. An earlier version of this chapter has appeared in French in Boyer and Saillard (1995).

1. Note, however, that there are a few 'aggregate' (that is, non-microfounded) models which are nonetheless 'evolutionary' in spirit (for a survey, see Silverberg and Verspagen (1995)).
2. On the notions of 'emergence' and 'metastability' cf. the discussion in Lane (1993).
3. Note that, given the above quite broad definition of the evolutionary research programme, it may well describe also the contributions of authors who would not call themselves 'evolutionist' in any strict sense.
4. To repeat, this is not meant to be a thorough review but just an approximate roadmap. Moreover, at least a partial overlap with the evolutionary archetype can be found in quite diverse fields of economic theory: see for example Aoki (1995) and Stiglitz (1994).
5. A related perspective, which it is not possible to discuss here, pursued especially by 'radical' American economists, is known as the theory of 'Social Structures of Accumulation'. See for example Bowles and Gintis (1993) and the references therein.
6. Note that we do not mean only formal, mathematically expressed, 'models', but also rigorous, albeit verbally expressed, theory-based propositions about whatever phenomena.

7. Broad historical interpretations building upon a *lato sensu* evolutionary microeconomics, such as Freeman and Perez (1988), might be considered as another point of departure of this dialogue.

8. A noticeable exception is Kirman and Vignes (1992) on the fish market in Marseille (!).

9. A simple adaptive learning mechanism nested in a macro model is presented in Silverberg and Verspagen (1995b). Much more constructive models of behavioural learning are in Marengo (1992), Marengo and Tordjman (1996) and Dosi *et al.* (1994c), but they are far from any macro model. Moreover, they, too, lack experiments on different institutional specifications.

   Note that, here, by routines we specifically mean those rules of thumb concerning such things as pricing, R&D, investments, and so on. It is a fundamental point of evolutionary theories that different techniques are intimately associated also with different production routines. And, indeed, the models provide a representation of the dynamics of the latter via a low-dimensional representation of search outcomes in the technology space. However, a major step forward would be an explicit account of the dynamics of the underlying problem-solving routines (see also below).

10. We also want to emphasize the fact that we share the requirement *in principle*, even if it might turn out that in many circumstances the micro–macro link turns out to be practically impossible. It is a circumstance familiar also to natural sciences where it is often the case that one can write the aggregate statistical properties (say, in a thermodynamic problem) without being able to derive them from an underlying micro description (say, detailed balance equations).

11. We have repeatedly stressed the *imperfect* adaptation of agents to the macro configurations of the system. A perfect adaptation would indeed imply a strong functionalist conjecture ('people do and think what they are supposed to do, given the functional requirements of the system itself'). In our view, on the contrary, it is precisely imperfect adaptation which is an important source of dynamics.

12. This notwithstanding the acknowledgment of their importance: cf. for example, Nelson and Winter's definition of routines as truces among conflicting interests (Nelson and Winter (1982)).

13. In turn, as known, once the problem is posed in these terms it can be formally handled by means, for example, of 'evolutionary games' (cf. Boyer and Orlean (1992) for such an attempt). Far from denying the usefulness of such exercises as sorts of gedankenexperiment on collective adaptation under potential conflict of interests (or conflicts between individual incentives and collective good), they still deliver a quite partial picture of the object of inquiry. For example, in the current state of the art we do not know of any model allowing for adaptation on preferences themselves (i.e. in game terms, endogenously evolving payoff matrices). Neither there is the discovery of new 'strategies' (with the exception of Lindgren (1992)). And finally, 'learning' tends to neglect any cognitive/problem-solving aspect and be reduced to a stimulus–response mechanism of reinforcement (possibly mitigated by stochastic search or mistakes).

14. A co-evolutionary view runs against, for example, 'technological determinism' (that is, technology proceeds exclusively according to its inner logics, and institutions ought simply to adjust, with varying lags) but also 'social determinism' (for example, technology is purely a 'social construction'). On the contrary, the co-evolutionary view does accept that technological change and social change have their own inner logics (possibly conflicting with each other) and does attempt to explain, for example, the emerging trajectories of technical change as the outcome of such a coupling.

15. Incidentally, 'Bayesian' and 'Pavlovian' learning have most characteristics in common since both claim (i) what Savage would have called a 'small world' hypothesis (the notional set of events and response strategies is given from the start); and (ii) there is a striking transparence of the links between actions and consequences. Hence, ultimately, the difference between the two just rests on what the theorist assumes the agent to consciously know, without much influence on the ultimate outcomes. So, for example, it is easy for biologists overwhelmed by economists' fascination to build models of rats who behave in equilibrium 'as if' understanding strategies involving first-order conditions and Lagrange multipliers, or conversely, respectable economists claiming 'Pavlovian' convergence to sophisticated Rational Expectation equilibria.

26   *Prospects for evolutionary and institutional theory*

16. By way of a comparison, recall that even in the most sophisticated state-of-the-art accounts, in economics, of behaviours and interactions (even under conditions of imperfect information) agents are assumed to *obviously* have the correct 'transparent' understanding of the causal links of the environment, and to *obviously* know how to solve the technical problems at hand.

REFERENCES

Abramovitz, M. (1989), *Thinking about Growth*, Cambridge/New York: Cambridge University Press.

Aglietta, M. (1974), *Accumulation et regulation du capitalisme en longue période. L'exemple des Etats-Unis (1870–1970)*, thesis, Paris, October.

Aglietta, M. (1982), *Regulation and Crisis of Capitalism*, New York, Monthly Review Press.

Aglietta, M. (1993), 'La finance au Japon, Changements de structures·et adaptations des comportements'. Communication au colloque, 'Mode de regulation au Japon et Relations Internationales: de l'histoire longue aux transformations recentes', *Japon in Extenso, Revue*, No. 33, 1994.

Amendola, G., G. Dosi and E. Papagni (1993), 'The dynamics of international competitiveness', *Weltwirtschaftliches Archiv*.

Aoki, M. (1995), 'Unintended Fit: Organisational Evolution and Government Design of Institutions in Japan', Working Paper, Department of Economics, Stanford University.

Arthur, B., Y. Ermoliev and Y. Kaniovski (1987), 'Path-dependent processes and the emergence of macrostructures', *European Journal of Operations Research*, 30, 294–303.

Basalla, G. (1988), *The Evolution of Technology*, Cambridge, Cambridge University Press.

Basle, M., J. Mazier and J.F. Vidal (1984), 'Quand les crise durent ... ', *Economica*, Paris.

Bowles, S. and H. Gintis (1993), 'The revenge of homo economicus: contested exchange and the revival of political economy', *Journal of Economic Perspectives*, 7, 83–102.

Boyer. R. (1978), 'La crise: une mise en perspective historique', *Critique de l'Economie Politique, Revue*, Paris.

Boyer, R. (1986a), *La Théorie de la Regulation, une analyse critique*, Paris: La Découverte.

Boyer, R. (1986b), *La Théorie du travail en Europe*, Paris: La Découverte.

Boyer, R. (1987), 'Regulation', in *The New Palgrave*, London: Macmillan.

Boyer, R. (1988a), 'Technical change and the theory of "Regulation"', in Dosi *et al.* (1988).

Boyer, R. (1988b), 'Formalizing growth regimes', in Dosi *et al.* (1988).

Boyer, R. (1990), *The Regulation School: A Critical Introduction*, New York, Columbia University Press.

Boyer, R. and J. Mistral (1978), *Accumulation, inflation et crise*, Paris: Puf.

Boyer, R. and A. Orlean (1991), 'Les transformations des conventions salariales entre Théorie et histoire. D'Henry Ford au fordisme', *Revue Economique*, 42(2) (Mars), 233–72.

Boyer, R. and A. Orlean (1992), 'How Do Conventions Evolve?', *Journal of Evolutionary Economics*.

Boyer, R. and Y. Saillard (eds) (1995), *Théorie de la Regulation. L'état des savoir*, Paris: La Découvert.

Caroli, E. (1995), *Formation, Institutions et Croissance Economique*, These IEP, Paris.

CEPREMAP (1977), *Approches de l'inflation: l'exemple francais*, Convention de recherches no. 22, mimeo, December.

Chiaromonte, F. and G. Dosi (1993), 'Heterogeneity, Competition and Macroeconomic Dynamics', *Structural Change and Economic Dynamics*, 4, 39–6.

Chiaromonte, F., G. Dosi and L. Orsenigo (1992), 'Innovative learning and institutions in the process of development: on the microfoundations of growth regimes', in R. Thomson (ed.), *Learning and Technological Change*, London, Macmillan.

Cohen, M. and P. Bacdayan (1994), 'Organizational routines as stored procedural memory: evidence from a laboratory study', *Organization Sciences*, 5, 554–68.

Commons, J.R. (1934), *Institutional Economics*, University of Wisconsin Press, Madison.

Conlisk, J. (1989), 'An aggregate model of technical change', *Quarterly Journal of Economics*, 104, 787–821.

Coriat, B. (1982), *L'atelier et le Chronomètre*, Paris: Bourgeois.

Coriat, B. (1990), *L'atelier et le Robot*, Paris: Bourgeois.

Coriat, B. (1991–94), *Penser à l'Envers – Travail et Organisation dans la firme Japonaise,* C. Bourgois; 2nd revised edition Bourgois/Choix 1994.

Coriat, B. (1993), 'L'hypothèse du Compagnie-isme', *Mondes en Developpement Revue*, no. 4, Paris.

Coriat, B. (1994a), 'La Théorie de la Régulation. Origines, Specificites, Enjeux', in *Future Antérieur,* Paris, L'Harmattan; special issue of *Théorie de la Regulation et critique de la Raison Economique.*

Coriat, B. (1994b), 'Variety, routines and networks: the metamorphosis of the Fordist firms', *Industrial and Corporate Change*, 4(1), Oxford University Press.

Coriat, B. and G. Dosi (1995), 'Learning How to Govern and Learning How to Solve Problems. On the Coevolution of Competences, Conflicts and Organisational Routines', IIASA Working Paper, WP-95-06, Laxenburg, Austria; forthcoming in A. Chandler, P. Hagström and Ö. Sölvell (eds), *The Dynamic Firm*, Oxford, Oxford University Press.

Coriat, B. and O. Weinstein (1995), *Les nouvelles Theories de l'Entreprise*, Paris: Hachette.

David, P. (1975), *Technical Choice, Innovation and Economic Growth*, Cambridge: Cambridge University Press.

David, P.A. (1985), 'Clio and the Economics of QWERTY', *American Economic Review. Papers and Proceedings*, (75), 332–7.

David, P.A. (1992), 'Heroes, herds and hysteresis in technological change: Thomas Edison and the battle of the systems', *Industrial and Corporate Change*, 1, 139–80.

David, P.A. (1994), 'Why are institutions the carriers of history?', *Structural Change and Economic Dynamics*.

Day, R. and G. Eliasson (eds) (1986), *The Dynamics of Market Economics*, Amsterdam: North Holland.

Delorme, R. and C. André (1983), *L'Etat et l'Economie*, Paris: Seuil.

DiMaggio, P.J. and W.W. Powell (1991), 'The iron cage revisited: institutional isomorphism and collective rationality in organisational fields', in W.W. Powell and P.J. DiMaggio (eds), *The New Institutionalism in Organisational Analysis*, Chicago: University of Chicago Press.

Dosi, G. (1982), 'Technical paradigms and technical trajectories. A suggested interpretation of the Determinants and Directions of technical change and the transformation of the economy', *Research Policy,* March.

Dosi, G. (1984), Technical Change and Industrial Transformation, London: Macmillan.

28   *Prospects for evolutionary and institutional theory*

Dosi, G. (1988), 'Sources, procedures and microeconomic effects of innovation', *Journal of Economic Literature*, 26, 126–73.

Dosi, G. (1991), 'Perspectives on evolutionary theory', *Science and Public Policy*.

Dosi, G. (1995), 'Hierarchies, markets and power: some foundational issues on the nature of contemporary economic organisations', *Industrial and Corporate Change*, (4), 1–19.

Dosi, G. and M. Egidi (1991), 'Substantive and procedural uncertainty. An exploration of economic behaviours in changing environments', *Journal of Evolutionary Economics*.

Dosi. G. and L. Marengo (1994), 'Some elements of an evolutionary theory of organisational competences', in R.W. England (ed.), *Evolutionary Concepts in Contemporary Economics*, Ann Arber: University of Michigan Press.

Dosi, G. and R.R. Nelson (1994), 'An introduction to evolutionary theories in economics', *Journal of Evolutionary Economics*, 4, 153–72.

Dosi, G., K. Pavitt and L. Soete (1990), *The Economics of Technological Change and International Trade*, Brighton: Wheatsheaf; New York: New York University Press.

Dosi, G., S. Fabiani, R. Aversi and M. Meacci (1994a), 'The dynamics of international differentiation: a multi-country evolutionary model', *Industrial and Corporate Change*, 3, 225–42.

Dosi, G., C. Freeman and S. Fabiani (1994b), 'The process of economic development: introducing some stylized facts and theories on technologies, firms and institutions', *Industrial and Corporate Change*, 3, 1–46.

Dosi, G., L. Marengo, A. Bassanini and M. Valente (1994c), 'Norms as Emergent Properties of Adaptive Learning. The Case of Economic Routines', Working Paper, WP-94 -73, Laxenburg, Austria.

Dosi, G., O. Marsili, L. Orsenigo and R. Salvatore (1995), 'Learning, market selection and the evolution of industrial structures', *Small Business Economics*.

Dosi, G., C. Freeman, R.R.Nelson, G. Silverberg and L. Soete (eds) (1988), *Technical Change and Economic Theory*, London: Francis Pinter; New York: Columbia University Press.

Dupuy, J.P. (1980), 'Convention et Common Knowledge', *Revue économique*, 40(2), 381–400.

Dupuy, J.P., F. Emard-Duvernay, O. Favereau, A. Orlean, R. Salais and L. Thevenot (1989), 'L'économie des conventions', *Revue economique*, 40(2).

Eggertsson, T. (1990), *Economic Behaviour and Institutions*, Cambridge: Cambridge University Press.

Egidi, M. (1994), 'Routines, Hierarchies of Problems, Procedural Behaviour: Some Evidence from Experiments', IIASA Working Paper WP-94-58, Laxenburg, Austria.

Eliasson, G. (1986), 'Micro-heterogeneity of firms and stability of industrial growth', in R. Day and G. Eliasson (eds), *The Dynamics of Market Economics*, Amsterdam: North Holland.

England, R.W. (ed.) (1994), *Evolutionary Concepts in Contemporary Economics*, Ann Arbor: University of Michigan Press.

Fagerberg, J. (1994), 'Technology and international differences in growth rates', *Journal of Economic Literature*, 32, 1147–75.

Favereau, O. (1986), 'La formalisation du role des conventions dans l'allocation des ressources', in R. Salais (ed.), *Le travail. Marches, règles, conventions*, Paris: INSEE-Economica.

Fontana, W. and L. Buss (1994a), '"The arrival of the fittest": toward a theory of biological organisation', *Bulletin of Mathematical Biology*, 1–64.

Fontana, W. and L. Buss (1994b), 'What would be conserved if the "Tape Were Run Twice!"', *Proc, Nat. Acad. Sci.*, USA.

Freeman, C. (1982), *The Economics of Industrial Innovation*, 2nd edn, London: Francis Pinter.

Freeman, C. (1994), 'The economics of technical change', *Cambridge Journal of Economics*, 18, 463–514.

Freeman. C. and C. Perez (1988), 'Structural crises of adjustment', in Dosi *et al.* (1988).

Granovetter, M. (1985), 'Economic action and social structure: the problem of embeddedness', *American Journal of Sociology*, 91, 481–510.

Granstrand, O. (ed.) (1994), *The Economics of Technology*, Amsterdam, Elsevier/North Holland.

Grendstad, G. and P. Selle (1995), 'Cultural theory and the new institutionalism', *Journal of Theoretical Politics*, (7), 5–27.

Hamilton, G.G. and R.C. Feenstra (1995), 'Variety of hierarchies and markets: an introduction', *Industrial and Corporate Change*, 4, 51–91.

Hanusch, H. (ed.) (1988), *Evolutionary Economics*, Cambridge: Cambridge University Press.

Hayek, F. (1937), 'Economics and Knowledge', *Economica*, 4.

Hodgson, G. (1988). *Economics and Institutions*, Cambridge: Polity Press; Philadelphia: University of Pennsylvania Press.

Hodgson, G. (1993), *Economics and Evolution*, Cambridge: Polity Press; Ann Arbor: Michigan University Press.

Holland, J.H., K.J. Holyoak, R.E. Nisbett and P.R. Thagaro (1986), *Induction*, Cambridge, Mass.: MIT Press.

Jessop, B. (1990), 'Regulation theories in retrospect and prospect', *Economy and Society*, 19(2), 153–216.

Kandori, M., G.J. Mailath and R. Rob (1993), 'Learning, mutation and long run equilibria in games', *Econometrica*, 61, 29–56.

Kaniovski, Y. and P. Young (1995), 'Learning Dynamics in Games with Stochastic Perturbations', *Games and Economic Behaviour*.

Kirman, A.P. and A. Vignes (1992), 'Price dispersion: theoretical considerations and empirical evidence from the Marseille fish market', in K. Arrow (ed.), *Issues in Contemporary Economics*, vol.I, London: Mcmillan.

Klepper, S. (1993), 'Entry, Exit, Growth and Innovation over the Product Cycle', Carnegie-Mellon University, Working Paper.

Kuran, T. (1991), 'Cognitive limitations and preference evolution', *Journal of Institutional and Theoretical Economics*.

Lane, D. (1993), 'Artificial worlds and economics', Parts I and II, *Journal of Evolutionary Economics*, 3, 89–107 and 177–97.

Langlois, R.N. (ed.) (1986), *Economics as a Process: Essays in the New Institutional Economics*, Cambridge/New York: Cambridge University Press.

Lesourne, J. (1991), *Ordre et Désordre*, Paris: Economica.

Levinthal, D. (1990), 'Organisational adaptation and environmental selection: interrelated processes of change', *Organisation Science*, 2, 140–5.

Lewis, D.K. (1969), *Convention: A Philosophical Study*, Cambridge, Mass.: Harvard University Press.

Lindgren, R. (1992), 'Evolutionary phenomena in simple dynamics', in C.G. Langton (ed.), *Artificial Life II.*, Redwood City: Addison-Wesley.

Lordon, F. (1993), 'Endogenous Structural Change and Crisis in a Multiple Time-Scales Growth Model', CEPREMAP Working Paper 9324, Paris.

Lundvall, B.-Å. (ed.) (1992), *National Systems of Innovation*, London: Francis Pinter.

Malerba, F. and L. Orsenigo (1994), 'The Dynamics and Evolution of Industries', Laxenburg, Austria, IIASA, Working Paper, WP-94-120.

March, J.G. and J.P. Olsen (1989), *Rediscovering Institutions: The Organizational Basis of Policies*, New York: Free Press.

Marengo, L. (1992), 'Coordination and organisational learning in the firm', *Journal of Evolutionary Economics*, 2, 313–26.

Marengo, L. and H. Tordjman (1996), 'Speculation, Heterogeneity and Learning: A Model of Exchange Rate Dynamics', Kyklos.

Metcalfe, S. (1992), 'Variety, structure and change: an evolutionary perspective on the competitive process', *Revue d'Economie Industrielle*, 65, 46–61.

Mokyr, J. (1990), *The Lever of Riches*, Oxford: Oxford University Press.

Nakicenovic, N. and A. Grübler (eds) (1992), *Diffusion of Technologies and Social Behaviour*, Berlin/Heidelberg/New York: Springer Verlag.

Nelson, R.R. (1987), *Understanding Technical Change As An Evolutionary Process*, Amsterdam: North Holland.

Nelson, R.R. (ed.) (1993), *National Innovation Systems: A Comparative Study*, Oxford/New York: Oxford University Press.

Nelson, R.R. (1994),' The co-evolution of technology, industrial structure, and supporting institutions', *Industrial and Corporate Change*, 3, 47–63.

Nelson, R. (1995), 'Recent evolutionary theorizing about economic change', *Journal of Economic Literature*, 33, 48–90.

Nelson, R. and S. Winter (1982), *An Evolutionary Theory of Economic Change*, Cambridge, Mass.: Bellkap Press of Harvard University Press.

Nelson, R.R. and G. Wright (1992), 'The rise and fall of American technological leadership: the post-war era in historical perspective', *Journal of Economic Literature*, 30, 1931–64.

North, D. (1990), *Institutions, Institutional Change and Economic Performance*, Cambridge: Cambridge University Press.

North, D. (1991), 'Institutions', *Journal of Economic Perspectives*, 75, 264–74.

Orlean, A. (ed.) (1994), *L'économie des conventions*, Paris: PUF.

Palmer, R.G., W.B. Arthur, J.H. Holland, B. LeBaron and P. Taylor (1994), 'Artificial economic life: a simple model of a stockmarket', *Physica D*, 75, 264–74.

Patel, P. and K. Pavitt (1994), 'Uneven (and divergent) technological accumulation among advanced countries: evidence and a framework of explanation', *Industrial and Corporate Change*, 3, 759.

Pavitt, I. (1984), 'Sectoral patterns of innovation: toward a taxonomy and a theory', *Research Policy*, 13, 343–75.

Reynaud, B. (1992), *Le Salaire, La règle et Le Marché*, C. Bourgois: Paris.

Reynaud, B. (1992c), *Les nouvelles Théories du Salaire*, Paris: La Découverte, Collection Repères.

Rosenberg, N. (1976), *Perspectives on Technology*, Cambridge: Cambridge University Press.

Rosenberg, N. (1982), *Inside the Black Box*, Cambridge: Cambridge University Press.

Saviotti, P. and S. Metcalfe (eds) (1991), *Evolutionary Economies*, London/Chur: Harwood Academic Press.

Schwartz, M. and M. Thompson (1990), *Divided We Stand: Redefining Politics, Technology and Social Choice*, Brighton: Harvester Wheatsheaf.

Silverberg, G. (1987), 'Technical progress, capital accumulation and effective demand: a self-organization model', in D. Batten, J. Casti and B. Johansson (eds), *Economic Evolution and Structural Adjustment*, Berlin/New York: Springer Verlag.

Silverberg, G. and L. Soete (eds) (1993), *The Economics of Growth and Technical Change: Technologies, Nations, Agents*, Aldershot: Edward Elgar.

Silverberg, G. and B. Verspagen (1994), 'Learning, innovation and economic growth: a long-run model of industrial dynamics', *Industrial and Corporate Change*, 3, 199–223.

Silverberg, G. and B. Verspagen (1995a), 'Evolutionary Theorizing on Economic Growth', IIASA Working Paper WP-95-78j; forthcoming in K. Dopfer (ed.), *The Evolutionary Principles of Economics*, Kluwer.

Silverberg, G. and B. Verspagen (1995b), 'From the Artificial to the Endogenous: Modelling Evolutionary Adaptation and Economic Growth', IIASA, Working Paper, WP-95-, Laxenburg, Austria.

Silverberg, G., G. Dosi and L. Orsenigo (1988), 'Innovation, diversity and diffusion: a self-organisation model', *Economic Journal*, 98, 1032–54.

Solow, J.A. (1990), *The Labour Market as a Social Institution*, Basil Blackwell.

Stiglitz, J.E. (1994), 'Economic growth revisited', *Industrial and Corporate Change*, 3, 65–110.

Tordjman, H. (1993), *Dynamiques spéculations, hétérogénéité des agents et apprentissage: le cas des taux de change*, Thèse CEFI, Universite d'Aix-Marseille II, Janvier 1994.

Utterback, J. and F. Suarez (1992), 'Innovation, Competition and Market Structure', *Research Policy*, 21, 1–21.

Veblen, T. (1898), 'Why is economics not an evolutionary science?', *Quarterly Journal of Economics*, 12.

Verspagen, B. (1993), *Uneven Growth Between Independent Economics: The Evolutionary Dynamics of Growth and Technology*, Aldershot: Avebury.

Vincenti, W. (1990), *What Do Engineers Do and How Do They Know It?*, Baltimore: Johns Hopkins University Press.

Warglien, M. (1995), 'Hierarchical selection and organisational adaptation', *Industrial and Corporate Change*, 4, 161–86.

Williamson, O.E. (1975), *Market and Hierarchies*, New York: Free Press.

Williamson, O.E. (1985). *The Economic Institutions of Capitalism*, New York: Free Press.

Williamson, O.E. (1990). 'The firm as a nexus of treaties: an introduction', in M. Aoki, B. Gustafsson and O.E. Williamson (eds), *The Firm as a Nexus of Treaties*, London: Sage.

Williamson, O.E. and W.G. Ouchi (1981), 'The markets and hierarchies and visible hand perspectives', in A.H. van de Ven and W.F. Joice (eds), *Perspectives on Organisational Design and Behaviour*, New York: Wiley.

Williamson, O.E. (1995), 'Hierarchies, market and power in the economy: an economic perspective', *Industrial and Corporate Change*, 4, 21–50.

Williamson, O.W. and S.G. Winter (1991), *The Nature of the Firm: Origins, Evolution, and Development*, Oxford University Press.

Winter, S.G. (1964), 'Economical natural selection and the theory of the firm', *Yale Economic Essays*.

Winter, S.G. (1982), 'An essay on the theory of production', in S.H. Hymans (ed.), *Economics and the World around It*, Ann Arbor: University of Michigan Press.

32   *Prospects for evolutionary and institutional theory*

Winter, S.G. (1984). 'Schumpeterian competition under alternative technological regimes', *Journal of Economic Behaviour and Organisation*, 5, 287–320.

Winter, S.G. (1986), 'The research program of the behavioural theory of the firm: orthodox critiques and evolutionary perspectives', in B. Gilad and S. Kaish (eds), *Handbook of Behavioural Economics*, Greenwich, Conn.: JAI Press.

Winter, S.G. (1987a), 'Natural selection and evolution', *New Palgrave*, 3, Macmillan.

Winter, S.G. (1987b), 'Competition and selection', *New Palgrave*, 2, Macmillan.

Winter, S.G. (1995), 'Four R's of Profitability: Rents, Resources, Routines and Replication', IIASA Working Paper, WP-95-07, Laxenburg, Austria.

Witt, U. (ed.) (1991), *Explaining Process and Change: Approaches to Evolutionary Economics*, Ann Arbor: University of Michigan Press.

Young, P. (1993), 'The evolution of conventions', *Econometrica*, 61, 59–84.

PART IV

LEARNING AND MARKET SELECTION: EVOLUTIONARY MODELS OF ECONOMIC CHANGE

[13]

J Evol Econ (1994) 4: 93–123

———Journal of———
Evolutionary Economics
© Springer-Verlag 1994

On "badly behaved" dynamics

Some applications of generalized urn schemes to technological and economic change

G. Dosi[1] and Y. Kaniovski[2]

[1] University of Rome "La Sapienza", Rome, Italy
[2] International Institute for Applied Systems Analysis, Laxenburg, Austria

Abstract. Adaptive (path dependent) processes of growth modeled by urn schemes are important for several fields of applications: biology, physics, chemistry, economics. In this paper we present a general introduction to urn schemes, together with some new results. We review the studies that have been done in the technological dynamics by means of such schemes. Also several other domains of economic dynamics are analysed by the same machinery and its new modifications allowing to tackle non-homogeneity of the phase space. We demonstrate the phenomena of multiple equilibria, different convergence rates for different limit patterns, locally positive and locally negative feedbacks, limit behavior associated with non-homogeneity of economic environment where producers (firms) are operating. It is also shown that the above urn processes represent a natural and convenient stochastic replicator dynamics which can be used in evolutionary games.

Key words: Urn scheme – Innovation – Ugly dynamics – Multiple limit states

JEL-classification: D83

1. Introduction

Microeconomic heterogeneity, non-equilibrium interactions and the co-existence of *negative* and *positive* feedbacks appear to be quite general characteristics of economic change. They are particularly evident in the case of technological innovation and diffusion – but by no means limited to them. Technical change typically involves diversity amongst the agents who generate or are effected by it; various forms of learning often based on trial-and-error procedures; and mechanisms of

Correspondence to: G. Dosi, Dipartimento di Science Economichie, Università degli Studi di Roma, Via Nomentana 41, I-00161 Rome, Italy selection which reward particular types of technologies, agents or behaviors at the expenses of others.

These appear to be, indeed, general features of the competitive process driving economic dynamics. "Competition" entails the interaction among heterogeneous firms embodying different technologies, different expectations and, quite often, displaying different behaviors. Moreover, it is often the case that technological and organizational learning is associated with various types of externalities and increasing returns.

Over the last two decades, at last, such dynamic phenomena have drawn an increasing attention within the economic discipline – especially with reference to technological change. A number of conceptual approaches and mathematical tools have been applied, often benefiting from contemporary developments in the analysis of dynamical systems in natural sciences.

In this work, we shall discuss some of these approaches and, in particular, present the basic structure and the interpretative scope of one "formal machinery", namely *generalized urn schemes*. This paper can be considered as an introduction to generalized urn models, containing both known and new results together with a sketch of some directions for the future research. In section 2, we shall outline some phenomena which are central to technological and economic dynamics, and briefly review alternative formal representations of them. Section 3 introduces the basics of urn schemes. In the following sections we illustrate some applications to relatively simple competitive environments (section 4), and further refinements, contemplating local feedback processes (section 5); phenomena of increasing returns deriving from system compatibility (section 6); non-homogeneous environments (section 7) and "evolutionary games" (section 8). Finally, in the conclusion we shall point out some promising areas of application of this formal apparatus, including the economics of innovation, industrial dynamics, macroeconomics, finance.

2. Processes of economic evolution

In very general terms, the impulses driving economic change stem, first, from variations in the knowledge and physical resources upon which individual agents can draw in order to pursue their activities; second, from the process by which agents learn, adapt, invent – on the grounds of whatever they perceive to be the available knowledge and resources, and, third, from the interactions amongst the agents themselves. Of course, these sources of change are by no means independent: for example, learning activities obviously affect the available knowledge and the efficiency by which resources are used; interactions might trigger learning and entail externalities; learning itself may be associated with particular forms of economic activity, such as learning-by-doning. The variety of sources and mechanisms of economic change highlighted by economic history, most likely, in our view, precludes the identification of some unique or archetypical dynamic form which could apply across industries, phases of development, historical contexts. Still, it might be possible (and indeed is a challenging area of research) to identify few relatively invariant characteristics of the process of change and, with them, also the "formal machineries" most apt to represent them.

Some basic features of economic evolution are the following: (i) imperfect and time-consuming microeconomic learning; (ii) microheterogeneity; (iii) most often, various form of increasing returns – especially in the accumulation of knowledge – and non-linearities; (iv) aggregate dynamics driven by both individual learning and collective selection mechanisms; (v) "orderly" structural properties resulting from non-equilibrium fluctuations.

Correspondingly, let us examine the formal representations which can account for at least some of these features of evolutionary dynamics. As a general reference, let us start from "order-through-fluctuation" dynamics (cf. Nicolis and Prigogine 1971 and 1989; Prigogine and Stengers 1984): it is a quite broad paradigm for the interpretation of complex non-linear processes, initially developed with reference to physical chemistry and molecular biology, but more generally emphasizing the properties of self-reinforcing mechanisms and out-of-equilibrium self-organization. Such systems turn out to be sensitive to (however small) early perturbations and display multiplicity of patterns in their long-term behaviour. The cumulation of small early disturbances (or small disturbances around unstable states) "pushes" the system toward one of these patterns and thus "select" the structure towards which the system will eventually tend. These properties apply to a very wide class of dynamical systems, highlighting, loosely speaking, some general "evolutionary" features well beyond the domain of social sciences and biology.

Further specifications of evolutionary dynamics come from mathematical biology (see Eigen and Schuster 1979). Evolution in many of such models occurs in a way that some integral characteristics (mean fitness for biological systems or mean "competitiveness" in the economic analogy) "improves" along the trajectory. In the simplest case of Fisher's selection model, "improvements" straightforwardly imply that the mean fitness increases along the path. However, even in biology this equivalence does not hold in general (due, for example, to phenomena of hyper-selection, co-evolution, symmetry-breaking: see Allen (1988) and Silverberg (1988) for discussions directly linked to economic applications). Even more so, this *non*-equivalence between "evolution" and "increasing fitness", however defined, is likely to emerge whenever there is no identifiable "fundamental law of nature" or conservation principle. Putting it another way: evolutionary dynamics – in biology as well in economics – involves some kind of selection process grounded on the relevant distributions of agents' characteristics, on the one hand, and on some environmental criterion of "adaptiveness", on the other. (Until recently, most economic models have avoided the issue simply by *assuming* that all the agents were perfectly "adapted", either via some unspecified selection process that occured just before the economist started looking at the world, or via some optimization process that occured in the head of the agents themselves.) Replicator dynamics is a common formal tool to represent such selection-driven adaptation (for applications to economics, see Silverberg (1988) and Silverberg et al. (1988); adaptation processes of various types in "evolutionary games" are discussed by Banerjee and Weibull (1992), Cabrales (1992), Kandori et al. (1993), Samuelson and Zhang (1992) Young (1993)). However, at least the simplest replicator process imposes quite stringent conditions on the way selection occurs. In essence, these restrictions turn out to be negative feedbacks, i.e. diminishing returns, deriving from some underlying "conservation principle".[1] On the contrary, positive feedbacks lead to multiple limit states and generate a much richer variety of trajectories which the system may follow. For example, it is increasingly acknowledged that technological innovations are likely

---

[1] Conventionally, in economics, profit (or utility) maximization under a constraint of given and scarce resources clearly performs this role.

to involve some forms of dynamic increasing returns – hence, positive feedbacks – along their development and diffusion (cf. Freeman (1982), Dosi et àl. (1988), Anderson et al. (1988), David (1988), and for an interpretation of the empirical evidence, Dosi (1988)). Relatedly, there is no guarantee that the particular economic outcome which happens to be historically selected amongst many notional alternatives will be the "best" one, irrespectively of the "fitness" or welfare yardsticks.[2]

Concerning the mathematical tools that have been proposed within and outside economics for the analysis of the competitive process, ordinary differential equations have a paramount importance (not surprisingly, since they are also the most common language of modern science and especially physics). They are applied to most analyses of economic and technological dynamics (for our purposes here, cf. Nelson and Winter (1982), Polterovich and Henkin (1988), Day (1992), and the works surveyed in Boldrin (1988); in general, cf. Brock and Malliaris (1989) and Rosser (1991)). In particular, ordinary differential equations with trajectories on the unit simplex – i.e. of the replicator type – borrow, as already mentioned, an idea of selection-driven evolution from biology (cf. Silverberg et al. 1988).[3] For stochastic (Markov) perturbations of these equations see Nicolis and Prigogine (1971) – for general equations –, and Foster and Young (1993), – for equations of the replicator type. However, while these continuous-time formulations work well, they involve a not so harmless approximation for events that are by nature discrete (the main example being a phase space which is discrete and changes by discrete increments). More intuitively, the continuous-time approximation is bound to take very literally the old saying that *natura non facet saltum*.

Moreover, from a technical point of view, the approximation carries unnecessary hypotheses of mathematical nature (a classical example is the Lipschitz condition on the coefficients of the differential equation describing the system) and specific difficulties (such as the requirement of rigorously defining the stochastic perturbations of replicator equations). In this respect, it might be worth mentioning here some recent results from so-called "evolutionary games" showing convergence to conventional Nash-type equilibria in the continuous approximation but not in the discrete formulation (Banerjee and Weibull 1992; Dekel and Scotchmer 1991). Moreover, formal representations of selection processes in economics often rely on replicator dynamics satisfying the weak monotonicity condition (Friedman 1991; Samuelson and Zhang 1992; Baherjee and Weibull 1992) (loosely speaking, the condition guarantees that, given an environment, there is no reversal in the "forces of selection" along the trajectory). However, even in simple cases the results on limit properties obtained under replicator dynamics might not hold under more general selection processes (see, for example, Cabrales 1992).

To summarize this brief overview of the formalisms applied to economic dynamics and evolution: ideally, one would like some machinery able to capture as

---

[2] In fact, even environments that are stationary in their "fundamentals" (e.g. best practice technologies) selection-driven adaptation yields convergence to equilibria associated with Pareto-optimal properties only under further (and quite demanding) restrictions on the nature of the interactions, the related payoffs and the adaptation dynamics. This is certainly true in presence of "strategic" interactions, but it applies also under (quasi) pure competition: on the latter, see the pioneering investigation in Winter (1971).

[3] Of course, this does not bear any implication for the sources of "mutation" upon which environmental selection operates. For example, Silverberg et al. (1988) assume an exogenous drift in innovative opportunities with learning-by-using and diffusion-related externalities.

adequately as possible (a) increasing-returns phenomena, i.e. positive feedbacks; (b) "ugly" and badly behaved selection dynamics, involving also "jumps" and discontinuities, co-evolutionary effects, etc.; (c) a large variety of individual processes of adaptation and innovation (and, thus, being quite agnostic on the processes driving the perturbations); and (d) the process of accumulation of agents' individual behaviors into the regularities driving the dynamics of the whole population.

In the following, we shall assess to what extent an alternative class of models, namely *generalized urn schemes*, can fulfill these tasks. These schemes, sometimes called *non-linear Pólya processes* or *adaptive processes* of *growth*, generate stochastic discrete-time dynamic systems with trajectories on the set of points with rational coordinates from the unit simplex (cf. Arthur 1988, Arthur et al. 1983 and 1987c; Glaziev and Kaniovski 1991; Dosi et al. 1994; Arthur and Ruszczinski 1992). Formally, they represent non-stationary Markov chains with growing numbers of states. This allows to reach, under corresponding conditions, any state from the unit simplex (which is, by definition, not the case for finite Markov chains). The mathematical background comes from Hill et al. (1980) and Arthur et al. (1983), (1987a) and (1988). It does not rely on notions common for Markov processes such as "master equations": this essentially simplifies the argument and allows to produce deeper results. Moreover, this formal apparatus enables one to handle positive and/or negative feedbacks, possibly coexisting in the same process: see Arthur (1988) and Arthur et al. (1987c). In particular, these feedbacks may have a "local" nature – in the sense that they may occur only under particular states on the trajectories (Dosi et al. (1994)). This approach allows also to treat complementaries and network externalities in the adoption of competing technologies (Arthur et al. 1987b), whereby individual commodities – say, computers or telecommunication equipment – operate within networks requiring compatibility.[4] It must be also emphasized that in this work we generally suggest examples of application of this formalism drawn from the economics of innovation, but similar properties can easily be found in many other economic domains: rather than technologies, one could also consider e.g. organizational forms or strategies in business economics; cognitive models and decision rules in finance; etc. (see the final section). Using the generalized urn schemes one can analyse the emergenece of random market structure with more than one limit state occuring with positive probability (cf. Arthur et al. 1983 and Glaziev and Kaniovski 1991). Moreover, one may determine the different convergence rates to the various limit states attainable with positive probability (Arthur et al. 1988).

Generalized urn schemes are well suited to analyse increasing returns phenomena and, generally, the interaction of individual behaviors of agents who have incomplete information about the environment and its mechanisms of evolution. The two points are most often related: dynamic increasing returns tend to imply unpredictability of the particular limit state that will be attained. Conversely, as we shall see, the process of information acquisition entails dynamic consequences similar to purely "technological" increasing returns. The rules driving the collective

---

[4] Systems compatibility implies that one ought to consider combinations amongst individual technologies. In turn, this can hardly be done by adding to the "technological space", where choices are made, all possible combinations of technologies existing at any moment in time. At the very least, this procedure would lead to an enormous growth in the dimension of the phase space. For example, if N new technologies come to the market, considering all their possible combinations would imply the "explosion" of the dimension of the phase space up to $2^N - 1$.

dynamics are the cumulated effects of individual behaviors. For each agent, the impact of his own action is negligible, but the sequence of all of them shape the evolution of the system. Hence, one looks for the long run properties when the size of the population or, equivalently, time go to infinity. This does not restrict the applicability of the results for finite, but large enough, populations (although some caution is obviously required). This formal machinery is also a simulation tool as convenient and effective as ordinary differential equations (we shall tackle this type of application in a future publication).

In this work we shall analyse some of the patterns of system evolution which can be discovered by means of generalized urn schemes. In order to do this, we shall use some known models of technological dynamics and also introduce some novel modification highlighting the complex limit structures that these models generate.

Let us start with the simplest definition of a generalized urn scheme.

3. The basic elements of the theory of generalized urn schemes

In this section we give the basic version of the generalized urn scheme and outline the main patterns of the asymptotic behavior which it can demonstrate: multiplicity of the limit states, attainability and unattainability of them, and different convergence rates to the attainable ones.

To simplify the presentation, let us restrict ourselves to the case of two competing technologies which corresponds to urn schemes with balls of two colors (Hill et al. 1980 and Arthur et al. 1983). As illustrations, think for example of two technologies whose efficiency improves together with its diffusion, due e.g. to increasing returns in its production or to "network externalities" for the adopters.

Consider an urn of infinite capacity with black and white balls. Starting with $n_w \geqslant 1$ white balls and $n_b \geqslant 1$ black balls into the urn, a new ball is added into the urn at time instants $t = 1, 2 \dots$. It will be white with probability $f_t(X_t)$ and black with probability $1 - f_t(X_t)$. By X_t we designate the proportion of white balls into the urn at time t. The general intuition is that, given the function $f_t(\cdot)$, one can build models of the stochastic evolution of X_t. The balls might be producers and white and black balls denote two technologies. The model is then one of adoption of competing innovations. Other interpretations might involve individuals selecting among products or even among "opinions". The path of X_t can take on a great variety of qualitative properties, depending on the specification of the function $f_t(\cdot)$: some of them will be explored in the following. Moreover, by allowing the addition of more than one ball, more than two colors, more than one urn, further urn models can be created. Here $f_t(\cdot)$ is a function,[5] which maps $R(0, 1)$ in $[0, 1]$ ($R(0, 1)$ stands for the set of rational numbers from $(0, 1)$). The dynamics of X_t is given by the relation

$$X_{t+1} = X_t + (t + n_w + n_b)^{-1}[\xi_t(X_t) - X_t], \quad t \geqslant 1, \quad X_1 = n_w(n_w + n_b)^{-1}.$$

Here $\xi_t(x)$, $t \geqslant 1$, are random variables independent in t, such that

$$\xi_t(x) = \begin{cases} 1 \text{ with probability } f_t(x), \\ 0 \text{ with probability } 1 - f_t(x). \end{cases}$$

---

[5] When it does not depend on t, it is called (Hill et al. (1980)) *urn function*.

Designate $\zeta_t(x) - E\xi_t(x) = \xi_t(x) - f_t(x)$ by $\zeta_t(x)$, where E stands for the mathematical expectation. Then we have

$$X_{t+1} = X_t + (t + n_w + n_b)^{-1}\{[f_t(X_t) - X_t] + \zeta_t(X_t)\}, \quad t \geqslant 1,$$
$$X_1 = n_w(n_w + n_b)^{-1}. \tag{1}$$

Due to $E\zeta(x) = 0$, the system (1) shifts on average at time $t \geqslant 1$ from a point x on the value $(t + n_w + n_b)^{-1}[f_t(x) - x]$. Consequently, limit points of the sequence $\{X_t\}$ have to belong to the "set of zeros" of the function $f_t(x) - x$ (for $x \in [0, 1]$). It will really be the set of zeros if $f_t(\cdot)$ does not depend on t, i.e. $f_t(\cdot) = f(\cdot), t \geqslant 1$, for $f(\cdot)$ being a continuous function.

In the general case one needs a specific mathematical machinery to describe this "set of zeros" (see Hill et al. (1980) for the case when the probabilities are discontinuous and do not depend on t; and Arthur et al. (1987b) for the case when the probabilities are discontinuous functions and depend on t).

To summarize the properties of the above urn scheme that are important for our purposes recall the following:

1. Representing a non-stationary Markov chain with growing number of states, the process X_t develops on the one-dimensional unit simplex $[0, 1]$ taking (discrete) values from the set $R(0, 1)$: at time $t + 1$, it can take the values $i(t + n_w + n_b)^{-1}$, where $n_w \leqslant i \leqslant n_w + t$;
2. Since in general we do not require any regularity of $f_t(\cdot), t \geqslant 1$, the process can display a very complicated behavior; for example, its trajectories can produce "persistent fluctuations",[6] or even can "sweep off" an interval with probability 1 (see Arthur et al. 1987b);
3. If for a sequence $\{f_t(\cdot)\}$ there is a function $f(\cdot)$ such that $f_t(\cdot) = f(\cdot) + \delta_t(\cdot)$ and $\sup_{x \in R(0,1)}|\delta_t(x)| \to 0$ sufficiently fast as $t \to \infty$, then for an isolated root θ of $f(x) - x$, one can have convergence of X_t to θ with positive or zero probability (we call such points *attainable*[7] or *unattainable*, correspondingly) depending upon

$$(f(x) - x)(x - \theta) \leqslant 0 \tag{2}$$

or

$$(f(x) - x)(x - \theta) \geqslant 0 \tag{3}$$

in a neighborhood of θ (see Hill et al. 1980) and Dosi et al. (1994)); similar results

---

[6] By "persistent fluctuations" we mean the following. Assume that $f_t(\cdot)$ does not depend on t. Also let the set of zeros of $f(x) - x$ on $[0, 1]$ contain an interval (α, β) and X_t converge with probability 1 to a limit X_0 as $t \to \infty$. Then $\mathscr{P}\{X_0 \in (\alpha, \beta)\} > 0$ (see Hill et al. (1980)). For a fixed elementary outcome ω, X_t would converge to a certain limit. But we cannot observe the whole path for a fixed ω. At each time instant $t \geqslant 1$ we pick up a new elementary outcome and, consequently, the trajectory is unlikely to have a limit. This phenomenon of chaotic behavior of an (observed) trajectory we interpret as a "persistent fluctuation". More complicated almost "bubble-type" fluctuations appear if there is no convergence of $X_t, t \geqslant 1$, with probability 1, as in the above mentioned case when a trajectory "sweeps off" an interval.

[7] Note that in the case of a deterministic model described by an ordinary differential equation, in order to speak about attainability of certain limit state, one would have to operate with such notions as "domain of attraction" of this state, whose practical implementation is not often clear (especially for systems of nonlinear ordinary differential equations).

are known also for touchpoints, i.e. solutions of the equation $f(x) - x = 0$, where this function does not change its sign (see Pemantle 1991);[8]

4. Under the above representation for $\{f_t(\cdot)\}$, the convergence rate to those θ, which belong to the support of the limit variable (i.e. are attainable), depends upon the smoothness of $f(\cdot)$ at θ. In particular, if the smoothness decreases from differentiability, i.e.

$$f(x) = f'(\theta)(x - \theta) + o(|x - \theta|) \quad \text{as} \quad x \to \theta,$$

to the Hölder differentiability of the order $\gamma > 1/2$, i.e.

$$f(x) = f'_H(\theta)\text{sgn}(x - \theta)|x - \theta|^\gamma + o(|x - \theta|^\gamma) \quad \text{as} \quad x \to \theta,$$

then the order of convergence of X_t to θ increases from $t^{-1/2}$ to $t^{-1/(1+\gamma)}$ (see Kaniovski and Pflug 1992).

The properties 1–3 listed above demonstrate the variety of possible long run behaviors of X_t, ranging from chaotic patterns to convergence to one of possibly multiple limit states. Therefore, it can describe an evolutionary process with many feasible outcomes. Developing in time, the process "selects" one of them. The different convergence rates mean that the rates of evolution are, in general, different for different limit states.

In order to show the analytical power of this formal apparatus, let us begin by considering some examples of technological dynamics in homogeneous economic environments, where competing firms, producing either one of the technologies, are operating.

4. Some examples of competition under global feedbacks in an homogeneous economic environment

We start with the simplest model which displays (global) positive feedback and, as a consequence, multiple patterns of limits behavior (two in this case). In this section we demonstrate in particular how the global forces ruling the dynamics of whole populations can be derived from the individual behavior of economic agents.

Suppose that we have two competing technologies, say, A and B, and a market with imperfectly informed and risk-averse adopters.[9] The two technologies have already been introduced in the market, say $n_A \geq 1$ units of A and $n_B \geq 1$ units of B. Let us study their diffusion on the market. At time instants $t = 1, 2, \ldots$ one new adopter enters the market. Since he is imperfectly informed and risk-averse, he uses some "boundedly rational" decision rule to make his choice.[10] For example,

---

[8] Depending upon whether $f(\cdot)$ attains or not the values 0 and 1, these properties can hold for X_1 belonging to a certain domain in $R(0, 1)$ or for any X_1 from $R(0, 1)$ (for details see Dosi et al. 1994).

[9] Note that some general system properties – such as the multiplicity of limit states under positive feedbacks – are independent from the exact characterization of microeconomic decision rules, although the latter influence both the processes and the nature of limit structures themselves.

[10] In any case, fascinating issues, which cannot be pursued here, regard the meaning of "rationality" in environments driven by positive feedbacks and showing multiple limit states. For example, even if the agents knew the "true" urn model, what use could they make of this cognitive representation? How could they be more than "boundedly rational"?

in Arthur et al. (1983) and Glaziev and Kaniovski (1991) the following rule was considered:

R1. Ask an odd number $r > 1$ of users which technology they adopt. If the majority of them use A, choose A. Otherwise choose B.

According to this rule, technologies are symmetric. Alternatively, suppose that they are not. For example, A comes from a well-known firm with a lot of "goodwill" and B from a new and unknown one. Hence, potential users perceive a different risk in this choice and require different evidence. Assume that this corresponds to the following rule:

R2. Fix $\alpha \in (0, 1)$. Ask $q \geqslant 3$ users of the technologies. If more than αq of them use A, choose A. Otherwise choose B.

Here α measures the relative uncertainty of the adopters concerning the two technologies. Clearly if $\alpha = 1/2$ and q is an odd number, then R2 converts into R1.

An alternative interpretation of the choice process described by R1 and R2 is in terms of increasing returns to the technologies, rather than risk-aversion of the adopters: the latter know that the greater the number of past adopters, the bigger are also the improvements which a technology has undergone (although the improvements themselves are not directly observable). Hence, in this case, sampling provides an indirect measure of unobservable technological characteristics.

Rule R1 generates the probability to choose A as a function of its current proportion on the market. Such probability is given by:

$$f_t(x) = p_{R1}(x) + \delta_t(x), \tag{4}$$

where

$$p_{R1}(x) = \sum_{i=(r+1)/2}^{r} C_r^i x^i (1-x)^{r-i},$$

$$\sup_{x \in R(0,1)} |\delta_t(x)| \leqslant \text{const} \min(x, 1-x) t^{-1},$$

and C_r^i stands for the number of combinations from r to i.

The function $p_{R1}(x) - x$ has three roots $0, 1/2$ and 1 on $[0, 1]$. The root $1/2$, satisfying (3), proves to be unattainable, i.e. there is no feasible asymptotic market structure corresponding to it or, speaking in mathematical terms, X_t converges to this root with zero probability as $t \to \infty$ (see Glaziev and Kaniovski (1991)), while the roots 0 and 1, satisfying (2), are indeed attainable, i.e. X_t converges to each of them with positive probability for any ratio between $n_A \geqslant 1$ and $n_B \geqslant 1$: in other words, they both identify a feasible asymptotic market structure. Moreover, the probability for $A(B)$ to dominate in the limit (i.e. that $X_t \to 1 (X_t \to 0)$ as $t \to \infty$) will be greater than $1/2$ if the initial number of units $n_A(n_B)$ of the technology is greater than the initial number of units of the alternative technology (for details see Glaziev and Kaniovski 1991).

Consequently, we observe here a mechanism of "selection" which is "history-dependent": the past shapes, in probability, the future, and this effect self-reinforces along the diffusion trajectory.

Quite similarly, rule R2 generates

$$f_t(x) = p_{R2}(x) + \delta_t(x), \tag{5}$$

where

$$p_{R2}(x) = \sum_{i=[\alpha q]+1}^{q} C_q^i x^i (1-x)^{q-i},$$

$$\sup_{x \in R(0,1)} |\delta_t(x)| \leqslant \text{const min}(x, 1-x)t^{-1}.$$

Here we designate by $[a]$ the integer part of a. The function $p_{R2}(x) - x$ has three roots $0, \theta$ and 1 on $[0, 1]$, where θ shifts to the right as α increases.[11] It can be shown, that similarly to the previous case, also this rule generates a mechanism for establishing the dominance of one of the competing technologies (and both have a positive probability to dominate). However, one cannot explicitly trace here the influence of the initial frequencies of the technologies on the probabilities to dominate.

In general, it is not true that a representation similar to (4) can be derived, with a function which does not depend on t ($p_{R1}(\cdot)$ in the case of (4)). To demonstrate this, consider the following example.

R3. At time $t \geqslant 1$ ask an odd number $r_t > 1$ of the users of alternative technologies. If the majority of them use A, choose A. Otherwise choose B.

Here each of the new adopters uses his own sample size to make his decision. Requiring that $r_t \leqslant N < \infty$ (i.e. that one can not infinitely increase the size of the sample used for decision making), we see that

$$f_t(x) = p_{R3}^t(x) + \delta_t(x),$$

where

$$p_{R3}^t(x) = \sum_{i=(r_t+1)/2}^{r_t} C_{r_t}^i x^i (1-x)^{r_t-i},$$

$$\sup_{x \in R(0,1)} |\delta_t(x)| \leqslant \text{const min}(x, 1-x)t^{-1}.$$

Generally speaking, $p_{R3}^t(\cdot)$ does not display any regularity as $t \to \infty$. Consequently, the representation from the previous section does not hold. At the same time, all the functions $p_{R3}^t(x) - x, t \geqslant 1$, have the same roots $0, 1/2$ and 1 on $[0, 1]$. Also, since $3 \leqslant r_t \leqslant N$, derivatives of these functions at $1/2$ are uniformly bounded from zero and from above. These properties imply that 0 and 1 are attainable, while $1/2$ turns out to be unattainable.[12] In contrast, assuming that the choice of the sample size is random according to a fixed distribution, i.e. that $r_t, t \geqslant 1$, are random variables and have the same distribution

$$\mathscr{P}\{r_t = 2i + 1\} = p_i > 0, \quad i = 1, 2, \ldots, n, \quad \sum_{i=1}^{n} p_i = 1,$$

---

[11] The above mentioned facts concerning the estimate for $\delta_t(\cdot)$ and the root θ hold true only for large enough q (depending on α). This becomes clear if notice that for $\alpha q < 1$ one gets $[\alpha q] = 0$ and $p_{R2}(x) - x$ has only two roots 0 and 1. The same is true for all other cases when asymmetric decision rules are involved (i.e. rules different from the simple majority/minority ones).

[12] Examples of essentially nonstationary functional sequences, i.e. $f_t(\cdot), t \geqslant 1$, that do not exhibit any regularity as $t \to \infty$, can be studied by means of a theory especially developed to tackle such issues (see Arthur et al. 1987a and 1988).

"Badly behaved" dynamics

we have

$$f_t(x) = \tilde{p}_{R3}(x) + \delta_t(x),$$

where

$$\tilde{p}_{R3}(x) = \sum_{i=1}^{n} p_i \sum_{j=(i+1)/2}^{2i+1} C_{2i+1}^{j} x^{j}(1-x)^{2i+1-j},$$

$$\sup_{x \in R(0,1)} |\delta_t(x)| \leqslant \text{const} \min(x, 1-x)t^{-1}.$$

The function $\tilde{p}_{R3}(\cdot)$, satisfying the representation from the previous section, also has three roots 0, 1/2 and 1, among which 0 and 1 are attainable and 1/2 is unattainable. Note that here stochasticity simplifies the problem by removing the intrinsic nonstationarity of the process.

The three foregoing examples display (global) positive feedbacks.[13] Examples of (global) negative feedbacks can be similarly derived.

Consider the following rules:

R4. Ask an odd number r of users which technology they adopt. If the majority of them use A, choose B. Otherwise choose A.

R5. Fix $\alpha \in (0, 1)$. Ask $q \geqslant 3$ users of the technologies. If more than αq of them use A, choose B. Otherwise choose A.

If $\alpha = 1/2$ and q is an odd number, then R5 converts into R4.

These rules may accommodate behaviors such as the search for diversity in consumption or implicitly capture the outcomes of strategic behaviors on the side of the producers of the technologies aimed at the exploitation of "market power" (cf. Dosi et al. 1994 and Glaziev and Kaniovski 1991). We have relations here similar to (4) and (5) with

$$p_{R4}(x) = \sum_{i=0}^{(r-1)/2} C_r^i x^i (1-x)^{r-1},$$

and

$$p_{R5}(x) = \sum_{i=0}^{[\alpha q]} C_q^i x^i (1-x)^{q-1}.$$

In both cases there is a unique solution of the corresponding equations $p_{R4}(x) - x = 0$ and $p_{R5}(x) - x = 0$. For R4 it is 1/2, and for R5 the root θ shifts to the right as α increases.[14] The negative feedback determines a limit market structure, whereby both technologies are represented in the market with equal share in R4, or they share the market in the proportion $\theta : (1 - \theta)$ (the limit for the ratio of the number of units of A to the number of units of B) in the case of R5.

---

[13] Actually this statement is not completely correct. Consider for example the rule R2. In the feasible domain $R(0, 1)$ (i.e. the set of points which can be attained with positive probability through a finite number of steps from the initial state) there is actually a global positive feedback with respect to θ. In other words, this root is a global repeller in $R(0, 1)$. But adding to this domain 0 and 1, two asymptotically attainable points, we see that there is a local negative feedback in $R(0, \theta)$ with respect to 0 and a local negative feedback in $R(\theta, 1)$ with respect to 1. Or, in other words, 0 is a local attractor in $R(0, \theta)$ and 1 is a local attractor in $R(\theta, 1)$.

[14] For a fixed α one can show that θ converges to α as $q \to \infty$.

For both rules, we know the rates of convergence of X_t to the root, i.e. $\sqrt{t}(X_t - 1/2)$ for $R4$ or $\sqrt{t}(X_t - \theta)$ for $R5$, are asymptotically normal as $t \to \infty$. The means of the limit normal distributions equal zero for both cases and one can also specify the corresponding variances (see Arthur et al. (1983) for the case of $R4$). Consequently, we can characterize the rate of emergence of the limit market structures.[15]

More complicated $f(\cdot)$ functions appear if we introduce additional hypotheses concerning the characteristics and/or dynamics of the pool of adopters. If we assume that adopters who use some decision rule R_i occur with frequency (probability) $\alpha_i > 0$, $i = 1, 2, \ldots, k$, ($\sum_{i=1}^{k} \alpha_i = 1$), then the function $f_t(\cdot)$, corresponding to the behavior of the whole pool, is a randomization with weights α_i of functions $f_t^i(\cdot)$ generated by the rules R_i, i.e.

$$f_t(x) = \sum_{i=1}^{k} \alpha_i f_t^i(x), \quad x \in R(0, 1), t \geqslant 1.$$

The simplest example, where adopters who use $R1$ come up with probability $\alpha > 0$, while those who use $R4$ come up with probability $1 - \alpha > 0$, has been considered in Dosi et al. (1994).

More generally, meaningful applications of generalized urn schemes to particular problems of technological and economic dynamics imply an "inductive" specification of the $f(\cdot)$ function, which, loosely speaking, "summarizes" the "intrinsic" or behavioral features of the agents and the nature of their interactions.

Beyond these properties of general positive and negative feedbacks, let us now consider those more complicated situations with *locally* positive and/or *locally* negative feedbacks.

5. Examples of technological dynamics under local feedbacks in homogeneous economic environments

In this section we deal with the situation when there are more than one interior attainable limit state (or root of the corresponding function). Conceptually it might mean for example that there are several patterns of the long run behavior which do not imply monopoly of either technology. Moreover, the second type of models considered in this section, suggests another interpretation of urn schemes. In contrast to the previous examples, where we assume that the uncertainty is due to imperfect information of individual adopters about the choices of the whole population, we shall introduce uncertainty generated by "imperfectness" of the adopters themselves (somewhat analogous to fluctuations of their preferences).

One of the simplest examples of technological dynamics under "local" feedbacks is the following.[16] Think of adopters of competing technologies who are risk-averse enough not to follow the choice of a minuscule minority of the pool of users, but,

---

[15] For this particular rules one can determine an even sharper asymptotic characterization – the law of iterated logarithm (see Arthur et al. 1983).

[16] In this section, by "local" we mean specific to particular states of the process, without however any "spatial" connotation. Feedbacks that the "local" in terms of some "topology" of the environment will be considered in section 7.

for some reasons, are not inclined to conform to the absolute majority of them (say, due to a preference for variety, "inwardedly" generated judgements, eccentricity, etc.). To trivialize, imagine the example of someone who might not want to buy a touch-tone phone instead of a classic rotary one when less than 10% of his friends do so, but may as well desire an old-fashioned rotary phone when more than 90% of his friends have touch-tone ones.

Somewhat similar dynamics are present also outside the domains of technology adoption and consumption patterns: for example, the "bullish" and "bearish" phases on financial markets retain some of these characteristics (although admittedly one should be cautious in applying without appropriate modifications the formal machinery presented here to speculative phenomena, since in the latter the "weight of history" might well be lower than that implied by these urn schemes).

This type of behavior gives rise to the following rule.

R6. Fix $\alpha \in (0, 1/2)$. Ask $q > 1/\alpha$ users of the technologies. If the number of those of them who use A is greater than αq and smaller than $(1 - \alpha)q$, choose A. Otherwise choose B.

Arguments similar to the ones given in the previous section show that an analog of the relation (4) in this case holds true and

$$p_{R6}(x) = \sum_{i = [\alpha q] + 1}^{[(1 - \alpha)q]} C_q^i x^i (1 - x)^{q - i}.$$

If α is small enough, then $p_{R6}(x) - x$ has three roots 0, θ_1 and θ_2 on $[0, 1]$. Here $0 < \theta_1 < 1/2 < \theta_2 < 1$.[17] Satisfying (3), the root θ_1 turns out to be unattainable, while 0 and θ_2 are attainable roots. Consequently, in the limit we can have either monopoly of B, or the situation when with positive probability the market is shared by A and B in the proportion $\theta_2 : (1 - \theta_2) > 1$. For large α close to $1/2$ there could be only one root 0, i.e. the corresponding limit market pattern is monopoly of B. For an intermediate value of α one can imagine a situation when $p_{R6}(x) - x$ has two roots on $[0, 1]$ – a crosspoint 0 and a touchpoint $\theta \in (0, 1/2)$. Then both are attainable with positive probability (for θ this follows from the results of Pemantle (1991)). Consequently, in the limit we have either monopoly of B, or the ratio between A and B equals to $\theta : (1 - \theta) < 1$.

We now turn to a different class of models.

Let us introduce a price dynamics for the two technologies. As in Dosi et al. (1994), assume that two firms (producers of A and B, respectively) use the following strategy: up to a certain market share, defined by the proportion of the product of the firm among all products which have been sold until the current time (usually greater than $1/2$), the firm reduces the price and above that level increases it. Let us consider the simplest (linear) case of this policy which is graphically represented in Fig. 1. Here $Pr_A(x_A)$ designates the dependence of the price of technology A as a function of its proportion x_A among adopters who are using either technology. $Pr_B(x_A)$ designates the dependence of the price of the technology B as a function of x_A. (Note that the proportions of the technologies A and B are related by: $x_A + x_B = 1$.) Define x_A^* and x_B^* as the "critical" market shares which switch from falling- to rising-price rules. Hence, the dependence of the price of the A (B)

---

[17] For a fixed α one can show that $\theta_1 \to \alpha$ and $\theta_2 \to 1 - \alpha$ as $r \to \infty$.

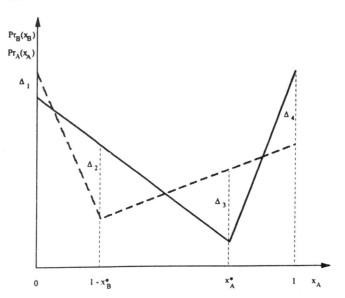

Fig. 1. Dependence of prices of A and B on the market share of A

technology on its proportion on the market $x_A(x_B)$ is given by four parameters: $Pr_A(0)$ x_A^*; $Pr_A(x_A^*)$; $Pr_A(1)(Pr_B(1)$; x_B^*; $Pr_B(1 - x_B^*)$; $Pr_B(0))$.[18]

This price dynamics embodies both positive and negative feedback mechanisms of diffusion. Within the domain of positive feedback the price falls with increasing market shares possibly due to learning economies, dynamic increasing returns, etc., and/or, on the behavioral side, to market-penetration strategies. Then, above a certain market share, the price starts to increase (hence entailing negative feedbacks), possibly due to monopolistic behaviors of the firm or to the progressive exhaustion of technological opportunities to lower production costs. Note that the model accounts also for those particular cases when firms follow different "non-symmetric" policies -- e.g. one increases the price and another lowers it, or both increase (lower) them,[19] or one increases (lowers) price and the other follows the above general strategy. These special cases can be obtained from the general one by simply changing the relations between $Pr_A(0)$, $Pr_A(x_A^*)$, $Pr_A(1)(Pr_B(1)$, $Pr_B(1 - x_B^*)$, $Pr_B(0))$.

It is natural to suppose that in the case when the "value" of the technologies for the users is approximately the same and potential adopters know about it, the technology which is cheaper has more chances to be sold, i.e. the A technology is bought if $Pr_A(x_A) - Pr_B(x_A) < 0$. However, if the prices only slightly differ or consumers have some specific preferences (which can be characterized only statistically or on average), that may sometimes lead to the adoption of the more expensive technology. Mathematically this case can be formalized in the following way (see

---

[18] Note that one accounts also for the circumstances when $Pr_A(1) \leqslant Pr_A(x_A^*)$ $(Pr_B(0) \leqslant Pr_B(1 - x_B^*))$, such as when $x_A^* = 1(x_B^* = 1)$: in this case, firm $A(B)$ still reduces the price on its product as its proportion on the market goes to one.

[19] For the case when both lower prices, see Glasiev and Kaniovski (1991) where formally the same situation is interpreted somewhat differently.

also Hanson 1985). The A technology is bought if $Pr_A(x_A) - Pr_B(x_A) + \xi < 0$, where ξ is a random variable. (Consequently, the B technology is bought if $Pr_A(x_A) - Pr_B(x_A) + \xi > 0$.) To preserve the symmetry of the decision rule we should avoid the situation when the event "$Pr_B(x_A) - Pr_A(x_A) = \xi$" has nonzero probability. This is definitely not the case when the distribution of ξ possesses a density with respect to the Lebesgue measure on the set of real numbers. Consequently, we will assume that the distribution ξ has a density in R^1. The probability $f(x_A)$ to choose the A technology, as a function of x_A, equals to $P\{\xi < Pr_B(x_A) - Pr_A(x_A)\}$. To avoid unnecessary sophistications of the model, we shall assume that ξ has a uniform distribution on $[-\alpha, \alpha]$. The probability to choose A as a function of x_A in this case has the form

$$f(x_A) = \begin{cases} 1 & \text{if } Pr_B(x_A) - Pr_A(x_A) \geqslant \alpha, \\ 0 & \text{if } Pr_B(x_A) - Pr_A(x_A) \leqslant -\alpha, \\ \dfrac{Pr_B(x_A) - Pr_A(x_A) + \alpha}{2\alpha} & \text{if } -\alpha < Pr_B(x_A) - Pr_A(x_A) < \alpha. \end{cases}$$

For $\alpha > \max_{i=1,2,3,4} \Delta_i$ this is graphically represented in Fig 2. Here we have three roots – θ_1, θ_2 and θ_3 – of the function $f(x) - x$ on $[0,1]$. Satisfying (3), the root θ_2 proves to be unattainable, while θ_1 and θ_3, satisfying (2), are attainable, i.e. the process X_t converges to each of them with positive probability for any initial proportions of the technologies on the market. Using results of Arthur et al. (1988),

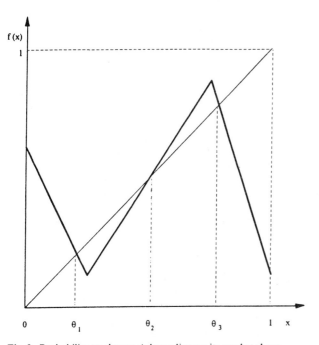

Fig. 2. Probability to choose A depending on its market share

we find the rates of convergence to the attainable roots

$$\theta_1 = \frac{(\alpha + \Delta_1)(1 - x_B^*)}{2\alpha(1 - x_B^*) + \Delta_1 + \Delta_2},$$

$$\theta_3 = 1 - \frac{(\alpha + \Delta_4)(1 - x_A^*)}{2\alpha(1 - x_A^*) + \Delta_3 + \Delta_4}.$$

In particular,

$$\lim_{t \to \infty} \mathscr{P}\{\sqrt{t}(X_t - \theta_i) < y, X_s \to \theta_i\} = \mathscr{P}\{X_s \to \theta_i\}\mathscr{P}\{\mathscr{N}(0, \sigma_i^2) < y\}. \tag{6}$$

Here $\mathscr{N}(0, \sigma_i^2)$ stands for a Gaussian distribution with zero mean and variance

$$\sigma_i^2 = \frac{\theta_i(1 - \theta_i)}{1 - 2f'(\theta_i)}, \tag{7}$$

where $f'(\cdot)$ designates the derivative of $f(\cdot)$. It can be shown that

$$f'(\theta_1) = -\frac{\Delta_1 + \Delta_2}{2\alpha(1 - x_B^*)} \tag{8}$$

and

$$f'(\theta_3) = -\frac{\Delta_3 + \Delta_4}{2\alpha(1 - x_A^*)}. \tag{9}$$

One sees from (6)–(9) that convergence to both θ_1 and θ_3 occurs with the rate $t^{-1/2}$ but the random fluctuations around this, which are determined by the variances of the corresponding limit distributions, can be different.

In this example, the above dynamics of prices together with the described behavior of adopters generate multiple limit patterns with slightly different rates of emergence. Under the same price dynamics and marginally more sophisticated assumptions concerning the behavior of adopters, one can have even more complicated limit market structures where the initial proportions of the technologies on the market influence those structures (see Dosi et al. 1994). Similar considerations concerning convergence rates also apply (with corresponding modifications).

The analytical procedure is to introduce further specifications on the statistical frequences (probabilities) of the producers of $A(B)$ to follow a particular shape of the above price dynamics and/or hypotheses concerning statistical frequences of the adopters who use variants of the above decision rules: thus, one can construct much more complicated functions $f_t(\cdot)$.

Next, let us discuss one important generalization of the urn scheme presented so far.

6. Urn schemes with multiple additions – a tool for analysis of system compatibilities

As mentioned in section 2, quite a few modern high-technology products require compatibility. Think for example of compatibility requirements of software packages and hardware in computers. Moreover, it is reasonable to expect that competing technologies might arrive in different "lumpy" quantities and in different combinations with each other. In this section we present the modification of the basic scheme apt to handle such phenomena. We have hinted earlier that considering all notional combinations of new technologies as a sort of "higher level" new technologies, although formally possible, does not look too attractive. An alternative method for handling inter-technological compatibilities has been introduced by Arthur et al. (1987a). For the case of two (A and B) competing technologies it looks like the following.

Consider Z_+^2, the set of two dimensional vectors with non-negative integer coordinates. Introduce $\vec{\xi}^t(x)$, $t \geq 1$, $x \in R(0,1)$, random vectors with values in Z_+^2 independent in t. If $\vec{\xi}^t(x) = (\xi_1^t(x), \xi_2^t(x))$ takes the value $\vec{i} = (i_1, i_2)$ we can interpret this both as additions of $i_1 \geq 0$ white and $i_2 \geq 0$ black balls into an urn of infinite capacity with black and white balls or, equivalently, as adoption in a market of infinite capacity of i_1 units of A and i_2 units of B.

Mathematical results similar to those presented in section 3 are obtained (see Arthur et al. 1987a, 1987b and 1988). An important property of this generalization is that $\vec{\xi}^t(x)$ can take the value $\vec{0} = (0,0)$ with nonzero probability. Consequently, no adoption might happen at time t. Taking into account that the scheme allows multiple adoptions, one sees that sequential instances of adoption do not coincide with physical time "periods". Hence, loosely speaking, history may "accelerate" by discrete jumps of variable length.

Designate by X_t the proportion of white balls in the urn at time $t \geq 1$. Then the number w_t of white balls and γ_t, the total number of balls in the urn at time t, follow the dynamics

$$w_{t+1} = w_t + \xi_1^t(X_t), \qquad t \geq 1, \tag{10}$$

$$\gamma_{t+1} = \gamma_t + \xi_1^t(X_t) + \xi_2^t(X_t), \quad t \geq 1. \tag{11}$$

Here $w_1 \geq 1$ and $b_1 \geq 1$ stand for the initial numbers of white and black balls in the urn. Also $\gamma_1 = w_1 + b_1$. Dividing (10) by (11), one has

$$X_{t+1} = X_t + \gamma_t^{-1} \frac{\xi_1^t(X_t) - X_t[\xi_1^t(X_t) + \xi_2^t(X_t)]}{1 + \gamma_t^{-1}[\xi_1^t(X_t) + \xi_2^t(X_t)]}, \quad t \geq 1, \quad X_1 = \frac{w_1}{\gamma_1}. \tag{12}$$

Let $p(\vec{i}, x)$, $\vec{i} \in Z_+^2$, $x \in R(0,1)$, be the distribution of $\vec{\xi}(x)$, i.e.[20]

$$\mathcal{P}\{\vec{\xi}^t(x) = \vec{i}\} = p(\vec{i}, x).$$

Since

$$E[\xi_1^t(X_t) + \xi_2^t(X_t)] = \sum_{\vec{i} \in Z_+^2} (i_1 + i_2) p(\vec{i}, x), \tag{13}$$

then, requiring that for all $x \in R(0,1)$

$$p(\vec{0}, x) \leq \alpha < 1 \quad \text{and} \quad \sum_{\vec{i} \in Z_+^2} (i_1 + i_2)^2 p(\vec{i}, x) \leq c_1, \tag{14}$$

---

[20] In general this distribution can also depend on t and/or the total current number of balls in the urn γ_t, but, to simplify the formulae, here we restrict ourselves to the simplest situation.

one has with probability 1

$$1 - \alpha \leqslant \liminf_{t \to \infty} \frac{\gamma_t}{t - 1} \leqslant \limsup_{t \to \infty} \frac{\gamma_t}{t - 1} \leqslant c_2. \tag{15}$$

Here $c_i, i = 1, 2$, stand for some constants. Notice that

$$\mathbf{E}\left\{ \gamma_t^{-1} \frac{\xi_1^t(X_t) - X_t[\xi_1^t(X_t) + \xi_2^t(X_t)]}{1 + \gamma_t^{-1}[\xi_1^t(X_t) + \xi_2^t(X_t)]} \,\Big|\, X_t = x, \gamma_t = \gamma \right\} =$$

$$= \gamma^{-1} \sum_{\vec{i} \in Z_+^2} \frac{i_1 - x(i_1 + i_2)}{1 + \gamma^{-1}(i_1 + i_2)} p(\vec{i}, x). \tag{16}$$

Relations (12), (15) and (16) allow to show that X_t converges with probabilitiy 1 as $t \to \infty$ to the properly defined (since the function involved may be discontinuous) set of zeros on $[0, 1]$ of the function

$$g(x) = \sum_{\vec{i} \in Z_+^2} [i_1 - x(i_1 + i_2)] p(\vec{i}, x). \tag{17}$$

Furthermore, if the function $G(\cdot)$ in the right hand side of (13) turns out to be continuous, and X_t a.s. converges to X^0, then, from (11) and (13), one has that $(t - 1)^{-1}\gamma_t$ converges with probability 1, and the limit γ^0 has the form $\gamma^0 = G(X^0)$.

For this case we can derive the same set of asymptotic statements as for the basic scheme.

As an example of how this modification of the basic scheme can work, let us consider the following generalizations of the decision rules R2 and R5 given in section 4.

R7. Fix $\alpha \in (1/2, 1)$. Ask $q \geqslant 3$ users of technologies. If more than αq of them use A, choose A. If not more than $(1 - \alpha)q$ of them use A, choose B. Otherwise do not choose any technology. This rule generates the following probability to choose A:

$$p((1, 0), x) = p_{R7}^{(1)}(x) + \delta_\gamma^{(1)}(x),$$

and, analogously, B:

$$p((0, 1), x) = p_{R7}^{(2)}(x) + \delta_\gamma^{(2)}(x).$$

Finally, the probability not to choose anything, i.e. $p((0, 0), x)$, is

$$p((0, 0), x) = p_{R7}^{(3)}(x) + \delta_\gamma^{(3)}(x).$$

Here γ stands for the total current number of balls in the urn,

$$p_{R7}^{(1)}(x) = \sum_{i = [\alpha q] + 1}^{q} C_q^i x^i (1 - x)^{q - i}, \quad p_{R7}^{(2)}(x) = \sum_{i = 0}^{[(1 - \alpha)q]} C_q^i x^i (1 - x)^{q - i},$$

$$p_{R7}^{(3)}(x) = 1 - p_{R7}^{(1)}(x) - p_{R7}^{(2)}(x) = \sum_{i = [(1 - \alpha)q] + 1}^{[\alpha q]} C_q^i x^i (1 - x)^{q - i},$$

$$\sup_{x \in R(0, 1)} |\delta_\gamma^{(i)}(x)| \leqslant \text{const} \min(x, 1 - x)\gamma^{-1}, i = 1, 2, 3.$$

Also $g(\cdot)$ in this case is

$$g(x) = p_{R7}^{(1)}(x) - x[p_{R7}^{(1)}(x) + p_{R7}^{(2)}(x)]$$

and the only root on $(0, 1)$ of $g(\cdot)$ is given by the equation

$$x = \frac{p_{R7}^{(1)}(x)}{p_{R7}^{(1)}(x) + p_{R7}^{(2)}(x)}.$$

Since $p_{R7}^{(1)}(x) + p_{R7}^{(2)}(x) < 1$ for $x \in R(0, 1)$, this root is smaller than the corresponding root of R2. But still it is unattainable. Two other roots, 0 and 1, are attainable.

Similarly to R7 we can introduce R8 – a counterpart of R5. In this case we have, as for R5, that there is only one attainable root. For reasons similar to those mentioned in the previous section, this root is larger than the corresponding one of R5 and for a fixed α it approaches α as $q \to \infty$.

As highlighted in all the foregoing examples, applications of urn schemes allow an analytical investigation of questions such as the possibility of "lock-in" into one of alternative technological systems or, conversely, the feasibility of their long-term co-existence. Clearly, in several of the examples, lock-in and history-dependent selection of a particular system does occur. But these models show also that the notional multiplicity of limit states and the evolutionary importance of early historical events depend upon the precise mechanics by which agents acquire information and change their preferences. (In the simple examples here these mechanics are captured by the different decision rules.) Similar considerations are likely to apply to more complex models allowing for learning processes also among suppliers of the technologies themselves. However, as already mentioned, it is not the purpose of this work to discuss the specific characteristics of market interactions and learning processes: rather, one of our major points here is that urn schemes, with the appropriate modifications, can be applied to a wide variety of them.

Further, let us introduce the urn model corresponding to the case when competition occurs in non-homogeneous economic environments, and thus interactions have "local" characteristics in some "spatial" sense.

7. Generalized urn schemes with non-homogeneous environments and their economic applications

In this section we introduce a new modification of the basic scheme allowing for a "distributed" economic system, composed of interacting parts which can be metaphorically understood as "regions". The parameters of the whole system are dynamically formed by all the regions, involving different kinds of non-linear interacting. Interestingly, the dynamics of the system proves to be much more complex than the behaviors of its components. In the following we shall mainly consider the technical aspect of this modification; however it is intuitive that obvious candidates for economic application are growth processes involving "local" learning.

Think of m urns of infinite capacity with black and white balls. Starting with $n_i^w \geqslant 1$ white balls and $n_i^b \geqslant 1$ black balls into the i-th urn, a ball is added in one of the urns at time instants $t = 1, 2, \dots$.[21] With probability $f_i(\vec{X}(t))$ it will be added into the i-th urn. It will be white with probability $f_i^w(\vec{X}(t))$ and black with probability

---

[21] In general one does not require that $n_i^w \geqslant 1$ and $n_i^b \geqslant 1$. The only thing one really needs is positiveness of $n_i^w + n_i^b$. Consequently, the process can start from zero number of balls of one of the colors into the urns. The same is true for all urn processes considered in the paper.

$f_j^b(\vec{X}(t))$. Here $\vec{f}(\cdot), \vec{f}^w(\cdot), \vec{f}^b(\cdot)$, are vector functions which map $R(\vec{0}, \vec{1})$ in S_m, and $\vec{f}^w(\cdot) + \vec{f}^b(\cdot) = \vec{f}(\cdot)$. By $R(\vec{0}, \vec{1})$ we designate the Cartesian product of m copies of $R(0, 1)$ and

$$S_m = \left\{ \vec{x} \in R^m : x_i \geq 0, \sum_{i=1}^{m} x_i = 1 \right\}.$$

$\vec{X}(t)$ stands for the vector whose i-th coordinate $X_i(t)$ represents the proportion of white balls in the i-th urn at time t. To introduce the dynamics of $\vec{X}(t)$ consider $\xi^t(\vec{x})$, $t \geq 1$, $\vec{x} \in R(\vec{0}, \vec{1})$, random $m \times 2$ matrices independent in t with the elements $\xi_{i,j}^t(\vec{x})$, $i = 1, 2, \ldots, m, . j = 1, 2$, such that $\mathscr{P}\{\xi_{i,1}^t(\vec{x}) = 1\} = f_i^w(\vec{x})$ and $\mathscr{P}\{\xi_{i,2}^t(\vec{x}) = 1\} = f_i^b(\vec{x})$. This means that a white (black) ball is added into the i-th urn at time t if $\xi_{i,1}(\vec{X}(t)) = 1(\xi_{i,2}(\vec{X}(t)) = 1)$. Then the total number γ_i^t of balls in i-th urn at time $t \geq 1$ follows the dynamics

$$\gamma_i^{t+1} = \gamma_i^t + \xi_{i,1}^t(\vec{X}(t)) + \xi_{i,2}^t(\vec{X}(t)), \quad t \geq 1, \quad \gamma_i^1 = n_i^w + n_i^b. \tag{18}$$

Since

$$E[\xi_{i,1}^t(\vec{x}) + \xi_{i,2}^t(\vec{x})] = f_i(\vec{x}), \tag{19}$$

then, requiring that

$$f_i(\vec{x}) \geq f_i^0 > 0, \tag{20}$$

one has

$$f_i^0 \leq \liminf_{t \to \infty} \frac{\gamma_i^t}{t} \leq \limsup_{t \to \infty} \frac{\gamma_i^t}{t} \leq 1. \tag{21}$$

The number w_i^t of white balls and the number b_i^t of black balls in the urn follow the dynamics

$$w_i^{t+1} = w_i^t + \xi_{i,1}^t(\vec{X}(t)), \quad t \geq 1, \quad w_i^1 = n_i^w, \tag{22}$$

$$b_i^{t+1} = b_i^t + \xi_{i,2}^t(\vec{X}(t)), \quad t \geq 1, \quad b_i^1 = n_i^b.$$

Dividing (22) by (18) one has the following dynamics for the proportion of white balls in the i-th urn

$$X_i(t+1) = X_i(t) + \frac{1}{\gamma_i^t} \frac{\xi_{i,1}^t(\vec{X}(t)) - X_i(t)[\xi_{i,1}^t(\vec{X}(t)) + \xi_{i,2}^t(\vec{X}(t))]}{1 + (\gamma_i^t)^{-1}[\xi_{i,1}^t(\vec{X}(t)) + \xi_{i,2}^t(\vec{X}(t))]},$$

$$t \geq 1, \quad X_i(1) = \frac{n_i^w}{\gamma_i^1}. \tag{23}$$

Since

$$E \left\{ \frac{1}{\gamma_i^t} \frac{\xi_{i,1}^t(\vec{X}(t)) - X_i(t)[\xi_{i,1}^t(\vec{X}(t)) + \xi_{i,2}^t(\vec{X}(t))]}{1 + (\gamma_i^t)^{-1}[\xi_{i,1}^t(\vec{X}(t)) + \xi_{i,2}^t(\vec{X}(t))]} \middle| \vec{X}(t) = \vec{x}, \vec{\gamma}^t = \vec{\gamma} \right\}$$

$$= \frac{1}{\gamma_i} \frac{f_i^w(\vec{x}) - x_i f_i(\vec{x})}{1 + (\gamma_i)^{-1} f_i(\vec{x})},$$

relations (21) and (23) allow to show that $\vec{X}(t)$ converges wth probability 1 as $t \to \infty$ to the set of zeros (properly defined) on $[\vec{0}, \vec{1}]$ of the m-dimensional vector-function $\vec{F}(\cdot)$ whose i-th coordinate is $f_i^w(\vec{x}) - x_i f_i(\vec{x})$. Assume that both $\vec{f}^w(\cdot)$ and $\vec{f}^b(\cdot)$ are continuous and there is a limit $\vec{X}^0$ *for* $\vec{X}(t)$. Then from equality (19) one can conclude that $t^{-1}\vec{\gamma}^t$ converges with probability 1 as $t \to \infty$ and the limit $\vec{\gamma}^0$ has the form

$$\gamma_i^0 = f_i(\vec{X}^0), \quad i = 1, 2, \ldots, m. \tag{24}$$

Using the above relations we can obtain analogs of the results listed in section 3 for the basic generalized urn scheme.

In principle, multiple urns models are capable of capturing positive (and, possibly, negative) feedback processes which are "local" on some appropriately defined space (it could be "regions" or "countries", but also groups of agents with particular features).

Consider a particular model of technological dynamics in a non-homogeneous economic environment which can be treated by means of the modification given here.

Suppose that we have two possible locations (which can be thought as urns), 1 and 2, for the producers of two competing technologies – A and B. At each of the locations (they could be understood as "economic regions" or "countries") there are one firm producing A and one firm producing B. Producers use the strategy described in section 5 (with their own sets of parameters). Suppose for example that there are (bounded) increasing returns and market-share dependent pricing strategies. Then for each of the locations there exists a minimal price of the technologies as a function of the current concentration of, say, A, i.e. $M(x_A) = \min(Pr_A(x_A), Pr_B(x_A))$. For the case represented by Fig. 1, the function is given in Fig. 3. Note that at points λ_i technologies reverse their order as the cheaper ones. Designate the proportion of A for the first and the second locations by x_1 and x_2 correspondingly. Also let λ_j^i, $j = 1, 2, 3, i = 1, 2$, be the points where the minimal prices switch from one technology to another. (Consequently, we consider the case when the minimal

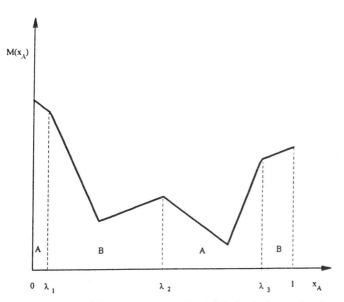

Fig. 3. The price of the cheapest among A and B technologies as a function of x_A

prices for both locations have a shape similar to that presented in figure 3.) Suppose that at time instants $t = 1, 2, \ldots$, a consumer buys a unit of either technology. (A "consumer", irrespectively of where he is located, can demand a technology produced in either region.) He adopts the cheapest among the technologies, but, as before (section 5), because of some specific preferences or other reasons which can be taken into account statistically, he measures the difference between $M_1(x_1)$ and $M_2(x_2)$ with a random error. Here $M_i(\cdot)$ stands for the minimal price for the i-th location as a function of the market-share of A at this location. A unit of the technologies from the first location is bought if $M_1(x_1) - M_2(x_2) + \zeta < 0$; otherwise, i.e. when $M_1(x_1) - M_2(x_2) + \zeta > 0$, a unit from the second location is bought. As before (section 5) to preserve the symmetry of the decision rule we should avoid the situation when the event "$M_2(x_2) - M_1(x_1) = \zeta$" has nonzero probability. Consequently, we should again assume that the distribution of ζ possesses a density with respect to the Lebesgue measure on the set of real numbers. The probability to choose the first location is $f_1(x_1, x_2) = \mathscr{P}\{\zeta < M_2(x_2) - M_1(x_1)\}$. To simplify our considerations let us suppose that ζ has a uniform distribution on $[-\beta, \beta]$. Then the probability to choose the first location is

$$
f_1(\vec{x}) = \begin{cases} 1 & \text{if} \quad M_2(x_2) - M_1(x_1) \geqslant \beta, \\ 0 & \text{if} \quad M_2(x_2) - M_1(x_1) \leqslant -\beta, \\ [M_2(x_2) - M_1(x_1) + \beta]/2\beta & \text{if} \quad -\beta < M_2(x_2) - M_1(x_1) < \beta. \end{cases}
$$

Suppose that $\beta > \max_{0 \leqslant x_i \leqslant 1, i = 1, 2} |M_2(x_2) - M_1(x_1)|$. Then (20) holds with

$$
f_1^0 = \left\{ \min_{0 \leqslant x_i \leqslant 1, i = 1, 2} [M_2(x_2) - M_1(x_1)] + \beta \right\} \Big/ 2\beta
$$

and

$$
f_2^0 = 1/2 - \left\{ \max_{0 \leqslant x_i \leqslant 1, i = 1, 2} [M_2(x_2) - M_1(x_1)] \right\} \Big/ 2\beta.
$$

The simplest decision rule for choosing a specific technology when a location has been chosen is the following: a unit of $A(B)$ is adopted at the i-th location if $x_i \in I_i^A (x_i \in I_i^B)$. Here $I_i^A = (0, \lambda_1^i) \cup (\lambda_2^i, \lambda_3^i)$ and $I_i^B = [\lambda_1^i, \lambda_2^i] \cup [\lambda_3^i, 1)$. The corresponding vector-function $F(\cdot)$ has the form

$$
F_i(\vec{x}) = \begin{cases} (1 - x_i) f_i(\vec{x}) & \text{for} \quad x_i \in I_i^A, \\ -x_i f_i(\vec{x}) & \text{for} \quad x_i \in I_i^B. \end{cases}
$$

We can show that $\vec{X}(t)$ converges (for any initial number of A and B at the both locations) with probability 1 as $t \to \infty$ to a random vector $\vec{X}$. The limit takes with positive probability four values: $(\lambda_1^1, \lambda_1^2), (\lambda_1^1, \lambda_3^2), (\lambda_3^1, \lambda_1^2), (\lambda_3^1, \lambda_3^2)$. Of course, one may easily refine these examples by introducing more complicated decision rules (e.g. mixed strategies randomizing the choice among technologies after having chosen the location, etc.), or by specifying the technological and behavioral relationships between location-specific prices and market-shares. In any case what is important to notice here is that this class of models is apt to analyse the dynamics of what can be interpreted as the inter-regional (or international) location of "production" of diverse technologies under non-constant returns and heterogeneous behaviors among producers. "Spatial" asymmetries in the limit distributions are the general outcome, while – as mentioned earlier – more precise long-term properties can be analysed by adding the appropriate "inductive" specifications on technological dynamics and behavioral responses.

Further along these lines, consider the application of this formal apparatus to a sort of "reduced form" model of international growth driven by investment in two alternative technologies, A and B. The "world economy" consists of m interacting parts (for example, economic regions) of infinite capacity. Technologies are capital-embodied so that each instance of adoption is associated with an investment decision. The time sequence $t = 1, 2, \ldots$, is defined by the sequence of investments (i.e. adoption decisions). This will not interfere with our considerations since we are interested in the proportions of the total capital stock embodying each of the technologies. Further, let us make the following assumptions:

1. Assume (in a quite non-Schumpeterian fashion) that there is no "creative destruction", and units of capital pile up on each other without depreciation.
2. Each technology yields a different productivity, which changes along the diffusion trajectory. The productivity of each technology in each region, and their shares by region, ultimately determines per capita incomes (along the process and in the limit). However, private agents do not select technologies on the grounds of productivities but in terms of their relative profitabilities.

For the i-th region we consider the following indicators: $x_i(1 - x_i)$ – the fraction of the capitals embodied by $A(B)$; $P_i^A(x_i)(P_i^B(x_i))$ – the cost of a unit of investments embodying $A(B)$ and dependent on x_i; $R_i^A(x_i)(R_i^B(x_i))$ – the overhead costs per unit of investment (which may include the cost of capital services) as a function of x_i; $W_i^A(x_i)(W_i^B(x_i))$ – the unit labour costs for a given x_i. (Note that the dynamics of $W_i^A(\cdot)(W_i^B(\cdot))$ may well depend on technology-specific changes in labour productivity associated with e.g. dynamic increasing returns, and region-specific changes in wage rates denominated in some constant unit of measure. However, in the most general formulation of the model we do not need to specify the exact form of these relationships.) For convenience, assume that each "investment" adds one unit of output. Thus, the profit $\pi_i^A(x_i)(\pi_i^B(x_i))$ from using $A(B)$ is

$$\pi_i^A(x_i) = P_i^A(x_i) - R_i^A(x_i) - W_i^A(x_i),$$
$$\pi_i^B(x_i) = P_i^B(x_i) - R_i^B(x_i) - W_i^B(x_i).$$

Also the total profit for the i-th region is

$$\pi_i(x_i) = \pi_i^A(x_i) + \pi_i^B(x_i).$$

Now we can consider the following mechanism of investment/adaptation. Suppose that $\pi_i^A(x_i) > 0$ and $\pi_i^B(x_i) > 0$ for $x_i \in [0, 1]$, $i = 1, 2, \ldots, m$ (i.e. all the technologies have non-negative profitabilities). Assuming that the current fractions of A in the regions are given by the corresponding coordinates of an m-dimensional vector $\vec{x} \in [\vec{0}, \vec{1}]$, a unit of $A(B)$ is adapted in the i-th region with probability

$$\frac{\pi_i^A(x_i)}{\sum_{k=1}^m \pi_k(x_k)} \left(\frac{\pi_i^B(x_i)}{\sum_{k=1}^m \pi_k(x_k)} \right). \tag{25}$$

The economic interpretation is a sort of "Ricardian" mechanism – whereby investment depends, in probability, on the net surplus generated by each technology –

jointly with less than perfect mobility of investment across technologies (say, due to technology-specific learning-by-doing and -by-using).[22]

By thinking of a unit of A as a white ball and a unit of B as a black ball, we obtain the above scheme with

$$f_i^w(\cdot) = \frac{\pi_i^A(\cdot)}{\sum_{k=1}^m \pi_k(\cdot)} \quad \text{and} \quad f_i^b(\cdot) = \frac{\pi_i^B(\cdot)}{\sum_{k=1}^m \pi_k(\cdot)}.$$

Further conceptual results can then be derived, for example, by imposing particular restrictions on the dynamics of labour productivity, wages, overheads and mark-ups, therefore determining the shape of the functions $\pi_i^A(\cdot)$ and $\pi_i^B(\cdot)$. Other refinements might involve the introduction of a stochastic element in the decisions governing the allocation of investment to regions and technologies. Assuming (small enough) random errors ε_i^A and ε_i^B, $i = 1, 2, \ldots, m$, instead of (25) we shall have

$$\frac{\pi_i^A(x_i) + \varepsilon_i^A}{\sum_{k=1}^m [\pi_k(x_k) + \varepsilon_k^A + \varepsilon_k^B]} \left(\frac{\pi_i^B(x_i) + \varepsilon_i^B}{\sum_{k=1}^m [\pi_k(x_k) + \varepsilon_k^A + \varepsilon_k^B]} \right).$$

In any case, whenever our assumption holds on the different (and endogenous) productivities associated with different technologies, our multiple urn scheme allows the analysis of the process of long-term differentiation in per capita incomes driven by "local" learning and other forms of "virtuous" and "vicious" circles – as Nicholas Kaldor would put it.[23] The limit shares of white and black balls in each urn, under a rather innocent hypothesis of monotonicity of productivities and incomes, determine also the limit distribution of the latter among countries or regions[24] (One may visualize this distribution as the shares into growing pie representing "world income" normalized with world population.)

8. Generalized urn process and evolutionary games

Generalized urn schemes generate stochastic replicator dynamics. In particular, all of the above urn process represent a kind of discrete time stochastic replicator equations and, consequently, can be used in the general setting of "evolutionary games" instead of deterministic ones (see Friedman (1991) for the corresponding construction with deterministic dynamics). Let us give a simple sketch of how this can be done, reserving to further works a more detailed analysis of this problem.

Following Friedman (1991), consider a set of interacting populations, indexed $k = 1, 2, \ldots, m$. If $m = 2$ they could be thought, for example, as "sellers" and "buyers". A member of each population has a finite number of available actions (or "behaviors" or "strategies"). Let us restrict ourselves for simplicity to the case of two possible actions, indexed $i = 1, 2$. Then, any point of the one dimensional

---

[22] This mechanism is somewhat analogous to the diffusion patterns of capital-embodied innovations modeled by Soete and Turner (1984). See also Metcalfe (1988).

[23] The formal apparatus presented here clearly allows generalizations in an explicit dynamic setting on the models of "local" learning put forward by Atkinson and Stiglitz (1969) and David (1975). Note that by "local" in this section we mean *both region- and technology-specific*.

[24] In this there is an intuitive link also with endogenously generated absolute advantages/disadvantages which shape the possibilities of growth in open economies as in Dosi et al. (1990).

simplex $[0, 1]$ represents a possible mixed strategy for an individual member of a population. Any point in the same simplex also represents the fraction of a population employing the first strategy. Hence $[\vec{0}, \vec{1}]$, the Cartesian product of m copies of the simplex $[0, 1]$, is the set of strategies profiles and also the state space under the maintained interpretation that interactions are anonymous.

Interactions are summarized in a fitness function which specifies the relevant evolutionary payoff for the individuals in each population as a function of their own strategy and the current state. Formally a fitness function consists of maps: $[0, 1] \times [\vec{0}, \vec{1}] \rightarrow R^1$, $k = 1, 2, \ldots, m$, which are assumed linear in the first (own strategy) argument and continuously differentiable in the second (population state) argument. If $m = 2$, the payoffs of a bi-matrix game give a simplest example of a fitness function.

The final basic element of the model, which radically departs from other models currently available (see Friedman 1991), is a stochastic replicator-type dynamic structure specifying how a state evolves over time. The urn machinery allows a quite general and powerful formalization. We postulate that

$$\vec{X}(t + 1) = \vec{Q}(t, \vec{X}(t), \vec{\xi}_t), \quad t \geqslant 1, \quad \vec{X}(1) \in [\vec{0}, \vec{1}]. \tag{26}$$

Here $\vec{X}(t)$ stands for the vector whose i-th coordinate $X_i(t)$ equals to the proportion of players in the i-th population who are using at time t the first strategy (then the proportion of players in the i-population who keep the second strategy is $1 - X_i(t)$). Moreover, $\vec{\xi}_t, t \geqslant 1$, m-dimensional random vectors are independent it t and $\vec{Q}(.,.,.)$ stands for a deterministic function, which:

(a) keeps $[\vec{0}, \vec{1}]$ invariant;

(b) is measurable with respect to the product of two σ-fields of Borel sets on R^m.

To illustrate this concept, let us consider the following example.

Assume a dynamics which satisfies the above requirements and consider two populations, say "buyers" and "sellers". Suppose the interaction concerns the exchange of some object under imperfect and incomplete information such that the two populations can undertake two (pure) strategies: "be honest" or "cheat" for the sellers and "inspect" or "trust" for the buyers (so $m = 2$). Assume that, starting from $b_1 \geqslant 1$ who inspect and $b_2 \geqslant 1$ who don't, at time instants $t = 1, 2, \ldots$, a new buyer joins that population. He can be of the inspecting or non-inspecting kinds and this depends upon the current frequencies of inspecting and non-inspecting buyers and of honest and cheating sellers. This dependency does not act deterministically, but randomly. In particular, there is a function $f_1(\cdot, \cdot): [\vec{0}, \vec{1}] \rightarrow [0, 1]$ and random variables $\xi_1(t, \cdot, \cdot)$, independent in $t \geqslant 1$, such that

$$\xi_1(t, x, y) = \begin{cases} 1 \text{ with probability } f_1(x, y), \\ 0 \text{ with probability } 1 - f_1(x, y), \end{cases}$$

where $(x, y) \in R(\vec{0}, \vec{1})$. Then $X(t)$, the proportion of buyers who inspects, evolves in the following way

$$X(t + 1) = X(t) + \frac{1}{t + b}[\xi_1(t, X(t), Y(t)) - X(t)], \quad t \geqslant 1,$$

$$X(1) = \frac{b_1}{b}, \quad (b = b_1 + b_2). \tag{27}$$

Consequently, at time t a new inspecting (non-inspecting) buyer joins the corresponding population if $\xi_1(t, X(t), Y(t)) = 1(0)$. Here $Y(t)$ stands for the current proportion of honest sellers. Similarly, the dynamics of the latter is

$$Y(t+1) = Y(t) + \frac{1}{t+s}[\xi_2(t, X(t), Y(t)) - Y(t)], \quad t \geq 1,$$

$$Y(1) = \frac{s_1}{s}, \quad (s = s_1 + s_2). \tag{28}$$

We set $s_1 \geq 1$ for the initial number of honest sellers and $s_2 \geq 1$ for the initial number of cheating ones. Also $\xi_2(t, \cdot, \cdot)$ are independent in $t \geq 1$ and such that

$$\xi_2(t, x, y) = \begin{cases} 1 & \text{with probability } f_2(x, y), \\ 0 & \text{with probability } 1 - f_2(x, y), \end{cases}$$

for $(x, y) \in R(\overrightarrow{0, 1})$. Therefore, at time t a new honest (cheating) seller joins the corresponding population if $\xi_2(t, X(t), Y(t)) = 1(0)$. The function $f_2(\cdot, \cdot)$ maps $[\overrightarrow{0, 1}]$ on $[0, 1]$. It is assumed that $\{\xi_1(t, \cdot, \cdot)\}$ and $\{\xi_2(t, \cdot, \cdot)\}$ are independent.

If we set $\overrightarrow{X}(t) = (X(t), Y(t))$, then (27) and (28) represents a dynamics of the form (26). Indeed, condition (a) here holds automatically and the measurability condition (b) is also met since $\overrightarrow{X}(\cdot)$ takes in this case at most a countable number of values.[25]

Taking the conditional expectations in (27) and (28), one gets

$$X(t+1) = X(t) + \frac{1}{t+b}[f_1(X(t), Y(t)) - X(t)]$$

$$+ \frac{1}{t+b}\zeta_1(t, X(t), Y(t)), \quad t \geq 1, \quad X(1) = \frac{b_1}{b} \tag{29}$$

and

$$Y(t+1) = Y(t) + \frac{1}{t+s}[f_2(X(t), Y(t)) - Y(t)]$$

$$+ \frac{1}{t+s}\zeta_2(t, X(t), Y(t)), \quad t \geq 1, \quad Y(1) = \frac{s_1}{s}. \tag{30}$$

Here $\zeta_i(t, x, y) = \xi_i(t, x, y) - E\xi_i(t, x, y)$, i.e. $E\zeta_i(t, x, y) = 0$. Hence, at time t the system shifts on average from a point (x, y) on

$$\left(\frac{1}{t+b}[f_1(x, y) - x], \frac{1}{t+s}[f_2(x, y) - y] \right).$$

This gives us two hints. First, that, under certain assumptions (see, for example, Ljung and Söderström 1983), the system of finite difference equations (29) and (30) asymptotically (as $t \to \infty$) behaves like the following system of ordinary differential

---

[25] Here $\overrightarrow{X}(\cdot)$ is a nonstationary Markov process with growing number of states. In particular, $\overrightarrow{X}(t)$ can attain only the following values: $\left(\frac{b_1 + i}{b + t - 1}, \frac{s_1 + j}{s + t - 1} \right)$, $0 \leq i \leq t - 1, 0 \leq j \leq t - 1$. If, for the purpose of the analysis, one would prefer populations which do not grow, then a number of conceptually interesting maps $\overrightarrow{Q}(\cdot, \cdot, \cdot)$ can be produced by means of finite state Markov chains (see, for example, Kandori et al. 1993 and Samuelson and Zhang 1992). An important feature of any dynamics like (26) developing in a discrete space is that condition (b) holds automatically.

equations

$$\dot{x} = f_1(x, y) - x, \quad \dot{y} = f_2(x, y) - y. \tag{31}$$

Second, possible limits of $\vec{X}(\cdot)$ are given as the solutions of the following system of nonlinear equations

$$f_1(x, y) - x = 0, \quad f_2(x, y) - y = 0, \tag{32}$$

where $(x, y) \in [\vec{0}, \vec{1}]$. Since, in general, we do not assume continuity of the functions $f_i(\cdot, \cdot)$, the solutions should be defined in the appropriate sense (see Arthur et al. 1987a).

So far, one has been totally agnostic in the form of the functions $f_i(\cdot, \cdot), i = 1, 2,$:[26] in our earlier example they depend on how buyers and sellers adjust their behaviors in the course of their interactions and, thus, on the fitness functions of the populations, $q_i(\cdot, \cdot), i = 1, 2$, but several other processes come easily to mind.[27] Note that, at one extreme, one can give a totally "ecological" interpretation of the link between the $f_i(\cdot, \cdot)$ and $q_i(\cdot, \cdot)$ functions: newly arriving agents do not "learn" anything by the observation of frequencies and payoffs, but relative fitness directly affects the probabilities of arrival of the cheating/non-cheating, inspecting/trusting types. In a crude biological analogy, relative fitness affects the rates of reproduction of the various "types". (In the economic domain, an analogy is the expansion/contraction of organizations characterized by fixed behavioral routines.) Alternatively, one may think also of various processes of adaptive learning. Models of this type are examined by Fudenberg and Kreps (1993) and Kaniovski and Young (1994). Hence, the dynamics of the form (27) and (28) will depend, of course, on the shape of the fitness functions[28] and also on the assumptions that one makes about the information agents are able to access – e.g. on the "true" fitness of their own population and the other ones, on the current combination of different types of agents (the "strategy profile") and also on the "cognitive" processes at work in adaptation. In this respect, the notion of "compatibility" (Friedman 1991) can be interpreted as a special restriction of the relationship between frequency dynamics and fitness functions, built on the deterministic analog (31) of the system (27) and (28).

9. Conclusions

Innovation and technology diffusion and more generally economic change involve competition among different technologies, and, most often, endogenous changes

---

[26] In general, they can also depend on t.

[27] Postponing a detailed analysis of the theoretical applications covered by this formalism to a separate publication, we only mention here the following examples. First, the agents, having no (explicit) fitness function, use a majority rule similar to the ones discussed in section 4. Second, playing a bi-matrix game, they use the corresponding payoffs as a fitness function. Since the proportions of players following a certain strategy from the opposite team are given by statistical estimates, opponents define the best reply strategy with a random error. Third, a combination of the previous two when the pool of players is not homogeneous, i.e. with positive probabilities new-comers can use both of the above decision rules.

[28] Incidentally, notice that for the purposes of this work, our "agnosticism" extends also to the precise form of the $q_i(\cdot, \cdot)$ functions.

in the costs/prices of technologies themselves and in adopters' choices. In the economic domain (as well as in other disciplines) the formal representation of such processes involves some dynamics of competing "populations" (i.e., technologies, firms, or even behavioral traits and "models" of expectation formation). A growing literature on such dynamics has begun studying the properties of those (generally non-linear) processes that innovation and diffusion entails. As by now robustly established, multiple equilibria are normally to be expected and "history matters", also in the sence that out-of-equilibrium fluctuations may bear system-level consequences on notional asymptotic outcomes. Developing on previous results showing – under dynamic increasing returns – the likely "lock-in" of diffusion trajectories onto particular technologies, we have presented a formal modeling apparatus aimed at handling the interaction between diffusion patterns, on the one hand, and technology learning or endogenous preferences formation or endogenous price formation, on the other. As examples, we presented three classes of stochastic models of shares dynamics on a market of infinite capacity by two competing new technologies. In the first of them, we assumed that the adoption dynamics is essentially driven by endogenous changes in the choices of risk-averse, imperfectly informed adopters (or, in a formally equivalent analogy, by some positive or negative externality imperfectly estimated by would-be users of alternative technologies). In the second example, we considered an endogenous price dynamics of two alternative technologies, driven by e.g., changes in their costs of production and/or by the intertemporal behaviors of their producers. In the third example we dealt with the same economic set-up as in the second one, but with an explicit "spatial" representation of the location of producers, and with location-specific selection of capital-embodied technologies (this latter case has interesting implications in terms of macroeconomic "lock-ins" into diverse patterns of growth). Finally, we sketched some possible applications of generalized urn schemes to the dynamics of selection and adaptation by interacting populations (including "evolutionary games").

In all of the cases, the process is allowed to embody some stochasticity, due to e.g., "imperfect" learning from other people's choices, marginal and formally undetectable differences in users' preferences, or some inertia in adjusting between different prices but identical-return technologies.

The formal apparatus presented here, based on the idea of the generalized urn scheme, allows, in the domain of its applicability, quite general analytical accounts of the relationships between some system-parameters (e.g., proxies for information "imperfection" by adopters; dynamic increasing returns and monopolistic exploitation of new technologies by their producers) and limit market shares. While path-dependency (i.e., "history matters") applies throughout, the foregoing analytical techniques appear to be able, at the very least, to discriminate those which turn out to be feasible limit equilibria (i.e., those which are attainable with positive probabilities) and, also, to discover the different rates of emergence of the limit patterns.

The apparatus can also be used for numerical simulation. In this case it proves to be as general as ordinary differential equations and as easy to implement. By means of numerical simulation one can also study much more complicated and "inductively rich" models. Still, the developed mathematical machinery serves in such numerical studies as a means of prediction and verification, showing the general kind of behavior one ought to expect. Yet another complementarity between the analytical exploration of these models and their numerical simulation concerns the study of their non-limit properties, e.g. the "transient" structures that might emerge along the trajectories and their degrees of persistence.

As the foregoing modeling illustrations show, "market imperfections" and "informational imperfections" often tend to foster technological variety, i.e., the equilibrium co-existence of different technologies and firms. Moreover, stochasticity in the choice process may well bifurcate limit market-shares outcomes. Finally, it is shown, corporate pricing strategies – possibly based on rationally-bounded procedures, imperfect information and systematically "wrong" expectation-formation mechanisms – are generally bound to influence long-term outcomes. Under all these circumstances, the foregoing modeling techniques allow, at the very least, a "qualitative" analytical assessment of diffusion/competition processes by no means restricted to those circumstances whereby microeconomic expectations, on average, represent unbiased estimations of the future.

If all this analytical representation is empirically adequate, then there seem to be no *a priori* reasons to restrict it to technological dynamics. In fact, under suitable modifications, it may apply as well to interdependent expectations, decisions and returns in many other economic domains. Just to give a few examples: the evolution of strategies and organizational forms in industrial dynamics; the dynamics of location in economic geography (Arthur 1990); adaptive processes and the emergence of social norms; "mimetic" effects on financial markets; macroeconomic coordination.[29] The list is likely to be indeed very long. Ultimately, what we have tried to implement is a relatively general analytical apparatus able to handle at least some qualitative properties of dynamic stochastic processes characterized by both positive, and, possibly negative, feedbacks of a functional form as "badly-behaved" as possible.

In principle, domains of applicability of generalized urn schemes correspond to the set of phenomena where not only "history matters" but the burden of the past increasingly shapes the present. Of course, we are far from claiming that this is always the case. However, we do indeed suggest that quite a few of the processes of economic change fall into this category.

Acknowledgments. We thank Sid Winter and two anonymous referees for their precious comments on earlier drafts. This research has benefitted at various stages from the support of the Italian Ministry of Research (MURST 40%); the Italian National Research Council (CNR); the Center for Research in Management, U.C. Berkeley; and throughout by the International Institute for Applied Systems Analysis (IIASA), Laxenburg, Austria.

References

Allen PM (1988) Evolution, Innovation and Economics. In: Dosi G, Freeman C, Nelson R, Silverberg G, Soete L. (eds) Technical Change and Economic Theory. Pinter Publishers, London and New York, pp 95–119

Anderson PW, Arrow KF, Pines R (eds) (1988) The Economy as an Evolving Complex System. SFI Studies in the Science of Complexity. Addison-Wesley, New York

Arthur WB, Ruszczinski A (1992) Strategic Pricing in Markets with Conformity Effects. Arch Control Sciences, 1: 7–31

Arthur WB (1983) On Competing Technologies and Historical Small Events: the Dynamics of Choice under Increasing Returns. International Institute for Applied Systems Analysis, Laxenburg, Austria WP-83-90, (Working paper)

---

[29] For some works in these different domains that link at least in spirit with the approach to economic dynamics suggested here, see among others, Kirman (1991), Kuran (1991), Boyer and Orléan (1992), Durlauf (1991).

Arthur WB (1990) "Silicon Valley" Location Clusters: When do Increasing Returns Imply Monopoly? Math Social Sci 19: 235–251

Arthur WB (1988) Self-Reinforcing Mechanisms in Economics. In: Anderson PW, Arrow KF, Pines R The Economy as an Evolving Complex System. SFI Studies in the Science of complexity. Addison-Wesley, New York, pp 9–31

Arthur WB, Ermoliev YM, Kaniovski YM (1983) The Generalized Urn Problem and Its Application. Kibernetika 1: 49–56 (in Russian)

Arthur WB, Ermoliev YM, Kaniovski YM (1987a) Adaptive Process of Growth Being Modeled by Urn Schemes. Kibernetika 6: 49–57 (in Russian)

Arthur WB, Ermoliev YM, Kaniovski YM (1987b) Nonlinear Urn Processes: Asymptotic Behavior and Applications. Interational Institute for Applied Systems Analysis, Laxenburg, Austria WP-87-85, (working paper)

Arthur WB, Ermoliev YM, Kaniovski YM (1987c) Path Dependent Processes and the Emergence of Macro-Structure. Eur J Operational Res 30: 294–303

Arthur WB, Ermoliev YM, Kaniovski YM (1988) Nonlinear adaptive Processes of Growth with General Increments: Attainable and Unattainable Components of Terminal Set. International Institute for Applied Systems Analysis, Laxenburg, Austria WP-88-86 (working paper)

Atkinson A, Stiglitz J (1969) A New View of Technological Change. Econ J 79: 573–578

Banerjee A, Weibull JW (1992) Evolution and Rationality: Some Recent Game-Theoretic Results. Presented at the Tenth World Congress of the International Economic Association, Moscow, August 1992

Boldrin M (1988) Persistent Oscillations and Chaos in Dynamic Economic Models: Notes for a Survey. In: Anderson PW, Arrow KF, Pines R (eds) The Economy as an Evolving Complex System. SFI Studies in the Science of Complexity. Addison-Wesley, New York, 49–75

Boyer R, Orléan A (1992) How do Conventions Evolve? J Evol Econ 2: 165–177

Brock WA, Malliaris AG (1989) Differential Equations, Stability and Chaos in Dynamic Economics. North Holland, Amsterdam

Cabrales A (1992) Stochastic Replicator Dynamics. Dept. of Economics, University of San Diego, California, mimeo

David PA (1985) Clio and the Economics of QWERTY. Am Econ Rev (Papers and Proceedings) 75: 332–337

David PA (1988) Path-Dependance: Putting the Past into the Future in Economics. Technical Report no. 533. Institute for Mathematical Studies in the Social Sciences, Stanford University

David PA (1975) Technical Choice, Innovation and Economic Growth. Cambridge University Press, Cambridge, Mass

Day R (1992) Irregular Growth Cycles. Am Econ Rev 72: 406–414

Dekel E, Scotchmer S (1991) On the evolution of Optimizing Behavior. J Econ Theory 59: 637–666

Dosi G (1988) Sources, Procedures and Microeconomic Effects of Innovation. J Econ Literature 26: 1120–1171

Dosi G, Freeman C, Nelson R, Silverberg G, Soete L (eds) (1988) Technical Change and Economic Theory. Francis Pinter, London and Columbia University Press, New York

Dosi G, Pavitt K, Soete L (eds) (1990) The Economics of Technological Change and International Trade. New York University Press, New York and Wheatsheaf, Brighton

Dosi G, Ermoliev Y, Kaniovski Y (1994) Generalized Urn Schemes and Technological Dynamics. J Math Econ 23: 1–19

Durlauf SN (1991) Non-Ergodic Economic Growth. Dept. of Economics, Stanford University, mimeo

Eigen M, Schuster P (1979) The Hypercycle: Principle of Natural Selforganization Springer, Berlin Heidelberg New York

Foster D, Young HP (1990) Stochastic Evolutionary Game Dynamics. Theoretical Population Biol 38: 219–232

Freeman C (1982) The Economics of Industrial Innovation, 2nd edn. Francis Pinter, London

Friedman D (1991) Evolutionary Games and Economics. Econometrica 59: 637–666

Frydman R (1982) Towards an Understanding of Market Processes: Individual Expectations, Learning and Convergence to Rational Expectations Equilibrium. Am Econ Rev 72: 652–668

Frydman R, Phelps ES (eds) (1983) Individual Forecasting and Aggregate Outcomes. Oxford University Press, Oxford

Fudenberg D, Kreps DM (1993) Learning Mixed Equilibria. Games Econ Behavior 4: 320–367

Glaziev SY, Kaniovski YM (1991) Diffusion of Innovations Under Conditions of Uncertainty: A Stochastic Approach. In: Nakicenovic N, Grubler A (eds), Diffusion of Technologies and Social Behavior. Springer, Berlin Heidelberg New York pp 231–246

Hanson WA (1985) Bandwagons and Orphans: Dynamic Pricing of Competing Systems Subject to Decreasing Costs. Ph.D. Dissertation, Standard University, Stanford

Hill BM, Lane D, Sudderth W (1980) A Strong Law for Some Generalized Urn Processes. Ann Probability 8: 214–226

Jordan J (1985) Learning Rational Expectation: The Finite State Case. J Econ Theory 36: pp 257–276

Kandori M, Mailath GJ, Rob R (1993) Learning, Mutation, and Long Run Equilibria in Games. Econometrica 61: 29–56

Kaniovski Y, Pflug G (1992) Non-standard Limit Theorems for Stochastic Approximation and Their Applications for Urn Schemes. International Institute for Applied Systems Analysis, Laxenburg, Austria WP-92-25 (working paper)

Kaniovski Y, Young HP (1994) Dynamic Equilibria Selection Under Incomplete Information. International Institute for applied Systems analysis, Laxenburg, Austria WP-94-30 (working paper)

Kirman A (1991) Epidemics of Opinion and Speculative Bubbles in Financial Markets. In: Taylor M (ed) Money and Financial Markets. Macmillan, London

Kuran T (1991) Congnitive Limitations and Preference Evolution. J Institutional Theoretical Econ 147: 241–273

Ljung L, Söderström T (1983) Theory and Practice of Recursive Identification. M.I.T. Press, Cambridge, Mass

Metcalfe JS (1988) The Diffusion of Innovations: an Interpretative Survey. In: Dosi G, Freeman C, Nelson R, Silverberg G, Soete L (eds) Technical Change and Economic Theory. Francis Pinter, London and Columbia University Press, New York, pp 560–589

Nelson R, Winter S (1982) An Evolutionary Theory of Economic Change. The Belknap Press of Harward University Press, Cambridge, Mass

Nicolis G, Prigogine I (1971) Self-Organization in Nonequilibrium Systems: From Dissipative Structures to Order through Fluctuations. Wiley, New York

Nicolis G, Prigogine I (1989) Exploring Complexity. An Introduction. Freeman, New York

Pemantle R (1991) When Are Touchpoints Limits for Generalized Pólya Urns? Proc Am Math Soc 113: 235–243

Polterovich VM, Henkin GM (1988) An Economic Model of Interaction of Processes of Creation and Leasing of Technologies. Ekonomika i Matematicheskie Metody 24: 1071–1083 (in Russian)

Prigogine I, Stengers I (1984) Order out of Chaos: Man's New Dialogue with Nature. Heinemann, London

Rosser JB, Jr (1991) From Catastrophe to Chaos: A General Theory of Economic Discontinuities. Kluwer, Boston Dordrecht London

Samuelson L, Zhang J (1992) Evolutionary Stability in Asymmetric Games. J Econ Theory 57: 363–391

Silverberg G, Dosi G, Orsenigo L (1988) Innovation, Diversity and Diffusion: a Self Organization Model. Econ J 98: 1032–1054

Silverberg G (1988) Modelling Economic Dynamics and Technical Change: Mathematical Models of Self-Organisation and Evolution. In: Dosi G, Freeman C, Nelson R, Silverberg G, Soete L (eds) Technical Change and Economic Theory. Francis Pinter, London and Columbia University Press, New York, pp 531–559

Soete L, Turner R (1984) Technological Diffusion and the Rate of Technical Change. Econ J 94: 612–623

Winter S (1971) Satisficing, Selection and the Innovating Remnant. Quarterly J Econ 85: pp 237–261

Young P (1993) The Evolution of Conventions. Econometrica 61: 57–84

[14]

The Economic Journal, **98** (*December* 1988), 1032–1054
Printed in Great Britain

INNOVATION, DIVERSITY AND DIFFUSION: A SELF-ORGANISATION MODEL*

Gerald Silverberg, Giovanni Dosi and Luigi Orsenigo

The diffusion of new products and new processes of production within and between business enterprises is clearly one of the fundamental aspects of the process of growth and transformation of contemporary economies.

It is well known that the diffusion of new products and processes takes varying lengths of time: some economic agents adopt very early after the development of an innovation while others sometimes do it only after decades. Moreover, during the diffusion process the competitive positions of the various agents (adopters and non-adopters) change. So do the economic incentives to adopt and the capabilities of the agents to make efficient use of the innovation. Finally, the innovation being adopted also changes over time, due to more or less incremental improvements in its performance characteristics which result in part from its more widespread use.

Contemporary analysis of diffusion has been essentially concerned with the following questions: (*a*) why is a new technology not instantaneously adopted by all potential users? (i.e. what are the 'retardation factors' preventing instantaneous diffusion?), (*b*) how can the dynamic paths of diffusion be represented?, and (*c*) what are the relevant variables driving the process?

However, innovation diffusion has rarely been formally treated as part of a more general theory of economic dynamics in which diversity of technological capabilities, business strategies, and expectations contribute to shape the evolutionary patterns of industries and countries (a remarkable exception is the evolutionary approach developed in particular by Nelson and Winter (1982) who, however, are more concerned with the general features of industrial dynamics than with the specific characteristics and implications of the diffusion process).

In this work, we shall analyse the nature of diffusion processes in evolutionary environments characterised by technological and behavioural diversity amongst the economic agents, basic uncertainty about the future, learning and disequilibrium dynamics.

First, we shall identify some fundamental characteristics of technology, innovation and diffusion which, we suggest, must be accounted for in theoretical models. Second, against this background, we shall briefly review

* We gratefully acknowledge comments on an earlier paper on which this work is partly based by several participants at the International Conference on Innovation Diffusion, Venice, 17–21 March 1986, and in particular those of Rlchard Nelson, as well as comments on earlier drafts by two anonymous referees and an Associate Editor. The work of one of us (Silverberg) was partially supported by a grant from the Deutsche Forschungsgemeinschaft, while the research of another one of us (Dosi) has been part of the activities of the Designated Research Centre, sponsored by the E.S.R.C. at the Science Policy Research Unit (SPRU), University of Sussex.

what we consider the major achievements and shortcomings of the current models of innovation diffusion. Third, we shall present what we call a 'self-organisation' model of innovation diffusion, that is, a model whereby relatively ordered paths of change emerge as the (partly) unintentional outcome of the dynamic interactions between individual agents and the changing characteristics of the technology. Fourth, the main properties and simulation results of the model will be discussed.

I. CHARACTERISTICS OF TECHNOLOGY AND DYNAMIC INDUSTRIAL ENVIRONMENTS

A renewed interest in the economics of innovation over the last two decades has brought considerable progress in the empirical description and theoretical conceptualisation of the sources, characteristics, directions and effects of technical change. We review these topics in Dosi (1988). Here, it suffices to summarise some of the major findings directly relevant to the diffusion of innovations concerning the nature of technology and the characteristics of firms and innovative environments.

(*a*) Technology – far from being a free good – is characterised by varying degrees of *appropriability*, of *uncertainty* about the technical and, *a fortiori*, commercial outcomes of innovative efforts, of *opportunity* for achieving technical advance, of *cumulativeness* in the patterns of innovation and exploitation of technological know-how and hardware, and of *tacitness* of the knowledge and expertise on which innovative activities are based. Particular search and learning processes draw on technology-specific knowledge bases, related to both freely available information (e.g. scientific results) and more 'local' and tacit skills, experience and problem-solving heuristics embodied in people and organisations.

(*b*) Technologies develop along relatively ordered paths (or 'trajectories') shaped by specific technical properties, search rules, 'technical imperatives' and cumulative expertise embodied in each 'technological paradigm' (cf. Dosi (1984); for similar arguments see Nelson and Winter (1977), Sahal (1981; 1985), Arthur (1985), Metcalfe (1985) and within somewhat different perspectives, Atkinson and Stiglitz (1969) and David (1975)). Relatedly, Winter (1984) defines different 'technological regimes' according to whether the knowledge base underpinning innovative search is primarily 'universal', and thus external to individual firms, or, alternatively, is primarily 'local' and firm-specific.

(*c*) As a consequence of (*a*) and (*b*), diversity between firms is a fundamental and permanent characteristic of industrial environments undergoing technical change (see also Metcalfe (1985) on this point). Inter-firm diversity (even *within* an industry) can fall into three major categories.

First, there are technological gaps related to different technological capabilities to innovate, different degrees of success in adopting and efficiently using product and process innovations developed elsewhere, and different costs of production of output. In Dosi (1984) we define these forms of diversity as *technological asymmetries*, meaning unequivocal gaps between firms which can be ranked as 'better' and 'worse' in terms of costs of production and product characteristics.

Second, diversity relates to differences between firms in their search procedures, input combinations and products, even with roughly similar production costs (on this point, see Nelson (1985)). Similarly, firms often search for their product innovations in different product-spaces and concentrate their effort on different sections of the market. Let us call this second set of sources of diversity *technological variety*, meaning all those technological differences which do not correspond to unequivocal hierarchies ('better' and 'worse' technologies and products).

Third, one generally observes within an industry (and even more so between industries) significant differences in the strategies of individual firms with respect to the level and composition of investment, scrapping, pricing, R & D, etc. Let us call these differences *behavioural diversity*.

Evolutionary processes in economic environments involving innovation and diffusion are governed to different degrees by *selection* mechanisms and *learning* mechanisms. Selection mechanisms tend to increase the economic dominance (e.g. profitability, market shares) of some firms with particular innovation characteristics at the expense of others. Learning mechanisms, on the other hand, may both spread innovative/imitative capabilities throughout the (possibly changing) set of potential adopters and reinforce existing disparities via cumulative mechanisms internal to the firm.

Learning processes generally occur via (*a*) the development of intra- and inter-industry 'externalities' (which include the diffusion of information and expertise, interfirm mobility of manpower, and growth of specialised services); (*b*) informal processes of technological accumulation within firms (of which learning-by-doing and learning-by-using are the best known examples of such 'internalised externalities'); and (*c*) processes of economically expensive search (R & D being, of course, the best example).

After a brief survey of the current state-of-the-art in the theory of innovation diffusion, we shall present a model which, in our view, makes a serious attempt to incorporate some of these features of innovative environments in a novel, yet consistent and realistic way.

II. DIFFUSION MODELS: RESULTS AND LIMITATIONS

Three basic approaches dominate current economic thought on innovation diffusion (cf. Stoneman (1983; 1986), Arcangeli (1986)). First, the line of enquiry pioneered by the seminal work of Mansfield (1961; 1968), and Griliches (1957) tries to identify the empirical regularities in diffusion paths, typically represented by S-shaped curves. In Mansfield's 'epidemic' approach, diffusion is generally found to be pushed by the expected profitability of the innovation and driven by the progressive dissemination of information about its technical and economic characteristics. Thus, diffusion is interpreted as a process of adjustment to some long-term equilibrium contingent upon learning by potential adopters.[1]

Empirical work on diffusion, however, whilst confirming the role of profitability in adoption decisions, has shown that differences in the characteristics of innovations, of product mixes, and of the potential adopters are also key factors in the diffusion process (see, for example, Nabseth and Ray (1974), Gold (1981), Davies (1979), David (1975)).

These findings, together with theoretical considerations about the crudely mechanical nature of epidemic diffusion models, lend support to a second approach, namely one based on 'equilibrium diffusion models'. Here, diffusion is seen as a sequence of equilibria determined by changes in the economic attributes of the innovation and the environment (see David (1969), Davies (1979), Stoneman and Ireland (1983), Ireland and Stoneman (1986), David and Olsen (1984), Reinganum (1981)). This approach has undoubtedly provided important insights into diffusion processes. Amongst other things, it has shown the importance of (i) differences (such as size) between potential adopters; (ii) the interactions between the supply decisions of the firms producing innovations and the pace of their adoption; (iii) the technological expectations of suppliers and adopters; (iv) the patterns of strategic interactions amongst both suppliers and adopters; (v) the market structure in both the supplying and using industries. However, these results are generally achieved at a high theoretical price. Radical uncertainty is *de facto* eliminated and maximising behaviour is assumed.[2] The analysis is often undertaken in terms of the existence and the properties of equilibria, while nothing is generally said about adjustment processes. Information about the techno-economic characteristics of the technologies is generally assumed to be freely available to all agents. The nature of 'technology' is radically simplified and assumed to be embodied in given technical features of production inputs.

A *third* approach is explicitly evolutionary and represents the diffusion of new techniques and new products under conditions of uncertainty, bounded rationality and endogeneity of market structures as a disequilibrium process (Nelson, 1968; Nelson and Winter, 1982; Metcalfe, 1985; Silverberg, 1984; Iwai, 1984a, b).[3]

The model that follows is in this evolutionary tradition, and thus allows for disequilibrium processes, endogeneity of market structures, etc. It also explicitly incorporates those assumptions of 'equilibrium' diffusion models which capture important empirical characteristics of innovative environments mentioned earlier, such as the relevance of expectations and differences between agents, as

---

[1] One may, for example, represent this diffusion process as the transition between two 'classical' long-term equilibrium positions: see Metcalfe and Gibbons (1988).

[2] To be precise, in Davies' original model adoption decisions are based on rules of thumb explicitly justified in terms of 'bounded rationality'. Yet, subsequent developments within this approach have been explicitly based on maximising behaviour of the agents.

[3] See also Eliasson (1982; 1986). On the connection to empirical analysis see Gort and Klepper (1982), Gort and Konakayma (1982) and Levin *et al.* (1985).

well as some features implicit in Mansfield-type models, such as imperfect information and asymmetric technological knowledge.[4]

III. A SELF-ORGANISATION MODEL OF THE DIFFUSION OF INNOVATIONS AND THE TRANSITION BETWEEN TECHNOLOGICAL TRAJECTORIES

In two previous papers, one of the present authors (Silverberg, 1984; 1987) attempted to demonstrate the relevance to economic theory of the self-organisational approach to dynamic modelling pioneered by Eigen, Haken, Prigogine and others.[5] In essence the argument proceeds from the observation that in complex interdependent dynamical systems unfolding in *historical*, i.e. *irreversible* time, economic agents, who have to make decisions today the correctness of which will only be revealed considerably later, are confronted with irreducible uncertainty and holistic interactions between each other and with aggregate variables. The *a priori* assumption of an 'equilibrium' solution to this problem to which all agents *ex ante* can subscribe and which makes their actions consistent and in some sense dynamically stable is a leap of methodological faith. Instead we proposed employing some of the recently developed methods of evolutionary modelling to show how the interaction of diverse capabilities, expectations and strategies with the thereby emerging selective pressures can drive a capitalistic economy along certain definite patterns of development.

Drawing on a dynamic model of market competition with embodied technical progress investigated in Silverberg (1987), we embed the question of diffusion into the larger one of the transition of an industry between two 'technological trajectories'. Choice of technique is no longer a choice between two pieces of equipment with given (but perhaps imperfectly known) characteristics, but now involves skills in using them which can be endogenously built up by learning by doing or by profiting from the experience of others, as well as expectations about future developments along the various competing trajectories. As we shall see, the diversity in firms' capabilities and expectations is an irreducible element driving the diffusion process.

In the sectoral approach taken here industry-level demand is taken as given and growing at some exponential rate. Firms command some market share of this demand at any given time, but market shares may change over time as a dynamic response with a characteristic time constant (reflecting the 'freeness' of competition and such factors as brand loyalty, information processing and search delays and costs, etc.) to disparities in the relative *competitiveness* of firms. This concept, so dear to close observers of the business scene, has to our knowledge evaded incorporation into a systematic economic theory until now.

---

[4] A more detailed discussion of the empirical basis of the hypotheses entering into the model presented below can be found in Dosi *et al.* (1988).

[5] For a multidisciplinary overview of self-organisational modelling and its methodological philosophy see Haken (1983), Nicolis and Prigogine (1977) and Prigogine (1976).

The evolution of market structure is governed in our approach by an equation relating the rate of change of a firm's market share to the difference between its competitiveness (defined below) and average industry competitiveness (averaged over all competing firms in an industry, weighted by their market shares). This equation is formally identical to the equation first introduced into mathematical biology by R. A. Fisher in 1930 and more recently applied in a variety of contexts and studied in considerable mathematical detail by Eigen (1971), Eigen and Schuster (1979), Ebeling and Feistel (1982), Hofbauer and Sigmund (1984), and Sigmund (1986). Our use of this equation differs from most biological applications, however, in that the competitiveness parameters, rather than being constants or simple functions of the other variables, themselves change over time in complex ways in response to the strategies pursued by firms and feedbacks from the rest of the system. In a systems theoretic sense this equation may be regarded as the fundamental mathematical description of competitive processes. It is worth emphasising the difference between our approach and standard theoretical conceptualisations of competition. The latter generally identify the circumstances under which no relative competitive shifts or profits can be realised (impossibility of arbitrage, uniform rate of profit, etc.) and then *assume* that the system must always be in or near this state.

If we denote by f_i the market share in percentage of real orders of the ith firm, by E_i its competitiveness and by $\langle E \rangle$ the average competitiveness of all firms in the industry ($= \Sigma f_i E_i$), then the evolution of market shares is governed by the following equation:

$$\dot{f}_i = A_9(E_i - \langle E \rangle) f_i. \qquad (1)$$

We define the competitiveness parameter as a linear combination of terms reflecting relative price and delivery delay differentials:

$$E_i = -\ln p_i - A_{10} dd_i, \qquad (2)$$

where p_i is the market price of the ith firm and dd_i its current delivery delay.[6]

Silverberg (1987) presents a basic dynamic structure for dealing with strategic investment in the face of uncertainty with respect to the future course of embodied technical progress, overall demand and changes in relative competitiveness. In this framework, entrepreneurs are seen as being fully conscious of the ongoing, process nature of economic growth and technological change, so that their decisions, particularly concerning fixed investment, take account of and try to anticipate these developments. Decision-making is incorporated on the one hand in certain robust rules of thumb (for the most part feedback rules dealing with oligopolistic pricing and production policies) and 'animal spirits' in the form of decision rules governing replacement policy (the payback period method) and expansion of capacity ('estimates' or 'guesses' of future demand growth corrected by experience). Technical change

---

[6] Product quality factors could also be included in this expression, but for simplicity we restrict the analysis here to markets with fully standardised commodities.

is embodied in vintages, and the resulting capital stocks are not assumed to start in, and in general need not converge to steady-state distributions.

The capital stock (measured in units of productive capacity) of each firm is represented as an aggregation over nondecaying vintages between the current period t and the scrapping date $T_i(t)$:

$$K_i(t) = \int_{T_i}^{t} K_i(t, t') \, dt', \qquad (3)$$

where $K_i(t, t)$ is gross investment at time t (in capacity units),

$$K_i(t, t') = K_i(t', t') \text{ if } T_i(t) < t' < t \text{ and}$$

$$= 0 \quad \text{otherwise.}$$

This aggregate capital stock may be a composite of different technologies as well as different vintages of a single technological trajectory. A payback calculation is performed by each firm with its desired payback period (which may differ between firms) to determine a desired scrapping date for its capital stock $T_{di}(t)$ by solving:

$$P(t)/[c(T_{di}) - c(t)] = b_i, \qquad (4)$$

where $P(t)$ is the price of new capital equipment per unit capacity, $c(\ldots)$ is the unit operating cost at time t of the vintage in question, and b_i is the target payback period of the ith firm.[7]

The actual scrapping date adjusts to this desired date via a first-order catch up procedure:

$$\dot{T}_i = z_i \max [A_{11}(T_{di} - T_i), 0] \qquad (5)$$

where z_i is a rationing parameter between 0 and 1 (the ratio of current cash flow to desired gross investment) which may arise if the ith firm, due to financial constraints, is not able to finance its desired investment programme fully (otherwise it is 1). The amount of capacity scrapped as a result of this decision (as well as a possible desire to reduce overall capacity) is

$$S_i = K_i(t, T_i) \, \dot{T}_i. \qquad (6)$$

Net expansion (or contraction) of capacity is governed by a desired expansion rate r_i for each firm:

$$N_i = r_i K_i. \qquad (7)$$

---

[7] In the economics literature a number of seemingly 'self-evident' rules have been applied to decide when technologically obsolete equipment should be replaced by new equipment. One calls for an old vintage to be replaced when its unit variable costs exceed total unit costs of current best practice. Another indicates replacement when unit variable costs exceed the price attained per unit of output. A substantial specialised literature exists, however, dealing with optimal replacement beginning with Terborgh (Terborgh, 1949; see also Smith, 1961). Under suitable assumptions about the rate of future technical progress this leads to the so-called square root rule.

Terborgh shows that the payback criterion is a reasonable approximation to the square root rule. Given that uncertain technological expectations (which are an extrapolation from past experience in this rule) play a major role, and that surveys of industrial practice consistently reveal rate of return or payback period calculations to be widely entrenched, we have opted for this simple criterion in our treatment of replacement. For a discussion of optimal replacement in the evolutionary framework employed here see Silverberg (1987).

The capital stock changes over time due to additions from gross investment and removals due to scrapping:

$$\dot{K}_i = N_i = K_i(t, t) - S_i. \tag{8}$$

The desired rate of capacity expansion may be set initially at any level ('animal spirits') but is revised over time using first-order feedback from the deviation of the rate of capacity utilisation u from its desired level u_0:

$$\dot{r}_i = A_{13}(u_i - u_0). \tag{9}$$

Labour is assumed to be the only current cost of production and can be decomposed into prime and overhead components.[8] The prime unit labour coefficient is an average over the historical technological labour/output coefficients $a(t)$ weighted by vintage (in the following the firm subscript i has been suppressed for simplicity):

$$\langle a \rangle = \int_T^t a(t') K(t, t') \, dt' / K(t). \tag{10}$$

It changes over time due to additions of more productive new equipment through investment and removal of marginal equipment through scrapping according to the following equation derived from (10) by differentiation:

$$\langle \dot{a} \rangle = \{K(t, t)[a(t) - \langle a \rangle] + S[\langle a \rangle - a(T)]\}/K. \tag{11}$$

If net investment is taking place, i.e. $N > 0$, then all scrapping serves the purpose of replacement investment R, so that $K(t, t) = N + R$, $S = R$ and

$$\langle \dot{a} \rangle = \{N[a(t) - \langle a \rangle] + R[a(t) - a(T)]\}/K, \tag{12}$$

which shows that replacement investment contributes more to lowering unit costs per unit of investment outlay than does expansion investment. Thus unit costs are determined by the age structure of the capital stock and the history of technological change it represents. They will vary over time as a result of the scrapping and expansion strategies of the firm under the constraint of its ability to finance its investment plans, itself a function of cost and profitability.[9]

Overhead labour per unit output at full operating capacity is assumed proportional to prime unit labour. Total overhead labour is then this value multiplied by total productive capacity K (and thus is independent of the rate of capacity utilisation, contrary to total prime labour, which is directly proportional to it).

The level of production is set such as to compensate for deviations of the current delivery delay (dd) from some industry-wide standard level (dd_0):

$$\dot{u} = A_5(dd - dd_0) u(1 \cdot 1 - u^2), u < 1,$$
$$= 0, u = 1 \text{ and rhs above} > 0. \tag{13}$$

[8] Other current costs of production could be incorporated by making the prime unit labour coefficient and nominal wage rate vectors.
[9] The exact functional relationship is reminiscent of Kaldor's technical progress function, but shows that the rate of change of *average* productivity is a function of the gaps between best practice, average and marginal vintage productivities *and* the division of gross investment between modernisation and expansion.

The quadratic saturation term is introduced to represent bottlenecks in the production process near the full capacity limit. Delivery delay dd is the ratio of order backlog L to current production y ($=uK$), and the order backlog is governed by the rate equation

$$\dot{L} = d - y, \tag{14}$$

where d is incoming orders ($=f_i \times$ total market demand).

Firms' prices are determined as a dynamic compromise between the desired mark-up on unit costs and relative competitiveness. Since only relative prices are of importance here, we take the logarithm of price variables throughout. Let p_i be the log of the ith firm's market price and p_{ci} its desired markup price based on its unit prime costs. Then

$$\dot{p}_i = A_7(p_{ci} - p_i) + A_8(E_i - \langle E \rangle). \tag{15}$$

Pricing policy is regarded as a compromise (depending on the 'degree of monopoly' characteristic of an industry) between strict cost-plus pricing and a concession to the 'prevailing' market price (the geometric mean of all prices weighted by market shares) via relative competitiveness. This structure of pricing allows the changing relative cost structure of firms to be transmitted through the market and makes intelligible such phenomena as price leadership or being under price pressure. Firms at a competitive (in general mostly cost) disadvantage are thus forced to lower their prices somewhat to prevent excessive losses of market share, while firms enjoying a competitive advantage are free to realise short-term profits by raising their prices. The ratio of A_8 to A_7 determines to what extent competitive pressures overrule the markup principle (which remains valid, however, at the aggregate level) and enables the model to span the entire range of market structures between pure monopoly and pure competition.[10]

As the model now stands, with a single vintage structure for each firm, it already accounts for the diffusion of new technology in the case in which a unique best practice technology is apparent to all agents (this perspective on diffusion was first introduced by Salter, 1962). The process of investment under the assumption of some long-term rate of technical progress implicit in the payback method ensures that advances in productivity will be continually incorporated into the capital stock, even if entrepreneurs differ in their assessment of the appropriate payback to use. Thus diffusion of technical progress is already guaranteed by the standard methods of investment policy at this first level of analysis.

However, in order to capture the collective dynamic of advance along different technological trajectories we propose the following additional structure. We compare two technological trajectories representing at any time the maximum productivities attainable in best practice vintages of the respective technologies. We assume that these are both changing at some rate, and that the second technology is always absolutely superior in productivity. Moreover, the relative price/capacity unit of the two technologies may also be

[10] For a more detailed discussion of the price interactions to which this system leads see Silverberg (1987).

changing. The actual productivities realised by firms are a product of this underlying value and the specific efficiency or skill with which firms master each technology (between o and 100%). For simplicity we assume all firms begin with technology 1, and technology 2 first becomes available at time t^*. Furthermore, technology 1 is already mature, i.e. skill levels are saturated at 100%. The firms initially possess lower (and possibly varying) efficiencies with technology 2, but the margin for further development is not knowable with any precision. Firms only know the product of this efficiency and the underlying potential. They may (and in fact must) make guesses about the rate at which further improvements in efficiency (equally applicable to previously installed vintages) and further embodied technical progress (only applicable to current investment) will be achieved. This formulation reflects the fact that the productivity of a technology realised in practice is not just a function of the presence of the requisite machines, but conjointly requires certain levels of specific expertise and experience (from specialised scientific and engineering training to shop floor apprenticeship and work discipline) both internal and external to the firm. Hence investment decisions are not merely a question of determining the best practice technology at a given time, but one of weighing the prospects for further development either by acquiring experience with it now to gain a jump on competitors or waiting for a more opportune moment and avoiding possible development costs.[11]

We identify the evolution of the efficiency parameter with movement down the well-known learning or experience curve using a logistic dynamic and a variable rate of change equal to the rate of growth of cumulative production with the technology (this corresponds to the classic power law learning curves on cumulative production reported in the literature for values well below saturation). This represents internal learning and is only achieved if the firm actually produces with the new technology. Writing s_i for the internal skill level of the ith firm using the new technology, P_i for its current production and CP_i for its cumulated production with the new technology, we have

$$\dot{s}_i = A_{15}[P_i/(CP_i + C)]\, s_i(1 - s_i), \qquad \text{if } s_i > s_p, \qquad (16)$$

where C is a constant proportional to the capital stock and s_p is the level of skill generally available in the industry even to those firms not yet producing on the new technological trajectory.

In addition, the experience acquired by individual firms can 'leak' out and become available to the rest of the industry. In practice this can take the form of skilled labour and management moving between firms (or setting up their own companies), manufacturers diffusing the results of experience gained with

---

[11] Thus in a very suggestive study of the diffusion of numerically controlled machine tools in German industry, Kleine (1983) reports that some firms invested in the new technology even though it did not yet satisfy their normal investment criteria because they hoped to build up superior skills specific to a technology which they anticipated would play a decisive role in the future. Others took a more conservative attitude, by no means irrational *prima facie*, and waited for the smoke to clear before buying into a more mature technology. The spread of knowledge about the availability and purported superiority of NC equipment played almost no role since the firms surveyed were well informed from the start by suppliers and trade publications. Similar observations on computer adoption decisions have been made by Stoneman (1976).

their equipment to other users in the form of operating instructions and the like, trade organisations and publications, educational institutions, or even industrial espionage. We represent this by having the level of generally available skill (public skill) lag behind the average of internal skill levels with an exponential delay:

$$\dot{s}_p = A_4(\langle s \rangle - s_p), \tag{17}$$

where

$$\langle s \rangle = \Sigma f_i s_i.$$

Firms profit from this learning externality because they 'float' on the rising general skill level even if they are not yet employing the new technology:

$$\dot{s}_i = \dot{s}_p \quad \text{if} \quad s_i = s_p. \tag{18}$$

In deciding on whether to switch to the new technology firms may want to abandon their normal investment criteria to take into consideration the gains in productivity they may be able to realise even after new equipment is installed as well as their desire to attain early proficiency in its use and thereby get on a possible virtuous circle. These will depend on how optimistic they are about the future development potential of the new trajectory and the extent to which temporary advantages can be appropriated (which is related to the relative rates of internal and external learning) as well as what their competitors are planning. To this end firms select an 'anticipation bonus' they award to the new technology in making their choice of technique. They multiply the current realisable productivity by their bonus for the new technology and compare it with the best practice productivity of the old in a payback calculation. This means that the new technology is preferred if its adjusted productivity is higher than that of the old and (i) it is cheaper per unit of capacity at the time of comparison or (ii) it is more expensive but the difference in price can be recouped within the desired pay-back period by the savings in labour cost. If c_1, P_1 and c_2, P_2 are the unit cost and price per efficiency unit of the old and the new technique, respectively, then the calculation is

$$(P_2 - P_1)/(c_1 - c_2/s_t X_t) \leqslant b_t, \tag{19}$$

where X_t is the anticipation bonus of the ith firm (cf. equation (4)). The last case in which its (adjusted) productivity is lower but its price is also lower is excluded here as being of limited empirical interest.

It remains to decide what changes this introduces into the replacement rule. The reference value entering into the payback calculation for replacement uses the maximum of the old best practice productivity and the currently realisable new best practice productivity. This ensures that scrapping does not fall below the rate that would have prevailed if investment had continued in the old technology, and that it only accelerates when the new technology actually proves its superior performance on the shop floor.

The above model represents a dynamical system which, due to the vintage structure, should be categorised as a set of differential-difference equations with age-dependent effects. This is a class of systems whose mathematical properties, even in the most simple cases, are still only poorly understood. Many of the mathematical elements going into the model, however, have a well-known pedigree, such as the replicator dynamics governing market shares (see, e.g. Sigmund, 1986). Consequently, we are forced to resort to 'experimental mathematics' in the form of a computer implementation to uncover some of the economic properties of the model.

IV. MARKET DYNAMICS, DIFFUSION, AND THE COLLECTIVE RATIONALITY OF THE ADOPTION DECISION

The system as described above admits several dimensions of structural and behavioural variability over time: firms can be of different sizes, characterised by different unit costs, delivery delays, rates of capacity utilisation, skill levels, age profiles of capital stock, etc. Of course, in this model as in a large part of the diffusion literature (e.g. David, 1969; Stoneman and Ireland, 1983), a distribution of initial characteristics of firms, with uniform expectations across firms, other things being equal, will lead to a distribution of adoption dates. In the general case of diverse firm characteristics and diverse technological expectations, the distribution of adoption decisions will both result from these initial distributions and contribute to their endogenous transformation. Thus firms' sizes, skill levels, and the like cannot be regarded as fixed characteristics to which the diffusion process can be referred, but rather must be seen themselves as in part products of that process. However, to focus more clearly on the strategic aspects of the diffusion process and the problem of the interdependence of behaviour even in the absence of diverse firm characteristics, we will neglect this dimension of the problem. Instead, we will single out the role of the anticipation bonus (reflecting expectations about the future course of the new trajectory) in relation to what we term dynamic appropriability and set all other characteristics identical across firms.

In the three runs we will now consider, technology 2 is potentially 100% more productive than technology 1 and both are advancing in the embodied sense at 4% p.a., as are nominal wages. Overall demand is growing at 5%. Technology 2 starts out being priced higher per capacity unit but this price declines at the rate of 1% p.a. All 10 firms employed in the first case (Figs. 1–4) start out identical in every respect except in their propensity to innovate, i.e. their innovation bonuses. The initial efficiency level on technology 2 is 30% for all firms. The anticipation bonuses range from 3·33 to 1·0 with a clustering around 1·33 (i.e. the firm evaluates the productivity of technology 2 in its choice of technique decision 33% higher than its actual present value). The vertical dotted lines indicate the date of adoption of the firm with the corresponding number.

Fig. 1 graphs three measures of diffusion. The curve marked with squares shows the classic measure of inter-firm diffusion discussed in the literature: the percentage of potential adopters already employing some quantity of the new technology. It shows the typical S-shape familiar to students of diffusion. Just near it (marked with a diamond) is a curve depicting the current market share of adopters. If this curve lies above/below the previous one, adopters as a whole

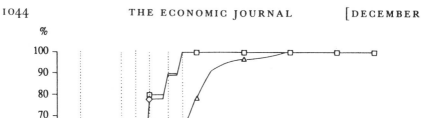

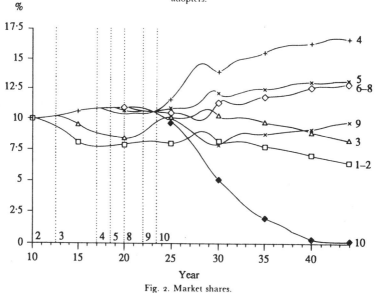

Fig. 1. Diffusion curves. □, Percentage of firms; △, percentage capacity; ◇, market share of adopters.

Fig. 2. Market shares.

have gained/lost market shares over time. The aggregation hides the fact that the vicissitudes of individual adopters can vary quite widely. The last curve represents the percentage of overall productive capacity embodied in the new technology. This results from both inter and intrafirm diffusion as well as shifts in the relative sizes of firms and is the key variable in analysing the impact of

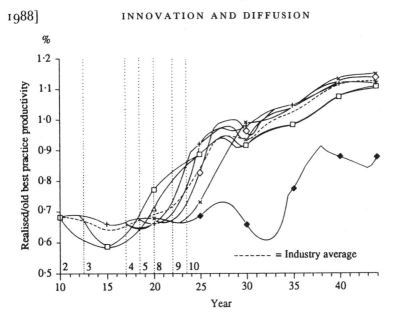

Fig. 3. Ratio of realised average productivity to best practice productivity of technique 1.

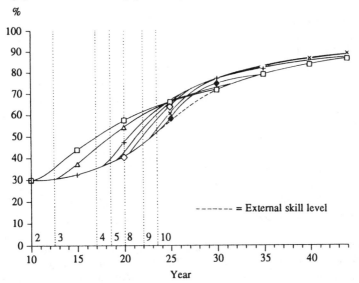

Fig. 4. Skill levels: firm-specific and external.

the innovation at the industry and the economy-wide levels. It displays the classic smooth S-shaped form Fisher and Pry (1971) found in measuring diffusion in capacity terms.

Fig. 2 plots market shares and reveals the microeconomic drama going on beneath the aggregation surface. Firms 1 and 2, which adopt as soon as the innovation appears on the market (year 10), just manage to maintain respectable market shares. Firm 3 innovates $2\frac{1}{2}$ years later and does around 2 percentage points better in holding on to market share. Firm 4 is the clear winner in this saga, benefitting from the mistakes of firms 1–3 but still getting in on the ground floor to increase its market share by over 50 %. Firms 5–8 are also net profiters from the market reshuffle to a small extent. Even firm 9, one of the laggards, manages to recover its initial market share after taking something of a beating. Firms 10 demonstrates the pitfalls of missing the boat by not providing for an anticipation bonus. It has evidently been pushed into a vicious downward spiral which completely eliminates it from the market.

Fig. 3 depicts the realised productivity of the entire capital stock of each firm, corrected for the rate of capacity utilisation, and divided by the old best practice productivity to eliminate the underlying exponential trend. The early adopters suffer a loss as they first go down the learning curve and then pull ahead. The middle adopters suffer only minor losses and soon overtake the early group, while the late adopters manage to get on the 'track' but consistently remain below the industry average (the dashed curve).[12] Firm 10, finally, is thrown completely off the track and never comes close to closing the gap.

The evolution of the firm-specific and external skill levels is shown in Fig. 4. The early adopters do indeed build up a lead in their internal efficiency, but the middle and late adopters start from a higher initial level due to external learning and eventually overtake them. Even firm 10 manages to rise above the public skill level for a while after it adopts.

If we now naively rerun history (in a run there is no point in plotting) by giving all 10 firms the anticipation bonus used by the winner of the first round (firm 4), something surprising occurs. The new technology is not adopted at all because no firm is willing to incur the development costs associated with bringing it to commercial maturity. This makes it clear that technological innovation and diffusion are characterised by collective effects and an inextricable tension between private and social gain.

This is further brought out in the third run (Figs. 5–8), which is an example of 'early adopters receive their just deserts'. All parameters of this run are identical to those of the first one except for a doubling of coefficient A_{15} in equation (14). This accelerates the rate of internal learning and thereby raises the dynamic appropriability of the innovation for the early adopters. Although the actual times of adoption have hardly changed, the relative fortunes of the competing firms change considerably. The first adopters (firms 1 and 2) are clear net beneficiaries, followed by firm 3. All of the middle adopters are huddled closely together with little change in their market shares, while the straggler firm 10 is once again catapulted from the market.

What story does this one sequence of runs out of many possible ones have to tell us about strategic behaviour in innovative environments? In some respects

---

[12] It should be borne in mind that productivity is only part of competitiveness. The response of delivery delays to production and capacity expansion decisions also contributes to changes in market shares and realised price margins.

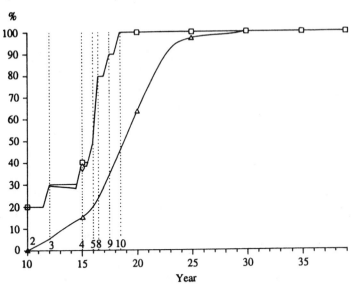

Fig. 5. Diffusion curves: □, Percentage of firms; △, capacity; ◇, market share of adopters.

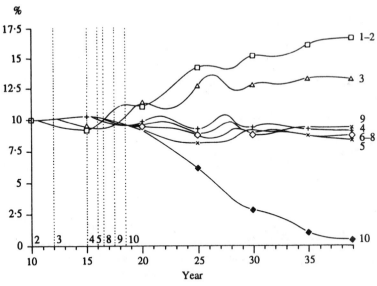

Fig. 6. Market shares.

the prospective shift of technological paradigm creates a Prisoner's Dilemma situation: conservative entrepreneurs would all prefer to avoid accelerated capital replacement and costly development expenditures. Yet profits may eventually be reaped and irreversible market share gains realised by adopting

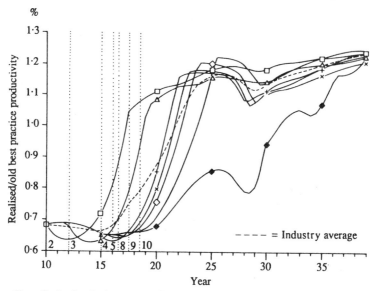

Fig. 7. Ratio of realised average productivity to best practice productivity of technique 1.

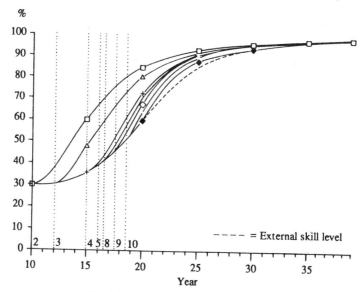

Fig. 8. Skill levels: firm-specific and external.

early. This threat thus forces entrepreneurs to take an anticipatory position and can be ultimately self-justifying, if the innovation is indeed potentially superior. This latter fact, of course, remains uncertain until the diffusion process is well underway. Moreover, the adoption decision is complicated by the learning externality. The dynamic appropriability of the new trajectory, as we have seen, serves as a bifurcation parameter. For high enough values a first-in strategy is preferable, for lower values a second-in one is. But a second-in strategy is only possible if there is a sacrificial lamb in the form of a first adopter. And first adopters exist because the precise value of the dynamic appropriability is unknown.

One might inquire whether some distribution of adoption times may not exist satisfying a Nash equilibrium, i.e. given that it is clear that adoption will actually take place in a certain sequence, no single entrepreneur has an incentive to deviate locally from his adoption decision. This is precisely what Reinganum (1981) has studied in a static context. In comparison with our model, however, it should first be noted that the payoffs to adoption cannot simply be expressed as a function of the percentage of the industry already adopting. This is because nonlinear cumulative causation (*a*) makes the form of the interaction between agents exceedingly complex and subject to bifurcations, and (*b*) in evolutionary games such as our own, outcomes are in terms of expansion, survival or extinction and not of one-time monetary payments.

In the biological literature the evolutionary stable strategy (ESS) concept corresponds to that of a Nash equilibrium.[13] Instead of the rationality postulate, the concept of noninvadability is used. The justification for this procedure is that interactions between strategies are microevents repeated sufficiently often against unchanging boundary conditions to ensure convergence. To what extent can such an argument be invoked to explain market dynamics? Routine rules such as the payback period investment criterion may become established historically through some such process, as is argued in Silverberg (1987). A shift between technological paradigms confronts us with an altogether different situation which is in some ways comparable to the lockin and standards phenomena discussed by Arthur (1985; 1988), David (1985), and Katz and Shapiro (1985; 1986). Because major innovations entailing a new endogenous skill regime occur infrequently, there can be no 'learning' process to ensure a convergence of strategies before the strategies have been irreversibly implemented. It is the diversity of positions adopted by firms that allows the potential superiority of a new technological regime to be developed and exploited. In that process losses and gains will almost invariably be made before routine procedures can reassert themselves. Rationality cannot be invoked to guarantee equilibrium because the system is not sufficiently transparent and there is no *ex ante* coordination mechanism. But if diversity may have inevitably negative consequences for some participants, at the system-level it is necessary to probe the development potential and trigger the collective development process. Lockin to an inferior technology of course is an associated danger. By the time another such decision arises, crucial parameters such as the dynamic appropriability will have almost certainly changed, so that

[13] For a discussion of the specific features of evolutionary games in various contexts see Axelrod (1984), Hofbauer and Sigmund (1984), Thomas (1984), and Zeeman (1979 and 1981).

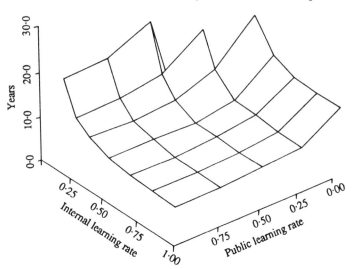

Fig. 9. Time to diffuse from 10–90%.

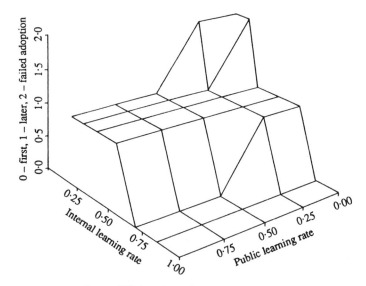

Fig. 10. Diffusion winner: first vs. later adopters.

the successful strategies of the last round may no longer be valid. Or they invalidate themselves because now they are being copied.

Figs. 9 and 10 and Tables 1 and 2 summarise the results of 35 runs conducted for the same distribution of anticipation bonuses as in Figs. 1–8 but for a range of values of the internal and public learning rates (A_{15} and A_4). Fig. 9 plots the time for the new technology to increase its share in total capacity from 10–90%

Table 1

Time for capacity share of new technology to diffuse from 10 to 90% for different values of parameters A_4 and A_{15}

A_{15}	A_4				
	0·1	0·325	0·55	0·775	1·00
0·2	*fd*	*fd*	29·51	25·53	21·50
0·3	*fd*	27·02	19·01	16·02	15·52
0·4	29·52	19·03	14·51	12·54	12·04
0·55	22·04	14·04	11·54	10·99	10·01
0·7	19·00	13·03	10·99	9·52	9·01
0·85	17·53	11·53	10·01	9·02	8·53
1·0	16·50	10·56	9·52	8·53	8·04

fd = failed diffusion.

Table 2

Asymptotic results of diffusion process in terms of relative market shares

A_{15}	A_4				
	0·1	0·325	0·55	0·775	1·00
0·2	*fd*	*fd*	*l*	*l*	*l*
0·3	*fd*	*l*	*l*	*l*	*l*
0·4	*l*	*l*	*l*	*l*	*l*
0·55	*l*	*l*	*l*	*l*	*l*
0·7	*l*	*l*	*f*	*f*	*f*
0·85	*f*	*f*	*f*	*f*	*f*
1·0	*f*	*f*	*f*	*f*	*f*

fd = failed diffusion and relative decline of adopting firms, *l* = later adopters attain largest market shares, *f* = first adopters attain largest market shares.

and is a measure of the speed of diffusion. A very regular pattern emerges, with the speed of diffusion increasing, but at a declining rate, as a function of both parameters. A threshold can be discerned in the region of low learning rates. Below it only a few pioneer firms adopt the new technology, but are then driven off the market. Non-adopters manage to dominate the industry, the diffusion process reverses, and the technology ultimately disappears, even though it is potentially superior.

In Fig. 10 the bifurcations in the qualitative nature of the market reshuffle become visible. As we have seen, for low values of the learning parameters, non-adopters eventually increase their market shares at the expense of adopters (the peak of the cliff). For a middle range of values some (but of course not all) of the later adopters profit most in terms of markets share gains from introducing the new technology (the plateau). As we suspected, a threshold exists in the A_4–A_{15} plane beyond which first adopters emerge with the largest gains in market share (the foot of the hill). This threshold is primarily a function of the internal learning rate but, surprisingly, declines somewhat with higher public learning rates. Tables 1 and 2 summarise the original data.

V. CONCLUSIONS

In the first part of this paper we underscored the role of technological expectations, cumulativeness, internal and public knowledge, and strategic competition in any discussion of the dynamics of innovation-induced technological change. We then went on to formulate a model based on a number of behavioural assumptions on the one hand, and a structure of feedback loops on the other. This removed the question of diffusion from the largely static framework in which it has traditionally been placed and led to a dynamic coupling between the behaviour of individual agents and the environment in which they are operating. Although, as we have argued, a considerable range of microeconomic diversity and disequilibrium must remain an irreducible feature of such a system, the diffusion process itself shows a rather stable and invariant structure. Thus our simulations show that while some firms may be incurring short-term losses for long-term gains in market share, and others are driven onto a vicious spiral towards backruptcy, nevertheless the S-shaped form of the diffusion curve (which, however, is not necessarily a logistic and may even decline during the early phases) stands out. It is this superposition of microeconomic drama and system-level logic which makes the Schumpeterian entrepreneur a crucial element in the innovation process.

MERIT, University of Limburg, Maastricht
University of Rome 'La Sapienza' and SPRU, University of Sussex)
Bocconi University, Milan and SPRU, University of Sussex
Date of receipt of final typescript: May 1988

REFERENCES

Arcangeli, F. (1986). 'Innovation diffusion: a cross-traditions state of the art.' University of Sussex: SPRU.
Arthur, W. B. (1985). 'On competing technologies and historical small events. The dynamics of choice under increasing returns,' Technological Innovation Programme Workshop Paper, Department of Economics, Stanford University.
—— (1988). 'Competing technologies: an overview.' In *Technical Change and Economic Theory* (eds. G. Dosi, C. Freeman, R. Nelson, G. Silverberg and L. Soete). London: Francis Pinter.
Atkinson, A. B. and Stiglitz, J. E. (1969). 'A new view of technological change.' ECONOMIC JOURNAL, vol. 79, pp. 573–8.
Axelrod, R. (1984). *The Evolution of Cooperation*. New York: Basic Books.
David, P. (1969). 'A contribution to the theory of diffusion', Stanford, Stanford Center for Research in Economic Growth, paper no. 71.
—— (1975). *Technical Choice, Innovation and Economic Growth*. Cambridge: Cambridge University Press.
—— (1985). 'Clio and the economics of QWERTY.' *American Economic Review, Papers and Proceedings*, vol. 75, pp. 332–7.
—— and Olsen, T. E. (1984) 'Anticipated automation: a rational expectations model of technological diffusion.' Stanford: Center for Economic Policy Research.
Davies, S. (1979). *The Diffusion of Process Innovations*. Cambridge: Cambridge University Press.
Dosi, G. (1984). *Technical Change and Industrial Transformation*. London: Macmillan.
—— (1988). 'The sources, procedures and microeconomic effects of innovation. An assessment of some recent findings.' *Journal of Economic Literature*. (In the press.)
——, Orsenigo, L and Silverberg, G. (1988). 'Innovation diffusion as a self-organizational process.' In *Innovation Diffusion* (eds. F. Arcangeli, P. David and G. Dosi). Oxford: Oxford University Press. (In the Press.)
Ebeling, W. and Feistel, R. (1982) *Physik der Selbstorganisation und Evolution*. East Berlin: Akademie Verlag.

Eigen, M. (1971). 'Selforganization of matter and the evolution of biological macromolecules.' *Die Naturwissenschaften*, vol. 58, pp. 465–523.
—— and Schuster, P. (1979). *The Hypercycle: A Principle of Natural Selforganization.* Berlin, Heidelberg, New York: Springer-Verlag.
Eliasson, G. (1982). 'On the optimal rate of structural adjustment.' Stockholm, Industrial Institute for Economic and Social Research, Working Paper no. 74.
—— (1986). 'Micro heterogeneity of firms and stability of industrial growth.' In *The Dynamics of Market Economies* (eds. R. Day and G. Eliasson). Amsterdam: North-Holland.
Fisher, J. C. and Pry, R. H. (1971). 'A simple substitution model of technological change.' *Technological Forecasting and Social Change*, vol. 3, pp. 75–88.
Gold, B. (1981). 'Technological diffusion in industry: research needs and shortcomings.' *Journal of Industrial Economics*, vol. 29, pp. 247–69.
Gort, M. and Klepper, S. (1982). 'Time paths in the diffusion of product innovation.' ECONOMIC JOURNAL, vol. 92, pp. 630–53.
—— and Konakayama, A. (1982). 'A model of diffusion in the production of an innovation.' *American Economic Review*, vol. 72, pp. 1111–20.
Griliches, Z. (1957). 'Hybrid corn: an exploration in the economics of technological change.' *Econometrica*, vol. 25, pp. 501–22.
Haken, H. (1983). *Synergetics: An Introduction*, 3rd ed. Berlin, Heidelberg, New York: Springer-Verlag.
Hofbauer, J. and Sigmund, K. (1984). *Evolutionstheorie und Dynamische Systeme.* Berlin and Hamburg: Verlag Paul Pavey.
Ireland, N. J. and Stoneman, P. (1986). 'Technological diffusion, expectations and welfare.' *Oxford Economic Papers*, vol. 38, pp. 283–304.
Iwai, K. (1984a). 'Schumpeterian dynamics. An evolutionary model of innovation and imitation. *Journal of Economic Behavior and Organization*, vol. 5, pp. 159–90.
—— (1984b). 'Schumpeterian dynamics. II. Technological progress, firm growth and "economic selection".' *Journal of Economic Behavior and Organization*, vol. 5, pp. 321–51.
Katz, M. L. and Shapiro, C. (1985). 'Network externalities, competition and compatibility.' *American Economic Review*, vol. 75, pp. 424–40.
—— and —— (1986). 'Technology adoption in the presence of network externalities.' *Journal of Political Economy*, vol. 94, pp. 822–41.
Kleine, J. (1983). *Investitionsverhalten bei Prozessinnovationen.* Frankfurt/New York: Campus Verlag.
Levin, R. C., Cohen, W. M. and Mowery, D. C. (1985). 'R & D appropriability, opportunity and market structure: new evidence on some Schumpeterian hypotheses.' *American Economic Review, Papers and Proceedings*, vol. 75, pp. 20–4.
Mansfield, E. (1961). 'Technical change and the rate of imitation.' *Econometrica*, vol. 29, pp. 741–66.
—— (1968). *Industrial Research and Technological Innovation.* New York: W. W. Norton.
—— (1985). 'On technological competition.' Manchester University.
Metcalfe, J. S. (1985). 'On technological competition.' Manchester University.
—— and Gibbons, M. (1988). 'On the economics of structural change and the evolution of technology.' In *Structural Change and Economic Interdependence* (eds. L. Pasinetti and P. Lloyd). London: Macmillan.
Nabseth, L. and Ray, G. (1974). *The Diffusion of New Industrial Processes: An International Study.* London: Cambridge University Press.
Nelson, R. (1968). 'A "diffusion" model of international productivity differences in manufacturing industry.' *American Economic Review*, vol. 58, pp. 1218–48.
—— (1985). 'Industry growth accounts and cost functions when techniques are proprietary.' Yale University, Institution for Social and Policy Studies Discussion Paper.
—— and Winter, S. (1977). 'In search of a useful theory of innovation.' *Research Policy*, vol. 6, pp. 36–76.
—— and —— (1982). *An Evolutionary Theory of Economic Change.* Cambridge, Mass.: The Belknap Press of Harvard University Press.
Nicolis, G. and Prigogine, I. (1977). *Self-Organization in Non-Equilibrium Systems.* New York: Wiley.
Prigogine, I. (1976). 'Order through fluctuation: self-organization and social system.' In *Evolution and Consciousness* (eds E. Jantsch and C. H. Waddington). Reading, Mass.: Addison-Wesley.
Reinganum, J. (1981). 'Market structure and the diffusion of new technology.' *Bell Journal of Economics*, vol. 12, pp. 618–24.
Sahal, D. (1981). *Patterns of Technological Innovation.* New York: Addison-Wesley.
—— (1985). 'Technology guide-posts and innovation avenues.' *Research Policy*, vol. 14, pp. 61–82.
Salter, W. (1962). *Productivity and Technical Change.* Cambridge: Cambridge University Press.
Sigmund, K. (1986). 'A survey of replicator equations.' In *Complexity, Language and Life: Mathematical Approaches* (eds. J. L. Casti and A. Karlqvist). Berlin, Heidelberg, New York, Tokyo: Springer-Verlag.

Silverberg, G. (1984). 'Embodied technical progress in a dynamic economic model: the self-organization paradigm.' In *Nonlinear Models of Fluctuating Growth* (eds. R. Goodwin, M. Krüger and A. Vercelli). Berlin, Heidelberg, New York: Springer-Verlag.

—— (1987). 'Technical progress, capital accumulation and effective demand: a self-organization model.' In *Economic Evolution and Structural Adjustment* (eds. D. Batten, J. Casti and B. Johansson). Berlin, Heidelberg, New York, Tokyo: Springer-Verlag.

Smith, V. (1961). *Investment and Production*. Cambridge: Harvard University Press.

Stoneman, P. (1976). *Technological Diffusion and the Computer Revolution*. Oxford: Clarendon Press.

—— (1983). *The Economic Analysis of Technological Change*. Oxford: Oxford University Press.

—— (1986). 'Technological diffusion: the viewpoint of economic theory.' Paper presented at the Conference on Innovation Diffusion, Venice, 17–21 March.

—— and Ireland, N. J. (1983). 'The role of supply factors in the diffusion of new process technology.' ECONOMIC JOURNAL, *Conference Papers*, vol. 93, pp. 65–77.

Terborgh, G. (1949). *Dynamic Equipment Policy*. New York: McGraw-Hill.

Thomas, L. C. (1984). *Games. Theory and Applications*. Chichester: Ellis Harwood.

Winter, S. (1984). 'Schumpeterian competition in alternative technological regimes.' *Journal of Economic Behavior and Organization*, vol. 5, pp. 137–58.

Zeeman, E. C. (1979). 'Population dynamics from game theory.' In *Global Theory of Dynamical Systems* (eds. Z. Neticki and C. Robinson). Berlin, Heidelberg, New York: Springer-Verlag.

—— (1981). 'Dynamics of the evolution of animal conflicts.' *Journal of Theoretical Biology*, vol. 89, pp. 249–70.

[15]

Learning, Market Selection and the Evolution of Industrial Structures*

Giovanni Dosi
Orietta Marsili
Luigi Orsenigo
Roberta Salvatore

ABSTRACT. Industrial economics is a rich source of 'puzzles' for economic theory. One of them – certainly the most discussed – regards the co-existence of firms (and plants) of different sizes, displaying rather invariant skewed distributions. Other 'puzzles', however, concern the sectoral specificities in industrial structures, the persistence of asymmetric corporate performances and the dynamics of entry and exit. The paper reports some preliminary results on evolutionary modeling of the links between the microeconomics of innovation, the patterns of industrial change and some observable invariances in industrial structures.

First, the paper reviews a few of these empirical regularities in structures and in the patterns of change. Second, the paper discusses the achievements and limits of interpretations of the evidence based on equilibrium theories. Finally, it presents a model where these regularities are explained as emergent properties deriving from non equilibrium interactions among technologically heterogeneous firms. Moreover, simulation exercises show that also the intersectoral variety in the observed industrial structures and dynamics can be interpreted on the grounds of underlying specificities in the processes of technological learning – which is called 'technological regimes' – and of the processes of market interactions – i.e. 'market regimes'.

Final version accepted on January 12, 1995

Giovanni Dosi
Department of Economics
University of Rome 'La Sapienza'

Orietta Marsili
Department of Economics
University of Rome 'La Sapienza'

Luigi Orsenigo
Department of Economics
Bocconi University
Milano

and

Roberta Salvatore
Tecsiel
Rome

I. Introduction

Industrial economics is a rich source of 'puzzles' for economic theory. One of them – certainly the most discussed – regards the co-existence of firms (and plants) of different sizes, displaying rather invariant skewed distributions, approximately Pareto-distributions for manufacturing as a whole.

Other 'puzzles', however, concern the sectoral specificities in industrial structures, the persistence of asymmetric corporate performances and the dynamics of entry and exit.

This paper reports some preliminary results on evolutionary modeling of the links between the microeconomics of innovation, the patterns of industrial change and some observable invariances in industrial structures.

At each of these levels of analysis many remarkable regularities have emerged, in principle demanding some unified account joining together what we know about the processes by which firms are born, grow, die – on the one hand – and what we know about some aggregate statistics (e.g. on size distributions) – on the other.

As an illustration, consider the puzzle provided by the coexistence of (a) an approximate stability of some skewed distribution of firm- (and plant-) sizes; (b) quite high degrees of market 'turbulence' (i.e. instability of market shares over time); (c) persistently high rates of entry and death; (d) persistence of non-average performances of individual firms (as measured by e.g. rates of innovation, production efficiency, profitability) in

This research has undertaken within an on going project sponsored by the Italian Research Council (CNR, 'Progetto strategico', *Cambiamento tecnologico e sviluppo economico*). Support by the Consortium on Competitiveness and Cooperation Centre for Research in Management, University of California at Berkeley is also gratefully acknowledged.

Small Business Economics 7: 411–436, 1995.
© 1995 *Kluwer Academic Publishers. Printed in the Netherlands.*

industrial structures. How can one reconcile the relative stability in the latter with apparently much more 'messy' microdynamics?

Conversely, from a cross-sectional point of view, how does one interpret the inter-industrial variety in structures (for example, significant departures from the aggregate size distribution) and also in underlying microbehaviours (for example, rates of innovation, entry, death, etc.)?

In the economic literature, the prevailing interpretations of observed industrial structures – described in term of size distributions of firms, and, less often by the rates of entry – fall within two major categories. The first include those models which assume the lack of any persistent effect of size, or for that matter any other systematic variable, upon growth and, thus, account for the observed size distributions as the outcome of a frequent, 'small' and unpredictable shocks on growth rates: 'Gibrat-type' processes of firm growth come under this heading (cf. Ijiri and Simon, 1977). The second category tries to interpret whatever observed structure as an equilibrium realization of some mechanism of optimal allocation of scarce managerial talents (Lucas, 1978), or of heterogeneous individual abilities under imperfect information (Jovanovic, 1982).

In this work, we depart from both approaches in many significant respects.

Neither of them, we suggest, is consistent with a few 'stylized facts' on the microeconomics of innovation and growth. For example, the former can hardly accommodate phenomena of persistence in individual corporate performances, and appears also to be at odds with cross-sectional observations on structural diversities. The latter approach, in our view, appears even more demanding on the microeconomics which generates aggregate observations, and, until now, has shown no easy way how to accommodate firm-specific innovations and the purported equilibrium dynamics in structures.

In the following, we shall try to interpret the regularities in industrial structures as emergent properties[1] deriving from non-equilibrium interactions amongst technologically heterogeneous firms. Here, we define 'structures' in terms of a set of statistics, including, of course, (i) size distributions, but also, (ii) degrees of asymmetries in performance among firms (which we shall

define below); (iii) rates of entry and exit; (iv) 'turbulence' in market shares.

Particular 'structures', we shall argue, can be interpreted on the grounds of underlying characteristics of the processes of technological learning – which we call *technological regimes* – and of the processes of interaction – i.e. *market regimes*.

Our general conjecture is that a few 'stylized facts' concerning time-series invariances in structures and their cross-sectional variety can be given an evolutionary explanation, as far-from-equilibrium outcomes of particular regimes of learning and market selection.

In Section II we review some empirical regularities and 'puzzles'. Section III discusses the achievements and limitations of economic theory in interpreting those regularities. Section IV sets forth an evolutionary account of industrial dynamics; a formal model is presented in Section V and some results are discussed in Section VI.

II. Some empirical regularities in industrial structures and dynamics

1. *General patterns*

Although the phenomena which we are going to review are quite familiar to the practitioners of the discipline, a fresh look at the theoretical issues involved in their interpretation is a good introduction to the rationale of the model which follows.

For the purposes of this work, it seems useful to distinguish between those empirical regularities which emerge in most or all industrial sectors and those which display a marked industry-specificity, and therefore differentiate different types of structures and different processes of industrial change.

Let us start from the former.

Skewed distributions and their stability

It is certainly the most known 'fact' in industrial demography: skewed distributions of both firm- and plant-sizes in manufacturing as a whole, following approximately Pareto distributions, appear relatively stable over all the industrial history for which data can be estimated. More technically, it remains rather controversial whether the cumulated distribution presents a concavity (while the theoretical Pareto distribution presents a straight line),[2] and it is also controversial how stable the distribution remained over time.[3] Two phenomena are in any case remarkable. First, the skewness implies the steady coexistence of plants and firms of different sizes, and with rather stable relative frequencies. Second, the relative stability of the distribution itself – despite the secular growth of industrial output and despite the secular tendency toward technical specialization among production tasks (i.e. an increasing division of labour) – implies also the approximate stability of the proportion of the activities of production and exchange occurring within organizations as compared to those mediated through the market.

Clearly, all this raises major questions concerning the nature of production technology and innovation. For example: what are the restrictions on returns to scale necessary to support the coexistence of widely different sizes of plants and firms? How plausible is an hypothesis of constant returns? What are the processes of innovation and diffusion consistent with the stability, in the aggregate of manufacturing, of particular skewed size distribution?

And other major questions relate to the processes of growth of individual firms.

Firms' growth

In principle, three fundamental mechanisms govern changes in firms' sizes, namely, first, variations in the market shares; second, variations in the size of the markets in which firm operate (holding shares constant); and, third, mergers, acquisitions, vertical integration/disintegration, horizontal diversification. While not much attention has been given to the separate effects of these mechanisms on firms' growth (or decline), a long tradition of studies, as known, has investigated the 'synthetic' statistical properties of firms' growth – the bench-mark being Gibrat's 'Law of Proportionate Effect'. In its simplest formulation the 'Law' states that growth rates are i.i.d. random variables independent from size. A handy property of the Law is that it generates log-normal or, under suitable modifications, Yule or Pareto distributions.[4]

In brief if $x_i(t)$ is the log of size of firm i at time t

$$x_i(t) = \alpha + \beta_i x_i(t-1) + \varepsilon_i(t), \qquad (1)$$

where α is a growth component common to all firms and $\varepsilon(\cdot)$ is a random term. Gibrat's law assumes that $\varepsilon(\cdot)$ is i.i.d. and the restriction $\beta_i = 1$, $\forall i$.

The evidence with respect to the Gibrat process is mixed, but it mostly tends to reject it, or restrict its applicability to particular size classes. Recent studies have found that both firms' growth rates and their variance tend to fall with size and with age (Hall, 1987; Evans, 1987a, 1987b; Bianco and Sestito, 1992). (However, Audretsch, 1995 finds some corroboration for the Law by including in the sample also firms exiting the industry.) Moreover, Gibrat's Law seems a more appropriate description of the growth process of relatively big firms.[5]

The statistical properties of growth dynamics add to the questions facing the theory. For example: under what circumstances is it safe to assume that randomness – whenever detected – simply means that differential growth is an outcome of a multiplicity of 'little' factors with low persistence? Does the evidence on the negative correlation between size and growth imply some form of decreasing returns – e.g. in production technology or managerial control? Or does it mainly reflect strategic traits of bigger firms (for example, higher desired mark-ups as in Nelson and Winter (1982) or in Sylos Labini (1967)). Does the negative correlation between age and growth reveal, from an evolutionary point of view, a fall in the 'average fitness' of firms in changing environments as time goes by? Further, how does one account for those outliers possibly too rare to show up in aggregate statistics but crucial archetypes in business economics – e.g. the Intels, the Sun Microsystems, or, on the opposite side, the British Leylands – which present persistent (positive or negative) differentials in growth rates?

Certainly, underlying whatever statistical regularities one detects in aggregate size distributions, a much more 'messy' microeconomics appears with respect to entries, exits and changes in market shares.

Entry, exits and market turbulence

A general 'stylized fact' concerns the significant degree of turbulence in all industries, due to entry, exit and changing shares of incumbents (Acs and Audretsch, 1990; Beesley and Hamilton, 1984).

In particular, gross entry is a pervasive phenomenon. Birth rates are quite high in most industries, even in those characterized by high degrees of capital intensity (Acs and Audretsch, 1989, 1991).

Most entrants are small firms, far below any measure of efficient minimum scale and a large percentage of new entrants exits the industry within few years after entry. However, an important source of entry are incumbents firms operating in other industries or countries which diversify. In this case, entry often occurs via acquisition of existing plants. The role of this second type of entry is limited in terms of number of firms, but much more important in terms of share of output or employment.

It must be remarked that we know very little about the degree of turbulence in the 'core' of the industry among large firms. Older studies (Kaplan, 1964; Collins and Preston, 1961; Mermelstein, 1969; Bond, 1975) suggested a relative stability in the hierarchy of large firms: rates of turnover among the largest corporations appeared to be small and declining over time. Acs and Audretsch (1991) confirm that turbulence among small firms is higher than among large firms by 35% in the 247 manufacturing industries included in their sample.

Mortality is however high too, so that the rates of net entry are much smaller than gross entry and significant turbulence characterizes industrial evolution. In general, the probability of survival appears to increase with age and with size.[6]

An interpretation of this evidence is that turbulence is primarily a characteristic of the fringe of each industry. This seems corroborated by the observation that substitution of 'old' firms with 'new' firms occurs to a much larger extent among small, young firms which are relatively similar to each other. In other words, entrants in the fringe often are not more efficient than the incumbents. Turbulence is much lower in the core of the industry and among larger firms. The latter appear to be relatively sheltered from selective pressures (Levinthal, 1991). In any case, one does not have yet any robust theory of what determines the birth of new firms: why do firms continue to enter despite their low probability of survival? Why is entry so high even in capital intensive sectors? Is current profitability driving entry? (Which does

not appear to stand empirical scrutiny.) Or is it the perception of some unexploited opportunity of innovation? What determines entry in new industries via diversification of existing firms?

Persistence of asymmetric performances

Whatever dynamics one observe, this is grounded in a collection of firms displaying persistent differences with each other. These differences (which we call elsewhere *asymmetries*, Dosi (1984)) concern significant differentials in productivity and costs (Nelson and Winter (1982), Contini and Revelli (1990), Baily (1987)); profitability (Mueller (1990), Geroski and Jacquemin (1988), Yamawaki (1970)); innovative output (Freeman (1982), Jaffe (1986), Griliches (1986), Patel and Pavitt (1991)).

What is particularly intriguing is the persistence of these asymmetries, so that, for example, firms enjoying higher (lower) profits can be expected to earn higher (lower) profits also in the future: that is to say, profits do not seem to converge to a common rate of return (and the same applies to e.g. rates of innovation).

It is hard to say to what extent the observed persistence in profitability differentials reflects the persistence of differential 'efficiencies' which are not eroded away by the competitive process or, conversely, the sluggishness of the competitive process itself. (However, the evidence seems to indicate that the adjustment of profits to their firm-specific 'permanent' values is rather quick, although a significant variability is observed across different countries.) Indeed, persistent asymmetries amongst firms – although no big news for business economists and practitioners – entail puzzling questions for the theorist. What are their sources? Why don't competitive interactions wither them away? And, also, what are their consequences for industrial dynamics?

'Life-cycle' patterns

The properties of industrial structures and dynamics discussed so far pertain to broad aggregates, such as 'manufacturing', or 'industries' – the way they are defined by conventional statistics, say, at 2- or 3-digit levels. However, the locus of innovation, competition, entry and exit is to be found at a much more disaggregated level of observation: it is not e.g. 'chemical' or even 'pharmaceuticals', but, say, 'antibiotics', 'β-blockers', or, within other industrial codes, 'integrated circuits', 'laser-printers', etc. Within micro sectors, one has identified some typical patterns of evolution along what is sometimes called the 'life cycle' of a particular technology or group of products.[7] These patterns (not entirely uncontroversial) are summarized by Klepper (1992) as follows:

(i)   There is an initial period of fairly steady growth in the number of producers followed by a period in which the number of producers declines sharply;

(ii) the time path in the number of entrants up to the peak number of producers does not follow a common pattern for all new products, with the number of entrants sometimes rising up to the peak whereas in other instances it reaches a maximum well before the peak. For all products, though, entry tends to peak at or before the peak in the number of producers and then falls off sharply and stays below exit throughout the shake-out;

(iii) the number of major product innovations tends to reach a peak during the period of growth in the number of producers and then falls over time;

(iv) during the period of growth in the number of producers, the most recent entrants account for a disproportionate share of product innovations;

(v)   over time, increasing effort by producers is devoted to process relative to product innovation;

(vi) over time, the rate of change of firm market shares slows. (Klepper, 1992, p. 7).

2. *Sector-specific phenomena*

Given these relatively general regularities in industrial structures and in the processes of change, at a finer level of detail one observes also significant cross-sectional differences.

Variety of industrial structures

Probably the oldest, albeit crude, exercise of sectoral classification has focused on the widely different degrees of concentration across sectors. Must likely, an undue emphasis has been put on the relationship between concentration and performance, but, still, the Schumpeterian question concerning the determinants of observed variety of industrial structures remains a crucial one.

In this respect, note also that the more disaggregate the observations on industrial structures are and the more likely is that one will observe size distributions departing from theoretical Pareto density functions.[8]

Moreover, industries widely differ in (a) the intensity of their innovative efforts and the ways they pursue innovation – as reflected, for example, by different propensities to undertake R&D; (b) their measurable innovative output – e.g. patents; and (c) their rates of productivity growth (for an interpretative survey, cf. Dosi, 1988).

Recently, sectoral taxonomies have been developed based on the size and organizational characteristics of innovating firms (Pavitt, 1984) and the nature of innovative opportunities, learning processes and appropriability conditions (Levin *et al.*, 1987; Malerba, 1992; Malerba and Orsenigo, 1990, 1992, 1993).

Different dynamic properties

Sectoral specificities appear to affect the processes of firms' growth, too. For example, Acs and Audretsch (1990) – one of the few recent studies which on average lends support to Gibrat's Law – find that growth rates are significantly different across firm-size classes in about 40% of the industries considered in their sample (and it is not intuitive to find together in the 'non-Gibrat group' a lot of sectors from e.g. petroleum, leather, paper, plastic; and in the 'Gibrat group', furniture, chemicals and transport equipment . . .).

Turbulence differs a lot across sectors, and tends to be relatively lower in industries characterized by high rates of innovation, high advertising, high capital intensity, low concentration, low growth (Acs and Audretsch, 1991).[9]

By further disentangling the sources of 'turbulence', it appears that, for example, advertising is a greater barrier than capital intensity to both gross and net entry, irrespectively of firm size. However, concentration inhibits entry of small firms but not of large companies. Similarly, high rates of innovation do not necessarily deter small firms from entry. On the contrary, in certain industries, in which small firms account for a significant share of total innovative activities, birth rates are rather high.

Evidence is less clear about the role played by variables like industry growth and profitability. The latter variable does not seem to have any significant effect in attracting entry, whilst mixed results are obtained for industry growth (in fact, the estimates of Acs and Audretsch (1990) would suggest that turbulence is higher in high-growth industries, but might be lower in high-profitability industries . . .).

Regarding the probability of survival of new small firms, it appears to be lower in capital-intensive industries, and in sectors characterized by high rates of innovation and high economies of scale. However, a further distinction needs to be made. Concentration, scale economies and capital intensity actually seem to be positively correlated with survival in the short run, but not in the long run. Indicators of innovativeness does not affect survival in the short run, but only in the long run. Moreover, survival is also easier in those industries in which small firms are important sources of innovation.[10]

Finally, it must be noted that surviving firms have either a higher initial size or higher growth rates. Bigger initial size implies lower growth, but higher survival probabilities. Surviving new firms tend to growth in the short run: surviving firms tend to grow faster in the early periods, but this property fades away in the long-run.

3. Empirical puzzles and economic theory

Many of the empirical regularities surveyed above are 'puzzles' for the theory in their own right – for example the relative aggregate stability of Pareto-type distributions. However, even more challenging is the explanation of how these different 'stylized facts' can stick together.

In very general terms, these puzzles have to do with a few major analytical questions, namely:

(i) The 'driving forces' of firms' growth. Are they multiple, small and temporary? Or conversely, can one identify deeper, more persistent°factors? And, what is the role of technological and organizational innovation in all that? What are the degrees of forward-looking rationality that one should attribute

to firms in their choice of entry, exit, expansion? And, does it matter, after all?

(ii) *Microheterogeneity and invariances in some aggregate statistics.* For example, how does one keep together the observations of persistent asymmetries among firms with that of relatively stable aggregate Pareto-type size distributions? How does one reconcile 'life-cycle' patterns at microsectoral level with apparently more stable structures at higher levels of aggregation?

(iii) *Cross-sectional variety in industrial structure and in the processes of change.* What determines these observed differences? Can one find some underlying variables which shape different evolutionary patterns? And, in that, what is the relative importance of technological factors, mechanisms of competitive interactions and demand conditions?

III. Industrial dynamics and economic theory

It is straightforward that the interpretation of foregoing regularities involves some underlying theory of production technology and innovation. In this respect, let us group the models proposed in the literature into three major approaches, which we shall call (a) neutral equilibria; (b) 'optimal control' equilibria; (c) (special) evolutionary equilibria. (In the next section we shall develop upon a fourth approach, namely, far-from- equilibrium evolution.)

Neutral equilibria
As already mentioned, one candidate theory for the interpretation of some aggregate invariances in industrial structures rests on the 'Law of Proportionate Growth' and has been explored, in different versions, by Herbert Simon and associates (cf. Ijiri and Simon, 1977).

The 'structure' (i.e. the relative invariant size distribution which data reveal) can be theoretically generated by some random process with little or no past memory, plus some auxiliary restrictions (such as on birth and death rates). In this case, the random process stands for a multiplicity of little factors which temporarily make one firm more (less) efficient than the competitors but are not persistent over time (these considerations, mutatis mutandis, apply also to stochastic models based on serial correlations of growth rates with decaying effects over time). Alternatively, one could also interpret the random process applied to growth rates not as the outcome of a multiplicity of small efficiency related 'shocks', but rather as random variations in corporate strategies. Relately, the most likely candidate for a theory of production compatible with Gibrat-type models implies constant returns to scale: no persistent scale-biased factor influences growth opportunities (an exception being Kalecki's model (Kalecki, 1945) with increasing constraints to growth related to financial factors). At the extreme, all possible conditions between organizations and market are neutral equilibria. That is, all possible distributions of industrial structures, ranging from monopoly to perfect competition, can be expected ex-ante to show identical efficiency properties.

As we see it, there are three major difficulties with this interpretation. First, we are rather sceptical of a general 'neutrality' hypothesis (i.e. 'all forms of industrial structures are identical in terms of efficiency'). To trivialize, it is difficult to image a Boeing aircraft produced with the same efficiency in an Italian industrial district by thousands of family-run firms, or, conversely, a (now defunct) East German Kombinat producing fashion garments with the same efficiency and creativity as an Italian district . . . More generally: microeconomic evidence, admittedly quite impressionistic, seems to suggest that in each industrial activity there are some 'typical ways' of organizing production. They can be more than one, but not very many. That is, there can be a few combinations between organization and markets that are 'neutral' in terms of efficiency, but the set is small and possibly not dense . . .

Second, and relatedly, at a disaggregated level, one does not often find either the structure or the Gibrat-type growth that one may observe in the aggregate (indeed, as discussed earlier, even for the manufacturing aggregate the evidence supporting a 'law of proportionate growth' is hardly overwhelming).

Third, it follows from the underlying theory of production that firms ought to almost identical – with scaling up or scaling down only affecting size – but, in turn, there seem no easy way to reconcile this assumption with the evidence on persistence of inter-firm asymmetries in revealed performances and – even more important – in innovative capabilities (cf. the foregoing section).

'Optimal control' equilibria
In Simon-type models of firm-size distributions, with the related Gibrat processes of growth, it does not make sense to ask whether the observed structure is the 'optimal' one: indeed, the implicit constant-return cum continuum of neutral equilibria hypothesis entails that the observed structures are some statistical outcome of history with nothing remarkable to be said for or against their allocative properties. And this is likely to fall well short of satisfaction for the true believer. Lucas (1978) handles the problem. He start with an optimal allocation problems, given a usual two-inputs production function to which one adds another factor ('managerial talents'), unevenly distributed across the workforce. This, together with ad-hoc auxiliary assumptions on managerial technology and on the distribution of such talents, yields the optimal size distribution of firms and the Gibrat-law as an empirically testable restriction on the production function.[11] With regards to the 'Gibrat restriction', we have already discussed above its likely empirical inconsistencies. More generally, it would take us too far to discuss the bizarre, albeit elegant and fashionable, epistemology involved in those modeling endeavours whereby the core assumptions of rationality and equilibrium are *ex hypotheses* shelved from refutation and the burden of the 'proof' is laid on testing some restrictions imaginatively derived on the grounds of some unobservable . . .

Let us just suggest that one does not seem to learn much more from these kind of exercises in rationalization than we didn't already know from 'inductive' observations (except, possibly, some Panglossian contentness, for those who can feel it). And, even more important for our purposes here, these exercises seem strictly unsuited to account for those phenomena of entry, exit, innovation and non-equilibrium learning which seem central in contemporary industrial change.

(Special) evolutionary equilibria
Recently a class of models has been proposed, which is explicitly dynamic and tries to explain the observed patterns of industrial dynamics as the

(equilibrium) outcome of processes of learning and selection.

Jovanovic (1982) attempts to explain the observed regularities in size distribution, together with the patterns of entry and exit as the result of a stochastic process of convergence to optimal techniques under imperfect information. New firms continuously enter the industry, with rational technological expectations but uncertain about their own production efficiency. By producing they acquire noisy information about their productivity. Those firms who discover that their efficiency exceeds their expectations expand their scale of output, while those who receive unfavourable signals contract or even exit from the industry. Thus, industry evolution is driven by noisy selection which fosters the growth of efficient firms and the decline of inefficient ones. Pakes and Ericson (1987) have extended this model to consider the possibility that firms can affect their productivity by investing in learning (e.g. R&D) activities, the outcome of which is however random. In the same vein, other models (Lambson, 1991) examine industry evolution and explains some of the stylised facts discussed above as the result of changing exogenous market conditions.

We have called these models as 'special evolutionary equilibria', because while they embody some evolutionary account of imperfect learning and market selection amongst heterogeneous agents they maintain stationary 'fundamentals' as far as best-practice technologies are concerned: biologists would say that the 'evolutionary landscape' upon which evolution occurs is fixed (another way of putting the same property is by assuming that changes in the evolutionary environment arrive at a rate that is much lower than that at which agents adjust to them). A consequence of all this, however, is that the models can hardly accommodate innovative processes, in general, and especially whenever they are idiosyncratic and firm-specific. Moreover, one finds difficult to accept that evolutionary pressures are so strong that each observation of e.g. size distributions, entry, exit, etc. is (nearly) an equilibrium one. Finally, the way selection dynamics works in e.g. Jovanovic (1992) heavily rests on very demanding assumptions on the rationality and forecasting abilities of individual agents (one is

not at all sure what the dynamics would be if every agents did not have rational technological expectations – indeed, a very heavy requirement in an evolutionary set-up).

Indeed, it might be worth exploring the properties of evolutionary models which are not constrained to particular equilibrium representations and which take full account of heterogeneous processes of innovation. This is what we shall try to do in the next section.

IV. Technological regimes, selection and industrial structures: far-from-equilibrium evolution

The evolutionary interpretation that we shall pursue in this work of empirical regularities discussed in section (ii) above, focuses on the nature of learning activities and on market interactions as selection mechanisms. It has in common with 'special evolutionary models' mentioned earlier the emphasis on microeconomic heterogeneity. However, it departs from them in several ways. First, it assumes that innovation – rather than adjustments to some unchanged technological landscape – is the driving force of industrial change. Second, it tries to specify an explicit market dynamics rather than assuming some limit state of the dynamics itself. Third, it conjectures that aggregate regularities are indeed the outcome of disequilibrium fluctuations.[12]

Let us start by characterizing learning activities. As emphasized especially by evolutionary and 'organizational' theories of the firms, the rates and direction of innovation depend on the competences that firms embody, on the internal and external knowledge they can draw upon, and the procedures by which they do it (see Nelson and Winter, 1982; Dosi, 1988; Teece *et al.*, 1993).

In particular, it has been suggested that various activities present different degrees of technological opportunity, that is a different scope for improvements in products and processes on the grounds of a given knowledge base, and also a different 'ease' in achieving these improvements. (One way of formalizing these differences is in terms of the probability distributions of achieving an $x\%$ improvement in some performance characteristics of a product or a process, given some search effort, say a one dollar investment in R&D.)

Technologies and sectors have also been found to differ in terms of appropriability conditions, i.e. the effectiveness through which innovations can be shielded from imitation by competitors.

According to the features of the process of innovative search and the knowledge upon which it draws, the innovative success of individual firms may show varying degrees of serial correlation, often referred to as the cumulativeness of innovative activities. Moreover, the degrees of tacitness and specificity of knowledge (or conversely, its universality and serendipity) influence the ease of access of entrants as compared to incumbents (Winter, 1984).

Finally, it has been argued elsewhere that radical changes in the knowledge bases, procedures and directions of technological change, i.e. a change in the 'technological paradigm' (Dosi, 1992) imply also significant changes in the relative innovative capabilities and growth potentials of firms embodying 'old' or 'new' competences.

In brief, we shall call particular combinations of these features of technological knowledge as *technological regimes* (Winter, 1984).

In line with Nelson and Winter (1982), Winter (1984), Dosi and Salvatore (1992), one of our central hypothesis is that these specificities of learning have a direct link with the explanation of why industrial structures are what they are and how they change. More in detail, some implications can be easily seen by comparison with the stochastic representation of firms' growth described by Equation (1), above.

(a) Differences across industries in technological opportunities (assuming some positive correlation between innovation and growth) imply different values for the constant and different means and variances of the stochastic term in Equation (1). Moreover, if 'opportunities' change over the development of each technology, one should also expect correlated change in the distribution of the ε_r.

(b) Appropriability of innovation, cumulativeness of technological advances, specificity of some elements of technological knowledge imply some firm-specificity in the factors which foster or hinder growth. The findings from the economics of innovation, as well as complementary findings from business studies, suggest that neither the stochastic process nor

the β in Equation (1) can be assumed to be identical across firms. Some firms may be persistently 'better' or 'worse' than others. In turns, that means that any evolution of industrial structures must not only be interpreted in terms of a multiplicity of little transitory shocks on individual growth opportunities, but also account for the interaction among firms that may be persistently different in their technological and organizational characteristics.

(c) Differential degrees of appropriability and cumulativeness, and different characteristics of the knowledge underlying innovative activities are also likely to imply different entry-conditions in each industry.

(d) Abandoning the assumption of single-product firms, the variegated sources and procedures of learning and innovations are bound to affect the corporate patterns of horizontal diversification and vertical integration and also the structure of individual industries and of manufacturing as a whole.

If the characteristics of learning are the first major building block of an evolutionary interpretation, some form of selection is the second one.

The intuition is quite straightforward. Technological (and organizational) heterogeneity implies diverse competitive abilities of each firm: that is, diverse levels of 'fitness' over some evolutionary landscape wherein firm interact (in the model which follows such landscape is restricted only to product-markets, but in actual fact it involves also other interactive domains, e.g. the market for finance). In turn, different competitive abilities affect the size and number of firms, i.e. the dynamics of market shares and of exit (mortality). It is important to notice that in any case the selection criteria are themselves endogenous, in that they are a collective property of the rates and directions of learning of each and every firm (and in more general versions of evolutionary models also of the patterns of learning of customers, suppliers, providers of finance, etc.). We distinguish *market selection regimes* according to the relative speed at which selection occurs – loosely speaking, analogous to what practitioners call 'the intensity of competition' – thus, market regimes determine, other things being equal, the 'intensity' of reward and penalties for the better (worse) competitors and the speed at which such rewards and penalties arrive.

Formally, selection processes are often captured by some dynamics on the unit simplex operating with respect to endogenous 'fitness' criteria.[13] However, irrespectively of the precise theoretical representation, the crucial point is that evolutionary processes generally embody some collective mechanism of ex-post selection amongst heterogeneous technologies, products, behaviours, organizations which can hardly be written out by assuming that agents perfectly anticipate the consequences of their actions and choose *ex ante* reciprocally consistent and symmetric behaviours.[14]

The model which follows formalizes these hypotheses about the dynamics of learning and selection.

V. An evolutionary model

Assume that 'industry' (say, the equivalent in recorded statistics of 'aggregate manufacturing') is composed of several 'sectors', each corresponding to particular technological and market regimes, which shall be defined below. In turn, any one 'sector' is composed of 'microsectors' (groups of relatively homogeneous products or technologies, loosely corresponding to the empirical analyses concerning 'technological cycles' and reviewed earlier in Section II). Hence, one has three levels of observation: most of the 'action' – i.e. learning, changes in market shares, entry and exit – occurs within 'microsectors'; but higher level statistical entities stochastically aggregate into 'sectors' (i.e. regimes) and the overall 'industry' (In fact, as we shall see, there is more than statistical aggregation since, in one of the regimes, firms may diversify across microsectors).

Each firm (j, if it is an incumbent; i, if it is an entrant) is defined by its age, a; size, s; and 'competitiveness', e. Size and competitiveness are endogenous variables dependent on learning, market selection and – regarding size – also on the dynamics of the markets to which the firms belong. 'Competitiveness' is a positive real number which in principle summarizes the technological and organizational capabilities of each firm. Hence, 'learning' yields positive increments to firm-specific competitiveness.

Learning dynamics

Each 'technological regime' is defined by the stochastic processes governing the transition probabilities $P(e_j(t+1)|e_j(t))$, for incumbents, and the draws on the competitiveness (i.e. the levels of initial knowledge) for entrants, $e_i(t)$.

Let us start with two extreme opposite archetypes, which we shall call 'Schumpeter Mark I' and 'Schumpeter Mark II': they are meant to capture some sort of limit configurations of the learning procedures discussed in the previous section.[15]

Under 'Schumpeter I' incumbents never learn: their competitiveness remains the one of their birth. Evolutionary dynamics is driven by the 'heroic entrepreneurship' of entrants.[16]

The competitiveness of entrants at time $(t+1)$ is

$$e_i(t+1) = \overline{e}(t)\left[1 - k + \frac{g}{\lambda_1}\right], \tag{2}$$

where $\overline{e}(\cdot)$ is the average competitiveness of incumbents, weighted with their market shares, f_j, $\overline{e} = \sum_j e_j f_j$, g is a random variable drawn from a Poisson distribution with mean g; k and λ_1 parametrize, respectively entry barriers (which might as well be absent) and levels of generically available opportunities, which, so to speak, 'rescale' the competitiveness jumps drawn from the stochastic process.

In the symmetric opposite model, 'Schumpeter II', learning by incumbents is highly cumulative – in probability, 'success breeds success':

$$e_j(t+1) = e_j(t)(1 + h_j(t)), \tag{3}$$

$$h_j(t+1) = \left[1 + \ln\left(1 + \frac{e_j(t)}{\overline{e}(t)}\right)\right]\frac{g_I}{\lambda_2}, \tag{4}$$

where, again, $g_I \approx$ Poisson (the subscript (I) here and throughout stands for incumbents, and (E) for entrants).

New firms enter with competitiveness

$$e_i(t+1) = \overline{e}(t)\left[1 - k + \frac{g_E}{\lambda_3}\right]. \tag{5}$$

Finally, let us define an 'Intermediate Regime' whereby incumbents learn via

$$e_j(t+1) = \overline{e}_j(t)\left[1 + \frac{g_I}{\lambda_4}\right], \tag{6}$$

and entrants are characterized by the same process as from Equation (5).

Note, incidentally, that even if learning for incumbents is a Gibrat-type process, this does not carry any straightforward implication for growth dynamics, since, as we shall see, the latter is also the collective outcome of market selection.

Birth of new firms

Let $n(t)$ the number of incumbents in any one microsectors at time t. The number of entrants, $b(t + 1)$ is the random variable

$$b(t + 1) = n(t)(h + \mu) \qquad (7)$$

(approximated to the nearest positive integer), where h (> 0) parametrizes the ease of entry, the possibility of spin-offs from incumbents, etc.; and μ is a random variable uniformly distributed on the support $-1 < -b \leq \mu \leq b < 1$.

Market selection and death rules

Market shares ($f_{(\cdot)}$) of individual firms (both incumbents and entrants) change according to a 'quasi-replicator' dynamic of the form

$$\Delta f_{(\cdot)}(t, t + 1) = A \left[\frac{e_{(\cdot)}(t)}{\bar{e}(t)} - 1 \right] f_{(\cdot)}(t). \qquad (8)$$

subject to the 'death rule'

$$\text{death}_{(\cdot)}(t) = 1 \text{ if } e_{(\cdot)}(t) < \psi \bar{e}(t) \text{ with } \psi \ll 1$$
$$\text{or if } f_{(\cdot)}(t) < \bar{f}e. \qquad (9)$$

That is, the event 'death' occurs if the competitiveness of the firm is below a certain fraction of the average competitiveness of the industry or if its market share falls below a certain minimum level ($\bar{f}e$).[17] The parameters A, ψ and $\bar{f}e$ capture the 'market regime': the higher their level, the higher also the 'selectiveness' of a market environment.

'Life cycles of microsectors'

The dynamics of the structure of each 'microsector' is endogenous and dependent on the processes described so far. However, we assume also a 'demand cycle' which determines the absolute size of the microsector itself, which we take as exogenously given. The level of output (i.e. the size of demand) for microsector k at the beginning and the end of its 'cycle' is conven-

tionally set equal to unity and peaks at $T/2$ with $M^k_{\tau = T/2} = m$, where T is the total length of the 'cycle'; we also assume that demand stays at unitary level thereafter.

New 'microsectors' are randomly born every ω times (with ω uniformly distributed on a finite support).

Hence, a cross-sectional observation of demand pattern, say at $t = t^*$, would impressionistically look like the one depicted in Figure 1.

Multi-product diversification

In contemporary economies, a good percentage of firms are multi-product. In Dosi, Teece and Winter

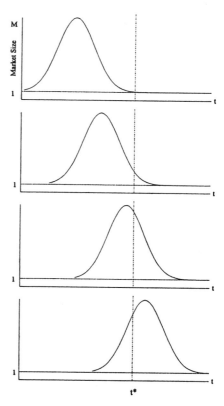

Fig. 1.

(1992), one argues that the patterns of horizontal diversification can be traced back to the 'core competences' which firms embody and to the nature of knowledge upon which the firms principal activities draw. Here we formalize some features of that intuition and assume that in the regime 'Schumpeter II' firms can cumulatively exploit their knowledge across different microsectors via entry and acquisition of incumbent firms.

Calling d, the event 'diversification' of a firm from microsector k,

$$\Pr(d = 1) = 1 - \theta \exp\left\{-\theta \frac{e_j^k}{\bar{e}_k}\right\}. \tag{10}$$

More successful firms face a higher probability of diversification, while θ captures the degrees of intersectoral 'serendipity' of knowledge.

If the event occurs, the microsector, l, toward which the firm moves is randomly drawn with a uniform distribution[18] over all sectors.[19] More precisely, in the experiments reported below we rule out $k = l$, that is intra-sectoral mergers/acquisitions. The impact of the later is on the agenda for future work. Next, the firm which is to be 'acquired' or 'founded' is selected, with uniform probability over all firms N^l of microsector l (if the firm draw is an incumbent, then diversification occurs via 'acquisition', otherwise it is an entry associated with establishment of a new unit – division – in that market).[20]

Regimes and structural properties
The foregoing model allows the determination of a quite rich set of endogenous variables and statistics characterizing industrial structures and their changes over time at the three levels of aggregation (microsectors, sectors/regimes, 'industry').[21]

For our purposes here we shall focus on the following ones:

(i)   size distributions and some statistics of industrial concentrations;
(ii)   asymmetries in firms' performances as proxied by some measure of dispersion in the level of 'competitiveness';
(iii) market turbulence (we shall define it in terms of market share changes involving incumbent, entrance and exiting firms: $\sum_{i,j} |f_{(\cdot)}(t + 1) - f_{(\cdot)}(t)|$;

(iv)   industrial demography indicators – e.g. gross and net entry, number of firms, age distributions;
(v)   industrial dynamics indicators – i.e. growth probabilities and death probabilities conditional on age and size;
(vi)   measures of persistence in the relative performance of individual firms.

Our basic analytical strategy is to try to 'map' the regularities in structures and dynamics highlighted by these indicators – into the underlying system parameters defining learning and selection regimes. We shall go further than that and claim that such a mapping represents, in a first approximation, also an explanation of the emerging patterns. This claim rests also on some additional – somewhat implicit – additional hypotheses.

First, readers (expecially economist readers) have probably noticed the lack of any behavioural assumption in our model. Quite a few evolutionary models embody indeed an array of ('boundedly rational') stylizations of behaviours (against which many orthodox criticisms dismiss their 'ad-hoc' nature and the unelegantly high number of supposedly 'free parameters'.[22] Here, we take a different methodological route and assume that, for the purposes of determining some general invariances in industrial structures, fine restrictions on microeconomic conducts exert, *on average*, only second-order system-level effects. It is obviously a very strong assumption, which can be justified either in terms of relatively uniform constraints which appear in relation to any one set of technological and market opportunities (i.e. each 'regime'), or in terms of behavioural norms and learning competences which co-evolve with the development of each regime itself (Nelson, 1992; Dosi and Orsenigo, 1988). In fact, we do believe that both processes are at work.

Second and relatedly, our modeling assumptions imply that some modal features of learning are *specific* to each particular 'regime' or, at least, change on a time scale which is longer than the time-scale of supposedly strategic interactions among agents: in our view, the evidence on the microeconomics of innovation supports this point (cf. Freeman, 1982, Dosi, 1982, 1988).[23]

Given both of these hypotheses, let us explore

some properties of the co-distributions between regime-parameters and characteristics of industrial structures.[24]

VI. Some simulation results

We present some simulation results of the three 'technological regimes' described earlier, parametrized with technological opportunities $g_{(I)}$ and $g_{(E)}$, ranging in different exercises between zero and 8; and selection between 1 and 5 (that is, the average Poisson draws for incumbents and entrants imply increments in 'competitiveness' between 0 and 8%, and 'selection' is captured by the parameter A in Equation (8).[25]

Microsectors

Number of firms. Not surprising in an evolutionary perspective, the number of firms is endogenous and depends on the characteristics of each 'regime'. Figure 2 presents the average

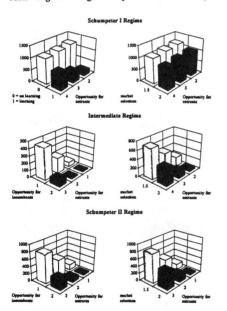

Fig. 2. Average number of firms in different regimes.

number of firms (over 10 simulations and 1000 iterations) under different regimes and parametrizations of learning opportunities and selection. Please note that the upper-left histogram in Figure 2 contrasts the Schumpeter I regime (no learning for incumbents) with the intermediate regime (opportunities for incumbents = 1). Ceteris paribus, those numbers decrease as the opportunities for incumbents grow, and as selection increases. Conversely, the number of firms grows in two out of the three technological regimes together with the technological opportunities for entrants.

All this is intuitively in line with the findings of Winter (1984) on the properties of what he calls 'entrepreneurial' and 'routinized' regimes. However, it is worth noting that, in our simulations, under 'Schumpeter I' – the regimes wherein incumbents do not learn and innovation is entirely associated with entry – greater opportunities are associated with a lower average number of firms. Our interpretative conjecture that increasing opportunities – even holding the selection parameter constant – implies a higher selective pressure by the most successful firms on the environment, and, also higher mortality rates (see below).

Concentration. Industrial concentration[26] is always a positive function of the opportunities of incumbents and of market selection, and, other things being equal, a negative one of the opportunities for entrants (see Figure 3).

Note that here concentration is an outcome of the uneven exploitation of learning opportunities by different firms, and, *ceteris paribus*, grows with the latter:[27] obviously, it has nothing to do in this model with 'market power' or collusive behaviours. Moreover, if the degrees of selection are interpreted as a proxy for 'how well markets work' – in the sense that they quickly reward winners and weed out losers – then more efficient markets tend to yield, in evolutionary environments, *more* concentrated market structures, rather than more 'perfect' ones in the standard sense.[28]

Asymmetries and turbulence. In general, higher opportunities for entrants are associated with higher market turbulence (as defined earlier) and higher interfirm asymmetries.[29] However, our simulations highlight remarkable non-linear inter-

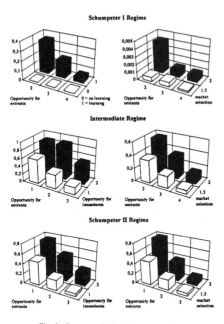

Fig. 3.   Degrees of industrial concentration.

actions between opportunity for entrants; opportunity for incumbents; and market selection. See Figures 4, 5, 6 and 7.

In particular, there seems to be a *negative* effect of learning opportunities for incumbents upon these two statistics which *decrease as general levels of opportunities increases.*

However, there seems to be a threshold in general learning and some 'critical ratio' between the learning potential of entrants *vis-à-vis* incumbents, above which the cumulative abilities of the latter do *not* 'stabilize the market' and do not render its suppliers more homogeneous. On the contrary, cumulative learning in these cases is likely to magnify over time the competitiveness of particularly skillful or particularly lucky entrants and incumbents alike. Let us illustrate the case with an impressionistic example. If these exercises tell something about empirical phenomena, one could argue that there has always been a high probability that IBM, even ruling out its own

organizational failures, was going to meet major competitive challenges by some entrants; that the most successful of these new firms would have exploited too the potential of fast and cumulative learning; and that all this would have generated persistent instabilities in market shares and persistent competitiveness gaps within the industry.

The effect of market selection upon these some indicators of industrial performance shows remarkable interactions with opportunities: as the latter grow, the market mechanisms which should supposedly reduce the interfirm variance in efficiency becomes less powerful (Figure 5).

Moreover, above some threshold in opportunities, faster selection appears to generate relatively more market turbulence and greater asymmetries.[30] Using the foregoing example, the intuition is that with rapid market selection – as one manager of a newly found company told one of us some years

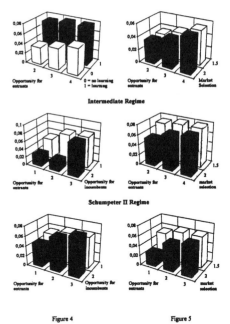

Figure 4   Figure 5

Figs. 4 and 5.   Degrees of industrial asymmetry.

ago – "soon we'll be able to cut one arm of the IBM giant . . ." Or, putting it another way, high selection jointly with high innovative opportunities make discrete evolutionary jumps easier. ('Jumps', in probability, may be bigger, even if over finite spans of time high opportunity and cumulativeness may well sustain the market dominance of one or few firms.)

Relatedly, it is worth emphasizing that higher degrees of selection – which, as mentioned earlier, formalizes the collective effectiveness of some 'quasi-Invisible Hand' of markets,[31] under circumstances of fast learning, seem to be associated with higher microeconomic disequilibrium and higher technological heterogeneity. That is, the competitive process allowing for fast changing technological fundamentals and relatively easy entry, is likely to bring the system *away* from any equilibrium where micro behaviours are consistent

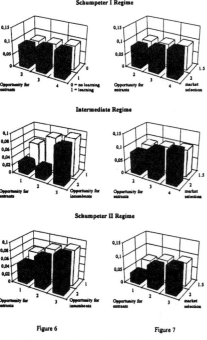

Figure 6

Figure 7

Figs. 6 and 7. Degrees of industrial turbulence.

with each other. On the contrary, the conjecture is that fast selection rapidly rewards 'hopeful monsters', to use a biological analogy. And above some opportunity threshold, these 'monsters' are so frequent that their (temporary) evolutionary superiority destabilizes the incumbent structure, notwithstanding cumulative learning by existing firms. Recall, however, that such a threshold is determined also by the *relative* learning abilities of incumbents and entrants. Thus, the model would predict that in 'high-tech' industries, for given general opportunities, market turbulence would be greater the lower is the ability of established firms to generate and competitively exploit the innovative opportunities. Pushing to the extreme a thesis argued in several works by Keith Pavitt at SPRU, University of Sussex, phenomena like the market volatility of the American electronics industries, the 'Silicon Valley', etc. should be interpreted at least as much in terms of persistent organizational *failures of established firms* to their innovative opportunities as in terms of entrepreneurial success of new firms fostered by favourable context conditions. (Indeed, a comparison with Japan is likely be quite revealing.)

Size distributions. The process of learning and selection modelled here generate skewed distributions of firms by size,[32] which, however, often depart significantly from a Pareto distribution with a density function

$$f(x) = qx^{-(1 + q)}$$

and a right-cumulated function

$$F(x) = x^{-q}. \tag{11}$$

Interestingly, the departures from the theoretical Pareto distribution (a) are systematic, (b) depend on the stage in the 'life cycle' in each micro sector, and (c) can be meaningfully 'mapped' into the underlying regime parameters. These departures are particularly marked at the level of microsectors but they carry over to regime-specific aggregations. Figures 8, 9 and 10 present the actual cumulated distribution and OLS estimates of the logs of Equation (11), concerning three somewhat archetypal cases of (i) a 'Schumpeter I' regime with very fast selection and extremely high opportunity for entrants (Figure 8); (ii) an 'intermediate' one with somewhat slower selection and

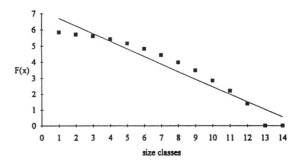

Schumpeter I (5,0,8)
(i.e. selection:5; opportunity for incumbents: 0; opportunity for entrants: 8)

Constant	Coefficient	Coef.Determination	F-ratio
1,9893	-0,6822	0,9284	155,6911

Fig. 8.

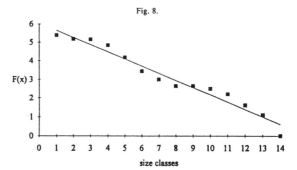

Intermediate (1.5,2,2)
(i.e. selection:1.5; opportunity for incumbents: 2; opportunity for entrants: 2)

Constant	Coefficient	Coef.Determination	F-ratio
1,7866	-0,5592	0,9600	319,30

Fig. 9.

relatively high opportunity for both incumbents and entrants (Figure 9); and (iii) a regime with a straightforward innovative advantage of incumbents and lower selection (Figure 10).[33]

It would seem, by qualitative inspection of these and other results not shown here, that 'Schumpeter I' regimes tend to display concavity of the actual distributions, yielding to 'double-humpted' ones for regimes where both incumbents and entrant access relatively rich learning opportunities, and, finally, to convex ones under 'Schumpeter II' regimes.

A remarkable property is that random aggregation over different microsectors and different regimes (i.e. 'aggregate manufacturing')[34] *does* display a size distribution quite close to a Pareto one (Figure 11). Our interpretation – already discussed in Dosi and Salvatore (1992) – is that, in the model and in the real world, this is a sheer outcome of aggregation. Moreover, as argued there, that aggregate distribution is likely to remain stable as long as *on average* the conditions of learning and selection do not dramatically change.[35]

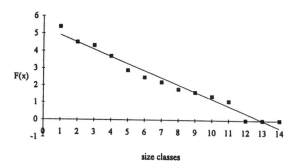

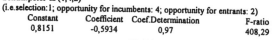

Schumpeter II (1,4,2)
(i.e.selection:1; opportunity for incumbents: 4; opportunity for entrants: 2)

Constant	Coefficient	Coef.Determination	F-ratio
0,8151	-0,5934	0,97	408,29

Fig. 10.

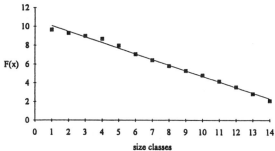

Industry

Constant	Coefficient	Coef.Determination	F-ratio
4,1219	-0,8612	0,99	1745,87

Fig. 11.

The invariance in structures. So far our interpretation of the simulation results has focused upon several properties of industrial structures which apply *on average* – over time and across different simulations of microsectors under the same parametrizations. Moreover, the results discussed above hold also for aggregations *within* learning regimes. Admittedly, at this stage of investigation of the properties of the model, we fall short of rigorous robustness tests. Still, standard deviations in the foregoing indicators of 'structures' across simulations turn out to be (surprisingly) low: at least a qualitative assessment of the results supports the hypothesis that relatively invariant, modal, patterns emerge.

Were these regularities corroborated by further modeling results and empirical taxonomic exercises, important theoretical implication would follow, too.

First, the microeconomics underlying the particular invariances in structures and performances appears to be fundamentally inconsistent with technological homogeneity and market equilibria. Rather, the model corroborates the view that it is the very existence of persistent inter-firm asymmetries which drives the process of change and, *together*, accounts for the statistical invariances in structures.

Second, a rather robust taxonomy of 'types' of industries emerge which can be mapped and, in some sense, 'explained' on the grounds of underlying system parameters governing particular regimes (and without invoking any particular behavioural assumption, either of the neoclassical or the 'institutionalist' kinds).

Evolutionary patterns. Another set of phenomena regards the time-series properties of microsectors, the performance over time of individual firms and their demography. Clearly, the matching between such properties of the model and the corresponding 'stylized facts' reviewed above are an important part of its corroboration. And, they also overlap with the predictions of other models suggested in the literature. For example, some relatively invariant non-linear dynamics in the number of firms, following temporally skewed distributions would fit well the prediction of 'organizational ecology' models. Conversely, theories emphasizing extreme cumulativeness and organizational routinization of innovative activities would predict a strong tendency toward monopoly.

What turns out is that (i) there seem to be relatively invariant patterns of evolution of microsectors, and (ii) they are quite *specific to the technological regimes* defining learning dynamics.

Interestingly, the cases which display an apparent convergence to some intertemporally stable structures are those emerging within a 'Schumpeter I' regime (cf. Figure 12 on the number of firms; similar consideration apply to concentration, asymmetries and turbulence).

As incumbents' learning is introduced, also an (irregular) long-term cyclicity shows up (cf. Figures 13 and 14 on number of firms and concentration within an 'intermediate' regime). The entire set of simulations that we have run suggests that the periodicity of these 'cycles', within each microsector, increases together with learning opportunities. The same applies to our other indicators.

Over sub-periods, the tendency toward oligopoly/monopoly driven by cumulative learning becomes stronger but, with probability one, 'creative destruction' by newly born innovative firms upsets established structures. Under strongly cumulative learning ('Schumpeter II' Regime) the average time that the sector spends in highly concentrated structures increases: 'disruptions' are less frequent but, when they occur, they induce major discontinuities in the statistics describing structures (Figures 15 and 16).

Growth and death of firms. A relatively familiar test concerns the relationships between growth and size, and, sometimes, age (see, for example Evans, 1987). In the literature, the analysis is often meant as a test of Gibrat-type laws of firm growth. Here, of course, we know the 'true law', by construction, but it is informative and theoretically interesting to know what econometric regularities emerge. We have estimated around fifty regres-

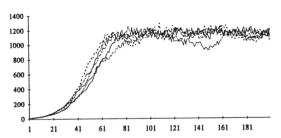

Schumpeter. I (1.5; 0; 3), plot of five simulations

Fig. 12. The dynamics of firms' populations: 'Schumpeter I'.

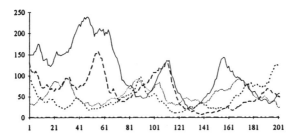

'Intermediate' (1.5; 1; 1), plot of five simulations

Fig. 13. The dynamics of firms' populations: 'Intermediate' Regime.

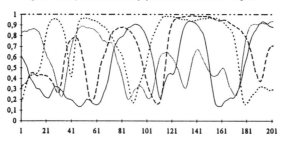

'Intermediate' (1.5; 1; 1), plot of five simulations

Fig. 14. The dynamics of concentration: 'Intermediate' Regime.

sions of the form

$$\log(g) = \alpha + \alpha_1 \log(s_0) + \alpha_2 \log(a_0) +$$
$$\alpha_3 [\log(a_0)\log(s_0)], \qquad (12)$$

where, for each firm, g ($= s_{10}/s_0$) is growth over 10 periods, s_0 is the initial size and a_0 is the initial age.[36]

Table I summarizes the signs and significance of coefficients for microsectors, regimes and 'aggregate manufacturing'.

At the level of microsectors a positive correlation often appears between size and growth. The effect is particularly evident under a 'Schumpeterian II' regime, but it shows up somewhat surprisingly also under 'Schumpeter I'. This effect fades away at the level of 'sectors' (i.e. aggregation within regimes) and turns out to be negative at the level of 'aggregate manufacturing'.

The age of firms is either uncorrelated or, much more often, exerts a negative impact on growth. This applies – more so – at higher levels of aggregation.

Regarding the interpretation of these tests, note, *first*, that at least in the aggregate our results correspond to the properties of historical data (see, for example Evans, 1987). That is, the model generates as *emergent properties* those empirical regularities which are often interpreted on the grounds of quite different microeconomics theories (cf. Section III, above).

Second, one ought to account for the somewhat puzzling positive links between size and growth which appear in several microsectors and one 'regime'. Of course, nothing in our model determines an advantage of size as such. On the contrary, it is the ex-post outcome of differential innovative success.

However, a particularly high competitiveness exerts its influence over relatively long periods,

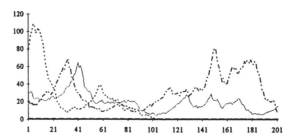

'Schumpeter II' (1.5; 2; 1), plot of five simulations

Fig. 15. The dynamics of firms' population: 'Schumpeter II'.

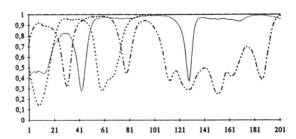

'Schumpeter II' (1.5; 2; 1), plot of five simulations

Fig. 16. The dynamics of concentration: 'Schumpeter II'.

TABLE I
Age, size and growth: a summary of regression results (dependent variable: firms growth over 10 periods)

	Schumpeter I		Intermediate		Schumpeter II		Aggregate manufac-turing
	Individual microsectors	Sector	Individual microsectors	Sector	Individual microsectors	Sector	
Initial size ln(s)	*non significant* with low opportunities for entrants; *positive* most often *significant* with high opportunities	negative, significant	*most often* *non significant,* *uncertain* *sign*	*non* *significant*	*positive,* *generally* *significant*	positive, often non significant	negative, not always significant
Initial age ln(a)	negative, non significant with low opportunities; *negative significantly* with high opportunity	*same* as micro-sectors	non significant uncertain sign	*negative,* *non* *significant*	negative, often significant	*negative,* significant	*negative,* significant
Interaction age and size ln(s)*ln(a)	non significant		non significant		negative often significant	negative sometimes significant	negative not always significant

especially in the 'cumulative regimes', but also under 'Schumpeter I', provided that opportunities are high. Hence, over finite spans of observation, one detects a positive link between size and growth which is spurious from a causal point of view, since it simply reveals a long autocorrelation structure in the growth of firms that happen to be at the extremes of the competitiveness distribution. Clearly, the causal link here goes from competitiveness to both growth *and* size.

Different regimes show quite different patterns of evolution of market shares and a different demography. Regarding the former, Figure 17 show the dynamics over 25 years, with some sort of 'Marshallian cycle' characterizing the most innovative entrants (the others die quite soon: see also below). Conversely, with cumulative learning one or few dominant firms emerge (Figure 18).

In these circumstances, the general properties of industrial dynamics are basically driven by an 'oligopolistic core' or a quasi-monopolist with a fringe of more or less numerous small marginal firms. Of course this occurs until with low but positive probability major disruptions in the competitive pecking order occur (as discussed earlier).[37] Even more so under 'Schumpeter II', where the tendency toward monopoly is particularly marked.

More generally, our results appear to suggest that evolutionary processes under most regimes show powerful monopolistic tendencies, curbed by (relatively infrequent) 'radical' innovations, and, probably more important, by the emergence of new microsectors (i.e. new markets and new lines of production activities) often explored by novel firms.

Regarding the demography of firms, Figure 19 show the probability of death conditional on age and Figure 20 conditional on size.

In general, mortality falls with size, but with

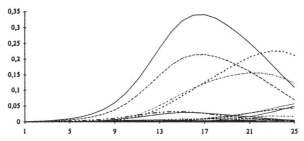

Fig. 17. The evolution of market shares, 'Schumpeter I'.

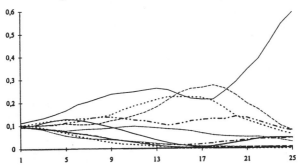

'Intermediate' regime (1.5; 2; 3)

Fig 18. Dynamics of market shares in a 'cumulative regime'.

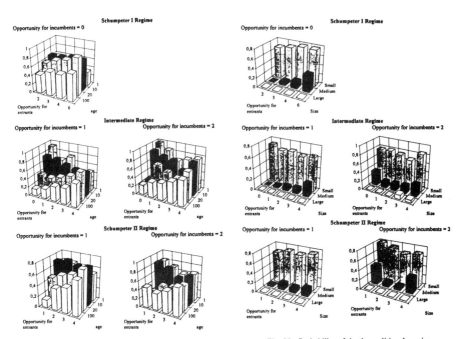

Fig. 19. Probability of death conditional on age.   Fig. 20. Probability of death conditional on size.

high learning opportunities also big firms have a positive probability to die.

Under a 'Schumpeter I' regime the probability of death increases during its youth, then falls and eventually starts rising again. Under all other regimes, mortality *falls* with age.

This property, together with the earlier one that growth also falls, loosely corresponds to the phenomena described in population-ecology models as adaptation to particular environmental niches. (Of course in our model there is no such behavioural feature.)

Interestingly, as the opportunity for entrants grows, *short-term* mortality *falls* and long-term one increases (which is also a phenomenon empirically noted by Audretsch (1991)).

VII. Conclusions

On the grounds of a rather simple evolutionary model, we have tried to show, one is able to generate a rich set of 'stylized facts' concerning several statistical invariances in industrial structures and in their dynamic properties, at different levels of aggregation. In the mode of analysis which we have followed here, the 'explanation' rests in the 'mapping' between aggregate properties and the system parameters governing learning processes and market selection, while being totally agnostic about specific behavioural assumptions.

The ability of the model of accounting for a multitude of regularities *together* is certainly a point of analytical strength (which indeed cannot be ascribed to most equilibrium models one finds in the literature). A preliminary comparison between the results of the model and the 'stylized facts' surveyed in Section II is indeed quite encouraging.

Relatedly, this approach can generate a rather long list of propositions that are at least in principle empirically testable, concerning for example the link between opportunities for learning – on the one hand – and size distributions, market turbulence, concentration, etc. – on the other; the links between degree of cumulativeness and market structures; the intertemporal patterns of industrial evolution; and many others. An increasing availability of time-series of micro data in recent years is making them testable not only in principle but also in practice.

In this respect this work ought to be considered only as an introductory exploration of the properties of evolutionary dynamics driven by various forms of learning and occurring, loosely speaking, over an 'evolutionary landscape' which the agents themselves continuously shape.

Acknowledgements

We thank Boyan Jovanovic and David Audretsch for their comments during conference presentations of the research, and Laura Porta for her helpful research assistantship.

Notes

[1]   More on this notion in Lane (1992).
[2]   Cf. Ijiri and Simon (1977). A detailed discussion is in Marsili (1992).
[3]   For example, Barca (1985) shows in the Italian case, for the '70s, significant departures from a Pareto distribution, biased in favour of small firms. In Dosi and Salvatore (1992) we show that this could well be a temporary phenomena associated with major technological discontinuities. See also below.
[4]   For example, Kalecki (1945) assumes a variance of the error term falling with size. Simon and Bonini (1958) account also for entry and Ijiri and Simon (1977) allow for a first-order Markov process on growth rates.
[5]   For example, Geroski and Machin (1992), on a sample of around 500 British firms while rejecting the null hypothesis that growth rates are random, find also that "one cannot say that the evidence against the null is very impressive" (p. 16). A somewhat contradictory evidence stems from earlier studies: see Hart and Prais (1956), Hymer and Pashigian (1962), Mansfield (1962) Singh and Whittington (1975), Simon and Bonini (1958), Hall (1987).
[6]   On entry and exit in different countries see Dunne, Roberts and Samuelson (1988), Baldwin and Gorecki (1991), Cable and Schwalbach (1991), Bianco and Sestito (1992), Aldrich and Auster (1986), Acs and Audretsch (1991) and (1992), Phillips and Kirchoff (1989), Audretsch and Mahmood (1991), Mahmood (1992), Geroski and Schwalbach (1991)).
[7]   On various features of the dynamics of entry, exit, innovation within 'life cycles' see Klepper (1992) and the works

surveyed therein: Suarez and Utterback (1991), Klepper and Graddy (1990), R. Henderson (1988), S. J. Lane (1989), W. G. Mitchell (1988).
Overlapping or complementary evidence stems from the growing field of 'organizational ecology': see Hannan and Freeman (1989) and Hannan and Carroll (1992).
[8]   In terms of plant-sizes, firms' market shares and total firms' sizes.
[9]   Note that 'turbulence' in the definition here may be low even if rates of gross entry are high, provided that entrants do not make any big impact on market shares – for example because many of them die young.
[10]   It must be also noted, however, that some studies have shown that mortality rates are much more stable over time and across sectors: the variance in mortality across industries is lower than the variance in birth rates.
[11]   An extension of the model incorporating different forms of learning is in Calvo and Wellisz (1980).
[12]   This conjecture, of course, is by no means restricted to the empirical domains one is considering here. On the contrary, it is germane to a general epistemological challenge to the 'equilibrium paradigm' underway in both natural and social sciences: see Nicolis and Pricogine (1989). Indeed, it happens that economics and theology hold out as the two disciplines most resilient to such a methodological shift.
[13]   In Nelson and Winter (1982) and Winter (1984), this 'quasi-replicator' dynamics is implicitly in the expansion rules of firms. For other examples of selection dynamics, see Iwai (1984a, 1984b), Conlisk (1980), Gibbons and Metcalfe (1986), Silverberg (1987), Silverberg, Dosi and Orsenigo (1988), Chiaromonte and Dosi (1992). Partly overlapping with this class of evolutionary models, recent studies of 'organizational ecology' have suggested that a selection pattern ('density dependent selection') is relatively invariant in all 'industry life cycles' (cf. Hannan and Freeman (1989) and Hannan and Carrol (1992)). Of course, whether such invariance holds is mainly an empirical question. Let us just note that these models do not involve an explicit learning dynamics. Moreover, they focus primarily on the demography of firms, rather than their characteristics – including their sizes. For our purposes here, 'density-dependence' could be regarded as one of the possible outcomes of evolutionary dynamics, and indeed a very interesting question is: which learning and selection regimes allow it to emerge? More generally, for a discussion of selection dynamics in evolutionary models, see Silverberg (1988) and in ecological models, see Winter (1990).
[14]   Moreover, even if agents were able to correctly forecast the consequences of their actions, still heterogeneous and changing technologies would imply some selection dynamics.
[15]   To some extent, this is also a caricatural version of the two quite different views of the innovative process which J. Schumpeter held during his life, cf. Freeman (1982).
[16]   Another, equivalent, way of saying it is that evolution is driven by mutation rather then by 'Lamarckian' transmission of acquired characters.
[17]   The modified version of the Fisher-Pry selection dynamics that we adopt in Equation (8) allows notional shares to become negative. Of course, in that case the death rule applies and actual market shares are recursively adjusted.
An advantage of the selection dynamics sub 8. is that,

given the non stationarity in the levels of competitiveness, it scales their affects on market shares to the dynamics of the mean: market adjustments are approximately invariant in the log differences in competitiveness.

[18] In a more sofisticated formulation, one should assume that the choice of the sectors of diversification depends on some measures of 'technological distance', as suggested in Dosi, Teece and Winter (1992). Indeed such an hypothesis of non-uniformly random processes of diversification appears corroborated by some preliminary evidence: cf. Teece *et al.* (1993). Here, however, we stick to the simpler, *and empirically false*, formulation since we are not so much interested in issues of internal coherence of firms, but rather on broader statistics on market structures.

[19] More precisely, in the experiments reported below we rule out $k = l$, that is intra-sectoral mergers/acquisitions. The impact of the later is on the agenda for future work.

[20] All the statistics that we shall present below on micro-sectors will consider such 'divisions' as indipendent firms. A proper account of multi-product firms will be given when describing 'sectors' and, of course, the whole 'industry'.

Moreover, note that the stochastic diversification process is recursively repeated across all microsectors, thus allowing firms to hold a number of activities ranging between 1 and $v(t)$ (the total number of microsectors that are active at that time).

[21] It might be worth emphasizing that within the notion of 'structure' adopted here one includes also variables that one would normally consider in industrial economics as describing the performance of particular industries – for example the dynamics and cross firms variances in 'competitiveness' – which can easily be interpreted to represent productivity or some combination between the latter and product innovation.

[22] Which, incidentally, is a quite ill-placed objection given their embeddedness in a well defined structure of interactions.

[23] More in line with microeconomic 'rationality', one could also assume to the same effect that regimes specific restrictions on our Markov processes of change in competitiveness are the outcomes of more sophisticated strategically motivated activities of innovative search: with little doubt, several Ph.D. are there to be written on the rationalization of intersectoral differences in innovation patterns . . .

[24] One should also mention some of the features which are missing in these modelling exercises: first, one does not account for any capital-embodied innovation and vintage-effect; second, the model does not account for any process of inter-firm imitation. Given these drawbacks, results on persistence concerning both sector-wide structures and firm-specific performance ought to be considered as sorts of lower bounds for the 'true' values, had one accounted for these additional sources of hysteresis and interdependences.

[25] Correspondinghly in the following, we shall describe each simulation by three indicators (A, $g_{(r)}$ and $g_{(E)}$).

[26] The index user here is $\{n_{(t)}\sum_i [f_i(t)]^2 - 1\}/[n(t) - 1]$ which is bound in [0; 1]; n is the number of firms and f_i are the market shares.

[27] The *ceteris paribus* implies also that the *relative* ability of entrants and incumbents is held constant.

[28] A line of inquiry which we cannot pursue here concerns

the normative implications of these results: it is straight-forward, for example, that for anti-trust purposes market share concentration measures might be highly biased indicators of the probability of collusion, while traditional pro-competition policies might imply 'perverse' effects on long-term improvements in products and processes of production, and competitiveness. In general, major normative questions concern the possible dilemmas between 'static' and 'dynamic' efficiency and one is only beginning to explore them (cf. Nelson and Winter (1982) and Dosi, Pavitt and Soete (1990)).

[29] The measure of asymmetry is the standard deviation in the degrees of competitiveness of the firm at t, $\sigma(E_{(t)}/\bar{E}_{(t)}$. This statistics is bound between zero and a finite value determined by one of the 'death rules': cf. Equation (9).

[30] Another direction of inquiry which, again, it is not possible to explore here concerns the link between selection on the product – and on the finance – markets. In Dosi (1991), one conjectures that, ceteris paribus, a higher 'efficiency' in the markets for ownership titles and corporate debt might lead to systematically lower rates of innovative exploration, given a plausible biased distribution of search effects toward mistakes. The model presented here neglects this issue by simply assuming – quite irrealistically – that the learning dynamics of individual firms is independent from finance.

[31] The 'Hand' is invisible in the sense that we assume that no agent explicitly tries to strategically influence its own payoffs, but, it might be quite 'visible' since 'atomlessness' hypotheses on the size of the agents *vis-à-vis* the market are largely violated and, ex-post, individual firms may well turn out to influence the selection process.

[32] Here, size is measured by the turnover of each firm.

[33] Each regime aggregates over five microsectors observed at different stages of their 'lifecycle' (i.e. different 'ages' of the microsectors themselves).

[34] The 'manufacturing aggregate' adds up over 80 'microsectors' randomly drawn from the three regimes.

[35] In Dosi and Salvatore (1992) we experiment with a generalized discontinuity in technological knowledge – an economy wide change in technological paradigms. This yields indeed an aggregate departure from a Pareto-type distribution, somewhat similar to that shown by actual data in the '70s in some countries. However, we also show that such a departure is likely to be a temporary phenomenon, unless one expects these generalized shocks to occur with high frequency.

[36] The tests exclude the firms which die within the 10-iteration period.

[37] Incidentally, note also that within the 'oligopolistic core', over finite periods, there might be *positive* correlation between age and growth for these outliers, but this property does not hold for the universe of firms.

References

Acs, Z. J. and D. B. Audretsch, 1989, 'Small-Firm Entry in U.S. Manufacturing', *Economica* 56, 255–265.

Acs, Z. J. and D. B. Audretsch, 1990, *Innovation and Small Firms*, Cambridge: MIT Press.

Aldrich, H. and E. Auster, 1986, 'Even Giants Started as Dwarves', *Research in Organizational Behaviour* 8, 46–61.

Audretsch, D. B., 1991, 'New-Firm Survival and the Technological Regime', *Review of Economics and Statistics* 60, 441–450.

Audretsch, D. B., 1995, *Innovation and Industry Evolution*, Cambridge: MIT Press.

Audretsch, D. B. and T. Mahmood, 1995, 'New Firm Survival: New Results Using a Hazard Function', *Review of Economics and Statistics* 64, forthcoming.

Baily, M. N. and A. K. Chakrabarty, 1985, 'Innovation and Productivity in US Industry', *Brookings Papers on Economic Activity* 2, 609–632.

Baldwin, J. R and P. K. Gorecki, 1991, 'Entry, Exit and Productivity Growth', in P. Geroski and J. Schwalbach (eds.), *Entry and Market Contestability: An International Comparison*, Oxford: Basil Blackwell, 244–256.

Barca, F., 1985, 'Tendenze nella Struttura Dimensionale dell'Industria Italiana: Una Verifica Empirica del "Modello di Specializzazione Flessibile"', *Politica Economica* 1, 71–109.

Beesley, M.E. and R. T. Hamilton, 1984, 'Small Firms' Seedbed Role and the Concept of Turbulence', *Journal of Industrial Economics* 33, 217–232.

Bianco, M. and P. Sestito, 1992, 'Entry, Growth and Market Structure: A Preliminary Analysis of the Italian Case', presented at the International Conference on 'Birth and Start-up of Small Firms', Milano.

Bond, R. S., 1975, 'Mergers and Mobility among the Largest Manufacturing Corporations, 1984 to 1988', *Antitrust Bullettin* 20, 505–519.

Cable, J. and J. Schwalbach, 1991, 'International Comparison of Entry and Exit', in P. Geroski and J. Schwalbach (eds.), *Entry and Market Contestability: An International Comparison*, Oxford: Basil Blackwell, 257–281.

Calvo, G. A. and S. Wellisz, 1980, 'Technology, Entrepreneurs and Firm Size', *Quarterly Journal of Economics* 95, 663–677.

Chiaromonte, F. and G. Dosi, 1992, 'The Microfoundations of Competitiveness and Their Macroeconomic Implications', in D. Foray and C. Freeman (eds.), *Technology and the Wealth of Nations*, London: Pinter Publishers.

Collins, N. R. and L. E. Preston, 1961, 'The Size Structure of the Largest Industrial Firms', *American Economic Review* 51, 986–1011.

Conlinsk, J., 1980, 'Costly Optimizers vs. Cheap Imitators', *Journal of Economic Behavior and Organization* 6, 46–61.

Dosi, G., 1982, 'Technological Paradigms and Technological Trejectories. A Suggested Interpretation of the Determinant and Direction of Technological Change', *Research Policy* 11, 147–162.

Dosi, G., 1984, *Technical Change and Industrial Transformation. The Theory and an Application to the Semiconductor Industry*, London: Macmillan.

Dosi, G., 1988, 'Sources, Procedures and Microeconomic Effect of Innovation', *Journal of Economic Literature* 26, 1120–1171.

Dosi, G. and L. Orsenigo, 1988, 'Industrial Structure and Technical Change', in A. Heertje (ed.), *Innovation, Technology and Finance*, Oxford: Blackwell, 14–37.

Dosi, G. and R. Salvatore, 1992, 'The Structure of Industrial Production and the Boundaries between Organization and Markets', in A. Scott and M. Stolper (eds.), *Pathways to Regional Development*, Boulder: Westview Press, 1–26.

Dosi, G., K. Pavitt and L. Soete, 1990, *The Economics of Technical Change and International Trade*, New York: New York University Press.

Dosi, G., D. J. Teece and S. Winter, 1992, 'Towards a Theory of Corporate Coherence: Preliminary Remarks', in G. Dosi, R. Giannetti and P.A. Toninelli (eds.), *Technology and Enterprises in a Historical Perspective*, Oxford: Oxford University Press, 185–211.

Dunne, T., M. J. Roberts and L. Samuelson, 1988, 'Patterns of Firm Entry and Exit in U.S. Manufacturing Industries', *Rand Journal of Economics* 19, 495–515.

Evans, D. S., 1987a, 'The Relationship Between Firm Growth, Size and Age: Estimates for 100 Manufacturing Industries', *Journal of Industrial Economics* 35, 567–581.

Evans, D. S., 1987b, 'Tests of Alternative Theories of Firm Growth', *Journal of Political Economy* 95, 657–674.

Foray. D. and C. Freeman, 1993, *Technology and the Wealth of Nations*, London: Pinter Publishers.

Freeman, C., 1982, *The Economics of Industrial Innovation*, London: Pinter Publishers.

Geroski, P. and A. Jacquemin, 1988, 'The Persistence of Profits: An International Comparison', *Economic Journal* 98, 375–390.

Geroski, P. and S. Machin, 1992, 'The Dynamics of Corporate Growth', mimeo, London Business School.

Geroski, P. and J. Schwalbach (eds.), 1991, *Entry and Market Contestability: An International Comparison*, Oxford: Basil Blackwell.

Gibbons, M. and J. S. Metcalfe, 1986, 'Technological Variety and the Process of Competition', mimeo, University of Manchester.

Griliches, Z., 1986, 'Productivity, R&D and Basic Research at the Firm Level in the 1970's', *American Economic Review* 76, 141–154.

Hall, B. H., 1987, 'The Relationship Between Firm Size and Firm Growth in the U.S. Manufacturing Sector', *Journal of Industrial Economics* 35, 583–600.

Hannan, M. T. and G. R. Carroll, 1991, *Dynamics of Organizational Populations: Density, Competition and Legitimation*, New York: Oxford University Press.

Hannan, M. T. and J. Freeman, 1989, *Organizational Ecology*, Cambridge, MA: Harvard University Press.

Hart, P. E. and S. J. Prais, 1956, 'The Analysis of Business Concentration: A Statistical Approach', *Journal of the Royal Statistical Society* 119, 150–191.

Henderson, R. M., 1988, *The Failure of Established Firms in the Face of Technical Change: A Study of Photolithographic Alignment Equipment*, Dept. of Business Economics, Harvard University Cambridge, Mass.

Hymer, S. and P. Pashigian, 1962, 'Firm Size and Rate of Growth', *Journal of Political Economy* 52, 556–569.

Ijiri, Y. and H. A. Simon, 1977, *Skew Distribution and the Size of Business Firms*, Amsterdam: North-Holland.

Iwai, K., 1984a, 'Schumpeterian Dynamics: An Evolutionary Model of Innovation and Imitation', *Journal of Economic Behavior and Organization* 5, 159–190.

Iwai, K., 1984b, 'Schumpeterian Dynamics, Part II: Technological Progress, Firm Growth and "Economic

Selection'", *Journal of Economic Behavior and Organization* 5, 321–351.

Jaffe, A. B., 1986, 'Technological Opportunity and Spillovers of R&D: Evidence from Firms' Patents, Profits and Market Value', *American Economic Review* 76, 984–1001.

Jovanovic, B., 1982, 'Selection and Evolution of Industry', *Econometrica* 50, 649–670.

Kalecki, M., 1945, 'On the Gibrat Law', *Econometrica* 13, 161–170.

Kaplan, A. D. H., 1954, *Big Enterprise in a Competitive System*, Washington, D.C.: The Brookings Institution.

Klepper, S., 1992, 'Entry, Exit and Innovation over the Product Life Cycle: The Dynamics of First Mover Advantages, Declining Product Innovation and Market Failure', paper presented at the International J.A. Schumpeter Society, Kyoto, August.

Klepper, S. and E. Graddy, 1990, 'The Evolution of New Industries and the Determinants of Market Structure', *Rand Journal of Economics* 21, 27–44.

Lambson, V.E., 1991, 'Industry Evolution with Sunk Costs and Uncertain Market Conditions', *International Journal of Industrial Organization* 9(2), 171–196.

Lane, S. J., 1989, *Entry and Industry Evolution in the ATM Manufacturers' Market*, Ann Arbor: UMI.

Lane, D. A., 1992, 'Artificial Worlds and Economics', SantaFe, SFI, Working Paper 92.09.048.

Levin, R., A. Klevorick, R. R. Nelson and S. Winter, 1987, 'Appropriating the Returns from Industrial Research and Development', *Brookings Papers on Economic Activity* 3, 147–163.

Lucas, R. E. Jr, 1978, 'On the Size Distribution of Business Firms', *Bell Journal of Economics* 9, 508–523.

Mahmood, T., 1992, 'Does the Hazard Rate of New Plants Vary Between Low- and High-Tech Industries?', *Small Business Economics* 4, 201–209.

Malerba, F., 1985, *The Semiconductor Business*, London: Pinter Publishers.

Malerba, F., 1992, 'Learning by Firms and Incremental Technical Change', *Economic Journal* 94, 213–228.

Malerba, F. and L. Orsenigo, 1989, 'Technological Regimes and Patterns of Innovation: A Theoretical and Empirical Investigation of the Italian Case', in A. Heertje and M. Perlman (eds), *Evolving Technology and Market Structure*, Ann Arbor: The University of Michigan Press.

Malerba, F. and L. Orsenigo, 1995, 'Schumpeterian Patterns of Innovation', *Cambridge Journal of Economics* 19, 47–66.

Malerba, F. and L. Orsenigo, 1993, 'Technological Regimes and Firm Behaviour', *Industrial and Corporate Change* 2(1), 74–89.

Mansfield, E., 1962, 'Entry, Gibrat's Law, Innovation and the Growth of Firms', *American Economic Review* 52, 1023–1051.

Marsili, O., 1992, *Apprendimento, Selezione e Dinamica delle Strutture Industriali*, Faculty of Statistics, Rome.

Mermelstein, D., 1969, 'Large Industrial Corporations and Asset Shares', *American Economic Review* 59, 531–541.

Mitchell, W. G., 1988, *Dynamic Commercialization: An Organizational Economic Analysis of Innovation in the Medical Diagnostic Imaging Industry*, University of California, Berkely, UMI.

Mueller, D. C., 1990, 'Profits and the Process of Competition',
in D. C. Mueller (ed.), *The Dynamics of Company Profits: An International Comparison*, Cambridge: Cambridge University Press, 1–14.

Nelson, R. R. and S. Winter, 1982, *An Evolutionary Theory of Economic Change*, Cambridge, Mass: Harvard University Press.

Nicolis and I. Prigogine, 1989, *Exploring Complexity An Instruction*, San Francisco: W.H. Freeman.

Odagiri, K. and H. Yamawaki, 1990, 'Persistence of Profits in Japan', in D. C. Mueller (ed.), *The Dynamics of Company Profits: An International Comparison*, Cambridge: Cambridge University Press, 169–186.

Pakes, A. and R. Ericson, 1987, 'Empirical Implications of Alternative Models of Firm Dynamics', Social System Research Institute Workshop series, University of Wisconsin.

Patel, P. and K. Pavitt, 1991, 'Europe's Technological Performance', in C. Freeman, M. Sharp and W. Walker (eds.), *Technology and the Future of Europe: Global Competition and the Environment in the 1990s*, London: Pinter Publisher, 37–58.

Pavitt, K., 1984, 'Sectoral Patterns of Technical Change: Towards a Taxonomy and a Theory', *Research Policy* 13, 343–373.

Phillips, B. D. and B. A. Kirchhoff, 1989, 'Formation, Growth and Survival: Small Firm Dynamics in the U.S. Economy', *Small Business Economics* 1, 65–74.

Silverberg, G., 1987, 'Technical Progress, Capital Accumulation and Effective Demand: A Self-Organization Model', in D. Batten, J. Casti and B. Johansson (eds.), *Economic Evolution and Structural Adjustment*, Berlin-Heidelberg-New York: Springer Verlag.

Silverberg, G., G. Dosi and L. Orsenigo, 1988, 'Innovation, diversity and Diffusion: A Self-Organization Model', *The Economic Journal* 98, 1032–1054.

Simon, H. A., 1955, 'On a Class of Skew Distribution Functions', *Biometrika* 42, 425–440.

Simon, H. A. and C. P. Bonini, 1958, 'The Size Distribution of Business Firms', *American Economic Review* 48, 607–617.

Singh, A. and G. Whittington, 1975, 'The Size and Growth of Firms', *Review of Economic Studies* 42, 15–26.

Suarez, F. F. and J. M. Utterback, 1991, 'Dominant Design and the Survival of Firms', WP, NO 42-91, International Center for Research on the Management of Technology, MIT.

Suarez, F. F. and J. M. Utterback, 1992, 'Innovation, Competition and Industry Structure', *Research Policy* 4, 67–74.

Sylos-Labini, P., 1967, *Oligopoly and Technical Progress*, Cambridge, Mass.: Harvard University Press.

Winter, S. G., 1984, 'Schumpeterian Competition in Alternative Technological Regimes', *Journal of Economic Behaviour and Organization* 5, 287–320.

Winter, S. G., 1990, 'Survival, Selection and Inheritance in Evolutionary Theories of Organization', in J. V. Singh (ed.), *Organizational Evolution: New Directions*, Newbury Park: Sage, 269–297.

[16]

Modeling Industrial Dynamics with Innovative Entrants

S.G. Winter (winter@upenn.edu)
The Wharton School, University of Pennsylvania
2000 Steinberg Hall-Dietrich Hall, Philadelphia, PA 19104.6370,
USA
Y.M. Kaniovski (kaniov@iiasa.ac.at and kaniov@cs.unitn.it)
The International Institute for Applied Systems Analysis
A-2361 Laxenburg, Austria
and
University of Trento
Via Inama 5, I-38100 Trento, Italy
G. Dosi (dosi@sssup.it)
The Sant'Anna School of Advanced Studies
Via Carducci 40, I-56127 Pisa, Italy

1   Introduction

In this work we explore the dynamic features of industries characterized by the persistent arrival of innovative entrants. The models which follow build upon and modify the *baseline model* presented in Winter et al.(1997). In an extreme synthesis, in the latter we develop a framework of analysis of the competitive dynamics of industries composed of heterogeneous firms and continuing stochastic entry. There, we show that despite the simplicity of the assumptions, the model is able to account for a rather rich set of empirical 'stylized facts', such as: (i) continuing turbulence in market shares; (ii) persistent inflows and outflows of firms; (iii) 'life cycle' phenomena – including, in particular, nearer the birth of an industry, relatively sudden 'shakeouts', yielding distinctly different industrial structure thereafter; and (iv) skewed size distributions of firms[1].

---

[1]This evidence is discussed at much greater length in the special issues of *Industrial and Corporate Change*, 5, 1997 and of *The International Journal of Industrial Organization*, 4, 1995. See also Baldwin (1995); Caroll and Hannan (1995); Davis et al. (1996); Dunne, Roberts and Samuelson (1988); Dosi et al. (1995); Geroski (1995); Hannan and Freeman (1989).

The 'heroic' simplicity of Winter et al. (1997) goes as far as assuming that the set of technological options among which entrants draw – as a formal metaphor of their diverse capabilities – is given from the start and is invariant throughout the unfolding evolution of the industry. While this assumption is certainly in tune with the spirit of most evolutionary game-theoretical set-ups, it is also at odds with an overwhelming empirical evidence highlighting the role of innovators as carriers of technological and organizational discoveries. Typically, these discoveries happen to be tapped at some point in the history of an industry on the grounds of the available knowledge base at that time, but would not have been possible earlier on, given the knowledge base at that earlier time.

More formally, this implies that what is commonly called the 'production possibility set' endogenously shifts, due to the cumulative (but stochastic) effects of exploration by potential innovators[2].

The model which follows studies the properties of industrial dynamics which correspond to that archetype of industrial evolution which some authors call *Schumpeter Mark I regime* (cf. Malerba and Orsenigo (1995) and Dosi et al. (1995)). In short, while of course both incumbents and new entrants empirically attempt to explore – to varying degrees – yet unexploited opportunities of innovation, here we focus upon the properties of that extreme archetype whereby only entrants have a positive probability of advancing the current state of technological knowledge. (Hence the name of such a 'regime', in analogy with the emphasis of Schumpeter (1934) upon novel entrepreneurial efforts as drivers of change.)

Compared with the cited 'baseline model' discussed in Winter et al. (1997), in the following we shall try to disentangle those properties which appear to be generic features of a wide class of processes of industrial dynamics simply resting upon persistently heterogeneous agents and market selection and, conversely, those properties which depend upon more specific forms of innovative learning, such as the *Schumpeter Mark I* regime considered here[3]. As we shall show below, some of the emerging 'stylized facts' of the modeled dynamics appear to robustly hold in both set-ups, with or without innovative entry. Other features, including some path-dependence properties, interestingly, appear only when 'open-ended' dynamics on technological opportunities is accounted for, as we do in this work.

---

[2]For more detailed empirical corroborations of these points, cf., among others, Dosi (1988) and Freeman and Soete (1997).

[3]See Winter et al. (1997) also for some comparative assessment of somewhat germane models of industrial dynamics based on much more stringent assumptions of individual forward-looking rationality and collective equilibrium, such as Jovanovic (1982), Hopenhayn (1992), Ericson and Pakes (1995).

Section 2 sets out the basic structure of the model, in a first specification with innovative learning by entrants directed at increasing capital productivity, and, conversely, in section 3, we study the properties of a symmetrical assumption of (stochastically) increasing labour efficiencies.

2 The basic framework of the model: a first setting with increasing capital efficiencies

Let us assume an industry evolving in discrete time $t = 0, 1, \ldots$. At $t = 0$ there are no firms ready to produce, but k firms arrive to the industry, ready to start manufacturing at $t = 1$. Techniques are capital-embodied and firm-specific. So, the model which follows can be interpreted as a vintage capital model, with heterogeneous techniques across firms also within each vintage.

At time $t \geq 1$ the industry consists of n_t firms which are involved in production and a number of new firms that enter at t and will participate in manufacturing from $t + 1$ onward. Uniformly for the whole industry we have:

v - price per unit of physical capital, $v > 0$,

d - depreciation rate of the capital stock, $0 < d \leq 1$.

In the first version of the model which follows the output is produced by capital alone. The competitiveness of any firm represented in the industry is ultimately determined by its capital per unit of output. Let us designate the latter by a_i for the i-th firm. As time goes on, the "best" capital/output ratio (in real terms) attainable in the industry stochastically decreases.

Let us further assume the following endogenous stochastic mechanism of learning by entrants. Take a random variable ξ with positive mean $E\xi$ and finite variance $D\xi$. Set ζ for a random variable distributed over $[a, b]$, $0 < a < b < \infty$. For each time instant $t \geq 0$ we allow for the industry to have $k \geq 1$ new firms whose levels of capital per unit of output are randomly determined as $\exp\{-A_t\}\zeta^i$, $tk + 1 \leq i \leq (t+1)k$. Here $A_{t+1} = A_t + \xi^{t+1}$, $t \geq 0$, $A_0 = \xi^0$. Also, ξ^t, $t \geq 0$, and ζ^i, $i \geq 1$, are mutually independent collections of realizations of ξ and ζ. Thus, all capital ratios feasible for newcomers at time t belong to $[\exp\{-A_t\}a, \exp\{-A_t\}b]$. Their distribution within this interval is governed by a realization of $\exp\{-A_t\}\zeta$. Consequently, A_t characterizes in a probabilistic way the highest productivity of capital attainable to newcomers in the industry at time t. Note that by construction *in this competitive environment only newcomers learn to improve the productivity of capital.*

It is important to notice that the assumption of a fixed number of entrants is just made here for expositional simplicity. The qualitative results do not change if one allows stochastic entry (as we in fact do in Winter et al. (1997)) and if entry probabilities were made dependent upon some state variable of the system, for example, the current level of profitability in the industry: see Remark 2.2. below.

The productive capacity of the i-th firm is $Q_t^i = K_i(t)/a_i$, where $K_i(t)$ stands for the capital of the i-th firm at time t. The total productive capacity of the industry involved in manufacturing at time t is

$$Q_t = \sum_{i=1}^{n_t} Q_t^i.$$

We assume a decreasing continuous demand function $p = H(q)$, mapping $[0, \infty)$ in $[0, H(0)]$ such that $H(0) < \infty$ and $H(q) \to 0$ as $q \to \infty$, where as usual, p stands for the price and q for demanded quantities. (Thus, the price at time t equals $H(Q_t)$.) The gross profit per unit of output at t is also $H(Q_t)$ since, without loss of generality we may also assume zero variable costs. The gross investment per unit of output at t is a share of the gross profit, i.e. $\lambda H(Q_t)$, where the constant λ captures the share of the gross profit which does not leak out as the interest payments and shareholders' dividends, and can be considered to be a measure for the propensity to invest. The total gross investment per unit of capital for the i-th firm at time t reads $\lambda H(Q_t)/va_i$.

For each capital ratio generated at t we shall allow a single entrant. Entrants' initial capitals are independent realizations θ^i, $i \geq 1$, of a random variable θ distributed over $[c, h]$, $0 < c < h < \infty$. (It is assumed that the realizations of ξ, ζ and θ are mutually independent random variables.)

To complete the description of the competitive environment we need some death mechanism. A firm is dead at time t and does not participate in the production process from $t + 1$ onward if its capital at t is less than ϵc, $\epsilon \in (0, 1]$[4].

We assume that all random elements are given on a probability space $\{\Omega, \mathcal{F}, P\}$.

In order to study the long run behavior of this industry, let us give a formal description of its evolution.

---

[4]The situation without mortality can be thought of as a limit case when $\epsilon = 0$. Conversely, for a possible refinement of the above mortality rule see Remark 2.3 below.

2.1 A dynamical setting of the model

Let firm i be manufacturing during time t. Our investment rule implies that at the end of this production period its capital is

$$Q_t^i a_i \left[1 - d + \frac{\lambda}{v a_i} H(Q_t) \right].$$

If this value does not drop below the death threshold ϵc, the firm continues to manufacture during time instant $t + 1$. Otherwise it dies. To capture these possibilities, we introduce $\chi_{Q_t^i[1-d+\frac{\lambda}{v a_i}H(Q_t)] \geq \epsilon c / a_i}$ the indicator function of the event that the firm continues to manufacture. As usual, for a relation $\mathcal{A}$ we set that

$$\chi_{\mathcal{A}} = \begin{cases} 1, & \text{if } \mathcal{A} \text{ is true,} \\ 0, & \text{otherwise.} \end{cases}$$

Now the evolution of the i-th firm (in terms of productive capacity) reads

$$Q_{t+1}^i = Q_t^i \left[1 - d + \frac{\lambda}{v a_i} H(Q_t) \right] \chi_{Q_t^i[1-d+\frac{\lambda}{v a_i}H(Q_t)] \geq \epsilon c / a_i}. \tag{2.1}$$

These equations are not handy for analysis. Mortality implies that n_t, the number of firms in business, changes over time. Thus, we have a system with a variable dimension. Moreover, these equations do not incorporate the entry process: hence (2.1) only captures a part of the evolution of the industry. In order to handle entry and variable numbers of incumbents one needs a dynamic representation of the model that leaves room for all feasible development paths. It is nested in an infinite dimensional space.

The intuition is the following. Even if at each time one assumes, quite naturally, a finite number of entrants, as time goes to infinity, one must allow for an infinite number of firms to visit the industry. Moreover, the number of firms is normally changing over time as the joint outcome of entry and selection (entailing mortality). Somewhat similar considerations apply to the input coefficients (i.e. the productivities) which the system explores. The rather novel formal machinery developed below is precisely aimed to rigorously capture these properties.

Introduce a space R_∞ of vectors with denumerably many coordinates. Set

$$R_\infty = R \bigotimes \left[\bigotimes_{i=1}^{\infty} R_i \right],$$

where $\bigotimes$ stands for the direct sum of a real line R and $2k$-dimensional real vector spaces R_i, $i \geq 1$. Thus, for every $\mathbf{q} \in R_\infty$

$$\mathbf{q} = q \bigotimes \left[\bigotimes_{i=1}^{\infty} \mathbf{q}^i \right] \tag{2.2}$$

with $q \in R$ and $\mathbf{q}^i \in R_i$, $i \geq 1$. Define an automorphism $\mathbf{D}(\cdot)$ on R_∞ such that

$$\mathbf{D}(\mathbf{q}) = \mathbf{D}^1(\mathbf{q}) \bigotimes \left[\bigotimes_{i=2}^{\infty} \mathbf{D}^i(\mathbf{q}) \right],$$

where $\mathbf{D}^1(\cdot): \ R_\infty \mapsto R \otimes R_1 \otimes R_2$ and $\mathbf{D}^i(\cdot): \ R_\infty \mapsto R_i$, $i \geq 3$. Let

$$D_1^1(\mathbf{q}) = q, \quad D_s^1(\mathbf{q}) = 0, \ \ 2 \leq s \leq 2k+1, \quad D_{2k+j+1}^1(\mathbf{q}) = q_j^1 \exp\{-q\} \chi_{A_j^1(\mathbf{q})},$$

$$D_{3k+j+1}^1(\mathbf{q}) = q_{k+j}^1 \left[1 - d + \frac{\lambda}{v} H \left(\sum_{s=1}^{k} [q_{k+s}^1 \exp\{q\}/q_s^1 + \sum_{i=2}^{\infty} q_{k+s}^i/q_s^i] \right) \exp\{q\}/q_j^1 \right] \chi_{A_j^1(\mathbf{q})},$$

$$D_j^i(\mathbf{q}) = q_j^i \chi_{A_j^i(\mathbf{q})}, \quad D_{k+j}^i(\mathbf{q}) = q_{k+j}^i \left[1 - d + \frac{\lambda}{v} H \left(\sum_{s=1}^{k} [q_{k+s}^1 \exp\{q\}/q_s^1 + \right. \right.$$

$$\left. \left. \sum_{p=2}^{\infty} q_{k+s}^p/q_s^p] \right)/q_j^i \right] \chi_{A_j^i(\mathbf{q})},$$

where $1 \leq j \leq k$, $i \geq 2$, $A_j^1(\mathbf{q})$ designates the relation

$$q_{k+j}^1 \left[1 - d + \frac{\lambda}{v} H \left(\sum_{s=1}^{k} [q_{k+s}^1 \exp\{q\}/q_s^1 + \sum_{i=2}^{\infty} q_{k+s}^i/q_s^i] \right) \exp\{q\}/q_j^1 \right] \geq \epsilon c$$

and $A_j^i(\mathbf{q})$ stands for the relation

$$q_{k+j}^i \left[1 - d + \frac{\lambda}{v} H \left(\sum_{s=1}^{k} [q_{k+s}^1 \exp\{q\}/q_s^1 + \sum_{p=2}^{\infty} q_{k+s}^p/q_s^p] \right)/q_j^i \right] \geq \epsilon c.$$

We restrict ourselves to vectors $\mathbf{q}$ defined by (2.2) belonging to

$$R_\infty^+ = [0, \infty) \bigotimes \left[\bigotimes_{i=1}^{\infty} R_i^+ \right]$$

and set $H(\infty) = 0$ for the case when the iterated sum involved in the above expressions is infinite. Here

$$R_i^+ = \{ \mathbf{q}^i \in R_i : \ q_j^i > 0, \ q_{k+j}^i \geq 0, \ j = 1, 2, \ldots, k, \}, \ \ i \geq 1.$$

Also, $D_s^i(\cdot)$ and q_s^i stand for the s-th coordinates of $\mathbf{D}^i(\cdot)$ and $\mathbf{q}^i$.

Define infinite dimensional random vectors $\mathbf{Y}^t$, $t \geq 0$, setting

$$Y_1^t = \xi^t, \quad Y_{i+1}^t = \zeta^{tk+i}, \quad Y_{k+i+1}^t = \theta^{tk+i}, \quad i = 1, 2, \ldots, k. \quad Y_j^t = 0 \ \ j \geq 2k+2.$$

(Note that here we number coordinates linearly rather than in terms of cohorts as above.)

The evolution of the industry is as follows

$$\mathbf{q}(t+1) = \mathbf{D}(\mathbf{q}(t)) + \mathbf{Y}^{t+1}, \ t \geq 0, \ \ \mathbf{q}(0) = \mathbf{Y}^0, \tag{2.3}$$

Since $\mathbf{Y}^t$ are independent in t, this expression defines a Markov process on R_∞^+. Moreover, since the deterministic operator $\mathbf{D}(\cdot)$ as well as the distribution of $\mathbf{Y}^t$ do not depend on time, the process is homogeneous in time.

Conceptually, this phase space is formed by the value characterizing the highest productivity which is potentially attainable at any time in the industry (the first coordinate), capitals per unit of output (the first k coordinates in each cohort, that is, a $2k$ box in the above structure) and individual capital stocks (the last k coordinates in each cohort: that is, to a capital ratio placed at the j-th position corresponds the capital placed at the $(k+j)$-th position) of all firms that stay alive. Therefore, if $q_{k+i}^n(t) > 0$ for some $i = 1, 2, \ldots, k$ and $n \leq t$, then a firm with $q_i^n(t)$ as capital per unit of output came to the industry at $t - n$ has been alive until t, that is, has manufactured $n - 1$ times, and continues to produce during the t-th time period. The representation via a direct sum seems to be a handy way of explicitly capturing the dynamic of cohorts.

The formulas for $\mathbf{D}^i(\cdot)$, $i \geq 2$, reflect our investment rule together with the assumption that the capital ratio remains constant through the life time of a firm. In analogy with (2.1), they are capturing the dynamic of capital stocks (but more precisely (2.1) refers to productive capacities). The indicators are needed because of the death rule[5]. The relation $\mathcal{A}_j^i(\mathbf{q})$ gives the criterion that a firm from the i-th box placed at the j-th position continues to manufacture given the state of the industry $\mathbf{q}$. As from above, the first coordinate carries the value determining the highest productivity attainable in the industry. The further $2k$ block is zero to host newcoming firms. The next k ones reflect the learning rule on improvement of productivity adopted by newcoming firms. Finally, the last k coordinates of $\mathbf{D}^1(\cdot)$ are defined according to our investment rule.

Given this formal description of this process of industry evolution, let us proceed to the analysis of its long run behavior.

2.2   Asymptotic properties of the industry

Define $\mathcal{B}^\infty$ the minimal σ-field in R_∞ generated by sets of the following form

$$\mathcal{A} = A \bigotimes \left[\bigotimes_{j=1}^{\infty} A^j \right], \qquad (2.4)$$

where A designates a set from the σ-field of Borel sets $\mathcal{B}$ on the real line, and A^j being a set from the σ-field of Borel sets $\mathcal{B}_j$ in R_j. For every such set $\mathcal{A}$ one step transition

---

[5]In particular, applied to the first k coordinates in a cohort, they prevent from carring over the capital ratios of firms that have died. However, the use of the death indicators to the first k coordinates is basically a matter of taste: without relevance for the conclusions, dropping them implies that the capital ratios of dead firms are in the structure of the model forever.

probability of process (2.3) reads

$$p^1(\mathbf{q}, \mathcal{A}) = P\{\mathbf{D}(\mathbf{q}) + \mathbf{Y} \in \mathcal{A}\} = P\{\mathbf{Y}^* \in \mathcal{A} \bigotimes A_1\} \chi_{\mathbf{D}(\mathbf{q}) \in \bigotimes_{i=2}^{\infty} A^i}. \tag{2.5}$$

Here $\mathbf{Y}^*$ stands for the $(2k+1)$-dimensional vector whose coordinates coincide with first $2k+1$ coordinates of a generic vector $\mathbf{Y}$ having the same distribution as $\mathbf{Y}^t$, $t \geq 0$.

To study the ergodic properties of process (2.3), we need the following condition which is due to Doeblin (see Doob (1953), p. 192).

There is a finite positive measure $\phi(\cdot)$ with $\phi(R_\infty^+) > 0$ and a positive number δ such that for all $\mathbf{q} \in R_\infty^+ p^1(\mathbf{q}, \mathcal{A}) \leq 1 - \delta$ if $\phi(\mathcal{A}) \leq \delta$.

For a set $\mathcal{A}$ as in (2.4) let $\phi(\mathcal{A}) = P\{\mathbf{Y}^* \in \mathcal{A} \bigotimes A_1\}$. From (2.4) it follows that $p^1(\mathbf{q}, \mathcal{A}) \leq \phi(\mathcal{A})$. Since $\phi(R_\infty^+) = P\{\mathbf{Y}^* \in [0, \infty) \bigotimes R_1^+\} = 1$, restricting ourselves to $\delta \leq 1/2$, we get that, if $\phi(\mathcal{A}) \leq \delta$, then $p^1(\mathbf{q}, \mathcal{A}) \leq \delta \leq 1 - \delta$. Thus, Doeblin's condition holds for this choice of $\phi(\cdot)$ and all $\delta \in (0, 1/2]$.

Now, by Theorem 5.7 from Doob (1953) (p. 214), we see that

$$\pi(\mathbf{q}, \mathcal{A}) = \lim_{n \to \infty} \frac{1}{n} \sum_{t=1}^{n} p^t(\mathbf{q}, \mathcal{A})$$

defines for each $\mathbf{q} \in R_\infty^+$ a stationary absolute distribution. Here $p^t(\mathbf{x}, \cdot)$ stands for the transition probability in t steps, that is,

$$p^t(\mathbf{q}, \mathcal{A}) = \int_{R_\infty^+} p^{t-1}(\mathbf{y}, \mathcal{A}) dp^1(\mathbf{q}, \mathbf{y}), \ t \geq 2.$$

The stationary distribution $\pi(\mathbf{q}, \cdot)$ turns out to be the same, that is $\pi_\mathcal{L}(\cdot)$, for all $\mathbf{q}$ belonging to the same ergodic set $\mathcal{L}$ (see Doob (1953), p. 210). It has the following generic property

$$\int_\mathcal{L} p^1(\mathbf{x}, \mathcal{A}) d\pi_\mathcal{L}(\mathbf{x}) = \pi_\mathcal{L}(\mathcal{A}).$$

In general, it is not possible to find an explicit expression for $\pi_\mathcal{L}(\cdot)$ from this relation.

Thus, we may only obtain the following result concerning ergodicity of process (2.3).

Theorem 2.1. *For every set $\mathcal{A}$ given by (2.4) with probability one*

$$\frac{1}{n} \sum_{t=1}^{n} p^t(\mathbf{Y}^0, \mathcal{A}) \to \pi(\mathbf{Y}^0, \mathcal{A}) \tag{2.6}$$

as $n \to \infty$. Here $\pi(\mathbf{Y}^0, \cdot)$ is a stochastic probability measure (since it depends on $\mathbf{Y}^0$), with $\pi_\mathcal{L}(\cdot)$ for any elementary outcome $\omega \in \Omega$, whereby $\mathbf{Y}^0$ belongs for this elementary outcome to an ergodic set $\mathcal{L}$.

Consider the implications of this result in terms of *path dependency*. On the one hand, Doeblin's condition implies that events occuring at t and $t + n$ are getting more and more statistically independent as n increases. Thus, the impact of the initial state vanishes as time goes on. Should one be able to prove that there is a single ergodic set, then the limit of time averages in (2.6) would not depend on the initial state, and hence the lack of path-dependency. On the other hand, the limit in (2.6), in general, does depend on the initial state. But the dependency acts in a way that such limit turns out to be the same for all initial states belonging to the same ergodic set. Therefore, there might indeed be some path-dependency which is governed by a partition of Ω. Note also that this partition, in general, turns out to be less fine than the one given by $\mathbf{Y}^0$.

Theorem 2.1 implies that, for every uniformly bounded characteristic of the industry, its time averages converge with probability one to a limit which is a deterministic function of the initial state in the sense given above. Unfortunately, – unlike for the model considered by Winter et al. (1997) –, some of the most important dynamic characteristics such as, for example, the total productive capacity, here are not uniformly bounded. Hence, Theorem 2.1 does not allow for immediate conceptual conclusions analogous to the ergodicity result presented in the foregoing work. On the other hand, one is still able to establish convergence of time averages of other aggregate variables such as the gross profit rate. Set

$$r_t = \frac{Q_t H(Q_t)}{\sum_{i=1}^{\infty} \sum_{j=1}^{k} q_{k+j}^i(t)}$$

for the gross profit rate at $t \geq 1$. Since there is no production at $t = 0$, $r_0 = 0$. As a consequence of Theorem 2.1 we have the following statement.

Corollary 2.1. *If* $xH(x) \leq const$ *for* $x \to \infty$, *then with probability one*

$$\frac{1}{n} \sum_{i=1}^{n} r_i \to \int_{R_{\infty}^+} \frac{Q(\mathbf{y}) H(Q(\mathbf{y}))}{\sum_{i=1}^{\infty} \sum_{j=1}^{k} y_{k+j}^i} d\pi(\mathbf{Y}^0, d\mathbf{y}) \tag{2.7}$$

as $n \to \infty$. *Here for a vector* $\mathbf{y}$ *of the form (2.2)*

$$Q(\mathbf{y}) = \sum_{s=1}^{k} \left[y_{k+s}^1 \exp\{y\}/y_s^1 + \sum_{i=2}^{\infty} y_{k+s}^i/y_s^i \right].$$

Indeed, $Q_t H(Q_t) \leq const$ by hypothesis. Also

$$\sum_{i=1}^{\infty} \sum_{j=1}^{k} q_{k+j}^i(t) \geq \sum_{i=1}^{k} \theta^{(t-1)k+i} \geq kc, \quad t \geq 1.$$

Hence $r_t \leq const/kc < \infty$. Which implies that (2.7) follows from (1.6).

Note that if $\lim_{x \to \infty} xH(x) = H$, then

$$\frac{1}{n} \sum_{i=1}^{n} r_i \to H \int_{R_{\infty}^+} \frac{d\pi(\mathbf{Y}^0, \mathbf{y})}{\sum_{i=1}^{\infty} \sum_{j=1}^{k} y_{k+j}^i}.$$

As mentioned, the total productive capacity of this industry unboundedly increases as time goes on. More precisely, we have the following statement.

Lemma 2.1. *The total productive capacity Q_t of the industry goes to infinity with probability one as $t \to \infty$.*

The lemma is proved in the Appendix.

Now let us study the mortality of firms in this competitive environment.

Theorem 2.2. *If $\epsilon > 0$, then every firm dies in a finite random time with probability one.*

The proof is given in the Appendix. The argument exploits the fact that the total productive capacity of the industry grows without bound, essentially due to the increasing capital efficiency embodied – in probability – in the new capital vintages, which implies that every firm with a fixed capital per unit of output starts shrinking from a finite random time with probability one.

Having shown the unbounded increase of productive capacity as time goes on, let us now characterize its rate of growth.

Theorem 2.3. *With probability one $\exp\{-\alpha t\}Q_t \to \infty$ as $t \to \infty$ for every $\alpha < E\xi$. Moreover, if*

$$\lim_{x \to \infty} H(x)x = 0, \tag{2.8}$$

then with probability one $\exp\{-\alpha t\}Q_t \to 0$ as $t \to \infty$ for every $\alpha > E\xi$.

The theorem is proved in the Appendix.

Remark 2.1. *The same result obtains if, instead of (2.8), we require that*

$$\limsup_{x \to \infty} H(x)x < d\frac{kvca}{\lambda b}. \tag{2.9}$$

Now, if for a positive number H a demand function decreases as H/x for $x \to \infty$, then, keeping all other parameters of the model involved in the right hand side of (2.9) fixed, one can ensure (2.9) just increasing k. Thus, for such demand functions the second statement of Theorem 2.3 always holds true if the number of newcoming firms is large enough.

Thus, we have showed that the productive capacity of the industry always grows faster than $\exp\{t\alpha\}$ for every $\alpha < E\xi$. If, additionally, the demand function declines fast enough (see (2.8) or (2.9)), then the productive capacity always grows slower than $\exp\{t\alpha\}$ for every $\alpha > E\xi$. Consequently, *the threshold value $E\xi$ is the only candidate for the growth rate in the class of exponential functions of time.* This growth is entirely due to the increasing efficiency of newcoming firms, and is not dependent upon the investment mechanism employed in the model. Interestingly, one is not able to prove that $\exp\{-tE\xi\}Q_t$ converges to a limit as t increases. Indeed, here we are facing with a *variety of growth regimes.* Each of them is determined probabilistically by the development path (i.e. also a particular "technological trajectory") and is deviating from the main trend, $\exp\{tE\xi\}$, by a value vanishing as $t \to \infty$ faster than $\exp\{-t\beta\}$ for every $\beta > 0$. Hence, *these deviations are not detectable if we restrict ourselves to the class of exponential functions of time.* To understand why this happens, let us consider the asymptotic behavior of the value V_t giving the lower bound for the total productive capacity since $Q_{t+1} \geq V_t$.

The random variable V_t is a product of the two other ones: $\exp\{A_t\}$ and Θ^t. The latter, Θ^t, does not contribute to the growth rate since its distribution does not depend on t, being a convolution of k copies of θ/ζ. Hence, let us focus on A_t. We have that

$$A_t = \sum_{i=0}^{t} \xi^i = (t+1)E\xi + \sum_{i=0}^{t} \xi_*^i,$$

where $\xi_*^i = \xi^i - E\xi^i$, $i \geq 0$. The law of iterated logarithm (see Loève (1955), p. 260) implies that

$$P\left\{\limsup_{t\to\infty} \frac{|\sum_{i=0}^{t}\xi_*^i|}{\sqrt{2D\xi(t+1)\ln\ln D\xi(t+1)}} = 1\right\} = 1,$$

taking into account that the random variables ξ and $\xi - E\xi$ have the same variance. Consequently, there are subsequencies t_n^+, $n \geq 1$, and t_n^-, $n \geq 1$, such that with probability one

$$\lim_{n\to\infty} \frac{\sum_{i=0}^{t_n^+}\xi_*^i}{\sqrt{2D\xi(t_n^+ + 1)\ln\ln D\xi(t_n^+ + 1)}} = 1$$

and

$$\lim_{n\to\infty} \frac{\sum_{i=0}^{t_n^-}\xi_*^i}{\sqrt{2D\xi(t_n^- + 1)\ln\ln D\xi(t_n^- + 1)}} = -1.$$

Consequently, as $n \to \infty$

$$\exp\{A_{t_n^+} - (t_n^+ + 1)E\xi\} \sim \exp\left\{\sqrt{2D\xi(t_n^+ + 1)\ln\ln D\xi(t_n^+ + 1)}\right\} \tag{2.10}$$

and

$$\exp\{A_{t_n^-} - (t_n^- + 1)E\xi\} \sim \exp\left\{-\sqrt{2D\xi(t_n^- + 1)\ln\ln D\xi(t_n^- + 1)}\right\}$$

with probability one. Thus, what remains in $\exp\{A_t\}$ if we remove its main part, $\exp\{(t+1)E\xi\}$, can be converging (along certain sequences) with probability one to both infinity and zero. Hence, the remaining value does not have any definite rate of growth as time goes on. Also, (2.10) shows that there is no hope to find a finite limit for $\exp\{-tE\xi\}Q_t$ as $t \to \infty$. Indeed, since $Q_{t+1} \geq V_t$, by (2.10) we get that with probability one

$$\exp\{-t_n^+ E\xi\}Q_{t_n^+} \geq \exp\{-t_n^+ E\xi\}V_{t_n^+ - 1} \to \infty \quad \text{as} \quad n \to \infty.$$

Hence, we find here a path-dependency property of the model. While we have proved that the threshold value of the rate of growth is exponential, it is history which selects the exact value of such rate.

Remark 2.2. *With the foregoing setting one may easily endogenize the entry rate by making it stochastically dependent on some system variable, e.g. current profitability, without qualitatively affecting the results. Let k be the maximum number of entrants. Fix positive numbers $p_0, p_1, \ldots, p_k$,*

$$\sum_{i=0}^{k} p_i = 1.$$

Let $\Phi(\cdot)$ be a decreasing function mapping $[0, \infty)$ to $[0, 1]$. For example, $\Phi(x) = \exp(-\Phi x)$, $\Phi > 0$. The random variable $\gamma^t(Q_t)$ governing the number of firms that enter the industry at t can be as follows

$$\gamma^t(x) = \begin{cases} 0, & \text{with probability } p_0 \Phi(H(x)), \\ s, & \text{with probability } \frac{p_s}{1-p_0}[1 - p_0 \Phi(H(x))], \end{cases}$$

where $1 \leq s \leq k$. For any deterministic x_t, the random variables $\gamma^t(x_t)$ are assumed to be stochastically independent in t. They also do not depend upon ξ, ζ and θ.

Remark 2.3. *Also death rules can be endogenized in this basic framework. For example, one could make it dependent on the total productive capacity of the industry at each t: that is, a firm is dead and does not participate in the industry evolution thereafter if its productive capacity is less than ϵQ_t, where $\epsilon \in (0, 1)$ denotes some critical threshold value. Somewhat relatedly, as we show in Winter et al. (1997), the model withholds extensions whereby the investment rates depend upon some threshold profit margins.*

2.3   Different time-scales of technological learning

So far one has assumed that production, entry and learning (by entrants) all take place on the same time-scale (i.e. at each "period"). However, the model can be extended to account also for a timing of innovative "events" asynchronous vis-à-vis production and entry. Suppose, for example, that the enlargement of innovative opportunities occurs at a slower pace.

This phenomenon may be formalized in the following way.

Let T_n, $n \geq 0$, be an increasing sequence of positive integers such that $T_0 = 0$ and $T_{n+1} - T_n \geq 1$. Also, let

$$A_{n+1} = A_n + \xi^{n+1}, \quad n \geq 0,$$

and levels of capital per unit of output of all firms coming during the time interval (T_n, T_{n+1}) from the distribution concentrated on $[\exp\{-A_n\}a, \exp\{-A_n\}b]$. So, capital ratios of the k-firms coming at time t are determined as $\exp\{-A_n\}\zeta^i$, $tk+1 \leq i \leq (t+1)k$ provided that $T_n \leq t < T_{n+1}$. Here ξ^n, $n \geq 0$, and ζ^i, $i \geq 1$, are mutually independent collections of realizations of ξ and ζ.

The sequence $T_n, n \geq 0$, characterizes the slower pace of generation of potential innovations as compared to the timing of manufacturing "periods". Hence the main component of the rate of growth of capital productivity for individual entrants and for the whole industry (under some additional assumptions cf. Theorem 2.3 and Remark 2.1) as $t \to \infty$ is determined by the function $\exp\{T^{-1}(t) \cdot E\xi\}$. Here $T^{-1}(\cdot)$ designates an inverse function to $T(\cdot) : n \to T_n$. For example, if $T_n = s \cdot n$ for an integer $s > 1$, then

$$\lim_{t \to \infty} \frac{\exp\{T^{-1}(t) \cdot E\xi\}}{\exp\{\frac{E\xi}{s}t\}} = 1.$$

Similarly, if T_n equals to the integer part of $\exp\{\alpha \cdot n\}$ for a real $\alpha > 0$ (and for sufficiently large n), then

$$\lim_{t \to \infty} t^{-\frac{E\xi}{\alpha}} \exp\{T^{-1}(t) \cdot E\xi\} = 1.$$

Clearly, asynchronous (and slower) paces of expansion of innovative opportunities will imply also slower rates of growth of output of the industry under consideration.

2.4 A computer simulation

To illustrate some quantitative properties of the model, let us consider a computer simulation[6]. The run presented here has the following parametrization: $k = 12$, $v = 1$, $d = 0.3$, $\lambda = 0.6$, $a = 2$, $b = 6$, $c = 0.02$, $h = 0.04$, $\epsilon = 0.5$. The demand function is $H(x) = 4.1667 \exp(-0.1x)$. The random variable ζ is uniformly distributed over $[a, b]$, ξ was uniformly distributed over $[0, 0.01]$, and the capitals of newcoming firms are uniformly distributed over $[c, h]$.

Figures 2.1 and 2.2 present the dynamic of prices. While prices decline to 0 with persistent fluctuations, the total productive capacity grows over time with qualitatively similar fluctuating patterns, whereby the amplitude of fluctuations themselves does not dampen out over time (in fact, in absolute terms, they increase): see Figures 2.3 and 2.4.

---

[6] A set of simulations of this kind has been undertaken based on a program from the Laboratory for Simulation Development (LSD), a package providing an environment for implementation of simulation models developed at the International Institute for Applied Systems Analysis (IIASA). It is publicly available via Internet (see also Valente (1997)). We have tried several runs with the same parametrization (since each 'history' is a particular sample path of the stochastic process defined by the above model) and we also experimented with different parametrizations. Even if we did not perform any more rigorous sensitivity analysis, the qualitative feature of the example which follows hold throughout all the performed experiments.

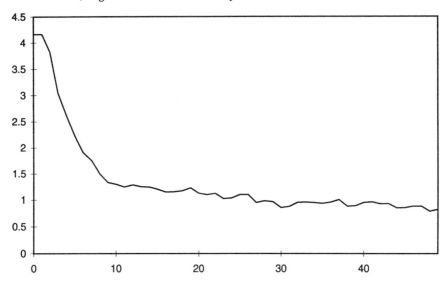

Figure 2.1: Price $H(Q_t)$ for $1 \leq t \leq 50$.

Figure 2.5 illustrates the dynamic of the number of firms in the industry. After an initial period of growth it declines, and then fluctuates around a fixed level. As already noted in Winter et al. (1997), phenomena looking like 'shakeouts' at some point in the early history of an industry appear to be a rather generic property plausibly associated with a changing selection regime. At the start, the 'carrying capacity' of the market exceeds the effective supply. So, in a sense, there is 'room for everyone'. At some point, as total supply increases, competitive conditions become more stringent and market selection rather quickly starts affecting growth and survival of lower-efficiency firms[7]. This change in "market selection regime" is illustrated also by the dynamics of the concentration measures of the industry (see Figure 2.6 for the "equivalent number" associated with the Hirfindhal index of concentration[8]: concentration falls (i.e. the equivalent number increases) up to the "shake out" phase and then increases thereafter). Figures 2.7 and 2.8 provide two snapshots, measured in terms of productive capacity for $t = 50$ and $t = 500$, where firms

---

[7]In many respects, the phenomenon recalls the "density dependent selection" emphasized in "organizational ecology" models (cf. among others Hannan and Freeman (1989) and Carroll (1997)).

[8]Calling $s_i(t)$ the market share of the i-th firm at t, the concentration index

$$H(t) = \sum_{i=1}^{n_t} s_i(t)^2.$$

The "equivalent number" $1/H(t)$ corresponds to the number of firms of equal size which would yield the same value of $H(t)$.

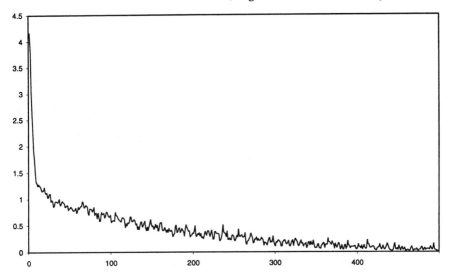

Figure 2.2: Price $H(Q_t)$ for $1 \le t \le 500$.

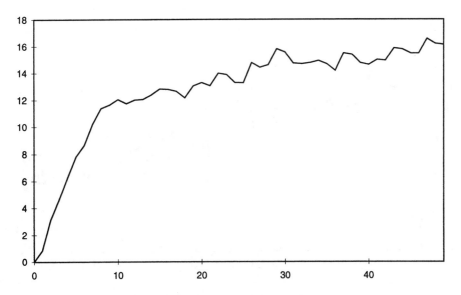

Figure 2.3: Productive capacity for $1 \le t \le 50$.

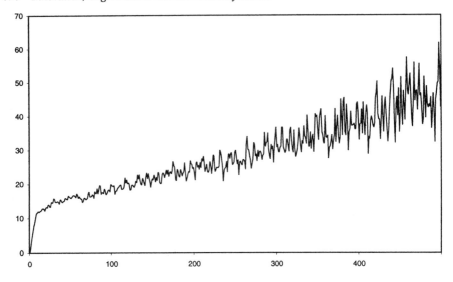

Figure 2.4: Productive capacity for $1 \leq t \leq 500$.

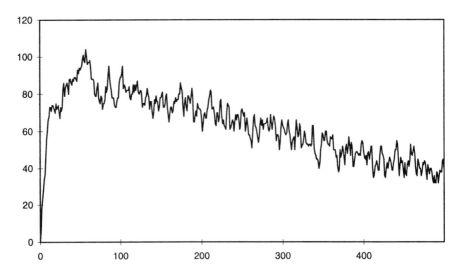

Figure 2.5: Total number of firms $0 \leq t \leq 500$.

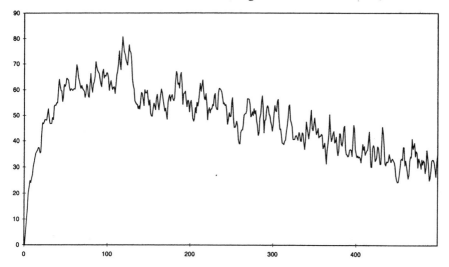

Figure 2.6: Equivalent number of firms from the Hirfindhal index $1 \leq t \leq 500$.

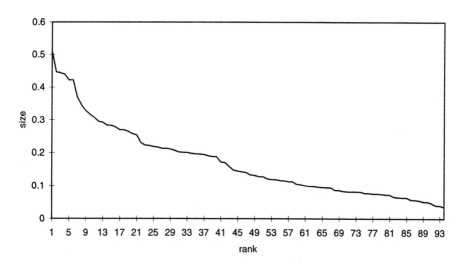

Figure 2.7: Size distribution for $t = 50$.

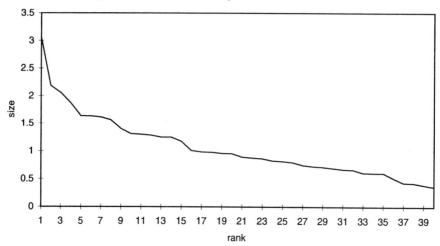

Figure 2.8: Size distribution for $t = 500$.

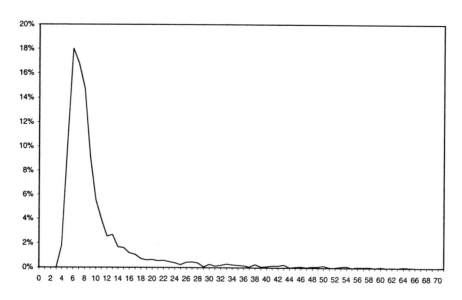

Figure 2.9: Life time distribution of firms for $1 \leq t \leq 500$.

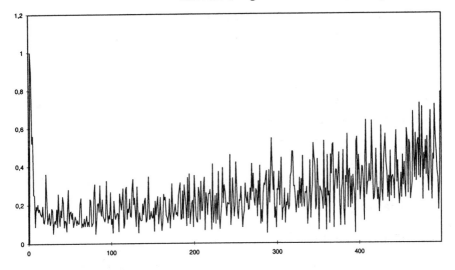

Figure 2.10: Turbulence index for $1 \leq t \leq 499$.

are ranked according to their size. What is observed here is something rather close to the Pareto law (see, for example, Ijiri and Simon (1974))[9]. Figure 2.9 provides with the life time distribution of firms for $1 \leq t \leq 500$ which died before $t = 500$. Life time here means the number of production cycles the firm performs before it dies. (So for example, in Figure 2.9, around 18% of all firms which where born and died before $t = 500$, did die when they where 6-periods old, etc.) Again, the mortality patterns appear to be quite in tune with the evidence, with high mortality rates shortly after birth and a (relative thin) tail of firms with much higher longevity (more on this type of evidence in Geroski (1995), Baldwin (1995), Hannan and Freeman (1989), and Carroll (1997)). As known, this survival patterns are sometimes interpreted – especially in the "organizational ecology" perspective – as the outcome of the differential adaptation of subsets of firms in the population. Notwithstanding the likely importance of the latter phenomena, our results here seem to suggest that a distribution of mortality rates which peaks in the early infancy, with a long but thin tale of old survivers might be a rather generic property of a large class of evolutionary processes characterized by heterogenous entry and market selection (cf. also the simulation results in Winter et al. (1997))[10].

Finally, Figure 2.10 vividly illustrates the evolutionary proposition that whatever per-

---

[9]Namely, in one of its versions, for a sample of firms ranked according to their size, the size s and the rank r of a firm are related in the following manner $sr^\beta = A$, where β and A are positive constants.

[10]*A fortiori*, one should expect this property to apply also to those circumstances wherein also incumbents are allowed to learn, as in a forthcoming model by the authors, currently in progress.

sistent regularity emerges in the aggregate, that is likely to be the collective outcome of an ever-lasting microeconomic turbulence. Define a "turbulence index"

$$T(t) = \sum_{i=1}^{n_t} |s_i(t) - s_i(t+1)| + \sum_{j=1}^{k} \exp\{A_t\}\theta^{tk+j}/\zeta^{tk+j}.$$

That is, the sum of the absolute values in the changes of market shares from one period to the next (including gross entry at t). As Figure 2.10 shows, market turbulence persists – and, if anything tends to increase, throughout the history of the industry.

3   An alternative dynamic setting: increasing productivity of labor

3.1   Main assumptions

Now we turn to symmetric opposite assumptions compared to the model above and assume that learning concerns only labor productivity[11]. As above, we have an industry evolving in discrete time $t = 0, 1, \ldots$. At $t = 0$ there are no firms ready to manufacture, but k firms come to the industry. They will start producing at $t = 1$. At time $t \geq 1$ the industry consists of n_t firms which are involved in manufacturing and new firms that enter at t and will participate in the production process from $t + 1$ on. As in the earlier version of the model we have uniformly for the whole industry:

   v - price per unit of physical capital, $v > 0$,

   d - depreciation rate, $0 < d \leq 1$,

   C - capital per unit of output, $C > 0$.

   Here, however, the competitiveness of any firm in the industry is determined by its variable costs per unit of output. Let us designate it by m_i for the i-th firm. *In this competitive environment only newcomers learn how to improve (in probability) the productivity of labor.* As time goes on the lowest variable costs present in the industry decreases. In particular, we have the following stochastic mechanism defined endogenously.

   Consider a random variable ξ with positive mean $E\xi$ and finite variance $D\xi$. Set ζ for a random variable distributed over $[a,b]$, $0 < a < b < \infty$. For each time instant $t \geq 0$ we allow for the industry to have $k \geq 1$ new firms whose variable costs are randomly determined as $\exp\{-A_t\}\zeta^i$, $tk+1 \leq i \leq (t+1)k$. Here $A_{t+1} = A_t + \xi^{t+1}$, $t \geq 0$, $A_0 = \xi^0$. Also, ξ^t, $t \geq 0$, and ζ^i, $i \geq 1$, are mutually independent collections of realizations of ξ and ζ. One sees that all variable costs feasible for newcomers at time t belong to $[\exp\{-A_t\}a, \exp\{-A_t\}b]$.

---

[11] An assumption, which together with the constancy of capital/output ratios, seems nearer the empirical evidence.

Their distribution over this interval is governed by a realization of $\exp\{-A_t\}\zeta$. Thus A_t characterizes in a probabilistic manner the highest productivity of labor attainable by newcomers in the industry at time t.

Alike in the model above there is a decreasing continuous demand function $p = H(q)$, mapping $[0, \infty)$ in $[0, H(0)]$ such that $H(0) < \infty$ and $H(q) \to 0$ as $q \to \infty$.

Set Q_t^i for the productive capacity of the i-th firm and m_i for its variable costs. Then

$$Q_t = \sum_{i=1}^{n_t} Q_t^i, \quad t \geq 1, \quad Q_0 = 0,$$

is the total productive capacity involved in manufacturing at t. The gross profit per unit of output at t for the i-th firm is obviously $H(Q_t) - m_i$. Its total gross investment per unit of capital is $\lambda \max[H(Q_t) - m_i, 0]/vC$. As above, the constant λ captures the share of the gross profit which is re-invested.

For each value of variable costs generated at t we shall allow a single entrant. The initial capitals of entrants are independent realizations θ^i, $i \geq 1$, of a random variable θ distributed over $[c, h]$, $0 < c < h < \infty$. It is assumed that the realizations of ξ, ζ and θ are mutually independent random variables.

Again, as above, the death mechanism implies that a firm is dead at time t and does not participate in manufacturing from $t + 1$ on if its capital at t is less than ϵc, $\epsilon \in (0, 1]$. The situation without mortality corresponds to the limit case when $\epsilon = 0$.

3.2   A dynamic balance equation for industry evolution

Consider a firm i that is manufacturing at time t. Our investment rule implies that at the end of this production period its capital reads

$$Q_t^i C \left\{ 1 - d + \frac{\lambda}{vC} \max[H(Q_t) - m_i, 0] \right\}.$$

If this value does not drop below the death threshold ϵc, the firm continues to manufacture at $t + 1$. Otherwise it dies.[12] Hence,

$$Q_{t+1}^i = Q_t^i \left\{ 1 - d + \frac{\lambda}{vC} \max[H(Q_t) - m_i, 0] \right\} \chi_{Q_t^i\{1-d+\frac{\lambda}{vC}\max[H(Q_t)-m_i,0]\}\geq\epsilon c/C}, \quad (3.1)$$

where $\chi_{Q_t^i\{1-d+\frac{\lambda}{vC}\max[H(Q_t)-m_i,0]\}\geq\epsilon c/C}$ is the indicator function of the event that the firm continues to manufacture given the above death rule and the total productive capacity of the industry involved in manufacturing.

---

[12] In a possibly more realistic setting one could add a sort of bankruptcy rule stating that firms die, even when their size is greater than ec , if their gross profits are negative (i.e. $[H(Q_t) - m_i] < 0$). However, this modification would not qualitatively change the results that follow: rather it would simply affect death rates of 'uncompetitive' firms.

This equation describes the evolution of a single firm in business. In analogy with the formalization of the foregoing section, let us proceed to a dynamic representation of the model that reserves room for all feasible development paths of the industry.

For the space R_∞ introduced in section 2, define an automorphism $\mathbf{D}(\cdot)$ on R_∞ such that

$$\mathbf{D}(\mathbf{q}) = \mathbf{D}^1(\mathbf{q}) \otimes \left[\bigotimes_{i=2}^{\infty} \mathbf{D}^i(\mathbf{q}) \right],$$

with $\mathbf{D}^1(\cdot):\ R_\infty \mapsto R \otimes R_1 \otimes R_2$ and $\mathbf{D}^i(\cdot):\ R_\infty \mapsto R_i,\ i \geq 3$. Set

$$D_1^1(\mathbf{q}) = q, \quad D_s^1(\mathbf{q}) = 0, \ 2 \leq s \leq 2k+1, \quad D_{2k+j+1}^1(\mathbf{q}) = q_j^1 \exp\{-q\} \chi_{A_j^1(\mathbf{q})},$$

$$D_{3k+j+1}^1(\mathbf{q}) = \left\{ q_{k+j}^1 \left[1 - d + \frac{\lambda}{vC} \max \left[H \left(\sum_{p=1}^{\infty} \sum_{s=1}^{k} q_{k+s}^p \right) - q_j^1 \exp\{-q\}, 0 \right] \right\} \chi_{A_j^1(\mathbf{q})},$$

$$D_j^i(\mathbf{q}) = q_j^i \chi_{A_j^i(\mathbf{q})}, \quad D_{k+j}^i(\mathbf{q}) = q_{k+j}^i \left\{ 1 - d + \frac{\lambda}{vC} \max \left[H \left(\sum_{p=1}^{\infty} \sum_{s=1}^{k} q_{k+s}^p \right) - q_j^i, 0 \right] \right\} \chi_{A_j^i(\mathbf{q})},$$

where $1 \leq j \leq k,\ i \geq 2$, $A_j^1(\mathbf{q})$ designates the relation

$$q_{k+j}^1 \left\{ 1 - d + \frac{\lambda}{vC} \max \left[H \left(\sum_{p=1}^{\infty} \sum_{s=1}^{k} q_{k+s}^p \right) - q_j^1 \exp\{-q\}, 0 \right] \right\} \geq \epsilon c / C$$

and $A_j^i(\mathbf{q})$ stands for the relation

$$q_{k+j}^i \left\{ 1 - d + \frac{\lambda C}{v} \max \left[H \left(\sum_{p=1}^{\infty} \sum_{s=1}^{k} q_{k+s}^p \right) - q_j^i, 0 \right] \right\} \geq \epsilon c / C.$$

We restrict ourselves to vectors $\mathbf{q}$ defined by (2.2) belonging to

$$R_\infty^+ = [0, \infty) \otimes \left[\bigotimes_{i=1}^{\infty} R_i^+ \right]$$

and set $H(\infty) = 0$ for the case when the iterated sum is infinite.

The conceptual interpretation of the automorphism is very similar to the one given earlier on. The $2k$ boxes contain data concerning cohorts, that is groups of firms which were born simultaneously. The only exception is the first box containing two cohorts and additionally (its first coordinate) the value capturing the highest productivity of labor attainable in the industry. In each cohort the first k coordinates are the variable costs and the last k coordinates represent productive capacities of corresponding firms. The adjustment rule for productive capacities is the same as in (3.1). (Again, the indicators prevent from carring over the data related dead firms.) The relation $A_j^i(\mathbf{q})$ means that a firm which is placed at the j-th position of the i-th cohort continues to manufacture given the state of the industry $\mathbf{q}$.

Define infinite dimensional random vectors $\mathbf{Y}^t$, $t \geq 0$, setting

$$Y_1^t = \xi^t, \ \ Y_{i+1}^t = \zeta^{tk+i}, \ \ Y_{k+i+1}^t = \theta^{tk+i}, \ \ i = 1, 2, \ldots, k. \ \ Y_j^t = 0 \ \ j \geq 2k+2.$$

The evolution of the industry is as follows

$$\mathbf{q}(t+1) = \mathbf{D}(\mathbf{q}(t)) + \mathbf{Y}^{t+1}, \ t \geq 0, \ \ \mathbf{q}(0) = \mathbf{Y}^0, \tag{3.2}$$

Since $\mathbf{Y}^t$ are independent in t, this expression defines a Markov process on R_∞^+. Moreover, it is homogeneous in time since the deterministic operator $\mathbf{D}(\cdot)$ as well as the distribution of $\mathbf{Y}^t$ do not depend on time.

This phase space is formed by the value characterizing the highest productivity which is potentially attainable so far in the industry, variable costs and productive capacities of all firms that stay alive.

3.3 Long run behavior of the industry

As above, Doeblin's condition holds here if we set $\phi(A) = P\{\mathbf{Y}^* \in A \otimes A_1\}$ for a set A given by (2.4). Here $\mathbf{Y}^*$ designates a $(2k+1)$-dimensional vector whose coordinates coincide with first $2k+1$ coordinates of a generic vector $\mathbf{Y}$ having the same distribution as $\mathbf{Y}^t$, $t \geq 0$. The following result establishes the ergodicity of process (3.1).

Theorem 3.1. *For every set A given by (2.4) with probability one*

$$\frac{1}{n} \sum_{t=1}^{n} p^t(\mathbf{Y}^0, A) \to \pi(\mathbf{Y}^0, A) \tag{3.3}$$

as $n \to \infty$. Here $\pi(\mathbf{Y}^0, \cdot)$ is a stochastic probability measure (since it depends on $\mathbf{Y}^0$), being $\pi_\mathcal{L}(\cdot)$ for an elementary outcome $\omega \in \Omega$ as long as $\mathbf{Y}^0$ belongs for this elementary outcome to an ergodic set $\mathcal{L}$. Moreover, $p^t(\cdot, \cdot)$ designates the transition probability in t steps of process (3.2).

The implications of this theorem in terms of path-dependency (or lack of it) are identical to those discussed above with reference to Theorem 2.1.

Theorem 3.1 implies that for every uniformly bounded characteristic of the industry its time averages converge with probability one to a limit which is a deterministic function of the initial state in the sense given above.

Let us now show that the total productive capacity of the industry is uniformly bounded. Since the minimal size of a firm is bounded by the death threshold, this implies uniform boundedness of the total number of firms in business (if $\epsilon > 0$). Hence, we shall be able to derive relations similar to those given in Winter et al. (1997) on convergence of time averages regarding some important characteristics of the industry.

Set $\bar{Q} = H^{-1}(dvC/2\lambda)$ and $\hat{Q} = \max(\bar{Q}, 2kh/Cd)$, where $H^{-1}(\cdot)$ designates the inverse function.

Lemma 3.1. *With certainty $Q_t \leq Q_*$ for $t \geq 1$, where $Q_* = \hat{Q}[1 + \lambda H(0)/vC] + kh/C$.*

Proof. Notice that $Q_1 \leq kh/C \leq Q_*$. Equations (3.1) and the assumption concerning the entry process imply that

$$Q_{t+1} \leq Q_t \left[1 - d + \frac{\lambda}{vC}H(Q_t)\right] + \frac{kh}{C}, \quad t \geq 1.$$

If $Q_t \geq \hat{Q}$ for some $t \geq 1$, we get that $Q_{t+1} \leq \hat{Q}$. Otherwise, if $Q_t < \hat{Q}$,

$$Q_{t+1} \leq Q_t \left[1 + \frac{\lambda}{vC}H(Q_t)\right] + \frac{kh}{C} < \hat{Q}\left[1 + \frac{\lambda}{vC}H(0)\right] + \frac{kh}{C}.$$

The lemma is proved.

As a simple consequence of Theorem 3.1 and Lemma 3.1 we have the following result.

Corollary 3.1. *With probability one*

$$\frac{1}{n}\sum_{t=1}^{n} Q_t \to \int_{\tilde{R}_+^\infty} \sum_{i=1}^\infty \sum_{p=1}^k y_{k+p}^i \, d\pi(\mathbf{Y}^0, \mathbf{y})$$

and, if $\epsilon > 0$,

$$\frac{1}{n}\sum_{t=1}^{n} \nu_t \to \int_{\tilde{R}_+^\infty} \sum_{i=1}^\infty \sum_{p=1}^k \chi_{A_p^i(\mathbf{y})} \, d\pi(\mathbf{Y}^0, \mathbf{y})$$

as $n \to \infty$. Here ν_t designates the number of firms in business at t. Also, for a vector $\mathbf{q}$ given by (2.2)

$$\tilde{R}_+^\infty = \left\{\mathbf{q} \in R_+^\infty : \sum_{i=1}^\infty \sum_{p=1}^k q_{k+p}^i \leq Q_*\right\}.$$

The relation $A_p^i(\mathbf{y})$ is defined as above.

Indeed, the infinite sum involved in the first limit is bounded by Q_* by Lemma 3.1. The sum involved in the second limit does not exceed $CQ_*/\epsilon c < \infty$ if $\epsilon > 0$.

Let us turn to the death process.

Theorem 3.2. *If $\epsilon > 0$, then each firm dies in a finite random time with probability one.*

The proof is given in the Appendix. The intuition is the following.

For simplicity let $\epsilon < 1$. (If $\epsilon = 1$, we need a more complicated argument.) Each firm comes with a capital that exceeds c. If it dies, at the moment when this happens its capital does not exceed ϵc. Since firms with lower variable costs per unit of output have higher investment rates, a notional firm that lives infinitely long would shrink at least ϵ times during the life time of a generic firm characterized by the lowest variable costs per unit of output at some particular time (which nonetheless dies in a finite time). Consequently, to prove that no firm can live infinitely long, it is enough to show that:

a) the capital of every alive firm is bounded from above by a constant;

b) for every level of variable costs per unit of output there is an infinite chain of firms with lower variable costs that are coming and dying one after another.

The capital of an alive firm is bounded from above by the total capital of the industry which, in turn, is bounded with certainty. Thus, a) holds. The capital of an alive firm is bounded from below by the death threshold and the total capital of the industry is bounded with certainty. Hence the total number of alive firms is bounded with certainty. Consequently, starting from a finite random time τ every newcoming firm dies in a finite time. According to the postulated learning rule, for every given level of variable costs per unit of output, all newcoming firms have lower variable costs starting from a finite random time τ'. Thus, from $\max(\tau, \tau')$ onward we have the chain required by b).

Interestingly, in this model the total productive capacity can be indefinitely growing if we drop the assumption that $\lim_{x\to\infty} H(x) = 0$. Namely, let $\lim_{x\to\infty} H(x) = H$ and $\lambda H/vC > d$. Then every firm whose variable costs are less than $H - vCd/\lambda$ will unboundedly grow. Hence, starting from a finite random time with probability one every newcomer will never die, but rather unboundedly grow. The intuition behind this property is the following. As $H(x)$ approaches its asymptotic value, demand elasticities grow and so does the "carring capacity" of the market. Correspondingly, selective presures get weaker. Since output prices have a positive lower bound, if gross margin are high enough (that is if variable costs are low enough) as to sustain positive net investments, then firms which fulfill these conditions will indefinitely survive (and indeed grow), irrespectively of the fact that an infinite number of even more efficient firms will enter thereafter. One will still observe a dynamic on market shares (with all firms having eventually their shares tending to zero), but given an infinitely expanding market, the number of firms will also be allowed to infinitely grow, and mortality will cease to operate as a selection device. Moreover, the total productive capacity of the economy will also grow in the foregoing circumstances faster than γ^t as $t \to \infty$ for every $0 < \gamma < 1 - d + \lambda H/vC$ but slower than $(1 - d + \lambda H/vC)^t$. In these circumstances, $(1 - d + \lambda H/vC)^t$ establishes the upper bound of all feasible rates of growth, with history selecting among them. Hence, some (bounded) path-dependency property of industrial dynamics reappears, as soon as the size of the market is allowed to endlessly grow.

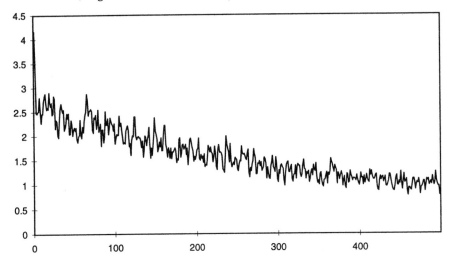

Figure 3.1: Price $H(Q_t)$ for $1 \leq t \leq 500$.

3.4   A numerical run of the model

Let us turn again to an illustration with a computer simulation (for details cf. footnote 6, above).

The run presented here has the following parametrization: $k = 12$, $v = 1$, $C = 2$, $d = 0.3$, $\lambda = 0.6$, $\epsilon = 0.5$. The demand function is $H(x) = 4.1667 \exp(-0.1x)$. The random variable ζ is uniformly distributed over $[2,6]$; ξ is uniformly distributed over $[0, 0.01]$, and the capitals of newcoming firms are uniformly distributed over $[0.02, 0.04]$. Figures 3.1 and 3.2 present the price dynamics, while Figures 3.3 and 3.4 show for the same time interval the dynamics of the total productive capacity. The evolution of the total number of firms is shown in Figures 3.5 and 3.6, with Figures 3.7 and 3.8 depicting size distributions at $t = 50$ and $t = 500$. (For prices, productive capacity and number of firms we report also longer simulation runs, with $t = 1000$, for a clearer illustration of the long term properties toward which the system tends to converge.) Figure 3.9 provides the life time distribution for firms that die before $t = 500$.

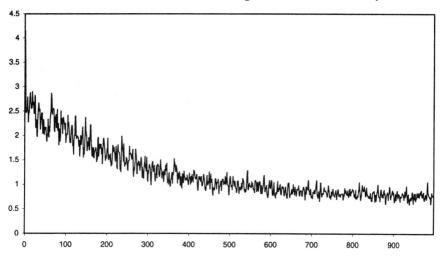

Figure 3.2: Price $H(Q_t)$ for $1 \leq t \leq 1000$.

Many qualitative properties of the dynamics are similar to those obtained earlier. For example, persistent fluctuations of prices and production capacities and persistent market share turbulence (Figure 3.10) are a robust feature of both set-ups. And so are Pareto-type size distributions and skewed age profiles. Interestingly, however, no "shake-out" seems to occur in the number of firms at some point in its infancy. In this set-up, notwithstanding the property – given appropriate demand conditions – that both productive capacity of the industry and the number of firms have upper bounds, the industry seems to approach them without any major structural discontinuities[13] with concentration falling in the long term (Figure 3.11).

4 Modeling learning on both capital and labour efficiencies

The two foregoing models may also be combined to account for those (empirically more plausible) circumstances whereby entrants are allowed to innovate, in probability, will respect to both capital and labour efficiencies. In order to define this set-up one needs four random variables: ξ_C, ξ_L, ζ_C, distributed over $[a_C, b_C]$, and ζ_L, distributed over $[a_L, b_L]$. Here $E\xi_i > 0$, $D\xi_i < \infty$, and $0 < a_i < b_i < \infty$, $i = C, L$.

Set for $t \geq 0$

$$A_{t+1}^{(C)} = A_t^{(C)} + \xi_C^{t+1}, \quad A_0^{(C)} = 0, \quad \text{and} \quad A_{t+1}^{(L)} = A_t^{(L)} + \xi_L^{t+1}, \quad A_0^{(L)} = 0.$$

---

[13]A similar profile in the evolution of the number of firms is also obtained, under somewhat similar *Schumpeter Mark I* regimes of learning, in Dosi et al. (1995).

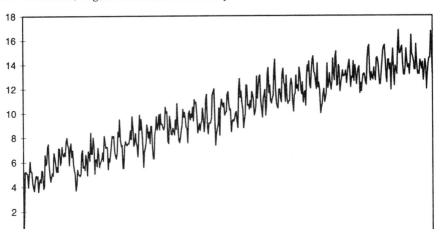

Figure 3.3: Total productive capacity Q_t for $1 \leq t \leq 500$.

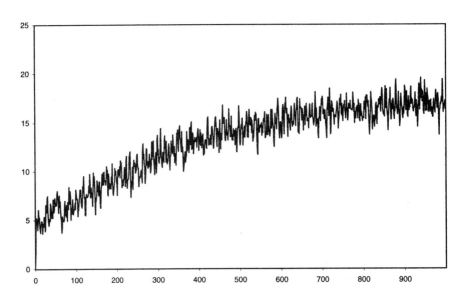

Figure 3.4: Total productive capacity Q_t for $1 \leq t \leq 1000$.

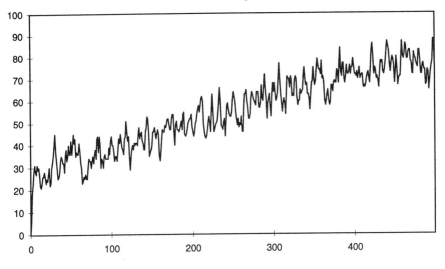

Figure 3.5: Total number of firms $0 \le t \le 500$.

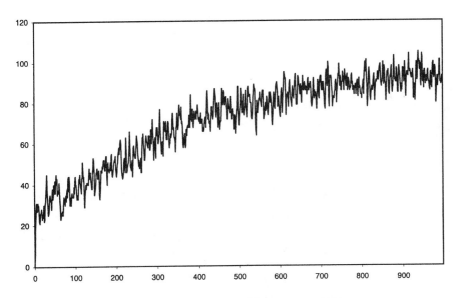

Figure 3.6: Total number of firms $0 \le t \le 1000$.

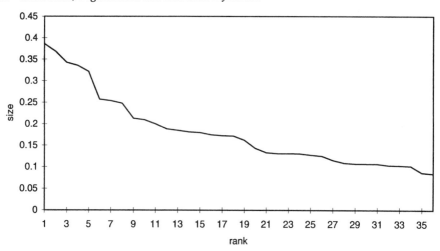

Figure 3.7: Size distribution at $t = 50$.

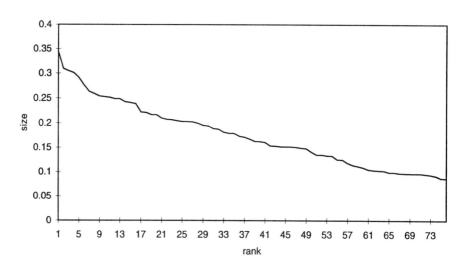

Figure 3.8: Size distribution at $t = 500$.

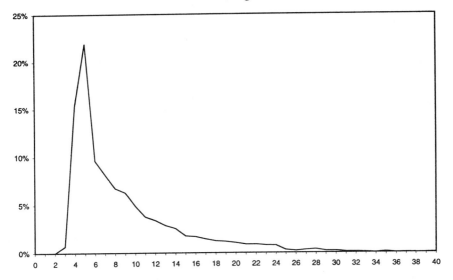

Figure 3.9: Life time distribution for $1 \leq t \leq 500$.

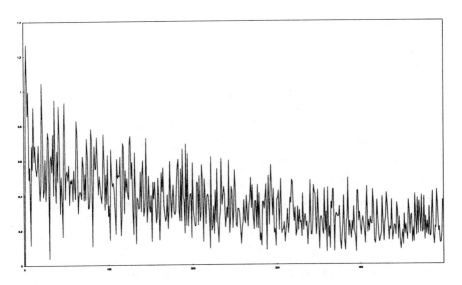

Figure 3.10: Turbulence index for $1 \leq t \leq 499$.

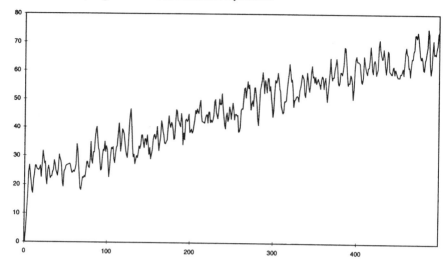

Figure 3.11: Equivalent number of firms from the Hirfindhal index for $1 \leq t \leq 500$.

Allowing for $k \geq 1$ newcomers at each time $t \geq 0$, define their capital ratios and variable costs as $\exp\{-A_t^{(C)}\}\zeta_C^i$ and $\exp\{-A_t^{(L)}\}\zeta_L^i$, $tk+1 \leq i \leq (t+1)k$. Here ζ_i^t, $t \geq 0$, $i = C, L$, and ζ_i^j, $j \geq 1$, $i = C, L$, are independent (in all indexes) realizations of the corresponding random variables.

For a firm i (whose capital ratio is a_i and variable costs m_i) manufacturing at time t we have as above

$$Q_{t+1}^i = Q_t^i\Big\{1 - d + \frac{\lambda}{va_i}\max[H(Q_t) - m_i, 0]\Big\}X_{Q_t^i\{1-d+\frac{\lambda}{va_i}\max[H(Q_t)-m_i,0]\}\geq \tau c/a_i}.$$

Interestingly, in this set-up productive capacities of newcomers grow to infinity in the same way as in the model with increasing productivity alone. So unboundedly grows the total productive capacity of the industry. Hence, the limit behavior of this industry turns out to be similar to the growth pattern of an industry where newcomers learn how to improve the productivity of capital alone, as in the first of the foregoing models.

5   Conclusions

In this work we have explored some dynamic properties of industrial dynamics driven by an ever-lasting flow of entrants which might, in probability, be carriers of technological innovations (that is, in our simple model, more efficient techniques of production).

Some properties of the ensuing industrial dynamics appear to be *generic* features of a wide class of evolutionary processes nested into microeconomic heterogeneity and market selection. In particular, a) persistent fluctuations of aggregate variables – such as price, production capacity, total output –; b) turbulence in market shares; and, c) skewed size distributions of firms appear to be robust features of the competitive process, irrespectively of any more detailed characterization of the origins and the bounds upon microeconomic heterogeneity. (In this respect compare the results presented here with Winter et al. (1997).) Other properties – corresponding to other empirically observable regularities – depend, on the contrary, upon more specific characterizations of the ways micro hetero-geneity is generated. That includes whether and how innovations are generated along the history of the industry.

First, and most intuitively, necessary (but not sufficient) condition for the industry to exponentially grow is the persistent enlargement of notional opportunities of innovation. In the foregoing model the process is represented as an endogenous drift in the set of input coefficients stochastically attainable at each time, conditional on the best-practise knowledge already achieved at such a time. It is an 'open-ended' dynamic insofar as, in the limit, there is no bound upon the possibilities of discovery, even if at each time what is attainable is ultimately constrained by what has been learned up to that time.

Second, as just mentioned, such open-endedness in in innovative opportunities is not sufficient to guarantee self-sustained growth. Rather, the latter stems from the interplay between learning opportunities and demand patterns. A significant implication of the foregoing modeling experiments – where, on purpose, we did not allow any exogenous demand drift – is that notionally unbounded dynamic increasing returns may fully exert their impact upon output growth only insofar as they are not limited by the extent of the market, to paraphrase the old *adagio* by Adam Smith. In the set-up with learning about capital efficiency, the market indefinitely grows in real terms because technical progress provides, for its nature, also a corresponding possibility of expansionary investment in productive capacity. Given the hypotheses of that specification of the model, even if the demand curve does not shift (in nominal terms) over time, capital costs of production per unit of output progressively wither away as time goes on, and, as a consequence, the benefits of increasing returns to knowledge accumulation can be fully reaped throughout.

Conversely, this might not be the case with learning occuring only with respect to labour efficiencies. Here, the long-term evolutionary outcomes depend upon the interplay between the shape of the demand curve and the level of fixed capital costs per unit of out-put. The latter obviously set a ceiling to the maximum expansion of production capacity from any t to $t + 1$ for whatever gross margin each firm is able to obtain. Whether such a ceiling to micro growth in any finite time carries over to the long-run *system* properties is, however, a quite different matter. As discussed above, under these circumstances, self-sustained growth of the industry can be attained only if the shape of the demand curve is such as to allow in the long-run an indefinite expansion of total gross surplus and of net investments in production capacity[14].

More generally, as both our analytical results and simulations show, the long-run dynamics of the industry depends also on the interplay between patterns of technological learning and demand conditions (this is a point emphasized also in more static set-ups by Sutton (1998), which turns out to apply even when disposing of any assumption of "rational" consistency amongst microbehaviors).

In the foregoing paper we focused upon a specific archetype of learning dynamics, which – in tune with earlier literature – we called *Schumpeter Mark I*. In such a stylized learning regime, one restricted a positive probability of learning to entrants, with inputs coefficients fixed thereafter for all incumbents. While an obvious violence to a much more messy empirical evidence, this modeling framework allows an easier identification of the properties of that subset of learning processes whereby incumbent knowledge is highly inertial and the dominant source of change is the arrival of new entrepreneurial trials.

Given the formal *Schumpeter Mark I* set-up, we show as our <u>third</u> major conclusion that generally the process of competition and collective growth must be fueled by an unending process of entry and exit, with each individual firm dying with probability one in finite time and, whereby, paraphrasing Geroski, the life of each firm tends to be "nasty, brutish and short" – cf. Geroski (1995) and Geroski and Schwalbach (1991). (The only exception we find is under some rather special demand patterns whereby an infinitely growing number of firms can survive, with non-decreasing absolute size, notwithstanding vanishingly small market shares, given exponentially growing markets).

<u>Fourth</u>, with the open-ended innovative dynamics considered here, the role of history – i.e., more formally, *path-dependence* – more forcefully appears in the account of long-term dynamics. As already noted in Winter et al. (1997), even in a 'closed' world of technological options, the expressions for long-term average statistics for the industry contains a possible dependence upon initial conditions (insofar as more than one ergodic set exists, determining the Markovian structure of industry evolution(s)). Here, however, path-dependency acquires much more straightforward implications. In essence, under all conditions whereby the industry unboundedly grows, what one is able to prove, *in a history-independent fashion*, is that a whole class of exponential functions may fit any pattern generated under these conditions. However, as we show above, path-dependence

---

[14]Clearly, the condition would be more easily met if one allowed some positive drift over time in demand curves themselves (and plausibly also negative drifts for 'shrinking' industries).

essentially affects *which growth rate* turns out to be selected also in the long-term.

Appendix

In the following, we provide the proofs omited in the text.

Lemma 2.1. *The total productive capacity Q_t of the industry goes to infinity with probability one as $t \to \infty$.*

Proof. We have to show that for every $\delta \in (0,1)$ and every positive Q there is a finite time instant $t(\delta, Q)$ such that

$$P\{Q_t \geq Q, \ t \geq t(\delta, Q)\} \geq 1 - \delta. \tag{a1}$$

By the strong law of large numbers (see, for example, Loève (1955), p. 239)

$$A_t = (t+1)[E\xi + o_t^1(1)]. \tag{a2}$$

Here $E\xi$ designates the expected value of ξ. Also, $o_t^1(1) \to 0$ with probability one as $t \to \infty$. Fix a $\delta \in (0,1)$ and a $Q \in (0, \infty)$. Since $o_t^1(1) \to 0$ with probability one, there is a finite time instant $t(\delta)$ such that

$$P\left\{|o_t^1(1)| < \frac{1}{2}E\xi, \ t \geq t(\delta)\right\} \geq 1 - \delta.$$

This implies

$$P\left\{A_t \geq \frac{t+1}{2}E\xi, \ t \geq t(\delta)\right\} \geq 1 - \delta.$$

Hence, capital ratios of firms coming from $t(\delta)$ onward do not exceed $\exp\{-\frac{t+1}{2}E\xi\}b$ with probability $1 - \delta$. Since initial capitals are always larger than c, the total productive capacity $V_t = \exp\{A_t\}\Theta^t$ of all firms coming at $t \geq t(\delta)$, exceeds $\exp\{\frac{t+1}{2}E\xi\}kc/b$ with probability $1 - \delta$. Here

$$\Theta^t = \sum_{i=1}^{k} \theta^{tk+i}/\zeta^{tk+i}.$$

Notice that

$$Q_{t+1} \geq V_t, \ t \geq 0. \tag{a3}$$

Hence,

$$P\left\{Q_t \geq \exp\left\{\frac{t}{2}E\xi\right\}kc/b, \ t \geq t(\delta)\right\} \geq 1 - \delta.$$

Set $t_Q = \min t :\ \exp\{\frac{t}{2}E\xi\}kc/b \geq Q$. For $t(\delta, Q) = \max[t(\delta), t_Q]$ inequality (a1) holds true.

The lemma is proved.

Theorem 2.2. *If $\epsilon > 0$, then every firm dies in a finite random time with probability one.*

Proof. Assume on the contrary that there is a firm surviving infinitely long with positive probability. Designating by q_t its capital at time t, we have

$$P\{q_t \geq \epsilon c, \ t \geq t_0\} > \delta > 0. \tag{a4}$$

Here $t_0 \geq 0$ stands for the time instant when the firm came to the industry. Also, take into account here that a firm stays alive as long as its capital does not drop below the death threshold ϵc.

Let $Q = \min x > 0 : \ 1 - d + \lambda H(x)/va_* \leq 1 - d/2$, where a_* designates the capital per unit of output of the firm surviving infinite time. By Lemma 2.1 there is a finite time instant $t(\delta/2, Q)$ such that

$$P\{Q_t \geq Q, \ t \geq t(\delta/2, Q)\} \geq 1 - \delta/2. \tag{a5}$$

For every pair of events $A, B \in \mathcal{F}$

$$P\{A \cap B\} = P\{A\} - P\{A \cap (\Omega \setminus B)\} \geq P\{A\} - P\{\Omega \setminus B\}. \tag{a6}$$

Taking this into account, we have by (a4) and (a5) that

$$P\{Q_t \geq Q, \ q_t \geq \epsilon c, \ t \geq t_1\} \geq P\{Q_t \geq Q, \ t \geq t_1\} - 1 + P\{q_t \geq \epsilon c, \ t \geq t_1\} > \delta/2,$$

where $t_1 = \max[t_0, t(\delta/2, Q)]$. Thus, the event $\{Q_t \geq Q, \ q_t \geq \epsilon c, \ t \geq t_1\}$ occurs with positive probability. But, if it happens, then simultaneously

$$q_{t+1} \leq q_t(1 - d/2) \quad \text{and} \quad q_t \geq \epsilon c$$

for $t \geq t_1$. These inequalities cannot hold simultaneously. Indeed, q_{t_1} is a finite value, namely,

$$q_{t_1} = q_{t_0} \prod_{i=t_0+1}^{t_1-1} \left[1 - d + \frac{\lambda}{v} H(Q_i)/a_*\right].$$

Since $1 - d/2 \in (0, 1)$, the first inequality implies that from t_1 onward the sequence $\{q_t\}$ is exponentially declining. The second inequality assumes that this sequence is uniformly bounded from below by $\epsilon c > 0$. This contradiction shows that there cannot be a firm surviving infinitely long with positive probability.

The theorem is proved.

Theorem 2.3. *With probability one $\exp\{-\alpha t\}Q_t \to \infty$ as $t \to \infty$ for every $\alpha < E\xi$. Moreover, if*

$$\lim_{x \to \infty} H(x)x = 0,$$

then with probability one $\exp\{-\alpha t\}Q_t \to 0$ *as* $t \to \infty$ *for every* $\alpha > E\xi$.

Proof. The first statement holds by (a3). Let us prove the second one. Notice that

$$Q_{t+1} = Q_t\left[1 - d + \frac{\lambda}{v}H(Q_t)\sum_{i=1}^{n_t}Q_t^i/Q_t a_i\right] + V_t - \mathcal{E}_t, \quad t \geq 1. \tag{a7}$$

Recall that a_i stands for the capital per unit of output of the i-th firm. Also, $\mathcal{E}_t \geq 0$ designates the total outflow of productive capacity at t due to mortality of inefficient firms. Dropping $\mathcal{E}_t$ in (a7), we get

$$Q_{t+1} \leq Q_t\left[1 - d + \frac{\lambda}{v}H(Q_t)\sum_{i=1}^{n_t}Q_t^i/Q_t a_i\right] + V_t, \quad t \geq 1.$$

Since $H(\cdot)$ decreases, by (a3) this inequality can be further relaxed

$$Q_{t+1} \leq Q_t\left[1 - d + \frac{\lambda}{v}H(V_{t-1})\sum_{i=1}^{n_t}Q_t^i/Q_t a_i\right] + V_t, \quad t \geq 1. \tag{a8}$$

We have that

$$\sum_{i=1}^{n_t}Q_t^i/Q_t a_i \leq \frac{1}{\min_{i=1,2\ldots,n_t} a_i}, \quad \min_{i=1,2\ldots,n_t} a_i \geq \exp\{-A_{t-1}\}a, \quad V_t \geq \exp\{A_t\}kc/b.$$

Consequently,

$$\sum_{i=1}^{n_t}Q_t^i/Q_t a_i \leq \frac{b}{kca}V_{t-1}.$$

Thus, by (a8), we get

$$Q_{t+1} \leq Q_t\left[1 - d + \frac{\lambda b}{kvca}H(V_{t-1})V_{t-1}\right] + V_t, \quad t \geq 1.$$

By (a2), $V_t \to \infty$ with probability one as $t \to \infty$. Hence, taking into account that $xH(x) \to 0$ as $x \to \infty$, the latter inequality can be rewritten as

$$Q_{t+1} \leq Q_t[1 - d + o_t^2(1)] + V_t, \quad t \geq 1, \tag{a9}$$

where $o_t^2(1) \to 0$ with probability one as $t \to \infty$.

Fix an $\alpha > E\xi$. Setting $X_t = \exp\{-\alpha t\}Q_t$ and $W_t = \exp\{-\alpha(t+1)\}V_t$, we get by (a9) that

$$X_{t+1} \leq \exp\{-\alpha\}X_t[1 - d + o_t^2(1)] + W_t \leq X_t[1 - d + o_t^2(1)] + W_t, \quad t \geq 1. \tag{a10}$$

We have to show that for every $\delta > 0$ and $\sigma \in (0,1)$ there is a finite time instant $t(\delta,\sigma)$ such that

$$P\{X_t \leq \delta, \ t \geq t(\delta,\sigma)\} \geq 1 - \sigma. \tag{a11}$$

Fix some $\delta > 0$ and $\sigma \in (0,1)$. Since $o_t^1(1)$ in (a2) converges to zero with probability one, there is a finite time instant $t_1(\sigma)$ such that

$$P\left\{|o_t^1(1)| \leq \frac{1}{2}(\alpha - E\xi),\ t \geq t_1(\sigma)\right\} \geq 1 - \sigma/2. \tag{a12}$$

Similarly, there is a finite time instant $t_2(\sigma)$ such that

$$P\left\{|o_t^2(1)| \leq \frac{d}{2},\ t \geq t_2(\sigma)\right\} \geq 1 - \sigma/2. \tag{a13}$$

By (a2) and (a12) we conclude that

$$P\left\{W_t \leq \frac{kh}{a}\exp\left\{-\frac{(\alpha - E\xi)(t+1)}{2}\right\},\ t \geq t_1(\sigma)\right\} \geq 1 - \sigma/2. \tag{a14}$$

Thus, setting $t(\sigma) = \max[t_1(\sigma), t_2(\sigma)]$ and taking into account (a10), (a13) and (a14), we get by (a6) that

$$P\left\{X_{t+1} \leq X_t(1 - d/2) + \frac{kh}{a}\exp\left\{-\frac{(\alpha - E\xi)(t+1)}{2}\right\},\ t \geq t(\sigma)\right\} \geq 1 - \sigma,$$

or, equivalently, for every finite $n \geq 1$

$$P\Big\{X_{t+n} \leq X_t(1 - d/2)^n +$$

$$\frac{kh}{a}\exp\left\{-\frac{(\alpha - E\xi)(t+1)}{2}\right\}\sum_{i=0}^{n-1}(1 - d/2)^{n-i-1}\exp\left\{-\frac{(\alpha - E\xi)i}{2}\right\},\ t \geq t(\sigma)\Big\} \geq 1 - \sigma.$$

Since

$$\sum_{i=0}^{n-1}(1 - d/2)^{n-i-1}\exp\left\{-\frac{(\alpha - E\xi)i}{2}\right\} \leq \sum_{i=0}^{n-1}(1 - d/2)^{n-i-1} = \frac{2}{d}[1 - (1 - d/2)^n] < \frac{2}{d},$$

the latter inequality implies that for every finite $n \geq 1$

$$P\left\{X_{t+n} \leq X_t(1 - d/2)^n + \frac{2kh}{ad}\exp\left\{-\frac{(\alpha - E\xi)(t+1)}{2}\right\},\ t \geq t(\sigma)\right\} \geq 1 - \sigma.$$

There is a finite t_δ such that for $t \geq t_\delta$

$$\frac{2kh}{ad}\exp\left\{-\frac{(\alpha - E\xi)(t+1)}{2}\right\} \leq \delta/2.$$

Hence, by the previous inequality we get that for every finite $n \geq 1$

$$P\{X_{t+n} \leq X_t(1 - d/2)^n + \delta/2,\ t \geq t_{\delta,\sigma}\} \geq 1 - \sigma, \tag{a15}$$

where $t_{\delta,\sigma} = \max[t(\sigma), t_\delta]$. By (a7), the random variable $Q_{t_{\delta,\sigma}}$ is finite with certainty. Hence, $X_{t_{\delta,\sigma}}$ is also a finite random variable with certainty. There is a finite number $n_{\delta,\sigma}$ such that

$$P\{X_{t_{\delta,\sigma}}(1 - d/2)^n \leq \delta/2,\ n \geq n_{\delta,\sigma}\} = 1. \tag{a16}$$

Setting $t(\delta, \sigma) = t_{\delta,\sigma} + n_{\delta,\sigma}$, by (a15) and (a16) we get (a11).

The theorem is proved.

Next, let us show that in the version of the model with growing labor productivity each firm dies in a finite random time with probability one.

Theorem 3.2. *If $\epsilon > 0$, then each firm dies in a finite random time with probability one.*

Proof. The death threshold implies that if a firm lives infinitely long, then its capital does not drop below ϵc. Since the total productive capacity of the industry is bounded with certainty, we conclude that starting from a finite random time τ with probability one every newcoming firm dies in a finite time. Indeed, otherwise we would have infinitely many firms living infinitely long. This, by boundness from below of their capitals, would imply that the total productive capacity goes to infinity.

At time $t \geq \tau$ consider two firms: one with capital c_t and variable costs per unit of output m, the other with capital c'_t and variable costs per unit of output m', $m > m'$. Then

$$\frac{c_{t+1}}{c'_{t+1}} = \frac{c_t\left\{1 - d + \frac{\lambda}{vC}\max[H(Q_t) - m, 0]\right\}\chi_{c_t\{1-d+\frac{\lambda}{vC}\max[H(Q_t)-m,0]\}\geq \epsilon c}}{c'_t\left\{1 - d + \frac{\lambda}{vC}\max[H(Q_t) - m', 0]\right\}\chi_{c'_t\{1-d+\frac{\lambda}{vC}\max[H(Q_t)-m',0]\}\geq \epsilon c}}. \tag{a17}$$

Assume that there is a firm living infinitely long with positive probability. Set c_t for its capital at t and m for its variable costs per unit of output. Then

$$P\{c_t \geq \epsilon c, \ t \geq \tau'\} = \delta > 0, \tag{a18}$$

where $\tau' < \tau$ stands for the time instant when it comes to the industry. By (a2) there is a time instant t_1 such that

$$P\{A_t > \frac{t+1}{2}E\xi, \ t \geq t_1\} \geq 1 - \delta/2.$$

Choose t_2 such that $\exp\{-\frac{t+1}{2}E\xi\}h < m$ for $t \geq t_2$. Then with probability exceeding $1 - \delta/2$ every firm coming after $t^* = \max(t_1, t_2)$ has variable costs less than m. Consider a time instant $t \geq \max(t^*, \tau)$. There is a firm coming at t. Set c'_t for its capital and m' for its variable costs. Since we are in the time domain where every entrant dies in a finite time, this new firm dies at a finite time instant $t' > t$ with probability one. Since $m' < m$, by (a17) we get that

$$c_{t'} \leq c_t\frac{c'_{t'}}{c_t} \leq c_t\frac{\epsilon c}{c} \leq \epsilon c_t. \tag{a19}$$

At t' another firm comes to the industry and, again, its variable costs are less than m. Similarly, it dies at t'' and we obtain that $c_{t''} \leq \epsilon c_{t'}$ or $c_{t''} \leq \epsilon^2 c_t$.

Let $\epsilon < 1$. Since $c_t \leq CQ_*$ for $t \geq \tau'$, we conclude that $c_{t_k} \to 0$ as $k \to \infty$ for some sequence of finite time instants t_k, $k \geq 1$, and this occurs with probability at least $1 - \delta/2$.

By (a6) and (a18) we see that with probability at least $\delta/2$ both the sequence c_t, $t \geq \tau$, is bounded from below by $\epsilon c > 0$ and has a subsequence c_{t_k}, $k \geq 1$, converging to zero. This is impossible.

Let $\epsilon = 1$. There are two possibilities, namely first, there is a sequence of finite time instants t_k, $k \geq 1$, such that $\lambda H(Q_{t_k})/vC - m \geq d$, or second, $\lambda H(Q_t)/vC - m < d$ starting from a finite time instant τ'' with probability one.

In the first case by (a17) we see that for every firm coming at some $t_k \geq \max(t^*, \tau)$

$$\frac{c_{t_k+1}}{c'_{t_k+1}} = \frac{c_{t_k}}{c'_{t_k}} \left\{ 1 - \frac{\lambda}{vC} \frac{m - m'}{1 - d + \frac{\lambda}{vC}[H(Q_{t_k}) - m']} \right\} \leq$$

$$\frac{c_{t_k}}{c'_{t_k}} \left\{ 1 - \frac{\lambda}{vC} \frac{m - m'}{1 - d + \frac{\lambda}{vC}[H(0) - m']} \right\} = \frac{c_{t_k}}{c'_{t_k}} r, \tag{a20}$$

where c'_{t_k} stands for the capital and m' for the variable costs of the newcomer. Since we are in the time domain where every entrant dies in a finite time, this firm dies at $t'_1 > t_k$. By (a17) and (a20) we see that

$$\frac{c_{t'_1}}{c'_{t'_1}} \leq \frac{c_{t'_1-1}}{c'_{t'_1-1}} \leq \cdots \leq \frac{c_{t_k+1}}{c'_{t_k+1}} \leq r \frac{c_{t_k}}{c'_{t_k}}.$$

Thus

$$c_{t'_1} \leq r c_{t_k} \frac{c'_{t'_1}}{c'_{t_k}} \leq r c_{t_k} \frac{\epsilon c}{c} \leq r c_{t_k}.$$

By (a19) we conclude that during the life time of any firm coming from $\max(t^*, \tau)$ onward, the firm living infinitely long at the very least does not gain anything in terms of capital stock. But it shrinks r times during the life times of firms coming at $t_k \geq \max(t^*, \tau)$. This occurs with probability not less than $1 - \delta/2$. Thus, with the same probability there is a sequence t'_k, $k \geq 1$, such that $c_{t'_k} \to 0$ as $k \to \infty$. By (a6) and (a18) we conclude that with probability at least $\delta/2$ both the sequence c_t, $t \geq \tau$, is bounded from below by $\epsilon c > 0$ and has a subsequence $c_{t'_k}$, $k \geq 1$, converging to zero. This is impossible.

Now let $\lambda H(Q_t)/vC - m < d$ starting from a finite time instant τ'' with probability one. Hence, from τ'' onward, the total productive capacity evolves in the domain where the notional firm surviving for infinite time shrinks. Consequently, we must have that $\lambda H(Q_t)/vC = d + m + o_t(1)$ where $o_t(1) \to 0$ with probability one as $t \to \infty$. This implies that with probability at least $1 - \delta/2$ every firm coming after $\max(t^*, \tau'')$ will be unboundedly growing (almost as $(1 + m - m')^t$ for $t \to \infty$) in contradiction with the uniform boundness of the total productive capacity.

Thus we have showed that assuming that there is a firm surviving infinitely long with positive probability yields a contradiction.

The theorem is proved.

References

Baldwin, J. R. (1995). *The Dynamics of Industrial Competition.* Cambridge: Cambridge University Press.

Carroll, G. R. (1997). "Long-term Evolutionary Changes in Organizational Populations: Theory, Models and Empirical Findings", *Industrial and Corporate Change,* **6**, pp. 119–143.

Carroll, G. R., and M. T. Hannan (eds.) (1995). *Organizations in Industry.* New York and Oxford: Oxford University Press.

Davis, S. T., J. C. Haltiwanger, and S. Schuh (1996). *Job Creation and Destruction.* Cambridge, Mass.: MIT Press.

Doob, J. L. (1953). *Stochastic Processes.* New York: John Wiley.

Dosi, G. (1988). "Sources, Procedures and Microeconomic Effects of Innovation", *Journal of Economic Literature,* **26**, No. 3, pp. 1120–1171.

Dosi, G., O. Marsili, L. Orsenigo, and R. Salvatore (1995). "Learning, Market Selection and the Evolution of Industrial Structures", *Small Business Economics,* **7**, pp. 411-436.

Dunne, T., M. J. Roberts, and L. Samuelson (1988). "Patterns of Firm Entry and Exit in U.S. Manufacturing Industries", *Rand Journal of Economics,* **19**, pp. 495-515.

Ericson, R., and A. Pakes (1995). "Markov-Perfect Industry Dynamics: A Framework for Empirical Work", *Review of Economic Studies,* **62**, pp. 53-82.

Freeman, C., and L. Soete (1997). *The Economics of Industrial Innovation.* Cambridge, Mass.: MIT Press, third edition.

Geroski, P.A. (1995). "What Do We Know About Entry?", *International Journal of Industrial Organisation,* **13**, pp. 421–440.

Geroski, P.A., and J. Schwalbach (eds.) (1991). *Entry and Market Contestability. An International Comparison.* Oxford: Basil Blackwell.

Hannan, M. T., and J. Freeman (1989). *Organizational Ecology.* Cambridge, Mass.: Harvard University Press.

Hopenhayn, H. A. (1992). "Entry, Exit and Firm Dynamics in Long Run Equilibrium", *Econometrica*, **60**, pp. 1127-1150.

Ijiri, Y. and H. A. Simon (1974). "Interpretations of Departures from the Pareto Curve Firm – Size Distributions", *Journal of Political Economy*, **82**, pp. 315-331.

Jovanovic, B. (1982). "Selection and Evolution of Industry", *Econometrica*, **50**, pp. 649-670.

Loève, M. (1955). *Probability Theory.* New York: D. van Nostrand Company.

Malerba, F., and L. Orsenigo (1995). "Schumpeterian Patterns of Innovation", *Cambridge Journal of Economics*, **19**, No.1, pp. 47–65.

Schumpeter, J. A. (1934). *Theory of Economic Development: an Inquiry into Profits, Capital, Interest and the Business Cycle.* Cambridge, Mass.: Harvard University Press.

Sutton, J. (1998). *Technology and Market Structure.* Cambridge, Mass.: MIT Press.

Valente, M. (1997). *Laboratory for Simulation Development. User Manual*, Interim Report IR-97-020/May 1997, International Institute for Applied Systems Analysis, Laxenburg, Austria.

Winter, S. G., Y. M. Kaniovski, and G. Dosi (1997). *A Baseline Model of Industry Evolution.* Interim Report IR-97-013/March, International Institute for Applied Systems Analysis, Laxenburg, Austria.

Acknowledgements

We are grateful to Andrea Bassanini, the participants to the Conference on Economic Models of Evolutionary Dynamics with Interacting Agents (The Abdus Salam International Centre for Theoretical Physics, Trieste, Italy, September 1998) and two anonymous referees for their comments on previous drafts. Mariele Berté and Marco Valente have been of crucial help for the simulation of the model. Francesca Chiaromonte preciously contributed to the endless discussions concerning both the fine details of the model and its computer simulations.

We thank the International Institute for Applied Systems Analysis, the Fujitsu Research Institute for Advanced Information (Japan), the University of Trento and the European Union (ESSI Project, TSER, DG XII) which at various stages supported the research leading to this work. Usual caveats apply.

[17]

Innovative Learning and Institutions in the Process of Development: On the Microfoundation of Growth Regimes

Francesca Chiaromonte, Giovanni Dosi and Luigi Orsenigo

INTRODUCTION

In his recent assessment of growth theories, Moses Abramovitz refers back to the *Wealth of Nations* as the illustrious ancestor of a long stream of investigations on the determinants of economic growth (Abramovitz, 1989). In fact, in the famous proposition on the dynamics linking division of labour, productivity and market growth, Adam Smith identifies one of many positive feedback loops between innovative learning and economic development. Since then, the evidence on the microeconomics of learning and innovation has got much richer, especially in recent years (a survey in Dosi, 1988). However, standard growth theory has proved to be hardly suitable to incorporate the microevidence on, for example, dynamic increasing returns, path dependent learning, 'disequilibrium' search processes, interfirm and international differences in technological capabilities and so on, notwithstanding recent increasing returns equilibrium models (see Romer, 1986, 1990; Lucas, 1988; Aghion and Howitt, 1989; Grossman and Helpman, 1991). Neither has standard theory focused on the institutions and behavioural norms underlying economic coordination and development: that is, what are the institutional mechanisms that allow the 'Invisible Hand' to operate in a world that continuosly innovates? Again, that question can be traced back to Adam Smith, where he asks – in the *Wealth of Nations* and, especially, in the *Theory of Moral Sentiments* – what are the 'moral inclinations', beliefs and behaviours that make non-destructive interactions possible in market societies. However, since Adam Smith, attempts at an answer have mainly been left to disciplines other than economics. In that, the typical economic assumptions of 'perfect rationality' and equilibrium have often hindered any proper account of the sociology and 'political economy' of development.

To be fair, one has observed in recent years a renewed interest in the relationships between technical change, institutions and economic dynamics. For example, trying to interpret long-term historical discontinuities in growth patterns, as well as the diversity of these patterns across countries and over time, scholars like Freeman and Perez have introduced notions such as 'techno-economic paradigms' (or 'regimes'). This notion historically links the phases of sustained growth with the establishment of appropriate institutions and corporate behaviour governing technological learning.

Moreover, Boyer and the (mainly French) 'Regulation Approach' (see, for example, Boyer, 1988a, 1988b) have extensively argued that the major phases of economic development, as well as ruptures and crises, can be interpreted in terms of compatibility or 'mis-matching' among the prevalent behaviours of main social actors (firms, workers, social institutions and so on). In that view, technology, economic variables and institutions cannot be separately analysed. Rather, technical change is dynamically coupled with institutional change, and the growth, decline, stability or instability of various economies has ultimately to be ascribed to specific relationships between technological progress, institutional change (or lack of it) and economic signals.

Finally, a variety of contributions broadly in the Schumpeterian tradition has emphasized the crucial role in technical change and growth of decentralized and mistake-ridden processes of search, innovation and imitation, undertaken by agents that are heterogeneous in their capabilities, expectations and behaviour (Freeman, 1982; Nelson and Winter, 1982; Dosi and Orsenigo, 1988; Silverberg, 1987; Silverberg, Dosi and Orsenigo, 1988).

The model which follows tries precisely to provide a theoretical account – albeit a highly stylized one – of the growth process, fuelled by technological learning of heterogenous competing agents and embedded in particular institutional regimes. In the model, learning takes different forms, involving innovation and imitation in products (the search for new 'machines' that are more efficient for their users), in processes of production (the search for more efficient methods of production of the 'machines' themselves), and learning by using (on the side of adopters of those same 'machines'). The 'institutional regime' is captured by the type of norms which guide the behaviour of (highly 'boundedly rational') agents and by system-level parameters which characterize market interactions (on the products and labour markets, for example).

We start by assuming a wide set of notional opportunities of innovation. Such a set is permanently expanding via an endogenous process. Further, we model individual agents that are motivated in their innovative attempt by economic incentives, but also constrained and 'locked' by their competences. Finally, we represent an 'out of equilibrium' environment wherein:

1. individual agents, characterized by various and permanent forms of diversity, compete on the grounds of their specific technological achievements and behavioural rules (in each 'industry');

2. market interactions determine also intersectoral adjustments in demand, prices and, ultimately, the levels and changes of macroeconomic variables.

Within such a microfoundation of the process of coordination and change – broadly in an evolutionary perspective, as pioneered by Nelson and Winter (1982) – we shall explore:

1. the conditions under which microtechnological learning yields relatively ordered aggregate patterns of growth;
2. the effect of particular *norms* of behaviour and interaction among agents upon aggregate dynamics.

A central hypothesis in our approach is that the processes of technological innovation and those of institutional change (including the emergence, establishment and change in the norms of behaviour of the agents) *co-evolve*, although via different mechanisms and at different paces. Hence, one would ideally like a dynamic model whereby not only individual agents search in the technology space, innovate, imitate and compete with each other, but also endogenously learn about decision rules. Here, we fall short of this task. In a first approximation, we assume that behavioural norms, no matter how they have developed, present a relatively high degree of inertia *vis-à-vis* the quicker pace of technological learning and, thus, can be taken as parameters. So, in simulation exercises of 'comparative dynamics', we experiment with different (and fixed) distributions of the parameters describing decision rules, and compare the aggregate dynamics that they generate.

Developing and modelling some of the ideas discussed at greater length in Coricelli, Dosi and Orsenigo (1989), we shall show that the possible regularities in the dynamics of aggregate variables (such as income and productivity growth) are *emergent properties* of a system which self-organizes far from equilibrium. Moreover, our preliminary results show that different 'institutional regimes' do indeed affect both the rates of technological learning and the patterns of growth: only particular combinations of behavioural rules and market interactions appear to be viable to sustain macroeconomic growth.

In the following section we outline the basic hypotheses and the qualitative structure of the model. The next section – which the non-technical reader might want to skip – presents its formal description. The properties of the model are then explored via simulations and the results are discussed.

INNOVATION, COMPETITION AND GROWTH[1]

Ideally, a satisfactory model of growth should account for, or be consistent with, a series of 'stylized facts' on macrodynamics and on the microecon-

omics of innovation and competition. Several of these empirical regularities
are discussed in Kaldor (1974), Simon (1984), Solow (1984), Maddison
(1982). Greenwald and Stiglitz (1988) and Coricelli, Dosi and Orsenigo
(1989). Let us briefly recall the stylized facts that are more directly relevant
to the model which follows.

At the macro level:

1. output per unit of employment grows at relatively stable rates over
   rather long periods, and so do per capitum incomes;
2. there are persistent economic-wide business cycles;
3. one can identify 'phases' of development intertwined by 'crisis' and
   discontinuities in the average rates of growth of income and labour
   productivity;
4. the levels and rates of growth of income and labour productivity significantly differ across countries;
5. there is no systematic trend in capital/output ratios, and neither are there
   systematic correlations across countries between such ratios and the level
   of development;
6. significant levels of unemployment may persist for quite a long time.

Moreover, at the micro level:

7. innovation in products and processes is to a good extent endogenous to
   the activity of the business sector, via firms' R&D activities and also via
   more informal mechanisms of learning by doing and by using;
8. firms (and countries) systematically differ in their commitment to innovation and in their ability to innovate;
9. forms of market interactions different from pure competition are prevalent. Market structures are endogenous to the process of innovation and
   competition, with a lot of variability in market shares, relative costs and
   relative profitabilities of individual firms.

The theoretical task is to model a process of innovation, competition and
growth whereby these 'stylized facts' can in principle hold together. The
model presented here consists of two vertically connected sectors. Sector 1
produces heterogeneous (durable) production inputs ('machines') with
labour alone. Sector 2 produces a homogeneous consumption good with
labour and 'machines'. The bi-sectoral structure is clearly more apt than
one-sector models to capture the transmission of demand and technological
impulses between agents that might not have any competitive interaction
with each other (that is, it may be taken as a metaphor for the input–output
structure of the economy). Moreover, it makes easier the representation of
both processes of endogenous innovation and diffusion. Labour is a
homogeneous input. Each sector is composed of a finite number of firms.
Their behaviour is represented as routinized, and they are characterized by
a persistent variety in behavioural rules and technological capabilities.
Firms' market shares endogenously change as a function of their relative

'competitiveness' (defined below), which, in turn, is connected with behavioural rules and technological capabilities. Firms of sector 1 innovate by developing new ('more efficient') types of machines and by finding more efficient techniques to produce them. Firms of sector 2 innovate by adopting and learning how to use the new types of machines. The collective outcomes of individual disequilibrium decisions determine also aggregate variables such as income growth, employment, wages and so on.

Innovative Opportunities

The very possibility of innovation must rest on the permanent existence of some unexploited technological opportunities, or the continuous emergence of new ones. In line with a growing body of evidence from the microeconomics of innovation (Rosenberg, 1976, 1982; Freeman, 1982; Dosi, 1988), we assume that unexploited opportunities permanently exist and that what is actually explored is much smaller than the set of notional possibilities. Furthermore, we draw a fundamental distinction between *knowledge* and *information*. Innovation, we suggest, does not imply only some processes of information acquisition about new products or techniques, but is grounded in pre-existing, partly tacit, forms of problem-solving knowledge embodied in the agents themselves. Innovation, in turn, augments this knowledge for individual agents or collections of them.

All this implies that, unlike the representation of technical change in the conventional growth or business cycle models, agents are not constrained by 'nature' in their innovative achievements, but rather by their own capabilities. More emphatically, paraphrasing Milton Friedman, there are always (semi-) 'free lunches', whose exploitation is primarily limited by agents' abilities.[2]

Our model of innovation incorporates the following major characteristics:

1. innovation involves changes in both products and production processes;
2. opportunities to innovate expand over time as a function of income growth (plausibly carrying with it more basic research, more scientific advancements and so on);
3. technical change is of two types, 'incremental' and 'radical';
4. abilities to innovate and imitate are firm-specific and depend on their past innovative record (that is, innovative learning is cumulative);
5. although some of the economic benefits from innovation and adoption of new products and processes can be appropriated by the innovators themselves, there are learning externalities: the ease of imitation varies with the number of incumbents already producing a certain commodity, and the skills in using a particular type of equipment partly 'leaks' from individual adopters to the whole industry.

In the model, as depicted in Figure 8.1, innovative opportunities in sector 1 correspond to 'machines', x, each of which corresponds to a technique of production for the final good, characterized by the labour productivity

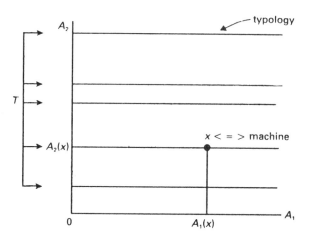

Figure 8.1   Innovative opportunities

coefficient $A_1(x)$, and to a technique of production for the machine itself, characterized by the labour productivity coefficient, $A_2(x)$. (Machines are 'measured' in terms of productive capacity, so that the machine input coefficient per unit of output is equal to one for each technique in sector 2 for each machine.)

In analogy with several empirical studies on innovation pointing out the difference between 'incremental' change – on the grounds of an unchanged knowledge base (a given 'paradigm') – and a 'radical' change (a new technological 'paradigm': see Dosi, 1984), we assume that the former is represented by increments in A_1, given A_2, while changes in both A_1 and A_2 correspond to 'qualitative' changes in technological competences and production organization (radical innovations). Hence, although empirically implausible, we assume for modelling simplicity that (within a paradigm) incremental innovation is only product-innovation for sector 1 agents (that is, it is the discovery of new machines embodying more efficient techniques for the final good production process – higher value of $A_1(x)$ – but produced with the same technique, a constant value of $A_2(x)$).

The 'notional opportunities', $T(\cdot)$, are defined by the set of achievable typologies (set of values for A_2) at each time $(\cdot)$. Over time, this set (containing old and new *potential* technological paradigms) grows via a stochastic process dependent on the level of economic (and scientific) development.

Note that the opportunity set always grows, or at least remains the same. However, as we shall see, the dynamics in potential opportunities does not directly influence the actual processes of innovation undertaken by individual agents. Agents' effective explorations generally remain well below the maximum notional opportunities.

Each agent, i ($i = 1, 2 \ldots n$), of sector 1 actually 'explores' the set of notional achievable typologies, $T(\cdot)$, via an expensive process based on R&D investments, assumed to be measured by the number of R&D workers that it employs. Such a search is represented as a stochastic process: when the search turns out to be successful the newly discovered machine will be a realization $(xg_i(t))$ of a probability distribution dependent on the production competences of the agents (as represented by the machine that is currently manufactured, $x_i(t)$), and on the opportunity set $T(t)$. Incremental progress within a typology of machines (elsewhere defined as the progress within a 'technological paradigm', or along a 'technological trajectory': see Dosi, 1984) is always possible, but subject to a progressive exhaustion of opportunities. This is like saying that any trajectory is characterized, in stochastic terms, by dynamic increasing returns, but at decreasing rates.

Conversely, the more a firm proceeds along a 'trajectory', the more its probability increases to jump on another one characterized by a higher value of A_2 (that is, to 'discover' a radical innovation). In turn, the discovery of a new 'paradigm' reopens the opportunities for further incremental improvements. Underlying this formalization, there is the idea that the progressive exhaustion of a trajectory is a 'focusing device' (Rosenberg, 1982) which triggers the search for new sources of innovative opportunities, while past experience on a trajectory also cumulatively built technological competence for the discovery of new trajectories.

The exploration process as a whole maintains its increasing returns and cumulative nature, with periods of incremental technical progress intertwined with more discrete jumps in both product and process technologies.

Moreover, technological knowledge, in most circumstances, is neither a purely public good nor an entirely appropriable blueprint or patent (such as in the formalization of 'patent races'), but rather can be reproduced and imitated in an expensive way (Mansfield, Schwartz and Wagner, 1981; Pavitt, 1987; Dosi, 1988). In the model we introduced the possibility, for each agent of sector 1, of imitating machines that are known, although not necessarily produced, by other agents.

We formalize imitation as a stochastic process whose success depends on the amount of imitative R&D investment undertaken by each firm. When such a search is successful, we further assume that, first, the probability of imitating any one type of machine is inversely related to the technological distance from the current capabilities of the imitating agent (given the partly tacit nature of technological knowledge, it is easier to imitate machines which are relatively similar to those that the agent already produces or knows). Second, the more widespread is the knowledge about a particular machine, the easier might be innovation: thus, we assume that the probability of imitating any one type of machine is directly proportional to the absolute frequency of agents who know it.

Through the search activity of sector 1 agents, the system continuously 'discovers' (and produces, under microeconomic decision rules specified further on) new capital-embodied opportunities for sector 2.

Innovation, for each agent j ($j = 1, 2 \ldots m$), of sector 2 is equivalent to the purchase of new types of machines, via expansion and scrapping decisions (whose rules, again, shall be specified below). However, producers of the (homogeneous) final good must learn how to use each machine type (A_2) up to the optimal use defined by the value of A_1 of the machines belonging to that type (that is, belonging to any one 'technological paradigm'). Similar to Silverberg, Dosi and Orsenigo (1988), we assume that each j embodies a *skill*, $s_j(A_2, t)$ (a coefficient between 0 and 1) in the use of machines belonging to the typology A_2, so that the actual labour productivity it can achieve on them at time t might well be less than the 'optimal' value. These skills improve via two learning processes. The first is a learning-by-using activity (as in Rosenberg, 1982), whereby the capabilities of using each typology of machines grow with the actual cumulated use of them. We assume that *private* firm-specific and technology-specific learning follow a logistic path. However, we assume also a second process of learning, through which part of the private skills 'leak out' to other potential adopters, via information diffusion, personnel mobility, consulting activities and so on (Silverberg, Dosi and Orsenigo, 1988); this part becomes a *public* skill shared by every firm.

Therefore, late-adopters of a particular typology A_2 in t will start by using only public skills, which in turn depend on previous adoption: that is, on the number of adoptions, the opportunities of private learning to use, and the appropriability of private capabilities (inversely related to the rate at which private skills become public).

To summarize: in the model, the economic system continuously explores new opportunities of capital-embodied technical progress, via R&D-based processes of generation and imitation of 'machines', undertaken by agents in sector 1. Moreover, the flow of new machines represents also a continuous opportunity of innovation for the agents in sector 2, via their adoption, the subsequent process of learning how to use them, and the learning externality that industry-wide diffusion of information and skills provides for late-adopters. Finally, the aggregate income dynamics, specified below, induces an endogenous increment of new potential avenues of innovation. All this defines an expanding universe of *notional* and (partly) *exploited* opportunities of technical progress.

However, in a microfounded model, activities of search, innovation, imitation and adoption by profit-motivated agents must be grounded in some economic incentive to do so and, more generally, in microeconomic decisions. This is what we shall discuss in the following.

Microeconomic Decision Rules

It is a standard practice in the economic profession to assume perfectly optimizing agents (and growth theory is no exception). It is impossible to discuss here the analytical status of that assumption. Suffice to say that such a representation of the decision processes, irrespective of its empirical plausibility under stationary conditions (that is, given technologies and preferences) becomes particularly demanding on the computational and forecasting capabilities of agents when innovations may occur endogenously. As Herbert Simon put it:

> [i]n a formal way, it is perfectly feasible to produce a theory of technical innovation based on the postulate of rationality. Since innovation is presumably produced by investment of human and capital resources, we introduce a new production function for innovation, and equate the value of marginal product of innovation with its cost. From a formal standpoint, we have simply replaced the task of estimating the parameters of a function, the production function for innovation. The only obvious gain from the replacement is that we can now rest comfortable in the knowledge that everything is proceeding rationally. Human rationality is now only bounded by the characteristics of the external environment: the quality of the ore that is mined by the innovation production process. Of course, if we examine the metaphor too closely, we see that 'quality' of the 'ore' is an euphemism for the 'effectiveness of the thought processes of human beings who are doing the innovating'. (Simon, 1984, pp. 41–2)

Indeed, if one sticks to a 'rational' microfoundation of economic dynamics *cum* endogenous innovation, one must subscribe to either (or both) of the following hypotheses, namely, (a) the actual 'thought processes' rather closely resemble optimizing procedures (and generally involve also 'rational' technological expectations), and, (b) if and when hypothesis (a) does not hold, the competitive process is such that the relative frequency of behaviours that *ex post* turn out to be 'optimizing' rapidly tends to 1.

In fact, good empirical and theoretical reasons – related to the nature of the innovation process, the associated uncertainty, the characteristics of innovation-based competition and so on – strongly suggest that hypothesis (a) does not generally hold (much more on that in Nelson and Winter, 1982; Simon, 1984; Winter, 1987; Dosi and Orsenigo, 1988; Dosi and Egidi, 1990). And, regarding hypothesis (b), its proponents have so far failed to deliver any proof of the general stability of rationally microfounded equilibrium dynamics whenever perturbed by 'disequilibrium behaviour'.

Here, we want to explore an opposite behavioural foundation. We assume that agents are characterized by *fixed decision rules* – generally different in their parameters among agents – concerning investments, research, pricing and so on.

In principle, these 'rules' must have developed via some *learning processes* over the history of individual firms and of the system as a whole. Here, however, we do not model such learning processes. We set ourselves the task of showing that some orderly aggregate properties may emerge even in those extreme conditions when *no* individual behaviour can be presumed to be an 'equilibrium' (optimizing) one, and also when no form of decision learning is going on. After all, the common modelling assumption of perfect rationality derives a good deal of the purported system properties from the forecasting and computing abilities of the 'representative' agent(s).

Moreover, whenever one adopts such a compact microfoundation (a single agent representing the whole of them), one also assumes by hypotheses perfect microeconomic coordination and precludes the possibility of analysing the long-term effects of those non-average behaviours that are typically associated with innovative entrepreneurship. In this respect, our agents are much less able to forecast and compute 'equilibrium behaviours' than commonly assumed, but they are continuously prepared to (imperfectly) adjust to the unexpected, and able to generate and imitate novelty. They are *different* in their decision parameters, although not in the rules themselves. Finally, they differ in their technological abilities and degrees of success in innovation and imitation, in line with the general finding from the innovation literature that technology presents highly firm-specific, tacit and idiosyncratic features.[3] In that, we entirely share and push further Greenwald and Stiglitz's suggestion that:

> [i]ndividuals do not have perfect foresight or rational expectations concerning the future. The events which they confront often appear to be unique, and there is no way that they can form a statistical model predicting the probability distributions of the outcomes. There is little evidence that they even attempt to do so. At the same time, individuals are not myopic. They do not simply assume that the future is like the present. (Greenwald and Stiglitz, 1987, p. 131)

Our decision rules implicitly embody also firm-specific 'theories' on how to cope with a changing world. This implies also that there is no common knowledge of either an 'innovation production function' or even a unique 'production function': both differ across firms and change over time according to agent-specific patterns.

Decision Rules: Sector 1

Machine producers do know that notional opportunities for 'better machines' always exist, and they know also the general procedure of discovering them (that is, by investing in R&D). Finally, they expect to derive some economic benefits from successful innovation or imitation. New machines are partly appropriated, due to various form of knowledge specificity (with or without a patent system), and indeed it turns out that some innovators increase their market shares and their profits. Similarly, successful imitation yields a form of 'business stealing'.[4] The fact that, *for some*, innovation and imitation result in differential profits and increasing market share, implies what we call *weak incentive compatibility* of search activities. However, agents do not know the actual probabilities of innovation or imitation, or the precise technical features of what they will discover. Furthermore, the product-market sales and profits of each firm depend on the performances and prices of every machine produced by all firms, which in turn are a function of the success in innovation and imitation by each of them. In such circumstances we make the extreme assumption that agents determine the level of their decision variables via fixed and firm-specific rules.

In sector 1, each firm is characterized by the following decision rules:

1. *desired* allocation of resources to R&D, via a fixed percentage of previous period turnover (note that here and throughout, individual agents may be unable to achieve their 'desired' rates of investment and production, given their maximum available liquidity determined by cash flow plus bank credit, the latter being a fixed proportion of the former);
2. a parameter distributing R&D between innovative and imitative search;
3. desired prices on each new machine that is or could be manufactured, via a mark-up on direct *costs* of production;
4. an evaluation function comparing prices and performances of currently produced machines with those stemming from innovation and imitation if any, in order to decide which one to manufacture (we assume single-product agents);
5. desired level of production for whatever machine is chosen.

Sticking to our general endeavour of exploring the possible orderly characteristics of system coordination and change in presence of highly routinized microbehaviours, we assume a very simple adaptive expectation which extrapolates from the demand of firm *i* over the previous two periods.

Given these five decision rules the desired demand for labour can also be automatically derived.

Decision Rules: Sector 2

The industry producing the final good is somewhat similar to what Pavitt (1984) calls a 'supply-dominated' sector: innovations are generated elsewhere in the system and introduced via decisions of scrapping and/or expansion. The levels of production and scrapping, jointly with the choice of the type of machine to purchase, influence also production efficiency, and thus unit costs of production.

Firms are characterized by the following decision rules.

1. *Desired level of production.* As in sector 2, it is derived from adaptive expectations on demand, based on their own demands of the previous two periods. (Given the existing capital stock, the rule allows also the automatic determination of desired net investment.)
2. *Desired price*, again, via a mark-up over direct unit costs.
3. A *choice function* which compares prices and performances of the new machines to purchase, if any.
4. A *scrapping rule*, based on a pay-back period criterion.

As in section 1, these rules are sufficient to determine also the desired demand for labour.

Competition, Coordination and Aggregate Dynamics

Firm-specific decision rules, together with the history of innovation, imitation and learning by individual agents, account for a permanent diversity among them. Firms differ in (a) the quality of products they offer (sector 1); (b) the prices they charge (both sectors); and (c) the parameters of the decision rules concerning their control variables (again in both sectors). All this, coupled with the fact that no agent is capable of correctly computing *ex ante* equilibria where individual actions are reciprocally consistent, implies that competition is a *permanent disequilibrium process*. Its outcomes are also variations in the market shares and profits of individual firms. Hence markets perform as *selection mechanisms*, acting upon the relative competitiveness of individual actors. In the model, as in common language, competitiveness is a relative concept: it implies a comparison among different agents. In sector 1, the competitiveness of each firm i is determined by (1) the production efficiency for the users of the machine offered on the market (as expressed by the value of $A_1(x)$); (b) its price (connected to the value of $A_2(x)$); and (c) the degree to which the firm might 'ration' the market since it might not be able to fulfil all demand given forecasting errors and/or liquidity constraints. Similarly, in sector 2, the competitiveness of each firm j is determined by (a) the price of the output (note that, despite the homogeneous good, we allow for prices that are different among firms); and (b) the possible degree of 'rationing' exercised by the firm (as described above for sector 1).

Firms with above-average competitiveness expand in their market shares, while firms below average shrink or even die. However, the selection criteria themselves are endogenous: they are the collective outcome of the dynamics of the competitiveness of each firm. Consider the selection process in sector 1, which is endogenous in two ways. First, it is determined by the individual dynamics of product innovation (that is, the changes in A_1 – and in the typologies A_2 – achieved by each i), in prices and in production capacity. Second, it is also determined by the evolution of the users' sector, via learning by using and expectations of machines users. Similarly, selection in sector 2 is shaped by the individual dynamics of capital-embodied process innovation, learning by using and the externality that all this entails.

In a biological analogy, the selection processes of the model represent the equivalent of a 'fitness function'. However, the 'landscape' over which 'fitness' is defined *co-evolves* with the behaviours and technological characteristics of individual agents in both sectors. In such an environment, individual abilities of forecasting the technology and the behaviours of the others is highly imperfect. Each agent can be expected to face unfulfilled expectations and lack of correspondence between *ex ante* plans and *ex post* realization. Therefore the agents must possess some adjustment rule in their control variables. In particular, with regard to prices, we model an (imperfect) adjustment rule whereby each firm changes *actual* prices while trying to strike some balance between desired (mark-up) prices and its relative competitiveness on the market (as revealed by the dynamics of market shares).

The system coordinates and evolves via competition among heterogeneous agents which continuously introduce, adopt and imitate technological innovations. In turn, the outcome of the competitive process feeds back to individual behaviours both directly, via price adjustments, and indirectly, via the effects that relative competitiveness exert on firm size and cash flow (and thus, also, on investments in R&D and machines).

Aggregate ('macro') variables are the endogenous outcomes of such processes of innovation and competition. Aggregate gross and net investment in machines sum, *ex post*, over the investments of individual firms. So does employment.

In line with the unorthodox spirit of this work, we further add the following assumptions: first, that labour supply is unlimited at any positive wage, and wages change, in the most general formulation, as a function of (a) previous period variations in labour demand; (b) changes in average system-level labour productivity; and (c) changes in the final good prices. Indeed, we shall represent different *labour market regimes* by allowing varying combinations of 'institutional' mechanisms of indexation of wages on cost-of-living and productivity of labour, and a 'classical' adjustment on net variations in labour demand.

Second, in an extreme and out-of-fashion 'Keynesian' simplification,[5] all wages are consumed (final good), profits are either invested (R&D or machines) or saved in the form of interest-yielding deposits; the interest rate is exogenously fixed, and does not have any effect on investment decisions. There is no credit ceiling at a system level.[6]

Indeed, these extreme assumptions, together with the earlier ones and the nature of technological change and rule-driven behaviour, define a system that is highly *unconstrained*. It is not bounded by 'nature' in its dynamics; unlike standard models, one cannot ultimately find a principle of order in the scarcities of primary inputs jointly with some objective technological constraint. Moreover, highly institutional (rule-driven) behaviour cannot provide by itself those ordering virtues which a perfectly rational 'representative agent' with foresight is assumed to possess.

These features of our model are instrumental in investigating the conditions under which a system that continuously 'explores' a wide and expanding set of possible states can self-organize despite, or *because of*, disequilibrium microbehaviour. Ideally, the non-linear dynamics of the system should be able to generate the 'stylized facts' recalled at the beginning of this section: here, we shall simply present some highly preliminary results. However, before doing that, we shall present more formally the structure of the model.

A SELF-ORGANIZATION MODEL

Innovation, imitation and Production: Sector 1

Machines are identified by couples of integers (A_1, A_2), corresponding to points in the non-negative subset of a bidimensional space ($\mathbb{R}_+^2$).[7]

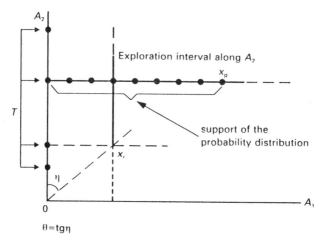

Figure 8.2   Innovation in sector 1

We define each 'typology' of machines belonging to the same paradigm as a set of points, $x = (A_1, A_2)$ in $\mathbb{R}_+^2$, given by

$$(x \in \mathbb{R}_+^2 : A_1 \in \mathbf{IN}, \text{ and } A_2 = a_2), a_2 \in \mathbf{IN}$$

in correspondence of various values of a_2 (see Figure 8.2). The set of achievable typologies, $T(\cdot)$, grows via a 'two-stage' stochastic process, the first stage determining the access to the second (see Nelson and Winter, 1982). In the first stage, the stochastic event 'access to the creation of a new paradigm' is determined as a draw from a Bernoulli distribution with probability

$$Pr\ (AT(t) = 1) = 1 - \exp\ (- r \cdot Y_m(t)) \tag{8.1}$$

where $Y_m(t)$ represents a moving average of aggregate income up to time t.

If access occurs, the system adds a new typology to the set, T, of the achievable ones, via an equiprobability draw in the set of the integers within the closed interval

$$[A_2^*(t - 1); (1 + h) \cdot A_2^*(t - 1)]$$

where $A_2^*(t - 1)$ is the maximum value in the set $T(t - 1)$. r in equation (8.1) and h are parameters that implicitly capture the general state of '*scientific*' opportunities and the effectiveness of their exploitation (translation into achievable paradigms). In order actually to access new 'machines', each agent, i, in sector 1 undertakes a two-step stochastic procedure, similar to the one above, through which it can access the generation of a new machine, in t, with probability

Francesca Chiaromonte, Giovanni Dosi and Luigi Orsenigo 131

$$Pr\,(AG_i(t) = 1) = 1 - exp\,(- r_g \cdot I_i^g(t)) \qquad (8.2)$$

where I_i^g represents i's investments in innovative search, in terms of number of R&D workers, and r_g is a system parameter. If the random access occurs, the new machine is drawn from a uniform probability distribution whose support is defined by the set of points with second coordinate (A_2) given by

$$A_{2i}^g(t) = \max\,(T(t) \cap [A_2(x_i(t)), A_2\,(x_i(t)) + \lambda \cdot \theta_i(t)]) \qquad (8.3)$$

and first coordinate given by the integers in

$$[\max\,(0;\, A_1(x_i(t)) - (1/\lambda) \cdot (A_{2i}^g(t)/A_1(x_i(t)));$$
$$A_1(x_i(t)) + (1/\lambda) \cdot (A_{2i}^g(t)/A_1(x_i(t)))] \qquad (8.4)$$

where λ is a system parameter and

$$\theta_i(t) = A_1(x_i(t))/A_2(x_i(t))$$

This formulation implies that exploration along a 'trajectory' (holding A_2 constant) induces a relative shrinkage of further opportunities of incremental innovation, but also expands the set of attainable 'machines' on the other 'trajectories'. An illustration of this is given in Figure 8.2.

Agents can also imitate each other's machines (again, via a two stages stochastic process). The probability of access to imitation is

$$Pr\,(AM_i(t) = 1) = 1 - exp\,(- r_m \cdot I_i^{m*}(t)) \qquad (8.5)$$

$I_i^m(t)$ is the investment in imitative search of agent i, and r_m is a system parameter which is lower the higher is the appropriability of innovations.

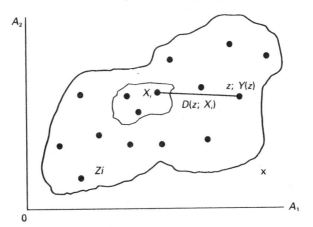

Figure 8.3   Imitation in sector 1

If access to imitation occurs, the imitated point (machine) will be a realization $(x_i^m(t))$ from a probability distribution defined over the set $Z_i(t) = X(t) \setminus X_i(t)$, where $X(t)$ is the set of the points known by the complex of the agents of sector 1, and $X_i(t)$ is the set of the points known by i (one rules out the possibility of imitating oneself!).

The probability of imitating any one type of machine in Z_i for i is inversely related to the distance, expressed in an orthogonal metric, between each point, $z \in Z_i(t)$, and the set $X_i(t)$.

$$D_{MET}(z, X_i(t)) = \min_{x \in X_i(t)} [(z - x)' \cdot MET \cdot (z - x)]^{1/2}$$

where *MET* is the matrix 2×2

$$MET = \begin{pmatrix} met1 & 0 \\ 0 & met2 \end{pmatrix}$$

The probability is also directly related to the frequency of agents knowing any one kind of machine in Z_i, $\gamma(z, t)$. Thus, the probability of imitating any one machine, $z \in Z_i(t)$, normalizing, is given by

$$Pr(x_i^m(t) = z) = \frac{\gamma(z, t) \cdot [D_{MET}(z; X_i(t))]^{-1}}{\sum_{x \in Z_i(t)} \gamma(x, t) \cdot [D_{MET}(x; X_i(t))]^{-1}} \tag{8.6}$$

An illustration of this is presented in Figure 8.3.

Each firm, i, determines its total desired allocation in R&D according to the rule

$$I_i^d(t) = \mu_i \cdot S_i(t - 1) / w(t) \tag{8.7}$$

where $S_i(t - 1)$ is the previous period turnover, μ_i is a firm-specific parameter and $w(t)$ is the current wage (hence, R&D investments are defined in terms of number of research workers). Actual investments, $I_i(t)$, as well as the actual values of the other decision variables of the firm, correspond to the desired ones up to the liquidity constraint.

A firm-specific parameter, ζ_i, distributes research between innovative and imitative activities, so that

$$I_i^g(t) = \zeta_i \cdot I_i(t) \text{ and } I_i^m(t) = (1 - \zeta_i) \cdot I_i(t)$$

At each time, each agent has to choose which machine to manufacture between the variety already in production, x_i, the machine discovered via innovative R&D, if any, x_i^g, and that imitated, if any, x_i^m. That choice involves an evaluation of the 'quality' of each machine for the users – approximated by the 'optimal' cost of production on the machines, given current wages – and also of the supply price of the machines themselves (p_i):

$$V_i(z, t) = \phi_1 \cdot ln \ (w(t)/A_1(z)) + \phi_2 \cdot ln \ (p_i(z, t)) \tag{8.8}$$

V_i is the notation for the evaluation functional, and it has to be applied to $z = x_i; x_i^g; x_i^m$.

For 'new' machines (candidates coming from innovation and/or imitation, and never manufactured before by the agent), prices are *desired* prices, calculated via a mark-up rule,

$$p_i^d(z, t) = m_i \cdot (w(t)/A_2(z)) \tag{8.9}$$

(m_i being the firm-specific mark-up parameter), while for the machine already in production, the price is the *actual* price applied by the agent in the previous period (which, as we shall see, may well be different from the desired one). If all three candidates for production belong to the same typology of machines (that is $A_2(x_i) = A_2(x_i^g) = A_2(x_i^m)$) the choice is straightforward, and will satisfy a simple minimization of $V_i(\cdot)$. However, if one or both the new candidates belongs to typologies that differ from that previously manufactured ($A_2(x_i)$), their evaluation V_i is multiplied by a 'prudential' firm-specific coefficient $\chi_i/w(t)$. The prudential correction requires that, in order to switch production to a new paradigm, with the consequent market uncertainty and learning costs for the users, the expected superiority of the new machine *vis-à-vis* the previously manufactured one must exceed a certain threshold, influenced by the 'animal spirits' of individual entrepreneurs.

Having chosen which machine to produce (the new x_i for the current period), each agent defines its desired level of production in relation to its demand expectations and its carried over inventories. Expected demand is extrapolated as

$$D_i^e(t) = \delta_i \ (D_i \ (t - 1), D_i(t - 2)) \tag{8.10}$$

where δ_i is a firm-specific function expressing demand expectations derived from the level of actual demand in the previous periods.[8]

Thus, the level of desired production is

$$Q_i^d(t) = D_i^e(t) - N_i(t - 1)$$

$N_i(t - 1)$ being the inventories carried over from the previous periods of production. As for research investment, actual production level ($Q_i(t)$) is equal to the desired one, unless adjusted via the liquidity constraint. Production occurs with labour alone, under constant returns to scale, at unit costs $w(t)/A_2(x)$.

Diffusion, Learning and Production: Sector 2[9]

The machines are purchased and used by sector 2 producers of the final good. Each agent, j ($j = 1, 2 \ldots m$), utilizes each machine with a skill level $s_j(A_2, t)$ (bounded between 0 and 1) specific to the agent and to the machine type (A_2). Thus actual labour productivity on each machine x, such that $A_2(x) = A_2$, is

$$s_j(A_2, t) \cdot A_1(x) \leq A_1(x) \tag{8.11}$$

Let us define the set of typologies actually produced at each time (.) by sector 1 as $T^s(t)$. On the new typologies offered on the market for the first time in t (that is, on $T^s(t)\backslash T^s(t-1)$), the initial using skills are assumed to be identical for all potential adopters of sector 2, and equal to the system parameter, σ. An agent that adopts any one type, A_2, of machines will grow in its using skill according to

$$s_j(A_2, t) - s_j(A_2, t-1) = \alpha_1 \cdot [Q_j(A_2, t)/(CQ_j(A_2, t) + a_2)] \tag{8.12}$$
$$\cdot [s_j(A_2, t-1) \cdot (1 - s_j(A_2, t-1))]$$

where Q stands for the production undertaken by j in t with machines of typology A_2, CQ is the correspondent cumulated production,

$$CQ_j(A_2, t) = \sum_{t=0 \ldots t} Q_j(A_2, t)$$

and α_1 is a system parameter capturing the level of learning by using opportunities.

Private skills, s_j, tend to partly diffuse to the whole industry. The *public* (commonly shared) machine using skill for each typology A_2 ($s_p(A_2, t)$), which starts at level σ when a typology is first introduced, grows over time according to

$$s_p(A_2, t) - s_p(A_2, t-1) = \beta_1 \cdot (s_m(A_2, t-1) - s_p(A_2, t-1)) \tag{8.13}$$

where s_m is the average of agents, j, private skills, weighted with their market shares, and β_1 is a parameter which is higher the lower is the private appropriability of machine using skills. Any new later-adopter of machines of a certain type (A_2) will start with public skill levels $s_p(.)$.

Each firm determines its levels of production based on a rough expectation rule on j's own demand

$$D_j^e(t) = \delta_j(D_j(t-1), D_j(t-2)) \tag{8.14}$$

(with a meaning analogous to that of equation (8.10) for sector 1), yielding desired production

$$Q_j^d(t) = D_j^e(t) - N_j(t)$$

N being, again, the inventories. The level of production allowed by the current capital stock is identical to the number of (heterogeneous) machines retained by the agent. Calling $\Gamma_j(t)$ the set of them (recall that they are measured in terms of units of production capacity), we have

$$K_j(t) = \sum_{x \,\in\, \Gamma_j(t)} g_j(x, t)$$

where $g_j(x, t)$ are the absolute frequencies of machines. The desired net investment (expansion) is

$$IE_j^d(t) = \max (0; \hat{K}_j^d(t))$$

$\hat{K}_j^d$ being the desired variation in capital stock, calculated as

$$\hat{K}_j^d(t) = v_j \cdot [Q_j^d(t) - u_j \cdot K_j(t)] \cdot (1/u_j) \qquad (8.15)$$

where u_j is the firm-specific level of desired capacity utilization ($0 \leq u_j \leq 1$), and v_j is a firm-specific parameter that can be taken to capture expectations about future levels of demand as compared to the past (note also that throughout the model own-demand expectations concern both industry-wide levels and one's own market share).

With a non-binding liquidity constraint, both actual production and actual expansion investment levels will equal the desired ones (otherwise, they are proportionally corrected).

Each j must choose within the set of machines currently offered by sector 1 producers ($X^s(t)$). It follows from the foregoing representation of technological learning that each agent, j, whenever choosing among different typologies, must account also for its specific skills in using them, $s_j(A_2, t)$. These skills imply a form of dynamic appropriability of learning by using. However, precisely because of such a partly appropriated learning opportunity, expectations of potential skill improvements enter the choice rule (like Silverberg, Dosi and Orsenigo, 1988). Call a_j the *'expectation bonus'*. The adjusted skills used for machines selection are

$$s_j^e(A_2, t) = s_j(A_2 t) + a_j \qquad \text{if } s_j(A_2, t) < 1 - a_j \qquad (8.16)$$

$$= 1 \qquad\qquad \text{otherwise}$$

Moreover, as we shall see below, nothing guarantees that markets for each type of machines clear: the degrees of 'rationing' by each machines supplier, $l_i(x, t)$, negatively influence preferences.

The choice of the machine depends on its price, the labour productivity that it entails and its possible levels of rationing. The chosen machine will be the one, among the supplied ($x \in X^s(t)$), that maximizes the evaluation functional

$$M_j(x, t) = \phi_3 \cdot ln \; (s_j^e(A_2(x), t) \cdot A_1(x)) -$$

$$\phi_4 \cdot ln \; (p_i(x, t)) - \phi_5 \cdot ln \; (l_i(x, t)) \quad\quad (8.17)$$

Call $x_j^*(t)$ the chosen machine.

Note that more than one producer may manufacture the same machine, but possibly offer it at a different price. The choice of sector 2 agents is therefore among 'couples' (machines-producers) which identify both the machine characteristics (typology A_2 and 'quality' A_1), and the supply price and 'rationing' conditions (p and 1, respectively). Since machines rationing can occur, each j may be forced to 'second best' options.

As regards scrapping, we assume that it follows a pay-back period rule. The current capital stock $K_j(t)$ is made of different kinds of machines, x, associated with *actual* labour productivities $\pi_j(x, t) = s_j(A_2(x), t) \cdot A_1(x)$, and actual unit labour costs $c_j(x, t) = w(t) \, / \, \pi_j(x, t)$ ('optimal' unit labour costs given the machines stock are simply $w(t) \, / \, A_1(x)$).

Correspondingly, call $c_j^*(t)$ the actual unit labour cost associated with $x_j^*(t)$.[10] The subset of the capital stock that j desires to scrap will be

$$OS_j(t) = (x \in \Gamma_j(t): [p(x_j^*(t))/(w(t)/A_1(x)) - c_j^*(t)]\leq b_j) \quad\quad (8.18)$$

where b_j is a firm-specific pay-back period parameter. Desired substitution investment will thus be

$$IS_j^d(t) = \sum_{x \in OS_j(t)} g_i(x, t)$$

Like producers of sector 1, also each j may be unable to meet its desired plans due to a liquidity constraint, in which case (in sector 2) we assume that firms will satisfy, in order, current production, expansion investments and replacement.

Production is characterized by constant returns to scale and the notional average productivity depends on the frequencies of different types of equipment

$$\pi_{mj}^n(t) = \sum_{x \in \Gamma_j(t)} (1/A_1(x)) \cdot (g_i(x, t)/K_j(t)) \qu\quad (8.19)$$

However, actual average productivities, and average unit labour costs (c_m) depend on such frequencies, but also on typology-specific and firm-specific skills[11]

$$c_{mj}(t) = \sum_{x \in \Gamma_j(t)} (w(t)/\pi_j(x, t)) \cdot (g_i(x, t)/K_j(t)) \qu\quad (8.20)$$

Finally, desired prices are determined via a mark-up over average labour unit costs, $p_j^d(t) = m_j \cdot c_{mj}(t)$.

Market Interactions and System Dynamics

Each sector 1 producer competes in the machine market for the demand stemming from expansion and replacement decisions of sector 2 manufacturers. Similarly, the latter compete on the final good market whose size is determined by the real wages of all employed workers.

In sector 1 the competitiveness of agent i ($E_i(t)$), manufacturing x, is defined as

$$E_i(t) = - \omega_1(t) \cdot ln \ (w(t)A_1(x)) - \omega_2(t) \cdot ln \ (p_i(x, t))$$
$$- \omega_3(t) \cdot ln \ (l_i(x, t - 1)) \qquad (8.21)$$

where $A_1(x)$ is the labour productivity of machine x for its users, $p_i(x, t)$ is the price charged for it by manufacturer i, and $l_i(x, t - 1)$ is the unfulfilled demand in the previous period.[12] As in Silverberg (1987), the selective bench-mark is the industry average competitiveness:

$$E_m^1(t) = \sum_{i=1 \ldots n} E_i(t) \cdot f_i(t)$$

that is, the average of individual levels of competitiveness weighted by market shares (f_i).

In sector 2, individual levels of competitiveness are

$$E_j(t) = - \omega_4 \cdot ln(p_j(t)) - w_5 \cdot ln(l_j(t - 1)) \qquad (8.22)$$

and $E_m^2(t)$ is the analogous average competitiveness in the final good industry.[13]

Moreover, notice – not surprisingly – the similarity between equation 8.21 (the competitiveness of machines producing firms) and equation 8.17 earlier, expressing the evaluation functions of different machines/machine suppliers by would-be customers. In fact, the arguments of both the functions are 'objective' supply-side parameters (labour productivity allowed by the machine, prices and degrees of 'rationing') which differentiate producers. However, the actual competitiveness of each producer is also the outcome of varying distributions of *heterogeneous users' skills and users' technological expectations*. These distributions, weighted by the demand shares of each customer, determine the $\omega(t)$s in equation 8.21.[14] Each market share, f_i, changes according to a non-linear process

$$f_i(t) - f_i(t - 1) = F^1(E_i(t - 1) - E_m^1(t - 1)) \qquad (8.23)$$

Indeed, in the structure of the simulation exercises presented here, the F function itself is constructed to be only the *ex post* aggregate outcome of (mistake-ridden) evaluation and choice rules by individual buyers.

Similarly, market shares for the final good change as a function of the difference between individual and average competitiveness

$$f_j(t) - f_j(t-1) = F^2(E_j(t-1) - E_m^2(t-1)) \tag{8.24}$$

In analogy with Silverberg, Dosi and Orsenigo (1988) we assumed the following adjustment dynamics of individual prices. In sector 1

$$ln(p_i(x, t)) - ln(p_i(x, t-1)) =$$
$$\psi_1 \cdot (ln(p_i^d(t)) - ln(p_i(x, t-1)) +$$
$$\psi_2 \cdot (E_i(t-1) - E_m^1(t-1)) \tag{8.25}$$

and similarly in sector 2

$$ln(p_j(t)) - ln(p_j(t-1)) =$$
$$\psi_3 \cdot (ln(p_j^d(t)) - ln(p_j(t-1)) +$$
$$\psi_4 \cdot (E_j(t) - E_m^2(t)) \tag{8.26}$$

That is, changes in actual prices when expressed in logs (different among firms, *also in the homogeneous good industry*) are influenced by desired (mark-up) prices, but they are also track the relative competitiveness of each firm in the market. The ψs are system parameters whose relative values capture the nature of the *product-market regime*: for example, a highly competitive regime is defined by relatively high ψ_2 and ψ_4 and near zero ψ_1 and ψ_3. The opposite applies to quasi-monopolistic markets.

Aggregate demand variables are emergent properties resulting from the microeconomic decision rules and interactions described so far. However, *ex post*, they are simply the sum of the corresponding realized decisions of individual units. Aggregate gross and net investments in machines (respectively $IE^T(t) + IS^T(t)$ and $IE^T(t)$) are the sum in j of individual investments. The same applies to employment. With fixed coefficient technologies and constant returns to scale, employment in the final good sector ($L^2(t)$) sums over the actual outputs compounded by labour productivities of each agent. In sector 1, employment is given by the sum of production employment and research employment (recalling that $I_i(t)$s – investments in research – are measured in labour: $L^2(t)$).

Of course, total employment is simply the sum over the two sectors $L^T(t) = L^1(t) + L^2(t)$.

Aggregate ('national') income, $Y^T(t)$, follows the standard accounting identities (it equals total production which equals total expenditure plus 'involuntary' changes in inventories). Finally, on the labour market we assume that wages (expressed in logs) change according to

$$\Delta ln(w(t)) = \zeta_1 \cdot \Delta ln(p_m^2(t-1)) + \zeta_2 \cdot \Delta ln(\Pi^T(t-1))$$
$$+ \zeta_3 \cdot \Delta ln(L^T(t-1)) \tag{8.27}$$

where p_m^2 is a price index for the final good and Π^T is the average labour productivity in the economy.

BEHAVIOURAL NORMS, TECHNOLOGICAL LEARNING AND
REGIMES OF GROWTH: SOME PRELIMINARY RESULTS

Clearly, the structure of the model with its complex thread of positive
feedbacks prevents analytical solutions so that inferences on its properties
can only be drawn from simulation exercises. In a first illustrative simulation
we assume 10 agents in each sector that start with identical technological
competences, but different parameters in their search rules (search investments, and propensity to innovate and imitate in sector 1) and in their
technological expectations ('confidence' in new products machines for the
agents of both sectors, and learning expectations in sector 2: see Appendix I
for a description of some parameters of the simulation). In the competitive
process, market interactions determine variation in the relative size and
profitability of each firm (they may also 'die' and, in sector 1 only, 're-enter'
with some probability, which is actually equivalent to the birth of new
firms).

  Figure 8.4 presents the dynamics of notional opportunities (those generated at aggregate level by income changes that yield new discoveries in
'basic science') and of opportunities that actually become technological
innovations. As the simulation shows, the innovative exploration of individual firms 'floats' in an expanding set of potential new 'technological
paradigms'. However, their path-dependent processes of technological

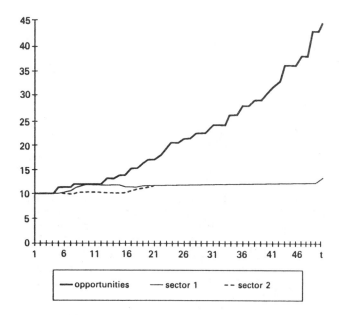

Figure 8.4   Distance between notional and realized opportunities

140   *Innovative Learning and Institutions*

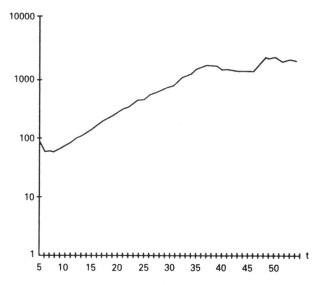

Figure 8.5   Income time series (logscale)

learning make them discover and develop only three of them, corresponding to the vertical steps along the otherwise horizontal line. Interestingly,
this property appears to be quite resistant to changes in the parameters
governing the probabilities of successful innovation by individual firms.
Whenever the economy sustains a flow of new notional opportunities (that
is, of 'scientific advancements') above a certain level, economic agents
appear to be unable – for a good range of search parameters – to 'keep up'
with them. All this illustrates also our earlier proposition that agents are not
limited in their innovativeness by some exogenously given 'natural' constraint, but rather by the history of their competences.

At this stage, one can only say that the generated series of income and
average productivity seem 'plausible' (see Figures 8.5 and 8.6): we conjecture that the model's aggregate dynamics might also show econometric
properties similar to the empirical ones. Indeed, in our view, what should be
surprising and, theoretically, encouraging is the very fact that relatively
ordered patterns of economic coordination and aggregate change emerge
without imposing either 'rational' *ex ante* consistency of microdecisions or
exogenous constraints on available technologies and resources.

Note also that, like 'Real Business Cycle' models, one cannot distinguish
between transitory and permanent (trend) components in the generated
time series. However, unlike the former models, innovations do not take
the form of exogenous stochastic shocks, but rather are generated endogenously by agents themselves.

Moreover, the transmission mechanism from innovation to aggregate
dynamics is neither the intertemporal adjustment of consumption plans by a

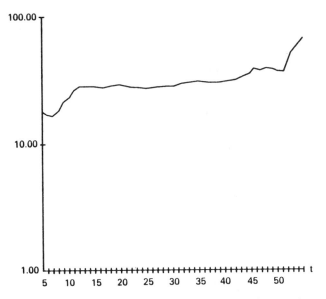

Figure 8.6   Labour productivity time series (logscale)

rational agent (see Long and Plosser, 1982), nor the optimal intertemporal distribution of investment plans (Schleifer, 1982). Indeed, in our model, innovation influences aggregate dynamics via two interrelated processes: *first*, via time-consuming diffusion among producers and users, and *second*, via the demand impulses that innovation and diffusion generate. The latter, 'Keynesian', feature of the model implies that, although (*endogenous*) 'shocks' have technological nature, the actual aggregate impact is determined by related *demand* shocks (via investment decisions, and levels of consumption).

Figure 8.6 shows the dynamics of labour productivity and illustrates also the possibility that the evolutionary dynamics may induce absolute decreases in average productivity even if best practice techniques may only improve (or remain the same): this is due to the learning lags of users and the possible fall in the market shares of early innovators. As with the results obtained by Silverberg, Dosi and Orsenigo (1988), innovators may sometimes be 'lambs' whose 'sacrifice' produces a learning externality for the whole system.

Finally, an 'impressionistic' consideration of both Figures 8.5 and 8.6 seems to hint at possibilities of major discontinuities in the relationship between income growth, productivity growth and, thus, also employment changes during different 'phases of growth' (compare, for example, the last 15 periods of both figures).

In a complementary work, Chiaromonte and Dosi (1990) analyse the essential role of *microdiversity* in aggregate growth. Contrary to the conventional microfoundations, one shows that the *form* of the distributions of microcharacteristics of the agents (technological competences and parameters of the decision rules) affect macrodynamics, *even for unchanged mean values*. For example, repetitions of the simulation shown in the above figures, assuming *identical* agents (with parameters equal to the mean values of the distributions as from the previous case), lead to very little technical progress and a long-term fall in aggregate income.

Collective learning and sustained income dynamics appear to find a necessary condition in technological and behavioural heterogeneity. Pushing the intuition to the extreme, what turn out to be 'mistakes' for individual agents might also represent positive externalities for the system as a whole.

Here, we want to focus upon the relationship between aggregate dynamics, on the one hand, and different institutional set-ups shaping behaviours and micro interactions, on the other.

In our model, these institutional features concern: (a) the *appropriability conditions of innovation*, as captured by the easiness of imitation in sector 1, and the speed at which private learning becomes a public externality in sector 2; (b) the *nature and parameters of decision rules* as they affect pricing, expansion, scrapping, R&D and so on; (c) the *nature of interaction processes* in the labour, product and financial markets.

As regards appropriability, corroborating Schumpeterian intuition, simulations not presented here show that some minimum appropriability threshold is a necessary condition for innovation. However, *variations* in appropriability, above a certain minimum threshold, have ambiguous effects on growth of income and productivity. For example, an increasing appropriability ensures the 'virtuous' feedback between innovation, profitability and growth for *individual* innovators, but may also slow down diffusion and, through that, *aggregate* growth in income and productivity.

More generally, in our model, 'institutions; are also the rules which govern adjustments in product and labour markets. Indeed, in the historical taxonomy of the various phases of capitalist development suggested by the French 'Regulation' approach, different 'regimes of growth' are also defined by different *average* adjustment parameters on the major markets. So, in an extreme archetype, a 'classical' ('competitive') regime is defined by the general absence of price-making power on the product markets and by the crucial dependence of real wage rates on unemployment level and changes. Conversely, the contemporary ('monopolistic') regime is defined – in that interpretation – also by various degrees of price-making behaviours on product markets and some (often union-led) indexation of wages on consumers' prices and on productivity increases. All that in our model implies that 'typical behaviours' in the product and labour markets would show up also in different adjustment parameters in equations 8.25, 8.26 and 8.27 above. In the highly constraint-free model defined here, the dependence of growth patterns upon particular institutional regimes would also appear through differences of dynamic patterns when variations occur in 'technological regimes' (that is, conditions of technological opportunity and appropriability) and in the average adjustment mechanisms on the various markets.

In fact, the simulation results shown earlier highlight a possible micro-foundation to 'Kaldorian' positive feedback between (a) expanding technological opportunities; (b) endogenous demand growth (also via old-fashioned 'accelerator' mechanisms and growing wage-based consumption); and subject to (c) some institutionally specific constraints on income distribution (via some price making power on both labour and products prices).

What would happen if one changes average 'institutional' rules of adjustment, while leaving technological conditions unchanged? If one assumes 'competitive' price-making on either markets of products or labour (but not both), then, in both cases, a few simulation runs suggest that a rather flat trend of aggregate income appears. In our interpretation, the absence of *one of the institutional adjustment rules* deprives the system of one of the 'virtuous' positive feedbacks, and thus 'locks it' into a less expansionary dynamics (see Figures 8.7–10).

In the case of 'competitive wages' (that is, wages reacting only to employment changes) and oligopolistic product pricing (as the standard simulation: see Figures 8.5 and 8.6) a deflationary tendency is likely to appear. It is somewhat similar to that sort of mature 'capitalism depression' early envisaged by 'Keynesian' and 'structuralist' scholars such as Hansen, Steindl and Sylos Labini. Indeed, in this scenario, growth conditions seem to depend crucially upon the 'animal spirits' of entrepreneurs: if their demand expectations are high and so are their beliefs in innovative opportunities, aggregate growth is high too. But their 'optimism' in expanding technological opportunities and demand must *increasingly* compensate for unfavourable conditions of aggregate demand generation (in an old language, changes in income distribution make the 'Keynesian multiplier' shrink).

Conversely, 'competitive rules' on product markets (that is, prices reacting only to competitive conditions with no 'desired' mark-up) with 'monopolistic rules' on the labour market (as in the standard simulation from Figures 8.5 and 8.6) constrain the capability of firms to expand productive capacity and also to explore new technological opportunities (compare Figures 8.9 and 8.10 with Figures 8.7 and 8.8, and all of them with Figures 8.5 and 8.6); in the present model, this is the case nearest to the classical/neoclassical hyphoteses on some binding system-level constraint to firms expansion and aggregate income growth, via 'rigidities' in income distribution.

In simulations not shown here, we tried various combinations of 'competitive' adjustment parameters on both labour and product markets: that is, some highly stylized representations of a 'classical' regime of growth. Under these conditions, it turns out that the crucial parameters influencing the rate of long-term income growth are the investment propensities, as represented by the δs in equations 8.13 and 8.14: that is, in the empirical equivalents of the theoretical metaphor, the *norms and beliefs* governing the *propensity to accumulate* of business firms.

144   *Innovative Learning and Institutions*

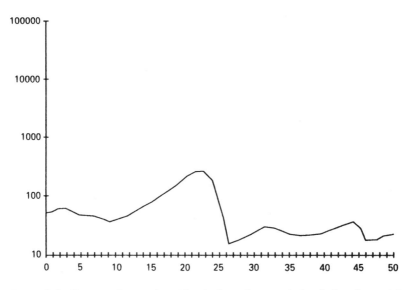

Figure 8.7   Income time series: 'classical employment' simulation (logscale)

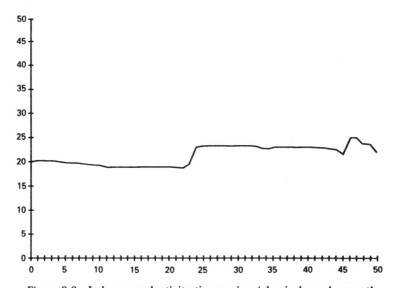

Figure 8.8   Labour productivity time series: 'classical employment'
simulation

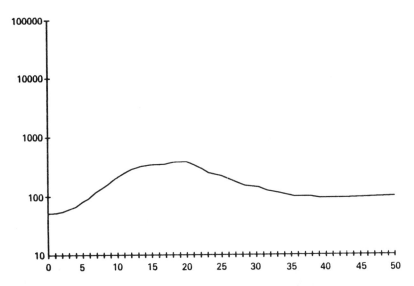

Figure 8.9   Income time series: 'competitive product-market' simulation
(logscale)

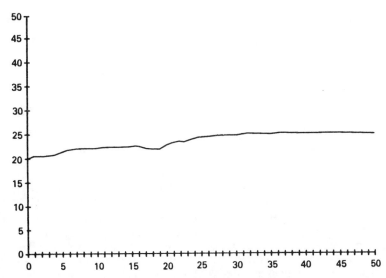

Figure 8.10   Labour productivity time series: 'competitive product-market'
simulation

SOME CONCLUSIONS

The 'evolutionary' model presented in this work explores some of the properties of aggregate economic dynamics whereby, *first*, innovative opportunities are permanently and abundantly generated as direct outcomes of 'scientific' search and collective, indirect outcomes of individual interest-motivated behaviours; and, *second*, decision-guiding *norms* shape individual behaviour and collective adjustment mechanisms. Highly nonlinear processes link individual strategies with aggregate outcomes. Moreover, in the *boundedly rational* environment depicted here, behavioural routines are rather inertial (at the very least, they change much more slowly than the notional technological opportunities which continuously emerge). Hence, the *rates and directions of individual learning might systematically differ from system-level learning*. And, also, one may well find *differences in the rates at which different institutional regimes exploit innovative and growth opportunities*.

We attempted to formalize a system dynamics as constraint-free as possible; therefore, the system could find a great (a priori unspecified) number of 'attractors' which it could lock-in according to its history and its technological and institutional characteristics. Our (admittedly very preliminary) investigation concerned some sort of mapping between technological *and institutional* set-ups, on the one hand, and system dynamics, on the other. In fact, a crucial feature of the model is to embed *endogenous* technological learning into specific behavioural and market institutions. We performed a few simulation exercises showing widely different aggregate outcomes of diverse conditions of microeconomic interaction which somewhat corroborate the conjecture that the various observed patterns of growth underlie *and require* highly specific combinations between collective technological learning and institutional forms of behavioural adjustments. As mentioned at the beginning, one would aim at a model wherein behavioural rules co-evolve with the system itself. Falling short of that, the present model is at the very least a 'theoretical tale' of the highly differentiated long-term outcomes to which varying combinations of technological learning and institutional norms can lead, whenever one abandons the modelling assumption of a world characterized by sophisticated calculating agents and binding 'natural' constraints to their actions. It can also be interpreted as a sort of *gedankenexperiment* (thought experiment) emphasizing some different system-level properties of learning and institutions (that is, different 'regimes') under increasing dynamic returns and much less than micro-optimizing rationality. In that, the model places the main burden of the explanation of 'why growth rates differ' over time and across countries upon the variegated ways by which innovative learning occurs. It also shows the importance of behavioural norms, even for *given* opportunities of technological learning. This is an old claim of development economics whose origin can be traced back to early political economists. The task of showing how different systems learn about institutions and rules has not been undertaken here: however, as difficult as it is, it seems within the reach of microfounded 'evolutionary' models.

Appendix I

Values attributed to the parameters defining the innovative microbehaviours in the simulation presented in the section on a self-organization model.

Parameters	Means	Distributed between:
Sector 1		
χ	0.15	0 and 0.3
μ	0.1	0 and 0.2
ζ	0.5	0.2 and 0.8
Sector 2		
a	0.2	0 and 0.4
b	5	3 and 7

The random distributions are of truncated normals around the above means.

Recall the meaning of the different parameters:

For sector 1 agents:

χ is a firm-specific 'prudential' coefficient in the decision rule about radical innovations in manufactured machines.

μ is the propensity to investments in technological search.

ζ is the parameter that distributes research investments between innovation and imitation (propensity to imitate).

For sector 2 agents:

a is the firm-specific learning expectation.

b is the pay-back period parameter used in the scrapping rule.

Notes

1. In this and the following sections we shall present only some basic features of the model: more details are in Chiaromonte (1990).
2. Compare this view with that of an exogenous random arrival of 'technological shocks', as in Long and Plosser (1982), or the steady flow of innovations in Schleifer (1986). Nearer to our approach, *prima facie*, are Romer (1990) and Aghion and Howitt (1989), where the rates of innovation depend on the 'human capital' (or, more generally, labour) invested in exploration. However, in our model, the *abilities* in exploring are themselves an endogenous variable, and are, to some extent, firm-specific.
3. Cf. Freeman (1982), Winter (1987), Pavitt (1987) and Dosi (1988).
4. Cf. Aghion and Howitt (1989) who, however, use the expression to refer only to the substitution among different generations of innovation.
5. Of course, the 'Keynesianism' of Cambridge, England!
6. Although there is for individual borrowers (firms), as a function of their cash flow.
7. The restriction to the integer values of A_1 and A_2, while not influencing any of the conclusions, allows a positive probability that two or more different agents may produce/use the same machine (see below).

8. In the simulations of the penultimate section we have distinguished demand expectations on new typologies of machines, correcting them with a firm-specific parameter of 'confidence' in new technologies.
9. The following part of the model draws significantly on the earlier model in Silverberg, Dosi and Orsenigo (1988).
10. In its calculation, as in Silverberg, Dosi and Orsenigo (1988), one uses the actual skill levels: it would be too adventurous to throw away good equipment simply on learning expectations. Moreover, if the new machine belongs to a typology not yet adopted by j, the initial skill level is the public one s_p (x, t).
11. In the model presented here there are no variable inputs other than labour, and overhead costs are independent from the levels of production.
12. Supposed equal to 0 if the currently manufactured machine is a new one.
13. Note, however, that, while the coefficients of the 'competitiveness' function of sector 1 agents are themselves functions of time, for sector 2 agents they are parameters (see below).
14. One cannot presume each producer would know the $\omega(t)$s. Rather, they result by aggregation over a heterogeneous population of customers.

References

Abramovitz, M. (1989) *Thinking about Growth* (Cambridge University Press).
Aghion, P. and Howitt, P. (1989) 'A Model of Growth through Creative Destruction' (Cambridge, Mass.: MIT Press), Dept of Economics, Discussion Paper.
Boyer, R. (1988a) 'Formalizing Growth Regime', in Dosi *et al.* (1988).
—— (1988b) *'Technical Change and the Theory of "Regulation"'*, in Dosi *et al.* (1988).
Chiaromonte, F. (1990) 'Processi di innovazione microeconomici e dinamiche macroeconomiche: un modello evolutivo bisettoriale' (Rome: Dept of Economics).
—— and Dosi, G. (1990) 'The Microfoundations of Competitiveness and their Macroeconomic Implications' (Paris: OECD/DSTI), presented at the Conference on 'Technology and Competitiveness', June.
Coricelli, F., Dosi, G. and Orsenigo, L. (1989) 'Microeconomic Dynamics and Macro-Regularities: An Evolutionary Approach to Technological and Institutional Change' (Paris: OECD/DSTI/SPR/89.7).
Dosi, G. (1984) *Technical Change and Industrial Transformation* (London: Macmillan).
—— (1988) 'Sources, Procedures and Microeconomic Effects of Innovation', *Journal of Economic Literature*, 26 (September).
—— and Egidi, M. (1990) 'Substantive and Procedural Uncertainty. An Exploration of Economic Behaviours in Changing Environments', *Journal of Evolutionary Economics*, 1.
—— Freeman, C., Nelson, R., Silverberg, G. and Soete, L. (eds) (1988) *Technical Change and Economic Theory* (London: Francis Pinter; New York: Columbia University Press).
—— and Orsenigo, L. (1988) 'Coordination and Transformation: An Overview of Structures, Behaviours and Change in Evolutionary Environments', in Dosi *et al.* (1988).
Freeman, C. (1982) *The Economics of Industrial Innovation*, 2nd edn (London: Francis Printer).

Greenwald, B. and Stiglitz, J. (1987) 'Keynesian, new-Keynesian and new-classical Economics', *Oxford Economic Papers*, 39.
—— and Stiglitz, J. (1988) 'Examining Alternative Macroeconomic Theories', *Brooking Papers on Economic Activity*, 11.
Grossman, G. and Helpman, H. (1991) 'Quality Ladders and Product Cycles', *The Quarterly Journal of Economics*, 106.
Kaldor, N. (1974) *Essays on Stability and Growth* (London: Duckworth).
Landes, D. (1969) *The Unbound Prometheus* (Cambridge University Press).
Long, J. and Plosser, C. (1982) 'Real business cycle', *Journal of Political Economy*, 91.
Lucas, R. (1988) 'On the Mechanics of Economic Development', *Journal of Monetary Economics*, 22.
Maddison, A. (1982) *Phases of Capitalist Development* (Oxford University Press).
Mansfield, E., Schwartz, M. and Wagner S. (1981) 'Imitation Costs and Patents: An Empirical Study', *Economic Journal*, 91.
Mokyr, J. (1990) *The Lever of Riches* (Oxford University Press).
Nelson, C. and Plosser, C. (1982) 'Trends and Random Walks in Macroeconomic time series', *Journal of Monetary Economics*, 10.
Nelson, R. and Winter, S. (1982) *An Evolutionary Theory of Economic Change* (Cambridge, Mass.: The Belknap Press of Harvard University Press).
Pavitt, K. (1984) 'Sectoral Patterns of Innovation: Towards a Taxonomy and a Theory', *Research Policy*, 13.
—— (1987) 'The Objective of Technology Policy', *Science and Public Policy*.
Romer, P. (1986) 'Increasing Returns and Long-Run Growth', *Journal of Political Economy*, 94.
—— (1990) 'Endogenous Technical Change', *Journal of Political Economy*, 98.
Rosenberg, N. (1976) *Perspectives on Technology* (Cambridge University Press).
—— (1982) *Inside the Black Box* (Cambridge University Press).
Schleifer, A. (1986) 'Implementation Cycles', *Journal of Political Economy*, 94.
Silverberg, G. (1987) 'Technical Progress, Capital Accumulation and Effective Demand: A Self-Organization Model', in D. Batten *et al.*, *Economic Evolution and Structural Change* (Berlin/New York, Springer Verlag).
——, Dosi, G. and Orsenigo, L. (1988) 'Innovation, Diversity and Diffusion: A Self-Organization Model', *Economic Journal*, 98.
Simon, H. (1984) 'On the Behavioural Foundations of Economic Dynamics', *Journal of Economic Behaviour and Organization*, 59.
Solow, R. (1984) *Growth Theory* (Oxford University Press).
Verspagen, B. (1990) '"New" neo-classical growth models and their relations to evolutionary theory of economic growth: an interpretative survey of some recent literature', Maastricht, University of Limburg, MERIT, Research Memorandum.
Winter, S. (1987) 'Natural Selection and Evolution', *The New Palgrave: A Dictionary of Economics* (London: Macmillan).

The Dynamics of International Differentiation: A Multi-country Evolutionary Model

GIOVANNI DOSI[a], SILVIA FABIANI[b], ROBERTA AVERSI[c]
and MARA MEACCI[d]

([a]Department of Economics, University of Rome, 'La Sapienza', Rome, Italy,
[b]University of Cambridge, UK, [c]Tecsiel, Rome, Italy
and [d]Faculty of Statistics, University of Rome, 'La Sapienza', Rome, Italy)

The paper presents some (admittedly preliminary) results on evolutionary modeling of open-economies interactions. The dynamics is microfounded in a multiplicity of boundedly rational agents who imperfectly learn how to innovate in environments characterized by notionally unlimited opportunities. Micro discoveries—it is shown—can generate persistent system-level effects. Despite the absence in the model of any institutional specificity of individual countries, processes of innovative exploration and imitation yield international divergence, (less often) convergence, catching-up, and falling-behind.

1. Introduction

Industrial and Corporate Change Volume 3 Number 1 1994

Are firm-specific activities of innovation sufficient to determine long-term country-level differentiation in the patterns of growth? Do the time series of the aggregate variables generated by evolutionary processes of learning and selection display statistical properties similar to the observed ones? Can one account also for convergence and divergence, forging ahead and falling behind in per capita incomes?

The model that follows addresses these questions and explores the properties of evolutionary microfoundations of growth in open economies which continuously undergo innovation and imitation by heterogeneous agents. As

——————— *The Dynamics of International Differentiation* ———————

such, it can be interpreted as an analysis of the ways in which each national economy self-organizes in its patterns of generation and exploitation of production knowledge. Indeed, the relationship between exploration of new sources of knowledge, accumulation and growth is increasingly acknowledged as a crucial one, well outside the evolution camp, e.g. in 'new' and refined versions of 'old' growth theories. For example, Benhabib and Jovanovic conclude their work by saying that:

> no doubt, a quantum leap in our understanding of growth will occur only when the engine of growth (namely the stochastic process driving country-specific technological shocks) is successfully endogenized (Benhabib and Jovanovic, 1991, p. 102).

This model tries to move some steps in this direction by microfounding country dynamics on some stylized company-specific processes of innovation and imitation.

We start from the Schumpeterian intuition that technical change is in its nature a disequilibrium phenomenon and we focus on the aggregate properties of economies where innovative learning is such that they are never able to reach a state wherein resources are allocated optimally and prices reveal relative efficiencies of inputs. In fact, we shall make our argument even more extreme and suppose that each economic system is never constrained by scarcities either in terms of notional technological opportunities or in terms of labour supply. Moreover, we shall neglect all those country-specific systematic influences, such as institutional specificities, policies, etc. which—one has argued in the introduction to this volume—exert a paramount influence on development patterns. Under these extreme circumstances, we shall ask, will each system self-organize through fluctuations far from equilibrium and generate some of those regularities which we empirically observe? (Of course, a positive result would only be reinforced by adding those country-specific factors mentioned above.)

More specifically, we shall show that:

(i)   Initially identical countries may well differentiate in ways that are persistent over time.

(ii) 'Local' (company-specific) fluctuations may determine long-term aggregate (country-wide) effects.

(iii) 'Evolutionary' microfoundations and heterogeneous learning are sufficient to sustain Kaldorian 'virtuous' and 'vicious' feedbacks.

(iv) According to different time-scales and different 'phases' one may observe 'catching up', forging ahead, divergence.

─────────────── *The Dynamics of International Differentiation* ───────────────

The modeling strategy finds a lot of inspiration in the seminal work of Nelson and Winter (1982) and draws from a previous (closed-economy) model by one of us (Chiaromonte and Dosi, 1992).[1]

2. *The Model*

In the general specification of the model, we consider a 'world' economy composed of L countries $(1...j...L)$, M sectors $(1...h...M)$ for each country and n $(1...i...n)$ firms per country per sector. By assumption every firm operates in the markets of all countries (we shall index with k each national market) and in only one sector of activity. Within each sector products are homogeneous. All countries and firms have exactly the same initial conditions. In a Schumpeterian vein, each firm can increase its productivity through innovation or imitation of already existing techniques. The probability of success in either activity depends on the firm's expenditures devoted to R&D and on a random component which captures the intrinsic uncertainty of the research process.

Labor is the only input in both search and production and by assumption there are no constraints in its supply. In the version of the model presented here for simplicity labor is homogeneous and can be applied indifferently to search and production. (Fixed) coefficients of production are company-specific, $1/\pi_{ij}(t)$, where π is labor productivity.

Search and Imitation

'Search' is a two-stages stochastic process and applies to both innovation and imitation.

A first stage determines whether search is successful:

$$\Pr\{I_{ij}(t) = 1\} = 1 - \exp\{-a_1 \, IN_{ij}(t)\}, \tag{1}$$

where I_{ij} is a binary variable which takes value one if the event 'success' occurs, IN_{ij} is the investment in search by firm i of country j measured in terms of a current and lagged number of searching workers (Inn):[2]

───

[1] Models within a similar evolutionary perspective are Iwai (1984a, 1984b); Metcalfe (1988); Silverberg *et al.* (1988); Conlisk (1991); Silverberg and Lehnert (1992). However, to our knowledge, this is the first attempt to explicitly represent a multi-economies dynamics. For greater detail on the model which follows, cf. Fabiani (1990) and Dosi *et al.* (1993).

[2] In another version of the model, not presented here, we have a learning externality, so that the probability of innovation depends also on the amount of search undertaken by all others firms within the country and in the world:

$$IN_{ij}(t) = \sum_{\tau=0}^{2} Inn_{ij}(t-\tau) + \alpha_{1j}\sum_{\tau=0}^{2} Inn_{tot j}(t-\tau) + \alpha_{2j}\sum_{\tau=0}^{2} Inn_{tot}(t-\tau).$$

——————— *The Dynamics of International Differentiation* ———————

$$\sum_{\tau = 0}^{2} Inn_{ij} (t - \tau)$$

The parameter a_1 captures the level of technological opportunities.

If 'success' is drawn, the firm adds a percentage productivity increment by accessing a Poisson distribution with mean λ:

$$E \left[\pi_{ij}^I (t + 1)\right] = \pi_{ij}(t) \left(1 + \frac{\lambda}{100}\right). \tag{2}$$

The value of λ, too, is a proxy for the richness of unexplored opportunities.

Technological knowledge, in our model, is neither a purely public good nor is perfectly appropriable. New techniques can be imitated but with a search cost. In analogy with innovation, imitation is a two stages stochastic process, dependent also on the 'technological gap' *vis-à-vis* the imitated technique.

Define the notional set of techniques that can be imitated as $\Pi(t) = U_{j=1}^{m} \pi_j(t)$. Next, define the differences (that is the 'distance') between the technique already used by firm i and any one technique belonging to Π:

$$d(\pi_{ij}(t); \pi(t)) = \max \{0; \pi - \pi_{ij}\} \qquad \text{if } \pi \ \varepsilon \ \Pi_j$$
$$= \xi \max \{0; \pi - \pi_{ij}\} \qquad \text{otherwise}$$

where $\zeta \ (> 1)$, so to speak, decreases the imitability of the techniques belonging to firms of other countries.

Hence, the imitation search set for the i-firm is defined by:

$$\Pi M_{ij} (t) = \{\forall \ \pi \ \varepsilon \ \Pi: d(\pi_{ij}(t), \pi) > 0\}.$$

Like the innovation process, success in imitation is a stochastic variable

$$\Pr\{M_{ij}(t) = 1\} = 1 - \exp \{- a_{2j} \ IM_{ij}(t)\}, \tag{3}$$

where, denoting the numbers of workers involved in imitative search at time t by $Imi(t)$,

$$IM_{ij} (t) = \sum_{\tau = 0}^{2} Imi_{ij} (t - \tau) + \alpha_{3j} \sum_{i} \sum_{\tau = 0}^{2} Imi_{ij} (t - \tau) + \alpha_{4j} \sum_{j} \sum_{\tau = 0}^{2} Imi_{ij} (t - \tau).$$

The parameter a_{2j} is an inverse measure of appropriability, while α_{3j} and α_{4j} capture country-wide and worldwide externalities, respectively. (In the simulations that we shall present below we shall put a_{3j} and a_{4j} equal to zero.) In the case of 'imitative success', the imitated technique is drawn from the imitation search set with a probability proportional to the distance from the technique currently used by firm i, $\forall \ \pi \ \varepsilon \ \Pi M_{ij}(t)$:

——————————— 228 ———————————

──────────── *The Dynamics of International Differentiation* ────────────

$$\Pr\{\pi_{ij}^{M}(t) = \pi\} = \frac{[\mathrm{d}\,(\pi,\pi_{ij})]^{-1}}{\displaystyle\sum_{\pi\varepsilon\Pi M_{ij}(t)}[\mathrm{d}\,(\pi,\pi_{ij})]^{-1}}. \tag{4}$$

The intuition behind this formulation is that learning is 'local' and knowledge is partly tacit, so that the probability of instantaneous catching up to best practice techniques is inversely proportional to the laggard's distance (although, of course, the scope for catching up is higher).

The rule determining the technique actually applied to production is straightforward:

$$\pi_{ij}(t+1) = \max\{\pi_{ij}(t);\ \pi I_{ij}(t);\ \pi M_{ij}(t)\}. \tag{5}$$

Behavioural Rules

In the model, we make the rather extreme and unorthodox assumption that behavior is totally 'routinized', that is, based on fixed and event-independent rules.

There are indeed good empirical and theoretical reasons to expect behaviors to be rather inertial in highly uncertain and non-stationary environments (see Nelson and Winter, 1982; Heiner, 1988; Dosi and Egidi, 1991) in addition, of course, to the 'behaviorist tradition' of Herbert Simon and James March). In any case, the reader who is more inclined to 'rational' characterizations of microbehaviors may well consider this assumption as an extreme version of bounded rationality with myopic expectations.

A first routine determines the quantity of investment in research by relating it to the firm's previous-period turnover:

$$\mathrm{R\&D}_{ij}(t) = a_{3ij}\,Y_{ij}(t-1). \tag{6}$$

The number of workers in research is defined by:

$$I_{ij}(t) = \frac{\mathrm{R\&D}_{ij}(t)}{w_j(t)}, \tag{7}$$

where $w_j(t)$ is the wage in country j at t.

Another rule divides research activity between innovation, Inn_{ij} and imitation, Imi_{ij}

$$Inn_{ij} = (1 - \mu_{ij})\,I_{ij}, \tag{8}$$

$$Imi_{ij} = \mu_{ij}\,I_{ij}. \tag{9}$$

──────────── 229 ────────────

——————— *The Dynamics of International Differentiation* ———————

The determination of the price within each firm is based on a two-stages process. First, the 'desired' price, $\tilde{p}_{ij}$, is calculated on the basis of a mark-up procedure, in relation to the wage level in the current and the previous period and the firm's productivity coefficient:

$$\tilde{p}_{ij}(t) = \frac{a_{4i}\,w_j(t) + a_{5i}\,w_j(t-1)}{\pi_{ij}(t)}(1 + m),\qquad(10)$$

where m is the mark-up coefficient and a_{4i} and a_{5i} are coefficients of adjustment ($a_{4i} + a_{5i} = 1$).

In the second stage, the actual price variation by each firm on its own domestic market is computed as:

$$\Delta p_i(t) = a_{6i}\,[\log\tilde{p}_i(t) - \log p_i(t-1)] + a_{7i}[\log f_i^*(t-1) - \log f_i(t-1)]$$
$$+ a_{8i}\,[\log f_i(t-2) - \log f_i(t-1)],\qquad(11)$$

where $f_i^*(t)$ is the desired market share of firm i (for simplicity here and throughout we drop the suffices whenever that does not engender confusion). (As it will be described in more detail in what follows, firms may happen to be in a situation of 'credit rationing'. In such cases, the actual market share, $f.(\ )$ is different from the desired one.)

Therefore, the actual price becomes:

$$p_i(t) = p_i(t-1)\,[1 + \Delta p_i(t)].\qquad(12)$$

The process of change of individual productivities jointly with the pricing procedure determine the level of firm-specific 'competitiveness', E_{ij}^k. A procedure of price variation similar to that described in equations (11) and (12) is applied for pricing in markets different from one's own market. Clearly, in these circumstances, the $p_{ij}(t)$'s are redefined with the current exchange rate in order to yield the desired and actual prices in local currencies. Thus, prices and exchange rates enter the determination of the competitiveness of each firm in each market:

$$E_{ij}^k(t) = \frac{1}{p_{ij}(t)}\rho_j(t),\qquad(13)$$

where ρ_j is the exchange rate of country j and k is the particular market where the firm operates.

Workers consume in $(t+1)$ all the wages that they have earned in t. Firms invest their surpluses in search via the mechanism of equation (6) and deposit their net cash flow in an interest-free account with the 'financial sector' which

——————————— 230 ———————————

———————— *The Dynamics of International Differentiation* ————————

is not modeled here. Or they can draw interest-free advances up to a limit proportional to their current turnover and past cash flows. This is like saying that credit is rationed for individual firms and may constrain individual growth. Note that, on the contrary, there is no aggregate ceiling to credit. That is, one may think of an endogenous money supply: the assumption is near the Kaldorian idea of 'endogenous money'. Call $C_{ij}(t)$ the net cash flows. The (credit-constrained) maximum growth of a firm is:

$$Y_i(t+1)_{max} \leq (1+a_{9i})\left(Y_i(t-1)\frac{p_i(t)}{p_i(t-1)} + a_{10i}\sum_0^t C_i(\tau)\right). \quad (14)$$

Market Dynamics

Domestic demand in each country (at current prices and exchange rates), D^j, aggregates *ex post* over the whole wage bill paid to workers employed in both production and search:

$$D^j(t) = \sum_i w_j(t) N_{ij}(t), \quad (15)$$

where N_{ij} is the total employment in firm i.

In this version of the model we also assume a constant-share demand function. For country j, we have:

$$D^{jb} = (1/M) D^j, \quad (16)$$

(M is the number of sectors).

Demand is distributed among individual producers (both domestic and foreign) according to their relative competitiveness. Demand can be thought of as 'orders' on the basis of which each firm determines its production decisions, according to the relation:

$$Y_{ij}(t) = \sum_k f_{ij}^k(t) D^{k_b}(t-1) \rho_j(t). \quad (17)$$

That is, the demand of firm i which produces in country j is the sum of the demands from all the national markets, k (in sector h where it operates), translated into its domestic currency via the exchange rate. In turn, the demand in each market is obviously identical to its market share, $f.$, multiplied by the size of the market itself, D.

Market share dynamics in each market is governed by:

$$\Delta f_i^k(t,t+1) = a_{11}\left(\frac{E_i^k(t)}{E^k(t)} - 1\right)f_i^k(t), \quad (18)$$

──────────── *The Dynamics of International Differentiation* ────────────

where $E^k(t)$ is the average competitiveness on market k and the coefficient a_{11} is a proxy for the 'selectiveness' of the market. Loosely speaking, it determines the speed at which success is rewarded and lags are punished. This replicator type dynamics associated with market selection entails, in general, the coexistence of firms characterized by different levels of efficiency and different behavioral rules.[3]

Firms die when their market shares are reduced below a certain critical level:

$$\sum_k f_{ij}^k < f_{min}.$$

The model also embodies entry of new firms. Dead firms are replaced by new entrants with an initial productivity equal to the average productivity in the sector and in the country where birth occurs, plus a white noise.

Demand for labor to be employed in production by firm i is:

$$N_{ij}^p(t) = \frac{1}{\pi_{ij}(t)} \sum_k \frac{Y_{ij}^k(t)}{p_{ij}^k(t)}. \tag{19}$$

That is, it is just the real output divided by labor productivity of the firm.

Aggregate Dynamics and National Accounts

National aggregate variables sum up (very much like national accounts) over their corresponding microeconomic values.

National income, at constant prices (Y^*) is:

$$Y_j^* = \sum_i \left(\frac{Y_{ij}}{p_{ij}} \right). \tag{20}$$

Exports are:

$$EXP_j = \sum_{k \neq j} \sum_h \sum_i (f_{ij}^k D^{kh}) \, p_j, \tag{21}$$

where we consider the market shares of firm i belonging to country j on each of the other k markets different from j (i.e. sales of domestic firms in every country different from their own).

---

[3] This selection dynamics draws from Silverberg (1987) and Silverberg *et al.* (1988). In that particular case when best practice techniques are stationary, it entails a sigmoid diffusion pattern. The particular formulation of the selection dynamics adopted here in its unconstrained form allows market shares to become negative. When that occurs, we constrain the share in the neighborhood of zero and shares of all others firms are rescaled proportionally.

———————————— *The Dynamics of International Differentiation* ————————————

Imports are:

$$IMP_j = D^j - \sum_{k=j}\sum_b\sum_i (f^k_{ij} D^{k_b})\, \rho_j, \qquad (22)$$

That is, imports are obviously the total domestic demand minus the domestic sales from domestic firms.

Trade balances (which in this model are taken to be identical to foreign payment balances) are:

$$B_j \equiv EXP_j - IMP_j.$$

The (monetary) wage dynamic is driven by labor productivity growth ($\bar{\pi}_j$), percentage consumer price changes ($\bar{p}_j$), and percentage changes in the levels of employment ($\dot{N}_j$):

$$\dot{w}_j\,(t,t+1) = a_{11j}\bar{\pi}_j\,(t-1,t) + a_{12j}\bar{p}_j\,(t-1,t) + a_{13j}\dot{N}_j\,(t-1,t). \qquad (23)$$

The variable $\bar{p}_j$ stands for a consumer price index; $\bar{\pi}_j$ is the average productivity across the M sectors weighted with the real product of each firm and the dots stand for rates of change. The coefficients are bounded in the interval $[0,1]$.

Exchange rates vary as a function of current and past cumulated foreign balances.[4]

Before discussing the simulation results, let us consider some general properties of this model. First, note that dynamics is driven by endogenously generated, company-specific technological shocks but the latter exert their influence on incomes via a 'Keynesian' mechanism of demand formation.

Second, the propagation of these shocks occurs via (i) imperfect adjustments on the product markets, through changes in market shares; and (ii) inter-firm imitation. This also implies, of course, that diffusion of innovation is never instantaneous and its rates depend jointly on market selection among heterogeneous firms and, in inverse fashion, on the appropriability of innovations. Further, financial market rationing may put a ceiling on the expansion of the most successful firms.

Third, the model embodies different sources of persistence: at company-

—————————————————————————————————

[4] Define an 'income-normalized' balance as $S_j = B_j/Y_j$. Then define:

$$\dot{r}\,(t,t+1) = a_{14}\,S_j\,(t)\exp\left\{a_{15}\left|\sum_{\tau=0}^{t} S_j\,(t)\right|\right\},$$

and:

$$r_j\,(t+1) = [1 + \dot{r}(t,t+1)]\, r_j\,(t)$$

level, (i) probabilities of innovation and imitation depend also on lagged expenditures in search; (ii) innovative success feeds on itself by increasing the amount of resources devoted to search in the future; and, of course, (iii) the dynamics of firm-specific levels of productivity implies a non-dissipating memory (indeed, productivity for the single firm displays a behavior like a random walk with drift).

Fourth, imitation plus market selection introduces non-linear processes of interactions among firms. Moreover, adjustments in wages and exchange rates can be considered as some sort of negative feedbacks which curb, at least to some extent, the ability of firms to expand indefinitely on the world market.

Fifth, the fact that new-born firms access on average the mean efficiency of the incumbent in the sector and country where they start up implies some sort of country-specific externality which contributes to differentiate national knowledge basis.

Finally, note also a few things that are missing in this model, although they are plausibly very important in reality and also crucial in determining the observed cross-sectional and time series regularities in incomes. There is no fixed investment and thus the model rules out all those sources of irreversibility associated with capital-embodied technical change and vintages effects (cf. Silverberg and Lehnert, 1992; Silverberg and Verspagen, this volume). There is no room for expectations formation and thus for the amplifying or dampening effects that they might exert *vis-à-vis* past dynamics and there is also no room for those general factors—i.e. education, levels and composition of investments, etc.—which, as argued in the introduction, have a paramount importance in development. Under these circumstances, one of the crucial questions is precisely whether firm-specific sources of persistence are sufficient to explain country-level differentiation, with persistent diversity in the levels and growth rates of incomes.

3. *Some Simulation Results*

Let us start by emphasizing that what we report in the following are highly preliminary results, which nonetheless suggest in our view the heuristic promises of evolutionary microfoundations of international growth and, together, of the time series properties of growth patterns.

The analytical strategy with the simulation exercises is to explore the major regularities which the model generates as emergent properties, that is, as aggregate outcomes of the thread of positive and negative feedback mechanisms embedded in the behaviors and interactions of micro units. We

—————————— *The Dynamics of International Differentiation* ——————————

TABLE 1. DF and ADF Tests for Per Capita Income Levels and Rates of Growth

Statistic	Sample	Observation	Without trend	With trend
Income levels				
DF	2–500	499	3.6547 (−2.8676)	−0.65283 (−3.4208)
ADF(1)	3–500	498	2.0329 (−2.8676)	−1.1399 (−3.4208)
Rates of growth				
DF	3–500	498	−12.6230 (−2.8676)	−12.8314 (−3.4208)
ADF(1)	4–500	497	−8.9219 (−2.8676)	−9.0954 (−3.4208)

Note: 95% critical values in brackets.

have experimented with a few different parametrizations: the results that we shall present appear to be robust to rather wide parameter variations.

A general feature of the model is that it reproduces persistent inter-firm asymmetries in productivities, profits and market shares, which certainly fit the microeconomic 'stylized facts' discussed in Dosi, Freeman and Fabiani (this volume).

In the simulations, we start by analyzing the time series properties in the closed economy case. The economy is composed of five sectors of production interacting with each other in terms of creation and distribution of the aggregate demand. Each sector is made of 100 initially identical firms.[5]

Concerning the aggregate properties of the generated time series, we have analyzed the dynamic behavior of income, prices, investment, employment, productivity and per capita income. In particular, testing for stationarity, these series appear to be non-stationary in the levels and frequently stationary in the first differences[6] and, therefore, appear to be integrated of order one. Figure 1 presents the dynamic pattern of the cyclical component of per capita income. The related autocorrelation function (Figure 2) indicates a high degree of persistence in aggregate fluctuations.[7]

Moreover, we have found mixed evidence concerning the presence of cointegrating vectors between income and each of the other variables. Cointegration seems to be highly sensitive to the different parametrizations.[8]

Next, we experimented with a simplified version of the multicountry case. We considered as a starting point a homogeneous world economy in a stationary equilibrium: all firms and all countries are identical, foreign account balances and all exchange rates are equal to one. In order to

[5] This part draws on Meacci (1993).

[6] DF and ADF tests have been carried out and the results are presented in Table 1.

[7] Following the method suggested by Cochrane (1988).

[8] In particular, the obtained time series appear to be cointegrated in the case of a high degree of market selection and a weak credit rationing.

—————————— 235 ——————————

─────────── *The Dynamics of International Differentiation* ───────────

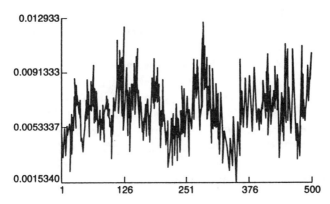

FIGURE 1. The cyclical component of per capita income.

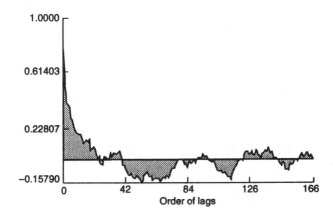

FIGURE 2. Autocorrelation function of the cyclical component of per capita income.

minimize any in-built bias toward differentiation, we have not allowed any country-wide externalities and we have assumed that the adjustment parameters (on the labor and product markets) and the behavioral parameters (e.g. mark-ups, propensity to invest in innovation, etc.) are identical across firms and across countries.[9]

Detailed analyses of the econometric properties of the time series gener-

─────────────────────────────────

[9] Moreover, for simplicity, unlike the closed economy exercises, we did not allow for 'inertial' price adjustments (cf. equations (11) and (12)) but we forced a straightforward mark-up pricing rule with mark-up identical across firms and countries:

$$P_{ij}(t) = \frac{w_j(t)}{\pi_{ij}(t)}(1 + a_4).$$

─────────────── *The Dynamics of International Differentiation* ───────────────

ated by the model are beyond the scope of this paper. However, let us just mention that persistence in shock propagation appears to be a general outcome. [10]

Clearly, the observer of the time series unaware of the process which generated them could easily interpret the strong trend component as the outcome of an exogenous technical progress (as in Solow-type production functions). However, it follows from the structure of the model outlined above that if anything this is an important aggregate property emerging from endogenous technical changes cum heterogeneous agents and far from equilibrium diffusion. This very structure yields also a very high persistence, without exogenously imposing autocorrelation in the shocks. (Note also our 'shocks' are firm-specific.)[11]

More central to the argument of this paper is the long-term convergence/divergence in per capita incomes. The experiment we show concerns a 'world' economy with two sectors and 55 countries. The evolutionary model generates increasing differentiation in both levels and rates of growth of per capita incomes: Figure 3 presents the dynamics of per capita incomes in a sample of simulated countries and Figure 4 the standard deviations in the rates of growth.

Simple tests on convergence from some intermediate date to the end period on the whole sample generally show divergence as the dominant pattern.

Estimates of the form:

$$\ln \frac{Y_i(t)}{Y_i(0)} = \alpha + \beta \ln Y_i(0),$$

on the periods 31–90 yield:

$$\ln (Y_i(t)/Y_i(0)) = -8.25 + 3.67 \ln Y(0) \qquad \overline{R^2} = 0.06$$
$$(5.07) \quad (1.76) \qquad\qquad F = 4.33$$

(the β is significant at 5% level).

───────────────

[10] Standard autocorrelation measures cannot always be applied to the first differences of the time series since they often appear to be distributed normally only for (relatively long) subperiods but not over the whole 'history' of the country. Note that this property is not necessarily a drawback of the model. Loosely speaking, the model generates in many cases a 'take off' process driving a country from near stagnation to sustained rates of growth or, conversely, 'vicious circles' from the latter persistent decline. As a consequence, for the statistical observer, the stochastic process describing growth undergoes a relatively sudden modification.

[11] It is also worth stressing that these basic properties hold for rather different 'technological opportunities' (we have experimented for different values of the λ in the Poisson distribution, between 4 and 16).

───────── *The Dynamics of International Differentiation* ─────────

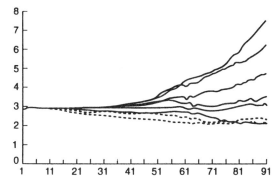

FIGURE 3. Per capita incomes in a sample of countries, simulation results.

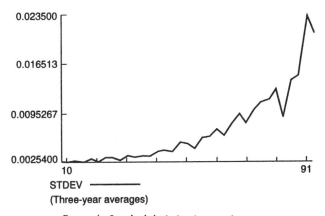

STDEV ─────
(Three-year averages)

FIGURE 4. Standard deviation in growth rates.

Of course, one can always explicitly introduce a 'post-selection bias' and test for the subgroups which turn out at the end to be 'developed' and 'undeveloped'. In the former case (same period, top 25 countries) we obtain a negative (-0.59) but statistically insignificant β coefficient (t-ratio: -0.23; $\overline{R^2} = -0.04$). For the bottom 20 countries β is positive (1.80) and highly significant (t: 3.06; $\overline{R^2} = 0.31$). If one were to infer some patterns from these estimates it is the relative weakness of systematic forces leading to convergence and, at the opposite side, the tendency of some countries to 'self-organize' in vicious circles of backwardness.

The dynamics of imports and exports are, in this model, the *ex post* outcome of sector specific international competition together with country-wide adjustments which in turn affect the competitiveness of single firms. Thus, 'comparative advantages' are the *ex post* outcome of innovation, imita-

─────────── *The Dynamics of International Differentiation* ───────────

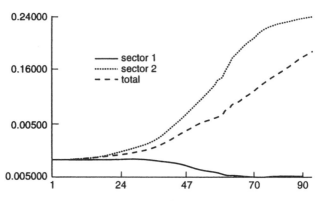

FIGURE 5. Sectoral and total exports of country *I*.

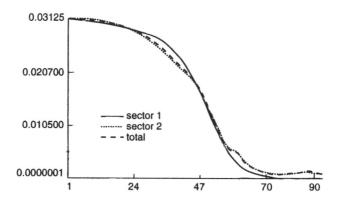

FIGURE 6. Sectoral and total exports of country *I*.

tion and selection. In some countries this process leads to specialization. Some other time, the dynamics of absolute advantages/disadvantages is similar across sectors (with an increasing technology gap rather homogeneous across the two sectors, see Figures 5 and 6).

4. *Microprocesses, Country Characteristics and Development Patterns: Some Conclusions*

What is somewhat surprising regarding the forgoing model is that, despite its rather simple structure, it generates a quite rich array of phenomena some-what isomorphic to the 'stylized facts' outlined in the introductory article by Dosi, Freeman and Fabiani: they concern, e.g. micro heterogeneity;

the cyclical and long-term behavior of aggregate time series; convergence and (more often) divergence in rates of innovation, diffusion, income levels and income growth; the endogenous emergence of absolute and comparative advantages. The story which the model tells is basically one of processes with no 'ingredients' or 'factors' to begin with: if anything, what at a certain point of the sequence appear to be such, are in fact the endogenous results of past self-organization processes. The two twin driving forces are learning and market selection.

We would like to consider this model as a sort of example of evolutionary microfoundation consistent, at least in principle, with other more structured, more aggregate and not necessarily microfounded analyses. For example, we suggest, an evolutionary microstructure is certainly consistent and complementary with the intuitions which inspired a lot of the developments in growth theory regarding country-specific characteristics and institutions, threshold effects, externalities. We suggest that these properties are, if anything, magnified whenever one does not superimpose or incorporate them within the standard micro scaffolding. Linking the current model with institutional richer analysis clearly would imply, among other things, some endogenization of behavioral rules, an explicit formalization of the effect of national characteristics such as education on search and production skill and differentiation among the regimes of governants of national markets. All this is beyond the aims of this work but certainly not unfeasible and indeed a promising frontier ahead.

Moreover, the emphasis on learning—decoupled from optimal allocation processes—is a common element between evolutionary models and models of Kaldorian inspiration. For example, it is easy to imagine co-evolutionary processes of innovation and capital accumulation (or lack of them), leading to self-reinforcing divergent patterns of development, which might rest on microfoundations of the kind outlined above. In a similar vein, one can conjecture fruitful links with models of cumulative divergence and catching up (see in particular, for non-linear formulations, Verspagen, 1991; Amable, 1992; and with respect to trade, Cimoli, 1988) and with growth models which derive the long-term properties of the economy from some general assumptions on the nature of learning and of innovation-embodying capital accumulation (like Pasinetti, 1982; Moss, 1990 and earlier, of course, Kaldor and development analysts such as Hirschman, Gerschenkron, Rosenstein-Rodan).

All this, of course, entails a rich research agenda; it overlaps with a few equilibrium-cum-rationality agendas (cf. new growth theories) in the thrust to place knowledge, innovation, increasing returns at the center of growth theory but it departs from them first of all in the assumptions about how

──────────── *The Dynamics of International Differentiation* ────────────

agents behave, how learning takes place and how markets work. Putting it somewhat loosely, evolutionary approaches focus on the analysis of what in standard production functions is the $A(t)$ dynamics and, further, claim that this is sufficient to incorporate also all the microeconomic action without invoking any underlying general equilibrium.

Also, the nature of 'explanation' and 'testing' is different between evolutionary and more standard growth models. The latter aim at 'explaining' by developing and testing particular formulations of and restrictions on the production function (the basic micro assumption underlying the production function itself being shielded from refutation). Conversely, evolutionary theories are often 'tested' (i) by comparing some statistical properties of the simulation they generate with those of observed data, and (ii) by mapping specific processes (e.g. on learning and market dynamics) into some relatively invariant aggregate outcomes (e.g. patterns of income growth, etc.).[12]

Any comparative assessment of the two approaches is likely to rest ultimately in the accuracy of empirical predictions and the width of the set of 'stylized facts' for which they are able to account. In this respect, this—still highly preliminary—work highlights, in our view, the promise of evolutionary approaches, even in their barest form, to interpret quite a few regularities in the development process.

References

Amable, B. (1992), 'National Effects of Learning, International Specialization and Growth Paths,' in C. Freeman and D. Foray (eds), *Technology and the Wealth of Nations*. Pinter Publishers: London and New York.

Azariadis, C. and A. Drazen (1990), 'Threshold Externalities in Economic Development,' *Quarterly Journal of Economics*, 105(2), 501–526.

Benhabib, J. and B. Jovanovic (1991), 'Externalities and Growth Accounting,' *American Economic Review*, 81 (1), 82–113.

Chiaromonte, F. and G. Dosi (1992), 'The Microfoundation of Competitiveness and Their Macro-economic Implications,' in C. Freeman and D. Foray (eds), *Technology and the Wealth of Nations*. Pinter Publishers: London and New York.

Cimoli, M. (1988), 'Technological Gaps and Industrial Asymmetries in a North–South Model with a Continuum of Goods,' *Metroeconomica*, 39 (3), 245–74.

Cochrane (1988), 'How big is the random walk in GNP?', *Journal of Political Economy*, 96(5), 893–920.

Conlisk, J. (1991), 'An Aggregate Model of Technical Change,' *Quarterly Journal of Economics* (November), 787–821.

---

[12] A good illustration possibly comes by a comparison between the model presented here with e.g. Azariadis and Drazen (1990) or Murphy *et al.* (1989). In common with the model presented here, they can easily account for persistent divergence in incomes (level and growth rates), due to 'technological externalities with threshold properties' (Azariadis and Drazen) or demand externalities (Murphy *et al.*). However, by accounting for observed divergences as equilibrium phenomena, they make it harder for the theory to interpret the dynamics across equilibria. The evolutionary view presented here takes the opposite view—admittedly at the price of much less elegance—and claims that most of the interesting phenomena that one observes can be explained as the outcome of disequilibrium processes.

──────────────── 241 ────────────────

Dosi, G., C. Freeman, R. Nelson, G. Silverberg and L. Soete (eds) (1988), *Technical Change and Economic Theory*. Pinter Publishers: London and New York.

Dosi, G. and M. Egidi (1991), 'Substantive and Procedural Uncertainty: an Exploration of Economic Behaviours in Changing Environments,' *Journal of Evolutionary Economics*, 1(2), 145–68.

Dosi, G., C. Freeman, S. Fabiani and R. Aversi (1993), 'On the Process of Economic Development,' CCC Working Paper, no. 93–2, Center for Research in Management, University of California at Berkeley.

Fabiani, S. (1990), *Dinamica tecnologica e commercio internazionale: Il processo di differenziazione tra paesi*. Graduation thesis, Dept of Economics: Rome.

Freeman, C. and D. Foray (eds) (1992) *Technology and the Wealth of Nations*. Pinter Publishers: London and New York.

Heiner, R. (1988), 'Imperfect Decisions and Routinized Production: Implications for Evolutionary Modelling and Inertial Technical Change,' in G. Dosi, C. Freeman, R. Nelson, G. Silverberg and L. Soete (eds), *Technical Change and Economic Theory*. Pinter Publishers: London and New York.

Iwai, K. (1984a), 'Schumpeterian Dynamics: An Evolutionary Model of Innovation and Imitation,' *Journal of Economic Behaviour and Organization*, 5(2), 159–90.

Iwai, K. (1984b), 'Schumpeterian Dynamics, Part II: Technological Progress, Firm Growth and "Economic Selection",' *Journal of Economic Behaviour and Organization*, 5(3–4), 321–51.

Kaldor, N. (1985), *Economics without Equilibrium*. University College Cardiff Press: Cardiff.

Meacci, M. (1993), *Origini e meccanismi di trasmissione delle fluttuazioni cicliche in economia. Un modello evolutivo*. Graduation thesis, Dept of Economics, University of Rome: Rome.

Metcalfe, S. (1988), 'The Diffusion of Innovation: An Interpretative Survey,' in G. Dosi, C. Freeman, R. Nelson, G. Silverberg and L. Soete (eds), *Technical Change and Economic Theory*. Pinter Publishers: London and New York.

Moss, S. (1990), 'Equilibrium, Evolution and Learning,' *Journal of Economic Behaviour and Organization*, 13(1), 97–115.

Murphy, K. M., A. Shleifer and R. W. Vishny (1989), 'Industrialization and the Big Push,' *Journal of Political Economy*, 97 (5) 1003–26.

Nelson, R. and S. Winter (1982), *An Evolutionary Theory of Economic Chance*. The Belknap Press of Harvard University Press: Cambridge MA.

Pasinetti, L. (1982), *Structural Change and Economic Growth*. Cambridge University Press: Cambridge.

Silverberg, G. (1987), 'Technical Progress, Capital Accumulation and Effective Demand: A Self-organization Model,' paper presented at the Fifth International Conference on Mathematical Modeling, Berkeley, June 1985, in D. Batten, J. Casti and B. Johansson (eds), *Economic Evolution and Structural Adjustment*. Springer-Verlag: Berlin, Heidelberg, New York, Tokyo.

Silverberg, G., G. Dosi and L. Orsenigo (1988), 'Innovation, Diversity and Diffusion. A Self-Organization Model,' *Economic Journal*, 98 (393), 1032–1054.

Silverberg, G. and D. Lehnert (1992), 'Long Waves and "Evolutionary Chaos" in a Simple Schumpeterian Model of Embodied Technical Change,' MERIT Working Paper, MERIT: Maastricht.

Solow, R. (1956), 'A Contribution to the Theory of Economic Growth,' *Quarterly Journal of Economics*, 70, 65–94.

Solow, R. (1957), 'Technical Change and the Aggregate Production Function,' *Review of Economics and Statistics*, (39), 312–20.

Verspagen, B. (1991), 'A New Empirical Approach to Catching Up or Falling Behind,' *Structural Change and Economic Dynamics*, 2 (2), 359–380.

Exploring the unknown. On entrepreneurship, coordination and innovation driven growth

Giovanni Dosi and Giorgio Fagiolo*

1. Introduction

The determinants of economic growth in general, and the possibility of a self-sustained process fueled by technological advances, have recently brought back the attention of the economic discipline, with respect to both formal theorizing and historical analysis. Concerning the former, 'Endogenous Growth' models (broadly in the spirit of Romer (1986, 1990) and Grossman and Helpman (1991a, 1991b)) and 'Schumpeterian' and 'Evolutionary' models (mainly building on Nelson and Winter (1982)) have been all trying – in different perspectives – to tell stories where per-capita incomes grow (also) as the outcome of positive feed-backs in knowledge accumulation. At the same time, a rapidly expanding empirically grounded literature on the economics of technological change has been exploring the drivers of innovation and diffusion; the mechanism through which they occur; and their effects – at the levels of firms, sectors and whole countries.[1]

Notwithstanding all that, we largely share the assessment spelled out in much more detail by Nelson (1998) of an enormous gap still remaining between what we historically know about technical change and its economic exploitation, on the one hand, and the ways we represent them in formal growth models, on the other.[2]

While some tensions between 'appreciative' (empirically drawn) generalizations and much more 'reduced forms' models are likely to always appear, our departing diagnostics is somewhat more pessimistic than that. In fact, a few general properties of the empirical patterns of innovation and diffusion seem to be neglected in a good deal of contemporary (formal) growth literature. Among them, and strictly related to the model presented here, in our view, there are the following.

First, aggregate formal accounts (in most of both the 'old' and 'new' growth models) tend to neglect the systematic heterogeneity in microeconomic technological competencies highlighted in the empirical literature. Relatedly, note that any 'representative agent' reduction might be highly misleading whenever the aggregate dynamics depends not only on the mean characteristics of any population but also on the distributions themselves and on the details of the interaction mechanisms among microentities.[3]

Second, there appears to be a striking conflict between the incredibly sophisticated forward-looking rationality one typically imputes to agents in aggregate formal stories and the messy experimentation which empirical students of innovation and business history usually find – full of stubborn mistakes, 'animal spirits' and unexpected discoveries.[4]

Third, partly as a consequence, it seems quite hard to interpret macrodynamics as equilibrium paths isomorphic to some underlying 'representative' behavioural pattern.

Fourth, economic change appears to be driven at least as much by time-consuming diffusion as from innovation.[5]

Here, we shall present a model of growth that builds on the foregoing properties, together with few other 'stylized facts' stemming from empirical analyses of technological change but often neglected in formal aggregate endeavours. In Section 2, we shall outline the building blocks and theoretical conjectures supporting the model presented in Section 3. Next, we discuss some simulations results (Section 4), and, finally, flag some research developments ahead (Section 5).

2. Decentralized knowledge accumulation and collective outcomes: some preliminaries

Technological advances, to a significant extent, are generated, *endogenously*, through resource-expensive search undertaken by a multiplicity of profit-motivated agents. Search itself is generally uncertain and innovative entrepreneurs (or, for that matter, incumbent firms undertaking innovative activities) are driven by the beliefs that 'there might be something profitable out there', but are generally unable to form probability distributions on the outcomes of their search efforts.

Innovations are not entirely appropriable: knowledge progressively diffuses to other agents who might well catch-up by investing in imitation – most likely, with a lag proportional to some measure of the distance between the knowledge which they master and that which they want to acquire.

Knowledge accumulation generally entails dynamic increasing returns both at the levels of individual agents (typically, business firms) and collection of them (i.e. industries), grounded upon collectively shared 'learning paradigms'. However, radically new technologies involve, to different degrees, ruptures and 'mismatchings', so that only part of the old knowledge might be useful to the exploitation of future technologies.[6]

On the grounds of these basic building blocks, the model that follows addresses three major issues.

First, under what circumstances processes of innovation and diffusion with the above characteristics can *self-organize* and yield aggregate outcomes with the properties corresponding to the empirically observed patterns of growth? Since the model does not rest on any *a priori* commitment to individual rationality and collective equilibria, the question involves an issue which could be called of Schumpeterian coordination, namely: can 'boundedly rational' agents, heterogeneous in their beliefs and technological competences, (imperfectly) coordinate their efforts of search for novel opportunities and of exploitation of what they already know such as to yield relatively ordered patterns of self-sustained aggregate growth?[7]

Second, we shall undertake some experiments of comparative dynamics and map different conditions of generation and diffusion of knowledge into the resulting growth patterns. For example, what happens to the mean (and higher moments) of the distribution of growth rates across independent sample paths as technological parameters change (including the richness of innovative opportunities, the easiness of imitation/ diffusion, and the degree of path-dependence in learning processes)?

Third, the model highlights a few sources of potential conflict between individual and collective rationality. It is an established result that in presence of externalities and dynamic increasing returns of some kind, one should not in general expect the dynamics generated by self-seeking agents to correspond with the socially optimal one. Abandoning 'representative agents' compression of the microeconomics of innovation makes the point even more vividly clear: there is no reason to expect that a decentralized economy would handle the dilemma between 'exploration' of novelty and 'exploitation' of incumbent knowledge the same way as an omniscient (and benign) planner would.[8] Moreover, by relaxing the assumption of hyper-rational agents with correct *technological* expectations, one is also able to consider those circumstances where collective growth finds its *necessary* condition in the presence of a number of 'irrational' entrepreneurs; that is, the vindication of innovative 'animal spirits' as public virtue, even when 'irrational acts' of private *hubris*...

In this work, we explicitly take on board four out of the five 'facts' that Paul Romer (1994) identifies as underlying New Growth Theories, namely: (i) multiplicity of agents; (ii) non-rivalry in the use of knowledge; (iii) replicability of physical production activities; (iv) endogeneity of discovery efforts. The fifth one – i.e. the rents associated with successful discoveries – is implicitly there but plays no role. On purpose, we mean to partly de-link the expectations on these rents from their actual average values (which is implied by the abandonment of any rational technological expectation hypothesis). Hence, while acknowledging that agents search for innovations because they can *sometimes* earn a rent on them, we do not assume any monotonic relation between the 'true' expected value of those rents and the propensity to innovate. As a first approximation, we prefer to study the ways the patterns of knowledge accumulation, together with institutionally nested 'animal spirits', affect growth – with rent-related incentives just as permissive conditions, above a minimum threshold.[9]

Moreover, well in the spirit of an evolutionary perspective, we assume: (i) heterogeneity among agents in their technological and behavioural features (e.g. their problem-solving knowledge and their propensity to search and to quickly imitate)[10]; (ii) diversity in the knowledge-bases upon which agents are able to draw; (iii) path-dependency in learning achievements; (iv) bounded rationality in both decisions to allocate resources to search and choices on the directions of search efforts (hence, unlike stochastic New Growth models of 'creative destruction' – such as Cheng and Dinopoulos (1991) and Aghion and Howitt (1992) – or 'hybrids' between 'old' and 'new' ones – such as Jovanovic and Rob (1990) and Jones and Newman (1994) – we shall not confine the analysis to those rather special cases whereby decentralized agents on average 'get it right'...);[11] (v) 'open-ended' dynamics in the technology space (so that learning opportunities are notionally unlimited, but what each agent can achieve at any one time is constrained by what one has learned in the past).

However, unlike full-fledged evolutionary models,[12] we do not account for any selection dynamics through which individual agents (*in primis*, firms) grow, shrink or die according to their revealed technological and market success. Hence, the following could be regarded as a reduced form 'toy model' of evolutionary growth, focusing upon the collective outcomes of decentralized patterns of knowledge accumulation, while suppressing – alike most traditional growth models – any explicit competitive interaction.

3. The model

Think of a *knowledge base* (i.e. a technological paradigm) as a metaphorical 'island' on a stochastic *n*-dimensional lattice (in the following 2-dimensional for simplicity). Each island is characterized by dynamic increasing returns, associated to knowledge-accumulation, which drive the exploitation of any knowledge base.

However, notionally unlimited opportunities exist – so that, as time goes to infinity, whatever economic performance measure may tend to infinity, too.

Relatedly, conflicts between 'exploration' of known technologies and 'exploration' of potentially superior ones might emerge (cf. March (1991) for an illuminating illustration of the dilemma).[13] Moreover, we assume that individual efforts of 'exploration' slowly yield a collective externality, via, first, diffusion of knowledge, and, second, incremental improvements upon specific knowledge bases.[14]

Search (i.e. exploration of new islands), as well as imitation, require a resource investment, which we assume to be proportional to the average current per capita output of the economy. Labour is the only formally accounted input – although one can easily think of a much higher dimensionality of the actual search and production input spaces as ultimately projected into labour productivity dynamics.

In this spirit, the economy is represented as a set of production activities, 'spatially' distributed on the 2-dimensional integer lattice $\aleph^2$ and it is composed of a fixed population of agents $I = \{1,2,...,N\}$, $N \ll \infty$, and a countable infinite number of islands, indexed by $j \in \aleph$. There is only one good, which can be 'extracted' from every island. Time is discrete and the generic time-period is denoted by $t \in \aleph \cup \{0\}$.

The lattice, i.e. the sea, is endowed by the 'Manhattan' metric d_1. Each node $(x,y) \in \aleph^2$ can be either an island or not, while each island has a size of one node. Let $\pi(x,y)$ be the probability that the node $(x,y) \in \aleph^2$ is an island. We will assume throughout that $\pi(x,y) = \pi$, all $(x,y) \in \aleph^2$, where $\pi \in (0, 1)$.[15]

Each island $j \in \aleph$ is completely characterized by its coordinates (x_j, y_j) in the lattice[16] together with an initial (or intrinsic) 'productivity' coefficient $s_j = s(x_j, y_j) \in \Re_+$.

Without loss of generality, we suppose that, at time $t = 0$, the population is randomly distributed on a (small) set of islands $L_0 = \{1,2,...,\ell_0\} \subset \aleph$. More precisely, assume that $d_1[(x_j, y_j)] \leq d_1[(x_{\ell_0}, y_{\ell_0})]$, all $j \in L_0$, and that each agent $i \in I$ has an initial location $(x_{i,0}, y_{i,0})$, such that, for all $i \in I$, there exists a $j \in L_0$: $(x_{i,0}, y_{i,0}) = (x_j, y_j)$. Furthermore, let initial productivity coefficients s_j to be uniformly distributed with mean $d_1[j] = d_1[(x_j, y_j)]$ $= x_j + y_j$, $j \in L_0$, and variance σ_s, so that, on average, the performance of a 'mine' increases with its distance from the origin of the lattice.

All agents are thus initially mining inside the smallest box containing islands in L_0, i.e. $B_0 = \{(x,y) \in \aleph^2: x \leq x_0^* \text{ and } y \leq y_0^*\}$, where $x_0^* = \max \{x_j, j \in L_0\}$ and $y_0^* = \max \{y_j, j \in L_0\}$.[17] In Figure 1 a very simple example of a conceivable initial configuration of the economy is depicted in order to make clearer the above assumptions.

Finally, assume that each agent $i \in I$ has an exogenously determined *willingness to explore* defined by the number $\varepsilon_i \in [0,1]$.[18]

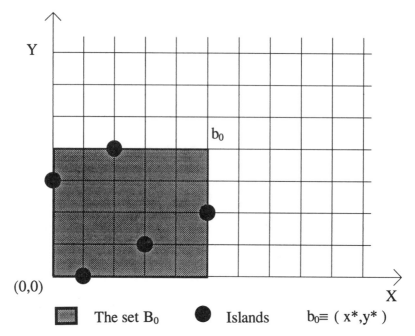

Figure 1   A simple example of initial distribution of islands ($\ell_0 = 5$)

Dynamics and endogenous novelty

Let us turn now to the description of how the economy evolves. At time $t=1,2,\ldots$ each agent can be in one of three different states, namely be a 'miner', an 'explorer' or an 'imitator'. Let $a_{i,t}$ the state of agent $i \in I$ at time t, where $a_{i,t} \in \{$'mi', 'ex', 'im'$\}$, and denote by $j \in \aleph$ the island currently occupied by the 'miner' $i \in I$, that is, the agent $i \in I$ such that $a_{i,t} =$ 'mi'.

Agents are allowed (with a certain probability) to leave the island they are working on, gradually explore the lattice around and, possibly, discover previously unexploited (and possibly more productive) islands. In order to illustrate how this is formalized, we need some additional notation.

Denote by $n_t(x_j, y_j)$ the number of miners working on island $j \in \aleph$ at time t. Then, define an island $j \in \aleph$ to be 'known' at time t if $n_\tau(x_j, y_j) > 0$ for at least a $0 \leq \tau \leq t$, that is, if it currently has some people on it or if it was so at least some finite time in the past. Accordingly, let the set of currently 'known' islands be given by:

$$L_t = \{ j \in N : \exists\ 0 \leq \tau \leq t :\ n_\tau(x_j, y_j) > 0 \}. \tag{1}$$

Among all known islands, let us call 'colonized' those currently exploited, i.e. all $j \in L_t : n_t(x_j, y_j) > 0$. Conversely, all islands in $\aleph \backslash L_t$ will be called 'unknown', since no agent has previously exploited them. Furthermore, denote the cardinality of L_t by ℓ_t, and the current location in the lattice of agent $i \in I$ by the pair $(x_{i,t}, y_{i,t})$.[19] Finally, as we did for L_0, consider the smallest box containing all islands in L_t, i.e. let

$$B_t = \{ (x,y) \in \aleph^2 :\ x \leq x_t^* \ \text{and} \ y \leq y_t^* \}, \tag{2}$$

where $x_t^* = \max\{x_j, j \in L_t\}$ and $y_t^* = \max\{y_j, j \in L_t\}$. Since the node $b_t^* \equiv (x_t^*, y_t^*)$ will only coincide by chance with a 'known' island, we can think of b_t^* just as a 'proxy' of the most efficient island (i.e. the best practice) currently exploited by the agents.[20]

The model allows for an endogenous dynamics on the set L_t and, consequently, on the box B_t, in the sense that the set L_t changes in time because of the actions of agents in I. A crucial distinction has to be made here between what we will call the 'currently realized' economy and the economy *tout court*. As the box B_t contains all exploited technologies up to time t, it therefore represents a proxy of what is actually at disposal of the economy, i.e. the current set of 'fundamentals' or the 'realized economy'.

However, outside B_t there is a whole – eventually better – world waiting to be discovered. The model depicts precisely the process of the gradual endogenous discovery of the economy by economic agents themselves.

Hence, given the endogenous nature of innovation/imitation activities, it is crucial to account for the process by which agents in different states make 'crucial decisions', i.e. irreversible choices that change forever the economic environment.[21] Let us consider the 'mining' process, first.

Mining
A 'miner' $i \in$ I currently located on island $j \in L_t$ with co-ordinates (x_j, y_j), will necessarily get, at no cost, a gross output $q_{i,t}$ according to the simple production function:

$$q_{i,t} = s(x_j, y_j) \, [n_t(x_j, y_j)]^{\alpha-1}, \tag{3}$$

where $s(x_j, y_j)$ is the initial 'productivity' coefficient defined above, $n_t(x_j, y_j)$ is the number of 'miners' currently working on island j and $\alpha > 1$. Returns to scale are thus increasing at the islands' level, since the current total gross output of island $j \in L_t$ is:

$$Q_t(x_j, y_j) = s(x_j, y_j) \, [n_t(x_j, y_j)]^{\alpha}. \tag{4}$$

The economy total gross output (GNP) will then be:

$$Q_t = \sum_{j \in L_t} Q_t(x_j, y_j). \tag{5}$$

As all agents are 'miners' at $t = 0$, then, all $i \in$ I:

$$q_{i,0} = s(x_{i,0}, y_{i,0}) \, [n_0(x_{i,0}, y_{i,0})]^{\alpha-1} \tag{6}$$

so that, aggregating, one obtains: $Q_0(x_j, y_j) = s(x_j, y_j) \, [n_0(x_j, y_j)]^{\alpha}$ for all $j \in L_0$ and $Q_0 = \sum_{j=1}^{t_0} Q_0(x_j, y_j)$.

Exploring
At time t, each miner has the opportunity to become 'explorer'. For sake of simplicity, we will assume here that this happens with probability $\varepsilon_i = \varepsilon$, for all $i \in$ I which are in

the state of 'miner'. As soon as a 'miner' currently working on island $j \in L_t$ decides to become 'explorer' (i.e. $a_{i,t+1}$ = 'ex'), it leaves its island, 'sailing' until it finds another one – possibly not known. Notice that up to now we have not endowed agents with any 'forecasting' skill. However, when a 'miner' leaves its island at time t, we let it to carry the memory of the last output which the agent was able to get in the state of 'miner' (i.e. its past knowledge and skills). We denote the memory of explorer $i \in I$ leaving island j at time τ by $q_{i,\tau}$. During the search, it does not extract any output but rather it pays a per-period 'transportation' cost equal to a given share $\beta \in [0,1)$ of the last-period per-capita GNP, raised to $\delta \geq 0$,[22] i.e. if $a_{i,t}$ = 'ex' then individual transportation cost in period t will be: $c_{i,t} = \beta \cdot [Q_{t-1}/N]^\delta$.

From time $t + 1$ on, it moves on the lattice following the 'naive' stochastic rule:

$$\text{Prob}\{ (x_{i,t+1}, y_{i,t+1}) = (x,y) \} = \begin{cases} 1/4 & \text{if } |x - x_{i,t}| + |y - y_{i,t}| = 1 \\ 0 & \text{otherwise} \end{cases} \quad , \text{ all } (x,y) \in \aleph^2. \quad (7)$$

That is, at each time period the 'explorer' moves from its current node $(x_{i,t}, y_{i,t})$ by randomly selecting one out of the four adjacent nodes. Notice that we are assuming that agents are not aware of the fact that islands are (on average) more and more productive the further away one goes from the origin of the lattice.

The new location of the explorer $(x_{i,t+1}, y_{i,t+1})$ might obviously be: (i) the 'sea'; (ii) a 'known' island $j \in L_t$; (iii) a 'new' island $j \in \aleph \backslash L_t$. In the first case, i.e. $(x_{i,t+1}, y_{i,t+1}) \neq (x_j,y_j)$ for all $j \in \aleph$, we still have $a_{i,t+1}$ = 'ex' and the exploration goes on. In the second case, there will be a $j \in L_t$ such that $(x_{i,t+1}, y_{i,t+1}) = (x_j,y_j)$ and hence the explorer $i \in I$ becomes miner on $j \in L_t$, i.e. $a_{i,t+1}$='mi'. The third case is the most important. Suppose, for simplicity, that at time t each explorer is allowed to find new islands only outside the box B_t.[23] As stated above, the node occupied by the 'explorer' $i \in I$ at time $t + 1$ could be a 'new' island with probability π. In case of discovery, the new island j^* with co-ordinates $(x_{j^*},y_{j^*})=(x_{i,t+1}, y_{i,t+1})$ is added to the set of 'known' islands, i.e. $L_{t+1} = L_t \cup \{ j^* \}$ and $\ell_{t+1} = \ell_t + 1$. Moreover, both the set $B_{(\cdot)}$ and the 'best practice' proxy $(x_{(\cdot)}^*, y_{(\cdot)}^*)$ are accordingly updated.

Path-dependence and 'ordinary' versus 'extraordinary' discoveries
In the model we allow discoveries to be either 'ordinary' or, to different extents, 'extraordinary'. In order to capture the distinction from the innovation literature between innovations within existing knowledge bases and the introduction of radically new 'technological paradigms' (Dosi, 1982), the 'initial' productivity coefficient of a 'new' island j^* discovered by the 'explorer' $i \in I$ carrying the output memory $q_{i,\tau}$, will be given by:

$$s_{j^*} = s(x_{j^*},y_{j^*}) = (1 + W) \cdot \{d_1[(x_{j^*},y_{j^*})] + \varphi\, q_{i,\tau} + \xi \}, \quad (8)$$

where $d_1[(x_{j^*},y_{j^*})] = x_{j^*} + y_{j^*}$ is, as usual, the distance of j^* from $(0,0)$; W is a random variable distributed as a Poisson with mean $\lambda > 0$; ξ is a uniformly distributed random variable, independent of W, with mean zero and variance σ_ξ and, finally, $\varphi \in [0,1]$. The interpretation of equation (8) is straightforward. The initial productivity of a 'new' island depends on four factors, namely: (i) its distance from the origin (as for initial islands); (ii) a cumulative learning effect directly linked to the past 'skills' of the discoverer, i.e. $\varphi \, q_{i,\tau}$; (iii) a random variable W which allows low probability 'jumps', that is, changes in technological paradigms;[24] (iv) a stochastic i.i.d. zero-mean noise ξ.

Two considerations are in order. First, the mechanism through which innovations are introduced in the economy is both path-dependent (Arthur, 1988 and 1994) and influenced by random (small) events (Arthur, 1989; David, 1992). On one hand, a large φ implies that more skilled 'explorers' (i.e. more efficient past 'miners') are likely to discover more productive islands and to produce more in the future, thanks to a sort of 'learning-to-learn' mechanism (Stiglitz, 1987). Moreover, the stochastic nature of innovation, together with increasing returns associated with learning by doing (as in Arrow (1962b) and Parente (1994)), allow even 'ordinary' discoveries to drive the process of growth. Second, notice that, as by independence:

$$\mathbf{E}s(x_{j*}, y_{j*}) = (1 + \lambda) \, [(x_{j*} + y_{j*}) + \varphi \, q_{i,\tau}], \tag{9}$$

then, on average, a larger λ lets 'extraordinary' discoveries to be more likely in the economy. The parameter λ, together with π, are measures of the degree of notional 'opportunities'. Indeed, a large λ lets, in expectation, the productivity of a newly discovered island to be sensibly larger than those associated to the currently 'known' islands; likewise, a larger π implies a larger average number of per-period discoveries.

Diffusion of knowledge and imitation

Due to the uncertainty of the exploration process and to within-island dynamic increasing returns, there is an incentive for both 'miners' and 'explorers' to imitate the most productive islands existing in the 'currently realized' economy. In the model we formalize a process of diffusion of knowledge which tries to capture some basic features of empirically observed patterns of imitation and diffusion (Nelson and Winter, 1982; David, 1975; Dosi, 1988 and 1991; Freeman, 1994; see also Jovanovic and Rob, 1989; Jovanovic and McDonald, 1994).

Let m_t be the number of 'miners' currently present in the economy. At time t, from each 'colonized' island $j \in L_t$ a signal is delivered and instantaneously[25] spread all around. Signals are characterized by an *intrinsic intensity* proportional to the share of miners present on $j \in L_t$ – i.e. $n_t(x_j, y_j) / m_t$ – and a *content* given by the actual productivity of the island – i.e. $Q_t(x_j, y_j) / n_t(x_j, y_j)$. Moreover, they decay exponentially with the distance from the source, so that the *actual intensity* with which a signal delivered from (x_j, y_j) reaches an agent currently located at (x, y) is given by:

$$w_t(x_j, y_j; x, y) = \frac{n_t(x_j, y_j)}{m_t} \, exp \, \{-\rho[\, |x-x_j| + |y-y_j| \,]\}, \qquad \rho \geq 0. \tag{10}$$

A signal delivered at (x_j, y_j) will be *received* by agent i located at (x, y) with a probability proportional to $w_t(x_j, y_j; x, y)$. Agent i will then collect the 'contents' of all *received* signals (those coming from, say, islands $j_{h_1}, \ldots, j_{h_M}$, where $M \leq \ell_t$ is a random variable) and contrast them with *its own performance*. The latter is simply agent i's current productivity if it is a 'miner' (say on island j), or the 'memory' on the productivity of its island of origin (say, j), if it is an 'explorer'. Hence, it will choose among the $M + 1$ available options by drawing from the set $\{ j, j_{h_1}, \ldots, j_{h_M} \} \subseteq L_i$, with probabilities proportional to the associate productivities. If the choice is j, then it will decide not to imitate any island but rather to remain in the current state. Otherwise, it will become an 'imitator' – i.e. $a_{i,t+1} = $ 'im' – and it will move toward the imitated island, say (x',y'), reaching it after $k = d_1[(x',y');(x,y)] = |x-x'| + |y-y'|$ time periods – i.e. making one step at each period and following the shortest path. During this lapse of time, an 'imitator' behaves as an 'explorer' for what concerns both production and transportation costs.[26] Finally, once the imitated island is reached, it will turn again its state into 'miner', i.e. $a_{i,t+k+1} = $ 'mi'.

Interactions
Interactions in our economy are basically 'local'.[27] Indeed, agents locally interact both deterministically through increasing returns in the mining process and stochastically through the process of knowledge diffusion. In the latter, the parameter $\rho \geq 0$ tunes the 'degree of locality' of the interactions: the larger ρ, the more the process of diffusion of knowledge is local, in the sense that signals tend to reach, in probability, only the nearest neighbours. Two extreme cases are: (i) $\rho = 0$, i.e. interactions are global, in that they do not depend on the distance between source and receiver; and (ii) $\rho = \infty$, i.e. no signal is spread, i.e. there is no diffusion of information.

Micro and macro system variables
At each time period $t = 0,1,2,\ldots$, the economy will be completely characterized by the following *micro variables*. Concerning *islands*: (a) the set of 'known' islands L_i; (b) the co-ordinates set: $Z_t = \{(x_j,y_j), j \in L_t\}$; (c) the initial productivity coefficients $S_t = \{s_j, j \in L_t\}$. Concerning *agents*, one might consider the mappings $A_t: I \rightarrow \{$ 'mi', 'ex', 'im' $\}$, $C_t: I \rightarrow \aleph^2$ and $\Theta_t: I \rightarrow \Re$, recording current states, coordinates and individual gross outputs.

The *macro variables* of interest are: (i) the triple $(m_t, e_t, i_t) \in \aleph^3$, $m_t + e_t + i_t = N$, i.e. the current number of 'miners', 'explorers' and 'imitators' in the economy; (ii) the pair $(\ell_t, \ell^C_t) \in \aleph^2$ (where ℓ_t is the number of currently *known* islands and $\ell^C_t \leq \ell_t$ is the number of the *colonized* ones), together with their coordinates and their initial productivity; (iii) the log of GNP, namely $q_t = log\ Q_t$; (iv) the growth rate of GNP, denoted by g_t.

4. Some results
Let us start with some qualitative results focusing on the different patterns of growth the model is able to generate. To begin, note that the model is an example of 'artificial economies', which one is bound to study mainly via computer simulations. Analytical solutions – at least as long as one looks at the model in its fully-fledged form – are indeed not achievable because of the underlying complexity of the stochastic processes which update micro – and accordingly macro – variables.[28]

Some other considerations are in order. First, we will mainly focus on the aggregate properties of simulated time series of (log of) GNP and growth rates. The main goal is to analyse how the model behaves in some 'benchmark' parametrizations, in order to assess the roles played by knowledge-specific increasing returns, imitation and exploration in the dynamics of the economy. In particular, we will address the question whether the model is able to display self-organizing patterns of persistent growth[29] and – if so – under which behavioural and system parametrizations (especially concerning innovation and diffusion rates). Second, let us emphasize the preliminary nature of the results which follow. In order to get a deeper understanding of the behaviour of the model, one should actually perform even more systematic searches of the parameter space and try accurately to map different regions of that space into (statistically) different behaviours of the variables of interest.[30]

4.1 A closed economy *without* exploration

Let us analyse a very simple 'stationary' case. Assume exploration is not allowed, i.e. let $\varepsilon_i = \varepsilon = 0, \forall i \in I$. In this set-up, the economy is 'closed', since agents can only exchange information about the initial set of islands and exploit them (i.e. act on the ground of *given* fundamentals), but are not supposed to endogenously introduce innovations. Without loss of generality, we can assume $\ell_0 = 2$ and $s_1 \le s_2$. In this case, given the initial productivities, the system is completely characterized by a stochastic process on $\underline{m} = (m_1, m_2)$, with $m_1 + m_2 = N$ (i.e. on the number of miners on island $j = 1,2$), which is a Markov chain with two absorbing states, namely $\underline{m}_{1,*} = (N,0)$ and $\underline{m}_{2,*} = (0,N)$. Accordingly, the GNP will converge with probability one to the attractor set $\Theta = \{s_1 N^\alpha, s_2 N^\alpha\}$. However, the process on $\underline{m}$ is not *ergodic*, implying also potential inefficiency of the economy.[31] Indeed, path-dependency entailed by increasing returns will tend to drive all agents, through waves of imitation, toward the island with the *actual* (not *initial*) best productivity. Hence both initial conditions $\{s_1, s_2$ and $(m_{10}, m_{20})\}$ – i.e. productivity coefficients and the initial distribution of miners on islands $j = 1,2$ – and 'small stochastic events' – i.e. stochastic imitation decisions – could lead agents to converge on the inefficient island $j = 1$.[32]

However, the probability that the system will be absorbed by the 'efficient' limit state, i.e. $p^* = \mathrm{Prob}\{\lim_{t \to \infty} Q_t = s_2 N^\alpha\}$, will be increasing in both $\Delta s_0 = s_2 - s_1$ and $\Delta m_0 = m_{20} - m_{10}$.[33] For what concerns GNP and growth rates one usually observes simulated time series as that in Figure 2. Hence, in this simple setting, growth is a transitory phenomenon because, once the lock-in on an island is achieved, no further dynamics is allowed in the system and no fluctuations will arise thereafter.

4.2 A closed economy *with* exploration

Suppose now that exploration is allowed, i.e. let $\varepsilon_i = \varepsilon > 0, \forall i \in I$, but only *inside* the initial 'realized economy', i.e. inside an unchanged set of 'knowledge bases'. This means that 'miners' can become 'explorers' but they can 'sail' only inside the box B_0. Hence, they are still not able to 'innovate' (i.e. to discover islands other than the already 'known' ones) and must necessarily exploit the existing technologies. However, unlike the previous case, they can always decide to leave the island they are working on, even though all agents are mining on it. All that introduces a potential source of 'exploration', or, more extremely, of 'irrationality' and 'idiosyncrasy' in individual behaviours. Although the decision to become explorer is not linked – in this version of the model – to any system variable, we are tempted to define this behaviour as a 'nonconformist' one, as in a few models of 'social interaction' and

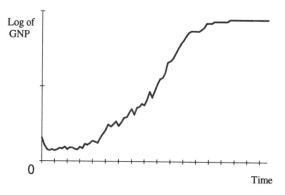

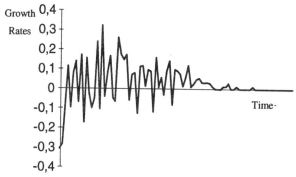

Figure 2   GNP (above) and growth rates in a closed economy without exploration
(N = 100, π = 0.1, σₛ = 0.1, ρ = 0.1, α = 1.5, β = 0.1)

'herd behaviour'.[34] Indeed, when exploration is allowed, the lock-in of the system will not generally, since there is always a positive probability that 'non conformist' decisions will induce phase transitions in the system.

In this setting, the economy can be described as before by a Markov process over the **m** states which the system can attain. However, unlike the previous case, the transition probabilities are not only influenced by the propensies to imitate technologies with a higher (revealed) efficiencies, but also involve a certain probability of 'exploring'. Islands represent here 'basins of attraction' among which the system persistently oscillates exhibiting the mentioned phenomena of phase transitions.[35] The stochastic process of exploration/imitation yields persistent output fluctuations. Indeed, as depicted in Figure 3, the simulated time-series of GNP display an auto-regressive stationary pattern – as econometric analyses (not reported) usually show. Note that, in this setting, over finite time periods, the number of miners working on each island obviously depends on earlier states of the system, as Figures 4(a) and 4(b) show for the two cases $s_1 = s_2$ and $s_1 < s_2$. Increasing returns and knowledge diffusion induces agents – on average – to move toward currently more efficient islands. However, exploration allows with positive probability 'de-locking' bursts, also toward notionally less efficient islands. In a sense, persistent fluctuations are in this case generated by a problem of *imperfect Schumpeterian coordination* in presence of dynamic increasing returns to learning.[36]

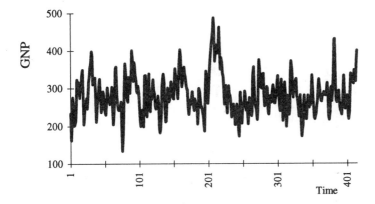

Figure 3   GNP in a closed economy with exploration (N = 100, π = 0.1, σ$_s$ = 0.1,
ρ = 0.1, α = 1.5, β = 0, ε = 0.1)

Moreover, here – as in the case closed-economy/no exploration case – as long as one does not allow for the possibility of endogenous novelty, self-sustaining growth could emerge only if one superimposes an exogenous Solow-like drift on the best-practice production function.

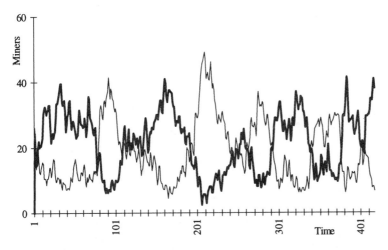

Figure 4(a)   Number of miners on islands j = 1,2 when s$_1$ = s$_2$ (thick line: Island 2)
(N = 100, π = 0.1, σ$_s$ = 0.1, ρ = 0.1, α = 1.5, β = 0)

4.3   Exploring in an open-ended economy: the emergence of self-sustaining growth

Consider now the more general case of exploration in an *open-ended* economy. In this set-up the economy displays, for a wide range of parameters, patterns of self-sustaining growth[37].

Typically, the simulated time-series of GNP are exponentially shaped (so that its logarithm displays a linear trend, as in Figure 5).

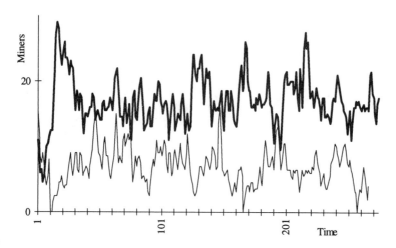

Figure 4(b)   Number of miners on islands j = 1,2 when s₁ < s₂ (thick line: Island 2)
(N = 100, π = 0.1, σ_s = 0.1, ρ = 0.1, α = 1.5, β = 0, ε = 0.1)

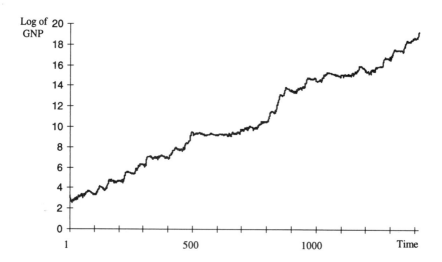

Figure 5   Exponential growth in an open-ended economy with exploration (log of
GNP) (N = 100, π = 0.1, σ_s = σ_ξ = 0.1, ρ = 0.1, α = 1.5, β = 0, ε = 0.1,
λ = 1, φ = 0.5)

More precisely, in the case of self-sustaining growth, the time-series of the (log of)
GNP turn out to be 'difference stationary', according to standard ADF tests[38] (see
Table 1). Indeed, irrespective of whether the constant and/or the trend terms are included
in the ADF regression, one is unable to reject at 5 per cent the null of a unit root,
which is on the contrary not accepted for both first differences Δq_t and growth rates
$g_t = (q_t - q_{t-1})/q_{t-1}$.[39]

Table 1(a) ADF tests on simulated series of log of GNP [q_t], first differences of log of GNP [Δq_t] and growth rates [$g_t = (q_t - q_{t-1})/q_{t-1}$]* (constant included)

(a) 1500 Obs., Critical values: 5% = –2.864, 1% = –3.438;

Variable	Lag	ADF t-test	σ	t-lag	t-probability
	5	0.1169	0.072001	1.3317	0.1832
	4	0.14585	0.072021	2.8253	0.0048
Log of GNP	3	0.20439	0.072199	1.1937	0.2328
q_t	2	0.22725	0.07221	–1.2462	0.2129
	1	0.20157	0.072225	0.49482	0.6208
	0	0.21226	0.072205		
	5	–13.397**	0.071939	–1.707	0.088
	4	–15.086**	0.071988	–1.2748	0.2026
First diff.	3	–17.190**	0.072004	–2.7825	0.0055
Δq_t	2	–21.328**	0.072176	–1.1552	0.2482
	1	–27.255**	0.072185	1.2672	0.2053
	0	–37.052**	0.072201		
	5	–15.046**	0.010963	–2.7796	0.0055
	4	–17.329**	0.010989	1.1188	0.2634
Growth rates	3	–18.595**	0.01099	–0.81087	0.4176
g_t	2	–21.829**	0.010989	–4.8012	0
	1	–32.801**	0.011075	7.3257	0
	0	–38.851**	0.01128		

Table 1(b) ADF tests on simulated series of log of GNP [q], first differences of log of GNP [Δq_t] and growth rates [$g_t = (q_t - q_{t-1})/q_{t-1}$]* (constant and trend included)

(b) 1500 Obs., Critical values: 5% = –3.415; 1% = –3.97;

Variable	Lag	ADF t-test	σ	t-lag	t-probability
	5	–2.4513	0.071869	1.4905	0.1363
	4	–2.3567	0.0719	2.9716	0.003
Log of GNP	3	–2.1664	0.0721	1.3261	0.185
q_t	2	–2.0876	0.072119	–1.1085	0.2678
	1	–2.1655	0.072125	0.6366	0.5245
	0	–2.1283	0.07211		
	5	–13.398**	0.071961	–1.7014	0.0891
	4	–15.086**	0.07201	–1.2704	0.2042
First Diff.	3	–17.190**	0.072025	–2.7771	0.0056
Δq_t	2	–21.326**	0.072197	–1.1506	0.2501
	1	–27.251**	0.072206	1.2718	0.2036
	0	–37.044**	0.072221		
	5	–15.313**	0.010939	–2.6601	0.0079
	4	–17.595**	0.010962	1.2743	0.2028
Growth rates	3	–18.837**	0.010965	–0.6385	0.5233
g_t	2	–22.057**	0.010963	–4.5807	0
	1	–33.052**	0.01104	7.5376	0
	0	–39.016**	0.011257		

Note: Econometric analyses refer to the following parametrization: N = 100, $\pi = 0.1$, $\sigma_z = \sigma_\xi = 0.1$, $\rho = 0.1$, $\alpha = 1.5$, $\beta = 0$, $\varepsilon = 0.1$, $\lambda = 1$, $\varphi = 0.5$.

In the appendix, some further results about persistence of output fluctuations are reported. In analogy with Campbell and Mankiw (1987, 1989), we address the question of whether fluctuations in GNP are characterized by a permanent component and how big such a component might be. They consider two different measures of persistence[40] based on sample estimates of auto-correlations of changes in log of GNP, finding that in 'six out of seven countries a 1 per cent shock to output should change the long-run univariate forecast of output by well over 1 per cent'. We computed the same statistics for both time-series of change in log of GNP (i.e. Δq_t) and growth rates (i.e. $g_t = (q_t - q_{t-1}) / q_{t-1}$), getting similar results. As Table 4 in the appendix shows, all estimated measures of persistence generally exceed unity, suggesting that our simulated GNP is characterized by non transitory fluctuations.[41]

However, exponential growth is not the sole regularity one can get from the simulated time-series of GNP. Indeed, for different parametrizations, the model is able to generate 'no growth' economies as in Section 4.2 – see Figure 6(a) – or 'low growth' ones,[42] as depicted in Figure 6(b).

Our conjecture is that necessary conditions for the model to exhibit exponential growth are, of course, the presence of increasing returns, but, moreover, the following ones – or a suitable mix of them – ought to apply, namely: (i) both the level of opportunities and the average number of current 'explorers' have to be sufficiently large; (ii) knowledge diffusion is not too 'local'; (iii) there is some path-dependency in innovation. Putting it another way, one should expect self-sustaining growth to emerge for large values of φ, π and λ and for small values of ρ.

In the following, some support to this conjecture will be shown.

The sources of self-sustaining growth: some 'qualitative' evidence
A basic insight stemming from a qualitative analysis of the behaviour of the model is that self-sustaining growth seems to be generated in the system – above certain thresholds – by non-linear interactions among innovation, path-dependency, increasing returns and diffusion of knowledge and *not* by any of these forces taken in isolation. In order to illustrate this point, assume to start from a fairly uniform distribution of the N agents on the initial 'known' islands L_0. On the one hand, diffusion of knowledge is likely to drive agents to concentrate on a relatively small cluster of 'known' islands – generally close to the frontier of the 'realized economy'– which, by dynamic increasing returns, might be, often but not always, the most efficient ones. On the other hand, some 'lucky' explorers – which have decided not to imitate one out of the cluster of colonized islands – will sometimes find intrinsically superior islands outside the 'realized economy'. Although they might not be able to adequately exploit the opportunities of the 'new' island by themselves, the 'extraordinary' character of their discovery might nevertheless induce other agents to move there in the future and, consequently, increase its actual productivities. Hence, a 'rare event' (i.e. the exceptional discovery), feeding path-dependently upon diffusion and incremental innovations thereafter, might be able to trigger a self-reinforcing process whose ultimate outcome might be a pattern of exponential growth.

The above conjecture can be further supported by looking at some other pieces of qualitative evidence on the dynamics of the model. Indeed, given a set-up yielding

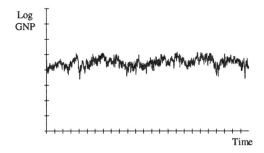

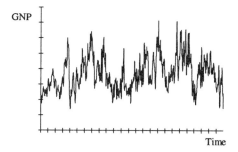

Figure 6(a)   No growth in an open-ended economy with exploration
(N = 100, π = 0.1, σₛ = σ_ξ = 0.1, ρ = 0.1, α = 1.5, β = 0, ε = 0.1,
λ = 1, φ = 0.1)

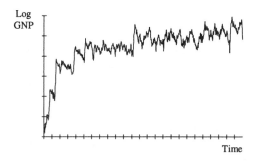

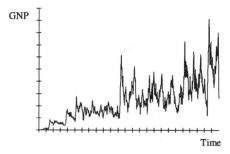

Figure 6(b)   'Linear' growth in an open-ended economy with exploration
(N = 100, π = 0.1, σₛ = σ_ξ = 0.1, ρ = 0.1, α = 1.5, β = 0, ε = 0.1,
λ = 1, φ = 0.2)

exponential growth,[43] the story that simulated time-series tell us might be rephrased as follows.

First, time series of the number of 'miners', 'explorers' and 'imitators' typically follows a stationary pattern, see Figure 7.

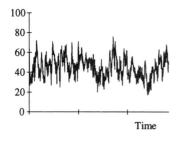

(a) Miners

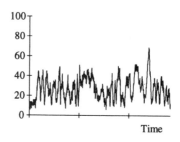

(b) Explorers

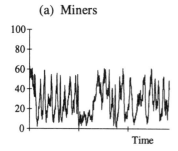

(c) Imitators

Figure 7   Number of miners, explorers and imitators in an open-ended economy displaying self-sustaining growth ($N = 100$, $\pi = 0.1$, $\sigma_s = \sigma_\xi = 0.1$, $\rho = 0.1$, $\alpha = 1.5$, $\beta = 0$, $\varepsilon = 0.1$, $\lambda = 1$, $\varphi = 0.5$)

Second, although the number of currently 'known' islands (at any τ) displays a linear trend, both the ratio 'colonized'/'known' islands and the number of 'colonized' ones – Figures 8(a) and 8(b) respectively – fall quickly and then follow a stationary process. Hence, imitation leads agents to exploit (i.e. to 'colonize') a small subset of islands (out of the 'known' ones).

Third, since the number of 'explorers' is a stationary process, the average per-period number of 'discoveries' keeps constant. Moreover, as the uniform nature of the 'exploration' rule should suggest – compare equation (7) – the distance from the origin of a new island increases linearly with the number of discovered islands (see Figure 9(a)). However, the path-dependent nature of innovation implies that the initial productivity of a new island (i.e. the coefficient s_{j*}) is generally greater than the average current productivity over all 'known' islands (see Figure 10) while the one-time push irregularly caused by the introduction of 'new paradigms' keeps the order of magnitude of initial productivity of new islands constantly above their distance from the origin (see Figure 9(b)).

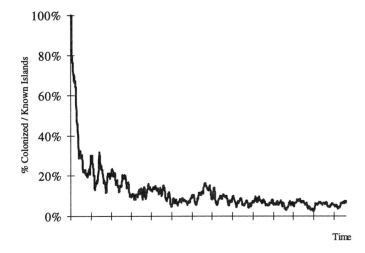

Figure 8(a)   *Percentage of colonized islands in an open-ended economy displaying self-sustaining growth (N = 100, π = 0.1, σ_s = σ_ξ = 0.1, ρ = 0.1, α = 1.5, β = 0, ε = 0.1, λ = 1, φ = 0.5)*

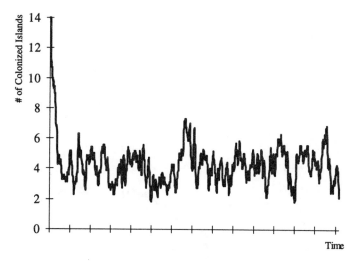

Figure 8(b)   *Number of colonized islands in an open-ended economy displaying self-sustaining growth (N = 100, π = 0.1, σ_s = σ_ξ = 0.1, ρ = 0.1, α = 1.5, β = 0, ε = 0.1, λ = 1, φ = 0.5)*

Finally, relatively ordered spatial patterns of colonized islands are likely to emerge, due to the local nature of both the exploration and imitation processes. In Figure 11 the path of expansion of the 'best practice' proxy b_t^* is plotted together with four 'snapshots' showing the locations of currently 'colonized' islands for different time periods $t = 0, 500, 1000, 1500$.

While in the early time periods of the simulation small (stochastic) events select the region of the lattice where the exploration is going to take place, the path-dependent

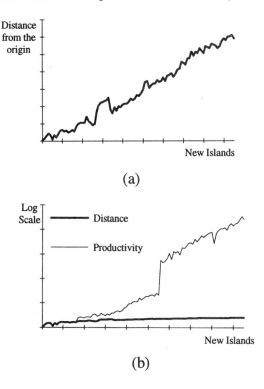

(a)

(b)

Figure 9   Distance from the origin and actual productivities of new islands (number of new islands on x-axis) in an economy displaying self-sustaining growth (N = 100, π = 0.1, $\sigma_s = \sigma_\xi = 0.1$, ρ = 0.1, α = 1.5, β = 0, ε = 0.1, λ = 1, φ = 0.5)

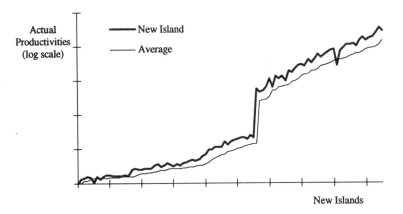

Figure 10   Actual productivity of new islands versus average current productivity of 'known' islands in an economy displaying self-sustaining growth (N = 100, π = 0.1, $\sigma_s = \sigma_\xi = 0.1$, ρ = 0.1, α = 1.5, β = 0, ε = 0.1, λ = 1, φ = 0.5)

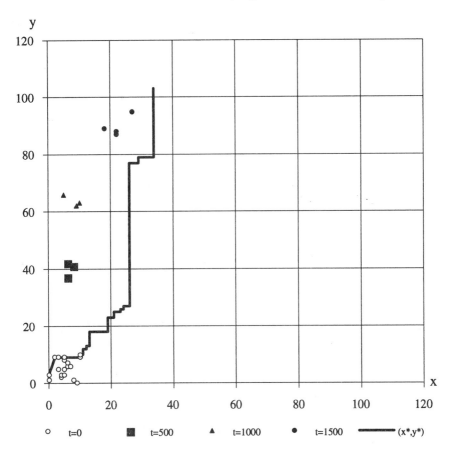

Figure 11   *Spatial diffusion patterns of colonized islands and 'best practice' proxy*
$b_t^* = (x_t^*, y_t^*)$ *in an economy displaying self-sustaining growth* ($N = 100$,
$\pi = 0.1$, $\sigma_s = \sigma_\xi = 0.1$, $\rho = 0.1$, $\alpha = 1.5$, $\beta = 0$, $\varepsilon = 0.1$, $\lambda = 1$, $\varphi = 0.5$)

nature of the overall process tends to keep the economy inside that region. At each
time period, only few islands are exploited and the economy is seldom producing
under the notionally most efficient conditions.

A Montecarlo analysis
In order to give strength to the above interpretation, we have performed some
Montecarlo (MC) studies with the goal of investigating (i) how behavioural and system
parameters affect average growth rates (AGRs); and (ii) the robustness of the results
across different sample paths, holding the parametrization constant.[44]

First, we have considered the role played by opportunities, path-dependency and
locality of knowledge diffusion in the emergence of 'self-sustained' growth.

For a given level of 'willingness to explore' ($\varepsilon = 0.1$), two benchmark cases,
namely a 'low opportunities' set-up (i.e. $\pi = 0.1$ and $\lambda = 1$) and a 'high opportunities'
one (i.e. $\pi = 0.4$ and $\lambda = 5$), have been analysed. For different combinations of 'path
dependency' and 'locality of knowledge diffusion',[45] a sufficiently large number of

independent simulations have been run, yielding correspondent distributions of AGRs.[46] In Figures 12(a) (low opportunities set-up) and 12(b) (high opportunities), MC mean values and variances of the distributions of AGRs are plotted. The histograms for mean values seem to confirm the above intuition. Mean values of AGRs are increasing in both path-dependency (φ) and globality of knowledge diffusion (ρ)[47] for a given level of opportunities, while high-opportunity AGRs are larger than low-opportunity ones for any given combination of path-dependency and globality of knowledge diffusion. Moreover, histograms of MC variances suggest an interesting emergent property of the model. Indeed, as a general result, one observes a strong positive correlation between high AGRs and larger variances in the MC distributions (see also below).[48]

Finally, a recursive analysis of the first four moments of AGRs MC distributions (not reported here) has been undertaken. For each combination in the above parameter grid, moments of MC distribution over the first M^* simulations – where $M^* = M_0, M_0 + 1, \ldots, M$ – have been computed and plotted against M^*. In all cases one can observe convergence of the first four moments after a number of simulations well below $M = 1000$.

Second, the net effect of 'willingness to explore' on AGRs (i.e. the effect of a change in ε, everything else being constant) has been investigated. For a given parametrization yielding as a usual outcome a pattern of self-sustaining growth[49], we have performed several simulations for varying ε, under the two above opportunities setups. An interesting emergent property is that MC means of AGRs seem to be small whenever the 'willingness to explore' is either very low or very large – see Figures 13(a) and 13(b). Furthermore, the system appears to be characterized – in both opportunities setups – by 'optimal' levels of 'willingness to explore', somehow increasing in the notional level of opportunities. The intuition here corresponds to that suggested in March (1991, p.71). As he points out, systems that engage in exploration to the exclusion of exploitation 'exhibit too many undeveloped new ideas and too little distinctive competences', while, conversely, at the opposite extreme, they 'are likely to find themselves trapped in sub-optimal stable equilibria'. Hence, in our model the losses stemming from the exploration-exploitation trade-off seem to be minimized by an appropriate balance between the two forces (March, 1991; Allen and McGlade, 1986), which, however, agents are generally unable to correctly evaluate ex-ante.

Third, in order to further investigate the emergence of some positive correlation between higher AGRs and larger variances in growth rates, we have computed, for different parametrizations, MC estimates of the frequency distribution of the simulated time-series of growth rates. This has been done by averaging, over $M = 100$ simulations, the frequency distributions of the time-series $\{h_t = (Q_t - Q_{t-1})/Q_{t-1}, t = 1, \ldots, 2500\}$. The results about the mean of those distributions (Table 2), together with those obtained before, suggest that 'self-sustaining' growth seems to be strongly related to a larger variability in the distributions of growth rates both *across* independent simulations and *within* a single sample path. The interpretation of this emergent property is strongly related to both the non-linear and self-reinforcing nature of the mechanisms involved. Indeed, what one usually gets by gradually increasing the strength of the sources of growth in the model is that the self-reinforcing mechanisms of exploration, innovation and production become somewhat explosive.

Means

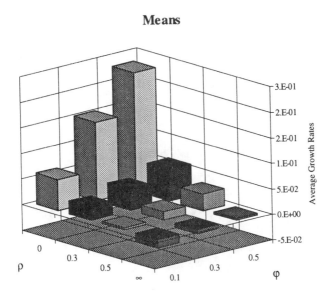

Variances

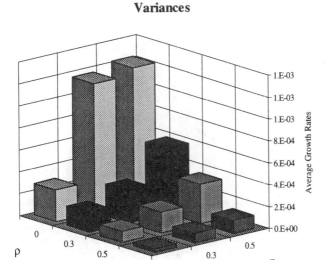

12(a)   Low opportunities ($\pi = 0.1$; $\lambda = 1$)

Figure 12   Montecarlo means and variances of the distributions of average rates of growth (1000 Sim., $N = 100$, $\sigma_s = \sigma_\xi = 0.1$, $\alpha = 1.5$, $\beta = 0$, $\varepsilon = 0.1$)

Means

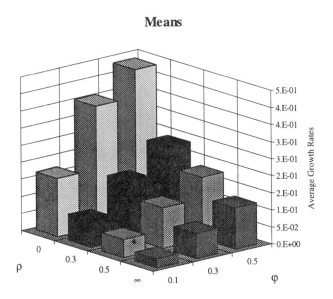

Variances

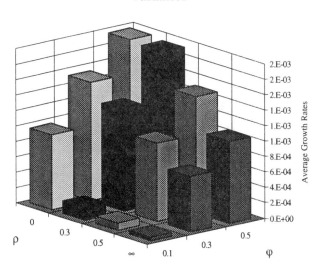

12(b)   High opportunities ($\pi = 0.4$; $\lambda = 5$)

Figure 12   Montecarlo means and variances of the distributions of average rates of growth (1000 Sim., N = 100, $\sigma_s = \sigma_\xi = 0.1$, $\alpha = 1.5$, $\beta = 0$, $\varepsilon = 0.1$)

(a) Low Opportunities (λ=1; π=0.1)

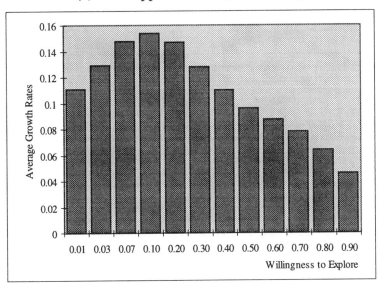

(b) High Opportunities (λ=5; π=0.4)

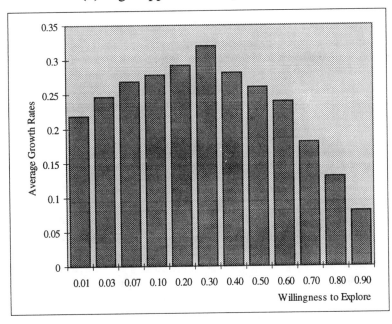

Figure 13   *Montecarlo means of average growth rates versus willingness to explore (ε) (1000 Simulations; N = 100, $\sigma_s = \sigma_\xi = 0.1$, $\beta = 0$, $\alpha = 1.5$, $\rho = 0.1$, $\varphi = 0.5$)*

Table 2   *Statistics of Montecarlo estimates of growth rates' frequency distributions* ***within*** *a simulation (100 Simulations; N = 100, $\sigma_s = \sigma_\xi = 0.1$, $\beta = 0$, $\varepsilon =$ 0.1, $\alpha = 1.5$)*

Path-dependency and globality of diffusion		Low opportunities ($\lambda = 1$; $\pi = 0.1$)		High opportunities ($\lambda = 5$; $\pi = 0.4$)	
φ	ρ	Means	Variances	Means	Variances
∞	0	0.4678	115.4997	0.4618	97.0392
0.7	0.1	0.4779	115.0756	0.4771	95.8557
0.6	0.2	0.4838	113.6873	0.5085.	97.3178
0.5	0.3	0.4961	112.6352	0.5518	98.0393
0.4	0.4	0.5157	111.9287	0.5946	95.7192
0.3	0.5	0.5440	112.1560	0.6801	94.3299
0.2	0.6	0.6230	113.9795	1.3825	188.0971
0.1	0.7	0.7124	112.7626	1.5167	187.7883
0	0.8	0.7905	113.0802	1.8653	229.5539

Self-sustaining growth appears to *imply* the co-existence of periods of moderate growth intertwined by 'jumps' caused by radical innovations (i.e. the arrival of new 'paradigms') which however diffuse through the economy thanks to a time-consuming process of adjustment of all agents to the new knowledge base. Hence, the model, despite its simplicity, is able to account for some of those 'retardation factors' emphasized by Abramovitz (1989, 1993) and David (1991), and, relatedly, for the appearance over finite time periods of distinct patterns (or 'phases') of development.

Moreover, higher average rates of growth entail *higher within-simulation* variability in the rates themselves and *also a higher cross-simulations variability* of AGRs.[50] The latter property seems to suggest a sort of path-dependency in growth patterns which becomes more marked the more one 'fuels' the economy with learning opportunities.

Size of the economy and growth
A well-known drawback of many models of endogenous growth based on some forms of increasing returns – involving dependence of a *flow* variable upon a *stock* variable, e.g. arrivals of technological 'blueprints' as a function of their levels – is that sheer size effects influence growth rates.[51] For instance, many one-factor models, such as Romer (1986), predict that growth rates are increasing, other things being equal, in the size of the population. Furthermore, when one considers extensions of these basic models – such as multi-factors models (Aghion and Howitt, 1992; Grossman and Helpman, 1991a; Romer, 1990) and with international trade (Grossman and Helpman, 1991b) – the standard result is that growth rates are increasing in the factor used intensively in the 'innovative' activity (e.g. skilled labour).[52]

The present model, notwithstanding increasing returns to learning, *does not* display that unreasonable property. To see this, we have computed MC mean values of AGRs across M = 100 simulations holding all parameters constant[53] but just increasing the size of the economy N, i.e. the number of agents. Moreover, in order to ascertain whether the time-length of observed histories affects our results, we have reported MC mean values of AGRs computed at different time-periods (i.e. for different econometric sample periods T). As Table 3 shows, there is a weak evidence on falling AGRs the larger the economy is *for a given time-length*, while AGRs do not display any monotone pattern even if one compares AGRs for N and T both increasing.

The intuition behind this is that, while *ceteris paribus* larger economies face potentially higher returns to knowledge exploitation, it is also true that they must cope, in probability, with higher 'adjustment lags' to new knowledge bases (as proxied in our model by the time it takes to move a certain fraction of the N agents to the notionally superior islands). Hence, larger economies which are potentially able to fuller exploit increasing returns to any one knowledge base need also a relative longer time to achieve persistently higher growth rates.

Table 3   *Montecarlo mean values of average growth rates (AGRs)$^{N\,54}$ as a function of the size of the economy (N) and the econometric sample size (T) (100 Simulations, $\pi = 0.4$, $\lambda = 5$, $\sigma_s = \sigma_\xi = 0.1$, $\beta = 0$, $\alpha = 1.5$, $\rho = 0.1$, $\varepsilon = 0.1$, and $\varphi = 0.5$)*

	Size of the Economy				
Sample size	N = 50	N = 100	N = 200	N = 500	N = 1000
T = 250	0.2526	0.2402	0.2454	0.2196	0.1275
T = 500	0.2879	0.2104	0.2278	0.1602	0.1563
T = 1000	0.2300	0.2262	0.1901	0.1889	0.1485
T = 1500	0.2448	0.2536	0.2287	0.2044	0.1895
T = 2500	0.2529	0.2048	0.2102	0.1707	0.1912
T = 5000	0.2347	0.2141	0.2163	0.2267	0.2156

4.4   Individual versus collective rationality: a simple example

As conjectured above, the model highlights a few sources of potential conflict between individual and collective rationality. In order to illustrate this point, consider the following simple example. Assume an economy characterized by: (i) constant returns to scale (i.e. $\alpha = 1$); (ii) no knowledge diffusion (i.e. $\rho = \infty$); (iii) no path-dependency in innovation (i.e. $\varphi = 0$); (iv) all N agents working at time $t = 0$ on a single island ($\ell_0 = 1$) with co-ordinates (x^*, y^*) and initial productivity $s^* = x^* + y^*$ [55]; (v) a constant positive transportation cost β (i.e. $\delta = 0$, $\beta \in [0,1)$, see Section 3.2).

Given the above parametrization, we will consider two different settings for what concerns behavioural assumptions.

In the first one, the population is composed of N agents behaving according to the behavioural rules defined in Section 3.

In the second one, we will introduce a 'representative individual' (RI) endowed by 'rational expectations'. More precisely, assume that the latter has unbounded computational skills and complete information, so that it knows: (i) the co-ordinates (x^*, y^*); (ii) the system parameters; (iii) the model of the economy. Although it knows that, on average, the initial productivity of a new island is increasing in its distance from the origin, it does not know where new islands are actually located. Hence, starting from the node (x,y), it will make use of an exploration rule which gives equal probability to the nodes $(x + 1, y)$ and $(x, y + 1)$. Finally, assume for simplicity that the intertemporal discount rate is zero.[56]

At time $t = 1$, the problem for the RI is to decide whether to continue to extract the good at time $t = 2$ or start to explore. In the first case, it will get a per-period net output from mining equal to $\theta_M = s^*$. In the second case, the expected per-period net output from exploration will be: $\theta_E = [(1 + \lambda)(s^* + \tau) - \beta\tau]/\tau$, where $\tau = 1/\pi$ is the expected length of exploration.[57] Then, the RI will decide to remain on island (x^*, y^*) if and only if $\theta_M > \theta_E$, i.e. iff:

$$\pi < \frac{1}{1 + \lambda} - \frac{1}{s^*} + \frac{\beta}{(1 + \lambda) \cdot s^*} = \pi^*(\beta, \lambda, s^*) \qquad (11)$$

As one can easily check, $\pi^*(\beta, \lambda, s^*)$ is decreasing in λ and increasing in s^* and β, as expected.[58] More generally, one could single out – for given values of s^* – a correspondent region in the space spanned by feasible values of (β, λ) satisfying (11) for some $\pi \in (0, 1)$.

For instance, assume for simplicity $\beta = 0$. Then, the pair $\pi = 0.15$ and $\lambda = 5$ satisfies equation (11) for $s^* = 100$. In this setup, the RI will decide to continue to work as a 'miner'. Hence, such an economy will get a net per-capita output $\theta^* = 100$. On the contrary, consider an economy characterized by the same parametrization,[59] composed of N = 100 agents, all starting as 'miners' on the island (x^*, y^*), $x^* + y^* = 100$, and behaving as described in Section 3. Notice that agents live here in a rather 'poor' environment, in which there is *neither* knowledge diffusion, *nor* path-dependency in innovation, *nor* increasing returns to scale. Furthermore, assume that agents are characterized by a very low 'willingness to explore' (i.e. $\varepsilon = 0.05$). Notwithstanding all that, simulations show (Figure 14) that the economy is able to get, as a general outcome, a per-capita net output persistently greater than $\theta^* = 100$.

Thus, even in this very simple setting, collective growth finds its necessary condition in the presence of a number of 'irrational' individuals.

Even more so, this potential conflict between individual rationality and collective welfare emerges in the general setting with unlimited notional opportunities of exploration and transportation costs born up front by the 'explorers' themselves.

Note that as mentioned earlier this property significantly expands upon the common result from e.g. New Growth literature that in presence of externalities or dynamic increasing returns a systematic divergence between endogenously generated growth rates and socially optimal ones (whatever the latter means…) is likely to emerge. Here, one may require indeed the presence of straightforwardly *irrational* agents in order to have endogenous growth at all.

5. Conclusions

The foregoing model presents a rather simple dynamics through which 'incremental' knowledge accumulation, diffusion and random discoveries of new technologies interact as to yield persistent – and persistently – fluctuating growth.

As mentioned, it could be considered as a sort of 'reduced form' evolutionary model, with an almost exclusive emphasis upon the learning/diffusion aspects of economic evolution, while repressing the competition/selection features of market interactions.

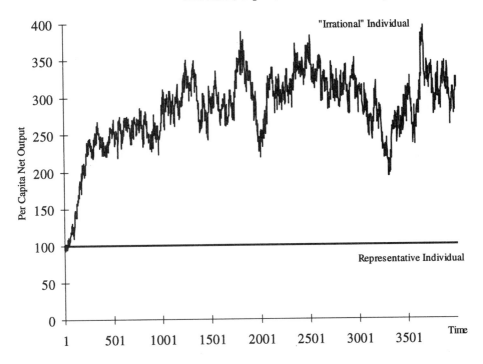

Figure 14   *Individual versus collective rationality: a simple example* ($s^* = 100$, $N = 100$, $\varepsilon = 0.05$, $\beta = 0$, $\delta = 0$, $\varphi = 0$, $\lambda = 5$, $\pi = 0.15$, $\rho = \infty$, $\sigma_s = \sigma_\xi = 0.1$, $\alpha = 1$)

While the limitations of this reduced form are quite obvious (for example, the 'microeconomics' is bound to be rather poor), on the upside, it still allows predictions on the dynamics of aggregate variables (and first of all growth rates of the economy), mapping them into system and behavioural parameters capturing the conditions of generations and diffusion of knowledge.

In particular, the model is able to study the effects upon the patterns of growth of: (a) *technological opportunities* (as captured by both the density of 'islands' and the probability of Poisson jumps to radically new paradigms); (b) *cumulativeness of learning* and *path-dependency* (i.e. the increasing return coefficient α, for each island, and the fraction of idiosyncratic knowledge, φ, that agents are able to carry over to newly discovered technologies); (c) *locality of learning* (i.e. an indirect inverse proxy for appropriability), captured by the diffusion parameter ρ; and, finally, on the behavioural side, (d) the *propensity to explore*, ε.

Note also, that, in principle, the above variables and parameters can find empirical (although inevitably rough) proxies. Therefore, one might not despair to test the qualitative properties generated by the model against actual data.

As simple as it is, the model is comparable with New Growth ones, with some overlappings and some major differences. It is similar to the former in that it identifies in knowledge diffusion *cum* dynamic increasing returns the primary sources of self-sustained growth. However, it departs from them in a few important respects.

First, knowledge is neither treated as entirely appropriable or a pure externality: rather, its benefits partly accrue to those who embody it and partly leak out as a sort of spillover.

Second, dynamic increasing returns to learning are, at least to some extent, technology-specific.

Third, diffusion takes time rather than being instantaneous (and indeed is a major source of growth).

Fourth, problems of 'Schumpeterian coordination' always emerge out of micro-economic heterogeneity in both technical knowledge and innovative decisions.

Finally, the radical uncertainty intrinsic in the innovation process involves the possibility that agents make *systematic* mistakes in innovative search and adoption.

Among other properties, our model shows how a decentralized economy with heterogeneous interacting agents, under certain technological and behavioural conditions, can *self-organize* into exponential growth,[60] without appealing to the forecasting powers of any far-sighted 'representative agent'. In fact the result is stronger than that, since the economy might require *non-average* (and individually irrational) behaviours in order to achieve such a self-sustained path.[61] Hence the permanent dilemma between *exploitation* of what one knows and *exploration* of the unknown (March, 1991) and, consequently, also the crucial collective role of entrepreneurial 'animal spirits', even when ill-grounded in the 'true' probability distributions of gains and losses stemming from innovative search.

As it stands, the model seems quite well suited to account for some generic properties of knowledge-driven growth. Nevertheless, further developments come easily to mind.

First, one could try to see how this basic story about growth is modified by the introduction also of a 'Keynesian' coordination problem affecting interdependent demand generation mechanisms.

Second, one might likewise study the relevance of adding explicit selection processes affecting the frequency in the population (i.e. the size) of different agents which are 'carriers' of different technologies.

And, on a methodological side, together with computer simulation, it might not be out of reach to study some analytical properties, at least in some special cases, of the Markovian process plausibly underlying the model presented here.

However, even before all that come, it seems to us that the foregoing work might contribute to the understanding of how endogenous learning processes, with imperfect collective adaptation and heterogeneous agents, drive growth notwithstanding (or rather *because of*) the absence of fantastically rational agents and equilibria fulfilled throughout.

Parameters of the model

N = Number of agents
ε = Willingness to explore
π = Probability that a node is an island
λ = Expected value of jumps in innovation
ρ = Globality of knowledge diffusion

φ = Path dependency in innovation
α = Returns to scale
β = Transportation cost (NB. $c_{i,t} = \beta \cdot [Q_{t-1}/N]^{\delta}$)
δ = Transportation cost (NB. $c_{i,t} = \beta \cdot [Q_{t-1}/N]^{\delta}$)
σ_s = Variance of the distribution of initial productivity coefficients for islands inside L_0
σ_ξ = Variance of the noise in the initial productivity coefficients for islands outside L_0

Appendix: some results on persistence of output fluctuations

Assume that the change in log of GNP follows a stationary process with moving average representation: $\Delta q_t = A(L)v_t$, where $A(L) = \sum_{j=0}^{\infty} A_j L^j$, $A_0 = 1$ and v_t is white noise. Following Campbell and Mankiw (1987, 1989) and Cochrane (1988), we computed estimates of the following persistence measures: (i) $V \equiv \lim_{k \to \infty} V^k$, where $V^k = [1 + 2 \sum_{j=1}^{k} (1 - \frac{j}{k+1})\rho_j]$ and ρ_j is the jth autocorrelation coefficient of Δq_t; (ii) $A(1) = \sum_{j=0}^{\infty} A_j$. An estimate of V^k (which consistently estimates V for large k) is found simply by replacing population auto-correlations with sample counterparts, while $A(1)$ must be estimated non-parametrically (for large k) by $\hat{A}^k(1) = \sqrt{\frac{\hat{V}^k}{1-\hat{\rho}_1^2}}$. Since both $\hat{V}^k$ and $\hat{A}^k(1)$ are downward biased, they have been multiplied by the correction factor T/$(T - k)$. For a random walk, $A(1)$ and V^k equal one, while for any series stationary around a deterministic trend $A(1)$ is zero and V^k approaches zero for large k. Thus, if both measures are above unity the output exhibits fluctuations with high persistence. Campbell and Mankiw (1987, 1989) and Cochrane (1988) provide Montecarlo studies on 90 per cent critical values of $\hat{V}$ and $\hat{A}^k(1)$ for different data generation processes and $k = 20, 40, 60$.

Sample autocorrelation functions for the change in log of GNP [Δq_t] and for growth rates [$g_t = (q_t - q_{t-1})/q_{t-1}$] are reported in Figure 15.[62] In Table 4 both statistics $\hat{V}^k$ and $\hat{A}^k(1)$ are computed for Δq_t and g_t and $k = 20, 40, 60$. Autocorrelation coefficients are quite small (in particular for Δq_t) but similar to those obtained in reality (see Campbell and Mankiw, 1989). Moreover, all estimates of persistence are greater than unity and quite similar to those obtained for empirical data. Comparing them with the corresponding 90% percentiles, one is able to reject all stationary processes with larger root less or equal to 0.9. In particular, the values of $\hat{V}^k$ for Δq_t fit quite well the case where q_t is generated by an AR(2) process with roots (1, 0.25).

Table 4   Estimates of persistence in simulated series of log GNP

k	g_t	Δq_t
	Bias corrected $\hat{V}^k$	
20	1.35	1.46
40	1.30	1.65
60	1.46	1.89
	Bias corrected $\hat{A}^k(1)$	
20	1.18	1.22
40	1.17	1.32
60	1.26	1.43

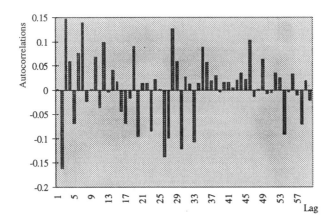

(a) Growth Rates $[g_t=(q_t- q_{t-1})/q_{t-1}]$

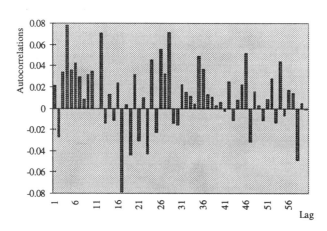

(b) Change in log of GNP $[\Delta q_t]$

Figure 15   *Sample autocorrelations*

Acknowledgements
Support for this research by the Italian National Research Council (CNR), the Italian Ministry of Research (MURST) and IIASA, Laxenburg, Austria is gratefully acknowledged. An early sketch of some ideas behind the model which follows is in Dosi and Orsenigo (1994). Comments by several participants to the Conference of CNAM, Paris, October 1996 helped a lot in sharpening the arguments. Usual caveats apply.

Notes
* European University Institute, S. Domenico de Fiesole (FI), Italy.
1. See, among others, Freeman (1982) and (1994), Rosenberg (1982) and (1994), David (1975), Dosi (1988), Nelson (1995), Lundvall (1993), Granstrand (1994), Stoneman (1995), and fair parts of Dosi *et al.* (1988) and Foray and Freeman (1992).
2. Cf. also Dosi, Freeman and Fabiani (1994), where one tries to outline a series of historical 'stylized facts' which the theory should ideally account for.
3. For highly pertinent considerations on this point cf. Kirman (1989) and (1992) and Allen (1988).

4. For example, on entry dynamics of new firms cf. the evidence discussed in Dosi and Lovallo (1997).
5. This point has indeed been emphasized within otherwise rather orthodox models by Jovanovic and Rob (1989), Jovanovic (1995), and, of course, is near the concerns of evolutionary modellers (cf. Nelson and Winter (1982), Silverberg *et al.* (1988), Metcalfe (1988) and (1996)).
6. On these points, see in particular Rosenberg (1982) and Freeman (1982) regarding technologies uncertainty; Freeman (1982), Levin *et al.* (1987), Nelson and Winter (1982) and the remarks in Dosi (1997) and Nelson (1998) on appropriability; Arrow (1962a), Arthur *et al.* (1987), David (1975) and (1988), Romer (1990); Atkinson and Stigliz (1969), Nelson and Winter (1982), Dosi (1988), Malerba and Orsenigo (1993) on different – theoretical and empirical – appreciations of dynamic increasing returns; Nelson and Winter (1977), Dosi (1982), Freeman and Perez (1988) on somewhat complementary notions of 'technological paradigms' and relatively ordered 'trajectories' in learning patterns.
7. For a thorough discussion on the exploitation-exploration trade-off arising in adaptive systems see March (1991), Schumpeter (1934), Holland (1975), Allen and McGlade (1986) and Kuran (1988). See also Levinthal and March (1981) and Levitt and March (1988) on the trade-off between the refinement of an existing technology and invention of a new one.
8. But any actual planner, too, would fall well short of that standard, being equally ignorant of long-run learning opportunities.
9. In fact, this is quite in tune with the empirical evidence. While it is obviously true that with zero appropriability of innovation no private actor has any incentive to undertake expensive search (e.g. for a long time agricultural research on new varieties of seeds, etc.), on the other side, to our knowledge, there is non convincing evidence, either cross-country or over time, that innovative efforts respond smoothly to the fine tuning of appropriability conditions.
10. Parts of the overwhelming evidence on this point are surveyed in Nelson (1981), Freeman (1982), Dosi (1988).
11. On this point, the empirical evidence indeed matches quite solid theoretical reasons on the impossibility of forming unbiased expectations on future technological advances. After all, innovation is about solving problems that one has been unable to solve so far. But if one could know, even in probability, how to solve them, that would mean that the solution algorithm has already been found! The issue bears on problem-solving complexity and, more generally, on the predictability of discovery. More on this is in Dosi and Egidi (1991) and Dosi, Marengo and Fagiolo (1996), within a vast literature.
12. See, among others, Nelson and Winter (1982), Winter (1984), Chiaromonte and Dosi (1993), Silverberg and Verspagen (1994), Dosi *et al.* (1994a, b), Silverberg and Lehnert (1994), Conlisk (1989) and Metcalfe (1988).
13. The distinction between 'incremental' and 'radical' technical progress (i.e. between paradigm changes and within-paradigm improvements) is increasingly accepted also in other modelling perspectives: cf. for example Cheng and Dinopoulos (1992), Jovanovic and Rob (1990), Jovanovic and McDonald (1994), Amable (1995).
14. Again, the issue of a time-consuming (and/or resource-consuming) adaptation and diffusion is beginning to make inroads also into equilibrium growth models: compare Jovanovic and McDonald (1994), Jovanovic (1995) and Jones and Newman (1994). In the model below we especially emphasize 'creative destruction' aspects of technological discontinuities, with relatively lower attention to the possible complementarities among them (on this point, in the formal growth literature, compare A. Young (1993)). However, note that the complementarity aspect is implicit in the possibility that we allow in our model for agents to 'carry over', so to speak, part of their previous production skills to new knowledge bases.
15. As Silverberg and Verspagen (1995) point out, following Nelson and Winter (1982), 'innovation should be modelled stochastically, to reflect the uncertainty in the link between effort and outcome'.
16. Notice that there is a one-to-one mapping between the index $j \in \aleph$ and the pair $(x_j, y_j) \in \aleph^2$, $j \in \aleph$.
17. This does not mean, however, that islands $j = 1, 2, \dots$ (both in L_0 and in $\aleph \backslash L_0$) are sorted (in some way) by their distance from the origin.
18. As we will see below, in each time period the 'miner' $i \in I$ decides to leave its island and explore around it with probability ε_i.
19. Notice that the location of an agent at time t will correspond to that of an island, say j, if only if currently there is at least one 'miner' on j, i.e.: for $t > 1$, $(x_{i,t}, y_{i,t}) = (x_j, y_j)$, some $j \in L_t$ if and only if $a_{i,t} =$ 'mi'.
20. Unlike most neoclassical models, generally based on technical change embodied in different vintages of equipment (Solow, 1960; Kaldor and Mirrlees, 1962), at any given moment in time there is not a single best-practice technique, but many competing technologies located near the frontier of the box B_t (see also Silverberg *et al.*, 1988).
21. See also Shackle (1955) and Davidson (1996) for some hints in a similar spirit.

22. This form of cost has been assumed for sake of normalization. However, since in this version of the model the willingness of explore is assumed to be independent of transportation costs, the latter have no effects on the dynamics of the model, but only on the magnitude of the total net output: see also Section 4.4.
23. This is not a necessary assumption, however. As we will see above, the economy is naturally driven, although only on average, toward more efficient islands by the process of diffusion of information, so that the event of finding a new island inside L_i is in fact irrelevant in our description.
24. As happens in Nelson and Winter (1982) or Silverberg and Verspagen (1994), innovation is a local process.
25. In an alternative version of the model, not discussed here, to every signal is also associated a 'speed' which measures how quickly the signal is spread around the economy.
26. For the sake of simplicity, notice that an imitator cannot be reached by any other signal while committed to a particular destination.
27. A more detailed discussion of local interaction models in Fagiolo (1998).
28. For a thorough discussion of 'artificial economies' models, see Lane (1993a,b).
29. More on the notion of self-organization is in Lesourne (1991). See also Silverberg *et al.* (1988) and the remarks in Coriat and Dosi (1995).
30. As shown below for the fully-fledged model, we did indeed begin this type of analysis.
31. For a more detailed discussion of these properties of path-dependency cf. Arthur (1994) and David (1988).
32. The behaviour of the model in this simple set-up is close to those obtained in different frameworks by David (1992), Arthur *et al.* (1987).
33. A Montecarlo study of the frequencies of absorption as functions of Δs_0 and Δm_0, not reported here, gives quantitative supports to intuition.
34. See Brock and Durlauf (1995), Hirshleifer (1993), Bikchandani *et al.* (1992), Scharfstein and Stein (1990), Kirman (1993).
35. These properties are quite similar to those displayed by models based on Fokker-Planck equations. Cf. also Kirman (1993) and Orléan (1992).
36. Notice here the loose analogy with the coordination-related dynamics treated by Cooper and John (1988) and Durlauf (1994).
37. In the following, a Montecarlo analysis giving a more precise meaning to this statement is presented.
38. The lag order $k = 5$ in the standard ADF regression $\Delta q_t = \mu + \gamma t + \theta_0 q_{t-1} + \theta_1 \Delta q_{t-1} + \ldots + \theta_{k-1} \Delta q_{t-k+1} + \zeta_t$ has been suggested by both Akaike and Schwarz criteria. All econometric analyses reported here refer, as an example, to a single time-series (i.e. that plotted in Figure 5). Nevertheless, the same conclusions appear to hold in all simulations displaying self-sustaining growth. However, in order to give more rigorous bases to the above outcomes, a Montecarlo study of the percentage of rejection of the null of a unit-root (for different parametrizations) has been undertaken.
39. The above results seem to match those obtained for GNP time-series for the US by Nelson and Plosser (1982) and Stock and Watson (1986). However, it is a well-known result that standard ADF tests for 'stochastic trend' (against 'deterministic trend' alternatives) suffer from very low power. In particular, many authors have recently shown that unit-root tests are unlikely to discriminate between difference- and trend-stationarity, (see Christiano and Eichenbaum (1989) and Rudebusch (1993)), giving birth to the so-called 'we don't know' literature. Conversely, many other contributions have recently appeared suggesting that unit-root tests can be nonetheless informative, at least over long spans (DeJong and Whiteman, 1991 and 1994). In this connection, Cochrane (1988) has pointed out that the use of longer GNP samples (as in our case) may produce sharper unit-root inference. Yet, evidence stemming from this strand of literature seems to conclude that U.S. aggregate output is *not* likely to be difference stationary (Diebold and Senhadji, 1996; Bernd, 1994). Hence, the question of deterministic versus stochastic trends in real economic aggregates remains open. Notice also that the distinction between trend- and difference-stationarity is potentially important only in economic forecasting, but might not be so critical in many other contexts.
40. See the appendix. For details, see also Cochrane (1988).
41. Notice, incidentally, that our estimates are very close to those of the US (log of) real GNP obtained by Campbell and Mankiw (1989). Again, there is no consensus in the literature about the size of the long-run response of actual real GNPs to an innovation. Christiano and Eichenbaum (1989), for instance, show that Campbell and Mankiw's results are very sensitive to the choice of the ARMA representation of the data.
42. By a 'low growth' economy we mean a situation where the GNP time-series fluctuates around a linear (stochastic) trend, while its log follows an '*s*-shaped' pattern, so that in the long run growth rates tend to become stationary around zero.
43. Unless differently stated, we refer throughout, as an example, to the basic parametrization: $N = 100$,

$\sigma_s = \sigma_\xi = 0.1$, $\beta = 0$, $\alpha = 1.5$. All results reported in this sub-section refer to: $\pi = 0.1$, $\rho = 0.1$, $\varepsilon = 0.1$, $\lambda = 1$, $\varphi = 0.5$.

44. For a given parametrization, let $\{g_m, m = 1,2,..,M\}$ be the Montecarlo sample of average growth rates, where, for a given simulated time series $\{q_t = logQ_t, t = 0,..,T\}_m$, we simply define $g_m = 100\cdot[(q_T/q_0)^{1/T}-1]$. In the following, T = 2500 and M = 1000.

45. In each case, a grid for ρ and φ has been prepared, namely: $\rho\in\{0, 0.1, 0.5, \infty\}$ and $\varphi\in\{0.1, 0.2, 0.3, 0.5\}$. Notice that if $\rho = 0$ the knowledge diffusion is 'global', while if $\rho = \infty$ it is absent.

46. The null of normality is accepted at 5 per cent for all AGR Montecarlo distributions (χ^2 test).

47. Notice that, as a 'rule of thumb', only mean values of AGR above 0.06 imply 'self-sustained growth', or, put it differently, a I(1) process for the log of GNP.

48. For a similar property of actual time series in a cross-section of countries, compare Fatas (1995).

49. The parametrization is $\rho = 0.1$ and $\varphi = 0.5$. For each value of $\varepsilon\in\{0.01, 0.03, 0.07, 0.10, 0.20, 0.30, 0.40, 0.50, 0.60, 0.70, 0.80, 0.90\}$, M = 1000 simulations have been run.

50. For similar findings, see Aghion and Howitt (1992).

51. We refer here to R&D-based models of endogenous growth, such as Aghion and Howitt (1992), Romer (1986, 1990), Grossman and Helpman, (1991a, 1991b). In these models, size-effects stem from three related assumptions, namely (i) technology is non rival, so that increases in the scale of the economy entail larger profits for all innovators; (ii) there are strong inter-temporal spillovers, i.e. each innovator can improve existing technology at any time; and (iii) new technologies are substitute for the old ones, so that returns to innovation are decreasing in the rate of innovation. Conversely, in many models in which growth is endogenously generated by the accumulation of human and physical *rival* capital, any increase in the scale of the economy has no impact on growth rates (cf. Lucas (1988), Jones and Manuelli (1990) and Rebelo (1991)). Furthermore, cf. Young (1995) and Jones (1995a) for recent examples of R&D-based models of endogenous growth *without* scale-effects.

52. Taken literally, they would predict India growing faster than, say, Singapore. See Jones (1995b) for a detailed discussion on empirical evidence on these points.

53. In what follows (see Table 3), we report as an example the results obtained considering a 'high-opportunity' set-up yielding 'exponential growth', i.e. we set $\pi = 0.4$, $\lambda = 5$, $\sigma_s = \sigma_\xi = 0.1$, $\beta = 0$, $\alpha = 1.5$, $\rho = 0.1$, $\varepsilon = 0.1$, and $\varphi = 0.5$. However, the same pattern holds also for other opportunity setups and different parametrizations of knowledge diffusion, path-dependency and dynamic increasing returns.

54. AGRs are defined as $g_m =100\cdot[(q_T/q_0)^{1/T}-1]$, where: $q_t = logQ_t$ is the log of the GNP at time $t = 0,...,$ T; $m = 1,2,...,M$ where M is the Montecarlo sample size; T is the econometric sample size.

55. Notice that with constant returns to scale the output of the agent working on island (x^*,y^*) is equal to its initial productivity s^*, irrespective of the number of agents are working on the island.

56. Our conjecture is that the following results will hold *a fortiori* for a strictly positive discount rate.

57. Notice that τ is also the expected distance between (x^*,y^*) and a new island.

58. If we allow β to be greater than the unity, then $\pi^*(\beta,\lambda,s^*)$ is increasing in s^* only if $\lambda>\beta-1$, i.e. if opportunities are large enough. Notice that if $s^*\rightarrow\infty$ the RI will always stay on (x^*,y^*), while if $\lambda^*\rightarrow\infty$ it will always leave.

59. That is $\beta = 0$, $\delta = 0$, $\varphi = 0$, $\lambda = 5$, $\pi = 0.15$, $\rho = \infty$, $\sigma_s = \sigma_\xi = 0.1$, $\alpha = 1$.

60. Cf. Lane (1993), Krugman (1996) and Fagiolo (1997).

61. A similar point on non-average behaviours inducing symmetry breaks in the distribution of particular features or performances of a population of agents is in Allen (1988).

62. As done in Table 1, econometric analyses refer to a simulation generated by the following parametrization: N = 100, $\pi = 0.1$, $\sigma_s = \sigma_\xi = 0.1$, $\rho = 0.1$, $\alpha = 1.5$, $\beta = 0$, $\varepsilon = 0.1$, $\lambda = 1$, $\varphi = 0.5$.

References

Abramovitz, M. (1989), *Thinking about Growth*, Cambridge: Cambridge University Press.

Abramovitz, M. (1993), 'The search for the sources of growth', *Journal of Economic History*, 53, 217–43.

Aghion, P. and P. Howitt (1992), 'A model of growth through creative destruction', *Econometrica*, **60**, 323–51.

Allen, P.M. (1988), 'Evolution, innovation and economics', in G. Dosi, C. Freeman, R.R. Nelson, G. Silverberg and L. Soete (eds), *Technical Change and Economic Theory*, London: Francis Pinter.

Allen, P.M. and J.M. McGlade 1986), 'Dynamics of discovery and exploitation: the case of the scotian shelf groundfish fisheries', *Canadian Journal of Fishery and Aquatic Sciences*, **43**, 1187–200.

Amable, B. (1995), 'Endogenous growth and cycles through radical incremental innovation', CEPREMAP, *Discussion Paper,* 9504.

Arrow, K.J. (1962a), 'Economic welfare and the allocation of resources to invention', in R.R.Nelson, (ed.), *The Rate and Direction of Inventive Activity*, Princeton: National Bureau of Economic Research.

Arrow, K.J. (1962b), 'The economic implications of learning by doing', *Review of Economic Studies*, **29**, 155–73.

Arthur, W.B. (1988), 'Self-reinforcing mechanisms in economics', in P.W. Anderson, K.J. Arrow and D. Pines (eds), *The Economy as an Evolving Complex System*, Santa Fe Institute, Santa Fe and Reading, MA: Addison-Wesley.

Arthur, W.B. (1989), 'Competing technologies, increasing returns and lock-in by historical small events: the dynamics of allocation under increasing returns to scale', *Economic Journal*, **99**, 116–31.

Arthur, W.B. (1994), *Increasing Returns and Path-Dependency in Economics,* Ann Arbor: University of Michigan Press.

Arthur, W.B., Yu. M. Ermoliev and Yu. M. Kaniovski (1987), 'Path-dependent processes and the emergence of macro-structure', *European Journal of Operational Research*, **30**, 294–303.

Atkinson, A. and J.E. Stiglitz (1969), 'A new view of technical change', *Economic Journal*, **79**, 573–78.

Bernd, L. (1994), 'Testing for unit-roots with income distribution data', *Empirical Economics*, **19**, 555–73.

Bikchandani, S.K., D. Hirshleifer and I. Welch (1992), 'A theory of fads, fashion, custom and cultural change as informational cascade', *Journal of Political Economy*, **100**, 992–1026.

Brock, W.A. and S.N. Durlauf (1995), 'Discrete choice with social interactions I: Theory', University of Wisconsin at Madison, SSRI Working Paper, 9521.

Campbell, J.Y. and N.G. Mankiw (1987), 'Are output fluctuations transitory?', *Quarterly Journal of Economics*, **102**, 857–80.

Campbell, J.Y. and N.G. Mankiw (1989), 'International evidences on the persistence of economic fluctuations', *Journal of Monetary Economics*, **23**, 319–33.

Cheng, L.K. and E. Dinopoulos (1991), 'Stochastic Schumpeterian economic fluctuations', University of Florida, mimeo.

Cheng, L.K. and E. Dinopoulos (1992), 'Schumpeterian growth and international business cycles', *American Economic Review*, **82**, 409–14.

Chiaromonte, F. and G. Dosi (1993), 'Heterogeneity, competition and macroeconomic dynamics', *Structural Change and Economic Dynamics*, **4**, 39–63.

Christiano, L.J. and M. Eichenbaum (1989), 'Unit roots in real GNP: Do we know and do we care?', NBER, Working Paper, 3130.

Cochrane, J.H. (1988), 'How big is the random walk in GNP?', *Journal of Political Economy*, **96**, 893–920.

Conlisk, J. (1989), 'An aggregate model of technical change', *Quarterly Journal of Economics*, **104**, 787–821.

Cooper, R. and A. John (1988), 'Coordinating coordination failures in Keynesian models', *Quarterly Journal of Economics*, **103**, 441–64.

David, P.A. (1975), *Technical Choice, Innovation and Economic Growth,* Cambridge: Cambridge University Press.

David, P.A. (1988), 'Path-dependence: putting the past into the future of economics', Stanford, Institute for Mathematical Studies in Social Sciences, Technical Report, 533.

David, P.A. (1991), 'Computer and dynamo: the modern productivity paradox in a not-too-distant mirror', in OECD (ed.), *Technology and Productivity*, Paris: OECD.

David, P.A. (1992), 'Path-dependence and predictability in dynamic systems with local externalities: a paradigm for historical economics', in D. Foray and C. Freeman (eds), *Technology and the Wealth of Nations*, London: Francis Pinter.

Davidson, P. (1996), 'Reality and economic theory', *Journal of Post-Keynesian Economics*, **18**, 479–508.

DeJong, D.N. and C.H. Whiteman (1991), 'The case for trend-stationarity is stronger than we thought', *Journal of Applied Econometrics*, **6**, 413–21.

DeJong, D.N. and C.H. Whiteman (1994), 'The forecasting attributes of trend- and difference-stationary representations for macroeconomic time-series', *Journal of Forecasting*, **13**, 279–97.

Diebold, F.X. and A.S. Senhadji (1996), 'The uncertain unit root in real GNP: Comment', *American Economic Review*, **86**, 1291–8.

Dosi, G. (1982), 'Technological paradigms and technological trajectories', *Research Policy*, **11**, 147–62.

Dosi, G. (1988), 'Sources, procedures and microeconomic effects of innovation', *Journal of Economic Literature*, **26**, 126–71.

Dosi, G. (1991), 'The research on innovation diffusion: an assessment', in A. Grubler and N. Nakicenovic (eds), *Diffusion of Technologies and Social Behavior*, New York: Springer Verlag.

Dosi, G. (1997), 'Opportunities, incentives and the collective patterns of technological change', *The Economic Journal*, **107**, 1530–47.

Dosi, G. and M. Egidi (1991), 'Substantive and procedural uncertainty. An exploration on economic behaviours in changing environments', *Journal of Evolutionary Economics*, **1**, 145–68.

Dosi, G. and D. Lovallo (1997), 'Rational entrepreneurs or optimistic martyrs? Some considerations on technological regimes', in R. Garud, P. Nayyar and Z. Shapiro (eds), *Foresights and Oversights in Technological Change*, Cambridge: Cambridge University Press.

Dosi, G. and L. Orsenigo (1994), 'Macrodynamics and microfoundations: an evolutionary perspective', in O. Granstrand (ed.), *The Economics of Technology*, Amsterdam: North Holland.

Dosi, G., S. Fabiani, R. Aversi and M. Meacci (1994a), 'The dynamics of international differentiation: a multi-country evolutionary model', *Industrial and Corporate Change*, **3**, 225–42.

Dosi, G., C. Freeman and S. Fabiani (1994b), 'The process of economic development: introducing some stylized facts and theories on technologies, firms and institutions', *Industrial and Corporate Change*, **3**, 1–46.

Dosi, G., C. Freeman, R.R. Nelson, G. Silverberg and L. Soete (eds) (1988), *Technical Change and Economic Theory*, London: Francis Pinter.

Dosi, G., L. Marengo and G. Fagiolo (1996), 'Learning in evolutionary environments', IIASA, Laxenburg, Austria, Working Paper, WP-96-124/Nov 1996.

Durlauf, S.N. (1994), 'Path-dependence in aggregate output', *Industrial and Corporate Change*, **3**, 149–71.

Fagiolo, G. (1997), 'An artificial model of coordination and innovation-driven growth in decentralized economies with heterogeneous interacting agents', European University Institute, mimeo.

Fagiolo, G. (1998), 'Spatial interactions in dynamic decentralized economies: a review', in P. Cohendet, P. Llerena, H. Stahn and G. Umbhauer (eds), *The Economics of Networks. Interaction and Behaviours*, Berlin - Heidelberg: Springer Verlag.

Fatas, A. (1995), 'Endogenous growth and stochastic trends', INSEAD, Working Paper, 95/85/EPS.

Foray, D. and C. Freeman (1992), *Technology and the Wealth of Nations*, Paris: OECD.

Freeman, C. (1982), *The Economics of Industrial Innovation*, London: Francis Pinter.

Freeman, C. (1994), 'The economics of technical change', *Cambridge Journal of Economics*, **18**, 463–514.

Freeman, C. and C. Perez (1988), 'Structural crisis of adjustment: business cycles and investment behavior', in G. Dosi, C. Freeman, R.R. Nelson., G. Silverberg and L. Soete (eds), *Technical Change and Economic Theory*, London: Francis Pinter.

Granstrand, O. (ed.) (1994), *The Economics of Technology*, Amsterdam: North Holland.

Grossman, G.M. and E. Helpman (1991a), 'Quality ladders and product cycles', *Review of Economic Studies*, **58**, 43-61.

Grossman, G.M. and E. Helpman (1991b), *Innovation and Growth in the Global Economy*, Cambridge: MIT Press.

Hirschleifer, D. (1993), 'The blind leading the blind: social influence, fads and informational cascades', UCLA, Los Angeles, Anderson Graduate School of Management, Working Paper, WP 24-93.

Holland, J.H. (1975), *Adaptation in Natural and Artificial Systems*, Cambridge: MIT Press.

Jones, C.I. (1995a), 'R&D-based models of economic growth', *Journal of Political Economy*, **103**, 759–84.

Jones, C.I. (1995b), 'Time series tests of endogenous growth models', *Quarterly Journal of Economics*, **110**, 495–525.

Jones, L.E. and R. Manvelli (1990), 'A convex model of equilibrium growth', *Journal of Political Economy*, **98**, 1008–38.

Jones, R. and G. Newman (1994), 'Economic growth as a coordination problem', University of British Columbia, Working Paper, 94/11.

Jovanovic, B. (1995), 'Learning and growth', NBER, Working Paper, 5383.

Jovanovic, B. and G.M. McDonald (1994), 'Competitive diffusion', *Journal of Political Economy*, **102**, 24-52.

Jovanovic, B. and R. Rob (1989), 'The growth and diffusion of knowledge', *Review of Economic Studies*, **56**, 569–82.

Jovanovic, B. and R. Rob, R. (1990), 'Long waves and short waves: growth through intensive and extensive search', *Econometrica*, **58**, 1391–409.

Kaldor, N. and J.A. Mirrlees (1962), 'A new model of economic growth', *Review of Economic Studies*, **29**, 174–92.

Kirman, A.P. (1989), 'The intrinsic limits of modern economic theory: the emperor has no clothes', *Economic Journal*, **99**, 126–39.

Kirman, A.P. (1992), 'Whom or what does the representative individual represent?', *Journal of Economic Perspectives*, **6**, 117–36.

Kirman, A.P. (1993), 'Ants, rationality and recruitment', *Quarterly Journal of Economics*, **108**, 137–56.

Krugman, P. (1996), *The Self-organizing Economy*, Cambridge: Blackwell.

Kuran, T. (1988), 'The tenacious past: theories of personal and collective conservatism', *Journal of Economic Behavior and Organization*, **10**, 143–71.

Lane, D. (1993a), 'Artificial worlds in economics : Part I', *Journal of Evolutionary Economics*, **3**, 89–107.

Lane, D. (1993b), 'Artificial worlds in economics : Part II', *Journal of Evolutionary Economics*, **3**, 177–97.

Lesourne, J. (1991), *Economie de l'ordre et du désordre,* Paris: Economica.

Levin, R.C., A. Klerovich, R.R. Nelson and S.G. Winter (1987), 'Appropriating the returns from industrial research and development', *Brookings Papers on Economic Activity*, **3**, 783–820.

Levinthal, D.A. and J.G. March (1981), 'A model of adaptive organizational search', *Journal of Economic Behavior and Organization*, **2**, 307–33.

Levitt, B. and J.G. March (1988), 'Organizational learning', *Annual Review of Sociology*, **14**, 319–40.

Lippi, M. and L. Reichlin, (1994), 'Diffusion of technical change and the decomposition of output into trend and cycle', *Review of Economic Studies*, **61**, 19–30.

Lucas, R.E. (1988), 'On the mechanics of economic development', *Journal of Monetary Economics*, **22**, 3–42.

Lundvall, B.A. (1993), *National Systems of Innovation,* London: Francis Pinter.

Malerba, F. and L. Orsenigo (1993), 'Technological regimes and firm behaviors', *Industrial and Corporate Change,* **2**, 54–71.

March, J.G. (1991), 'Exploration and exploitation in organizational learning', *Organization Science*, **2**, 71–87.

Metcalfe, J.S. (1988), 'Trade, technology and evolutionary change', Manchester: Manchester University, mimeo.

Metcalfe, J.S. (1996), 'Lectures on evolutionary theory', Manchester: Manchester University, mimeo.

Nelson, C.R. and C.I. Plosser (1982), 'Trends and random walks in macroeconomic time series', *Journal of Monetary Economics*, **10**, 139–62.

Nelson, R.R. (1981), 'Research on productivity growth and differences', *Journal of Economic Literature*, **19**, 1029–64.

Nelson, R.R. (1994), 'What has been the matter with Neoclassical Growth Theory?', in G. Silverberg and L. Soete (eds), *The Economics of Growth and Technical Change*, Cheltenham: Edward Elgar.

Nelson, R.R. (1995), 'Recent evolutionary theorizing about economic change', *Journal of Economic Literature*, **33**, 48–90.

Nelson, R.R. (1998), 'The agenda for growth theory: a different point of view', *Cambridge Journal of Economics*, **22**, 497–520.

Nelson, R.R. and S.G. Winter (1977), 'Simulation of Schumpeterian competition', *American Economic Review*, **67**, 271–6.

Nelson, R.R. and S.G. Winter (1982), *An Evolutionary Theory of Economic Change,* Cambridge: The Belknap Press of Harvard University Press.

Orléan, A. (1992), 'Contagion des opinions et fonctionnement des marchés financiers', *Revue Economiques*, **43**, 685–97.

Parente, S.L. (1994), 'Technology adoption, learning by doing and economic growth', *Journal of Economic Theory*, **63**, 346–69.

Rebelo, S.T. (1991), 'Long run policy analysis and long run growth', *Journal of Political Economy*, **99**, 500–521.

Romer, P.M. (1986), 'Increasing returns and long-run growth', *Journal of Political Economy*, **94**, 1002–37.

Romer, P.M. (1990), 'Endogenous technological change', *Journal of Political Economy*, **98**, 71–102.

Romer, P.M. (1994), 'The origins of endogenous growth', *Journal of Economic Perspectives*, **8**, 3–22.

Rosenberg, N. (1982), *Inside the Blackbox,* Cambridge: Cambridge University Press.

Rosenberg, N. (1994), *Exploring the Black Box : Technology, Economics and History,* Cambridge: Cambridge University Press.

Rudebusch, G.D. (1993), 'The uncertain unit root in real GNP', *American Economic Review*, **83**, 264–72.

Scharfstein, D.S. and J.C. Stein (1990), 'Herd behaviour and investment', *American Economic Review*, **80**, 465–79.

Schumpeter, J.A. (1934), *The Theory of Economic Development,* Cambridge, MA: Harvard University Press.

Shackle, G.L.S. (1955), *Uncertainty in Economics,* Cambridge: Cambridge University Press.

Silverberg, G. and D. Lehnert (1994), 'Growth fluctuations in an evolutionary model of creative destruction', in G. Silverberg and L. Soete (eds), *The Economics of Growth and Technical Change*, Cheltenham: Edward Elgar.

Silverberg, G. and B. Verspagen (1994), 'Collective learning, innovation and growth in a boundedly rational, evolutionary world', *Journal of Evolutionary Economics*, **4**, 207–26.

Silverberg, G. and B. Verspagen (1995), 'Evolutionary theorizing on economic growth', IIASA, Laxenburg, Austria, Working Paper, WP-95-78.

Silverberg, G., G. Dosi and L. Orsenigo (1988), 'Innovation, diversity and diffusion: a self-organization model', *Economic Journal*, **98**, 1032–54.

Solow, R.M. (1960), 'Investment and technical progress', in K.J. Arrow, S. Korbin and P. Suppes (eds), *Mathematical Methods in Social Sciences 1959*, Stanford: Stanford University Press.

Stiglitz, J.E. (1987), 'Learning to learn, localized learning and technological progress', in P. Dasgupta and P. Stoneman (eds), *Economic Policy and Technological Performance*, Cambridge: Cambridge University Press.

Stock, J.H. and M.W. Watson (1986), 'Does GNP have a unit root', *Economic Letters*, **22**, 147–51.

Stoneman, P. (ed.) (1995), *Handbook of the Economics of Innovation and Technological Change*, Oxford: Blackwell.

Winter, S.G. (1984), 'Schumpeterian competition in alternative technological regimes', *Journal of Economic Behavior and Organization*, **5**, 287–320.

Young, A. (1993), 'Substitution and complementarity in endogenous innovation', *Quarterly Journal of Economics*, **108**, 775–807.

Young, A. (1995), 'Growth without scale effects', NBER, Working Paper, 5211.

PART V

INSTITUTIONS AND
ECONOMIC DYNAMICS

[20]

The Manchester School Vol LVI No. 2   June 1988
0025–2034 $2.50   00–00

INSTITUTIONS AND MARKETS IN A DYNAMIC WORLD*

by

GIOVANNI DOSI†

DEAST, Venice and
SPRU, University of Sussex

I INTRODUCTION

This article concerns the role of institutions and policies and their relationship with market processes in open economies characterized by various forms of technological change.

The approach which is most familiar to the contemporary economic discipline essentially consists of a process of reduction of institutional and policy issues to exceptions, anomalies and particular cases of a general framework centred around the equilibrium conditions of the economic system postulated by the theory. The impact of policies and institutions is evaluated on the grounds of a yardstick — the equilibrium which the economy would achieve if left to itself — under very special and sometimes rather awkward hypotheses, whose properties, nonetheless, are such as to yield "optimal" outcomes. In this well worked-out and widely-accepted strategy, any normative issue, phenomenon or behaviour is compared with that fundamental yardstick and, *by difference*, one also defines the role and impact of policies. Thus, the economist commonly uses concepts like "externalities", "market failures", "limited information", "imperfect markets", etc., to categorize the most common "sub-optimal" features of the empirical world as compared with the theoretical model. In a very peculiar overlapping of positive and normative judgements, these "imperfections" of the real world also delimit the domain of institutional intervention, which — it is claimed — should make the world more similar to the theory. Generally, the economics profession likewise treats in a similar fashion the problems related to technological and economic change, assessing, for example, the degree of "market failure" associated with technological uncertainty, the "market imperfection" stemming from property rights on innovation, etc.

*Manuscript received 12.7.85; final version received 10.4.87.
†Useful comments on previous drafts by H. Ergas, L. Orsenigo and S. Winter, the participants at the Special Session on Industrial Policies of the 7th World Congress of Political Science (Paris, 14–20 July, 1985) and two anonymous referees are gratefully acknowledged.
This research has been undertaken at the Science Policy Research Unit (SPRU) of the University of Sussex as part of the research programme of the Designated Research Centre funded by the Economic and Social Research Council (ESRC). Since December 1987, the author has held a post at the University of Rome "La Sapienza".

The leap from the core theoretical model on which welfare conclusions are generally based to the properties of actual economic systems is a tremendous one: yet, the correspondence between the fundamental hypotheses of the model (on behaviours, technology, interactions between the agents, etc.) and the "stylized facts" of the world is often treated rather casually, and sometimes with the irritation that discussions on methodological issues provoke among the practitioners of the discipline.[1] Yet, in the history of the economic discipline this has not always been so.

Two to three centuries ago, when political economy was emerging as an autonomous discipline, more or less contemporary to the emergence of a "market society"[2] and of a capitalist mode of production, one of the intellectual concerns was the status, function and social implications of the free pursuit of private interests and their relationship with other forms of social coordination. Adam Smith's Invisible Hand related to a fundamental conjecture on the mechanisms of impersonal coordination occurring in decentralized markets. Yet, it was clear among classical writers that strictly non-economic variables and institutions established particular rules of interaction and "meta-codes" of behaviours which were necessary conditions for a satisfactory collective outcome of individual self-seeking attitudes, in terms of collective welfare and dynamic performance of the economy.[3] However, those background conditions which allow the consistency of individual behaviours and their dynamic progressiveness (in a sense, the factors accounting for the "moral" and political constitution of relatively efficient market societies) generally remained a concern of political thinkers, philosophers, sociologists and anthropologists (from the Scottish social thinkers to Hegel and Tocqueville and, later, Weber, Polanyi and Luhmann) but steadily disappeared from the explicit attention of economics.

---

[1] Notably, the "Founding Fathers" of modern General Equilibrium Analysis are generally well aware of the gap between the core theory and the interpretation of empirical economic phenomena. However, one finds much less caution amongst the "normal scientists"—in a Kuhian sense—of the discipline: compare, for example, Hahn (1984) with a random sample of articles in the main economic journals.

[2] *Cf.* Polanyi (1944) and (1971). See also Hirschman (1982).

[3] *Cf.*, for example, Adam Smith's *Theory of Moral Sentiments* (1976) and the discussion in Cropsey (1957). (For fascinating analyses of the "economic anthropology" of the modern economy, see Dumont, 1977, and Hirschman, 1977.) Other challenging (and very different) analyses of the functions and characteristics of the economic domain within the general social fabric are the classic work of de Tocqueville (1969) and, by contemporary authors, Luhmann (1975) and Hirsch (1976). These are only few examples of several ambitious attempts of modern social sciences to answer two fundamental questions which have puzzled Western thought at least since the eighteenth century, namely (a) under what conditions is the free pursuit of private interests consistent with the orderly reproduction of society and what kinds of social organization does it produce; and conversely (b) what are the forms of social organization and norms which allow an orderly expansion of the economy? However, contemporary economic discipline has been conspicuously absent from the debate. (For one of the few cases of dialogue between economics and other social disciplines on these challenges, see the review by Hahn of the cited work of Hirsch, in Hahn, 1984.)

In tune with some insights of early political economists and drawing from a few more recent contributions, we are going to suggest a framework of analysis of institutions which is in its essence *non-reductionist*. The heuristics of this second class of approaches we are thinking of are based on four fundamental hypotheses, namely (a) behaviours (and their outcomes) cannot adequately be represented by the simple and universal rationality of the *homo oeconomicus* postulated by the prevailing economic theory; (b) markets and economic processes occurring within them are themselves institutional set-ups specific to historical periods, cultures, countries, etc.; (c) there are particular combinations between *lato sensu* institutions and market processes which efficiently "match" in terms of some (but most likely not all) performance yardsticks; (d) non-market variables (including, of course, policies in the strict sense) are a permanent feature of the *constitution* of the economic system and an essential part of the ways the economic machine is "tuned" and evolves.[4]

Innovation, change, transformation represent almost a crucial experiment for the relative adequacy of the "reductionist" and "non-reductionist" approaches. For example, is the prevailing frame of economic thought capable of accounting for the process of technological innovation? Can we elaborate non-trivial propositions, on both positive and normative levels, regarding the role and effect of policies in relation to economic change? What accounts for the fact that different countries show systematically different capabilities of innovating and economically exploiting the innovations?

By way of an introduction, consider two rather well-known examples against which the achievements and limitations of the "reductionist" and "non-reductionist" approaches can be assessed.

To illustrate, consider one of the most famous explanations of the differences in the growth record of developed economies, namely the so-called "growth accounting exercises".[5] For this purpose, one uses all the variables strictly consistent with the "proper" economic model (the primary endowments of each economy and their change through time), some variables which in the theoretical model would be considered "imperfections" (economies of scale, etc.) and some spurious variables which can be squeezed into economies with some considerable unease (the "endowment of education", etc.). Here, one can see the reductionist programme at its best: paraphrasing Kindleberger, one tries to account for the degree to which the higher efficiency of the "endowment" École Politechnique in France compensates for the lower throughput of French coal mines, or the ways the Italian

---

[4]These issues are discussed at greater length, with different perspectives, in Nelson and Winter (1982); Boyer and Mistral (1983); and Dosi and Orsenigo (1985).
[5]*Cf.* Denison (1967). For a discussion of the same example within an analysis of economic methodology, *cf.* Salvati (1985).

entrepreneurship compensates for the lower endowments of "capital" or "civil service competence"....[6] Yet, one is left with a large unexplained residual, sometimes called "technical change". In actual fact, the questions one begins with remain mostly unanswered: why the disappointing British economic performance or the impressive Japanese growth? Why did Italy not become another Japan? Is the U.S. technological and economic performance getting weaker? And so on.

The second example, even more fundamental and nearer to the concerns of this paper, concerns technical change. It is well recognized in the economic literature that the very existence of innovation *requires* a "market failure" in the static allocative sense: in decentralized markets, the incentive to innovate needs some kind of asymmetric information and super-normal profits.

Certainly, in the history of economic thought, there are "heretic" attempts to investigate the phenomena of innovation and change as central features of modern economic systems—notably Schumpeter (1961) and (1975)—and in contemporary economics—Nelson and Winter (1982).

However, in a curious paradox, most policy analyses remain based on a theoretical yardstick—the efficiency properties of decentralized processes of allocation under very special and generally stationary conditions—which seems strikingly inappropriate for dealing with innately dynamic phenomena such as technical change over time and across countries.[7]

In what follows here, we will suggest some propositions on the relationship between technical change and market processes (Section II) and explore the role of policies and institutions in both closed and open economies under all those circumstances when change and transformation are permanent and fundamental features of the system (Section III).

II Seven Propositions on Technical Change, Markets and Institutions

Proposition 1

Building on the works on technical change, among others, of Freeman (1974); Nelson and Winter (1977); Nelson (1982); and Rosenberg (1976), we have tried to show elsewhere that the process of technological change is an activity characterized by partly tacit knowledge and highly selective heuristics. Technical progress generally proceeds along rather precise "trajectories", linked by major discontinuities associated with the emergence of new "technological paradigms".[8] Whenever new paradigms emerge, the material

---

[6]*Cf.* Salvati (1985).

[7]See, for example, standard industrial economics textbooks. A similar observation is discussed in Silva (1984).

[8]*Cf.* Dosi (1984) and Dosi and Orsenigo (1985) for a more analytical discussion of this and the following points.

technology, the relevant tasks which are meant to be fulfilled, the heuristics ("where to go" and "where not to go"), the required knowledge skills and equipment, the relevant dimensions of "progress", all contextually change. *Technology, far from being a free good, involves a fundamental learning aspect, characterized*—following Nelson and Winter (1982)—*by varying degrees of cumulativeness, opportunity, appropriability.* This is our first proposition. Both appropriability and cumulativeness of technical change are affected by the degrees of *tacitness* and the degrees of *formal understanding* of each technology (see Nelson and Winter, 1982). The more a technology is tacit (i.e., it involves idiosyncratic capabilities—e.g., the experience-based skills of designing particular machines for particular conditions of use, etc.), the higher the difficulty in transmitting it in the form of blueprints or even to imitate it without a painstaking process of informal learning. (For a discussion of the underlying theory of production, see Winter, 1982.) An implication is that, at any point in time, different companies and countries are likely to be characterized by different technical coefficients and product technologies. These differences do not essentially relate to different factor combinations along a single production function, but to proper technological gaps/leads in relation to a given trajectory of technological progress. In another work,[9] we discuss some empirical evidence on the subject: even within the group of OECD countries, the general case is (i) relatively wide international gaps in labour productivity and innovative capabilities, and (ii) the absence of any significant relationship between these gaps and international differences in the capital/output ratios. This is to say that differences in input coefficients generally represent different techniques which can often be unequivocally ranked irrespective of relative prices. The process of development is strictly associated with the inter- and intra-national diffusion of "superior" techniques (see Nelson, 1968). Thus, at each point in time, there are, in general, one or very few "best practice" techniques of production which correspond to the "technological frontier". Relatedly, the description of the production structure in the short term, by means of fixed coefficients, is a reasonable approximation to the *irreversibility properties* of evolutionary economic processes that occur in real time.

Proposition 2

A fundamental implication of such a view of technology and technical change is that there are *widespread asymmetries in the technological capabilities, input efficiencies and product performances between firms and between countries*; these asymmetries correspond to *equally uneven patterns of economic signals facing the economic agents.* This is our second proposition. The asymmetries in capabilities are a direct consequence of the cumulative idiosyncratic and

---

[9]See Dosi, Pavitt and Soete (1988).

partly appropriable nature of technological advances. The more cumulative are technological advances at firm-level, the higher the likelihood of "success breeding success" (*cf.* Nelson and Winter, 1982, for a formalization). Moreover, the higher the opportunity for technological progress, *ceteris paribus*, the higher the possibility of relatively bigger "technological gaps" between successful innovators and laggard firms. In general, the evolution over time of these asymmetries will depend on the relative rates of innovation and of diffusion and, thus, on the degrees of innovative opportunity, cumulativeness and appropriability which characterizes any one particular technology. Notably, the standard textbook case of industries composed of technologically identical firms is the limiting case in which innovation stops and thus evolutionary dynamics ceases to be relevant.

These features of technical change also determine the nature of the economic signals that firms face, so that, for example, a high technological opportunity, associated with a high degree of appropriability of technological innovation may well perform as a powerful incentive to innovate (related to high expected profitabilities and market shares) for a company which is on or near the technological frontier, being at the same time a powerful *negative* signal (an entry barrier) for a company with relatively lower technological capability.

Proposition 3

In a world characterized by technical change and transformation, the behaviours of the agents are most adequately represented by routines, strategies, meta-rules, search processes (see the seminal work of Nelson and Winter, 1982). That is to say that in an environment which is complex, changing and uncertain, firms do not and cannot adopt maximizing behaviours (and, in many circumstances, might not find it dynamically efficient to try to do so, even if they could).[10] This is our third proposition.

Moreover, behaviours cannot be entirely deduced from the sole knowledge of a generic self-seeking goal of the agent and of the economic structure (taken to include the asymmetries in technological capabilities, the nature of the technology, the patterns of economic signals, etc.).

A specific but very important case concerns the nature of the adjustment processes each firm undertakes in a changing environment. As an illustration, take a firm producing any one particular product. The "signals" that the firm receives, in an extreme synthesis, are of three kinds, namely (i) the technological opportunities (and expected economic benefits) associated with technical change in that and other products; (ii) the rate of growth of demand in that and other products; (iii) the changes in costs, prices, quantities, profitabilities in its markets (and also other markets). These signals loosely

---

[10]*Cf.* Nelson and Winter (1982); Heiner (1983); Dosi (1984); Dosi and Orsenigo (1985).

correspond to three notional adjustment strategies. The first one relates to innovation/imitation/technological upgrading. Let us call it "Schumpeterian adjustment". The second one relates to the search of the most promising growth opportunities. Call it "growth adjustment". The third one refers to price/quantity changes on the basis of an *unchanged* technology. Let us—improperly—call it "Ricardian" or "classical" adjustment.

Clearly, most firms will choose varying combinations of all three adjustment processes. However, the fundamental point is that we have here "open-exit" alternatives (that is, alternatives subject to discretionary decisions) whose outcome cannot be deduced from either the knowledge of the state-of-the-world and/or of an unchanging rationality principle.

Notably, a maximization approach would not lead us very far in explaining the choices. Even *if* we knew that the considered firm will choose the option which maximizes the integral of the expected discounted profits, for a *given* time horizon, the analytical content of such a statement would be practically nil: the indeterminacy about the ways technological and market expectations are formed, and about the time horizon and the intertemporal preferences, is another way of describing our theoretical ignorance. A more fruitful approach, in our view, considers the behavioural regularities (the "routines" and "meta-routines", *à la* Nelson–Winter) in relation to (i) the nature of the signals and (ii) the technological assets firms possess (in terms of technological capabilities, knowledge, expertise, etc.) which—among other things—determine different capabilities of "seeing" and reacting to any given set of signals. Clearly, the structure of the industry and the nature of the technology constrains the set of feasible behavioural rules: for example, investment and R&D commitments will be constrained by the ability to finance them; the adjustments in prices/quantities/market shares will be constrained by minimum profitability requirements, etc. However, the crucial point is that, within these structural and technological constraints, there are varying spaces for *discretionary choices*, related to the propensities to accumulate, to take risks, to trade-off present profits for market shares, to commit more or less resources to innovative search, to search in some directions and not in others, etc.[11]

This applies to both intertemporal comparisons within the same country or, even more so, to inter-country comparisons. In a purely anecdotal way, the reader is invited to think of the specific *weltanschauung* which informed

---

[11]On these points, see Metcalfe (1985, p. 4), who discusses the "differences in the capacity and willingness of the firm to expand market share and accumulate productive capacity with respect to current products and processes". The analysis of these strategic choices is—as known—also the domain of game-theoretical approaches to oligopolistic interactions. Our view is that they certainly highlight some important features of strategic interdependencies; however, they are subject to the same objections to the "maximization" representation of behaviours, mentioned above: simply they move the problem one step backward (how are the "rules of the games" established? How are expectations formed?, etc.). For some comments, see Dosi, Orsenigo and Silverberg (1986).

the strategies of the entrepreneurship in some of the most successful late-coming industrializers, such as Germany in the last century (Veblen, 1915) and Japan in this one (Johnson, 1982). Even if the nature of the economic context might go a long way towards the explanation of such performances, it does not exhaust it. More institutional explanations (in the broad sociological sense, including established behaviours and fundamental cultural traits) are required in order to account for the relative emphasis in the most successful countries upon processes of "growth adjustment" and "Schumpeterian adjustments" as compared to simple short-term allocative efficiency. If this is so, one must relate to this socio-institutional level of analysis any proper investigation of statements—which are part of the conventional wisdom of practical economists—such as "... the trouble with British industry is that it is led by accountants, while German firms are led by engineers...", etc. Or, one certainly realizes by reading a work like Dore's *British Factory, Japanese Factory*[12] that the difference in economic performances stemming from different institutional contexts is much greater than, and irreducible to, the set of economic signals markets deliver. Another related example—almost entirely neglected among economists, with the outstanding exception of Hirschman (1970)—is the economic importance of loyalty:[13] to trivialize, it is intuitive that such commonplace notions as Japanese mechanisms of loyalty to the company and to the state, the Italian sole loyalty to their families and lack of collective loyalties, or, at a more general level, the general perception of the "moral boundaries" in behaviours toward competitors, customers, suppliers, government officials, etc., must have a profound influence on the adjustment processes the economic agents undertake.

Evidence of this "institutional constitution of markets" emerges indirectly also from the highly simplified context of so-called "experimental markets": even under quasi-laboratory conditions, "the institutional organisation of a market has been an important treatment variable. The mechanics of how buyers and sellers get together can substantially influence market performance. That is, *for the same underlying incentives*, the market performance is affected by a change of institutions".[14] There is no reason to believe that this does not *a fortiori* apply to the much more complex real markets. In general, these phenomena hint at suggestions present among the early analyses of "market societies", from Locke, Ferguson and Smith to Hegel, about the "moral" and "ethical" preconditions of modern economies. An interpretation of the different ethical constitutions or, at least, a taxonomy is still to come. Yet, we see here a first fundamental role of non-market institutions (including strictly political ones) in that they are instrumental in *shaping and selecting* the fundamental rules of behaviour and interactions of

---

[12]*Cf.* Dore (1973). We owe this observation to M. Salvati.
[13]On the issue, see also Pizzorno (1985).
[14]Plott (1982, p. 1489), our emphasis.

the economic agents: policies, implicit social rules, dominant forms of organizing the links within and between the various groups of economic agents (e.g., between firms and banks, between management and workers, etc.), levels and forms of industrial conflict, have a paramount importance in determining the relative mix and the direction of microeconomic adjustment processes, for any *given* set of economic signals and structural conditions.[15]

The importance of this point also from a normative perspective should be clear: it might not be enough to influence the patterns of signals if microeconomic strategies are biased in directions conflicting with the policy objectives (e.g., if the fundamental strategic rules of private agents are heavily biased against "Schumpeterian adjustments", public incentives might not be very effective in promoting a sufficient rate of innovation: see also below).

Proposition 4

Another (and related) aspect of the role of non-market variables in economic performance and technological dynamism refers to the *patterns and organization* of *externalities and the unintentional outcomes of market processes*. In economic theory, externalities are generally considered a fastidious source of non-convexity while strongly counter-intentional outcomes disturb the rationality assumptions of the theory. However, *untraded interdependencies* between sectors, technologies, firms have a primary importance in the process of technological change (see, among others, Freeman, 1974; Rosenberg, 1976 and 1982; Dosi, Pavitt and Soete, 1988). For example, knowledge and expertise about continuous chemical processes may allow technological innovations in food processing even when the latter do not involve any chemical inputs; "arms-length" relationships between producers and users of industrial equipment are often a fundamental element in the innovative process even if sometimes no economic transaction is involved; the production of bicycles originally drew technological knowledge from the production of shotguns, even though neither product is an output or an input in the other activity. Technological complementarities, untraded technological interdependencies and information flows which do

---

[15]Notably, somewhat similar conclusions can be reached through the exploration of the properties of markets still characterized by maximizing agents, who, however, have only limited information about the outcomes of different courses of action: then, it can be shown, the institutional architecture of the system shapes choices, outcomes and economic performances (see Sah and Stiglitz, 1985). Moreover, even in the unlikely world of rational expectations, one can show the necessity both of "social norms (in particular business practices) imposing some restrictions and coherence on the individual decisions and [of] information generated by institutions external to the market" (Frydman, 1982, p. 662).

A fortiori, institutions which shape behaviours, patterns of interactions and expectation formation are *required* in the more complex environments—characterized by technical change, multi-level decision processes, etc.—discussed here. (On the relationship between expectation formation, behaviours and institutional specializations of the economic agents, see also Kaldor, 1972.)

not entirely correspond to the flows of commodities, all represent a structured set of technological externalities which is in a *collective asset* of groups of firms/industries within countries/regions and/or tends to be internalized within individual companies (see, for example, Teece, 1982). In other words, technological bottlenecks and opportunities, experiences and skills embodied in people and organizations, capabilities and "memories" overflowing from one economic activity to another, etc., tend to organize *context conditions* which (i) are country-specific, region-specific or even company-specific; (ii) are a fundamental ingredient in the innovative process; and, (iii) as such, determine different opportunities/stimuli/constraints to the innovation process for any given set of strictly economic signals. This is our fourth proposition.

These untraded interdependencies and context conditions are, to different degrees, the *unintentional outcome* of decentralized (but irreversible) processes of environmental organization (one obvious example is the "Silicon Valley") and/or the result of explicit strategies of public and private institutions (in this sense one can interpret, for example, the strategies of vertical and horizontal integration of electrical oligopolies into microelectronics technologies or the efforts of various governments to create "science parks", etc.).

Proposition 5

We mentioned above our hypothesis that technical change is organized by "technological paradigms". It is useful to distinguish between that "normal" technical progress which proceeds along the trajectories defined by an established paradigm and those "extraordinary" technological advances which relate to the emergence of radically new paradigms. As regards the latter, we try to show elsewhere (Dosi, 1984, and Dosi and Orsenigo, 1985) that market processes are generally rather weak in directing the emergence and selection of these radical technological discontinuities. When the process of innovation is highly exploratory, its direct responsiveness to economic signals is looser and—especially in this century—the linkages with strictly scientific knowledge are greater.

Then, institutional factors play a direct role, providing the necessary conditions for new scientific developments and performing as *ex ante* selectors of the explored technological paradigms from within a much wider set of potential ones. One can cite, for example, the cases of semiconductors and computer technologies and the influence of both military/space agencies and big electrical corporations in the early days of the development of these new technological paradigms.[16] Somewhat similar cases can be found in the early developments of synthetic chemistry (especially in Germany). In a

---

[16]On these points, *cf.* Dosi (1984).

less apparent way, strictly non-economic stimuli and "selectors" act in the present development of new technologies, such as bioengineering or new materials.

In general, the features of the process of search and selection of new technological paradigms is such that the *institutional and scientific contexts and public policies are fundamental insofar as they affect* (a) *the bridging mechanisms between pure science and technological developments;* (b) *the criteria and capabilities of search by the economic agents;* and (c) *the constraints, incentives and uncertainty facing would-be innovators.* This is our fifth proposition.

Its counterpart on an international level is that when new technologies emerge, the relative success of the various countries depends on the successful matching between (a) one country's scientific context and technological capabilities (*cf.* Propositions 2 and 4 above); (b) the nature of its "bridging institutions"; (c) its strictly economic conditions (relative prices, nature and size of the markets, availability/scarcity of raw materials, etc.); (d) the nature of the dominant rules of behaviour, strategies, forms of organization of the economic actors (*cf.* Proposition 3 above).

Clearly, all these sets of variables are, to different degrees, affected by public policies, either directly (e.g., procurement policies or R&D subsidies which obviously influence the economic signals facing individual firms), or indirectly (e.g., through the influence of the education system upon scientific and technological capabilities, etc.).

In particular, as regards the "normal" functioning of markets and industries and the "normal" technological activities (as opposed to the extraordinary ones related to the emergence of new technological paradigms), it must be noticed that each sector embodies a different balance between institutions and markets. This appears to be true in two senses.

First, there is a technology- and country-specificity of the balance between what is coordinated and organized through the visible hand of corporate structures and what is left to the invisible hand of the markets (for discussions on the issue, *cf.* Marris and Mueller, 1980; Williamson, 1979 and 1981; Chandler, 1966 and 1977; and Teece, 1982).

Second, there is an analogous differentiation in the balance between public institutions and private organization in the process of innovation (*cf.* Nelson, 1984). For example, some sectors rely on an endogenous process of technological advances (e.g., several manufacturing sectors) while others depend heavily on public sources of innovation (e.g., agriculture).[17]

If anything, one could suggest the following empirical generalization: other things being equal, the higher the role of the *visible* hand of oligopolistic organizations, the lower the requirement for strictly public institutions in the

---

[17]For sectoral analyses of the sources and uses of innovations, see Scherer (1982) and Pavitt (1984).

processes of economic coordination and technological advance and, *vice versa*, the nearer one activity is to the economist's model of "pure competition", the higher also appears to be its need for strictly institutional organization of its "externalities" and technological advances. Agriculture is a case in point: historically a significant part of its technological advances, in the U.S.A., Europe and, also, in the Third World, has been provided by government-sponsored research (*cf.* Nelson, 1984) and even its price–quantity adjustments have been increasingly regulated, both in the U.S.A. and in Europe, by institutional intervention. Conversely, oligopoly-dominated manufacturing produces a good part of its "normal" technological advances endogenously and, apart from major crises, seems to coordinate rather well its price/quantity adjustments.

Proposition 6

We have so far focused on the relationship between *lato sensu* institutional factors, economic processes and technological change without much attention to the consequences induced by the very fact that all economies are, more or less, open economies: they trade with each other and, by doing so, undergo changes in the economic signals each of them faces. One of the few conclusions on which the economic profession agrees is that, under conditions of non-increasing returns, absence of externalities and for given rates of macroeconomic activity, the patterns of allocation stemming from international trade are generally efficient. In other words, there are generally gains from trade for all partners based on "comparative advantages". Let us call this *allocative* (or "Ricardian") *efficiency*, to mean the likely outcome of short-term adjustment processes (essentially linked to relative prices and relative profitabilities) on the grounds of *given* technologies and *given* levels of macroeconomic activity. However, the fundamental question concerns the effect that such a pattern of allocation has upon technological dynamism and upon long-term macroeconomic rates of activity. Let us call the performance criterion related to the former, *Schumpeterian efficiency*, and that related to the latter, *growth efficiency*. Now, the crucial point is that there is nothing in the mechanisms leading to Ricardian efficiency which guarantees also the fulfilment of the other two criteria of efficiency.

The reasons for possible trade-offs amongst these different efficiency criteria is a consequence of the features of technological change mentioned above (for a more detailed discussion, see Dosi, Pavitt and Soete, 1988), namely (a) the cumulative, (partly) appropriable and local nature of technological advances (Atkinson and Stiglitz, 1969; David, 1975; and Arthur, 1985); (b) the widespread existence of static and dynamic economies of scale; (c) the influence that technological gaps between firms and between countries have upon the economic signals faced by the economic agents; (d) the importance of country-specific and area-specific untraded interdependencies.

As discussed by Kaldor (1980), if different commodities or sectors possess significant differences in their "dynamic potential" (in terms of economies of scale, technical progress, possibilities of Smithian division of labour, learning-by-doing, etc.), then specializations which are efficient in terms of the comparison of a given set of input coefficients may not be so in terms of a longer-term assessment of the notional patterns of technological dynamism related to these specializations. This is more than a special case related to infant industries: it is the general condition of an economic system whereby *technological opportunities vary across products and across sectors.* More precisely, within each technology and each sector the technological capabilities and learning processes of each firm and each country are generally associated with the actual process of production in that same activity. Thus, the mechanisms regarding international specialization have a dynamic effect in that they also *select* the areas where technical skills will be accumulated, (possibly) innovation undertaken, economies of scale reaped, etc. However, the potential for these effects is widely different between technologies and sectors. This is another aspect of the irreversibility features of economic processes: present allocative choices influence the direction and rate of the future evolution of technological coefficients. Whenever we abandon the idea of technology as a set of blueprints and we conceive technical progress as a *joint production* with manufacturing itself, then it is possible to imagine an economic system which is dynamically better off (in terms of productivity, innovativeness, etc.) if it always operates in disequilibrium *vis-à-vis* "Ricardian" conditions of allocative efficiency. On the grounds of the foregoing propositions on the nature of technology, it is possible to establish when a trade-off between "allocative efficiency" and "Schumpeterian efficiency" can emerge. "Ricardian" patterns of specialization (with their properties of allocative efficiency) are determined, for each country, by the relative size of the sector-specific technology gaps (or leads).[18] Whenever the gap is higher in the most dynamic technologies (i.e., those characterized by the highest technological opportunities), then allocative efficiency directly conflicts with dynamic efficiency. This is our sixth proposition.

Since this point has important analytical and normative implications, related to the long-term consequences of the patterns of allocation stemming from decentralized market processes, let us consider it in some detail.

By way of an introduction, the reader is invited to think of the case of increasing returns and indivisibilities; as known in the economic literature,[19] multiple equilibria are likely to emerge, without the possibility—for the analyst and *a fortiori* for the economic agents—to establish which one will be selected. As thoroughly discussed in Arthur (1985), increasing returns

[18]*Cf.* Dosi, Pavitt and Soete (1988).
[19]See, for example, Arrow and Hahn (1971); Katz and Shapiro (1983); Arthur (1985).

generally show the properties of (i) non-predictability of equilibria; (ii) non-ergodicity (the past is not "forgotten" by the future and strong hysteresis effects emerge); and (iii) potential inefficiency (a particular equilibrium, or, dynamically, a particular path might be "inferior" in terms of any welfare measure but still the system may be "locked" in it).

Somewhat similarly, trade analyses show that, with non-convexities, decentralized processes of allocation may not lead to mutual gains from trade (see, for example, Krugman 1984; Markusen and Melvin, 1984; and Helpman and Krugman, 1985).

Now, generalize these results by considering the fact that (a) technical change always represents a form of increasing returns over time, and (b) most often, technological advances are associated with the actual process of production (see above) and, thus, cannot be treated parametrically (e.g., as exogenous shocks which switch the value of equilibria of time t to those of time $(t + 1)$). One is bound to account for an interaction between decisions of production at time t and technical coefficients at time $(t + 1)$, conceptually similar to the interaction between technical coefficients and levels of production of static analyses of increasing returns. The fundamental point is that, with increasing returns, the market cannot signal to the agents the unintentional outcome of their collective behaviour (think—as the clearest example—of economies of scale external to the firm and internal to the industry). Even more so, markets *cannot* signal the (at least partly) *uncertain*, *unintentional* and *future* technological advances made possible/fostered/hindered by the present decentralized allocative decisions of a relatively high number of independent profit-motivated agents.[20] *A fortiori* Arthur's conclusions on non-predictability, inflexibility, non-ergodicity and potential inefficiency apply to this case, too.

As an illustration,[21] consider the case of two countries which—before trade—produce, under conditions of non-decreasing returns, two commodities, characterized by different future opportunities of learning and technical progress. As argued earlier, suppose that learning occurs only (or primarily) together with the actual process of production. Now, allow trade to take place. The resulting patterns of specialization, as trade theory predicts, will generally entail a better allocation of resources and, thus, "gains from trade". However, one of the two countries may well be "locked" into an activity where the scope of technical progress is relatively limited. Under such circumstances, in order to have gains from trade in the long term the relative gain stemming from a better allocation of resources must exceed the

---

[20]This independence concerns, of course, decision-making. However, the point is that each agent contributes to creating an "externality" for the whole of them.

[21]At the time of the second revision of this work, a paper by P. Dasgupta and J. Stiglitz on "Exercises in Learning-by-Doing", which shows some similarity with the example that follows, was presented at the Conference on Innovation Diffusion, Venice, 17–21 March, 1986.

productivity increases which would have been obtained by producing also (or more of) a commodity characterized by a higher technological opportunity. Conversely, for the other country the gains from a better "Ricardian" allocation of resources will sum up with the gains from relatively higher technical progress in the commodity in which it is specialized. Thus, the other country will always enjoy gains-from-trade, both in the short and the long term.

If one considers a sufficiently long time span, thus allowing for a significant technical progress to take place, it is plausible that the once-for-all gains in resource allocation coming from the decentralized search of minimum-cost opportunities of production may well fall short of the cumulative gains in productivity which would have been obtained over time with "sub-optimal" allocations (in a static sense) biased in favour of activities characterized by higher technological opportunities (for a similar point, see Pasinetti, 1981).

As an historical illustration, it is not necessary to think of developing countries: it is even possible that the technological leadership in "old" technological paradigms (and, thus, a strong "comparative advantage" in the related commodities) may be a hindrance to a quick allocation of resources to new ones. One could think, as examples, of the relative British delay in electro-mechanical technologies, as compared with Germany and the U.S.A., at the turn of the century, or the European delay in electronics technologies, as compared to Japan, in the post-war period.

As a related empirical generalization, we suggest that the *likelihood of such trade-offs between allocative and Schumpeterian efficiencies is proportional to the distance of each country from the technological frontier* in the newest and most promising technologies, where a high rate of innovation, idiosyncratic processes of learning and appropriation tend to prevent any easy endogenous process of international technological diffusion.[22]

Proposition 7

A somewhat similar argument applies to the possibility of trade-offs between allocative and growth efficiencies. Generally, the analysis of the outcome of the notional transition from autarky to trade is undertaken by focusing upon the adjustments in relative prices and relative quantities on the assumption of unchanged rates of macroeconomic activity.

This condition of *constancy* of the aggregate level of macroeconomic activity before and after trade, is already stated from the start by Ricardo[23]

---

[22]For an analysis also of the forces that, on the contrary, tend to induce technological diffusion and convergence between countries, *cf.* Dosi, Pavitt and Soete (1988). See also Perez (1983) and Metcalfe and Soete (1984).

[23]*Cf.* Ricardo (1951, p. 129).

and it is maintained by modern classical reappraisals *à la* Sraffa–Steedman, whereby the analysis is undertaken in terms of steady-growth paths. This applies—even more so—to neoclassical trade theories, whereby the hypothesis of full-employment of all factors of production is possibly the *core* assumption of the model.

The easiest way to see this condition at work is to imagine that each trading nation operates at full employment rates of activity. In this case, whenever all the other assumptions hold, we can see the full operation of the theorem of comparative advantage: each trading partner "gains from trade" since it can get from abroad more commodities of a certain kind than it would otherwise be able to manufacture domestically without foregoing any amount of consumption of the commodities in which that country is specialized.

Modern economic systems, however, do not often present full employment rates of activity. In these cases the *macroeconomic* efficiency of specialization based on comparative advantages depends on the income intensity (and, dynamically, on income elasticities) of the various commodities in world income. As a first approximation, let us suppose that:

(a) price elasticities, in the generality of the traded commodities for the corresponding world industry as a whole, are relatively low;[24]

(b) commodities present a relatively wide range of income elasticities which are *commodity-specific* and *country-specific*.

Let us also add that, in general, price-related substitution in consumption is limited and the patterns of demand are essentially related to income levels, long-run trends in income distribution and institutional and social factors (more on this point is in Pasinetti, 1981).

Now, under conditions of non-decreasing returns, there is no straightforward way in which markets can relate the varying future growth-efficiencies of the various commodities to relative-profitability signals for the microeconomic agents. In other words, microeconomic units may well find it relatively profitable to produce commodities which a decreasing number of people on the world market wants to buy. The reader may think, as extreme examples, of the dynamic outcomes of patterns of comparative advantages in "inferior" commodities (say, jute, mechanical typewriters or black and white TVs) as compared to income-dynamic ones (say, synthetic fibres, word processors, or colour TVs).

A limited price-induced substitution between commodities and a relatively stable evolution in the baskets of consumption may well imply painful trade-offs between microeconomic mechanisms leading to Ricardian efficiency and those patterns of production which could yield comparatively

---

[24]This statement must not be confused with price elasticities for individual countries which might well be higher. In other words, relatively small price changes may induce significant changes in the international competitiveness of individual countries even when the overall world demand for the corresponding commodity shows a very low price elasticity. There is, however, an essential "beggar-my-neighbour" element in this process.

higher rates of macroeconomic activity compatible with the foreign balance constraint (via higher foreign-trade multipliers).[25]

This is our seventh proposition.

Possible trade-offs between allocative, Schumpeterian and growth efficiencies have nothing to do with exceptional cases of "infant industry" conditions, but are structurally at the core of the signalling and allocative mechanisms of our economic system.[26]

Remarkably, markets may well work efficiently, deliver all the information they can and even discount contingencies for future states of the world to which probabilities can notionally be attached (although, empirically, these markets rarely exist). What markets *cannot* do is to deliver information about or discount the possibility of future states of the world whose occurrence is itself an "externality" resulting unintentionally from the interaction of present decisions of behaviourally unrelated agents. As we saw, this is precisely one of the characteristics of these particular "increasing returns" over time which are associated with technological learning. In this respect, conflicts between short-term allocative efficiency and Schumpeterian efficiency, as defined earlier, could emerge even if markets were complete (in a neoclassical sense: if all contingencies about future *states of nature* could be discounted).[27]

Somewhat similarly, the possibility of conflict between allocative efficiency and growth efficiency is not associated with any "market imperfection". On the contrary, it is due to the fact that, lacking both generalized substitution in consumption with respect to prices and homotheticity of the patterns of demand in income—as we believe to be the

---

[25]Again, for a more thorough discussion along these lines, we must refer to Dosi, Pavitt and Soete (1988). There, and in Cimoli, Dosi and Soete (1986), we formalize a two-country model with "Ricardian" processes of inter-commodity specialization and "Keynesian adjustments" in the rates of macroeconomic activity under a foreign balance constraint, showing also that, *ceteris paribus*, the rates of growth of any one economy consistent with the foreign accounts will be higher, the higher the income intensity (i.e., dynamically, the income elasticity) of the commodities in which that country is specialized. Under certain conditions, this property is approximated by the Kaldor–Thirlwall foreign trade multiplier, whereby the rate of growth of each economy is determined by the world income elasticity of its exports compared to the domestic income elasticity of its imports (see Thirlwall, 1980).

[26]A way of restating Propositions 6 and 7 which is possibly more familiar to the economist is by saying that the *general case*, in our view, is the non-convexity of production- and consumption-possibility sets (more rigorously, their *non-existence*, except perhaps in the very small). In general, the conclusions we draw from Propositions 6 and 7 are consistent with and broadly similar to the analyses of international competitiveness of Cohen *et al.* (1984) and of Mistral (1982).

[27]It is conceivable, if implausible, to discount states of nature such as "tomorrow it will rain". This is clearly very different from the possibility of trading guesses about states of the world which, in turn, depend on one's own expectations on what all the others are doing, let alone all the problems related to the indivisibilities and public-good features of technological knowledge (Keynes's "beauty contest" parable somewhat resembles this set of "market failures" related to interdependencies between expectations, behaviours and states-of-the-world; see also Schelling, 1978).

general case—there is no general way in which markets can transform "information" about long-term trends in income elasticities of the various commodities into economic incentives for competitive producers who tend to treat the states of the world parametrically.

Incidentally, one might notice that both these sources of conflict between static (allocative) efficiency and the two criteria of dynamic efficiency hint at the possible advantages of oligopoly as compared to free competition. In world oligopolistic markets the "dynamic externalities" associated with technical learning-through-production can be (partly) appropriated by individual firms. Thus, current allocative decisions may take account, to different degrees, of their effects upon future technological advances. Similarly, for oligopolistic agents the slope of and the movements over time in demand schedules matter and so present patterns of allocation may account for different expected income elasticities of demand. To give an example, a few European electrical companies (such as Philips and Siemens) decided in the early 'seventies to increase their involvement in microelectronics, despite heavy losses (i.e., despite "allocative inefficiency" and "comparative disadvantage"). Amongst the motivations, there were the expected very high rates of growth of the market and the technological capabilities which could have been acquired and would perform as an "internalized externality" for technologically-related productions. One could not expect the same behaviour from competitive producers.

The trade-offs that we have discussed between allocative efficiency, growth efficiency and technological dynamism may clearly be one of the determinants of the emergence of vicious and virtuous circles in national patterns of growth. Notably, this conclusion is similar to those which are well established in development theory. However, its determinants do not bear any direct relationship with phenomena specific to developing countries (such as several kinds of supposed "market failures"). For our purposes here, developed and developing countries could be placed on some kind of continuum, according to their distance from the technological frontiers and to the differences between their patterns of production and the long-term patterns of world demand.

Whenever any one country happens to present its highest technological lead (or the lowest technological gap) in new technological paradigms, then its pattern of intersectoral profitability signals points in the directions of activities which generally also present the highest demand growth and the highest potential of future product- and process-innovations. Conversely, countries well behind the technological frontiers may be "dynamically penalized" by their present patterns of intersectoral allocative efficiency. This property, in our view, contributes to explain the relative stability of the "pecking order" between countries in terms of technological innovativeness and international competitiveness and also the relatively ordered ways in which this "pecking order" changes in the long term. The interaction between present economic signals, patterns of specializations and dynamics of the sectoral technology gaps provides the basis for cumulative processes. Significantly, major changes in the international competitiveness of each economy are often associated with the emergence of new technological paradigms. This occurrence reshapes the patterns of technological advantages/disadvantages between countries, often demands different organizational and institutional set-ups and sometimes presents a unique opportunity for the emergence of new technological and economic leaders.

More generally, we may restate the foregoing argument in the following way. Markets characterized by decentralized decision-making fulfil two fundamental functions. First, they provide a mechanism of coordination between individual economic decisions and, in doing so, they reallocate resources in ways, which—under the conditions specified by the theory— have efficiency properties of varying degrees. Second, whenever we allow technological progress to take place (with its features of search, uncertainty, etc.), markets provide an incentive to innovate through the possibility of private appropriation of some economic benefit stemming from technical progress itself. Relatedly, they provide a selection environment for the innovations. It is remarkable that as soon as these second functions of markets are considered in the theoretical picture, their efficiency properties become more blurred and complicated to assess, even in a closed economy context: allocative efficiency in a static sense may conflict with dynamic efficiency in terms of incentives to technological progress. It is not the purpose of this work to analyse in depth these "Schumpeterian trade-offs", which are discussed by Nelson (1981) and Nelson and Winter (1982). Overlapping with, and adding to, the "Schumpeterian trade-offs" of the closed economy case, there is—we argued here—the possibility of a statics *vs.* dynamics trade-off originating from the patterns of economic signals in the international market. In a way, the open economy case induces a *structural distortion* upon that pattern of signals which would have been generated in autarky conditions. In doing so, they may either overrule upon the domestic "Schumpeterian trade-offs" or amplify them. The substantive hypothesis, we suggested, is that this depends on the relative distance of each country *vis-à-vis* the technological frontiers in those technological paradigms showing the highest opportunities of innovation and demand growth.

III ECONOMIC AND TECHNOLOGICAL DYNAMISM: THE ROLE OF
     INSTITUTIONS AND POLICIES

The seven propositions discussed above jointly highlight a picture of the process of coordination of economic activities and generation of technological advances whereby institutions (both "micro" institutions, e.g., complex corporate structures embodying specific capabilities, rules of behaviours, "rationalities", modes of institutional organization of market interactions, etc.; and "macro" institutions, such as strictly public agencies) enter as a set of crucial factors irreducible to simple economic mechanisms. On the contrary, *lato sensu* institutional factors appear to shape the *constitution of behavioural rules, learning processes, patterns of environmental selection, context conditions* under which economic mechanisms operate—in general, and *a fortiori* with reference to technological change. To put it another way, there appears to be *no* meaningful possibility of (a) separating the strictly economic variables from their institutional context and then assessing the former in relation to their performance outcome, neglecting the latter; (b) assuming that strictly economic variables overdetermine their institutional contexts to such an extent that the latter tend to converge to a unique pattern; (c) simply reducing all extra economic elements to either interferences or exceptional corrections to a supposedly "optimally-performing", self-contained and well-tuned economic machine. That is to say that, if the propositions suggested above are correct, then also any assessment of the role of policies based on the "reductionist" approach is bound to be, at best, incomplete.[28]

In these circumstances, complex normative issues emerge in relation to the definition and assessment of the efficiency of various combinations between institutional set-ups, nature of the technologies and economic processes. Here, we are simply going to suggest some conjectures and methodological remarks.

First, let us start from a classification of the variables upon which policies may act—in general and with particular reference to technological progress. On the grounds of the foregoing discussion they can be categorized as:

(a) the capability of the scientific/technological system of providing major innovative advances and of organizing the technological *context conditions* (ranging from infrastructure to the ways the different varieties of externalities are organized);

(b) the *capabilities of the economic agents*, in terms of the technology they embody, the effectiveness and speed with which they search for new technological and organizational advances, etc.;

(c) the patterns of *signals* (which, as we saw, depend also on inter-firm and inter-national technological asymmetries, and, in turn, shape the boundaries

---

[28]Remarkably, somewhat similar conclusions can be implicitly reached by the exploration of the properties and heuristic limitations of general equilibrium models with externalities, indivisibilities, limited and/or market dependent information (*cf.*, for example, Hahn, 1984 and 1985; Kornai, 1971; and Stiglitz, 1984). The institutional "architecture" of the system must be accounted for as one of the determinants of the performance of the system (Stiglitz, 1984). Once we recognize that (a) externalities, uncertainty, increasing returns, etc. are *general* and *permanent* features of economies characterized by change in general and technical change in particular, and (b) institutions are necessary to explain economic performance at any time and the relative order of economic change over time, then, in our view, not much is left to interpretative powers of the "reductionist" research programme.

of the set of possible microeconomic responses that are economically feasible for agents which—irrespective of their precise strategies—have profitability among their behavioural considerations);

(d) the *forms of organization* within and between markets (e.g., the relationship between financial structures and industry, the forms of industrial relations, the varying balance between cooperation and competition, the degree and forms of corporate internalization of transactions, etc.);

(e) the incentives/stimuli/constraints facing the agents in their adjustment and innovative processes (e.g., the degree of private appropriability of the benefits of innovating, the intensity of competitive threats, the cost and profitability of innovation, etc.).

These categories, we suggest, allow a taxonomy of policies according to their implications in terms of the corresponding groups of variables. Our general conjectures are that (i) all major Western countries indeed present relatively high degrees of intervention—whether consciously conceived as industrial policies or not—that affect all the above variables; (ii) probably, if one simply considers the impact of various forms of financial transfer and public procurement, no striking difference is likely to be detected between most OECD countries (possibly with a relatively lower importance in Japan); and (iii) what primarily differentiates the various countries are the instruments, the institutional arrangements and the philosophy of intervention. As an illustration, consider the case of Japanese policies, especially in relation to electronics technologies. Interestingly, Japan appears to have acted comprehensively upon all the variables categorized in our taxonomy above. A heavy discretionary intervention upon the structure of signals (by means of formal and informal protection against imports and foreign investments and through an investment policy of financial institutions consistent with growth and Schumpeterian efficiencies) recreated the "vacuum environment" that is generally enjoyed only by the technological leader(s). However, this was matched by a pattern of fierce oligopolistic rivalry between Japanese companies and a heavy export orientation which fostered technological dynamism and prevented any exploitation of protection simply in terms of collusive monopolistic pricing.

It is tempting to compare this Japanese experience with others, much less successful, such as the European ones, which heavily relied upon one single instrument, financial transfers (especially R&D subsidies and transfers on capital account), leaving to the endogenous working of the international market both the determination of the patterns of signals and the response capabilities of individual firms. Certainly, there are country-specific features of the Japanese example which are hardly transferable. However, that case, in its striking outcome, points at a general possibility of reshaping the patterns of "comparative advantages" as they emerge from the endogenous evolution of the international markets.

There is a general point here. Historically, a successful catching-up effort in terms of per capita income and wages has always been accompanied by technological catching-up in the new and most dynamic technological paradigms, irrespective of the initial patterns of comparative advantages, specializations and market-generated signals.

Second, from a normative point of view, the foregoing discussion highlights the general role that policies and/or institutions play in technological change. The innovative process *necessarily* embodies a complex and differentiated mixture of private appropriation and public-good aspects (see Nelson, 1981 and 1984) and involves an unavoidable "market failure", to use the language familiar to economists. Thus, the normative counterpart of this phenomenon does not regard *if* but *how* and *to what degree* policies should affect the innovative activities. Moreover, the existence of possible trade-offs between "static" efficiency, on the one hand, and growth/"Schumpeterian" efficiencies, on the other, sometimes amplified by the ways technological gaps feed back on market signals in the international market, implies that policies affecting also economic signals may be required—on whatever welfare criterion is chosen (e.g., income growth, innovativeness, employment, etc.)—in a much wider set of cases than those prescribed by traditional "infant industry" arguments.

Our conjecture is that, *ceteris paribus*, the structural need for policies affecting *also* the patterns of economic signals (including relative prices and relative profitabilities) as they emerge from the international market will be greater, the higher the distance of any one country from the technological frontier. Conversely, endogenous market mechanisms tend to behave in a "virtuous" manner for those countries that happen to be on the frontier, especially in the newest/most promising technologies. This is broadly confirmed by historical experience: unconditional free trade often happened to be advocated and fully exploited only by the leading countries.

Third, as regards the time-profile of technological developments, a fundamental divide can be traced between policies related to the *emergence* of new technological paradigms and policies apt to sustain technological activities along relatively established paths. In the former case, policies should (i) provide a satisfactory flow of scientific advances; (ii) establish "bridging institutions" between scientific developments and their economic exploitation; (iii) develop conducive financial structures to support the trial-and-error procedures generally involved in the search for new technological paradigms; and (iv) act as "focusing devices"[29] in the process of selection of the directions of technological development. As regards "normal" technical progress, important policy tasks appear to be the maintenance of a relatively fluid supply of techno-scientific advances, coupled with "balanced" conditions of private appropriability of the benefits of innovating.

[29] *Cf.* Rosenberg (1976).

Conversely, countries well below the technological frontier may find it necessary also to act directly upon both the capability levels of the domestic companies and *against* the appropriability features of the related technologies insofar as they perform as an *entry barrier* for laggard companies/countries.

Fourth, there is a fundamental policy dimension which relates to context conditions, the organization of externalities and infrastructures. These are likely to be particularly important in the process of transition between different technological regimes (different clusters of technological paradigms), whereby the new set-ups involve new patterns of intersectoral flows of commodities and information, new common infrastructures (think of the role of motorways in relation to the automotive industries or the role of telecommunications in relation to electronics), and a different set of untraded interdependencies between companies and sectors.

Fifth, public policies, whether intentionally or not, affect the fundamental "rationalities" of the agents, the ways their expectations and objectives are formed. By means of an illustration, one may think of the role of military spending. In addition to obvious effects upon the composition of demand and the pattern of economic signals, another indirect, but equally important, implication regards the way it is likely to shape the strategies and the managerial outlooks: almost certainly, public agencies tend to be perceived as a "guarantee of last resort",[30] while the skills of detecting and influencing procurement authorities are likely to become dominant upon the capabilities of understanding and anticipating market trends in competitive environments. Clearly, this is only one—possibly the most straightforward— example of a set of influences that the political structures exert upon the *behavioural constitution* of market processes.[31]

IV   SOME CONCLUSIONS

In a world characterized by technical change (both "continuous" change along defined technological trajectories and "discontinuous" ones related to the emergence of new technological paradigms), technological lags and leads shape the patterns of intersectoral and interproduct profitability signals and, thus, also the patterns of microeconomic allocation. The latter, however, may affect the long-term macroeconomic dynamism of each country, in terms of both rates of growth of income consistent with the foreign balance constraint and of technological innovativeness. In the last resort, this happens because the effects of a multiplicity of signals (related to profitability, long-term demand growth and technological opportunities) upon microeconomic

---

[30]We owe this observation to a discussion with H. Minsky.

[31]Another important example, analysed by Zysman (1983), concerns the effects of country-specific institutional organizations of the financial markets upon the allocation of resources and the industrial attitudes toward risk, growth, innovation, etc.

processes of adjustments are likely to be *asymmetric*. Whenever trade-offs between different notions of efficiency arise, "sub-optimal" or "perverse" macroeconomic outcomes may emerge. Since the *future* pattern of technological advantages/disadvantages is also related to the *present* allocative patterns, we can see at work here dynamic processes which Kaldor calls of "circular causation": economic signals related to intersectoral profitabilities—which lead in a straightforward manner to "comparative advantages" and relative specializations—certainly control and check the allocative efficiency of the various productive employments, but may also play a more ambiguous or even perverse role in relation to long-term macroeconomic trends.

The ("vicious" or "virtuous") circular processes we have discussed concern the very nature of allocative mechanisms, insofar as the economy is characterized by technical change showing varying degrees of sector-specific opportunity, cumulativeness, appropriability, dynamic technological externalities and local and idiosyncratic learning.

This defines also a fundamental domain for policies.

Moreover, we argued, institutional factors—including, of course, policies—are part of the very *constitution* of economic processes, i.e., the ways economic activities are organized and coordinated, technical change is generated and used, the dominant behavioural regularities emerge, etc. This is another fundamental domain for policies.

A detailed understanding of, and intervention upon, patterns of signals, rules of allocative responses and forms of institutional organization of the "economic machine" are particularly important in those phases of transition from a technological regime (based on old technological paradigms) to a new one. These historical periods define a new set of opportunities and threats for each country: the patterns of international generation and diffusion of technologies become more fluid as do, consequently, the international trade flows and the relative levels of per capita income.

The contemporary economy—we believe—is undergoing such a change, in the transition toward an electronics-based technological regime. In the process, comparative advantages become the self-fulfilling prophecy of a successful set of institutional actions and private strategies: *ex post*, technological and economic success makes "optimal" from the point of view of the economist what *ex ante* is a political dream.

One decade after the Second World War, no economist would have suggested that electronics was one of the Japanese comparative advantages. Now it certainly is. If one would have taken the relative allocative efficiency of the different industrial sectors thirty years ago as the ground for normative prescriptions, Japan would still probably be exporting silk ties. In a sense, the use of comparative-advantage criteria as the final and sole ground for normative prescriptions is a luxury that only countries on the technological frontier can afford: *rebus sic stantibus*, it will not take long before Japanese economists will learn and preach Ricardo or even Heckscher–Ohlin while it may well be that the Americans and the Europeans will rediscover Hamilton, List and Ferrier.

REFERENCES

Arrow, K. and Hahn, F. (1971). *General Competitive Analysis*, San Francisco, Ca., Holden-Day.

Arthur, W. B. (1985). "Competing Technologies and Lock-in by Historical Events: The Dynamics of Allocation Under Increasing Returns", *Stanford University, CEPR, Discussion Paper*.

Atkinson, A. B. and Stiglitz, J. (1969). "A New View of Technological Change", *Economic Journal*, Vol. 79, No. 3, pp. 573–578.

Boyer, R. and Mistral, J. (1983). *Accumulation, Inflation, Crises* (2nd Edition), Paris, Presses Universitaires de France.

Chandler, A. D. (1966). *Strategy and Structure*, New York, Anchor Books.

Chandler, A. D. (1977). *The Visible Hand. The Managerial Revolution in American Business*, Cambridge, Mass., The Belknap Press.

Cimoli, M., Dosi, G. and Soete, L. (1986). "Technology Gaps, Institutional Differences and Patterns of Trade: A North–South Model, *SPRU, University of Sussex, DRC Discussion Paper*.

Cohen, S., Teece, D., Tyson, L. and Zysman, J. (1984). "Competitiveness", *University of California at Berkeley, BRIE Working Paper*.

Cropsey, J. (1957). *Policy and the Economy. An Interpretation of the Principles of Adam Smith*, The Hague, M. Nijhoff.

Dalton, G. (Ed.) (1971). *Primitive, Archaic and Modern Economies*, Boston, Ma., Beacon Press.

David, P. (1975). *Technical Change, Innovation and Economic Growth*, Cambridge, Cambridge University Press.

Denison, E. F. (1967). *Why Growth Rates Differ*, Washington, D.C., Brookings Institution.

Dore, R. (1973). *British Factory—Japanese Factory*, London, Allen and Unwin.

Dosi, G. (1984). *Technical Change and Industrial Transformation*, London, Macmillan.

Dosi, G. and Orsenigo, L. (1985). "Market Processes, Rules and Institutions in Technical Change and Economic Dynamics", presented at the Conference on "The Impact of Technology, Labour Processes and Financial Structures on Economic Progress and Stability", St. Louis, Missouri, May 1985, forthcoming in H. Minsky and P. Ferri (eds.), *Innovation, Financial Structures and Growth Stability*, New York, Sharp, 1988.

Dosi, G., Orsenigo, L. and Silverberg, G. (1986). "Innovation, Diversity and Diffusion: A Self-Organisation Model", *SPRU, University of Sussex, DRC Discussion Paper*.

Dosi, G., Pavitt, K. and Soete, L. (1988). *The Economics of Technical Change and International Trade*, Brighton, Wheatsheaf, forthcoming.

Dumont, L. (1977). *Homo Aequalis. Genèse et Épanouissement de l'Idéologie Économique*, Paris, Gallimard.

Freeman, C. (1982). *The Economics of Industrial Innovations* (Second Edition), London, Francis Pinter.

Frydman, R. (1982). "Toward an Understanding of Market Processes", *American Economic Review*, Vol. 72, No. 4, pp. 652–668.

Gibbons, M., Gummett, P. and Udgaonkar, B. M. (Eds.) (1984). *Science and Technology Policy in the 1980's and Beyond*, London, Longmans.

Hahn, F. (1984). *Equilibrium and Macroeconomics*, Oxford, Basil Blackwell.

Hahn, F. (1985). "On Equilibrium with Market-Dependent Information" in *Money, Growth and Stability*, Oxford, Basil Blackwell.

Heiner, R. A. (1983). "The Origin of Predictable Behavior", *American Economic Review*, Vol. 73, No. 4, pp. 560–595.

Helpman, E. and Krugman, P. (1985). *Market Structure and Foreign Trade*, Cambridge, Mass., MIT Press.

Hirsch, F. (1976). *Social Limits to Growth*, Cambridge, Mass., Harvard University Press.

Hirschman, A. (1970). *Exit, Voice and Loyalty*, Cambridge, Mass., Harvard University Press.

Hirschman, A. (1977). *The Passion and the Interests*, Princeton, N.J., Princeton University Press.

Hirschman, A. (1982). "Rival Interpretations of Market Society: Civilising, Destructive or Feeble?", *Journal of Economic Literature*, Vol. 20, No. 4, pp. 1463–1484.

Johnson, C. A. (1982). *MITI and the Japanese Miracle: The Growth of Industrial Policies, 1925–1975*, Stanford, Ca., Stanford University Press.

Kaldor, N. (1972). "The Irrelevance of Equilibrium Economics", *Economic Journal*, Vol. 82, No. 4, pp. 1237–1255.

Kaldor, N. (1980). *The Role of Increasing Returns, Technical Progress and Cumulative Causation in the Theory of International Trade*, Paris, ISMEA.

Katz, N. L. and Shapiro, C. (1983). "Network Externalities, Competition and Compatibility", *Princeton University, Woodrow Wilson School, Discussion Paper No. 54*.

Kierzkowski, H. (Ed.) (1984). *Monopolistic Competition and International Trade*, Oxford, Oxford University Press.

Kornai, J. (1971). *Anti-Equilibrium*, Amsterdam, North-Holland.

Krugman, P. (1984). "Import Protection as Export Promotion: International Competition in the Presence of Oligopoly and Economies of Scale" in Kierzkowski (ed.), *op. cit.*

Levin, R., Klevarick, A. J., Nelson, R. and Winter, S. (1984). "Survey Research on R&D Appropriability and Technological Opportunity. Part I: Appropriability", Yale University, mimeo.

Luhman, N. (1975). *Macht*, Stuttgart, Ferdinand Euke Verlag.

Markusen, J. R. and Melvin, J. R. (1984). "The Gains-from-Trade Theorem with Increasing Returns to Scale" in Kierzkowski (ed.), *op. cit.*

Marris, R. and Mueller, D. C. (1980). "Corporation, Competition and the Invisible Hand", *Journal of Economic Literature*, Vol. 18, No. 1, pp. 32–63.

Metcalfe, J. S. (1985). "On Technological Competition", Manchester University, mimeo.

Metcalfe, J. S. and Soete, L. (1984). "Diffusion in Innovations and International Competitiveness" in Gibbons, Gummett and Udgaonkar (eds.), *op. cit.*

Mistral, J. (1982). "La Diffusion Inter-national Inégal de l'Accumulation et ses Crises" in Reiffers (ed.), *op. cit.*

Nelson, R. (1968). "A 'Diffusion' Model of International Productivity Differences in Manufacturing Industry", *American Economic Review*, Vol. 58, No. 5, pp. 1219–1248.

Nelson, R. (1981). "Assessing Private Enterprise", *Bell Journal of Economics*, Vol. 12, No. 1, pp. 93–111.

Nelson, R. (1982). "The Role of Knowledge in R&D Efficiency", *Quarterly Journal of Economics*, Vol. 97, No. 3, pp. 453–470.

Nelson, R. (Ed.) (1982a). *The Government and Technical Progress*, New York, Pergamon Press.

Nelson R. (1984). *High Technology Policies: A Five Nations Comparison*, Washington, D.C., American Enterprise Institute.

Nelson, R. and Winter, S. (1977). "In Search of a Useful Theory of Innovation", *Research Policy*, Vol. 6, No. 1, pp. 36–76.

Nelson, R. and Winter, S. (1982). *An Evolutionary Theory of Economic Change*, Cambridge, Mass., The Belknap Press.

Noble, D. F. (1977). *America by Design*, Oxford, Oxford University Press.

Pasinetti, L. L. (1981). *Structural Change and Economic Growth*, Cambridge, Cambridge University Press.

Pavitt, K. (1984). "Sectoral Patterns of Technical Change: Towards a Taxonomy and a Theory", *Research Policy*, Vol. 13, No. 6, pp. 343–373.

Perez, C. (1983). "Structural Change and New Technologies", *Futures*, Vol. 15, No. 5, pp. 357–375.

Pizzorno, A. (1985). "Some Other Kinds of Otherness", Harvard University, Department of Sociology, mimeo.

Plott, C. R. (1982). "Industrial Organisation Theory and Experimental Economics", *Journal of Economic Literature*, Vol. 20, No. 4, pp. 1485–1527.

Polanyi, K. (1944). *The Great Transformation*, Boston, Ma., Beacon Press.

Polanyi, K. (1971). "Our Obsolete Market Mentality" in Dalton (ed.), *op. cit.*

Reiffers, J. L. (Ed.) (1982). *Économie et Finance Internationale*, Paris, Dunod.

Ricardo, D. (1951). *On the Principles of Political Economy and Taxation*, P. Sraffa (ed.), Cambridge, Cambridge University Press.

Rosenberg, N. (1976). *Perspectives in Technology*, Cambridge, Cambridge University Press.

Rosenberg, N. (1982). *Inside the Black Box*, Cambridge, Cambridge University Press.

Sah, R. K. and Stiglitz, J. E. (1985). "Human Fallibility and Economic Organisation", *American Economic Review*, Papers and Proceedings, Vol. 75, No. 2, pp. 292–297.

Salvati, M. (1985). "Diversita' e mutamento", *Economia Politica*, Vol. 2, No. 2, pp. 249–292.

Schelling, T. C. (1978). *Micromotives and Macrobehavior*, New York, Norton.

Scherer, F. M. (1980). *Industrial Market Structure and Economic Performance* (2nd Edition), Chicago, Rand McNally.

Scherer, F. M. (1982). "Inter-Industry Technology Flows in the U.S.", *Research Policy*, Vol. 11, No. 3, pp. 227–245.

Schumpeter, J. A. (1961). *The Theory of Economic Development*, Oxford, Oxford University Press.

Schumpeter, J. A. (1975). *Capitalism, Socialism, Democracy*, New York, Harper and Row.

Shonfield, A. (1965). *Modern Capitalism. The Changing Balance of Public and Private Power*, Oxford, Oxford University Press.

Silva, F. (1984). "Some Comparison in the Fields of Industrial Policy: Theory, the U.S., Italy", *Yale University, Institution for Social and Policy Studies, Working Paper No. 1016*.

Smith, A. (1976). *The Theory of Moral Sentiments*, Oxford, Oxford University Press.

Stiglitz, J. E. (1984). "Information and Economic Analysis: A Perspective", *Economic Journal, Conference Papers*, Vol. 95, pp. 21–41.

Teece, D. (1982). "Toward an Economic Theory of the Multiproduct Firms", *Journal of Economic Behavior and Organisation*, Vol. 3, No. 1, pp. 39–63.

Thirlwall, A. P. (1980). *Balance-of-Payment Theory and the United Kingdom Experience*, London, Macmillan.

de Tocqueville, A. (1969). *Democracy in America*, New York, Anchor Books.

Veblen, T. (1915). *Imperial Germany and the Industrial Revolution*, London, Macmillan.

Williamson, O. (1979). *Markets and Hierarchies*, New York, Free Press.

Williamson, O. (1981). "The Modern Corporation: Origin, Evolution, Attributes", *Journal of Economic Literature*, Vol. 19, No. 4, pp. 1537–1568.

Winter, S. (1982). "An Essay on the Theory of Production" in S. H. Hymans (ed.), *Economics and the World Around It*, Ann Arbor, Mich., University of Michigan Press.

Zysman, J. (1983). *Governments, Markets and Growth. Financial Systems and the Politics of Industrial Change*, Ithaca, N.Y., Cornell University Press.

[21]

Journal of Economic Behavior and Organization 13 (1990) 299–319. North-Holland.

FINANCE, INNOVATION AND INDUSTRIAL CHANGE*

Giovanni DOSI

University of Rome 'La Sapienza', 00100, Rome, Italy

University of Sussex, BN1 9RH, Brighton, UK

Received August 1988, final version received February 1990

This paper investigates the impact financial structures upon industrial dynamics whenever the system is permanently characterized by unexploited opportunities for innovation, (highly) 'bounded' rationality and trial-and-error search processes. In these circumstances, it is argued, specific financial set-ups – such as 'market-based' vs. 'credit-based' mechanisms of allocation, control and ownership transfer – are likely to exert different influences on the rates and modes of industrial innovation. Relatedly, one suggests some hypotheses on the links between financial systems and features of industrial evolution, and some tentative taxonomies.

1. Introduction

In a very general sense, innovation concerns processes of learning and discovery about new products, new production processes and new forms of economic organisation, about which, ex ante, economic actors often possess only rather unstructured beliefs on some unexploited opportunities, and which, ex post, are generally checked and selected, in non-centrally planned economies, by some competitive interactions, of whatever form, in product markets. However, in addition, and complementary, to product market competition, innovative efforts are shaped and selected also by the rates and criteria by which financial markets and financial institutions, such as stock markets and banks, allocate resources to business enterprises. Irrespectively of whether resources are attributed to business units ('firms') or individual projects, allocative criteria and rates of allocation should plausibly affect the amount of resources which the real sector (call it the 'industry') devotes to the innovative search, and also the directions in which the agents search.

*Prepared for the Conference on 'The Markets for Innovation, Ownership and Control', IUI, Stockholm, 12–15 June 1988. Comments by the participants at the Conference and in particular the discussants, L. Bjuggrenn and G. Eliasson and by two anonymous referees are gratefully acknowledged.

Support to part of the research which lead to this work has been kindly provided by the Designated Research Center of the ESRC, at the Science Policy Research Unit (SPRU), University of Sussex, and by the Italian Ministry of Public Education ('Progetti 40%').

This work is a tentative and highly conjectural investigation of these issues. I shall first provide a brief assessment of a few theoretical and historical findings on the relationships between finance and economic change (section 2). Then I shall discuss some stylised features of those environments which are permanently characterised by technological and organisational change, and in particular, the features of their *learning processes* and *selection processes* (section 3). Section 4 will analyse some properties that distinguish 'market-based' and 'credit-based' systems of financial allocation. Next, section 5 will advance some hypotheses on the relationship between the financial domain and real economic evolution.

2. Finance, information and economic change: History and theory

Let me introduce the analysis that follows by straightly focusing on a fundamental issue, namely: *Do financial institutions matter in terms of levels and changes in real aggregate variables?* There has been a rich, insightful, tradition in economic history, that has focused on this question in terms of specific financial institutions and actual modes for financing corporate growth. *First*, it has been argued that particular financial institutions (or lack of them) may foster or, *other things being equal*, impede long term economic development [see e.g. Cameron et al. (1967) and Kindleberger (1983)]. In this respect, one brings forward rather convincing – although necessarily indirect – evidence on the role that particular financial institutions, e.g., banks, emerging stock markets, central banks, clearing houses, etc., did (or did not) play in the development of the manufacturing sector and the growth of its modern part, especially in the early phases of industrialisation. *Second*, even today, one observes significant international differences in the modes through which industrial growth is financed. In particular, Rybczynsky (1974) and Zysman (1983) have put forward a broadly similar taxonomy which distinguishes between 'market-based' and 'institution-oriented' (or 'credit-based') systems. In a stylised representation of the former, stock markets, equity issues and, more so, bonds and retained profits are the dominant forms of corporate growth; bank loans serve mainly short-term purposes; allocation criteria are typically non-discretionary. Certainly, empirical examples nearest to the 'market-based' archetype are the U.S.A. and the U.K. Conversely, in an equally stylised credit- (or institution-) based system, long-term bank loans and long-term ownership titles by banks, other financial institutions and/or governments, represent the major sources of corporate growth; allocation processes are much more discretionary and depend also on long-term relationships between particular firms and particular banks. *Third*, at a general level, it is argued that particular forms of organisation of ownership, production, finance, influence allocations and performance outcomes, even for the *same* set of economic incentives.[1] Underpinning all these historical interpretations there has been the (explicit or implicit) general hypothesis that *institutions,* in our case here financial institutions, *affect* (i) *the rates at which resources are accumulated,* (ii) *their employments,* and (iii) the *economic efficiency of their uses.*

Conversely, a significant stream of theoretical and econometric literature has purported the claim that specific financial institutions *do not matter* in terms of real aggregate dynamics, because the latter is led by a largely *exogenous* dynamics of the 'fundamentals' of the economy (technology and individual preferences) and because individual rationality is sufficient to guarantee the exploitation of all available opportunities, equated to all available information, at any single point in time.[2] However, a few, quite different, modelling methodologies agree at least on the broad conclusion that imperfect/asymmetric information implies/requires some sort of institutions governing information transfers, incentives, resource allocation. In this respect, the 'information and economics' literature is a powerful point of departure for the argument that follows. Let me recall some related theoretical results, namely (a) incentives, allocation patterns and system performances generally depend upon the institutional set-up of each system (e.g., hierarchy versus decentralisation); (b) there are equilibria that involve resource rationing; (c) equilibria depend on the particular sequences of information flows and on agents' beliefs; (d) learning processes may lead to non-convexities in the technology sets and possibly also to the non-existence of equilibria.[3] All these results bear three major implications.

First, they imply some *de-linking between patterns of resource allocation,* on the one hand, *and the 'fundamentals' of the economy,* on the other. As a consequence, institutions – in our case, in particular, financial institutions – governing information and incentives, *do matter* in terms of micro resource allocation and aggregate performances. *Second,* any empirical evidence – even when properly and successfully detected – on 'financial market efficiency' must, therefore, be interpreted simply as a corroboration of the 'weak' hypothesis that *on average* financial agents try to make the best use of the information they have, but that this imperfect and possibly asymmetric information is not independent from the institutional 'architecture' of that particular system. Moreover, there is little ground for the hypothesis that

---

[1]See, e.g., Gerschenkron (1953), Zysman (1983), Dosi (1988).

[2]Broadly speaking, such an hypothesis is shared by rather diverse analytical approaches, ranging from Modigliani and Miller (1958) to more recent 'strong' versions of market efficiency/ rational expectation models [for a symposium mainly supporting the hypothesis, cf. Jensen et al. (1978) and for a critical appraisal cf. Summers (1986); some critical remarks concerning more directly industrial analysis are in Teece (1983)].

[3]On all these points, cf., e.g., Sah and Stiglitz (1985), Stiglitz (1984), Stiglitz and Weiss (1986), Aoki (1986) and (1988), Hahn (1987), Atkinson and Stiglitz (1969), David (1975) and (1985), Arrow (1987), Radner (1987), Williamson (1988), Arthur (1983) and (1988).

agents adjust to some underlying 'real' equilibrium uniquely determined by fundamentals [Summers (1986)]. *Third*, if actual patterns of resource allocation are allowed to exert an influence on the future dynamics of the 'fundamentals' themselves, especially technology, then any assumptions on stationarity, or on an exogenous technological change turns out to be rather doubtful.

All these analytical conclusions are also a good start for the analysis of those environments which are *explicitly* assumed to be non-stationary (technologies, organisations and preferences endogenously (change over time).

In such non-stationary environments, I shall assume that agents continuously try to exploit 'opportunities', which they believe – rightly or wrongly – that 'are there', or might be created by their own actions. In the broadest sense, an 'opportunity' is a chance of getting a 'better' product in terms of some price weighted performance characteristics, a more efficient production process (given ruling inputs costs, or even better, irrespectively of relative prices), and a more efficient organisational set-up (e.g., new organisational networks which increase the completeness of information without affecting the incentives facing organisation members). Of course, an 'opportunity' will be pursued if agents believe that the cost of doing so will be lower than the expected economic benefit from its successful exploitation.

Well, in order to represent this process, a theoretical strategy with a noble pedigree is to work, so to speak, 'backward', from probability distributions of notional states-of-the-world, to actions and expected pay-offs [cf. Arrow (1983)]. Add to this also the assumptions that agents will (a) try to estimate as accurately as possible the 'true' probability distributions, and (b) push up their search costs until they equalise the expected returns discounted by some risk factor. One gets at the end a theoretical representation whereby one is able to separately analyse some sort of 'drift' in opportunities available at each time, and the equilibria that rational agents could achieve at such times, given the incentive- and information-architectures in which they operate. Possibly, the exploitation of an oil field is a good example. Once its possible existence is known – i.e., an 'opportunity' emerges – rational agents will try to 'tap' it. The ways in which they will try to do this will depend also on their belief-ridden expectations, on institutions (e.g. property rights), on information flows. In all this, however, oil fields are there, whether we know about their existence or not: Any new 'opportunity' can be reasonably represented as improved information about a 'true' state of the world which, as such, is stationary (any omniscient God-like agent would have the complete map of world oil fields, which were the same also a thousand years ago ...). The non-stationarity is only the characteristics of economic environments composed of less than perfectly informed agents who are, so to speak, 'shocked' by any novel piece of news. Here, on the contrary, I would like to investigate some properties of environments whereby *previously unknown states-of-the-world are themselves the result of the actions of the agents.* To put it paradoxically, I shall focus on environments wherein the very existence of an oil field depends on the process of searching for it: It is created a few thousand metres below the earth surface by the very process of thinking about its existence, planning for its exploration, setting up the drilling equipment, and, finally, tapping it ... It is obviously absurd for an oil field, but, I suggest, it captures a fundamental feature of contemporary processes of technological and organisational innovation. What is believed to be possible to achieve, what is in fact achieved, and the capabilities of achieving it are dynamically coupled so that no easy separation is possible between 'opportunity drifts' and 'economic adjustments'. In the interpretation that I am proposing here, technological innovations such as the transistor, the electrical motor or the zipper are more akin to Newton's and Leibniz' development of differential calculus than the discovery of oil fields, iron mines and, even less so, to gambling on a lottery.

If this interpretation is correct, *first*, 'events' did not properly 'exist' before their very discovery: States-of-the-world and agents' behaviours are not separable. The fact that both technological and scientific discoveries are grounded on some natural phenomena is irrelevant for the argument here: The process that led to them is largely independent from the ex ante perception of the underlying natural properties or 'laws'; indeed, the latter emerge together with the discoveries themselves. *Second*, there is a fundamental *problem-solving feature* of innovative activities, based also on uncodified, tacit, cumulative elements of knowledge [cf. Nelson and Winter (1982) and Dosi (1988a)]. Loosely speaking, innovative activities both 'pose the problem' and try to solve it. The uncertainty about its solution does not relate only to imperfect information but to the inherently 'ill-structured' nature of the problem itself [Simon (1982)]. Let me put it more provocatively. The economic profession is generally inclined to represent decision problems as trivial ones. They may be computationally very complex but they are still trivial: A powerful computer could handle them equally well or better than any human actor [Stiglitz (1984)]. Conversely, innovation-related problems could *not in general* be handled by any computer, irrespectively of the information that we feed into it, falling short of any complete infomation about the solution itself.[4] *Third*, the foregoing conjectures add further weight to the hypothesis that innovative processes are *path-dependent* and *institution-dependent*. It may well be that where an agent searches depends on where one has already found something in the past and on where its knowledge is. Moreover, past successes and failures can plausibly feed back upon the incentives to search in some directions and not in others,

---

[4]A more detailed argument on these topics, and some theoretical implications are in Dosi and Egidi (1987).

irrespectively of the *notional* opportunities that might exist elsewhere [Arthur (1983, 1988) and David (1990)]. In other works[5] I have tried to conceptualise these processes of innovation in terms of what I call *technological paradigms* and *technological trajectories*, based on specific bodies of knowledge and search heuristics; and showing varying degrees of opportunity, cumulativeness of technological capabilities, appropriability of innovation-based economic advantages. An important implication of all this for the present discussion is that innovative processes are intimately associated with *persistent* non-convexities in what are commonly called production possibility sets.[6] *Fourth*, a theoretical corollary is that something crucial is missing by representing the innovative process as some sort of 'hill-climbing', whereby the 'hill' is postulated to be already there from the start, and agents – Bayesians or not – try to get to the top, and to converge to some equilibrium (equilibria) notionally independent from their own actions.[7] Rather, innovative patterns might be more accurately represented by dynamic processes whereby opportunities, incentives and capabilities endogenously evolve: Hill-shapes change while climbing them, and new higher hills are continuously generated.

Hence, I propose a theoretical representation of non-stationary environments, *cum* technological and organisational change, as *evolutionary systems*. In general, I define the latter as systems where:

(i) Agents are explicitly allowed to search, make mistakes, sometimes obtain unexpected successes, and try to learn throughout such processes.

(ii) Product- and financial markets operate also as selection devices amongst different firms and different technologies.

(iii) Notwithstanding any generic economic motivation ('... make as much money as possible ...'), agents' behaviours have to be further characterised by empirically-based, context-specific, decision rules. And finally,

(iv) aggregate performances of the system change over time as *self-organising* (collective) properties of the interactions amongst diverse agents which permanently show disequilibrium behaviours.[8]

In short, I propose that innovative environments are characterised by the twin fundamental properties of *learning and selection*. Relatedly, I suggest

---

[5]Dosi (1984) and (1988a), broadly in line with a growing literature on the economics of innovation [cf. Freeman (1982), Rosenberg (1975) and (1982), Nelson and Winter (1977) and (1982)].

[6]In this respect several innovation studies corroborate and extend an earlier conjecture of Atkinson and Stiglitz (1969). See also David (1975).

[7]Incidentally, note that such an account of environmental dynamics might turn out to be misleading even in biological environments that, plausibly, present much higher structural stability than social ones: cf. Allen (1988).

[8]On these points, cf. Nelson and Winter (1982), Iwai (1984), Day (1984), Eliasson (1986), Silverberg (1987) and (1988), Dosi, Orsenigo and Silverberg (1990); Silverberg, Dosi and Orsenigo (1988).

that differences in *structures* (e.g. firms' size, levels and distributions of technological capabilities, etc.) and *performances* (e.g. rates of innovation, productivity growth) can *be mapped into different underlying balances between, and modes of, learning and selection.* Thus, the question of the influence of financial structures on innovation and industrial dynamics turns out to concern the influence that financial structures exert on the rates and modes at which firms learn and the rates and criteria on which particular environments select among firms and among technologies.

In general, in such environments, one would expect the major conclusions achieved in the 'imperfect information' literature, *a fortiori* to hold. For example, non-stationarity adds further factors making rationing a permanent phenomenon. The subtle combination between imperfect/asymmetric information and possible incentive incompatibilities (e.g. moral hazard and adverse selection) is obviously enlarged by innovation activities about which, *by definition,* contracts cannot be completely specified and performances cannot be completely monitored [Teece (1988)]. The continuous emergence of unknown events (which after all, innovations are too) deepens the uncertainty facing decision processes and magnifies the importance of the particular institutions guiding behaviours. However, in addition to all that, when analysing evolutionary environments, one must also explicitly consider the effects that current patterns of finance allocation have on the *future capabilities* of any one economic system to *generate, and adjust to,* new events (innovations), at present largely unpredictable.

3. Learning and selection: Finance, diversity and evolution

A seemingly robust hypothesis about non-stationary environments – which applies when exogenous 'shocks' appear, and, more so, when changes in economic fundamentals are endogenously produced – is that *diversity* amongst agents, in terms of technological competences, behaviours, expectations is positively correlated with the 'resiliance' and long-term performance of any one economic system. In turn, this implies some quite subtle demands on the allocative criteria of the financial system.

Of course, a rather weak and general criterion of efficiency of resource allocation by the financial system is that it should be biased against firms and 'projects' which have shown and are expected to show a future economic performance worse than others. By that, the financial system operates as a *selection device.* It does obviously so when it is a direct source of financial resources to individual firms. Indirectly, it does this too when an overwhelming role is played by capital markets, whose main function – it appears – is the exchange of ownership titles. Yet, it can be reasonably claimed that it still exerts a 'disciplining' influence on management behaviours and performances. In fact one may conceive also financial systems in which allocative selection operates *against* efficiency.[9] However, I shall assume that financial selection satisfies the weak efficiency criterion, just defined, and ask, loosely speaking, whether 'more efficiency' necessarily implies also 'better evolutionary performance' (e.g. more innovation, more productivity growth, easier long-term adjustment capabilities). The crucial point, here, is that, under non-stationarity, long-term aggregate performance might not be monotonic into the efficiency of the selection rules by which financial investors, on the grounds of all presently available information, discriminate among alternative employments of their funds. This is a possible outcome of the characteristics of innovation discussed earlier: Efficiency on the grounds of past/ present performances and past/present technologies might not be necessarily taken as an unbiased predictor of future performances – at the levels of both single firms and aggregates of them. Allen's point [Allen (1988)], on a somewhat analogous biological equivalent to this problem, is a revealing illustration. A greater average 'fitness' of a population, he shows, may still imply a lower dynamic 'fitness' vis-a-vis some other species that, *on average*, are 'worse' – require more environmental resources in order to survive, have a lower rate of successful reproduction, and make more 'mistakes' in their genetic transmission. Still, despite the skewedness in the frequency distribution of mutation between 'mistakes' and revealed 'improvements', biased in favour of the former, species which are ecologically 'less efficient' at any one time might turn out to be dynamically 'fitter' than species which are better at optimising within any given environment. I certainly do not want to draw any one-to-one correspondence with social sciences. However, in analogy with these examples, I *do* suggest that *some departures* (of magnitudes which still wait to be theoretically assessed) from the technological and economic efficiency revealed on the grounds of past and present environments are *necessary* in order to ensure future innovativeness and adaptiveness.[10]

In all that, financial markets may well face permanent dilemmas between *efficiency* – as assessed on the grounds of all available information – and *evolutionary viability* – defined here by (a) the probability that some innovation will emerge at a future time t, which will turn out to be 'fitter' in the t-environment, and (b) the probability that they system will smoothly adjust to any shock at some future time. Quite independently, Eliasson (1986) and the author [Dosi (1988)], broadly in line with Nelson (1981) and Nelson and Winter (1982), have tried to define the nature of the trade-offs between 'static efficiency' (roughly, the opportunity cost of given resources at any one time), on the one hand, and 'Schumpeterian-' and 'growth-' efficiencies, on the other, related to the varying potential for *future* explorations of technological and market opportunities which *current* patterns of

[9]There is indeed some evidence especially from centrally-planned economies but also from Western ones, that this can be empirically plausible. However, this issue cannot be pursued here.
[10]This is also an implication of the model suggested in Amendola and Gaffard (1988).

allocation entail.[11] Indeed, it is nearly tautological that the tighter the discipline which financial institutions exert on business firms, the higher 'static efficiency' will be. For example, in market economies, financial structures set boundaries to the revealed distribution in production efficiencies and market competitiveness of firms within each industry [that is, on what I call in Dosi (1984) the 'degree of industrial asymmetry']. And they also set limits to the length of adjustment time for industrial 'lame ducks'. Improvements in 'static efficiency' increase the mean and decrease the variance in the performances of micro units. However, in an evolutionary perspective, the mean performance of the system at some future time t may not be monotonic into its mean performance at time zero, but, possibly into its *time zero variance*. Note, moreover, that any increase in the variance may well imply a *lowering of the mean* (given 'deviant' behaviours heavily biased toward 'mistakes'). Hence, we have here one of the grounds for the fundamental trade-offs introduced above. In order to illustrate this point, following Silverberg (1987), suppose that the fundamental competition/ selection process in the product markets results in changes of market shares of individual firms, such as

$$\dot{f_i} = A[E_i - \bar{E}]f_i,\tag{1}$$

where the dots stand for the rates of change; f_i is the market share of firm i; E_i is the 'competitiveness' of the i-firm and $\bar{E}$ is the 'average competitiveness' of the industry $(=\sum f_i E_i)$. For the purposes of this work suppose also that the competitiveness of each firm is linear in its 'performance', which, in turn, is some combination of the elements of a vector μ describing its process technology, product characteristics, organisational set-ups, learning economies, etc. Of course, other things being equal, any criteria of allocation of financial resources which is positive in the E_i's satisfies 'static efficiency'. However, 'Schumpeterian efficiency', will depend also on the transition probabilities in the μ's. Interestingly, with *complete* cumulativeness of technological progress, no trade-off between 'static' and 'Schumpeterian' efficiencies would emerge: The technological winner(s) today would also be the winner(s) tomorrow. Conversely, in a dramatised version of the 'early Schumpeter' [Schumpeter (1934)], today's winners are going to be tomorrow's losers and the financial system (the 'banker') is permanently facing a dilemma between making the best out of what is revealed by experience, and some sort of 'heroic trust' in unexplored opportunities. In this respect, the 'optimistic

[11]The reader should notice that, here and throughout, 'dynamic' or 'Schumpeterian' efficiency is defined in terms of the capabilities of economic organisations or systems to continuously generate innovations and adapt to unforeseen changes, but does not carry any normative implication, e.g. on whether a greater innovativeness is also normatively 'better'.

irrationality' of the Schumpeterian entrepreneurs requires a symmetric counterpart amongst 'bankers'.

Obviously, empirical environments are likely to fall somewhere in between these two extremes. Hence, the possibility of a tension between static allocative efficiency and evolutionary performance. Ceteris paribus, the evolutionary viability of any one system may indeed be positively related to the diversity of its processes of search, its (sometimes 'useful') mistakes, its diversity in competences and expectations.[12] As a consequence, any financial system in order to be evolutionarily viable must allow for the possibility of rather numerous 'gambles' on unexplored opportunities, about which little is known ex ante, but which can be reasonably expected to be, *on average, failures.* With a probability one that some currently unknown events will emerge at some future date, the higher the selective efficiency of financial allocation to firms and technologies that are 'optimal' in a certain environment, the higher might also be the probability of a future 'dynosaurs syndrome'. Indeed, the tension between present and future performances, at both levels of individual enterprises and whole industries is also what underlies the arguments on the 'myopia' of financial structures, which ex-post sometimes appear to reveal 'conservatism' and an anti-innovation bias – as it is often claimed, for example, in the British case – or, and, some other time, 'optimistic irrationality' – as Sahlman and Stevenson (1985) argue on the case study of the American disk drive industry.

Historically, observable financial systems differ also in the *ways* they seem to trade-off 'static efficiency' for 'evolutionary viability' and also in the apparent success in doing so. I propose that those historical conjectures mentioned earlier on the importance of financial structures for long-term economic performance are strictly consistent with the following propositions, namely: (a) different institutional set-ups, governing the exchange of ownership of real assets and the channels of corporate finance, embody also different balances between 'efficient selection' and innovative search, and (b) the institutional *modes* by which financial allocations occur affects both 'static' and 'Schumpeterian' efficiencies.

4. Financial institutions and innovative learning: A taxonomic exercise

On the grounds of the foregoing framework, one can highlight some dynamic properties of the two stylised 'market-based' and 'credit-based' financial systems sketched above. *First,* one may recall that 'market-based' systems tend to be relatively biased toward 'impersonal' exchanges of ownership titles; and 'credit-based systems toward more 'institutionalised'

---

[12]More on these points in Nelson and Winter (1982), Winter (1971), Eliasson (1986), Metcalfe (1986), Gibbons and Metcalfe (1990), Silverberg (1988), Dosi and Orsenigo (1988), Silverberg, Dosi and Orsenigo (1988).

ownership/control relationships. Moreover, in the latter, information flows tend to be more specific and restricted to particular suppliers and users of financial resources. Zysman (1983) applies Hirschman's dychotomy to financial systems and argues that the former mainly rely on *entry/exit* mechanisms of selection, while the latter rest on *'voice'* mechanisms, – that is, explicit purposeful intervention and guidance [Hirschman (1970)]. *Second*, the features of innovation, as from the earlier discussion, lend support to the conjecture that the processes of financial allocation themselves involve specific *competences* [Pelikan (1988)] which plausibly grow cumulatively over time, logically pre-exist information detection and guide its processing.

Thus, in credit-based systems learning is going to be relatively more important than selection. However, the 'paradigmatic' nature of knowledge (see earlier) generally implies that learning entails a powerful *exclusion effect*: Specific competences and 'visions' in a certain domain may well make it harder to see things in other directions. This property is often found in individual behaviours and, even more frequently, in collective organisations where 'knowledge' is also stored in repeated and rather sticky organisational routines. Hence, there may well be a trade-off between the 'width' of the information set that is processed in allocative decisions and the 'depth' of processing competences. Relatedly, one may expect some trade-off between the evolutionary efficiency of allocations by specialised financial operators – such as business-managing universal banks – along *rather established technological trajectories* versus their capability of allowing highly uncertain experiments on new technological paradigms.[13] Conversely, 'market-based' systems may be more conducive to the exploration of new technological paradigms whenever (a) innovative opportunities are high, and, *jointly,* (b) innovative competences are quite diffused throughout the economy.

These asymmetric allocative properties of financial systems may be possibly illustrated in the following way. Suppose that the environment is non-stationary, and consider two extreme possibilities. In environment A, learning by individual firms and by the financial operators which allocates funds to them is negligible. In turn this implies that, given non-stationarity, the innovative capabilities and economic performances of any one firm will, sooner or later, become worse ('less-fit') than some other newer firms. Thus, the evolutionary dynamics is led by a sort of pure selection process, whereby the mean performance of the system at any one time is a function of the efficiency at which selection (also financial selection) occurs. The performance dynamics is a function of the rate of entry of new firms and the distribution amongst them of fruitful innovations and 'mistakes'. All this involves the purest 'market-based' mode of financing. Only *common,* and low, *knowledge*

[13]See also Ergas (1986).

is available to financial investors and they can only assess incumbent companies by their past/present performances. No assessment at all is possible on entrants: investors can only spread risks by diversifying their portfolios.[14]

Conversely, consider environment B, wherein knowledge is quite specific and cumulative on both sides of firms and investors. Firms are so good that they possess powerful 'meta-rules' of innovative search which let them efficiently cope with non-stationary environments. Financial investors know that, and, in fact, are sharing part of that knowledge and steadily help in building it up. Unlike the previous case investors will not select allocations only on the grounds of current performances. Indeed, they may well see any current performance failure as 'bad luck', or as a learning investment for the future, or else as 'management mistakes' which call them to step in and take positive actions. Moreover, the relevant knowledge is highly idiosynchratic and specific to these agents. At the extreme, this is a pure 'learning mode', wherein variety and selection among agents would become redundant. In fact, it would be a sheer resource waste.

Long-term dynamism requires also the continuous exploration of new potential paradigms, new 'trajectories', new products. In that, trial-and-error processes of exploration are an important ingredient of technological progress. In some 'market-led' systems allocation to innovative search, insofar as the latter involves novel firms, have increasingly become institutionally separated: via venture capital markets. The latter are, in this light, an institutional innovation which augments the allocating competence of 'specialised' investors; reduces innovative uncertainty by spreading risks over investment portfolios; and institutionally separates *allocation-by-selection* among revealed performances and part of the *allocations-to-exploration*. In other more 'credit-based' countries, the financing channels are much less split-up. Banks are important for both processes and allocative criteria may differ. For example, in some countries much higher requirements on collaterals may be required for new innovative ventures.[15] Yet in other countries (e.g. Japan), the exploration of new products, processes and organisational arrangements is, to a good extent, *inbuilt* within the organisational routines/ strategies of established companies. Moreover, note that irrespectively of whether a financial system is nearer the 'credit-based' or the 'market-based' archetype, an overwhelming part of business-performed innovative search goes on in *established firms*. In turn, these firms normally access financial

---

[14]Of course, one must assume also that investors know that on large numbers the success of some companies will eventually reward their total investment.

[15]I come from a country, Italy, where it is not surprising to know that an innovative venture has been financed by mortgaging the houses of uncles and grandmothers ...

resources as whole entities and not with respect to individual projects. In different systems they may rely more on bankloans or, alternatively, on bonds, or retained profits, etc., but still, it is, e.g. General Motors, Siemens, ICI etc. which acquire a certain amount of financial resources on the grounds of their *global* performance. In relation to innovative learning, there are particularly good reasons for that, since part of the economic value of a successful search is precisely in that it remains private and appropriable.

Irrespectively of the institutional archetype, the 'Schumpeterian efficiency' of any one system requires that financial institutions operate a relocation of resources toward the new activities much quicker than that which would normally occur through the product markets. After all new technologies often start by occupying small but rapidly growing markets. Different institutional set-ups appear to do it in quite different ways: in market-based systems by quickly capitalising future revenues in the current stock exchange valuation; in credit-based systems, by an explicit targetting of resources. In that, opposite examples are the U.S.A. and Japan. Finally, the taxonomy of systems of financial allocation based on the relative importance of learning *versus* selection; voice *versus* exit; discretional *versus* non-discriminatory allocative rule may also be applied to intra-national differences. For example, irrespectively of whether a country tends to be more 'market-based' or 'credit-based', it seems plausible that bigger firms, quoted on the Stock Exchange, can have more access to non-discriminatory 'impersonal' channels of finance, while smaller firms (e.g. partnerships) ought to rely more on discretionary relationships with their providers of financial resources (e.g. banks or individual investors) and on 'voice' mechanisms of control.

5. On the evolutionary properties of different financial systems

Can one make general statements on the welfare properties of different architectures of the finance-industry links? How would one judge the relative efficiency of different combinations between the pure 'learning' and 'selection' modes? Obviously a satisfactory answer is enormously difficult to give. More modestly, let me simply consider some properties of these processes.

First, the more knowledge is asymmetric, appropriable, and 'scarce', the more also 'institutionalised' processes of finance allocation will be conducive to 'evolutionary viability'. Knowledge specificity and asymmetry are, in fact, plausibly higher in catching-up countries, and in the early phases of industrialisation. Indeed, rather formal bank-industry relationships have historically appeared to be the general case in industrialising countries, which often require long-term commitments of resources to the accumulation of technological competences, often despite absolute and comparative disadvantages and despite unfavourable short-term profitabilities, especially in the newest technological paradigms [Dosi (1988)].[16] *Second*, I suggest that a *necessary* (but *not sufficient*) condition for the 'Schumpeterian efficiency' of a 'market-oriented' system is that it must operate in a country which is on, or near, the 'technological frontier'. In these circumstances, current efficiencies of business units, as revealed by their economic results, may on average be a roughly unbiased predictor of their future learning potential *within the technological paradigms* whose knowledge they embody. Moreover, in countries on the technological frontier current profits often happen to be sufficient to finance growth and innovative efforts.

In general, one can hardly resolve the dilemma between processes of allocation which foster path-dependent learning on particular 'trajectories' and the seemingly 'wasteful' exploration of other ones. The former process – as B. Arthur and P. David show – may well present increasing returns, strengthen the microeconomic incentives to go further down the path, but, most likely, may also lock-in the system onto that path. And no one knows precisely what there could have been on another path without actually having walked on it for a while. There is no a priori reason to expect that a 'universal banker' (say, of the German type) who has a vested interest in the long-term viability of a particular company should allocate financial resources any worse – in terms of 'Schumpeterian efficiency' – than a market which can only allocate on the grounds of *average* performances and *common* knowledge. This, in fact, does not require financial institutions to 'know much more than the market' in terms of long-term perspectives of particular technologies. It simply requires them to know more about the internal competences, innovative projects, etc. of individual firms, which they are likely to do.

On the other hand, whenever there are plenty of (actual and perceived) opportunities around, and diffused capabilities of economically exploiting them, non-discretionary patterns of allocations are likely to be instrumental in exploring yet unknown 'paths'. Or, seeing it from the opposite angle, the more a 'credit-based' system needs to explore new paradigms, the *higher must also be the technological competences and strategic flexibility of both its firms and its interlinked financial institutions*. In essence, firms are required to 'simulate' internally to their organisations part of those processes of trial-and-error which in 'market-based' systems generally occur via much more 'decentralised' search endeavours, often associated with the emergence of new 'Schumpeterian' firms. In this respect, a good illustration of these points is the case of Japan as compared to the U.S.A.[17]

[16]Such an argument is also supported by those models showing the beneficial outcomes for economic growth of the 'pooling' of otherwise private information: See, e.g. Greenwood and Jovanovic (1988).

[17]On the Japanese firm as an 'innovative laboratory', cf., for example, Baba (1988), Aoki and Rosenberg (1987). Such differences in the patterns of development of new technologies is corroborated by industry case studies, e.g. microelectronics [Dosi (1984)].

In this perspective, one may also reinterpret the often-heard claims on 'stock-market short-sightedness'. Given market expectations inevitably based on revealed performances and common knowledge and beliefs, 'short-sightedness' does not necessarily require the inability of the market to correctly forecast future corporate performances. Corporate behaviours, may be 'rational', given the institutional context, but systematically neglect all those innovative opportunities involving high current learning costs and short-term fall in profitability. If all firms do that and investors interpret falls in profitability as sheer inefficiencies, then the market is indeed 'forecasting correctly'. This simply means that a sort of structural shortsightedness has become self-fulfilling in the system.[18] Conversely, one may plausibly conceive financial set-ups whereby evolutionary 'far-sightedness' is precisely the outcome of the *imperfection* of capital markets [Aoki (1988)]. That 'imperfection' may force upon financial institutions the burden of learning about the specific conditions under which resources are employed, and also impose a long-term commitment to the 'Schumpeterian viability' of firms whose future is interlinked with the future of the lenders themselves. Of course, there is no intrinsic necessity for financial markets to be always 'short-sighted', in the evolutionary sense used here. However, the degrees of 'short-' or 'far-sightedness' are unlikely to depend on the nature of the relevant common knowledge – plausibly quite low in any case –, but rather on the nature of *common beliefs*. Anecdotally, recall that it has often happened that drug companies were allowed quite high price/earning ratios because the general view embodied *a belief* in high innovative opportunities; or, recall the changing fashions by which the stock markets have reacted to varying propensities to invest in R&D.[19]

I have argued so far that different institutional arrangements governing the allocation of financial resources *may* indeed turn out to show roughly comparable degrees of overall 'Schumpeterian efficiency'. Of course, one can also find plenty of empirical examples where such a rough equivalence does not seem to be there. For instance, based on little more than an 'informed guess', I would pick the Italian and the British cases as illustrations of the worse of 'credit-based' and 'market-based' worlds. In the Italian case, a pattern of finance mainly based on discretionary allocations by banks does not seem to have fostered the development of particular competences of the latter. Thus, one has here the disadvantage of weak selection processes,

---

[18]For some empirical evidence along these lines, in a U.K.–Germany comparison, see Prais (1981). In general, and on the U.S.A. case, cf. B. Klein (1988).

[19]On 'market myopia', cf., e.g., Lorenz (1979), Carrington and Edward (1979), Crotty (1985). Interestingly, one may consider as a 'market myopia' also those cases where collective 'irrational' optimism eventually disappoints financial investors even though, it could be reasonably argued, foster rapid rates of innovation and, thus, 'Schumpeterian efficiency' for the industry as a whole [see, again, Sahlman and Stevenson (1985)].

without the advantages of cumulative allocative competences of financial institutions. The 'market-based' British case, while revealing all the dangers of 'short-sightedness' that such an arrangement entails, has not developed to any satisfactory degree mechanisms of allocation to innovative search, neither – until recently – to new ventures, nor through the internal rules of allocation of established firms.

The topics discussed so far re-appear also in relation to the internal organisation and strategies of individual firms, which face the same dilemmas between 'static' and 'Schumpeterian' efficiencies. Each firm, too, must embody procedures which makes it as efficient as possible in allocating resources to currently known employments, monitor current transactions, etc., but also procedures which allow it to adapt to future possibly unpredictable changes in the environment and produce these changes itself, by innovating. Since, as argued so far, no simple relationship can be postulated between current efficiency and innovative learning, each firm is likely to embody a *permanent tension* between its different behavioural rules. In particular, it is likely to embody different combinations between organisational procedures which 'make it good at doing what it is already doing', and procedures aimed at 'doing new things', or 'doing the same things in different ways'. Moreover, this tension is going to influence also the horizontal and vertical boundaries of each firm. In a work, currently in progress, by D. Rumelt, D. Teece, S. Winter and the author,[20] we interpret these varying boundaries in terms of three fundamental dimensions, namely (a) the *learning opportunities* offered by its core business(es); (b) the *degrees of path-dependency/cumulativeness* of such learning; (c) the *'toughness'* of the *selection environment(s)* in which the firm operates.

What do patterns of finance allocation have to do with all this? Some properties of different 'stylised' financial systems are outlined in table 1. *First*, financial structures affect the *selectiveness* of the environment of the firm and its rules of allocation to learning activities. Inevitably, firms embody varying degrees of 'efficiency slack'. Some of this slack may be 'progressive' in evolutionary terms in so far as apparently 'wasteful' activities are instrumental in the exploration of new market opportunities and also provide useful technological knowledge for other activities in which the firm is involved. Some slack is sheer inefficiency, shielded behind the 'indivisibility' of the firm. Well, one could expect that the more a system is 'market-based', the more it allows easy transfer of ownership claims, the more also it will increase environmental selection. Thus, over-diversified companies will be slowly

---

[20]Some preliminary results have been presented in Dosi, Teece and Winter (1987). Corroborating evidence can be found in Pavitt (1987), who independently developed a broadly similar interpretation.

Table 1

A taxonomy of features and properties of 'stylised' financial systems

Properties systems	'Market-based' systems	'Credit-based' systems
Selective pressure on the grounds of revealed performances	higher	lower
Trial-and-error processes through birth of new firms	higher	lower
'Voice' versus 'exit' processes of change	exit	voice
Opportunities of cumulative learning	lower	higher
Discretionality of allocative processes	lower	higher
Specialisation of competences by financial allocators	lower	higher
'Specialisation' versus diversification of incumbent firms	more specialisation	more diversification

weeded out, firms with below-average competitiveness will show a higher probability of being taken-over by other ones.[21]

However, this may only be part of the picture, since an increased volatility of ownership (i.e., a higher 'perfection' in the market for industrial assets) may also imply more ambiguous evolutionary effects. This leads to my *second* point. The potential conflict between 'static efficiency' and 'Schumpeterian efficiency', discussed above with reference to whole industries, may also apply at the level of individual companies. There are two clear cases in which this sort of trade-off occurs, namely: (a) whenever the protection of a certain ownership structure is amongst the management objectives, so that the firms employ resources simply to protect itself, and (b) whenever learning costs depress current profitability and the market is unable to capitalise future opportunities. Under these circumstances high levels of financial discipline may in fact jeopardise the long-term viability of a company or lower its future learning potential. Relatedly, I suggest that similar financial indicators across different financial systems entail quite different implications for dynamic performances. For example, the current rise of debt–equity ratios in U.S. companies might well have very different effects from the historically high debt ratios in Japan. In the latter a highly leveraged system has certainly been instrumental in financing rates of growth above the rates at

[21]This is, in my view, *part* of the story behind the recurrent waves of mergers and take-overs in the U.S.A. and other countries, probably favoured by financial innovations such as securitisation, etc. In turn, mergers and take-overs appear to have often led to *disintegration*, selling-off of non-core business, specialisation [Carlsson (1988)].

which cash flows were internally generated. In the U.S.A. the current debt growth may simply imply an increased emphasis on 'speculative' strategies, in the attempt of discovering/exploiting arbitrage opportunities on existing real assets or, conversely, building 'insurances' against supposed attempts of arbitrage by rivals. *Third*, and more generally, one would expect that, other things being equal, in credit-based systems, industrial growth will occur more via diversification of existing companies, while in market-based systems the pressure to specialise in highly profitable activities will be greater.[22]

One can presume that, in general, the more capital markets matter and the more 'efficient' they are, the higher also will be the pressure against uncompetitive activities and uncompetitive firms. However, from the point of view of long-term performances this higher market efficiency is not sufficient for normative judgements. Most likely, there is more than one pattern of corporate change that is evolutionarily viable and such viability cannot be presumed to bear a monotonic relationship with the 'perfection' of the markets in which the ownership titles of the companies are traded.

6. Conclusions

In this largely exploratory work, I have tried to suggest some conjectures on the properties of financial institutions in environments where innovations continuously occur, where 'opportunities are always there', and where the degrees to which agents actually exploit them are primarily constrained by their own capabilities. In turn, I have argued, the performance of financial systems must be assessed on the grounds of the double, and possibly conflicting, roles of selecting resource employments based on revealed relative efficiencies and fostering learning capabilities. In these non-stationary environments several of the properties identified by the economic analysis of imperfect information apply and are indeed amplified. Other properties emerge as the outcome of innovative activities. Forms of plausibly non-Bayesian learning and market 'disequilibrium' selection have a paramount importance. Also puzzling issues emerge. For example, no simple relationship can be established between the revealed efficiency of any one allocating system and its evolutionary performance. In that, finance is a crucial bridge between the present and the future, between what 'has proved to work' and the exploration of 'what is possible': The present work has tried to highlight some features of such tension between continuity and change, efficiency and mistake-ridden explorations, cumulative learning and discrete ruptures, and the importance of financial structures in all this.

---

[22]Some evidence showing the higher degrees of diversification of European and Japanese companies as compared to American ones is in Mariotti (1987).

References

Allen, P., 1988, Evolution, innovation and economics, in: Dosi et al., eds.

Amendola, M. and J.L. Gaffard, 1988, The innovative choice (Basil Blackwell, Oxford).

Aoki, M., 1986, Horizontal vs. vertical information structure of the firm, American Economic Review 76, no. 5, 971–983.

Aoki, M., 1988, Information, incentives and bargaining in the Japanese Economy (Cambridge University Press, Cambridge).

Aoki, M. and N. Rosenberg, 1987, The Japanese firm as an innovating institution, Paper presented at the IEA Roundtable Conference, Tokyo, Sept.

Arcangeli, F., P. David and G. Dosi, eds., 1990, Innovation diffusion (Oxford University Press, Oxford) forthcoming.

Arrow, K., 1983, Innovation in large and small firms, in: Ronen, ed.

Arrow, K., 1987, Technical information, returns to scale and the existence of competitive equilibrium, in: Groves, et al., ed.

Arthur, B., 1983, Competing techniques and lock-in by historical events. The dynamics of allocation under increasing returns, Laxenburg, IIASA, Working paper WP-83-90-; rev. ed: 1985 (Stanford University, Stanford, CA).

Arthur, B, 1988, Competing technologies: An overview, in: Dosi et al.

Atkinson, A.B. and J.E. Stiglitz, 1969, A new view of technological change, Economic Journal 79, no. 3, 573–578.

Baba, Y., 1988, The dynamics of continuous innovation in scale-intensive industries, Brighton, SPRU, University of Sussex, DRC Discussion paper; Presented at the 2nd Conference of the Schumpeter Society, Siena, Italy, May.

Cable, J., 1985, Capital market information and industrial performance: The role of West German banks, The Economic Journal.

Cameron, R., et al., 1967, Banking in the early stages of industrialization (Oxford University Press, Oxford).

Carlsson, B., 1988, The evolution of manufacturing technology and its impact on industrial structure: An international study, Paper presented at the 2nd Conference of the Schumpeter Society, Siena, Italy, May.

Carrington, J.C. and G.T. Edward, 1979, Financing industrial development (Macmillan, London).

Ciocca, P., 1982, Interesse e profitto (Il Mulino, Bologna).

Coricelli, F. and G. Dosi, 1988, Coordination, order in economic change, and the interpretative power of economic theory, in: Dosi et al., ed.

Crotty, J., 1985, Real and financial sector interaction in macromodels: Reflections on monocausal theories of investment instability; Paper presented at the Conference on 'The impact of technology labor markets and financial structures on economic progress and stability (Washington University, St. Louis, MO).

David, P., 1975, Technical choice, innovation and economic growth (Cambridge University Press, Cambridge).

David, P., 1985, Clio and the economics of QWERTY, American Economic Review. Papers and Proceedings 75, 332–337.

David, P., 1990, Narrow windows, blind giants and angry orphans: The dynamics of system rivalries and dilemmas of technology policy, in: Arcangeli et al., eds., forthcoming.

Day, R., 1984, Disequilibrium economic dynamics. A Post-Schumpeterian contribution , Journal of Economic Behavior and Organization 5, no. 1, 57–76.

Dosi, G., 1984, Technical change and industrial transformation (Macmillan, London; St. Martin Press, New York).

Dosi, G., 1988, Institutions and markets in a dynamic world, The Manchester School 56, no. 2.

Dosi, G., 1988a, Sources, procedures, microeconomic effects of innovation, Journal of Economic Literature, Sept.

Dosi, G. and M. Egidi, 1987, Substantive and procedural uncertainty. An exploration of economic behaviours in complex and changing environments, SPRU, DRC discussion paper (University of Sussex, Brighton).

Dosi, G., C. Freeman, R. Nelson, G. Silverberg and L. Soete, eds., 1988, Technical change and economic theory (Francis Pinter, London; Columbia University Press, New York).

Dosi, G. and L. Orsenigo, 1988, Coordination and transformation: An overview of structures, behaviours and change in evolutionary environments, in: Dosi et al., eds.

Dosi, G. and L. Orsenigo, 1988a, Industrial structures and technical progress, in: A. Heertje, ed., Technology, innovation and finance (Basil Blackwell, Oxford).

Dosi, G., L. Orsenigo and G. Silverberg, 1990, A self-organisation approach to innovation diffusion, in: Arcangeli et al., ed.

Dosi, G., D. Teece and S. Winter, 1987, Toward a theory of firm coherence, Presented at the conference on 'Technology and the enterprise in an historical perspective', forthcoming in: G. Dosi, R. Giannetti and P.A. Toninelli, eds., Technology and the enterprise in a historical perspective (Oxford University Press, Oxford).

Edwards, J., J. Franks, C. Mayer and S. Schaeffer, eds., 1986, Recent developments in corporate finance (Cambridge University Press, Cambridge).

Eliasson, G., 1986, The firm and financial markets (Almquist and Wicksell, Stockholm).

Ergas, H., 1986, Why do some countries innovate more than others?, Paper no. 5 (Center for European Policy Studies, Brussels).

Ergas, H., 1988, Financial/environmental interaction in a changing productive system (F. Angeli, Milan).

Freeman, C., 1982, The economics of industrial innovation, 2nd ed. (Francis Pinter, London).

Gerschenkron, A., 1953, Social attitudes, enterpreneurship and economic development, Explorations in entrepreneurial history.

Gibbons, M. and S. Metcalfe, 1990, Technological variety and the process of competition, in: Arcangeli et al., eds.

Gonenc, R., 1988, Capital market changes and corporate strategies (F. Angeli, Milan).

Greenwood, J. and B. Jovanovic, 1988, Financial development, growth and the distribution of income, Economic Research Report 88–12 (New York University, New York).

Grossman, S.J. and J.E. Stiglitz, 1980, On the impossibility of informationally efficient markets, American Economic Review 70, 393–408.

Groves, T., R. Radner and S. Reiter, eds., 1987, Information, incentives and economic mechanisms – Essays in honour of Leonid Hurwicz (Basil Blackwell, Oxford).

Hahn, F., 1987, Information, dynamics and equilibrium, Scottish Journal of Economics.

Hirschman, A., 1970, Exit, voice and loyalty (Harvard University Press, Cambridge, MA).

Hurwicz, L., 1989, Mechanisms and institutions, Paper presented at the IEA Roundtable, Tokyo, Sept.

Iwai, K., 1984, Schumpeterian dynamics. I: An evolutionary model of innovation and imitation, and II: Technological progress, firm growth and economic selection, Journal of Economic Behavior and Organization 5, no. 2, 159–190.

Jensen, M.C., et al., 1978, Symposium on some anomolous evidence regarding market efficiency, Journal of Financial Economics.

Kindleberger, C.P., 1983, Financial institutions and economic development: A comparison of Great Britain and France in the eighteenth and nineteenth centuries, Seminar paper no. 234 (Institute for International Economic Studies, Stockholm).

Klein, B., 1988, Luck, necessity and dynamic flexibility, in: H. Hanusch, ed., Evolutionary economics (Cambridge University Press, Cambridge).

Lorenz, C., 1979, Investing in success. How to profit from design and innovation, the Anglo-American foundation for the study of industrial society.

Mariotti, S., 1987, La diversificazione delle imprese industriali europee e statunitensi: Una comparazione, Economia e Politica Industriale.

Metcalfe, S., 1986, On technological competition, Mimeo. (Manchester University, Manchester).

Modigliani, F. and M.H. Miller, 1958, The cost of capital, corporate finance and the theory of investment, American Economic Review 48, no. 3, 261–297.

Nelson, R., 1981, Assessing private enterprise, Bell Journal of Economics.

Nelson, R., 1987, The roles of firms in technical advance: A perspective from evolutionary theory; Paper presented at the conference on technology and the enterprise in an historical perspective, Terni, Oct.; forthcoming in: G. Dosi, R. Giannetti and P.A. Toninelli, eds., Technology and the enterprise in a historical perspective (Oxford University Press, Oxford).

Nelson, R. and S. Winter, 1977, In search of a useful theory of innovation, Research policy.

Nelson, R. and S. Winter, 1982, An evolutionary theory of economic change (The Belknap Press of Harvard University Press, Cambridge, MA).

Nelson, R., S. Winter and H.I. Schuette, 1976, Technical change in an evolutionary model, Quarterly Journal of Economics.

Pavitt, K., M. Robson and J. Townsend, 1988, Technological accumulation, diversification and organization in U.K. companies, DRC discussion paper, SPRU, University of Sussex, Brighton.

Pelikan, P., 1988, Can the innovation system of capitalism be outperformed?, in: Dosi et al., eds.

Prais, S., 1981, Productivity and industrial structure (Cambridge University Press, Cambridge).

Radner, R., 1987, Decentralization and incentives, in: Groves et al., eds.

Ronen, J., ed., 1983, Entrepreneurship (Lexington Books, Lexington, MA).

Rosenberg, N., 1975, Perspectives on technology (Cambridge University Press, Cambridge).

Rosenberg, N., 1982, Inside the black box (Cambridge University Press, Cambridge).

Rybczynsky, T., 1974, Business finance in the EEC, U.S.A and Japan, Three Banks Review.

Sah, R.K. and J.E. Stiglitz, 1985, Human fallibility and economic organization, Papers and proceedings, American Economic Review.

Sahlman, A. and H.H. Stevenson, 1985, Capital market myopia, Journal of Business Venturing.

Scherer, F.M., 1986, Takeovers: Present and future advantages, Brookings papers on economic activity.

Schumpeter, J., 1934, The theory of economic development (Harvard University Press, Cambridge, MA).

Schumpeter, J., 1954, History of economic analysis (Allen and Unwin, London).

Silverberg, G., 1987, Technical progress, capital accumulation and effective demand: A self-organization model, in: D. Batten, J. Casti and B. Johansson, eds., Economic evolution and structural adjustment (Springer Verlag, Berlin).

Silverberg, G., 1988, Modeling economic dynamics, in: Dosi et al., eds.

Silverberg, G., G. Dosi and L. Orsenigo, 1988, Innovation, diversity and diffusion: A self-organisation model, Economic Journal.

Simon, H., 1982, On the structure of ill-structured problems, Artificial intelligence.

Stiglitz, J., 1982, Information and capital markets in financial economics, in: W. Sharpe and C. Lootner, eds., Essays in honor of P. Lootner (Prentice Hall, Englewood Cliffs, NJ).

Stiglitz, J., 1988, Learning to learn, in: P. Dasgupta and P. Stoneman, eds., The economic theory of technology policy (Cambridge University Press, Cambridge).

Stiglitz, J. and A. Weiss, 1986, Credit rationing and collateral, in: Edwards et al., eds.

Stiglitz, J.E., 1984, Information and economic analysis: A perspective, Economic Journal.

Stiglitz, J.E., 1985, Credit markets and the control of capital, Journal of Money, Credit and Banking 17, no. 2.

Summers, L.H., 1986, Do we really know that markets are efficient?, in: Edwards et al., eds.

Teece, D., 1982, Towards an economic theory of multiproduct firm, Journal of Economic Behavior and Organization 3, no. 1, 39–63.

Teece, D., 1988, Technological change and the nature of the firm, in: Dosi et al., eds.

Williamson, O., 1988, The economic institutions of capitalism (Free Press, New York).

Winter, S., 1971, Satisficing, selection and the innovative remnant, Quarterly Journal of Economics.

Winter, S., 1987, Natural selection and evolution, The new pelgrave: A dictionary of economics (Macmillan, London).

Zysman, J., 1983, Governments, markets and growth (Cornell University Press, Ithaca, NY).

[22]

Corporate Organization, Finance and Innovation[1]

MASAHIKO AOKI AND GIOVANNI DOSI

Introduction

This chapter deals with some theoretical issues concerning the relationship between financial institutions and business (non financial) corporations and its implications for innovation and other corporate behavior in contemporary economies. Let us introduce it with three broad empirical historical phenomena which are relevant. First, the forms of financing of production activities have changed impressively in most of the industrialized countries over the development process. Second, significant differences in financial institutions and in their relative importance among industrialized countries (and, more so, in developing countries) have persisted. Third, a widespread claim, albeit not uncontroversial as an accepted "stylized fact," is that different financial set-ups have historically been an important conducive factor, or alternatively an important obstacle, to industrialization and growth.

In relation to the foregoing issues, the following major theoretical questions emerge. What is the importance of financial institutions in long-term growth? Do they significantly influence the rates and patterns of resource allocation? How do they influence the rates and directions of innovation? How do they influence the forms of corporate organization? Did they evolve simply within a trend toward higher and increasingly common levels of efficiency? Can particular financial institutions be related historically with particular patterns of corporate organization and behavior? The financial institutions simultaneously play the roles of a provider of investment funds, a monitor of corporate behavior and management, and a selection mechanism for would-be innovative endeavors. Hence, one is likely to find in the relationship between finance and industrial activity a powerful influence on the performance and paths of evolution of different economic systems.

We shall propose a few theoretical hypotheses on the basis of some of the above questions. The two authors have converged on broadly similar and complementary perceptions of those questions, via different routes. One of us (Aoki) has extensively studied the information and incentive properties of diverse institutional arrangements for corporate firms. Specifically, the comparative organizational analysis of highly stylized "American" (A) and "Japanese" (J) firms has clarified some reasonable conditions under which either of them might perform better than the other in efficiency terms, due to different informational and incentive characteristics. Quite concise theoretical abstractions on the A and J firms as two polar archetypes, however, suggest a need for the extension of the analysis to cover other empirical cases. In this comparative organizational perspective, specific cultural traits and sociological variables, together with particular sequences of historical events, would certainly be considered fundamental to explaining why a particular set of organizational forms and rules emerged: but once they emerged, no matter what the historical reason, their workings may be analyzed in terms familiar to economists, i.e., equilibrium properties arising out of their information, incentive, and financial control characteristics (Aoki, 1986, 1988, 1990b). The other author (Dosi) has focused on the features of the processes of evolution, in particular on those features of technological and institutional innovation which are difficult to study in terms of their final equilibrium properties. On the bases of these different methodologies, however, we have come to a common appreciation, for instance, of the importance of a theoretical analysis of the permanent tension that each economic system embodies, between incentives and information flows which make it more or less efficient at performing a given set of tasks, versus its potential for discovering and developing new things (products, processes, forms of organization); or that of the differential influence of a variety of financial institutions upon the innovative behavior of business organizations.

This chapter is organized as follows: in the next section we shall review the general functions which corporate organizations, as well as markets, perform – to varying degrees and with varying success – irrespective of the particular institutional design. How do financial institutions influence those various functions of the firm? Preliminary to any answer to the question is, of course, a theoretical understanding of the internal structure and performance of the firm. In this regard we suggest that the framework of standard agency theory of the firm prevents a unified account of diverse links between finance and industry. The next section then attempts to develop what we believe to be a potentially richer theoretical framework, and examines the informational and incentive properties of different archetypes of organization and finance. The final section enlarges the proposed theoretical framework to account for innovation and environmental non stationarity.

Markets, Firms, and Finance: A Taxonomy of Functions and their Theoretical Interpretations

Whether economic activities occur through market exchanges or within organizations, they obviously involve a resource allocating function. Indeed, this property of economic interaction has been one of the central concerns of economic theory since its origin. However, as well as resource allocation, both markets and organizations perform other equally important functions. First, they involve a structure of information flows. Even the simplest exchange communicates information: after all, it is widely held that prices are a parsimonious device for communicating information in decentralized economic systems. This, however, applies under quite strict assumptions (e.g. market completeness and rational expectations). Moreover, the way information is distributed among agents affects their behavior: various sorts of asymmetric information models have highlighted the multiplicity of equilibria that can arise under different informational assumptions. In reality, things are even more complicated. Some information flows transit through the market. Many others do not; a lot of information flows occur within organizations. One can reasonably presume that the nature of such flows depends also on the structures of the organizations themselves, the "channels" they allow, the kinds of information they select. Also information flows are mediated between organizations by a variety of financial institutions. As a result, different financial systems are likely to generate different distributions of information across organizations.

Second, both markets and organizations involve incentive structures. Markets, in a Williamsonian terminology, involve "high power" incentives, in that they provide rather direct rewards and sanctions to economic behaviors. However, with asymmetric information and, more so, with environmental non stationarity, even market incentives are affected by information that the agents hold, their beliefs, their past experience, their problem-solving competences. A multiplicity of incentive structures is generated by the multiplicity of possible contractual arrangements. As illustrations, think of the different incentive structures associated with crop sharing versus land tenure (Stiglitz, 1974a), or in risk-sharing versus cost-plus contracts in R & D (Teece, 1988). Such a multiplicity of incentive structures is further expanded within organizations with different hierarchical ladders, promotion schemes, forms of reward, etc. Incentives for management at the apex of internal hierarchies may be varied depending on types of financial contracts provided by financial institutions.

Third, economic interaction involves forms of monitoring and control. Again, even if markets can be thought to provide more "high powered" forms of performance monitoring, this is not always so with asymmetric information: Akerlofs "market for lemons" is a good example (Akerlof, 1970). Within organizations, particular procedures of monitoring and control are associated with specific authority structures. Whether one believes (as most social scientists do) or not (as most economists do not) that power represents an autonomous dimension motivating behavior, it appears to hold that the variety of hierarchies in organizations implies differentiated criteria by which subordinates' behaviors are selected, performances are monitored, decisions are transmitted and implemented. Further, the variety of financial institutions exercises differentiated modes of financial control and monitoring on the behaviors and decisions of management at the apex of internal hierarchies.

Fourth, and finally, individuals and organizations learn, in the sense that they do not only refine their information about an unchanged external environment, but they also discover new products and production processes, new problems and new problem-solving rules. In a word, they innovate, and by doing so they also continuously change the environment in which they operate. Various financial institutions affect these evolutionary processes in differentiated ways by encouraging/discouraging different types of innovative activities on the part of individuals and organizations.

Let us emphasize that most of the economic theories of the firm have not dealt consistently with the entire set of functions as enumerated above and, less so, with the observed variety in their institutional arrangements of business organizations combining these functions.

The Marshallian tradition largely focuses on the allocative properties of the firm, whose very existence is justified mainly in terms of some asset indivisibilities and (bounded) economies of scale. Incentives and information issues are largely neglected.

The new contractual approach to the study of the firm, in which the firm is regarded as a nexus of principal-agency contracts involving investors, employees, and business partners, has made inroads since the early 1970s. What are the information and control relationships among these contracts? How are the incentives of agents aligned in the nexus? Agency theory regards the incentive content of contracts forming a nexus as essentially preconditioned by markets, in the sense that reservation utilities of contracting partners are exogenously given, and the pecuniary rewards for the supply of resources are *ex ante* specified in contracts, except for one class of contracting partners. This exception applies to residual claimants who receive the residual after all other contractual payments are made, that is, stockholders in the case of publicly held corporations. Because of their unique position, residual claimants are regarded as accountable as the principal designer of the nexus of contracts for the purpose of efficiency. However, details of management and operating decisions need not be specified in contracts, and the drawing of actual contracts with other agents may be delegated to management, if management is effectively placed under market-oriented financial control. This can be done in the following hierarchical order.

First, top management may be controlled directly through the board of directors providing proper incentive contracts for managers and monitoring management decisions on behalf of residual claimants. But who monitors the monitor? There is the market for corporate control (i.e., the selection of the board) and, if the incumbent board fails to meet stockholders' interests, takeover discipline may be imposed on it. Thus corporate management decisions of the firm, such as on investment, employment, corporate finance and the like, are assumed to be effectively controlled in the direction of maximizing the present value of residuals. Management control over operating activities, in turn, may be hierarchically decomposed by means of hierarchical layers of incentive contracts. At a higher level, management acts as a surrogate for residual claimants (the principal) *vis-à-vis* management at a lower level, as well as outside agents such as suppliers and distributors. At the bottom level of the hierarchy, operating employees control only their own effort level, within the framework of incentive contracts provided by management.

The assumed information structure within the hierarchical nexus is roughly as follows: in designing incentive contracts, the principal is supposed to know *ex ante* the probability distribution of relevant events affecting the outcome of the agent's action, whereas only the agent is able to have access *ex post* to the eventual realization of events. The prior knowledge of the principal may be thought as deriving from formal learning exogenous to the nexus, as well as from the principal's own higher order decisions that shape the action environment of the lower level. Because of this information asymmetry, any incentive-compatible contract has to accrue information rents to the agent who has on-site information regarding its action environment. But within this inevitable "agency loss," the principal may be able to control the agent's action in its own interests by properly designing incentive schemes consistent with market constraints. Thus, according to principal–agency theorists, the firm is nothing but a "legal fiction which serves as a focus for processes in which conflicting objectives of individuals are brought into equilibrium within a contractual framework" (Jensen and Meckling, 1976). Actions of agents are induced by incentive contracts consistent with market competition, and the control-monitoring function of the firm is only tacit.

Interestingly, Coase (1988), regarded as the pioneer of the contractual approach, recently criticized such a state of contractual theory. He held that because of contractual theorists' preoccupation with the incentive provision function of the firm, another important aspect of the firm, i.e., "organizational coordination" – which saves on costs of market transactions – has largely been left unexplored. Coase maintains that this gap is undesirable, and unsatisfactory for understanding "the institutional structure of production in the system as a whole." In the nexus-of-contracts approach, hierarchical ordering of information distribution and flow within the firm seems to be taken for granted: on the contrary, we argue later that modern firms need to be analyzed within a richer informational variety.

From the evolutionary perspective, the neglect of explicit treatment of the specificities of control/authority mechanisms associated with organizational hierarchies is equally unsatisfactory. Even if one accepts that any one particular organizational structure has emerged as the result of some original contractual process, one must at least admit that, thereafter, this same structure has some inertia: it is largely event-independent, and resilient to recontracting on the grounds of subsequent information acquired by the contracting parties. Indeed, with generalized asymmetric information and transaction costs, Williamson's model has shown that discretionary behavior within the context of hierarchies may outperform markets precisely because of their irreversibility features. Relatively sticky organizational rules moderate the risk of opportunistic behavior by introducing some combination of incentives and administrative control, with limited recontracting possibilities.

Finally, we want to emphasize the almost complete neglect in most contemporary industrial organization theories of the specificities of competences and skills that each firm embodies and that obviously affect performances. It is true that some competence-related issues have been addressed in "human capital" models and in "incentives-to-learn" models. However, a fundamental dimension is still missing, namely those relatively tacit and changing organizational capabilities which cannot be imputed to individual workers, but, rather, are the collective outcome of particular interactive procedures within the firm. As one of us has discussed at greater length elsewhere (Dosi, Teece and Winter (1991)), this lack of attention to specific firm competences impedes any satisfactory analysis of the innovative capabilities of different firms. Somewhat complementarily, as the other author has shown, it also obscures one of the main sources of differential performance between firms and countries (Aoki, 1986, 1990b).

Our endeavor, in the following, is to proceed some modest steps toward a deeper theoretical understanding of the nature of the firm, which can account for the coexistence of the functions discussed above in a unified framework and recognize an observable variety of their combination. In doing so, we specifically emphasize the following points:

(a) Different patterns of business organization and different modes of interaction with other agents imply diverse combinations amongst those functions, and thus different performances. There might be some different organizational designs which are roughly equivalent in terms of performance. However, others may be shown to present specific or general "inferior"/"superior" characteristics.

(b) An intrinsic tension may appear amongst the above organizational functions: in particular between those combinations which are conducive to relatively high performances on the grounds of current technologies and markets, and those other combinations which are more conducive to learning and innovation, possibly at the expense of current performances.

(c) The modes of financing and the link between business firms and various financial actors influence the ways firms combine their various functions, and also their long-term innovative success.

Coordination, Incentives, and Financial Control

There are alternative ways to represent different institutional combinations of the functions performed by the firm, depending on particular methodological inclinations. Even the authors of this work have pursued the inquiry with rather different approaches. One of us has interpreted the general properties of the firm in terms of outcomes of bargaining games. That is, the distribution of quasi-rents arising out of firm-specific coordination are subject to explicit/implicit bargaining among constituent members of the firm. Therefore institutional interdependence between, for example, employees, corporate management, other firms, and financial institutions, needs to be explicitly specified. Some institutional arrangements may be able to approximate the rational outcome as described by the cooperative game theory under certain environmental conditions, but others may not (Aoki, 1986).

The other author has been inclined to a much more "institutionalist" representation of business organizations, with more emphasis on "routinization" and on the role of extraeconomic, highly inertial, variables as guides to economic behavior (Dosi, 1984, 1988a; Dosi and Orsenigo, 1988). Organizations are viewed, following Nelson and Winter (1982), as involving also some sort of "truce" between conflicting interests: hence, the precarious status of any incentive-compatibility that is possibly achieved, and also a big allowance for "disequilibrium" behavior.

However, for the purposes of this chapter, the two views are not inconsistent and somewhat complement each other, in that together they highlight the economic properties of specific institutional arrangements as well as the "rationality" of different micro-behaviors under different organizational set-ups. For our purposes here it does not matter whether one believes that some contractual agreements between rational individuals are the ultimate "philosophical" foundation of organizations, or alternatively that various institutions "philosophically" exist prior to the individual perception of self-seeking goals, and shape their "economic rationality." What is crucial is that different behaviors may be informationally feasible and incentive-compatible under different forms of economic organization. Hence, no matter what the general theoretical preference, one may take any comparative exercise on the equilibrium performance of different organizational regimes, at least as a "thought experiment" on the economic viability of particular institutional developments.

With these premises, let us proceed to a simple comparative analysis by presenting archetype models of a combination of internal coordination, incentives, and financial control (and innovation in the next section), and compare them with the alternative principal/agent model discussed in the previous section. This analysis is inspired by the comparative analysis of stylized archetypes of the "American" and the "Japanese" firm discussed by one of the authors (Aoki, 1986, 1988, 1990b). However, the following presentation may suggest a broader applicability of the analysis than to those two extreme archetypes.

Coordination: hierarchies versus knowledge-sharing

First, we compare two archetype modes of internal coordination of activities pursuing given strategic business decisions on investment, sales targets, etc. (We will consider modes of financial and other possible controls over strategic business decision later.) Suppose that predetermined strategic decisions need to be implemented as a joint effort by multiple subunits of an organization (say, a chain of shops), technologically mutually interrelated. The costs of each shop performing a certain task depend upon uncertain events. In order to achieve the overall organizational goal most efficiently, however, it is not necessarily good for each shop to select the cost-minimizing method of doing its own task in a decentralized way, for this might overburden other shops. The choice of operating methods by individual shops must be coordinated.

One archetype mode of coordination, which we call the hierarchical mode and shall refer to as the *H-mode*, is implicit in the agency model of the firm, and its essence may be reiterated simply as follows. Management has knowledge concerning the prior probability distributions of events affecting the cost conditions of shops, and chooses the tasks for all shops that will jointly minimize the total expected cost of achieving the strategic goal. Each shop is required to perform the task chosen by management. As events evolve, the chosen set of tasks may not achieve *ex post* the minimization of total cost. But since there has been already an effort to minimize such discrepancy, operating task should proceed as planned and *ex post* information available at shops is to be communicated to (or be monitored by) management for the revision of its subjective probability distributions of events, which may be utilized only for the improvement of next-round centralized planning.

An alternative archetype mode is more participatory. Suppose that the centralized planning by management only sets a preliminary framework for actual operations of each shop. Suppose that, as time goes by, each shop utilizes its own observation on-site for the revision of its prior probability distribution of events (in a Bayesian manner) and communicates this information horizontally with other shops (possibly with the help of centralized communication facilities) for the purpose of fine-tuning the coordination of tasks. This coordination mode based on information sharing, referred to as the *S-mode*, can improve on cost performance per time because of better utilization of on-site information. Such gains cannot be without cost, however. The participation of each shop in learning (the revision of prior distributions) and communications involves costs in terms of effort expenditure, and the diversion of attention to non-routine kinds of operations, including possible bargaining among shops over operational coordination.

Thus, the contrast of two archetype modes involves a tension almost universally present in any organization, i.e. the tension between economies of specialization (specialization in specific operational tasks as well as the separation of planning and operational tasks), versus gains from learning and knowledge-sharing. The comparative analysis of informational efficiency of the two modes has been recently tried by various authors (Aoki, 1986, 1990b; Cremer, 1990; Itoh, 1987). According to those studies, the H-mode outperforms the S-mode when operational environments for shops are relatively stable or drastically changing. In both cases, decentralized learning may not add so much information value (saving of costs), and the sacrifice of economies of specialization may not be worthwhile. In the intermediate case where environments are continually changing (but in relatively recognizable ways), the S-mode may outperform the H-mode, provided that the learning capability of each shop and the communicability among shops are high enough. In this case, gains from decentralized learning and knowledge-sharing may be greater than losses from the sacrifice of economies of specialization.

In actual organizations, elements of both H-mode and S-mode may be combined in varying degrees and in complex ways. However, the results of a comparative analysis based on simple archetype models is not entirely devoid of empirical implications. For example, the American automobile and steel industries, which dominated world markets up to the end of the 1960s with a relatively small set of homogeneous products, predominantly exhibited aspects of the H-mode, whereas the Italian textile and garment industry, as well as the Japanese automobile and steel industries, attuned to small-to-medium batch production of a large variety of products, predominantly exhibit aspects of the S-mode. We shall postpone discussion of the implications for innovation to the next section.

Incentives: markets versus promotional hierarchies.

As discussed in the previous section, the essence of the incentive structure captured by the agency model of the nexus of contracts is its market orientation, in spite of its preoccupation with incentive design. It is assumed that there is only one type of residual claimant, and the agency theory explores various types of incentive schemes precisely to extract the maximum residual, while guaranteeing the exogenously determined expected utility levels for agents. The market-oriented incentive mode, referred to as the *M-mode*, may be thought as being well aligned with the H-mode of coordination, because the information efficiency of the latter depends upon specialized skills of operation and planning. Specialized skills which can be acquired through formal training and are universally applicable may be supplied through well-defined job markets. If an agent can acquire a firm-specific information-processing capacity (skill) through internal training, the principal may have to accrue information rent to the agent in designing an incentive-compatible contract. However, the principal can offer long-term contracts to newcomers such that the amount equivalent to the discounted present value of the information rent is extracted as a training cost in the training period (Riordan, 1990), since the new agent does not have any bargaining power to prevent the principal from doing so before the acquisition of firm-specific skills themselves.

Conversely, as soon as elements of the S-mode of coordination set in, the exclusive reliance on the archetypical M-mode of incentive structure becomes problematic. Since the S-mode involves inter-shop communication of learned results by shops (or employees) to coordinate their operations, the information-value net of training and communication costs created by the S-mode is of a collective nature, and not decomposable into individual contributions. In other words, the skills of participants in the S-mode can be accumulated and are useful only within the context of the S-mode and may be appropriately characterized as "network-specific" (as distinguished from "firm-specific," Mailath and Postlewaite, 1990). Accordingly, market-transferable, individual contracts cannot be written *ex ante* for individuals.

An archetype model of incentive structure combined with the archetype S-mode coordination may be constructed in two steps: the collective level and then the individual level. First, and collectively, the net information value created by the S-mode may be subject to internal distribution between the participants of the S-mode (the employees of the firm) as a whole, on one hand, and the "firm," on the other. Since the net information value can be generated by the active involvement of all employees in learning on-site, and by communications among themselves, they are likely to have credible collective bargaining power for a share in the value by the threat of withdrawal of cooperation (Aoki, 1990a). Conversely, if the information value is to be snatched away by the competitors of the firm unless the evolving information is utilized effectively on-site as well as between shops, it is incentive-compatible for both the employees and the firm immediately to agree on the sharing of information value to be created and cooperatively to engage in the S-mode of coordination (Binmore, Rubinstein and Wolinsky, 1986).

An interesting question is why the employees cannot appropriate the whole value of the network by themselves. Why cannot they purchase the network (the S-mode) collectively and replicate it, guaranteeing themselves the whole value? Mailath and Postlewaite (1990) pose this question and argue that, if there are intangible benefits which individual employees receive from the "firm" and which are not verifiable by each other, a share of the information-value created by the network is likely to go to the firm, as the size of the network becomes larger. There are many possibilities for the emergence of such intangible benefits. The firm's provision of the incentive-monitoring mechanism for individual performance within the S-mode may in fact realize such a possibility. That is, the guarantee of a share in information value to the employees as a whole does not automatically induce the level and kind of efforts by individual shops and employees appropriate for the efficient operation of the S-mode. Individuals may try to free-ride, whereas individual shops may develop and assert their own group-centric goal (a larger share in information value) wastefully, taking up time and resources. The collective sharing of information-value needs to be supplemented by a proper mechanism for monitoring individual performance.

In order to achieve individual efforts appropriate for the S-mode which are incentive-compatible, the incentive-monitoring mechanism needs to have the following properties. First, since the S-mode relies upon decentralized information-processing (and problem-solving) based on knowledge sharing, participating employees need to be encouraged to develop information processing capacities appropriate for a specific network built in the firm (learning). Second, shops and individuals need to be encouraged to cooperate and to restrain the assertion of subgroup-centric interests. As Koike has emphasized in a series of works (1984, 1988) in the Japanese context, the nurturing of network-specific skills in general, and the capacity for problem-solving on-site in particular, may require a wider-range understanding of the working of the network. Skills versed only in a specific component task of the organization may not contribute to the informational efficiency of the S-mode as under the H-mode. Such wider-range understanding may be nurtured by experiencing various interrelated tasks, through the rotation of jobs. The rotation of employees between shops may also facilitate knowledge-sharing among shops, and restrain the development of an egocentric coherent subgroup.

One possible way to encourage wide-range learning and cooperative efforts may be to create promotional hierarchies of ranks (there may be multiple hierarchies for various job categories, such as clerical employees, blue-collar employees, engineers, etc.) and administer them from the organizational perspective. Suppose that new employees not trained for network-specific skills are placed at the bottom rank of an appropriate hierarchy and that they are promoted to higher ranks over time according to their learning achievements evaluated in relatively wide dimensions as well as their cooperative contributions (e.g. in teaching junior employees, communications ability, teamwork, etc.). A particular level of compensation and other benefits is associated with each rank, but not with a specific task. Imagine that employees are rotated over various jobs through administrative assignments by the management. Employees of the same rank may be assigned to different tasks, while employees assigned to the same tasks may be of different rank because of differences in general learning achievements. There are elements of seniority in ranking, because learning takes time. But employees of the same job tenure may well be ranked differently according to their learning achievements. One who fails to progress in rank hierarchy, because of failure in learning and/or poor cooperativeness may be ousted from the rank hierarchy and have to seek another job elsewhere. Since this might represent a negative signal concerning the person's qualities, he might be unable to obtain another position of equivalent rank, and a substantial loss in income may be inflicted upon him. Thus the organizational "administration" of rank hierarchies and job assignments might function as an effective incentive-monitoring mechanism to induce learning and cooperation useful for the S-mode (MacLeod and Malcomson (1986)). Let us denote this mechanism as the *R-mode*.

It may be appropriate to comment here on the so-called "internal labor market," as this is often confused with the R-mode incentive structure. It is certainly true that both share a feature, in that employees are made mobile among jobs within the firm. But the internal labor market is characterized by "job ladders," i.e. the progression over mutually related but well-defined job categories, not by mere ranks of pay and status. Also, the mobility of employees over job ladders is realized by the matching of the posting of vacant jobs by the employer with the applications of employees. Only if there is an excess of demand for jobs by equally qualified employees is selection to be made on the basis of seniority. On the other hand, only when the supply of jobs exceeds the internal supply, the market is made open externally. In the R-mode, on the contrary, task assignments as well as rank assignments are administered by the personnel department of the firm. For these reasons, the internal labor market may be classified as a variant of the M-mode, rather than of the R-mode.

There tends to be a rigidity in the level of employment under the R-mode, as it is designed to promote internal learning over time. Within this rigid framework, however, employees' skills may be flexibly utilized because of the relative ease of rotation and transfer of employees through administrative job assignment. On the other hand, the M-mode incentive system can be relatively flexible in the adjustment of employment, as it can absorb and release workers through labor markets as needs arise. Conversely, the internal reallocation of employees is rigidly limited, as job categories are defined in external labor markets. We will discuss below some implications of the rigidity–flexibility dilemma in terms of innovative activities of the firm under each mode.

As in the case of the coordination mechanism, real-world firms tend to combine elements of both archetype modes of incentive structure. Generally speaking, however, in Western economies the incentive systems tend to be relatively more characteristic of the M-mode, whereas in Japan the R-mode tends to dominate.

Modes of finance and corporate control: markets versus banks

It has been argued by several authors that, historically, one can distinguish between two basic modes of finance-industry links, often classified as the market-oriented system and as the bank (credit)-oriented system (Rybczynsky, 1985; Berglof, 1990; Dosi, 1990). In the market-oriented system, historically approximated by Britain and the USA, ownership titles are traded relatively freely on stock markets, and variations in the stock values are taken to represent the main impersonal disciplining mechanism on corporate behavior. Growth is financed mainly through retained profits and, to a lesser extent, by bonds and new equity issues. In the bank-oriented system, historically observed in Continental Europe and in Japan, banks and other financial organizations have played a more direct role in industrial growth. They have holdings of company shares, and their holdings are relatively stable and concentrated; the ratio of bank credit to total assets of the nonfinancial corporate sector is relatively high, and a "voice" mechanism of control – in Hirschman's terminology – is often exercised to influence the strategic decisions of management. Recently, as the internally accumulated financial resources of nonfinancial companies have grown, the importance of bank credits in financing growth, as well as the frequency and strength of the banks' "voice," have tended to decline, but stable stockholding on the part of banks still insulates corporate firms in the bank-oriented system from hostile takeovers through the market for corporate control.

Let us discuss the finance–firm links in terms of financial control over strategic decisions of the firm by distinguishing four archetype modes – the M-mode, as envisioned in the agency theory discussed in the foregoing section, an RB-mode, a WB-mode and an SB-mode, which are introduced below.

The now classic treatment by Modigliani and Miller of finance theory distinguishes debt financing and equity financing only in terms of return characteristics (i.e., fixed returns with a probability of default, versus residual claim). As is well known, they argued that in the absence of taxes, and with perfectly competitive markets, the choice between these two methods of finance does not matter, from the viewpoint of stockholders. Implicit in this claim is the assumption that the inside manager who enters into debt contracts (possibly in the form of a bond) is the agent of stockholders. But are bank credits essentially the same as bond issues from the viewpoint of corporate control? The Modigliani-Miller theory assumes that there is a clear-cut point of bankruptcy, at which stockholders' control and liquidation are separated. But it is often observed that bankruptcy does not necessarily lead to liquidation, but rather to reorganization attempts by specialists (often the bank as creditor cum stockholder). How can we analyze the implications of this phenomenon?

Recently Aghion and Bolton (1988) have suggested an interesting incomplete contract model of finance, trying to answer these and other questions. They argue that the essence of debt contracts does not lie in their return characteristics, as commonly believed, but in the *ex ante* arrangements regarding the distribution of control. As long as good profitability continues, the outside investor (the bank) does not intervene, and the inside manager keeps managing; otherwise the outside investor (bank) takes over management and reorganizes or liquidates. Within the specific context of their model, they showed that such a contract can achieve *ex ante* Pareto optimality when the inside manager has a strong preference for carrying on business as usual (rather than "liquidating" in a bad profit state or "innovating" in a good profit state). An external investor with control rights may be excessively "innovative" in good profit states (as in the case of a takeover raider), while inside management may try to survive wastefully on other people's money in bad profit states. Indeed, Aghion and Bolton's model of debt contracts captures some important elements of financial control in a "mature" bank-oriented system in which, in the normal state of affairs, the bank's voice within the corporate governance structure is not loud, and inside managers' discretionary power is strong, while in crisis situations the bank's power becomes visible and plays an essential role in the reorganization or liquidation of failing companies. In such a bank-oriented system, the takeover of failing companies can occur, but takeover is usually exercised by banks, rather than occurring via the market for corporate control, as in market-oriented systems. Thus the financial control mode, in which there is an *ex ante* agreement between management and the bank about the transfer of control contingent upon profit states as described by Aghion and Bolton, may be distinguished from *relational banking*, which we often observe in developing countries. In the latter setting, banks are often owned and controlled by industrialists, and are used as instruments for raising funds for their firms. Moreover, risk diversification is limited in such circumstances. We refer to this relational banking system as the *RB-mode*, which, for our purposes, also includes all those cases where a bank formally owns one or a few firms, but is completely "tied-in" with them: the future of the bank goes together with the fortune of the companies with which it is linked. On the other hand, in the developed banking system *à la* Aghion and Bolton, not only control rights shift between banks and industrial firms, depending upon the latter's wealth position, but also banks normally diversify their lending among many industrial firms. We refer to this system as the *WB-mode* (the weak bank control mode). Finally, we refer to those banking systems in which strong financial control by banks is exercised over industrial firms regardless of the latter's wealth position as the *SB-mode* (the strong bank control mode).

Types of modal combination

Empirically, one can easily observe varying combinations among the dichotomic organizational characteristics discussed so far. Some of these combinations may turn out to be plausibly "inferior" to others in efficiency terms, but they can historically persist, due precisely to that same institutional inertia which makes the continuity of "superior" combinations easier. Among "superior" ones, however, there may not be simple ranking. One combination may be superior in certain technological, market and cultural conditions, but not in others. It is quite likely, therefore, that any observed structure of a corporate economy will be quite complex, barring simple stylizations. However, let us list a few representative archetypical combinations below, at the risk of oversimplification, in an attempt to provide a sort of comparative taxonomy.

(a) H-M-M. This is the combination of the hierarchical internal coordination with the market-oriented incentive structure and market-based financial control. This archetype is the one which more closely corresponds to the model of the firm as a nexus of agency contracts discussed in the previous sections, and may be referred to as the A-model of the firm hereafter. One may say that this model represents a sort of "neoclassical image" of Anglo-American firms.

(b) H-M-RB. The H-mode internal coordination and the M-mode incentives are combined with "relational" banking. One is likely to observe something similar to this combination in several developing countries (authoritarian coordination, segmented and localized labor markets, and oligarchic industrial control), which tend to hinder participating behavior on the part of the labour force and to make firm-specific development of skills more difficult, while fostering collusive rent-seeking strategies by firms.

(c) H-R-SB. This is the combination of hierarchies in both coordination and incentives (rank hierarchies) with strong bank control. If banks degenerate into a single monolithic national system, this model may come somewhat to resemble the socialist firm (the S-model) under central planning. Note that, for corporate organizations to be effective (in terms of whatever organizational goals) while at the same time utilizing individual initiatives, they may need to combine centralization (the H-mode or the R-mode) and decentralization (the S-mode or the M-mode) in coordination and incentives. If the coordination mechanism and incentive structures are both centralized, as in this model, organizations may be stifled by bureaucratic burdens and lack of individual initiative. Moreover, in the single monolithic banking system, the allocation of financial resources is apt to be guided by political expediency, and financially failing firms are often salvaged by refinancing, leading to an excessive survival rate for inefficient firms, a phenomenon known as the "soft-budgeting problem" (Kornai, 1980).

(d) S-R-WB. The S-mode mechanism of internal coordination and the R-mode incentive structure are combined with the WB mode of financial control. This combination is related to the archetypical Japanese model (the J-model) as developed by one of the present authors (Aoki, 1988, 1990b), but it need not be limited to it. We have already mentioned that the S-R combination is effective for the development of network-specific skills geared towards continually changing market and technological environments. But what about its combination with the WB-mode? Is it accidental or not? Whose interests does the "inside" manager represent in the J-model? We argue, first, that the combination is essential and second, that the "inside" manager represents the dual interests of financial investors and employees embodying network-specific skills.

Let us begin with the first proposition. You will recall that in the S-mode coordination, within the framework of strategic decisions, problem-solving is delegated to the lower level of functional hierarchy, while relatively free communication among constituent units at the lower level is practiced. However, in order to guarantee that the constituent units at the lower level do not engage in collusive behavior aimed at rent-seeking, sacrificing the organizational strategic goals, the actions of lower units must be properly monitored. This monitoring requires more than just checking whether they perform hierarchically decomposed directives. It needs to be assessed whether economically meaningful information is created and efficiently utilized on a shared basis at the lower level. In turn, on the side of monitoring, this requires the knowledge of how the internal information network operates. Such knowledge may be most effectively nurtured by the experience of active participation in the network. Under the M-mode of financial control, however, top management is likely to be selected from the "external" market of managers, separated from the internal network of information. Thus, from the information-monitoring point of view, the WB-mode of financial control, which assures the control of the internal management on the conditions of internal informational efficiency, is more likely to be consistent with the S-mode of internal coordination.

Second, note that for rank hierarchies to work as an effective incentive mechanism, it is desirable that ranks extend "indefinitely" upward. If progression in rank hierarchy is known to cease at a certain rank, shirking may occur at that point (e.g. in the form of the lack of effort sometimes observed among middle management in the S-firm). Of course, the indefinite extension of rank hierarchy in a literal sense is not feasible. Suppose, nonetheless, that internal rank hierarchy could extend up to the top management. What about the incentives of top management then? We have suggested that under the WB-mode of financial control the degree of discretionary power of top management is positively correlated with the level of profit. Top managers of J-model firms are thus likely to be engaged in competition over profit ranking, subsequent to the successful completion of internal competition over promotion. Competition over ranking is thus made open-ended through the combination of the R-mode of incentive structure with the WB-mode of financial control.

Let us now turn to the second proposition. We have already argued that some sharing of the net value of information is more likely in the S-R combination. But strategic management decisions – such as on investment, diversification, and employment levels – obviously exert an impact on the lifetime earnings of employees by affecting their positions in rank hierarchies in the short run as well as in the long run. Therefore it is rational for them to negotiate with management regarding possible trade-offs between the current pay level, the level of their own effort, and, generally, management policy decisions. Such negotiation may be in the interests of investors as well. The "negotiation" between the financial investor and employees need not be direct and explicit, but may be mediated by management. In fact, we can prove the following interesting result: if, on the one hand, employees are committed to the level of effort expenditure at which total information value (albeit not their share therein) net of the total disutility from work is maximized, and, if, on the other hand, management strikes some balance in its decisions between the interests of financial investors (as represented by the bank) and employees – with distributive shares as weights – then, from the viewpoint of both financial investors and employees, Pareto efficient and incentive-compatible outcomes are likely to emerge (as it approximates the generalized Nash bargaining solution cum subgame perfect equilibrium; cf. Aoki, 1986, 1988).

Note that in the WB-mode, the bank cum stockholding does not place pressure on management for continual share price maximization, yet is committed to the supply of financial resources as far as the delivery of satisfactory yields, defined in the debt contracts, is secured. On the other hand, internally promoted management may be more effective in identifying employees' interests and their bargaining power in striking some balance of interests between them and the shareholders.

Forms of Corporate Organization, Finance and Innovation

So far, we have suggested that different institutional combinations between modes of coordination, incentives, and financial control may well lead to different forms of behavior and economic performance of firms. This is even more so if one allows for the innovative activities of business firms. Already, in the previous section, we have considered the potential for learning under different organizational set-ups. However, we purposely limited the representation of "learning" to those activities involving information-processing, somewhat akin to Bayesian procedures of estimating random variables with stationary means and finite variance. What happens if there is some largely unknown dynamic in these variables, or if agents may "create" new events by their own actions? After all, as argued elsewhere (Dosi, 1990), these are precisely the consequences of innovative activities. More formally, these activities imply the discovery and/or the adjustment to events which *ex ante* are "unique" (and thus hardly allow Bayesian learning) and are not enumerable.

In dynamic terms, firms are required to develop skills allowing them to explore an ever-expanding opportunity domain (Dosi and Orsenigo, 1988; Nelson and Winter, 1982; Amendola and Gaffard, 1988). In turn, these skills may be highly specific to particular technological tasks and particular networks within firms. They may well seem redundant and uneconomical on the grounds of given technological and market conditions, yet still be crucial to the long-term viability of a firm. Here, a possible tension emerges between short-term performance optimization regarding existing products and known technologies, on the one hand, and learning about radically new opportunities, on the other. Contemporary firms always face some aspects of this dilemma and try to deal with it in ways that can hardly be managed, *ex ante*, with optimizing criteria. Rather, firms will develop various forms of innovative *loci* and procedures without being able to precisely attribute pay-offs to individual activities and projects. Firms in a few industrial sectors undertake part of their research activities in specialized units (typically R & D laboratories). Others do not. Even those which happen to undertake formal R & D-based research, also rely on more "informal" activities of innovation diffused throughout the firm, including the shopfloor (for sectoral evidence and taxonomies, see Pavitt, 1984; Levin *et al.*, 1987; Dosi, 1988a).

This represents a general informational and competence dilemma: the ability to develop innovations with some bearing on the general organization and strategies of the firm differs, and indeed is likely to be separate from the ability to conduct and perform "business as usual." In turn, the latter ability may imply a potential absence of innovative capabilities by many members of the organization, neglect of potentially useful information and, ultimately, loss of opportunities.

This is where the analysis of the coordination, incentive, and finance properties of firms links with the evolutionary analyses of non stationary environments. For example, it is straightforward that in the archetypical A-model of the firm – with its high degree of functional hierarchy and specialization, decisions concerning the directions of innovative search, the introduction of new products and techniques, or even the modification of existing ones must be placed quite high in the strategic management. In such an institutional set-up, efficiency via specialization has precisely the corollary of positively avoiding changes in individual behaviors which are not planned *ex ante* in the design of the organization. In the case of the J-firm, more decentralized information-processing and knowledge-sharing among related functional units appears to be more conducive to local innovative adjustments on the basis of in-house knowledge (e.g. on shop-wide production procedures, on particular product characteristics, etc.). However, it does not seem to provide any strong endogenous incentives to approach R & D activities which may require a new firm-wide organizational set-ups, new researchers and scientists acquired from external markets, etc. In all cases, the very nature of organizations which make the latter, to different degrees, informationally viable and incentive-compatible (hence, efficient) under conditions of limited (or relatively predictable) innovative opportunities, limits the incentive to experiment with radically new ideas. It is hard to imagine an organization with positive incentives for all its members stopping them doing what they are "supposed" to do and fiddling around with their brilliant ideas on how to reorganize the firm, its production mix, etc.! All this is for good efficiency reasons, but these same reasons may well also represent an evolutionary limitation, in that they restrict the incentive to innovate.

This limitation is strengthened by the very nature of the innovative process. As several works have shown (Freeman, 1982; Rosenberg, 1974 and 1982; Dosi, 1988; Aoki and Rosenberg, 1989), innovation cannot generally be represented as a linear process, stemming from exogenous scientific discovery and ending with economic exploitation. Rather, it most often involves complicated forms of feedback among notional technological opportunities, perceived market opportunities, and organizational responses. That is, there is a good part of innovative opportunities which are endogenous to corporate dynamics. Different organizational frameworks imply diverse links with customers, suppliers, competitors; diverse degrees of reliance on endogenous skills versus exogenous (especially scientific) sources; and diverse degrees of exploitation of new technological paradigms via the formation of new firms. In addition, the allocative criteria associated with bank- or market-oriented finance are plausibly important, too. We want to touch only on the last factor here.

Any system must rely for its evolutionary potential on its capabilities of innovative exploration. As argued elsewhere (Dosi, 1990), the distribution of innovative trials may well be biased toward "mistakes," and thus any system which selectively operates too quickly against below-average performing companies may actually discourage innovation. On the other hand, less "selectiveness" means more inefficient slacks and lower average performances. It is a fundamental evolutionary dilemma. Relatively big and diversified firms somewhat mitigate this dilemma internally, through their rules for fund allocation across divisions and across products. Bank-oriented systems, in a few cases (e.g., Japan, Germany and Sweden), appear to allow more internal experimentation by established companies, as the banks tend to have more detailed and differential knowledge about those firms and do not have to draw too heavily on their current and/or average performances. Market-oriented systems, on the other hand, tend to value existing firms largely on the grounds of common knowledge, inevitably drawing on current performance. However, they seem more frequently to give opportunities to new innovative firms to explore new technological trajectories. Relatedly, these systems have generated new financial organizations, such as venture capital firms, which, interestingly, embody some "special" management knowledge and play an active ("voice") role toward customer firms, similar to that observed in many bank-oriented systems.

More generally, the institutions governing the allocation of financial resources to business firms influence the criteria and speed of selection among agents displaying different economic performances; the variety of directions in the exploration of yet unexploited technological opportunities; and the rate at which innovative capabilities are accumulated within firms. There is no easy way to map these "evolutionary" properties into the comparative taxonomy developed earlier in the previous section. Indeed, this is a major field of research, namely: how effectively do those different archetypical models handle the dilemma between informational coordination and incentive-compatibility, on the one hand, and innovative exploration, on the other? Building on the foregoing analysis, one can advance some tentative conjectures.

First, as argued at greater length in Dosi (1990), bank-based financial systems are likely to be more conducive to "far-sighted" corporate strategies of incremental accumulation of innovative competences, even when they involve relatively uncertain returns and in a relatively far-away future. A weaker selection force on the financial side puts less pressure on the management for short-term profitability. This, together with rank-based incentives and relatively low management mobility, makes corporate commitment to long-term competence accumulation incentive-compatible for the members of the firm.

Second, there might be some "critical threshold" in the richness of innovative opportunities which any one environment provides that makes the A-model evolutionarily viable. That is, only when the probabilities (not necessarily known to the agents) are high enough that new discoveries can be economically exploited, market-based financial systems are able to foster innovative research via venture-backing and market selection of new innovative firms. This is possibly also the reason why the A-model has not historically been particularly successful in technologically less-developed countries. In fact, an M-incentive mode requires a pre-existing abundant availability of skills, a developed market for them, and, equally important, an allocation of financial resources to technological activities which – on the grounds of sheer common knowledge – present, especially, in laggard countries, an extremely high probability of failure. Conversely, WB-modes of financing appear to be more conducive to the accumulation and "targeting" of initially scarce innovative skills, partly sheltered from short-term profitability evaluations on the grounds of market "common knowledge."

Third, environments which are permanently characterized by unexploited opportunities and unexpected innovations somewhat distort the notion of incentive-compatibility as discussed earlier. Under technological stationarity or quasi-predictable change, incentive-compatible behavior within firms, or for that matter by firms *vis-à-vis* financial investors, can be measured against some widely shared yardstick of efficiency. However, in an innovative world, evolutionary viability must involve some incentive to "break the rules," both within firms and by the firm as whole. In so far as each corporate organization, no matter how "innovative," can innovate only to a limited degree without dramatically losing its efficiency, some financial institution must back "deviant" exploratory behavior. Notionally, both market-based and bank-based financial systems could do this equally well. Empirical evidence so far apparently suggests that the A-model (in the American, but not in the British case) has adapted rather flexibly to that function. However, some analysts interpret the same phenomenon in an opposite way: Keith Pavitt, for example, suggests that widespread innovative exploration via the birth of new firms is in fact a by-product of the failure of the A-model to foster innovative behavior within incumbent firms (a related argument is in Pavitt, 1991).

Conclusions

Building on the analysis of different functions performed by corporate organizations – in terms of information coordination, incentives, performance control and innovative learning – we have suggested a sort of comparative institutional taxonomy (see Fig. 2.1). Each archetype of firm, in order to be economically viable, defines its information-efficiency and incentive-compatibility in relation to both its internal organizational mechanisms and its relationship with external institutions such as those governing the labour market and finance (e.g. with stockholders, banks, etc.). Hence one can theoretically describe various notional combinations between internal governance structures and industry-finance links. In that context we have tried to present four basic "models" or archetypes, ranging from one characterized by market-based incentives, hierarchical information flows, and market-based finance, on the one hand, to an opposite type of

	S Information sharing / H Hierarchical	M Market-oriented incentives	R Rank hierarchies	Financial regime	Institutional archetype
C O O R D I N A T I O N	S			M (Market based)	A-model (The "anglo-american" model)
	H	X			
	S			RB (Relational banking)	D-model ("Developing countries" model)
	H	X			
	S		X	WB (Weak bank-based)	J-model (The Japanese archetype)
	H				
	S			SB (Strong bank-based)	S-model (The centrally planned economy)
	H		X		

Figure 2.1 A comparative taxonomy.

model based on generalized hierarchical relations, on the other. Then, we explicitly added the requirement of innovative learning in each firm, and of financial allocations to innovative research. Permanent innovative opportunities, we have argued, may well introduce a permanent dilemma between the revealed efficiency of each institutional set-up and its evolutionary viability, as manifested by its ability to successfully generate innovations.

In a continuously changing world, internal governance structures of firms and industry–finance links must be assessed on their dual, and possibly conflicting, roles of determining efficient performances – on the grounds of given technologies and innovative exploration. Our taxonomic exercise of basic archetypes of such corporate structures and finance modes certainly falls short of any explicit analysis of their different evolutionary properties, and lacks a thorough historical investigation highlighting particular empirical examples closer to each theoretical model. Indeed, the foregoing discussion should be considered as a theoretical introduction to a comparative analysis of the differentiated patterns of change of corporate and financial institutions: in a biological analogy, a sort of "Linnean" exercise of classification, in the perspective of an evolutionary theory of their origins and change.

Note

[1] M. Aoki's research was supported by the Japanese Ministry of Education and by the grant of the Research Institute of System Analysis, NTT Data, to the Japanese Economy Program at the Center for Economic Policy Research, Stanford. Giovanni Dosi's research was supported by the Designated Research Center of the ESRC at SPRU, University of Sussex, and by the Italian Ministry of Education ("Progetti 40%").

References

Aghion, P. and Bolton, P. (1988), *An Incomplete Contract Approach to Bankruptcy and the Financial Structure of the Firm*, MIT, Department of Economics Working Paper 484.

Akerlof, G. (1970), "The Market for 'Lemons': Quality Uncertainty and the Market Mechanism," *Quarterly Journal of Economics*, 90: 488–500.

Amendola, M. and Gaffard, J.L. (1988), *The Innovative Choice. An Economic Analysis of the Dynamics of Technology*, Basil Blackwell, Oxford and New York.

Aoki, M. (1986), "Horizontal versus Vertical Information Structure of the Firm," *American Economic Review*, 76 (5), Dec: pp. 193–224.

Aoki, M. (1988), *Information, Incentives and Bargaining in the Japanese Economy*, Cambridge University Press, Cambridge.

Aoki, M. (1990a), "The Participatory Generation of Information Rents and the Theory of the Firm," in Aoki, M., Gustafsson, B. and Williamson, O.E. (eds), *The Firm as a Nexus of Treaties*, Sage Publications, London: pp. 26–51.

Aoki, M. (1990b), "Towards an Economic Model of the Japanese Firm," *Journal of Economic Literature*, XXVIII, March: pp.1–27.

Aoki, M. and Rosenberg, N. (1989), "The Japanese Firm as an Innovating Institution," in Shiraishi, T. and Tsuru, S. (eds), *Economic Institutions in a Dynamic Society*, Macmillan, London: pp. 137–54.

Berglof, E. (1990), "Capital Structure as a Mechanism of Control: a Comparison of Financial Systems," in Aoki, M., Gustafsson, B. and Williamson, O.E. (eds), *The Firm as a Nexus of Treaties*, Sage Publications, London: pp. 26–51.

Binmore, K., Rubinstein, A. and Wolinsky, A. (1986), "The Nash Bargaining Solution in Economic Modelling," *Rand Journal of Economics*, 17 (2), Summer: pp. 176–88.

Coase, R. (1988), *The Firm, the Market and the Law*, Chicago University Press, Chicago.

Cremer, J. (1990), "Common Knowledge and the Coordination of Economic Activities," in Aoki, M., Gustafsson, B. and Williamson, O.E. (eds), *The Firm as a Nexus of Treaties*, Sage Publications, London, pp. 53–76.

Dosi, G. (1984), *Technical Change and Industrial Transformation*, Macmillan, London and St. Martin's Press, New York.

Dosi, G. (1988a), *Institutions and Markets in a Dynamic World*, The Manchester School.

Dosi, G. (1988b), "Sources, Procedures, and Microeconomic Effects of Innovation," *Journal of Economic Literature*, 26: pp. 1120–71.

Dosi, G. (1990), "Finance, Innovation and Industrial Change," *Journal of Economic Behavior and Organization*, 13, 299–319.

Dosi, G. and Orsenigo, L. (1988), "Coordination and Transformation: an Overview of Structures, Behavior and Change in Evolutionary Environments," in Dosi, G., Freeman, C., Nelson, R., Silverberg, G. and Soete, L. (eds), *Technical Change and Economic Theory*, Francis Pinter, London and Columbia University Press, New York.

Dosi, G., Teece, D.J. and Winter, S. (1991), "Toward a Theory of Corporate Coherence: Preliminary Remarks," in Dosi, G., Toninelli, P.A. and

Giannetti, R., *Technology and Enterprise in a Historical Perspective*, Oxford University Press, Oxford.

Freeman, C. (1982), *The Economics of Industrial Innovation*, Francis Pinter, London.

Itoh, I. (1987), "Information Processing Capacities of the Firm," *Journal of Japanese and International Economics*, Sept. (3): pp. 299–326.

Jensen, M. and Meckling, W. (1976), "Theory of the Firm: Managerial Behavior, Agency Costs and Ownership Structure," *Journal of Financial Economics*, 3: pp. 305–60.

Koike, K. (1984), "Skill Formative Systems in the US and Japan: a Comparative Study," in Aoki, M. (ed.), *The Economic Analysis of the Japanese Firm*, North-Holland, Amsterdam: pp. 47–75.

Koike, K. (1988), *Understanding Industrial Relations in Modern Japan*, Macmillan, London.

Kornai, J. (1980), *The Economics of Shortage*, North-Holland, Amsterdam.

Levin, R., Klevorick, A., Nelson, R. and Winter, S. (1987), "Appropriating the Returns from Industrial R&D," *Brookings Papers on Economic Activity*: pp. 783–820.

MacLeod, B. and Malcomson, J. (1986), "Reputation and Hierarchy in Dynamic Models of Employment," mimeo, University of Southampton.

Mailath, G. and Postlewaite, A. (1990), "Workers versus Firms: Bargaining over a Firm's Value," *Review of Economic Studies*, 57: pp. 369–80.

Modigliani, F. and Miller, M. (1958), "The Cost of Capital, Corporation Finance and the Theory of Investment," *American Economic Review*, 48, June: pp. 261–7.

Nelson, R.L. and Winter, S. (1982), *An Evolutionary Theory of Economic Change*, The Belknap Press of Harvard University Press, Cambridge, MA.

Pavitt, K. (1984), "Sectoral Patterns of Innovation. Toward a taxonomy and a theory," *Research Policy*.

Pavitt, K. (1991), "Some Foundations for a Theory of the Large Innovative Firm," in Dosi, G., Toninelli, P.A. and Giannetti, R., *Technology and Enterprise in a Historical Perspective*, Oxford University Press, Oxford.

Riordan, M. (1990), "What is Vertical Integration?," in Aoki, M., Gustafsson, B. and Williamson, O.E. (eds), *The Firm as a Nexus of Treaties*, Sage Publications, London, pp. 53–76.

Rosenberg, N. (1974), *Perspectives on Technology*, Cambridge University Press, Cambridge.

Rosenberg, N. (1982), *Inside the Black Box*, Cambridge University Press, Cambridge.

Rybczinski, T.M. (1985), "Financial Systems, Risk and Public Policy," *The Royal Bank of Scotland Review*: n. 148, pp. 35–45.

Stiglitz, J. (1974a), "Incentives and Risk Sharing in Sharecropping," *Review of Economic Studies*, 41, April: pp. 219–55.

Teece, D. (1988), "Technological Change and the Nature of the Firm," in Dosi, G., Freeman, C., Nelson, R., Silverberg, G. and Soete, L. (eds), *Technical Change and Economic Theory*, Francis Pinter, London, and Columbia University Press, New York.

[23]

Hierarchies, Markets and Power: Some Foundational Issues on the Nature of Contemporary Economic Organizations

GIOVANNI DOSI

(Dipartimento di Scienze Economiche, Università degli Studi de Roma
'La Sapienza', Via A. Cesalpino, 12/14, I-00161 Roma, Italy)

1. Introduction

An adequate summary of the multiple lines of discourse, results and controversies offered by the papers which follow is obviously beyond the scope of
a short introduction. Rather, what I shall try to do is to outline some major
themes which cut across many of the contributions. Indeed, many topics
addressed in this special issue of *Industrial and Corporate Change* touch the
very foundations of modern social sciences. And the time is probably ripe
for a fresh reassessment. After all, the identification of specific foundations
and methodologies with specific disciplines has become increasingly blurred.
For example, a trend that many consider a form of 'economists' imperialism'
has forced the archetype of *Homo economicus* and the mainstream economist's
toolkit (with rational choice, equilibrium, etc.) into other disciplines such
as political science and sociology.[1] Many scholars, in different quarters, have
begun sharing similar formal instruments, such as game-theoretic models,
whose use was originally confined mainly to economics. The challenge of
methodological individualism is felt, with excitement or apprehension, well
beyond the boundaries of economic theory.[2]

However, at the same time, theses and conjectures traditionally pertaining
to disciplines other than economics have started penetrating the latter. Issues
such as path-dependence, boundaries between organizations and markets,
institutions, endogenous preferences and self-reinforcing collective phenomena
are increasingly part of the discourse of economists (and not only of those
who call themselves 'evolutionists' or 'institutionalists'). Organizational

---

[1] For an excellent discussion of 'the impact of economics on contemporary sociology', see Baron and Hannan (1994).

[2] Just to name two examples of excitement, cf. Coleman (1990) in sociology and Milgrom and Roberts (1992) with respect to organization theory and management.

Industrial and Corporate Change   Volume 4   Number 1   1995 studies have become a fruitful crossroads among practitioners from different disciplinary origins. We thus have the studies of technological and organizational innovation. At last one is starting to follow up Simon's invitation to study what actually goes on in the heads of people and in the (metaphorical) 'heads' of organizations, if such exist. Hence, also, issues of learning, cognition and adaptation have gained importance outside the domains of cognitive and social psychology. Models of path-dependency of various sorts have started 'bringing history into economics', as David puts it. And the list goes on.

In brief, the strong impression that one gets from contemporary developments in social science is that themes increasingly overlap disciplines. To some extent, this also applies to methodologies and basic analytical 'paradigms'. (For example, it is nowadays rather common to find 'neoclassical' sociologists and political scientists, or, conversely, evolutionary economists who talk a language which is more familiar to sociologists than to their own mainstream colleagues.) For all these reasons it might be fruitful to reflect on the 'basics', while at the same time referring to a relatively precise, albeit very broad and complex, domain, namely the forms of economic organization in contemporary economies, their nature and their origins.

Certainly, in the articles contained in this issue, the balance between 'inductive reasoning' [i.e. what Nelson and Winter (1982) have called 'appreciative theories'] and more explicitly theory-based propositions varies a great deal. And the underlying theoretical assumptions differ profoundly. Possible axes of classification concern the (implicit or explicit) role attributed to individual rationality in the development of collective institutions; the inertia (or 'path-dependency') of the latter; the analytical importance of 'choice' as compared with 'constraints' in explaining individual and collective behaviors; the degrees to which preferences and actions are shaped by history and institutions; and the very nature of the organizations within which most human beings operate.

In turn, with regard to the forms of economic organization, these interpretative dimensions obviously influence the units of analysis that one selects (are they 'information partitions', 'transactions', 'specific resources', 'social roles', 'utilities and endowments' or 'cognitive frames'?), the description of both individual actors and aggregate entities (such as 'institutions'), and the interactions between the two.

The extreme boundaries on the distribution of 'primitive' theoretical building-blocks are set, on the one side, by nearly theological axiomatizations of human behavior derived from simple invariant principles (resulting in an unconditionally self-seeking forward-looking rationality *à la* Becker, or older religious theories on grace, predestination and temptation) and, on the opposite side, purely 'functionalist' or holistic theories of collective dynamics. Indeed, while there might be little scope for a constructive debate with fundamentalist believers, most of the challenging controversies concern precisely the relative interpretative merits of theories, all acknowledging some role to both motivational microfoundations and system-level effects, which, however, differ profoundly in the ways they describe and combine these two levels of analysis. In my view, a fruitful reassessment of 'foundations' rests precisely at this level (which is where the 'grand' debates in social sciences have found their ultimate ground — from Hobbes to Smith, Durkheim, Weber and Schumpeter). Without any ambition of thoroughness, let me try to highlight some of these foundational issues.

2. On the 'Ultimate Primitives'

Behind each specific interpretative story, there is a set of *ceteris paribus* assumptions and also some fictitious tale on a 'once upon a time' reconstruction of the theoretical primitives of the story itself. Needless to say, most of (but not all!) scholars realize that the tales are just tales, but they still influence the way that interpretative stories are told, the selection of dominant variables, the modeling assumptions, etc.

Pushing it to the extreme, as I see it, there are in the social sciences two archetypal (meta) tales. The first says, more or less, that 'once upon a time' there were individuals with reasonably structured and coherent preferences, with adequate cognitive algorithms to solve the decision–action problems at hand, and (in most cases) with self-seeking restrictions on preferences themselves. They met in some openings in the forest and, conditional on the technologies available, undertook some sort of general equilibrium trading or, as an unavoidable second best, built organizations in order to deal with technological non-convexities, trading difficulties, contract enforcements, etc. Here, clearly, the rough 'primitives' of the tale are preferences, endowments and given technologies (of production and exchange), while 'institutions' or 'organizations' are derived entities.

In a second and alternative tale, 'once upon a time' there were immediately factors of socialization and preference-formation of individuals, institutions like families shaping desires, representations and, possibly, cognitive abilities. Non-exchange mechanisms of interactions appear in the explanation from the start: authority, violence and persuasion of parents upon children; obedience; tribes; schools; churches; and, generally, the adaptation to particular social roles. Here 'institutions' are the primitives, while 'preferences' and the very notion of 'rationality' are derived entities.

Certainly, with enough refinements, both basic tales become analytically respectable and in many variations observationally indistinguishable. So, for example, in the 'rational' tale one can easily admit that preferences, too, are endogenous, but on a longer time scale. However, in principle, institutions and organizations ought to be considered relatively plastic and adaptable, while the interests, motivations and menus of strategies available to the agents ought to be relatively invariant. Conversely, in the 'institutionalist' tale it is easy to account for the influence of individual preferences and strategies upon the evolution of social organizations. However, one is inclined to view institutions as the relatively inertial entities and agents' motivations and behaviors as comparatively flexible and adaptive.

Foundational tales obviously influence also the derived interpretive heuristics. Consider the problem of 'why does one observe organization x at time t?'. In the first perspective, one would start answering by focusing upon the interests of the agents involved in such an organization, the tasks that the organization is meant to handle and the technologies available, and then try to impute its existence to the intentional efforts of the agents to 'do their best', given the constraints. (The exercise, as Granovetter remarks in his contribution, is often riddled with a good deal of teleological reasoning; see also below.) In contrast, in the second perspective, one would look much more carefully at the organization(s) that existed at time $(t - 1)$, at the linkages between organization x and other institutional entities, and then try to tell an explicitly dynamic story on how one got from the state at $(t - 1)$ to the state at t. In this respect, the answer to 'why something exists' relies a good deal on the account of how it came about.

Note that I am not suggesting that the first story is institution-free and the second is agent-free. Consider, for example, Williamson's contribution to this issue (which certainly belongs to the 'rationalist' camp as defined here): he emphasizes that institutions intervene in the parametrization of the economic problem at hand — in his case, the transaction-governance problem — and also exert a (weak) influence on the characteristics of the agents. Of course, they play a more prominent role in any 'institutionalist' story, and they do so by shaping and constraining the opportunities, incentives and motivations of the actors (cf. Granovetter in this issue).[3] I would add that they also help shape the representations that agents hold of what their interests are and of the instruments at their disposal to pursue them (i.e. their 'rationality').

The presumption in strong versions of the 'rationalist tale' is that agents

---

[3] A version of the 'institutionalist tale' trying to make a detailed link between the behavioral motivations traditionally emphasized by 'rationalists' (such as sheer utility maximization), on the one hand, and other motivational factors (including moral and ethical ones), on the other, is 'socio-economics' (see Etzioni, 1988). Incidentally, note that, as the latter approach shows, non-utilitarian motivations can be brought into the picture without giving up 'rational' (at least in the sense of purposeful and coherent) decision-making. But see also below.

somehow possess a kit of algorithmic devices sufficient to adequately represent the environment in which they operate and to choose the appropriate courses of action. 'Boundedly rational' versions — such as Williamson's in this issue or the contributions that come under the heading of 'evolutionary games' in economics — relax the assumption by allowing computational and memory limitations, but still tend to define 'bounded' rationality as an imperfect approximation to the 'unbounded' one.

At the opposite end of the spectrum, the 'institutionalist tale' finds intuitive links with all those inquiries, such as cognitive psychology and artificial sciences, which start from the presumption of general (nearly ontological) gaps (a) between what one sees and believes, and 'what is really out there'; and (b) between what one could notionally do, given the environmental constraints and opportunities, and what one is actually capable of doing. As a consequence, in this perspective, the challenge to the theory is to investigate the nature and process of emergence of particular cognitive frames, interpretative categories, patterns of behaviors, routines, etc. [Within an enormous and diverse interdisciplinary literature, examples Shafir Tversky (1992) on reasoning and choice; Holland *et al.* (1986) and Lakoff (1987) on adaptive learning and category formation; and the analyses of behavioral routines in Nelson and Winter (1982), Cohen (1987), Cohen and Bacdayan (1991) and Dosi and Egidi (1991).]

Related issues concern the separability between cognitive and motivational dimensions of decision-making. Clearly, the 'rationalist tale' demands such separation between 'what one desires' (i.e. goals, utilities, etc.) and 'what one knows' (i.e. the assessment of the status of the environment and the means available to achieve given goals). Conversely, the 'institutionalist tale' is comfortable also with blurred coupled dynamics between the two, possibly yielding endogenous preferences, coexisting contradictory models of cognition and action in the heads of the same individuals, phenomena of cognitive dissonance, etc.[4]

I mention these basic dichotomies in the underlying views of social interactions because they also cut across the contributions that follow and might be where some of the interpretative divergences ultimately rest (compare, for example, Williamson and Ostrom on the one hand, and Granovetter and Hamilton-Feenstra on the other).[5] Differences at such a deep method-

---

[4] Relevant discussions in these respects are Cohen *et al.* (1972), Earl (1983, 1988, 1992), Elster (1979, 1983). A thorough introduction is in March (1994).

[5] Clearly, the majority of economists tend to be more comfortable with the first tale and sociologists with the second. However, it is deeply misleading, in my view, to identify the dichotomy with disciplinary boundaries (a bit along the lines of Pareto, who equated economics and sociology with the study of 'rational' and 'irrational' behaviors respectively). In fact, I personally consider it good news that these diverse perspectives increasingly affect *all* social disciplines.

ological level are most likely undecidable, but they also influence propositions and conjectures at lower levels of abstraction that in principle may be assessed against the empirical evidence. Indeed, the papers in this issue provide a rich and solid point of departure for this type of exercise.

3. Power, Authority and Hierarchies

Another major 'foundational' issue concerns the nature of hierarchies, the notion of authority and the associated notion of power. Again, for the sake of simplicity, let me suggest two caricaturally simple archetypes.

The first one (represented by Williamson in the issue with much higher sophistication) proposes that (a) the notion of 'power' does not have any clear analytical status; (b) the basic unit of analysis ought to remain as much as possible that of transactions; and (c) organizations are primarily governance structures. Call this model the *exchange view* of interactions and organizations. The second, which I shall (improperly) call the *political view*, holds on the contrary that (a) an essential, although not unique, feature of organizations is their authoritative structure (cf. Hamilton-Feenstra in this issue); (b) authority relations are inherently different from exchange relations; and (c) power must be considered an autonomous interpretative dimension.

Some definitions are in order. Consider the following: authority involves 'the transfer of the locus of decision from the subordinate or follower to the authority' itself (Kemp, 1993, p. 161). Authority entails domination, as Weber would put it, so that the conduct of the 'ruled' is such that it is 'as if the ruled had made the content of the command the maxim of their conduct for its very own sake' (Weber, 1968, p. 946; also cited in Kemp, 1993). Therefore, obedience and identification with the authority, and not self-interest, are the motivational drives.

Related to this, let me define power as the ability of some agent (the 'ruler' or authority) to determine the set of actions available to other agents (the ruled) and to influence or command the choice within this set according to the deliberations of the ruler himself [this definition echoes in many ways the analysis of Luhmann (1979)]. Hence, the units of analysis are the dimensionality and boundaries of the 'choice sets', and the mechanisms by which 'domination' by means of authority is enforced.

The political view, of course, does not claim to be exhaustive: command and exchange coexist in different forms within and outside organizations. But it claims—at least as I interpret it—that the sole consideration of exchange relations prevents a full understanding of what goes on within the 'organizational black box', of the boundaries between organizations and of organizational dynamics.

Note also that the dichotomy between the exchange and political views is not entirely orthogonal to the previous one between 'rationalist' and 'institutionalist' foundations. In fact, the political view demands microfoundations involving socially adaptive preferences and behavioral modes (such as 'obedience' or 'identification with the role' and with the authority)[6] quite at odds with the rationalist tale. Conversely, any strong version of the latter almost inevitably leads to the interpretation of seemingly authoritative relations as the outcome of some sort of voluntary meta-exchange by self-seeking, forward-looking agents.

Ultimately, the rationalist tale-cum-exchange view entails a sort of unitary and invariant anthropology, based on well-formed, consistent interests as the basic motivational drives and criteria for action. At the other extreme, the institutionalist tale-cum-political view is naturally consistent with the idea of an irreducible multiplicity of motivational dimensions, and, possibly, with multiple 'identities' coexisting within the same agent. So, for example, the latter perspective builds upon broad historical generalizations such as Hirschman's account of the changing balance between 'passions' and 'interests' in modern Western culture (Hirschman, 1977) or Sen's fascinating discussion of the (sometimes uneasy) coexistence between 'ethical' and 'economic' motives (Sen, 1987). The same phenomena would be interpreted in rationalist/exchange perspectives as varying restrictions on some sort of 'enlarged utility functions' or changing 'social technologies' for the governance of exchanges and production.[7]

Moreover, the 'institutionalist' perspective would see exchanges themselves as embedded in particular institutions (e.g. 'the markets') whose origins and characteristics demand to be explained [on the notion of embeddedness, cf. Granovetter (1985) and this issue]. Finally, note that the political view is quite in tune with the picture of business firms provided by most organizational theorists and business economists alike (cf. Pfeffer, 1981; March and Simon, 1993).

4. Origins, Dynamics and Efficiency Property of Organizations

Let me go back to the question of 'why organization x exists'. As already mentioned, there are two types of answer. One involves an explicit account of the dynamics (i.e. how it got to become what it is). The second answer

---

[6] Classic discussions of these processes are in Milgram (1974), Simon (1976) and Lindblom (1977).

[7] Of course, pushing the interpretation to the extreme, one reaches a Becker-type anthropology whereby, for example, the only remarkable difference between Adolf Hitler and Sister Theresa of Calcutta rests on diverse weights of the arguments of their (dimensionally identical) utility function and, analogously, the differences between Micronesian civilizations and L. A. yuppies can be reduced to differences in available social technologies.

derives necessary and sufficient reasons for its existence from the tasks it performs and its efficiency properties. With the former methodology, admittedly it might be quite difficult to achieve general theoretical propositions, since it involves the identification of classes of processes and sets of initial conditions yielding specific classes of outcomes. But, with the second methodology, functionalist or teleological fallacies are an easy temptation, as vigorously argued by Granovetter in this issue (i.e. 'organization x exists because it is good at performing function a'). This need not necessarily be the case, but then the challenge is to show that functional efficiency is a robust outcome of either intentional constructive processes or collective, unintentional mechanisms of selection among a variety of alternative organizational solutions. It is fair to say that, so far, neither proof is available.

On the constructive, intentional side, the game-theoretic route does not seem able to deliver the goods. Without entering into any detailed discussion of the state of the art, one should just recall the hurdles facing selection among multiple equilibria or the implications of the Folk theorem in repeated games (which basically says that any behavioral sequence that one observes can be interpreted as an equilibrium strategy).[8] All this applies to interactive setups involving individual agents and, plausibly, even more to collective entities such as formal organizations or institutions in general.

Alternatively, the selection route is the most rudimentary form of a dynamic, evolutionary argument. It dates back at least to Friedman's 'as ... if' proposition, according to which, due to some unspecified selection mechanism, observed behavioral traits (and, implicitly, also organizational forms) can be interpreted as if they were the outcome of an explicit optimization process, since no other behavior would survive in equilibrium. However, apart from a lot of hand waving, the analytical results are mainly negative: only under quite restrictive conditions on the selection space, selection mechanisms and initial conditions does such an outcome obtain [cf. Winter (1971), and the critical surveys in Silverberg (1988) and Hodgson (1993)].

To sum up, it seems to me that no matter what kind of explanation one offers as to why particular organizations exist, an answer to the 'how' question is unavoidable. This, in turn, implies some explicit dynamic account of how formal organizations — and, more generally, institutions — emerge and change over time. To be brief, I shall continue to reason in terms

---

[8] Incidentally, I would like to point out that these critical remarks primarily refer to game theory as both an analytical device and a *weltanschauung* (including all ontological commitments to rationality, common knowledge, etc.). A much more cavalier use might be also heuristically much more useful, especially in the exploration of incentive–compatibility problems: see Ostrom (this issue), or Schelling's pioneering work (Schelling, 1960).

of dichotomous archetypes. The first archetype — call it the *constitutional model* — is based on the idea of intentional interactions among purposeful, forward-looking agents who try to establish ground rules for their co-operative endeavors (Ostrom's paper in this issue is a good example of that methodology). In opposition, one may conceive the origin and evolution of organizations primarily in terms of collective, largely unintentional outcomes of interactions — call this the *self-organization model* (with respect to organizational evolution, see Warglien in this issue). Needless to say, empirical processes of organizational formation are likely to involve different mixtures between the two modes, but the formal study of the properties of each archetype adds important insights to the understanding of which kinds of interaction mechanism yield which kinds of feasible outcome.

The question of origins and change of organizations inevitably demands an account of the mechanisms of adaptation and selection (Levinthal, 1990, 1992; Warglien, this issue). This is straightforward under the self-organization model, but it applies also to the constitutional model, unless one assumes that one gets it perfectly right every time (i.e. that agents are always able to construct 'optimal' organizational arrangements, whatever that means). Crucial issues, in this respect, are (a) the processes of organizational learning; and (b) the criteria and mechanisms of selection within and among organizations. (In fact, there might not be such a clearcut distinction between the two since organizational learning and adaptation may be seen as resting on intra-organizational selection of behaviors, skills, etc.; see Warglien in this issue.) In any case, organizational learning directly links with the current debate on the nature of organizational competences [cf., among others, Dosi and Marengo (1992) and Teece *et al.* (1994), and the ways they are modified over time]. Warglien's work in this issue contributes a novel view of this dynamics, based on hierarchically nested processes of learning and selection within each organization that unfold on multiple temporal and spatial scales.

Can one univocally define the criteria of selection? And what is the dimensionality of the selection space? The dynamic story implicit in Williamson's contribution to this issue is that there is only one dominant selection criterion (i.e. cost-minimizing efficiency). Interestingly, an implicit one-dimensional selection is shared also by some of the most vocal critics of Williamson's transaction–cost theory, namely American 'radical political economists', but the fundamental criterion for them concerns power over the labor process and income distribution (cf. Bowles and Gintis, 1993). A fascinating perspective, however, stems from the possibility of multiple selection criteria within and among organizations: organizational dynamics in that case could be understood as the imperfect outcome of adaptation and selection according to possibly conflicting objectives of the members of the organization and of the organization as a whole.

Think, for example, of the following 'toy model'. Suppose that an organization could be actually described according to the following five dimensions:

- the distribution of (formal) authority;
- the distribution of (actual) power (in the above definition);
- the incentive structure;
- the structure of information flows;
- the distribution of knowledge and competence.

Note that even with one-dimensional selection (e.g. based on some efficiency criterion) one should expect to observe imperfect alignment among the five dimensions whenever organizational traits appear in a correlated form (so that, for example, the 'most efficient' distribution of knowledge and competences comes together with a highly 'suboptimal' incentive structure; or, conversely, an efficient exercise of authority is correlated with a high frequency of idiots in the organization).[9] Hence (bounded) variety of organizational forms might coexist. Moreover the hypothesis of one-dimensional selection is not sufficient to guarantee that being 'more efficient' at any one point in time is necessarily monotonic into 'dynamic efficiency' [e.g. survival probabilities; there is more on these topics in Levinthal (1992)].

These considerations apply to a greater degree under multiple selection criteria (e.g. cost-minimizing efficiency with innovative capabilities and 'political' coherence). Then, one starts having a co-evolutionary picture whereby the changes of particular organizational traits — say, those impinging upon the forms of transaction governance — are shaped and constrained by other organizational characteristics related, for example, to the reproduction of power within the organization or to its past strategic commitments.[10] At a broader level of analysis, this co-evolutionary view holds also in the case of multiple organizations and institutions; indeed, the idea that adaptation and selection are nested into broader institutional environments — which might themselves change but on a different timescale — seems quite in tune with the spirit of Granovetter's concept of embeddedness (cf. also Nelson, 1994; Granovetter and Hamilton-Feenstra, this issue).

———————————————————

[9] The idea comes from a recent suggestion by Levinthal on 'epistatic correlation' among organizational characteristics.

[10] For a thorough reconstruction of the 'coevolutionary' processes between technical change and market orientation in the case of AT&T, see Lipartito (1994).

5. *Path-dependency and Discontinuities*

Whatever dynamic story one tells, it naturally involves the question of where the dynamics is leading to (which economists, perhaps too easily, confine to the nature of asymptotic properties of the process). And, symmetrically, one may ask the question of whether one would have got to a certain observed state, say, a certain organizational setup at time *t*, irrespectively of any initial conditions, further back in time. As is known, when initial conditions matter and their effect is not vanishing but possibly self-reinforcing over time, one says that the process is path-dependent. Hence, simplifying to the extreme, an integral part of the explanation of 'where one is going' or 'why we are here' is the account of 'where we come from'. Conversely, note that a necessary (although not sufficient) condition for a 'teleological' interpretation of an observed organizational phenomenon is the lack of path-dependency. As David puts it,

> whether the focus falls upon the supposed evolutionary tendency toward efficiency in the development of property rights and other macro-institutional arrangements, or upon the conceptualization of a firm's internal organization and mode of doing business as the consequence of rational, optimizing decisions, the implicit presumption [is] that institutional arrangements are perfectly malleable . . . (David, 1992, p. 3).

David suggests at least four reasons why one should expect path-dependency in organizations and institutions. First, they incorporate shared conventions and mutually consistent expectations grounded in 'shared historical experiences and conscious perceptions of the shared past' (David, 1992, p. 9). Second, they provide 'role-typing' and acculturation mechanisms which is a sort of 'sunk capital' of organizations (on this point, see also Douglas, 1986). Third, they embody 'codes' for communication and information processing (and it is precisely their irreversibility which make them useful: if a language could be frequently changed it would become worthless for communication with the others!). Fourth, the interrelatedness of different organizational functions — in terms of information processing, incentives, roles, etc. (see also above) — self-reinforces specific organizational structures, possibly well beyond the time of their purported usefulness.[11]

Other complementary reasons are implicit in the earlier discussion. In particular, 'the processes of adaptive learning may result in a competency trap whereby increasing skill at the current procedures makes experimentation with alternatives less attractive. In this sense, organizational learning contributes to organizational inertia' (Levinthal, 1992, p. 432).

———

[11] David (1992) uses, appropriately, the analogy with technological interrelatedness, whereby technical interdependencies within complex systems make it hard to change any one component without affecting the whole structure.

——————————————————— *Hierarchies, Markets and Power* ———————————————

Organizational routines, while being an effective way of storing and reproducing organizational knowledge (Nelson and Winter, 1982; Cohen, 1987), are by their very nature a source of organizational inertia (cf. also Robertson and Langlois, 1994). And finally, entrenched, socially shared expectations, such as particular forms of trust or lack of it, underlie the reproduction over time of behavioral patterns, irrespectively of their collective efficiency [cf. Lorenz (1994) on the lack of trust, conflict and competitive decline in the British industry]. All these factors enhance the importance of path-dependent development and lock-in in particular self-reinforcing institutions and organizations. History, so to speak, solidifies into structures which constrain future developments.

The co-evolutionary view briefly discussed above, however, entails also some potentially 'de-locking' factors. First, the imperfect alignment of different functions within organizations always implies the possibility of far-reaching changes in the overall organizational structure triggered by the accumulation of adjustments on single dimensions.

Similar properties are likely to apply also at more macroscopic levels to the co-evolution of networks of interrelated organizations and the institutional context in which they operate.[12] Several contributions to this issue present rich examples of this general point.

Coriat studies the cumulative changes in intra- and inter-organizational routines induced by adjustments to increasing product variety. Ultimately, this has led to significantly different forms of inter-firm networking — with different types of hierarchical relations between final producers of goods (in this case automobiles) and component suppliers; a different distribution of knowledge within the network; and different combinations between contractual and trust-based relations.

Lazonick and West show in a comparative perspective how embedding roughly similar technologies into different organizational structures might yield quite diverse performances: long-term competitiveness is the outcome of the interactions between institutions, industries and firm. Part of the argument strengthens the view of path-dependency and (limited) lock-in. But they also show examples of how an institutional context — e.g. the American — can, so to speak, be successfully 'invaded' by alternative organizational arrangements — in this case, more 'integrated' and participatory firms.

Galambos' paper raises puzzling questions on the influence of the changing

---

[12] In a different analytical context, Padgett and Ansell (1993) show how the simultaneous membership of agents within multiple social networks is a source of opportunities and dynamics. The illustration that they provide of this point is a fascinating reconstruction of the rise of the Medicis in Renaissance Florence.

balance between 'authority' and 'responsibility' of CEOs in the USA upon the strategic capabilities of top management and ultimately upon the internal structure and boundaries of large enterprises. [13] Finally, Chavance's article vividly illustrates the dynamics toward collapse engendered in centrally planned economies by deep-seated mismatchings between formal hierarchies, incentives and actual decision powers.

More generally, a major theoretical challenge concerns the determinants of 'de-locking' (that is, ultimately, of major discontinuities, 'revolutions', etc.) even in the presence of path-dependent, cumulative dynamics. Of course, there is the easy answer: try to trivialize them as much as possible in terms of unforeseen exogenous shocks. [14] However, for those who do not take that as a serious explanation, the much more difficult task is to understand, in different social domains, how 'success contains also the seeds of its own demise'. Clearly, it is the domain of Schumpeter's 'creative destruction', and of Moore's (1978) analysis of the social bases of obedience and revolt, to name but two famous examples, and it applies also to the dynamics of economic organizations and institutions at large.

6. *Some 'Grand' Empirical Questions*

Foundational issues — such as 'rationalist' versus 'institutionalist' primitive tales; *Homo economicus* versus *Homo politicus*; history and path-dependency; role-determined versus 'free-choice'-determined behaviors, and the ultimate sources of social dynamics — stand also behind the kind of 'grand' empirical questions that one asks and the ways one answers them. By that I mean broad questions, in principle, of a historical nature, covering, for example, the nature of contemporary socio-economic organizations or the long-term patterns of development.

One of these grand questions, namely the 'Coasian' question, 'why do firms exist?', is one of the points of departure of three papers in this issue (Williamson, Granovetter and Hamilton-Feenstra). And highly related themes concern the boundaries of organization themselves and the ways they

---

[13] The author concludes that the recent movements toward deregulation, LBOs, and dismantling of the welfare state have brought about a closer identification of responsibility and authority, thus improving the performance of top managers. However, quite opposite conclusions could be drawn from that same evidence. For example, the fall in the domains of 'responsibility' may well lower the pressure to build 'integrated' organizational structures, with an active involvement of the labor force, which Lazonick and West identify as a major ingredient of long-term competitiveness. And it could strengthen financial skills — as many have argued — at the expense of more idiosyncratic competences related to production and innovation.

[14] Interestingly, note that both those believing in purely teleological, hyperrationalist rules and those standing for purely functionalist, agent-free rules are the most likely candidates to be satisfied with such an answer.

———————————— *Hierarchies, Markets and Power* ————————————

internally operate. Williamson's (approximate) identification of organizations with hierarchies, on the one hand, and what is not a formal organization with markets, on the other, is already part of his own answer. Granovetter and Hamilton-Feenstra challenge, at least partly, that interpretation and suggest that there are many more 'non-market' relations among firms and between firms and individual agents than Williamson's theory is acknowledging.[15]

In fact, one could push the argument further and ask a sort of 'anti-Coasian' question, namely why do markets exist? How do they actually function? How did they come about? Incidentally, notice the relevance of these issues also from a normative point of view with respect to the transition of previously centrally planned economies (cf. the conclusions of Chavance in this issue). It seems to me that it is an unforgivable negligence to allow the field to be monopolized by apprentice sorcerers, with very little knowledge of how Western capitalist economies actually work, but ready to miraculously promise to do in a few hundred days what in the West was imperfectly accomplished in a century or two.

Another grand question that is implicit in some of the papers that follow (compare, for example, Lazonick-West and Galambos) concerns the ordering properties that institutions and non-market relations retain *vis-à-vis* purely economic exchanges and purely self-seeking behaviors.[16] In a sense, it is the grand question on the destiny of contemporary societies. It has been asked, in several perspectives, since the birth of modern social sciences. For example, Smith inquired into the nature of 'moral sentiments' which would allow the invisible hand of markets to yield non-disruptive collective outcomes. Weber asked what the collective outcomes of the diffusion of means–end (i.e. instrumental) rationality would be. And an illustrious tradition — ranging from Tocqueville to Lindblom — investigated the relations between politics and economics which made democracy viable and self-reproducing. Ultimately, to paraphrase Hirschman (1982), is the very process of economic development self-destructive in the sense that it progressively eats out the institutional base upon which it can operate in an orderly manner? Is it plausible to think that those forms of capitalism that work 'better' — in the sense that they deliver more competitiveness, growth, employment — are also those that present organizational forms which deviate more systematically from pure self-seeking motivations (the way I read Lazonick-West, this is not far from their perspective)? Or, conversely, is a greater incentive-

---

[15] The point that what we call markets are themselves institutional constructions and, conversely, organizations embody as well a lot of exchange relations is also emphasized by Hodgson's 'impurity principle' (Hodgson, 1988).

[16] Much more on these issues will be found in Polanyi (1944), Hirsch (1976), Lindblom (1977), Hirschman (1982) and Redner (1993). I discuss some of them at greater length in Dosi (1988).

alignment monotonic into 'better' collective performances (as seems implicit in parts of Galambos' analysis)?

Pushing it to the extreme, one can see here, again, two opposite archetypes of the way contemporary societies operate. The first one is inclined to assume self-adjusting, ordering properties of various sorts of invisible (or visible) hands, even outside the economic arena, grounded into purposeful, utility-maximizing, forward-looking agents. Purposefulness and rationality — irrespectively of whether via market interactions or via the construction of organizations and institutions — carries over to the collective domain (with some caveats stemming from the possibility of multiple, Pareto-rankable, equilibria). Vice versa, the alternative archetype is much more gloomy on the self-adjusting properties of these same visible or invisible hands, and is inclined to point at institutions as the 'primitive' glue which keeps society, and also the economy, together.[17]

7. *An Invitation to a Debate, by Way of a Conclusion*

Needless to say, the general issues and questions that I have tried to raise in these introductory notes go well beyond what can be thoroughly discussed in a dozen articles, even if of the extremely high quality found in this issue. But the editors of *Industrial and Corporate Change* would like to see them as the beginning of a debate ambitiously tackling some of the core themes in social sciences, civilized, robustly grounded in empirical inquiries and theoretical models. In this respect, the articles that follow are nearly a paradigm of the genre. After all, the ways economic activities are organized and the ways they link up with other institutions provide crucial ingredients of the setup of the whole social fabric. I do not think one is exaggerating by suggesting that understanding them better will give us also a better understanding of how contemporary democratic systems work, and also better ways to preserve and defend them.

Acknowledgements

Support for this work at different stages by the Italian Ministry of University Research (MURST, 'Progetti 40%'), the Italian National Research Council ('Progetto Strategico'), the International Institute of Applied Systems Analysis (IIASA, Laxenburg, Austria) and INRA (Ivry, France) is gratefully acknowledged.

---

[17] Within this archetype fit also many investigations of the 'institutional architecture' of the socio-economic system which make growth viable or, alternatively, engender 'mismatching' and crises (cf. Boyer, 1988a, b).

———————————————— *Hierarchies, Markets and Power* ————————————————

References

Akerlof, G. (1984), *An Economic Theorist's Book of Tales*. Cambridge University Press: New York.

Aoki, M. (1988), *Information, Incentive and Bargaining in the Japanese Economy*. Cambridge University Press: Cambridge.

Aronson, E. (1972), *The Social Animal*. W. H. Freeman: San Francisco, CA.

Arrow, K. (1974), *The Limits of Organization*. Norton: New York.

Arthur, B. (1988), 'Competing Technologies. An Overview,' in G. Dosi, C. Freemen, R. Nelson, G. Silverberg and L. Soete (eds), *Technical Change and Economic Theory*. Francis Pinter: London; Columbia University Press: New York.

Baron, J. N. and R. T. Hannan (1994), 'The Impact of Economics on Contemporary Sociology,' *Journal of Economic Literature*, 32, 1111–1146.

Becker, G. S. (1993), 'Nobel Lecture: The Economic Way of Looking at Behavior,' *Journal of Political Economy*, 101, 385–409.

Bourdieu, P. (1977), *Outline of a Theory of Practice*. Cambridge University Press: Cambridge.

Bowles, S. and H. Gintis (1993), 'The Revenge of Homo Economicus: Contested Exchange and the Revival of Political Economy,' *Journal of Economic Perspectives*, 7, 83–114.

Boyer, R. (1988a), 'Technical Change and the Theory of Regulation,' in G. Dosi, C. Freeman, R. Nelson, G. Silverberg and L. Soete (eds), *Technical Change and Economic Theory*. Francis Pinter: London; Columbia University Press: New York.

Boyer, R. (1988b), 'Formalizing Growth Regimes,' in G. Dosi, C. Freeman, R. Nelson, G. Silverberg and L. Soete (eds), *Technical Change and Economic Theory*. Francis Pinter: London; Columbia University Press: New York.

Coase, R. (1937), 'The Nature of the Firm,' *Economica*, 4, 386–405.

Cohen, M. D. (1987), 'Adaptation and Organizational Routines,' working paper, University of Michigan, Institute of Public Policy Studies, Ann Arbor, MI.

Cohen, M. D. and P. Bacdayan (1991). 'Organizational Routines are Stored as Procedural Memory: Evidence from a Laboratory Study,' working paper, University of Michigan, Institute of Public Policy Studies, Ann Arbor, MI.

Cohen, M., J. March and J. P. Olson (1972), 'A Garbage Can Model of Organizational Choice,' *Administrative Science Quarterly*, 17, 1–25.

Coleman, J. S. (1990), *Foundations of Social Theory*. Harvard University Press: Cambridge, MA.

David, P. (1992), 'Why are Institutions the Carriers of History?: Notes on Path-dependence and the Evolution of Conventions, Organizations and Institutions,' working paper, Stanford University, Department of Economics, Stanford, CA.

Denzau, A. T. and D. C. North (1994), 'Shared Mental Models: Ideologies and Institutions,' *Kyklos*, 47, 3–31.

DiMaggio, P. and W. Powell (1985), 'The Iron Cage Revisited: Institutional Isomorphism and Collective Rationality in Organizational Fields,' *American Journal of Sociology*, 48, 147–160.

Dosi, G. (1988), 'Institutions and Markets in a Dynamic World,' *The Manchester School*, 56, 119–146.

Dosi, G. and M. Egidi (1991), 'Substantive and Procedural Uncertainty: An Exploration on Economic Behaviours in Changing Environments,' *Journal of Evolutionary Economics*.

Dosi, G. and L. Marengo (1992), 'Towards a Theory of Organizational Competences,' in R. W. England (ed.), *Evolutionary Concepts in Contemporary Economics*. Michigan University Press: Ann Arbor, MI.

Dosi, G., L. Marengo, A. Bassanini and M. Valente (1994), 'Norms as Emergent Properties of Adaptive Learning: The Case of Economic Routines,' working paper, International Institute for Applied Systems Analysis (IIASA), Laxenburg, Austria.

Douglas, M. (1986), *How Institutions Think*. Syracuse University Press: Syracuse, NY.

Earl, P. E. (ed.) (1988), *Psychological Economics*. Kluwer: Boston, MA.

———————————————— 16 ————————————————

Earl, P. E. (1983), *The Economic Imagination: Toward a Behavioural Analysis of Choice*. Wheatsheaf: Brighton.

Earl, P. E. (1992), 'On the Complementarity of Economic Applications of Cognitive Dissonance Theory and Personal Construct Psychology,' in S. E. G. Lea, P. Webley and B. M. Young (eds), *New Directions in Economic Psychology*. Edward Elgar: Aldershot.

Egidi, M. (1994), 'Routines, Hierarchies of Problems, Procedural Behaviour: Some Evidence from Experiments,' working paper, International Institute for Applied Systems Analysis (IIASA), Laxenburg, Austria.

Elster, J. (1983), *Sour Grapes: Studies in the Subversion of Rationality*. Cambridge University Press: Cambridge.

Elster, J. (1979), *Ulysses and the Sirens*. Cambridge University Press: Cambridge.

Etzioni, A. (1988), *The Moral Dimension*. The Free Press: New York.

Festinger, L. (1957), *A Theory of Cognitive Dissonance*. Stanford University Press: Stanford, CA.

Friedman, M. (1953), *Essays in Positive Economics*. University of Chicago Press: Chicago, IL.

Geertz, C. (1963), *Peddlars and Princes*. University of Chicago Press: Chicago, IL.

Granovetter, M. S. (1985), 'Economic Action and Social Structure: The Problem of Embeddedness,' *American Journal of Sociology*, 51, 481–510.

Hirsch, F. (1976), *Social Limits to Growth*. Harvard University Press: Cambridge, MA.

Hirschman, A. O. (1965), 'Obstacles to Development: A Clarification and a Quasi-vanishing Act,' *Economic Development and Cultural Change*, 13, 385–393.

Hirschman, A. O. (1970), *Exit, Voice and Loyalty*. Harvard University Press: Cambridge, MA.

Hirschman, A. O. (1977), *The Passions and the Interests*. Princeton University Press: Princeton, NJ.

Hirschman, A. O. (1982), 'Rival Interpretations of Market Society: Civilizing, Destructive or Feeble?' *Journal of Economic Literature*, 20, 1463–1484.

Hodgson, G. (1988), *Economics and Institutions*. Polity Press: Cambridge; University of Pennsylvania Press: Philadelphia, PA.

Hodgson, G. (1993), *Economics and Evolution*. Polity Press: Cambridge; Michigan University Press: Ann Arbor, MI.

Holland, J. H., K. J. Holyoak, R. E. Nisbett and P. R. Thagard (1986), *Induction: Processes of Inference. Learning and Discovery*. MIT Press: Cambridge, MA.

Johnson-Laird, P. N. (1983), *Mental Models*. Harvard University Press: Cambridge, MA.

Kemp, D. A. (1993), 'Authority and Public Policy: Solving the Political Problem,' in H. Redner (ed.), *An Heretical Heir of the Enlightenment: Politics, Policy and Science in the Work of Charles E. Lindblom*. Westview Press: Boulder, CO.

Lakoff, G. (1987), *Women, Fire and Dangerous Things: What Categories Reveal about the Mind*. University of Chicago Press: Chicago, IL.

Levinthal, D. (1990), 'Organizational Adaptation and Environmental Selection: Interrelated Processes of Change,' *Management Science*, 2, 140–145.

Levinthal, D. (1992), 'Surviving Schumpeterian Environments: An Evolutionary Perspective,' *Industrial and Corporate Change*, 2, 427–443.

Lewis, D. K. (1969). *Convention*. Harvard University Press: Cambridge, MA.

Lieberman, S. (1956), 'The Effects of Changes in Roles on the Attitudes of Role Occupants,' *Human Relations*, 9, 385–402.

Lindblom, C. E. (1977), *Politics and Markets*. Basic Books: New York.

Lipartito, K. (1994), 'Component Innovation: The Case of Automatic Telephone Switching, 1891–1920,' *Industrial and Corporate Change*, 3, 325–357.

———————————— *Hierarchies, Markets and Power* ————————————

Lorenz, E. (1994), 'Organizational Inertia and Competitive Decline: The British Cotton, Shipbuilding and Car Industries,' *Industrial and Corporate Change*, 3, 405–434.

Luhmann, N. (1979), *Trust and Power*. Wiley: Chichester.

March, J. and H. Simon (1993), *Organizations*, 2nd edn. Blackwell: Cambridge, MA.

March, J. G. (1994), *A Primer in Decision Making*. The Free Press: New York.

Milgram, S. (1974), *Obedience to Authority; An Experimental View*. Tavistock Institute: London.

Milgrom, P. and J. Roberts (1992), *Economics, Organization and Management*. Prentice-Hall: Englewood Cliffs, NJ.

Moore, B., Jr (1978), *Injustice: The Social Bases of Obedience and Revolt*. Pantheon Books: New York.

Nelson, R. (1994), 'The Co-evolution of Technology, Industrial Structures and Supporting Institutions,' *Industrial and Corporate Change*, 3, 47–63.

Nelson, R. and S. Winter (1982), *An Evolutionary Theory of Economic Change*. Harvard University Press: Cambridge, MA.

Ostrom, E. (1990), *Governing the Commons: The Evolution of Institutions for Collective Action*. Cambridge University Press: New York.

Padgett, J. F. and C. K. Ansell (1993), 'Robust Action and the Rise of the Medici, 1400–1434,' *American Journal of Sociology*, 98, 1259–1319.

Pfeffer, J. (1981), *Power in Organizations*. Pitman Publishers: Marshfield, MA.

Polanyi, K. (1944), *The Great Transformation*. Beacon Press: Boston, MA.

Putterman L. (ed.) (1986), *The Economic Nature of the Firm: A Reader*. Cambridge University Press: Cambridge.

Redner, H. (ed.) (1993), *An Heretical Heir of the Enlightenment: Politics, Policy and Science in the Work of Charles E. Lindblom*. Westview Press: Boulder, CO.

Robertson, P. L. and R. N. Langlois (1994), 'Institutions, Inertia and Changing Industrial Leadership,' *Industrial and Corporate Change*, 3, 359–378.

Schelling, T. C. (1960), *The Strategy of Conflict*. Oxford University Press: Oxford.

Schwarz, M. and M. Thompson, (1990), *Divided We Stand: Redefining Politics, Technology and Social Choice*. University of Pennsylvania Press: Philadelphia, PA.

Sen, A. (1977), 'Rational Fools: A Critique of the Behavioral Foundations of Economic Theory,' *Philosophy and Public Affairs*, 6, 317–344.

Sen, A. (1987), *On Ethics and Economics*. Blackwell: New York.

Shafir, E. and A. Tversky (1992), 'Thinking through Uncertainty: Unconsequential Reasoning and Choice,' *Cognitive Psychology*, 24, 449–474.

Silverberg, G. (1988), 'Modeling Economic Dynamics and Technical Change: Mathematical Approaches to Self-organization and Evolution,' in G. Dosi, C. Freeman, R. Nelson, G. Silverberg and L. Soete (eds), *Technical Change and Economic Theory*. Francis Pinter: London; Columbia University Press: New York.

Simon, H. (1976), *Administrative Behavior: A Study of Decision-making Processes in Administrative Organization*. The Free Press: New York.

Simon, H. (1983), *Reason in Human Affairs*. Stanford University Press: Stanford, CA.

Teece, D., R. Rumelt, G. Dosi and S. Winter (1994), 'Understanding Corporate Coherence: Theory and Evidence,' *Journal of Economic Behavior and Organization*, 22, 1–24.

Thompson, M., R. Ellis and A. Wildawsky (1990), *Cultural Theory*. Westview Press: Boulder, CO.

Tocqueville, A. de (1969), *Democracy in America*. Anchor Books: New York.

Weber, M. (1968), *Economy and Society*. University of California Press: Berkeley, CA.

———————————— 18 ————————————

————————————— *Hierarchies, Markets and Power* —————————

White, H. C., S. A. Boorman and R. L. Breiger (1976), 'Social Structure from Multiple Networks: I. Block Models of Roles and Positions,' *American Journal of Sociology*, 81, 730–780.

Williamson, O. E. (1985), *The Economic Institution of Capitalism*. The Free Press: New York.

Williamson, O. E. and S. Winter (eds) (1991), *The Nature of the Firm: Origins, Evolution and Development*. Oxford University Press: Oxford.

Winter, S. (1971), 'Satisfying, Selection and the Innovating Remnant,' *Quarterly Journal of Economics*, 85, 237–261.

Works and publications of Giovanni Dosi

'La "Teoria Generale": Saggio sulla Rivoluzione Keynesiana', in M.C. Marcuzzo (ed.), *Problemi e storia delle teorie economiche*, Milano: Mazzotta, 1976.

'Sul ruolo della teoria del Valore-Lavoro in Marx', *Quaderni della Fondazione Feltrinelli*, n. 3, 1978.

'Una stima del contributo del bilancio della Pubblica Amministrazione alla formazione della domanda in sei paesi OECD, 1967–74', *Rivista Internazionale di Scienze Economiche e Commerciali*, June 1979.

'A simple illustrative model of the impact of increasingly labour-saving technical progress on employment in an open economy', SERC (Sussex European Research Centre), University of Sussex, 1979, mimeo.

'De-industrializzazione e politiche economiche: il caso Inglese', *L'Industria – Rivista di Economia e Politica Industriale*, n. 1, 1980.

'The European process plant industry', *Interim Report*, SERC, University of Sussex, 1981 (in collaboration with Tibor Barna, Jonathan Aylen, Daniel Jones), Report to EEC Commission.

'Technical change and survival: the European semiconductor industry', Brighton: *Sussex European Papers*, 1981.

'Trade, international adjustment, technical innovation', SERC, University of Sussex, 1981, mimeo.

'Institutions and markets in high-technology: government support for microelectronics in Europe', in C. Carter (ed.), *Industrial Policies and Innovation*, London: NIESR/ Heinemann, 1981.

'Technology, industrial structures and international economic performance', Paris, OECD, DSTI/SPR/81.43, 1981.

'Direzione e tasso di innovazione, struttura industriale e indicatori di performance economica', in F. Onida (ed.), *Valutazioni Preliminari per uno Studio su Vincolo Energetico, Innovazione Tecnologica e Collocazione Internazionale dell'Industria Italiana*, Milano: Istituto di Ricerca Sociale, 1981.

'On engines, thermostats, bicycles and tandems, or, moving some steps towards economic dynamics', Brighton: SPRU (Science Policy Research Unit), mimeo, 1982.

'La circolarità tra crescita del reddito e produttività: alcune note sulla "Legge di Verdoorn-Kaldor"', *L'Industria*, 1982.

'International specialisation, technical change and industrial interdependencies. Some notes on economic signals and context conditions', Brighton: SPRU, mimeo, 1982.

'Technological paradigms and technological trajectories. A suggested interpretation of the determinants and directions of technical change', *Research Policy*, 1982.

'Technological paradigms and technological trajectories. The determinants and directions of technical change and the transformation of the economy', in C. Freeman (ed.), *Long Waves in the World Economy*, London: Butterworth, 1983 (second edn: London: Francis Pinter, 1984).

(With L. Soete), *Technology and Employment in the Electronics Industry*, London: Francis Pinter, 1983.

'Tecnologia, struttura industriale e performance economica internazionale: alcune ipotesi teoriche', in F. Momigliano and G. Dosi, *Tecnologia e Organizzazione Industriale*, Bologna: Il Mulino, 1983.

(With L. Soete), 'Technology and cost-based adjustments: some explorations on the determinants of international competitiveness', *Metroeconomica*, 1983.

'Sul rapporto tra sistema delle tecnologie e condizioni di sviluppo macroeconomico', in (various authors), *Le Trasformazioni del Welfare State tra Storia e Prospezione del Futuro*, Bari: De Donato, 1984.

'Technology and conditions of macroeconomic development. Some notes on adjustment mechanism and discontinuities in the transformation of capitalist economies', in C. Freeman (ed.), *Innovation, Design and Long-Cycles in Economic Development*, London: Royal College of Arts, 1984.

Technical Change and Industrial Transformation – The Theory and an Application to the Semiconductor Industry, London: Macmillan, 1984; American Edition: New York: St. Martin Press, 1984.

'Economic signals in a changing world. A note on new technologies, comparative advantages and growth, and some policy implications', Brighton: SPRU, University of Sussex, 1984.

'Semiconductors: Europe's precarious survival in high technology', in G. Shepherd, F. Duchêne, C. Saunders (eds), *Europe's Industries. Public and Private Strategies for Change*, London, Francis Pinter, 1984.

'Technology gaps, cost-based adjustments and industrial organizations. A theoretical exploration of the determinants of international competitiveness', Brighton: SPRU, mimeo, 1984.

'Economic signals in a changing world. An introductory view of technologies, comparative advantages and growth', Brighton: SPRU, mimeo, 1984.

'International differences in labour productivities and international gaps in technology', Brighton: SPRU, mimeo, 1984.

'Absolute and comparative advantages in international trade: some empirical evidence', Brighton: SPRU, mimeo, 1984.

'Le politiche industriali: interventi istituzionali e meccanismi di mercato', *Politica ed Economia*, 1984.

(With L. Orsenigo), 'Regulation, dominance and market processes in the theory of technical change', prepared for the Conference *The Impact of Technology, Labour Market Processes and Financial Structures on Economic Stability and Progress*, George Washington University, Saint Louis, May 1985, Working Paper.

'Asimmetrie tecnologiche e costi relativi: alcune note di teoria', in F. Onida (ed.), *Innovazione, Competitività e Vincolo Energetico*, Bologna: Il Mulino, 1985.

(With L. Soete), 'Vantaggi assoluti e vantaggi comparati nel commercio internazionale: alcuni elementi di evidenza empirica', in F. Onida (ed.), *Innovazione, Competitività e Vincolo Energetico*, Bologna: Il Mulino, 1985.

'Technology gaps, international specialization and patterns of growth in open economies', Brighton: SPRU, University of Sussex, DRC Discussion Paper, 1986.

(With M. Cimoli and L. Soete), 'Innovation diffusion, institutional differences and patterns of trade: a north–south model', Brighton: SPRU, DRC Discussion Paper, 1986.

(With M. Moggi), 'La capacità innovativa italiana: alcuni confronti internazionali, inter-settoriali e inter-regionali', in F. Onida (ed.), *Vincolo Estero, Struttura Industriale e Credito all'Esportazione*, Bologna: Il Mulino, 1986.

'Tendenze dei processi d'innovazione e scenari socio-economici', *Oltre il Ponte*, n. 13, 1986.

'Institutions and markets in a dynamic world', *The Manchester School*, 1988.

'Innovazione e dinamica industriale', in G. Zanetti (ed.), *Alle Radici della Struttura Produttiva Italiana*, Roma: Editore SIPI, 1988.

'Alcune riflessioni su mutamento tecnico e fabbisogni energetici', in C.M. Guerci and G. Zanetti (eds), *Sviluppo Economico e Vincolo Energetico*, Bologna: Il Mulino, 1988.

(With M. Moggi), 'Diffusione delle tecnologie elettroniche ed evoluzione della struttura industriale contemporanea', in G.P. Barbetta and F. Silva (eds), *Trasformazioni Strutturali dell'Industria Italiana*, Bologna: Il Mulino, 1988.

(With G. Silverberg and L. Orsenigo), 'Innovation, diversity and diffusion: a self-organising model', *Economic Journal*, 1988.

'Sources, procedures and microeconomic effects of innovation', *Journal of Economic Literature*, 1988.

(With C. Freeman, R. Nelson, G. Silverberg and L. Soete), *Technical Change and Economic Theory*, London: Francis Pinter, and New York: Columbia University Press, 1988.

(With L. Orsenigo), 'Industrial structures and technological progress', in A. Heertje (ed.), *Technology, Innovation and Finance*, Oxford: Basil Blackwell, 1988.

(With L. Orsenigo), 'Coordination and transformation: an overview of structures, behaviours and change in evolutionary environments', in G. Dosi *et al.* (eds), *Technical Change and Economic Theory*, 1988.

'The nature of innovative process', in G. Dosi *et al.* (eds), *Technical Change and Economic Theory*, 1988.

(With F. Coricelli), 'Coordination and order in economic change, and the interpretative power of economic theory', in G. Dosi *et al.* (eds), *Technical Change and Economic Theory*, 1988.

(With L. Soete), 'Technical change and international trade', in G. Dosi *et al.* (eds), *Technical Change and Economic Theory*, 1988.

(With M. Egidi), 'A bounded rationality approach to uncertainty and innovation', in M. Campanella (ed.), *Between Rationality and Cognition,* Torino-Geneve: A. Maynier, 1988.

(With M. Cimoli), 'Technology and development: some implications of recent advances in the economics of innovation for the process of development', in D. Ernst and A. Wad (eds), *Science, Technology and Development*, Boulder (Col.): Westview Press, 1988.

'Economia dell'innovazione ed evoluzione economica', in M. Amendola (ed.), *Innovazione e Progresso Tecnico*, Bologna: Il Mulino, 1989.

'Comments on Aoki and Rosenberg', in T. Shiraishi and S. Tsuru (eds), *Economic Institutions in a Dynamic Society*, London: Macmillan, 1989.

(With L. D'Andrea Tyson and J. Zysman), 'Trade, technologies and development: a framework for discussing Japan', in C. Johnson, L. D'Andrea Tyson and J. Zysman (eds), *Politics and Productivity. The Real Story of How Japan Works*, Cambridge (Mass.): Ballinger, 1989.

'Innovacion, difusion y dinamica industrial', in D. Chudnovsky and J.C. Del Bello (eds), *Las Economias de Argentina e Italia*, Buenos Aires and Mexico City: Fondo de Cultura Economica, 1989.

(With J. Zysman and L. D'Andrea Tyson), 'Technology, trade policies and Schumpeterian efficiency', in J. De La Mothe and L.M. Ducharme (eds), *Science, Technology and Free Trade*, London: Francis Pinter, 1990.

(With D. Teece and S. Winter), 'Les frontières des entreprises: vers une théorie de la cohérence de la grande entreprise', *Revue d'Economie Industrielle*, 1990.

(With M. Cimoli), 'The characteristics of technology and the development process: some introductory notes', in M. Chatterji (ed.), *Technology Transfer in Developing Countries*, London: Macmillan, 1990.

'Innovazione, diffusione, apprendimento nell'industria in Europa: una valutazione delle capacità tecnologiche dell'Europa occidentale', in A. Ruberti (ed.), *Europa e Tecnologia a Confronto,* Bari: SEAT/Laterza, 1990.

'Finance, innovation and industrial change', *Journal of Economic Behaviour and Organization*, 1990.

(With K. Pavitt and L. Soete), *The Economics of Technical Change and International Trade*, Brighton: Wheatsheaf, and New York: New York University Press, 1990.

'Economic change and its interpretation, or, is there a "Schumpeterian approach?"', in A. Heertje and M. Perlman (eds), *Evolving Technology and Market Structure*, Ann Arbor: Michigan University Press, 1990.

(With F. Coricelli and L. Orsenigo), 'Microeconomic dynamics and macro-regularities: an evolutionary approach to technological and institutional change', in OECD, *Technology and Productivity*, Paris: OECD, 1991.

(With M. Egidi), 'Substantive and procedural uncertainty. An exploration of economic behaviours in changing environments', *Journal of Evolutionary Economics*, 1991.

(With F. Arcangeli and M. Moggi), 'Patterns of diffusion of electronics technologies: an international comparison with special reference to the Italian case', *Research Policy*, 1991.

(With J.S. Metcalfe), 'On some notions of irreversibility in economics', in P. Saviotti and J.S. Metcalfe (eds), *Evolutionary Economics*, London: Harwood Academic Press, 1991.

'Approches de l'irréversibilité en théorie économique', in R. Boyer and B. Chavance (eds), *Les figures de l'irréversibilité en économie*, Paris: Édition de l'École des Hautes Etudes en Sciences Sociales, 1991.

'Perspectives on evolutionary theory', *Science and Public Policy*, 1991.

'Una reconsideracion de las condiciones y los modelos del desarollo. Una perspectiva "evolucionista" de la innovacion, el comercio y el crecimiento', *Pensamiento Iberoamericano*, n. 20, 1991.

(With F. Chiaromonte), 'The microfoundations of competitiveness and their macroeconomic implications', in D. Foray and C. Freeman (eds), *Technology and The Wealth of Nations*, London: Francis Pinter, 1992.

(With R. Giannetti and P.A. Toninelli), 'Theory and history of technology and business firms: the microeconomics of industrial development', in G. Dosi, R. Giannetti and P.A. Toninelli (eds), *Technology and the Enterprise in a Historical Perspective*, Oxford: Clarendon Press of Oxford University Press, 1992.

(With D. Teece and S. Winter), 'Toward a theory of corporate coherence: preliminary remarks', in G. Dosi, R. Giannetti and P.A. Toninelli (eds), *Technology and the Enterprise in a Historical Perspective*, Oxford: Clarendon Press of Oxford University Press, 1992.

'Performances, interactions and evolution in the theory of industrial organisation', in A. Del Monte (ed.), *Recent Developments in Industrial Organization*, London: Macmillan, and Ann Arbor: University of Michigan Press, 1992.

(With M. Aoki), 'Corporate organization, finance and innovation', in V. Zamagni (ed.), *Finance and the Enterprise. Facts and Theories*, New York: Academic Press, 1992.

(With R. Salvatore), 'The structure of industrial production and the boundaries between firms and markets', in A. Scott and M. Storper (eds), *Pathways to Industrialization and Regional Development*, London: Routledge, 1992.

(With M. Moggi), 'Piccole e medie imprese e innovazione in Italia', *L'Industria*, 1992.

'Industrial organisation, competitiveness and growth', *Revue d'Economie Industrielle*, 1992.

'Research on innovation diffusion: an assessment', in A. Grübler and N. Nakićenović (eds), *Diffusion of Technologies and Social Behavior*, Heidelberg/Berlin/New York: Springer-Verlag, 1991.

'Evolutionare ansätze der industrieökonomik – konsequenzen für eine industrie- und technologiepolitik', in F. Meyer-Kramer (ed.), *Innovations-ökonomie und Technologie-politik*, Heidelberg: Phisica-Verlag, 1993.

(With B. Kogut), 'National specificities and the context of change: the co-evolution of organization and technology', in B. Kogut (ed.), *Country Competitiveness – Technology and Re-organization of Work*, Oxford: Oxford University Press, 1993.

(With F. Chiaromonte and L. Orsenigo), 'Innovative learning and institutions in the process of development: on the microfoundations of growth regimes', in R. Thomson (ed.), *Learning and Technological Change*, London: Macmillan, 1993.

(With G. Amendola and E. Papagni), 'The dynamics of international competitiveness', *Weltwirtschaftliches Archiv*, 1993.

(With D. Teece), 'Organizational competences and the boundaries of the firm', University of California, Berkeley, Graduate Business School, CCC Working Paper, 1993, published in R. Arena and C. Longhi (eds), *Markets and Organizations*, Berlin/Heidelberg/New York: Springer-Verlag, 1998.

(With F. Chiaromonte), 'Heterogeneity, competition and macroeconomic dynamics', *Structural Change and Economic Dynamics*, 1993.

(With L. Marengo), 'Some elements of an evolutionary theory of organizational competence', in R.W. England (ed.), *Evolutionary Concepts in Contemporary Economics*, Ann Arbor: University of Michigan Press, 1994.

(With R. Nelson), 'An introduction to evolutionary theories in economics', *Journal of Evolutionary Economics*, 1994.

(With Yu. Ermoliev and Yu. Kaniovski), 'Generalized urn schemes and technological dynamics', *Journal of Mathematical Economics*, 1994.

(With C. Freeman and S. Fabiani), 'The process of economic development. Introducing some stylized facts and theories on technologies, firms and institutions', *Industrial and Corporate Change*, 1994.

(With S. Fabiani, R. Aversi and M. Meacci), 'The dynamics of international differentiation. A multi-country evolutionary model', *Industrial and Corporate Change*, 1994.

(With C. Freeman, S. Fabiani and R. Aversi), 'The diversity of development patterns: catching-up, forging ahead and falling behind', in L.L. Pasinetti and R.M. Solow (eds), *Economic Growth and the Structure of Long-Term Development*, London: Macmillan, 1994.

(With S. Fabiani), 'Convergence and divergence in the long-term growth of open economies', in G. Silverberg and L. Soete (eds), *The Economics of Growth and Technological Change*, Aldershot: Edward Elgar, 1994.

(With D. Teece, R. Rumelt and S. Winter), 'Understanding corporate coherence: theory and evidence', *Journal of Economic Behavior and Organization*, 1994.

(With F. Malerba and L. Orsenigo), 'Evolutionary regimes and industrial dynamics', in L. Magnusson (ed.), *Evolutionary Approaches to Economics*, Boston: Kluwer, 1994.

(With L. Orsenigo), 'Macrodynamics and microfoundations: an evolutionary perspective', in O. Granstrand (ed.), *Economics of Technology*, Amsterdam: Elsevier North Holland, 1994.

(With B. Coriat), 'Learning how to govern and learning how to solve problems. On the co-evolution of competences, conflicts and organizational routines', Presented at the Prince Bertil Symposium, Stockholm School of Economics, June 1994, published in A. Chandler, P. Hagström and Ö. Sölvell (eds), *The Dynamic Firm*, Cambridge: Cambridge University Press, 1998.

(With B. Coriat), 'Evolutionisme et regulationisme: differences et convergences', in R. Boyer and F. Saillard (eds), *Theorie de la Regulation: Etat du Savoir*, Paris: La Decouverte, 1994.

(With Y. Kaniovski), 'On "badly behaved" dynamics. Some applications of generalized urn schemes to technological and economic change', *Journal of Evolutionary Economics*, 1994.

(With M. Cimoli), 'Technological paradigms, patterns of learning and development: an introductory roadmap', *Journal of Evolutionary Economics*, 1995.

(With O. Marsili, L. Orsenigo and R. Salvatore), 'Learning, market selection and the evolution of industrial structures', *Small Business Economics*, 1995.

'Hierarchies, markets and power: some foundational issues on the nature of contemporary economic organizations', *Industrial and Corporate Change*, 1995.

'The contribution of economic theory to the understanding of a knowledge-based economy', IIASA, Laxenburg, Austria, Working Paper, 1995; revised version published in D. Foray and B.A. Lundvall (eds), *Knowledge, Employment and Growth*, Paris: OECD, 1996.

(With F. Malerba), 'Organizational learning and institutional embeddedness. An introduction to the diverse evolutionary paths of modern corporations', in G. Dosi and F. Malerba (eds), *Organization and Strategy in the Evolution of the Enterprise*, London: Macmillan, 1996.

(Edited with F. Malerba), *Organization and Strategy in the Evolution of the Enterprise*, London: Macmillan, 1996.

(With M.D. Cohen, R. Burkhart, M. Egidi, L. Marengo, M. Warglien and S. Winter), 'Routines and other recurring action patterns of organizations: contemporary research issues', *Industrial and Corporate Change*, 1996.

(With D. Lovallo), 'Rational entrepreneurs or optimistic martyrs? Some considerations on technological regimes, corporate entries and the evolutionary role of decision biases', in R. Garud, P.R. Nayyar and Z.B. Shapira (eds), *Technological Innovation: Oversights and Foresights*, Cambridge/New York: Cambridge University Press, 1997.

'Organizational competences, size and The Wealth of Nations: some comments from a comparative perspective', in A. Chandler, F. Amatori and T. Hikino (eds), *Big Business and the Wealth of Nations*, Cambridge: Cambridge University Press, 1997.

(With L. Marengo and G. Fagiolo), 'Learning in evolutionary environments', Laxenburg, Austria, IIASA Working Paper, 1996, forthcoming in K. Dopfer (ed.), *Principles of Evolutionary Economics*, Cambridge: Cambridge University Press, 2000.

(With Yu. Kaniovski and S. Winter), 'A baseline model of industry evolution', Laxenburg, Austria, IIASA Working Paper, 1997.

'Opportunities, incentives and the collective patterns of technical change', *Economic Journal*, 1997.

(With F. Malerba, O. Marsili and L. Orsenigo), 'Industrial structures and dynamics: evidence, interpretations and puzzles', *Industrial and Corporate Change*, **6** (1), 1997.

(With R. Nelson), 'Evolutionary theories', in R. Arena and C. Longhi (eds), *Markets and Organizations*, Berlin/Heidelberg/New York: Springer-Verlag, 1998.

(With G. Fagiolo), 'Exploring the unknown. On entrepreneurship, coordination and innovation driven growth', in J. Lesourne and A. Orléan (eds), *Advances in Self-Organization and Evolutionary Economics*, Paris: Economica, 1998.

(With B. Coriat), 'The institutional embeddedness of economic change. An appraisal of the "evolutionary" and the "regulationist" research programmes', in K. Nielsen and B. Johnson (eds), *Institutions and Economic Change*, Cheltenham, UK and Northampton, MA: Edward Elgar, 1998.

(With A. Bassanini), 'Competing technologies, technological monopolies and the rate of convergence to a stable market structure', Laxenburg, Austria, IIASA Interim Report, 1998.

(With D. Teece and J. Chytry) (eds), *Technology, Organization and Competitiveness*, Oxford/New York: Oxford University Press, 1998.

(With G. Fagiolo and L. Marengo), 'Modelli ed evidenza empirica su quel poco che sappiamo dell'apprendimento in mondi che cambiano', in A. Vercelli (ed.), *Incertezza, razionalità e decisioni economiche*, Bologna: Il Mulino, 1998.

(With F. Chiaromonte), 'Modeling a decentralized asset market: an introduction to the financial "toy-room"', Laxenburg, Austria, IIASA, Interim Report, 1998.

(With S. Winter), 'Interpreting economic change: evolution, structures and games', St Anna School of Advanced Studies, Pisa, Working Paper, 1999.

(With S. Winter and Y. Kaniovski), 'Modeling industrial dynamics with innovative entrants', *Structural Change and Economic Dynamics*, 1999, forthcoming.

(With A. Bassanini), 'When and how chance and human will can twist the arm of Clio', in R. Garud and P. Karnoe (eds), *Path Dependence and Creation*, Nahwah, NY: Lawrence Erlbaum Publishers, 1999, forthcoming.

(With A. Bassanini), 'Heterogeneous agents, complementarities and diffusion: do increasing returns imply convergence to international technological monopolies?', in D. Delli Gatti, M. Gallegati and A. Kirman (eds), *Market Structure, Aggregation and Heterogeneity*, Cambridge: Cambridge University Press, 1999, forthcoming.

(With G. Fagiolo, R. Aversi, M. Meacci and C. Olivetti), 'Cognitive processes, social adaptation and innovation in consumption patterns: from stylized facts to demand theory', in S.C. Dow and P.E. Earl (eds), *Economic Organization and Economic Knowledge: Essays in Honour of Brian J. Loasby, Volume 1*, Cheltenham, UK and Northampton, MA: Edward Elgar, 1999.

(With R. Aversi, G. Fagiolo, M. Meacci and C. Olivetti), 'Demand dynamics with socially evolving preferences', *Industrial and Corporate Change*, 1999.

'Some notes on national systems of innovation and production, and their implications for economic analysis', in D. Archibugi, J. Howells and J. Michie (eds), *Innovation Policy in a Global Economy*, Cambridge: Cambridge University Press, 1999.

(With R. Nelson and S. Winter) (eds), *The Nature and Dynamics of Organizational Capabilities*, Oxford/New York: Oxford University Press, 2000, forthcoming.

Name index

Abernathy, W.J. 59, 68, 339
Abramovitz, M. 3, 150, 315, 501, 576
Abreu, D. 218
Acs, Z.J. 435–8
Adler, P. 310
Aghion, P. 501, 531, 554, 576, 656–7
Aglietta, M. 37, 353–4, 357
Aitken, H.G.J. 308
Akerlof, G. 154, 645
Alchian, A.A. 172
Allen, P. 8, 135, 381, 572, 628
Altshuler, A. 93, 101
Amable, B. 355, 360, 549
Amendola, G. 2, 21, 358
Amendola, M. 135, 628, 661
Anderson, P. 27, 283, 327, 340, 382
Andre, C. 354
Ansell, C.K. 680
Aoki, M. 18, 19, 37, 212, 220, 229, 231–2, 296, 302, 312, 314, 635, 643, 648–51, 653, 659–60, 661
Arcangeli, F. 5, 22, 98, 117, 120, 135, 138, 412
Arena, R. 90
Argote, L. 239
Arifovic, J. 197
Arnold, J. 239
Arrow, K.J. 10, 11, 18, 22, 27, 58, 68, 73, 82, 89, 118, 153, 169, 172, 190, 197, 211, 223, 250, 297, 327, 559, 624
Arthur, W.B. 27, 31, 33, 86–7, 89–91, 119, 129, 135, 154, 196, 298, 340–41, 349, 383–5, 390, 393, 395, 405, 407, 411, 427, 559, 604–5, 626, 634
Asanuma, B. 312
Ashton, P. 78, 101
Atkinson, A.B. 86, 118, 411, 604
Audretsch, D.B. 435–8, 454
Aversi, R. 2, 21, 31, 38
Axelrod, R. 206
Azariadis, C. 550

Bacdayan, P. 368, 673
Baily, M.N. 436
Bain, J. 145
Baldwin, J.R. 252, 477
Banerjee, A. 381–2
Barca, F. 97, 455

Barna, T. 3, 4
Basalla, G. 14, 334, 349
Bassanini, A. 21, 31
Bateman, T. 238
Baumol, W.J. 175
Bazerman, M.H. 238
Becker, G.S. 670
Beer, J. 79
Beesley, M.E. 434
Benhabib, J. 535
Bercovitz, J. 254
Berglof, E. 655
Bernal, J. 79
Bernd, L. 584
Bernoulli 167
Berry, C.H. 267
Bertè, M. 34
Bianco, M. 435
Billandot 355
Binmore, K. 653
Boeker, W. 273
Boldrin, M. 382
Bolton, P. 656–7
Bond, R.S. 436
Bonfiglioli, A. 52
Bonini, C.P. 455
Bound, J. 95
Bowles, S. 677
Boyer, R. 5, 22, 37, 138, 317, 353–5, 360–61, 363, 502
Braun, E. 79
Breznev, L. 32
Brock, W.A. 23, 27, 382
Brooks, H. 122
Brüderl, J. 247
Buer, T.C. 93
Burns, A.F. 80
Buss, L.W. 198

Cabrales, A. 381–2
Cairnarca, G. 98
Camerer, C. 30
Cameron, R. 622
Campbell, J.Y. 566, 581, 584
Cantwell, J. 139, 300
Carlsson, B. 637
Caroli, E. 355
Carroll, G.R. 245, 477

Carter, C. 100, 124
Caves, R. 99, 267
Chandler, A.D. 35, 229, 265, 295, 300, 307, 313, 334, 353, 603
Chavance, B. 681–2
Cheng, L.K. 554
Chesnais, F. 5, 69, 80, 82, 101, 125
Chiaromonte, F. 21, 34, 147, 253, 330, 349, 353, 361, 525, 536
Christiano, L.J. 584
Cimoli, M. 2, 21, 99, 139, 549, 609
Clark, J. 60
Clark, K.B. 247, 251, 282, 340
Coase, R. 647
Cochrane, J.H. 581, 584
Cohen, M.D. 6, 23, 34, 222, 368, 673, 680
Cohen, W.N. 94, 101, 145, 147, 249
Cohendet, P. 90
Collins, N.R. 436
Colombo, M. 98
Commons, J.R. 350
Conlisk, J. 147, 359
Constant, E.W. 68, 84
Contini, B. 99, 436
Cooper, R. 74
Coriat, B. 5, 22, 36, 87, 96, 138, 147, 295–6, 308–9, 312–13, 317–19, 353, 355, 364–5, 680
Coricelli, F. 138, 503–4
Crémer, J. 212, 222, 651
Curzon-Price, T. 192
Cutland, N.J. 176–7, 196, 217
Cyert, R. 9, 31, 34, 216, 248, 302

Dahmen, E. 5
Dasgupta, P. 73, 101, 119, 138
David, P.A. 13, 22–3, 31, 68, 73–4, 84, 86–7, 89, 91, 104, 118–19, 122–3, 129, 131–2, 135, 139, 150, 152, 154, 159, 255, 280, 298, 340–42, 349, 351, 382, 411, 413, 421, 427, 559, 576, 626, 634, 670, 679
Davies, S. 121–3, 129, 131–2, 413
Day, R. 147, 327, 349, 382
De Janosi, P. 34
De Tocqueville, A. 594, 682
De Tournemine, R.L. 90
DeBresson, C. 327
DeJong, D.N. 584
Dekel, E. 382
Delorme, R. 354
Diebold, F.X. 584
DiMaggio, P.J. 351
Dinopoulos, E. 554
Doeblin 466
Doob, J.L. 466

Dore, R. 303, 600
Dosi, G. 2, 5–8, 14, 19, 21, 23, 29–31, 33–4, 37, 68, 70–72, 74, 76–9, 84, 86–8, 92–3, 98–102, 105, 107, 118–20, 125, 129, 134–5, 139, 145, 147–8, 156, 159, 183–5, 191, 194, 197, 212–13, 216–17, 219–20, 229, 232, 239, 246, 248–53, 284, 295, 297–8, 300, 303–4, 317, 327, 330–31, 334–5, 339, 341, 348–9, 351, 353, 358–9, 364–5, 368–9, 382–3, 385, 389–91, 394, 411–12, 436–7, 440–41, 443–4, 448, 460, 502–9, 519, 522, 525, 536, 538, 544, 548, 558–9, 601–2, 604, 609, 625, 628–9, 634, 636, 648–9, 655, 661–3, 673, 677
Douglas, M. 679
Drazen, A. 550
Dubois, D. 222
Dûchene, F. 4
Dulude, L.S. 81
Dunne, T. 236, 245
Dunning, J. 139
Durkheim, E. 37, 671
Durlauf, S. 27
Dyer, L. 239

Ebeling, W. 415
Egan, P.T. 78, 101
Egidi, M. 23, 69, 77, 191, 194, 197, 212, 216–17, 248, 297, 331, 368, 509, 538, 673
Eichenbaum, M. 584
Eigen, M. 381, 414–15
Eliasson, G. 23, 101, 147, 327, 349, 628
Enos, J.L. 74, 93
Ergas, H. 5, 85, 92
Erikson, R. 440
Ermoliev, Y. 33, 298
Evans, D.S. 435
Everett, M. 327

Fabiani, S. 2, 8, 21, 159, 544, 548
Fagerberg, I. 14, 358
Fagiolo, G. 2, 5, 19, 21, 26
Farrell, J. 129, 135
Feenstra, R.C. 673–4, 678, 681–2
Feistel, R. 415
Feyerabend, P.K. 55
Figuereido, J. 254
Fisher, J.C. 423
Fleck, J. 151
Fontana, W. 27, 198
Foray, D. 341
Forni, M. 8
Forrest, S. 218

Foster, D. 382
Fox, F.V. 238
Frankel, M. 90
Freeman, C. 2, 4–5, 8, 13, 14, 17, 22, 48, 51,
    55, 59, 60, 68–9, 77–9, 84, 87, 99, 100,
    123, 134, 145, 147–8, 150–51, 156,
    159, 213, 239, 334, 341, 349, 353, 382,
    436, 502, 505, 544, 548, 559, 596, 601,
    662
Freeman, J. 245, 273, 477
Friedman, D. 382, 402–3, 405
Friedman, M. 10, 172, 196, 328, 505
Frydman, R. 601
Fuà, G. 3
Fudenberg, D. 30, 133, 405
Fujimoto, T. 282
Fuller, J.K. 99

Gaffard, J.L. 135, 628, 661
Galambos 680, 682–3
Gardiner, P. 74
Garegnani 4
Garud, R. 254
Garvin, D.A. 282
Geanakoplos, J. 27, 215
Gell-Mann, M. 27
Geneen, H. 266
Geroski, P. 38, 99, 213, 244, 252, 436, 455,
    477, 492
Gerschenkron, A. 21, 153, 549
Gibbons, M. 69, 101, 106, 110, 337
Gilboa, I. 223
Gintis, H. 677
Glaziev, S.Y. 383, 387, 389
Gold, B. 99, 122–3, 413
Gollop, F.M. 268
Gonenc, M. 98
Gordon, T. 71
Gort, M. 81, 101, 105, 124–5, 250, 267, 339
Grady, E. 339
Granovetter, M. 37, 295, 319, 350, 672–3,
    675–6, 678, 681–2
Granstrand, O. 101, 145, 349
Greenwald, B. 12, 504, 510
Grenstad, G. 351
Griliches, Z. 68, 77, 94, 120, 129, 412, 436
Grossman, G. 153, 501, 552, 576
Grübler, A. 349

Habukkuk, H. 86
Hahn, F. 11, 172, 174, 594
Haken, H. 431
Hall, B.H. 435
Hamilton, G.G. 673–4, 678, 681–2
Hamilton, R.T. 435

Hannan, M.T. 245, 477
Hansen, A.H. 527
Hanusch, H. 23
Harlow, C.J. 99
Harris, D.J. 18
Hay, D. 99
Hegel, W.F. 191, 594, 600
Heiner, R.A. 78, 168, 170, 197, 248, 538
Helpman, E. 153, 501, 552, 576, 606
Henderson, R.M. 247, 250–51, 340
Henkin, C.M. 382
Herrera, A. 21
Hicks, J. 355
Hill, B.M. 383–5
Hirsch, F. 594
Hirschman, A.O. 21, 90, 153, 303, 549, 600,
    631, 655, 675, 682
Hobbes, T. 671
Hodgson, G. 23, 348, 676, 682
Hofbauer, J. 415
Hogart, R.M. 169
Holland, J.H. 27, 185, 190, 192, 197–9, 218,
    220, 224, 673
Hollander, S. 68
Howitt, P. 501, 531, 554, 576
Hufbauer, G.C. 99
Hughes, T.P. 14, 54, 71–2, 89
Husserl, G. 182

Ijiri, Y. 434, 438, 477
Ireland, N.J. 413, 421
Itoh, I. 651
Iwai, K. 17, 101, 413

Jacquemin, A. 90, 99, 213, 436
Jaffe, A.B. 436
Jakumar, R. 282
Janis, I.L. 238
Jelle, P. 351
Jensen, R.A. 132
Jenson, M. 623, 647
Jessop, B. 353
Jewkes, J. 50, 57
Johnson, C.A. 600
Johnston, R. 69
Jones, D. 4
Jones, R. 554
Jovanovic, B. 133, 136, 214, 434, 440, 535,
    554, 559
Juillard, M. 355, 360

Kahnemann, D. 169–70, 236, 238–9
Kaldor, N. 3, 7, 8, 153, 298, 504, 549, 605
Kalecki, M. 439, 455
Kamien, M. 94, 119

Kandori, M. 349, 381
Kaniovski, Y. 33, 298, 349, 383, 386–7, 389, 405
Kaplan, A.D.H. 436
Katz, G. 101
Katz, J. 21
Katz, M.L. 427
Katzner, D.W. 174
Kauffman, S. 27–8
Kay, N. 76
Kelley 122
Kemp, D.A. 674
Keynes, J.M. 3, 8, 167–8, 237
Kindleberger, C.P. 595, 622
Kirman, A. 8, 23
Klavans, R. 268
Kleene 195
Kleiman, H.S. 79
Klein, B. 68
Kleine, P. 124, 419
Klepper, S. 101, 105, 124–5, 245, 250, 339, 437
Klevorick, A.K. 147
Kline, S.J. 151
Knight, F.H. 167, 282
Kogut, B. 2, 37, 313
Koike, K. 653
Konakayama, A. 101, 124
Kornai, J. 658
Koza, J.R. 192, 198–9
Kreps, David 11, 220, 301, 405
Krugman, P. 606
Kuhn, T. 14, 52–3
Kuznets, S. 7, 80

Lach, S. 133, 136
Lakatos, I. 52
Lakoff, G. 673
Lambson, V.E. 440
Lancaster, K. 70
Landes, D. 72, 359
Lane, D. 27, 245, 328
Langlois, R. 23, 254, 327, 680
Langrish, J. 69
Lazonick, W. 72, 303, 319, 680–82
Le Bas, C. 124
Lehnert, D. 543
Leibniz, G. 625
Lemelin, A. 267
Leroy, C. 360
Lesourne, J. 23, 38, 349
Levin, R. 54, 82–3, 91, 94, 101, 119, 125, 148, 661
Levine, D.K. 30
Levinthal, D. 147, 248–9, 254, 349, 436, 677–9

Lewis, A. 173, 181, 194–5, 217
Liebowitz, S.J. 158
Lindblom, C.E. 682
Lindgren, K. 197, 349
Lippi, L. 8, 21, 23
Lipsey, R. 40
Ljung, L. 404
Loève, M. 469, 493
Locke, J. 600
Long, J. 525, 531
Lordon, F. 355
Lorenz, E. 313, 680
Lovallo, D. 236, 238–9, 242, 244
Lucas, R. 185, 214, 434, 439, 501
Luhmann, N. 594, 674
Lundvall, B.-Å. 17, 89, 123, 148, 353, 367
Lunghini, G. 3

MacDonald, S. 79
Machin, S. 455
Machlup, F. 172
MacLeod, B. 654
Maddison, A. 504
Maidique, M. 74
Mailath, G. 652–3
Malcomson, J. 654
Malecki, E.J. 90
Malerba, F. 6, 93, 101, 147–8, 156, 246, 349, 361, 437, 460
Malliaris, A.G. 382
Malthus, T. 327
Mankiw, N.G. 566, 581, 584
Mansfield, E. 74, 77, 83, 120–23, 129, 412, 507
Marais, M.L. 239
March, J. 9, 31, 34, 216, 218, 226, 228, 238, 248, 252, 302, 305, 307, 331, 351, 538, 555, 572, 580, 675
Marcuzzo, C. 3
Marengo, L. 2, 5, 19, 31, 197, 224–5, 228, 239, 248–50, 295, 303–4, 349, 368, 677
Marglin, S. 316
Margolis, S.E. 158
Mariotti, S. 98, 638
Markusen, J.R. 606
Marris, R. 603
Marshall, A. 328
Marsili, O. 21
Martino, J. 71
Marx, K. 2, 8, 13, 18, 327
McDonald, G.M. 559
McGlade, J.M. 572
McLean, M. 5
Meacci, M. 21

Meckling, W. 647
Melvin, J.R. 606
Mermelstein, D. 436
Merrow, E. 239
Metcalfe, J.S. 22–3, 26, 38, 70, 71, 100, 101,
    106, 120, 122, 129, 252, 327, 330, 337,
    349, 411, 413, 599
Miles, R.E. 287
Miller, J.H. 197
Miller, M.H. 623, 656
Minsky, M. 177, 180
Mirrlees, J.A. 7
Mistral, J. 353–4
Mitchell, W. 245, 283
Modigliani, F. 623, 656
Moggi, M. 98
Mokyr, J. 14, 334, 349
Momigliano, F. 5, 83, 87, 101
Monahan, J.L. 268
Moore, B. 681
Morgenstern, O. 190
Morris, D. 99
Moss, S. 549
Mowery, D. 49–50, 75, 77, 84–5, 101, 151
Mueller, D. 99, 213, 339, 436, 603
Müller, J. 4
Munson, T. 71
Murphy, K.M. 550
Myrdal, G. 3, 21, 153, 298

Nabseth, L. 121, 413
Nakicenovic, N. 349
Nayyar, P.R. 254
Needham, D. 58
Nelson, R. 2, 6, 7, 9, 12, 13, 17, 22–3, 26,
    31, 33–4, 49, 53–6, 59, 60, 68–9, 71,
    73–5, 77, 79, 81–2, 84, 86, 90–93, 96,
    99–101, 103, 107, 118–19, 129, 134–5,
    139, 145, 147–8, 151–2, 154, 172, 183,
    212, 216, 218–19, 221, 228, 237, 248,
    250, 278, 300, 302, 304–5, 317, 327,
    329–31, 333–6, 348–9, 353, 357, 359,
    361, 367, 382, 410, 412–13, 435–6,
    440–41, 444, 455, 502–3, 509, 514,
    536, 538, 552, 559, 584, 596–9, 603–4,
    611, 614, 625, 628, 649, 661, 670, 673,
    678, 680
Newell, A. 175, 190
Newman, G. 554
Newton, I. 625
Nicolis, G. 381–2
Nillson, N.J. 175
Noble, D. 71
North, D. 350
Nurske, R. 21

Oakey, R.P. 90
Odigiri, Y. 99
Ohno, T. 309, 311
Olivetti, C. 21
Olsen, J.P. 351
Olsen, T. 129, 131, 135, 413
Orsenigo, L. 5, 7, 78–80, 87, 100–102, 120,
    129, 135, 148, 185, 253, 287, 330, 349,
    361, 437, 444, 460, 502–4, 508–9, 519,
    522, 525, 602, 649, 661
Ostrom, E. 673, 676–7

Paci, E. 3
Padgett, J.F. 680
Paez, B. 290
Pakes, A. 77, 80, 94, 440
Palepu, K. 267
Palmer, R.G. 349
Papagni, E. 2
Parante, S.L. 559
Pareto, V. 673
Pasinetti, L.L. 4, 7, 18, 549, 607–8
Patel, P. 13, 213, 300, 357, 436
Pavitt, K. 2, 5, 13–15, 17, 18, 22, 35, 37–8,
    51, 65, 68–9, 74, 76–8, 81, 87–9, 91–2,
    94, 98–9, 104, 118, 213, 219, 230, 250,
    265, 297, 300, 349, 357, 436–7, 447,
    507, 511, 601, 604, 609, 636 661,
    664–5
Pelikan, P. 282, 631
Pelkey, J. 27, 246
Pemantle, R. 386
Penrose, E. 34
Peracchi, F. 3
Perez, C. 17, 134, 150, 502
Petit, P. 5, 22
Pfeffer, J. 675
Pflug, G. 386
Phillips, A. 101, 125
Pines, D. 327
Piore, M. 96, 316
Pisano, G. 287
Pizzuto, G. 3
Plosser, C. 525, 531, 584
Plott, C.R. 600
Polanyi, K. 594
Polanyi, M. 69, 74
Polterovich, V.M. 382
Porter, M. 99, 299, 300
Possas, M. 21
Post, E. 195
Postlewaite, A. 652–3
Powell, W.W. 351
Prade, H. 222
Pratten, C. 99

Prebish, R. 21
Preisendorfer, P. 247
Preston, L.E. 436
Price, D. de S. 79
Prigogine, I. 27, 381–2, 414
Pry, R.H. 423

Quandt, R.E. 175
Quinn, J.B. 280

Rabin, M.O. 195
Radner, R. 169–70, 314
Rainelli, M. 90
Ranci, P. 5
Ray, G.F. 121, 413
Reich, L. 75
Reichlin, P. 21
Reinganum, J.F. 129, 132–3, 250, 413, 427
Revelli, R. 436
Ricardo, D. 607
Richardson, G.B. 34
Riordan, M. 652
Rob, R. 554, 559
Roberts, M.J. 236
Robertson, P.L. 680
Robinson, J. 4, 51
Robson, M. 76, 94, 265
Rogers, E.M. 120, 130
Romeo, A.A. 120, 122
Romer, P.M. 153, 156, 501, 531, 552, 554, 576
Roncaglia, A. 21
Rosenberg, N. 13, 14, 34, 49, 50, 53–4, 59, 68, 70, 72, 74–5, 78–9, 81, 84–9, 120–23, 134, 147, 149, 151, 156, 308, 314, 334, 349, 505, 507–8, 596, 601, 662
Rosenstein-Rodan, P.N. 549
Ross, J. 238
Rosser, J.B. 382
Rothbarth, E. 86
Rothwell, R. 74, 78
Rubinstein, A. 218, 653
Rumelt, R. 34, 213, 267, 636
Rustichini, A. 3
Ruszczinski, A. 385
Ruttan, V. 145, 148–9, 152, 159
Rybczynsky, T. 622, 655

Sabel, C. 35, 96, 316
Sah, R. 212, 314
Sahal, D. 16, 54, 59, 68, 70–72, 74, 84, 134, 411
Sahlman, A. 630
Saillard, Y. 353–5, 360, 363

Saloner, G. 129, 135
Salter, W. 99, 124, 132, 418
Salvati, M. 3, 58
Salvatore, R. 21, 251, 441, 448
Samuelson, L. 29, 30, 236, 381–2
Samuelson, P. 4
Sanders, L. 290
Savage, L.J. 190
Saviotti, P. 16, 70–72, 252, 327
Schankerman, M. 80
Schelling, T.C. 30, 676
Scherer, F.M. 67, 80, 81, 91, 94, 99
Schleifer, A. 525, 531
Schmalensee, R. 213
Schmookler, J. 59, 78, 82, 84, 150
Schoemaker, P.J.H. 239
Schumpeter, J. 13, 18, 50, 57, 77, 106, 117, 170, 328, 335, 460, 596, 629, 671, 681
Schuster, P. 381, 415
Schwalbach, J. 492
Schwartz, M. 83, 351, 507
Schwartz, N. 94, 119
Sciberras, E. 101
Scotchmer, S. 382
Seabright, M.A. 239
Sen, A. 675
Senhadji, A.S. 584
Sestito, P. 435
Shackle, G.L.S. 167–8, 174
Shafir, E. 236, 673
Shan, W. 287
Shapira, Z.B. 238, 254
Shapiro, C. 427
Shen, T.-Y. 99
Shepherd, G. 4
Sigmund, K. 415, 421
Silberston, A. 99
Silverberg, G. 2, 22–3, 87, 100–102, 129, 135–6, 147, 172, 253, 330, 337–8, 340, 348–9, 359, 381–2, 413–15, 427, 502, 508, 519, 521–2, 525, 541, 543, 583, 629, 676
Simon, H.A. 9, 12, 20, 31, 34, 69, 118, 166, 170–71, 175, 182, 190, 194, 211, 215–16, 237, 248, 274, 278, 302, 304–5, 307, 331–2, 434, 438, 455, 477, 504, 509, 538, 625, 675
Smith, A. 8, 13, 18, 76, 153, 267, 491, 501, 594, 600, 671
Snow, C.C. 287
Söderström, T. 404
Soete, L. 2, 5, 13, 14, 22, 51, 58, 60, 74, 86–8, 92, 94, 99, 147, 297, 337, 349, 402, 601, 609

Solow, R.M. 7, 18, 145, 504
Soskice, D. 37, 319
Spaventa, L. 21
Sraffa, P. 4, 608
Starbuck, W.H. 156
Staw, B. 238
Steedman, I. 608
Steindl, J. 527
Stengers, I. 381
Stevenson, H.H. 630
Stigler, G. 75, 268
Stiglitz, J. 11, 12, 18, 40, 86, 101, 118, 138, 171, 212, 314, 327, 411, 504, 510, 559, 604, 612, 625, 645
Stock, J.H. 584
Stoneman, P. 118, 120, 124, 129, 132, 134, 412–13, 421
Suarez, F. 250, 339, 349
Summers, L.H. 623–4
Sutton, J. 38, 492
Svenilsson, T. 3
Swaminathan, A. 245
Sylos Labini, P. 6, 21, 99, 435, 527

Taylor, F.W. 305–6, 308–10, 317
Teece, D.J. 15, 34–5, 38, 68, 73, 75–6, 83, 89, 90, 102, 125, 184, 219, 232, 250, 254, 264, 273, 280–81, 283–4, 286–7, 295, 299, 300, 317, 440, 443, 456, 602–3, 627, 636, 645, 648–9, 677
Temin, P. 86
Terborgh, G. 416
Teubal, M. 57, 74
Thirlwall, A.P. 609
Thomas, M.D. 90
Thompson, M. 351
Thwaites, A.T. 90
Tidd, J. 38
Tiger, L. 255
Tilton, J. 101, 339
Tirole, J. 118, 133, 265, 273
Toledano, J. 90
Tordjman, H. 27, 349, 368
Torre, A. 90
Townsend, J. 76, 94, 265
Traktenbrot, B.A. 180
Truel, J.L. 5, 90
Turner, R. 337, 402
Tushman, M. 283, 340
Tversky, A. 169, 236, 238–9, 673

Utterback, J.M. 59, 68, 250, 339, 349

Valente, M. 21, 33
Varaldo, R. 21
Veblen, T. 328, 350, 352, 600

Veca, S. 3
Vercelli, A. 182
Verspagen, B. 23, 147, 348–9, 358–9, 543, 549, 583
Vincenti, W. 14, 334, 337, 349
Von Hayek, F.A. 328
Von Hippel, E. 68
Von Neumann, J. 190
Von Tunzelman, G.N. 13, 72, 121

Wagner, S. 83, 507
Wald, S. 51
Walker, W. 5
Wall, R.A. 81
Walsh, V.M. 55, 59, 151
Warglien, M. 349, 677
Watson, M.W. 584
Weber, M. 37, 594, 671, 674
Weibull, J.W. 381–2
West, J. 680–82
Whiteman, C.H. 584
Williams, B. 100, 124
Williams, J. 290
Williamson, O. 15, 36, 75, 93, 184, 212, 237, 279, 289–90, 314, 350, 603, 672, 674, 681–2
Wilson, R. 78, 101
Winter, S. 6, 7, 9, 10, 13, 17, 22–4, 26, 28, 31, 33–4, 49, 53–6, 59, 60, 68–9, 71, 73–4, 76–7, 81, 86, 96, 100–103, 107, 118, 129, 134–5, 146–8, 151–2, 154, 170, 172–3, 183–4, 196, 212, 216, 218–19, 221, 228, 232, 237, 248, 250, 278, 297, 301–2, 304–5, 317, 327, 330–36, 339, 341, 348–9, 359, 361, 382, 410, 413, 435–6, 440–41, 443, 445, 455–6, 459–60, 462, 467, 472, 477, 481, 491–2, 502–3, 509, 514, 536, 538, 552, 559, 596–9, 611, 625, 628, 636, 648, 661, 670, 673, 680
Witt, U. 23, 327
Wolinsky, A. 653
Wright, G. 152, 357

Yamawaki, H. 99, 436
Yelle, L. 68
Young, A. 153
Young, H.P. 382, 405
Young, P. 349, 381

Zeithami, C. 238
Zeitlin, J. 35
Zhang, J. 381–2
Ziegler, R. 247
Zuscovitch, E. 90
Zysman, J. 303, 319, 622, 631